Y0-CAS-118

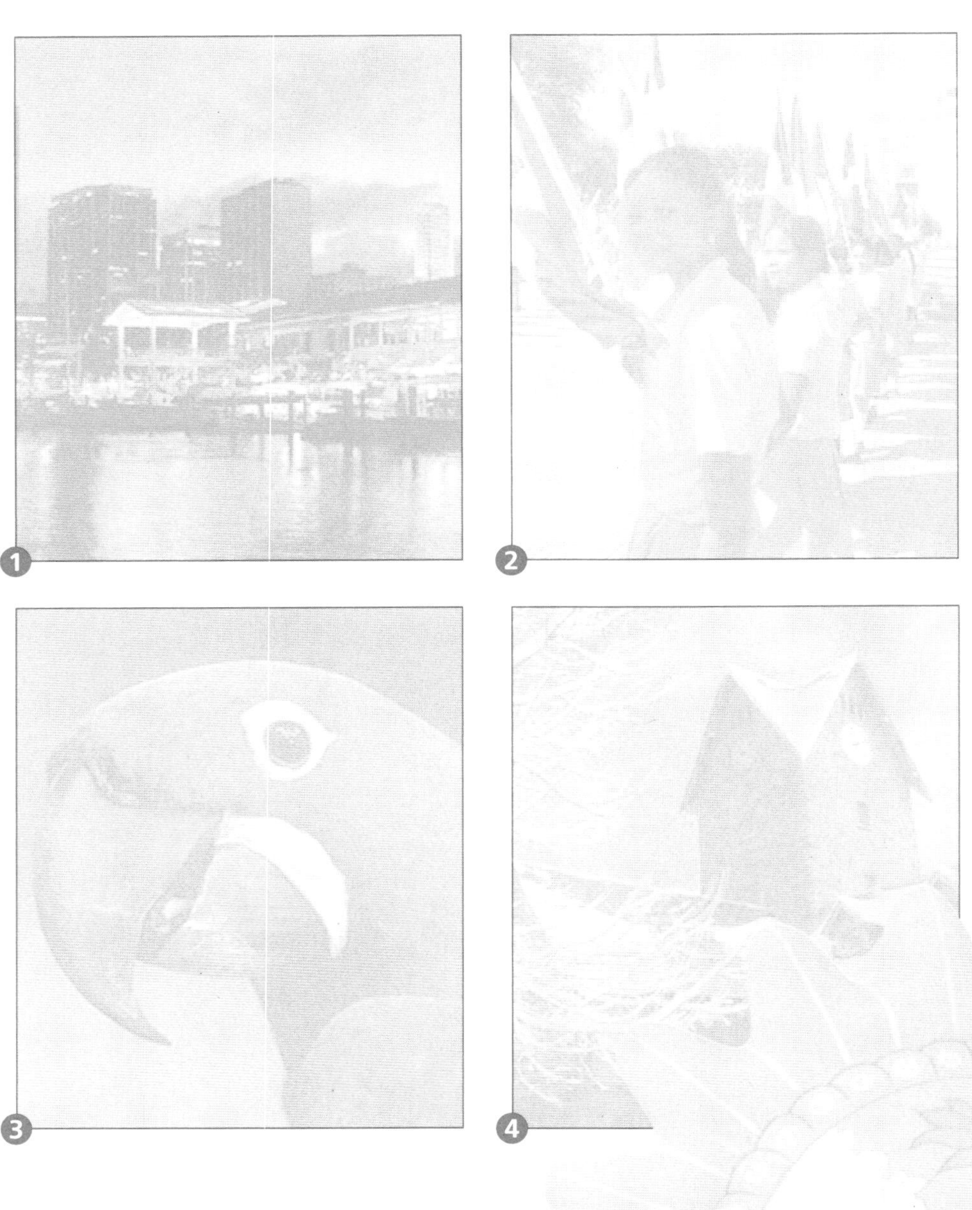

1 **Florida** Miami Beach skyline after dark
2 **Dominican Republic** Girls in Independence Day parade
3 **Peru** Hyacinth macaw
4 **Argentina** Bariloche civic center in winter
5 **Mexico** Decorative pottery sun face

(Back cover: **Peru** Teens in Indepedence Day parade, Lima)

TEACHER'S EDITION

HOLT SPANISH 1B

¡Exprésate!®

Nancy Humbach

Sylvia Madrigal Velasco

Ana Beatriz Chiquito

Stuart Smith

John McMinn

HOLT, RINEHART AND WINSTON

A Harcourt Education Company

Orlando • Austin • New York • San Diego • Toronto • London

Holt Teacher Advisory Panel

As members of the **Holt World Languages Teacher Advisory Panel,** the following teachers made a unique and invaluable contribution to the ***¡Exprésate!*** Spanish program. They generously shared their experience and expertise in a collaborative group setting and helped refine early materials into the program design represented in this book. We wish to thank them for the many hours of work they put into the development of this program and for the many ideas they shared.

¡Muchísimas gracias a todos!

Erick Ekker
Bob Miller Middle School
Henderson, NV

Dulce Goldenberg
Miami Senior High School
Miami, FL

Beckie Gurnish
Ellet High School
Akron, OH

Bill Heller
Perry High School
Perry, NY

MilyBett Llanos
Westwood High School
Austin, TX

Rosanna Perez
Communications Arts
High School
San Antonio, TX

Jo Schuler
Central Bucks High School East
Doylestown, PA

Leticia Schweigert
Science Academy
Mercedes, TX

Claudia Sloan
Lake Park High School
Roselle, IL

Judy Smock
Gilbert High School
Gilbert, AZ

Catriona Stavropoulos
West Springfield High School
Springfield, VA

Nina Wilson
Burnet Middle School
Austin, TX

Janet Wohlers
Weston Middle School
Weston, MA

COVER PHOTOGRAPHY CREDITS

FRONT COVER (from top left to bottom right): ©Royalty Free/CORBIS; John Langford/HRW; ©Frans Lanting/Minden Pictures; ARGENPHOTO S.A./Luis Rosendo Productions/Image Bank Argentina; ©Creatas.

BACK COVER: Don Couch/HRW.

Acknowledgments appear on page R60, which is an extension of the copyright page.

Printed in the United States of America

ISBN 0-03-074358-3

2 3 4 5 6 7 048 07 06 05 04

Authors

Nancy Humbach

Nancy Humbach is Associate Professor and Coordinator of Languages Education at Miami University, Oxford, Ohio. She has authored or co-authored over a dozen textbooks in Spanish. A former Fulbright-Hays Scholar, she has lived and studied in Colombia and Mexico and has traveled and conducted research throughout the Spanish-speaking world. She is a recipient of many honors, including the Florence Steiner Award for Leadership in the Foreign Language Profession and the Nelson Brooks Award for the Teaching of Culture.

Sylvia Madrigal Velasco

Sylvia Madrigal Velasco was born in San Benito, Texas. The youngest of four siblings, she grew up in the Rio Grande Valley, between two cultures and languages. Her lifelong fascination with Spanish has led her to travel in many Spanish-speaking countries. She graduated from Yale University in 1979 and has worked for over 20 years as a textbook editor and author at various publishing companies. She has written bilingual materials, video scripts, workbooks, CD-ROMs, and readers.

Ana Beatriz Chiquito

Professor Ana Beatriz Chiquito is a native of Colombia. She teaches Spanish linguistics and Latin American culture at the University of Bergen, Norway, and conducts research and develops applications for language learning at the Center for Educational Computing Initiatives at the Massachusetts Institute of Technology. She has taught Spanish for more than thirty years and has authored numerous textbooks, CD-ROMs, videos, and on-line materials for college and high school students of Spanish.

Stuart Smith

Stuart Smith began her teaching career at the University of Texas at Austin from where she received her degrees. She has been a professor of foreign languages at Austin Community College, Austin, Texas, for over 20 years and has been writing textbook and teaching materials for almost as long. She has given presentations on language teaching methodology at ACTFL, SWCOLT, and TCCTA.

John McMinn

John McMinn is Professor of Spanish and French at Austin Community College, where he has taught since 1986. After completing his M.A. in Romance Linguistics at the University of Texas at Austin, he also taught Spanish and French at the secondary level and was a Senior Editor of World Languages at Holt, Rinehart and Winston. He is co-author of both Spanish and French textbooks at the college level.

Student Edition

Contributing Writers

Jeff Cole
Tucson, AZ

Jodee Costello
Gunnison, CO

Jabier Elorrieta
The University of Texas at Austin

Karin Fajardo
Englewood, CO

Catherine Gavin
New York City, NY

Pablo Muirhead
Shorewood High School
Shorewood, WI

Gloria Munguía
Austin, TX

Marci Reed
Austin, TX

Mayanne Wright
Austin, TX

Reviewers

Elizabeth Baird
Independence High School
Independence, OH

Johnnie Eng
Alamo Heights High School
San Antonio, TX

Patricia Gander
Berkeley High School
Moncks Corner, SC

Laura Grable
Riverhead Central School District
Riverhead, NY

Mani Hernandez
Presentation High School
San Jose, CA

Yoscelina Hernandez
Socorro High School
El Paso, TX

Jorge Muñoz
St. Stephen's Episcopal School
Austin, TX

Jessica Shrader
Charlotte High School
Punta Gorda, FL

Sharlene Soto
D.C. Everest Jr. and Sr. High Schools
Wausau, WI

Paula Camardella Twomey
Ithaca High School
Ithaca, NY

Nancy Walker de Llanas
George C. Marshall High School
Falls Church, VA

Teacher's Edition

Contributing Writers

Elizabeth Baird
Independence, OH

Valorie E. Brown
START Educational Consulting
Washington, DC

Dana Chicchelly
Florence, MT

Jodee Costello
Gunnison, CO

Ruthie Ford
Johnston HS
Austin, TX

Alisa Glick Trachtenberg
Weston Middle School
Weston, CT

Dianne Harwood
Austin, TX

Bill Heller
Perry HS
Perry, NY

Marci Reed
Austin, TX

Marcia Tugendhat
Austin, TX

Reviewers

Elizabeth Baird
Independence, OH

Luis Carmona
Odessa, TX

Teresa Duffus
Campbell MS
Houston, TX

Beckie Gurnish
Ellet HS
Akron, OH

Bill Heller
Perry High School
Perry, NY

Grace Holmen
Highland Park HS
Dallas, TX

Milybett Llanos
Westwood HS
Austin, TX

Jodi Mahlmann
Stafford HS
Houston, TX

Mary Alice Mora
Franklin High School
El Paso, TX

Josephine Schuler
Central Bucks HS East
Doylestown, PA

Catriona Stavropoulos
West Springfield HS
Fairfax Station, VA

Claudia Sloan
Lake Park High School
Roselle, IL

Judy Smock
Gilbert High School
Gilbert, AZ

Nina Wilson
Burnet Middle School
Austin, TX

Field Test Participants

Tom Burel
West Middle School
Rockford, IL

Liliana Camarena
Gueillen Middle School
El Paso, TX

Mariluz Julio
Clover Junior High School
Clover, SC

Patrice Kahn
Noel Grisham Middle School
Round Rock, TX

Rebekah Lindsey
Campbell Middle School
Daytona Beach, FL

Estela Morel
Corlears Middle School 56
New York, NY

Linda Schell
Landmark Middle School
Jacksonville, FL

Sarah Taylor
Richland Middle School
Richmond, VA

Rebecca Taylor-Norton
Beechwood Middle School
Cleveland, OH

Amanda York
George Washington Carver Academy
Waco, TX

Teacher's Edition

Contenido

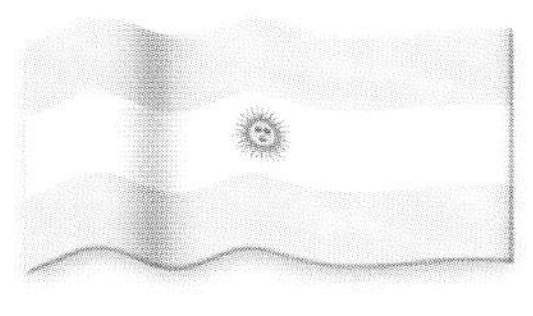

To the Teacher

¡Exprésate!—a new program with real-world photos, on-location video, animated grammar, and solid pedagogy—is an exciting, motivational, and effective Spanish series that will appeal to all types of learners and keep them coming back for more. Based on the "five C's" of the national standards, this new program has an easy-to-use format that allows students to achieve success, and gives teachers a host of teaching tools to make sure all students can focus on each lesson's goals.

Communication

¡Exprésate! engages students right from the start of each lesson and carefully leads them from structured practice to open-ended communication. Unique image-based **Vocabulario** presentations introduce a thematic context and provide a reason and motivation for using the language. Colorful **Gramática** presentations, accompanied by **animated grammar** explanations, help students achieve accuracy in their communication.

Culture

The **Geocultura** feature that precedes each chapter, realia-based readings and activities, and culture notes in each chapter offer high-interest cultural information and a chance to learn about the **products**, **practices** and **perspectives** of the target cultures.

Connections

Links to other subject areas, such as social studies, math, language arts, music, and fine arts are found throughout each chapter of *¡Exprésate!*. Additional opportunities for connections are found at point of use in the *Teacher's Edition*.

Comparisons

To enable students to acquire a broader and a deeper understanding of language and culture *¡Exprésate!* offers them multiple opportunities to compare the new language and culture with their own.

Communities

The ultimate goal of learning to communicate in a new language should be the ability to function in an increasingly diverse community and an increasingly demanding world market. *¡Exprésate!* is built on the theory that the global community has its roots in the second language classroom. If learning language and culture is enjoyable and accessible, all students will become productive members of their community.

For any language program to be successful, the needs of teachers and students have to be the primary consideration. From suggestions for differentiated instruction to the latest in technology products, *¡Exprésate!* provides an abundance of teacher support and learning tools to help ensure success for all teachers and students.

Contenido en breve

Capítulo puente

Capítulo 6 ¡A comer!

Geocultura

En video

Geocultura	GeoVisión
Vocabulario 1 y 2	ExpresaVisión
Gramática 1 y 2	GramaVisión
Cultura	VideoCultura
Video Novela	¿Quién será?
	Variedades

Visit Holt Online
go.hrw.com
KEYWORD: EXP1B CH6
Online Edition

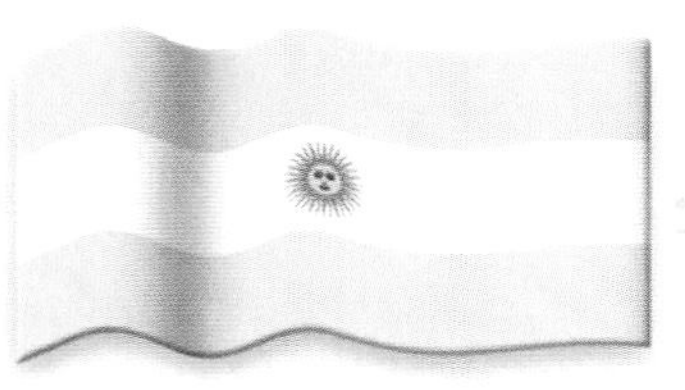

Argentina

Capítulo 7 Cuerpo sano, mente sana 84

Geocultura

En video

Geocultura	**GeoVisión**
Vocabulario 1 y 2	**ExpresaVisión**
Gramática 1 y 2	**GramaVisión**
Cultura	**VideoCultura**
Video Novela	**¿Quién será?**
	Variedades

Visit Holt Online

go.hrw.com

KEYWORD: EXP1B CH7

Online Edition

Capítulo 8 Vamos de compras 130

En video

Geocultura	GeoVisión
Vocabulario 1 y 2	ExpresaVisión
Gramática 1 y 2	GramaVisión
Cultura	VideoCultura
Video Novela	¿Quién será?
	Variedades

Visit Holt Online
go.hrw.com
KEYWORD: EXP1B CH8
Online Edition

La República Dominicana

Capítulo 9 ¡Festejemos! 176

Geocultura

En video

Geocultura	GeoVisión
Vocabulario 1 y 2	ExpresaVisión
Gramática 1 y 2	GramaVisión
Cultura	VideoCultura
Video Novela	¿Quién será?
	Variedades

Visit Holt Online

go.hrw.com

KEYWORD: EXP1B CH9

Online Edition

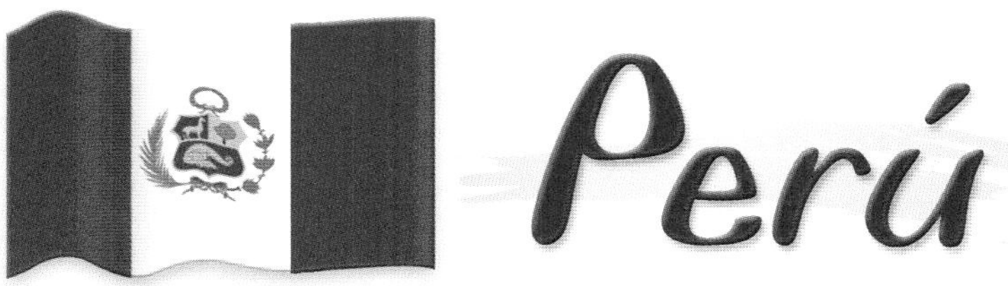

Capítulo 10 ¡A viajar! 222

En video

Geocultura	GeoVisión
Vocabulario 1 y 2	ExpresaVisión
Gramática 1 y 2	GramaVisión
Cultura	VideoCultura
Video Novela	¿Quién será?
	Variedades

Visit Holt Online
go.hrw.com
KEYWORD: EXP1B CH10
Online Edition

Base your pacing on your schedule...

If you are teaching on a traditional schedule, base your instruction on the following plan.

Traditional Schedule

Days of Instruction: 180		
Capítulo puente	10 days of instruction	10 days
Geocultura	4 days of instruction per Geocultura x 5 Geoculturas	20 days
Chapter	30 days per chapter (including assessment) x 5	150 days
Total days of instruction using ¡Exprésate!:		**180 days**

Block Schedule

Blocks of instruction: 90		
Capítulo puente	5 blocks of instruction	5 blocks
Geocultura	3 blocks of instruction per Geocultura x 5 Geoculturas	15 blocks
Chapter	14 blocks per chapter (including assessment) x 5	70 blocks
Total blocks of instruction using ¡Exprésate!:		**90 blocks**

If you are teaching on a block schedule, spend three blocks on each **Geocultura** and fourteen blocks on each chapter.

...and plan your lessons to fit.

Pacing Tips

In this chapter, there is more review in **Gramática 2,** so you might spend more time on the concepts presented in **Gramática 1.** For complete lesson plan suggestions, see pages 221G–221N.

Suggested pacing:	Traditional Schedule	Block Schedule
Vocabulario 1/Gramática 1	10 1/2 days	5 1/3 blocks
Cultura	1 day	1/2 block
Vocabulario 2/Gramática 2	11 1/4 days	5 1/3 blocks
Conexiones culturales	1 day	1/2 block
Novela	3/4 day	1/3 block
Leamos y escribamos	1 1/2 days	1/2 block
Repaso	2 days	1 block
Chapter Test	1 day	1/2 block
Integración	1 day	1/2 block

Planning

One-Stop Planner® CD-ROM

Use the One-Stop Planner to make *¡Exprésate!* work for you...

- **Calendar planning tool** for both short-term and long-term planning
- **PDF format lesson plans** with links to **all** teaching resources, including video and audio
- **Examview Pro® Test Generator**
- **Clip art Library**

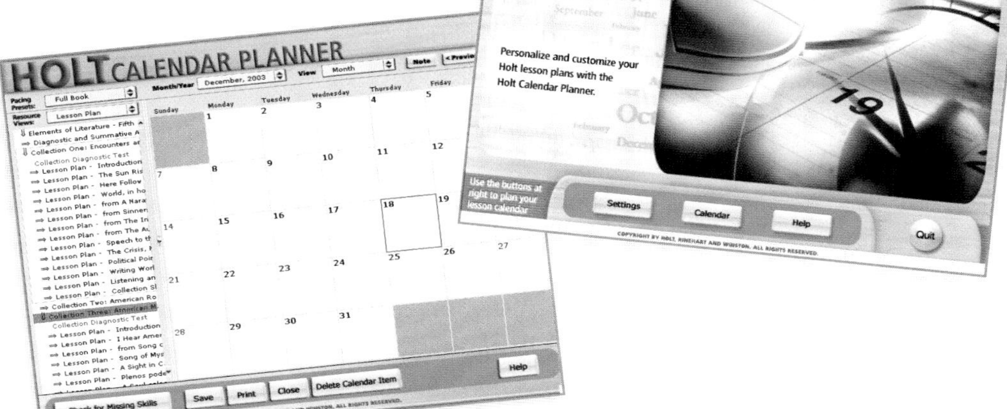

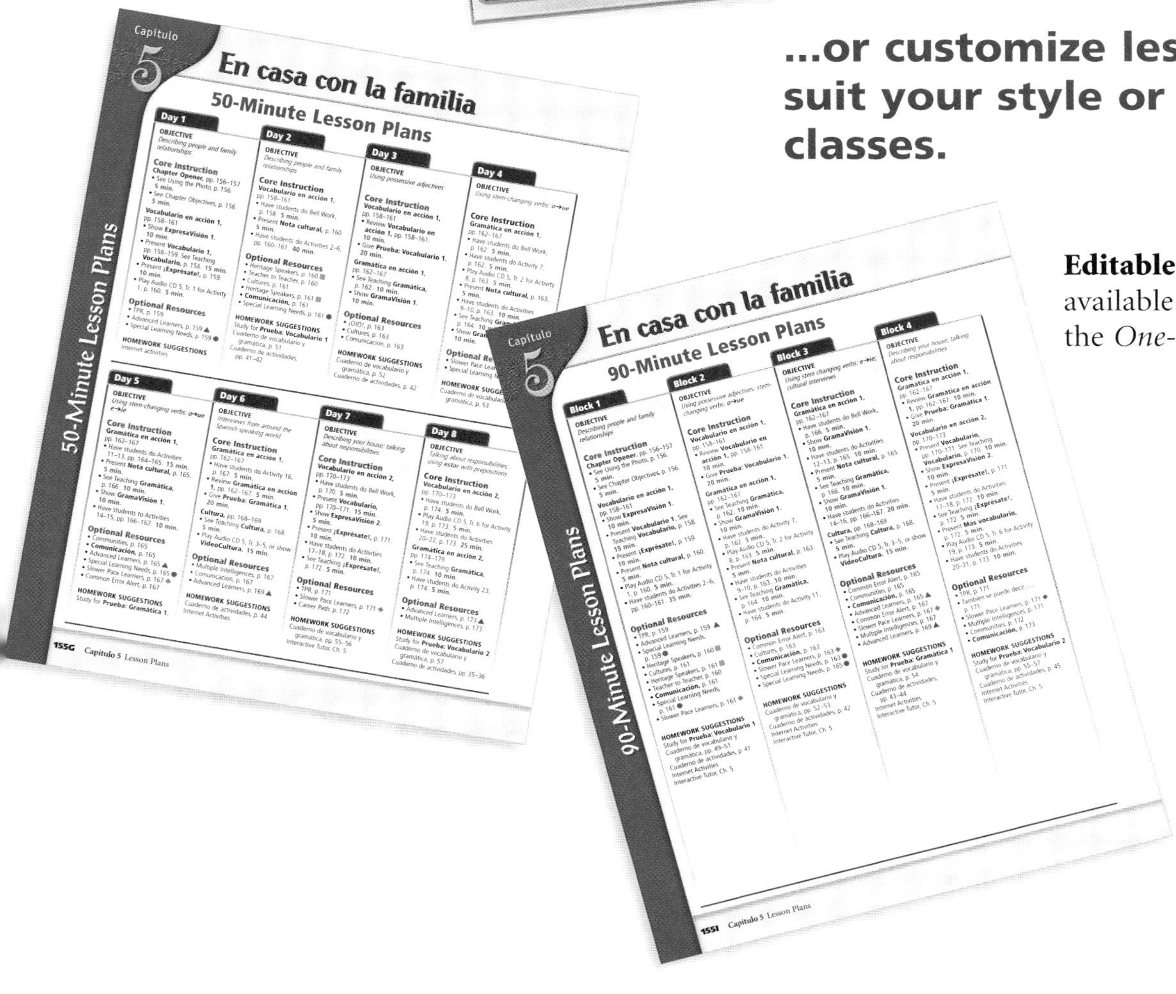

...or customize lesson plans to suit your style or individual classes.

Editable lesson plans are available for all chapters on the *One-Stop Planner*.

Articulation Across Levels

From Middle School through Advanced Placement

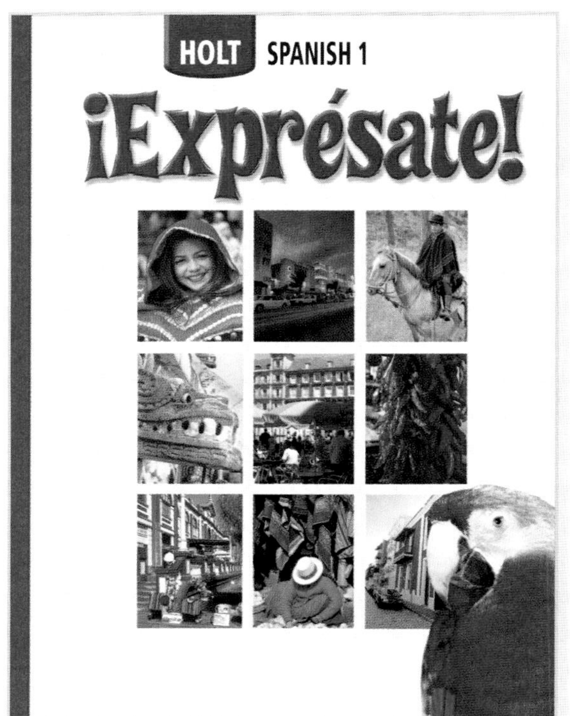

Level 1

Begin the learning experience with **Level 1** ...

...or

set a slower pace for middle school with **Level 1A** and **Level 1B**

Level 1A

Level 1B

Level 2 thoroughly reviews the basics and continues to build a solid foundation for communication.

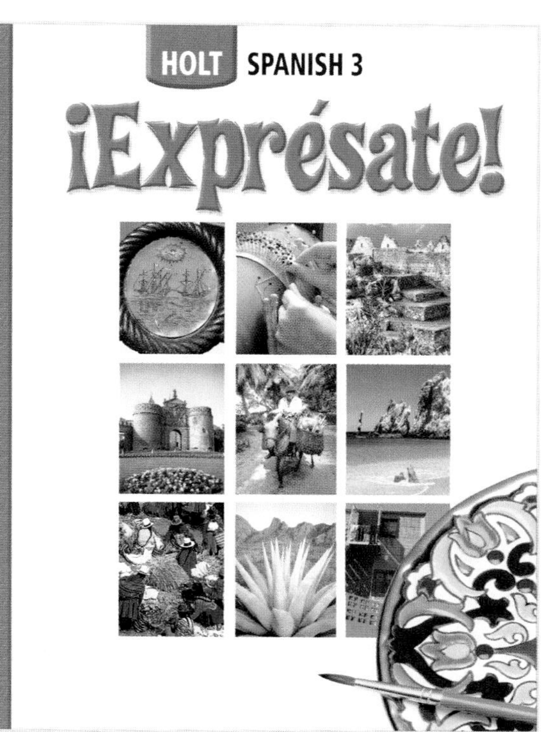

Level 3 begins with a review of the major points covered in Level 2, then builds student skills to the Intermediate Proficiency level.

NUEVAS VISTAS
Curso de introducción
(Level 4)

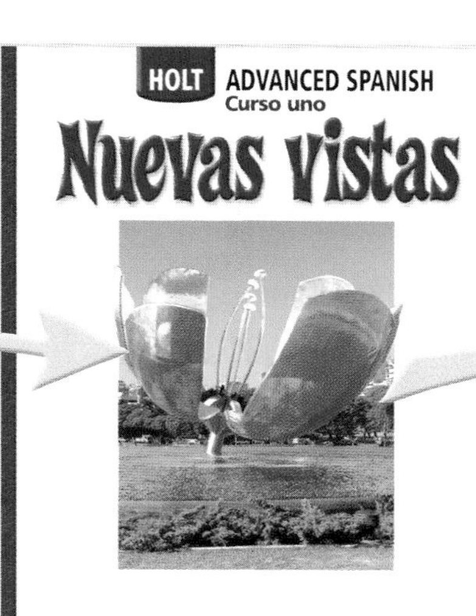

NUEVAS VISTAS
Curso uno
(Level 5)

NUEVAS VISTAS
Curso dos
(Level 6)

Nuevas Vistas will prepare your students for the AP* exams. It is especially effective in preparing Heritage Speakers for the challenges they will face in the workplace and as members of the global Spanish-speaking community.

*Advanced Placement Program and AP are registered trademarks of the College Entrance Examination Board, which was not involved in the production of, and does not endorse, this product.

Scope and Sequence

¡Exprésate! Level 1A

	Vocabulary	Functions	Grammar	Culture	Strategies
Capítulo 1 ¡Empecemos! pp. 4–37					
España **La geografía** **Las celebraciones** **La comida** **La arquitectura** **El arte**	• Greetings and Goodbyes	• Asking someone's name • Asking how some-one is • Introducing someone • Saying where you and others are from	• Subjects and verbs in sentences • Subject pronouns	• Diminutives and nicknames • How students address teachers • **Comparaciones:** Greetings and goodbyes • **Comunidad:** What's in a name?	• **Video Strategy:** Making connections • **Reading Strategy:** Recognizing cognates • **Writing Strategy:** Making lists
	• Numbers 0–31 • Telling time • Days of the week and months of the year • Alphabet	• Giving phone numbers • Giving the time, the date, and the day • Spelling words and giving e-mail addresses	• Present tense of the verb **ser** • Punctuation marks and written accents	FINE ART • ***La persistencia de la memoria,*** Salvador Dalí	
Review/Re-Entry	• **Integración,** pp. 40–41				
Capítulo 2 A conocernos pp. 46–83					
Puerto Rico **La geografía** **La comida** **El arte** **Las celebraciones** **La arquitectura**	• Describing friends • Numbers 32–100	• Describing people • Asking someone's age and birthday	• **Ser** with adjectives • Gender and adjective agreement • Question formation	• Ways to describe people • Legal driving and voting age • **Comparaciones:** Describing yourself and your best friend • **Comunidad:** Teaching what we know	• **Video Strategy:** Drawing conclusions • **Reading Strategy:** Making inferences • **Writing Strategy:** Cluster diagrams
	• Likes and dislikes	• Talking about what you and others like • Describing things	• Nouns and definite articles • The verb **gustar, ¿por qué?,** and **porque** • The preposition **de**	• Puerto Rican musicians FINE ART • ***Día lluvioso en El Viejo San Juan,*** Orlando Santiago Correa	
Review/Re-Entry	• **ser** • **Integración,** pp. 86–87				

Capítulo 3 ¿Qué te gusta hacer? pp. 92–129

Texas
La geografía
La arquitectura
El arte
La comida
Las celebraciones

Vocabulary	Functions	Grammar	Culture	Strategies
• Sports and leisure activities	• Talking about what you and others like to do • Talking about what you want to do	• **Gustar** with infinitives • Pronouns after prepositions • Present tense of **querer** with infinitives 	• Participating team in sports in Latin America • Introducing your friends to your parents • **Comparaciones:** What you and your friends like to do during weekends • **Comunidad:** What's the weather?	• **Video Strategy:** Understanding subtext • **Reading Strategy:** Making predictions • **Writing Strategy:** Arranging ideas chronologically
• Weekend activities	• Talking about every-day activities • Saying how often you do things	• Present tense of regular **-ar** verbs • Present tense of **ir** and **jugar** • Weather expressions	• Who pays when going out with friends  FINE ART • ***La feria en Reynosa,*** Carmen Lomas Garza	

Review/Re-Entry • Subject pronouns • **Integración,** pp. 132–133

Capítulo 4 La vida escolar pp. 138–175

Costa Rica
La geografía
Las celebraciones
El arte
La comida
Las criaturas

Vocabulary	Functions	Grammar	Culture	Strategies
• School supplies and items needed for school • Classes	• Saying what you have and what you need • Talking about classes	• Indefinite articles; **¿cuánto?, mucho,** and **poco** • Present tense of **tener** and **tener** idioms • **Venir** and **a** + time	• Beginning of the school year • Elective classes and tracking • **Comparaciones:** A typical day at school • **Comunidad:** ¿Cómo se dice . . . en español?	• **Video Strategy:** Comparing and contrasting • **Reading Strategy:** Who, what, where, when, and why questions • **Writing Strategy:** Using drawings
• School events • Places at school 	• Talking about plans • Inviting others to do something	• **Ir** + **a** + infinitives • Present tense of **-er** and **-ir** verbs • Tag questions • **-er/-ir** verbs with irregular **yo** forms	• Passing and failing courses • School schedules and sessions  FINE ART • ***Domingueando,*** Tomás Povedano	

Review/Re-Entry • **los** + days of the week • **Integración,** pp. 178–179

Capítulo 5 En casa con la familia pp. 184–221

Chile
La geografía
La arquitectura
La comida
Las celebraciones
Las bellas artes

Vocabulary	Functions	Grammar	Culture	Strategies
• Family members • Describing people (physical and personality)	• Describing people and family relationships	• Possessive adjectives • Stem-changing verbs **o → ue** • Stem-changing verbs **e → ie**	• Hispanic surnames • Extended family • **Comparaciones:** Describing family • **Comunidad:** Las escuelas del mundo	• **Video Strategy:** Understanding humor • **Reading Strategy:** Scanning • **Writing Strategy:** Graphic organizers
• Rooms in the house • Furniture and accessories • Chores • Where you live	• Talking about where you and others live • Talking about your responsibilities	• **Estar** with prepositions • Negation with **nunca, tampoco, nadie,** and **nada** • **Tocar** and **parecer**	• Climate and houses  FINE ART • ***Esperando a los pescadores,*** Isidoro Molleda	

Review/Re-Entry • **querer** and **tener** • Negation • **Integración,** pp. 224–225

Scope and Sequence

¡Exprésate! Level 1B

REPASO

Vocabulary	Functions	Grammar
Capítulo puente ¡Exprésate! pp. xxii–33		
• Introducing and meeting others • Talking about likes and dislikes • Talking about what you and others like to do • Talking about plans • Talking about classes and school supplies • Talking about your home and family members	• To ask for personal information and to respond • To ask for descriptions and to respond • To ask what someone likes or wants to do and to respond • To talk about your plans • To talk about school and classes and to respond • To ask about home and family and to respond	• The verbs **ser** and **estar** • The verbs **gustar** and **tener** • **querer, ir a** + infinitive, and pronouns • Regular **-ar** verbs and possessive adjectives • The present tense of **-er** and **-ir** verbs • Stem-changing verbs

México

La geografía
El arte
La arquitectura
Las celebraciones
La comida

Vocabulary	Functions	Grammar	Culture	Strategies
Capítulo 6 ¡A comer! pp. 38–75				
• Lunch foods • Foods you might order in a restaurant • Condiments • Describing food • Table setting	• Commenting on food • Making polite requests	• **Ser** and **estar** • **Pedir** and **servir** • **Preferir, poder,** and **probar**	• Mexican food; **atole** • Corn as a staple food • **Comparaciones:** Favorite dishes • **Comunidad:** ¡Tacos, enchiladas y más!	• **Video Strategy:** Recognizing a make-believe situation • **Reading Strategy:** Considering genre • **Writing Strategy:** Arranging your ideas in chronological order
• Breakfast and dinner foods	• Talking about meals • Offering help • Giving instructions 	• Direct objects and direct object pronouns • Affirmative informal commands • Affirmative informal commands with pronouns	• Main meal of the day • Snacks  FINE ART • ***The Market of Cuernavaca in the Age of the Spanish Conquest,*** Diego Rivera	
Review/Re-Entry	• Stem-changing verbs	• Definition of pronouns; subject pronouns	• **Integración,** pp. 78–79	

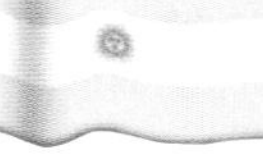

Argentina

La geografía
La arquitectura
El arte
Las celebraciones
La comida

Vocabulary	Functions	Grammar	Culture	Strategies
Capítulo 7 Cuerpo sano, mente sana pp. 84–121				
• Daily routine • Personal items • Parts of the body	• Talking about your daily routine • Talking about staying fit and healthy	• Verbs with reflexive pronouns • Using infinitives • Stem-changing verbs	• Argentina's ski resorts • **Comparaciones:** Keeping in shape • **Comunidad:** Spanish in health care careers	• **Video Strategy:** Understanding a character's motives • **Reading Strategy:** Using background knowledge
• Telling how you feel • More parts of the body • Healthful advice	• Talking about how you feel • Giving advice 	• **Estar, sentirse,** and **tener** • Negative informal commands • Object pronouns and informal commands	• Argentine food • **Mate** FINE ART • ***Un alto en el campo,*** Prilidiano Pueyrredón	• **Writing Strategy:** Graphic organizers
Review/Re-Entry	• **querer, jugar, poder,** and **pedir**	• Rules for written accents	• **Integración,** pp. 124–125	

Florida

La geografía
La comida
El arte
La arquitectura
Las celebraciones

Capítulo 8 Vamos de compras pp. 130–167

Vocabulary	Functions	Grammar	Culture	Strategies
• Clothing • Colors	• Asking for and giving opinions • Asking for and offering help in a store	• The verb **costar** • Numbers to 1 million • Demonstrative adjectives and comparisons • The verb **quedar**	• Clothing sizes • **Guayaberas** • **Comparaciones:** Shopping • **Comunidad:** Import stores	• **Video Strategy:** Recognizing different points of view • **Reading Strategy:** Visualizing what you read • **Writing Strategy:** Creating sharp, clear contrasts
• Stores and the things you buy there • Expressions of time 	• Saying where you went and what you did • Talking on the phone	• Preterite of **-ar** verbs • Preterite of **ir** • Preterite of **-ar** verbs with reflexive pronouns	• Spanish speakers' buying power in the USA • Open-air markets and bargaining  FINE ART • ***Mercado caribeño,*** Dra. Dominica Alcántara	
Review/Re-Entry	• **Integración,** pp. 170–171			

República Dominicana

La geografía
La arquitectura
El arte
Las celebraciones
La comida

Capítulo 9 ¡Festejemos! pp. 176–213

Vocabulary	Functions	Grammar	Culture	Strategies
• Holidays • Holiday activities	• Talking about your plans • Talking about past holidays	• Preterite of **-er** and **-ir** verbs • **Pensar que** and **pensar** with infinitives	• Dominican **carnaval** • **Pasteles en hoja** • **Comparaciones:** Holidays and celebrations • **Comunidad:** ¿Cómo celebramos?	• **Video Strategy:** Predicting • **Reading Strategy:** Using context and grammatical clues • **Writing Strategy:** Using descriptive details
• Party activities • Getting ready for a party 	• Preparing for a party • Greetings, introducing others, and saying goodbye	• Direct object pronouns • **Conocer** and personal **a** • Present progressive	• Special birthdays: **quinceañeras** • Dancing at parties  FINE ART • ***Merengue,*** Jaime Colson	
Review/Re-Entry	• Greetings	• **Integración,** pp. 216–217		

Perú

La geografía
La arquitectura
El arte
Las celebraciones
La comida

Capítulo 10 ¡A viajar! pp. 222–259

Vocabulary	Functions	Grammar	Culture	Strategies
• Airport and travel terms	• Asking for and giving information • Reminding and reassuring	• Review of the preterite • Preterite of **-car, -gar,** and **-zar** verbs • Preterite of **hacer**	• Uros islands • Quinoa • **Comparaciones:** Traveling • **Comunidad:** Spanish: Your World Passport	• **Video Strategy:** Summarizing • **Reading Strategy:** Reading with a purpose • **Writing Strategy:** Using transitional phrases
• Vacation activities • Transportation • Reacting to news 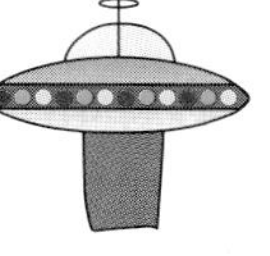	• Talking about a trip • Expressing hopes and wishes 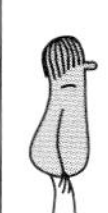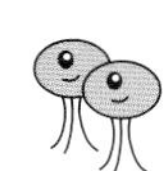	• Informal commands of verbs ending in **-ger, -gir, -guir, -car, -gar, -zar** and of irregular verbs • Review of direct object pronouns • Review of verbs with infinitives	• Traveling by train in Peru • Peru's Manu rainforest  FINE ART • ***La vendedora de Anticuchos,*** Juan de la Cruz Machicado	
Review/Re-Entry	• Preterite of **ir**	• Informal affirmative and negative commands	• **Integración,** pp. 262–263	

Scope and Sequence

¡Exprésate! Level 2

Capítulo 1 Familiares y amigos pp. 4–39

Ciudad de México

La geografía
El arte
Las celebraciones
La historia
La arqueología

Vocabulary	Functions	Grammar	Culture	Strategies
• Describing friends and family members	• Asking about people, routines, and activities • Expressing likes and dislikes	• Nouns, adjectives, and **gustar** • Present tense of regular and stem-changing verbs • Present tense of **e → i** stem-changing verbs and irregular verbs • Reflexive pronouns	• Xochimilco gardens • Mexico's Independence Day, September 16 • **Comparaciones:** Studying world languages • **Comunidad y oficio:** World languages at school and work	• **Video Strategy:** Looking for clues • **Reading Strategy:** Looking for key words • **Writing Strategy:** Using a prewriting list
• Celebrations and preparations • Parts of the house • Household chores • Family members • Travel plans and activities	• Offering help and talking about chores • Talking about plans and places	• Idioms with **tener** • Verbs followed by infinitives • Present progressive • **Ir a** with infinitives • Direct object pronouns • Affirmative and negative informal commands	• Shopping in Mexico City • Aztec ruins in Mexico City FINE ART • ***Mis sobrinas,*** María Izquierdo	

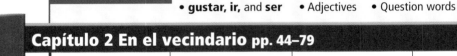

Review/Re-Entry
• Family and home • **gustar, ir,** and **ser** • Nouns • Adjectives • Present tense • Question words • Informal commands • **Integración,** pp. 38–39

Capítulo 2 En el vecindario pp. 44–79

Cuzco

La geografía
Las celebraciones
La arqueología
El arte y la artesanía
La arquitectura

Vocabulary	Functions	Grammar	Culture	Strategies
• Professions • Work-related verbs	• Talking about what people do for a living • Introducing people	• Indirect objects and indirect object pronouns • **Dar** • **Decir** • **Saber** and **conocer** • Uses of **ser**	• Terrace farming in Peru • Llamas • **Comparaciones:** Preparing for a profession • **Comunidad y oficio:** Bilingualism in the workplace	• **Video Strategy:** Resolving problems • **Reading Strategy:** Looking for cognates • **Writing Strategy:** Creating a clear setting
• Parts of the house • Furniture • Chores	• Describing a house • Saying what needs to be done and complaining	• Prepositions • **Ser** and **estar** • Expressions followed by infinitives • Preterite of regular verbs, **hacer,** and **ir**	• Potatoes and **el chuño**  FINE ART • ***La caserita*** Gladys Martínez Nosiglia	

Review/Re-Entry
• Personal **a** • Uses of **ser** • Adjectives of nationality • **tocar** • Preterite of regular verbs, **hacer,** and **ir** • **Integración,** pp. 78–79

Capítulo 3 Pueblos y ciudades pp. 84–119

Santo Domingo

La geografía
La comida
Las artes
La naturaleza
La historia

Vocabulary	Functions	Grammar	Culture	Strategies
• Names of stores • Places around town	• Asking for information • Asking where someone went and what he or she did	• Impersonal **se** and passive **se** • Preterite of **-car, -gar,** and **-zar** verbs • Preterite of **conocer** • Irregular verbs in the preterite: **andar, tener, venir, dar, ver**	• **Bachata** music • **Comparaciones:** Plazas and other gathering places • **Comunidad y oficio:** Businesses and services	• **Video Strategy:** Gathering information • **Reading Strategy:** Focusing on ideas • **Writing Strategy:** Using dialog
• Places in the city • Ordinal numbers	• Asking for and giving directions • Asking for clarification	• Formal commands • Irregular formal commands • Commands with pronouns • Object and reflexive pronouns with commands	• Growth of Santo Domingo • Author Julia Álvarez • **Merengue**  FINE ART • ***Merengue en el pueblo,*** José Morillo	

Review/Re-Entry

- **haber**
- Informal commands
- Present tense of **conocer**
- **hay que, deber,** and **tener que**
- Spelling-change verbs in the preterite
- Preterite tense of **hacer** and **ir**
- **Integración,** pp. 118–119

Capítulo 4 ¡Mantente en forma! pp. 124–159

Miami

La geografía
Las bellas artes
Las celebraciones
La vida latina
Los deportes

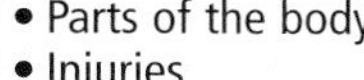

Vocabulary	Functions	Grammar	Culture	Strategies
• Competitions • Emotional reactions	• Talking about how something turned out • Talking about reacting to events	• Irregular preterites **ponerse, decir, ser** and **estar** • Preterite of stem-changing **-ir** verbs	• **Calle Ocho** festival • **Jai-alai** • **Comparaciones:** School/club sports • **Comunidad y oficio:** Spanish in medical fields	• **Video Strategy:** Asking questions • **Reading Strategy:** Using graphic organizers • **Writing Strategy:** Providing specific details
• Parts of the body • Injuries • Illnesses • Treatments and advice	• Talking about getting hurt • Asking for and giving advice	• Verbs with reflexive pronouns and direct objects • Past participles used as adjectives • Use of articles with parts of the body • Preterite of **caerse**	• Latin American Art • Tourism in Miami FINE ART • ***La zumba, el mamey y otras frutas tropicales,*** Tere Pastoriza	

Review/Re-Entry

- Reflexive pronouns
- Noun and adjective agreement
- Preterite of **-ar** and **-er** verbs and **dar**
- **Integración,** pp. 158–159

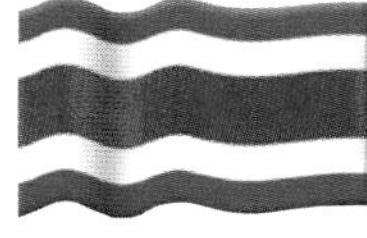

Capítulo 5 Día a día pp. 164–199

San José

La geografía
Los museos
Los parques
Los festivales
Las bellas artes

Vocabulary	Functions	Grammar	Culture	Strategies
• Routine activities • Getting ready	• Telling someone to hurry • Reminding someone to do something	• Preterite of **poder** and **traer** • More verbs with reflexive pronouns • Reflexive and direct object pronouns • Possessive pronouns	• African heritage • **quetzal** bird • **Comparaciones:** Being on time • **Comunidad y oficio:** Marketing to Spanish speakers	• **Video Strategy:** Understanding relationships • **Reading Strategy:** Making predictions • **Writing Strategy:** Transitional phrases
• Pastimes and interests • Time expressions	• Expressing interest and disinterest • Talking about how long something has been going on	• Negative expressions • **Hace** with time expressions • **Pero** and **sino**	• Costa Rican oxcarts • Music in San José FINE ART • ***Casa de adobes,*** Ezequiel Jiménez	

Review/Re-Entry

- Preterite of **decir**
- Possessive adjectives
- Reflexive pronouns
- **no** in negative expressions
- **Integración,** pp. 198–199

Capítulo 6 Recuerdos pp. 204–239

Segovia
La geografía
La historia
La arquitectura
Más geografía
La moneda

Vocabulary	Functions	Grammar	Culture	Strategies
• Childhood activities • Toys and games	• Talking about what you used to like and dislike • Saying what you used to do and what you wanted to be	• Imperfect tense • Imperfect of **ir** and **ver** • Verbs with reciprocal actions	• Segovia's **Alcázar** • Winter sports in the Guadarrama Mountains • Outdoor cafes • **Comparaciones:** Childhood likes and dislikes • **Comunidad y oficio:** Researching the past	**Video Strategy:** Comparing attitudes **Reading Strategy:** Using context **Writing Strategy:** Avoiding repetition
• Adjectives to describe people • Life events	• Describing people and things in the past • Talking about an emotional reaction	• Imperfect of **ser** and **haber** • Preterite with mental and emotional states • Preterite of **creer, construir, leer, and oír** • **caerle a uno**	• Roman aqueduct FINE ART • ***Clotilde y Elena en las rocas, Jávea,*** Joaquín Sorolla Y Bastida	

Review/Re-Entry
- **hay**
- Preterite of **estar** and **ponerse**
- Present of **oír**
- **Integración,** pp. 238–239

Capítulo 7 ¡Buen provecho! pp. 244–279

San Juan
La geografía
La arquitectura
La vida cultural
La vida contemporánea
La historia

Vocabulary	Functions	Grammar	Culture	Strategies
• Menu words • Restaurant terms • Foods • Adjectives to describe food	• Ordering in a restaurant • Talking about how food tastes	• Double object pronouns • Commands with double object pronouns • Reflexive pronouns with a direct object • Adverbs	• **Yuca** and **casabe** • Puerto Rican cooking • **Comparaciones:** Festivals and holidays • **Comunidad y oficio:** Spanish in the food industry	**Video Strategy:** Understanding subtext **Reading Strategy:** Looking for organizational clues **Writing Strategy:** Using adjectives that focus on the senses
• Food terms • Measurements • More adjectives to describe food	• Talking about your diet • Describing the preparation of food	• More uses of the imperfect • Past participles used as adjectives	• **El gofio,** a Puerto Rican sweet  FINE ART • ***El pan nuestro,*** Ramón Frade	

Review/Re-Entry
- Direct and indirect object pronouns
- Pronouns with affirmative and negative commands
- Using the imperfect in descriptions
- Adjective agreement
- **Integración,** pp. 278–279

Capítulo 8 Tiendas y puestos pp. 284–319

Santiago
La geografía
La historia
La arquitectura
Los barrios
Más geografía

Vocabulary	Functions	Grammar	Culture	Strategies
• Buying and selling terms • Adjectives to describe clothing	• Talking about trying on clothes and how they fit • Talking about shopping for clothes	• Imperfect and preterite • Using the imperfect of **ir a** + infinitive • Comparatives and superlatives	• Europeans in Chile • **Arpilleras** • **Comparaciones:** Dressing up to go out • **Comunidad y oficio:** Spanish in the fashion world	**Video Strategy:** Following the plot **Reading Strategy:** Using background knowledge **Writing Strategy:** Comparing and contrasting
• Handicrafts • Jewelry • Materials	• Bargaining in a market • Stating preferences	• **Por** and **para** • Demonstrative adjectives **ese** and **aquel** • Adverbs of place • Adjectives as nouns	• Chilean handicrafts • Foods from Chile FINE ART • ***El mercado,*** Ana Cortés	

Review/Re-Entry
- Comparison with adjectives
- Irregular comparatives
- **este** and **ese**
- **Integración,** pp. 318–319

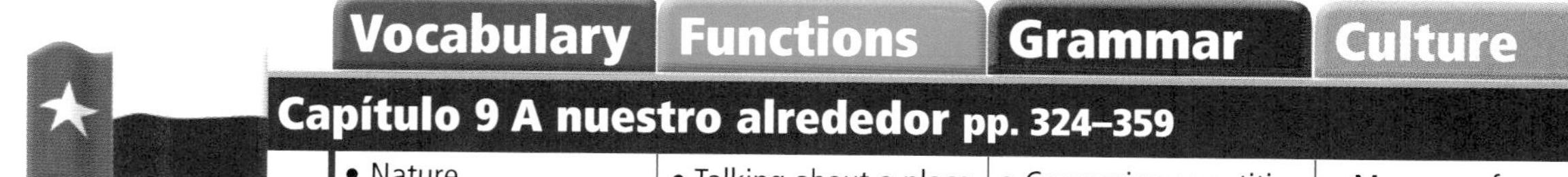

	Vocabulary	Functions	Grammar	Culture	Strategies
Capítulo 9 A nuestro alrededor pp. 324–359					
 **El Paso** **La geografía** **El arte** **La arquitectura** **Las celebraciones** **La economía**	• Nature • Animals and plants • Weather and natural events	• Talking about a place and its climate • Telling a story	• Comparing quantities • Adjectives as nouns • Preterite and imperfect to begin a story • Preterite and imperfect to continue and end a story	• Museum of Archaeology in El Paso • Ysleta and Spanish missions • **Comparaciones:** How climate and geography affect a region • **Comunidad y oficio:** Spanish in the sciences	**Video Strategy:** Making deductions **Reading Strategy:** Taking notes **Writing Strategy:** Establishing the tone and mood
	• Camping terms • Outdoor activities	• Talking about what you and others will do • Wondering out loud	• Subjunctive for hopes and wishes • Subjunctive of stem-changing **-ir** and irregular verbs • Future tense	• Conserving water in El Paso • Hueco Tanks  FINE ART • ***El Paso antes de su fundación,*** José Cisneros	
Review/Re-Entry	• **tanto** • Infinitives after **querer** and **poder**	• Weather expressions • **Integración,** pp. 358–359			
Capítulo 10 De vacaciones pp. 364–399					
 **Buenos Aires** **La geografía** **Gente famosa** **Las costumbres** **Las compras** **La música**	• Travel words • Methods of payment	• Asking for and making recommendations • Asking for and giving information	• Present perfect • Irregular past participles • Subjunctive for giving advice and opinions • Subjunctive of **-car, -gar, -zar, -ger,** and **-guir** verbs	• Mar del Plata and Bariloche in Argentina • Vacations in the Spanish-speaking world • **Comparaciones:** Popular tourist attractions • **Comunidad y oficio:** Spanish and tourism	**Video Strategy:** Putting the story together **Reading Strategy:** Making inferences **Writing Strategy:** Using conjunctions and transitional phrases
	• Places to visit • Things to do • Writing a letter or e-mail	• Talking about where you went and what you did • Talking about the latest news	• Preterite and imperfect • Present progressive and future • Subjunctive	• Eva Perón • Origins of the **tango**  FINE ART • ***Libertad,*** Marilyn Itrat	
Review/Re-Entry	• Past participles • Subjunctive	• Present progressive and future • **Integración,** pp. 398–399			

Scope and Sequence

¡Exprésate! Spanish Level 3

Castilla-La Mancha

La geografía
La historia
El arte

Vocabulary	Functions	Grammar	Culture	Strategies
Capítulo 1 ¡Adiós al verano! pp. 6–47				
• Vacation activities and destinations • Weather	• Talking about the past • Saying what you liked and used to do	• Preterite and imperfect • **Ser** and **estar** • Subjunctive mood	• Culture and folklore of Castilla-La Mancha • The town of Cuenca • **Mazapán** and **queso manchego** • **Comparaciones:** Summer trips • **Comunidad y oficio:** Spanish in the tourism industry	• **Video Strategy:** Analyzing the opening • **Reading Strategy:** Determining the point of view • **Writing Strategy:** Using point of view in a story
• Activities • Advice	• Asking for and giving advice • Asking about the future	• Pronouns • Comparisons, demonstrative adjectives, and demonstrative pronouns • Negative words and time constructions	• How Castilla-La Mancha was named • Languages in Spain FINE ART • ***Torero y toro,*** Óscar Domínguez	
Review/Re-Entry	• Preterite and imperfect • Pronouns	• **Ser** and **estar** • Reciprocal actions	• Past participles • Negative words	• Subjunctive mood • **Integración,** pp. 46–47
Capítulo 2 ¡A pasarlo bien! pp. 48–89				
• Pastimes • Sports	• Expressing interest and displeasure • Inviting someone to do something and responding	• Imperfect • **Ir a** + infinitive in the imperfect • **Nosotros** commands	• Hiking in Spain • **El jai-alai** • **Comparaciones:** Friendships • **Comunidad y oficio:** Broadcasting in Spanish in the U. S.	• **Video Strategy:** Looking for personality traits • **Reading Strategy:** Looking for the main idea • **Writing Strategy:** Writing an outline
• Friendships and relationships • Adjectives to describe friends	• Describing the ideal friend • Expressing happiness and unhappiness	• Object pronouns • Subjunctive with the unknown or nonexistent • Subjunctive with expressions of feelings	• **La Ruta de Don Quijote** FINE ART • ***Feria de Santiponce,*** Manuel Rodríguez de Guzmán	
Review/Re-Entry	• Imperfect • Subjunctive **nosotros** forms of **-zar, -gar, -car** verbs • Verbs used with indirect object pronouns	• **Ir a** + infinitive in the imperfect • Subjunctive endings • Object pronouns		• **Integración,** pp. 88–89

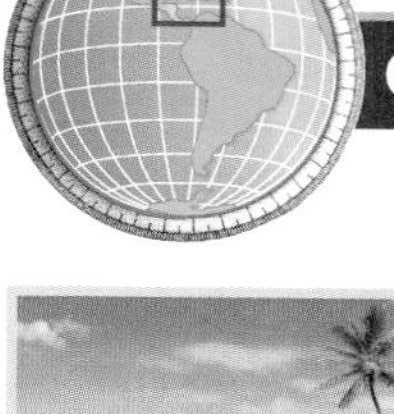

El Caribe
La geografía
La historia
El arte

Capítulo 3 Todo tiene solución pp. 96–137

Vocabulary	Functions	Grammar	Culture	Strategies
• Attitudes and opinions • School courses	• Complaining • Expressing an opinion and disagreeing	• Verb + infinitive • Subjunctive with will or wish • Subjunctive with negation or denial	• Study of English and private schools in Puerto Rico • Schools in Cuba • **Comparaciones:** Family conflicts • **Comunidad y oficio:** Studying abroad	• **Video Strategy:** Making deductions • **Reading Strategy:** Paraphrasing • **Writing Strategy:** Brainstorming
• Relationship problems and solutions	• Making suggestions • Apologizing	• Future tense • Conditional	• **Telenovelas** in Latin America  FINE ART • ***Cometas y habitantes,*** José Morillo	

Review/Re-Entry
- Verb + infinitive
- Future tense
- Subjunctive with will or wish
- Irregular stems in the future
- **Saber** and **haber** in the subjunctive
- **Integración,** pp. 136–137

Capítulo 4 Entre familia pp. 138–179

Vocabulary	Functions	Grammar	Culture	Strategies
• Family members and relationships • Family events	• Asking about and responding to the latest news • Reacting to news	• Present progressive • Present perfect indicative • Present perfect subjunctive	• Caribbean family ties • Typical Cuban dishes • Weddings in Latin America • **Comparaciones:** Keeping in touch with relatives • **Comunidad y oficio:** Specialty food stores	• **Video Strategy:** Connecting the dots • **Reading Strategy:** Using context • **Writing Strategy:** Using rhyme in poetry
• Foods	• Commenting on food • Explaining and giving excuses	• Preterite • **Se** + indirect object pronouns • Past progressive	• Popular Caribbean dishes • **Sancocho**  FINE ART • ***Baile en la playa,*** Julio Marcano	

Review/Re-Entry
- Present progressive
- Imperfect of **estar**
- Present perfect indicative
- Object pronouns and participles
- Irregular past participles
- **Integración,** pp. 178–179
- Preterite

Capítulo 5 El arte y la música pp. 186–227

El Suroeste y el Norte de México
La geografía
La historia
El arte

Vocabulary	Functions	Grammar	Culture	Strategies
• Arts and architecture • Adjectives to describe art	• Asking for and giving opinions • Introducing and changing a topic of conversation	• Comparatives of equality and superlatives • Passive **se** • Passive voice with **ser**	• Spanish influence in Mexican architecture • **Comparaciones:** Art and architecture in Mexico and Costa Rica • **Comunidad y oficio:** Hispanic artists	• **Video Strategy:** Getting confirmation • **Reading Strategy:** Drawing inferences • **Writing Strategy:** Making a writing plan
• Music and dramatic arts • Adjectives to describe art	• Making suggestions and recommendations • Inviting someone to do something and turning down an invitation	• Subjunctive with hopes and wishes • Past perfect	• **Norteña** music • Frida Kahlo FINE ART • ***Unidad Panamericana,*** Diego Rivera	

Review/Re-Entry
- Comparatives of equality
- **Se impersonal**
- Subjunctive with hopes and wishes
- Superlatives
- Past participles
- **Integración,** pp. 226–227
- Demonstrative adjectives

Capítulo 6 ¡Ponte al día! pp. 228–269

Vocabulary	Functions	Grammar	Culture	Strategies
• Electronic media terms • Adjectives to describe media	• Expressing certainty • Expressing doubt and disbelief	• Indicative after expressions of certainty • Subjunctive after expressions of doubt and disbelief • Uses of **haber**	• Programs in Spanish • Latin American news • **Comparaciones:** Means of communication • **Comunidad y oficio:** Radio and TV in Spanish	• **Video Strategy:** Analyzing viewpoints • **Reading Strategy:** Determining chrono-logical order • **Writing Strategy:** Putting events in order
• Print media terms	• Asking about information and explaining where you found it • Talking about what you know and don't know	• Indefinite expressions • Gender of nouns • Indicative in compound sentences	• Latin American game shows FINE ART • ***Códice Mendoza***	

Review/Re-Entry
- Present perfect subjunctive
- **Decir** with the subjunctive
- **Haber**
- Indefinite expressions
- **Integración,** pp. 268–269

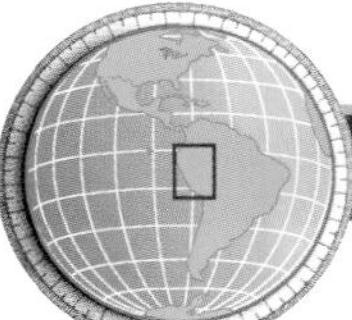

Capítulo 7 Mis aspiraciones pp. 276–317

Los Andes: Ecuador, Perú, y Bolivia

La geografía
La historia
El arte

Vocabulary	Functions	Grammar	Culture	Strategies
• Challenges • Cultural heritage	• Talking about challenges • Talking about accomplishments	• Preterite and imperfect of stative verbs • Grammatical reflexives • **Lo** and **lo que**	• Indigenous words • Otavalo • **Comparaciones:** Future plans • **Comunidad y oficio:** Hispanics in the U.S.	• **Video Strategy:** Separating the essential from the non-essential • **Reading Strategy:** Making inferences • **Writing Strategy:** Leading readers to make inferences
• Hopes and plans	• Talking about future plans • Expressing cause and effect	• Subjunctive after adverbial conjunctions • Subjunctive with future actions • Indicative with habitual or past actions	• Andean peoples and artefacts • Incan roads  FINE ART • ***Benito's Village*** Benito Huillcahuaman	

Review/Re-Entry
- **Conocer, saber,** and **querer**
- Subjunctive
- Preterite and imperfect
- Indicative
- Reflexive actions
- **Integración,** pp. 316–317

Capítulo 8 ¿A qué te dedicas? pp. 318–359

Vocabulary	Functions	Grammar	Culture	Strategies
• Jobs and business terms • Volunteerism • Technology	• Saying what you can and cannot do • Talking about what you do and do not understand	• Verbs with indirect object pronouns • Verbs that express "to become" • Uses of **se**	• Internet in Peru • **Comparaciones:** Using technology • **Comunidad y oficio:** Spanish in the business world	• **Video Strategy:** Evaluating choices • **Reading Strategy:** Determining the author's purpose • **Writing Strategy:** Using dialogue
• Professions • Workplace terms	• Writing a formal letter • Talking about your plans	• Conditional • Past subjunctive with hypothetical statements • Past subjunctive (with past tense)	• **La licenciatura** • Business hours FINE ART • ***Mujer en un puesto de frutas,*** A.S. Forrest	

Review/Re-Entry

- Indirect object pronouns
- Subjunctive uses
- Conditional
- **Integración,** pp. 358–359

Scope and Sequence

El Cono Sur

La geografía
La historia
El arte

Capítulo 9 Huellas del pasado pp. 366–407

Vocabulary	Functions	Grammar	Culture	Strategies
• Legends, folk tales and fairy tales	• Setting the scene for a story • Continuing and ending a story	• Preterite and imperfect in storytelling • Preterite and imperfect contrasted • **Por** and **para**	• Indigenous peoples in Argentina • Iguazú National Park • **Comparaciones:** Legends • **Comunidad y oficio:** Spanish place names in the Americas	• **Video Strategy:** Predicting • **Reading Strategy:** Determining the main idea • **Writing Strategy:** Using detailed descriptions
• Historical events	• Talking about your hopes and wishes • Expressing regret and gratitude	• Uses of subjunctive • Sequence of tenses	• Chilean flag • Chilean political history FINE ART • ***Revista de Rancagua,*** Juan Manuel Blanes	
Review/Re-Entry	• Preterite and imperfect • Verbs with special meanings in the preterite		• **Por** and **para** • Subjunctive	• Impersonal expressions • **Integración,** pp. 406–407

Capítulo 10 El mundo en que vivimos pp. 408–449

Vocabulary	Functions	Grammar	Culture	Strategies
• Historical events • Natural disasters	• Talking about a past event • Expressing and supporting a point of view	• Present and past progressive • **Haber** • Expressions of time	• Argentina's economy • Buenos Aires • Natural disasters in Chile • **Comparaciones:** Experiencing historical events • **Comunidad y oficio:** Pesticides in Latin America	• **Video Strategy:** Tying together all the events • **Reading Strategy:** Understanding figures of speech and dialect • **Writing Strategy:** Using rhetorical devices
• Environment	• Making predictions and giving warnings • Expressing assumptions	• Future tense • Subjunctive with doubt, denial, and feelings • Subjunctive and indicative with adverbial clauses	• Natural resources of Argentina • Environmental issues in Argentina • Buenos Aires • Chile's business relationship with the U.S. FINE ART • ***Mirando un paracaídas,*** Patricia Figueroa	
Review/Re-Entry	• Present and past progressive • Expressions of time • Subjunctive use	• Present participles • Ordinal numbers • Indicative	• **Haber** • Future tense • **Integración,** pp. 448–449	• Perfect tense

Scope and Sequence

Nuevas vistas Curso de introducción

	Lectura	Comunicación oral	Cultura	Comunicación escrita
Colección 1 ¡Así somos! págs. XX–47				
	**Julio Cortázar** "Yo soy, tú eres, él es…" y "Viajes" "…Y así nos distraemos" **Estrategia** Comparación y contraste; Impresiones del texto	**Vocabulario** Los sinónimos Los antónimos **Gramática** El modo indicativo Ser, estar y gustar El adjetivo El presente progresivo El presente perfecto Los comparativos	***Contigo en la distancia:*** Telenovela ¿Qué hicisteis en México? (Episodio 1) Desde que se fueron los muchachos . . . (Episodio 2) **Cultura y comparaciones** Ritmo y folclor del mundo hispano	**Ortografía** **Acentuación:** El acento tónico **Letra y sonido:** La **h** y el sonido */y/* **Taller del escritor** La correspondencia informal La correspondencia formal **Así se dice** Para escribir cartas: el saludo, el cuerpo y la despedida
Colección 2 La niñez págs. 48–95				
	**Carmen Kurtz** "El nacimiento de *Veva*" **Elena Poniatowska** "Los juegos de Lilus" **Estrategia** Pensar en voz alta; Las deducciones	**Vocabulario** Pistas del contexto El registro léxico **Gramática** El pasado del indicativo: el pretérito y el imperfecto; El pasado continuo, el pluscuamperfecto Variantes pronominales: los pronombres del complemento directo e indirecto	***Contigo en la distancia:*** Telenovela El mundo es un balón de fútbol (Episodio 3) ¡Qué sabroso! (Episodio 4) **Cultura y comparaciones** Datos históricos del mundo hispano	**Ortografía** **Acentuación:** El acento ortográfico: palabras agudas y llanas **Letra y sonido:** La *b* y la *v*, la *m* y la *n* **Taller del escritor** Una semblanza Un episodio autobiográfico **Así se dice** Para escribir sobre la vida de una persona Para hacer una descripción
Colección 3 El mundo en que vivimos págs. 96–147				
	Tecnología: Rumbo al futuro Protejamos nuestra Tierra **Estrategia** Pistas gráficas, Reacciones en cadena	**Vocabulario** Los neologismos Los cognados y los cognados falsos **Gramática** El futuro; el futuro perfecto; el condicional; los verbos reflexivos; El modo imperativo; uso simultáneo de los pronombres de complemento directo e indirecto; oraciones simples y compuestas	***Contigo en la distancia:*** Telenovela El poder del amor (Episodio 5) La obra maestra (Episodio 6) **Cultura y comparaciones** Diversidad geográfica del mundo hispano	**Ortografía** **Acentuación:** El diptongo y el hiato **Letra y sonido:** El sonido */s/* **Taller del escritor** El anuncio publicitario La exposición **Así se dice** Para escribir un anuncio publicitario Para hablar de causas y efectos

For Beginning Heritage Speakers or Level 4

Lectura	Comunicación oral	Cultura	Comunicación escrita
Colección 4 El misterio y la fantasía págs. 148–199			
 **Guillermo Samperio** "Tiempo libre" **Carlos Fuentes** "Chac Mool" **Estrategia** La palabra principal, Guía de anticipación	**Vocabulario** Las familias de palabras La formación de palabras (prefijos y sufijos) **Gramática** El modo subjuntivo: usos y conjugación del presente del subjuntivo El subjuntivo en cláusulas nominales: expresiones de influencia y emoción, duda y juicios impersonales El presente perfecto del subjuntivo El subjuntivo en cláusulas adjetivas Las preposiciones y los adverbios	***Contigo en la distancia*** Telenovela: ¡Mira, tienes una carta! (Episodio 7) Al mundo le hace falta más romance (Episodio 8) **Cultura y comparaciones** Arquitectura del mundo hispano	**Ortografía** **Acentuación:** El acento ortográfico: palabras esdrújulas y sobreesdrújulas **Letra y sonido:** El sonido */k/* **(c, qu, k)** **Taller del escritor** La fantasía Un artículo informativo **Así se dice** Para expresar asombro Para presentar información
Colección 5 El amor págs. 200–255			
 **Laura Esquivel** "Enero: tortas de navidad de *Como agua para chocolate*" **Horacio Quiroga** "El hijo" **Estrategia** Un té; Lee, evalúa y vuelve a leer	**Vocabulario** Más prefijos y sufijos **Gramática** Las cláusulas adverbiales: el indicativo y el subjuntivo en cláusulas adverbiales de modo, lugar tiempo, causa, condición y finalidad Las cláusulas de relativo El imperfecto del subjuntivo en cláusulas nominales, adjetivas y adverbiales; Las oraciones condicionales	***Contigo en la distancia*** Telenovela: En casa del tío Guadalupe (Episodio 9) Cuando sea mayor… (Episodio 10) **Cultura y comparaciones** Sabor culinario del mundo hispano	**Ortografía** **Acentuación:** El acento diacrítico **Letra y sonido:** El sonido */x/* **Taller del escritor** Un escrito persuasivo Un guión **Así se dice** Para persuadir o convencer Para escribir un guión
Colección 6 El poder de la palabra págs. 256–305			
 **Julia de Burgos** "A Julia de Burgos" **Miguel de Cervantes** De *Don Quijote de la Mancha* **Estrategia** El contraste; Las pistas del contexto	**Vocabulario** El lenguaje figurado: metáfora y comparación Símbolos e hipérboles **Gramática** El pluscuamperfecto del subjuntivo en cláusulas nominales y en oraciones condicionales La voz pasiva y la pasiva refleja El infinitivo, el gerundio y el participio La correlación de los tiempos verbales	***Contigo en la distancia*** Telenovela: Si yo fuera presidenta (Episodio 11) El tiempo vuela, ¿no? (Episodio 12) **Cultura y comparaciones** Arte del mundo hispano: el muralismo	**Ortografía** Signos de puntuación **Letra y sonido:** Los sonidos */r/* y */rr/* **Taller del escritor** La poesía El cuento **Así se dice** Para escribir símiles Para enlazar los hechos y las ideas

Scope and Sequence

Nuevas vistas Curso uno

	Lectura	Cultura	Comunicación	Escritura
Colección 1 ¡Viva la juventud! págs. xxii–57				
	**Rubén Darío** "Mis primeros versos" **Gary Soto** "Primero de secundaria" **Gabriel García Márquez** "Un cuentecillo triste" **Estrategia para leer** Comparing and contrasting **Elementos de literatura** Biographies, autobiographies, essays, and articles	**Cultura y lengua** Nicaragua **Panorama cultural** What do you do to get the attention of a boy or girl you like? **Comunidad y oficio** Spanish speakers in the United States	**Así se dice** Expressing feelings Talking about causes and effects Narrating an experience in the past Combining sentences Evaluating a written work Reflecting about a written work **Vocabulario** Prefixes and suffixes **Gramática** Nouns Definite and indefinite articles Adjectives **Comparación y contraste** Definite and indefinite articles in Spanish and English	**Prepara tu portafolio** Writing notebook Creative writing Speaking and listening Art **Ortografía** The letter **h** The */y/* sound Diacritics **Taller del escritor** Autobiographical writing
Colección 2 Habla con los animales págs. 58–125				
	**Horacio Quiroga** "La guerra de los yacarés" **Juan Ramón Jiménez** de *Platero y yo* **Rigoberta Menchú** de *Me llamo Rigoberta Menchú* **Estrategia para leer** Using context clues **Elementos de literatura** Plot, characterization, setting, point of view, irony, and theme	**Cultura y lengua** Uruguay **Panorama cultural** In your country, how are animals treated? Are there laws that protect them? **Comunidad y oficio** Spanish and preservation of the environment	**Así se dice** Giving a description Comparing and contrasting Talking about what one should do Combining sentences Evaluating a written work **Vocabulario** Word families **Gramática** Verbs Present tense Imperfect tense Preterite tense Uses of the preterite and imperfect **Comparación y contraste** The past in Spanish and English	**Prepara tu portafolio** Writing notebook Investigation Speaking and listening Drawing Creative writing **Ortografía** The letters **b** and **v** Division of words into syllables **Taller del escritor** Writing a short story
Colección 3 Fábulas y leyendas págs. 126–183				
	**Ana María Shua** "Posada de las Tres Cuerdas" **Antonio Landaura** "La puerta del infierno" **Ciro Alegría** "Güeso y Pellejo" **Estategia para leer** Making predictions **Elementos de literatura** Myths, legends, folktales, and fables	**Cultura y lengua** Argentina **Panorama cultural** Have you ever heard a chilling story? Can you tell it to us? **Comunidad y oficio** Protecting the cultural heritage of the Americas	**Así se dice** Expressing certainty Presenting and connecting ideas Expressing certainty or doubt Talking about cause and effect Evaluating a written work **Vocabulario** Synonyms and antonyms **Gramática** Mood Forms of the present subjunctive Present subjunctive in noun and adverbial clauses **Comparación y contraste** Infinitives and noun clauses in Spanish and English	**Prepara tu portafolio** Writing notebook Creative writing Speaking and listening Investigation **Ortografía** The */s/* sound The tonic accent **Taller del escritor** Writing an essay

For Intermediate Heritage Speakers or Level 5

Lectura	Cultura	Comunicación	Escritura
Colección 4 Dentro del corazón págs. 184–243			
 **Serafín y Joaquín Álvarez Quintero** "Mañana de sol" **Isabel Allende** de *Paula* **José Martí** de *Versos sencillos* **Antonio Cabán Vale** "Verde luz" **Estrategia para leer** Recognizing cause and effect **Elementos de literatura** Drama	**Cultura y lengua** Spain **Panorama cultural** When you feel overwhelmed by problems, what do you do to relax? **Comunidad y oficio** Pioneer Latino artists in the United States	**Así se dice** Talking about the past Asking for and clarifying an opinion Talking about hypothetical situations Combining sentences Evaluating a written work **Vocabulario** Idiomatic expressions **Gramática** Imperfect subjunctive; Conditional; Future **Comparación y contraste** Future Modals in Spanish and English	**Prepara tu portafolio** Writing notebook Creative writing Dramatization Art **Ortografía** The */k/* sound Tonic stress **Taller del escritor** Persuasive writing
Colección 5 Caminos págs. 244–303			
 **Alfonso Quijada Urías** "Hay un naranjo ahí" **Pablo Neruda** "La tortuga" **Sabine R. Ulibarrí** "El forastero gentil" **Jorge Manrique** de *Coplas por la muerte de su padre* **Antonio Machado** de *Soledades* y de *Campos de Castilla* **Estrategia para leer** Evaluating **Elementos de literatura** Poetry: rhyme, imagery, and similes	**Cultura y lengua** Chile **Panorama cultural** Have you ever felt like a stranger in the midst of people you know? **Comunidad y oficio** Traveling in a multilingual world	**Así se dice** Talking about poetry Presenting and supporting an opinion Talking about someone in the past Evaluating a written work **Vocabulario** Specialized vocabulary **Gramática** Present perfect indicative Present perfect subjunctive Past perfect indicative Past perfect subjunctive Sequence of verb tenses **Comparación y contraste** Infinitives and tenses in Spanish and English	**Prepara tu portafolio** Writing notebook Speaking and listening Investigation Creative revising Art **Ortografía** The */x/* sound Accentuation **Taller del escritor** Persuasive writing
Colección 6 Tierra, sol y mar págs. 304–363			
 **Alejandro Balaguer** de "Valle del Fuego" **Jordi Sierra i Fabra** de *Aydin* **Federico García Lorca** "Romance sonámbulo" **Estrategia para leer** Writing a summary **Elementos de literatura** The novel	**Cultura y lengua** Peru **Panorama cultural** Is there any place that you will always remember, either for its beauty or for the significance it has for you? **Comunidad y oficio** Spanish in the media	**Así se dice** Expressing similarities and differences Combining sentences Evaluating a written work Reflecting about a written work **Vocabulario** Cognates **Gramática** Infinitives Gerunds Prepositions **Comparación y contraste** Gerunds, infinitives, and prepositions in Spanish and English	**Prepara tu portafolio** Writing notebook Creative revising Investigation Speaking and listening **Ortografía** The sounds */r/* and */rr/* Diphthongs and hiatuses **Taller del escritor** Informative writing

Scope and Sequence

Nuevas vistas Curso dos

	Lectura	Cultura	Comunicación	Escritura
Colección 1 Esfuerzos heroicos págs. xxii–73				
	**Juan Francisco Manzano** de *Autobiografía de un esclavo* **Horacio Quiroga** "En la noche" **Rose del Castillo Guilbault** "Trabajo de campo" **Sor Juana Inés de la Cruz** "Soneto 149" **Estrategia para leer** Using context clues **Elementos de literatura** Biographies, autobiographies, essays, and articles **Enlaces** La prosa didáctica medieval	**Cultura y lengua** Cuba **Panorama cultural** Have you ever done something heroic or witnessed an act of heroism? **Comunidad y oficio** Humanitarian services for refugees	**Así se dice** Talking about feelings and actions in the past Talking about causes and effects Describing in the past Expressing your point of view Evaluating a written work Reflecting on a written work **Vocabulario** Synonyms; Tone and register **Gramática** Personal pronouns Direct and indirect object pronouns Prepositional pronouns Reflexive pronouns Possessive pronouns Demonstrative pronouns **Comparación y contraste** The indirect object in Spanish and English	**Prepara tu portafolio** Research and oral report Adventure story Creative writing **Ortografía** Capitalization Diacritical marks; Dieresis **Taller del escritor** Autobiographical writing
Colección 2 Lazos de amistad págs. 80–139				
	**Gary Soto** "Cadena rota" y "Naranjas" **Gregorio López y Fuentes** "Una carta a Dios" **Nicolás Guillén** "La muralla" **Estrategia para leer** Drawing conclusions **Elementos de literatura** Short story: plot, characterization, and setting **Enlaces** El soneto del Siglo de Oro	**Cultura y lengua** The Mexican Americans **Panorama cultural** Have you ever done a generous deed anonymously, or known someone who has? **Comunidad y oficio** Spanish in emergency services	**Así se dice** Relating physical appearance to personality Presenting and supporting an opinion Writing a letter of apology Reflecting on a written work **Vocabulario** Anglicisms: loanwords, calques, and false cognates **Gramática** Adjectives Adverbs Comparatives **Comparación y contraste** Diminutives and augmentatives in Spanish	**Prepara tu portafolio** Writing/Solving a problem Creative writing **Ortografía** The */r/* and */rr/* sounds The */y/* sound Accent marks **Taller del escritor** Biographical sketch
Colección 3 El frágil medio ambiente págs. 146–215				
	**Mistral:** de "La fiesta del árbol" **Paz:** "Arbol adentro" **García Lorca:** "Paisaje" **Mistral:** "Meciendo" **Denevi:** "Las abejas de bronce" **de Castro:** "Dicen que no hablan las plantas" **Estategia para leer** Distinguishing fact and opinion **Elementos de literatura** Poetry; Rhetorical devices; style **Enlaces** La poesía del siglo XIX	**Cultura y lengua** Chile **Panorama cultural** Where are you from? What do you think of your city? Is it an ideal place to live and work? **Comunidad y oficio** Business opportunities in the national and international markets	**Así se dice** Explaining a point of view Talking about nature using comparisons Contrasting two ideas Talking about what should be done Reflecting on a written work **Vocabulario** Figurative language **Gramática** The uses of **se** Passive voice **Comparación y contraste** Passive and active voice in Spanish and English	**Prepara tu portafolio** Research and presentation Publication and poetry Dramatization **Ortografía** The letters **b** and **v** Diphthongs and hiatuses **Taller del escritor** Informative report

For Advanced Heritage Speakers or Level 6

Lectura	Cultura	Comunicación	Escritura
Colección 4 Pruebas págs. 222–295			
 **Josefina Niggli** "El anillo del general Macías" **Francisco Jiménez** "Cajas de cartón" **Jorge Luis Borges** "Los dos reyes y los dos laberintos" **Estrategia para leer** Writing a summary **Elementos de literatura** Drama **Enlaces** La poesía latinoamericana del siglo XX	**Cultura y lengua** Mexico **Panorama cultural** Have you ever been faced with a dilemma where you had to make a difficult decision? **Comunidad y oficio** Achievement through education	**Así se dice** Talking about how things really are Taking about the consequences of an historical event Talking about hypothetical situations Reflecting on a written work **Vocabulario** Regionalisms **Gramática** Relative clauses and relative pronouns The use of relative pronouns **Comparación y contraste** Relative clauses in Spanish and English	**Prepara tu portafolio** Journalism Literature and history **Ortografía** The letters **m** and **n** Accent marks and suffixes **Taller del escritor** Persuasive writing
Colección 5 Mitos págs. 302–363			
 Versión de **Jorge Luis Arriola** *El Popol Vuh* Versión de **Douglas Gifford** "Tres mitos latinoamericanos" Versión de **Américo Paredes** "El corrido de Gregorio Cortez" **Estrategia para leer** Evaluating **Elementos de literatura** Myths, legends, and folktales **Enlaces** La nueva narrativa latinoamericana del siglo XX	**Cultura y lengua** The Mayans **Panorama cultural** If you could put something in a time capsule to show the progress of our civilization, what would it be? **Comunidad y oficio** Preserving oral traditions	**Así se dice** Evaluating a literary text Making conjectures Making comparisons Evaluating a written work Reflecting on a written work **Vocabulario** Loanwords from indigenous American languages **Gramática** Review of relative clauses Mood with relative clauses The subjunctive in adverbial clauses **Comparación y contraste** Relative clauses with indefinite antecedents in Spanish and English	**Prepara tu portafolio** Art Posters **Ortografía** The */s/* sound Verb forms and accent marks **Taller del escritor** Persuasive writing
Colección 6 Perspectivas humorísticas págs. 376–427			
 **Miguel de Cervantes** de *Don Quijote de la Mancha* **Pedro Antonio de Alarcón** "El libro talonario" **Lope de Vega** *"El Soneto"* **Estrategia para leer** Cause and effect **Elementos de literatura** The novel **Enlaces** El teatro latinoamericano del siglo XX	**Cultura y lengua** Spain **Panorama cultural** Have you ever done something that was embarrassing at the time but that now makes you laugh? **Comunidad y oficio** Bilingualism in law	**Así se dice** Talking about hypothetical situations in the past Talking about the arts Making conjectures Evaluating a written work **Vocabulario** Learned words **Gramática** Aspect Perfective aspect Imperfective aspect Progressive aspect **Comparación y contraste** The imperfect and the preterite progressive in Spanish	**Prepara tu portafolio** Creative writing and drawing Creative writing **Ortografía** Verbs that end in **-ear** Minimal pairs **Taller del escritor** Writing an essay

Student Edition

¡*Exprésate!* gives students the confidence to express themselves!

With ever-growing class sizes and more ability levels than ever before in the Spanish classroom, it takes a special Spanish program to engage your students. ***¡Exprésate!*** immerses students in the Spanish-speaking world and makes them want to communicate!

Cross-curricular connections make material relevant to students

The ***Geocultura*** pages that come before each chapter introduce students to a new country. Students make connections with geography, art, architecture, food, and celebrations.

The **GeoVisión** video brings each location to life.

Colorful and vivid presentations hold students' attention

Objetivos
Talking about everyday activities, saying how often you do things

Vocabulario en acción 2

Video/DVD
ExpresaVisión

Los fines de semana me gusta...

estudiar
descansar
trabajar
practicar deportes
tocar el piano
hablar por teléfono
bailar

108 *ciento ocho*

Capítulo 3 • ¿Qué te gust…

Vocabulary and functional phrases are the foundation of meaningful communication. The large, real-life photos in the vocabulary sections help students connect learning Spanish to their world.

ExpresaVisión video presentations reinforce key vocabulary.

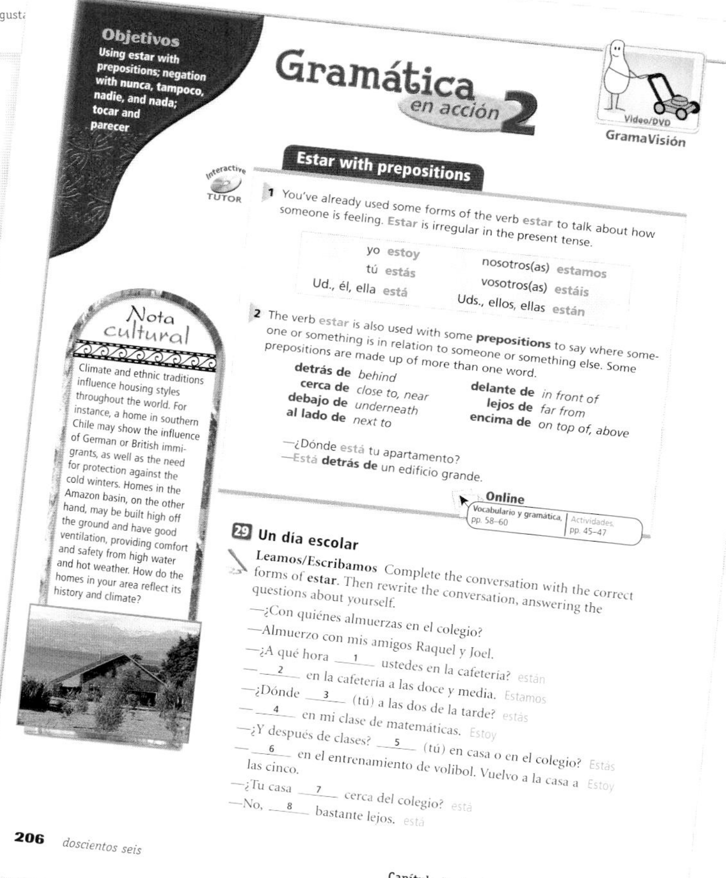

Objetivos
Using estar with prepositions; negation with nunca, tampoco, nadie, and nada; tocar and parecer

Gramática en acción 2

Video/DVD
GramaVisión

Estar with prepositions

Interactive TUTOR

1 You've already used some forms of the verb **estar** to talk about how someone is feeling. **Estar** is irregular in the present tense.

yo **estoy**	nosotros(as) **estamos**
tú **estás**	vosotros(as) **estáis**
Ud., él, ella **está**	Uds., ellos, ellas **están**

2 The verb **estar** is also used with some **prepositions** to say where someone or something is in relation to someone or something else. Some prepositions are made up of more than one word.

detrás de	*behind*	**delante de**	*in front of*
cerca de	*close to, near*	**lejos de**	*far from*
debajo de	*underneath*	**encima de**	*on top of, above*
al lado de	*next to*		

—¿Dónde **está** tu apartamento?
—**Está detrás de** un edificio grande.

Online
Vocabulario y gramática, pp. 58–60
Actividades, pp. 45–47

Nota cultural

Climate and ethnic traditions influence housing styles throughout the world. For instance, a home in southern Chile may show the influence of German or British immigrants, as well as the need for protection against the cold winters. Homes in the Amazon basin, on the other hand, may be built high off the ground and have good ventilation, providing comfort and safety from high water and hot weather. How do the homes in your area reflect its history and climate?

29 Un día escolar

Leamos/Escribamos Complete the conversation with the correct forms of **estar**. Then rewrite the conversation, answering the questions about yourself.

—¿Con quiénes almuerzas en el colegio?
—Almuerzo con mis amigos Raquel y Joel.
—¿A qué hora __1__ ustedes en la cafetería? están
—__2__ en la cafetería a las doce y media. Estamos
—¿Dónde __3__ (tú) a las dos de la tarde? estás
—__4__ en mi clase de matemáticas. Estoy
—¿Y después de clases? __5__ (tú) en casa o en el colegio? Estás
—__6__ en el entrenamiento de volibol. Vuelvo a la casa a las cinco. Estoy
—¿Tu casa __7__ cerca del colegio? está
—No, __8__ bastante lejos. está

206 *doscientos seis*

Capítulo 5 • En casa con la familia

Grammar presentations are color-coded with graphics and highlighting to emphasize the important points.

GramaVisión animation makes even the most abstract concepts accessible to all students.

A consistent lesson format balances grammar and communication

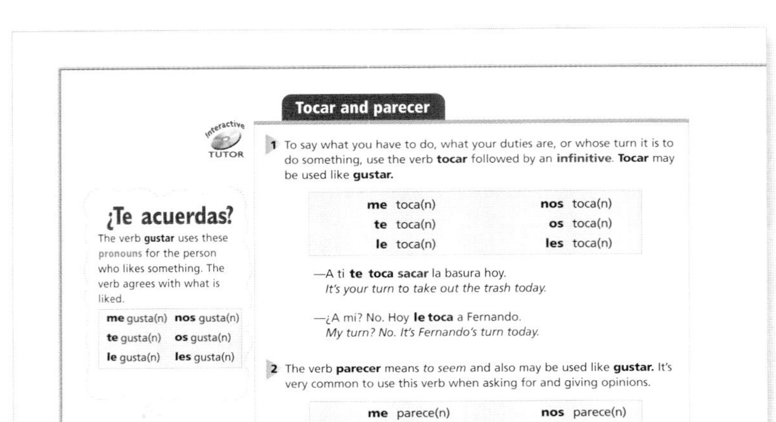

Tocar and parecer

Interactive TUTOR

1 To say what you have to do, what your duties are, or whose turn it is to do something, use the verb **tocar** followed by an **infinitive**. **Tocar** may be used like **gustar.**

me toca(n)	**nos** toca(n)
te toca(n)	**os** toca(n)
le toca(n)	**les** toca(n)

—A ti **te toca sacar** la basura hoy.
It's your turn to take out the trash today.

—¿A mí? No. Hoy **le toca** a Fernando.
My turn? No. It's Fernando's turn today.

2 The verb **parecer** means *to seem* and also may be used like **gustar.** It's very common to use this verb when asking for and giving opinions.

me parece(n)	**nos** parece(n)
te parece(n)	**os** parece(n)
le parece(n)	**les** parece(n)

Siempre me toca a mí lavar los platos. **Me parece** injusto.
I always have to wash the dishes. It seems unfair to me.

A mi papá **le** parece una lata **cortar** el césped pero a mí me gusta mucho.
My dad thinks cutting the grass is a pain, but I like it a lot.

Online Vocabulario y gramática, pp. 58–60 | Actividades, pp. 45–47

¿Te acuerdas?

The verb **gustar** uses these pronouns for the person who likes something. The verb agrees with what is liked.

me gusta(n)	**nos** gusta(n)
te gusta(n)	**os** gusta(n)
le gusta(n)	**les** gusta(n)

CD 5, Tr. 8

31 ¡Qué lata!

Escuchemos Based on the pictures below, decide whether the statements you hear are **cierto** or **falso.** 1. falso 2. cierto 3. cierto 4. cierto 5. cierto 6. f...

mi hermana — mi hermano — mi papá y mi hermano menor — mi mamá y ...

210 *doscientos diez* — **Capítulo 5** • En casa con ...

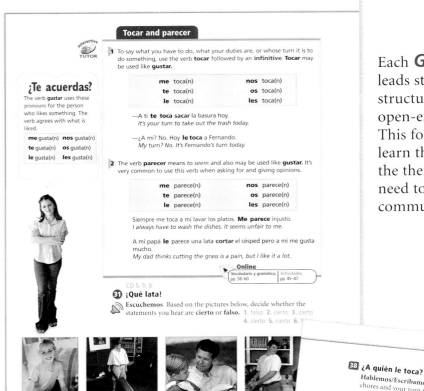

Each ***Grammar*** section leads students from closed-ended, structured practice through open-ended communication. This format allows students to learn the grammar rules using the thematic vocabulary they need to participate actively in a communicative situation.

38 ¿A quién le toca?

Hablemos/Escribamos Tell your sister it's her turn to do the chores and your turn to have fun.

MODELO **A ti te toca limpiar el baño. A mí me toca jugar.**

1. descansar/cortar el césped
2. lavar los platos/ir de compras
3. cocinar/ver televisión
4. jugar/hacer la cama
5. leer/limpiar la casa
6. limpiar el baño/cantar

39 ¿Qué les parece?

Hablemos/Escribamos Say how the following activities seem to you. Then name someone you know who has a different opinion.

MODELO **A mí me parece divertido ir de compras. Pero a mi padre le parece aburrido.**

divertido difícil	fácil aburrido	muy bien fenomenal	interesante pésimo

1. trabajar en el jardín
2. vivir en el campo
3. jugar con los perros
4. ir al centro comercial
5. jugar a videojuegos
6. hablar por teléfono
7. bailar
8. hacer ejercicio

Comunicación

40 Mi familia

Hablemos Take turns with a partner. Imagine that one of you is the teenage girl in the drawings below. Ask and anwer questions about the girl's family, her house, and family's activities.

a. b. nuestra casa — la casa de abuela c.

Chile

Gramática 2

doscientos once **211**

Communication is the goal of every presentation. The consistent placement of features helps all students recognize the pattern and easily comprehend the chapter format.

Student Edition

Cultural interviews introduce students to people from around the Spanish-speaking world

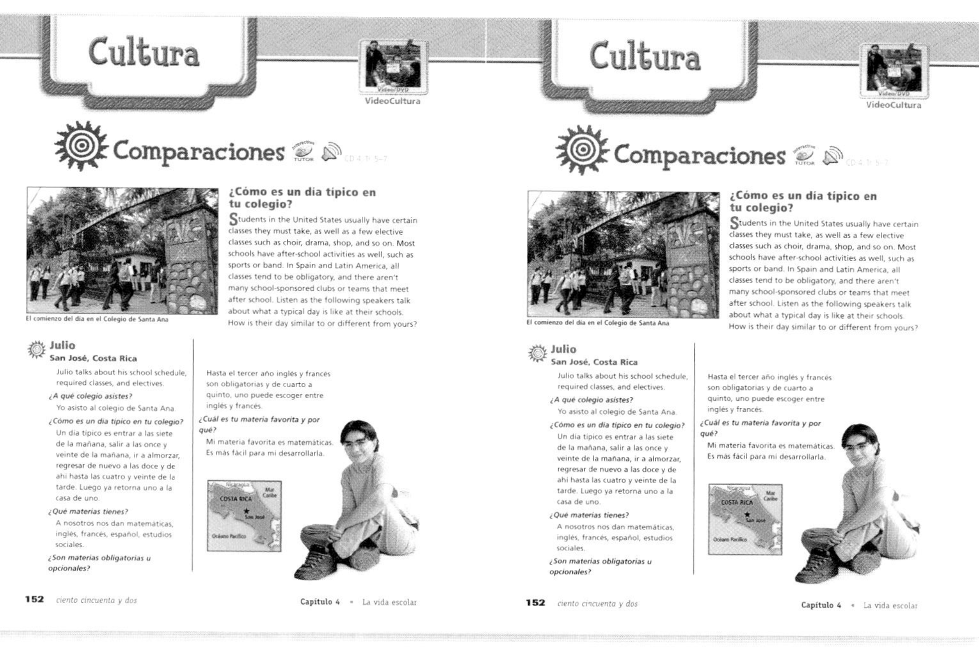
Cultura

VideoCultura

Comparaciones

¿Cómo es un día típico en tu colegio?

Students in the United States usually have certain classes they must take, as well as a few elective classes such as choir, drama, shop, and so on. Most schools have after-school activities as well, such as sports or band. In Spain and Latin America, all classes tend to be obligatory, and there aren't many school-sponsored clubs or teams that meet after school. Listen as the following speakers talk about what a typical day is like at their schools. How is their day similar to or different from yours?

El comienzo del día en el Colegio de Santa Ana

Julio
San José, Costa Rica

Julio talks about his school schedule, required classes, and electives.

¿A qué colegio asistes?
Yo asisto al colegio de Santa Ana.

¿Cómo es un día típico en tu colegio?
Un día típico es entrar a las siete de la mañana, salir a las once y veinte de la mañana, ir a almorzar, regresar de nuevo a las doce y de ahí hasta las cuatro y veinte de la tarde. Luego ya retorna uno a la casa de uno.

¿Qué materias tienes?
A nosotros nos dan matemáticas, inglés, francés, español, estudios sociales.

¿Son materias obligatorias u opcionales?
Hasta el tercer año inglés y francés son obligatorias y de cuarto a quinto, uno puede escoger entre inglés y francés.

¿Cuál es tu materia favorita y por qué?
Mi materia favorita es matemáticas. Es más fácil para mi desarrollarla.

152 ciento cincuenta y dos

Capítulo 4 • La vida escolar

In every *Cultura* section, students meet people from different countries and learn more about culture in the Spanish-speaking world.

VideoCultura presents interviews shot on location and helps students become accustomed to different accents.

Integrated technology puts language in context for students

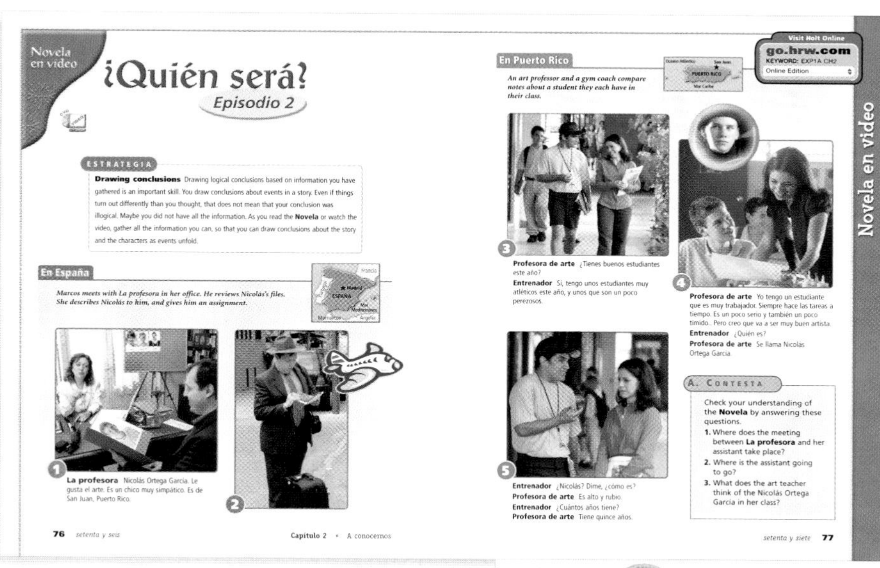
Novela en video

¿Quién será?
Episodio 2

ESTRATEGIA
Drawing conclusions Drawing logical conclusions based on information you have gathered is an important skill. You draw conclusions about events in a story. Even if things turn out differently than you thought, that does not mean that your conclusion was illogical. Maybe you did not have all the information. As you read the **Novela** or watch the video, gather all the information you can, so that you can draw conclusions about the story and the characters as events unfold.

En España
Marcos meets with La profesora in her office. He reviews Nicolás's files. She describes Nicolás to him, and gives him an assignment.

1 **La profesora** Nicolás Ortega García. Le gusta el arte. Es un chico muy simpático. Es de San Juan, Puerto Rico.

2

En Puerto Rico
An art professor and a gym coach compare notes about a student they each have in their class.

3 **Profesora de arte** ¿Tienes buenos estudiantes este año?
Entrenador Sí, tengo unos estudiantes muy atléticos este año, y unos que son un poco perezosos.

4 **Profesora de arte** Yo tengo un estudiante que es muy trabajador. Siempre hace las tareas a tiempo. Es un poco serio y también un poco tímido... Pero creo que va a ser muy buen artista.
Entrenador ¿Quién es?
Profesora de arte Se llama Nicolás Ortega García.

5 **Entrenador** ¿Nicolás? Dime, ¿cómo es?
Profesora de arte Es alto y rubio.
Entrenador ¿Cuántos años tiene?
Profesora de arte Tiene quince años.

A. CONTESTA
Check your understanding of the **Novela** by answering these questions.
1. Where does the meeting between **La profesora** and her assistant take place?
2. Where is the assistant going to go?
3. What does the art teacher think of the Nicolás Ortega García in her class?

Visit Holt Online go.hrw.com KEYWORD: EXP1A CH2 Online Edition

76 setenta y seis

Capítulo 2 • A conocernos

setenta y siete 77

¿Quién será?, an intriguing video story, will have students guessing all year long. While trying to predict what will happen next, students learn the language in context as the story progresses with each chapter.

VideoNovela provides optional Spanish captions if you choose to give students some "text support" as they watch the story unfold.

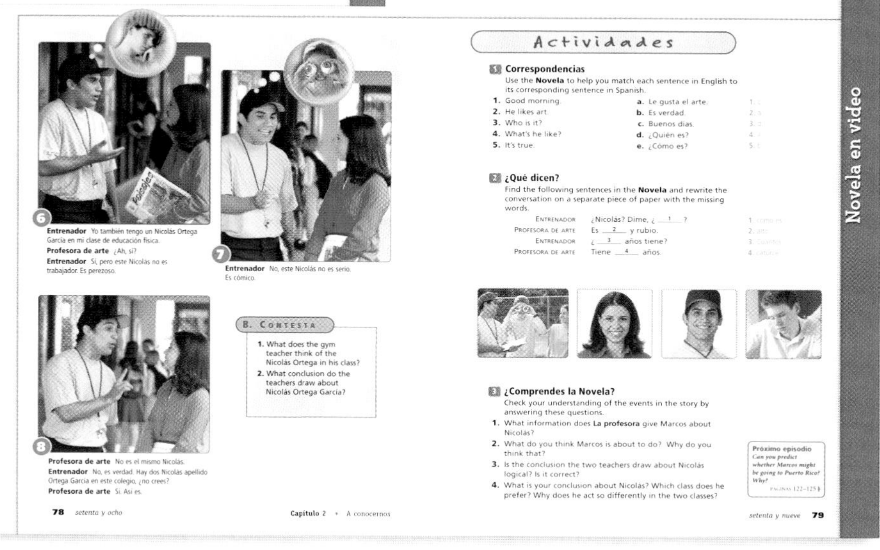
6 **Entrenador** Yo también tengo un Nicolás Ortega García en mi clase de educación física.
Profesora de arte ¿Ah, sí?
Entrenador Sí, pero este Nicolás no es trabajador. Es perezoso.

7 **Entrenador** No, este Nicolás no es serio. Es cómico.

8 **Profesora de arte** No es el mismo Nicolás.
Entrenador No, es verdad. Hay dos Nicolás apellido Ortega García en este colegio, ¿no crees?
Profesora de arte Sí. Así es.

B. CONTESTA
1. What does the gym teacher think of the Nicolás Ortega in his class?
2. What conclusion do the teachers draw about Nicolás Ortega García?

Actividades

1 Correspondencias
Use the **Novela** to help you match each sentence in English to its corresponding sentence in Spanish.
1. Good morning. — a. Le gusta el arte.
2. He likes art. — b. Es verdad.
3. Who is it? — c. Buenos días.
4. What's he like? — d. ¿Quién es?
5. It's true. — e. ¿Cómo es?

2 ¿Qué dicen?
Find the following sentences in the **Novela** and rewrite the conversation on a separate piece of paper with the missing words.
ENTRENADOR ¿Nicolás? Dime, ¿ 1 ?
PROFESORA DE ARTE Es 2 y rubio.
ENTRENADOR ¿ 3 años tiene?
PROFESORA DE ARTE Tiene 4 años.

3 ¿Comprendes la Novela?
Check your understanding of the events in the story by answering these questions.
1. What information does **La profesora** give Marcos about Nicolás?
2. What do you think Marcos is about to do? Why do you think that?
3. Is the conclusion the two teachers draw about Nicolás logical? Is it correct?
4. What is your conclusion about Nicolás? Which class does he prefer? Why does he act so differently in the two classes?

Próximo episodio
Can you predict whether Marcos might be going to Puerto Rico? Why?

78 setenta y ocho

Capítulo 2 • A conocernos

setenta y nueve 79

Student Edition

Student Edition *continued*

Reading and writing practice build student comprehension and written communication

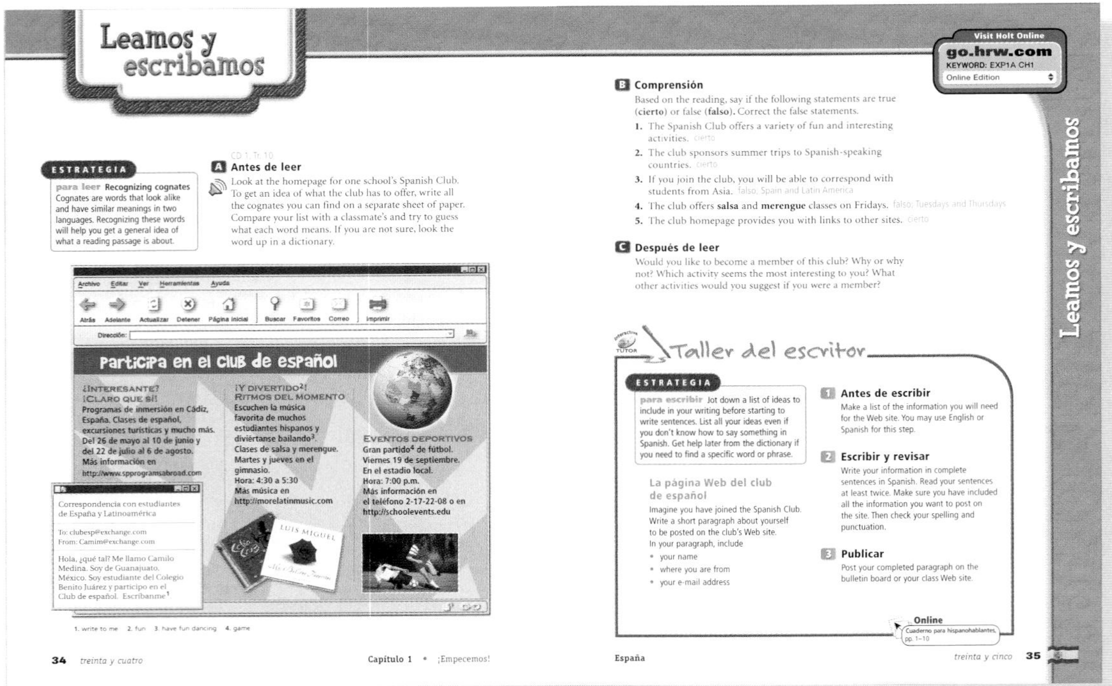

Leamos y escribamos

Visit Holt Online
go.hrw.com
KEYWORD: EXP1A CH1
Online Edition

ESTRATEGIA

para leer **Recognizing cognates** Cognates are words that look alike and have similar meanings in two languages. Recognizing these words will help you get a general idea of what a reading passage is about.

CD 1, Tr. 10

A Antes de leer

Look at the homepage for one school's Spanish Club. To get an idea of what the club has to offer, write all the cognates you can find on a separate sheet of paper. Compare your list with a classmate's and try to guess what each word means. If you are not sure, look the word up in a dictionary.

1. write to me 2. fun 3. have fun dancing 4. game

B Comprensión

Based on the reading, say if the following statements are true (**cierto**) or false (**falso**). Correct the false statements.

1. The Spanish Club offers a variety of fun and interesting activities. cierto
2. The club sponsors summer trips to Spanish-speaking countries. cierto
3. If you join the club, you will be able to correspond with students from Asia. falso; Spain and Latin America
4. The club offers **salsa** and **merengue** classes on Fridays. falso; Tuesdays and Thursdays
5. The club homepage provides you with links to other sites. cierto

C Después de leer

Would you like to become a member of this club? Why or why not? Which activity seems the most interesting to you? What other activities would you suggest if you were a member?

Interactive TUTOR

Taller del escritor

ESTRATEGIA

para escribir Jot down a list of ideas to include in your writing before starting to write sentences. List all your ideas even if you don't know how to say something in Spanish. Get help later from the dictionary if you need to find a specific word or phrase.

La página Web del club de español

Imagine you have joined the Spanish Club. Write a short paragraph about yourself to be posted on the club's Web site. In your paragraph, include
- your name
- where you are from
- your e-mail address

1 Antes de escribir

Make a list of the information you will need for the Web site. You may use English or Spanish for this step.

2 Escribir y revisar

Write your information in complete sentences in Spanish. Read your sentences at least twice. Make sure you have included all the information you want to post on the site. Then check your spelling and punctuation.

3 Publicar

Post your completed paragraph on the bulletin board or your class Web site.

Online
Cuaderno para hispanohablantes, pp. 1–10

34 *treinta y cuatro* **Capítulo 1** • ¡Empecemos!

España *treinta y cinco* **35**

The ***Leamos*** section provides students with readings from informational texts to literature. Every reading has a corresponding strategy to help students tackle reading confidently as well as pre- and post-reading activities.

Taller del escritor follows each reading and steps students through the writing process, gradually building their writing skills in Spanish.

Interdisciplinary activities increase cultural awareness and relate Spanish to other subject areas

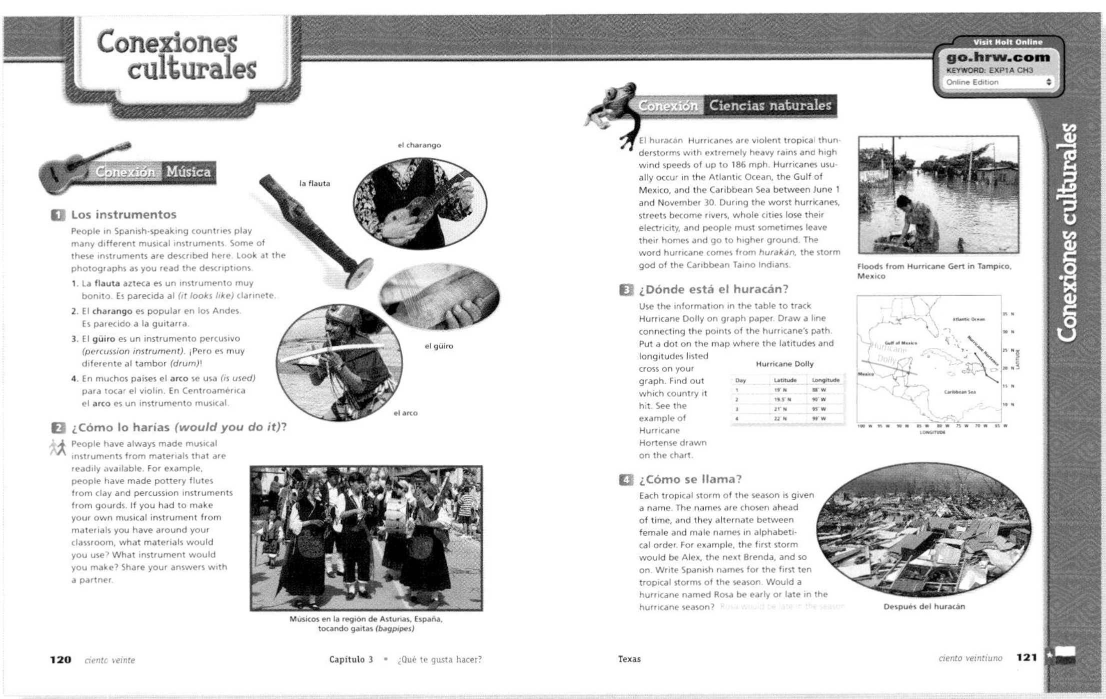

Conexiones culturales

Visit Holt Online
go.hrw.com
KEYWORD: EXP1A CH3
Online Edition

Conexión Música

1 Los instrumentos

People in Spanish-speaking countries play many different musical instruments. Some of these instruments are described here. Look at the photographs as you read the descriptions.

1. La **flauta** azteca es un instrumento muy bonito. Es parecida al *(it looks like)* clarinete.
2. El **charango** es popular en los Andes. Es parecido a la guitarra.
3. El **güiro** es un instrumento percusivo *(percussion instrument)*. ¡Pero es muy diferente al tambor *(drum)*!
4. En muchos países el **arco** se usa *(is used)* para tocar el violín. En Centroamérica el **arco** es un instrumento musical.

2 ¿Cómo lo harías *(would you do it)*?

People have always made musical instruments from materials that are readily available. For example, people have made pottery flutes from clay and percussion instruments from gourds. If you had to make your own musical instrument from materials you have around your classroom, what materials would you use? What instrument would you make? Share your answers with a partner.

Músicos en la región de Asturias, España, tocando gaitas *(bagpipes)*

Conexión Ciencias naturales

El huracán Hurricanes are violent tropical thunderstorms with extremely heavy rains and high wind speeds of up to 186 mph. Hurricanes usually occur in the Atlantic Ocean, the Gulf of Mexico, and the Caribbean Sea between June 1 and November 30. During the worst hurricanes, streets become rivers, whole cities lose their electricity, and people must sometimes leave their homes and go to higher ground. The word hurricane comes from *hurakán*, the storm god of the Caribbean Taino Indians.

Floods from Hurricane Gert in Tampico, Mexico

3 ¿Dónde está el huracán?

Use the information in the table to track Hurricane Dolly on graph paper. Draw a line connecting the points of the hurricane's path. Put a dot on the map where the latitudes and longitudes listed cross on your graph. Find out which country it hit. See the example of Hurricane Hortense drawn on the chart.

Hurricane Dolly

Day	Latitude	Longitude
1	19° N	88° W
2	19.5° N	90° W
3	21° N	95° W
4	22° N	99° W

4 ¿Cómo se llama?

Each tropical storm of the season is given a name. The names are chosen ahead of time, and they alternate between female and male names in alphabetical order. For example, the first storm would be Alex, the next Brenda, and so on. Write Spanish names for the first ten tropical storms of the season. Would a hurricane named Rosa be early or late in the hurricane season? Rosa would be late in the season.

Después del huracán

120 *ciento veinte* **Capítulo 3** • ¿Qué te gusta hacer?

Texas *ciento veintiuno* **121**

Conexiones culturales provides high-interest interdisciplinary activities on a variety of topics. Each ***Conexión*** presents a new aspect of Spanish-speaking culture and relates it to another academic subject.

Two types of review boost students' retention

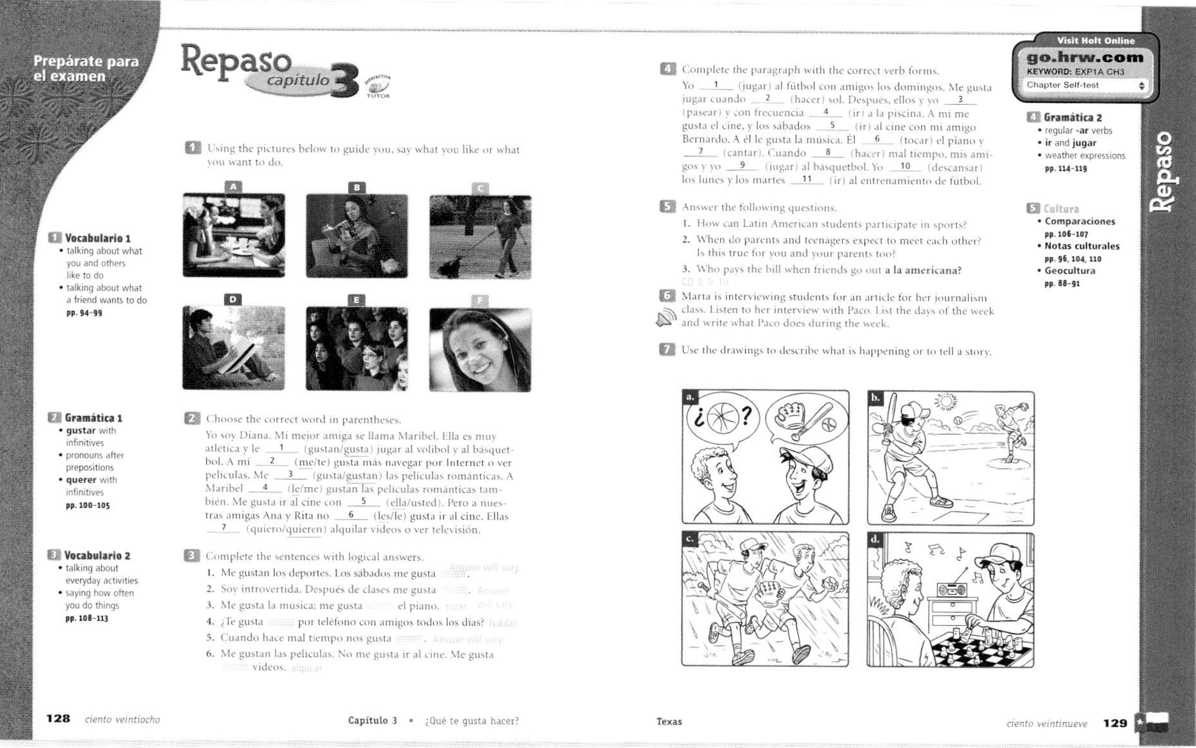

Preparate para el examen

Repaso capítulo 3

1 Using the pictures below to guide you, say what you like or what you want to do.

A B C D E F

1 **Vocabulario 1**
- talking about what you and others like to do
- talking about what a friend wants to do

pp. 94–99

2 Choose the correct word in parentheses.

Yo soy Diana. Mi mejor amiga se llama Maribel. Ella es muy atlética y le __1__ (gustan/gusta) jugar al volibol y al básquetbol. A mí __2__ (me/te) gusta más navegar por Internet o ver películas. Me __3__ (gusta/gustan) las películas románticas. A Maribel __4__ (le/me) gustan las películas románticas también. Me gusta ir al cine con __5__ (ella/usted). Pero a nuestras amigas Ana y Rita no __6__ (les/le) gusta ir al cine. Ellas __7__ (quiero/quieren) alquilar videos o ver televisión.

2 **Gramática 1**
- **gustar** with infinitives
- pronouns after prepositions
- **querer** with infinitives

pp. 100–105

3 Complete the sentences with logical answers.

1. Me gustan los deportes. Los sábados me gusta ____. Answer will vary.
2. Soy introvertida. Después de clases me gusta ____. Answer will vary.
3. Me gusta la música; me gusta ____ el piano. tocar
4. ¿Te gusta ____ por teléfono con amigos todos los días? hablar
5. Cuando hace mal tiempo nos gusta ____. Answer will vary.
6. Me gustan las películas. No me gusta ir al cine. Me gusta ____ videos. alquilar

3 **Vocabulario 2**
- talking about everyday activities
- saying how often you do things

pp. 108–113

4 Complete the paragraph with the correct verb forms.

Yo __1__ (jugar) al fútbol con amigos los domingos. Me gusta jugar cuando __2__ (hacer) sol. Después, ellos y yo __3__ (pasear) y con frecuencia __4__ (ir) a la piscina. A mí me gusta el cine, y los sábados __5__ (ir) al cine con mi amigo Bernardo. A él le gusta la música. Él __6__ (tocar) el piano y __7__ (cantar). Cuando __8__ (hacer) mal tiempo, mis amigos y yo __9__ (jugar) al básquetbol. Yo __10__ (descansar) los lunes y los martes __11__ (ir) al entrenamiento de fútbol.

5 Answer the following questions.

1. How can Latin American students participate in sports?
2. When do parents and teenagers expect to meet each other? Is this true for you and your parents too?
3. Who pays the bill when friends go out **a la americana?**

CD 3, Tr. 10

6 Marta is interviewing students for an article for her journalism class. Listen to her interview with Paco. List the days of the week and write what Paco does during the week.

7 Use the drawings to describe what is happening or to tell a story.

a. b. c. d.

Visit Holt Online
go.hrw.com
KEYWORD: EXP1A CH3
Chapter Self-test

4 **Gramática 2**
- regular **-ar** verbs
- **ir** and **jugar**
- weather expressions

pp. 114–119

5 **Cultura**
- **Comparaciones** pp. 106–107
- **Notas culturales** pp. 96, 104, 110
- **Geocultura** pp. 88–91

Repaso

128 ciento veintiocho · Capítulo 3 • ¿Qué te gusta hacer? · Texas · ciento veintinueve 129

The ***Repaso*** review section offers discrete, **chapter-specific practice** with references back into the chapter if students need further review.

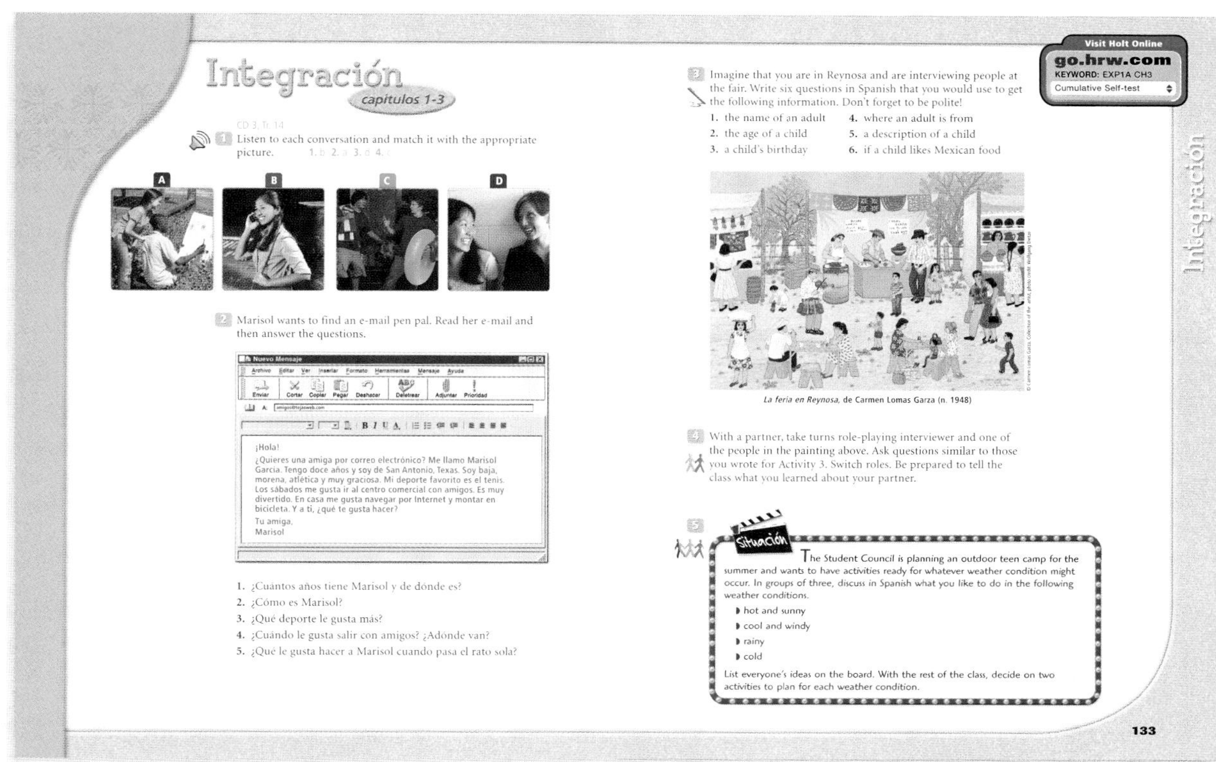

Integración capítulos 1-3

CD 3, Tr. 14

1 Listen to each conversation and match it with the appropriate picture. 1. b 2. a 3. d 4. c

A B C D

2 Marisol wants to find an e-mail pen pal. Read her e-mail and then answer the questions.

Nuevo Mensaje

Archivo Editar Ver Insertar Formato Herramientas Mensaje Ayuda

Enviar Cortar Copiar Pegar Deshacer Deletrear Adjuntar Prioridad

A: amigos@tejasweb.com

¡Hola!

¿Quieres una amiga por correo electrónico? Me llamo Marisol García. Tengo doce años y soy de San Antonio, Texas. Soy baja, morena, atlética y muy graciosa. Mi deporte favorito es el tenis. Los sábados me gusta ir al centro comercial con amigos. Es muy divertido. En casa me gusta navegar por Internet y montar en bicicleta. Y a ti, ¿qué te gusta hacer?

Tu amiga,
Marisol

1. ¿Cuántos años tiene Marisol y de dónde es?
2. ¿Cómo es Marisol?
3. ¿Qué deporte le gusta más?
4. ¿Cuándo le gusta salir con amigos? ¿Adónde van?
5. ¿Qué le gusta hacer a Marisol cuando pasa el rato sola?

3 Imagine that you are in Reynosa and are interviewing people at the fair. Write six questions in Spanish that you would use to get the following information. Don't forget to be polite!

1. the name of an adult
2. the age of a child
3. a child's birthday
4. where an adult is from
5. a description of a child
6. if a child likes Mexican food

La feria en Reynosa, de Carmen Lomas Garza (n. 1948)

4 With a partner, take turns role-playing interviewer and one of the people in the painting above. Ask questions similar to those you wrote for Activity 3. Switch roles. Be prepared to tell the class what you learned about your partner.

5 **Situación**

The Student Council is planning an outdoor teen camp for the summer and wants to have activities ready for whatever weather condition might occur. In groups of three, discuss in Spanish what you like to do in the following weather conditions.

- hot and sunny
- cool and windy
- rainy
- cold

List everyone's ideas on the board. With the rest of the class, decide on two activities to plan for each weather condition.

Visit Holt Online
go.hrw.com
KEYWORD: EXP1A CH3
Cumulative Self-test

Integración

133

The ***Integración*** section provides students with **cumulative practice after every chapter.** Students are ready for a cumulative test at any time.

Student Edition

Teacher's Edition

Using the Chapter Interleaf

Each chapter of the ***¡Exprésate!*** *Teacher's Edition* includes interleaf pages to help you plan, teach, and expand your lessons.

Overview and Resources at the beginning of each chapter provide a snapshot of the material presented and the resources available for additional practice with each chapter section.

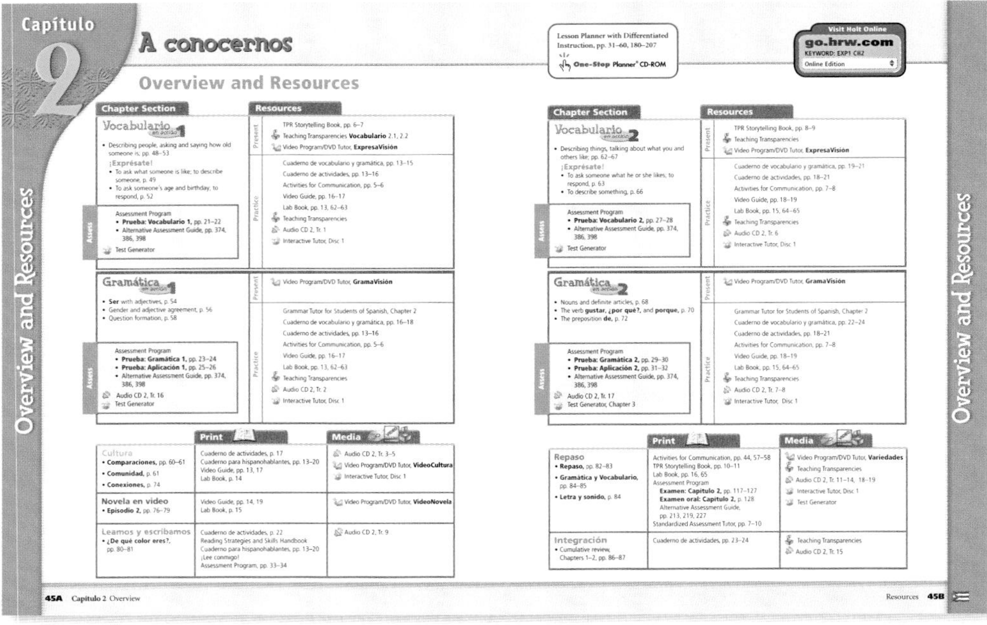

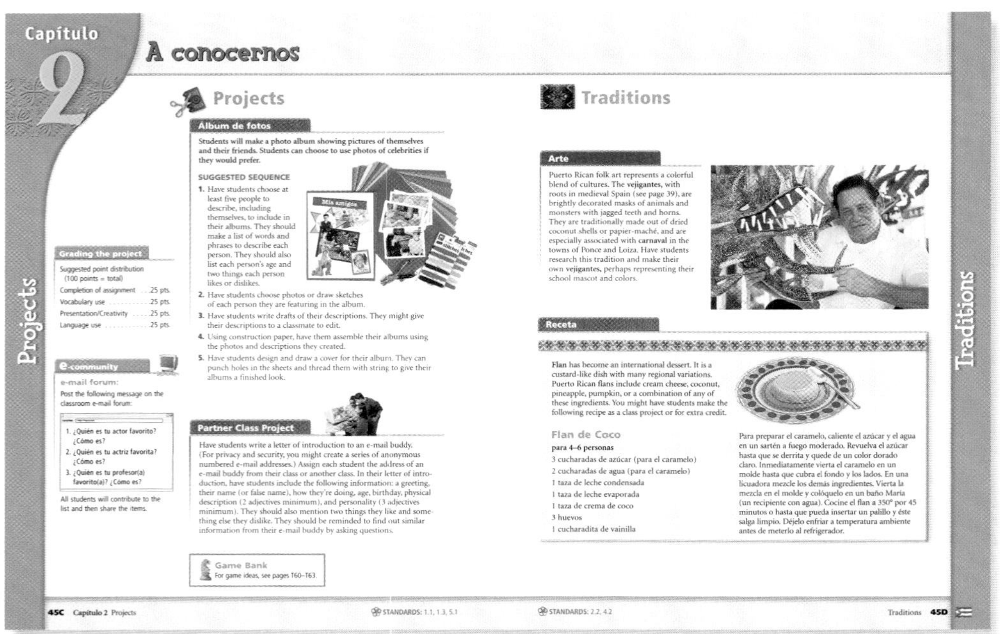

Projects and Traditions allow students to work at several different levels to expand on the information in the chapter—individually, in pairs or groups, or with a partner class.

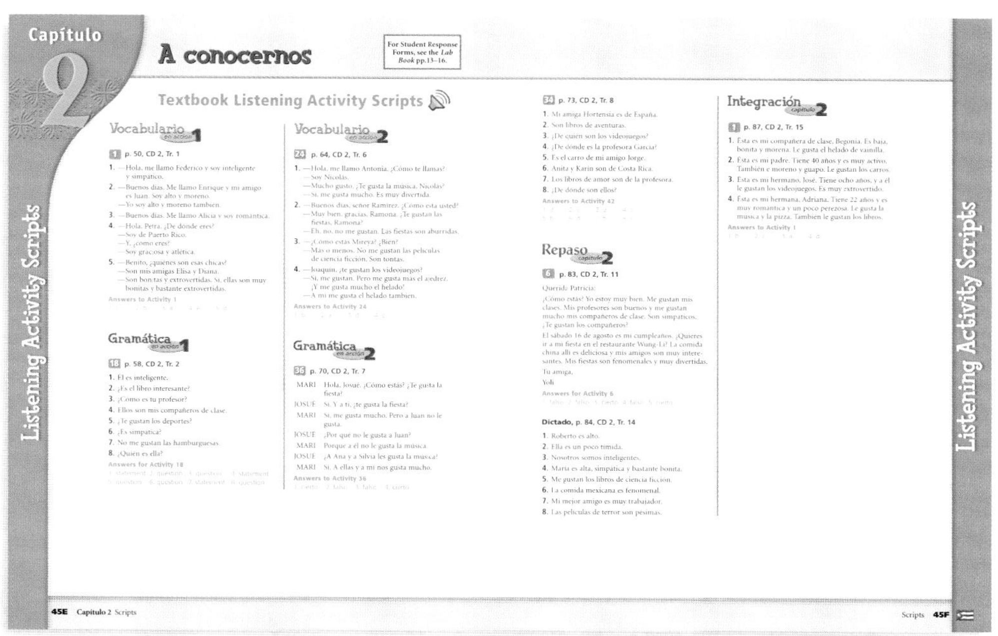

Textbook Listening Activity Scripts are placed at point of use throughout each chapter. In addition, all scripts and answers for listening activities are found on these pages for easy reference. The activity masters for listening activities are found in the Lab Book.

Suggested Lesson Plans provide a logical sequence of instruction, along with suggestions for optional practice and homework. Both **50–minute** and **90–minute block** plans are provided.

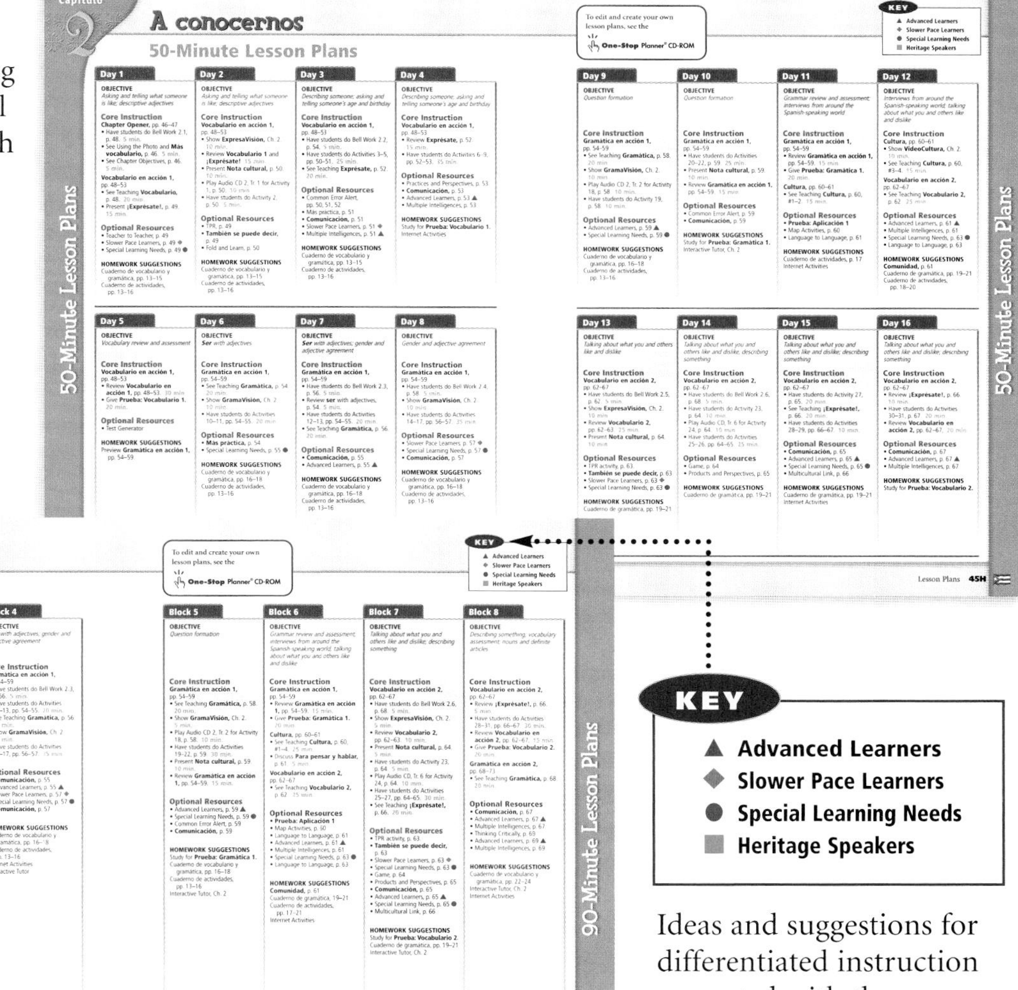

KEY

- ▲ Advanced Learners
- ◆ Slower Pace Learners
- ● Special Learning Needs
- ■ Heritage Speakers

Ideas and suggestions for differentiated instruction are noted with these icons ▲ ◆ ● ■ .

Teacher's Edition *continued*

Using the Wrap-Around Teacher Text

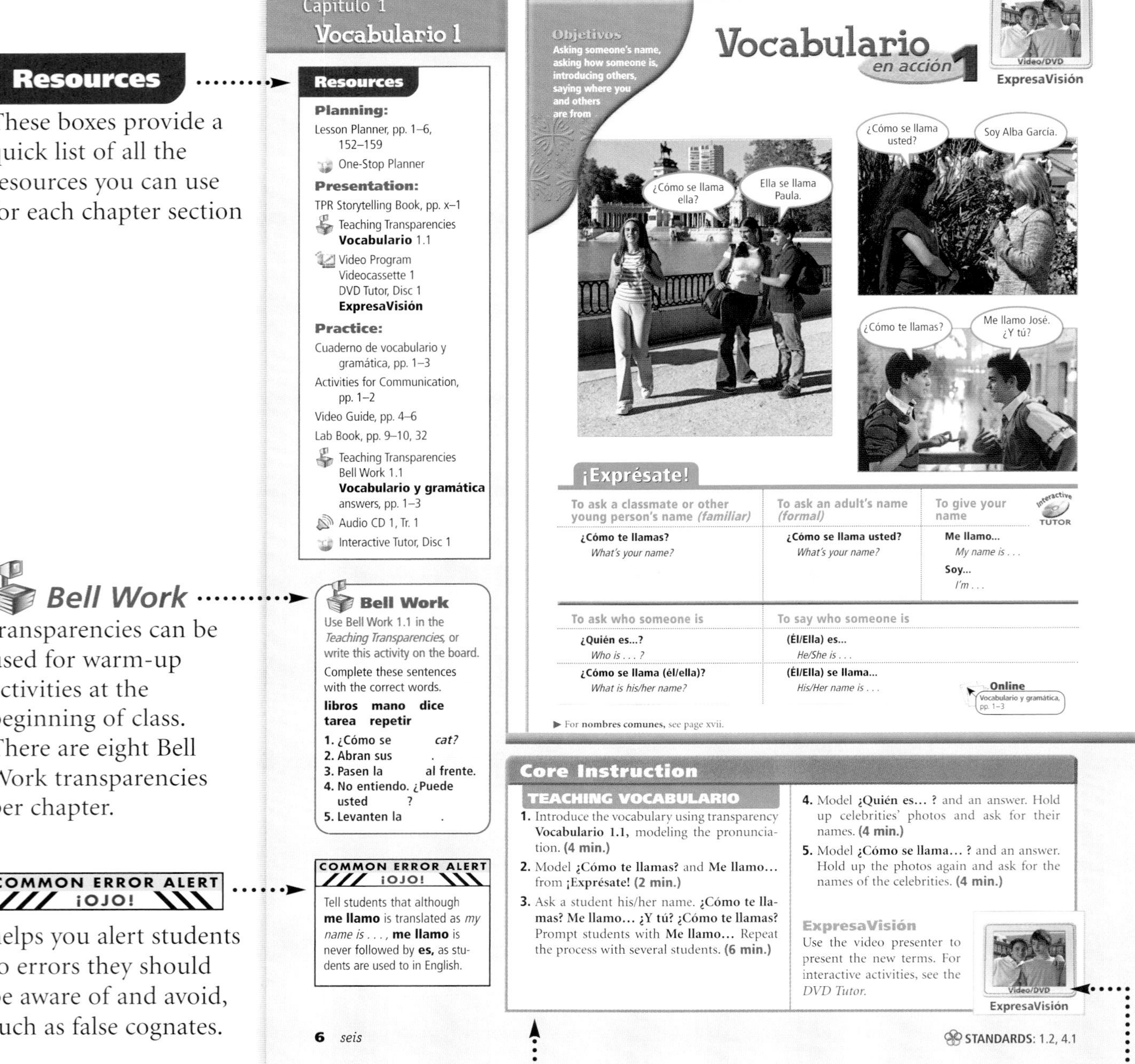

Capítulo 1

Vocabulario 1

Resources

Planning:

Lesson Planner, pp. 1–6, 152–159

One-Stop Planner

Presentation:

TPR Storytelling Book, pp. x–1

Teaching Transparencies **Vocabulario** 1.1

Video Program
Videocassette 1
DVD Tutor, Disc 1
ExpresaVisión

Practice:

Cuaderno de vocabulario y gramática, pp. 1–3

Activities for Communication, pp. 1–2

Video Guide, pp. 4–6

Lab Book, pp. 9–10, 32

Teaching Transparencies
Bell Work 1.1
Vocabulario y gramática answers, pp. 1–3

Audio CD 1, Tr. 1

Interactive Tutor, Disc 1

Bell Work

Use Bell Work 1.1 in the *Teaching Transparencies*, or write this activity on the board.

Complete these sentences with the correct words.

libros mano dice tarea repetir

1. ¿Cómo se _____ *cat?*
2. Abran sus _____.
3. Pasen la _____ al frente.
4. No entiendo. ¿Puede usted _____?
5. Levanten la _____.

COMMON ERROR ALERT ¡OJO!

Tell students that although **me llamo** is translated as *my name is . . .*, **me llamo** is never followed by **es,** as students are used to in English.

Objetivos

Asking someone's name, asking how someone is, introducing others, saying where you and others are from

Vocabulario en acción 1

Video/DVD ExpresaVisión

¿Cómo se llama ella?
Ella se llama Paula.
¿Cómo se llama usted?
Soy Alba García.
¿Cómo te llamas?
Me llamo José. ¿Y tú?

¡Exprésate!

To ask a classmate or other young person's name *(familiar)*	To ask an adult's name *(formal)*	To give your name
¿Cómo te llamas? *What's your name?*	**¿Cómo se llama usted?** *What's your name?*	**Me llamo...** *My name is . . .* **Soy...** *I'm . . .*

To ask who someone is	To say who someone is
¿Quién es...? *Who is . . . ?*	**(Él/Ella) es...** *He/She is . . .*
¿Cómo se llama (él/ella)? *What is his/her name?*	**(Él/Ella) se llama...** *His/Her name is . . .*

Interactive TUTOR

Online Vocabulario y gramática, pp. 1–3

▶ For **nombres comunes,** see page xvii.

Core Instruction

TEACHING VOCABULARIO

1. Introduce the vocabulary using transparency **Vocabulario 1.1,** modeling the pronunciation. **(4 min.)**
2. Model **¿Cómo te llamas?** and **Me llamo...** from **¡Exprésate! (2 min.)**
3. Ask a student his/her name. **¿Cómo te llamas? Me llamo... ¿Y tú? ¿Cómo te llamas?** Prompt students with **Me llamo...** Repeat the process with several students. **(6 min.)**
4. Model **¿Quién es... ?** and an answer. Hold up celebrities' photos and ask for their names. **(4 min.)**
5. Model **¿Cómo se llama... ?** and an answer. Hold up the photos again and ask for the names of the celebrities. **(4 min.)**

ExpresaVisión

Use the video presenter to present the new terms. For interactive activities, see the *DVD Tutor.*

Video/DVD ExpresaVisión

6 *seis*

STANDARDS: 1.2, 4.1

Resources

These boxes provide a quick list of all the resources you can use for each chapter section

Bell Work transparencies can be used for warm-up activities at the beginning of class. There are eight Bell Work transparencies per chapter.

COMMON ERROR ALERT ¡OJO!

helps you alert students to errors they should be aware of and avoid, such as false cognates.

Core Instruction

TEACHING VOCABULARIO

Timed suggestions for each presentation in the chapter provide guidance to newer teachers, and a quick reference for more experienced teachers.

Video Support is provided for each presentation in ***¡Exprésate!*** Native speakers and master teachers help you reach all students.

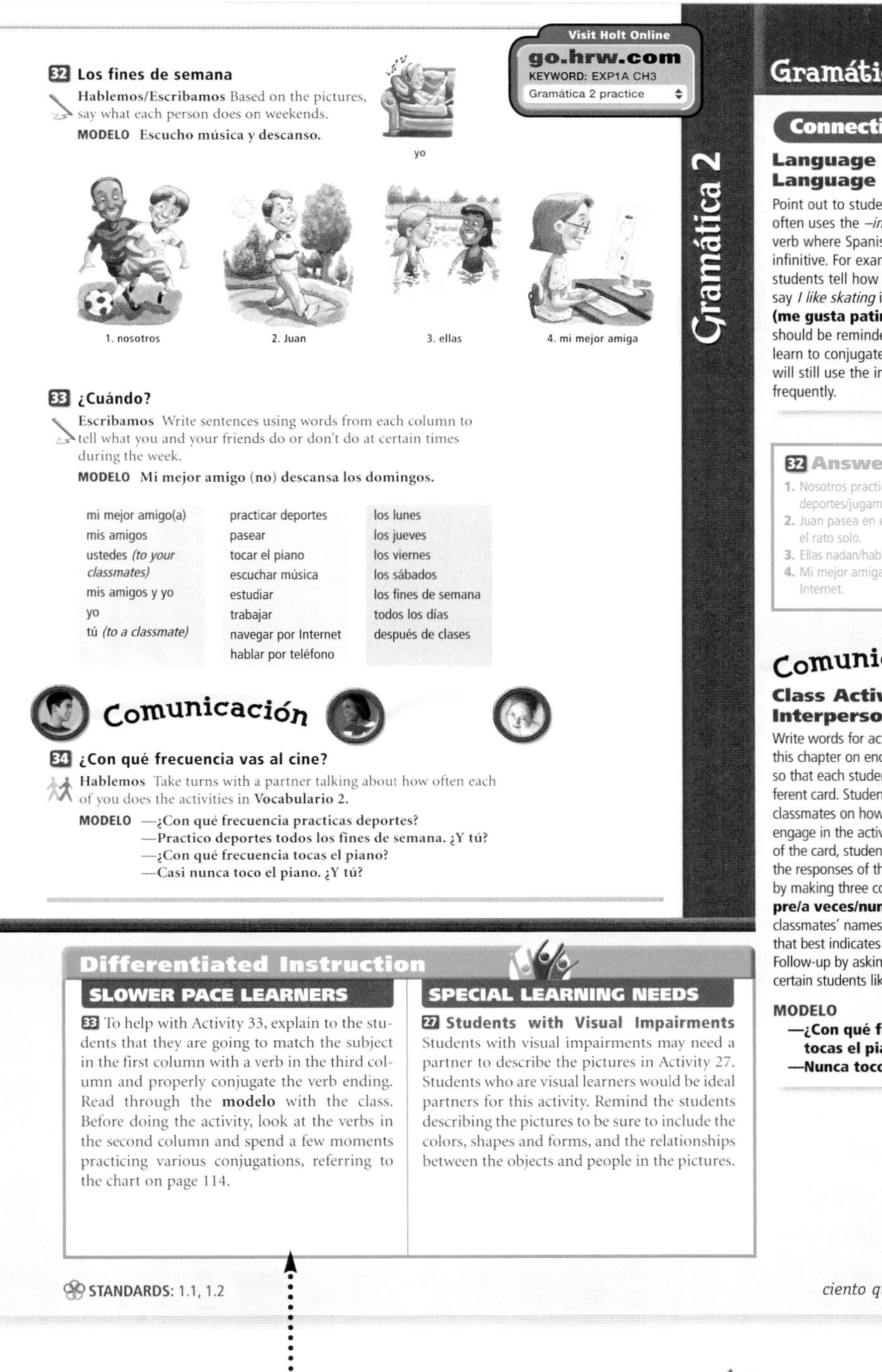

Visit Holt Online
go.hrw.com
KEYWORD: EXP1A CH3
Gramática 2 practice

Capítulo 3
Gramática 2

32 Los fines de semana

Hablemos/Escribamos Based on the pictures, say what each person does on weekends.

MODELO Escucho música y descanso.

yo

1. nosotros 2. Juan 3. ellas 4. mi mejor amiga

33 ¿Cuándo?

Escribamos Write sentences using words from each column to tell what you and your friends do or don't do at certain times during the week.

MODELO Mi mejor amigo (no) descansa los domingos.

mi mejor amigo(a)	practicar deportes	los lunes
mis amigos	pasear	los jueves
ustedes *(to your classmates)*	tocar el piano	los viernes
mis amigos y yo	escuchar música	los sábados
yo	estudiar	los fines de semana
tú *(to a classmate)*	trabajar	todos los días
	navegar por Internet	después de clases
	hablar por teléfono	

Comunicación

34 ¿Con qué frecuencia vas al cine?

Hablemos Take turns with a partner talking about how often each of you does the activities in **Vocabulario 2**.

MODELO —¿Con qué frecuencia practicas deportes?
—Practico deportes todos los fines de semana. ¿Y tú?
—¿Con qué frecuencia tocas el piano?
—Casi nunca toco el piano. ¿Y tú?

Connections

Language to Language

Point out to students that English often uses the *–ing* form of the verb where Spanish uses the infinitive. For example, have students tell how they would say *I like skating* in Spanish **(me gusta patinar).** Students should be reminded that as they learn to conjugate verbs, they will still use the infinitive form frequently.

32 Answers

1. Nosotros practicamos deportes/jugamos al fútbol.
2. Juan pasea en el parque/pasa el rato solo.
3. Ellas nadan/hablan en la piscina.
4. Mi mejor amiga navega por Internet.

Comunicación

Class Activity: Interpersonal

Write words for activities learned in this chapter on enough index cards, so that each student can have a different card. Students will poll their classmates on how often they engage in the activity. On the back of the card, students should record the responses of their classmates by making three columns: **siempre/a veces/nunca** and writing classmates' names in the column that best indicates their response. Follow-up by asking the class what certain students like to do.

MODELO
—**¿Con qué frecuencia tocas el piano?**
—**Nunca toco el piano.**

Differentiated Instruction

SLOWER PACE LEARNERS

33 To help with Activity 33, explain to the students that they are going to match the subject in the first column with a verb in the third column and properly conjugate the verb ending. Read through the **modelo** with the class. Before doing the activity, look at the verbs in the second column and spend a few moments practicing various conjugations, referring to the chart on page 114.

SPECIAL LEARNING NEEDS

27 Students with Visual Impairments Students with visual impairments may need a partner to describe the pictures in Activity 27. Students who are visual learners would be ideal partners for this activity. Remind the students describing the pictures to be sure to include the colors, shapes and forms, and the relationships between the objects and people in the pictures.

STANDARDS: 1.1, 1.2

ciento quince **115**

"Five-C's" suggestions for enhancing or extending the material on the student page focus on the **national standards.**

Scripts and ***Answers*** at point of use are a quick reference for all *Student Edition* listening activities.

Comunicación

The activities suggested here focus on one of the three kinds of communication: **interpersonal, interpretative,** or **presentational**.

Differentiated Instruction suggests ways to address the diversity of any classroom. The suggestions on the left are for either advanced or slower-paced learners, and those on the right are suggested actvities for special-needs learners or multiple intelligences.

Any time, from any computer, access *¡Exprésate!* online.

All Online Editions include

- Audio Recordings
- Practice activities, Projects, and Self-tests
- Searchable Spanish-English/English-Spanish Glossaries
- Searchable Grammar Summary
- Photo-Tour slide shows

Also available with each Online Edition

- Online Voice Recording
- Complete Video Program
- Online Workbooks
- Photo Projects
- Four-skills Online Assessment

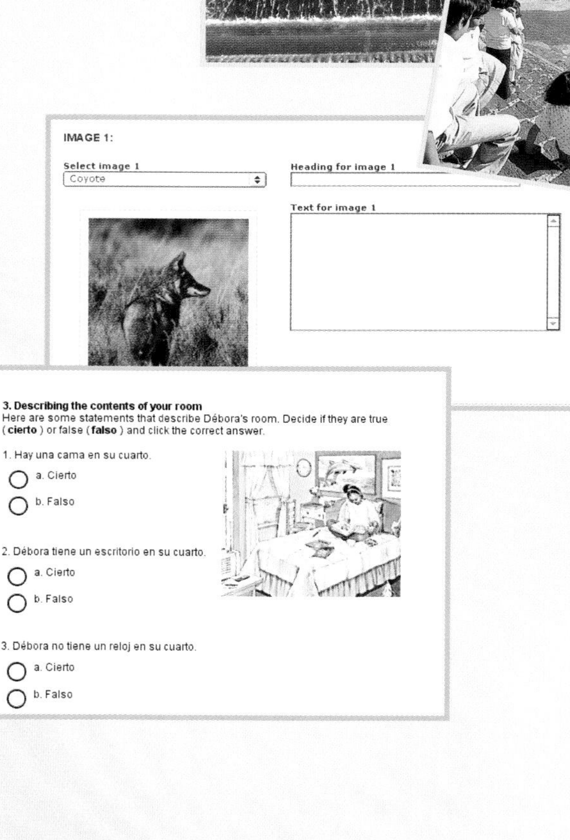

IMAGE 1:
Select image 1
Coyote
Heading for image 1
Text for image 1
3. Describing the contents of your room
Here are some statements that describe Débora's room. Decide if they are true (cierto) or false (falso) and click the correct answer.
1. Hay una cama en su cuarto.
a. Cierto
b. Falso
2. Débora tiene un escritorio en su cuarto.
a. Cierto
b. Falso
3. Débora no tiene un reloj en su cuarto.
a. Cierto
b. Falso

Video Takes You There!

GeoVisión

ExpresaVisión

GramaVisión

VideoCultura

VideoNovela

Video Program

Shot on location around the Spanish-speaking world, the Video Program provides video support for you and your students for every section of the book

- **GeoVisión** Video tours of the Spanish-speaking world
- **ExpresaVisión** Contextualized vocabulary presentations shot in each chapter location
- **GramaVisión** Animated grammar presentations with Master Teacher presentations, modeling, and practice activities
- **VideoCultura** Interviews with Spanish-speakers from around the world
- **VideoNovela** An exciting, ongoing story modeling vocabulary, functional expressions, and grammar in every chapter

Tutors Increase Student Success!

DVD Tutor

- The entire Video Program with all grammar presentations
- Optional captions for all video segments
- Comprehension activities
- Additional cultural footage
- Additional scenes modeling language in context

Interactive Tutor

- Games to practice all chapter material
- Writing and Recording Workshops
- Spanish-English and English-Spanish glossaries
- A grammar reference tool
- Teacher Management System

Ancillaries

¡Exprésate! offers a comprehensive ancillary package that meets the needs of today's classroom

Planning

One-Stop Planner with ExamView® Pro Test Generator

- **Editable lesson plans**
- **Printable worksheets** from resource books
- Direct link to HRW internet activities
- **Entire video** and **audio** programs
- **Clip art** library
- **Calendar planning tool** for customizing lesson plans

Lesson Planner with Differentiated Instruction

- **50-minute** and **90-minute Block** lesson plans for every chapter
- Block scheduling suggestions
- **Standards for Foreign Language Learning** correlations
- **Homework calendar**
- **Substitute Teacher** lesson plans for each chapter

Listening and Speaking

Lab Book

- Online resource activities for every chapter
- Student Response Forms for the listening activities in the *Student Edition*
- Activity masters for video-related activities

Audio Compact Discs

Listening activities for the Student Edition, the Testing Program, recorded reading selections, and songs

Activities for Communication

- **Information gap activities**
- **Situation cards** to practice interviews and role-plays
- **Picture sequences** for practice narrating a story

TPR Storytelling Book

- Step-by-step explanation of the TPR storytelling method
- Illustrated stories for each section of the chapter, with vocabulary lists and suggestions for gestures
- Teaching suggestions

Vocabulary & Grammar Practice

PuzzlePro®

Crossword puzzle, Word Search and Word Jumble maker with chapter-by-chapter vocabulary banks

Cuaderno de vocabulario y gramática

- Alternate presentations of major grammar points
- Additional focused practice
- *Teacher's Edition* with overprinted answers

Grammar Tutor for Students of Spanish

- Comparisons of basic grammar concepts in English and Spanish
- Comprehension check activities in both languages
- Discovery and application activities

Teaching Transparencies

- Colorful transparencies and blackline masters that help present and practice vocabulary, grammar, culture, and a variety of communicative functions
- Suggested activities for using the transparencies
- Answer transparencies

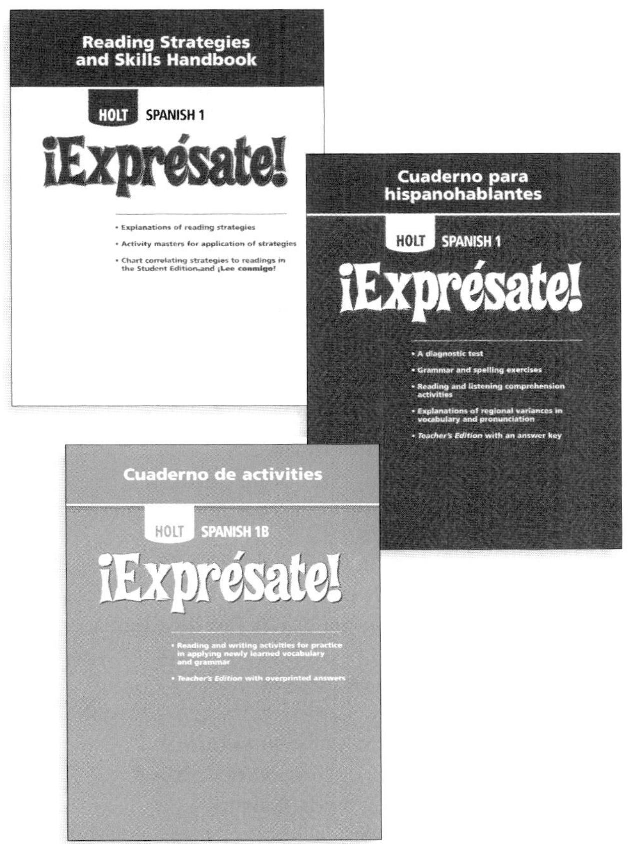

Reading and Writing

Reading Strategies and Skills Handbook

- Explanations of reading strategies
- Activity masters for application of strategies
- Chart correlating strategies to readings in the *Student Edition* and ***¡Lee conmigo!***

¡Lee conmigo!

- Readings on familiar topics
- Cultural information
- Additional vocabulary
- Interesting and engaging activities

Cuaderno de actividades

- Reading and writing activities for practice in applying newly learned vocabulary and grammar
- *Teacher's Edition* with overprinted answers

Heritage Speakers

Cuaderno para hispanohablantes

- Grammar and spelling exercises
- An engaging **novela** with comprehension activities
- **Workplace readiness** vocabulary presentations and activities
- *Teacher's Edition* with an answer key

Assessment

Assessment Program

Core Assessment:

- Nine quizzes per chapter (vocabulary, grammar, skills-based, reading, writing, **Geocultura**)
- Chapter Tests
- Speaking tests for each chapter
- Midterm and Final Exams
- Score sheets, scripts, answers

Alternative Assessment:

- Suggestions for oral and written portfolio assessment
- Suggestions for performance assessment
- Picture sequences (for testing student's ability to tell a story based on images)
- Rubrics, portfolio checklists, and evaluation forms

Standardized Assessment Tutor

Reading, writing, and math tests in a standardized, multiple-choice format

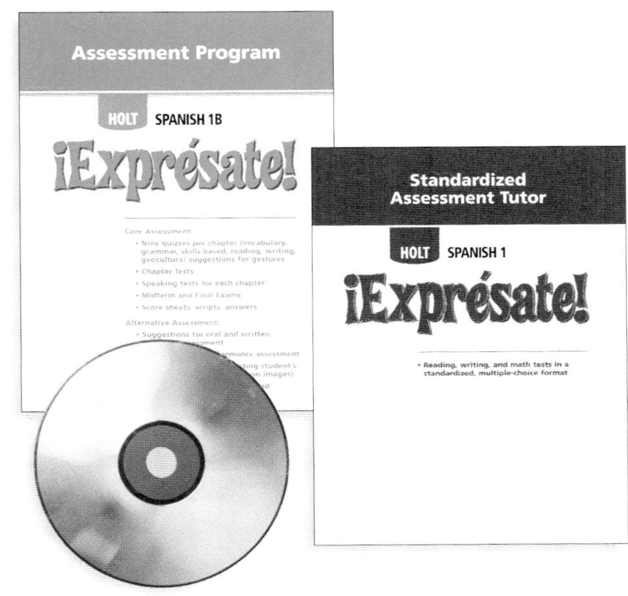

Cultural References

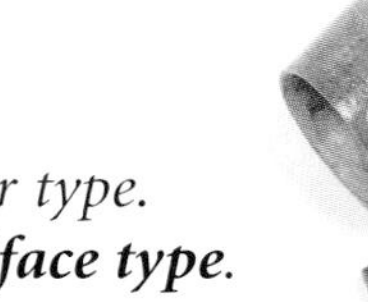

Page numbers referring to material in the Student Edition appear in regular type. For material located in the Teacher's Edition, page numbers appear in ***boldface type.***

ADVERTISEMENTS

ANIMALS AND NATURE

ART

BIRTHDAYS

ENTERTAINMENT

FASHION

FOOD

GEOGRAPHY AND MAPS

HISTORY

HOLIDAYS

HOME AND FAMILY LIFE

LANGUAGE

PARKS

PEOPLE

POINTS OF INTEREST

PRODUCTS AND ECONOMY

RECIPES

SEASONS, WEATHER, AND TIME

SHOPPING

SOCIAL CUSTOMS

SPORTS AND FITNESS

TRADITIONS

TRANSPORTATION

Professional Development

Holt, Rinehart and Winston is dedicated to enabling America's students to study world languages and culture. The educators who developed *¡Exprésate!* know that professional development begins with the instructional resources that teachers use every day. To that end, *¡Exprésate! Teacher's Editions* include:

Differentiated Instruction

ADVANCED LEARNERS

Extension Have students role-play a conversation between two friends at the mall. They

SPECIAL LEARNING NEEDS

Students with AD(H)D Before doing Activity 5, have students list the items they need for

- Instructions for adapting activities to meet the needs of a diverse student population with a wide range of ability levels and interests

TPR

TOTAL PHYSICAL RESPONSE

Bring to class or have students bring to class items from the Vocabulary. Try to find like items in different colors.

- Instructions for using methods, such as TPR, that appeal to specific types of learners

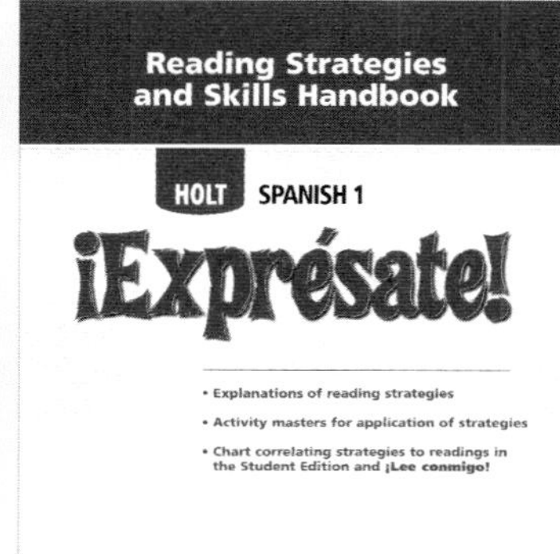

Reading Strategies and Skills Handbook
HOLT SPANISH 1
¡Exprésate!

- Ancillaries such as the Reading Strategies and Skills Handbook, help teachers learn to use reading strategies to help struggling readers become more effective readers

Meeting the National Standards

Communication

Comunicación, pp. 43, 45, 47, 49, 51, 57, 59, 61, 63, 65

Situación, p. 79

- Specific suggestions for building the national standards into the instructional program

The No Child Left Behind (NCLB) legislation considers foreign language a "core academic subject," which means foreign language teachers must be "highly qualified"; therefore states and districts can use their Title II teacher quality grant money (nearly $3 billion) on professional development and other initiatives to get their teachers, including foreign language teachers, to become highly qualified in their field.

Last year, ACTFL introduced policy directives to increase the international focus of the Department of Education. In response, the Fulbright-Hays Group Projects Abroad includes a request for seminars that develop and improve foreign language and area studies at elementary and secondary schools. Holt Speaker's Bureau Institutes can help local schools and districts increase their focus.

For the first time, the Title VI Undergraduate International Studies and Foreign Language competition has asked for projects that provide in-service training for K-12 teachers in foreign languages and international studies. Holt Professional Development courses can provide teachers with research-based, data-driven teacher education programs that are highly effective in improving performance.

Several Holt Professional Development Workshops are available for foreign language teachers.

Holt Professional Development Workshops

- **TPR Storytelling**
- **Teaching for Proficiency**
- **Culture in the World Languages Classroom**
- **Meeting the Needs of Diverse Learners and Students with Special Needs**
- **Assessment Options for World Languages**
- **Balancing the Four Skills and Culture**
- **The "What, Why, and How" of No Child Left Behind**
- **Teaching and Technology**

Implementing National Standards

Paul Sandrock
World Language Consultant, Wisconsin Department of Public Instruction Madison, Wisconsin

RESEARCH

National Standards in Foreign Language Education Project. (1999) *Standards for Foreign Language Learning in the 21st Century.* Lawrence, KS: Allen Press.

Phillips, June K., ed. (1999) *Foreign Language Standards: Linking Research, Theories, and Practice.* Lincolnwood, IL: National Textbook Company. (ACTFL Foreign Language Education Series)

Sandrock, Paul. (2002) *Planning Curriculum for Learning World Languages.* Madison, WI: Wisconsin Department of Public Instruction.

Shrum, Judith and Eileen Glisan. (2000) *Teacher's Handbook: Contextualized Language Instruction,* 2nd Edition. Heinle & Heinle.

Wiggins, Grant, and Jay McTighe. (1998) *Understanding by Design.* Alexandria, VA: Association for Supervision and Curriculum Development.

To implement the five goals of the national standards—communication, cultures, connections, comparisons, and communities—requires a shift from emphasizing the means to focusing on the ends.

Instead of simply planning a series of activities, today's world language teacher focuses on what and how the student is learning. Rather than teaching and testing the four skills of listening, speaking, reading, and writing in isolation, teachers need to make their instructional decisions based on the three purposes directing the communication (interpersonal, interpretive, and presentational) and within a cultural context. Our standards answer why we are teaching various components of language.

Since the publication of the standards, many states have developed more specific performance standards that provide evidence of the application of the national content standards, and teachers have carried the standards into the classroom. Textbook writers and materials providers are also responding to the shift brought about by the standards, providing an organization, creating a context, and modeling the kind of instruction that leads students to successfully demonstrate the communication strategies envisioned in our standards. Textbooks can bring authentic materials into the classroom, real cultural examples that avoid stereotypes, and a broader exposure to the variety of people who speak the language being studied. Standards provide the ends; teachers use textbooks and materials to help students practice the means.

Assessment is the jigsaw puzzle that shows students what they can do with their new language. If we only test students on the means of vocabulary and grammar, students simply collect random puzzle pieces. We have to test, and students have to practice, putting the pieces together in meaningful and purposeful ways. When they are truly communicating, students will know they've achieved the standards.

Goal	Standards
Communication Communicate in Languages Other Than English	**Standard 1.1 Interpersonal** Students engage in conversations, provide and obtain information, express feelings and emotions, and exchange opinions. **Standard 1.2 Interpretive** Students understand and interpret written and spoken language on a variety of topics. **Standard 1.3 Presentational** Students present information, concepts, and ideas to an audience of listeners or readers on a variety of topics.
Cultures Gain knowledge and understanding of Other Cultures	**Standard 2.1 Practices** Students demonstrate an understanding of the relationship between the practices and perspectives of the culture studied. **Standard 2.2 Products** Students demonstrate an understanding of the relationship between the products and perspectives of the culture studied.
Connections Connect with other disciplines and Acquire information	**Standard 3.1 Across Discipline** Students reinforce and further their knowledge of other disciplines through the foreign language. **Standard 3.2 Added Perspective** Students acquire information and recognize the distinctive viewpoints that are only available through the foreign language and its cultures.
Comparisons Develop Insight into the Nature of Language and Culture	**Standard 4.1 Language** Students demonstrate understanding of the nature of language through comparisons of the language studied and their own. **Standard 4.2 Culture** Students demonstrate understanding of the concept of culture through comparisons of the cultures studied and their own.
Communities Participate in Multilingual Communities at Home and Around the World	**Standard 5.1 Practical Applications** Students use the language both within and beyond the school setting. **Standard 5.2 Personal Enrichment** Students show evidence of becoming life-long learners by using the language for personal enjoyment and enrichment.

Kylene Beers, PhD.
Clinical Associate Professor
University of Houston
Houston, Texas

RESEARCH

Baumann, J. 1984
"Effectiveness of a Direct Instruction Paradigm for Teaching Main Idea Comprehension." *Reading Research Quarterly,* 20: 93–108.

Beers, K. 2002.
When Kids Can't Read—What Teachers Can Do. Portsmouth: Heinemann.

Dole, J., Brown, K., and Trathen, W. 1996.
"The Effects of Strategy Instruction on the Comprehension Performance of At-Risk Students," *Reading Research Quarterly,* 31: 62–89.

Duffy, G. 2002
"The Case for Direct Explanation of Strategies." *Comprehension Instruction: Research-Based Best Practices.* Eds. C. Block and M. Pressley. New York: Guilford Press. 28–41.

Pearson, P. D. 1984
"Direct Explicit Teaching of Reading Comprehension." *Comprehension Instruction: Perspectives and Suggestions.* Eds. G. Duffy, L. Roehler, and J. Mason. New York: Longman, 222–233.

Teaching Comprehension

"Comprehension is both a product and a process, something that requires purposeful, strategic effort on the reader's part as he or she predicts, visualizes, clarifies, questions, connects, summarizes, and infers."

—Kylene Beers

When the Text is Tough

"Comprehension is only tough when you can't do it," explained the eleventh grader. I almost dismissed his words until I realized what truth they offered. We aren't aware of all the thinking we do to comprehend a text until faced with a difficult text. Then, all too clearly, we're aware of what words we don't understand, what syntax seems convoluted, what ideas are beyond our immediate grasp. As skilled readers, we know what to do; we slow our pace, re-read, ask questions, connect whatever we do understand to what we don't understand, summarize what we've read thus far, make inferences about what the author is saying. In short, we make that invisible act of comprehension visible as we consciously push our way through the difficult text. At those times, we realize that, indeed, comprehension is tough.

Reading Strategies for Struggling Readers

It's even tougher if you lack strategies that would help you through the difficult text. Many struggling readers believe they aren't successful readers because that's just the way things are (Beers, 2002); they believe successful readers know some secret that they haven't been told (Duffy, 2002). While we don't mean to keep comprehension a secret, at times we do. For instance, though we tell students to "re-read," we haven't shown them how to alter their reading. We tell them to "make inferences," or "make predictions," but we haven't taught them how to do such things. In other words, we tell them what to do, but don't show them how to do it, in spite of several decades of research showing the benefit of direct instruction in reading strategies to struggling readers. (Baumann, 1984; Pearson, P.D., 1984; Dole, et al., 1996; Beers, 2002).

Direct Instruction

Direct instruction means telling students what you are going to teach them, modeling it for them, providing assistance as they practice it, then letting them practice it on their own. It's not saying, "Visualize while you read," but, instead, explaining, "Today, I'm going to read this part aloud to you. I'm going to focus on seeing some of the action in my mind as I read. I'm going to stop occasiionally and tell you what I'm seeing and what in the text helped me see that." When we directly teach comprehension strategies to students via modeling and repeated practice, we show students that good readers don't just get it. They work hard to get it. **¡Exprésate!** takes the secret out of comprehension as it provides teachers the support they need to reach struggling readers.

Differentiated Instruction

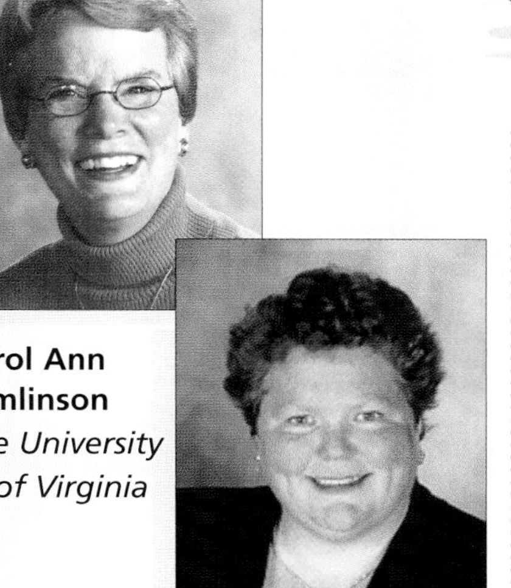

rol Ann
mlinson
e University
of Virginia

Cindy Strickland
The University of Virginia

Teachers who differentiate their instruction recognize that students are at different points in their learning journeys, will grow at different rates, and will need different kinds and amounts of support to reach their goals.

Differentiation and Varied Approaches

Differentiated classrooms offer varied approaches to **content** (what students learn), **process** (how students go about making sense of essential knowledge and practicing essential skills), **product** (how students demonstrate what they have learned), and **learning environment** (the setting in which students learn). Differentiation is based on an ongoing diagnosis of student interest, learning profile, and readiness.

Differentiation and the World-Language Teacher

World language teachers are natural differentiators for learning profile. We provide opportunities for students to acquire proficiency in the target language through a variety of means: speaking, listening, writing, and reading. Through this variety of approaches, we recognize that students' proficiency in each of these skill areas will vary. Good language teachers work hard to help students improve in areas in which they struggle, and revel in areas of strength.

Systematic differentiation for readiness provides many world-language teachers with a bit more of a challenge. Students come to us with a huge range in amount and type of language experience, including, for example, first-year students who have had no exposure to the target language, who have had an exploratory class, who have studied another target language, or who are native speakers.

Key Principles of Differentiated Instruction

There are several key principles to follow when differentiating instruction in the language classroom. First, start by clearly defining what is most essential for students to know, understand, and be able to do in the target language. Second, hold high expectations for all students and make sure that they are engaged in **respectful work**. Third, use **flexible grouping,** an excellent tool to ensure that all students learn to work independently, cooperatively and collaboratively in a variety of settings and with a variety of peers.

A final principle of differentiated instruction is **ongoing assessment**. To this end, the teacher constantly monitors student interest, learning profile, and readiness in order to adjust to the growing and changing learner. Teachers must not assume that a student will have the same readiness or interest in every unit of study or in every skill area. Preassessment is a must, particularly in the areas of knowledge and facility with vocabulary and grammatical constructions.

The Role of the Teacher in Academically Diverse Classrooms

Good teachers have always recognized that "one size fits all" instruction does not serve students well. To be effective, teachers must find ways consistently to **reach more kinds of learners more often**—by recognizing and responding to students' varied readiness levels, by honoring their diverse interests, and by understanding their preferences for how they learn information and practice new skills.

RESEARCH

Tomlinson, C., and Eidson, C. *Design for Differentiation: Curriculum for the Differentiated Classroom,* Grades 5–9. Alexandria, VA: Association for Supervision and Curriculum Development (in press).

Tomlinson, C. 2001. *How to Differentiate Instruction in Mixed-Ability Classrooms,* 2/e. Alexandria, VA: Association for Supervision and Curriculum Development

Tomlinson, C. and Allan, S. 2001. *Leadership for Differentiating Schools and Classrooms.* Alexandria, VA: Association for Supervision and Curriculum Development, 2000.

Winebrenner, S. 1996. *Teaching Kids with Learning Difficulties in the Regular Classroom.* Minneapolis, MN: Free Spirit, 1996.

Technology and Foreign Language Instruction

Robert Ponterio,
Professor of French, SUNY Cortland

Jean W. LeLoup,
Professor of Spanish, SUNY Cortland

New technologies make it possible for foreign language teachers to bring the world into their classroom as never before and to make direct connections between their students and the speakers and culture of the target language.

From the World to the Classroom

Communication technologies are of prime interest to foreign language professionals because communication is the main thrust in foreign language teaching (Omaggio Hadley, 2001; Phillips, 1998). The present emphasis on *using* language, not just *learning about* language, calls for materials that prepare students for authentic communicative situations and lead them quickly to work with real information in the target language. In addition, the ready access to authentic materials, native speakers, and rich target language input that these new media can provide facilitates the creation of lessons that have tremendous potential in the foreign language classroom for directly addressing many of the goal areas of the national Standards for Foreign Language Learning (Shrum & Glisan, 2000).

The Standards, Cultural Knowledge, and Multimedia

The Standards stress the importance of cultural knowledge as an integral part of language learning; the tri-part examination of cultural products, practices and the perspectives underlying them is greatly enhanced by using Internet materials that help students better connect with different cultural realities (Standards, 1999). Multimedia, mixing together realia, photos, video, and sounds from the native environment, contributes significantly to creating a culturally and linguistically authentic context for language learning. Multimedia visual materials also offer a window to nonlinguistic cues that are vital to second language comprehension and learning (Binkley, 2003).

Technology Is a Tool

Technology is a powerful tool when properly integrated in the curriculum (LeLoup & Ponterio, 2003). Computers, audio, and video are an adjunct to language learning objectives and not an end in themselves; they offer many benefits for expanding options in the instructional process. Access to the materials through Internet sites can significantly increase the time spent working with the language as well as the quality of homework activities. Electronic materials are easily updated for continued accuracy and adapted to correspond to current lesson topics and themes. Computer-based exercises that offer immediate feedback to the learner reflect a student-centered approach to language instruction that can help reinforce accuracy in the written language and provide for self-paced learning. For example, the use of hypertext allows an individual to find clarification of meaning or to examine an idea in more depth by connecting to additional materials beyond the text. It puts the power to control this exploration squarely in the student's hands. Current writing tools, both assisted writing environments and word processors, help develop the skills needed for communication in the real world (Scott, 1996). Finally, because of its flexibility and ease of use, technology provides the optimal vehicle for creating authentic assessments, which parallels the use of authentic materials and complements a proficiency-based orientation (Terry, 1998).

RESEARCH

Binkley, S. C. (2004). "Using digital video of native speakers to enhance listening comprehension and cultural competence." In Lomicka, L., & Cooke-Plagwitz, J., Eds. *Teaching with Technology.* Boston, MA: Heinle & Heinle; 115–120.

LeLoup, J. W. & Ponterio, R. (2003). *Second Language Acquisition and Technology: A Review of the Research.* ERIC Digest EDO-FL-03-11.

Omaggio Hadley, A. (2001). *Teaching language in context.* Boston, MA: Heinle & Heinle.

Phillips, J. K. (1998). "Changing teacher/learner roles in Standards-driven contexts." In Harper, J., Lively, M., & Wiliams, M., Eds. *The coming of age of the profession: Issues and emerging ideas for the teaching of foreign languages.* Boston, MA: Heinle & Heinle; 3–14.

Scott, V. M. (1996). *Rethinking foreign language writing.* Boston, MA: Heinle & Heinle.

Nancy Humbach

Classroom Management

Successful classes are created by teachers who are motivated, have high expectations, demonstrate enthusiasm for their students and for content, and who maintain organization, flexibility, and the ability to mediate.

Managing Your Class Successfully

Managing the classroom so that students stay on task, understand the concepts being taught, and have their needs addressed is one of the most daunting challenges facing a teacher. The beginning of the year is the best time to let students know what you expect of them and what they can expect of you. Inform students what they will need to bring to class and discuss with them required behaviors, such as respect for others. For more effective participation, allow students to brainstorm behaviors that would help them learn.

Present your expectations in writing and on your website, if you have one, keeping rules and regulations simple and clear. State them in positive terms, such as "Come to class with textbook, paper, etc.," instead of "Don't come to class without..."

Plans and Organization

To keep your class running smoothly, create lesson plans that have a variety of activities, plans for transitions between activities, a varied pace, and attention to time-on-task. Effective lesson plans take into account the ability level of the students. They present a challenge that is within reach of the students but holds their interest, and they include advance organizers, presentations, checks, and evaluations.

Begin class on a positive note by having an activity (some type of advance organizer) on the board, the overhead, or on paper. Such an activity will allow you to take attendance and check homework and still be ready to begin class as the bell rings.

Task-based activities enlist the creativity of students and may be done either alone, in pairs, or in groups. Problem-solving tasks with time limits allow students to be involved actively in learning, as do those that require students to discover solutions or outcomes.

Pair and Group Work

Group work is important in a language class. If you plan well, train students to work in groups, and have a sound evaluation plan, group work can be rewarding and a highly productive part of the learning process. No matter how you establish your groups, the process of moving into groups must be rapid and cause as little disruption as possible. Systematic monitoring is essential for successful pair and group work, evaluation, and teacher feedback.

Be Prepared—But Stay Flexible

No two teaching situations are alike. What works for one teacher or one class may not work in all situations. However, motivation, preparation, interest in the students and in the content, and sensible ground rules for such things as pair and group work can help you maintain a successful class.

RESEARCH

Cangelosi, James (1997). *Classroom Management Strategies: Gaining and Maintaining Students' Cooperation.* New York: Addison Wesley Longman. Third Edition.

Danforth, Scot and Joseph R. Boyle (2000). *Cases in Behavior Management.* Upper Saddle River: Pearson Education (Merrill Prentice Hall).

McEwan Landau, Barbara (2004). *The Art of Classroom Management: Building Equitable Learning Communities.* Pearson Education (Merrill Prentice Hall).

McEwan, Barbara (2000). *The Art of Classroom Management: Effective Practices for Buiding Equitable Learning Communities.* Upper Saddle River: Pearson Education (Merrill Prentice Hall).

Palmer, Parker (1998). *The Courage to Teach: Exploring the Inner Landscape of a Teacher's Life.* San Francisco: Jossey-Bass Publishers.

Schmuck, Richard A. and Patricia A. Schmuck (2001). *Group Processes in the Classroom.* Boston: McGraw Hill. Eighth Edition.

Shrum, Judith and Eileen Glisan. *Teachers' Handbook: Contextualized Language Instruction.* Boston: Heinle and Heinle. Any edition.

¡Ponga!

P	O	N	G	A
12	18	41	47	66
7	26	39	54	70
6	27	LIBRE	49	63
5	23	35	58	73
3	30	36	52	75

This game, played much like Bingo, lets students practice numbers, colors, body parts, clothing, or other objects in Spanish.

Materials Index cards (or paper) and markers

Procedure Students prepare their own Ponga card by drawing a card similar to a Bingo card with four horizontal and vertical spaces. Students write a number, color a square a certain color, or draw a body part, piece of clothing, or other object in each space. Read a number or one of the other themed vocabulary words in Spanish and record it. Students cover or cross off the spaces as the items in them are called until a player has filled an entire row or column. He or she then says **¡Ponga!** The student who reads the vocabulary back correctly wins. You may laminate the cards for later use with water-based markers, or use paper scraps to cover the numbers.

Cerebro

This game, played like Concentration®, helps students learn and review through concentration and recall. This game can be used to reinforce vocabulary, questions and answers, and verbs.

Les gusta comer pizza.

Materials Index cards

Procedure Have students make three pairs of cards. On a card have them write a question, a verb, or a vocabulary word. On the card's mate, the student writes the answer to the question, draws the action of the verb, or draws the vocabulary item. Divide the class into pairs or small groups. Have one student combine and shuffle all the group's cards together and then lay them out in a grid on the desk, blank side up. Players take turns turning over two cards each. If they match, the player takes them. If they don't, they are returned, face down, to their original place. Play continues until all the cards are paired. The player with the most matches wins.

Categorías

This game is patterned after the game Scattergories®. It should be played in teams and is good for reinforcing vocabulary from various categories.

Materials A timer, index cards, and pencils and paper for scoring

Procedure Make index cards with the letters of the alphabet on them. Write a list of three categories on the board that the class has learned: classes, school supplies, names, descriptive adjectives or other themed vocabulary. Have teams prepare a paper with three columns, one for each category. One team chooses a letter from the stack of index cards and calls out the letter to be used in this round. The timer is set for one minute and the round begins. For each category, teams quickly fill in the answer sheet with vocabulary words that begin with the key letter. When the timer rings, students must stop writing. Have one team read its answers. If any other team has that word, everyone crosses it off their list. The next team reads any words remaining on their lists, and again any duplicates are crossed off all lists. Repeat this process for the remaining teams. The winning team is the one with the highest number of unique, unduplicated words.

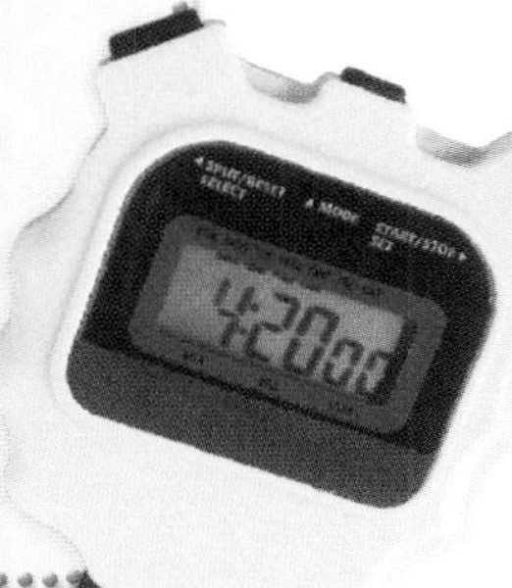

Arreglar palabras

Similar to Scrabble®, this game is excellent for review of all learned vocabulary and verbs.

Materials Heavy paper or card stock.

Procedure Cut the paper into one-inch squares. Leave a third of them blank and write the Spanish alphabet on the rest. Make extra squares with the most common letters: vowels, s, t, etc. A blank may serve as any letter. Place the letters face down in one pile and the blanks in another pile. Each student picks ten letters and five blanks. Using learned vocabulary, students arrange letters and blanks to form as many words as possible on their desk. The student with the most words, and the student with the longest word, are the winners. This game may be played in pairs with students taking turns and building their words off of the already played words on the desk.

Mímica

Played like charades, this game reviews active verbs. It is an excellent activity for kinesthetic learners.

Materials Index cards

Procedure Write action verbs or phrases from chapter themes on index cards, (things you like to do, school activities, preparing for a party, preparing and serving food, staying healthy, or vacation activities). Divide the class into teams and give one card to each student. Taking turns, students act out their word or phrase without speaking, while the other team guesses in Spanish. You may consider limiting the time that each team has to guess. As a challenge, have the teams combine a number of students' cards to created sentences, assigning nouns and other necessary parts of speech to individuals. The team acts out its string of words while the other team tries to figure out the sentence that is being presented.

levantar pesas

ir al cine

jugar a los videojuegos

La papa caliente

This exciting game quickly practices vocabulary and phrases while getting the entire class involved.

Materials A small box, a wind up timer or battery operated alarm clock

Procedure Make a **papa caliente** by placing an alarm clock or a timer in a small box. Be sure the alarm or timer ticks loudly. Have students sit in a circle. Call out a category based on a vocabulary category, (**frutas, comida del desayuno,** etc.). As you name the category hand the **papa** to a student who must then say a related vocabulary word. After saying a word, that student then passes the **papa** to the student to the right, who is to name a different item from the category. If a student is left holding the **papa** when the timer goes off, they are out of the game. You decide when a category has been exhausted and change it accordingly. The winner is the last student remaining who could think of new vocabulary, and pass the **papa** on with out getting caught by the buzzer.

Palabras revueltas

This game is good for tactile learners. The goal is for students to construct Spanish vocabulary words from scrambled letters.

Materials Small squares of paper for each student

Procedure Divide the class into two teams. Each person on the team finds a different Spanish vocabulary word from the chapter and writes each letter of that word on one of the pieces of paper. After everyone is finished, team members exchange their letters with a person on the other team. Students quickly try to arrange the letters to form the word. The student who unscrambles a word before his or her counterpart wins a point for his or her team.

Una palabra más

This game helps students build on words and ideas to make complete sentences. The sentences can be odd or funny, but they should be grammatically correct.

Procedure Create any number of teams. Begin a sentence on the board with a word. For example, (**Mi**). Have one player write a word to continue the sentence, (**papá**). The next team's player writes another word, (**tiene**). Once the sentence becomes complicated, students may add words before or after others. For example, **inteligente** could go between **papá** and **tiene**. Players score one point for each logical contribution.

Mi papá tiene ...

¡Dibújalo!

This game provides a thorough review of nouns, verbs, and adjectives and creates team spirit within the class.

Materials Index cards and colored markers

Procedure Divide the class into five equal groups of students. Each group selects 10 vocabulary items from a chapter or various chapters already learned and writes one vocabulary word on each card. A more challenging version can be played with phrases or short sentences. Combine all cards from each group and shuffle. Divide the class into two teams. You will need one scorekeeper and one timekeeper. Give the first team a card with the Spanish word written on it. That team member goes to the board and must illustrate the word within 15 seconds. The next three people in line from that person's team are allowed one guess each. If one of the three people guesses correctly, the team scores a point. If they cannot guess, the question goes to the next person on the other team. The other team is allowed only one guess. If the student shown the card does not know what the Spanish word means, the team defaults its turn, and the opportunity to play the word goes to the other team. ***¡Dibújalo!*** can be played by the whole class, or a small group for vocabulary review.

9-13
El trece
de septiembre
es mi cumpleaños.

De sílabas a palabras

This game provides an opportunity to practice pronunciation and can be used to review vocabulary from any chapter.

Materials Index cards and pens or markers

Procedure Review the definition of a syllable as a short unit of speech. Break up the vocabulary words from the chapter into syllables and have the students write each syllable on an index card using large letters. For example, make three cards for **cua – der – no,** two cards for **com – prar,** etc. Shuffle the cards and pass them out among students. Say **"De sílabás a palabras"**. Give the students a specific amount of time (one minute), to find other people with whom they can form a word. Tell students to call out **"¡Palabra!"** when they have formed a word. The group must say their word in unison as you point to them. Collect all the index cards, shuffle them, and redistribute to play again.

cua

der

no

Béisbol con palabras

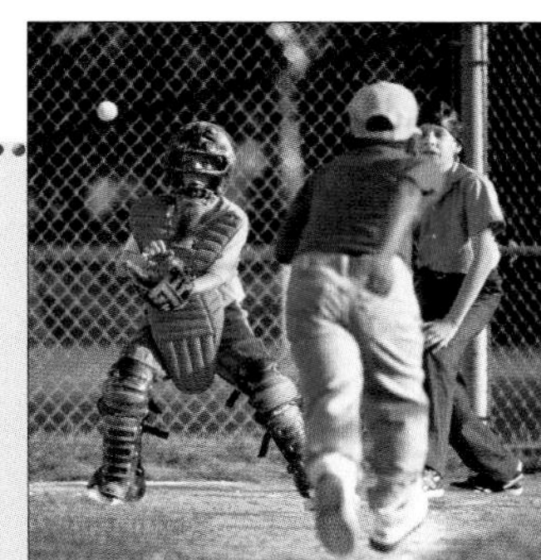

With this game students will practice the new vocabulary words and expressions and review previously learned vocabulary.

Preparation Develop a list of questions whose answers require the students to use words and phrases from the current and previous chapters. (Examples: **Para evitar el estrés yo practico ______. Para tener músculos grandes hay que levantar ______. Debes dormir para no estar ______. Antes de hacer ejercicio hay que ______.**)

Procedure Divide the class into two teams. Assign a student scorekeeper. Draw a baseball diamond with bases on the board. Set a number of innings for playing. The batter is the first player on Team A. You serve as the pitcher and ask the batter a question. If the batter gives a correct answer, he or she moves to first base. The scorekeeper places a mark on first base. If the batter cannot answer, he or she is out. You then ask a question of the second batter on Team A. If the second batter answers correctly, he or she goes to first base. If there is a player on first base, he or she advances to second base and the scorekeeper places a mark on second base. A team scores a run by advancing a player to home plate. Team A continues batting until it has three outs. Then Team B goes to bat. When Team B has three outs, the first inning is over. Teams get one point for each run, and the team with the most points wins.

Cadena

This game, which helps students review vocabulary, is good for auditory learners.

Procedure Have all students stand up. Announce a vocabulary theme, (school classes, clothing, housing items, etc.). Say a sentence with one word from the theme. For example, **En el colegio estudio matemáticas**. The first student then repeats the sentence saying what you said and adding another word that follows the theme, (**En el colegio estudio matemáticas y español**). When someone says the "chain" incorrectly, he or she sits down. This sequence continues until no one can add any more words to the sentence. At this time you might select another theme. The winners are the last three students to be left standing.

El español, ¿por qué?
Why Study Spanish?

Por lo mundial *Because it's worldwide*

Spanish is the fourth most commonly spoken language in the world. You can visit any one of 21 countries in the world that speak Spanish and feel at home. Even in the United States, knowing Spanish can open doors to you.

So whether you're in Europe, North, Central, or South America, or even Africa, as a Spanish speaker you won't have to rely on someone else to watch television or read a newspaper. You'll learn things on your own. You'll truly be a citizen of the world.

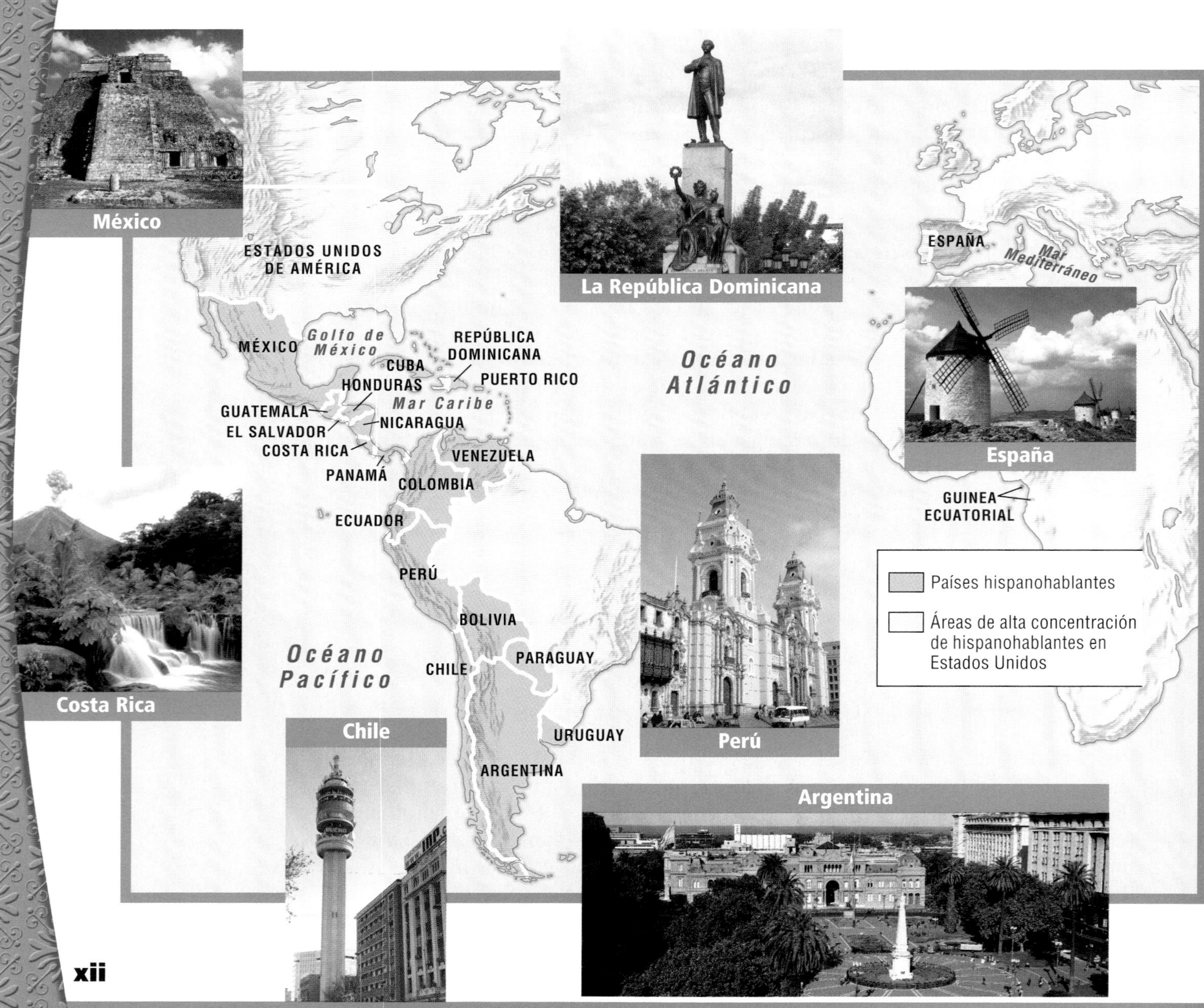

Por lo bello *Because it's beautiful*

You'll be amazed to discover how rich the Spanish-speaking world is in works of music, literature, science, religion, and art. The novels of Miguel de Cervantes or Isabel Allende, the paintings of Fernando Botero or Frida Kahlo, the poetry of Gabriela Mistral or Pablo Neruda: all these treasures and many more await you as you explore the Spanish-speaking world.

Ceramic tiles form this mural by Dominican artist Said Musa.

Traditional painted carts in Costa Rica are a part of **El Festival de las Carretas.**

The fountain of Cibeles, named after the goddess Cybele, is one of Madrid's best-known landmarks.

These young Costa Ricans are wearing traditional dance costumes.

Why Study Spanish?

Por lo práctico *Because it's practical*

You're living in the country with the fifth-largest Hispanic population in the world, more than 33 million people. And whether they're originally from Mexico, Puerto Rico, or Cuba—or from any other part of Latin America or Spain—almost nine out of ten are Spanish speakers.

Businesses, government agencies, educational institutions, and other employers will be looking for more bilingual employees every year. Give yourself an edge in the job market with Spanish!

Bilingual doctors, nurses, and others in the field of medicine provide care for Spanish-speaking patients.

Patricia Janiot is a popular anchor at the Spanish language news department of CNN En Español.

Miami is an international center and a multicultural hub for Latin American trade.

Why Study Spanish?

¡Porque puedes! *Because you can do it!*

Applying your learning skills to a new language will be challenging at first. But you have the tools you need to do the job. And you're lucky to be living at a time when there are almost no limits to your opportunities to practice Spanish. You can interact with Spanish speakers not just in your community but all over the world, via pen pal organizations, the library, or a multitude of resources and online networks.

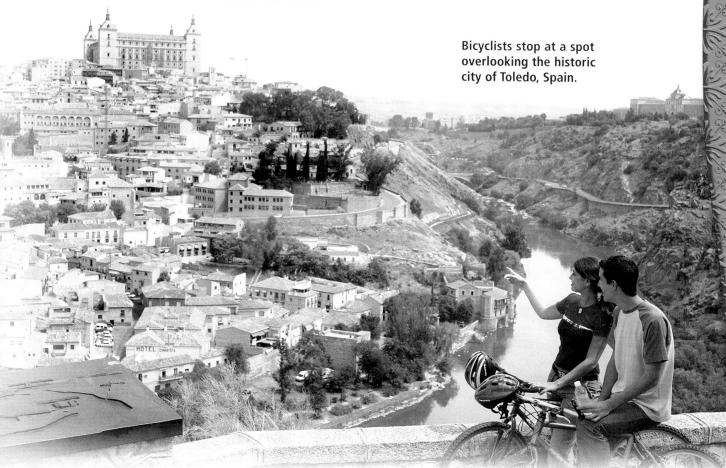

Bicyclists stop at a spot overlooking the historic city of Toledo, Spain.

En fin, porque sí *Finally, just because...*

The best reason of all to study Spanish is because you want to! You know better than anyone what motivated you to enroll for Spanish class. It might be one of the reasons given here, such as getting a job, learning about world issues, or enjoying works of art. Or it might be something more personal, like wanting to communicate with Spanish-speaking friends and family, or travel. So pat yourself on the back and **¡Exprésate!**

En la clase de español
In Spanish Class

Here are some phrases you'll probably hear in your classroom, along with some responses.

Phrases:	Responses:
Tengo una pregunta. *I have a question.*	**¿Sí? Dime.** *Yes? What is it?*
¿Cómo se dice...? *How do you say . . .?*	**Se dice...** *You say . . .*
¿Cómo se escribe...? *How do you spell . . .?*	**Se escribe...** *It's spelled . . .*
No entiendo. ¿Puede repetir? *I don't understand. Could you repeat that?* **Más despacio, por favor.** *More slowly, please.*	**Claro que sí.** *Yes, of course.*
¿Sabes qué significa (quiere decir)...? *Do you know what . . . means?*	**No, no sé.** *No, I don't know.* **Sí, significa (quiere decir)...** *Yes, it means . . .*
Gracias. *Thank you.*	**De nada.** *You're welcome.*
Perdón. *I'm sorry.*	**Está bien.** *It's okay.*

Here are some things your teacher might ask you to do.

Levanten la mano.
Raise your hand.

Escuchen.
Listen.

¡Su atención, por favor!
Attention, please.

Silencio, por favor.
Silence, please.

Abran sus libros en la página...
Open your books to page . . .

Cierren los libros.
Close your books.

Estamos en la página...
We're on page . . .

Miren la pizarra (la transparencia).
Look at the board (transparency).

Saquen una hoja de papel.
Take out a sheet of paper.

Pasen la tarea (los papeles) al frente.
Pass the homework (the papers) to the front.

Levántense, por favor.
Stand up, please.

Siéntense, por favor.
Sit down, please.

Repitan después de mí.
Repeat after me.

Nombres comunes
Common Names

Here are some common names from Spanish-speaking countries.

Nombres de muchachas		
Ana	Inés	Patricia
Bárbara	Irene	Pilar
Beatriz	Isabel	Rosalía
Cecilia	Josefina	Rosario
Cristina	Lourdes	Sonia
Dolores	María	Susana
Elena	Maribel	Tamara
Elisa	Marisol	Teresa
Emilia	Nuria	Vanesa
Fátima	Olga	Yolanda

Nombres de muchachos		
Alfredo	Francisco	Óscar
Antonio	Gilberto	Pablo
Arturo	Héctor	Pedro
Bruno	Javier	Rafael
Carlos	Julio	Ramón
Daniel	Lorenzo	Roberto
Eduardo	Luis	Sergio
Enrique	Manuel	Tomás
Esteban	Marcos	Vicente
Fernando	Miguel	Víctor

Instrucciones
Directions

Throughout the book, many activities will have directions in Spanish. Here are some of the directions you'll see, along with their English translations.

Completa... con una palabra del cuadro.
Complete . . . with a word from the box.

Completa el párrafo con...
Complete the paragraph with . . .

Completa las oraciones con la forma correcta del verbo.
Complete the sentences with the correct form of the verb.

Con base en..., contesta cierto o falso. Corrige las oraciones falsas.
Based on . . ., respond with true or false. Correct the false sentences.

Con un(a) compañero(a), dramatiza...
With a classmate, act out . . .

Contesta las preguntas usando...
Answer the questions, using . . .

Contesta (Completa) las siguientes preguntas (oraciones)...
Answer (Complete) the following questions (sentences) . . .

En parejas (grupos de tres), dramaticen...
In pairs (groups of three), act out . . .

Escoge el dibujo (la respuesta) que corresponde (mejor completa)...
Choose the drawing (the answer) that goes with (best completes) . . .

Escribe..., usando el vocabulario de la página...
Write . . ., using the vocabulary on page . . .

Escucha las conversaciones. Decide qué conversación (diálogo) corresponde a cada dibujo (foto).
Listen to the conversations. Decide which conversation (dialog) corresponds to each drawing (photo).

Mira las fotos (los dibujos) y decide (di, indica)...
Look at the photos (drawings) and decide (say, indicate) . . .

Pon en orden...
Put . . . in order.

Pregúntale a tu compañero(a)...
Ask your partner . . .

Sigue el modelo.
Follow the model.

Túrnense para...
Take turns . . .

Usa el vocabulario de... para completar...
Use the vocabulary from . . . to complete . . .

Usa una palabra o expresión de cada columna para escribir...
Use one word or expression from each column to write . . .

Usa los dibujos para decir lo que pasa.
Use the drawings to say what is happening.

Sugerencias para aprender el español
Tips for learning Spanish

Listen

Listen carefully in class and ask questions if you don't understand. You won't be able to understand everything you hear at first, but don't feel frustrated. You are actually absorbing a lot even when you don't realize it.

Visualize

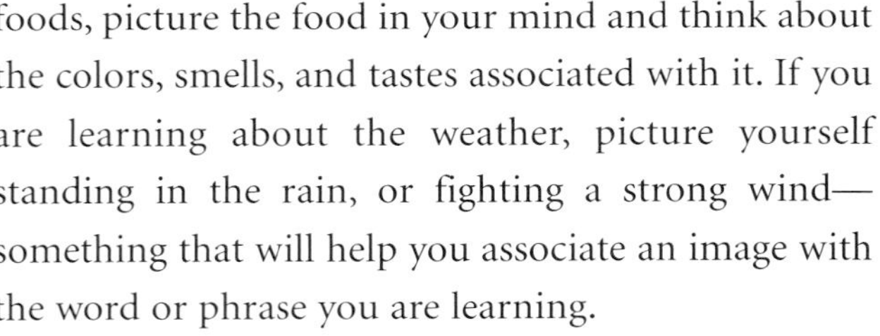

It may help you to visualize the words you are learning. Associate each new word, sentence, or phrase with a mental picture. For example, if you're learning words for foods, picture the food in your mind and think about the colors, smells, and tastes associated with it. If you are learning about the weather, picture yourself standing in the rain, or fighting a strong wind—something that will help you associate an image with the word or phrase you are learning.

Practice

Short, daily practice sessions are more effective than long, once-a-week sessions. Also, try to practice with a friend or a classmate. After all, language is about communication, and it takes two to communicate.

Speak

Practice speaking Spanish aloud every day. Don't be afraid to experiment. Your mistakes will help identify problems, and they will show you important differences in the way English and Spanish work as languages.

Explore

Increase your contact with Spanish outside class in every way you can. Maybe someone living near you speaks Spanish. It's easy to find Spanish-language programs on TV, on the radio, or at the video store, and many magazines and newspapers in Spanish are published or sold in the United States and are on the Internet. Don't be afraid to read, watch, or listen, even if you don't understand every word.

Connect

Making connections between what you learn in other subject areas and what you are learning in your Spanish class will increase your understanding of the new material, help you retain it longer, and enrich your learning experience.

Have fun!

Above all, remember to have fun! Learn as much as you can, because the more you know, the easier it will be for you to relax—and that will make your learning easier and more effective.

¡Buena suerte! (Good luck!)

Ven a conocer más del
mundo hispanohablante y...
¡Exprésate!

Capítulo puente

Overview and Resources

Primera parte

Vocabulario en acción 1

- Introducing and meeting others, talking about likes and dislikes, pp. 2–5

¡Exprésate!

- To ask for and respond to personal information p. 3
- To ask for descriptions and respond, p. 4

Assess

Assessment Program
- **Prueba: Vocabulario 1,** pp. 1–2

Test Generator

Resources

Present

Teaching Transparencies

Practice

Cuaderno de vocabulario y gramática, pp. 1–2
Lab Book, pp. 9–10
Teaching Transparencies
Audio CD 6, Tr. 1
Interactive Tutor, Disc 1

Gramática en acción 1

- The verbs **ser** and **estar,** p. 6
- The verbs **gustar** and **tener,** p. 8

Assess

Assessment Program
- **Prueba: Gramática 1,** pp. 3–4

Test Generator

Present

Video Program, Videocassette 1 and 3, DVD Tutor, Disc 1, **GramaVisión**

Practice

Grammar Tutor for Students of Spanish, Chapters 1–5
Cuaderno de vocabulario y gramática, pp. 3–5
Cuaderno de actividades, pp. 1–4
Lab Book, pp. 9–10
Teaching Transparencies
Audio CD 6, Tr. 2
Interactive Tutor, Disc 1

Segunda parte

Vocabulario en acción 2

- Talking about what you and others like to do, pp. 12–15

¡Exprésate!

- To ask what someone likes or wants to do, p. 13
- To talk about your plans, p. 14

Assess

Assessment Program
- **Prueba: Vocabulario 2,** pp. 5–6

Test Generator

Resources

Present

Teaching Transparencies

Practice

Cuaderno de vocabulario y gramática, pp. 6–7
Lab Book, pp. 11–12
Teaching Transparencies
Audio CD 6, Tr. 3
Interactive Tutor, Disc 1

Gramática en acción 2

- **Querer, ir a** + infinitive, and pronouns, p. 16
- Regular **–ar** verbs and possessive adjectives, p. 18

Assess

Assessment Program
- **Pruebas: Gramática 2,** pp. 7–8

Test Generator

Present

Teaching Transparencies
Video Program, Videocassette 2, DVD Tutor, Disc 1, **GramaVisión**

Practice

Grammar Tutor for Students of Spanish, Chapters 1–5
Cuaderno de vocabulario y gramática, pp. 8–10
Cuaderno de actividades, pp. 5–8
Lab Book, pp. 11–12
Audio CD 6, Tr. 4

Lesson Planner with Differentiated Instruction, pp. 1–10, 162–171

One-Stop Planner® CD-ROM

Visit Holt Online
go.hrw.com
KEYWORD: DKG K30
Online Edition

Tercera parte

Vocabulario en acción 3

- Talking about classes and school supplies, talking about your home and family members, pp. 22–25

¡Exprésate!
- To ask about school and classes, p. 23
- To ask about home and family, p. 24

Assess
Assessment Program
- **Prueba: Vocabulario 3,** pp. 9–10

Test Generator

Resources

Present
- Teaching Transparencies
- Video Program, Videocassette 1/DVD Tutor, **ExpresaVisión**

Practice
- Cuaderno de vocabulario y gramática, pp. 11–12
- Lab Book, pp. 13–14
- Teaching Transparencies
- Audio CD 6, Tr. 5
- Interactive Tutor, Disc 1

Gramática en acción 3

- The present tense of **–er** and **–ir** verbs, p. 26
- Stem-changing verbs, p. 28

Assess
Assessment Program
- **Pruebas: Gramática 3,** pp. 11–12

Test Generator

Present
- Video Program, Videocassettes 1and 2, DVD Tutor, Disc 1, **GramaVisión**

Practice
- Grammar Tutor for Students of Spanish, Chapters 1–5
- Cuaderno de vocabulario y gramática, pp. 13–15
- Cuaderno de actividades, pp. 9–12
- Lab Book, pp. 13–14
- Teaching Transparencies
- Audio CD 6, Tr. 6
- Interactive Tutor, Disc 1

Repaso	Print	Media
El mundo hispanohablante pp. 30–31	Cuaderno de Actividades, pp. 13–14	Interactive Tutor, Disc 1
• **¿Quién eres?** pp. 32–33	Cuaderno de Actividades, p. 14 Assessment Program, pp. 121–131, 132 **Examen: Capítulo 1,** pp. 121–131 **Examen oral: Capítulo 1,** p. 132	Teaching Transparencies Audio CD 6, Trs.7, 8 Interactive Tutor, Disc 1 Test Generator

Capítulo puente

Projects

¡A conocerte mejor!

Students role-play an interview in which one student responds to a neighbor's ad for doing odd jobs, such as babysitting, yardwork, and housecleaning. Students will videotape their interviews and present them to the class.

SUGGESTED SEQUENCE

1. Discuss with students the kind of information the neighbor would want to know about the job applicant.
2. Divide the class into pairs to brainstorm the neighbor's questions. Students should include questions that ask who the applicant is, what his or her telephone number and e-mail address are, what he or she is like, what the applicant likes to do, what types of chores he or she does at home, and when the applicant is available to work on the weekends.
3. Review students' list of questions. Have students write a script for their interview.
4. Have pairs proofread and critique one another's scripts.
5. Students rehearse and videotape their interviews.
6. Students present their videos to the class.

Grading the project

Suggested point distribution (100 points total)

Contents 40
Correct vocabulary and grammar 20
Originality and effort 20
Oral presentation 20

Partner Class Project

Have students pretend that they are opening a small store next to their partner class's school. To decide what to stock in their store, have them prepare a questionnaire for their partner class about the items they need in school every day. Students should write the questionnaire so that the partner class can answer specific questions. For example: **¿Cuántas personas necesitan una regla?** Have students attach the questionnaire and e-mail it to their partner class. When the questionnaire comes back, students should create a list of the items they should stock in their store and how many of each item they need. Then they should compare what their partner class needs to what they need.

e-community

e-mail forum:

Post the following message on the classroom e-mail forum:

Location: http://spanish

¿Qué te gusta hacer… ?

a. ¿por las tardes después de las clases?
b. ¿los sábados por la mañana?
c. ¿los sábados por la noche?

Game Bank

For game ideas, see pages T60–T63.

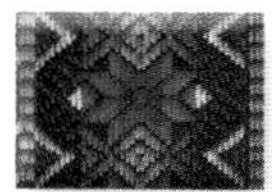

Traditions

Festivales

Every fall the Mapuche people of Chile celebrate the harvest with the **Ngillatan** ceremony. In this ceremony, the Mapuche pay homage to **Pillán,** a representative of the tribal ancestors. A female leader called a **machi** directs the ceremony. Entire towns participate in the **Ngillatan,** with everyone painting his or her face blue. Blue is symbolic of the cosmic place of the ancestors. During the ceremony, there is music featuring the **trutruka,** a long trumpet made of bamboo and a bull's horn. The **trutruka** is believed to have special powers. There is also dancing and singing during the **Ngillatan** ceremony, followed by a party with plenty of food and drink for everyone. Discuss with students the role music plays in local festivals as compared to the role it plays during **Ngillatan.** Then have students make a **trutruka** using a long piece of hose and a plastic bottle. The hose or pipe should be nearly as long as the player. Remove the bottom of the plastic bottle and attach the bottleneck to the tube using masking tape. To play the **trutruka,** hold the trumpet with the bottle on the floor and blow hard into the tube to make a deep, loud sound.

Receta

Guacamole, served as a salad with many Tex-Mex dishes or as a dip for corn tortilla chips, is made using avocados. Avocados lose their green color when exposed to air. Lemon or lime juice not only enhances the flavor, but helps preserve the green color by preventing oxidation. The dish can be spiced up or down according to taste by altering the amount of jalapeño pepper.

Guacamole

para 4 personas

1 tomate fresco

1/2 cebolla pequeña

3 ramas de cilantro fresco

1 jalapeño fresco

3 aguacates maduros

1 cucharada de jugo de limón

sal al gusto

Pique el tomate, la cebolla, el cilantro y el jalapeño en trocitos. Use guantes para cortar el jalapeño para evitar la irritación de la piel o los ojos. Coloque todo en un recipiente hondo. Corte los aguacates por la mitad y quite la semilla. Pele los aguacates y agréguelos al recipiente con las verduras picadas. Machaque todo bien. Agregue el jugo de limón y sal. Sírvalo con tortillitas de maíz o como ensalada.

Capítulo puente

For Student Response Forms, see Lab book.

Textbook Listening Activity Scripts

Vocabulario en acción 1

1 **p. 4, CD 6, Tr. 1**

1. Me llamo Juan.
2. ¿Cómo se llama ella?
3. ¿Cómo te llamas?
4. Ella se llama Laura.
5. Me llamo Liliana.
6. ¿Cómo se llama usted?
7. Me llamo Jorge Acevedo.

Answers to Activity 1

1. b 2. a 3. a 4. b 5. b 6. a 7. b

Gramática en acción 1

11 **p. 9, CD 6, Tr. 2**

1. Son las cuatro y cuarto. Lorenzo regresa a casa.
2. Él tiene un examen de historia el jueves.
3. Lorenzo tiene prisa porque va a llegar tarde al partido de fútbol.
4. Lorenzo tiene mucha tarea para la clase de inglés. Tiene que leer muchos libros.

Answers to Activity 11

A. 2 B. 4 C. 3 D. 1

Vocabulario en acción 2

14 **p. 14, CD 6, Tr. 3**

1. A Carla le gusta pasar el rato sola.
2. A Eduardo le gusta ver televisión.
3. A José le gusta hacer la tarea.
4. A mis amigos les gusta jugar al volibol.
5. A Janet le gusta leer y hacer la tarea.
6. A mis amigas les gusta ir a fiestas y alquilar videos.

Answers to Activity 14

1. tímida
2. perezoso
3. trabajador
4. atléticos
5. seria
6. divertidas

Gramática en acción 2

19 **p. 16, CD 6, Tr. 4**

Juan: Sofía, ¿quieres ir a patinar en el centro comercial conmigo?

Sofía: Está bien. También quiero leer revistas.

Juan: Y yo quiero jugar a los videojuegos.

Sofía: No me gustan los videojuegos. Son aburridos.

Juan: ¿Quieres comer comida italiana en el centro comercial?

Sofía: No, gracias. Quiero una hamburguesa.

Juan: ¡Fenomenal! Las hamburguesas del centro comercial son muy buenas. Yo también quiero comer una hamburguesa.

Answers to Activity 19

b and e

Vocabulario en acción 3

29 p. 25, CD 6, Tr. 5

1. Beatriz es la hija de Federico y Olga.
2. Ricardo es el nieto de Alberto.
3. Lorenzo y Mercedes son los padres de Ana.
4. Beatriz es la tía de Carlos.
5. Olga es la madre de Ana.
6. Ana es la sobrina de Ricardo.
7. Mercedes es la abuela de Ricardo.
8. Ana es la hermana de Carlos.

Answers to Activity 29

1. cierta
2. falsa
3. cierta
4. cierta
5. falsa
6. falsa
7. falsa
8. cierta

Gramática en acción 3

36 p. 28, CD 6, Tr. 6

1. A mi hermana no le parece fácil hacer la tarea.
2. A mi hermana le toca hacer la tarea por la tarde, pero no es gran cosa.
3. A mi hermano le toca pasar la aspiradora.
4. A mi hermano le parece aburrido pasar la aspiradora.
5. A mi papá le toca leer con mi hermano menor.
6. A mi papá no le parece una lata leer con mi hermano menor.
7. A mí me toca lavar los platos. Me parece bien.
8. A mi mamá no le gusta cocinar. Le parece injusto.

Answers to Activity 36

1. falso
2. cierto
3. cierto
4. cierto
5. cierto
6. cierto
7. cierto
8. falso

Capítulo puente

50-Minute Lesson Plans

Day 1

OBJECTIVE
Introducing and meeting others, talking about likes and dislikes

Core Instruction
Chapter Opener, pp. xxii–1
- Using the photo, p. T88. 5 min.

Vocabulario en acción 1, pp. 2–5
- See Teaching **Vocabulario 1,** p. 2. 15 min.
- Play Audio CD 6, Tr. 1 for Activity 1, p. 4. 10 min.
- Have students do Activities 2, 3, and 4 pp. 4–5. 20 min.

Optional Resources
- TPR, p. 3
- Slower Pace Learners, p. 3 ◆
- Special Learning Needs, p. 3 ●

HOMEWORK SUGGESTIONS
Activity 4, p. 5
Cuaderno de vocabulario y gramática, pp. 1–5
Interactive Tutor, Disc 1
Holt Online, **Vocabulario 1** practice

Day 2

OBJECTIVE
*Using the verbs **ser** and **estar***

Core Instruction
- Give **Prueba: Vocabulario 1** 10 min.

Gramática 1, pp. 6–9
- Have students do Bell Work CP.2, p. 6 5 min.
- See Teaching **Gramática 1,** p. 6. 15 min.
- Have students do Activities 6, 7, and 9, p. 7. 20 min.

Optional Resources
- Show **Gramavision,** Level 1A, Ch. 2, 5
- Slower Pace Learning, p. 7 ◆
- **Comunicación,** p. 7

HOMEWORK SUGGESTIONS
Activity 8, p. 7
Cuaderno de vocabulario y gramática, pp. 1–5
Interactive Tutor, Disc 1
Holt Online, **Gramática 1** practice

Day 3

OBJECTIVE
*Using the verbs **gustar** and **tener***

Core Instruction
Gramática 1, pp. 6–9
- Have students do Bell Work CP. 3, p. 8. 5 min.
- See Teaching **Gramática 1,** p. 8. 15 min.
- Have students do Activity 10, p. 8 5 min.
- Play Audio CD 6, Tr. 2 for Activity 11, p. 9. 10 min.
- Have students do Activity 12, p. 9. 5 min.
- Have students do Activity 13, p. 9. 10 min.

Optional Resources
- Advanced Learners, p. 9 ▲
- Multiple Intelligences, p. 9
- **Comunicación**, p. 9

HOMEWORK SUGGESTIONS
Cuaderno de vocabulario y gramática, pp. 1–5
Interactive Tutor, Disc 1
Holt Online, **Gramática 1** practice

Day 4

OBJECTIVE
Talking about what you and others like to do; talking about plans

Core Instruction
- Have students do Bell Work CP.4, p. 12. 5 min.
- **Prueba: Gramática 1** 20 min.

Vocabulario 2, pp. 12–13
- See Teaching **Vocabulario 2,** p. 6 10 min.
- Have students do Activity 16 and 18, p. 15 15 min.

Optional Resources
- TPR, p. 13
- Slower Pace Learners, p. 13 ◆
- Special Learning Needs, p. 13 ●

HOMEWORK SUGGESTIONS
Activity 17, p. 15
Cuaderno de vocabulario y gramática, pp. 1–5
Interactive Tutor, Disc 1
Holt Online, **Vocabulario 2** practice

Day 5

OBJECTIVE
*Using the verbs **querer, ir a** + infinitive, and pronouns after prepositions*

Core Instruction
Gramática 2, pp. 16–19
- Have students do Bell Work CP.5, p. 16. 5 min.
- See Teaching **Gramática 2,** p. 16. 20 min.
- Play Audio CD 6, Tr. 4 for Activity 19, p. 16. 10 min.
- Have students do Activity 20, p. 17. 5 min.
- Have students do Activity 22, p. 17. 10 min.

Optional Resources
- Slower Pace Learners, p. 17 ◆
- Special Learning Needs, p. 17 ●
- **Comunicación**, p. 17

HOMEWORK SUGGESTIONS
Activity 21, p. 17
Cuaderno de vocabulario y gramática, pp. 1–5
Interactive Tutor, Disc 1
Holt Online, **Gramática 2** practice

To edit and create your own lesson plans, see the **One-Stop** Planner® CD-ROM

KEY
- ▲ Advanced Learners
- ◆ Slower Pace Learners
- ● Special Learning Needs
- ■ Heritage Speakers

Day 6

OBJECTIVE
*Using regular **-ar** and possessive adjectives*

Core Instruction

Gramática 2, pp. 16–19
- Have students do Bell Work CP.6, p. 18. 5 min.
- Give **Prueba: Vocabulario 2** 20 min.
- See Teaching **Gramática 2,** p. 16 (Point 3) 5 min.
- Have students do Activities 23 and 24, pp. 18 and 19. 10 min.
- Have students do Activity 26, p. 19. 10 min.

Optional Resources
- Special Learning Needs, p. 19 ●
- **Comunicación,** p. 19

HOMEWORK SUGGESTIONS
Activity 25, p. 19
Cuaderno de vocabulario y gramática, pp. 1–5
Interactive Tutor, Disc 1
Holt Online, **Gramática 2** practice

Day 7

OBJECTIVE
Talking about classes, school supplies, home, and family members

Core Instruction

Vocabulario 3, pp. 22–25
- Have students do Bell Work CP.7, p. 22. 5 min.
- Give **Prueba: Gramática 2** 20 min.
- See Teaching **Vocabulario 3,** p. 22. 10 min.
- Have students do Activities 27 and 28, p. 24. 10 min.
- Play Audio CD 6, Tr. 5 for Activity 29, p. 25. 5 min.

Optional Resources
- Activity 30, p. 25
- TPR, p. 23
- Slower Pace Learners, p. 23 ◆

HOMEWORK SUGGESTIONS
Activity 30, p. 25
Cuaderno de vocabulario y gramática, pp. 1–5
Interactive Tutor, Disc 1
Holt Online, **Vocabulario 3** practice

Day 8

OBJECTIVE
*Using **-er** and **-ir** verbs*

Core Instruction

Gramática 3, pp. 26–29
- Have students do Bell Work CP.8, p. 26. 5 min.
- Have students do Activity 31, p. 25. 10 min.
- Give **Prueba: Vocabulario 3** 10 min.
- See Teaching **Gramática 3,** Points 1 and 2, p. 26. 10 min.
- Have students do Activities 32 and 33, pp. 26 and 27. 10 min.
- Have students do Activity 34, p. 27. 5 min.

Optional Resources
- Slower Pace Learners, p. 27 ◆
- **Comunicación,** p. 27

HOMEWORK SUGGESTIONS
Activity 35, p. 27 (written part)
Cuaderno de vocabulario y gramática, pp. 1–5
Interactive Tutor, Disc 1
Holt Online, **Gramática 3** practice

Day 9

OBJECTIVE
Using stem-changing verbs

Core Instruction

Gramática 3, pp. 26–29
- Have students do Bell Work CP.9, p. 28 5 min.
- See Teaching **Gramática 3,** p. 28 20 min.
- Play Audio CD 6, Tr. 6 for Activity 36, p. 28. 10 min.
- Have students do Activity 37, p. 29. 5 min.
- Have students do Activity 39, p. 29. 10 min.

Optional Resources
- Advanced Learners, p. 29 ▲
- Special Learning Needs, p. 29 ●
- **Comunicación,** p. 29
- **¿Quién eres?,** pp. 32–33

HOMEWORK SUGGESTIONS
Activity 38, p. 29
Review for Chapter Test

Day 10

OBJECTIVE
Assessment

Core Instruction
- Give Chapter Test. 50 min.

Optional Resources
- **Cultura: El mundo hispanohablantes,** pp. 30–31

HOMEWORK SUGGESTIONS
Preview **Geocultura: Mexico,** pp. 34–37
Interactive Tutor, Disc 1
Holt Online, **Geocultura: Mexico**

Capítulo puente

90-Minute Lesson Plans

Block 1

OBJECTIVE
Introducing and meeting others, talking about likes and dislikes; Using the verbs ***ser*** *and* ***estar***

Core Instruction

Chapter Opener, pp. xxii–1
- Using the photo, p. T88. 5 min.

Vocabulario en acción 1, pp. 2–5
- See Teaching **Vocabulario 1,** p. 2. 15 min.
- Play Audio CD 6, Tr. 1 for Activity 1, p. 4. 10 min.
- Have students do Activity 2, p. 4. 5 min.
- Have students do Activity 3, p. 4. 5 min.
- Have students do Activity 5, p. 5. 10 min.

Gramática 1, pp. 6–9
- Have students do Bell Work CP.2, p. 6 5 min.
- See Teaching **Gramática 1,** p. 6. 15 min.
- Have students do Activities 6 and 7, p. 7. 10 min.
- Have students do Activity 9, p. 7. 10 min.

Optional Resources
- Show **Gramavision,** Level 1A, Ch. 2, 5
- Learning Tip, p. 1
- TPR, p. 3
- Slower Pace Learners, pp. 3, 7 ◆
- Special Learning Needs, pp. 3, 7 ●
- **Comunicación,** p. 7

HOMEWORK SUGGESTIONS
Activity 4, p. 5 and Activity 8, p. 7
Cuaderno de vocabulario y gramática, pp. 1–5
Interactive Tutor, Disc 1
Holt Online, **Vocabulario 1** and **Gramática 1** practice

Block 2

OBJECTIVE
Using the verbs ***gustar*** *and* ***tener;*** *Talking about what you and others like to do; talking about plans*

Core Instruction
- Give **Prueba: Vocabulario 1** 15 min.

Gramática 1, pp. 6–9
- Have students do Bell Work CP. 3, p. 8. 5 min.
- See Teaching **Gramática 1,** p. 8. 15 min.
- Have students do Activity 10, p. 8 5 min.
- Play Audio CD 6, Tr. 2 for Activity 11, p. 9. 10 min.
- Have students do Activity 12, p. 9. 5 min.
- Have students do Activity 13, p. 9. 10 min.

Vocabulario 2, pp. 12–13
- See Teaching **Vocabulario 2,** p. 6. 10 min.
- Have students do Activity 16, p. 15. 5 min.
- Have students do Activity 18, p. 15. 10 min.

Optional Resources
- Advanced Learners, p. 9 ▲
- Multiple Intelligences, p. 9
- **Comunicación,** p. 9
- TPR, p. 13
- Slower Pace Learners, p. 13 ◆
- Special Learning Needs, p. 13 ●
- **También se puede decir...**, p. 13

HOMEWORK SUGGESTIONS
Activity 17, p. 15
Cuaderno de vocabulario y gramática, pp. 1–5
Interactive Tutor, Disc 1
Holt Online, **Gramática 1** and **Vocabulario 2** practice

Block 3

OBJECTIVE
Using the verbs ***querer, ir a*** *+ infinitive, and pronouns after prepositions; Using regular* ***-ar*** *and possessive adjectives*

Core Instruction

Gramática 2, pp. 16–19
- Have students do Bell Work CP.5, p. 16. 5 min.
- Give **Prueba: Gramática 1** 20 min.
- See Teaching **Gramática 2 (querer, ir a),** p. 16. 15 min.
- Play Audio CD 6, Tr. 4 for Activity 19, p. 16. 10 min.
- Have students do Activity 20, p. 17. 5 min.
- Have students do Activity 22, p. 17. 10 min.

Gramática 2, pp. 16–19
- Have students do Bell Work CP.6, p. 18. 5 min.
- See Teaching **Gramática 2 (-ar verbs),** p. 16 (Point 3) 5 min.
- Have students do Activity 23, p. 18. 5 min.
- Have students do Activity 26, p. 19. 10 min.

Optional Resources
- Slower Pace Learners, p. 17 ◆
- Special Learning Needs, p. 17 ●
- **Comunicación,** pp. 17, 19
- Advanced Learners, p. 19 ▲
- Special Learning Needs, p. 19 ●

HOMEWORK SUGGESTIONS
Activity 21, p. 17; Activity 24, p. 19; or Activity 25, p. 19
Cuaderno de vocabulario y gramática, pp. 1–5
Interactive Tutor, Disc 1
Holt Online, **Gramática 2** practice

To edit and create your own lesson plans, see the **One-Stop** Planner® CD-ROM

KEY
- ▲ Advanced Learners
- ◆ Slower Pace Learners
- ● Special Learning Needs
- ■ Heritage Speakers

Block 4

OBJECTIVE
Talking about classes, school supplies, home, and family members; using ***-er*** *and* ***-ir*** *verbs*

Core Instruction

Vocabulario 3, pp. 22–25
- Have students do Bell Work CP.7, p. 22. 5 min.
- Give **Prueba: Gramática 2** 20 min.
- See Teaching **Vocabulario 3,** p. 22. 10 min.
- Have students do Activities 27 and 28, p. 24. 10 min.
- Play Audio CD 6, Tr. 5 for Activity 29, p. 25 5 min.

Gramática 3, pp. 26–29
- Have students do Bell Work CP.8, p. 26. 5 min.
- Have students do Activity 31, p. 25. 10 min.
- See Teaching **Gramática 3,** Points 1 and 2, p. 26. 10 min.
- Have students do Activities 32 and 33, pp. 26 and 27. 10 min.
- Have students do Activity 34, p. 27. 5 min.

Optional Resources
- Activity 30, p. 25
- TPR, p. 23
- Cultures, p. 24
- Slower Pace Learners, p. 23 ◆
- Slower Pace Learners, p. 27 ◆
- Multiple Intelligences, p. 27
- **Comunicación,** p. 27

HOMEWORK SUGGESTIONS
Activity 30, p. 25; Activity 35, p. 27 (written part)
Prueba: Vocabulario 3 (take-home quiz)
Cuaderno de vocabulario y gramática, pp. 1–5
Interactive Tutor, Disc 1
Holt Online, **Vocabulario 3** and **Gramática 3** practice

Block 5

OBJECTIVE
Using stem-changing verbs

Core Instruction

Gramática 3, pp. 26–29
- Have students do Bell Work CP.9, p. 28 5 min.
- See Teaching **Gramática 3,** p. 28 20 min.
- Play Audio CD 6, Tr. 6 for Activity 36, p. 28. 5 min.
- Have students do Activity 37, p. 29. 5 min.
- Have students do Activity 39, p. 29. 5 min.
- Give Chapter Test. 50 min.

Optional Resources
- **Cultura: El mundo hispanohablantes,** pp. 30–31
- Advanced Learners, p. 29 ▲
- Special Learning Needs, p. 29 ●
- **Comunicación,** p. 29
- **¿Quién eres?,** pp. 32–33

HOMEWORK SUGGESTIONS
Preview **Geocultura: Mexico,** pp. 34–37
Interactive Tutor, Disc 1
Holt Online, **Geocultura: Mexico**

Meeting the National Standards

Communication
Comunicación, pp. 5, 7, 9, 15, 17, 19, 25, 27

Cultures
Practices and Perspectives, pp. 11, 24
Products and Perspectives, pp. 10, 30

Connections
Interdisciplinary Links, pp. 9, 20
Social Studies Link, p. 31

Comparisions
Comparing and Contrasting, pp. 19, 21

Communities
Career Path, p. 29
Using Technology, p. 31

Using the Photo

Tell students this photo was taken in the bedroom of a new student at their school. Ask students yes-no and either-or questions based on the photo to see how much information they can tell about the student: **¿Es un muchacho o una muchacha? ¿Están seguros? ¿A esta persona le gusta el béisbol? (Sí.) ¿El 4 de octubre es el cumpleaños de esta persona o de otra persona?**

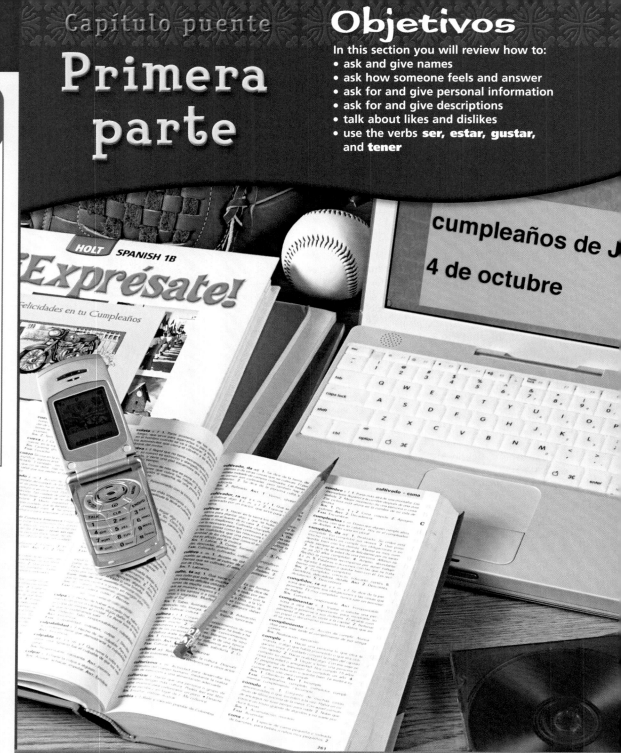

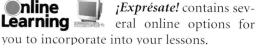

Capítulo puente

Primera parte

Objetivos

In this section you will review how to:
- ask and give names
- ask how someone feels and answer
- ask for and give personal information
- ask for and give descriptions
- talk about likes and dislikes
- use the verbs **ser, estar, gustar,** and **tener**

Holt Online Learning *¡Exprésate!* contains several online options for you to incorporate into your lessons.

¡Exprésate! Student Edition **online at my.hrw.com**
At this site, you will find the online version of *¡Exprésate!* All concepts presented in the textbook are presented and practiced in this online version of your textbook. This online version can be used as a supplement to or as a replacement for your texbook.

Practice activities at go.hrw.com
These activities provide additional practice for major concepts presented in each chapter. Practice items include structured practice as well as research topics.

Teacher resources at www.hrw.com
This site provides additional information that teachers might find useful about the *¡Exprésate!* program.

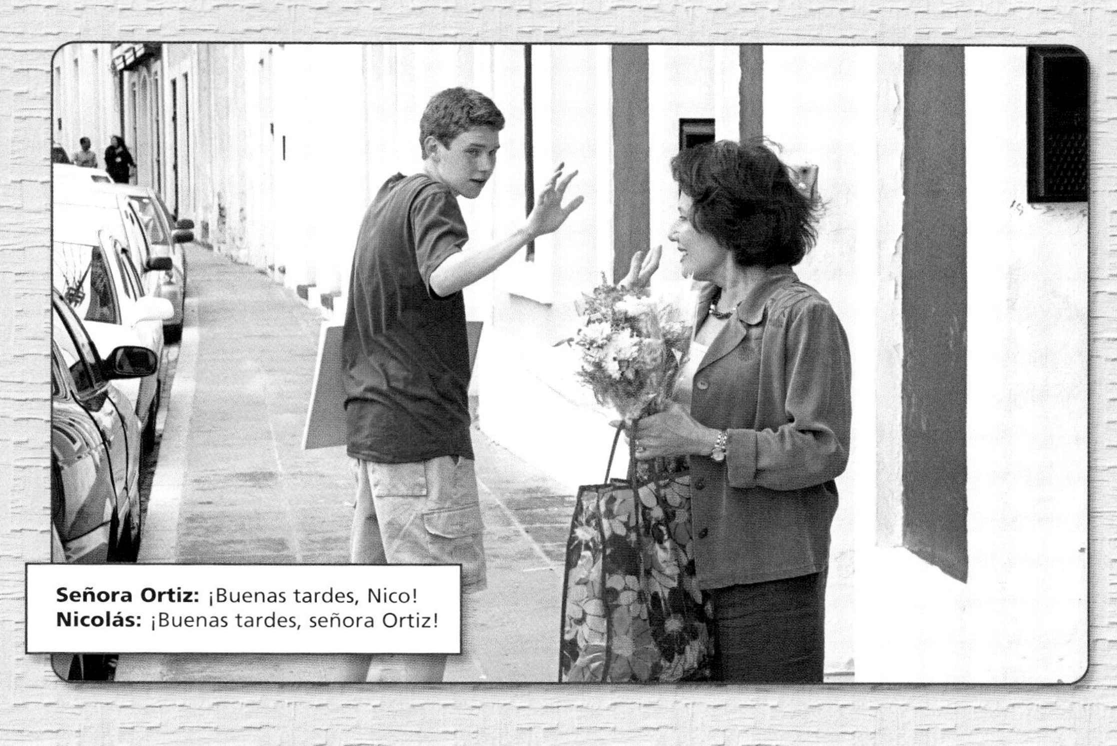

Señora Ortiz: ¡Buenas tardes, Nico!
Nicolás: ¡Buenas tardes, señora Ortiz!

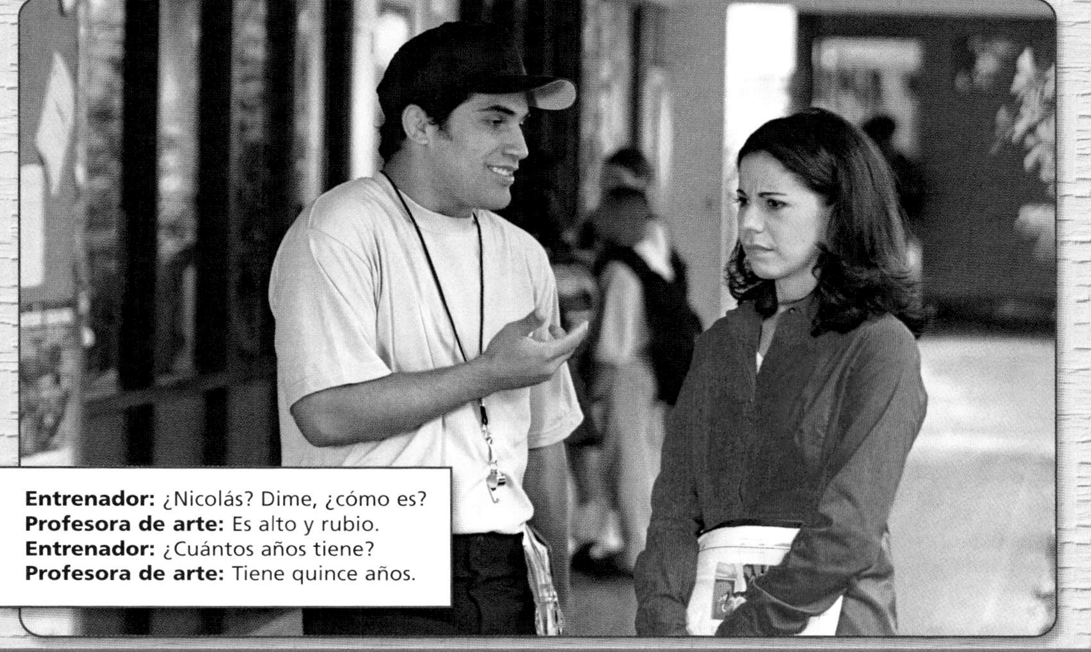

Entrenador: ¿Nicolás? Dime, ¿cómo es?
Profesora de arte: Es alto y rubio.
Entrenador: ¿Cuántos años tiene?
Profesora de arte: Tiene quince años.

Primera parte Opener

Learning Tips

The photos here and on pages 11 and 21 are scenes from the **1A Novela en video.** They can be used to briefly refresh students' memory of the communicative functions and grammatical structures they learned last year and to prepare them for the more in-depth review of the **Capítulo puente.**

To use the photos, you might:

- ask students to recall in English the plot of the two episodes shown (See Video Synopses below.)
- read each dialogue and check comprehension by asking yes-no and either-or questions
- review vocabulary, functions, and structures by asking students yes-no and either-or questions related to the dialog

Video Synopses

Top photo:
In Chapter 1, **Episodio 1,** of **¿Quién será?** Nicolás, one of the main characters, is shown hurrying home from school with a sketch pad under his arm. He bumps into and greets señora Ortiz and don Pablo on his way home.

Bottom photo:
In Chapter 2, **Episodio 2**, a gym teacher and an art teacher at Nicolás's school in Puerto Rico discuss their students. They have different opinions of Nicolás and they conclude that there must be two students named Nicolás Ortega García.

Pacing Tips

In this chapter, the **Gramática** sections contain key grammar points that might require extra time. You might allot more time for each **Gramática** presentation and use more of the optional resources to ensure that students have a solid grasp of each grammar concept before presenting the next **Gramática** or **Vocabulario** section. For complete lesson plan suggestions, see pages T73G–T73J.

Suggested pacing:	Traditional Schedule	Block Schedule
Vocabulario 1/Gramática 1	2 1/2 days	1 1/4 blocks
Vocabulario 2/Gramática 2	2 1/2 days	1 1/4 blocks
Vocabulario 3/Gramática 3	2 1/2 days	1 block
El mundo hispanohablante/Repaso	2 days	1 block
Chapter Test	1/2 day	1/2 block

Resources

Planning:

Lesson Planner, pp. 1–2, 162–165

 One-Stop Planner

Practice:

Cuaderno de vocabulario y gramática, pp. 1–2

Lab Book, pp. 9–10

 Teaching Transparencies
Bell Work CP.1
Vocabulario y gramática answers, pp. 1–2

Interactive Tutor, Disc 1

Bell Work

Use Bell Work CP.1 in the *Teaching Transparencies,* or write this activity on the board.

Complete these sentences with one of the words below.

1. ¡_____ tardes, Eduardo!
2. ¿Cuántos _____ tienes?
3. Juan es _____ y rubio.
4. ¿Cómo es la _____ García?
5. Teresa tiene _____ años, ¿verdad?

a. señora
b. trece
c. años
d. Buenas
e. alto

Objetivos
Introducing and meeting others, talking about likes and dislikes

Vocabulario en acción 1

Core Instruction

TEACHING VOCABULARIO

1. Review the vocabulary and model its pronunciation. **(2 min.)**
2. Before class prepare an **"¡Hóla! Me llamo _____ ."** sticker with a new Spanish name for each of your students. Make some of the names **señor/señora** + last name to indicate adults. You might include some celebrity names, such as Enrique Iglesias. Distribute the stickers to students. Then call up different students and use them as "props" to present the five short dialogues shown in the photos. **(10 min.)**
3. Write the ***¡Exprésate!*** questions on index cards. Model the pronunciation of the questions. Then have students imagine that you are the new student whose desk is shown on page T88. Distribute the cards and have students ask you the questions. **(8 min.)**

STANDARDS: 1.2

Visit Holt Online
go.hrw.com
KEYWORD: EXP1B PUENTE
Vocabulario 1 practice

Buenos días, Paco. ¿Qué tal?
Estoy bien, gracias. ¿Y usted?

Hola. ¿Cómo estás?
Más o menos. ¿Y tú?

¡Exprésate!

To ask for personal information	To respond
¿De dónde eres? *Where are you from?*	**Soy de Estados Unidos.** *I'm from the United States.*
¿Cuál es tu teléfono? *What is your telephone number?*	**Es tres-veintiséis-ochenta y nueve.** *It's three, twenty-six, eighty-nine.*
¿Cuál es el correo electrónico de Marisa? *What is Marisa's e-mail address?*	**Es eme punto a-ere-ce-e arroba ce-o-ele-e punto e-de-u.** *It's m.arce@cole.edu.*
¿Cuándo es tu cumpleaños? *When is your birthday?*	**Es el catorce de febrero.** *It's the fourteenth of February.*

Interactive TUTOR

Online
Vocabulario y gramática, pp. 1–5

▶ **Vocabulario adicional** — For nombres comunes, see page xvii

Vocabulario 1

TPR
Total Physical Response

Set up props on a table at the front of the room: a globe, a phone book, a "laptop computer" (made out of two pieces of cardboard), and a calendar. Have different groups of students stand by the table. Ask the questions from **¡Exprésate!** and have students touch the item related to that question. (**¿De dónde eres?** Students touch the globe. **¿Cuál es tu teléfono?** Students touch the phone book.) You might make this a **"Simón dice..."** game.

Differentiated Instruction

SLOWER PACE LEARNERS

Bring in photos of younger and older people. First, show each picture and ask, **¿Pregunto '¿Cómo te llamas?' or '¿Cómo se llama?'** Then, show each picture again and ask, **¿Pregunto '¿Cómo estás?' o '¿Cómo está?'** Then review numbers 1–99, the alphabet, and months of the year before presenting the ***¡Exprésate!*** questions and responses.

SPECIAL LEARNING NEEDS

Students with Learning Disabilities/ Dyslexia Remind students that Spanish cannot always be translated word-for-word into English. Point out that **¿Cómo te llamas?** means literally *How / yourself / do you call?* and **¿De dónde eres?** translates word-for-word as *From / where / are (you)?* Encourage students to learn phrases as a whole, rather than try to translate word-for-word meaning.

Resources

Planning:

Lesson Planner, pp. 1–2, 162–165

 One-Stop Planner

Practice:

Cuaderno de vocabulario y gramática, pp. 1–2

Lab Book, pp. 9–10

 Teaching Transparencies **Vocabulario y gramática** answers, pp. 1–2

 Audio CD 6, Tr. 1

 Interactive Tutor, Disc 1

1 Script

—Me llamo Juan.
—¿Cómo se llama ella?
—¿Cómo te llamas?
—Ella se llama Laura.
—Me llamo Liliana.
—¿Cómo se llama usted?
—Me llamo Jorge Acevedo.

Más vocabulario...

¿Quién es el muchacho?
Who is the boy?
(Él) es mi mejor amigo.
He is my best friend.
(Él) es estudiante.
He is a student.
¿Quién es la muchacha?
Who is the girl?
(Ella) es mi mejor amiga.
She is my best friend.
(Ella) es estudiante.
She is a student.

CD 6, Tr. 1

1 ¿Qué hacen?

Escuchemos As you listen, decide whether the people speaking are **a**) asking someone's name or **b**) giving a name.

1. b 2. a 3. a 4. b 5. b 6. a 7. b

2 Preguntas y más preguntas

Leamos Match each question to the correct response. There may be more than one correct answer.

1. ¿Qué tal Jorge? c	**a.** Me llamo Manuel Solís Hidalgo.
2. ¿Quién es él? g	**b.** Es guajiro@planeta.net
3. ¿Cómo se llama usted? a	**c.** Muy bien, ¿y tú?
4. ¿Cuál es tu correo electrónico? b	**d.** Soy de España.
5. ¿De dónde eres? d	**e.** Es el tres de enero.
6. ¿Cuándo es tu cumpleaños? e	**f.** Más o menos, ¿y usted?
7. ¿Cómo está usted? f	**g.** Es Alberto Gutiérrez.

3 ¿Cuál es?

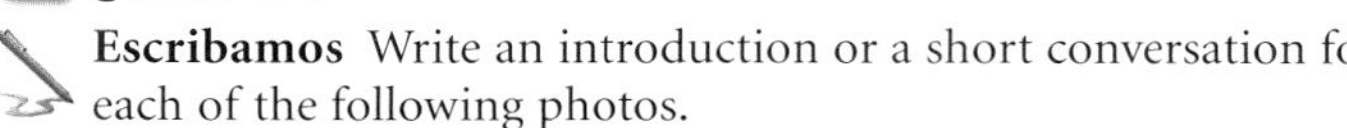

Escribamos Write an introduction or a short conversation for each of the following photos.

1

2

3

4

¡Exprésate!

To ask for descriptions	To respond
¿Cómo es Paco? *What is Paco like?*	**Paco es moreno. También es inteligente y un poco tímido.** *Paco has dark hair/a dark complexion. He is also intelligent and a little shy.*
¿Cómo eres? ¿Eres romántico(a)? *What are you like? Are you romantic?*	**Sí, soy bastante romántico(a).** *Yes, I am quite romantic.*
¿Cómo es la comida china? *What is Chinese food like?*	**Es muy deliciosa.** *It's very delicious.*

Interactive TUTOR

Online
Vocabulario y gramática, pp. 1–2

Core Instruction

TEACHING ¡EXPRÉSATE!

1. Model the pronunciation of the questions and answers in ***¡Exprésate!*** **(2 min.)**

2. Bring in your own class yearbook and use it to present the questions and answers in **Más vocabulario.** Point out different students and teachers and ask yourself who they are, as if you cannot remember their names, then suddenly remember and explain what that person is like. **(8 min.)**

3. Bring in your school's yearbook from last year and use the questions in **Más vocabulario** and **¡Exprésate!** to ask students about students and teachers they recognize in the photos. Phrase the questions as yes-no, or either-or: **¿Quién es la muchacha, Alyssa o Kaitlin? ¿Es alta? ¿Es rubia o morena?** **(10 min.)**

STANDARDS: 1.2

4 Mucho gusto

Leamos Carla and Miguel are talking to a new student, Ana, on the first day of school. Complete the conversation using phrases from the word box.

Estoy	Igualmente	estás	Encantado	cuál
Regular	Son	Es	Cómo	Es de

MIGUEL ¡Hola, Carla! ¿Cómo __1__? estás
CARLA ¡Hola Miguel! __2__ bien. ¿Y tú? Estoy
MIGUEL __3__. Regular
CARLA Miguel, ésta es Ana. __4__ Perú. Es de
MIGUEL __5__. Encantado
ANA __6__. Igualmente
MIGUEL ¿__7__ son tus clases Ana? Cómo
ANA __8__ buenas. Son
CARLA Ana, ¿__9__ es tu correo electrónico? Cuál
ANA __10__ apaloma@mundo.net. Es

Comunicación

5 Encantado

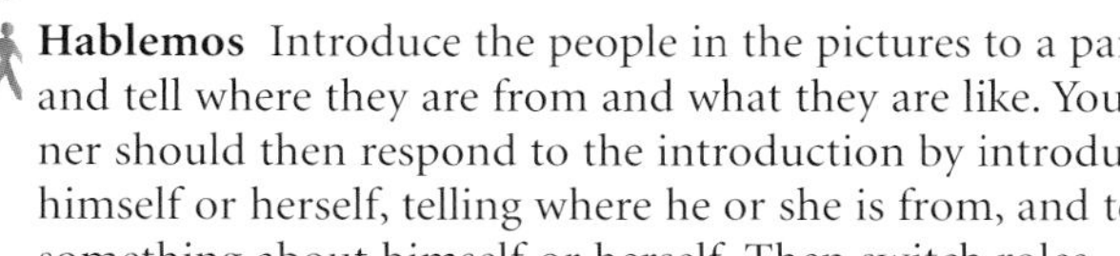

Hablemos Introduce the people in the pictures to a partner and tell where they are from and what they are like. Your partner should then respond to the introduction by introducing himself or herself, telling where he or she is from, and telling something about himself or herself. Then switch roles.

Juan, España

MODELO **—Éste es mi amigo Juan. Él es de España. Es moreno y...**

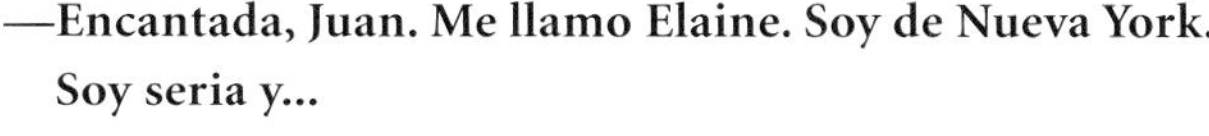

—Encantada, Juan. Me llamo Elaine. Soy de Nueva York. Soy seria y...

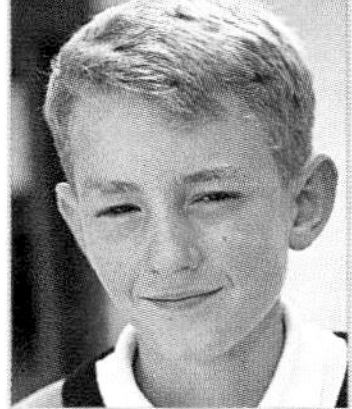

1. Arturo, Perú

2. Benito, Costa Rica

3. Timoteo, México

4. Sra. Galván, Chile

5. Sr. Cárdenas, Venezuela

Differentiated Instruction

ADVANCED LEARNERS

Challenge students to see if they can find a person in the community from a Spanish-speaking country who would like to visit the class to talk about themselves and their country of origin. The student who invites a particular guest will be responsible for introducing him or her in Spanish and preparing a few questions in English.

SPECIAL LEARNING NEEDS

Students with Auditory Impairments Consider allowing students with auditory impairments to choose their own partners for pair activities to ensure that they work with students with whom they feel comfortable interacting. You might make sure that the preferred partner is in the same group as the student when doing group activities.

COMMON ERROR ALERT ¡OJO!

Ask students to guess why **tú** in Carla's first line has an accent mark, but **tu** in Carla's last line does not have an accent. Explain to students that accent marks serve different purposes. In this case, the accent on **tú** shows that it means "you," not "yours." You might point out that in Miguel's first line **cómo** has an accent because it is a question word, and **estás** has an accent to show how it should be pronounced. Write the sentence "I want to present you with a present," on the board and ask students if they think accent marks would help make this sentence easier for people to pronounce.

Comunicación

Group Work: Interpersonal

Socializing Have students form a circle and redo Activity 5 with the first student introducing the student on his or her left to the student on his or her right. The student on the right then introduces the first student and so forth. Take notes on the students' introductions. After all students have been introduced, form teams and ask questions about the students based on your notes. **(¿Quién es de Chicago? ¿Cómo es Julia?)** The team that answers the most questions correctly wins.

Assess

Assessment Program

Prueba: Vocabulario 1, pp. 1–2

Test Generator 

STANDARDS: 1.1, 1.2, 4.1

Resources

Planning:

Lesson Planner, pp. 2–4, 162–167

 One-Stop Planner

Practice:

Cuaderno de vocabulario y gramática, pp. 3–5

Cuaderno de actividades, pp. 1–4

Lab Book, pp. 9–10

 Teaching Transparencies Bell Work CP.2
Vocabulario y gramática answers, pp. 3–5

Interactive Tutor, Disc 1

Bell Work

Use Bell Work CP.2 in the *Teaching Transparencies*, or write this activity on the board.

Match each question with the correct response.

1. ¿Cómo estás?
2. ¿Quién es el muchacho?
3. ¿Cómo es Ana?
4. ¿Cómo eres?
5. ¿Quién es ella?

a. Es bastante seria.
b. Es mi mejor amiga.
c. Soy muy romántico.
d. Más o menos, ¿y tú?
e. Es mi mejor amigo.

Objetivos
Using the verbs ser, estar, gustar, and tener

Gramática en acción 1

Interactive TUTOR

The verbs ser and estar

1 Use the irregular verb **ser** to identify or describe a person or thing. Also use the verb **ser** with **de** to tell where someone is from.

soy *I am*	**somos** *we are*
eres *you are*	**sois** *you are*
es *he is, she is, you are*	**son** *you are, they are*

Las películas **son** divertidas.
Movies are fun.

Juan **es de** Cuba.
Juan is from Cuba.

2 Use the irregular verb **estar** to say how you or someone else feels. You can also use the verb **estar** with **prepositions** to say where someone or something is in relation to another person or thing.

estoy *I am*	**estamos** *we are*
estás *you are*	**estáis** *you are*
está *he is, she is, you are*	**están** *you are, they are*

¿Cómo **está** usted?
How are you?

Estoy bien gracias.
I am fine, thank you.

¿Dónde **está** mi libro?
Where is my book?

Está encima de la mesa.
It's on top of the table.

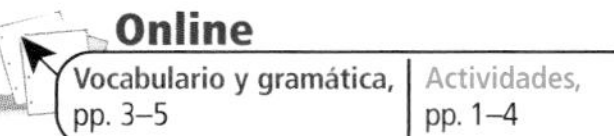

Online
Vocabulario y gramática, pp. 3–5 | Actividades, pp. 1–4

6 Juan y yo

Leamos Complete each sentence with the correct form of either the verb **ser** or **estar.**

1. Juan y yo ____ en casa. estamos
2. Él y yo ____ amigos. somos
3. Yo ____ de Chile. soy
4. Él ____ de Perú. es
5. Juan va al parque hoy. ____ cerca de su casa. Está
6. No voy al parque con Juan porque yo no ____ bien. estoy
7. Laura y Manolo ____ en la clase de inglés con Juan. están
8. Juan ____ alto, pero yo ____ bajo. es, soy
9. Yo ____ moreno y gracioso. soy
10. Tú ____ en la clase de biología conmigo y con Juan. estás

Amigos en Cuzco, Perú

Core Instruction

TEACHING GRAMÁTICA

1. Ask students how to say "I am intelligent," and "I am from Mexico," in Spanish. Write the sentences on the board and underline each **soy.** Ask how to say "I am fine," and "I am here," Write the sentences on the board and underline each **estoy.** Then act puzzled and argue that **estoy** should be **soy** since in English you say "I am" each time. **(5 min.)**
2. Then read over points 1 and 2 of **Gramática** and concede that the students were right with **Estoy bien** and **Estoy aquí. (10 min.)**
3. Have students write **ser** and **estar** on two pieces of paper. Give them scenarios and have them hold up the verb they would use in each situation. ("What if I'm a pirate and I want to tell my parrot *where* the treasure is?" Students hold up **estar.**) **(5 min.)**

STANDARDS: 1.2

Visit Holt Online
go.hrw.com
KEYWORD: EXP1B PUENTE
Gramática 1 practice

7 Somos así

Escribamos Use the sentence starters below to write descriptions of yourself, your friends, your family, and your home. Also tell how you are feeling.

MODELO **Mi hermano es...**
Mi hermano es alto y divertido.

1. Yo estoy...
2. Mis amigos y yo somos...
3. Nuestra casa está...
4. Nuestro carro es...
5. Mis abuelos son...
6. Mis hermanos son...
7. Mi casa es...
8. Mi mejor amigo y yo somos...

8 ¿Cómo son?

Escribamos/Hablemos Look at the pictures below and say how each person feels. Also say what each person is like.

MODELO **María está más o menos.**
María es inteligente, seria y rubia.

María

1. Ernesto

2. Pablo y Javier

3. Catarina y Miguel

4. Esmeralda

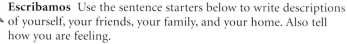

Comunicación

9 Mi amigo por correspondencia

Escribamos Write a letter or an e-mail to a new pen pal to introduce yourself. Include your name, age, birthday, where you are from, a description of yourself, what you like or don't like, and how you are feeling today. Ask your pen pal to tell you about himself or herself. Exchange letters with a classmate and respond in writing to your classmate's letter.

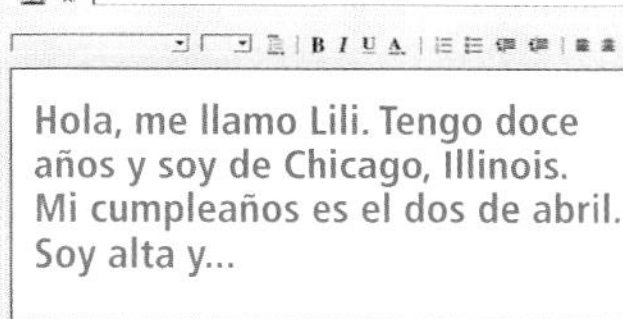

Nuevo Mensaje
Hola, me llamo Lili. Tengo doce años y soy de Chicago, Illinois. Mi cumpleaños es el dos de abril. Soy alta y...

8 Possible answers:

1. Ernesto está más o menos. El es moreno. A él le gusta la música.
2. Pablo y Javier están muy bien. Ellos son morenos. A ellos les gusta jugar al fútbol.
3. Catarina y Miguel están muy bien. Ellos son morenos. A ellos les gusta jugar videojuegos.
4. Esmeralda está bien. Ella es romántica. A ella le gusta leer.

Comunicación

Individual Activity: Presentational

Presenting information Have each student read her or his classmate's pen pal letter aloud and have the rest of the students guess the writer's identity. If they cannot guess, have the student provide clues by giving additional descriptions of the writer. Or, have the class ask questions about the letter writer until they are able to guess who it is.

Differentiated Instruction

SLOWER PACE LEARNERS

Students may have difficulty with activity items that are different from the model given. For example, in Activities 7 and 8, the model shows a singular subject. You might want to do an additional model on the board showing students how to do items with plural subjects.

SPECIAL LEARNING NEEDS

8 Students with Visual Impairments If you have a student with a visual impairment, do activities like Activity 8 as a class. Have volunteers take turns describing the model and each of the images in the activity in English. Give students time between each description to write their responses.

STANDARDS: 1.1, 1.2, 1.3

Resources

Planning:

Lesson Planner, pp. 2–4, 162–167

 One-Stop Planner

Practice:

Cuaderno de vocabulario y gramática, pp. 3–5

Cuaderno de actividades, pp. 1–4

Lab Book, pp. 9–10

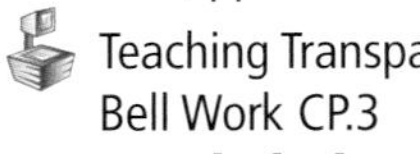 Teaching Transparencies Bell Work CP.3 **Vocabulario y gramática** answers, pp. 3–5

 Audio CD 6, Tr. 2

 Interactive Tutor, Disc 1

Bell Work

Use Bell Work CP.3 in the *Teaching Transparencies*, or write this activity on the board.

Complete each sentence with the correct form of **ser** or **estar.** Then write the letter of the reason for using that verb.

1. Mi libro _____ encima de la cama.
2. _____ bien, gracias.
3. Miguel _____ de Perú.
4. Sofía y Ana _____ rubias.

a. to tell where someone is from
b. to tell where something is
c. to describe people
d. to tell how someone is feeling

The verbs gustar and tener

1 Use the verb **gustar** to say what people like. If the thing they like is singular, use **gusta**; if it is plural use **gustan**. Put one of these **pronouns** before **gustar** to say who likes something.

me gusta(n)	*I like*	**nos** gusta(n)	*we like*
te gusta(n)	*you* **(tú)** *like*	**os** gusta(n)	*you* **(vosotros)** *like*
le gusta(n)	*you* **(usted)** *like, he/she/it likes*	**les** gusta(n)	*you* **(ustedes)** *like, they like*

2 Use the verb **tener** to tell what someone has. To conjugate the yo form drop the **-er** ending and add **-go** . The **-e** in the stem of **tener** changes to **-ie** in all forms except **yo, nosotros,** and **vosotros.**

yo ten**go**	nosotros(as) tenemos
tú t**ie**nes	vosotros(as) tenéis
Ud., él, ella t**ie**ne	Uds., ellos, ellas t**ie**nen

3 **Tener** is also used in these common expressions.

tener que + infinitive	*to have to do something*
tener ganas de + infinitive	*to feel like doing something*
tener prisa	*to be in a hurry*
tener (mucha) hambre	*to be (very) hungry*
tener (mucha) sed	*to be (very) thirsty*

Tengo prisa. Tengo que ir a un ensayo.
I'm in a hurry. I have to go to a rehearsal.

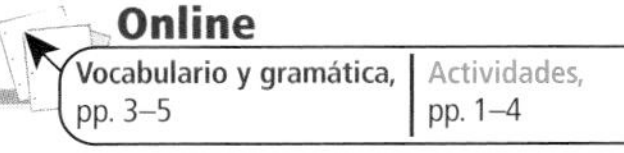
Online
Vocabulario y gramática, pp. 3–5 | Actividades, pp. 1–4

Un día en la playa, Santo Domingo, República Dominicana

10 Vacaciones de verano

Leamos Some friends are going to camp this summer. Complete their conversations with the pronouns **me, te, le, nos,** or **les.**

FELICIA ¡Hola! Me llamo Felicia y éste es Roberto. A nosotros __1__ gusta la comida china. ¿A ustedes __2__ gusta la comida china?

JUAN Sí, a mi hermana Raquel y a mí __3__ gustan la comida china y las hamburguesas. ¿A ustedes __4__ gustan las hamburguesas?

FELICIA A mí __5__ gustan, pero a Roberto no __6__ gustan.

ROBERTO Sí, es verdad, pero __7__ gustan la pizza y el helado. Raquel, ¿a ti __8__ gusta el helado?

RAQUEL Sí, a Juan y a mí __9__ gusta el helado de chocolate.

1. nos
2. les
3. nos
4. les
5. me
6. le
7. me
8. te
9. nos

Core Instruction

TEACHING GRAMÁTICA

1. Say, **¡Tengo mucha hambre y tengo mucha sed! Tengo ganas de comer algo.** Pull out an apple and a small bottle of orange juice from a bag. Begin eating and drinking. Say how much you like apples and orange juice. Then apologize and ask different students if they are hungry and thirsty, too. Guide their responses. **(5 min.)**
2. Then pull out a grapefruit and give it to a student. Ask **"¿No te gusta la toronja?"** Next, pass out plastic glasses and pull out a bottle of prune juice. Ask different students, **¿Te gusta el jugo de ciruela pasa?** In the end, serve up apple slices and orange juice for students to munch on while reading points 1 and 2 of the **Gramática. (10 min.)**
3. Use the grapefruit as a prop to practice the **tener** forms. Then say different sentences using **tener** expressions and have the students you name act them out. (**Josh y Quentin tienen que estudiar.**) **(5 min.)**

STANDARDS: 1.2

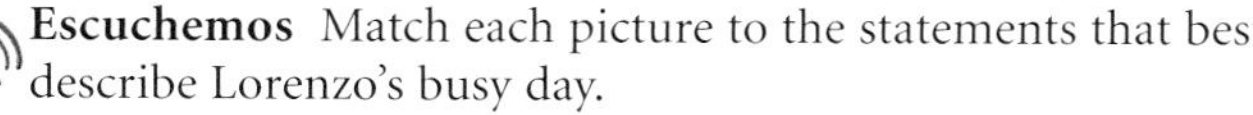

CD 6, Tr. 2

11 El día de Lorenzo

Escuchemos Match each picture to the statements that best describe Lorenzo's busy day.

a. 3

b. 2

c. 1

d. 4

12 ¿A quién le gusta?

Leamos Look at the pictures and complete the sentences with the name(s) of the people and the correct pronouns.

a. Juan y Beto

b. Laura

c. Pati y Tere

d. Memo

1. A ____ gusta el helado. Laura le
2. A ____ gusta la música. Juan y a Beto les
3. A ____ gustan los libros. Memo le
4. A ____ gustan los videojuegos. Pati y aTere les

Comunicación

13 ¿Quién es ella?

Hablemos In groups of four, role-play a situation where you know one person, but you don't know the other two. Take turns greeting everyone and introducing yourself and the person you know. Find out as much as you can about the other people.

MODELO —**Hola. Me llamo... ¿Cómo te llamas?**
—**Me llamo... y éste es mi amigo...**
—**¿De dónde eres?**
—**Soy de...**

Gramática 1

11 Script

1. Son las cuatro y cuarto. Lorenzo regresa a casa.
2. Él tiene un examen de historia el jueves.
3. Lorenzo tiene prisa porque va a llegar tarde al partido de fútbol.
4. Lorenzo tiene mucha tarea para la clase de inglés. Tiene que leer muchos libros.

Comunicación

Pair Work: Interpersonal

Socializing Ask students to bring a picture of a friend to class. Have them refer to the photo as they redo Activity 13 with a partner. You might have students expand the model by asking about and describing the friends in the photographs.

Differentiated Instruction

ADVANCED LEARNERS

Have students write and perform a skit about friends who want to order a pizza but who all like different toppings. Supply the words for the toppings to the students or have them do research in the community or on the Internet to find out how to say *pepperoni, anchovies,* and so forth.

MULTIPLE INTELLIGENCES

Logical/Mathematical Students may benefit from an explanation of why **gustar** has two forms, **gusta** and **gustan** (when used to express what people like), while other verbs such as **tener, ser,** and **estar** have many forms. Tell them that with **gustar,** the person is not *doing* the action, but *receiving* the action. Spanish speakers don't say, for example, "*I* like to swim," but rather "To swim is pleasing *to me.*"

Assess

Assessment Program
Prueba: Vocabulario 1, pp. 3–4
Test Generator 

STANDARDS: 1.1, 1.2

Cultures

Practices and Perspectives

Food Bring different kinds of tortilla chips to class and have students sample them. Tell students that tortilla chips are made by cutting tortillas into triangles and deep-frying them. Originally, all tortillas were made from corn, which has been a major food crop in Mexico since the time of the Aztecs and Mayans. Flour tortillas originated only after the Spanish introduced wheat to the region. It is estimated today that around 100 billion tortillas are eaten in Mexico each year. Have students research and report on how tortillas are traditionally made.

Using the Photo

Copy the day planner page shown in the photo on the board. Make statements about other activities the person might do that day. Have students give a thumbs-up sign if the person would be likely to do an activity, based on the objects shown in the photo, and a thumbs-down if he or she would be unlikely to do an activity. Write the likely activities on the day planner.

Capítulo puente

Segunda parte

Objetivos

In this section you will review how to:

- talk about what you and others like to do
- ask what a friend wants to do and answer for yourself
- use the verb **querer** with infinitives
- use **ir a** + an infinitive to talk about the future
- form and use regular **-ar** verbs
- place pronouns after prepositions

Interdisciplinary Links

La comida

History Link Ask students to name the main ingredient of **salsa.** (tomatoes) Tell students that the prehistoric peoples of the Andes were the first to grow tomatoes. When they traveled north to Central America and Mexico, they brought tomato seeds with them. The tomato was not eaten in Europe until the 16th century, when the Spanish brought back tomato seeds from Mexico. Have students do research to learn other foods the Spanish brought back to Europe and what foods they introduced into the Americas.

Mexican Handblown Bubble Glass

Art Link The glass shown in the photo is an example of Mexican handblown bubble glass. Glassmaking was introduced to Mexico by the Spanish in the 16th century. Handblown glass is created by heating glass in a special oven, then blowing it into a glob of molten glass through a pipe, while shaping it into different forms. It is called "bubble glass" because of the bubbles that sometimes form in the glass during the process.

Roque: Hace muy buen tiempo hoy. ¿Por qué no vamos a la piscina a nadar?
Celeste: No, no quiero nadar. Quiero ir al cine.
Sofía: Pero no quiero ir a la piscina. Y tampoco quiero ir al cine. Voy a casa a estudiar.
Celeste: ¿Qué te pasa, Sofía? ¡Nunca estudias los viernes por la tarde!

Mateo: ¿Qué tal si vamos al partido de béisbol después de clases?
Julia: Claro que sí.
Nicolás: No, no tengo ganas.
Mateo: ¿No tienes ganas? ¿Qué vas a hacer?

Teaching the Novela

1. Have students recall in English the plots of **Episodio 3** and **4. (2 min.)**
2. Have students count off by 3s and read the top dialog as a class: the 1s read Roque's line all together, the 2s Celeste's lines, and the 3s Sofías lines. Repeat with the bottom dialog: the 1s read Mateo's lines, the 2s read Julia's line, and the 3s read Nicolás's line. **(3 min.)**
3. Write other places and activities students have learned on the board. Repeat Step 2, but replace the places and activities in the dialog with places and activities from the board. **(5 min.)**
4. Have students write an activity on a piece of paper and place it face down on their desks: **nadar, ir al partido de béisbol.** Your goal is to invite each student to do the activity he or she has written. Ask, **¿Por qué no vamos a nadar?** If the student wrote **nadar,** he or she must accept the invitation saying, **Claro que sí,** and is out of the game. If you ask about an activity that is not on the paper, the student declines by saying **No, no quiero** ______ , and remains in the game. The last student to accept your invitation wins. **(10 min.)**

Segunda parte Opener

Cultures

Practices and Perspectives

Uniforms Ask students what they notice about how the students are dressed in the photos. Review with students that many schools in Spanish-speaking countries require students to wear uniforms. Ask students why they think schools might want their students to wear uniforms and whether or not they think school uniforms are a good idea.

Video Suggestion

Episodio 3 Estrategia: Understanding subtext Ask students why Sofía didn't tell her friends the truth and how her friends knew she wasn't telling the truth. Then ask students if they have a friend who can "see right through them" and how it makes them feel when their friend makes them "come clean."

Episodio 4 Estrategia: Comparing and contrasting Have students compare and contrast Sofía's and Nicolas's behavior and their friends' reactions.

Video Synopses

Top photo: In **Episodio 3,** Sofía's mother surprises her with ballet lessons. Sofía is horrified at the idea of becoming a ballerina. When her friends invite her to go swimming or to the movies, Sofía says she has to go home to study rather than telling them that she has dance class. Her friends are surprised at Sofía's strange behavior.

Bottom photo: In **Episodio 4,** Nicolas and Mateo discuss what Mateo needs for math class. Then Mateo asks if Nicolas and Julia want to go to a baseball game after school. Julia accepts, but Nicolas declines without giving a good reason. Mateo and Julia become suspicious and wonder what Nicolas is up to. They spot the college professor's assistant, Marcos, taking pictures of Nicolas.

Resources

Planning:

Lesson Planner, pp. 4–6, 164–165

 One-Stop Planner

Practice:

Cuaderno de vocabulario y gramática, pp. 6–7

Lab Book, pp. 11–12

 Teaching Transparencies
Bell Work CP.4
Vocabulario y gramática answers, pp. 6–7

 Interactive Tutor, Disc 1

Bell Work

Use Bell Work CP.4 in the *Teaching Transparencies,* or write this activity on the board.

Match the activity with the logical place to do the activity. Use each place one time.

1. nadar
2. estudiar
3. ver una película
4. descansar y escuchar música
5. jugar al béisbol

a. en el cine
b. en la biblioteca
c. en casa
d. en el parque
e. en la piscina

Objetivos
Talking about what you and others like to do, talking about plans

Vocabulario en acción 2

A mis amigos y a mí nos gusta...

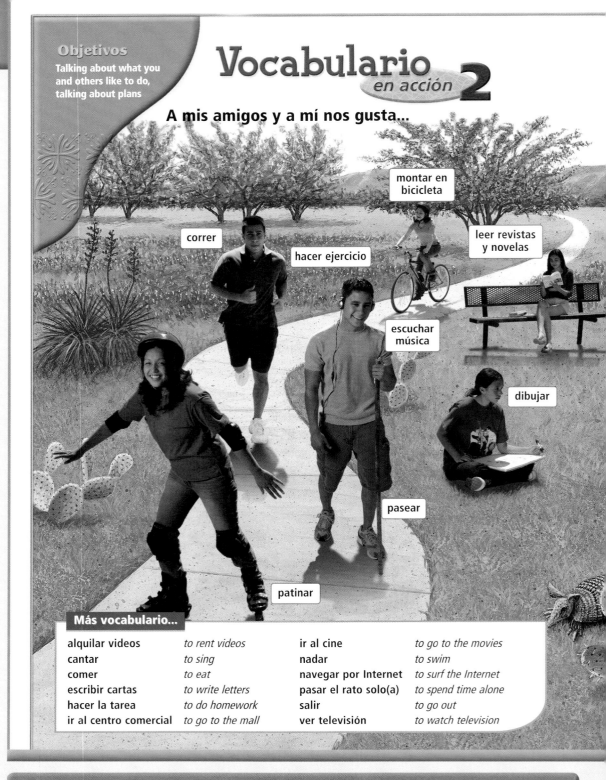

Más vocabulario...

alquilar videos	*to rent videos*	ir al cine	*to go to the movies*
cantar	*to sing*	nadar	*to swim*
comer	*to eat*	navegar por Internet	*to surf the Internet*
escribir cartas	*to write letters*	pasar el rato solo(a)	*to spend time alone*
hacer la tarea	*to do homework*	salir	*to go out*
ir al centro comercial	*to go to the mall*	ver televisión	*to watch television*

Core Instruction

TEACHING VOCABULARIO

1. Review the vocabulary and model the pronunciation. **(2 min.)**
2. Write the days of the week across the board, spaced three feet apart. Say that you are already planning your winter break. Have seven students stand at the board, one student under each day of the week. Tell the activities you plan to do each day. The student standing under the day you describe will draw you doing the activities you mention. Have seven other students take their places and tell your plans for spring break, and then the first week of summer vacation. **(10 min.)**
3. Have three students sit at the front of the room. Interview them with the ***¡Exprésate!*** question, **¿Qué quieres hacer hoy?** Also, find out with whom they would like to do the activities they mention. Then ask the rest of the class questions about what the students said. Model your questions on the ***¡Exprésate!*** question, **¿A Lili le gusta ir al centro comercial? (8 min.)**

STANDARDS: 1.2

Visit Holt Online
go.hrw.com
KEYWORD: EXP1B PUENTE
Vocabulario 2 practice

¿Qué te gusta hacer?

A mí me gusta...

hablar por teléfono

bailar

descansar

Y me gusta jugar...

a juegos de mesa

al básquetbol

al béisbol

al fútbol

Más vocabulario...

¿Con quién?	
conmigo	*with me*
contigo	*with you*
con mi familia	*with my family*

También se puede decir...

Spanish speakers in Mexico say **el baloncesto** instead of **el básquetbol,** and **andar en bicicleta** instead of **montar en bicicleta.**

¡Exprésate!

To ask what someone likes or wants to do	To respond
¿Qué quieres hacer hoy? *What do you want to do today?*	**Ni idea.** *I have no idea.*
¿Quieres ir al cine conmigo? *Do you want to go to the movies with me?*	**Está bien./No, no quiero ir.** *All right./No, I don't want to go.*
¿A Lili le gusta ir al centro comercial? *Does Lili like to go to the mall?*	**Sí, porque le gusta ir de compras.** *Yes, because she likes to go shopping.*

Interactive TUTOR

Online
Vocabulario y gramática, pp. 6–7

▶ Vocabulario adicional — Deportes y pasatiempos, p. R12

Vocabulario 2

TPR

TOTAL PHYSICAL RESPONSE

Ask students what they would like to do today, giving them two alternative activities. **(¿Qué quieres hacer hoy, bailar o cantar?)** Have the students act out their choice of activity.

También se puede decir...

Have students hypothesize on why there are language differences between the Spanish spoken in different countries. Explain that languages evolve over time and if two groups of people who speak the same language are separated geographically, the same language will evolve in different ways. Spanish was brought to the Americas in the 16th century. The vast distances between Spain and its colonies, and between the various colonies themselves, resulted in language differences. Ask students to think of an instance of colonialism that resulted in linguistic variations in English. (e.g., British and American English)

Differentiated Instruction

SLOWER PACE LEARNERS

Slower paced learners may be overwhelmed by the number of activities in the **Vocabulario.** Help students organize the vocabulary into different types of activities. As a class, come up with categories (for example, team sports, individual sports, things to do when going out with friends, things to do alone at home) and decide where to place each activity.

SPECIAL LEARNING NEEDS

Students with Physical Impairments Be sensitive when discussing physical activities that some of your students are unable to do because of a physical impairment. Ask them what their favorite activities are and provide them with the Spanish vocabulary they need to talk about them.

Resources

Planning:

Lesson Planner, pp. 4–6, 164–165

One-Stop Planner

Practice:

Cuaderno de vocabulario y gramática, pp. 6–7

Lab Book, pp. 11–12

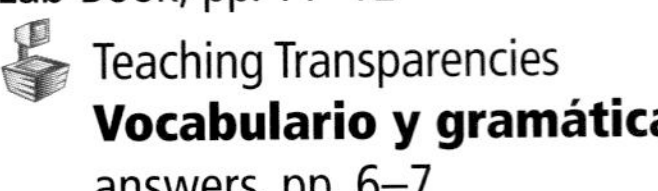Teaching Transparencies **Vocabulario y gramática** answers, pp. 6–7

Audio CD 6, Tr. 3

Interactive Tutor, Disc 1

14 Script

1. A Carla le gusta pasar el rato sola.
2. A Eduardo le gusta ver televisión.
3. A José le gusta hacer la tarea.
4. A mis amigos les gusta jugar al volibol.
5. A Janet le gusta leer y hacer la tarea.
6. A mis amigas les gusta ir a fiestas y alquilar videos.

CD 6, Tr. 3

14 Les gusta...

**Escuchemos** Choose the most logical description based on the sentences you hear.

1. Es (extrovertida/tímida).
2. Es (muy activo/perezoso).
3. Es (trabajador/perezoso).
4. Son (atléticos/intelectuales).
5. Es (activa/seria).
6. Son (divertidas/serias).

15 ¿Qué les gusta?

Leamos Match the sentences with the pictures.

1. A Tere le gusta hacer ejercicio. f
2. A Nico le gusta cantar. d
3. A Mila le gusta ver televisión. e
4. A Beto y a Toño les gusta jugar al básquetbol. a
5. A José y a Ana les gusta bailar. b
6. A Paco y a Lalo les gusta jugar al fútbol. c

A

B
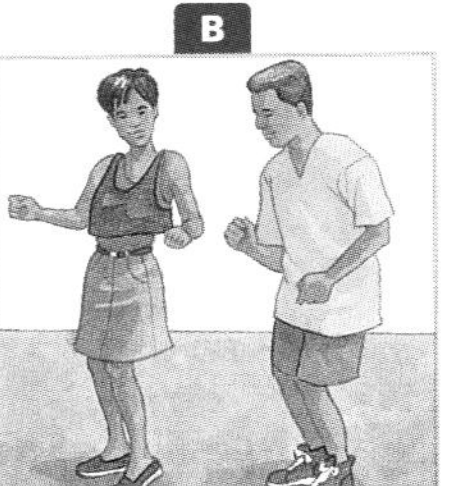
C

D

E

F

¡Exprésate!

To talk about your plans

Interactive TUTOR

¿Qué haces los fines de semana? *What do you do on the weekends?*	**Cuando hace buen tiempo, voy al parque.** *When the weather is nice, I go to the park.*
¿Qué vas a hacer el viernes próximo? *What are you going to do next Friday?*	**Voy a ir a una fiesta.** *I'm going to go to a party.*

Core Instruction

TEACHING ¡EXPRÉSATE!

1. Bring in pictures of the activities on pages 12–13 and pictures of celebrities for Steps 2–4. Model the pronunciation of the questions and responses. **(2 min.)**
2. Ask students, **¿Qué haces los fines de semana cuando hace buen tiempo?** and hold up a picture of an activity for students to use in their response. **(6 min.)**
3. Then ask, **¿Qué haces los fines de semana cuando no hace buen tiempo?** and hold up a picture of an activity for students to use in their response. **(6 min.)**
4. Next, ask students **¿Qué vas a hacer el viernes próximo? Y, ¿con quién?** Hold up an activity picture and the picture of a celebrity for students to use in their response. (**¡Voy a ir al cine con Brad Pitt!**) **(6 min.)**

16 ¿Qué tal si...?

Leamos Lupe is calling her friend Tomás from the mall. Read the sentences of their conversation, and then put them in the most logical order.

Lupe	Tomás
—Estoy en el centro comercial. ¿Quieres ir al cine conmigo? 3	—¡Hola, Lupe! Nada. ¿Dónde estás? 2
—Buena idea, Tomás. Nos vemos en diez minutos. 7	—Adiós. Hasta luego. 8
—¡Excelente! Y después de la película, ¿qué quieres hacer? 5	—¿Qué tal si vamos al parque? Hace buen tiempo hoy. 6
—Hola. ¿Tomás? Soy Lupe. ¿Qué haces? 1	—Sí, quiero ir. Voy a llegar en diez minutos. 4

17 ¿Quieres ir?

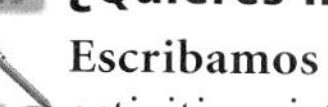

Escribamos Write a sentence inviting a friend to do the activities pictured below. Then write what you think your friend will say in response.

MODELO **—¿Quieres pasear en el parque conmigo?**
—Sí, quiero pasear. Hace buen tiempo hoy.
(—No, no quiero. No me gusta el parque.)

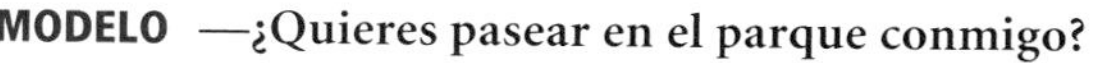

1 

2 

3 

4 

5 

Comunicación

18 Una invitación personal

Hablemos Think of a place you'd like to go and something you'd like to do there. Invite two or three of your classmates to do the activity with you, and see how they respond. If they don't want to do the activity, be sure to ask them why.

MODELO **—Jorge, ¿quieres ir al cine conmigo?**
—No, no quiero ir al cine hoy.
—¿Por qué no?
—No me gusta ir al cine. Es aburrido.

COMMON ERROR ALERT ¡OJO!

Write **viernes próximo** on the board and have students tell you what each word means individually. (Friday / next) Ask students how it sounds in English to say, "What are you doing Friday next?" Remind them that in English, words that describe other words usually come before the word they describe, while in Spanish, they can come before or after. Students will need to remember the correct position of the describing words they learn.

Comunicación

Individual Activity: Presentational

Providing information Ask students to bring in two objects that represent their favorite activity and least favorite activity and have a Show-and-Tell Day. Students tell in Spanish which activity they like, which activity they don't like, and why. You might have them research additional Spanish vocabulary to talk further about each activity.

Differentiated Instruction

ADVANCED LEARNERS

In pairs, have students write and perform a skit about a teenager trying to get his or her "couch potato" friend to do something with him or her. Students should include in their skits several possible activities, some indoor, some outside.

MULTIPLE INTELLIGENCES

Musical/Rhythmic Have students write a song titled, **¡No quiero hacer la tarea!** about a student having a hard time doing his or her homework because the weather is so nice outside. In the song, students should mention the other activities the student would rather be doing. Provide them with a familiar melody to set their lyrics to, or let them come up with their own melody.

Assess

Assessment Program

Prueba: Vocabulario 2, pp. 5–6

Test Generator 

STANDARDS: 1.1, 1.2, 1.3

Resources

Planning:

Lesson Planner, pp. 5–7, 166–169

One-Stop Planner

Practice:

Cuaderno de vocabulario y gramática, pp. 8–10

Cuaderno de actividades, pp. 5–8

Lab Book, pp. 11–12

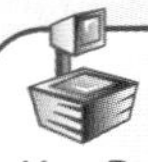

Teaching Transparencies Bell Work CP.5 **Vocabulario y gramática** answers, pp. 8–10

Interactive Tutor, Disc 1

Audio CD 6, Tr. 4

Bell Work

Use Bell Work CP.5 in the *Teaching Transparencies,* or write this activity on the board.

Unscramble the conversation.

—¿Con quién?
—Voy a ir al cine.
—¡Está bien! Buena idea.
—Ni idea. Y tú, ¿qué vas a hacer?
—¡Contigo!
—Marcos, ¿qué vas a hacer este viernes?

Objetivos
Using the verbs **querer, ir a** + infinitive, pronouns after prepositions, regular **-ar** verbs, and possessive adjectives

Gramática en acción 2

Interactive TUTOR

querer, ir a + infinitive, and pronouns

1 To say what you or others want or want to do, use a form of the verb **querer.** The form you use depends on the subject.

yo	qu**ie**ro	nosotros	queremos
tú	qu**ie**res	vosotros	queréis
Ud., él, ella	qu**ie**re	Uds., ellos, ellas	qu**ie**ren

2 To talk about what someone is or isn't going to do, use the present tense of **ir** with **a** followed by an **infinitive**.

¿**Vas a estudiar**? *Are you going to study?*
No, **voy a descansar**. *No, I'm going to rest.*

3 **Pronouns** have a different form when they come after prepositions such as **a** *(to),* **de** *(of, from),* **con** *(with)* and **en** *(in, on, at).*

mí	nosotros(as)
ti	vosotros(as)
usted, él, ella	ustedes, ellos, ellas

4 With **gustar,** the phrase formed by **a** and a **pronoun** can be added to a sentence to clarify or emphasize the pronoun that's already there.

adds emphasis ¿**A ti** te gusta dibujar? *adds emphasis* **A mí** no me gusta. *clarifies* **A ella** le gusta.

Online
Vocabulario y gramática, pp. 8–10 | Actividades, pp. 5–8

¿Te acuerdas?

The verb **querer** is a stem changing verb. The **e** in the stem changes to **ie** in all forms except **nosotros** and **vosotros.** Other **e** → **ie** stem changing verbs are **empezar** and **merendar.**

CD 6, Tr. 4

19 Vamos al centro comercial

Escuchemos Listen to the conversation between Juan and Sofía and decide which photos show what they both want to do. b and e

A

B

C

D

E

Core Instruction

TEACHING GRAMÁTICA

1. Read over the first point and the **¿Te acuerdas?** Then tell students dramatically, **¡Yo quiero... cantar!** and sing a few **La, la, la's.** Point to a student and say, **¡Tú quieres cantar!** and encourage him or her to sing a little bit. Repeat with other students to model the **usted, él, ella, nosotros, vosotros, ellos,** and **ellas** forms. **(8 min.)**
2. Read over the second point and announce, **¡Voy a... bailar!** and do a little jig. Repeat the procedure above to practice the rest of the pronouns with the present tense of **ir** with **a** and **bailar. (8 min.)**
3. Read over the third and fourth points. Then discuss whether your students like or dislike singing and dancing based on their reactions to Steps 1 and 2. (**¡A mí me gusta bailar, pero a él** [point to a student who chose not to dance] **no le gusta bailar!**) **(4 min.)**

STANDARDS: 1.2

Visit Holt Online
go.hrw.com
KEYWORD: EXP1B PUENTE
Gramática 2 practice

20 ¿Cuál es la pregunta?

Leamos Choose the question that best matches the answer given.

1. Juan no quiere ver televisión porque tiene mucha tarea.
   (a.) ¿Por qué Juan no quiere ver televisión?
   b. ¿Por qué a Juan no le gusta ver televisión?
2. Porque queremos alquilar un video.
   a. ¿Por qué no quiere ir al cine?
   (b.) ¿Por qué no quieren ir al cine?
3. No, a mí me gusta salir con amigos.
   (a.) Profesora, ¿a usted le gusta pasar el rato sola?
   b. Profesora, ¿a ella le gusta pasar el rato sola?
4. No, no quiero.
   a. ¿Quieren jugar a un videojuego?
   (b.) ¿Quieres jugar a un videojuego?

21 ¿Qué van a hacer?

Escribamos Write five questions using a word or phrase from each column. Then write an answer to each of your questions.

MODELO **—¿Vas a jugar al básquetbol?**
—No, a mí no me gustan los deportes.

Tú	ir a	asistir a un concierto
Sr. González (Ud.)	querer	estudiar el español
Mi amiga		trabajar
Los estudiantes		visitar al abuelo
Ustedes		jugar en el parque
Ellas		ir a la escuela

Niños en el parque, Santo Domingo, República Dominicana

Comunicación

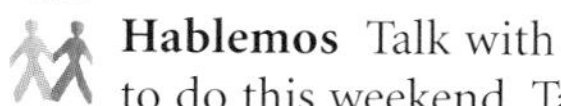

22 El fin de semana

Hablemos Talk with a classmate about things you like to do or want to do this weekend. Take turns suggesting weekend activities based on what the other person says that he or she likes.

—A mí me gustan los deportes.
—¿Quieres jugar al básquetbol en el parque el sábado?
—Sí, quiero jugar al básquetbol contigo.

19 Script

Juan: Sofía, ¿quieres ir a patinar en el centro comercial conmigo?
Sofía: Está bien. También quiero leer revistas.
Juan: Y yo quiero jugar a los videojuegos.
Sofía: No me gustan los videojuegos. Son aburridos.
Juan: ¿Quieres comer comida italiana en el centro comercial?
Sofía: No, gracias. Quiero una hamburguesa.
Juan: ¡Fenomenal! Las hamburguesas del centro son muy buenas. Yo también quiero comer una hamburguesa.

21 Answers

Possible answers

1. —¿Tú vas a asistir a un concierto?
   —Sí, a mí me gusta escuchar música.
2. —¿El Sr. González quiere trabajar?
   —Sí, a él le gusta trabajar.
3. —¿Los estudiantes van a estudiar el español?
   —No, a ellos no les gusta estudiar español.
4. —¿Ustedes quieren visitar al abuelo?
   —Sí, a nosotros nos gusta visitar al abuelo.
5. —¿Ellas van a asistir a un concierto?
   —Sí, a mí me gusta escuchar la música.

Differentiated Instruction

SLOWER PACE LEARNERS

21 Write the forms of **ir** on the board and review them with students before they begin Activity 21. Also, students might have problems deciding which verb form to use when a proper noun or noun is given instead of a pronoun. Make sure they understand that they will use the **él** form with **Sr. González,** the **ella** form with **mi amiga,** and the **ellos** form with **los estudiantes.**

SPECIAL LEARNING NEEDS

19 Students with Auditory Impairments Provide students with a copy of the script to help them do Activity 19. You might also allow students with auditory impairments to read the script aloud as they complete the activity.

Comunicación

Group Activity: Interpersonal

Socializing Distribute to students index cards that have either **básquetbol** or **béisbol** written on them. Have students circulate around the room and invite their classmates to do the sport on their card. If that student has the same sport on his or her card, the invitation is accepted and both students write each other's names on the card. If the student has a different sport, the invitation is declined and both students move on. The goal is to find enough students to form a team.

STANDARDS: 1.1, 1.2, 1.3

Resources

Planning:

Lesson Planner, pp. 5–7, 166–169

One-Stop Planner

Practice:

Cuaderno de vocabulario y gramática, pp. 8–10

Cuaderno de actividades, pp. 5–8

Lab Book, pp. 11–12

Teaching Transparencies Bell Work CP.6 **Vocabulario y gramática** answers, pp. 8–10

Interactive Tutor, Disc 1

Bell Work

Use Bell Work CP.6 in the *Teaching Transparencies,* or write this activity on the board.

Write five sentences telling what you are going to do next weekend. Use **Voy** + **a** + infinitive in your sentences.

En inglés

In Spanish, verb conjugations in the present tense have six forms. The **subject pronouns (yo, tú, usted, él, ella, nosotros, vosotros, ustedes, ellos, ellas)** are often left out because the subject is understood from the ending of the verb.

In English, most verb conjugations in the present tense have only two forms. The **subject pronouns** are not left out.

I sing	**we** sing
you sing	**you** sing
he, she, it sings	**they** sing

Regular -ar verbs and possessive adjectives

1 Every verb has a stem followed by some kind of **ending**. The stem tells the verb's meaning. An infinitive ending means the verb has no subject.

verb stem → **habl** **-ar** ← *infinitive ending*

2 To give the verb a subject you conjugate it. To conjugate a regular **-ar** verb in the present tense, drop the **-ar** ending of the infinitive and add these other **endings**. Each ending goes with a particular subject.

yo	cant**o**	nosotros(as)	cant**amos**
tú	cant**as**	vosotros(as)	cant**áis**
Ud., él, ella	cant**a**	Uds., ellos, ellas	cant**an**

¿Te gusta **cantar**? Sí, cant**o** todos los días.

3 Possessive adjectives show ownership or relationships between people. They are placed before the **noun.**

Owner			Owner				
yo	**mi**	**libro**	nosotros(as)	**nuestro**	**libro**	**nuestra**	**casa**
	mis	**libros**		**nuestros**	**libros**	**nuestras**	**casas**
tú	**tu**	**libro**	vosotros(as)	**vuestro**	**libro**	**vuestra**	**casa**
	tus	**libros**		**vuestros**	**libros**	**vuestras**	**casas**
usted, él/ella	**su**	**libro**	ustedes, ellos/ellas	**su**	**libro**		
	sus	**libros**		**sus**	**libros**		

4 Possessive adjectives agree with the **noun** that comes after them.

refers to / *agrees grammatically*

Martín vive con **nuestros abuelos.**

Online
Vocabulario y gramática, pp. 8–10 | Actividades, pp. 5–8

23 En mi familia

Leamos Choose the correct verb forms to complete the conversation.

—Mariana, ¿cómo (paso/pasas) el fin de semana?
—Los sábados mis amigos y yo (pasan/pasamos) el rato juntos.
—¿Y es todo?
—No. A veces yo (patino/patinas) en el parque con José.
—Y tus padres, ¿cómo (pasan/pasamos) el fin de semana?
—Ellos (montan/montamos) en bicicleta.
—¿Y tu hermano Javier?
—Él siempre (practicas/practica) deportes. Es muy atlético.

Core Instruction

TEACHING GRAMÁTICA

1. Have students read **En inglés** and points 1 and 2 of **Gramática.** Then line up six chairs at the front of the classroom. On the back of each chair, tape one of the **–ar** endings. Divide the class into two teams and have a student from each team stand in back of the chairs. Call out an infinitive and a pronoun. The first student to sit in the chair with the correct ending and say the verb form correctly wins a point for his or her team. **(8 min.)**

2. Read over points 3 and 4 of **Gramática.** Then have students fold two pieces of paper in half to represent two book covers. Tell them to write the titles of two books they would like to write some day on the book covers. Have them write their name and a quick sketch on each cover that suggests what each book is about. Have your own books prepared ahead of time. Collect all the book covers and use them to demonstrate the possessive pronouns. (**—¿Cómo se llama el libro de Justin? —Su libro se llama** *Skateboarding for Fun and Profit.*) **(12 min.)**

24 El fin de semana

Hablemos Based on the pictures, say what each person does on the weekend.

MODELO **Estudio matemáticas.**

Yo

1. Luisa

2. Mi papá

3. Nosotros

4. Mi hermana

5. Ellos

6. Gisela

7. Pati y Arturo

8. Mis amigos

25 La familia de Gregorio

Leamos Gregorio is talking about his family with a friend. On a separate piece of paper, write the missing possessive adjectives.

—¿Cuántas personas hay en __1__ familia?

—Somos seis en __2__ familia: __3__ padres, __4__ dos hermanas, __5__ hermano y yo.

—¿Dónde trabajan __6__ padres?

—__7__ madre es profesora. __8__ trabajo es muy interesante. __9__ padre trabaja con __10__ padre, mi abuelo.

—Ustedes tienen una casa azul, ¿verdad?

—No, __11__ casa no es azul, pero __12__ carro es azul.

1. tu **2.** mi **3.** mis **4.** mis **5.** mi **6.** tus **7.** Mi **8.** Su **9.** Mi **10.** su **11.** nuestra **12.** nuestro

Comunicación

26 ¿Y qué haces tú?

Hablemos/Escribamos Make a list of five things you do with your friends or family on the weekends. Ask a classmate if he or she does the same things. Then answer your classmate's questions.

MODELO **—Yo nado con mis amigos. Y tú, ¿nadas con tus amigos?**
—No, mis amigos y yo no nadamos. Vemos televisión.

Gramática 2

24 Answers

1. Luisa nada.
2. Mi papá trabaja.
3. Nosotros estudiamos.
4. Mi hermano arregla su carro.
5. Ellos montan en bicicleta.
6. Gisela patina.
7. Pati y Arturo bailan.
8. Mis amigos cantan.

Comunicación

Pair Work: Interpersonal

26 Socializing Have students expand Activity 26 by inviting their partner to participate in the activities on their list. They should respond, taking turns inviting and responding.

MODELO
—¿Quieres nadar con nosotros este sábado?
—Gracias, sí. ¿A qué hora?

Differentiated Instruction

ADVANCED LEARNERS

Have students create a board game that helps students learning Spanish to conjugate the verbs reviewed in the **Segunda parte** and the vocabulary reviewed on pages 12–13.

SPECIAL LEARNING NEEDS

25 Students with Learning Disabilities/ Dyslexia Students with dyslexia may need extra help deciding which noun they should use when choosing a possessive pronoun. Before students do Activity 25 independently, as a class, have them identify all the nouns in each sentence and then tell which noun the possessive pronoun should agree with.

Assess

Assessment Program
Prueba: Gramática 2, pp. 7–8
Test Generator 

Tercera parte Opener

Comparisons

Comparing and Contrasting

Have students guess the relationships of the people in the photo. Remind them that in Spanish-speaking countries, people consider their grandparents, aunts and uncles, and cousins as part of their "family unit" as well as their mother, father, brothers, and sisters. Ask the class: When someone asks how many people are in your family, who do you typically count? Do you include relatives such as your grandparents? Why do you suppose different cultures include or exclude extended relatives in their perception of 'family'?

Using the Photo

Ask students if they think you can tell what people value by the photos they keep around them. Have students say what this student's desk tells us about his or her values. Ask students what photos they have in their room at home and if they carry any photos in their wallets. Invite students to show their photos to the rest of the class, telling in Spanish who the people in the photos are.

Capítulo puente

Tercera parte

Objetivos

In this section you will review how to:

- say what you have and need
- talk about classes and school supplies
- describe and talk about family relationships
- ask about other's responsibilities and talk about yours
- form **-er** and **-ir** verbs in the present tense
- form and use stem-changing verbs
- form and use the verbs **hacer, poner,** and **tocar**

Interdisciplinary Links

La tecnología

Math Link Ask students to guess when calculators were invented. Tell them the very first "personal calculator" was the abacus, a calculating tool invented in China around 3,000 B.C. Another ancient counting system was the **quipu,** a system of colored strings tied into knots that was used by the Incas. Have interested students research the abacus or the **quipu** and present their findings to the class.

La familia

Social Studies Link Ask students if it is easy or hard for them to ask for help when they have a problem. Comment that in U.S. culture, many people find it hard to ask for help. Tell them that this is not true in many Hispanic cultures, where people depend more on their family and friends for help with life's problems. In fact, people who try to solve their own problems might be seen as cold or superior-acting. Ask students if they think it is good or bad to depend on other people, and explain why.

STANDARDS: 2.1, 3.1, 4.2

Nicolás: ¿Qué necesitas?
Mateo: A ver, necesito un lápiz... una goma... una regla... y papel.

Sofía: Ese niño travieso es mi hermano Quique. A Quique no le toca hacer los quehaceres. ¡Me parece injusto!

Teaching the Novela

1. Have students recall the episodes in English (see Video Synopses in side column). **(2 min.)**
2. Read the first dialogue. Then give each student a pencil, an eraser, a ruler, or a piece of paper. Ask students, **¿Qué necesitas?** Students will respond with the three items they do not have. **(8 min.)**
3. Read Sofía's monologue aloud, focusing the students' attention on the phrase **A Quique no le toca hacer los quehaceres.** Make sure they understand the meaning of the phrase (He doesn't have to/it's never his turn to...) Then play a game of "Hangman" (**el Ahorcado**) with the class. Randomly distribute cards numbered from 1 to however many students you have. Selecting words from the chapter, write blanks for the letters on the board. Students take turns guessing letters according to the number they received. Call out a number, and then ask students each time, **¿A quién le toca jugar ahora?** and have students respond, **A mí me toca jugar. (10 min.)**

Tercera parte Opener

Comparisons

Comparing and Contrasting

Ask students what **A ver...** means *(Let's see . . .)*. Ask students if Mateo is really inviting Nicolás to look at something or if he is just stalling for time while he thinks of the school supplies he needs. Tell students that Spanish speakers also say **Bueno,...** *(Well, . . .)* when they pause to think what they are going to say. Ask students what words English speakers say to fill up pauses while they're speaking. (Um . . ., Uh . . .) Then challenge students to see if they can talk on a given topic for one minute without saying "Um . . ." or "Uh . . ."

Video Synopses

Top photo: In **Episodio 4,** Nicolas and Mateo discuss what Mateo needs for math class. Then Mateo asks if Nicolas and Julia want to go to a baseball game after school. Julia accepts, but Nicolas declines without giving a good reason. Mateo and Julia become suspicious and wonder what Nicolas is up to. They spot the college assistant Marcos taking pictures of Nicolas.

Bottom photo: In **Episodio 5,** Sofía tells why she doesn't like Saturdays very much: It is the day she must do chores around the house. Sofía introduces her mother, her father, and her little brother who all remind her of the chores she must do.

Resources

Planning:

Lesson Planner, pp. 7–8, 168–169

 One-Stop Planner

Practice:

Cuaderno de vocabulario y gramática, pp. 11–12

Lab Book, pp. 13–14

 Teaching Transparencies
Bell Work CP.7
Vocabulario y gramática answers, pp. 11–12

 Interactive Tutor, Disc 1

Bell Work

Use Bell Work CP.7 in the *Teaching Transparencies*, or write this activity on the board.

Complete each sentence with the correct form of **necesitar.**

1. **Yo _____ un lápiz.**
2. **Jorge _____ una regla.**
3. **Tú _____ una bicicleta.**
4. **Lupita y Yolanda _____ unas gomas.**
5. **Nosotros _____ papel.**

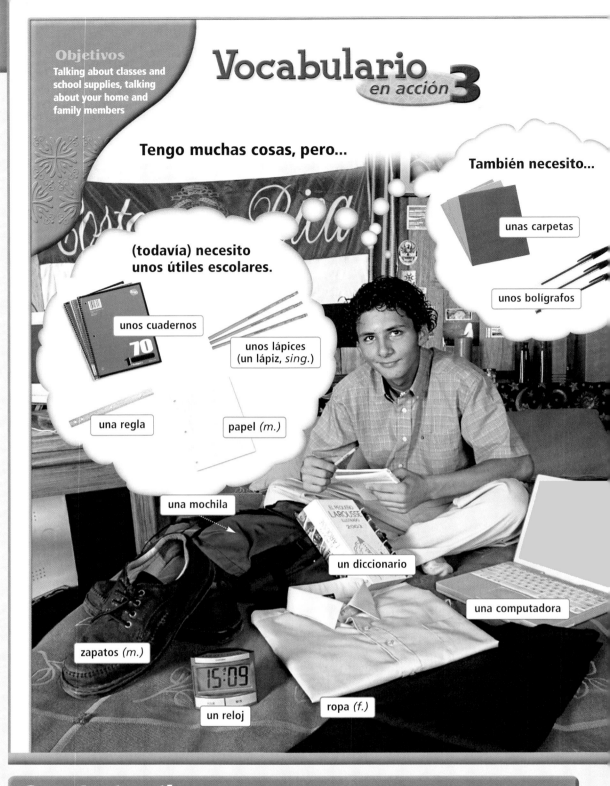

Objetivos
Talking about classes and school supplies, talking about your home and family members

Vocabulario en acción 3

Tengo muchas cosas, pero...

(todavía) necesito unos útiles escolares.

unos cuadernos

unos lápices (un lápiz, *sing.*)

una regla

papel *(m.)*

También necesito...

unas carpetas

unos bolígrafos

una mochila

un diccionario

una computadora

zapatos *(m.)*

un reloj

ropa *(f.)*

Core Instruction

TEACHING VOCABULARIO

1. Model the pronunciation of the school supplies on page 22 and the first question and answer in **¡Exprésate!** Have students point in their books to each item as you pronounce it. Read over the **También se puede decir…** on page 23. **(2 min.)**
2. Have each student draw a large backpack and a large shopping cart. Tell them to draw three school supplies in the backpack and three items in the shopping cart. Ask students **¿Qué tienes todavía?** and **¿Necesitas algo para el colegio?** Have them respond based on the contents of their backpack and shopping cart. **(10 min.)**
3. Model the pronunciation of the sentences in speech bubbles and **Más vocabulario** and the last two questions and answers in **¡Exprésate!** Have three students write their own schedules on the board. Ask the students questions about their schedules and then ask the rest of the class about the students' schedules. **(8 min.)**

Vocabulario 3

Visit Holt Online
go.hrw.com
KEYWORD: EXP1B PUENTE
Vocabulario 3 practice

Horas	Clases
8:00	*matemáticas*
8:50	*arte*
9:40	*biología*
10:30	*español*
11:20	*educación física*
12:10	*almuerzo*
13:00	*historia*
13:50	*inglés*

Más vocabulario...

las materias	*school subjects*
el alemán	*German*
el francés	*French*
las ciencias	*science*
la química	*chemistry*
el taller	*workshop*
la computación	*computer science*

También se puede decir...

In Spain, a computer is called **un ordenador,** while in Colombia, the word is **computador.**

In Latin America, many speakers say **una pluma,** or **un lapicero,** instead of **bolígrafo.** In Spain, **lapicero** is a pencil case.

¡Exprésate!

To ask about school and classes	To respond
¿Necesitas algo para el colegio? *Do you need anything for school?*	**Sí, necesito muchas cosas./No, no necesito nada.** *Yes, I need a lot of things./No, I don't need anything.*
¿Qué clases tienes esta tarde después del almuerzo? *What clases do you have this afternoon after lunch?*	**Primero tengo español y después tengo computación.** *First I have Spanish and afterwards I have computer science.*
¿A qué hora tienes la clase de francés? *What time do you have French class?*	**Tengo francés a las dos y media.** *I have French at two-thirty.*

Interactive TUTOR

Online
Vocabulario y gramática, pp. 11–12

▶ Vocabulario adicional — Materias, p. R11

TPR

TOTAL PHYSICAL RESPONSE

Place three backpacks and the school supplies from page 22 on a table at the front of the room. Have three students at a time stand at the table and follow your directions to put different items into their backpack, take them out, give them to each other, and so forth.

También se puede decir...

Tell students that another name for the language we call "Spanish" is Castilian **(castellano),** as the language originated in Castile, a province of Spain. Other languages native to Spain are Catalan **(catalán),** spoken in northeastern Spain in the Catalan province; Galician **(gallego),** spoken in Galicia, a province in northwestern Spain; and Basque **(euskera),** spoken in the western Pyrenees that border France and Spain. Spaniards who speak Castilian as their native language tend to call it **español.** Spaniards whose native language is not Spanish may call the same language **castellano,** as they feel that their regional languages are **español,** too. Ask students to consider why people feel so strongly about their native language.

Differentiated Instruction

SLOWER PACE LEARNERS

Before presenting the **¡Exprésate!** question **¿Qué clases tienes esta tarde después del almuerzo?,** review the names of school subjects by holding up different props for the courses and having students identify them. Before presenting **¿A qué hora tienes la clase de francés?,** review telling time by calling out different times and having students draw clocks showing those times.

SPECIAL LEARNING NEEDS

Students with Visual Impairments Do a chain activity to present the school supplies in **Vocabulario.** Pick up one of the school supplies, say the Spanish word for the item, pass it to a student who repeats the Spanish word and passes the item to the next student who repeats the word, and so forth.

STANDARDS: 1.2

Resources

Planning:

Lesson Planner, pp. 7–8, 168–169

 One-Stop Planner

Practice:

Cuaderno de vocabulario y gramática, pp. 11–12

Lab Book, pp. 13–14

 Teaching Transparencies
Vocabulario y gramática answers, pp. 11–12

 Audio CD 6, Tr. 5

 Interactive Tutor, Disc 1

Cultures

Practices and Perspectives

Ask students if they think people in the United States tend to be very open and informal, even with people they don't know. Comment that people from Spanish-speaking countries may be reluctant to answer personal questions such as those in **¡Exprésate!** until they get to know someone well. Ask students if they would feel comfortable answering the questions if someone they didn't know asked them. Remind students there are also cultural differences in body language. For example, people from South America tend to stand closer to each other when they are talking than North Americans do. If you step back, the person may think you are being rude or may subconsciously try to close the gap by moving forward. With a volunteer, perform a humorous skit in which a student from the United States has a conversation with you, a student from South America, who "invades" his or her "space."

Entre clases en Costa Rica

27 ¡No lo tengo!

Leamos Jorge says Lili has taken his dictionary without asking. Complete Lili's response using the words from the box.

diccionario	papel	mochila	carpetas
lápices	calculadora	cuaderno	comida

Tengo en mi __1__ unos __2__, unas __3__, y un __4__. También tengo una __5__, y mucho __6__. ¡No tengo tu __7__!

1. mochila 2. lápices 3. carpetas 4. cuaderno 5. calculadora 6. papel 7. diccionario

28 ¿Qué clase tengo?

Leamos/Escribamos Ana can't remember her class schedule. Based on the schedule below, answer Ana's questions.

Día	lunes	martes	miércoles	jue
Horario				
8:45	*historia*	*biología*	*historia*	*bio*
9:40	*matemáticas*	*computación*	*matemáticas*	*con*
10:35	*ed. física*	*arte*	*ed. física*	*arte*
11:30	*español*	*ciencias*	*español*	*cie*
12:25	*almuerzo*	*almuerzo*	*almuerzo*	*alm*
12:55	*química*	*inglés*	*química*	*ing*
1:50	*taller*	*francés*	*taller*	*fra*

1. ¿Qué clase tengo después del almuerzo los lunes? química
2. ¿Qué clase tengo los martes a las once y media? ciencias
3. ¿Qué clase tengo después de historia los miércoles? matemáticas
4. ¿Qué clase tengo los martes a las dos menos diez? francés

¡Exprésate!

To ask about home and family	To respond
¿Cuántas personas hay en tu familia? *How many people are in your family?*	**En mi familia somos cuatro. Mi madre, mi padre, mi hermana y yo.** *In my family, there are four of us. My mother, my father, my sister, and I.*
¿Cómo son tus hermanos? *What are your brothers and sisters like?*	**Ellos son delgados y altos. Usan lentes.** *They are thin and tall. They wear glasses.*
¿Dónde viven ustedes? *Where do you live?*	**Vivimos en un apartamento.** *We live in an apartment.*
¿Qué haces para ayudar en casa? *What do you do to help out around the house?*	**A mí me toca cocinar la cena.** *I have to cook dinner.*

Interactive TUTOR

Online
Vocabulario y gramática, pp. 11–12

▶ **Vocabulario adicional** — Profesiones, p. R14

Core Instruction

TEACHING ¡EXPRÉSATE!

1. Model the pronunciation of the questions and responses. **(2 min.)**
2. Before class, research TV shows your students are likely to watch that center around a family. Take notes on the family members' names and relationships, their appearance, where they live, and any chores the children would logically do. Then take on the roles of different characters and use the responses in **¡Exprésate!** to describe your TV family. Have students guess who you are and the name of the show. **(8 min.)**
3. Randomly form groups of four or five students. Tell students that their group is their new family and that they must decide who will be the father, mother, and children and each family member's name. Then ask the groups the **¡Exprésate!** questions. Each student will answer at least one of the questions about his or her new family. **(10 min.)**

CD 6, Tr. 5

29 ¿Cierto o falso?

Escuchemos Mira el árbol genealógico *(family tree)* y escucha las oraciones. Indica si cada oración es **cierta** o **falsa.**

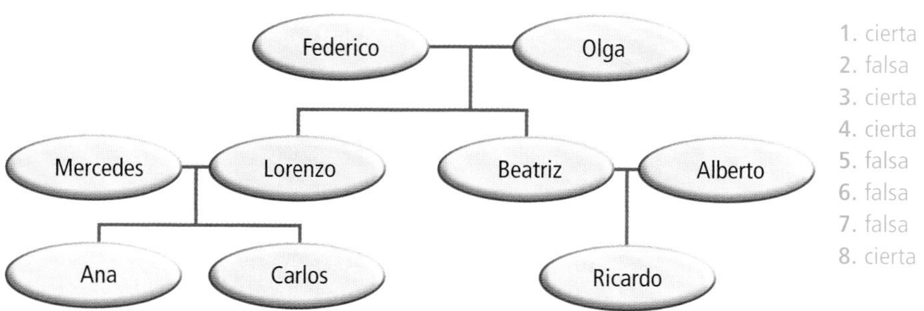

1. cierta
2. falsa
3. cierta
4. cierta
5. falsa
6. falsa
7. falsa
8. cierta

30 Son hermanos

Leamos/Escribamos Answer the questions based on the family tree in Activity 29.

1. ¿Quién es la hermana de Lorenzo? Beatriz
2. ¿Quién es la madre de Carlos? Mercedes
3. ¿Cómo se llama el padre de Ricardo? Alberto
4. ¿Cómo se llama la abuela de Ana? Olga
5. ¿Quién es la hermana de Carlos? Ana
6. ¿Quién es el abuelo de Ricardo? Federico
7. ¿Es Ana la hermana de Ricardo? No.
8. ¿Es Carlos el hermano de Ana? Sí.
9. ¿Son primos Carlos y Ricardo? Sí.

Comunicación

31 ¿Y a quién le toca en tu casa?

Hablemos Ask three classmates the following questions to find out who is most like you. Report your findings to the class.

1. ¿Cuántas personas hay en tu familia?
2. ¿Cuántos hermanos mayores tienes? ¿Cuántos menores? ¿Cómo son?
3. ¿Qué quehaceres casi siempre haces en casa?
4. ¿A quién le toca lavar los platos?, ¿cortar el césped?, ¿hacer las camas?, ¿sacar la basura?

Differentiated Instruction

ADVANCED LEARNERS

Have students working individually or in small groups create and videotape a commercial for a new reality show that follows a family around as they go about their daily lives. In their commercial, students will introduce their families (real or fictional) using the **¡Exprésate!** responses and tell which chores different family members do.

MULTIPLE INTELLIGENCES

Intrapersonal Intelligence Have students write a journal entry about the person in their family who is *most* like them and/or *least* like them. Have them focus on the likes and dislikes they share (or do not share) with this person and encourage them to write as much of their journal entry in Spanish as they are able.

Vocabulario 3

29 Script

1. Beatriz es la hija de Federico y Olga.
2. Ricardo es el nieto de Alberto.
3. Lorenzo y Mercedes son los padres de Ana.
4. Beatriz es la tía de Carlos.
5. Olga es la madre de Ana.
6. Ana es la sobrina de Ricardo.
7. Mercedes es la abuela de Ricardo.
8. Ana es la hermana de Carlos.

COMMON ERROR ALERT ¡OJO!

Ask students what **¿Cómo son tus hermanos?** and **¿Cómo están tus hermanos?** both mean and how they would say each question in English. *(What are your brothers like?* and *How are your brothers?).* Ask students both types of questions about a brother or sister and have them respond by telling what he or she is like or how he or she is.

Comunicación

Pair Activity: Interpersonal

31 Obtaining information

Have students imagine that they are going to go live with a family in a Spanish-speaking country and they want to learn more about the family. Have them write a letter using the questions in Activity 31, and at least two original questions. Have them "mail" their letters to a student in one of your other Spanish classes, and then read aloud to the class the letter they get in return.

Assess

Assessment Program

Prueba: Vocabulario 3, pp. 9–10

Test Generator 

STANDARDS: 1.1, 1.2, 1.3, 2.1, 4.1

Resources

Planning:

Lesson Planner, pp. 8–9, 168–171

One-Stop Planner

Practice:

Cuaderno de vocabulario y gramática, pp. 13–15

Cuaderno de actividades, pp. 9–12

Lab Book, pp. 13–14

Teaching Transparencies Bell Work CP.8 **Vocabulario y gramática** answers, pp. 13–15

Interactive Tutor, Disc 1

Bell Work

Use Bell Work CP.8 in the *Teaching Transparencies*, or write this activity on the board.

Paco is describing his family. Complete the sentences with the correct family member.

1. **El hijo de mi madre es mi _____ .**
2. **La hija de mi tío es mi _____ .**
3. **El esposo de mi madre es mi _____ .**
4. **La esposa de mi abuelo es mi _____ .**
5. **El padre de mi padre es mi _____ .**

Objetivos
Using **-er** and **-ir** verbs and stem changing **-ar, -er,** and **-ir** verbs

Gramática en acción 3

Interactive TUTOR

The present tense of -er and -ir verbs

1 To conjugate a regular **-er** or **-ir** verb in the present tense, drop the **-er** or **-ir** of the infinitive and add these **endings**.

	comer	**escribir**
yo	com**o**	escrib**o**
tú	com**es**	escrib**es**
Ud., él, ella	com**e**	escrib**e**
nosotros(as)	com**emos**	escrib**imos**
vosotros(as)	com**éis**	escrib**ís**
Uds., ellos, ellas	com**en**	escrib**en**

2 The following **-er** and **-ir** verbs have irregular **yo** forms.

hacer → yo ha**go**	poner → yo pon**go**
traer → yo trai**go**	saber → yo **sé**
ver → yo v**eo**	salir → yo sal**go**

Online
Vocabulario y gramática, pp. 13–15 | Actividades, pp. 9–12

32 Conversaciones en la clase

Leamos Complete each sentence with the correct form of one of the verbs from the word box. In some sentences more than one verb is possible.

salir	escribir	tener	ver	poner	comer
hacer	saber	asistir	leer	abrir	traer

1. —¿Ustedes ═══ cartas en la clase de español?
   —Sí. Nosotros ═══ muchas cartas.
2. —¿Tú ═══ con tus amigos todos los fines de semana?
   —No, no ═══. No hay tiempo. ¿Cuándo ═══ la tarea?
3. —¿═══ cuál es el número de teléfono de Paco?
   —No, no ═══.
4. —Profesor Álvarez, ═══ a los conciertos, ¿verdad?
   —No, no ═══ tiempo porque ═══ novelas todos los días.
5. —¿Dónde ═══ todos tus útiles escolares?
   —═══ todos mis útiles escolares en mi mochila.

1. escriben, escribimos
2. sales, salgo, hago
3. Sabes, sé
4. asiste, tengo, leo
5. pones/tienes, Pongo/Tengo

Core Instruction

TEACHING GRAMÁTICA

1. Read over the first point and model the pronunciation of each verb form. **(1 min.)**
2. Write a chart on the board with the headings: **Comer mi comida favorita** and **Escribir a mi tía/tío favorita(o).** Down the side write: **nunca, a veces, cada mes, cada semana, cada día.** Ask students how often they eat their favorite food and write to their favorite aunt or uncle. Write their names on the chart in the squares that correspond to their responses. Then use the chart to ask students about their classmates' responses. Have them use the correct form of **comer** or **escribir** in their answers. **(8 min.)**
3. Read over the second point and then have the students call out the complete conjugations of the irregular verbs as you write them on the board. Review the meanings of the verbs. **(5 min.)**
4. Divide the class into two teams. Have two people from each team stand at the board. Call out a pronoun and one of the irregular verbs. The partners will work together to write a complete sentence of at least five words, using the correct form of the verb. **(6 min.)**

STANDARDS: 1.2

Visit Holt Online
go.hrw.com
KEYWORD: EXP1B PUENTE
Gramática 3 practice

33 ¿Con qué frecuencia...?

Hablemos/Escribamos Tell how often you do the following things.

MODELO **Cocino todos los días.**

cocinar

1. salir a patinar con amigos

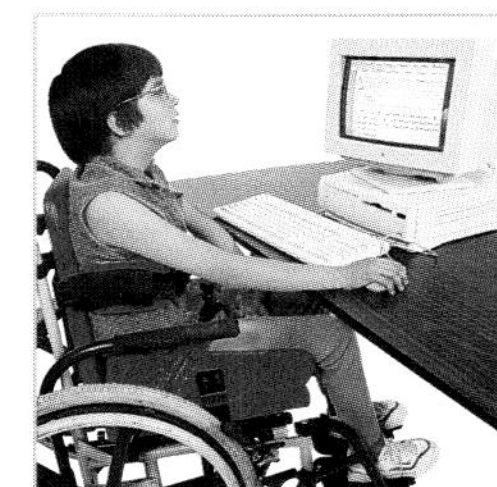
2. hacer la tarea en la computadora

3. comer con la familia

4. hacer ejercicio

5. correr con un(a) amigo(a)

6. escribir en el parque

7. beber algo después de clases

8. traer algo especial

Comunicación

34 Entrevista

Hablemos/Escribamos Work in groups of four. Ask one member of your group how often he or she does the activities pictured above. Then tell the group what your partner said.

MODELO JORGE —**¿Con qué frecuencia corres?**
SUSANA —**Corro todos los días.**

35 Hacemos cosas diferentes

Escribamos/Hablemos Write about things you always do, sometimes do, and never do. Then compare your activities with a partner's.

MODELO **Yo siempre lavo los platos. A veces saco la basura.**

Gramática 3

33 Answers

Possible answers:

1. Salgo a patinar con amigos cada fin de semana.
2. Hago la tarea por Internet cada noche.
3. Como con la familia todos los días.
4. Hago ejercicio a veces.
5. Corro con un amigo cada sábado.
6. Nunca escribo en el parque.
7. A veces bebo algo después de clases.
8. Traigo algo especial a la clase.

Comunicación

Individual Activity: Presentational

Presenting information Have students create a calendar page and write in the activities they normally do during the month. Have them present their calendars to the class, telling how often they do different activities.

Differentiated Instruction

SLOWER PACE LEARNERS

Practice the conjugations of **–er** and **–ir** verbs "horizontally" instead of "vertically" by saying different infinitives, but repeating the same pronoun and having students tell you the correct conjugation. (**—Comer: yo —Como. —Asistir: yo —Asisto.**) By practicing one pronoun at a time, students will have a chance to get a solid grasp of the endings that go with each pronoun.

MULTIPLE INTELLIGENCES

Musical Intelligence Have students choreograph and videotape a music video in which they present one of the **–er** or **–ir** verbs. Bring CDs for them to choose a song from or allow them to use their own CD. Be sure to screen the backgound music they choose for inappropriate language.

STANDARDS: 1.1, 1.2, 1.3

Resources

Planning:

Lesson Planner, pp. 8–9, 168–171

 One-Stop Planner

Practice:

Cuaderno de vocabulario y gramática, pp. 13–15

Cuaderno de actividades, pp. 9–12

Lab Book, pp. 13–14

 Teaching Transparencies
Bell Work CP.9
Vocabulario y gramática answers, pp. 13–15

 Audio CD 6, Tr. 6

 Interactive Tutor, Disc 1

Bell Work

Use Bell Work CP.9 in the *Teaching Transparencies*, or write this activity on the board.

Complete each sentence with the **yo** form of one of these irregular **–er** and **–ir** verbs: **hacer, traer, ver, poner, saber, salir.**

1. No _____ cómo se llama esa profesora.
2. _____ un pastel a la fiesta.
3. _____ la tarea cada día después de las clases.
4. _____ mis útiles escolares en mi mochila.
5. Este fin de semana, _____ con mis amigos.
6. _____ perfectamente con mis lentes, pero no _____ nada sin mis lentes.

36 Script

1. A mi hermana no le parece fácil hacer la tarea.
2. A mi hermano menor le toca pasar la aspiradora.
3. A mi hermano menor le parece aburrido pasar la aspiradora.
4. A papá le toca leer a mi hermano menor.
5. A mí me toca lavar los platos. Me parece bien.
6. A mamá no le gusta cocinar. Le parece injusto

Interactive TUTOR

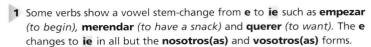

Stem-changing verbs

1 Some verbs show a vowel stem-change from **e** to **ie** such as **empezar** *(to begin)*, **merendar** *(to have a snack)* and **querer** *(to want).* The **e** changes to **ie** in all but the **nosotros(as)** and **vosotros(as)** forms.

yo	emp**ie**zo	nosotros(as)	empezamos
tú	emp**ie**zas	vosotros(as)	empezáis
Ud., él, ella	emp**ie**za	Uds., ellos, ellas	emp**ie**zan

—¿A qué hora **empieza** la película? —**Empieza** a las siete.

2 **Dormir** *(to sleep)* is also a stem-changing verb. The **o** of the stem changes to **ue** in all forms except **nosotros(as)** and **vosotros(as).**

yo	d**ue**rmo	nosotros(as)	dormimos
tú	d**ue**rmes	vosotros(as)	dormís
Ud., él, ella	d**ue**rme	Uds., ellos, ellas	d**ue**rmen

El perro **duerme** poco. Ana y yo **dormimos** mucho.

3 Other verbs that follow this pattern are **almorzar** *(to have lunch)*, **volver** *(to go or come back)*, and **llover** *(to rain).*

Yo **almuerzo** poco. Tu perro **vuelve** a su casa. Hoy **llueve**.

4 To say what you have to do or whose turn it is to do something, use the verb **tocar** followed by an infinitive. **Tocar** may be used like **gustar.** The verb **parecer** means *to seem* and may also be used like **gustar** to ask for or give an opinion.

A mí siempre me **toca** sacar la basura. Me **parece** injusto.

Online
Vocabulario y gramática, pp. 13–15
Actividades, pp. 9–12

¿Te acuerdas?

In Spanish, regular verbs have **regular stems** and regular endings.

-ar	**habl**o	**habl**amos
	hablas	**habl**áis
	habla	**habl**an
-er	**com**o	**com**emos
	comes	**com**éis
	come	**com**en
-ir	**escrib**o	**escrib**imos
	escribes	**escrib**ís
	escribe	**escrib**en

1. falso 2. cierto 3. cierto 4. cierto 5. cierto 6. cierto 7. cierto 8. falso

CD 6, Tr. 6

36 ¡Qué lata!

Escuchemos For each picture you will hear two sentences. Tell whether they are **cierto** or **falso.**

mi hermana

mi hermano

mi papá y mi hermano menor

mi mamá y yo

Core Instruction

TEACHING GRAMÁTICA

1. Have students read the four points of **Gramática.** Model the pronunciation of each of the verb forms. Read **¿Te acuerdas?** and have students state in their own words the difference between a regular verb and a stem-changing verb. **(4 min.)**
2. Have students imagine that the class will be raising money for a field trip by having a car wash. Begin by asking students how late they sleep in on Saturdays to practice the forms of **dormir.** Then plan the times that students will begin their work (**empezar**), when they will have a snack (**merendar**), when they will have lunch (**almorzar**), what to do if it rains (**llover**), and what time they will return to their house (**volver**). Write the work schedule on the board. **(10 min.)**
3. Coach students into giving their opinion of the work schedule. Have them make statements like, **¡Me toca trabajar hasta las cinco y media! ¡Me parece injusto! (6 min.)**
4. You might consider actually having a car wash or other activity to provide students the chance to practice the verbs in a real-life setting.

STANDARDS: 1.2

37 El sábado yo...

Leamos Use the correct forms of the verbs in parentheses to complete the conversation.

PACO ¿Qué haces los sábados, Roberto?
ROBERTO Siempre ___ (dormir) hasta las once. duermo
PACO Yo no. Siempre ___ (empezar) el día a las siete. empiezo
ROBERTO Bueno, ¿___ (querer) jugar al fútbol el sábado? Quieres
PACO Sí. Si no ___ (llover), ___ (querer) jugar al fútbol. llueve, quiero
ROBERTO Y si ___ (llover), ¿___ (querer) ir al cine? llueve, quieres
PACO Sí, está bien. ___ (Querer) ver "El gato negro". Quiero
ROBERTO Y después tú y yo ___ (volver) a mi casa. volvemos, merienda
Mi familia ___ (merendar) a las cuatro.

38 ¿Cómo les parece?

Hablemos/Escribamos Everyone in the Ruíz family has something to do today. Write what José would say about their activities and how they feel about them.

MODELO **A mi papá le toca trabajar. Le parece bien.**

mi papá

1. mis hermanos

2. mi prima Zoraida

3. mis abuelos

4. mi tío, mi primo y yo

Comunicación

39 ¿Qué quieres hacer este fin de semana?

Hablemos A classmate asks you if you want to do something on the weekend. Answer and say that the plans seem good, but you can't do anything until the afternoon because of your chores.

MODELO **—¿Qué tal si vamos al parque para jugar al tenis?**
—Me parece fenomenal. Hoy me toca limpiar la sala. ¿Qué te parece si vamos a las cuatro?

Differentiated Instruction

ADVANCED LEARNERS

Have students in groups of three write a skit about a teenager who is interviewing another teenager to be his or her housekeeper so that the first teenager won't have to do chores around the house. Everything works out fine—until the parents find out!

SPECIAL LEARNING NEEDS

Students with Learning Disabilities/ Dyslexia Ask students if they know the expression "*i* before *e*, except after *c*." Explain that memory tricks like this phrase are called mnemonic devices. Tell them that when they are writing the forms of stem-changing verbs, the same rule can be applied, with a slight difference: "*i* before *e*, and *u* before *e*." Have students come up with their own mnemonic devices to remember that the **nosotros(as)** and the **vosotros(as)** forms do not undergo a stem change.

Gramática 3

38 Answers

Possible answers:
1. A mis hermanos les toca lavar los platos. Les parece bien.
2. A mi prima Zoraida le toca limpiar su cuarto. Le parece injusto.
3. A mis abuelos les toca ir al parque con mi hermano menor. Les parece muy bien.
4. A nosotros nos toca jugar al béisbol. Nos parece bien.

Communities

Career Path

Invite Spanish-speaking members of the community to your class to talk about their jobs. Have each student prepare at least three questions for the guest speaker about his or her typical work day: how late in morning the speaker gets to sleep, when the speaker starts his or her work day, breaks for lunch, returns home, and what tasks the speaker does during his or her day.

Comunicación

Group Work: Interpersonal

Providing information Set up four messy living rooms in four parts of the classroom. Divide the class into four teams and give each team a list of chores that need to be done in their living room. Have them decide who will do each chore. Circulate and ask students about their chores. Then have the teams race to see which team can complete their chores first. Inspect the living rooms and ask who did different chores. Praise them or jokingly scold them for how well they carried out their chores.

Assess

Assessment Program
Prueba: Gramática 3, pp. 11–12
Test Generator 

Resources

Planning:

Lesson Planner, pp. 9, 170–171

 One-Stop Planner

Practice:

Cuaderno de actividades, p. 13

 Interactive Tutor, Disc 1

VideoCultura

For a video presentation of the interviews as well as for additional interviews, see Chapter 2 **VideoCultura** for Yaz's and Chapter 3 **VideoCultura** for Roberto's interviews on videocassette or on DVD. For interactive practice, see the *DVD Tutor.*

Cultures

Products and Perspectives

El Palacio de Bellas Artes
Mexico's national opera, national theater, National Symphony Orchestra, and **Ballet Folklórico,** the official national dance company of Mexico all call **El Palacio de Bellas Artes** their home. The construction of this building was an international collaboration. An Italian architect designed the plans. An American construction firm laid the foundation and created the metal framework for the building. Italian and Spanish sculptors provided artwork for the facades and the front plaza. German firms installed the complex stage equipment. Ask students to discuss the pros and cons of such a collaboration. Ask if they can think of other examples of international projects. (e.g., the International Space Station)

REPASO

El mundo hispanohablante

Yaz
Ciudad de México, México

—*¿Conoces la expresión, "Dime con quien andas y te diré quien eres"?*
—Sí, la conozco.

—*¿Cómo eres tú?*
—Yo soy bajita, inteligente y amigable.

—*¿Qué cosas te gustan?*
—Me gusta el cine, el teatro y las películas.

—*¿Cómo es tu mejor amigo?*
—Mi mejor amigo as alto, moreno, amigable y muy inteligente.

—*¿Qué cosas le gustan a él?*
—Le gustan el teatro, las películas y los libros.

—*¿Cómo son ustedes?*
—Somos inteligentes y muy amigables.

—*¿Qué cosas les gustan a ustedes?*
—Nos gusta el cine, las películas y los libros.

—*¿La expresión se aplica en su caso?*
—Sí, sí se aplica porque siempre estamos juntos y porque somos muy inteligentes.

Core Instruction

TEACHING EL MUNDO HISPANOHABLANTE

1. Play the **VideoCultura** section of the Video Program/DVD Tutor for Chapter 2 to view Yaz's interview. Roberto's interview is on the **VideoCultura** for Chapter 3. Stop periodically and ask students to predict what kinds of questions the interviewer is likely to ask during the interview—questions about what Roberto and his friends are like, for example. **(2 min.)**
2. Write a chart on the board with **¿Cómo es?, ¿Qué le gusta?,** and **¿Qué no le gusta?** across the top. Write **Yaz, El mejor amigo de Yaz,** and **Roberto** down the left side. Replay the videos or read the rest of the interview straight through. Have students supply as much information as they can to fill the chart. Then replay the interviews one more time, this time stopping after each response to a question. Have students add information they missed to the chart. **(8 min.)**
3. Do the **Para comprender** and **Para pensar y hablar** activities as a class or as independent writing activities. Leave the chart on the board for students' reference. **(20 min.)**

STANDARDS: 2.2

Roberto
Madrid, España

—*¿Dime, ¿adónde vas cuando hace buen tiempo?*

—Cuando hace buen tiempo, me gusta ir a la piscina o a bañarme con mis amigos a la playa.

—*¿Vas solo o vas con amigos?*

—Con mis amigos.

—*¿Qué te gusta hacer en ese lugar?*

—Jugar a la pelota y nadar.

—*¿Qué no te gusta hacer?*

—No me gusta nada estudiar.

—*¿Por qué no te gusta?*

—Porque es aburrido y prefiero patinar.

Para comprender

1. ¿Cómo es Yaz?
2. ¿Cómo es el mejor amigo de Yaz?
3. ¿Qué les gusta hacer a Yaz y a su mejor amigo?
4. ¿Qué le gusta hacer a Roberto cuando hace buen tiempo?
5. ¿Qué le gusta hacer en la playa?
6. ¿A Roberto le gusta estudiar? ¿Por qué sí o por qué no?

Para pensar y hablar

What do you like to do when the weather is good? Are your outdoor activities similar to or different from Roberto's?

What characteristics or interests do you have in common with your friends? Are your friends very similar to you or very different?

Differentiated Instruction

ADVANCED LEARNERS

Challenge Have students brainstorm sayings in English related to friendship and do research to find out if there is a Spanish equivalent. (*A friend in need is a friend indeed.* **En las malas se conocen a los amigos.**) Have them create a poster that illustrates the meaning of the saying.

MULTIPLE INTELLIGENCES

Interpersonal/Intrapersonal Intelligence Have students create a chart similar to the one described in Step 2 of **Teaching El mundo hispanohablante,** but replacing the names with their own name and two friends' names. Have them exchange charts with a classmate and interview each other to fill in the charts.

Para comprender Answers

Possible answers:

1. Yaz es bajita, inteligente y amigable.
2. El mejor amigo de Yaz es alto, moreno, amigable, y muy inteligente.
3. A Yaz y a su mejor amigo les gusta ir al cine, ver películas y leer libros.
4. Cuando hace buen tiempo, a Roberto le gusta ir a la piscina o a la playa.
5. En la playa o en la piscina, Roberto juega a la pelota y nada.
6. A Roberto, no le gusta estudiar. Es aburrido.

Connections

Social Studies

Have students interview at least three members of your community: one from a Spanish-speaking culture and two from other cultures to see if there are any differences in how they view friendship. Brainstorm questions for students to ask, such as: What is a good friend? What is your best friend like? What do you and your friends like to do together? Have them present the results of their interviews to the class.

Communities

Using Technology

Pen pals Many websites exist for people interested in finding pen pals from a different country. Locate one that is appropriate for your students to visit. Have them find a pen pal who shares similar interests and write an e-mail message to him or her.

Resources

Planning:

Lesson Planner, pp. 9, 170–171

One-Stop Planner

Practice:

Interactive Tutor, Disc 1

Grammar Review

For more practice with the review grammar topics in this chapter, see the *Grammar Tutor,* the *DVD Tutor,* the *Interactive Tutor,* or the *Cuaderno de vocabulario y gramática.*

Online Edition 

Students might use the online textbook to review for the exam.

Más práctica

Arrange it so that two students from your other Spanish classes can visit your class for approximately ten minutes. Smuggle them into the room without the students seeing them and have them stand behind a screen to hide their identity. Divide your class into teams. Have the teams take turns asking the mystery students questions from the **Primera** and **Segunda parte** of **¿Quién eres?**

REPASO

¿Quién eres?

Contesta las siguientes preguntas.

Primera PARTE

1. ¿Cómo te llamas?
2. ¿Cómo se llama tu profesor de español?
3. ¿De dónde eres?
4. ¿Cuál es tu correo electrónico?
5. ¿Cuándo es tu cumpleaños?
6. ¿Cuántos años tienes?
7. ¿Cómo eres?

Segunda PARTE

8. ¿Qué te gusta hacer?
9. ¿Qué haces los fines de semana?
10. ¿Cuáles deportes te gustan?
11. ¿Te gusta más pasar el rato solo(a) o salir con amigos?
12. ¿Qué te gusta más el fútbol o el básquetbol?
13. ¿Qué vas a hacer el viernes próximo?
14. ¿Vas a ir al cine este fin de semana? ¿Con quién vas a ir?

FOLD-N-LEARN

Question/Answer book

1. Have students fold a sheet of paper in half from left to right to create a book.
2. On the cover of the book, students draw ten lines from the right edge of the paper to the center fold at one inch intervals. Have students cut each line, on the cover only, to make eleven tabs.
3. Students write the questions from **¡Exprésate!**, pp. 13, 14, 23, and 24. Students should have eleven different questions in all.
4. Students lift each tab and write an appropriate answer to the question underneath the tab.

For example: On the first tab, students write **¿Qué quieres hacer hoy?** Underneath the tab, they write **Ni idea.**

Repaso

Vocabulary Review

For more practice with the vocabulary in this chapter, see the *DVD Tutor,* the *Interactive Tutor,* or the *Cuaderno de vocabulario y gramática.*

Más práctica

Before class, prepare logical answers to each question in the **Tercera parte.** Read your answers at random to the class and have students guess which question you are answering. You might also divide the class into two teams and do this activity as a game. Place two bells on a table at the front of the room and have a member of each team stand by the table. Read an answer. The first student to ring his or her bell gets to guess which question the answer is for.

Tercera PARTE

15 ¿Qué necesitas para el colegio?

16 ¿Con qué frecuencia estudias matemáticas?

17 ¿A qué hora vas al colegio?

18 ¿A qué hora tienes la clase de inglés?

19 ¿Qué clase tienes después de español?

20 ¿Qué clases tienes esta tarde?

21 ¿Cuántas personas hay en tu familia?

22 ¿Cómo son tus hermanos?

23 ¿Dónde viven ustedes?

24 ¿Qué haces para ayudar en casa?

25 ¿Tienes ganas de ir al parque?

ENCUESTA

26 Ask three classmates questions 3, 6, 9, 13, 20, and 24. Write their responses to your questions and turn them in to your teacher.

Game

¿Quién es? en diez preguntas

1. Write the names of ten well known people on the board. Use nationally famous people, as well as local or school personalities that are well known. Choose one person from the list to be "it."
2. Divide the students into teams.
3. Each team will take turns asking a **sí–no** question to determine the identity of the person. For example, **¿Es rubio?**
4. Remind students that they can ask a wide variety of questions about the person, including physical description, personality, origin, likes and dislikes, and family.
5. Tell teams to take notes about the answers. At the end of ten questions, (five from each team), ask Team A to guess the mystery identity. If they guess right they get a point. If not, allow Team B an opportunity to guess and win a point.
6. Continue the game for nine of the ten people on the board. The team with the most points wins.

Assess

Assessment Program

Examen: Capítulo puente, pp. 121–131

Examen oral: Capítulo puente, p. 132

Test Generator 

Resources

Planning:

Lesson Planner, p. xv

 One-Stop Planner

Presentation:

 Teaching Transparencies
Mapa 5

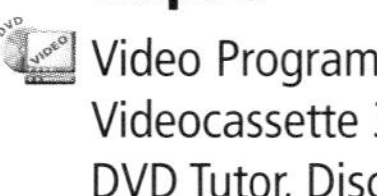 Video Program,
Videocassette 3
DVD Tutor, Disc 2
GeoVisión

Practice:

Video Guide, pp. 51–52

Lab Book, p. 37

 Interactive Tutor, Disc 2

Atlas INTERACTIVO MUNDIAL

Have students use the interactive atlas at **go.hrw.com** to find out more about the geography of Mexico and to complete the Map Activities below.

Map Activities

1. Have students locate Mexico and its bordering countries. **(Estados Unidos, Guatemala, Belize)** Ask students to identify the surrounding bodies of water. **(Golfo de México, Océano Pacífico)**
2. Have students locate and name Mexico's two peninsulas. **(Baja California, la Península de Yucatán)**
3. Point out that most of Mexico's border with the U.S. is formed by a river. What is the name of the river? **(Río Bravo del Norte)**

GeoVisión

Geocultura México

▲ **El volcán Popocatépetl** This active volcano, nicknamed **El Popo,** is in Mexico's central valley. At 5,465 meters, it is the second-highest peak in Mexico.

► **México, D.F.** Mexicans often refer to Mexico City as **el D.F. (Distrito Federal).** It is one of the largest cities in the world.

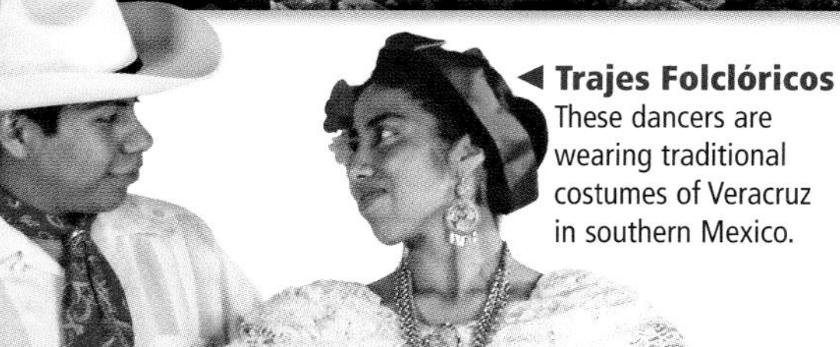

◄ **Trajes Folclóricos** These dancers are wearing traditional costumes of Veracruz in southern Mexico.

Almanaque

Población
103.400.165

Capital
La Ciudad de México

Gobierno
república federal

Idioma oficial
español

Moneda
peso mexicano

Código Internet
www.[ ].mx

¿Sabías que...?

The volcano Popocatépetl cannot be climbed anymore because of its eruptions.

Background Information

History

By the early 1500s, the Aztecs had solidified power among the indigenous groups in Mexico. The Aztec empire fell to Cortés, a Spanish explorer, in 1521. Mexico was a Spanish colony until 1821. After independence, a half century of political chaos ensued. In 1858, Mexico suffered through a civil war led by Benito Juárez. In 1910, the Mexican Revolution started. It lasted for 10 years. In 1929, the National Revolutionary Party became the governing party of Mexico until losing the presidential election for the first time in 2000.

Geography

El Valle Central around Mexico City is home to more than one fifth of Mexico's population. It also offers much of the nation's most fertile farmland.

La Reserva de la Biósfera Calakmul in the Yucatan Peninsula is Mexico's largest remaining tropical forest and home to many endangered species such as the jaguar.

Popocatépetl, one of Mexico's active volcanoes, has rumbled as recently as 1993 causing the evacuation of 25,000 people. More than 20 million people live within 50 miles of this legend-inspiring mountain.

◀ **La Barranca del Cobre** Chihuahua's spectacular Copper Canyon, in the Sierra Madre mountains, resembles Arizona's Grand Canyon in scale.

▲ **Agua Azul** Agua Azul in Chiapas has turquoise-colored waterfalls and swimming holes.

▲ **Tulum** These ruins are one of many sites left by the Maya people on the Yucatan Peninsula. The name **Tulum** means *wall* in the Yucatec Mayan language.

▼ **Teotihuacán** The ruins of this ancient city show what civilization in Mexico was like before the Aztecs came to power. Its Pyramid of the Sun is the third-largest pyramid in the world.

¿Qué tanto sabes?

What major volcano lies close to Mexico City?

México

Cultures

Practices and Perspectives

Family Life In Mexico, family is very important. Often, extended families live under the same roof, including children, parents, grandparents and sometimes aunts, uncles, and cousins. Everyone contributes in some way to maintaining the home. During the week, the family eats lunch together. The special family day is Sunday when friends and more family get together for a big meal or a picnic at a park. Have students compare Mexican family life to that of families in the United States. What are some of the differences and similarities? Why do they think family life in the two countries might differ?

Communities

Celebrations

December 12 is the day that millions of Mexicans make a pilgrimage to the **Villa de Guadalupe** to pay homage and celebrate the appearance of their beloved **Virgen de Guadalupe. Conchero** dancers don costumes imitating the Aztec traditional festival dress, with brightly colored feather headdresses, and bells and shells around their ankles. Young boys dress up like peasants, wearing a **sarape,** sandals, and a false mustache to imitate Juan Diego, the Mexican peasant who first saw the **Virgen** in 1531. Approximately fifteen million people go to the **Villa de Guadalupe** each year. Ask students to use the Internet to find out what the words **conchero** and **sarape** mean.

CNN enEspañol.com

Have students check the **CNN en español** website for news on Mexico.

¿Sabías que... ?

Students might be interested in knowing the following facts about Mexico.

- **Baja California** comprises 3,000 miles (4,800 km) of Mexico's 5,320 miles (8,560 km) of coastline.
- **Tenochtitlán,** the ancient Aztec capital, astounded Cortés with palaces, markets, and finely dressed lords and ladies. Today it is the site of Mexico City.
- **Chichén Itzá,** a Mayan pyramid located in the Yucatan Peninsula, is one of Mexico's most studied and revered archeological sites.

Preguntas

You might choose to present these questions in English.

1. **¿Dónde se encuentra el volcán Popocatéptl? (En el valle central)**
2. **¿Qué región tiene muchos sitios arqueológicos de las civilizaciones mayas? (La Península de Yucatán)**
3. **¿Qué reflejan las ruinas de Teotihuacán? (La civilización antes de los aztecas)**
4. **¿Qué sitio se parece al Gran Cañón en Arizona? (La Barranca del Cobre)**

Cultures

Products and Perspectives

Food Mexican food, usually simple and subtle, varies greatly by geographic region and culture. With an extensive coastline, many places in Mexico are known for their delicious fresh fish. **Ceviche,** a Mexican standard, is any white fish "cooked" by letting it sit overnight in a marinade of lime juice, then diced with onion, **chile,** tomato, and cilantro. In the north of Mexico, meat and beans provide the mainstay of typical meals. Almost all meals are served with **tortillas,** (ground flour or corn grilled on a hot griddle), and some kind of **chile** made into a **salsa.** There are dozens of varieties of **chiles,** and their flavor and name changes when they are dried. For example, the mouth burning **jalapeño** becomes the smoky tasting **chipotle** in its dried form. Have students tasted foods with these ingredients?

Connections

Thinking Critically

Native Languages
Approximately thirty percent of the Mexican population is comprised of indigenous peoples, while another sixty to seventy percent is comprised of **mestizos** (of mixed indigenous and European heritage). The primary language for more than five million Mexicans is one of several indigenous dialects, not Spanish. The main indigenous dialects are Mayan, Mixtec, Náhuatl, and Zapotec. Have students reflect on the fact that many of the citizens of Mexico don't speak the official national language, Spanish, as their first language or primary conversational language. Why and how do students think maintaining their native language has helped the Mexicans maintain their indigenous culture? What are some of the benefits and inconveniences of maintaining a group's dialect?

A conocer México

El arte

► ***Vendedora de Alcatraces*** Diego Rivera (1886–1957) painted this picture, *Calla Lily Vendor*, in 1938. Rivera is also known for his many public murals.

◄ **Los antiguos murales mayas** These Mayan murals in Bonampak, Chiapas, are preserved in an ancient building.

► **La biblioteca de la Universidad Nacional Autónoma de México** The library at the National Autonomous University of Mexico is decorated with a giant mosaic showing the history of Mexico. Juan O'Gorman, a well-known Mexican architect, planned and built the library in the 1950s.

La arquitectura

► **Taxco** The city of Taxco in the state of Puebla is famous for its Spanish colonial architecture.

Interdisciplinary Links

El arte

History Link The muralist movement in Mexico lasted over 50 years. Artists such as Diego Rivera, José Clemente Orozco, and David Alfaro Siqueiros covered Mexico's public buildings with murals depicting the entire history of their nation. This group art was not for self-expression, but for public education. Have students choose one of the painters mentioned and research one of their murals on the Internet or at the library. What historical event does the mural portray? Where is the mural? Why did the muralists feel that art needed to be public?

La arquitectura

Economics Link Contemporary Mexican architects, like Ricardo Legorreta, use large walls covered with vivid colors. The Camino Real hotel in Mexico City has walls painted pink, yellow, and lavender. Using bright colors has become a defining element in Mexican architecture and advertising. Brightly colored billboards, public service announcements, and political slogans are found on homes, public buildings, and retaining walls. Have students analyze the architecture in their own neighborhood. Is it bold or subtle? Is the advertising bold or subtle? Does the advertising reflect the local style of architecture in any way?

Las celebraciones

Visit Holt Online
go.hrw.com
KEYWORD: EXP1B CH6
Photo Tour

▲ **El festival de La Guelaguetza** Every July, the city of Oaxaca hosts the **Festival de La Guelaguetza.** This celebration of dance and music dates to pre-Columbian times.

¿Sabías que...?

About one-fourth of Mexico's population lives in or near Mexico City. Look at the **Almanaque** and calculate how many people that is.

► **El festival del 16 de septiembre** September 16 is Independence Day, commemorating Mexico's independence from Spain. Mexicans all over the country celebrate with parades, parties, and fireworks.

La comida

► **Las empanadas de flor de calabaza** This **empanada,** or turnover, is made with pumpkin flowers.

► **Chiles en nogada** These green chili peppers stuffed with meat and nuts, with walnut sauce, are usually eaten in December.

► **El mole poblano** **Mole** is a sauce made from lots of ingredients, including chocolate, chili peppers, seeds, and nuts. It is often served over chicken or turkey.

México

Cultures

Products and Perspectives

Farming Some people in Mexico own their own plots of land and practice subsistence farming, but the vast majority of land is still owned by a few people and large corporations. Farming is big business and employs many workers. These agri-businesses grow fruit, corn, cotton, sugar cane, and coffee. Many of these products are exported to other countries. Mexico produces most of its own food. Slash-and-burn agriculture is still practiced today despite laws to prohibit it. Ecotourism appears to be one way to end such practices. Although it is still in a development phase, it is beginning to provide deprived communities with a practical substitute for income.

¿Comprendes?

You can use the following questions to check students' comprehension of the **Geocultura.**

1. What does the library at the National Autonomous University of Mexico have on its walls? (A mosaic showing the history of Mexico)
2. When does Mexico celebrate Independence Day? (September 16)
3. What is the woman in Rivera's painting selling? (Flowers/lilies)
4. Where can you find Mayan murals? (In Bonampak, Chiapas, on an ancient building)
5. What is in **mole?** (Chocolate, chiles, seeds, nuts)

Las celebraciones

Music Link No celebration in Mexico would be complete without music. Music varies by region, from the country style **norteña** bands in the north, to the tropical sounding **cumbia** and **salsa** sounds heard in Veracruz. The **mariachi** sounds have become a national anthem. Have students research at the library or on the Internet, a Mexican celebration and the type of music that is played for that occasion. What is the celebration? In what region do they celebrate the holiday? What music is associated with it? What instruments are used to play that type of music?

La comida

History Link Christopher Columbus took cacao beans, from which we make chocolate, back to Europe. Twenty-seven years later Montezuma, the ruler of the Aztecs, shared his chocolate drink recipe—**chocolatl**—with Cortez, who took it to the Spanish king and queen. The Spanish did not share the chocolate recipe with other Europeans for about one hundred years, when Queen María Teresa decided to divulge the secret to her husband, King Louis XIV of France.

Assess

Assessment Program
Prueba: Geocultura, pp. 15–16
Test Generator 

Capítulo 6

¡A comer!

Overview and Resources

Overview and Resources

Chapter Section		Resources
Vocabulario en acción 1 • Commenting on food; taking someone's order; making polite requests, pp. 40–45 **¡Exprésate!** • To comment on food, p. 41 • To take someone's order, to make polite requests, p. 44	Present	TPR Storytelling Book, pp. 30–31 Teaching Transparencies  Video Program/DVD Tutor, **ExpresaVisión**
Assess Assessment Program • **Prueba: Vocabulario 1,** pp. 17–18 • Alternative Assessment Guide, pp. 241, 249, 257  Test Generator	Practice	Cuaderno de vocabulario y gramática, pp. 17–19 Activities for Communication, pp. 21–22 Video Guide, pp. 54–56 Lab Book, pp. 1, 15–18, 38 Teaching Transparenc. ies Audio CD 6, Tr. 11 Interactive Tutor, Disc 2
Gramática en acción 1 • **Ser** and **estar,** p. 46 • **Pedir** and **servir,** p. 48 • **Preferir, poder,** and **probar,** p. 50	Present	Video Program/DVD Tutor, **GramaVisión**
Assess Assessment Program • **Prueba: Gramática 1,** pp. 19–20 • **Prueba: Aplicación 1,** pp. 21–22 • Alternative Assessment Guide, pp. 241, 249, 257  Audio CD 6, Tr. 25  Test Generator	Practice	Grammar Tutor for Students of Spanish, Chapter 6 Cuaderno de vocabulario y gramática, pp. 20–22 Cuaderno de actividades, pp. 15–17 Activities for Communication, pp. 21–22 Video Guide, pp. 54–55 Lab Book, pp. 1, 15–18 Teaching Transparencies Audio CD 6, Tr. 12 Interactive Tutor, Disc 2

	Print	Media
Cultura • **Comparaciones,** pp. 52–53 • **Comunidad,** p. 53 • **Conexiones,** pp. 66–67	Cuaderno de actividades, p. 18 Cuaderno para hispanohablantes, pp. 45–52 Video Guide, pp. 54–55, 57 Lab Book, p. 39	Audio CD 6, Tr. 13–15 Video Program/DVD Tutor, **VideoCultura** Interactive Tutor, Disc 2
Novela en video • **Episodio 6,** pp. 68–71	Video Guide, pp. 54–55, 59 Lab Book, p. 41	Video Program/DVD Tutor, **VideoNovela**
Leamos y escribamos • **La montaña del alimento,** pp. 72–73	Cuaderno de actividades, p. 22 Reading Strategies and Skills Handbook Cuaderno para hispanohablantes, pp. 45–52 ¡Lee conmigo! Assessment Program, pp. 29–30	Audio CD 6, Tr. 18

Lesson Planner with Differentiated Instruction, pp. 11–40, 172–199

One-Stop Planner® CD-ROM

Visit Holt Online
go.hrw.com
KEYWORD: EXP1B CH6
Online Edition

Chapter Section / Resources

Vocabulario en acción 2

- Talking about meals; offering help; giving instructions, pp. 54–59

¡Exprésate!
- To talk about meals, p. 55
- To offer help; to give instructions, p. 58

Assess

Assessment Program
- **Prueba: Vocabulario 2,** pp. 23–24
- Alternative Assessment Guide, pp. 241, 249, 257

 Test Generator

Present
- TPR Storytelling Book, pp. 32–33
- Teaching Transparencies
- Video Program/DVD Tutor, **ExpresaVisión**

Practice
- Cuaderno de vocabulario y gramática, pp. 23–25
- Activities for Communication, pp. 23–24
- Video Guide, pp. 54–55, 58
- Lab Book, pp. 1, 15–18, 40
- Teaching Transparencies
- Audio CD 6, Tr. 16
- Interactive Tutor, Disc 2

Gramática en acción 2

- Direct objects and direct object pronouns, p. 60
- Affirmative informal commands, p. 62
- Affirmative informal commands with pronouns, p. 64

Assess

Assessment Program
- **Prueba: Gramática 2,** pp. 25–26
- **Prueba: Aplicación 2,** pp. 27–28
- Alternative Assessment Guide, pp. 241, 249, 257

 Audio CD 6, Tr. 26

 Test Generator

Present
- Video Program/DVD Tutor, **GramaVisión**

Practice

- Grammar Tutor for Students of Spanish, Chapter 6
- Cuaderno de vocabulario y gramática, pp. 26–28
- Cuaderno de actividades, pp. 19–21
- Activities for Communication, pp. 23–24
- Video Guide, pp. 54–55
- Lab Book, pp. 1, 15–18
- Teaching Transparencies
- Audio CD 6, Tr. 17
- Interactive Tutor, Disc 2

Print  / Media 

	Print	Media
Repaso • **Repaso,** pp. 74–75 • **Gramática y Vocabulario,** pp. 76–77 • **Letra y sonido,** p. 76	Activities for Communication, pp. 48, 65–66 TPR Storytelling Book, pp. 34–35 Lab Book, pp. 15–18, 42 Assessment Program, pp. 133–143, 144 Alternative Assessment Guide, pp. 241, 249, 257 Standardized Assessment Tutor, pp. 25–28	Video Program/DVD Tutor, **Variedades** Teaching Transparencies Audio CD 6, Tr. 20–23 Interactive Tutor, Disc 2 Test Generator
Integración • Cumulative review, Chapters 1–6, pp. 78–79	Cuaderno de actividades, pp. 23–24 Lab Book, pp. 15–18	 Teaching Transparencies Audio CD 6, Tr. 24

¡A comer!

Projects

Una fiesta internacional

In this activity, students plan a tasting party (**una fiesta internacional**) of everyday dishes from Spanish-speaking countries. They write invitations, cook, then sample dishes, and converse in Spanish at the **fiesta.**

SUGGESTED SEQUENCE

1. Have students work in groups of four. Each group selects a recipe to prepare. If students are unfamiliar with foods in Spanish-speaking countries, have them find recipes on the Internet or in cookbooks at a local library. You might also share the **recetas** provided in the interleaf of each chapter of your *Teacher's Edition.*
2. Set a date for the **fiesta.**
3. Have students divide the responsibilities for the preparation and decide how they will accomplish everything. Dishes should be prepared outside of class. Students only need to prepare enough for everyone to have a taste.
4. Each group designs and writes an invitation in Spanish. Have groups exchange invitations with each other. Or, invitations can be given to administrators or parents who might like to join the party.
5. At the **fiesta,** students sample the different items and use Spanish to converse and comment on the various dishes.

Grading the project

Suggested point distribution (100 points total)

Written invitation 30

Selecting recipe and preparing food 40

Using Spanish at the fiesta . . .30

e-community

e-mail forum:

Post the following questions on the classroom e-mail forum:

1. ¿Cuál es tu restaurante favorito?
2. ¿Qué tipo de comida sirve?
3. Por lo general, ¿qué pides allí?

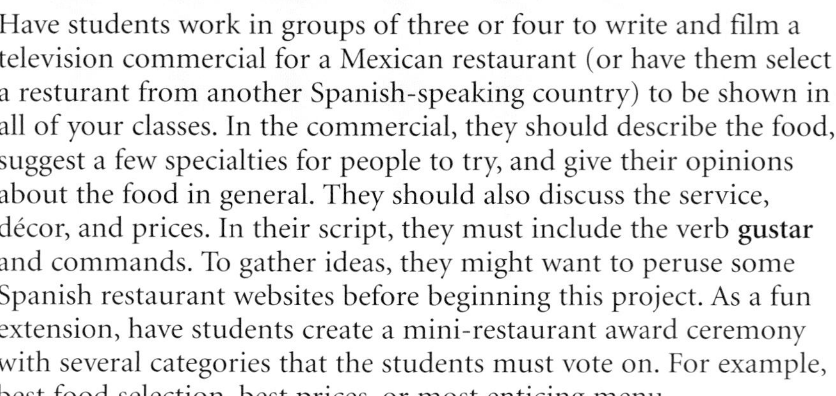

Partner Class Project

Have students work in groups of three or four to write and film a television commercial for a Mexican restaurant (or have them select a resturant from another Spanish-speaking country) to be shown in all of your classes. In the commercial, they should describe the food, suggest a few specialties for people to try, and give their opinions about the food in general. They should also discuss the service, décor, and prices. In their script, they must include the verb **gustar** and commands. To gather ideas, they might want to peruse some Spanish restaurant websites before beginning this project. As a fun extension, have students create a mini-restaurant award ceremony with several categories that the students must vote on. For example, best food selection, best prices, or most enticing menu.

Game Bank

For game ideas, see pages T60–T63.

STANDARDS: 1.3, 3.2, 5.1

Traditions

Las Piñatas

It is said that **piñatas** originated in China, where they were made of colored paper and adorned with ribbons. After breaking them, people picked up the pieces for good luck. This tradition then took root in Italy and later on in Spain, where a clay container was used instead. Spanish missionaries in the New World used the **piñata** for religious instruction. For them, the pot (**olla**) symbolized the Devil and his attempts to lure human souls, and the fruits and candies represented temptation. In recent times, **piñatas** filled with good things to eat and with toys have lost much of their religious symbolism, and are intended only for fun. Have students make their own **piñatas** as individual or group projects. They will need balloons, newspaper, colored construction paper, scissors, and glue. Instruct them to inflate the balloons and cover them with papier-mâché. Then they'll make a design with the construction paper. The final step is to fill the **piñata** with candy!

Receta

The practice of grinding corn into tortillas in present-day Mexico and Central America dates back to pre-Columbian civilizations. The corn was boiled with lime before it was ground on a **metate,** or flat stone. The resulting lime-whitened corn dough was then pressed into thin round pieces and cooked on a dry surface. In recent times, factories produce most tortillas, and flour is a popular alternative to corn. Homemade tortillas no longer involve boiling and grinding corn; the dough is sold at stores as **masa para tortillas** or **masa harina.** You might have students make the following recipe as a class project or for extra credit.

Las tortillas de maíz

12 tortillas

1 libra de masa harina

4 cucharaditas de sal

agua fría

Añada suficiente agua a la masa harina y sal para que la masa no se deshaga en la prensa *(tortilla press)*. Abra la prensa y cubra la parte superior e inferior con plástico transparente. Ponga una bolita de masa entre el plástico y aplástela con la prensa. Coloque la tortilla en un comal *(griddle)* caliente. Voltee la tortilla varias veces hasta que se dore. ¡Las tortillas recién hechas son riquísimas!

¡A comer!

For Student Response Forms, see the *Lab Book*, pp. 15–18.

Textbook Listening Activity Scripts

Vocabulario en acción 1

2 p. 42, CD 6, Tr. 11

1. —¿Qué tal está la sopa?
   —Está muy fría.
2. —Aquí preparan muy bien las hamburguesas.
   —Sí, estoy de acuerdo.
3. —¡Qué rico está el sándwich de jamón!
   —Sí, me encanta.
4. —¿Qué tal está la ensalada?
   —Está horrible.
5. —¿Qué tal está el sándwich de atún?
   —Está muy salado. No me gusta.
6. —¡Qué ricas están las papas fritas!
   —Sí, me encantan.
7. —¿Qué tal si pruebas la sopa de verduras?
   —¡Ay no! ¡Aquí preparan muy mal la sopa de verduras!
8. —¿Qué tal el helado?
   —¡Está riquísimo!

Answers to Activity 2

1. mal
2. bien
3. bien
4. mal
5. mal
6. bien
7. mal
8. bien

Gramática en acción 1

16 p. 48, CD 6, Tr. 12

1. Cuando tengo sed, pido agua.
2. Siempre pedimos flan de postre.
3. Para comer una ensalada, pido un tenedor.
4. Cuando hace frío, pedimos sopa.
5. Siempre pides muchas papas fritas con tu hamburguesa.
6. Primero sirven los refrescos.
7. En mi casa servimos frutas y helado de postre.

Answers to Activity 16

1. a 2. b 3. a 4. b 5. d 6. c 7. b

Vocabulario en acción 2

32 p. 58, CD 6, Tr. 16

1. —¿En qué puedo ayudar?
   —Saca el bróculi del refrigerador.
2. —¿Pongo el bróculi en el horno?
   —No, ponlo en el microondas.
3. —¿En qué puedo ayudar?
   —Pon la mesa, por favor.
4. —¿Necesitas ayuda?
   —Sí, saca las zanahorias del refrigerador, por favor.
5. —¿Pongo el bróculi en la mesa?
   —Sí, ponlo en la mesa.

Answers to Activity 32

1. C 3. B 5. E
2. A 4. D

Gramática en acción 2

47 p. 65, CD 6, Tr. 17

1. ¿Qué hago con el arroz con pollo?
2. ¿Te ayudo con las zanahorias?
3. ¿Y los refrescos? ¿Qué hago con ellos?
4. ¿Qué debo hacer con las frutas?
5. ¿Tienen la leche los niños?

Answers to Activity 47

1. a
2. d
3. b
4. e
5. c

Repaso capítulo 6

6 p. 75, CD 6, Tr. 20

—Verónica, ¿qué vas a pedir?

—No sé, Antonio. No tengo mucha hambre.

—¿Qué tal si pruebas un sándwich de atún? Aquí preparan sándwiches muy buenos.

—No me gusta el atún. Tengo mucha sed. Creo que voy a pedir un jugo de tomate y un vaso de agua.

—Bueno. Voy a pedir un sándwich de jamón y queso y un refresco. Carlos, ¿qué vas a pedir?

—Me encanta la sopa de verduras aquí. Es muy rica. También me gustan las papas.

—¿Sabes? Voy a pedir una ensalada de frutas también.

—Verónica, siempre almuerzas frutas. Prueba un sándwich.

—Pues, bien. Voy a pedir un sándwich de queso.

Answers to Activity 6

1. Verónica
2. Antonio
3. la sopa de verduras y las papas
4. Es my rica.
5. sí

Dictado, p. 76, CD 6, Tr. 23

1. Yo estudio por la tarde al lado del estadio.
2. En el diccionario no hay nada delicioso.
3. Está delgado: solo come un durazno y helado.
4. Los domingos veo un partido aburrido.
5. Puedo dormir detrás del jardín.
6. Yo no desayuno el día doce de diciembre
7. Vive en un edificio de diez pisos en la ciudad.
8. Dibujo una aspiradora grande y verde.

Integración capítulos 1-6

1 p. 78, CD 6, Tr. 24

1. Hace calor y tengo mucha sed. ¿Quieres ir a tomar algo conmigo?
2. Aquí preparan unos sándwiches deliciosos. Yo prefiero los sándwiches de jamón y queso.
3. Mis amigos dicen que aquí sirven un pescado muy bueno, pero a mí no me gusta para nada.
4. Están un poco saladas, pero me encantan. Las como con hamburguesas.

Answers to Activity 1

1. C
2. B
3. D
4. A

¡A comer!

50-Minute Lesson Plans

Day 1

OBJECTIVE
Commenting on food

Core Instruction
Chapter Opener, pp. 38–39
- See Using the Photo and **Más vocabulario,** p. 38. 5 min.
- See Chapter Objectives, p. 38. 5 min.

Vocabulario en acción 1, pp. 40–45
- See Teaching Vocabulario, p. 40. 30 min.
- Present other expressions from **¡Exprésate!,** p. 41. 10 min.

Optional Resources
- Common Error Alert, pp. 40, 41
- **También se puede decir,** p. 41
- Advanced Learners, p. 41 ▲
- Multiple Intelligences, p. 41

HOMEWORK SUGGESTIONS
Cuaderno de vocabulario y gramática, pp. 17–19

Day 2

OBJECTIVE
Commenting on food

Core Instruction
Vocabulario en acción 1, pp. 40–45
- Have students do Bell Work 6.1, p. 40. 5 min.
- Show **ExpresaVisión,** Ch. 6. 10 min.
- Review **Vocabulario 1** and **¡Exprésate!,** pp. 40–41 10 min.
- Present **Nota cultural,** p. 42. 5 min.
- Have students do Activity 1, p. 42. 10 min.
- Play Audio CD 6, Tr. 11 for Activity 2, p. 42. 10 min.

Optional Resources
- **Más práctica,** p. 42
- Fold-n-Learn, p. 42

HOMEWORK SUGGESTIONS
Cuaderno de vocabulario y gramática, pp. 17–19

Day 3

OBJECTIVE
Commenting on food; taking someone's order; making polite requests

Core Instruction
Vocabulario en acción 1, pp. 40–45
- Have students do Activities 3–6, pp. 42–43. 35 min.
- See Teaching **¡Exprésate!,** p. 44. 15 min.

Optional Resources
- Slower Pace Learners, p. 43 ◆
- Special Learning Needs, p. 43 ●
- **Comunicación,** p. 43
- Language Note, p. 45

HOMEWORK SUGGESTIONS
Cuaderno de vocabulario y gramática, pp. 17–1

Day 4

OBJECTIVE
Taking someone's order; making polite requests

Core Instruction
Vocabulario en acción 1, pp. 40–45
- Have students do Bell Work 6.2, p. 46. 5 min.
- Review **¡Exprésate!,** p. 44. 10 min.
- Have students do Activities 7–10, pp. 44–45. 35 min.

Optional Resources
- Extension, p. 44
- Advanced Learners, p. 45 ▲
- Multiple Intelligences, p. 45
- **Comunicación,** p. 45

HOMEWORK SUGGESTIONS
Study for **Prueba: Vocabulario 1.**
Internet Activities

Day 5

OBJECTIVE
Vocabulary review and assessment

Core Instruction
Vocabulario en acción 1, pp. 40–45
- Review **Vocabulario en acción 1,** pp. 40–45. 30 min.
- Give **Prueba: Vocabulario 1.** 20 min.

Optional Resources
- Test Generator

HOMEWORK SUGGESTIONS
Preview **Gramática en acción 1,** pp. 46–51.

Day 6

OBJECTIVE
Ser *and* ***estar***

Core Instruction
Gramática en acción 1, pp. 46–51
- See Teaching **Gramática,** p. 46. 30 min.
- Have students do Activity 11, p. 46. 10 min.
- Present **Nota cultural,** p. 46. 10 min.

Optional Resources
- Special Learning Needs, p. 47 ●
- Career Path, p. 47

HOMEWORK SUGGESTIONS
Cuaderno de vocabulario y gramática, pp. 20–22
Cuaderno de actividades, pp. 15–18

Day 7

OBJECTIVE
Ser *and* ***estar***

Core Instruction
Gramática en acción 1, pp. 46–51
- Have students do Bell Work 6.3, p. 48. 5 min.
- Show **GramaVisión,** Ch. 6. 10 min.
- Have students do Activities 12–15, p. 47. 35 min.

Optional Resources
- **Comunicación,** p. 47
- Slower Pace Learners, p. 47 ◆

HOMEWORK SUGGESTIONS
Cuaderno de vocabulario y gramática, pp. 20–22
Cuaderno de actividades, pp. 15–18

Day 8

OBJECTIVE
Pedir *and* ***servir***

Core Instruction
Gramática en acción 1, pp. 46–51
- Show **GramaVisión,** Ch. 6. 5 min.
- See Teaching **Gramática,** p. 48. 25 min.
- Play Audio CD 6, Tr. 12 for Activity 16, p. 48. 10 min.
- Have students do Activity 17, p. 48. 10 min.

Optional Resources
- Practices and Perspectives, p. 49
- **Comunicación,** p. 49

HOMEWORK SUGGESTIONS
Cuaderno de vocabulario y gramática, pp. 20–22
Cuaderno de actividades, pp. 15–18

To edit and create your own lesson plans, see the

One-Stop Planner® CD-ROM

KEY
- ▲ Advanced Learners
- ◆ Slower Pace Learners
- ● Special Learning Needs
- ■ Heritage Speakers

Day 9

OBJECTIVE
Pedir** and **servir; preferir, poder,** and **probar

Core Instruction
Gramática en acción 1, pp. 46–51
- Have students do Activities 18–20, p. 49. 25 min.
- See Teaching **Gramática,** p. 50. 25 min.

Optional Resources
- Advanced Learners, p. 49 ▲
- Multiple Intelligences, p. 49

HOMEWORK SUGGESTIONS
Cuaderno de vocabulario y gramática, pp. 20–22
Cuaderno de actividades, pp. 15–18
Internet Activities
Interactive Tutor, Ch. 6

Day 10

OBJECTIVE
Preferir, poder,** and **probar

Core Instruction
Gramática en acción 1, pp. 46–51
- Have students do Bell Work 6.5, p. 54. 5 min.
- Review **preferir, poder,** and **probar,** p. 50. 10 min.
- Have students do Activities 21–24, pp. 50–51. 35 min.

Optional Resources
- Slower Pace Learners, p. 51 ◆
- Special Learning Needs, p, 51 ●
- **Comunicación,** p. 51

HOMEWORK SUGGESTIONS
Study for **Prueba: Gramática 1.**
Interactive Tutor, Ch. 6

Day 11

OBJECTIVE
Grammar assessment; interviews from around the Spanish-speaking world

Core Instruction
Gramática en acción 1, pp. 46–51
- Review **Gramática en acción 1,** pp. 46–51. 10 min.
- Give **Prueba: Gramática 1.** 20 min.

Cultura, pp. 52–53
- See Teaching **Cultura**, #1–2, p. 52. 20 min.

Optional Resources
- Map Activities, p. 52
- Heritage Speakers, p. 52 ■
- Special Learning Needs, p. 53 ●

HOMEWORK SUGGESTIONS
Cuaderno de actividades, p. 19
Advanced Learners, p. 53 ▲

Day 12

OBJECTIVE
Interviews from around the Spanish-speaking world; talking about meals

Core Instruction
Cultura, pp. 52–53
- Have students read the interviews, pp. 52–53. 10 min.
- See Teaching **Cultura,** #3, p. 52. 10 min.
- Present and assign **Comunidad,** p. 53. 5 min.

Vocabulario en acción 2, pp. 54–59
- See Teaching **Vocabulario 2,** p. 54. 25 min.

Optional Resources
- Products and Perspectives, p. 53
- Language Note, p. 55
- **También se puede decir,** p. 55
- Special Learning Needs, p. 55 ●

HOMEWORK SUGGESTIONS
Comunidad, p. 53
Community Link, p. 53
Cuaderno de vocabulario y gramática, pp. 23–25

Day 13

OBJECTIVE
Talking about meals

Core Instruction
Vocabulario en acción 2, pp. 54–59
- Show **ExpresaVisión,** Ch. 6. 10 min.
- Review **Vocabulario 2,** pp. 54–59. 15 min.
- Present **Nota cultural,** p. 56. 10 min.
- Have students do Activities 25–26, p. 56. 15 min.

Optional Resources
- TPR activity, p. 55.
- Advanced Learners, p. 55 ▲
- Practices and Perspectives, p. 56
- Game, p. 56

HOMEWORK SUGGESTIONS
Cuaderno de vocabulario y gramática, pp. 23–25
Internet Activities

Day 14

OBJECTIVE
Talking about meals

Core Instruction
Vocabulario en acción 2, pp. 54–59
- Have students do Bell Work 6.6, p. 60. 5 min.
- Have students do Activities 27–31, pp. 56–57. 45 min.

Optional Resources
- Language Note, p. 57
- Slower Pace Learners, p. 57 ◆
- Multiple Intelligences, p. 57
- **Comunicación,** p. 57

HOMEWORK SUGGESTIONS
Cuaderno de vocabulario y gramática, pp. 23–25

Day 15

OBJECTIVE
Offering to help and giving instructions

Core Instruction
Vocabulario en acción 2, pp. 54–59
- See Teaching **¡Exprésate!,** p. 58. 15 min.
- Play Audio CD 6, Tr. 16 for Activity 32, p. 58. 10 min.
- Have students do Activities 33–35, pp. 204–205. 25 min.

Optional Resources
- Language to Language, p. 58
- Extension, p. 59
- Slower Pace Learners, p. 59 ◆
- Special Learning Needs, p. 59 ●

HOMEWORK SUGGESTIONS
Cuaderno de vocabulario y gramática, pp. 23–25
Internet Activities

Day 16

OBJECTIVE
Offering to help and giving instructions; vocabulary review

Core Instruction
Vocabulario en acción 2, pp. 54–59
- Have students do Activity 36, p. 59. 20 min.
- Review **Vocabulario en acción 2,** pp. 54–59. 30 min.

Optional Resources
- **Comunicación,** p. 59
- Game, p. 56

HOMEWORK SUGGESTIONS
Study for **Prueba: Vocabulario 2.**

50-Minute Lesson Plans, continued

Day 17

OBJECTIVE
Vocabulary assessment; direct objects and direct object pronouns

Core Instruction
Vocabulario en acción 2, pp. 54–59
- Review **Vocabulario en acción 2,** pp. 54–59. 5 min.
- Give **Prueba: Vocabulario 2.** 20 min.

Gramática en acción 2, pp. 60–65
- See Teaching **Gramática,** p. 60. 25 min.

Optional Resources
- Test Generator
- Common Error Alert, p. 60

HOMEWORK SUGGESTIONS
Cuaderno de vocabulario y gramática, pp. 26–28
Cuaderno de actividades, pp. 20–23
Internet Activities
Interactive Tutor, Ch. 6

Day 18

OBJECTIVE
Direct objects and direct object pronouns

Core Instruction
Gramática en acción 2, pp. 60–65
- Show **GramaVisión**, Ch. 6. 10 min.
- Review direct objects and direct object pronouns, p. 60. 15 min.
- Have students do Activities 37–39, pp. 60–61. 25 min.

Optional Resources
- Teacher to Teacher, p. 61
- Slower Pace Learners, p. 61 ◆

HOMEWORK SUGGESTIONS
Cuaderno de vocabulario y gramática, pp. 26–28
Cuaderno de actividades, pp. 20–23
Internet Activities

Day 19

OBJECTIVE
Direct objects and direct object pronouns; affirmative informal commands

Core Instruction
Gramática en acción 2, pp. 60–65
- Have students do Bell Work 6.7, p. 62. 5 min.
- Have students do Activity 40, p. 61. 15 min.
- See Teaching **Gramática,** p. 62. 30 min.

Optional Resources
- **Comunicación,** p. 61
- Multiple Intelligences, p. 61
- Teacher to Teacher, p. 63

HOMEWORK SUGGESTIONS
Cuaderno de vocabulario y gramática, pp. 26–28
Cuaderno de actividades, pp. 20–23

Day 20

OBJECTIVE
Affirmative informal commands

Core Instruction
Gramática en acción 2, pp. 60–65
- Show **GramaVisión,** Ch. 6. 5 min.
- Review affirmative informal commands, p. 62. 10 min.
- Present **Nota cultural,** p. 62. 10 min.
- Have students do Activities 41–43, pp. 62–63. 25 min.

Optional Resources
- Teacher to Teacher, p. 63
- Advanced Learners, p. 63 ▲

HOMEWORK SUGGESTIONS
Cuaderno de vocabulario y gramática, pp. 26–28
Cuaderno de actividades, pp. 20–23
Interactive Tutor, Ch. 6

Day 21

OBJECTIVE
Affirmative informal commands with pronouns

Core Instruction
Gramática en acción 2, pp. 60–65
- See Teaching **Gramática,** p. 64. 25 min.
- Present **Nota Cultural,** p. 64. 10 min.
- Have students do Activities 45–46, p. 64. 15 min.

Optional Resources
- **Comunicación,** p. 63

HOMEWORK SUGGESTIONS
Cuaderno de vocabulario y gramática, pp. 26–28
Cuaderno de actividades, pp. 20–23
Internet Activities
Interactive Tutor, Ch. 6

Day 22

OBJECTIVE
Affirmative informal commands with pronouns

Core Instruction
Gramática en acción 2, pp. 60–65
- Show **GramaVisión,** Ch. 6. 5 min.
- Play Audio CD 6, Tr. 17 for Activity 47, p. 65. 10 min.
- Have students do Activities 48–49, p. 65. 20 min.
- Review **Gramática en acción 2,** pp. 60–65. 15 min.

Optional Resources
- Slower Pace Learners, p. 65 ◆
- Multiple Intelligences, p. 65

HOMEWORK SUGGESTIONS
Study for **Prueba: Gramática 2.**
Interactive Tutor, Ch. 6

Day 23

OBJECTIVE
Grammar assessment; food exchange between the New World and Europe

Core Instruction
Gramática en acción 2, pp. 60–65
- Review **Gramática en acción 2,** pp. 60–65. 15 min.
- Give **Prueba: Gramática 2.** 20 min.

Conexiones culturales, pp. 66–67
- See Teaching **Conexiones culturales,** #1–2, p. 66. 15 min.

Optional Resources
- **Prueba: Aplicación 2**
- Test Generator
- Advanced Learners, p. 67 ▲
- Multiple Intelligences, p. 67

HOMEWORK SUGGESTIONS
Internet Activities

Day 24

OBJECTIVE
Food exchange between the New World and Europe; developing listening and reading skills

Core Instruction
Conexiones culturales, pp. 66–67
- See Teaching **Conexiones culturales,** #3–5, p. 66. 25 min.
- Have students do Activity 3, p. 67. 10 min.

Novela en video, pp. 68–71
- See Teaching **Novela en video**, #1–2, p. 68. 15 min.

Optional Resources
- Practices and Perspectives, p. 67
- Suggestion, p. 67
- Gestures, p. 68
- Visual Learners, p. 68
- Comparing and Contrasting, p. 69

HOMEWORK SUGGESTIONS
Culminating Project, p. 70

To edit and create your own lesson plans, see the

One-Stop Planner® CD-ROM

KEY

- ▲ Advanced Learners
- ◆ Slower Pace Learners
- ● Special Learning Needs
- ■ Heritage Speakers

Day 25

OBJECTIVE
Developing listening and reading skills

Core Instruction

Novela en video, pp. 68–71

- See Teaching **Novela en video,** #3–5, p. 68 30 min.

Leamos y escribamos, pp. 72–73

- See Teaching **Leamos,** #1–2, p. 72. 20 min.

Optional Resources

- Language Note, p. 70
- **Más práctica,** p. 71
- Applying the Strategies, p. 72
- Practices and Perspectives, p. 73

HOMEWORK SUGGESTIONS
Cuaderno de actividades, p. 24

Day 26

OBJECTIVE
Developing reading and writing skills

Core Instruction

Leamos y escribamos, pp. 72–73

- Have students read **Leamos** silently, p. 72. 10 min.
- See Teaching **Leamos,** #3, p. 72. 15 min.
- See Teaching **Escribamos,** #1–2, p. 72. 10 min.
- Have students complete the first part of step 2 in **Taller del escritor,** p. 73. 15 min.

Optional Resources

- Advanced Learners, p. 73 ▲
- Special Learning Needs, p. 73 ●
- Additional Reading, pp. 266–267

HOMEWORK SUGGESTIONS
Cuaderno de actividades, p. 24
Taller del escritor, p. 73
Additional Reading, pp. 266–267

Day 27

OBJECTIVE
Chapter review

Core Instruction

Leamos y escribamos, pp. 72–73

- Have students complete the second half of step 2 and step 3, **Taller del escritor,** p. 73. 15 min.

Repaso, pp. 74–75

- Have students do Activities 1–4, pp. 74–75. 35 min.

Optional Resources

- Fold-n-Learn, p. 74
- Reteaching, p. 74

HOMEWORK SUGGESTIONS
Internet Activities
Interactive Tutor, Ch. 6

Day 28

OBJECTIVE
Chapter review

Core Instruction

Repaso, pp. 74–75

- Have students do Activity 5, p. 75. 10 min.
- Play Audio CD 6, Tr. 20 for Activity 6, p. 75. 10 min.
- Have students do Activity 7, p. 75. 15 min.
- Play Audio CD 6, Tr. 21–23 for **Letra y sonido,** p. 76. 15 min.

Optional Resources

- Letra y sonido, p. 76
- Game, p. 77

HOMEWORK SUGGESTIONS
Study for Chapter Test.
Interactive Tutor, Ch. 6

Day 29

OBJECTIVE
Chapter review

Core Instruction

Integración, pp. 78–79

- Play Audio CD 6, Tr. 24 for Activity 1, p. 78. 10 min.
- Have students do Activities 2–4, pp. 78–79. 40 min.

Optional Resources

- **Más práctica,** p. 78
- Culture Project, p. 76
- Fine Art Connection, p. 77

HOMEWORK SUGGESTIONS
Study for Chapter Test.
Cuaderno de actividades, pp. 25–26

Day 30

OBJECTIVE
Assessment

Core Instruction

Chapter Test 50 min.

Optional Resources

Assessment Program:

- **Prueba: Lectura**
- **Prueba: Escritura**
- Alternative Assessment
- Test Generator

HOMEWORK SUGGESTIONS
Cuaderno de actividades, pp. 78–79

90-Minute Lesson Plans

Block 1

OBJECTIVE
Commenting on food

Core Instruction

Chapter Opener, pp. 38–39
- See Using the Photo and **Más vocabulario,** p. 38. 5 min.
- See Chapter Objectives, p. 38. 5 min.

Vocabulario en acción 1, pp. 40–45
- Show **ExpresaVisión,** Ch. 6. 10 min.
- See Teaching **Vocabulario,** p. 40. 30 min.
- Present other expressions from **¡Exprésate!,** p. 41. 10 min.
- Present **Nota cultural,** p. 42. 10 min.
- Have students do Activity 1, p. 42. 10 min.
- Play Audio CD 6, Tr. 11 for Activity 2, p. 42. 10 min.

Optional Resources

- Common Error Alert, pp. 40, 41
- **También se puede decir,** p. 41
- TPR, p. 41
- Advanced Learners, p. 41 ▲
- Multiple Intelligences, p. 41
- **Más práctica,** p. 42
- Fold-n-Learn, p. 42

HOMEWORK SUGGESTIONS
Cuaderno de vocabulario y gramática, pp. 17–19

Block 2

OBJECTIVE
Commenting on food; taking someone's order; making polite requests

Core Instruction

Vocabulario en acción 1, pp. 40–45
- Have students do Bell Work 6.1, p. 40. 5 min.
- Review **Vocabulario 1** and **¡Exprésate!,** pp. 40–41. 15 min.
- Have students do Activities 3–6, pp. 42–43. 30 min.
- See Teaching **¡Exprésate!**, p. 44. 15 min.
- Have students do Activities 7–10, pp. 44–45. 25 min.

Optional Resources

- Game, p. 42
- Slower Pace Learners, p. 43 ◆
- Special Learning Needs, p. 43 ●
- **Comunicación,** p. 43
- Language Note, p. 45
- Extension, p. 44
- Advanced Learners, p. 45 ▲
- Multiple Intelligences, p. 45
- **Comunicación,** p. 45

HOMEWORK SUGGESTIONS
Study for **Prueba: Vocabulario 1.**
Cuaderno de vocabulario y gramática, pp. 17–19
Internet Activities

Block 3

OBJECTIVE
Vocabulary review and assessment; ***ser*** *and* ***estar***

Core Instruction

Vocabulario en acción 1, pp. 40–45
- Have students do Bell Work 6.2, p. 46. 5 min.
- Review **Vocabulario en acción 1,** pp. 40–45. 20 min.
- Give **Prueba: Vocabulario 1.** 20 min.

Gramática en acción 1, pp. 46–51
- See Teaching **Gramática,** p. 46. 30 min.
- Have students do Activity 11, p. 46. 10 min.
- Present **Nota cultural,** p. 46. 5 min.

Optional Resources

- Test Generator
- Special Learning Needs, p. 47 ●
- Career Path, p. 47

HOMEWORK SUGGESTIONS
Cuaderno de vocabulario y gramática, pp. 20–22
Cuaderno de actividades, pp. 15–18

Block 4

OBJECTIVE
Ser *and* ***estar; pedir*** *and* ***servir***

Core Instruction

Gramática en acción 1, pp. 46–51
- Have students do Bell Work 6.3, p. 48. 5 min.
- Review **ser** and **estar,** p. 46. 10 min.
- Have students do Activities 12–15, p. 47. 30 min.
- See Teaching **Gramática,** p. 48. 25 min.
- Play Audio CD 6, Tr. 12 for Activity 16, p. 48. 10 min.
- Have students do Activity 17, p. 48. 10 min.

Optional Resources

- **Comunicación,** p. 47
- Slower Pace Learners, p. 47 ◆
- **GramaVisión,** Ch. 6
- Practices and Perspectives, p. 49
- **Comunicación,** p. 49

HOMEWORK SUGGESTIONS
Cuaderno de vocabulario y gramática, pp. 20–22
Cuaderno de actividades, pp. 15–18

To edit and create your own lesson plans, see the **One-Stop** Planner® CD-ROM

KEY
- ▲ Advanced Learners
- ◆ Slower Pace Learners
- ● Special Learning Needs
- ■ Heritage Speakers

Block 5

OBJECTIVE
Pedir *and* ***servir; preferir, poder,*** *and* ***probar***

Core Instruction
Gramática en acción 1, pp. 46–51
- Have students do Activities 18–20, p. 49. 25 min.
- Show **GramaVisión,** Ch. 6. 10 min.
- See Teaching **Gramática,** p. 50. 25 min.
- Have students do Activities 21–24, p. 50–51. 30 min.

Optional Resources
- Advanced Learners, p. 49 ▲
- Multiple Intelligences, p. 49
- Slower Pace Learners, p. 51 ◆
- Special Learning Needs, p. 51 ●
- **Comunicación,** p. 51

HOMEWORK SUGGESTIONS
Study for **Prueba: Gramática 1.**
Cuaderno de vocabulario y gramática, pp. 20–22
Cuaderno de actividades, pp. 15–18
Interactive Tutor, Ch. 6

Block 6

OBJECTIVE
Grammar assessment; interviews from around the Spanish-speaking world; talking about meals

Core Instruction
Gramática en acción 1, pp. 46–51
- Review **Gramática en acción 1,** pp. 46–51. 10 min.
- Give **Prueba: Gramática 1.** 20 min.

Cultura, pp. 52–53
- See Teaching **Cultura,** p. 52. 30 min.
- Present and assign **Comunidad,** p. 53. 5 min.

Vocabulario en acción 2, pp. 54–59
- See Teaching **Vocabulario 2,** p. 54. 25 min.

Optional Resources
- Map Activities, p. 52
- Heritage Speakers, p. 52 ■
- Special Learning Needs, p. 53 ●
- Products and Perspectives, p. 53
- Language Note, p. 55
- **También se puede decir,** p. 55
- Special Learning Needs, p. 55 ●

HOMEWORK SUGGESTIONS
Cuaderno de actividades, p. 19
Advanced Learners, p. 53 ▲
Comunidad, p. 53
Community Link, p. 53
Cuaderno de vocabulario y gramática, pp. 23–25

Block 7

OBJECTIVE
Talking about meals

Core Instruction
Vocabulario en acción 2, pp. 54–59
- Show **ExpresaVisión,** Ch. 6. 10 min.
- Review **Vocabulario 2,** pp. 54–59. 10 min.
- Present **Nota cultural,** p. 56. 10 min.
- Have students do Activities 25–31, pp. 56–57. 45 min.
- See Teaching **¡Exprésate!,** p. 58. 15 min.

Optional Resources
- TPR activity, p. 55.
- Advanced Learners, p. 55 ▲
- Practices and Perspectives, p. 56
- Game, p. 56
- Language Note, p. 57
- Slower Pace Learners, p. 57 ◆
- Multiple Intelligences, p. 57
- **Comunicación,** p. 57

HOMEWORK SUGGESTIONS
Cuaderno de vocabulario y gramática, pp. 23–25
Internet Activities

Block 8

OBJECTIVE
Offering to help and giving instructions; direct objects and direct object pronouns

Core Instruction
Vocabulario en acción 2, pp. 54–59
- Review **¡Exprésate!,** p. 58. 5 min.
- Play Audio CD 6, Tr. 16 for Activity 32, p. 58. 10 min.
- Have students do Activities 33–36, pp. 204–205. 35 min.

Gramática en acción 2, pp. 60–65
- See Teaching **Gramática,** p. 60. 25 min.
- Have students do Activities 37–38, pp. 60–61. 15 min.

Optional Resources
- Language to Language, p. 58
- Extension, p. 59
- Slower Pace Learners, p. 59 ◆
- Special Learning Needs, p. 59 ●
- **Comunicación,** p. 59
- **GramaVisión,** Ch. 6.
- Common Error Alert, p. 60

HOMEWORK SUGGESTIONS
Study for **Prueba: Vocabulario 2.**
Cuaderno de vocabulario y gramática, pp. 23–25
Cuaderno de actividades, pp. 20–23
Interactive Tutor, Ch. 6

90-Minute Lesson Plans, continued

Block 9

OBJECTIVE
Vocabulary assessment; direct objects and direct object pronouns; affirmative informal commands

Core Instruction
Vocabulario en acción 2, pp. 54–59
- Review **Vocabulario en acción 2,** pp. 54–59. 10 min.
- Give **Prueba: Vocabulario 2.** 20 min.

Gramática en acción 2, pp. 60–65
- Review direct objects and direct object pronouns, p. 60. 10 min.
- Have students do Activities 39–40, pp. 60–61. 20 min.
- See Teaching **Gramática,** p. 62. 30 min.

Optional Resources
- Test Generator
- Teacher to Teacher, p. 61
- **Comunicación,** p. 61
- Slower Pace Learners, p. 61 ◆
- Multiple Intelligences, p. 61

HOMEWORK SUGGESTIONS
Cuaderno de vocabulario y gramática, pp. 26–28
Cuaderno de actividades, pp. 20–23
Internet Activities
Interactive Tutor, Ch. 6

Block 10

OBJECTIVE
Affirmative informal commands; affirmative informal commands with pronouns

Core Instruction
Gramática en acción 2, pp. 60–65
- Review affirmative informal commands, p. 60. 10 min.
- Present **Nota cultural,** p. 62. 5 min.
- Have students do Activities 41–44, pp. 62–63. 25 min.
- See Teaching **Gramática,** p. 64. 25 min.
- Present **Nota Cultural,** p. 64. 5 min.
- Have students do Activities 45–46, p. 64. 10 min.
- Play Audio CD 6, Tr. 7 for Activity 47, p. 65. 10 min.

Optional Resources
- Teacher to Teacher, p. 63
- Advanced Learners, p. 63 ▲
- **Comunicación,** p. 63
- **GramaVisión,** Ch. 6. 5 min.

HOMEWORK SUGGESTIONS
Study for **Prueba: Gramática 2.**
Cuaderno de vocabulario y gramática, pp. 26–28
Cuaderno de actividades, pp. 20–23
Internet Activities
Interactive Tutor, Ch. 6

Block 11

OBJECTIVE
Grammar assessment; food exchange between the New World and Europe

Core Instruction
Gramática en acción 2, pp. 60–65
- Have students do Activities 48–49, p. 65. 15 min.
- Review **Gramática en acción 2,** pp. 60–65. 15 min.
- Give **Prueba: Gramática 1.** 20 min.

Conexiones culturales, pp. 66–67
- See Teaching **Conexiones culturales,** #1–5, p. 66. 40 min.

Optional Resources
- **Prueba: Aplicación 2**
- Test Generator
- Slower Pace Learners, p. 65 ◆
- Multiple Intelligences, p. 65
- Advanced Learners, p. 67 ▲
- Multiple Intelligences, p. 67
- Practices and Perspectives, p. 67
- Suggestion, p. 67

HOMEWORK SUGGESTIONS
Conexiones, Activity 3, p. 67
Interactive Tutor, Ch. 6

To edit and create your own lesson plans, see the

One-Stop Planner® CD-ROM

KEY
- ▲ Advanced Learners
- ◆ Slower Pace Learners
- ● Special Learning Needs
- ■ Heritage Speakers

Block 12

OBJECTIVE
Developing listening, reading, and writing skills

Core Instruction

Novela en video, pp. 68–71
- See Teaching **Novela en video,** p. 68. 40 min.

Leamos y escribamos, pp. 72–73
- See Teaching **Leamos,** p. 72. 35 min.
- See Teaching **Escribamos,** #1–2, p. 72 10 min.
- Have students begin **Taller del escritor,** step 1, p. 73 5 min.

Optional Resources
- Gestures, p. 68
- Visual Learners, p. 68
- Comparing and Contrasting, p. 69
- Language Note, p. 70
- **Más práctica,** p. 71
- Applying the Strategies, p. 72
- Practices and Perspectives, p. 73

HOMEWORK SUGGESTIONS
Taller del ecritor, p. 73
Culminating Project, p. 70
Cuaderno de actividades, p. 24
Additional Reading, pp. 266–267

Block 13

OBJECTIVE
Developing writing skills; chapter review

Core Instruction

Leamos y escribamos, pp. 72–73
- See Teaching **Escribamos,** #3, p. 72. 30 min.

Repaso, pp. 74–75
- Have students do Activities 1–5, pp. 74–75. 25 min.
- Have students do Activity 5, p. 75. 10 min.
- Play Audio CD 6, Tr. 20 for Activity 6, p. 75. 5 min.
- Have students do Activity 7, p. 75. 10 min.
- Play Audio CD 6, Tr. 21–23 for **Letra y sonido,** p. 76. 10 min.

Optional Resources
- Advanced Learners, p. 73 ▲
- Special Learning Needs, p. 73 ●
- Fold-n-Learn, p. 74
- Reteaching, p. 74
- **Letra y sonido,** p. 76
- Game, p. 77

HOMEWORK SUGGESTIONS
Study for Chapter Test.
Interactive Tutor, Ch. 6

Block 14

OBJECTIVE
Assessment

Core Instruction

Chapter Test 50 min.

Integración, pp. 78–79
- Play Audio CD 6, Tr. 24 for Activity 1, p. 78. 10 min.
- Have students do Activities 2–4, pp. 78–79. 30 min.

Optional Resources

Assessment Program:
- **Prueba: Lectura**
- **Prueba: Escritura**
- Alternative Assessment
- Test Generator
- **Más práctica,** p. 78
- Culture Project, p. 76
- Fine Art Connection, p. 77

HOMEWORK SUGGESTIONS
Cuaderno de actividades, pp. 25–26, 78–79

Chapter Opener

Meeting the National Standards

Communication
Comunicación, pp. 43, 45, 47, 49, 51, 57, 59, 61, 63, 65

Situación, p. 79

Cultures
Comparaciones, pp. 52–53

Nota cultural, pp. 42, 46, 56, 62, 64

Conexiones culturales, pp. 66–67

Practices and Perspectives, pp. 35, 49

Products and Perspectives, p. 53

Connections
Background Information, pp. 34–35

Interdisciplinary Links, p. 36

Visual Learners, p. 68

Comparisons
Comparaciones, pp. 52–53

Language Note, p. 45

Comparing and Contrasting, p. 69

Communities
Career Path, p. 47

Comunidad, p. 53

Using the Photo
Read the caption and have students study the photo. Tell them that many building interiors and exteriors in Mexico are painted bright vibrant colors, such as yellow, pink, and turquoise. Have students compare the restaurant decor in the photo with that of a restaurant in which they have eaten. Use the questions in **¿Qué ves en la foto?** and the words in **Más vocabulario** to discuss the restaurant decor in more detail. Have students point to each of the decorative details listed in **Más vocabulario.**

Más vocabulario

el papel picado *cut paper art*
el mantel *tablecloth*
el azulejo *tile*
el arco *archway*
la reja *grille*

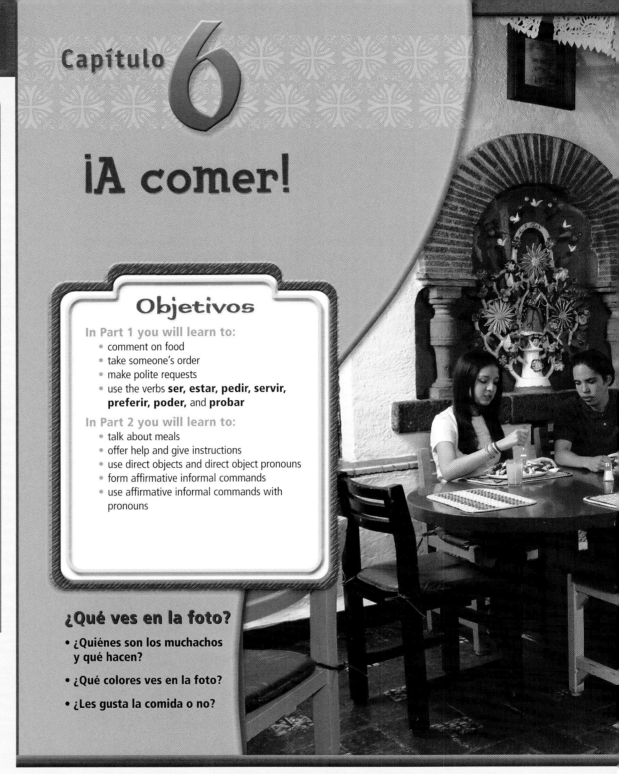

Capítulo 6

¡A comer!

Objetivos

In Part 1 you will learn to:
- comment on food
- take someone's order
- make polite requests
- use the verbs **ser, estar, pedir, servir, preferir, poder,** and **probar**

In Part 2 you will learn to:
- talk about meals
- offer help and give instructions
- use direct objects and direct object pronouns
- form affirmative informal commands
- use affirmative informal commands with pronouns

¿Qué ves en la foto?
- **¿Quiénes son los muchachos y qué hacen?**
- **¿Qué colores ves en la foto?**
- **¿Les gusta la comida o no?**

Holt Online Learning *¡Exprésate!* contains several online options for you to incorporate into your lessons.

***¡Exprésate!* Student Edition online at my.hrw.com**
At this site, you will find the online version of *¡Exprésate!* All concepts presented in the textbook are presented and practiced in this online version of your textbook. This online version can be used as a supplement to or as a replacement of your textbook.

Practice activities at go.hrw.com
These activities provide additional practice for major concepts presented in each chapter. Practice items include structured practice as well as research topics.

Teacher resources at www.hrw.com
This site provides additional information that teachers might find useful about the *¡Exprésate!* program.

STANDARDS: 1.2

Visit Holt Online
go.hrw.com
KEYWORD: EXP1B CH6
Online Edition

El restaurante Las Lupitas en Coyoacán, Ciudad de México

Chapter Opener

Learning Tips

Tell students that learning a foreign language is like any other long-term project, such as getting into shape or taking up a new sport: it may take some time to see the results they want. They should stay motivated by setting short-term, realistic goals. Once they have learned more Spanish, they could make a goal of going to a store or restaurant in a Spanish-speaking part of town and shopping or ordering a meal entirely in Spanish.

- **ExpresaVisión 1**
- **GramaVisión 1**
  Ser and **estar; pedir, servir; preferir, poder,** and **probar**
- **VideoCultura**
- **ExpresaVisión 2**
- **GramaVisión 2**
  Direct objects and direct object pronouns; affirmative informal commands; affirmative informal commands with pronouns
- **VideoNovela**
- **Variedades**

Pacing Tips

In this chapter, the amount of vocabulary and grammar presented is balanced in both chapter sections. Many food items are cognates, so students can more easily master the new items.

For complete lesson plan suggestions, see pages 37G–37N.

Suggested pacing:	Traditional Schedule	Block Schedule
Vocabulario 1/Gramática 1	10 1/2 days	5 1/3 blocks
Cultura	1 day	1/2 block
Vocabulario 2/Gramática 2	11 1/4 days	5 1/3 blocks
Conexiones culturales	1 day	1/2 block
Novela	3/4 day	1/3 block
Leamos y escribamos	1 1/2 days	1/2 block
Repaso	2 days	1/2 block
Chapter Test	1 day	1/2 block
Integración	1 day	1/2 block

Resources

Planning:

Lesson Planner, pp. 11–15, 172–177

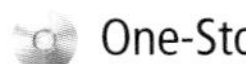 One-Stop Planner

Presentation:

TPR Storytelling Book, pp. 30–31

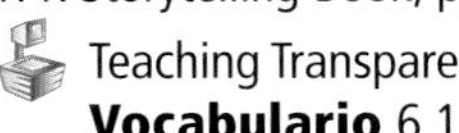 Teaching Transparencies **Vocabulario** 6.1, 6.2

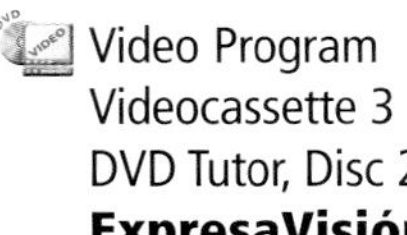 Video Program
Videocassette 3
DVD Tutor, Disc 2
ExpresaVisión

Practice:

Cuaderno de vocabulario y gramática, pp. 17–19

Activities for Communication, pp. 21–22

Video Guide, pp. 54–56

Lab Book, pp. 15–16, 38

Teaching Transparencies
Bell Work 6.1
Vocabulario y gramática answers, pp. 17–19

Interactive Tutor, Disc 2

Bell Work

Use Bell Work 6.1 in the *Teaching Transparencies,* or write this activity on the board.

Match each chore to the place it occurs.

1. Ana corta el césped.
2. Ana hace la cama.
3. Ana cocina el almuerzo.
4. Ana arregla el sofá.
5. Ana limpia el baño.

a. la cocina **b.** el baño
c. el jardín **d.** la sala
e. el cuarto

COMMON ERROR ALERT ¡OJO!

Remind students that **la papa** is feminine and has no accent. Its stress falls on the first syllable. Changing its gender or stress changes its meaning. **Los papas** means *popes;* **los papás** means *parents.*

Objetivos
Commenting on food, taking someone's order, making polite requests

Vocabulario en acción 1

Video/DVD
ExpresaVisión

¿Qué vas a pedir?

¿Qué prefieres pedir de almuerzo en este restaurante?

un sándwich de atún
una ensalada
una ensalada de frutas
la salsa
unas papas fritas
un sándwich de jamón con queso

Más vocabulario...

Está...

riquísimo(a)	*very good (tasty)*
salado(a)	*salty*
picante	*spicy*
frío(a)	*cold*
(muy) caliente	*(very) hot*

También se puede decir...

In the Southwestern United States, **el lonche** is a common way to say *lunch,* while in Spain, Mexico, and much of Latin America, **la comida** is used. **El almuerzo** is commonly used in many rural areas to mean *breakfast.*

A sandwich made with French bread is **un bocadillo** in Spain, and **una torta** in Mexico. You may also hear **un emparedado.**

In Spain, **el jugo** is usually called **el zumo.**

Core Instruction

TEACHING VOCABULARIO

1. Introduce the food and table setting vocabulary, using transparencies **Vocabulario 6.1** and **6.2.** Model the pronunciation of each word. **(12 min.)**
2. Ask students which foods they like, using **¿Te gusta(n)...? (5 min.)**
3. Ask students which utensils, plates, etc. you need to eat certain foods. For example, **—Para comer la sopa, ¿necesitas un tenedor? —No, necesito una cuchara y un plato hondo. (5 min.)**
4. Encourage students to try various foods using **¿Qué tal si pruebas...?** Model some possible answers for students such as **¡Ay no! Nunca pido..., No me gusta(n),** and **Sí, me encanta(n). (8 min.)**

ExpresaVisión

Use the video presenter to teach the new mealtime vocabulary. For interactive activities, see the *DVD Tutor.*

ExpresaVisión

Visit Holt Online
go.hrw.com
KEYWORD: EXP1B CH6
Vocabulario 1 practice

Para tomar, puedes pedir...

En la mesa hay...

¡Exprésate!

To comment on food

Interactive TUTOR

¿Qué tal si pruebas un sándwich de atún? Son muy buenos aquí. *How about trying a tuna sandwich? They're very good here.*	**¡Ay no! Nunca pido atún. No me gusta.** *Oh no! I never order tuna. I don't like it.*
Aquí preparan muy bien (mal) la salsa picante. *They make very good (bad) hot sauce here.*	**(No) estoy de acuerdo.** *I (don't) agree.*
¡Qué ricas están las papas! *The potatoes are really good (tasty)!*	**Sí, me encantan.** *Yes, I love them.*
¿Qué tal está la sopa (de verduras)? *How's the (vegetable) soup?*	**Está un poco salada.** *It's a little salty.*

Online
Vocabulario y gramática, pp. 17–19

TPR
Total Physical Response

Have students help you collect items for a place setting and photos or illustrations of each of the food items presented. Present and model the commands and then have individual students respond.

Pon el plato y la servilleta en la mesa.

Pon el tenedor sobre la servilleta.

Sirve el flan en el plato hondo.

Tráele a... el flan.

Prueba la sopa de verduras con la cuchara.

Sírvele el sándwich de queso a...

Busca las comidas picantes.

Busca las cosas que se sirven en un vaso.

... quiere irse. Tráele la cuenta.

También se puede decir...

Students may hear **papas (papitas) fritas** (Dominican Republic, Venezuela) or **patatas fritas** (Spain). They are also likely to hear many different words for *bowl.* In Puerto Rico, a *soup bowl* is referred to as a **sopera,** and in Venezuela as a **plato de sopa.** Although **sopa** is a term commonly used for a cream soup or one that is primarily broth, many terms are used for soup with pieces of meat or vegetables. In Venezuela, this is called an **hervido** and a **sancocho** in Perú.

Common Error Alert ¡Ojo!

Although **agua** is feminine, it uses the definite article **el.** Students often confuse the words **jugo** *(juice)* and **juego** *(I play, game)* since they look similar, so you might take time to remind students about the difference.

Differentiated Instruction

Advanced Learners

Bring a variety of empty food packages to class, such as an empty ice-cream container, a green-bean can, a tea bag, a macaroni-and-cheese box, etc. Hold up each food item one at a time and ask student volunteers to create a sentence about the food using the adjectives from **Más vocabulario...** on page 40.

Multiple Intelligences

Logical-Mathematical Have students solve this problem: Juanita and Pablo went to lunch, and they ordered these items: **un sándwich de atún (45 pesos), un sándwich de jamón con queso (60 pesos), papas fritas (20 pesos), una ensalada (20 pesos), y dos refrescos (20 pesos total).** They have decided to split the cost evenly. If they tip 15% of the total bill, what is the amount that they will each need to pay, in **pesos?** Have students look up the conversion rate to find out the total in dollars.

2 Script

1. —¿Qué tal está la sopa?
—Está muy fría.
2. —Aquí preparan muy bien las hamburguesas.
—Sí, estoy de acuerdo.
3. ¡Qué rico está el sándwich de jamón!
—Sí, me encanta.
4. —¿Qué tal está la ensalada?
—Está horrible.
5. —¿Qué tal está el sándwich de atún?
—Está muy salado. No me gusta.
6. —¡Qué ricas están las papas fritas!
—Sí, me encantan.
7. —¿Qué tal si pruebas la sopa de verduras?
—¡Ay no! ¡Aquí preparan muy mal la sopa de verduras!
8. —¿Qué tal el helado?
—¡Está riquísimo!

Más práctica

1 After finishing Activity 1, have students arrange the foods and drinks in three groups. In the first group, they'll draw or write all the foods and drinks that are very healthful. In the second group, they'll include the foods and drinks that are somewhat healthful; and in the third, the ones that they should not eat or drink very often. Then have them arrange in three groups which foods they eat most frequently, least frequently, or never. How healthful are their eating habits?

Game

Carreras Divide students into three groups. Have one student from each group go to the board. Instruct students to draw or write on the board the more healthful food or drink that you call out. Choose one item from pages 40–41 that is healthful and another that is not. The student who draws or writes the correct item first, wins and his or her team gets a point.

Nota cultural

The foods we eat often reflect our ethnic traditions and history. In Mexico, many foods trace their origins to pre-Columbian times. **Atole,** a drink first enjoyed by the Aztecs, combines corn meal, milk or water, and a flavoring such as chocolate, fruit, or even chile peppers. **Atole** is so popular that it even comes packaged like instant hot chocolate. What foods do we eat in the United States that were part of the Native American diet?

1 Una dieta balanceada

Leamos Choose the more healthful food item from each pair.

MODELO **la pizza/la ensalada**
la ensalada

1. las papas fritas/las verduras
2. el refresco/el agua
3. la sopa de verduras/el helado
4. la pizza/la ensalada de frutas
5. el jugo de naranja/el refresco
6. el helado/las frutas
7. el sándwich de jamón/la ensalada
8. el sándwich de atún/la hamburguesa con queso
9. el refresco/la leche
10. las papas fritas/el sándwich de atún
11. la pizza/las verduras

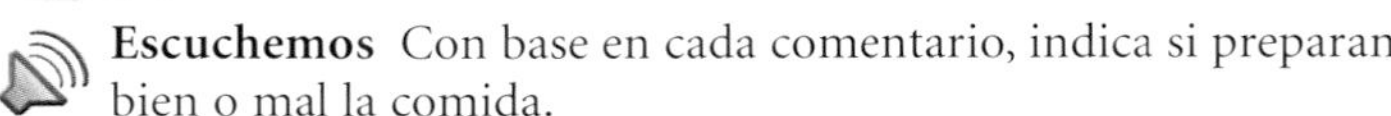

CD 6, Tr. 11

2 ¿Qué tal está la comida?

Escuchemos Con base en cada comentario, indica si preparan bien o mal la comida.

1. la sopa mal
2. las hamburguesas bien
3. el sándwich de jamón bien
4. la ensalada mal
5. el sándwich de atún mal
6. las papas fritas bien
7. la sopa de verduras mal
8. el helado bien

3 ¿Cómo está la comida?

Leamos/Hablemos Read each question. Then look at the pictures and pretend you are the person answering the question.

Soledad

MODELO **—Soledad, ¿cómo están los refrescos?**
—¡Están buenos!

1. Cristóbal, ¿cómo está el sándwich de queso? El sándwich está...
2. Gloria, ¿cómo está la comida mexicana? La comida está...
3. Mariano, ¿cómo está la sopa de papas? La sopa está...
4. Leticia, ¿cómo está el helado? El helado está...

Cristóbal

Gloria

Mariano

Leticia

FOLD-N-LEARN

The Flower

1. Have students fold together opposite corners of an 8"x 8" paper to make a diagonal crease; then unfold the paper and fold together the other two corners. They now have a triangle with a center crease. Students mark the folded edge at 1 and 3 inches on either side of the crease; then cut the paper from the marked points on the fold toward the center crease on an angle, stopping 1/4 and 1/2 inch before the crease. Students unfold the paper; then fold it along the opposite diagonal crease and cut at 2 and 4 inches from the fold toward the center crease. Students unfold the paper and bend the points of the four inner cuts together to form petals.
2. Students draw a food or drink on one side of each 'petal' and its name in Spanish on the other side. On the opposite 'petal' they write an adjective to describe it in English and Spanish. Students turn the 'petals' over to check their vocabulary.

STANDARDS: 1.2, 2.1, 3.1, 4.2

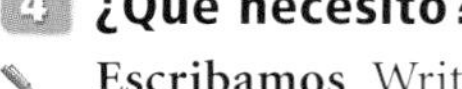

4 ¿Qué necesito?

Escribamos Write a sentence for each photo that tells what you need to eat or to serve that food or drink.

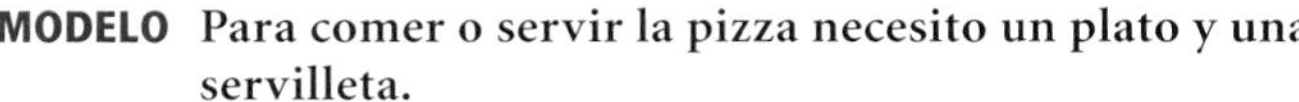

MODELO **Para comer o servir la pizza necesito un plato y una servilleta.**

1

2.

3.

4.

5.

Comunicación

5 Comidas diferentes

Hablemos Work with two partners to come up with some unusual foods for a contest. Think up two foods for each category. Choose a spokesperson and present your creative food ideas to the class.

MODELO **comidas frías:**
helado de atún y...

comidas frías	comidas calientes
comidas malas	comidas picantes

6 Comidas preferidas

Hablemos Take turns with your partner asking what he or she likes to eat and drink at various times of day. When you answer your partner, include the reason for your choices.

MODELO después de clases —**¿Qué te gusta comer/beber después de clases?**
—**Me gusta beber leche porque es buena.**

1. antes de ir al colegio
2. cuando hace mucho calor
3. cuando hace frío
4. para el almuerzo los sábados

4 Possible Answers

1. Para comer una ensalada de frutas necesito un plato y un tenedor.
2. Para servir el agua necesito un vaso.
3. Para comer una ensalada necesito un plato, un tenedor y una servilleta.
4. Para servir la salsa picante necesito un plato hondo y una cuchara.
5. Para comer la cena necesito un plato, un tenedor, una cuchara, un cuchillo y una servilleta.

Comunicación

Group Activity: Interpersonal

Write this list of foods and drinks on the board.

la pizza de jamón y fruta
las hamburguesas con queso y tomate
las papas fritas con salsa picante
el sándwich de atún
la comida china con muchas verduras
el sándwich de queso
el jugo de naranja con leche
el refresco de naranja

Tell students to imagine that they are tasting the foods and drinks listed. Have them work in pairs to take turns asking each other how they like each food or drink. Ask some of the pairs to share their comments with the class. As a wrap up ask them to tell the class which food or drink they like the most.

MODELO
—¿Qué tal está la pizza de jamón y fruta?
—Está muy caliente pero ¡riquísima!...
—A mí me gusta más el sándwich de queso.

Differentiated Instruction

SLOWER PACE LEARNERS

Additional Practice Ask students to work with a partner and pretend that they are in a favorite restaurant or snack shop. Have them act out a conversation about the food there by using the expressions in **¡Exprésate!** on page 41. After they practice, have them act out the conversation for the class.

SPECIAL LEARNING NEEDS

Students with Visual Impairments
Additional Practice Photocopy the vocabulary pictures from pages 40 and 41. Enlarge each picture and glue it to a sheet of construction paper. Write the vocabulary word in large, bright letters on the reverse side of each picture. Let students with visual impairments work with a partner and use these large flash cards for vocabulary practice.

STANDARDS: 1.1, 1.3

Resources

Planning:

Lesson Planner, pp. 11–15, 172–177

 One-Stop Planner

Presentation:

TPR Storytelling Book, pp. 30–31

 Teaching Transparencies **Vocabulario** 6.1, 6.2

Video Program
Videocassette 3
DVD Tutor, Disc 2
ExpresaVisión

Practice:

Cuaderno de vocabulario y gramática, pp. 17–19

Activities for Communication, pp. 21–22

Video Guide, pp. 54–56

Lab Book, pp. 15–16, 38

 Teaching Transparencies **Vocabulario y gramática** answers, pp. 17–19

Interactive Tutor, Disc 2

7 Extension

Have students write about a situation in a restaurant between a waiter and a customer, using expressions from **¡Exprésate!** and Activity 7. Instruct them to use as many of those expressions as possible. Then have students act out their conversations with you in front of the class.

¡Exprésate!

To take someone's order	To request something
¿Qué desea usted? *What would you (formal) like?*	**Quisiera un sándwich de queso.** *I would like a cheese sandwich.*
¿Y para tomar? *And to drink?*	**Para tomar, quiero jugo de tomate.** *To drink, I want tomato juice.*
¿Desea algo de postre? *Would you like something for dessert?*	**Sí, ¿me trae un flan?** *Yes, could you bring me a flan?*
¿Algo más? *Anything else?*	**¿Nos trae la cuenta, por favor?** *Could you bring us the bill, please?*

Interactive TUTOR

Online
Vocabulario y gramática, pp. 17–19

7 ¡Camarero!

Leamos Look at the drawings and match each one with what the people are probably saying to the waiter.

a. ¿Nos trae unas servilletas, por favor? 2
b. ¿Nos trae un sandwich de atún y una ensalada, por favor? 3
c. ¿Me trae un plato, por favor? 4
d. ¿Me trae un vaso de agua, por favor? 1

1.

2.

3.

4.

Core Instruction

TEACHING ¡EXPRÉSATE!

1. Use the expressions in **¡Exprésate!** to act out a conversation between a server and a customer at a restaurant. **(6 min.)**
2. Read aloud some of the expressions and ask students whether the speaker is most likely a server or customer. **(4 min.)**
3. Put up transparencies **Vocabulario 6.1** and **6.2.** Ask volunteers what they would like to eat and drink. Point to an item on the transparencies to cue their answers. You may also suggest food items students learned in earlier chapters, such as **el helado. (5 min.)**

8 En el restaurante

Hablemos Ask a server politely for these items.

1.

2.

3.

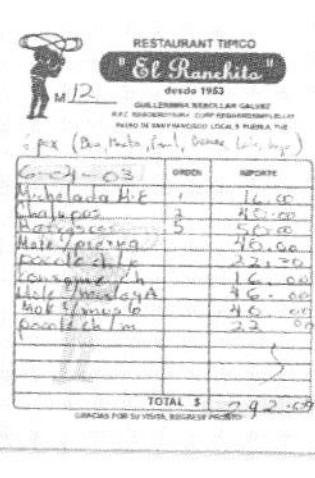
4.

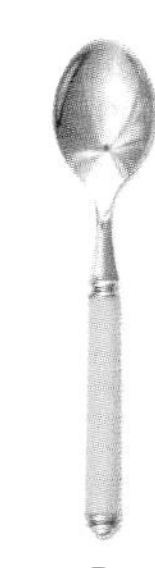
5.

9 ¿Cómo se dice?

Escribamos You are in a restaurant with a friend. Write how you would say the following in Spanish. Possible answers:

MODELO **Ask your friend how the ham sandwich is.**
¿Qué tal está el sándwich de jamón?

1. Suggest that your friend try the fruit salad. ¿Qué tal si pruebas la ensalada de frutas?
2. Tell the server you would like a flan. Quisiera un flan, por favor.
3. Say that the soup is a little spicy. La sopa está un poco picante.
4. Say that the French fries are delicious. Las papas fritas están riquísimas.
5. Say that they make very good desserts here. Preparan muy bien los postres aquí.
6. Ask the server to bring the bill. ¿Me trae la cuenta, por favor?

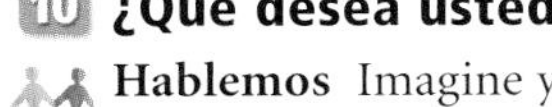

Comunicación

10 ¿Qué desea usted?

Hablemos Imagine you are in a restaurant. You and your partner will play the roles of the server and the customer. Be sure to include the following information in your dialog.

MODELO **—¿Qué desea usted?**
—Quisiera...

1. what you want to eat
2. what you want to drink
3. what you think of the food
4. whether you want dessert
5. whether there's anything else you need

Differentiated Instruction

ADVANCED LEARNERS

Challenge Have students scramble five words from Vocabulario 1. Tell them not to include the articles in the scramble. Ask them to practice scrambling on a piece of scrap paper until they get a version they like. Have them write the final version on an index card. Shuffle all of the scrambled word cards together, then hand out five to each student. Time the activity and have them unscramble the words without using notes.

MULTIPLE INTELLIGENCES

Mathematical Ask students to write up an imaginary **cuenta,** like the one in Activity 8, for a restaurant meal that includes food, drink, and desserts for two people. First have them find the current exchange rate for Mexican pesos on the Internet or in a newspaper. Tell students to list the foods and drinks with appropriate prices in pesos. Then have them add all the prices to total up the bill. Ask each student to tell his or her total in Spanish to find out who has the most or the least expensive meal.

Comparisons

Language Note

It is common, especially in Caribbean countries, for people to use the diminutive to talk about food. This is especially true when someone is requesting food, as it seems more polite to ask for something small. So one might hear a guest ask for **un vasito de agua, un juguito,** or **un sandwichito.** Ask students if they do the same thing when requesting food.

8 Answers

1. ¿Me trae una servilleta por favor?
2. Para tomar, quiero un jugo de naranja.
3. Quisiera una sopa de verduras.
4. ¿Nos trae la cuenta, por favor?
5. ¿Me trae una cuchara, por favor?

Comunicación

Pair Activity: Interpersonal

Have students work in pairs and use the sentences they wrote for Activity 9 to prompt a conversation. Ask one student to read a sentence, then have the other student make an appropriate comment or response in the role of either diner or waiter.

MODELO
—¿Qué tal si pruebas la ensalada de frutas?
—¡Ay, no! Nunca pido ensalada. No me gustan las frutas.

Assess

Assessment Program

Prueba: Vocabulario 1, pp. 17–18

Alternative Assessment Guide, pp. 241, 249, 257

Test Generator

STANDARDS: 1.1, 1.2, 1.3, 4.2

Resources

Planning:

Lesson Planner, pp. 16–21, 176–183

 One-Stop Planner

Presentation:

 Video Program
Videocassette 3
DVD Tutor, Disc 2
GramaVisión

Practice:

Grammar Tutor for Students of Spanish, Chapter 6

Cuaderno de vocabulario y gramática, pp. 20–22

Cuaderno de actividades, pp. 15–17

Activities for Communication, pp. 21–22

Video Guide, pp. 54–55

Lab Book, pp. 15–16

Teaching Transparencies
Bell Work 6.2
Vocabulario y gramática answers, pp. 20–22

 Interactive Tutor, Disc 2

Bell Work

Use Bell Work 6.2 in the *Teaching Transparencies,* or write this activity on the board.

Rewrite the conversation in logical order.

1. **¿Y para tomar?**
2. **Quisiera una ensalada.**
3. **¿Algo más?**
4. **¿Qué desea usted?**
5. **Para tomar, quiero un vaso de agua.**

Objetivos
Using ser and estar, pedir and servir, preferir, poder, and probar

Gramática en acción 1

GramaVisión

Interactive TUTOR

Ser and estar

1 Both **ser** and **estar** mean *to be*, but they have different uses. Use **estar** to say where someone is or where something is located, and to ask and say how people are doing.

La servilleta **está** en la mesa. *The napkin is on the table.*
Estoy bien, gracias. *I'm fine, thanks.*

2 You have used **ser** to identify people and things; to say where they are from; to describe what someone or something is like; and to give the day, date, and time.

Ricardo **es** mi amigo. **Es** de México. **Es** alto y simpático.
Es lunes. **Es** el 2 de marzo. **Son** las cuatro en punto.

3 Both **ser** and **estar** can be used to describe foods and drinks. Use **ser** to describe what foods and drinks are normally like.

—¿Cómo **es** el arroz con pollo? *What is chicken and rice like?*
—**Es** riquísimo. *It's delicious.*

To say how something looks, tastes, or feels at a particular moment, use **estar**.

—¿Cómo **está** tu sopa? *How is your soup?*
—**Está** fría. *It's cold.*

Online
Vocabulario y gramática, pp. 20–22 | Actividades, pp. 15–17

Nota cultural

Corn is a food staple in many Spanish-speaking countries, but Mexico claims it as its own. The first varieties of corn were grown near the present-day capital, Mexico City, and can be seen in the National Museum of Anthropology. In Nahuatl, the language of the Aztecs, one word for corn was **elotl** *(eh'-lotl)*, which became **elote** in Mexican Spanish. What traditional dishes in the United States use corn as a staple ingredient?

11 ¿Cómo son? ¿Cómo están?

Leamos Decide if these people are talking:
a) about the characteristics of a dish, or
b) about the flavor at a specific moment.

1. La sopa de verduras es buena para ti. a
2. ¡Ay! ¡Qué caliente está la sopa! b
3. Me gusta el flan de la tía Elena. Está rico. b
4. No me gusta el atún. Es muy salado. a
5. Preparan muy bien la salsa aquí. Está deliciosa, ¿verdad? b
6. No nos gusta la salsa. Es muy picante. a
7. ¿Quieres probar mi sándwich? Está rico. b

Core Instruction

TEACHING GRAMÁTICA

1. Review the forms of **ser** and **estar.** **(5 min.)**
2. Go over Point 1. Ask students to suggest additional sentences using the verb **estar.** **(4 min.)**
3. Go over Point 2. Ask students to suggest additional sentences using the verb **ser.** **(5 min.)**
4. Go over Point 3. Give students descriptions of foods, like **Está picante** and have students tell whether you are describing what the food normally tastes like or tastes like right now. **(6 min.)**
5. Have students start a section in their notebooks listing the uses of **ser** and **estar.** Under each use of the verbs, have students include an example sentence. **(10 min.)**

GramaVisión

For a video presentation of **ser** and **estar**, use **el joven G.** For interactive activities, see the *DVD Tutor.*

GramaVisión

Visit Holt Online
go.hrw.com
KEYWORD: EXP1B CH6
Gramática 1 practice

12 ¿Ser o estar?

Leamos/Escribamos Your new pen pal, Carla, has just written to you. Complete the letter with the correct form of the verb in parentheses. Then tell why **ser** or **estar** is used in each item.

Hola. ¿Cómo __1__ (eres/estás)? __2__ (Soy/Estoy) Carla. __3__ (Soy/Estoy) de Chicago. Y tú, ¿de dónde __4__ (eres/estás)? Hoy __5__ (es/está) lunes. __6__ (Son/Están) las diez de la mañana y mis compañeros y yo __7__ (somos/estamos) en la clase de español. La profesora __8__ (es/está) la señora Gámez. La clase de español __9__ (es/está) un poco difícil, pero me gusta.

13 ¿Cómo estás tú?

Escribamos Now write to Carla, answering her questions. Also, tell her about your day, using **ser** and **estar** correctly.

14 ¿Qué tal está...?

Hablemos Imagine you are in a restaurant. The server asks you how the food is. Answer, imagining the flavor of each dish.

MODELO —¿Qué tal el flan?
—Está muy rico.

1.

2.

3.

4.

5.

6.

Comunicación

15 ¿Te gustan?

Hablemos Choose five foods. Take turns with a partner asking each other if you like each of the foods and giving a reason.

MODELO —¿Te gustan los sándwiches de atún?
—Sí, me gustan mucho. Son deliciosos.

Differentiated Instruction

SLOWER PACE LEARNERS

13 To prepare students for Activity 13, read Activity 12 together. Point out the two questions that they must answer and the correct use of **ser** and **estar.** Then, guide them through the description of the class schedule. Tell them that they must describe at least one class, including the time, the teacher's name, and give an opinion about the class. If necessary, write the five steps of the writing activity on the board.

SPECIAL LEARNING NEEDS

Students with Language Impairments Some terms in the cultural text may be challenging for students with language impairments. Their inability to understand these terms may keep them from fully understanding the key concepts. In the **Nota Cultural,** for example, an understanding of the terms *staple, present-day, anthropology,* and *traditional* is necessary to fully understand this cultural concept. You might preview and define these words for students who may struggle with higher-level vocabulary.

12 Answers

1. **estás;** how someone feels
2. **Soy;** identifies a person
3. **Soy;** tells where someone is from
4. **eres;** asks where someone is from
5. **es;** tells day
6. **Son;** tells time
7. **estamos;** tells where someone is
8. **es;** identifies person
9. **es;** describes something

Comunicación

Pair Activity: Interpersonal

Have a taste testing event with small samples of typical foods and juices from Spanish-speaking countries. Label the cups with the names of the food. Have students make a chart to write down words they would use to describe each food or beverage and their opinion of it. After the tasting, allow students to give their opinions and give brief identifications and explanations about the foods that were tasted. Make sure to check district policies about using, handling, and preparing foods for students before planning this activity. Also, check with the school nurse for students who may have serious food allergies.

Communities

Career Path

Ask students to list food-related careers in which they can use Spanish. Many companies do international business; others have a growing Spanish-speaking clientele. You might have students research the Internet to see what American companies in food-related industries have a presence in Spanish-speaking countries. Some ideas are: restaurants, retail companies, wholesale companies, health fields, and science fields.

Resources

Planning:

Lesson Planner, pp. 16–21, 176–183

One-Stop Planner

Presentation:

Video Program
Videocassette 3
DVD Tutor, Disc 2
GramaVisión

Practice:

Grammar Tutor for Students of Spanish, Chapter 6

Cuaderno de vocabulario y gramática, pp. 20–22

Cuaderno de actividades, pp. 15–17

Activities for Communication, pp. 21–22

Video Guide, pp. 54–55

Lab Book, pp. 15–16

Teaching Transparencies
Bell Work 6.3
Vocabulario y gramática answers, pp. 20–22

Audio CD 6, Tr. 12

Interactive Tutor, Disc 2

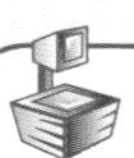

Bell Work

Use Bell Work 6.3 in the *Teaching Transparencies*, or write this activity on the board.

Complete the sentences with the correct form of **ser** or **estar.**

1. La sopa _____ fría. No quiero esta sopa.
2. Mi madre y yo _____ altas.
3. El lápiz _____ encima del escritorio.
4. Los postres de aquí _____ ricos.
5. Es muy tarde. _____ las nueve y media.

Pedir and servir

1 In some **-ir** verbs with an **e** in the stem, this **e** changes to **i** in all the present-tense forms except those of **nosotros(as)** and **vosotros(as).** Two such verbs are **pedir** *(to ask for, to order)* and **servir** *(to serve).*

yo **pido**	nosotros(as) **pedimos**
tú **pides**	vosotros(as) **pedís**
Ud., él, ella **pide**	Uds., ellos, ellas **piden**

—¿Qué vas a **pedir**?
What are you going to order?

—Siempre **pido** una ensalada.
I always order a salad.

yo **sirvo**	nosotros(as) **servimos**
tú **sirves**	vosotros(as) **servís**
Ud., él, ella **sirve**	Uds., ellos, ellas **sirven**

—¿Qué **sirven** en la cafetería?
What do they serve in the cafeteria?

—**Sirven** muchas comidas diferentes.
They serve many different foods.

Online
Vocabulario y gramática, pp. 20–22 | Actividades, pp. 15–17

¿Te acuerdas?

Stem-changing verbs like **dormir** and **querer** do not change in the **nosotros(as)** and **vosotros(as)** forms.

d**ue**rmo	dormimos
d**ue**rmes	dormís
d**ue**rme	d**ue**rmen
qui**e**ro	queremos
qui**e**res	queréis
qui**e**re	qui**e**ren

CD 6, Tr. 12

16 ¿De quién habla?

1. a 2. b 3. a 4. b 5. d 6. c 7. b

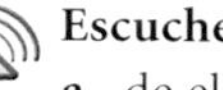

Escuchemos En cada oración, decide si la persona habla...

a. de ella misma *(herself)*
b. de otras personas y ella misma
c. de otras personas
d. de otra persona

17 ¿Qué pedimos?

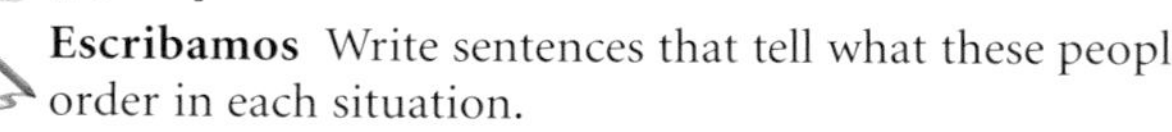

Escribamos Write sentences that tell what these people might order in each situation.

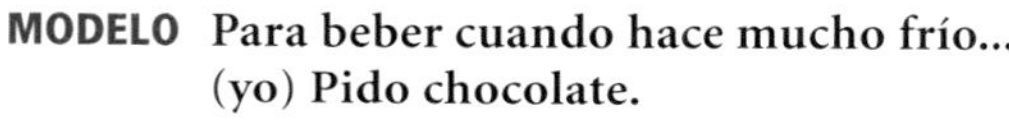

MODELO **Para beber cuando hace mucho frío...**
(yo) Pido chocolate.

Para beber cuando hace mucho calor...

1. yo
2. mis amigos
3. mi familia y yo
4. mi mejor amigo(a)

Para almorzar cuando todos tenemos mucha hambre...

5. yo
6. mi mejor amigo(a)
7. mis padres
8. mis amigos y yo

Core Instruction

TEACHING GRAMÁTICA

1. Go over **¿Te acuerdas?** Ask each student to come up with two or three sentences using stem-changing verbs they've already learned **(almorzar, dormir, empezar, merendar, querer, tener, volver).** Spot check the sentences by having volunteers write their sentences on the board. **(10 min.)**
2. Go over point 1. **(5 min.)**
3. Ask students to add the conjugation of an **e** to **i** stem-changing verb to the verb conjugation chart in their notebooks. **(5 min.)**
4. Review the forms of all of the stem-changing verbs students have learned by calling out a subject pronoun and an infinitive. Ask a volunteer to use the correct form of the verb in a simple sentence. **(5 min.)**

GramaVisión

For a video presentation of **pedir** and **servir,** use **el joven G.** For interactive activities, see the *DVD Tutor.*

GramaVisión

STANDARDS: 1.2

18 ¿Qué servimos?

Hablemos Carlos is telling a friend what these people serve at parties. What is he saying? Use the correct form of the verb **servir** in your answers.

MODELO nosotros
Siempre servimos helado.

nosotros

1. yo

2. tú

3. tus amigos y tú

4. mi hermano y yo

5. mis amigos

6. mi madre

19 ¿Servir o pedir?

Escribamos/Hablemos Completa las preguntas con la forma correcta de **pedir** o **servir**.

1. En un restaurante, ¿ ═══ (pedir/tú) una ensalada o un sándwich? pides
2. ¿Qué refresco generalmente ═══ (pedir) usted? pide
3. ¿Qué ═══ (servir/ellos) en tu restaurante preferido? sirven
4. ¿Qué ═══ (servir/tú) en una fiesta? sirves
5. ¿Qué ═══ (pedir) tus padres en un restaurante mexicano? piden
6. ¿Quién ═══ (servir) la cena *(dinner)* en tu casa? sirve
7. ¿Qué tipo de sándwich ═══ (pedir) tu amigo(a)? pide

Comunicación

20 Una entrevista

Hablemos Use the questions in Activity 19 to interview your partner. Then let your partner ask you the questions.

Gramática 1

16 Script

1. Cuando tengo sed, pido agua.
2. Siempre pedimos flan de postre.
3. Para comer una ensalada, pido un tenedor.
4. Cuando hace frío, pedimos sopa.
5. Siempre pides muchas papas fritas con tu hamburguesa.
6. Primero sirven los refrescos.
7. En mi casa servimos frutas y helado de postre.

18 Answers

1. (Yo) Siempre sirvo sándwiches de jamón y queso.
2. (Tú) Siempre sirves sopa de verduras y ensalada.
3. Siempre sirven pizza.
4. Siempre servimos hamburguesas y papas fritas.
5. Para beber, siempre sirven agua, jugo y refrescos.
6. De postre, siempre sirve ensalada de frutas.

Cultures

Practices and Perspectives

In certain restaurants in some Spanish-speaking countries, an inexpensive lunch menu consists of choosing between two or three complete meals for which substitutions cannot be made. The **menú del día,** or **comidas corridas,** often include a soup, a salad, an appetizer, an entrée, and dessert. The price of the meal usually includes bread and a beverage. Have students experienced a similar practice when dining out in the United States?

Differentiated Instruction

ADVANCED LEARNERS

20 Have students write down their partner's answers for the Activity 20 interview. Call on student volunteers to report to the class their partner's answers, being careful to change the verb form to match the subject **él** or **ella.**

MULTIPLE INTELLIGENCES

20 Linguistic Students with strengths in the linguistic areas of intelligence tend to be skilled at persuasive speaking. Instead of using Activity 19 to interview a partner in Activity 20, allow these students to pair together and pretend that they are having a party, and are trying to convince their friend to choose a particular food or drink item for the party. Their partner can respond with reasons why they don't think that the food/drink item is a good choice.

Comunicación

Individual Activity: Presentational

Students should plan and present a menu for a special occasion. Use the following questions to guide student thinking:
¿Qué vas a celebrar? ¿Qué para comer y beber quieres servir?

STANDARDS: 1.1, 1.2, 1.3, 2.1

Resources

Planning:

Lesson Planner, pp. 16–21, 176–183

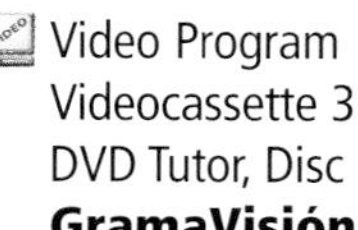

One-Stop Planner

Presentation:

Video Program
Videocassette 3
DVD Tutor, Disc 2
GramaVisión

Practice:

Grammar Tutor for Students of Spanish, Chapter 6

Cuaderno de vocabulario y gramática, pp. 20–22

Cuaderno de actividades, pp. 15–17

Activities for Communication, pp. 21–22

Video Guide, pp. 54–55

Lab Book, pp. 15–16

Teaching Transparencies
Bell Work 6.4
Vocabulario y gramática answers, pp. 20–22

Interactive Tutor, Disc 2

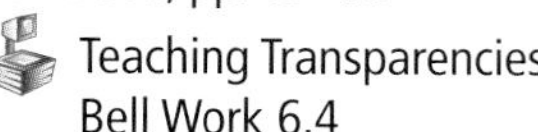

Bell Work

Use Bell Work 6.4 in the *Teaching Transparencies*, or write this activity on the board.

Write the correct form of **pedir** or **servir** in the following sentences.

1. Conchita siempre _____ agua para tomar en los restaurantes.
2. Esteban y Carlos nunca _____ salsa. No les gusta comer nada picante.
3. Mi madre _____ la cena a las ocho todos los días.
4. Javier y yo _____ un sándwich de jamón al mediodía.
5. Los restaurantes mexicanos _____ comida riquísima.

Preferir, poder, and probar

1 The verb **preferir** has an **e** → **ie** stem change. It can be followed by a noun to say what someone *prefers* or by an **infinitive** to say what someone *would rather do* or *prefers to do*.

yo	pref**ie**ro	nosotros(as)	preferimos
tú	pref**ie**res	vosotros(as)	preferís
Ud., él, ella	pref**ie**re	Uds., ellos, ellas	pref**ie**ren

¿**Prefieres** jugo o leche en el almuerzo?
¿**Prefieres salir** o **ver** televisión?

2 The verbs **poder** and **probar** have an **o** → **ue** stem change. **Poder** is normally followed by an **infinitive** to say what someone *may, is able to,* or *can do*. **Probar** means *to try* something, as in *to taste*.

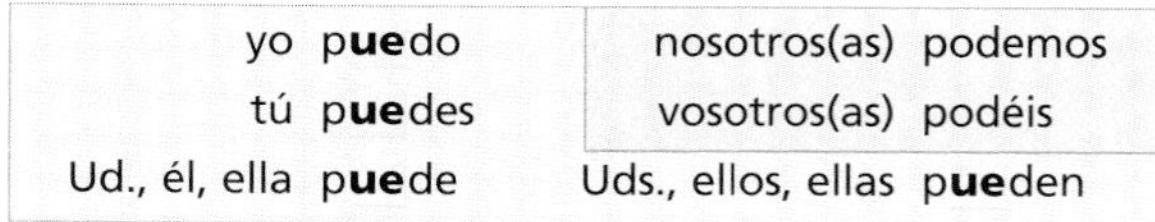

yo	p**ue**do	nosotros(as)	podemos
tú	p**ue**des	vosotros(as)	podéis
Ud., él, ella	p**ue**de	Uds., ellos, ellas	p**ue**den

¿Nos **puede traer** otra silla? *Can you bring us another chair?*

yo	pr**ue**bo	nosotros(as)	probamos
tú	pr**ue**bas	vosotros(as)	probáis
Ud., él, ella	pr**ue**ba	Uds., ellos, ellas	pr**ue**ban

¿Qué tal si **pruebas** la sopa? *How about trying the soup?*

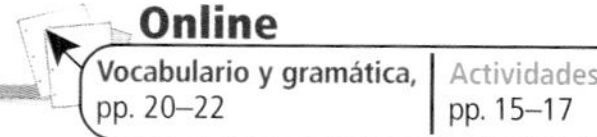

Online
Vocabulario y gramática, pp. 20–22 | Actividades, pp. 15–17

¿Te acuerdas?

Tener and **dormir** are also stem-changing verbs.

Ella t**ie**ne 16 años.
Tú d**ue**rmes mucho.

The **nosotros** and **vosotros** forms do not have stem changes.

Tenéis un perro bonito.
Dormimos más los sábados.

21 Preferir, poder o probar

Escribamos Complete each sentence with the correct form of the verb in parentheses. Then write your own sentence using that same verb and the subject in parentheses.

MODELO Mi tío no _____ (poder) comer flan. (nosotros)
Mi tío no puede comer flan.
No podemos comer hamburguesas.

1. Analisa _____ (preferir) el flan más que el helado. (mis amigos)
2. Yo siempre _____ (probar) la sopa cuando _____ (comer) en restaurantes. (mis amigos y yo)
3. Mi abuela no _____ (poder) comer salsa picante. (mis padres)
4. Nosotros _____ (preferir) almorzar en la cafetería. (usted)
5. Mis hermanas nunca _____ (probar) los postres. No les gustan. (yo)

Core Instruction

TEACHING GRAMÁTICA

1. Go over **¿Te acuerdas? (2 min.)**
2. Go over point 1. What similar verbs have students already learned? (**empezar, merendar, querer, tener, venir**) **(4 min.)**
3. Have each student use **preferir** in a sentence. Ask volunteers to write their sentences on the board for the class to check. **(7 min.)**
4. Go over point 2. What similar verbs have students already learned? (**almorzar, dormir, llover, volver**) **(4 min.)**
5. Have each student use **poder** and **probar** in a sentence. Ask volunteers to write their sentences on the board for the class to check. **(8 min.)**

GramaVisión

For a video presentation of **preferir, poder,** and **probar,** use **el joven G.** For interactive activities, see the *DVD Tutor.*

GramaVisión

22 ¿Qué prueban?

Escribamos/Hablemos Based on what these people like, say what dish they always try when they go to a new restaurant.

MODELO **A Lucinda le gustan los postres. Ella... Ella siempre prueba el flan.**

1. A Andrés le gusta el atún. Él...
2. A ustedes les gusta el postre. Ustedes...
3. A Linda y a Jorge les gusta el jamón. Ellos...
4. A Elsa y a mí nos gustan las frutas. Nosotras...
5. Lucinda, a ti te gustan las verduras. Tú...
6. A mí me gustan el queso y la salsa de tomate. Yo...

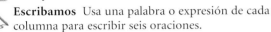

Probando platos en un restaurante, Ciudad de México

23 Rompecabezas

Escribamos Usa una palabra o expresión de cada columna para escribir seis oraciones.

MODELO **Prefiero tomar jugo.**

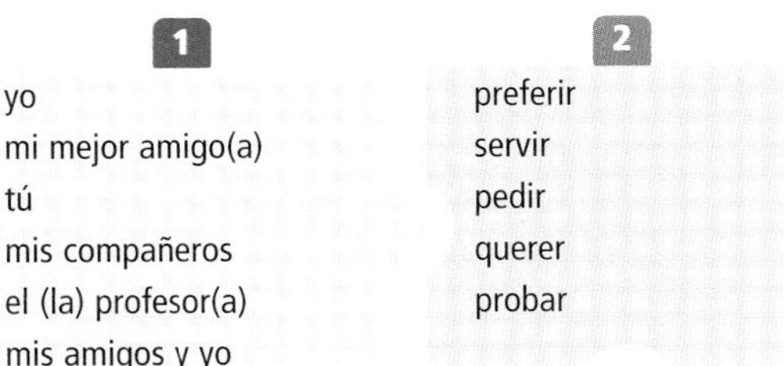

1	2	3
yo	preferir	la cuenta
mi mejor amigo(a)	servir	tomar jugo o leche
tú	pedir	una sopa de...
mis compañeros	querer	comida italiana
el (la) profesor(a)	probar	una ensalada de...
mis amigos y yo		algo de postre

Comunicación

24 ¿Qué prefieres hacer?

Escribamos/Hablemos Write what you like to do at each of the indicated times. Then ask three classmates what they like to do. Try to find someone who likes the same things that you like.

MODELO **—¿Qué prefieres hacer los viernes por la noche?**
—Prefiero... ¿Y tú?

1. los jueves por la noche
2. los sábados por la tarde
3. los sábados por la mañana
4. los domingos por la mañana
5. los domingos por la noche
6. los martes por la tarde
7. los miércoles por la noche
8. los lunes por la mañana

Gramática 1

21 Answers

Sentences will vary.
1. prefiere
2. pruebas
3. puede
4. preferimos
5. prueban

22 Answers

1. ...prueba el sándwich de atún.
2. ...prueban el helado.
3. ...prueban el sándwich de jamón.
4. ...probamos la ensalada de frutas.
5. ...pruebas la sopa de verduras.
6. ...pruebo el sándwich de queso.

Comunicación

Class Activity: Interpersonal

Develop a set of forced choice questions. **(¿Prefieres la leche o el jugo de naranja? ¿Prefieres el atún o el jamón?)** Give each student an index card with a different question on it. Organize the students into two concentric circles facing each other. Students should take turns asking the person facing them the question on their card. Give a signal and instruct one of the circles to rotate. As a follow-up, ask some of the questions to the entire class.

Differentiated Instruction

SLOWER PACE LEARNERS

23 Before assigning Activity 23, go over the verb conjugations together in class. Use the subjects in column one and have volunteers conjugate the verbs in column 2 for each of the different subjects. Read the phrases in column 3 together. Ask students which verbs would mostly likely be used with each phrase.

SPECIAL LEARNING NEEDS

21 Students with Learning Disabilities/ Dyslexia To modify Activity 21 so that students focus on the correct conjugation of the new verbs (without stumbling over writing out the full sentences), provide a "fill in the blank" format for students to complete. Each item will have two sentences, each with a blank where the verb should be written correctly.

Assess

Assessment Program

Prueba: Gramática 1, pp. 19–20

Prueba: Aplicación 1, pp. 21–22

Alternative Assessment Guide, pp. 241, 249, 257

Audio CD 6, Tr. 25

Test Generator

STANDARDS: 1.1, 1.2, 1.3

Cultura

VideoCultura

Resources

Planning:

Lesson Planner, pp. 21–22, 182–183

 One-Stop Planner

Presentation:

Audio CD 6, Tr. 13–15

 Video Program
Videocassette 3
DVD Tutor, Disc 2
VideoCultura

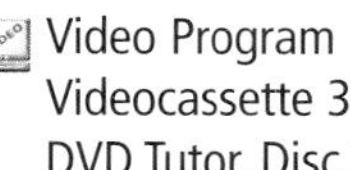

Practice:

Cuaderno de actividades, p. 18

Cuaderno para hispanohablantes, pp. 45–52

Video Guide, pp. 54–55, 57

Lab Book, p. 39

 Interactive Tutor, Disc 2

Atlas INTERACTIVO MUNDIAL

Have students use the interactive atlas at **go.hrw.com.**

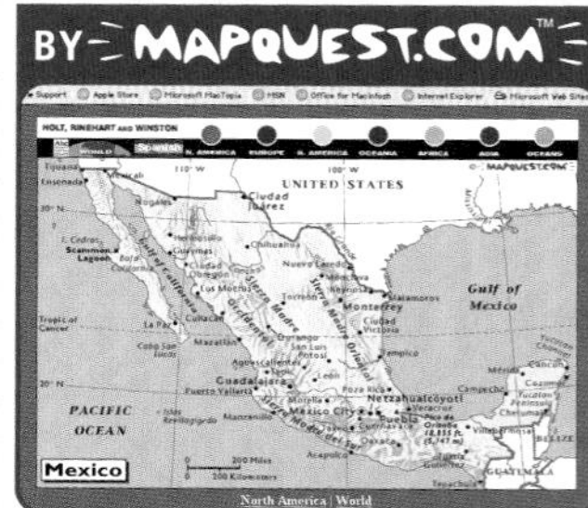

Map Activities

Using Map Transparencies 4 and 5 for reference, have students tell what they know about Mexico and the Dominican Republic. Have them locate Mexico City and Santo Domingo on these maps.

Heritage Speakers

Ask heritage speakers or students who have lived in or traveled to a Spanish-speaking country to help compile a list of foods that are generally unknown in the U.S.

Comparaciones

CD 6, Trs. 13–15

Platos típicos mexicanos

¿Cuál es tu plato preferido y cómo es?

«A buena hambre no hay mal pan» dice el refrán, y ¿qué mejor pan que un plato que nos encanta? Todos tenemos un plato preferido que no sólo es delicioso sino que muchas veces nos hace recordar a nuestra familia, nuestro país de origen y nuestras costumbres. En Estados Unidos, ¿qué platos son regionales o nacionales? ¿Son éstos algunos de tus platos preferidos? ¿Cuáles son algunos platos preferidos de los jóvenes en otros países?

Angélica
Ciudad de México, México

Angélica describes her favorite dish and how it is made. Are any of your favorite dishes similar to the ones Angélica describes?

Dime, ¿cuáles son dos o tres platos típicos de México?

Bueno, está el mole, el pozole y los chiles en nogada.

¿Cuál es tu plato favorito?

Los chiles en nogada.

Dime cómo es.

Son muy ricos porque además de ser picantes, también son dulces.

¿Qué llevan?

Bueno, tiene el chile poblano, la carne molida, pasitas, acitrón, crema, nueces y un poquito de granada.

¿Es un plato típico de la región donde vives?

Claro, en el Distrito Federal se consume mucho.

Muchas gracias, Angélica.

No hay de qué, al contrario.

Core Instruction

TEACHING CULTURA

1. Read and discuss the introductory paragraph as a class. How would students answer the question about their own favorite foods? **(10 min.)**
2. Have students watch the two interviews on video using the *Video Program* or the *DVD Tutor.* Have students listen for the food items they are familiar with that the interviewees mention. **(10 min.)**
3. Have students answer the questions in the **Para comprender** section with a partner. Discuss **Para pensar y hablar** with the class. **(10 min.)**

VideoCultura

For a video presentation of the interviews as well as for additional interviews, see Chapter 6 **VideoCultura** on Videocassette or on DVD. For interactive practice, see the *DVD Tutor.*

VideoCultura

Visit Holt Online
go.hrw.com
KEYWORD: EXP1B CH6
Online Edition

Paula
Santo Domingo, República Dominicana

Paula describes typical Dominican dishes. Are any typical dishes from where you live similar to Dominican dishes?

Dime, ¿cuáles son unos platos típicos en la República Dominicana?
El plato más típico de la República Dominicana es el arroz con habichuela y carne, que puede ser de res o pollo.

¿Cuál es tu plato favorito?
El moro de guandules con pescado.

¿Me puedes decir cómo es?
El moro de guandules es una mezcla de guandules con arroz y un poco de salsa para el color. Y el pescado se hace con el limón y sal y ajo.

¿Es un plato típico de tu región?
Sí, es muy típico.

Muchas gracias, Paula.
Gracias a ti.

Cultura

Para comprender

1. ¿Qué plato se come mucho en el Distrito Federal?
2. ¿Cómo es el plato preferido de Paula?
3. ¿Cuáles son tres platos típicos de México?
4. ¿Cómo son los chiles en nogada?
5. ¿Qué se come con el arroz con habichuelas?
6. ¿Cuál es el plato más típico de la República Dominicana?

Para pensar y hablar

Angélica and Paula tell us about their favorite dishes, both of which are typical of their countries. How are their favorite dishes different? Do they seem simple to make or do they seem rather complicated? Are there foods unique to where you live? What are they?

Cuaderno para hispanohablantes, pp. 57–68

Comunidad

¡Tacos, enchiladas y más!

Thousands of restaurants serve international food in the United States. Immigrants can keep cultural traditions alive by serving familiar foods. How many restaurants from Spanish-speaking countries are there in your town? Visit one of these restaurants with your family or friends.

- Is the menu in English, Spanish, or both languages?
- Ask the server if there is a specialty of the house.
- Order your meal and ask for the check in Spanish.
- Write a paragraph about the meal to share with the class.

Un restaurante, tex-mex en Austin, Texas

Differentiated Instruction

ADVANCED LEARNERS

Have students select a Spanish-speaking country and research foods typical of that country. Tell them to list the typical dishes and have them choose a recipe for one of those dishes. They can present the dishes and recipe using real foods or illustrations. Ask them to share their findings with the rest of the class.

SPECIAL LEARNING NEEDS

Students with Learning Disabilities Some new terms in the interview may be challenging for students with learning disabilities. Before playing the video, make a list of the key dishes each interviewee will mention. Play the video one time, and have students mark an "A" for the foods Angélica mentions and a "P" for the foods Paula mentions. Then, play the video again for students and have them tell what they could understand. You might use the captioned version from the DVD to help further their understanding.

Para comprender Answers

1. Chiles en nogada.
2. Es gandules con arroz y salsa con pescado.
3. El mole, el pozole y los chiles en nogada.
4. Son dulces y picantes
5. La carne.
6. Arroz con habichuela y carne.

Cultures

Products and Perspectives

Along streets in Mexico, one finds many fruit, ice cream, **paleta,** and **jugo** stands. The iced **paletas** can be any flavor—even corn or avocado. While smoothies shops in the United States are a newer phenomenon, they have long been popular in Mexico. **Licuados** of fruit and egg, in a base of orange or carrot juice, **alfalfa y limón, betabel,** or milk (called an **eskimo**), are enjoyed throughout Mexico. Ask students how mass production of food and the proliferation of "chains" in the United States have affected our consumption habits.

Communities

Community Link

Ask students to interview someone in your school or community who is from another country. Instruct them to get the following information:

- where the person is from
- the names of two typical dishes from his or her country
- what is in each dish
- a description of any unknown ingredients
- if the dish is usually prepared for special occasions
- which of the dishes the person prefers and why
- if any restaurants in your community serve these dishes

STANDARDS: 1.2, 2.2, 4.2, 5.1, 5.2

Resources

Planning:

Lesson Planner, pp. 22–27, 182–189

One-Stop Planner

Presentation:

TPR Storytelling Book, pp. 32–33

Teaching Transparencies **Vocabulario** 6.3, 6.4

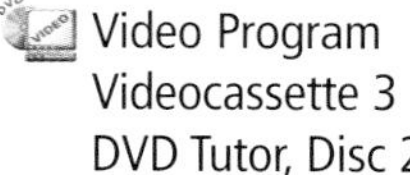
Video Program
Videocassette 3
DVD Tutor, Disc 2
ExpresaVisión

Practice:

Cuaderno de vocabulario y gramática, pp. 23–25

Activities for Communication, pp. 23–24

Video Guide, pp. 54–55, 58

Lab Book, pp. 17–18, 40

Teaching Transparencies
Bell Work 6.5
Vocabulario y gramática answers, pp. 23–25

Interactive Tutor, Disc 2

Bell Work

Use Bell Work 6.5 in the *Teaching Transparencies*, or write this activity on the board.

Unscramble the words and conjugate the verbs to write logical sentences.

1. **amigo/ensalada/Andrés/mi/preferir/la**
2. **nuestra/helado/poder/familia/no/comer**
3. **hermano/probar/tu/nuevo/nunca/nada**
4. **yo/siempre/los/probar/todos/postres**
5. **padre/comida/la/nuestro/preferir/caliente**

Objetivos
Talking about meals, offering help, giving instructions

Vocabulario en acción 2

Video/DVD
ExpresaVisión

El desayuno en casa

los cereales
el durazno
el chocolate
la naranja
la manzana
el café con leche
el pan dulce
el pan tostado
el tocino
los huevos

También se puede decir...

Some Spanish speakers say **un melocotón** instead of **un durazno.**

In some parts of Mexico and Central America, speakers refer to an egg as **un blanquillo.**

Core Instruction

TEACHING VOCABULARIO

1. Introduce the vocabulary, using transparencies **Vocabulario 6.3** and **6.4.** Model the pronunciation of each item as you point to the appropriate picture. **(12 min.)**
2. Call out the names of foods (including those students learned previously), and have volunteers tell whether they normally eat the food at breakfast or at lunch/dinner. For example, if you call out **los cereales,** a student might respond **Siempre desayuno cereales** or **Como cereales para el desayuno. (6 min.)**
3. Tell students what you usually have for breakfast, then ask what they have, using **¿Qué desayunas?** Then ask students what they would like to have for lunch and dinner today using **¿Qué quieres hoy de almuerzo/cena? (7 min.)**

ExpresaVisión

Use the video presenter to teach the new food and meal vocabulary. For interactive activities, see the *DVD Tutor.*

ExpresaVisión

STANDARDS: 1.2

Visit Holt Online
go.hrw.com
KEYWORD: EXP1B CH6
Vocabulario 2 practice

¿Qué hay de cena?

el pollo

la carne

el maíz

las zanahorias

el bróculi

las espinacas

el pastel

También se puede decir...

For many Spanish speakers, *corn on the cob* is **la mazorca.** In Mexico and Central America, it is **el elote.** And in Andean countries, such as Bolivia and Ecuador, it is called **el choclo.**

¡Exprésate!

To talk about meals

Interactive TUTOR

¿Qué desayunas? *What do you have for breakfast?*	**Siempre desayuno cereales con leche.** *I always have cereal with milk for breakfast.*
¿Qué quieres hoy de almuerzo? *What do you want for lunch today?*	**¿Qué tal si almorzamos ensalada de pollo?** *How about we have chicken salad for lunch?*
¿Qué hay de cena? Tengo mucha hambre. *What is there for dinner? I'm very hungry.*	**Vamos a cenar pescado, arroz y espinacas.** *We're going to have fish, rice, and spinach for dinner.*

Online
Vocabulario y gramática, pp. 23–25

▶ **Vocabulario adicional** — Comida, p. R11

Vocabulario 2

T P R
Total Physical Response

Present and model the commands. Point out to students how to do a good role-play, for example, when asked to try a coffee, they could blow on it first and then hold the handle of the cup to taste it.

Prueba las papas fritas. Ten cuidado. Están calientes.

Prepara cereales con leche.

Dale media naranja a...

Prepara un huevo para tu desayuno.

Prueba el tocino que está muy salado.

Sírvele un café a...

Connections

Language Note

In Central and South America there are a number of different terms for coffee and the way it is served. A **cafecito** is served in a very small cup containing only a few sips, while a **grande** is served in a normal size coffee cup. A **marrón (marroncito)** has a little milk, and **café con leche** is quite milky, and is often served with steamed milk. A **negro (negrito)** is served black. Ask students if they know different terms for coffee in English.

Differentiated Instruction

Advanced Learners

Give students a copy of a food pyramid, available from the U.S. Department of Agriculture website (www.usda.gov). Have them write the Spanish names for different kinds of foods and drinks into the sections of the pyramid. Some foods, such as **quesadillas,** will fit into more than one section of the food pyramid (dairy and breads).

Special Learning Needs

Students with Learning Disabilities Reinforce the vocabulary by asking students to group the food under different categories like vegetables, fruits, meats, beverages etc.

También se puede decir...

Students may hear various terms for *cake*. In Puerto Rico and the Dominican Republic, they could hear **bizcocho,** while in Venezuela, Argentina, and Uruguay the word **torta** is used. Puerto Ricans generally refer to an *orange* as a **china** while reserving the word **naranja** for a much more sour variant.

27 Possible Answers

1. Juana, ¿por qué no pruebas los tacos de pollo?
2. Julio, ¿qué tal si pruebas el helado de mango?
3. ¿Por qué no prueben Uds. el jugo de...?
4. ¿Qué tal si probamos el arroz con pollo?
5. Carmen, ¿qué tal si pruebas los tacos de verduras?
6. Julio, ¿por qué no pruebas la sopa de pescado?
7. Tere, ¿qué tal si pruebas el pastel de chocolate?
8. ¿Qué tal si Uds. prueban la ensalada de atún?
9. Eduardo, ¿por qué no pruebas una ensalada, una sopa, el arroz con pollo y....

Cultures

Practices and Perspectives

Eating Lunch at Home Many students in Spanish-speaking countries such as Mexico and Spain leave school to eat lunch at home. These students take a much longer lunch break than is common in the United States, but they get to spend more time with their families and probably eat a healthier lunch than many American students eat. Ask students to discuss some pros and cons of eating lunch at home. Also, ask them what conclusions they might be able to draw about the importance of family time in the Spanish-speaking world.

Nota cultural

In the United States, dinner is considered the main meal of the day, while lunch is a lighter meal. In Mexico and Spain, the biggest meal of the day, **la comida,** is served around 2:00 P.M. Family members come home from work and school to eat together. **La cena,** a light meal, ends the day around 9:00 P.M. For Chileans and Colombians, **la cena** is a formal evening meal for special occasions. Most days they eat a light supper early in the evening. How do your meal times compare?

25 Tengo mucha hambre

Leamos Completa las oraciones con las palabras más lógicas.

1. ¿Qué hay de ____ ? Tengo mucha hambre.
   a. tomar **(b.)** cena **c.** pastel
2. Hoy vamos a almorzar ____.
   a. cereales **b.** pan dulce **(c.)** pollo
3. No me gustan los postres. Voy a comer ____.
   a. flan **b.** pastel **(c.)** un durazno
4. Ricardo siempre desayuna cereales con ____.
   (a.) leche **b.** zanahorias **c.** arroz
5. Me encantan las verduras. Siempre como muchas ____.
   a. naranjas **(b.)** espinacas **c.** manzanas
6. No me gusta el ____. Es muy salado.
   (a.) tocino **b.** pastel **c.** durazno

26 ¿Desayuno o cena?

Hablemos Which of these foods do you eat for breakfast and which ones do you eat for dinner?

MODELO **los huevos**
Siempre como huevos para el desayuno.

1. el tocino desayuno
2. el pescado cena
3. las espinacas cena
4. las zanahorias cena
5. el arroz con pollo cena
6. el pan tostado desayuno
7. el maíz cena
8. el bróculi cena
9. el café con leche desayuno
10. los cereales con leche desayuno

Restaurante Don José

PLATOS DEL DÍA
Ensalada de atún
Arroz con pollo
Tacos de pollo
Sopa de pescado
Tacos de verduras

BEBIDAS
Refrescos
Jugos
(de manzana, de naranja, de zanahoria)

POSTRES
Pastel de chocolate
Helado de mango

27 En el restaurante

Leamos/Escribamos Suggest something for each of the following people from the menu at **Restaurante Don José.**

MODELO **A Alicia le gustan los postres.**
Alicia, ¿qué tal si pruebas el pastel?

1. Juana quiere probar comida mexicana.
2. De postre, Julio prefiere comer algo muy frío.
3. De tomar, Elena y su amigo quieren un jugo.
4. A Manolo y a mí nos gusta el pollo.
5. Carmen nunca pide carne.
6. A Julio le gusta el pescado.
7. Tere siempre pide algo con chocolate para el postre.
8. Pablo y María quieren cenar pero no pueden comer carne.
9. Eduardo tiene mucha hambre. Quiere una cena grande.

Game

Sobre la mesa

1. Bring in as many items or photos of items from **Vocabulario 2,** pp. 54–55, as possible. **2.** Place the items on a table or desk and cover them with a cloth. Divide the students into teams. **3.** Have all students gather around the table or desk as you remove the cloth. Give students two minutes to study the items on the table. **4.** At the end of two minutes, replace the cloth and have students regroup into their teams. **5.** Give teams three minutes to make a list in Spanish of as many of the items as they can remember. **6.** The team with the most complete list wins.

STANDARDS: 1.2, 2.1

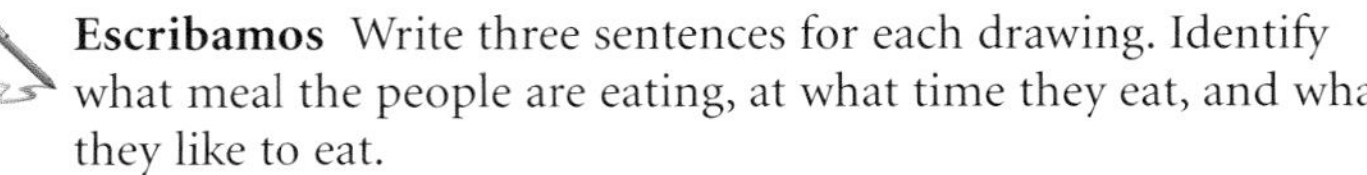

28 Tienen hambre

Escribamos Write three sentences for each drawing. Identify what meal the people are eating, at what time they eat, and what they like to eat.

8:00

13:00

19:00

29 Y yo como...

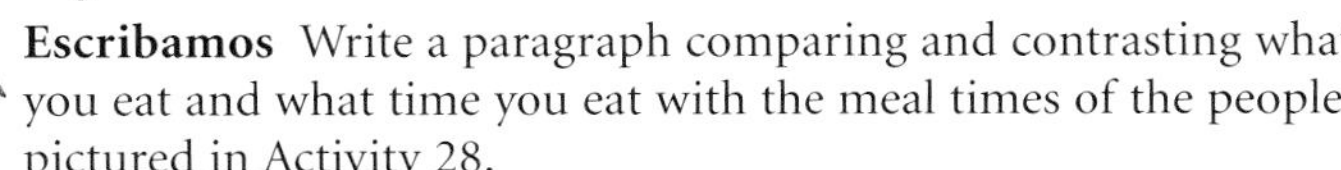

Escribamos Write a paragraph comparing and contrasting what you eat and what time you eat with the meal times of the people pictured in Activity 28.

Comunicación

30 ¿Qué comes tú?

Hablemos Work with a partner. Take turns asking and answering the following questions.

1. ¿Qué desayunas?
2. ¿Dónde almuerzas?
3. ¿A qué hora cenas?
4. ¿Qué vas a cenar esta noche?
5. ¿Te gustan las comidas picantes?
6. ¿Cuál es tu jugo preferido?

31 ¿Qué van a pedir?

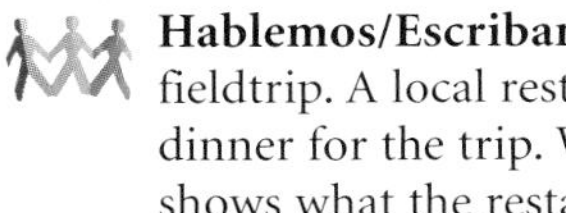

Hablemos/Escribamos Imagine that you are going on an all-day fieldtrip. A local restaurant is going to cater breakfast, lunch, and dinner for the trip. With a group of classmates, make a menu that shows what the restaurant will offer for each meal. Then ask two members of your group what they are going to order. (**¿Qué vas a pedir?**) Be prepared to role-play a scene where you order meals, pretend to eat the meal, and comment on the food.

Vocabulario 2

28 Possible Answers

1. Ella desayuna. Son las 8:00 de la mañana. Le gusta comer los cereales con leche, café,...
2. Los muchachos almuerzan. Es la una de la tarde. Ellos comen sándwiches, manzanas y beben leche.
3. Ella cena. Son las 7:00 de la noche. Le gusta comer una hamburguesa y papas fritas. Ella bebe...

Connections

Language Note

The Spanish language has many verbs that refer to eating. **Desayunar** means *to eat breakfast.* **Almorzar** means *to eat lunch,* and **cenar** means *to eat dinner.* **Merendar** is a verb that means *to eat a snack.* **La merienda** is a snack or picnic.

Comunicación

Pair Work: Interpersonal

Ask students to work with a partner to compare:

- breakfasts they eat on school days with those they eat on weekends
- lunches they eat on school days with those they eat on weekends

Ask them to note similarities and differences (meal time, foods eaten, with whom, where).

Differentiated Instruction

SLOWER PACE LEARNERS

Slower Pace Have students create a poster that illustrates the foods they like to eat/drink at their favorite meal. Instruct them to write the name of the meal (DESAYUNO, ALMUERZO, CENA) in large, colorful letters vertically in the center of the paper, then to use the letters of that word to make words of foods they like. Ask them to display their posters in class.

MODELO Carne
lEche
flaN
Arroz

MULTIPLE INTELLIGENCES

Naturalist Ask students to imagine they are chefs in a new restaurant. Their first job is to create a dish that will become the house specialty. Have them follow these instructions:

- create and name the dish
- list the ingredients in English and Spanish
- look up any ingredient words you do not know in Spanish
- give a short description of the dish (**Es rico, un poco salado y picante**).

Ask each student to introduce his or her new creation to the class.

STANDARDS: 1.1, 1.3, 4.1

Resources

Planning:

Lesson Planner, pp. 22–27, 182–189

 One-Stop Planner

Presentation:

TPR Storytelling Book, pp. 32–33

 Teaching Transparencies **Vocabulario** 6.3, 6.4

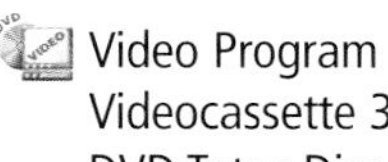 Video Program
Videocassette 3
DVD Tutor, Disc 2
ExpresaVisión

Practice:

Cuaderno de vocabulario y gramática, pp. 23–25

Activities for Communication, pp. 23–24

Video Guide, pp. 54–55, 58

Lab Book, pp. 17–18, 40

 Teaching Transparencies **Vocabulario y gramática** answers, pp. 23–25

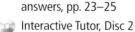

 Interactive Tutor, Disc 2

Connections

Language to Language

You might tell students that there are many history lessons contained in the names for foods. **Café** is thought to come from Kaffa, the name of the Ethiopian province where coffee was first discovered. An indigenous plant in the Ethiopian highlands and other parts of tropical Africa, it is now cultivated in many parts of the world. **Arroz** comes from an Arabic word. Rice was first cultivated more than 6000 years ago in China, where Arab traders encountered it. It was introduced to Spain by the Moors during their rule, which began in 711 AD. The Spaniards then brought it to the Americas in colonial times.

¡Exprésate!

Interactive TUTOR

To offer help	To give instructions
¿Necesitas ayuda? *Do you need help?*	**Sí, saca el pollo y ponlo en el horno (el microondas).** *Yes, get out the chicken and put it in the oven (the microwave).*
¿Puedo ayudar? *Can I help?*	**Saca el flan del refrigerador.** *Take the flan out of the refrigerator.* **¿Por qué no preparas los sándwiches?** *Why don't you make the sandwiches?*
¿Pongo la mesa? *Shall I set the table?*	**Sí, ponla, por favor.** *Yes, set it, please.*

Online
Vocabulario y gramática, pp. 23–25

CD 6, Tr. 16

32 ¿En qué puedo ayudar?

Escuchemos Mira las fotos y escucha la conversación entre Patricia y su madre. Decide qué parte del diálogo corresponde a cada foto.

1. C 2. A 3. B 4. D 5. E

A 
B 
C 
D 
E 

33 La cena

Leamos Marlena and her mother are talking about how she can help with the dinner preparations. For each of Marlena's questions, choose her mother's probable response.

Marlena	La madre
1. ¿Necesitas ayuda, mamá? c	a. Sí, ponlo en el horno.
2. ¿Saco las frutas del refrigerador? g	b. Sí, ¿por qué no preparas el flan?
3. ¿Necesitas un plato hondo? f	c. Sí, hija, necesito ayuda.
4. ¿Pongo el pollo en el horno? a	d. Sí, y tenedores también.
5. ¿Pongo la mesa en la cocina? e	e. No, ponla en el comedor, por favor.
6. ¿Necesito poner cuchillos? d	f. Sí. ¿Me traes un plato hondo?
7. ¿Puedo ayudar con el postre? b	g. Sí, saca las frutas, por favor.

Core Instruction

TEACHING ¡EXPRÉSATE!

1. Introduce the new expressions in **¡Exprésate!**, modeling the pronunciation of each new word and phrase. **(10 min.)**
2. Ask students what they can deduce about the words **saca** and **ponla.** What are the infinitives of these verbs? How are they being used? What does the **lo** on the end of **ponlo** probably refer to? What about the **la** on the end of **ponla** in the sentence: **Sí, ponla, por favor.** Tell students they will learn more about commands and pronouns later in the chapter. **(5 min.)**

STANDARDS: 1.2

34 Mucha ayuda

Leamos Read the questions and match them with a picture.

1. ¿Necesitas ayuda con tus hermanos? b
2. ¿Por qué no sacas más leche del refrigerador? d
3. Hijo, ¿me traes el libro, por favor? a
4. ¿Puedo ayudar con la tarea? c

A

B

C

D

35 ¿Cómo te ayudo?

Escribamos Write this conversation between Rita and José who are preparing a special breakfast for their mother's birthday.

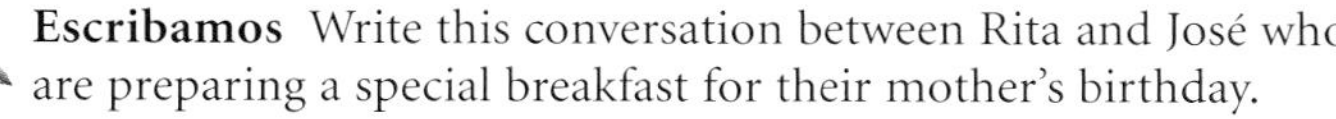

tocino	refrigerador	duraznos	saca
ponla	pongo	ayudar	preparas

José ¿Puedo ___ con el desayuno? ayudar
Rita Sí, ¿por qué no ___ el pan tostado? preparas
José Bueno. ¿Saco el jugo de naranja del ___ también? refrigerador
Rita Sí, ___ el jugo, y ponlo en la mesa. saca
José ¿Preparas huevos con ___? tocino
Rita No, mamá prefiere cereales con ___. duraznos
José ¿___ la mesa en la cocina? Pongo
Rita No, ___ en el patio, porque hace buen tiempo. ponla

Comunicación

36 Sí, por favor

Escribamos/Hablemos With a partner, write a dialog between a child and parent getting ready to serve a meal. Then take turns with another pair of classmates role-playing your dialogs. You can say . . .

¿Cómo puedo ayudar?	¿Por qué no me ayudas con...?
¿Pongo...?	Pon..., por favor.
¿Saco... del refrigerador?	Sí, saca... del refrigerador.

Vocabulario 2

32 Scripts

1. —¿En qué puedo ayudar?
—Saca el bróculi del refrigerador.
2. —¿Pongo el bróculi en el horno?
—No, ponlo en el microondas.
3. —¿En qué puedo ayudar?
— Pon la mesa, por favor.
4. —¿Necesitas ayuda?
—Sí, saca las zanahorias del refrigerador, por favor.
5. —¿Pongo el bróculi en la mesa?
—Sí, ponlo en la mesa.

Extension

35 Have students act out the conversation with a partner.

Comunicación

Pair Activity: Interpersonal

Photocopy the statements below and give one to each pair of students. For part A, instruct one partner to read a statement **(Quiero preparer el pollo).** The other partner responds by giving instructions **(Pon el pollo en el horno).** For part B, the first partner again reads a statement **(¡Tengo mucha tarea!)** and the other partner responds with a question offering help **(¿Necesitas ayuda con la tarea?)** Then have the partners switch roles.

A. Quiero...preparar el pollo.
...beber un vaso de leche.
...cenar en casa.

B. ¡Tengo mucha tarea!
No hay platos en las mesa.
Tengo sed.
Tengo tres hermanos, ¡y mamá no está en casa!

Differentiated Instruction

SLOWER PACE LEARNERS

Extension Ask pairs of students to rewrite the conversation in Activity 35, changing the name of the meal and the food items mentioned. Then have them act out the new conversation.

Variety Write out the conversation in Activity 35 as a cloze activity, leaving out every 4th or 5th word. Give copies to students and ask them to fill in words that complete the conversation.

SPECIAL LEARNING NEEDS

Students with ADD To help your ADD students more successfully complete the activities on these pages, read the instructions out loud, slowly, and do an example for each activity. Then pair the students with a partner to complete the activities together. Allow extra time if needed.

Assess

Assessment Program

Prueba: Vocabulario 2, pp. 23–24

Alternative Assessment Guide, pp. 241, 249, 257

Test Generator

STANDARDS: 1.1, 1.2, 1.3

Resources

Planning:

Lesson Planner, pp. 27–33, 186–193

 One-Stop Planner

Presentation:

 Video Program
Videocassette 3,
DVD Tutor, Disc 2
GramaVisión

Practice:

Grammar Tutor for Students of Spanish, Chapter 6

Cuaderno de vocabulario y gramática, pp. 26–28

Cuaderno de actividades, pp. 19–21

Activities for Communication, pp. 23–24

Video Guide, pp. 54–55

Lab Book, pp. 17–18

 Teaching Transparencies
Bell Work 6.6
Vocabulario y gramática answers, pp. 26–28

Interactive Tutor, Disc 2

Bell Work

Use Bell Work 6.6 in the *Teaching Transparencies*, or write this activity on the board.

For each list, give the correct category of food or meal.

1. los huevos, el pan tostado, el tocino
2. el sándwich, la sopa, la manzana
3. la manzana, la naranja, el durazno
4. el arroz con pollo, las zanahorias
5. el flan, el helado

COMMON ERROR ALERT ¡OJO!

Since the direct object pronouns **la, los,** and **las** look exactly like definite articles, students may replace the direct object **el libro** with the definite article **el** instead of the direct object pronoun **lo**.

Objetivos
Using direct objects, direct object pronouns, and affirmative informal commands with pronouns

Gramática en acción 2

GramaVisión

Interactive TUTOR

Direct objects and direct object pronouns

1 Verbs can be followed by **direct objects**, the person or thing receiving the action of the verb.

Rafaela pone **la mesa**. Siempre pido **la sopa**.

2 A **direct object** can be a noun or a pronoun. Use **direct object pronouns** to avoid repeating nouns that have already been mentioned. These pronouns must agree with the nouns they stand for.

	Masculine	Feminine
SINGULAR	**lo** *him, it*	**la** *her, it*
PLURAL	**los** *them*	**las** *them*

—¿Quién va a pedir el flan? —Yo **lo** voy a pedir.

3 **Direct object pronouns** go before the conjugated verb. If there is an infinitive in the sentence, the pronouns go before the conjugated verb or are attached to the end of the infinitive.

—¿Quién prepara los sándwiches? —Yo **los** preparo.
—¿Quién va a preparar la cena? —Mi padre **la** va a preparar.
—Mi padre va a preparar**la**.

Online
Vocabulario y gramática, pp. 26–28 | Actividades, pp. 19–21

¿Te acuerdas?

Pronouns take the place of nouns. They have different forms depending on how they're being used in the sentence.

Ana es mi amiga. **Ella** es muy simpática. **La** llamo por teléfono todos los días.

37 ¿Qué comes?

Leamos/Escribamos Answer the questions, using the correct direct object pronoun.

1. —¿Comes huevos en el desayuno?
   —Sí, ____ como todos los días. los
2. —¿Pides tocino con los huevos?
   —No, nunca ____ pido. lo
3. —¿Tomas leche en el desayuno?
   —No, nunca ____ tomo. la
4. —¿Comes naranjas por la mañana?
   —Sí, siempre ____ como. las

Core Instruction

TEACHING GRAMÁTICA

1. Go over **¿Te acuerdas?** **(2 min.)**
2. Go over Point 1. Have students suggest first English sentences, then Spanish sentences that have direct objects. **(6 min.)**
3. Go over Point 2. Ask students what words we use for direct object pronouns in English *(me, you, him, her, it,* etc.*)* Give students a variety of nouns in Spanish, including masculine singular and plural and feminine singular and plural nouns. For each noun, have students give the corresponding direct object pronouns. **(7 min.)**
4. Go over Point 3. Write four or five Spanish sentences on the board. Have students underline the direct object, tell which pronoun they would use to replace the direct object, and finally, write the sentence with the direct object in place. **(10 min.)**

GramaVisión

For a video presentation of direct object pronouns, use **el joven G.** For interactive activities, see the *DVD Tutor.*

STANDARDS: 1.2

Visit Holt Online
go.hrw.com
KEYWORD: EXP1B CH6
Gramática 2 practice

38 ¿A quién le tocan los quehaceres?

Escribamos Who does the following chores at your house? Use the correct direct object pronoun in your answers.

MODELO **¿Quién prepara la cena?**
Yo la preparo. (Mi hermano la prepara.)

1. ¿Quién limpia la casa?
2. ¿Quién pone la mesa?
3. ¿Quién corta el césped?
4. ¿Quién hace las camas?
5. ¿Quién sirve el desayuno?
6. ¿Quién arregla los cuartos?
7. ¿Quién saca la basura?
8. ¿Quién pasa la aspiradora?

39 ¿Qué van a traer?

Escribamos Write a question and answer about who is going to bring which foods to the Spanish Club party.

MODELO **—¿Quién va a traer el pastel?**
—Yo lo voy a traer. (Yo voy a traerlo.)

yo

1. Miguel

2. Tomás y Raquel

3. Elsa y yo

4. Tú

Comunicación

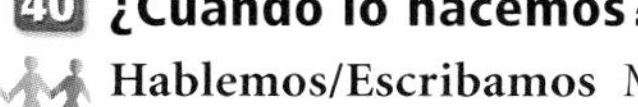

40 ¿Cuándo lo hacemos?

Hablemos/Escribamos Make a chart like the one pictured. Then in small groups, take turns asking and answering each other about how frequently you do the following things. Use direct object pronouns in your answers.

MODELO **preparar tu almuerzo**
—¿Cón qué frecuencia preparas tu almuerzo?
—Lo preparo a veces.

1. preparar el desayuno
2. beber refrescos
3. comer pizza
4. comer el almuerzo en la cafetería
5. poner la mesa
6. almorzar hamburguesas y papas fritas

todos los días	a veces	nunca

39 Answers

1. ¿Quién va a traer los duraznos? Miguel los va a traer. (Va a traerlos.)
2. ¿Quién va a traer los refrescos? Tomás y Raquel los van a traer. (Van a traerlos.)
3. ¿Quién va a traer la carne? Elsa y yo la vamos a traer. (Vamos a traerla.)
4. ¿Quién va a traer el pollo? Tú lo vas a traer. (Vas a traerlo.)

Teacher to Teacher

Jodi Mahlmann
Stafford High School
Stafford, TX

My students make human sentences to practice direct-object pronouns. First, I write sentences on strips of paper and cut out each word, for example, **Juan lava el carro.** Then I assign each word to a student and have them stand in sentence order in front of the class. I assign other students the words **lo, la, los,** and **las.** I ask the class what the direct object is. They should answer **el carro.** Then the student holding the word **lo** goes to the appropriate place to replace the student holding **el carro.** The activity continues with different sentences.

Differentiated Instruction

SLOWER PACE LEARNERS

39 Before assigning Activity 39 have students name the direct object pronoun for each item shown. Read the **Modelo** together as a class. Tell them that they must use the subject given for each sentence, and that they will always use the verb **ir.** Have them write the sentences as homework.

MULTIPLE INTELLIGENCES

40 **Intrapersonal** Students with intrapersonal strengths have the ability to accurately describe themselves and their habits, and to act adaptively. As an alternative to Activity 40, allow students to keep a written or oral (on videotape or audiotape) food journal of what they eat in one day, who prepares the food, and what they think of the food. Ask students to think about and describe their eating habits, and to think of any changes that might make them healthier.

Comunicación

Pair Activity: Interpretive

Prepare a list of 12–15 foods or dishes from the chapter. Have students work in pairs to interview each other about when their partner eats each of the foods, using direct object pronouns in their answers.

STANDARDS: 1.1, 1.2, 1.3

Resources

Planning:

Lesson Planner, pp. 27–33, 186–193

 One-Stop Planner

Presentation:

 Video Program
Videocassette 3,
DVD Tutor, Disc 2
GramaVisión

Practice:

Grammar Tutor for Students of Spanish, Chapter 6

Cuaderno de vocabulario y gramática, pp. 26–28

Cuaderno de actividades, pp. 19–21

Activities for Communication, pp. 23–24

Video Guide, pp. 54–55

Lab Book, pp. 17–18

 Teaching Transparencies
Bell Work 6.7
Vocabulario y gramática answers, pp. 26–28

Interactive Tutor, Disc 2

Bell Work

Use Bell Work 6.7 in the *Teaching Transparencies*, or write this activity on the board.

Write the answer to each question, using a direct object pronoun.

1. ¿Quién pide el café? Iñaki ____.
2. ¿Quién limpia la casa hoy? Tú ____.
3. ¿Quién sirve la cena en tu casa? Mis padres ____.
4. ¿Quién prepara los postres? Nosotros ____.
5. ¿Quién va a sacar la basura esta noche? Yo ____.

Affirmative informal commands

1 To tell someone you address as **tú** to do something, use an **affirmative informal command**.

2 To form the affirmative informal command of regular or stem-changing verb, just drop the final **s** off the end of the **tú** form of the verb.

(tú) hablas → **habla**	*you speak → speak*
(tú) comes → **come**	*you eat → eat*
(tú) pides → **pide**	*you ask (for) → ask (for)*
Pide un sándwich de pollo.	*Order a chicken sandwich.*

3 Some verbs have irregular affirmative informal command forms.

tener → **ten** *(have)*	ir → **ve** *(go)*	hacer → **haz** *(do, make)*
venir → **ven** *(come)*	ser → **sé** *(be)*	salir → **sal** *(go out, leave)*
poner → **pon** *(put)*		

4 Here are some verbs you might use to ask someone to help you in the kitchen. They all have regular command forms. Note that **calentar** is an **e → ie** stem-changing verb.

abrir *to open*	calentar (ie) *to heat up*	mezclar *to mix*
añadir *to add*	cortar *to cut*	sacar *to take out*

Corta las zanahorias, por favor. *Cut the carrots, please.*
Calienta el chocolate. *Heat the chocolate.*

Online
Vocabulario y gramática, pp. 26–28 | Actividades, pp. 19–21

Nota cultural

In Mexico many people buy snacks like cucumbers or roasted corn with chile powder, mango, pineapple, or watermelon from street vendors. For their afternoon snack, Argentines, Chileans, Uruguayans, and Colombians meet in tearooms to drink tea or coffee and eat sandwiches or pastries. Spaniards and Mexicans have a **merienda** around 6:00 P.M., a small snack such as **chocolate** and **churros** or **pan.** Compare your snacks to those in Spanish-speaking countries. Do you snack with your friends or family at a particular time? What do you eat?

41 La ensalada de frutas

Leamos/Escribamos Graciela is helping her brother prepare a fruit salad. Complete each sentence with the correct informal command. Then reorder the sentences logically.

1. (Servir) ____ la ensalada fría. Sirve, 8
2. (Lavar) ____ las frutas. Lava, 1
3. (Probar) ____ la ensalada para ver qué tal está. Prueba, 7
4. (Añadir) ____ un poco de azúcar *(sugar)* a las frutas. Añade, 6
5. (Cortar) ____ las frutas en trozos *(pieces)* con el cuchillo. Corta, 2
6. (Poner) ____ los trozos en un plato hondo. Pon, 4
7. (Tener) ____ cuidado con el cuchillo. Ten, 3
8. (Mezclar) ____ las frutas con un poco de jugo de naranja. Mezcla, 5

Core Instruction

TEACHING GRAMÁTICA

1. Go over Point 1. Have students suggest some English sentences using commands. **(4 min.)**
2. Go over Point 2. Call out the infinitive of several regular verbs and ask students for the informal affirmative command form. **(8 min.)**
3. Go over Point 3. Have students give each other commands like **¡Pon el lápiz en la mesa! (10 min.)**
4. Go over Point 4. Have students practice the new verbs by suggesting steps they might see in a recipe. **(8 min.)**

GramaVisión

To present the affirmative informal commands, use **el joven G** from the *Video Program*. For interactive activities, see the *DVD Tutor.*

GramaVisión

STANDARDS: 1.2, 2.1, 4.2

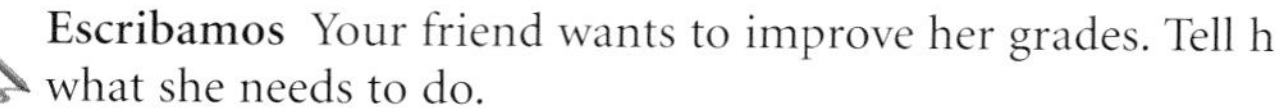

42 ¡Sé buena estudiante!

Escribamos Your friend wants to improve her grades. Tell her what she needs to do.

MODELO **estudiar mucho**
Estudia mucho.

1. hacer la tarea
2. ir a clase todos los días
3. salir temprano para el colegio
4. escuchar bien en clase
5. trabajar en clase
6. venir conmigo a la biblioteca
7. ser trabajadora
8. tener los útiles contigo

1. Haz la tarea.
2. Ve a clase todos los días.
3. Sal temprano para el colegio.
4. Escucha bien en clase.
5. Trabaja en clase.
6. Ven conmigo a la biblioteca.
7. Sé trabajadora.
8. Ten los útiles contigo.

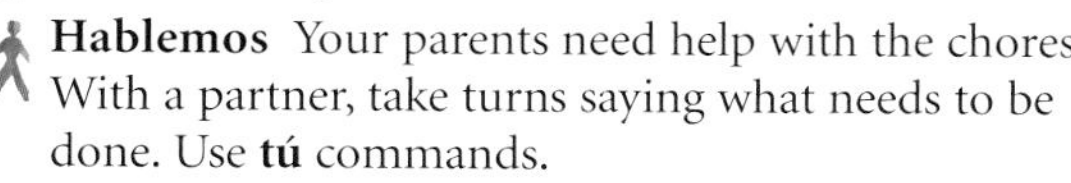

Comunicación

43 Necesito ayuda

Hablemos Your parents need help with the chores. With a partner, take turns saying what needs to be done. Use **tú** commands.

MODELO **Lava los platos.**

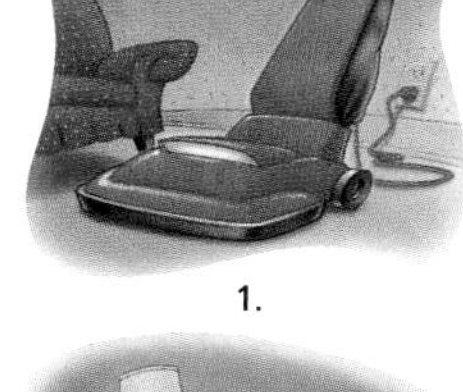

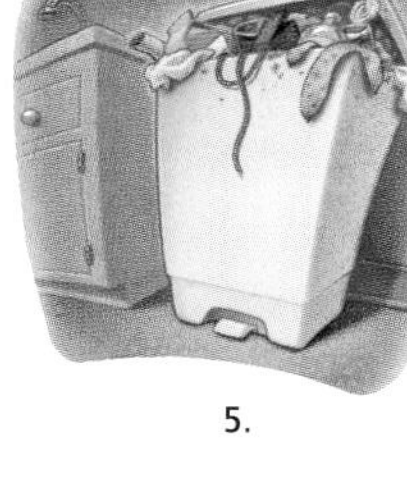

1. 2. 3. 4. 5. 6.

1. Pasa la aspiradora.
2. Haz la cama.
3. Corta el césped.
4. Arregla la sala.
5. Saca la basura.
6. Lava el perro.

44 Te toca a ti

Hablemos Imagine that you and your partner are doing each other's chores. Take turns giving each other instructions, using **tú** commands.

MODELO **—Lava el carro.**
—Saca la basura.

Teacher to Teacher

Sarah Vorrhees
Saratoga HS, Saratoga, CA

To practice familiar commands, I have each student first hide a piece of candy somewhere on campus before coming to class the next day. Students may hide candy near lockers, near the cafeteria or auditorium. In class, students write commands as clues to find the hidden candy. They give the clues to another student who has to go find the candy. The students can't believe that I am permitting them to leave the classroom!

Comunicación

Pair Activity: Interpersonal

Present students with a variety of situations to role-play in which familiar commands would naturally be necessary. You can organize the students into concentric circles or have students prepare and present their dialogues to the entire class. Some might include:

- A parent tells a child to clean his or her bedroom.
- A child tells a parent what he or she wants to do for his/her birthday.

Differentiated Instruction

ADVANCED LEARNERS

Have students create a work chart calendar in Spanish that shows their responsibilities at home. They should list at least six responsibilities and write them using informal commands down the left side of their paper. Across the top of their paper have them write the days of the week. Tell them to fill in the chart during the week putting a check on each activity as they complete it. Have them turn it in at the end of the week and keep it in the portfolio.

SPECIAL LEARNING NEEDS

42 Students with Learning Disabilities To modify Activity 42, make copies of the section and underline or highlight the word that needs to be changed to its correct form. Then, instruct students to rewrite that word in its correct form, without rewriting the entire sentence. This will allow students to focus on the key information in the activity, and will reduce the amount of writing that is required.

STANDARDS: 1.1, 1.2, 1.3

Resources

Planning:

Lesson Planner, pp. 27–33, 186–193

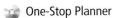

One-Stop Planner

Presentation:

Video Program
Videocassette 3,
DVD Tutor, Disc 2
GramaVisión

Practice:

Grammar Tutor for Students of Spanish, Chapter 6

Cuaderno de vocabulario y gramática, pp. 26–28

Cuaderno de actividades, pp. 19–21

Activities for Communication, pp. 23–24

Video Guide, pp. 54–55

Lab Book, pp. 17–18

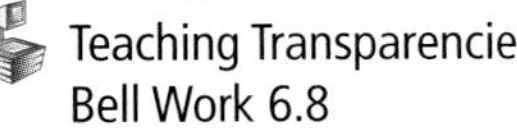

Teaching Transparencies
Bell Work 6.8
Vocabulario y gramática answers, pp. 26–28

Audio CD 6, Tr. 17

Interactive Tutor, Disc 2

Bell Work

Use Bell Work 6.8 in the *Teaching Transparencies*, or write this activity on the board.

Tell this person how to remedy each problem.

1. **Tengo mucha hambre.**
2. **Mis notas son malas.**
3. **Estoy aburrido en casa.**
4. **No me gusta la sopa.**
5. **Tengo sed.**

46 Answers

1. Ponla en la habitación.
2. Ponla en la sala.
3. Ponla en la cocina.
4. Ponlos en la cocina.
5. Ponlo en la cocina.
6. Ponlos en la sala.
7. Ponlos en la sala.
8. Ponlas en la sala/comedor.
9. Ponla en el comedor.

Affirmative informal commands with pronouns

1 You know that the **direct object pronoun** goes immediately before the conjugated verb. It can also be attached to the end of an infinitive.

—¿Siempre preparas **la cena**?
—No, no **la** preparo siempre, pero hoy sí voy a preparar**la**.

2 When you use a pronoun with an affirmative informal command, attach it to the end of the verb. Then add an accent to the stressed vowel of the verb, unless the verb is only one syllable long.

—¿Preparo **la carne**? —Sí, prepára**la**.
—¿Pongo **los vasos** en la mesa? —Sí, pon**los** allí.

Online
Vocabulario y gramática, pp. 26–28 | Actividades, pp. 19–21

45 ¿De qué hablas?

Leamos Identify the direct object pronoun in each sentence. Then decide which item it refers to.

1. Ponlo en el refrigerador.
   a. el queso **b.** la leche **c.** el libro
2. Sácala del horno.
   a. la basura **b.** el tocino **c.** la pizza
3. Ábrelo otra vez.
   a. el durazno **b.** el refrigerador **c.** la aspiradora
4. Córtalas con el cuchillo.
   a. las zanahorias **b.** las servilletas **c.** la manzana
5. Sírvela en el plato hondo.
   a. los cereales **b.** la sopa **c.** los refrescos
6. Mézclalo con el bróculi.
   a. el queso **b.** el flan **c.** los huevos
7. Mézclalos en el plato hondo.
   a. los huevos **b.** las naranjas **c.** los tenedores

Los colores de un mercado, México

46 Ponlas aquí

Hablemos A friend is helping you move. Tell him where to put these things.

MODELO **el refrigerador**
Ponlo en la cocina.

1. la cama
2. la televisión
3. la comida
4. los vasos
5. el microondas
6. los libros
7. los videojuegos
8. las sillas
9. la mesa

Core Instruction

TEACHING GRAMÁTICA

1. Go over Point 1. **(2 min.)**
2. Review the use of direct object pronouns by having students answer questions using a direct object pronoun. **—¿Quién tiene mi bolígrafo? —Yo lo tengo. (5 min.)**
3. Go over Point 2. **(5 min.)**
4. Have students practice using direct object pronouns and commands. Give students commands with direct objects and have them rewrite the sentences using direct object pronouns. **(13 min.)**

GramaVisión

For a video presentation of affirmative informal commands with pronouns, use **el joven G.** For interactive activities, see the *DVD Tutor.*

GramaVisión

STANDARDS: 1.2, 2.2

CD 6, Tr. 17

47 **¿Qué hago?**

Escuchemos Escucha las preguntas de Nuria y escoge la respuesta más lógica. 1. a 2. d 3. b 4. e 5. c

a. Caliéntalo en el horno.
b. Sácalos del refrigerador y ponlos en la mesa.
c. No, todavía no. Ponla con las otras bebidas.
d. Sí, ponlas a calentar en el microondas.
e. Córtalas y mézclalas en un plato hondo.

48 **El amigo desesperado**

Escribamos Your friend wants to prepare supper for his parents, but he doesn't know how to cook! Answer his questions, using **tú** commands and direct object pronouns.

1. ¿Caliento la sopa antes de preparar el pollo o después?
2. ¿Pongo las servilletas al lado de los platos o encima de ellos?
3. ¿Saco el flan del refrigerador antes de comer o después?
4. ¿Mezclo el café con leche o con agua?
5. ¿Preparo el pollo con zanahorias o con espinacas?
6. ¿Sirvo el helado con la comida o con el postre?
7. ¿Pruebo la ensalada antes de añadir el atún o después?

Comunicación

49 **¡Arregla la casa!**

Hablemos With a partner, take turns playing the roles of **el señor Gonzaga** and his daughter. She asks what she should do in each picture, and he answers, using **tú** commands.

MODELO —**Papá, ¿qué hago primero?**
—**¡Lava los platos!**

Capítulo 6

Gramática 2

47 **Script**

See page 37E for scripts

48 **Answers**

1. Caliéntala después de preparar el pollo.
2. Ponlas al lado del plato.
3. Sácalo del refrigerador después de comer.
4. Mézclalo (prepáralo) con agua.
5. Prepáralo con zanahorias.
6. Sírvelo con el postre.
7. Pruébala después de añadir el atún.

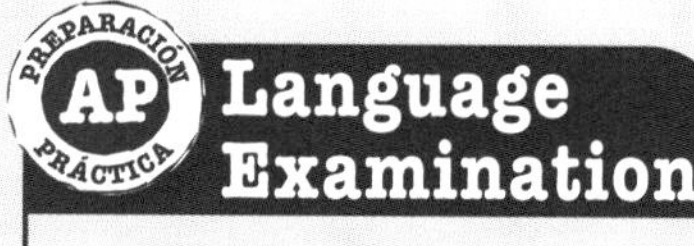

49 Below is a sample answer for the picture description activity.

—¿Qué hago con la leche?
—Ponla en el refrigerador.
—¿Qué hago con la basura?
—Sácala.
—¿Debo lavar los platos?
—Sí, lávalos.
—¿Paso la aspiradora en la sala?
—Sí, pásala.
—¿Tengo que hacer la cama?
—Sí, hazla.
—¿Y también debo organizar el cuarto?
—Sí, organízalo.

To display the drawings to the class, use the *Picture Sequences Transparency* for Chapter 6.

Differentiated Instruction

SLOWER PACE LEARNERS

48 Before assigning Activity 48, read each question together in class. Have students point out the verb and convert it to an informal command. Then have students determine the direct object and state the correct direct object pronoun. Do the first sentence on the board as a written model before assigning the rest of the activity as homework.

MULTIPLE INTELLIGENCES

48 **Bodily-Kinesthetic** After completing Activity 48, allow students to prepare a dish to take home to their parents. Divide students into small groups, based on their skills. Choose certain students to read the recipe(s), certain students to measure the ingredients, certain students to mix and prepare the food, certain students to take photographs of the steps in the process, and certain students to taste the food and write a report of how the food tastes.

Assess

Assessment Program

Prueba: Gramática 2, pp. 25–26

Prueba: Aplicación 2, pp. 27–28

Alternative Assessment Guide, pp. 241, 249, 257

Audio CD 6, Tr. 26

Test Generator

STANDARDS: 1.1, 1.2

Conexiones culturales

Bienvenido al nuevo mundo de comida Some believe that the New World's most important gift to Europe was not gold, silver, or jewels, but food. In the 1400s, Europeans were used to a bland diet with little variety. After the Spaniards brought back fruits and vegetables from the Americas, the eating habits of Europeans changed forever. The Spaniards, in turn, brought the first cattle, sheep, pigs, and chickens to the Americas.

NUEVO MUNDO
blueberries
chili peppers
cacao
corn
cranberries
pecans
pinto beans
potatoes
pumpkins
squash
string beans
sunflowers
tomatoes
turkeys
VIEJO MUNDO
apples
chickens
cattle
grapes
lemons
lettuce
limes
mangoes
oranges
pigs
sheep
wheat

Resources

Planning:

Lesson Planner, pp. 33–34, 192–193

 One-Stop Planner

Connections

History Link

- The Mayans were the first to make chewing gum, taking **chicle** sap from the **chicozapote** tree found in the Yucatan Peninsula.
- The word tomato **(tomate)** comes from the náhuatl language that was spoken by the Aztecs, who called it **xitomatl.** In some regions in Mexico today a tomato is called **jitomate.** It is believed that tomatoes have been cultivated in Mexico and Central America for more than 5,000 years.

Connections

Language Arts Link

Corn has been the center of Mexican food for over five thousand years. Many of the Mesoamerican tribes gave corn a religious significance and a heightened status in their societies. Ask students to think about the significance of food in celebrations, holidays, and other special occasions in their own lives. Have students write a brief paragraph in English about a special food in their region, culture, or religion. If they can't think of one, have them make up a short myth for a regional or national food that they think is important.

Core Instruction

TEACHING CONEXIONES CULTURALES

1. Read out loud the information on this page. Have students look at the lists of foods and ask them if any of these are among their favorites. Make sure they recognize where their favorite foods originated. **(5 min.)**
2. Present History Links and get student questions and comments. **(10 min.)**
3. Do Activity 1 with entire class. Which of these foods do they eat at Thanksgiving? Do they have any favorites? **(5 min.)**
4. Discuss the Language Arts Link with students before assigning the paragraph for homework. **(5 min.)**
5. Present Thinking Critically. **(10 min.)**
6. Read **Tostadas** and do Activity 2 in class. **(5 min.)**
7. You may want to assign Activity 3 as homework. As an extension, ask students to rewrite the recipe in English using their converted measurements.

STANDARDS: 4.2

Visit Holt Online
go.hrw.com
KEYWORD: EXP1B CH6
Online Edition

Conexiones culturales

1 El día de acción de gracias

Below are some foods you might find at a typical Thanksgiving meal. Based on the information on p. 66, which of these foods in boldface come from the "Old World" and which from the Americas? Answers in side column

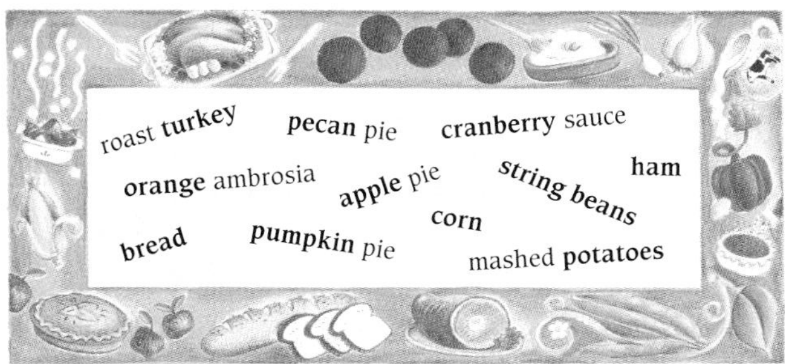

Tostadas El origen del maíz The cultivation of corn was developed by the Mayas in what is now Mexico. Corn tortillas, made from ground corn flour, were central to the daily diet of the Mayas.

2 ¿De dónde son?

¿Cuáles de los ingredientes para las tostadas son originalmente de Europa y cuáles son de las Américas?

Answers in side column

Tostadas

24 tostadas
1/2 kg de frijoles refritos
1 kg de queso
8 chiles
2 kg de pollo cocido
2 cabezas de lechuga
4 tomates

Procedimiento. Pon los frijoles, el queso, los chiles y el pollo encima de las tostadas. Entonces, pon las tostadas en el horno a 400° F por tres minutos. Ponles la lechuga y los tomates.

3 ¿Cuánto necesito?

Convert the kilogram measurements for refried beans, cheese, and chicken to pounds using the conversion formula. For example, if a recipe called for 3 kilograms (kg) of flour, then you would multiply 2.2 x 3 to find out you need 6.6 lbs. of flour.

1.1 lbs. refried beans, 2.2 lbs. cheese, 4.4 lbs. chicken

Conversions
1 kilogram (kg) = 2.2 pounds (lbs.)

Differentiated Instruction

ADVANCED LEARNERS

Challenge Have students use a dictionary to look up the Spanish words for the food items on page 66. Ask them to write the English words in a column on the left side of a sheet of paper, and write the corresponding Spanish words on the right. Have them fold the sheets in half, looking only at the Spanish side. Ask them to work with a partner to practice pronouncing and guessing the meaning of the Spanish terms.

MULTIPLE INTELLIGENCES

Bodily/Kinesthetic Get two blank poster boards. Label one **"Nuevo mundo"** and the other **"Viejo mundo."** Attach these to the board. Ask students to draw pictures of the foods listed on page 66 on small index cards. Call on students one at a time and ask them to attach their picture to the correct poster with a small piece of tape, and identify the food. Display the posters in the classroom.

Conexiones culturales

1 Answers

Old World: orange ambrosia, bread, apple pie, ham
Americas: cranberry sauce, turkey, pecan pie, pumpkin pie, corn, mashed potatoes, string beans

2 Answers

de Europa: pollo, lechuga, queso
de las Américas: maíz (para las tostadas), tomates, frijoles, chiles

Cultures

Practices and Perspectives

The Mayans also grew many other crops and hunted turkey, duck, pheasant, and deer for meat.

Suggestion

1 Before checking the correct answers to Activity 1, have students compare answers with those of other classmates. Were they surprised to learn that some foods associated with tropical countries and islands were actually brought to the Americas by Europeans?

Thinking Critically

Ask students what they are having for lunch today. Which foods are American and which are European in origin? Do any of the dishes combine ingredients from both the Americas and Europe? For example: spaghetti with meatballs: beef (Europe), wheat noodles (Europe), tomatoes (Americas). What parts of their lunches come from the "Old World" and what parts are from the Americas?

STANDARDS: 1.2, 2.1, 2.2, 3.1

Resources

Planning:

Lesson Planner, pp. 34–35, 194–195

 One-Stop Planner

Presentation:

 Video Program, Videocassette 3
DVD Tutor, Disc 2
VideoNovela

Practice:

Video Guide, pp. 54–55, 59
Lab Book, p. 41

Connections

Visual Learners

To help students compare what is real and what is imaginary in this episode of **Novela en video,** have them create a Venn diagram. Guide them through the diagram on the board. First, create a circle labeled REAL. Have students tell what is really happening to Sofía. Then, create a circle for the imaginary activities. In the overlapping part, list where the imaginary and the real lives of Sofía intersect.

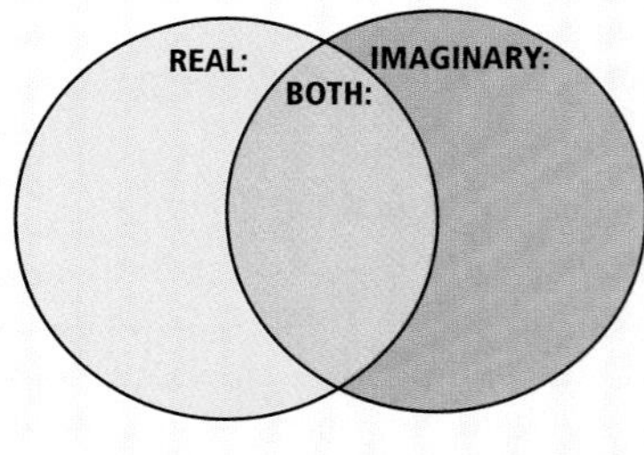

Gestures

Sofía's body language is different in her real life and her imaginary role. Compare Sofía's gestures when she is talking with her brother with her behavior when she pretends to be a waitress. Where are her hands when she is trying to explain the situation to her brother? Where are they when she is greeting her parents at the door? What does this difference reveal? Are her imaginary gestures as a waitress convincing?

Novela en video

¿Quién será?

Episodio 6

ESTRATEGIA

Recognizing a make-believe situation In order to understand this episode, it is helpful to recognize that certain parts are make-believe. With the help of her little brother, a little imagination, and the cooperation of her parents, Sofía turns an ordinary event into a more interesting experience. As you read the **Novela** or watch the video, figure out which parts are make-believe and then see what problem Sofía's make-believe situation creates for her.

En México

Sofía va a casa a preparar la cena. Marcos la mira para ver adónde va.

1

2

Quique Sofía, ¡es tarde! Mamá y papá están por llegar.
Sofía Ya sé, Quique.
Quique ¿Y la cena?
Sofía No te preocupes, Quique. No es tu problema. Yo la voy a preparar.

Core Instruction

TEACHING NOVELA EN VIDEO

1. Have students scan the **Novela en video** text, looking at the pictures. **(3 min.)**
2. Play the video, stopping at each scene change. Ask general comprehension questions for each scene. **(12 min.)**
3. Play the video a second time without stopping. Have students read the **Novela en video** text out loud, using dramatics as they read. **(15 min.)**
4. Have students work in pairs to complete the **¿Contesta?** questions on page 69. **(10 min.)**
5. Have students complete the **Actividades** on page 71. **(10 min.)**

Captioned Video/DVD

As an alternative, you might use the captioned version.

STANDARDS: 1.2, 3.2

Visit Holt Online
go.hrw.com
KEYWORD: EXP1B CH6
Online Edition

3
Quique ¿En qué puedo ayudar? ¿Pongo la mesa?
Sofía Sí, ponla.
Quique ¿Y el menú?
Sofía Ponlo en el comedor.

4
Sofía Señor y señora Corona. Bienvenidos al **Restaurante Sofía**. Veo aquí que tienen una reservación para dos personas a las ocho en punto.
Sr. Corona Sí, señorita.

5
Sra. Corona Señorita, ¿nos puede traer los menús, por favor?
Quique Aquí están los menús, señor, señora.
Sr. Corona ¿Qué tal están los tamales oaxaqueños hoy?
Sofía Riquísimos, señor, pero, malas noticias, no quedan tamales oaxaqueños.

6
Sra. Corona Óscar, a mí me apetece pollo con mole con arroz y tortillas de maíz azul. ¿Qué tal está el pollo con mole hoy, señorita?
Sofía No lo recomiendo. Está un poco salado.

Novela en video

A. Contesta

Check your understanding of the **Novela** by answering these questions.

1. Why is Sofía hurrying home after ballet class?
2. Why did Quique make menus?
3. What special occasion is being celebrated?
4. What foods do her parents ask about?

A. Contesta Answers

1. To prepare a special dinner for her parents
2. To help Sofía with the "make-believe" restaurant
3. Their parents' anniversary
4. Tamales oaxaqueños, pollo en mole con arroz y tortillas de maíz azul, bistec con puré de papa y unas zanahorias

Comparisons

Comparing and Contrasting

Restaurants that deliver food are quite unusual in the Spanish-speaking world. Today a few major chains have begun to deliver in large urban areas, but in general, if people want to eat restaurant food, they go out to a restaurant. Ask students why they think people in the U.S. like to have food delivered to their home? Why might it be different in Spanish-speaking countries? What are the advantages and disadvantages of having home delivery?

¿Quién será?

In Chapter 5, Sofía and Nicolás spent their Saturday morning doing chores. In this episode, Sofía decides to prepare her parents' anniversary dinner. She arrives home late and is approached by her brother, who has prepared menus for tonight's dinner. Sofía has him set the table and then tries to figure out what to prepare. Realizing she doesn't have much time, she orders from a restaurant. When Mr. and Mrs. Corona arrive, they are greeted by Sofía and Quique, who pretend to be restaurant workers. They seat their parents at a "special" table and show them the menu. Unfortunately, the restaurant doesn't have anything that the parents order. When they finally ask what is available, the food delivery arrives. Her dad is handed the bill. At the end of the episode **la profesora,** in Spain, decides that the next "candidate" should be from Argentina.

STANDARDS: 1.2, 3.2, 4.2

B. Contesta Answers

1. Flautas
2. In Mexico
3. To Argentina
4. To research another student candidate

Connections

Language Note

Have students reflect on the conversation between Sofía and her parents. How is it different from how Sofía and her brother talk to each other? How do Sofía and Quique address each other? What does Sofía's mom call her dad? What kind of a relationship does Sofía have with her parents in this episode, formal or informal? Ask students for examples of formal and informal speech in this episode. Have them rewrite the conversation between Sofía and her parents using the same type of language Sofía uses with her brother Quique.What effect does the change have on the make-believe situation?

7

Sr. Corona Y ¿el bistec, señorita? Aquí dice que viene con puré de papa y zanahoria.

Sofía Sí, señor, buena elección, el bistec está delicioso, pero… hoy es viernes, y los viernes, no sirvo bistecs.

8

Un poco más tarde.

9

Sra. Corona Pues, dígame, señorita, ¿cuál es la especialidad de la casa?

Sofía La especialidad de la casa son ¡LAS FLAUTAS! Y si no le importa, señor, aquí tiene la cuenta. ¿Me la puede pagar ahora?

En España

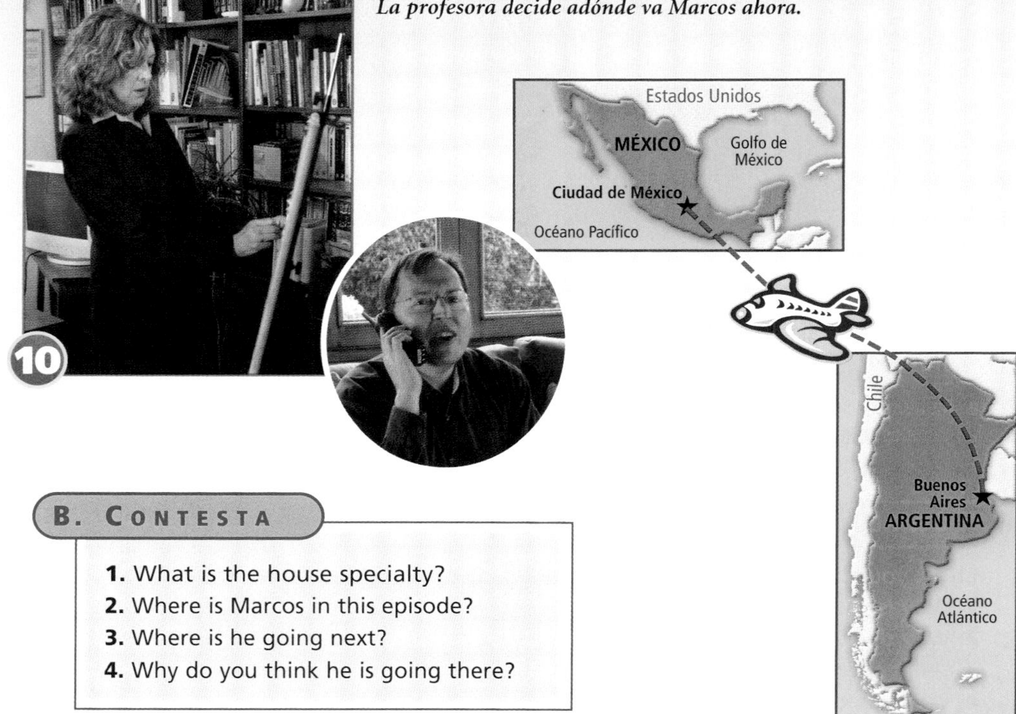

10

La profesora decide adónde va Marcos ahora.

B. Contesta

1. What is the house specialty?
2. Where is Marcos in this episode?
3. Where is he going next?
4. Why do you think he is going there?

Culminating Project

El restaurante

1. Tell students to imagine that they work for a restaurant in a luxury hotel. The hotel is offering a special weekend package that includes all meals: breakfast, lunch, and dinner.
2. Divide the class into groups of four and have them brainstorm a name for their restaurant.
3. Distribute two blank sheets of white construction paper to each group. Explain to students that they will create fixed-meal menus for both Saturday and Sunday. Each menu will show the three full meals offered in the package. Each meal should include at least four items. Some items may be repeated, but students should plan their menus to have as much variety as possible.
4. Have the groups prepare and design the menus using colored markers or pencils. They should include additional art work to enhance the appearance of their menus.
5. Have each group present their menus to the class.

STANDARDS: 2.1

Actividades

1 El menú de Quique

Match the food from the menu with the best description.

1. El pollo con mole — a. not available on Fridays
2. las flautas — b. it's a little salty
3. el bistec con papas — c. they are all gone
4. los tamales oaxaqueños — d. the house specialty

1. b
2. d
3. a
4. c

2 ¿Quién lo diría?

According to the **Novela**, who would most likely say each of the following things?

1. Pon los menús en el comedor.
2. Me gusta el pollo con mole.
3. ¡Bienvenidos a mi restaurante!
4. Aquí tienen ustedes los menús, señores.
5. Ahora vas a Argentina.

1. Sofía
2. Sra. Corona
3. Sofía
4. Quique
5. La profesora

3 ¿Comprendes la Novela?

Check your understanding of the events in the story by answering these questions.

1. What is the make-believe situation in this episode?
2. What role does Quique play in the make-believe situation?
3. What excuses does Sofía offer for the foods they order? Why?
4. Why does she finally offer them **las flautas**? Do you think she made them herself? Why or why not?

Próximo episodio
Marcos leaves to go to another country. How many more countries does he have to visit?
PÁGINAS 114–117

Novela en video

1 Answers

1. b
2. d
3. a
4. c

2 Answers

1. Sofía
2. La Sra. Corona
3. Sofía
4. Quique
5. La profesora

3 Answers

1. That Sofía and Quique are serving their parents at a restaurant
2. He sets the table and brings the menus to his parents.
3. Tamales: no longer available; chicken: too salty; steak: not served on Friday. She only has one dish available.
4. That's the only dish she has. She gets them delivered and has her dad pay the bill.

Próximo episodio:

After Argentina, three more (total of 10)

Más práctica

1 As a follow-up to Activity 1, have students write true/false statements in Spanish about the dishes listed in 1–4.

MODELO
1. El pollo en mole (no) está...

Comunicación

Pair Work: Interpersonal

After students have seen the **VideoNovela,** have them work in pairs, role-playing an imaginary restaurant scene. They are babysitting a small child who is very picky. To get him or her to eat, they pretend that they are waiters/waitresses. The child doesn't want anything they offer. The waiter/waitress must offer at least three different dishes and say why they are good. Have students switch roles.

Differentiated Instruction

SLOWER PACE LEARNERS

Extension Have students work in pairs to create a conversation to go with Photo 8 on page 70. Ask them to imagine that Sofía has just answered a knock on the door, and to begin the conversation there. Instruct students to make up at least 2 lines each for Sofiá and the boy at the door. Ask a few pairs to volunteer to read their conversations to the class.

MULTIPLE INTELLIGENCES

Logical/Mathematical Ask students to research this information:

- distance from Mexico City to Buenos Aires
- flight time between the two cities
- time zones for Mexico City, Madrid, and Buenos Aires, and hours of difference

Have them answer these questions:

1. If Marcos leaves Mexico City at noon, what time will he arrive in Buenos Aires?
2. What time will it be in Madrid when he arrives in Buenos Aires?

STANDARDS: 1.1

Leamos y escribamos

Resources

Planning:

Lesson Planner, pp. 35–37, 194–197

One-Stop Planner

Presentation:

Audio CD 6, Tr. 18

Practice:

Cuaderno de actividades, p. 22

Cuaderno para hispanohablantes, pp. 45–52

Reading Strategies and Skills Handbook, Chapter 6

¡Lee conmigo!

Applying The Strategies

Have students use the "Sketch to Stretch" strategy from the *Reading Strategies and Skills Handbook.*

READING PRACTICE

Strategy: Sketch to Stretch

STRATEGIES

Reading Skill	When can I use this strategy?		
	Prereading	During Reading	Postreading
Drawing Conclusions			✓
Making Generalizations			✓
Analyzing Cause and Effect			✓
Summarizing			✓

Strategy at a Glance: Sketch to Stretch

- The teacher introduces **Sketch to Stretch** to students by showing and discussing symbolic pictures based on a text.
- After reading a selection, students work independently or with a partner to create their own symbolic sketches. On the back of the sketches, students write why they drew what they did, using evidence from the text to support their opinions.
- Students share their sketches in small groups, allowing others to comment before revealing their explanations of their work.

Many students find it difficult to go beyond the reading selection to talk about the theme, or the symbolism, or to express a generalization about the story that can be applied to their lives. But some students who have difficulty talking about a text can express their ideas visually, far beyond what even they themselves imagine. This strategy, **Sketch to Stretch**, gives students the opportunity to formulate images that represent the ideas they cannot otherwise express. For some students, putting ideas into pictures, rather than words, is the best way to express their responses to the text.

This is a postreading strategy in which students think about what a passage or entire selection means to them and then draw symbolic representations of their interpretations of the text. As students discuss the text and decide what to draw, they think about the theme, draw conclusions, form generalizations, recognize cause-and-effect relationships, and summarize.

38 Reading Strategies and Skills Handbook — Sketch to Stretch

Additional Practice

For more reading practice, use the **Literatura y variedades** reading for Chapter 6 on pages 266–267.

Leamos y escribamos

ESTRATEGIA

para leer The *genre* of a reading tells you what kind of writing to expect. Some examples of different genres are legend, short story, novel, poem, essay, and play. Knowing the genre of a text will help you predict what it's about.

CD 6, Tr. 18

A Antes de leer

The following is a version of a legend about Quetzalcoatl, a god of the Aztec, Maya, and other cultures in Mexico and Central America. Before reading it, write a list of the characteristics you would expect to find in a legend.

La montaña del alimento[1]

Es una época muy difícil en la tierra[2]. Los hombres están desesperados porque no hay alimento y todos tienen mucha hambre. Van a hablar con Quetzalcóatl, la serpiente emplumada[3] y le explican que no tienen nada que comer.

Quetzalcóatl, dios compasivo[4], noble y generoso, decide ayudar a los hombres. Va a la montaña del alimento. Allí ve a un grupo de hormigas[5] gigantes que cuidan una fabulosa cantidad de maíz, la comida de los dioses. Quetzalcóatl les pide a las hormigas unos granos de maíz.

—¿Por qué quieres tú el maíz? —preguntan ellas.

—Mi gente tiene hambre —explica Quetzalcóatl.

—¿Son dioses tu gente? —dice una de las hormigas.

—No —responde Quetzalcóatl. —Son simplemente gente con hambre que vive sobre la tierra.

—Este maíz es sólo para los dioses —dicen las hormigas. —Busca[6] comida en otra parte.

Quetzalcóatl se va, pero no se da por vencido[7]. Vuelve a la montaña en la forma de una inmensa e imponente hormiga. Las hormigas le permiten entrar y el dios ve con admiración que hay granos de maíz de muchos colores. Les dice que nunca ha visto[8] granos rojos, amarillos, azules o morados y las hormigas, orgullosas[9] de su maíz, le dan un grano de cada color.

El dios vuelve rápidamente a la tierra y les enseña a todos a cultivar el maíz. Después de un tiempo hay mucho alimento y la gente de la tierra no vuelve a tener hambre nunca más.

1 food 2 earth 3 the feathered serpent 4 compassionate god 5 ants
6 Look for 7 doesn't give up 8 he has never seen 9 proud

Core Instruction

TEACHING LEAMOS

1. Read the **Estrategia para leer** with students and have students do Activity A. **(5 min.)**
2. Have students read the legend in pairs. Have them stop after every section to paraphrase what they have just read in order to monitor comprehension. You might have pairs volunteer after each section to share their results with the rest of the class. **(15 min.)**
3. Have students complete Activities B and C on page 73. **(15 min.)**

TEACHING ESCRIBAMOS

1. Discuss with students foods they would enjoy at potlucks before beginning their recipe. **(5 min.)**
2. Discuss the **Estrategia para escribir** as a group. **(5 min.)**
3. Have students complete sections 1–3. You might have a "recipe swap" at the end of class or prepare a "cookbook" as a gift for parents. **(30 min.)**

STANDARDS: 3.1, 3.2

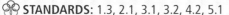

Visit Holt Online
go.hrw.com
KEYWORD: EXP1B CH6
Online Edition

B Comprensión

Answer the following questions in complete sentences.

1. ¿Qué problema tienen los hombres de la tierra?
2. ¿Quién va a ayudar a los hombres? ¿Por qué?
3. ¿Qué les dice Quetzalcóatl a las hormigas y qué responden ellas?
4. ¿Qué pasa cuando Quetzalcóatl vuelve a la montaña?
5. ¿Qué hace el dios al regresar a la tierra?

C Después de leer

Legends often reflect the values and beliefs of a culture. What values are reflected in this legend? Explain your choices. What are some similarities between this legend and other legends or stories you have read?

Taller del escritor

ESTRATEGIA

para escribir Arranging your writing in the order in which events happen helps you write more clearly. When you give written instructions such as recipes, the ordering of elements is important.

SALSA (para 4 personas)
4 tomates grandes
1 cebolla mediana
2 cucharadas de cilantro fresco
1 cucharada de vinagre
1 latita de chiles verdes
Corta el tomate, la cebolla y el cilantro. Añade sal al gusto. Mezcla todos los ingredientes. Sirve con tostadas.

¿Cómo lo preparas?

Imagine you are invited to a Spanish club potluck lunch where you are asked to exchange your favorite recipe from a Spanish-speaking country with other guests. Write a simple recipe for a dish with clear instructions on how to prepare it.

1 Antes de escribir

- List the foods you need to prepare your dish.
- Arrange them in the order you will need them.
- Write a command telling what needs to be done with each ingredient.

2 Escribir y revisar

After listing your ingredients, use command forms and adjectives to describe in detail the different steps in the preparation.
Para hacer una ensalada de frutas muy rica, usa muchas frutas diferentes.
Exchange your recipe with a classmate to see if it sounds appetizing to him or her. Your classmate may suggest an addition to your dish. Check for spelling and punctuation as well as for logical order.

3 Publicar

You may want to illustrate your recipe and display it on a poster board in class or post it on a school-sponsored web site. Consider trying a few in class or at home.

Online
Cuaderno para hispanohablantes, pp. 57–68

Leamos y escribamos

B Answers

1. No hay alimento y todos tienen mucha hambre.
2. Quetzalcóatl va a ayudar a la gente. Es compasivo, noble y generoso.
3. Les pide a las hormigas unos granos de maíz. Dicen que el maíz es sólo para los dioses.
4. Las hormigas le permiten entrar.
5. Les enseña a todos a cultivar el maíz.

Cultures

Practices and Perspectives

Quetzalcóatl Quetzalcóatl is one of the most important deities of ancient Mexico and a critical connection to the past for the Mexican people. Ask students to research a story about Quetzalcóatl and relate it to the class.

Writing Assessment

To assess the **Taller del escritor,** you can use the following rubric.

Writing Rubric	4	3	2	1
Content (Complete—Incomplete)				
Comprehensibility (Comprehensible—Seldom comprehensible)				
Accuracy (Accurate—Seldom accurate)				
Organization (Well-organized—Poorly organized)				
Effort (Excellent effort—Minimal effort)				

18–20: A 14–15: C Under
16–17: B 12–13: D 12: F

Assess

Assessment Program
Prueba: Lectura, p. 29
Prueba: Escritura, p. 30
Standardized Assessment Tutor, pp. 25–27
Test Generator 

Differentiated Instruction

ADVANCED LEARNERS

Discuss with students what food they think is most representative of their family's eating habits. What is served at almost every dinner? Is it rice, beans, bread, tortillas, or something entirely different? Have students write a short paragraph describing their family's typical or traditional meals.

SPECIAL LEARNING NEEDS

Students with Learning Disabilities To modify the **Taller del escritor** activity, change the order of the steps. Rather than having students write out their recipe (step 1) and then illustrate it (step 3), allow them to illustrate the steps of the recipe first, and then write steps as captions to go with each picture. This will give them a visual cue as they think of the correct sequence and complete the rest of the activity.

 **STANDARDS:** 1.3, 2.1, 3.1, 3.2, 4.2, 5.1

Resources

Planning:

Lesson Planner, pp. 37–38, 196–197

One-Stop Planner

Presentation:

Video Program
Videocassette 3
DVD Tutor, Disc 2
Variedades

Teaching Transparencies
Situación, Capítulo 6
Picture Sequences, Chapter 6

Practice:

Activities for Communication, pp. 48, 65–66

TPR Storytelling Book, pp. 34–35

Video Guide, pp. 54–55, 60

Lab Book, pp. 17–18, 42

Audio CD 6, Tr. 10–13

Interactive Tutor, Disc 2

3 Answers

Possible Answers:

1. Desayuno huevos, tocino y pan tostado.
2. Hoy voy a almorzar un sándwich de jamón y queso y una naranja. No, no me gusta la comida de la cafetería.
3. Esta noche quiero cenar arroz con pollo.
4. Cuando voy a un restaurante me gusta pedir sopa y pescado.
5. Prefiero pescado.
6. De cena, servimos pollo, arroz, y zanahorias.

Reteaching

Have students make a placemat and flatware using construction paper to represent a correct table setting. Have them each cut out a different colored plate, napkin, fork, spoon, knife, and glass. Have them each label each item in Spanish. If possible, laminate the place mats for display and later use at home.

Prepárate para el examen

1 Vocabulario 1
- commenting on food
- taking someone's order
- making polite requests

pp. 40–45

1 Write a dialog between two friends and a server in a restaurant. In the dialog, include comments on the food and polite requests for the items in the photos below.

1.

2.

3.

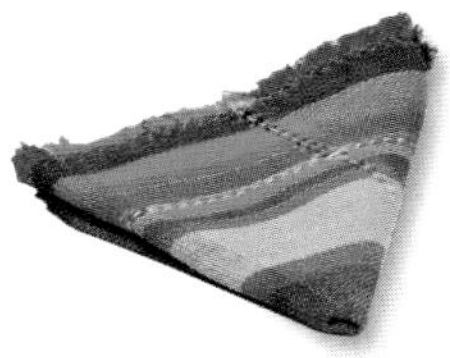

4.

5.

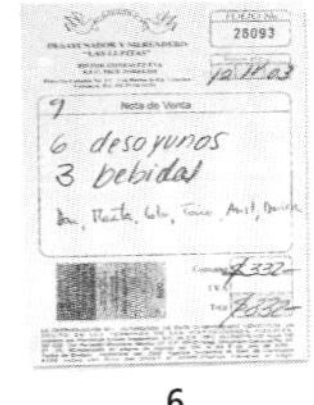
6.

2 Gramática 1
- **ser** and **estar**
- **pedir** and **servir**
- **preferir, poder,** and **probar**

pp. 46–51

2 Completa el párrafo con las formas correctas de los verbos del cuadro.

1. podemos 2. estamos 3. preferimos 4. es 5. pido 6. está 7. prefieren/piden 8. sirve

poder	estar	pedir
ser	preferir	servir

Mis amigos y yo no __1__ almorzar en casa porque siempre __2__ en el colegio, pero los fines de semana __3__ cenar en el Restaurante Don Carlos. La comida __4__ muy deliciosa allí. Yo siempre __5__ una ensalada y me gusta también la sopa porque siempre __6__ caliente. Mis amigos __7__ el pescado porque les encanta. También __8__ unos sándwiches riquísimos en el restaurante.

3 Vocabulario 2
- talking about meals
- offering help and giving instructions

pp. 54–59

3 Answer the questions about what you eat.

1. ¿Qué desayunas?
2. ¿Qué vas a almorzar hoy? ¿Te gusta la comida de la cafetería?
3. ¿Qué quieres cenar esta noche?
4. ¿Qué te gusta pedir cuando vas a un restaurante?
5. ¿Qué prefieres, la carne o el pescado?
6. ¿Qué sirven ustedes de cena en casa los fines de semana?

Preparing for the Exam

FOLD-N-LEARN

Layered Book

1. To help students prepare for the Chapter Test, have them create a **Fold-n-Learn** study aid as shown here using two sheets of paper, a stapler, and a pen or pencil.

2. Once the Layered Book template is completed, ask students to create a booklet practicing food and meal vocabulary. One page of the booklet can represent a meal, or students could create different food groups on different pages. Encourage students to find their own way to organize the new concepts.
3. Have students use their templates to help quiz themselves while preparing for the Chapter Test.

STANDARDS: 1.2, 1.3

Repaso

Visit Holt Online
go.hrw.com
KEYWORD: EXP1B CH6
Chapter Self-test

4 Tell your friends what to do to help you get ready for a party. Use **tú** commands and direct object pronouns.

1. ¿La sala? (limpiar)
2. ¿Las frutas? (poner)
3. ¿Los sándwiches? (hacer)
4. ¿Los refrescos? (sacar)
5. ¿La carne? (calentar)
6. ¿El cuarto? (arreglar)
7. ¿Las zanahorias? (cortar)
8. ¿El café? (servir)

5 Contesta las siguientes preguntas en español.

1. What are some foods that reflect Mexico's indigenous heritage?
2. In most Spanish-speaking countries, when is the big meal of the day?
3. What are some popular snack foods in Mexico? In other Spanish-speaking countries?

CD 6, Tr. 10

6 Verónica, Antonio y Carlos están en un restaurante. Escucha mientras hablan de lo que van a comer. Luego contesta las preguntas.

1. ¿Quién tiene sed? Verónica
2. ¿Quién pide un refresco? Antonio
3. ¿Qué prefiere Carlos? la sopa de verduras y las papas
4. ¿Cómo es la sopa? Es muy rica.
5. ¿Van a pedir unos sándwiches? sí

7 Usa los dibujos para decir *(to tell)* qué pasa.

a.

b.

c.

d.

4 Gramática 2
- direct objects and direct object pronouns
- affirmative informal commands with pronouns
pp. 60–65

5 Cultura
- **Comparaciones** pp. 52–53
- **Notas culturales** pp. 42, 46, 56, 62
- **Geocultura** pp. 34–37

Repaso

4 Answers
1. Límpiala.
2. Ponlas en la mesa.
3. Hazlos ahora, por favor.
4. Sácalos del refrigerador.
5. Caliéntala, por favor.
6. Arréglalo.
7. Córtalas para la ensalada.
8. Sírvelo después de la cena.

5 Answers
1. corn, tortillas
2. midday
3. cucumbers, roasted corn, fruits, quesadillas, sandwiches, pastries

6 Script
See script on p. 37F.

AP Language Examination
PREPARACIÓN PRÁCTICA

7 Below is a sample answer for the picture description activity.

Al señor Gonzaga le gusta el pescado y lo prepara con frecuencia. A su hija Josefina no le gusta mucho y prefiere no comerlo. En el comedor los dos empiezan a comer y Josefina prueba el pescado. Para ella, está muy picante y no sabe qué hacer. Su padre le sirve leche en un vaso. Josefina la toma y puede terminar su cena.

To display the drawings to the class, use the *Picture Sequences Transparency* for Chapter 6.

Oral Assessment

To assess the speaking activities in this section, you might use the following rubric. For additional speaking rubrics, see the *Alternative Assessment Guide.*

Speaking Rubric	4	3	2	1
Content (Complete—Incomplete)				
Comprehension (Total—Little)				
Comprehensibility (Comprehensible—Incomprehensible)				
Accuracy (Accurate—Seldom Accurate)				
Fluency (Fluent—Not Fluent)				

18–20: A 16–17: B 14–15: C 12–13: D Under 12: F

Repaso

Grammar Review

For more practice with the grammar topics in the chapter, see the *Grammar Tutor*, the *DVD Tutor*, the *Interactive Tutor*, or the *Cuaderno de vocabulario y gramática*.

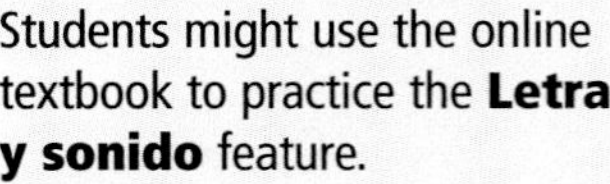

Online Edition

Students might use the online textbook to practice the **Letra y sonido** feature.

Letra y sonido

To reinforce writing skills, have students write the tongue twister in the **Letra y sonido** as you dictate it. You might create a cloze passage for the text to make the task less challenging. After they have finished, ask them to look at the text to correct their work.

Dictado Script

1. Yo estudio por la tarde al lado del estadio.
2. En el diccionario no hay nada delicioso.
3. Está delgado: sólo come un durazno y helado.
4. Los domingos veo un partido aburrido.
5. Puedo dormir detrás del jardín.
6. Yo no desayuno el día doce de diciembre.
7. Vive en un edificio de diez pisos en la ciudad.
8. Dibujo una aspiradora grande y verde.

Gramática 1
- uses of **ser** and **estar** **pp. 46–47**
- **pedir** and **servir** **pp. 48–49**
- **preferir, poder** and **probar** **pp. 50–51**

Repaso de Gramática 1

Uses of ser	Uses of estar
• to say where people are from	• to talk about location
• to tell the day, date, and time	• to say how people are doing
• to identify people and things by what they're normally like	• to say how something looks, feels, tastes at a given time

pedir e → i	
pido	pedimos
pides	pedís
pide	piden

servir e → i	
sirvo	servimos
sirves	servís
sirve	sirven

The verbs **poder** and **probar** are **o → ue** stem-changing verbs. The verb **preferir** is an **e → ie** stem-changing verb. See page 50.

Gramática 2
- direct objects and direct object pronouns **pp. 60–61**
- affirmative informal commands **pp. 62–63**
- affirmative informal commands with pronouns **pp. 64–65**

Repaso de Gramática 2

Direct object pronouns	Masculine	Feminine
SINGULAR	lo	la
PLURAL	los	las

Affirmative informal commands

Regular	Irregular		
habla	ten	ve	haz
come	ven	sé	sal
pide	pon		

Attach direct object pronouns to affirmative commands.

Letra y sonido d

La letra d CD 6, Tr. 11–13

- At the beginning of a phrase, or after **n** or **l**, the letter **d** is similar to the English *d* in *Daniel:* **d**elicioso, hon**d**o, an**d**ar, un **d**ía, el **d**eporte.
- After other consonants and especially after a vowel, it is much like English *th* in *then:* na**d**ar, me**d**ia, cua**d**erno, ma**d**re, uste**d**, aburri**d**o, tar**d**e, ver**d**e, la**d**o, a **d**ormir.

Trabalenguas

Me han dicho
que has dicho un dicho,
un dicho que he dicho yo,
ese dicho que te han dicho
que yo he dicho, no lo he dicho;
y si yo lo hubiera dicho,
estaría muy bien dicho.

Dictado

Escribe las oraciones de la grabación.

Chapter Review

Bringing It All Together

You might have students review the chapter using the following practice items and transparencies.

Interactive DVD Program

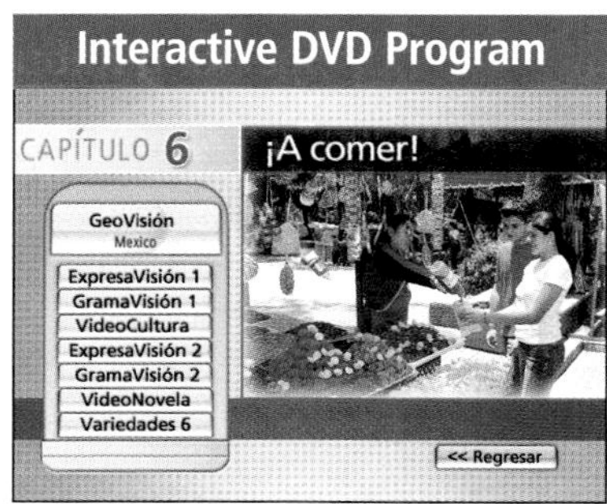

Interactive Tutor

STANDARDS: 1.2, 1.3

Repaso de Vocabulario 1

Commenting on food

el agua *(f.)*	*water*
el atún	*tuna*
(muy) caliente	*(very) hot*
encantar	*to really like, to love*
En la mesa hay...	*There is (are) . . . on the table.*
la ensalada (de frutas)	*(fruit) salad*
Esta (un poco) salado(a).	*It's (a little) salty.*
(No) estoy de acuerdo.	*I (don't) agree.*
el flan	*flan, custard*
frío(a)	*cold*
el jamón	*ham*
el jugo de...	*. . . juice*
la leche	*milk*
las papas	*potatoes*
las papas fritas	*French fries*
Para tomar puedes pedir...	*You can order . . . to drink.*
pedir (i)	*to ask for, to order*
picante	*spicy*
preferir	*to prefer*
preparar	*prepare, to make*
probar (ue)	*to try, to taste*
¿Qué prefieres pedir de...?	*What would you rather have for . . .?*
¿Qué tal está(n)...?	*How is (are) the . . .?*
¿Qué vas a pedir?	*What are you going to order?*
el queso	*cheese*
el refresco	*soft drink*
el restaurante	*restaurant*
riquísimo(a)	*delicious*
la salsa	*sauce, gravy*
el sándwich de...	*. . . sandwich*
servir (i)	*to serve*
la sopa (de verduras)	*(vegetable) soup*
el tomate	*tomato*

Making polite requests

la cuchara	*spoon*
el cuchillo	*knife*
la cuenta	*bill*
desear	*to want, to wish for, to desire*
el plato	*dish, plate*
el plato hondo	*bowl*
poder	*to be able to, can*
el postre	*dessert*
querer	*to want*
Quisiera...	*I would like . . .*
la servilleta	*napkin*
el tenedor	*fork*
tomar	*to drink, to take*
traer	*to bring*
el vaso	*glass*

Repaso de Vocabulario 2

Talking about meals

almorzar(ue)	*to eat lunch*
el arroz	*rice*
el bróculi	*broccoli*
el café (con leche)	*coffee (with milk)*
la carne	*meat*
la cena	*dinner*
cenar	*to eat dinner*
los cereales	*cereal*
el chocolate	*chocolate*
desayunar	*to eat breakfast*
el desayuno	*breakfast*
el durazno	*peach*
las espinacas	*spinach*
el huevo	*egg*
el maíz	*corn*
la manzana	*apple*
la naranja	*orange*
el pan	*bread*
el pan dulce	*pastries*
el pan tostado	*toast*
el pastel	*cake*
el pescado	*fish*
el pollo	*chicken*
el tocino	*bacon*
la zanahoria	*carrot*

Offering help

la ayuda	*help*
ayudar	*to help*
¿Puedo...?	*Can I . . .?*
el refrigerador	*refrigerator*

Useful verbs for cooking

añadir	*to add*
calentar (ie)	*to heat up*
cortar	*to cut*
mezclar	*to mix*

Repaso

Repaso

Vocabulary Review

For more practice with the vocabulary in this chapter, see the *DVD Tutor*, the *Interactive Tutor*, or the *Cuaderno de vocabulario y gramática.*

ExpresaVisión

Online Practice

For students to hear the vocabulary on audio, have them access the online textbook.

Game

Tirar palabras Bring a foam ball to class. Call out a category based on the chapter vocabulary **(frutas, comida para el desayuno, comida en general, etc.).** As you name the category, toss the ball to a student. The student says a related vocabulary word and tosses the ball to another student, who names a different item from that category. When a student cannot come up with a word, he or she is out of the game. The winners are the last players remaining in each round. You decide when a category has been exhausted. At that time, change the category and have all the students resume play.

Online Edition

Transparency Vocabulario 6.1

Transparency Situación 6.2

Assess

Assessment Program

Examen: Capítulo 6, pp. 133–143

Examen oral: Capítulo 6, p. 144

Alternative Assessment Guide, pp. 241, 249, 257

Standardized Assessment Tutor, pp. 25–28

Audio CD 6, Tr. 17–18

Test Generator

Resources

Planning:

Lesson Planner, pp. 38–39, 198–199

 One-Stop Planner

Presentation:

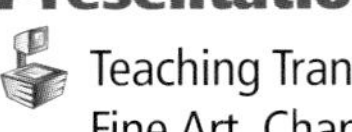 Teaching Transparencies Fine Art, Chapter 6

Practice:

Cuaderno de actividades, pp. 23–24

Lab Book, pp. 17–18

Audio CD 6, Tr. 14

 Interactive Tutor, Disc 2

1 Script

1. Hace calor y tengo mucha sed. ¿Quieres ir a tomar algo conmigo?
2. Aquí preparan unos sándwiches deliciosos. Yo prefiero los sándwiches de jamón y queso.
3. Mis amigos dicen que aquí sirven un pescado muy bueno, pero a mí no me gusta para nada.
4. Están un poco saladas, pero me encantan. Las como con hamburguesas.

2 Answers

1. onion
2. Answer may vary. onion, lettuce, carrots, potatoes, tomatos
3. Cut the potatoes and onion into small pieces.
4. oil, vinegar, salt and pepper
5. six to eight people
6. forty-five minutes (more or less)

Más practica

For more practice with recipes, consult the interleaf pages of your *Annotated Teacher's Edition.* Each chapter presents a recipe from the location students are studying in that chapter.

Integración

capítulos 1-6

CD 6, Tr. 14

1 Escucha los comentarios sobre la comida y escoge la foto correspondiente. **1.** c **2.** b **3.** d **4.** a

A
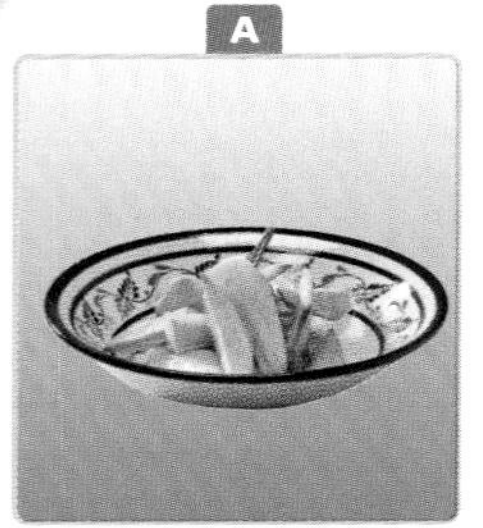

B

C

D

2 Mrs. Ramírez is going to fix supper. Read the recipes and answer the questions that follow. Write your answers in Spanish.

ENSALADA MIXTA

1 lechuga grande
4 tomates
1 taza de arroz cocido
100 g atún de lata
1/2 zanahoria rallada
1/2 cebolla picada

Se limpian las verduras y se cortan en trozos. Se mezcla todo junto y se sirve con aceite, vinagre, sal y pimienta.
Raciones 6–8
Tiempo–15 minutos

TORTILLA ESPAÑOLA

4 huevos
4 papas medianas
1/2 cebolla
sal y aceite de oliva

Corta las papas y la cebolla en pedacitos. Fríe con aceite en una sartén. Bate los huevos y mézclalos con las papas. Agrega la sal. Tapa con otra sartén y fríe al gusto. Dale la vuelta con la sartén superior y cocina el otro lado.
Raciones 6–8
Tiempo–30 minutos

1. What vegetable do the two recipes have in common?
2. Name three vegetables Mrs. Ramírez needs to fix supper.
3. What is the first step in the recipe for the **tortilla española**?
4. Name two extra ingredients in the **ensalada mixta** that are not listed in the ingredients at the top of the recipe.
5. How many people can Mrs. Ramírez feed with these recipes?
6. How much time should she plan on to cook supper?

Culture Project

Have students create a web site about a fictious restaurant that serves food from a Spanish-speaking country or area they have studied. The web site can be done on paper or using a word-processing program for students who cannot create a web site. On their site, they should promote their restaurant by listing menu items and prices (using the correct currency from the area they selected) and special features. They should also include positive comments from customers about how they enjoyed their meal. Have students share their restaurant sites with their classmates.

STANDARDS: 1.2, 1.3, 5.1

3 Discuss this painting by Mexican muralist Diego Rivera with a partner. The Spanish sentence prompts will guide your conversation. After you have completed the sentences, write a short paragraph in Spanish together describing the painting in your own words.

1. Las mujeres son... *(description)*
2. Ellas traen...
3. Los hombres son... *(description)*
4. Ellos tienen...
5. El señor español quiere comprar...

The Market of Cuernavaca in the Age of the Spanish Conquest, Diego Rivera (1886–1957)

4 **Situación**

Imagine you are interviewing a Mexican exchange student about typical daily meals in Mexico. With a partner, take turns playing the roles of the exchange student and interviewer. Your conversation should cover the following topics.

- What is the student's favorite food and beverage?
- Which foods and drinks does she or he typically have for each meal?
- At what time are meals served?
- Is there a favorite dish the family eats for dinner?
- Does the student usually eat dessert? If so, what does he or she prefer?

Integración

Fine Art Connection

Introduction Diego Rivera (1886–1957) is one of Mexico's well-known muralists. His murals chronicle the events and personalities of Mexican history from indigenous times to the modern age. Many of these murals are on the walls of public buildings on the Zócalo of Mexico City, including the Palacio Nacional. One of his best known murals is in Detroit, Michigan in the Detroit Institute of Fine Arts. *The Market of Cuernavaca in the Age of the Spanish Conquest* is painted at the Palacio de Cortés, also known as the Museo Cuauhnahuac in Cuernavaca. Rivera was married to artist Frida Kahlo (1907–1954), also a well-known Mexican painter.

Analyzing To help students discuss the photo, you might use the following questions.

1. **¿Dónde compran Uds. la comida? ¿Cuántas veces a la semana van al supermercado? ¿Van alguna vez a un mercado al aire libre?**
2. **¿Qué se vende en este mercado?**
3. **En tu opinión, ¿las personas en el mercado van allí muchas veces a la semana? ¿Por qué?**
4. **¿Qué más hace la gente en la pintura?**
5. **¿Hay un mercado como éste donde vives tú? ¿Dónde se reúne la gente?**

Extension As an enrichment activity, challenge students to create a mural of a scene at a local mall or other community gathering place.

ACTFL Performance Standards

The activities in Chapter 6 target the communicative modes as described in the Standards.

Interpersonal	Two-way communication using receptive skills and productive skills	**Comunicación (SE),** pp. 43, 45, 47, 49, 51, 57, 59, 61, 65 **Situación,** p. 79 **Comunicación (TE),** pp. 43, 45, 47, 51, 57, 59, 63, 71
Interpretive	One-way communication using receptive skills	**Comparaciones,** pp. 52–53 **Novela en video,** pp. 68–70 **Leamos,** p. 72
Presentational	One-way communication using productive skills	**Comunicación (SE),** pp. 43, 57, 59, 63 **Comunicación (TE),** p. 49

STANDARDS: 1.1, 1.3

Argentina

Resources

Planning:

Lesson Planner, p. xv

 One-Stop Planner

Presentation:

Teaching Transparencies **Mapa 3**

Video Program, Videocassette 4
DVD Tutor, Disc 2
GeoVisión

Practice:

Video Guide, pp. 61–62

Lab Book, p. 43

Interactive Tutor, Disc 2

Atlas INTERACTIVO MUNDIAL

Have students use the interactive atlas at **go.hrw.com** to find out more about the geography of Argentina and to complete the Map Activities below.

Map Activities

1. Have students locate Argentina and name the bordering countries. **(Chile, Bolivia, Paraguay, Brazil, Uruguay)**
2. Argentina's tallest peak is also the highest mountain in the Western Hemisphere. Have students locate Mt. Aconcagua and say to what mountain range it belongs. **(la cordillera de los Andes)**
3. Have students locate Argentina's largest region, Patagonia. What is the southernmost tip of Argentina called? **(Tierra del Fuego)**

GeoVisión

▲ **Buenos Aires** The capital of Argentina is located at the mouth of the **Río de la Plata** estuary on the Atlantic coast.

Geocultura Argentina

► **San Carlos de Bariloche** The town of San Carlos de Bariloche on **Lago Nahuel Huapí** is in the Andes Mountains. This area is known as "the Switzerland of the Andes."

► **La Pampa** The Pampa region is the land of **gauchos** and the center of livestock raising in Argentina. The flat, fertile land is similar to the Great Plains of North America.

Almanaque

Población
37.812.817

Capital
Buenos Aires

Gobierno
república

Idioma oficial
español

Moneda
peso argentino

Código Internet
www.[ ].ar

◄ **Trajes folclóricos** These young Argentines sport traditional dress.

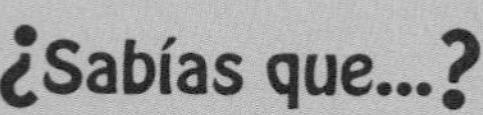

¿Sabías que...?

The highest peak in the Western Hemisphere is Mount Aconcagua in the Andes Mountains. Mount Aconcagua lies close to the Chilean border and is 6,960 meters high.

Background Information

History

Around twenty major indigenous groups lived in Argentina from 10,000 B.C., farming and hunting. The Spanish explorer, Juan Díaz de Solís, arrived in 1516 and Spain quickly appropriated the land. Argentina won independence from Spain in 1816. Through the 1800s, Argentina enjoyed prosperity and a wave of European immigration from Germany, England, and Italy. Argentina was under military rule from 1976 to 1983. Today, Argentina is governed by a democratic government.

Geography

Iguazu Falls, situated on Argentina's border with Brazil, is more than two miles wide.

Las Pampas, the grassy central plains, are home to more than half of Argentina's population and thousands of head of cattle.

Perito Moreno, in Patagonia, is the world's only inland glacier. Still growing, the river of blue ice moves forward about 30 feet a year.

▶ **La Garganta del Diablo** The "Devil's Throat" is an enormous waterfall of the **Río Iguazú** on the border between Argentina and Brazil. It is the most impressive of a series of waterfalls called the **Cataratas del Iguazú**.

BOLIVIA
Nevado de Chani (6200 m)
San Salvador de Jujuy
Salta
Río Pilcomayo
Gran Chaco
La Garganta del Diablo
Cataratas del Iguazú
erro Galán (6600 m)
Los Andes
San Miguel de Tucumán
ro Ojos Salado 30 m)
Santiago del Estero
Río Paraná
Río Paraná
Posadas
BRASIL
Mesopotamia
Parque Provincial Ischigualasto
Salinas Grandes
Laguna Mar Chiquita
Río Uruguay
Cerro de Olivares (6252 m)
Córdoba
Santa Fé
Paraná
San Juan
Cerro Aconcagua (6960 m)
Mendoza
URUGUAY
San Antonio de Areco
BUENOS AIRES
Pampa
ARGENTINA
Río de la Plata
Mar del Plata
Los Andes
Río Colorado
Río Negro
OCÉANO ATLÁNTICO
San Carlos de Bariloche
Lago Colhué Huapí
Río Deseado
Cueva de las Manos
Patagonia
afate
Tierra del Fuego
Ushuaia

▼ **El Parque Provincial Ischigualasto** This area of unusual rock formations contains fossils from the Triassic Period. Remains of one of the earliest known dinosaurs, *Eoraptor lunensis*, have been found here.

▼ **Los pingüinos** Magellanic penguins live in large colonies in the far south of Argentina.

▼ **Ushuaia** The southernmost town in the world, Ushuaia, gets up to 20 hours of sunlight a day during the summer months of December and January.

¿Qué tanto sabes?
Using the map, find three mountains in Argentina that are over 6,000 meters high.

Argentina

Cultures

Products and Perspectives

Argentina's first nuclear power plant was built in 1974 at Atucha, about 70 miles north of Buenos Aires. The plant handles seven percent of Argentina's power needs. Other nuclear power plants were built throughout the 1980s and 1990s. Disposal of the nuclear waste from the new power plants has created ongoing problems for Argentina. Although construction was started in 1986 for a medium to high-level nuclear-waste disposal site, it met public opposition. Angry citizens have protested the dumping of waste near their own homes. The project has been delayed until 2030 and disposal of nuclear waste in Argentina remains problematic.

Communities

Celebrations

Each December **gauchos** are honored in a National Gaucho Festival in Buenos Aires. Boys wear baggy pants, called **bombachas.** Parades, floats, vintage cars, and horses begin the celebration. Throughout the city, winners of nationwide contests gather to recite their poetry and tell **gaucho** campfire stories. The **sortija** is a **gaucho** game in which players attempt to thread a pin through a small ring hung from a pole, while galloping toward it on their horses at full speed. Ask students to name other cowboy-related celebrations.

¿Sabías que... ?

Students might be interested in knowing the following facts about Argentina.

- **Avenida 9 de Julio** is the world's widest street. It is 425 feet wide.
- **María Estela (Isabel) Martínez de Perón,** president of Argentina from 1974 to 1976, was the first woman to head any nation in the Americas.
- **Quebracho** trees are grown in the Chaco region of Argentina. This tree's rare wood is so hard it is known as the "ax breaker."
- Argentina is the eighth largest nation in the world, second only to Brazil in South America.

Preguntas

You might want to present these questions in English.

1. **¿Dónde se encuentra Buenos Aires? (En la boca del Río de la Plata en la costa del Océano Atlántico)**
2. **¿Qué región es la tierra de los gauchos y de la ganadería? (Las Pampas)**
3. **¿Qué fue descubierto en el Parque Provincial Ischigualasto? (El *Eoraptor lunensis*, uno de los dinosaurios más antiguos)**
4. **¿Cuál es la ciudad más sureña del mundo? ¿Dónde está? (Ushuaia, en Tierra del Fuego)**

CNN enEspañol.com
Have students check the **CNN en español** website for news on Argentina.

STANDARDS: 2.1, 3.1

Cultures

Products and Perspectives

Given the success of the cattle industry of the **Pampas,** it is not surprising that meat, primarily beef, is the backbone of Argentine cuisine. Argentines eat beef nearly every day. **Chorizos, morcillas,** and **salchichas** are a few of the kinds of sausage made from beef. A popular stew-like dish called **locro** is found in the north, again made with beef, pumpkin, and other vegetables. Ask students what areas of the United States are influenced by the cattle industry.

Connections

Thinking Critically

The Spanish spoken in Argentina is very different from that of Spain. In Argentina, every region has its own dialect. Argentine Spanish is also heavily influenced by Italian. People often greet each other with the Italian **buongiorno,** rather than **buenos días,** and **ciao,** for *goodbye.* The second person **tú** is rarely used, replaced by the characteristic Argentine **vos.** Finally, another completely unique language called **lunfardo,** a mix of many immigrant languages built around **castellano,** allows people of diverse backgrounds to communicate. Have students reflect on the dynamic nature of Argentina's Spanish. Is the English language of the United States evolving in any similar ways? Is there a language similar to the concept of **lunfardo** anywhere in the U.S.?

A conocer Argentina

La arquitectura

◄ **Iglesia y Convento de San Francisco de Salta** The Church of St. Francis is in Salta, a city in northwest Argentina. The 53-meter-high tower, one of the highest in South America, was designed by Spanish and Italian architects.

▲ **La Boca, Buenos Aires** This neighborhood was originally home to Italian immigrants who used parts of abandoned ships to build their houses. **La Boca** is famous for the tango music that echoes in its streets.

El arte

▼ **La Cueva de las Manos** The Cave of the Hands in Patagonia is decorated with outlines of hands painted over 10,000 years ago.

▲ ***Vuel Villa* (1936)** This painting is by Xul Solar (1887–1963), an Argentine artist of German heritage. He had great influence on the development of modern art in Argentina.

Interdisciplinary Links

El arte

Economics Link For hundreds of years, European immigrants imported paintings from Europe or they persuaded painters from Europe to come to Argentina and work. It wasn't until the 19th century that native Argentines began to develop a name in the fine arts. Today, some countries have placed import limitations on art forms such as film, to ensure that their own film industry continues to develop. In light of the delayed artistic development in Argentina, have students reflect on the import/export of art and its economic impact.

La arquitectura

History Link The imposing architecture of Buenos Aires is a perfect example of how Argentines adapted European styles to fit the needs of an entirely new culture. Most of downtown was built in the 19th century, to accommodate the population increase of European immigrants. Have students choose a building or a neighborhood of Buenos Aires and research its history on the Internet or at the library. What is the principal architectural style? What European country does this style originate from? How has the architectural style changed or adapted to fit the new Argentine culture?

Las celebraciones

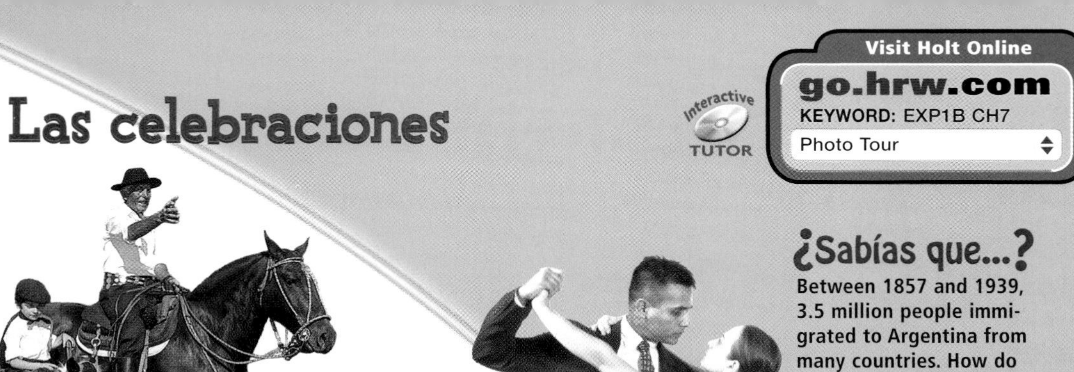

◄ **La Fiesta de la Semana de la Tradición** This major festival held in **San Antonio de Areco** is dedicated to **gauchos** and their traditions.

► **Tango** The tango originated in immigrant neighborhoods of Buenos Aires in the 1880s. The music is a combination of African rhythms, European folk music, and popular **gaucho** songs.

¿Sabías que...?

Between 1857 and 1939, 3.5 million people immigrated to Argentina from many countries. How do you see the cultures of immigrants reflected in the cities, architecture, festivals, and customs of Argentina?

La comida

► **Las picadas** A **picada** is a restaurant that serves a huge variety of appetizers prepared with cheese, meat, seafood, and nuts.

◄ **El mate** Between four o'clock and six o'clock in the afternoon, Argentines young and old drink **mate,** a tea made from leaves of the **yerba** plant. **Mate** is served in a hollowed-out gourd **(calabacita)** with a metal straw **(bombilla)**.

▼ **Calabacitas de mate con bombilla**

Las celebraciones

Music Link The tango is the national dance of Argentina. It was created in poor, immigrant neighborhoods in Buenos Aires in the early twentieth century. By 1920, tango recordings had reached a worldwide audience, and upper and lower-class Argentines alike danced to the melodic music. Have students research at the library or on the Internet one of the early tango musicians, like Carlos Gardel, Francisco Canaro, or Edmundo Leonel Rivero. What were the composer's principal themes? Which were the musician's favorite instruments?

El arte

Math Link **Las picadas** serve a wide variety of appetizers. At these restaurants, people make an entire meal out of many different, but smaller, servings of food. Have students compare the price of making a meal out of appetizers to ordering a main dish. Copy a to-go menu. Tell them to select three appetizers, add their prices, and calculate 15% for gratuity. Then have them select a main dish and calculate 15% for the tip. Which meal is more economical? Why do they think the idea of **picadas** isn't as popular in the U.S.? Is it because of value, quantity, perception, or culture?

Cultures

Practices and Perspectives

Yerba mate The national drink of Argentina is a bitter tea called **yerba mate.** The tea leaves, taken from a tree with the same name, are placed in a special wooden cup called a **mate.** The leaves steep for several minutes with hot, boiling water. Finally, the sweetened drink is sipped through a metal straw called a **bombilla.** The **yerba mate** is passed around a group of drinkers in a circle, each taking a sip from the **bombilla.** Have students reflect on the social and group nature of sipping **yerba mate.** Ask students if such a custom (sharing the **bombilla**) indicated anything about the social attitudes of Argentines.

¿Comprendes?

You can use the following questions to check students' comprehension of the **Geocultura.**

1. What is **La Boca, Buenos Aires,** famous for? (tango music)
2. How old are the hand prints in **la cueva de las manos**? (10,000 years old)
3. Around what time did the tango originate? (1880s)
4. What is served in a **picada** restaurant? (a variety of appetizers)
5. What is needed in order to drink yerba mate? (**calabacita, bombilla,** leaves of yerba plant)

Assess

Assessment Program
Prueba: Geocultura, pp. 135–136
Test Generator

Capítulo 7

Cuerpo sano, mente sana

Overview and Resources

Chapter Section		Resources
Vocabulario en acción 1 • Talking about your daily routine; talking about staying fit and healthy, pp. 86–91 **¡Exprésate!** • To talk about your daily routine, p. 87 • To talk about staying fit and healthy, p. 90	Present	TPR Storytelling Book, pp. 36–37 Teaching Transparencies Video Program/DVD Tutor, **ExpresaVisión**
Assess Assessment Program • **Prueba: Vocabulario 1,** pp. 37–38 • Alternative Assessment Guide, pp. 242, 250, 258 Test Generator	Practice	Cuaderno de vocabulario y gramática, pp. 29–31 Activities for Communication, pp. 25–26 Video Guide, pp. 64–66 Lab Book, pp. 2, 19–22, 44 Teaching Transparencies Audio CD 7, Tr. 1 Interactive Tutor, Disc 2
Gramática en acción 1 • Verbs with reflexive pronouns, p. 92 • Using infinitives, p. 94 • Stem-changing verbs, p. 96	Present	Video Program/DVD Tutor, **GramaVisión**
Assess Assessment Program • **Prueba: Gramática 1,** pp. 39–40 • **Prueba: Aplicación 1,** pp. 41–42 • Alternative Assessment Guide, pp. 242, 250, 258 Audio CD 7, Tr. 16 Test Generator	Practice	Grammar Tutor for Students of Spanish, Chapter 7 Cuaderno de vocabulario y gramática, pp. 32–34 Cuaderno de actividades, pp. 25–27 Activities for Communication, pp. 25–26 Video Guide, pp. 64–65 Lab Book, pp. 2, 19–22 Teaching Transparencies Audio CD 7, Tr. 2–3 Interactive Tutor, Disc 2

	Print	Media 
Cultura • **Comparaciones,** pp. 98–99 • **Comunidad,** p. 99 • **Conexiones,** pp. 112–113	Cuaderno de actividades, p. 28 Cuaderno para hispanohablantes, pp. 53–60 Video Guide, pp. 64–65, 67 Lab Book, p. 45	Audio CD 7, Tr. 4–6 Video Program/DVD Tutor, **VideoCultura** Interactive Tutor, Disc 2
Novela en video • **Episodio 7,** pp. 114–117	Video Guide, pp. 64–65, 69 Lab Book, p. 47	Video Program/DVD Tutor, **VideoNovela**
Leamos y escribamos • **¡En buena salud!,** pp. 118–119	Cuaderno de actividades, p. 32 Reading Strategies and Skills Handbook Cuaderno para hispanohablantes, pp. 53–60 ¡Lee conmigo! Assessment Program, pp. 49–50	Audio CD 7, Tr. 9

Lesson Planner with Differentiated Instruction, pp. 41–70, 200–227

One-Stop Planner® CD-ROM

Visit Holt Online
go.hrw.com
KEYWORD: EXP1B CH7
Online Edition

Chapter Section		Resources
Vocabulario en acción 2 • Talking about how you feel; giving advice, pp. 100–105 **¡Exprésate!** • To ask how someone feels; to respond, p. 101 • To give advice, p. 104	Present	TPR Storytelling Book, pp. 38–39 Teaching Transparencies Video Program/DVD Tutor, **ExpresaVisión**
Assess Assessment Program • **Prueba: Vocabulario 2,** pp. 43–44 • Alternative Assessment Guide, pp. 242, 250, 258  Test Generator	Practice	Cuaderno de vocabulario y gramática, pp. 35–37 Activities for Communication, pp. 27–28 Video Guide, pp. 64–65, 68 Lab Book, pp. 2, 19–22, 46 Teaching Transparencies Audio CD 7, Tr. 7 Interactive Tutor, Disc 2
Gramática en acción 2 • **Estar, sentirse,** and **tener,** p. 106 • Negative informal commands, p. 108 • Object and reflexive pronouns with commands, p. 110	Present	Video Program/DVD Tutor, **GramaVisión**
Assess Assessment Program • **Prueba: Gramática 2,** pp. 45–46 • **Prueba: Aplicación 2,** pp. 47–48 • Alternative Assessment Guide, pp. 242, 250, 258  Audio CD 7, Tr. 17  Test Generator	Practice	Grammar Tutor for Students of Spanish, Chapter 7 Cuaderno de vocabulario y gramática, pp. 38–40 Cuaderno de actividades, pp. 29–31 Activities for Communication, pp. 27–28 Video Guide, pp. 64–65 Lab Book, pp. 2, 19–22  Teaching Transparencies Audio CD 7, Tr. 8 Interactive Tutor, Disc 2

	Print 	Media 
Repaso • **Repaso,** pp. 120–121 • **Gramática y Vocabulario,** pp. 122–123 • **Letra y sonido,** p. 122	Activities for Communication, pp. 49, 67–68 TPR Storytelling Book, pp. 40–41 Lab Book, pp. 19–22, 48 Assessment Program, pp. 145–155, 156 Alternative Assessment Guide, pp. 242, 250, 258 Standardized Assessment Tutor, pp. 29–32	 Video Program/DVD Tutor, **Variedades**  Teaching Transparencies Audio CD 7, Tr. 11–14  Interactive Tutor, Disc 2   Test Generator
Integración • Cumulative review, Chapters 1–7, pp. 124–125	Cuaderno de actividades, pp. 33–34 Lab Book, pp. 19–22	 Teaching Transparencies Audio CD 7, Tr. 15

Capítulo 7

Cuerpo sano, mente sana

Projects

¡A tu salud!

In this activity, groups of students will create a "slide" presentation to promote a fictitious health resort. The presentation is intended for Spanish-speaking clients in the United States. Students can use PowerPoint® or other presentation software, or create "slides" using overhead transparencies that they can project to the classroom.

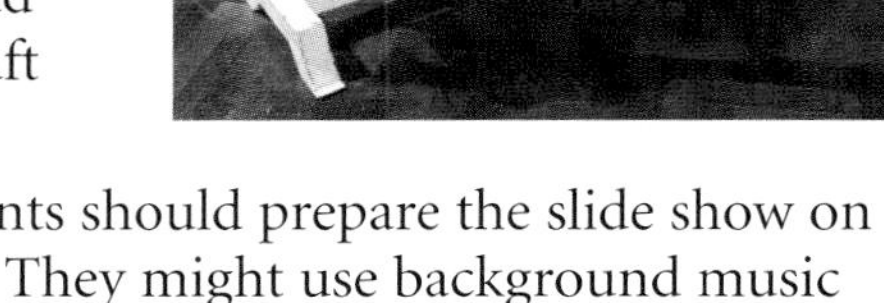

SUGGESTED SEQUENCE

1. Have groups of 3–4 students name their resort and choose its location.
2. Group members decide what features to highlight in their presentation. They should describe the meals served and the activities offered, telling how each is beneficial to the participants.
3. Students write the script for the presentation. All group members proofread the script. Students write a final draft and hand it in.
4. While you correct the scripts, students should prepare the slide show on the computer or on transparencies. They might use background music or sound effects as long as it doesn't render their speech inaudible.
5. Using the scripts they created, students present their slide show to the class.

Grading the project

Suggested point distribution (100 points total)

Content	20
Accuracy of written script	20
Creativity/Presentation	20
Comprehensibility	20
Effort/Participation	20

e-community

e-mail forum:

Post the following questions on the classroom e-mail forum:

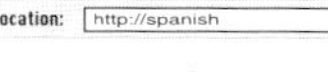

1. En tu familia, ¿quién necesita más tiempo para prepararse?
2. ¿Para quién en tu familia es difícil despertarse por la mañana?

Partner Class Project

Have individual students make a video (or digital movie) to share with a partner from another class. Students should play the role of patients. If possible, designate one or two students to be responsible for filming the actual segment. In the video, students tell what is bothering them, discuss related symptoms, and present other information that would be helpful for a doctor to know, including how they usually feel, their daily routine, their eating, sleeping, exercise habits, and things that might contribute to stress. Encourage students to present creative scenarios. Then, videos are shared with the students in the partner class to create the doctor's response. In the movie response, the doctor will give advice. You might have students vote on the most creative scenarios.

Game Bank

For game ideas, see pages T60–T63.

STANDARDS: 1.3, 3.2

Traditions

Los gauchos

Gauchos are among the most famous cultural symbols of Argentina, personifying pride, courage, honor, and a love of liberty. The word **gaucho** comes from the Quechua word for orphan. In the eighteenth century, the first **gauchos** were **mestizos,** or people of mixed indigenous and Spanish descent. **Gauchos** live out of doors, sleeping on their **recados,** which are both saddle and bedding. The **gauchos'** diet consists mainly of beef and **mate,** the traditional tea-like drink of Argentina. With his horse and his **recado,** the **gaucho** is well adapted to the environment and can be categorized as a **rastreador,** capable of interpreting imprints left by horses; a **boleador,** who hunts on horseback with **bolas** (three stones covered with leather, attached by long leather cords); or a **gato moro,** running from justice. **Gaucho** games were designed to measure the value of horsemanship, much like the rodeo of the American cowboy. Have students compare and contrast the customs and cultural significance of **gauchos** and cowboys and present their findings to the class.

Receta

Gauchos were the originators of the famous Argentine **parrillada** *(barbecue),* but Italian immigrants gave the **parrillada** its distinctive sauce, **chimichurri.** It is very similar to the Italian **salsa verde,** but substitutes cilantro for the capers that give the sauce its green color and makes steaks, other cuts of beef, even **empanadas,** taste delicious. You might have students make this recipe as a class project or for extra credit.

Chimichurri

para 4 personas

1/2 taza de aceite de oliva

1/2 taza de vinagre

2 cucharadas de perejil, picado

1 cucharada de hojas frescas de orégano, picadas

1 cucharada de cilantro, picado

1 cucharadita de ajo, picado fino

jugo de un limón (o limón verde)

1/2 cucharadita de pimienta, recién molida

1 cucharadita de sal

Combine todos los ingredientes en un recipiente. Se puede usar la mezcla inmediatamente, pero sabe mejor después de 24 horas. Si no se usa en seguida, guarde en el refrigerador, bien tapada, unos 2 días. Remuévalo bien antes de servir. Se puede emplear como un remojo para carnes o pescados antes de cocinar a la parrilla, o más tradicionalmente como una salsa.

STANDARDS: 2.2, 4.2

Capítulo 7

Cuerpo sano, mente sana

For Student Response Forms, see the *Lab Book*, pp. 19–22.

Textbook Listening Activity Scripts

Listening Activity Scripts

Vocabulario en acción 1

6 p. 90, CD 7, Tr. 1

JUAN ¿Vas a dormir tarde el sábado?

LUISA No, voy a levantarme a las siete. Siempre me entreno los sábados por la mañana.

JUAN ¿Cómo te mantienes en forma? ¿Corres?

LUISA No, no corro. Me estiro y hago ejercicio en casa y luego voy al gimnasio a levantar pesas.

JUAN ¿Y qué vas a hacer por la tarde?

LUISA Bueno, casi siempre almuerzo cuando vuelvo a casa. Siempre tengo mucha hambre después de hacer ejercicio. Luego voy a bañarme y relajarme.

JUAN ¿Qué haces para relajarte?

LUISA Leo una revista o a veces duermo la siesta.

Answers to Activity 6

1. temprano
2. Levanto pesas
3. Casi siempre
4. por la tarde
5. relajarme
6. A veces
7. leer

Gramática en acción 1

11 p. 92, CD 7, Tr. 2

Tengo mucho que hacer. Primero tengo que hacer la tarea. Después voy a bañarme. Luego me lavo los dientes y me pongo el piyama. A las nueve me acuesto. Tengo que acostarme temprano porque mañana me levanto a las seis y media.

Answer to Activity 11

Manuel se acuesta.

19 p. 96, CD 7, Tr. 3

En mi familia todos nos acostamos tarde. Generalmente, mi padre se acuesta a las diez y mi madre se acuesta un poco más tarde. Mi hermano prefiere acostarse después de su programa de televisión preferido. Me acuesto después de todos porque juego al ajedrez por Internet y luego empiezo mi tarea. Por la mañana no tenemos mucho tiempo para desayunar porque no nos gusta levantarnos temprano. Por eso, mi madre sólo sirve cereales para el desayuno. Después de desayunar, quiero dormir más pero no puedo. Tengo que salir para el colegio. Voy a mi cuarto y me visto y me maquillo en menos de diez minutos.

Answers to Activity 19

1. cierta
2. falsa
3. falsa
4. cierta
5. cierta

Vocabulario en acción 2

29 p. 104, CD 7, Tr. 7

1. —¿Qué te pasa? Te veo muy cansado.
   —Sí, me siento muy cansado. Veo televisión hasta tarde todas las noches y tengo que levantarme temprano por la mañana.
2. —¿Qué te pasa?
   —Me duelen mucho los pies. Me gusta mantenerme en forma pero si corro todos los días me duelen.
3. —Siempre te veo muy nervioso. ¿Estás bien?
   —No sé qué me pasa. No puedo relajarme.
4. —¿Qué tienes?
   —Ay, me duele mucho el estómago. Acabo de comer una pizza y muchos dulces.
5. —¿Qué tienes? ¿Te duele algo?
   —Sí. Siempre me duelen las piernas cuando levanto pesas.
6. —¿Estás enferma?
   —No. Es que siempre me duele la garganta después de fumar.
7. —¿Qué te pasa? ¿Por qué no haces la tarea?
   —Me duelen los ojos cuando leo.

Answers to Activity 29

1. b
2. c
3. d
4. e
5. g
6. f
7. a

34 **p. 106, CD 7, Tr. 8**

1. No me siento muy bien. Estoy enferma.
2. ¡Qué bonito día! Hace sol y me siento muy bien.
3. ¿Qué voy a hacer? Hay un examen en mi clase de matemáticas mañana. Las matemáticas son muy difíciles para mí.
4. Acabo de trabajar todo el día. Estoy muy cansado y tengo mucho sueño.
5. No hay nada interesante en la televisión y no puedo salir esta noche.
6. Tengo catarro. Me duelen los ojos, la nariz y la garganta.
7. Hoy tengo que cantar solo en el concierto. Siempre tengo miedo de cantar mal.

Answers to Activity 34

1. c 2. a 3. d 4. b 5. e 6. c 7. d

6 **p. 121, CD 7, Tr. 11**

ROBERTO Hola Laura, ¿Cómo estás?

LAURA Ay, Roberto. No me siento muy bien.

ROBERTO ¿Por qué? ¿Qué tienes?

LAURA Tengo catarro y me duele mucho la garganta.

ROBERTO Pobrecita. Debes tomar mucho jugo de naranja y dormir más.

LAURA No puedo dormir más mañana porque tengo que levantarme temprano. Tengo que ayudar a mi madre con los quehaceres.

ROBERTO ¡Qué lata! ¿Cuándo puedes descansar?

LAURA Voy a descansar después de hacer los quehaceres.

ROBERTO ¿Y por qué no haces algo para relajarte hoy?

LAURA Sí, buena idea. Voy a ver televisión o leer porque acabo de hacer la tarea.

ROBERTO Me parece bien. Descansa y hasta mañana.

LAURA Adiós, Roberto y gracias.

1. Laura se siente bien.
2. Laura debe tomar jugo y dormir más.
3. Laura no puede dormir hasta tarde mañana.
4. Laura va a descansar después de jugar al tenis.
5. Roberto dice que Laura debe seguir una dieta sana.

Answers to Activity 6

1. falsa
2. cierta
3. cierta
4. falsa
5. falsa

Dictado, p. 122, CD 7, Tr. 14

1. Me gusta jugar con juegos graciosos.
2. Los domingos hago dieta para mi estómago.
3. Como poca grasa, bebo jugo y hago yoga en grupo.
4. Mi amigo delgado sigue una dieta sana.
5. Muchas gracias, pero no tengo ganas de arreglar el garaje.
6. El gato negro está algo gordo.
7. A la muchacha guapa le duele la garganta.
8. Mis amigos son muy inteligentes y graciosos.

Integración capítulos 1-7

1 **p. 124, CD 7, Tr. 15**

1. Nuestra familia tiene la misma rutina todas las mañanas. Papá y mamá se despiertan a las seis. Mamá se lava la cara y va a la cocina a preparar el desayuno.
2. Papá se afeita y luego se baña. Mi hermano y yo nos vestimos antes de comer.
3. Todos desayunamos juntos en el comedor. Hay pan, fruta y jugo de naranja.
4. Por fin salimos para el colegio.

Answers to Activity 1

1. b 2. d 3. a 4. c

Cuerpo sano, mente sana

50-Minute Lesson Plans

Day 1

OBJECTIVE
Talking about your daily routine

Core Instruction
Chapter Opener, pp. 84–85
- See Using the Photo and **Más vocabulario,** p. 84. 5 min.
- See Chapter Objectives, p. 84. 5 min.

Vocabulario en acción 1, pp. 86–91
- See Teaching **Vocabulario,** p. 86. 40 min.

Optional Resources
- Common Error Alert, p. 87
- **También se puede decir,** p. 87
- Advanced Learners, p. 87 ▲
- Multiple Intelligences, p. 87

HOMEWORK SUGGESTIONS
Cuaderno de vocabulario y gramática, pp. 29–31
Internet Activities

Day 2

OBJECTIVE
Talking about your daily routine

Core Instruction
Vocabulario en acción 1, pp. 86–91
- Show **ExpresaVisión,** Ch. 7. 10 min.
- Review **Vocabulario 1** and **¡Exprésate!,** pp. 86–87. 15 min.
- Have students do Activities 1–3, p. 88. 25 min.

Optional Resources
- TPR, p. 87
- Fold-n-Learn, p. 88
- **Más práctica,** p. 88

HOMEWORK SUGGESTIONS
Cuaderno de vocabulario y gramática, pp. 29–31
Internet Activities

Day 3

OBJECTIVE
Talking about your daily routine; talking about staying fit and healthy

Core Instruction
Vocabulario en acción 1, pp. 86–91
- Have students do Activities 4–5, p. 89. 30 min.
- See Teaching **¡Exprésate!,** p. 90. 20 min.

Optional Resources
- **Comunicación,** p. 89
- Slower Pace Learners, p. 89 ◆
- Multiple Intelligences, p. 89

HOMEWORK SUGGESTIONS
Cuaderno de vocabulario y gramática, pp. 29–31
Internet Activities

Day 4

OBJECTIVE
Talking about staying fit and healthy

Core Instruction
Vocabulario en acción 1, pp. 86–91
- Review **¡Exprésate!,** p. 90. 5 min.
- Play Audio CD 7, Tr. 1 for Activity 6, p. 90. 10 min.
- Present **Nota cultural,** p. 90. 10 min.
- Have students do Activities 7–9, pp. 90–91. 25 min.

Optional Resources
- Science Link, p. 90
- Geography Link, p. 90
- **Comunicación,** p. 91
- Special Learning Needs, p. 91 ●

HOMEWORK SUGGESTIONS
Study for **Prueba: Vocabulario 1.**

Day 5

OBJECTIVE
Vocabulary review and assessment

Core Instruction
Vocabulario en acción 1, pp. 86–91
- Have students do Activity 10, p. 91. 15 min.
- Review **Vocabulario en acción 1,** pp. 86–91. 15 min.
- Give **Prueba: Vocabulario 1.** 20 min.

Optional Resources
- Advanced Learners, p. 91 ▲
- Test Generator

HOMEWORK SUGGESTIONS
Preview **Gramática en acción 1,** pp. 92–97.

Day 6

OBJECTIVE
Verbs with reflexive pronouns

Core Instruction
Gramática en acción 1, pp. 92–97
- Have students do the Bell Work 7.2, p. 92. 5 min.
- See Teaching **Gramática,** p. 92. 30 min.
- Play Audio CD 7, Tr. 2 for Activity 11, p. 92. 5 min.
- Have students do Activity 12, p. 193. 10 min.

Optional Resources
- Slower Pace Learners, p. 93 ◆
- Special Learning Needs, p. 93 ●

HOMEWORK SUGGESTIONS
Cuaderno de vocabulario y gramática, pp. 32–34
Cuaderno de actividades, pp. 27–30

Day 7

OBJECTIVE
Verbs with reflexive pronouns

Core Instruction
Gramática en acción 1, pp. 92–97
- Have students do the Bell Work 7.3, p. 94. 5 min.
- Present **Nota cultural,** p. 92. 5 min.
- Show **GramaVisión,** Ch. 7. 10 min.
- Review verbs with reflexive pronouns p. 92. 15 min.
- Have students do Activities 13–14, p. 93. 15 min.

Optional Resources
- Teacher to Teacher, p. 93
- **Comunicación,** p. 93

HOMEWORK SUGGESTIONS
Cuaderno de vocabulario y gramática, pp. 32–34
Cuaderno de actividades, pp. 27–30

Day 8

OBJECTIVE
Using infinitives

Core Instruction
Gramática en acción 1, pp. 92–97
- See Teaching **Gramática,** p. 94. 30 min.
- Have students do Activities 15–17, pp. 94–95. 20 min.

Optional Resources
- Common Error Alert, p. 95
- Circumlocution, p. 95
- Advanced Learners, p. 95 ▲

HOMEWORK SUGGESTIONS
Cuaderno de vocabulario y gramática, pp. 32–34
Cuaderno de actividades, pp. 27–30
Interactive Tutor, Ch. 7

To edit and create your own lesson plans, see the **One-Stop** Planner® CD-ROM

KEY
- ▲ Advanced Learners
- ◆ Slower Pace Learners
- ● Special Learning Needs
- ■ Heritage Speakers

Day 9

OBJECTIVE
Using infinitives

Core Instruction
Gramática en acción 1, pp. 92–97
- Review using infinitives p. 94. 10 min.
- Have students do Activity 18, p. 95. 15 min.
- See Teaching **Gramática,** p. 96. 25 min.

Optional Resources
- **GramaVisión,** Ch. 7.
- Multiple Intelligences, p. 95
- **Comunicación,** p. 95

HOMEWORK SUGGESTIONS
Cuaderno de vocabulario y gramática, pp. 32–34
Cuaderno de actividades, pp. 27–30
Internet Activities
Interactive Tutor, Ch. 7

Day 10

OBJECTIVE
Review of stem-changing verbs

Core Instruction
Gramática en acción 1, pp. 92–97
- Review stem-changing verbs, p. 96. 10 min.
- Play Audio CD 7, Tr. 3 for Activity 19, p. 96. 5 min.
- Have students do Activities 20–23, pp. 96–97. 35 min.

Optional Resources
- **Comunicación,** p. 97
- Slower Pace Learners, p. 97 ◆
- Special Learning Needs, p. 97 ●

HOMEWORK SUGGESTIONS
Study for **Prueba: Gramática 1.**
Interactive Tutor, Ch. 7

Day 11

OBJECTIVE
Grammar assessment; interviews from around the Spanish-speaking world

Core Instruction
Gramática en acción 1, pp. 92–97
- Review **Gramática en acción 1,** pp. 92–97. 10 min.
- Give **Prueba: Gramática 1.** 20 min.

Cultura, pp. 98–99
- See Teaching **Cultura,** #1–2, p. 98. 20 min.

Optional Resources
- Test Generator
- **Prueba: Aplicación 1**
- Map Activities, p. 98
- Slower Pace Learners, p. 99 ◆
- Special Learning Needs, p. 99 ●

HOMEWORK SUGGESTIONS
Read **Comparaciones,** pp. 98–99.
Cuaderno de actividades, p. 31

Day 12

OBJECTIVE
Interviews from around the Spanish-speaking world; talking about how you feel

Core Instruction
Cultura, pp. 98–99
- See Teaching **Cultura,** #3, p. 98. 15 min.
- Present and assign **Comunidad,** p. 99. 10 min.

Vocabulario en acción 2, pp. 100–105
- See Teaching **Vocabulario 2,** p. 100. 25 min.

Optional Resources
- Interdisciplinary Link, p. 99
- **También se puede decir,** p. 101
- Language Note, p. 101
- Advanced Learners, p. 101 ▲

HOMEWORK SUGGESTIONS
Comunidad, p. 99
Community Link, p. 99
Cuaderno de gramática, pp. 35–37

Day 13

OBJECTIVE
Talking about how you feel

Core Instruction
Vocabulario en acción 2, pp. 100–105
- Show **ExpresaVisión,** Ch. 7. 10 min.
- Review **Vocabulario 2** and **¡Exprésate!,** pp. 100–101. 15 min.
- Present **Nota cultural,** p. 102. 10 min.
- Have students do Activity 24–25, p. 102. 15 min.

Optional Resources
- TPR, p. 101
- Multiple Intelligences, p. 101
- Teacher to Teacher, p. 102
- Game, p. 102

HOMEWORK SUGGESTIONS
Cuaderno de gramática, pp. 35–37

Day 14

OBJECTIVE
Talking about how you feel; giving advice

Core Instruction
Vocabulario en acción 2, pp. 100–105
- Have students do Activities 26–28, pp. 102–103. 25 min.
- See Teaching **¡Exprésate!,** p. 104. 15 min.
- Present **Nota cultural,** p. 104. 10 min.

Optional Resources
- Extension, p. 103
- **Comunicación,** p. 103
- Advanced Learners, p. 103 ▲
- Special Learning Needs, p. 103 ●

HOMEWORK SUGGESTIONS
Cuaderno de gramática, pp. 35–37
Internet Activities

Day 15

OBJECTIVE
Giving advice

Core Instruction
Vocabulario en acción 2, pp. 100–105
- Have students do Bell Work 7.6, p. 106. 5 min.
- Review **¡Exprésate!,** p. 104. 10 min.
- Play Audio CD 7, Tr. 7 for Activity 29, p. 104. 10 min.
- Have students do Activities 30–32, pp. 104–105. 25 min.

Optional Resources
- **Comunicación,** p. 105
- Slower Pace Learners, p. 105 ◆

HOMEWORK SUGGESTIONS
Study for **Prueba: Vocabulario 2.**
Cuaderno de gramática, pp. 35–37
Internet Activities

Day 16

OBJECTIVE
Vocabulary review and assessment

Core Instruction
Vocabulario en acción 2, pp. 100–105
- Have students do Activity 33, p. 105. 15 min.
- Review **Vocabulario en acción 2,** pp. 100–105. 15 min.
- Give **Prueba: Vocabulario 2.** 20 min.

Optional Resources
- Multiple Intelligences, p. 105
- Test Generator

HOMEWORK SUGGESTIONS
Preview **Gramática en acción 2,** pp. 106–111.

50-Minute Lesson Plans, continued

Day 17

OBJECTIVE
Estar, sentirse, *and* ***tener***

Core Instruction
Gramática en acción 2,
pp. 106–111
- Show **GramaVisión,** Ch. 7. 10 min.
- See Teaching **Gramática,** p. 106. 30 min.
- Play Audio CD 7, Tr. 8 for Activity 34, p. 106. 10 min.

Optional Resources
- Heritage Speakers, p. 107 ■

HOMEWORK SUGGESTIONS
Cuaderno de vocabulario y gramática, pp. 38–40
Cuaderno de actividades, pp. 32–35

Day 18

OBJECTIVE
Estar, sentirse, *and* ***tener***

Core Instruction
Gramática en acción 2,
pp. 106–111
- Review **Estar, sentirse,** and **tener,** p. 106. 15 min.
- Have students do Activities 35–37, p. 107. 35 min.

Optional Resources
- Special Learning Needs, p. 107 ●
- Advanced Learners, p. 107 ▲
- **Comunicación,** p. 107

HOMEWORK SUGGESTIONS
Cuaderno de vocabulario y gramática, pp. 38–40
Cuaderno de actividades, pp. 32–35
Internet Activities

Day 19

OBJECTIVE
Negative informal commands

Core Instruction
Gramática en acción 2,
pp. 106–111
- Have students do Bell Work 7.7, p. 108. 5 min.
- See Teaching **Gramática,** p. 108. 25 min.
- Have students do Activities 38–39, pp. 108–109. 20 min.

Optional Resources
- Language to Language, p. 109

HOMEWORK SUGGESTIONS
Cuaderno de vocabulario y gramática, pp. 38–40
Cuaderno de actividades, pp. 32–35
Internet Activities

Day 20

OBJECTIVE
Negative informal commands

Core Instruction
Gramática en acción 2,
pp. 106–111
- Show **GramaVisión,** Ch. 7. 10 min.
- Review negative informal commands, p. 108. 15 min.
- Have students do Activities 40–41, pp. 108–109. 25 min.

Optional Resources
- **Comunicación,** p. 109
- Advanced Learners, p. 109 ▲
- Special Learning Needs, p. 109 ●

HOMEWORK SUGGESTIONS
Cuaderno de vocabulario y gramática, pp. 38–40
Cuaderno de actividades, pp. 32–35
Interactive Tutor, Ch. 7

Day 21

OBJECTIVE
Object pronouns and informal commands

Core Instruction
Gramática en acción 2,
pp. 106–111
- Have students do Bell Work 7.8, p. 110. 5 min.
- Show **GramaVisión,** Ch. 7. 5 min.
- See Teaching **Gramática,** p. 110. 20 min.
- Have students do Activities 42–43, pp. 110–111. 20 min.

Optional Resources
- Slower Pace Learners, p. 111 ◆
- Special Learning Needs, p. 111 ●

HOMEWORK SUGGESTIONS
Cuaderno de vocabulario y gramática, pp. 38–40
Cuaderno de actividades, pp. 32–35
Internet Activities
Interactive Tutor, Ch. 7

Day 22

OBJECTIVE
Object pronouns and informal commands

Core Instruction
Gramática en acción 2,
pp. 106–111
- Review object pronouns and informal commands, p. 110. 10 min.
- Have students do Activities 44–45, p. 111. 20 min.
- Review **Gramática en acción 2,** pp. 106–111. 20 min.

Optional Resources
- **Comunicación,** p. 111
- Slower Pace Learners, p. 111 ◆

HOMEWORK SUGGESTIONS
Study for **Prueba: Gramática 2.**
Interactive Tutor, Ch. 7

Day 23

OBJECTIVE
Grammar assessment; baseball in Latin America

Core Instruction
Gramática en acción 2,
pp. 106–111
- Review **Gramática en acción 2,** pp. 106–111. 15 min.
- Give **Prueba: Gramática 2.** 20 min.

Conexiones culturales,
pp. 112–113
- See Teaching **Conexiones culturales,** #1–2, p. 112. 15 min.

Optional Resources
- **Prueba: Aplicación 2**
- Test Generator
- Slower Pace Learners, p. 113 ◆

HOMEWORK SUGGESTIONS
Internet Activities
Multiple Intelligences, p. 113

Day 24

OBJECTIVE
Baseball in Latin America; developing listening and reading skills

Core Instruction
Conexiones culturales,
pp. 112–113
- See Teaching **Conexiones culturales,** #3–5, p. 112. 25 min.

Novela en video, pp. 114–117
- See Teaching **Novela en video,** #1–3, p. 114. 25 min.

Optional Resources
- Practices and Perspectives, p. 113
- Multiple Intelligences, p. 113
- Visual Learners, p. 114
- Gestures, p. 114
- Special Learning Needs, p. 117 ●

HOMEWORK SUGGESTIONS
Culminating Project, p. 116
Internet Activities

To edit and create your own lesson plans, see the **One-Stop** Planner® CD-ROM

KEY
- ▲ Advanced Learners
- ◆ Slower Pace Learners
- ● Special Learning Needs
- ■ Heritage Speakers

Day 25

OBJECTIVE
Developing listening and reading skills

Core Instruction
Novela en video, pp. 114–117
- Show **VideoNovela,** Ch. 7. 10 min.
- See Teaching **Novela en video,** #4, p. 114 20 min.

Leamos y escribamos, pp. 118–119
- See Teaching **Leamos,** #1–3, p. 118. 20 min.

Optional Resources
- Practices and Perspectives, p. 115
- **Comunicación,** p. 117
- Advanced Learners, p. 117 ▲
- Applying the Strategies, p. 118

HOMEWORK SUGGESTIONS
Leamos Activity B, p. 119
Cuaderno de actividades, p. 36

Day 26

OBJECTIVE
Developing reading and writing skills

Core Instruction
Leamos y escribamos, pp. 118–119
- Have students skim **Leamos** text, p. 118. 5 min.
- See Teaching **Leamos,** #4, p. 118. 10 min.
- See Teaching **Escribamos,** #1–3, p. 118. 35 min.

Optional Resources
- Advanced Learners, p. 119 ▲
- Special Learning Needs, p. 119 ●

HOMEWORK SUGGESTIONS
Taller del escritor, p. 119
Cuaderno de actividades, p. 36

Day 27

OBJECTIVE
Chapter review

Core Instruction
Leamos y escribamos, pp. 118–119
- See **Teaching Escribamos,** #4, p. 118. 10 min.

Repaso, pp. 120–121
- Have students do Activities 1–4, pp. 120–121. 40 min.

Optional Resources
- Fold-n-Learn, p. 120
- Career Path, p. 120

HOMEWORK SUGGESTIONS
Internet Activities
Interactive Tutor, Ch. 7

Day 28

OBJECTIVE
Chapter review

Core Instruction
Repaso, pp. 120–121
- Have students do Activity 5, p. 121. 10 min.
- Play Audio CD 7, Tr. 11 for Activity 6, p. 121. 10 min.
- Have students do Activity 7, p. 121. 15 min.
- Play Audio CD 7, Tr. 12–14 for **Letra y sonido,** p. 122. 15 min.

Optional Resources
- **Letra y sonido,** p. 122
- Game, p. 123

HOMEWORK SUGGESTIONS
Study for Chapter Test.
Interactive Tutor, Ch. 7

Day 29

OBJECTIVE
Chapter review

Core Instruction
Integración, pp. 124–125
- Play Audio CD 7, Tr. 15 for Activity 1, p. 124. 10 min.
- Have students do Activities 2–4, pp. 124–125. 40 min.

Optional Resources
- Slower Pace Learners, p. 124 ◆
- Culture Project, p. 124
- Fine Art Connection, p. 125

HOMEWORK SUGGESTIONS
Study for Chapter Test.
Cuaderno de actividades, pp. 37–38

Day 30

OBJECTIVE
Assessment

Core Instruction
Chapter Test 50 min.

Optional Resources
Assessment Program:
- **Prueba: Lectura**
- **Prueba: Escritura**
- Alternative Assessment
- Test Generator

HOMEWORK SUGGESTIONS
Cuaderno de actividades, pp. 37–38, 80–81

Cuerpo sano, mente sana

90-Minute Lesson Plans

Block 1

OBJECTIVE
Talking about your daily routine

Core Instruction

Chapter Opener, pp. 84–85
- See Using the Photo and **Más vocabulario,** p. 84. 5 min.
- See Chapter Objectives, p. 84. 5 min.

Vocabulario en acción 1, pp. 86–91
- See Teaching **Vocabulario,** p. 86. 40 min.
- Have students do Activities 1–5, pp. 88–89. 40 min.

Optional Resources
- Common Error Alert, p. 87
- **También se puede decir,** p. 87
- Advanced Learners, p. 87 ▲
- Multiple Intelligences, p. 87
- **Más práctica,** p. 88
- **Comunicación,** p. 89
- Slower Pace Learners, p. 89 ◆

HOMEWORK SUGGESTIONS
Cuaderno de vocabulario y gramática, pp. 29–31
Internet Activities

Block 2

OBJECTIVE
Talking about your daily routine; talking about staying fit and healthy

Core Instruction

Vocabulario en acción 1, pp. 86–91
- Show **ExpresaVisión,** Ch. 7. 5 min.
- Review **Vocabulario 1** and **¡Exprésate!,** pp. 86–87. 15 min.
- See Teaching **¡Exprésate!,** p. 90. 20 min.
- Play Audio CD 7, Tr. 1 for Activity 6, p. 90. 10 min.
- Present **Nota cultural,** p. 90. 10 min.
- Have students do Activities 7–10, pp. 90–91. 30 min.

Optional Resources
- TPR, p. 87
- Fold-n-Learn, p. 88
- Multiple Intelligences, p. 89
- Science Link, p. 90
- Geography Link, p. 90
- **Comunicación,** p. 91
- Advanced Learners, p. 91 ▲
- Special Learning Needs, p. 91 ●

HOMEWORK SUGGESTIONS
Study for **Prueba: Vocabulario 1.**
Cuaderno de vocabulario y gramática, pp. 29–31
Internet Activities

Block 3

OBJECTIVE
Vocabulary review and assessment; verbs with reflexive pronouns

Core Instruction

Vocabulario en acción 1, pp. 86–91
- Review **Vocabulario en acción 1,** pp. 86–91. 20 min.
- Give **Prueba: Vocabulario 1.** 20 min.

Gramática en acción 1, pp. 92–97
- See Teaching **Gramática,** p. 92. 30 min.
- Play Audio CD 7, Tr. 2 for Activity 11, p. 92. 5 min.
- Present **Nota cultural,** p. 92. 5 min.
- Have students do Activity 12, p. 193. 10 min.

Optional Resources
- Test Generator
- Slower Pace Learners, p. 93 ◆
- Special Learning Needs, p. 93 ●

HOMEWORK SUGGESTIONS
Cuaderno de vocabulario y gramática, pp. 32–34
Cuaderno de actividades, pp. 27–30

Block 4

OBJECTIVE
Verbs with reflexive pronouns; using infinitives

Core Instruction

Gramática en acción 1, pp. 92–97
- Have students do Bell Work 7.3, p. 94. 5 min.
- Show **GramaVisión,** Ch. 7. 10 min.
- Review verbs with reflexive pronouns p. 92. 20 min.
- Have students do Activities 13–14, p. 93. 25 min.
- See Teaching **Gramática,** p. 94. 30 min.

Optional Resources
- Teacher to Teacher, p. 93
- **Comunicación,** p. 93
- Common Error Alert, p. 95

HOMEWORK SUGGESTIONS
Cuaderno de vocabulario y gramática, pp. 32–34
Cuaderno de actividades, pp. 27–30
Internet Activities
Interactive Tutor, Ch. 7

To edit and create your own lesson plans, see the **One-Stop** Planner® CD-ROM

KEY
- ▲ Advanced Learners
- ◆ Slower Pace Learners
- ● Special Learning Needs
- ■ Heritage Speakers

Block 5

OBJECTIVE
Using infinitives; review of stem-changing verbs

Core Instruction

Gramática en acción 1, pp. 92–97
- Review using infinitives, p. 94. 10 min.
- Have students do Activities 15–18, p. 94–95. 30 min.
- See Teaching **Gramática,** p. 96. 25 min.
- Play Audio CD 7, Tr. 3 for Activity 19, p. 96. 5 min.
- Have students do Activities 20–22, pp. 96–97. 20 min.

Optional Resources
- **GramaVisión,** Ch. 7.
- Circumlocution, p. 95
- **Comunicación,** p. 95
- Advanced Learners, p. 95 ▲
- Multiple Intelligences, p. 95
- Slower Pace Learners, p. 97 ◆

HOMEWORK SUGGESTIONS
Study for **Prueba: Gramática 1.**
Finish Activity 22, p. 97.
Cuaderno de vocabulario y gramática, pp. 32–34
Cuaderno de actividades, pp. 27–30

Block 6

OBJECTIVE
Grammar review and assessment; interviews from around the Spanish-speaking world; talking about how you feel

Core Instruction

Gramática en acción 1, pp. 92–97
- Have students do Activity 23, p. 97. 10 min.
- Review **Gramática en acción 1,** pp. 92–97. 10 min.
- Give **Prueba: Gramática 1.** 20 min.

Cultura, pp. 98–99
- See Teaching **Cultura,** p. 98. 35 min.
- Present and assign **Comunidad,** p. 99. 5 min.

Vocabulario en acción 2, pp. 100–105
- See Teaching **Vocabulario 2,** #1, p. 100. 10 min.

Optional Resources
- **Comunicación,** p. 97
- Special Learning Needs, p. 97 ●
- Test Generator
- **Prueba: Aplicación 1**
- Map Activities, p. 98
- Interdisciplinary Link, p. 99
- Slower Pace Learners, p. 99 ◆
- Special Learning Needs, p. 99 ●
- **También se puede decir,** p. 101
- Language Note, p. 101

HOMEWORK SUGGESTIONS
Comunidad, p. 99
Community Link, p. 99
Cuaderno de actividades, p. 31

Block 7

OBJECTIVE
Talking about how you feel; giving advice

Core Instruction

Vocabulario en acción 2, pp. 100–105
- Show **ExpresaVisión,** Ch. 7. 5 min.
- Review **Vocabulario 2,** p. 100–101. 10 min.
- See Teaching **Vocabulario 2,** #2–3, p. 100. 15 min.
- Present **Nota cultural,** p. 102. 5 min.
- Have students do Activity 24–28, pp. 102–103 30 min.
- See Teaching **¡Exprésate!,** p. 104. 15 min.
- Present **Nota cultural,** p. 104. 10 min.

Optional Resources
- Advanced Learners, p. 101 ▲
- TPR, p. 101
- Multiple Intelligences, p. 101
- Teacher to Teacher, p. 102
- Extension, p. 103
- **Comunicación,** p. 103
- Advanced Learners, p. 103 ▲
- Special Learning Needs, p. 103 ●

HOMEWORK SUGGESTIONS
Cuaderno de gramática, pp. 35–37
Internet Activities

Block 8

OBJECTIVE
Giving advice; ***estar, sentirse,*** *and* ***tener***

Core Instruction

Vocabulario en acción 2, pp. 100–105
- Review **Vocabulario 2** and **¡Exprésate!,** p. 104. 15 min.
- Play Audio CD 7, Tr. 7 for Activity 29, p. 104. 5 min.
- Have students do Activities 30–33, pp. 104–105. 30 min.

Gramática en acción 2, pp. 106–111
- See Teaching **Gramática,** p. 106. 30 min.
- Play Audio CD 7, Tr. 8 for Activity 34, p. 106. 10 min.

Optional Resources
- Game, p. 102
- **Comunicación,** p. 105
- Slower Pace Learners, p. 105 ◆
- Multiple Intelligences, p. 105
- **GramaVisión,** Ch. 7.
- Heritage Speakers, p. 107 ■

HOMEWORK SUGGESTIONS
Study for **Prueba: Vocabulario 2.**
Cuaderno de vocabulario y gramática, pp. 38–40
Cuaderno de actividades, pp. 32–35

90-Minute Lesson Plans, continued

Block 9

OBJECTIVE
Vocabulary review and assessment; ***estar, sentirse,*** *and* ***tener;*** *negative informal commands*

Core Instruction

Vocabulario en acción 2, pp. 100–105
- Review **Vocabulario en acción 2,** pp. 100–105. 10 min.
- Give **Prueba: Vocabulario 2.** 20 min.

Gramática en acción 2, pp. 106–111
- Review **Estar, sentirse,** and **tener,** p. 106. 10 min.
- Have students do Activities 35–37, p. 107. 25 min.
- See Teaching **Gramática,** p. 108. 25 min.

Optional Resources
- Test Generator
- Special Learning Needs, p. 107 ●
- Advanced Learners, p. 107 ▲
- **Comunicación,** p. 107

HOMEWORK SUGGESTIONS
Cuaderno de vocabulario y gramática, pp. 38–40
Cuaderno de actividades, pp. 32–35
Internet Activities
Interactive Tutor, Ch. 7

Block 10

OBJECTIVE
Negative informal commands; object pronouns and informal commands

Core Instruction

Gramática en acción 2, pp. 106–111
- Have students do Bell Work 7.8, p. 110. 5 min.
- Show **GramaVisión,** Ch. 7. 5 min.
- Review negative informal commands, p. 108. 10 min.
- Have students do Activities 38–41, pp. 108–109. 30 min.
- See Teaching **Gramática,** p. 110. 20 min.
- Have students do Activities 42–43, pp. 110–111. 20 min.

Optional Resources
- Language to Language, p. 109
- **Comunicación,** p. 109
- Advanced Learners, p. 109 ▲
- Special Learning Needs, p. 109 ●
- Slower Pace Learners, p. 111 ◆
- Special Learning Needs, p. 111 ●

HOMEWORK SUGGESTIONS
Study for **Prueba: Gramática 2.**
Cuaderno de vocabulario y gramática, pp. 38–40
Cuaderno de actividades, pp. 32–35
Internet Activities
Interactive Tutor, Ch. 7

Block 11

OBJECTIVE
Grammar review and assessment; baseball in Latin America

Core Instruction

Gramática en acción 2, pp. 106–111
- Have students do Activities 44–45, p. 111. 15 min.
- Review **Gramática en acción 2,** pp. 106–111. 30 min.
- Give **Prueba: Gramática 2.** 20 min.

Conexiones culturales, pp. 112–113
- See Teaching **Conexiones culturales,** #1–3, p. 112. 25 min.

Optional Resources
- **Comunicación,** p. 111
- Slower Pace Learners, p. 111 ◆
- **Prueba: Aplicación 2**
- Test Generator
- Slower Pace Learners, p. 113 ◆

HOMEWORK SUGGESTIONS
Internet Activities
Multiple Intelligences, p. 113

To edit and create your own lesson plans, see the

One-Stop Planner® CD-ROM

KEY

- ▲ Advanced Learners
- ◆ Slower Pace Learners
- ● Special Learning Needs
- ■ Heritage Speakers

Block 12

OBJECTIVE
Baseball in Latin America; developing listening and reading skills

Core Instruction

Conexiones culturales, pp. 112–113
- See Teaching **Conexiones culturales,** #4–5, p. 112. 20 min.

Novela en video, pp. 114–117
- See Teaching **Novela en video,** #1–3, p. 114. 40 min.

Leamos y escribamos, pp. 118–119
- See Teaching **Leamos,** p. 118. 30 min.

Optional Resources

- Practices and Perspectives, p. 113
- Multiple Intelligences, p. 113
- Visual Learners, p. 114
- Gestures, p. 114
- Special Learning Needs, p. 117 ●
- Practices and Perspectives, p. 115
- **Comunicación,** p. 117
- Advanced Learners, p. 117 ▲
- Heritage Speakers, p. 118 ■
- Applying the Strategies, p. 118
- Advanced Learners, p. 119 ▲

HOMEWORK SUGGESTIONS
Culminating Project, p. 116
Cuaderno de actividades, p. 36

Block 13

OBJECTIVE
Developing writing skills; chapter review

Core Instruction

Leamos y escribamos, pp. 118–119
- See Teaching **Escribamos,** #1–3, p. 118. 35 min.

Repaso, pp. 120–121
- Have students do Activities 1–5, pp. 120–121. 30 min.
- Play Audio CD 7, Tr. 11 for Activity 6, p. 121. 5 min.
- Have students do Activity 7, p. 121. 10 min.
- Play Audio CD 7, Tr. 12–14 for **Letra y sonido,** p. 122. 10 min.

Optional Resources

- Special Learning Needs, p. 119 ●
- Fold-n-Learn, p. 120
- Career Path, p. 120
- **Letra y sonido,** p. 122
- Game, p. 123

HOMEWORK SUGGESTIONS
Study for Chapter Test.
Taller del escritor, p. 119
Interactive Tutor, Ch. 7

Block 14

OBJECTIVE
Assessment

Core Instruction

Chapter Test 50 min.

Leamos y escribamos, pp. 118–119
- See Teaching **Escribamos,** #4, p. 118. 10 min.

Integración, pp. 124–125
- Play Audio CD 7, Tr. 15 for Activity 1, p. 124. 5 min.
- Have students do Activities 2–4, pp. 124–125. 25 min.

Optional Resources

Assessment Program:
- **Prueba: Lectura**
- **Prueba: Escritura**
- Alternative Assessment
- Test Generator
- Slower Pace Learners, p. 124 ◆
- Culture Project, p. 124
- Fine Art Connection, p. 125

HOMEWORK SUGGESTIONS
Cuaderno de actividades, pp. 37–38, 80–81

Chapter Opener

Meeting the National Standards

Communication
Comunicación, pp. 89, 91, 93, 95, 97, 103, 105, 107, 109, 111, 115
Situación, p. 171

Cultures
Practices and Perspectives, pp. 81, 115
Products and Perspectives, pp. 82, 83
Comparaciones, pp. 98–99
Nota cultural, pp. 90, 102, 104
Conexiones culturales, pp. 112–113

Connections
Background Information, pp. 80 –81
Interdiciplinary Links, pp. 82–83
Thinking Critically, p. 82
Science Link, p. 90
Geography Link, pp. 90, 99, 113
Language Note, p. 101
Language-to-Language, p. 109
History Link, p. 112
Visual Learners, p. 114
Fine Art, p. 125

Comparisons
Comparaciones, pp. 98–99

Communities
Celebrations, p. 81
Comunidad, p. 99
Community Link, p. 99
Career Path, p. 120

Using the Photo

The Andes Mountains are a popular destination in South America for mountain biking and climbing, hiking, rafting, and kayaking. In pairs, have students answer the questions in **¿Qué ves en la foto?**, then discuss the cycling equipment in the photo.

Capítulo 7

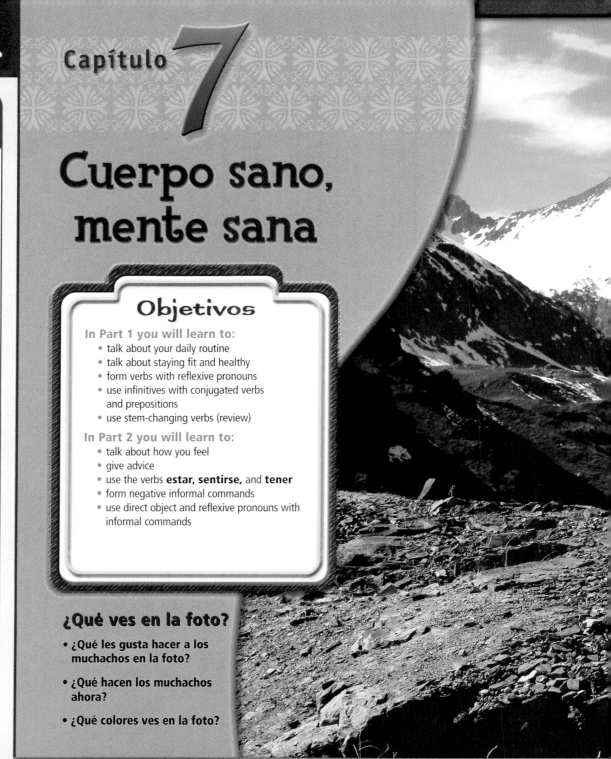

Cuerpo sano, mente sana

Objetivos

In Part 1 you will learn to:
- talk about your daily routine
- talk about staying fit and healthy
- form verbs with reflexive pronouns
- use infinitives with conjugated verbs and prepositions
- use stem-changing verbs (review)

In Part 2 you will learn to:
- talk about how you feel
- give advice
- use the verbs **estar, sentirse,** and **tener**
- form negative informal commands
- use direct object and reflexive pronouns with informal commands

¿Qué ves en la foto?

- ¿Qué les gusta hacer a los muchachos en la foto?
- ¿Qué hacen los muchachos ahora?
- ¿Qué colores ves en la foto?

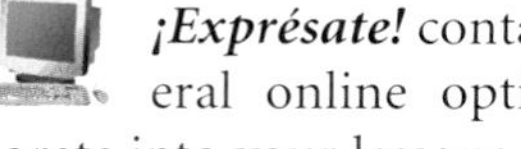

¡Exprésate! contains several online options for you to incorporate into your lessons.

¡Exprésate! Student Edition online at my.hrw.com
At this site, you will find the online version of *¡Exprésate!* All concepts presented in the textbook are presented and practiced in this online version of your textbook. This online version can be used as a supplement to or as a replacement of your textbook.

Practice activities at go.hrw.com
These activities provide additional practice for major concepts presented in each chapter. Practice items include structured practice as well as research topics.

Teacher resources at www.hrw.com
This site provides additional information that teachers might find useful about the *¡Exprésate!* program.

La cordillera de los Andes entre Argentina y Chile

Chapter Opener

Learning Tips

Encourage students to talk in Spanish to classmates outside of class whenever possible. In this chapter, students will learn how to talk about their daily routines and tell how they feel, giving them more vocabulary to talk about what is relevant to their daily lives.

VIDEO OPTIONS

- **ExpresaVisión 1**
- **GramaVisión 1**
  Verbs with reflexive pronouns; using infinitives; review of stem-changing verbs
- **VideoCultura**
- **ExpresaVisión 2**
- **GramaVisión 2**
  Estar, sentirse, and **tener;** negative informal commands; object pronouns and informal commands
- **VideoNovela**
- **Variedades**

Pacing Tips

In this chapter, students will learn the vocabulary for body parts in both sections of the chapter. Since there is a lot of new vocabulary in this chapter, you might spend extra time on the **Vocabulario** sections. For complete lesson plan suggestions, see pages 83G–83N.

Suggested pacing:	Traditional Schedule	Block Schedule
Vocabulario 1/Gramática 1	11 days	5 1/3 blocks
Cultura	1 day	1/2 block
Vocabulario 2/Gramática 2	10 3/4 days	5 1/3 blocks
Conexiones culturales	1 day	1/2 block
Novela	3/4 day	1/3 block
Leamos y escribamos	1 1/2 days	1/2 block
Repaso	2 days	1/2 block
Chapter Test	1 day	1/2 block
Integración	1 day	1/2 block

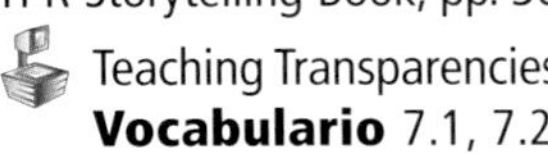

Resources

Planning:

Lesson Planner, pp. 41–45, 200–205

One-Stop Planner

Presentation:

TPR Storytelling Book, pp. 36–37

Teaching Transparencies **Vocabulario** 7.1, 7.2

Video Program
Videocassette 4
DVD Tutor, Disc 2
ExpresaVisión

Practice:

Cuaderno de vocabulario y gramática, pp. 29–31

Activities for Communication, pp. 25–26

Video Guide, pp. 64–66

Lab Book, pp. 19–20, 44

Teaching Transparencies
Bell Work 7.1
Vocabulario y gramática answers, pp. 29–31

Interactive Tutor, Disc 2

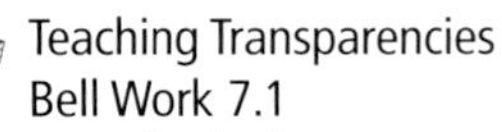

Bell Work

Use Bell Work 7.1 in the *Teaching Transparencies,* or write this activity on the board.

Write the name of the meal in which you would most likely eat the following foods.

el desayuno el almuerzo la cena

1. **un sándwich de jamón**
2. **una ensalada de atún y sopa**
3. **cereales con leche**
4. **un bistec, pan, espinacas y una papa al horno**
5. **dos huevos fritos, tocino y café con leche**

Objetivos

Talking about your daily routine, talking about staying fit and healthy

Vocabulario en acción 1

ExpresaVisión

Por la mañana, tengo que...

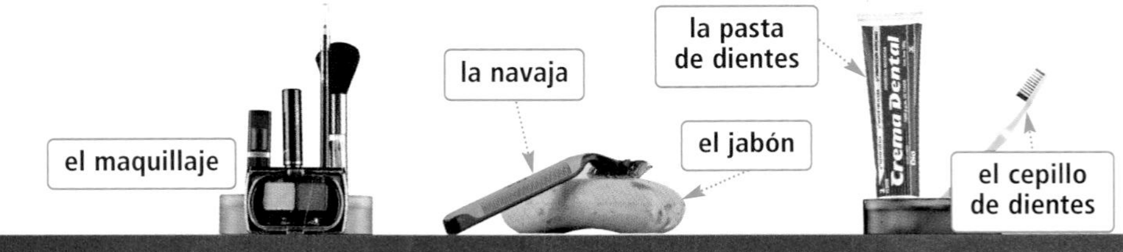

Core Instruction

TEACHING VOCABULARIO

1. Introduce the vocabulary using transparencies **Vocabulario 7.1** and **7.2**. **(20 min.)**
2. Tell students your morning or bedtime routine, using **Tengo que...** As you list each activity in your routine, act it out. **(3 min.)**
3. Tell students something you have to do to get ready (**Tengo que afeitarme**) and have students act out the activity. Name parts of the face/body, and have students point to the appropriate part of their face/body. **(10 min.)**
4. Finally, point to a part of your face/body and ask a volunteer to name the body part. You can also act out one of the activities in the **Vocabulario** and ask a volunteer to tell that he or she needs to do that activity to get ready. **(7 min.)**

ExpresaVisión

To teach the new vocabulary, use the video presenter. For interactive activities, see the *DVD Tutor.*

ExpresaVisión

STANDARDS: 1.2

Visit Holt Online
go.hrw.com
KEYWORD: EXP1B CH7
Vocabulario 1 practice

Por la tarde, después de clases, voy a...

estirarme antes de hacer ejercicio.
el brazo
la pierna
la pantorrilla

entrenarme. Me gusta levantar pesas.
el hombro
el pecho
la espalda

Por la noche, necesito...

quitarme la ropa,

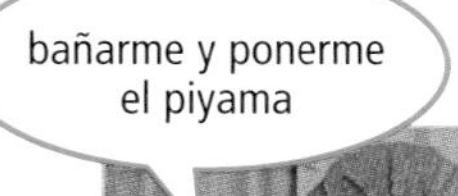
bañarme y ponerme el piyama

y acostarme temprano.

¡Exprésate!

To talk about your daily routine

Interactive TUTOR

¿Estás listo? ¿Qué te falta hacer? *Are you ready? What do you still have to do?*	**¡Ay, no! Acabo de levantarme. Tengo que lavarme la cara antes de desayunar.** *Oh, no! I just got up. I have to wash my face before I eat breakfast.*
¿Qué tienes que hacer para prepararte? *What do you have to do to get ready?*	**Tengo que secarme el pelo, pero no encuentro la secadora de pelo.** *I have to dry my hair, but I can't find the hair dryer.*

Online
Vocabulario y gramática, pp. 29–31

▶ **Vocabulario adicional** — Partes del cuerpo, p. R14

Differentiated Instruction

ADVANCED LEARNERS

Write **Por la mañana, tengo que...** on the board and tell the class to write a paragraph describing their personal morning routine in the proper order of events. You might write your own morning routine on the board to guide them. For example, **Tengo que despertarme a las seis, hacer ejercicio, bañarme, vestirme, secarme el pelo, comer el desayuno, lavarme los dientes y salir para el trabajo a las siete y media.** Ask volunteers to share their routines.

MULTIPLE INTELLIGENCES

Bodily-Kinesthetic Write each of the following verbs/verb phrases on a strip of paper, fold them in half, and put them in a container from which students can take turns choosing: **encontrar, afeitarse, bañarse, entrenarse, estirarse, lavarse, levantarse, levantar pesas, maquillarse, peinarse, vestirse, secarse.** The student who chooses the verb should act it out, while other students in the class guess the verb, based on the charades. The student who guesses correctly can take a turn acting out the next verb/verb phrase.

TPR
Total Physical Response

Have students help you collect items or illustrations of the items. Include some clothing and pajamas and an alarm clock. Present the commands and then have individual students respond.

Busca lo que necesitas para peinarte.

Dale a... lo que necesita para lavarse la cara.

Pon la toalla con el jabón.

Tráeme el cepillo de dientes y la pasta de dientes.

Busca lo que necesitas para bañarte.

Busca lo que necesitas para vestirte.

Dale a... lo que necesita para levantarse temprano.

Busca lo que te pones antes de acostarte.

COMMON ERROR ALERT
¡OJO!

Caution students about the use of **el piyama.** Even though it ends in **–a,** it is a masculine noun. In Spanish, it is used as a singular noun, whereas in English it is plural.

También se puede decir...

In Peru and Puerto Rico, toothpaste is often referred to as **pasta dental** and in Colombia it may be called **crema dental. Dentífrico** is another term they may hear. **Limpiarse el cutis** is sometimes used instead of **lavarse la cara,** especially by women. Instead of **peine, peineta** is sometimes used in Chile, and **peinilla** can be heard in Puerto Rico, Ecuador, and Panama. Other terms for **navaja** include **rasuradora, cuchilla de afeitar** which is often used in Cuba and Spain, and **rastrillo** which can be heard in Mexico.

STANDARDS: 1.2

2 Answers

1. Primero voy a levantarme y luego voy a bañarme.
2. Primero voy a bañarme y luego voy a secarme el pelo.
3. Primero voy a lavarme la cara y luego voy a maquillarme.
4. Primero voy a lavarme el pelo y luego voy a peinarme.
5. Primero voy a bañarme y luego voy a ponerme la ropa.
6. Primero voy a ponerme el piyama y luego voy a acostarme.
7. Primero voy a quitarme la ropa y luego voy a ponerme el piyama.
8. Primero voy a vestirme y luego voy a salir para el colegio.

Más práctica

1 After completing Activity 1 ask students to work with a partner and take turns reading the sentences out loud. Then ask them to read the sentences again, this time using the other word in parentheses and changing parts of the sentence to go with that choice.

MODELO

(as is) Quiero lavarme las manos antes de cenar.
(changed) Quiero lavarme la pantorrilla después de hacer ejercicio.

Dos muchachas hacen ejercicio en Buenos Aires

1 ¿Qué te falta hacer?

Leamos Escoge la palabra más apropiada y completa las oraciones.

1. Quiero lavarme (las manos/la pantorrilla) antes de cenar.
2. Me gusta (acostarme/entrenarme) temprano por la mañana.
3. Tengo que estirar (la boca/los brazos) antes de levantar pesas.
4. Necesito lavarme (los dientes/la nariz) después de comer.
5. ¿Dónde está (la navaja/la secadora)? Tengo que secarme el pelo.

2 ¿Qué vas a hacer primero?

Hablemos ¿En qué orden vas a hacer las siguientes cosas?

MODELO **vestirme/bañarme**
Primero voy a bañarme y luego voy a vestirme.

1. bañarme/levantarme
2. secarme el pelo/bañarme
3. lavarme la cara/maquillarme
4. lavarme el pelo/peinarme
5. ponerme la ropa/bañarme
6. acostarme/ponerme el piyama
7. quitarme la ropa/ponerme el piyama
8. vestirme/salir para el colegio

3 La familia López

Leamos The López family is getting ready for the day. Match each sentence with one of the pictures below.

1. Primero voy a lavarme los dientes y luego voy a lavarme las manos. la señora López
2. Primero voy a leer y luego voy a afeitarme. el señor López
3. Voy a levantarme primero. Luego voy a bañarme y vestirme. Ernesto
4. Voy a maquillarme y peinarme. Adela

a. el señor López

b. Ernesto

c. la señora López

d. Adela

FOLD-N-LEARN

The Pyramid

1. Have students fold opposite corners of an 8"x 8" paper to make a diagonal crease and then unfold the paper and repeat step 1 with the other two corners. **2.** Have students write questions from **¡Exprésate!,** p. 87, in one of the triangles. In the next triangle, they write the beginning of the answer (For example: **¡Ay no! Tengo que...**) and draw an item that represents the verbs from **Vocabulario 1,** pp. 87–88, to conclude the answer. **3.** In the third triangle, students write a verb that matches each of their illustrations. **4.** Students cut along the crease next to the empty triangle, stopping at the center point, and tape or glue the blank triangle under the adjacent flap, forming a pyramid. **5.** To study, students read the questions from the pyramid, rotate it to look at the illustration, answer the questions, and rotate it again to check their answers.

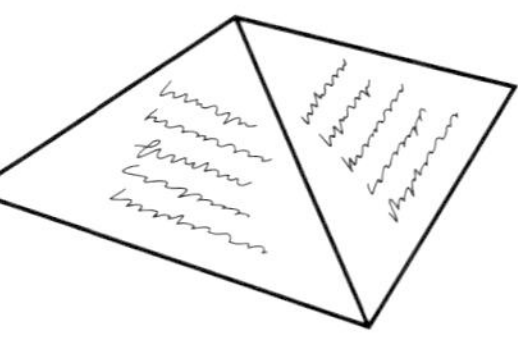

4 ¿Estás listo?

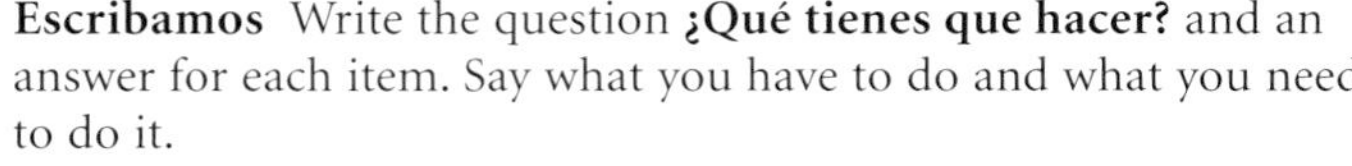

Escribamos Write the question **¿Qué tienes que hacer?** and an answer for each item. Say what you have to do and what you need to do it.

MODELO **¿Qué tienes que hacer?**
Tengo que afeitarme, pero primero tengo que encontrar la navaja.

1. 2. 3. 4.

5. 6. 7. 8.

Comunicación

5 Mi rutina

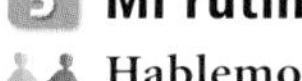

Hablemos Work with a partner. Write eight sentences each about your daily routine, using **necesito** or **me gusta** with the following verbs. Then read your sentences aloud, asking each other questions about your routines. Include phrases such as **¿a qué hora?, a veces, por la mañana, por la noche,** and days of the week.

MODELO **—Me gusta entrenarme por la mañana.**
—¿A qué hora?

despertarme	bañarme	estirarme	lavarme los dientes
levantarme	vestirme	entrenarme	acostarme

Vocabulario 1

4 Answers

1. Tengo que vestirme, pero primero tengo que encontrar la camisa y los pantalones.
2. Tengo que secarme el pelo, pero primero necesito encontrar la secadora de pelo.
3. Tengo que lavarme los dientes con el cepillo de dientes.
4. Tengo que secarme; necesito unas toallas.
5. Tengo que lavarme la cara; necesito el jabón.
6. Tengo que peinarme el pelo, pero primero tengo que encontrar el peine.
7. Tengo que maquillarme; necesito el maquillaje.
8. Tengo que acostarme, pero primero tengo que ponerme el piyama.

Comunicación

Class Activity: Interpersonal

Collect real items that represent the vocabulary in Activity 4. Place all items on a table. Have students, one at a time, go to the table, pick up an item and state that he or she needs that item **(Necesito el cepillo de dientes).** Then have someone ask **¿Qué tienes que hacer?** Instruct the student at the table to answer what he or she has to do **(Tengo que lavarme los dientes.).** Continue until each student has had a chance to get to the table.

Differentiated Instruction

SLOWER PACE LEARNERS

Variety Have students work with a partner and use the items pictured or brought in for Activity 4. Instruct the first student to point to or pick up an item (e.g. the hairdryer) and then name it (**la secadora de pelo**). Tell the second student to ask why that item is needed (**¿Por qué necesitas la secadora de pelo?**) Then have the first student answer by telling what he or she is going to do and when (**Voy a secarme el pelo antes de vestirme**).

MULTIPLE INTELLIGENCES

Auditory Learners Write vocabulary words in English and Spanish all over a sheet of paper and make a copy to give to each student. Call out 10–12 words in either language. If you say a word in Spanish, tell students to circle the word in English. If you say it in English tell them to circle it in Spanish. Check at the end to see who has the most correct circles.

Resources

Planning:

Lesson Planner, pp. 41–45, 200–205

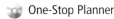

 One-Stop Planner

Presentation:

TPR Storytelling Book, pp. 36–37

 Teaching Transparencies **Vocabulario** 7.1, 7.2

Video Program
Videocassette 4
DVD Tutor, Disc 2
ExpresaVisión

Practice:

Cuaderno de vocabulario y gramática, pp. 29–31

Activities for Communication, pp. 25–26

Video Guide, pp. 64–66

Lab Book, pp. 19–20, 44

 Teaching Transparencies **Vocabulario y gramática** answers, pp. 29–31

 Audio CD 7, Tr. 1

Interactive Tutor, Disc 2

Connections

Science Link

Ask students to explain why the seasons occur at opposite times of the year in the Southern and Northern Hemispheres. (Due to the tilt of the earth's axis, sunlight is more direct in the Southern Hemisphere in December and more direct in the Northern Hemisphere in June.)

Geography Link

Ask students to write a short description of the current week's weather in Ushuaia, Argentina, using information they find on the Internet or in newspapers. Then have them compare it with the weather where you are.

¡Exprésate!

To talk about staying fit and healthy — Interactive TUTOR

¿Cómo te mantienes en forma? *How do you stay in shape?*	**Corro y levanto pesas. Entreno las piernas y los brazos.** *I run and lift weights. I work out my legs and my arms.*
¿Qué haces para relajarte? *What do you do to relax?*	**Me entreno. También duermo la siesta o escucho música.** *I work out. I also take a nap or listen to music.*

Online
Vocabulario y gramática, pp. 29–31

CD 7, Tr. 1

6 El sábado

 **Escuchemos** Escucha la conversación entre Juan y Laura sobre los planes de ella para el sábado. Luego completa las oraciones con las palabras correctas.

1. Voy a levantarme (temprano/tarde) este sábado.
2. (Corro/Levanto pesas/No me entreno) los sábados.
3. (Casi siempre/A veces/Nunca) almuerzo en casa los sábados.
4. Voy a bañarme (por la mañana/por la tarde) este sábado.
5. Quiero (relajarme/salir con mis amigos) este sábado por la tarde.
6. Para relajarme, prefiero (leer/escuchar música/ir de compras).
7. (Siempre/A veces/Nunca) duermo la siesta por la tarde los sábados.

Nota cultural

Argentina boasts some of the finest ski resorts in the world. Argentina's city of Bariloche is well known for its July ski season. Each August, Bariloche celebrates the National Snow Party, a week of winter celebrations. Why do you think the ski season is in July and August in Argentina?

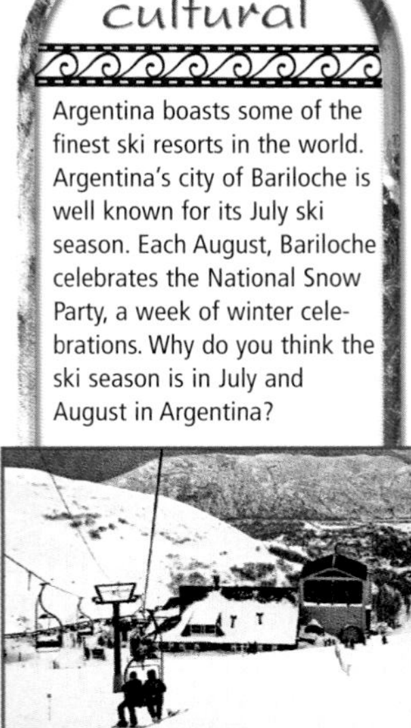

7 Una rutina sana

Leamos A student in Argentina has written telling how he stays in shape. Complete his letter with the best choice of words.

1. forma 2. levanto 3. entreno/estiro 4. corro 5. duermo 6. escucho 7. mantienes

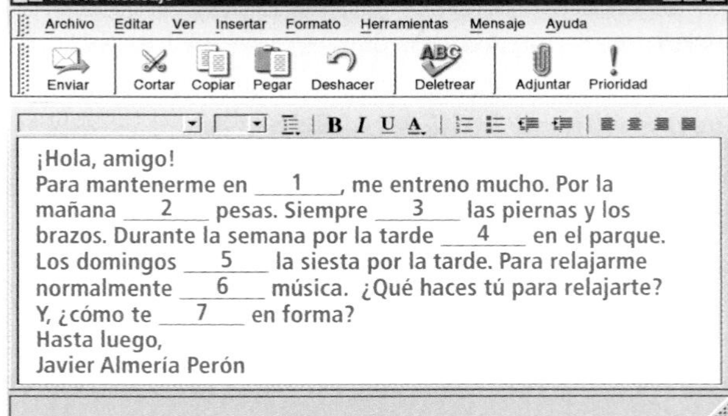
Nuevo Mensaje
Archivo Editar Ver Insertar Formato Herramientas Mensaje Ayuda
Enviar Cortar Copiar Pegar Deshacer Deletrear Adjuntar Prioridad

¡Hola, amigo!
Para mantenerme en __1__, me entreno mucho. Por la mañana __2__ pesas. Siempre __3__ las piernas y los brazos. Durante la semana por la tarde __4__ en el parque. Los domingos __5__ la siesta por la tarde. Para relajarme normalmente __6__ música. ¿Qué haces tú para relajarte? Y, ¿cómo te __7__ en forma?
Hasta luego,
Javier Almería Perón

Core Instruction

TEACHING ¡EXPRÉSATE!

1. Review **levantar pesas, entrenarme,** and **estirarme** from **Vocabulario** and the sports and activities from **Chapter 3** by acting out an activity, and then asking students to tell you that they also like to do that activity. For example, if you pretend to stretch, students will say **Me gusta estirarme también. (8 min.)**
2. Act out both sides of a conversation using expressions from **¡Exprésate!** When you answer **¿Cómo te mantienes en forma?** and **¿Qué haces para relajarte?,** recycle **levantar pesas** and sports and activities from **Chapter 3. (5 min.)**
3. Take turns asking volunteers both questions from **¡Exprésate! (7 min.)**

STANDARDS: 1.2, 2.1

8 **Y tú, ¿qué haces?**

Escribamos Write an answer to Javier's letter in Activity 7 and tell him about your own ways of staying fit and healthy. Use his letter as a model.

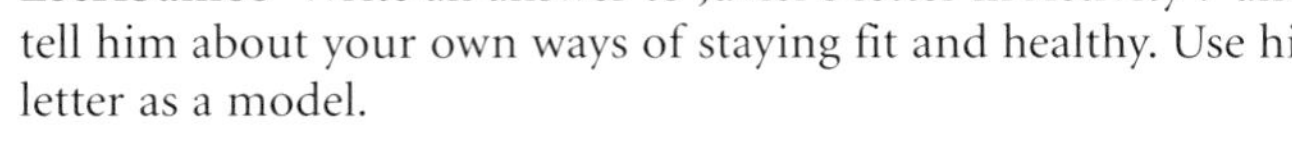

Comunicación

9 **Y a ti, ¿qué te gusta?**

Hablemos Take turns with a partner pretending you are the person in the following photos. Ask each other how you stay in shape, answer with the activity, and tell what parts of the body you work out.

MODELO —¿Cómo te mantienes en forma?
—**Hago ejercicio. Entreno las piernas y el estómago.**

1.

2.

3.

4.

5.

6.

10 **¿Cómo te mantienes en forma?**

Escribamos/Hablemos First write the following questions and your answers on a piece of paper. Then ask the questions to two or three classmates, and jot down their answers. Are their answers similar to yours or different? Be prepared to report your survey to the class.

1. ¿Cómo te mantienes en forma?
2. ¿Te gusta hacer ejercicio?
3. ¿Qué haces para relajarte?
4. ¿Prefieres entrenarte o relajarte?

6 Script

—¿Vas a dormir tarde el sábado?
—No, voy a levantarme a las siete. Siempre me entreno los sábados por la mañana.
—¿Cómo te mantienes en forma? ¿Corres?
—No, no corro. Me estiro y hago ejercicios en casa y luego voy al gimnasio a levantar pesas.
—¿Y qué vas a hacer por la tarde?
—Bueno, casi siempre almuerzo cuando vuelvo a casa. Siempre tengo mucha hambre después de hacer ejercicio. Luego voy a bañarme y relajarme.
—¿Qué haces para relajarte?
—Leo una revista o a veces duermo la siesta.

Comunicación

Pair Activity: Interpersonal

Have students interview a partner and take turns asking about the activities pictured in Activity 9. Instruct them to ask if the partner likes that activity and why/why not.

Individual Activity: Presentational

Ask students to prepare a written report about their preferred method of staying in shape. Have them include:

- which activity they like best to stay in shape
- why they prefer it
- what parts of the body they train with this activity
- what they like to do to relax after completing the activity

Then have them exchange reports with a classmate and read each others' comments.

Differentiated Instruction

ADVANCED LEARNERS

Challenge Ask students to write out a daily schedule for a healthy lifestyle that includes the time of the day for each activity. Ask them to include times for getting up and going to bed, times and activities for getting/keeping in shape, and also ideas for healthy meals and eating times. Then have them compare schedules with classmates and choose the three most appealing schedules to post in the classroom.

SPECIAL LEARNING NEEDS

Students with Learning Disabilities Use the pictures in Activity 9 to provide extra practice with vocabulary and verb usage for students with learning disabilities. Write sentences on the board that explain what each pictured person is doing, without using names (**Juega al béisbol todos los sábados.**). Read each sentence aloud and ask students to identify which person it is, and then to repeat the sentence using **él** or **ella** (**Es número uno. Él juega al béisbol...**)

Assess

Assessment Program

Prueba: Vocabulario 1, pp. 37–38

Alternative Assessment Guide, pp. 242, 250, 258

Test Generator

STANDARDS: 1.1, 1.2, 2.1

Resources

Planning:

Lesson Planner, pp. 46–51, 204–211

 One-Stop Planner

Presentation:

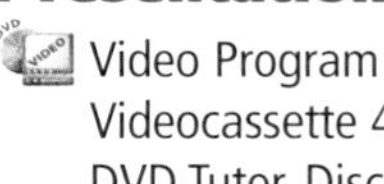 Video Program
Videocassette 4
DVD Tutor, Disc 2
GramaVisión

Practice:

Grammar Tutor for Students of Spanish, Chapter 7

Cuaderno de vocabulario y gramática, pp. 32–34

Cuaderno de actividades, pp. 25–27

Activities for Communication, pp. 25–26

Video Guide, pp. 64–65

Lab Book, pp. 19–20

 Teaching Transparencies
Bell Work 7.2
Vocabulario y gramática answers, pp. 32–34

 Audio CD 7, Tr. 2

 Interactive Tutor, Disc 2

Bell Work

Use Bell Work 7.2 in the *Teaching Transparencies,* or write this activity on the board.

Identify the part of the body each person will use for these activities.

1. Voy a maquillarme.
2. Manolo levanta pesas.
3. El muchacho corre.
4. La profesora habla.
5. Luisa va a lavarse los dientes.

11 Script

Tengo mucho que hacer. Primero tengo que hacer la tarea. Después voy a bañarme. Luego me lavo los dientes y me pongo el piyama. A las nueve me acuesto. Tengo que acostarme temprano porque mañana me levanto a las seis y media.

Objetivos
Verbs with reflexive pronouns, infinitives, review of stem-changing verbs

Gramática en acción 1

GramaVisión

Interactive TUTOR

Verbs with reflexive pronouns

1 If the subject and object of a verb are the same, a **reflexive pronoun** can be used. The reflexive pronoun shows that the subject acts upon itself. When you conjugate a verb like **lavarse,** include the reflexive pronoun that agrees with the subject.

yo **me** lavo	nosotros(as) **nos** lavamos
tú **te** lavas	vosotros(as) **os** laváis
Ud., él, ella **se** lava	Uds., ellos(as) **se** lavan

2 **Reflexive pronouns** can go before a conjugated verb or can be joined to the end of an **infinitive**. After reflexive verbs, use **el, la, los** or **las** with parts of the body or clothing.

(Yo) **Me** voy a **lavar** la cara.
I'm going to wash my face.

(Yo) Voy a **lavarme** la cara.
I'm going to wash my face.

3 Verbs such as **acostar (ue)** can be used with **reflexive pronouns** that refer to the subject or with direct objects that are different from the subject.

different from the subject
Juan **acuesta** a los niños.
Juan puts the children to bed.

refers to the subject
Juan **se acuesta.**
Juan goes to bed.

4 These are some other verbs with **reflexive pronouns**.

afeitar**se**	levantar**se**	preparar**se**
bañar**se**	mantener**se** (ie)	quitar**se**
despertar**se** (ie)	maquillar**se**	relajar**se**
entrenar**se**	peinar**se**	secar**se**
estirar**se**	poner**se**	vestir**se** (i)

Online
Vocabulario y gramática, pp. 32–34 | Actividades, pp. 25–27

Manteniéndose en forma, Buenos Aires, Argentina

CD 7, Tr. 2

11 ¿Qué hace Manuel?

Escuchemos Escucha lo que dice Manuel. ¿Va al colegio o se acuesta? Manuel se acuesta.

Core Instruction

TEACHING GRAMÁTICA

1. Go over point 1. Read each form of **lavarse** aloud, modeling pronunciation. **(5 min.)**
2. Go over point 2. Point to parts of your face/body and ask students to tell you that they are washing that body part. **(7 min.)**
3. Go over point 3. Show students more examples of the two different uses by pretending to comb your hair (**Me peino**), and then pretending to comb someone else's hair (**Peino a Carmen**). **(7 min.)**
4. Go over point 4, modeling the pronunciation of each verb. Ask students to use three of the verbs in sentences. Then ask volunteers to put their sentences on the board for the class to check. **(11 min.)**

GramaVisión

For a video presentation of reflexive verbs, use **el joven G.** For interactive activities, see the *DVD Tutor.*

GramaVisión

STANDARDS: 1.2

Visit Holt Online
go.hrw.com
KEYWORD: EXP1B CH7
Gramática 1 practice

12 Por la mañana

Leamos María is talking about her typical day. Read the paragraph and decide if the reflexive pronoun is needed with each verb.

Mis padres __1__ (levantan/se levantan) a las seis todos los días. Mientras mi padre __2__ (prepara/se prepara) para ir al trabajo, mi madre va a la cocina, __3__ (lava/se lava) las manos y __4__ (prepara/se prepara) el desayuno para la familia. Mi hermano menor y yo __5__ (levantamos/nos levantamos) a las siete. Mientras mamá y yo __6__ (vestimos/nos vestimos), papá __7__ (viste/se viste) a mi hermano. Después del desayuno, mamá __8__ (lava/se lava) los platos rápidamente mientras mi hermano y yo __9__ (lavamos/nos lavamos) los dientes antes de salir de la casa.

13 ¿Qué y cuándo?

Escribamos Mira las fotos. Escribe una oración para cada foto.

MODELO **El señor Vargas se afeita por la mañana.**

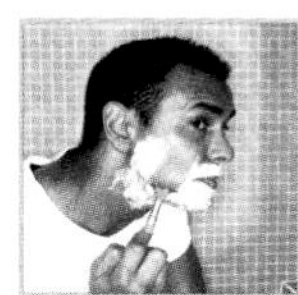
el señor Vargas por la mañana

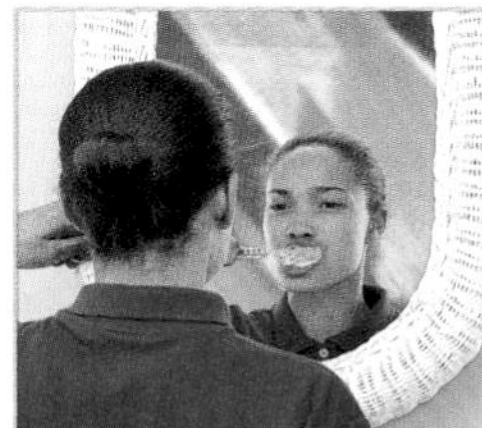
1. Laura 7:00 A.M.

2. ellas por la tarde

3. nosotros los fines de semana

4. tú por la noche

Comunicación

14 Cuéntame de ti

Hablemos Work in small groups. Use these phrases to ask each other what you do on Saturdays. Answer, adding details of your routine.

MODELO **—Berta, ¿qué haces los sábados?**
—Me levanto tarde y veo televisión.

relajarse	entrenarse en el gimnasio
levantarse temprano	ponerse ropa vieja
maquillarse/afeitarse	salir con los amigos

13 Answers

1. Laura se lava los dientes a las siete de la mañana.
2. Ellas se maquillan por la tarde.
3. Nos entrenamos/Levantamos pesas los fines de semana.
4. Te lavas el pelo por la noche.

Teacher to Teacher

Dena Bachman
Lafayette High School
St. Joseph, MO

Reflexives race Divide students into two teams. Assign a reflexive pronoun to each of the first five students on each team (same pronouns on each team) and a reflexive verb to each student remaining on each team (same verbs on each team). Call out a phrase in English that is reflexive in Spanish; for example, "I take a bath." The students on each team who have **me** and **bañar** rush to the board and write the phrase in Spanish: **Me baño.** The first pair to write the correct pronoun and verb form earn a point for their team.

Comunicación

Pair Activity: Presentational

Assign pairs of students one of the reflexive verbs listed on page 92. Challenge each pair to come up with a three or four-exchange dialogue to present from memory to the class which uses both the reflexive and non-reflexive uses for the verb.

Differentiated Instruction

SLOWER PACE LEARNERS

12 To prepare students for Activity 12, read each sentence of the paragraph together as a class. Have students name the subject in each sentence. Then have them name the object of the verb. Ask them "who" or "what" is receiving the action. Remind students that if the subject and the object are the same, they will use the reflexive pronoun.

SPECIAL LEARNING NEEDS

Students with Learning Disabilities It may be tricky for students to understand that reflexive pronouns may be written before a conjugated verb or may be joined to the end of an infinitive. To help reinforce this concept, instruct students to practice writing the reflexive pronouns both ways by writing the conjugation of each verb listed in point 4 of **Gramática,** with each reflexive pronoun.

STANDARDS: 1.1, 1.2, 1.3, 2.1

Resources

Planning:

Lesson Planner, pp. 46–51, 204–211

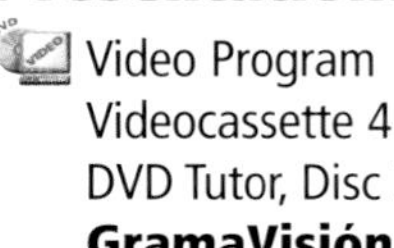

One-Stop Planner

Presentation:

Video Program
Videocassette 4
DVD Tutor, Disc 2
GramaVisión

Practice:

Grammar Tutor for Students of Spanish, Chapter 7

Cuaderno de vocabulario y gramática, pp. 32–34

Cuaderno de actividades, pp. 25–27

Activities for Communication, pp. 25–26

Video Guide, pp. 64–65

Lab Book, pp. 19–20

Teaching Transparencies
Bell Work 7.3
Vocabulario y gramática answers, pp. 32–34

Interactive Tutor, Disc 2

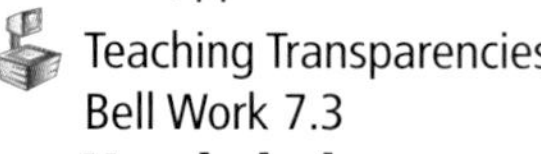

Bell Work

Use Bell Work 7.3 in the *Teaching Transparencies,* or write this activity on the board.

Complete the sentences with the correct reflexive pronoun.

me te se nos

1. Elena siempre _____ levanta a las siete de la mañana.
2. Mi padre y yo _____ relajamos con un juego de mesa los sábados.
3. ¿_____ estiras antes de levantar pesas?
4. Laura y Esteban _____ mantienen en buena forma.
5. Yo _____ baño por la noche.

Using infinitives

1 A **reflexive pronoun** can go at the end of an **infinitive** or before a conjugated verb. The meaning does not change.

Yo no quiero **estirarme** hoy. = Yo no **me** quiero **estirar** hoy.
I don't want to stretch today.

2 To say what someone just did, use the present tense of **acabar de** followed by an **infinitive.**

Acabo de lavar el carro. *I just washed the car.*

Los niños **acaban de acostarse.** *The children just went to bed.*

3 Use the preposition **para** before an **infinitive** to explain your purpose for doing something. Prepositions and prepositional phrases such as **a**, **para**, **antes de**, and **después de** are followed by verbs in the **infinitive.**

Tengo que levantarme temprano **para presentar** un examen.
I have to get up early (in order) to take an exam.

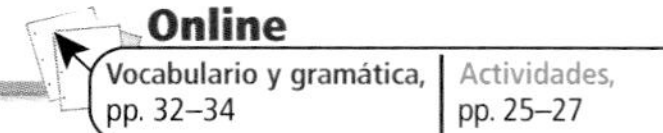

Online
Vocabulario y gramática, pp. 32–34 | Actividades, pp. 25–27

En inglés

In English, you can say **in order to** or just **to** to explain your purpose for doing something.

I need to call John (**in order**) **to** *see* how he's doing.

In Spanish, you can use **para** followed by an infinitive to explain your purpose for doing something. If you're talking about going somewhere to do something, use **a** followed by an infinitive.

Necesito llamar a Juan **para** saber cómo está.

Necesito ir al gimnasio **a** levantar pesas.

Manteniéndose en forma en un gimnasio

15 ¿Qué sigue?

Escribamos Choose the correct form of the verb in parentheses to complete each sentence.

1. **(se levanta, se levantan, me levanto, levantarse, levantarme)**
   a. Mis padres ═══ a las seis de la mañana. se levantan
   b. Mi padre ═══ primero. se levanta
   c. (Yo) ═══ temprano todos los días también, pero prefiero ═══ a las nueve o diez. me levanto, levantarme
2. **(se viste, me visto, vestirse, vestirme)**
   a. Mi madre desayuna antes de ═══. vestirse
   b. (Yo) prefiero desayunar después de ═══. vestirme
   c. (Yo) siempre ═══ en el baño. me visto
3. **(me lavo, nos lavamos, lavarme, lavarnos)**
   a. Después de desayunar voy al baño a ═══ los dientes. lavarme
   b. (Yo) siempre ═══ los dientes por la mañana. me lavo
   c. En el colegio no nos gusta ═══ los dientes. lavarnos
4. **(se acuesta, me acuesto, nos acostamos, acostarse, acostarme)**
   a. Nosotros ═══ tarde en mi familia. nos acostamos
   b. (Yo) ═══ primero, a las once. me acuesto
   c. Mi padre no ═══ hasta la medianoche porque prefiere leer un poco antes de ═══. se acuesta, acostarse

Core Instruction

TEACHING GRAMÁTICA

1. Go over point 1. Ask students to write 3 sentences using verbs with an infinitive and a reflexive pronoun. Have students choose one of their sentences to read aloud for the class to check. **(15 min.)**
2. Go over point 2. Ask students to suggest something they just did, using **acabar de.** You may also wish to have them imagine what various other people just did, to practice other forms of **acabar de. (9 min.)**
3. Go over point 3 and **En inglés. (6 min.)**

GramaVisión

To present different ways of using infinitives, use **el joven G** from the *Video Program.* For interactive activities, see the *DVD Tutor.*

GramaVisión

STANDARDS: 1.1, 1.3

16 Antes de acostarte

Hablemos Tell when you are going to do the following things.

MODELO **bañarme**
Me voy a bañar esta noche antes de acostarme.

1. levantarme
2. acostarme
3. ponerme el piyama
4. relajarme
5. entrenarme
6. vestirme

17 ¿Cuál es la situación?

Escribamos/Hablemos Look at the photos. Indicate what these people have just done or what they are going to do.

MODELO **Yo me voy a acostar.**

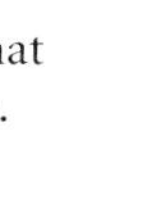
yo

1. ella

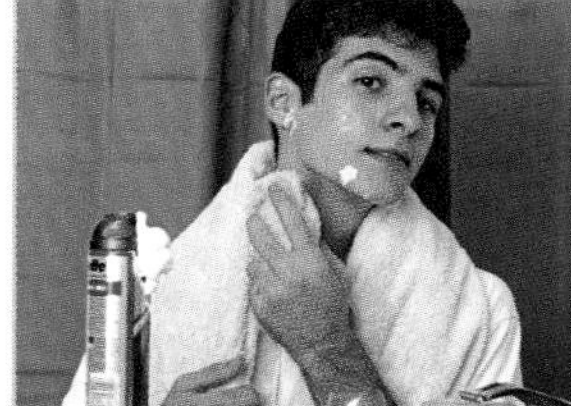
2. él

3. tú

4. Juan

Comunicación

18 ¿Cómo es tu rutina?

Escribamos/Hablemos Prepare five questions to ask a classmate, using words from each group. Then answer your classmate's questions. Be prepared to report what your partner says to the class.

MODELO **—Luis, ¿vas a levantarte temprano mañana?**
—No, mañana es sábado. Voy a levantarme tarde.
—Luis va a levantarse tarde mañana.

ir a	acostarse	todos los días
necesitar	despertarse	temprano
tener que	entrenarse	tarde
querer	estirarse	por la mañana
poder	levantarse	por la noche
	mantenerse en forma	por la tarde
	peinarse	mañana
	ponerse	el sábado
	relajarse	antes de desayunar
	vestirse	después de estudiar

Differentiated Instruction

ADVANCED LEARNERS

15 After students have finished Activity 15, have them change the statements to make them true for themselves and their families. Ask volunteers to read their answers for the class.

MULTIPLE INTELLIGENCES

18 Spatial Allow students to draw cartoons of their daily routines, writing the phrases in captions or dialogue bubbles, rather than simply writing out the sentences. You might allow them to use alternative forms of media, such as a drawing tool on the computer or transparency sheets and transparency markers. When they have finished the activity, you might also encourage students to share the cartoon drawings with the entire class.

17 Possible Answers

a. Ella acaba de lavarse el pelo./ Ella va a secarse el pelo.
b. Él acaba de leer un libro./ Él va a acostarse.
c. Tú acabas de bañarte,/Tú vas a vestirte.
d. Juan acaba de lavarse los dientes./ Juan va a peinarse.

COMMON ERROR ALERT ¡OJO!

Remind students that when using reflexives in an infinitive construction, the attached reflexive pronoun must agree with the subject of the sentence. Students will often leave **-se** at the end of the infinitive, resulting in **Yo quiero acostarse** instead of **Yo quiero acostarme.**

Circumlocution

Have students practice the vocabulary and reflexive verbs in this section by using circumlocution to play a guessing game with a partner. You might want to teach the expression **Se usa para...** to get students started.

Comunicación

Individual Activity: Presentational

As a homework assignment, ask students to describe the daily routine of a famous singer, actor, politician, or cartoon character. Students should write at least 8 sentences and use reflexive verbs and vocabulary from this section. The following day, call on several students to present their descriptions to the class. Ask several other students to comment on the plausibility of each description which is read. Collect all of the descriptions for a quick informal assessment of how students are using the reflexive verbs.

STANDARDS: 1.1, 1.2, 1.3

Resources

Planning:

Lesson Planner, pp. 46–51, 204–211

One-Stop Planner

Presentation:

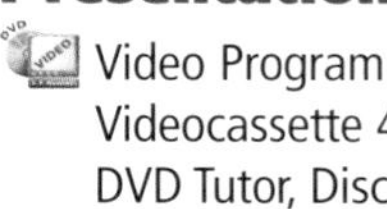
Video Program
Videocassette 4
DVD Tutor, Disc 2
GramaVisión

Practice:

Grammar Tutor for Students of Spanish, Chapter 7

Cuaderno de vocabulario y gramática, pp. 32–34

Cuaderno de actividades, pp. 25–27

Activities for Communication, pp. 25–26

Video Guide, pp. 64–65

Lab Book, pp. 19–20

Teaching Transparencies
Bell Work 7.4
Vocabulario y gramática answers, pp. 32–34

Audio CD 7, Tr. 3

Interactive Tutor, Disc 2

Bell Work

Use Bell Work 7.4 in the *Teaching Transparencies,* or write this activity on the board.

Unscramble the words to write logical sentences.

1. **acaba / pesas / Julio / de / levantar**
2. **mi / se / correr / de / estira / padre / antes**
3. **levantarme / no / las / a / siete / quiero / yo**
4. **bañarse / Laura / se / para / temprano / levanta**
5. **madre / maquilla / no / de / antes / se / salir / mi**

Repaso Stem-changing verbs

1 In the present tense, some verbs have one of three types of stem changes: (**e ➝ ie**), (**o/u ➝ ue**), or (**e ➝ i**) in all but the **nosotros** and **vosotros** forms.

2 The new verbs **despertarse** *(to wake up),* **mantenerse** *(to stay in shape),* **acostarse** *(to go to bed),* **encontrar** *(to find),* and **vestirse** *(to get dressed)* all have stem changes in the present tense.

acostarse (o ➝ ue)			
yo	me ac**ue**sto	nosotros (as)	nos acostamos
tú	te ac**ue**stas	vosotros (as)	os acostáis
Ud., él, ella	se ac**ue**sta	Uds., ellos, ellas	se ac**ue**stan

Mi hermana y yo **nos acostamos** a las diez.

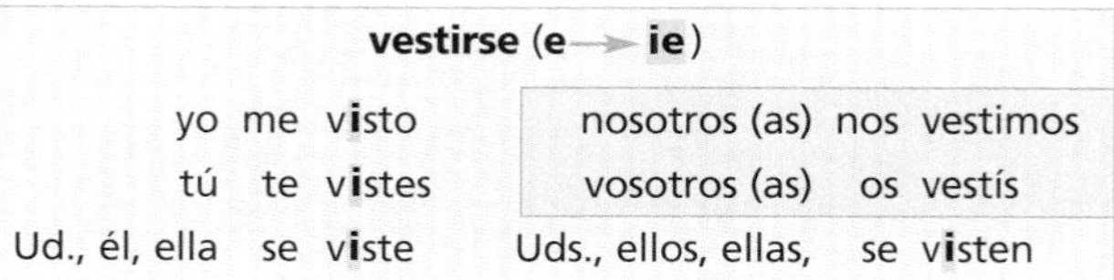

vestirse (e ➝ ie)			
yo	me v**i**sto	nosotros (as)	nos vestimos
tú	te v**i**stes	vosotros (as)	os vestís
Ud., él, ella	se v**i**ste	Uds., ellos, ellas,	se v**i**sten

Mi abuela **se viste** con ropa elegante.

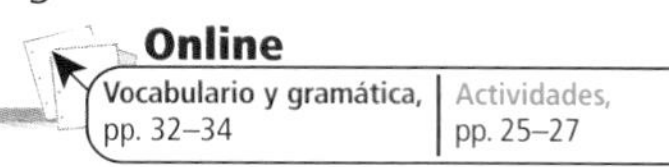

Online
Vocabulario y gramática, pp. 32–34
Actividades, pp. 25–27

¿Te acuerdas?

Here are some of the **stem-changing verbs** you have seen so far.

querer (e ➝ **ie**)

poder (o ➝ **ue**)

jugar (u ➝ **ue**)

pedir (e ➝ **i**)

CD 7, Tr. 3

19 Nuestra rutina

Escuchemos Decide si estas oraciones son **ciertas** o **falsas.**

1. El papá de Camila se acuesta antes que su mamá. cierta
2. Su hermano se acuesta después de jugar al ajedrez por Internet. falsa
3. Su mamá sirve huevos, tocino y pan tostado para el desayuno. falsa
4. Por la mañana, Camila y su hermano se levantan tarde. cierta
5. Después de desayunar, Camila se viste y se maquilla. cierta

20 La rutina familiar

Leamos/Escribamos Escoge el verbo apropiado y usa la forma correcta para completar cada oración.

Por la tarde mi hermana __1__ (servir/jugar) videojuegos pero yo __2__ (probar/empezar) mi tarea a las tres. Nosotras __3__ (servir/almorzar) la cena todos los días. Mis padres __4__ (acostar/preferir) cenar temprano. Mi padre siempre __5__ (querer/servir) leer un libro después de cenar pero mi madre __6__ (dormir/preferir) escuchar música. Yo siempre __7__ (levantarse/acostarse) antes de las diez de la noche.

1. juega
2. empiezo
3. servimos
4. prefieren
5. quiere
6. prefiere
7. me acuesto

Core Instruction

TEACHING GRAMÁTICA

1. Go over **¿Te acuerdas?** Ask volunteers to write sentences using **querer, poder, jugar,** and **pedir** on the board. **(10 min.)**
2. Go over point 1. **(7 min.)**
3. To review stem-changing verbs, give a student a stem-changing verb and a subject pronoun and ask the student to conjugate the verb. For example, if you say **yo** and **pedir,** the student would say **pido.** Continue, varying the pronouns and verbs until all students have had a chance to participate. **(8 min.)**

GramaVisión

For a video presentation of stem-changing verbs, use **el joven G** from the *Video Program.* For interactive activities, see the *DVD Tutor.*

GramaVisión

STANDARDS: 1.2

21 **¿Cuándo lo hacen?**

Escribamos Write sentences telling when everyone does the following activities.

MODELO **Luis/acostarse** ______
Luis se acuesta temprano.

1. mis amigos y yo/acostarse ______
2. los sábados/Carlitos/vestirse ______
3. mi amigo/no/encontrar/su tarea ______
4. ¿tú/encontrar/secadora de pelo ______?
5. mis padres/ siempre/acostarse ______
6. mis amigos y yo/vestirse/rápido ______

22 **¿Qué pasa en casa?**

Escribamos Write two short paragraphs. Use the verbs given to describe what is happening in each drawing.

1.

2.

jugar	llover
poder	querer

probar	servir
preferir	vestirse

Comunicación

23 **Tu rutina diaria**

Hablemos Use these phrases to interview a classmate about a typical school day.

despertarse temprano/tarde	vestirse en menos de veinte minutos
dormir mucho/poco	dormir la siesta
jugar a(l)...	encontrar tu mochila/libro de español
volver a casa	empezar la tarea

Gramática 1

19 **Script**

En mi familia todos nos acostamos tarde. Generalmente, mi padre se acuesta a las diez y mi madre se acuesta un poco más tarde. Mi hermano prefiere acostarse después de su programa de televisión preferido. Me acuesto después de todos porque juego al ajedrez por Internet y luego empiezo mi tarea. Por la mañana no tenemos mucho tiempo para desayunar porque no nos gusta levantarnos temprano. Por eso, mi madre sólo sirve cereales para el desayuno. Después de desayunar, quiero dormir más pero no puedo. Tengo que salir para el colegio. Voy a mi cuarto y me visto y me maquillo en menos de diez minutos.

Comunicación

Individual Activity: Presentational

Think-Draw-Speak Give students ten minutes to sketch pictures or symbols on a sheet of paper to represent ten activities that they do each morning before school. After ten minutes, have students use their drawings as cue cards to describe their morning routine. To help students connect their ideas, it may be helpful to brainstorm a list of time sequencing words and write them on the board or on a transparency. Ask students to present their drawings to the class.

Differentiated Instruction

SLOWER PACE LEARNERS

19 Before playing the audio, read each of the statements with the class so that they know what activities they might need to listen for. Play the entire audio straight through. Play the audio a second time, pausing after each statement. Allow the students to write their answers.

SPECIAL LEARNING NEEDS

23 **Students with Dyslexia** Students with dyslexia often have challenges with sequencing. As a modification for Activity 23, instruct students to write each of the action phrases listed on a separate 3 x 5 card. Then, have students rearrange the order of the actions to show the sequence that they follow on the days that they go to school.

Assess

Assessment Program

Prueba: Gramática 1, pp. 39–40

Prueba: Aplicación 1, pp. 41–42

Alternative Assessment Guide, pp. 242, 250, 258

Audio CD 7, Tr. 16

Test Generator

STANDARDS: 1.1, 1.2, 1.3

Cultura

VideoCultura

Resources

Planning:

Lesson Planner, pp. 51–52
210–211

 One-Stop Planner

Presentation:

 Teaching Transparencies
Mapa 3

 Audio CD 7, Tr. 4–6

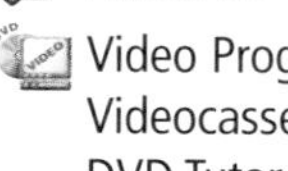 Video Program
Videocassette 4
DVD Tutor, Disc 2
VideoCultura

Practice:

Cuaderno de actividades, p. 28

Cuaderno para hispanohablantes, pp. 53–60

Video Guide, pp. 64–65, 67

Lab Book, p. 45

 Interactive Tutor, Disc 2

Atlas INTERACTIVO MUNDIAL

Have students use the interactive atlas at **go.hrw.com.**

BY MAPQUEST.COM™

Map Activities

Using transparencies **Mapa 3** and **4,** have students gage the distance between Costa Rica and Argentina. Remind them that Spanish-speaking cultures are spread out across the globe and that, even if peoples from various countries share a language, they might be very different, due to diverse historical backgrounds and geographical situations. Ask students to reflect on possible differences between people from Argentina and Costa Rica, based on where their respective countries are located.

Comparaciones

CD 7, Tr. 4–6

Parque Palermo, Argentina

¿Cómo te mantienes en forma?

La necesidad de mantenerse en forma es universal. En Argentina los jóvenes prefieren mantenerse en forma practicando el esquí, el patinaje en hielo y el hockey, también el ciclismo, la natación, el windsurf, el taekwondo, el alpinismo y, desde luego, el fútbol. Muchos jóvenes se mantienen en forma con la práctica del fútbol todos los fines de semana. ¿Qué diferencia hay entre lo que hacen estos jóvenes y lo que haces tú para mantenerte en forma?

Miguel
Buenos Aires, Argentina

Miguel talks about what he does to stay in shape. What kinds of exercise do you do?

¿Crees que estás en forma ahora?

Eh, sí creo que estoy en forma, me mantengo, trato siempre de salir a correr, cosas por el estilo, cosas de mantenerme siempre en forma.

¿Cómo te mantienes en forma?

Practico gimnasia acrobática desde hace nueve años. Este, salgo a correr, distintos tipos de deportes... me gusta un poquitito de todo, muy variado.

Para ti, ¿qué es lo difícil de mantenerte en forma?

Lo difícil de mantenerse en forma, yo creo que es mantener una constancia en un entrenamiento, fijarse objetivos y a partir de ahí, bueno, a ver qué pasa.

¿Qué haces para relajarte?

Me gusta leer. Me gusta escuchar música, especialmente leer porque como quien dice, este, en un cuerpo sano, mente sana.

Core Instruction

TEACHING CULTURA

1. Read and discuss the introductory paragraph and photo as a class. **(10 min.)**
2. Have students watch the two interviews on video using the *Video Program* or the *DVD Tutor.* Pause the video periodically and check for comprehension. **(15 min.)**
3. Have students answer the questions in the **Para comprender** section with a partner. Discuss **Para pensar y hablar** with the class. **(15 min.)**

VideoCultura

For a video presentation of the interviews as well as for additional interviews, see Chapter 7 **VideoCultura** on Videocassette or on DVD. For interactive practice, see the *DVD Tutor.*

VideoCultura

STANDARDS: 1.2, 2.1, 4.2

Visit Holt Online
go.hrw.com
KEYWORD: EXP1B CH7
Online Edition

Ivania
San José, Costa Rica

Ivania talks about how exercise and diet help her stay in shape. How do diet and exercise affect the way you feel?

¿Crees que estás en forma en este momento?

Sí, sí creo que estoy en forma.

¿Cómo te mantienes en forma?

Yo para mantenerme en forma camino, corro o voy al gimnasio.

Para ti, ¿qué es lo difícil de mantenerte en forma?

Para mí, lo difícil de mantenerme es poder evitar comer chocolate, picaditas o helados.

¿Qué haces para relajarte?

Yo para relajarme hago muchas cosas, leo poemas, hablo con mis amigos, salgo a pasear.

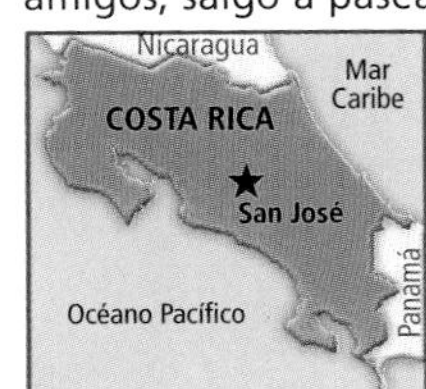

Para comprender

1. ¿Qué hace Miguel para mantenerse en forma? ¿Qué deportes le gustan a Miguel?
2. ¿Por qué es difícil para Miguel mantenerse en forma?
3. ¿Cómo se mantiene en forma Ivania? ¿Qué le gusta comer a Ivania?
4. ¿Qué hacen Miguel e Ivania para relajarse? ¿Qué cosa hacen los dos? En tu opinión, ¿es cierto lo que dice Miguel, "en un cuerpo sano, mente sana"? ¿Por qué?

Para pensar y hablar

Very often exercise involves going to the gym. But, simple things like walking or riding a bike to places can be enough exercise. Both Miguel and Ivania live in cities in their home countries where places are often within walking distance. Are places easy to walk to in your community, or are they spread out so you have to ride there in a car or bus? How can the way a city is built make it easy or hard for a person to get exercise?

Cuaderno para hispanohablantes, pp. 69–80

Comunidad

Spanish in health care careers

The medical field needs health care workers who know Spanish. In small groups, write a letter to the Personnel Manager of a nearby health care facility. Ask these questions in your letter.

- What percentage of their patients speak Spanish?
- How many bilingual employees do they have?
- Is Spanish a requirement for any of their job positions?
- Do they have printed signs in English and Spanish?

When you receive replies to your letters, share them with the class.

En la oficina de la dentista

Differentiated Instruction

SLOWER PACE LEARNERS

Before showing the video, have students make a list in Spanish of what they do to stay in shape or live a healthy life. Tell them that they should write at least three things. Explain to them that they are going to hear how Spanish-speaking teens stay fit. As they are watching the video, tell them to put a check next to any item in their list that the kids in the video mention. Also tell them to write down at least two things that the interviewees do that are not on their list. Use these written lists to guide discussion at the end of the video.

SPECIAL LEARNING NEEDS

Students with Learning Disabilities To help students read and comprehend this section, it might help to give them extra prompts such as the following for more pre-reading work: Look at the pictures. What clues do they give you about each paragraph? There are words here that are the same or very similar in English and Spanish. What are those words? Based on those words and the picture, what do you think that the paragraphs are about?

Para Comprender Answers

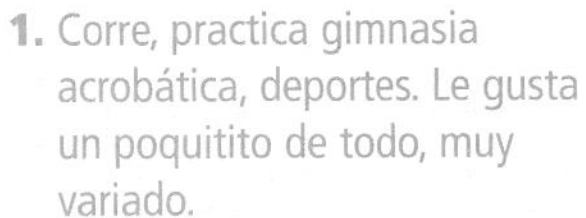

1. Corre, practica gimnasia acrobática, deportes. Le gusta un poquitito de todo, muy variado.
2. Es difícil mantener una constancia en un entrenamiento y fijarse en objetivos.
3. Camina, corre, va al gimnasio. Le gusta comer chocolate, picaditas o helados.
4. Miguel lee, escucha música. Ivania lee poemas, habla con sus amigos, sale a pasear. Los dos leen.

Connections

Interdisciplinary Link

Geography

Ask student to identify the geographical feature which is referred to in the term **alpinismo.** You may want to tell them that other sports such as **esquí alpino** and **esquí nórdico** also refer to geographical features or regions. Have students use inference to tell why these terms are used. (Downhill skiing originated in the Alps, and cross-country skiing originated in Norway. Mountain climbing first became recognized as a sport in the Alps.)

Communities

Community Link

Ask students to start compiling a class list of businesses in your community where Spanish is used or needed. Have them look for signs in Spanish in places they visit with their families. Ask them if they can talk to employees at various businesses and ask if they often have Spanish-speaking customers. Do the employees speak Spanish? Are there certain things the business does to help Spanish-speaking customers? Have students add the information they find to a poster to be placed in the classroom.

STANDARDS: 1.2, 2.1, 3.1, 4.2, 5.1

Resources

Planning:

Lesson Planner, pp. 52–56, 210–217

 One-Stop Planner

Presentation:

TPR Storytelling Book, pp. 38–39

Teaching Transparencies **Vocabulario** 7.3, 7.4

 Video Program
Videocassette 4
DVD Tutor, Disc 2
ExpresaVisión

Practice:

Cuaderno de vocabulario y gramática, pp. 35–37

Activities for Communication, pp. 27–28

Video Guide, pp. 64–65, 68

Lab Book, pp. 21–22, 46

 Teaching Transparencies
Bell Work 7.5
Vocabulario y gramática answers, pp. 35–37

 Interactive Tutor, Disc 2

Bell Work

Use Bell Work 7.5 in the *Teaching Transparencies*, or write this activity on the board.

Choose the logical verb for each sentence and write the correct form in the blank.

acostarse vestirse
encontrar pedir jugar

1. **Yo no _____ mi cepillo de dientes.**
2. **Mi hermano y yo _____ tarde todos los días. Por eso estamos cansados.**
3. **Hernán y Pablo siempre quieren _____ al básquetbol.**
4. **Tu madre _____ muy bien.**
5. **Tú nunca _____ sopa en los restaurantes.**

Objetivos
Talking about how you feel, giving advice

Vocabulario en acción 2

Video/DVD
ExpresaVisión

¿Te duele algo?

LOS MUSCULOS

¿Qué te pasa?

Me duele...

la cabeza

el oído

la garganta

el estómago

la mano

el pie

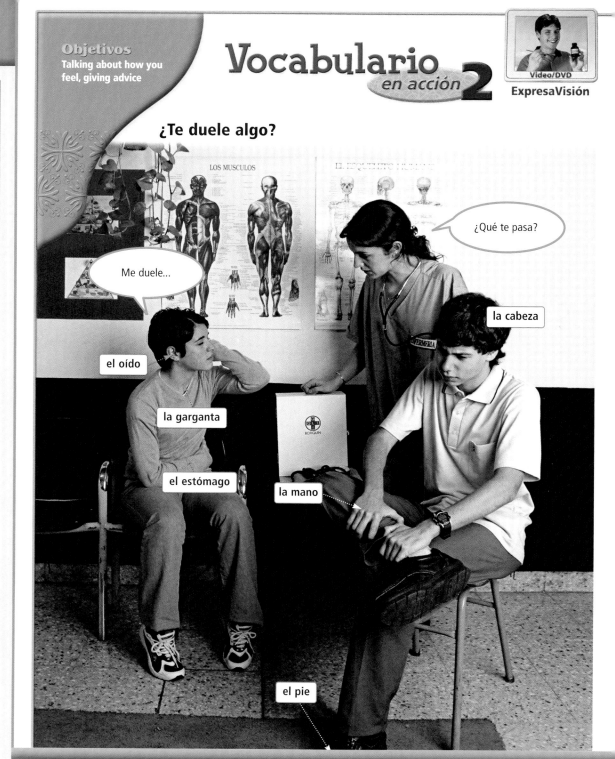

Core Instruction

TEACHING VOCABULARIO

1. Introduce the vocabulary using transparencies **Vocabulario 7.3** and **7.4.** Model the pronunciation of each word as you point to the appropriate picture. **(10 min.)**
2. Act out both sides of a conversation in which you ask **¿Qué te pasa? ¿Te duele algo?** As you respond with **Me duele(n)...,** point to the appropriate part of the body. Then, point to a student and tell the class **Le duele...,** while the student points to the appropriate body part. **(7 min.)**
3. Read the new expressions using **estar** or use the phrases **seguir una dieta sana, hacer yoga,** and **caminar** in a sentence, and have a volunteer act out the meaning. **(8 min.)**

ExpresaVisión

To teach health-related vocabulary, use the video presenter. For interactive activities, see the *DVD Tutor.*

ExpresaVisión

STANDARDS: 1.2

¿Cómo se sienten?

Visit Holt Online
go.hrw.com
KEYWORD: EXP1B CH7
Vocabulario 2 practice

Está cansada.

Está aburrido.

Está nerviosa.

Está triste.

Para cuidar la salud debes...

hacer yoga

caminar

seguir una dieta sana

Más vocabulario...

bajar de peso	*to lose weight*
buscar un pasatiempo	*to find a hobby*
dejar de fumar	*to stop smoking*
enojarse	*to get angry*
estar contento (a)	*to be happy*
subir de peso	*to gain weight*

¡Exprésate!

To ask how someone feels	To respond
Te veo mal. *You don't look well.*	**Es que estoy enferma. Tengo catarro.** *I'm sick. I have a cold.*
¿Qué te pasa? ¿Te duele algo? *What's wrong with you? Does something hurt?*	**Me siento (un poco) cansado y me duelen los pies (las manos).** *I feel (a little) tired and my feet (hands) hurt.*
¿Qué tiene Rosa? ¿Está enojada? *What's the matter with Rosa? Is she angry?*	**Le duele el cuello.** *Her neck hurts.*

Interactive TUTOR

Online
Vocabulario y gramática, pp. 35–37

▶ Vocabulario adicional — En el consultorio, p. R12

TPR
Total Physical Response

Present and model the commands before having students respond. You might have students play this in a "Simon Says..." format for fun. Continue to practice the other related items.

Pon la mano encima de la cabeza.

Pon la mano cerca del estómago.

Levanta los brazos por encima de la cabeza.

Párate en un solo pie.

Pon la mano cerca del oído.

Levanta sólo un pie.

Then practice the rest of the vocabulary. You will need some items to represent healthy and less healthy food items, a symbolic representation of stopping smoking, signs with a numerical weight and an arrow up or down to represent weight gain and loss.

Eres una persona nerviosa.

Eres una persona cansada.

Connections

Language Note

You may want to explain to students about onomatopoeia and tell them that **garganta** is an example. **Garganta** comes from the root **garg-** which imitates the sound of expectoration and other sounds made by the throat.

También se puede decir...

Students may hear **reducir** or **adelgazar** *(to become thinner)* instead of **bajar de peso.** In addition to **subir de peso, aumentar de peso** *(to increase in weight)* and **engordar** *(to become fatter)* are also commonly used.

Differentiated Instruction

Advanced Learners

To reinforce the vocabulary ask the students **¿Qué me pasa?** Then, pantomime one of the illnesses or problems, such as holding your stomach, rubbing your neck, or tapping your fingers on the desk. Allow the student that has correctly stated what is wrong with you to come to the front of the class and pantomime an action. Continue until you have circulated through all the vocabulary.

Multiple Intelligences

Linguistic/Interpersonal/Spatial Students with linguistic strengths are usually skilled in persuasive writing, students with interpersonal strengths tend to be good at inspiring people, and people with spatial strengths are often skilled artists. This activity allows students with different strengths to work together. Have groups create an advertisement showing one of these messages: *eat a balanced diet, stop smoking, do yoga, lose weight, be happy, get enough sleep.* Bring some advertisements to class to use as examples.

Teacher to Teacher

Carol Chadwick
Taipei American School
Taipei, Taiwan

Before the students enter the room, I tape 20 small pictures of different parts of the body around the room, numbered 1–20, visible but not too obvious. The first five students to write down all 20 correctly get a small prize or extra points. This totally engages the students!

26 Possible Answers

1. No puedo hablar. Me duele la garganta.
2. No puedo levantar pesas. Me duele la espalda.
3. No puedo comer. Me duele la boca.
4. No puedo escribir. Me duele la mano.
5. No puedo oír. Me duele el oído.
6. No puedo estudiar. Me duele la cabeza.
7. No puedo bailar. Me duelen los pies.
8. No puedo leer. Me duelen los ojos.
9. No puedo jugar al tenis. Me duelen los hombros.
10. No puedo patinar. Me duele la pantorrilla.

Nota cultural

Argentina is famous for its **parrilladas**—steaks and other grilled meats. Another important element in Argentine cooking is the influence of Spain and Italy. You might be surprised to find a **milanesa napolitana** (veal cutlet, a dish from Naples, Italy) served in Buenos Aires. How does Argentine food compare to your diet?

24 Debes cuidarte mejor

Leamos Lee lo que varios amigos te dicen sobre sus problemas. Escoge la mejor respuesta para cada situación.

1. Me duelen mucho los ojos. c
2. Siempre estoy aburrido. d
3. Me siento muy cansada. g
4. Nunca como frutas ni verduras. b
5. Siempre me duele la garganta. a
6. Quiero bajar de peso. e
7. Tengo catarro. h
8. ¡Estoy enojada! i
9. Me duelen los pies. f

a. Debes dejar de fumar.
b. Necesitas seguir una dieta sana.
c. ¡Usa tus lentes!
d. ¿Qué tal si buscas un pasatiempo?
e. Debes comer menos y hacer ejercicio.
f. No debes correr sin *(without)* zapatos.
g. Debes dormir lo suficiente.
h. Toma jugo de naranja y descansa.
i. Debes relajarte. ¿Por qué no haces yoga?

25 ¿Estás bien?

Leamos A teacher has noticed that you don't look well. After class you have a conversation. Refer to **Exprésate** on page 101 to complete your part of the conversation. 1. enfermo(a) 2. catarro 3. cansado(a) 4. la cabeza 5. enferma 6. Answers will vary.

La profesora	Tú
Te veo mal.	Es que estoy __1__.
¿Qué te pasa?	Tengo __2__ y me siento un poco __3__.
¿Te duele algo?	Sí, me duele __4__.
Debes llamar a tu mamá por teléfono.	No puedo, ella está __5__ también.
Y, ¿qué tiene ella?	Le duele __6__.

26 ¿Qué te duele?

Hablemos Explain that you can't do the folllowing activities because something hurts.

MODELO correr
No puedo correr. Me duelen las piernas y los pies.

1. hablar
2. levantar pesas
3. comer
4. escribir
5. oír *(to hear)*
6. estudiar
7. bailar
8. leer
9. jugar al tenis
10. patinar

Game

¿Qué te pasa?

1. Make large, simple drawings on sheets of paper, or enlarge clip art, to show different ways that people feel. Use the illustrations to review **Vocabulario 2,** pp. 101–102, so students know which vocabulary expression is represented by each illustration. **2.** Divide students into two teams and explain that only one player from each team will compete in each round of the game. **3.** Call up a player from each team to the front of the room. Hold up an illustration for both teams to see and ask, **¿Qué te pasa? 4.** The first player to raise his or her hand answers the question by stating how he or she is feeling according to the illustration. **5.** If the answer is correct, that player's team earns a point and two more players are called to the front for the next illustration. If the answer is incorrect, the other player gets a chance to earn a point. **6.** The team with the most points after viewing all the illustrations wins.

STANDARDS: 1.2, 1.3, 2.1, 4.2

27 ¿Cómo estamos?

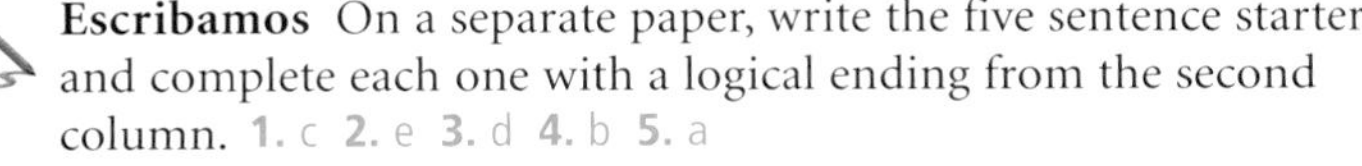

Escribamos On a separate paper, write the five sentence starters and complete each one with a logical ending from the second column. 1. c 2. e 3. d 4. b 5. a

1. Yo estoy triste porque...	a. ella no duerme bien.
2. Juan está enfermo y...	b. no tienen nada que hacer.
3. Maricarmen está nerviosa porque...	c. mi perro está enfermo.
4. Los niños están aburridos porque...	d. tiene que presentar un examen.
5. La Sra. Romero está cansada porque...	e. le duele el estómago.

Comunicación

28 ¿Cómo se siente?

Hablemos Look at the drawings. With a partner, take turns asking what is wrong with each person and answering with what hurts.

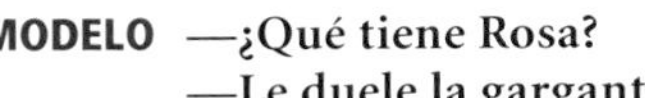

MODELO —¿Qué tiene Rosa?
—**Le duele la garganta.**

Rosa

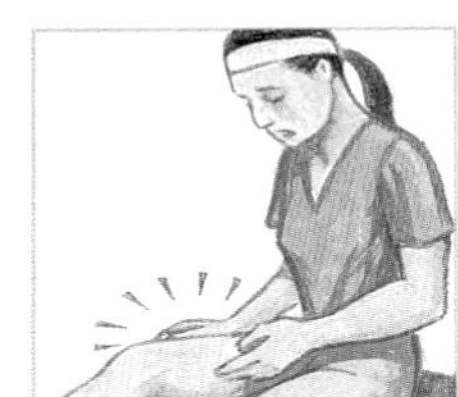
Midori

Conchita

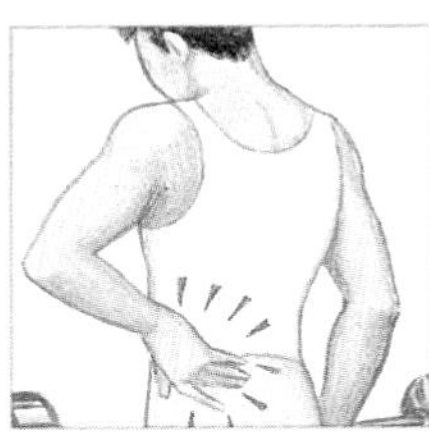
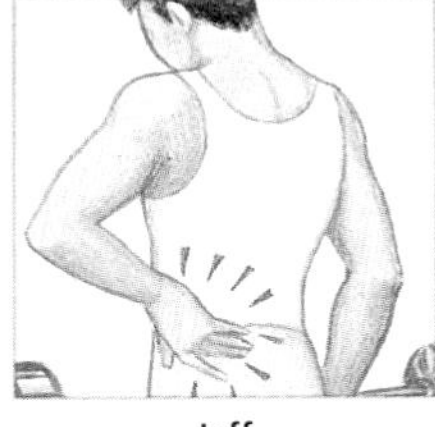
Jeff

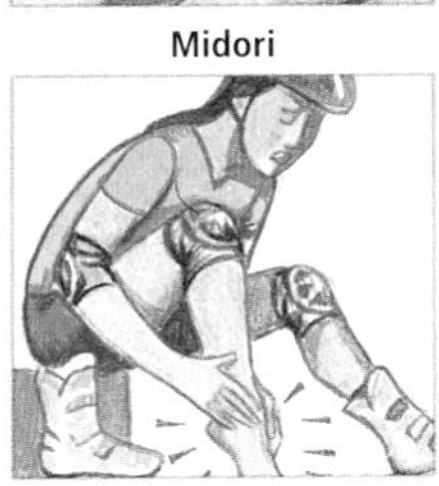
Linda

Donna

Benito

Now take turns with your partner playing the roles of the people above. Ask each other what's wrong, and answer as if you were the person in the drawing.

MODELO —**Jeff, te veo mal. ¿Qué tienes?**
—**Es que me duele...**

28 Answers

—¿Qué tiene Midori? Le duele la pierna.
—¿Qué tiene Conchita? Le duele el brazo.
—¿Qué tiene Jeff? Le duele la espalda.
—¿Qué tiene Linda? Le duele la pantorrilla.
—¿Qué tiene Donna? Le duele la cabeza.
—¿Qué tiene Benito? Le duele la mano.

Extension

27 Have students check their answers to Activity 27 with a partner. Then ask them to work together to write different endings for the sentence starters. Have them get together with another pair and read their new sentences.

Comunicación

Pair Activity: Presentational

Have students play the roles of a doctor and a patient. Ask the patient to make up a health scenario: how he or she feels, what hurts and why. Have the doctor ask questions to the patient to get the information, and then tell the patient what to do about the condition. Instruct students to be prepared to act out the scene for the rest of the class.

MODELO

Dr: Te veo mal. ¿Qué tienes?
Pt: Es que tengo catarro.
Dr: ¿Te duele algo?
Pt: Sí, me duele la garganta.
Dr: Necesitas beber jugo de naranja y descansar.

Differentiated Instruction

ADVANCED LEARNERS

Challenge Have students work in pairs to write reasons why the people pictured in Activity 28 are hurting. Then conduct a question and answer period with the entire class to get a variety of reasons.

MODELO

—**¿Por qué le duele a Midori la pierna?**
—**Porque ella corre mucho y hace ejercicio.**

SPECIAL LEARNING NEEDS

Students with ADD To make sure ADD students understand the vocabulary, write 7 sentences on the board that describe the conditions of the people in Activity 28. Do not include names (**Le duele la garganta**). Read a sentence out loud and have students point to the corresponding picture. Then ask **¿A quién le duele la garganta?** and have a student volunteer the name on the picture (**José**). Respond with **Sí, a José le duele la garganta** and have students repeat after you.

STANDARDS: 1.1, 1.2, 1.3

Resources

Planning:

Lesson Planner, pp. 51–52, 210–217

 One-Stop Planner

Presentation:

TPR Storytelling Book, pp. 38–39

 Teaching Transparencies **Vocabulario** 7.3, 7.4

 Video Program
Videocassette 4
DVD Tutor, Disc 2
ExpresaVisión

Practice:

Cuaderno de vocabulario y gramática, pp. 35–37

Activities for Communication, pp. 27–28

Video Guide, pp. 64–65, 68

Lab Book, pp. 21–22, 46

 Teaching Transparencies **Vocabulario y gramática** answers, pp. 35–37

 Audio CD 7, Tr. 7

Interactive Tutor, Disc 2

29 Script

1. —¿Qué te pasa? Te veo muy cansado.
—Sí, me siento muy cansado. Veo televisión hasta tarde cada noche y tengo que levantarme temprano por la mañana.
2. —¿Qué te pasa?
—Me duelen mucho los pies. Me gusta mantenerme en forma pero si corro todos los días me duelen.
3. —Siempre te veo muy nervioso. ¿Estás bien?
—No sé qué me pasa. No puedo relajarme.
4. —¿Qué tienes?
—Ay, me duele mucho el estómago. Acabo de comer una pizza y muchos dulces.
5. —¿Qué tienes? ¿Te duele algo?
—Sí. Siempre me duelen las piernas cuando levanto pesas.
6. —¿Estás enferma?
—No. Es que siempre me duele la garganta después de fumar.
7. —¿Qué te pasa? ¿Por qué no haces la tarea?
—Me duelen los ojos cuando leo.

Nota cultural

Mate is a popular South American drink made from an herb called **yerba mate.** The dried herb is placed in a gourd or metal cup, also called a **mate,** and hot water is slowly poured from a kettle called a **pava. Mate** is sipped through a metal straw called a **bombilla** that filters out the loose tea. When the cup of **mate** is finished, more water is added to the leaves. What kinds of herbal teas or other drinks are popular where you live? Is coffee more popular than tea in your community?

¡Exprésate!

To give advice

¿Sabes qué? Comes muy mal. No debes comer tanto dulce ni grasa.
You know what? You eat very badly. You shouldn't eat so many sweets nor so much fat.

Para cuidarte mejor, debes dormir lo suficiente. ¿Por qué no te acuestas más temprano?
To take better care of yourself, you should get enough sleep. Why don't you go to bed earlier?

No debes ver demasiada televisión.
You shouldn't watch too much television.

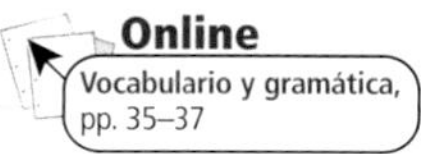

CD 7, Tr. 7

29 ¿Qué te pasa?

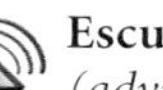

Escuchemos Escucha las conversaciones. Escoge el consejo *(advice)* apropiado. 1. b 2. c 3. d 4. e 5. g 6. f 7. a

a. Debes usar lentes.
b. Necesitas dormir lo suficiente.
c. ¿Qué tal si caminas o montas en bicicleta?
d. Tienes que relajarte. Debes hacer yoga.
e. Hombre, ¡debes seguir una dieta sana!
f. ¡Deja de fumar!
g. Debes estirarte antes de hacer ejercicios.

30 Consuelo y sus hábitos

Leamos/Escribamos Read these notes that Consuelo has made about her health and eating habits. For each comment, write some advice on what she should or should not do to improve her health.

Como mucho chocolate y hamburguesas.
A veces estoy cansada.
Me duelen los ojos por la noche.
Estoy aburrida por la mañana.
No hago ejercicio.

Core Instruction

TEACHING ¡EXPRÉSATE!

1. Introduce the new expressions in **¡Exprésate!**, modeling the pronunciation. Point out to students the use of **ni**, meaning *nor*. **(5 min.)**
2. Show pictures of people engaging in activities that are bad for their health such as eating sweets or chips, staying up late, looking tired, watching a lot of television. Give the people in the pictures advice using the expressions in **¡Exprésate! (5 min.)**
3. Put the pictures of people engaged in unhealthful activities where all the students can see them. Give health advice and ask a volunteer to indicate which "person" the advice is for. **(5 min.)**

STANDARDS: 1.2, 1.3, 2.1, 4.2

31 ¿Sano o no?

Leamos Read the paragraphs about Leo and Juan, and then decide whether the statements that follow are **cierto** or **falso.** If a statement is **falso,** change it to make it read **cierto.**

LEO	JUAN
Leo es un hombre de 50 años. Se levanta por la mañana a las 6:00 y corre por una hora. Come frutas, verduras y toma leche. No come carne. Por la tarde levanta pesas. Se acuesta a las 10:00 de la noche.	Juan tiene 35 años. No hace ejercicio nunca. Come mucha pizza y toma refrescos todos los días. Ve televisión por la noche. Fuma mucho y siempre está cansado. Se acuesta a la 1:00 de la mañana.

1. Juan no debe comer tanta grasa. cierto
2. Leo no duerme lo suficiente. falso, Juan no duerme lo suficiente.
3. Juan debe dejar de fumar. cierto
4. Leo come muy mal. falso, Leo sigue una dieta sana.
5. Juan no se cuida. cierto
6. Leo levanta pesas por la mañana. falso, Levanta pesas por la tarde.

Comunicación

32 ¿Cómo te sientes?

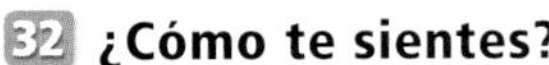
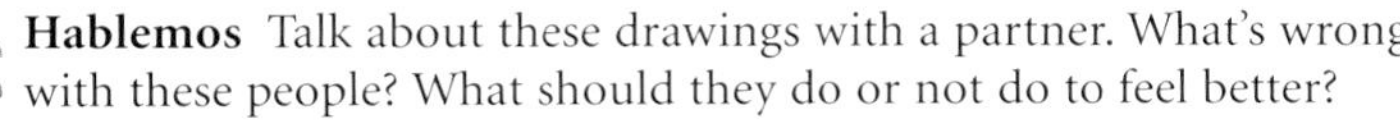

Hablemos Talk about these drawings with a partner. What's wrong with these people? What should they do or not do to feel better?

1. Selena

2. Víctor

3. Anastasio

33 Un cuestionario

Escribamos/Hablemos Write a questionnaire in Spanish to find out how three of your classmates are doing today. Ask how each person is feeling, if anything hurts, what kind of mood he or she is in, and why. Also ask what each person usually eats for breakfast. Then, offer advice about how he or she might feel better.

Comunicación

Group Activity: Interpersonal

Divide students into groups of three and have each play the role of one of the people pictured in Activity 32. Instruct them to take turns asking each other how they feel, what is wrong, and what hurts. Then have them offer advice to make the other feel better.

Individual Activity: Presentation

Ask each student to prepare a **Cuerpo sano** poster. Instruct them to include information about:

- a healthy diet
- exercise and activity recommendations
- hours of sleep needed

Ask them to include illustrations and captions to make the poster visually appealing while also imparting good advice about health. Have students present the posters to the class, and then display them in the classroom.

Differentiated Instruction

SLOWER PACE LEARNERS

Variation Have students write three **Cierto/Falso** statements about each of the pictures in Activity 32. Then ask them to exchange papers with a classmate and mark the statements either **C** or **F.** Have them go over the answers with their partners, and then restate any **Falso** statements to make them **Cierto.**

MULTIPLE INTELLIGENCES

Bodily/Kinesthetic Set up a clinic (**clínica**) in the classroom. Choose some students to play the roles of doctors (**médicos**), and others to play the roles of patients (**enfermos**). Instruct the patients to act out what is wrong while describing symptoms. Have the doctors ask questions and give advice about what the patients need to do to feel better.

Assess

Assessment Program

Prueba: Vocabulario 2, pp. 43–44

Alternative Assessment Guide, pp. 242, 250, 258

Test Generator 

Resources

Planning:

Lesson Planner, pp. 57–63, 214–221

One-Stop Planner

Presentation:

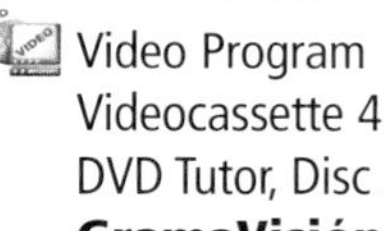

Video Program
Videocassette 4
DVD Tutor, Disc 2
GramaVisión

Practice:

Grammar Tutor for Students of Spanish, Chapter 7

Cuaderno de vocabulario y gramática, pp. 38–40

Cuaderno de actividades, pp. 29–31

Activities for Communication, pp. 27–28

Video Guide, pp. 64–65

Lab Book, pp. 21–22

Teaching Transparencies
Bell Work 7.6
Vocabulario y gramática answers, pp. 38–40

Audio CD 7, Tr. 8

Interactive Tutor, Disc 2

Bell Work

Use Bell Work 7.6 in the *Teaching Transparencies*, or write this activity on the board.

Find the correct answer to help these people solve their problems.

1. Estoy cansado.
2. Necesito bajar de peso.
3. Estoy aburrida.
4. Estoy nervioso.
5. Quiero subir de peso.

a. Relájate con un libro.
b. Come una dieta sana.
c. Acuéstate más temprano.
d. Pide postre con todas las comidas.
e. Busca un pasatiempo.

Objetivos
Estar, sentirse, and **tener,** negative informal commands, object and reflexive pronouns with commands

Gramática en acción 2

GramaVisión

Estar, sentirse, and tener

Interactive TUTOR

1 You have used **ser** to tell what people and things are normally like. Use **estar** with adjectives describing mental or physical states or conditions.

Mi amigo **es** joven. *My friend is young.*
Está muy cansado. *He's very tired.*

2 Like **estar**, **sentirse** *(to feel)* can be used with adverbs **bien/mal** or with adjectives to describe mental or physical states The verb **sentirse** is an **e → ie** stem-changing verb.

yo me s**ie**nto	nosotros(as) nos sentimos
tú te s**ie**ntes	vosotros(as) os sentís
Ud., él, ella se s**ie**nte	Uds., ellos(as) se s**ie**nten

Nos sentimos cansados. *We feel tired.*
No **se sienten** bien. *They don't feel well.*

3 The following **tener expressions** with a **noun** describe a mental or physical state.

tener frío *to be cold*
tener calor *to be hot*
tener miedo *to be afraid*
tener sueño *to be sleepy*

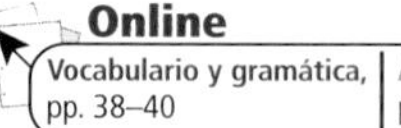
Online
Vocabulario y gramática, pp. 38–40 | Actividades, pp. 29–31

CD 7, Tr. 8

34 ¿Cómo están?

Escuchemos Escucha las oraciones y decide qué dibujo corresponde a cada oración. Algunos dibujos se usan más de una vez. 1. c 2. a 3. d 4. b 5. e 6. c 7. d

a.

b.

c.

d.

e.

Core Instruction

TEACHING GRAMÁTICA

1. Go over point 1. Ask students to add these points to the **ser/estar** chart in their notebooks. Write several sentences using **ser** or **estar** on an overhead, leaving the verb blank. Have students read the sentences aloud, filling in the correct form of the appropriate verb. **(10 min.)**
2. Go over point 2, modeling the pronunciation of each form of **sentirse.** Ask a few volunteers to write sentences using **sentirse** on the board for the class to check. **(10 min.)**
3. Go over point 3. Review conjugation of **tener.** Act out feeling cold, hot, hungry, thirsty, sleepy, or afraid and have students guess how you feel. For example, if you shiver, students should say **¡Tiene frío! (10 min.)**

GramaVisión

For a video presentation of **estar, sentirse,** and **tener,** use **el joven G.** For interactive activities, see the *DVD Tutor.*

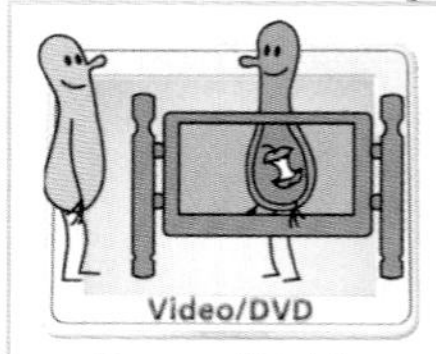

GramaVisión

STANDARDS: 1.2

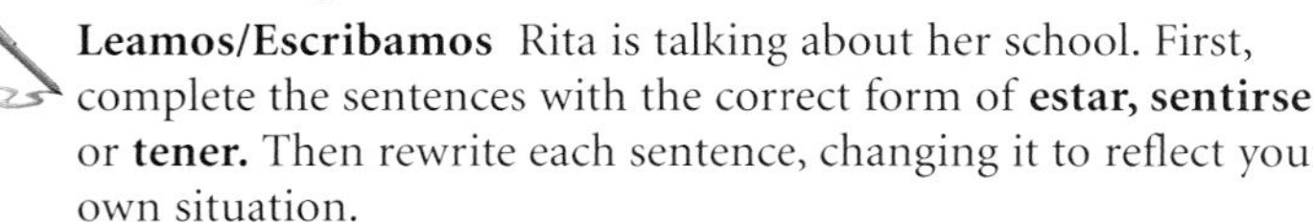

Visit Holt Online
go.hrw.com
KEYWORD: EXP1B CH7
Gramática 2 practice

35 En el colegio

Leamos/Escribamos Rita is talking about her school. First, complete the sentences with the correct form of **estar, sentirse,** or **tener.** Then rewrite each sentence, changing it to reflect your own situation.

MODELO **A veces Luis está aburrido en la clase de matemáticas. Casi nunca estoy aburrido(a) en mis clases.**

1. Muchos estudiantes ___ miedo de los exámenes de inglés. tienen
2. Joaquín y Mateo ___ nerviosos cuando presentan un examen. están/se sienten
3. Muchos estudiantes ___ calor cuando practican deportes. tienen
4. Nos gusta mucho el arte y ___ contentos en la clase de arte. estamos
5. Mi amiga Matilde siempre ___ hambre antes del almuerzo. tiene
6. A veces nosotros ___ sueño después de almorzar. tenemos
7. Mis profesores no ___ enfermos casi nunca. están/se sienten

36 ¿Quién es?

Escribamos Use **estar, sentirse,** or **tener** and the adjective for each number to write sentences describing how these people are feeling.

Leti

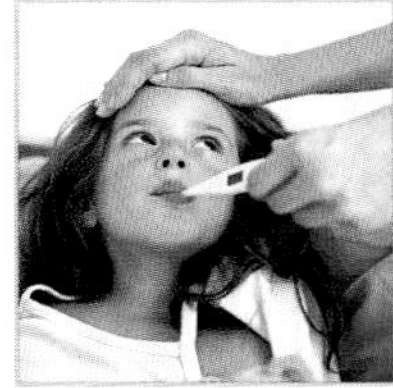
Marta

Ricardo

Vicente

1. sueño
2. enfermo(a)
3. sed
4. nervioso(a)
5. miedo
6. mal
7. calor
8. cansado

Comunicación

37 Un catarro

Hablemos With a classmate, act out the following situation. You have a cold and are describing how you feel. A friend gives you advice about how you should take care of yourself. Use at least five of the following words in your role-play.

enfermo(a)	frío	calor	sed
cansado(a)	mal	sueño	me duele(n)

Gramática 2

34 Script

1. No me siento muy bien. Estoy enferma.
2. ¡Qué bonito día! Hace sol y me siento muy bien.
3. ¿Qué voy a hacer? Hay un examen en mi clase de matemáticas mañana. Las matemáticas son muy difíciles para mí.
4. Acabo de trabajar todo el día. Estoy muy cansado y tengo mucho sueño.
5. No hay nada interesante en la televisión y no puedo salir esta noche.
6. Tengo catarro. Me duelen los ojos, la nariz y la garganta.
7. Hoy tengo que cantar solo en el concierto. Siempre tengo miedo de cantar mal.

36 Answers

1. Vicente se siente/está cansado.
2. Marta está enferma.
3. Leti tiene sed.
4. Ricardo está/se siente nervioso.
5. Ricardo tiene miedo.
6. Leti/Marta tiene calor.
7. Marta se siente mal.
8. Vicente tiene sueño.

Heritage Speakers

Ask heritage speakers to share with the class various expressions related to how one is feeling: **tener resfrío** *(to have a cold);* **tener ansias** *(to feel anxious);* **tener calambre** *(to have a cramp);* **tener náuseas** *(to feel nauseated).*

Differentiated Instruction

ADVANCED LEARNERS

37 Allow students to work in groups of three to prepare a skit for Activity 37. Tell them that they are going to write and perform a skit set in a doctor's office. One person will be the patient, another the nurse, and the other the doctor. Write down various illnesses on slips of paper and tell the groups that they will draw their ailment randomly. Allow the groups to write down their lines and practice their skits before performing for the rest of the class.

SPECIAL LEARNING NEEDS

35 Students with Learning Disabilities Students with learning disabilities tend to struggle with multiple directions for one activity. As a result, they often overlook part of the activity. For Activity 35, remind students that there are two tasks for this activity: filling in the blank correctly and writing a new sentence to comment on their own situation. To remind students to complete both parts, it may be helpful to rewrite the example on the board, with each part given a letter (**a** for the first sentence and **b** for the second).

Comunicación

Class Activity: Interpersonal

Prepare for this activity by listing phrases on a transparency for expressing how someone feels. Then, arrange the class into two circles with students in the inner circle facing the students in the outer circle. Give the students an expression using the verb **sentirse.** Students in the inner circle tell how they are feeling. Students in the outer circle sympathize and give advice. When students have completed the dialogue, they rotate and repeat the dialogue.

STANDARDS: 1.1, 1.2

Resources

Planning:

Lesson Planner, pp. 57–63, 214–221

One-Stop Planner

Presentation:

Video Program
Videocassette 4
DVD Tutor, Disc 2
GramaVisión

Practice:

Grammar Tutor for Students of Spanish, Chapter 7

Cuaderno de vocabulario y gramática, pp. 38–40

Cuaderno de actividades, pp. 29–31

Activities for Communication, pp. 27–28

Video Guide, pp. 64–65

Lab Book, pp. 21–22

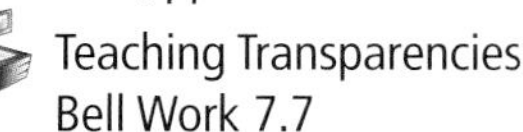
Teaching Transparencies
Bell Work 7.7
Vocabulario y gramática answers, pp. 38–40

Interactive Tutor, Disc 2

Bell Work

Use Bell Work 7.7 in the *Teaching Transparencies,* or write this activity on the board.

Write the correct **tener** expression to describe the situation.

1. Nieva y camino al colegio. Yo...
2. Es muy tarde y la hermana de Jaime no está en casa. Él...
3. Hace mucho sol y nosotros tenemos que hacer ejercicio. Nosotros...
4. Tú acabas de levantarte. (Son las cinco de la mañana.) Tú...
5. No hay agua y acabo de correr mucho. Yo...

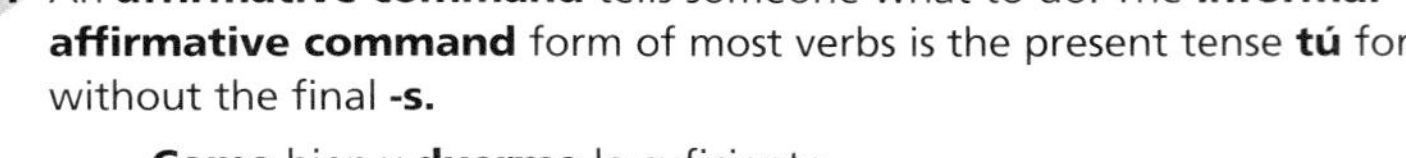

Negative informal commands

1 An **affirmative command** tells someone what to do. The **informal affirmative command** form of most verbs is the present tense **tú** form without the final **-s.**

Come bien y **duerme** lo suficiente.
Eat right and get enough sleep.

2 A **negative command** tells someone not to do something. To form the **negative informal command** of most **-ar** verbs, drop the final **o** of the **yo** form and add **-es**.

(yo) fum**o** → no fum**es**
(yo) trabaj**o** → no trabaj**es**

No trabajes tanto. *Don't work so much.*

3 To form the **negative informal command** of most **-er** and **-ir** verbs, drop the final **o** of the **yo** form and add **-as**.

(yo) veng**o** → no veng**as**
(yo) com**o** → no com**as**
(yo) duerm**o** → no duerm**as**

No duermas hasta tarde. *Don't sleep late.*
No pongas las frutas en la sopa. *Don't put . . .*

4 These verbs have irregular **negative informal command** forms.

dar → **no des**
ir → **no vayas**
ser → **no seas**

¿Te acuerdas?

These verbs have irregular **affirmative informal command forms.**

hacer	haz
ir	ve
poner	pon
salir	sal
ser	sé
tener	ten
venir	ven

Online
Vocabulario y gramática, pp. 38–40 | Actividades, pp. 29–31

¡No corras Lalo!

38 Consejos

Leamos/Hablemos Por lo general, ¿qué le dicen los padres a su hijo?

1. (Come/No comas) verduras.
2. (Compra/No compres) muchos dulces.
3. (Sal/No salgas) tarde para el colegio.
4. (Haz/No hagas) tu tarea.
5. (Pon/No pongas) los pies en la mesa.
6. (Vuelve/No vuelvas) tarde a casa.
7. (Ve/No vayas) al colegio.
8. (Sé/No seas) bueno.
9. (Arregla/No arregles) tu cuarto.

Core Instruction

TEACHING GRAMÁTICA

1. Go over point 1 and **¿Te acuerdas?** Practice the affirmative informal commands by giving students simple orders. **(5 min.)**
2. Go over point 2. Give students some regular **–ar** verbs and have them make the negative informal command forms. **(7 min.)**
3. Go over point 3. Ask students what they noticed about the endings. (The **–as** ending goes with **–er/–ir** verbs and the **–es** ending goes with **–ar** verbs.) Give students some regular **–er/–ir** verbs and have them make the negative informal command forms. **(7 min.)**
4. Go over point 4. Review all of the verbs by giving students an infinitive and asking them for the negative informal command forms. **(6 min.)**

GramaVisión

For a video presentation of negative informal commands, use **el joven G.** For interactive activities, see the *DVD Tutor.*

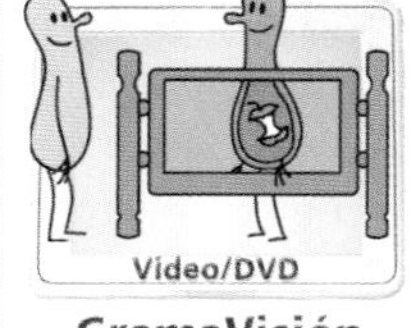

GramaVisión

STANDARDS: 1.2

39 ¿Qué deben hacer?

Escribamos Using commands, tell a friend if he or she should or should not do the things in parentheses.

MODELO **Si siempre estás enfermo... (fumar/dormir lo suficiente/comer dulces)**
No fumes. Duerme lo suficiente. No comas dulces.

1. Si quieres cuidarte la salud... (comer verduras/hacer ejercicio/pasar el día delante de la televisión) Come verduras. Haz ejercicio. No pases el día delante de la televisión.
2. Si te duelen los pies... (correr/descansar/ir a bailar) No corras. Descansa más. No vayas a bailar.
3. Si siempre estás aburrido... (dormir tanto/salir con los amigos/buscar un pasatiempo) No duermas tanto. Sal con los amigos. Busca un pasatiempo.
4. Si no entiendes algo en la clase de matemáticas... (estudiar más/hacer la tarea/ver tanta televisión) Estudia más. Haz la tarea. No veas tanta televisión.
5. Si siempre estás cansado... (volver tarde a casa/dormir más/salir con los amigos todas las noches) No vuelvas tarde a casa. Duerme más. No salgas con los amigos todas las noches.

40 Para salir bien

Escribamos Imagine a younger friend of yours is going to attend your school next year. Give the friend some advice about what he or she should do or not do in order to have a good year.

MODELO **comer en clase**
No comas en clase nunca.

1. correr en clase
2. participar en un deporte o club
3. interrumpir a los profesores
4. ser tímido
5. estudiar todos los días

1. No corras en clase nunca. 2. Participa en un deporte o club. 3. No interrumpas a los profesores. 4. No seas tímido. 5. Estudia todos los días.

Un colegio en Argentina

Comunicación

41 Nuestros problemas

Escribamos/Hablemos On a separate sheet of paper, write a real or imaginary problem. Hand all the "problems" to the teacher, who will write some of them on the board. In pairs, prepare some solutions to the problems. Be prepared to role-play your conversation about problems and solutions for the class.

MODELO **—Siempre tengo sueño en mi primera clase.**
—¡Duerme más en casa!

Differentiated Instruction

ADVANCED LEARNERS

41 As an extension to Activity 41, tell students to choose one of the problems that you wrote on the board. They are now going to write an answer in the form of an advice column. Have them write the problem down in the form of a letter. Then tell them to write a short response with at least two pieces of advice using positive commands and two pieces of advice using negative commands.

SPECIAL LEARNING NEEDS

41 Students with AD(H)D To help keep students with AD(H)D on task for Activity 41, it might be a good idea to let those students copy the problems on the board or on an overhead transparency, rather than having them wait and likely become distracted while the teacher does so.

39 Answers

1. Come verduras. Haz ejercicio. No pases el día delante de la televisión.
2. No corras. Descansa. No vayas a bailar.
3. No duermas tanto. Sal con los amigos. Busca un pasatiempo.
4. Estudia más. Haz la tarea. No veas tanta televisión.
5. No vuelvas tarde a casa. Duerme más. No salgas con los amigos todas las noches.

40 Answers

1. No corras en clase nunca.
2. Participa en un deporte o club.
3. No interrumpas a...
4. No seas tímido(a).
5. Estudia todos los días.

Connections

Language to Language

You may want to tell students that the word **dedo** comes from the Latin *digitus.* **Dígito,** a word for *number,* is so called because numbers can be counted on fingers. **Subir** is composed of **sub-** meaning "under" and **ir** meaning "to go." It is therefore used to mean *to go towards something high from below.* The term **fumar** derives from the Latin word *fumus* as does the word **humo** or smoke.

Comunicación

Group Activity: Interpersonal

El amigo Bueno, el amigo Malo Divide students into groups of three. Give each group a situation to dramatize in which one student has to make decisions about what to do. One friend, the "good friend," gives good advice. The "bad friend" gives bad advice. Have volunteers present their scenarios to the class.

STANDARDS: 1.1, 1.2, 1.3

Resources

Planning:

Lesson Planner, pp. 57–63, 214–221

 One-Stop Planner

Presentation:

 Video Program
Videocassette 4
DVD Tutor, Disc 2
GramaVisión

Practice:

Grammar Tutor for Students of Spanish, Chapter 7

Cuaderno de vocabulario y gramática, pp. 38–40

Cuaderno de actividades, pp. 29–31

Activities for Communication, pp. 27–28

Video Guide, pp. 64–65

Lab Book, pp. 21–22

 Teaching Transparencies
Bell Work 7.8
Vocabulario y gramática answers, pp. 38–40

 Interactive Tutor, Disc 2

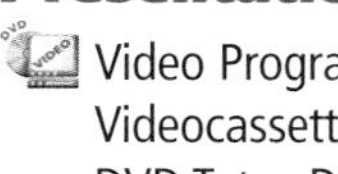

Bell Work

Use Bell Work 7.8 in the *Teaching Transparencies,* or write this activity on the board.

Write a negative command responding to each problem.

1. Necesito bajar de peso.
2. Tengo calor.
3. Estoy cansada.
4. Tengo miedo de los exámenes.
5. Me duele la espalda.

Object and reflexive pronouns with commands

1 Direct object pronouns and reflexive pronouns are attached to the end of **affirmative commands**. A written accent mark goes over the stressed vowel of the verb, unless the verb is only one syllable long.

Levántate y **ponte** los zapatos.
Get up and put your shoes on.

2 Direct object pronouns and reflexive pronouns go in between **no** and the verb in the **negative command form**.

Ese libro es pésimo. **No lo leas.**
That book is awful. Don't read it.

No te levantes muy tarde.
Don't get up too late.

Online
Vocabulario y gramática, pp. 38–40 | Actividades, pp. 29–31

¿Te acuerdas?

Words ending in a **vowel, -n,** or **-s** are normally stressed on the next-to-last syllable. If another syllable is stressed, there must be a written accent on its vowel.

está	**esta**
teléfonos	**lentes**
jóvenes	**joven**

42 Más consejos

Leamos/Hablemos Escoge el consejo apropiado.

1. ¿Tienes sueño?
   (a.) ¡Acuéstate! **b.** ¡No te acuestes!
2. ¿Te duelen los pies?
   a. ¡No te quites los zapatos! **(b.)** ¡Quítate los zapatos!
3. Vamos a comer.
   (a.) ¡Lávate las manos! **b.** ¡No te laves las manos!
4. Necesitas dormir más.
   a. ¡Levántate! **(b.)** ¡No te levantes!
5. ¿Tienes frío?
   (a.) ¡Vístete! **b.** ¡No te vistas!
6. ¿Estás nervioso?
   (a.) ¡Relájate! **b.** ¡No te estires!
7. ¿Tienes catarro?
   a. ¡No te cuides! **(b.)** ¡Cuídate!
8. Los libros son muy aburridos.
   (a.) ¡No los leas! **b.** ¡Léelos!
9. ¿Los pies?
   a. Ponlos en la mesa. **(b.)** ¡No los pongas en la mesa!
10. ¿Llegar al colegio por la mañana?
    (a.) Sal temprano. **b.** No salgas temprano, sal tarde.
11. A mi hermano no le tocan los quehaceres.
    a. ¡Limpia el baño! **(b.)** ¡No te enojes!

Core Instruction

TEACHING GRAMÁTICA

1. Go over **¿Te acuerdas? (2 min.)**
2. Go over point 1. Give examples by first saying that you are doing something (**Me pongo el reloj**), then telling a student to do the same thing (**Ponte el reloj**). **(7 min.)**
3. Go over point 2. Give the students pairs of words with which to make affirmative and negative commands. (**escuchar/música, servir/flan, traer/cuenta, escribir/cartas, hacer/tarea**) Have volunteers write their sentences on the board for the class to check. **(11 min.)**

GramaVisión

For a video presentation of object pronouns and informal commands, use **el joven G** from the *Video Program.* For interactive activities, see the *DVD Tutor.*

GramaVisión

43 El hombre prehistórico

Leamos/Escribamos A caveman has arrived in your classroom through a time warp. He does the following things. Use informal commands to explain to him how these things are done.

MODELO **Se baña en la cocina.**
¡No te bañes en la cocina! ¡Báñate en el baño!

1. Se pone el piyama para salir.
2. Se lava los dientes con una toalla.
3. Se levanta a las once de la noche.
4. Se baña con la pasta de dientes.
5. Se viste en el patio.
6. Se acuesta en la mesa.
7. Se peina con el jabón.
8. Se afeita con un cuchillo.

1. ¡No te pongas el piyama para salir! ¡Ponte la ropa!
2. ¡No te laves los dientes con una toalla! ¡Lávate los dientes con cepillo de dientes!
3. ¡No te levantes tarde! ¡Levántate temprano!
4. ¡No te bañes con la pasta de dientes! ¡Báñate con jabón!
5. ¡No te vistas en el patio! ¡Vístete en el cuarto!
6. ¡No te acuestes en la mesa! ¡Acuéstate en la cama!
7. ¡No te peines con el jabón! ¡Péinate con el peine!
8. ¡No te afeites con el cuchillo! ¡Aféitate con la navaja!

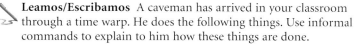

44 ¿Qué hago con esto?

Escribamos/Hablemos Follow the **modelo** to tell the caveman what he should or should not do with the following items.

MODELO **poner los platos (en el piso/en la mesa)**
¡No los pongas en el piso! ¡Ponlos en la mesa!

1. lavar la ropa (en la casa/en el carro)
2. usar los lentes (para cortar/para leer)
3. limpiar las ventanas (con jugo/con agua y jabón)
4. pasar la aspiradora (en la sala/en el césped)
5. poner la computadora (en el escritorio/en el microondas)
6. el arroz con pollo (comer con los pies/con un tenedor)

Comunicación

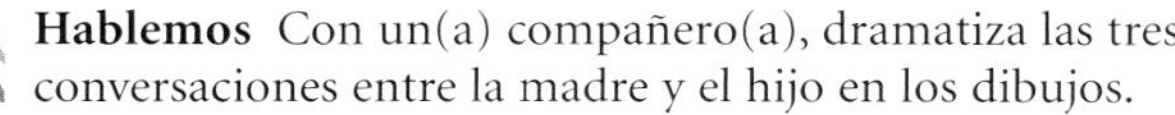

45 La madre cansada

Hablemos Con un(a) compañero(a), dramatiza las tres conversaciones entre la madre y el hijo en los dibujos.

Language Examination

AP Preparación Práctica

45 Below is a sample answer for the picture description activity.

—Hijo, son las siete y media. Báñate y vístete.
—Ay, mamá, tengo mucho sueño.
—Tienes que salir para el colegio en quince minutos. Ten tu camisa y ve a bañarte.
—Mamá, me duele el estómago. No me siento bien.
—No debes comer tantos dulces. Y por favor, quítate los zapatos.

—Hijo, son las diez y media. Deja de leer y ponte el piyama.
—Este libro es muy bueno y no tengo sueño.

To display the drawings use the *Picture Sequences Transparency* for Chapter 7.

Comunicación

Group Work: Interpersonal

Review the verbs and expressions in this chapter. Prepare index cards so that each student gets a different card. On each card, write a question for students to ask their classmates.

Differentiated Instruction

SLOWER PACE LEARNERS

43/44 Read through the **modelo** with the class. Explain that each of their answers will have two commands, first a negative command followed by a logical positive command. Read through the statements with the class and discuss what is wrong with each one. Allow students to suggest possible positive solutions in English.

SPECIAL LEARNING NEEDS

43 Students with Learning Disabilities/ Language Impairments In order to complete Activity 43, students will have to determine the meaning of the sentences, then think of the logical actions for modern times, and then write grammatically correct sentences. This multi-level activity can challenge students with learning disabilities. To modify this activity, first make sure students understand the meaning of the original sentences. Have them decide what would be more logical today. Then, have students write their responses.

Assess

Assessment Program

Prueba: Gramática 2, pp. 45–46

Prueba: Aplicación, pp. 47–48

Alternative Assessment Guide, pp. 242, 250, 258

Audio CD 7, Tr. 17 

Test Generator

STANDARDS: 1.1, 1.2

Conexiones culturales

Resources

Planning:

Lesson Planner, pp. 63–64, 220–223

 One-Stop Planner

Connections

English Link

2 English has borrowed words from many different languages. Some examples of words borrowed from French are **ballet, hors d'oeuvre, déjà vu, croquet,** and **chic.** Words borrowed from German include **frankfurter, hamburger, bratwurst, kaput(t)** and **kindergarten.**

History Link

Explain that, although baseball originated in the United States, it is very popular in Latin America as well. Three examples of Latin American athletes who play for baseball teams in the United States are Sandy Alomar, who was voted Most Valuable Player for his seventh-inning home run in the All-Star Game in 1997; Ramón Martínez, who finished the 1996 season with a seven-game winning streak, and Wilson Álvarez, a left-handed pitcher who in 1991 was the first Venezuelan to throw a no-hitter.

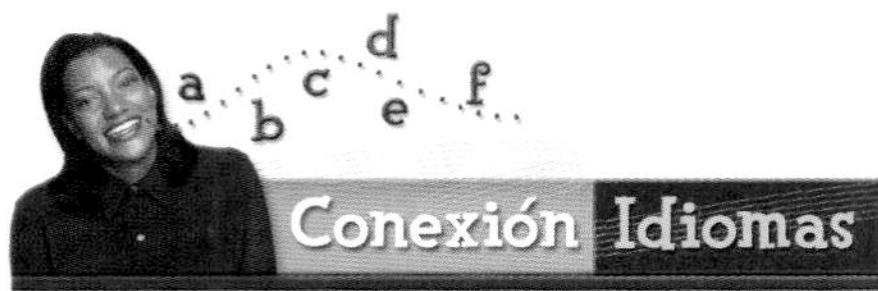

El béisbol Baseball is very popular in Latin America, especially in the Caribbean. Many players from Caribbean countries have gone on to play in the major leagues in the United States. Because baseball originated in the U.S., many of the Spanish words for the sport come from the English words. Words borrowed directly from one language to another are called loanwords.

1 El lenguaje del béisbol

Work with a group to identify which of the baseball terms below are borrowed from English. Decide which English word each comes from.

el pelotero/la pelotera	batear	el récord
el jardinero/la jardinera	el hit	pichear
el lanzador/la lanzadora	la pelota	el cuadrangular
bases robadas	el jonrón	ranqueado

2 Palabras del español

English has also borrowed words from Spanish. Below are some Spanish loanwords found in English. What does each word mean? Use a dictionary if you're not sure.

patio	adobe	tornado
rodeo	lasso	poncho
salsa	arroyo	mosquito

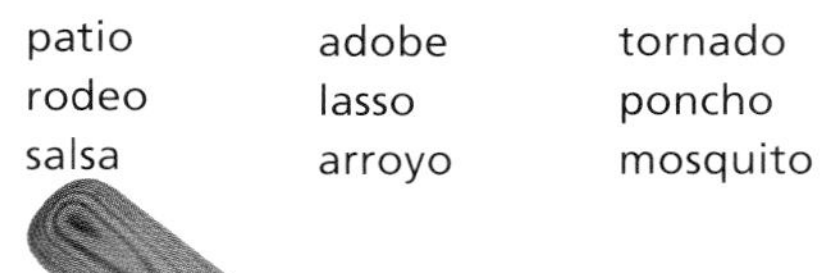

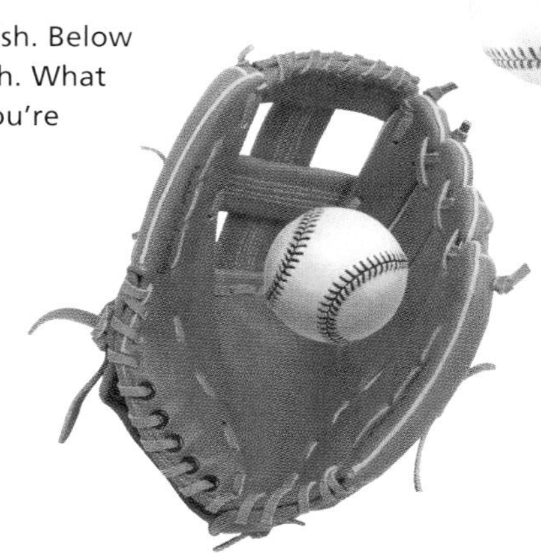

Core Instruction

TEACHING CONEXIONES CULTURALES

1. Ask students who their favorite baseball teams and players are. Have them think of common baseball terms and list them on the board. **(5 min.)**
2. Read **El béisbol** aloud and present English Link. Do Activity 1 in small groups. **(10 min.)**
3. Have students work in pairs to do Activity 3. **(10 min.)**
4. Read aloud **Los peloteros latinoamericanos** and present History Link. Ask students if they know the names of other Hispanic baseball players. **(10 min.)**
5. Present Geography Link and Practices and Perspectives. Do Activities 3 and 4 as a class. **(10 min.)**

Visit Holt Online
go.hrw.com
KEYWORD: EXP1B CH7
Online Edition

Conexión Ciencias sociales

Los peloteros latinoamericanos Approximately one out of every six players in the major leagues in the United States is from Latin America.

Juan Antonio (Sánchez) Marichal, dominicano
Lanzador, Los Gigantes de San Francisco
Electo al Salón de la Fama en 1983

Atanasio 'Tony' Pérez Regal, cubano
Primera base, Los Rojos de Cincinnati
Electo al Salón de la Fama en 2000

Roberto Clemente Walker, puertorriqueño
Jardinero derecho, Los Piratas de Pittsburgh
Electo al Salón de la Fama en 1973

3 El clima y el béisbol

Read the photo captions to find out where these three players are from. Look at the maps on pages R5–R6 to find their countries. Where are these countries in relation to the equator? In relation to the U.S.? Based on what you know about weather and seasons, would the climate in the Caribbean be good for playing baseball?

4 Las temporadas

Many Latin American baseball teams play in the Caribbean Series every February. This event ends the winter baseball season for those countries. How does this compare with the baseball season in the U.S.?

Conexiones culturales

Differentiated Instruction

SLOWER PACE LEARNERS

Extension Draw a large diamond on the board to represent a baseball field. Label the bases, the pitcher, and catcher. Divide the students into two teams and have them choose a Spanish name. To play, have students from Team 1 take turns playing pitcher by asking a student from Team 2 (the batter) any vocabulary word from this chapter. Place a post-it note on first base for a right answer, and bring a new student up to bat. If a player misses an answer, it is an "out". Three outs end the inning and the other team gets up to bat.

MULTIPLE INTELLIGENCES

Spatial Have students research the Internet to find a picture of a Hispanic baseball player and then make a baseball card for that player, using the picture and other information they found. On the front of the card have them place the picture, the player's name, team, and position. On the back of the card instruct them to write any other information or statistics they found, using Spanish whenever possible. Then have a card-trading session where students can talk about their cards with classmates and perhaps trade for different players.

Conexiones culturales

Connections

Geography Link

3 Explain that the tropics are between the Tropic of Cancer and the Tropic of Capricorn. Have students look at the maps of Central and South America in their books and find the tropics. **(trópico de Cáncer, trópico de Capricornio)** In tropical areas there is an almost constant temperature year round. The weather alternates between rainy and dry seasons.

Cultures

Practices and Perspectives

Mexico, Puerto Rico, the Dominican Republic, and Venezuela play in **la Serie del Caribe,** a Latin American winter baseball championship. Many major league players from the U.S. join the Caribbean teams after the U.S. season is over, and continue to play through the winter. Many players return to their home countries to play. The first Caribbean Series was held in Cuba in 1949, although Cuba does not currently participate. Venezuelan teams began participating in 1970, but were unable to send a team to the 2003 playoffs because of political unrest in their country. Ask students to figure out what some of these team names mean: **Águilas del Cibao, Tigres del Licey** (Dominican Republic); **Indios de Mayagüez, San Juan Senadores** (Puerto Rico); **Caracas Leones, La Guaira Tiburones** (Venezuela). Have students research team names in the Mexican League.

STANDARDS: 2.1, 3.2

Resources

Planning:

Lesson Planner, pp. 64–65, 222–223

 One-Stop Planner

Presentation:

 Video Program, Videocassette 4
DVD Tutor, Disc 2
VideoNovela

Practice:

Video Guide, pp. 64–65, 69
Lab Book, p. 47

Connections

Visual Learners

To help students understand the motivation of Nicolás in this episode of **Novela en video,** have them create a mind map. Guide students through the map on the board. First create a square in the middle labeled **Nicolás.** Draw lines extending from **Nicolás** for each of the following categories: who, what, when, why. Have students help you fill in the blanks. Who is influencing **Nicolás** in this episode? What do they want him to do?

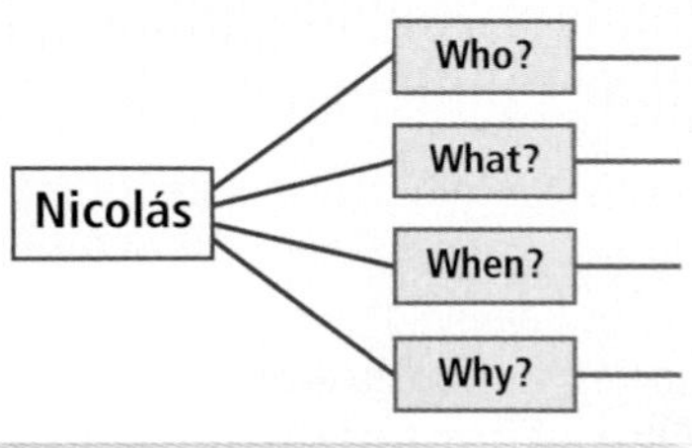

Cultures

Practices and Perspectives

Nicolás has a television in his bedroom. In general, there are fewer televisions per capita in Spanish-speaking countries than in the U.S. It isn't nearly as common for children to have a television set in their bedroom. Ask students why they think it's less common in Spanish-speaking countries than in the U.S.

Novela en video

¿Quién será?

Episodio 7

ESTRATEGIA

Understanding a character's motives To understand a character, you must first understand motives—why he or she is doing something or acting a certain way. To understand someone's motives, you must watch behavior. Nicolás has to get ready to go to his grandmother's birthday lunch. Can you tell from his actions whether he really wants to go? When he tells his grandmother he is sick, what is his motive? As you read the **Novela** or watch the video, notice what he does and decide what his motive is.

En Puerto Rico

La mamá de Nicolás quiere hablar con él. Él tiene que alistarse para el almuerzo de cumpleaños de su abuela.

1 **Sra. Ortega** ¿Nicolás? ¿Hijo?

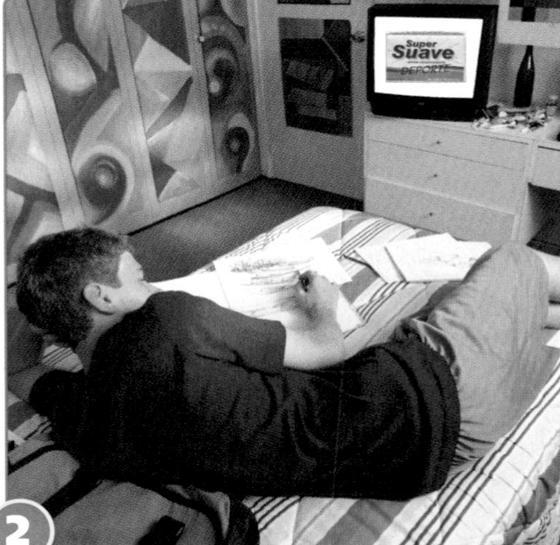

2 **Sra. Ortega** ¿Nicolás, estás listo? Hijo, ya sabes que hoy es el cumpleaños de tu abuela y tenemos que ir a almorzar con ella.

Core Instruction

TEACHING NOVELA EN VIDEO

1. Have students read the **Novela en video** text to themselves and study the pictures. Ask general comprehension questions. Who is the principal character in this episode? **(10 min.)**
2. Play the video without stopping. **(5 min.)**
3. Play the video a second time, stopping after each scene. Have students repeat the conversation lines with you, frame by frame. **(10 min.)**
4. Have students write the answers for the **Contesta** questions on page 115. Then discuss them in class. **(15 min.)**

Captioned Video/DVD

As an alternative, you might use the captioned version on Videocassette 5 or on DVD.

STANDARDS: 1.2, 3.2

Visit Holt Online
go.hrw.com
KEYWORD: EXP1B CH7
Online Edition

Báñate con SuperSuave, el jabón que te hace sentir ¡súper suave!

3 **Sra. Ortega** ¡Nicolás, por favor! ¡Levántate, hijo! Tienes que bañarte. Aquí está el jabón.

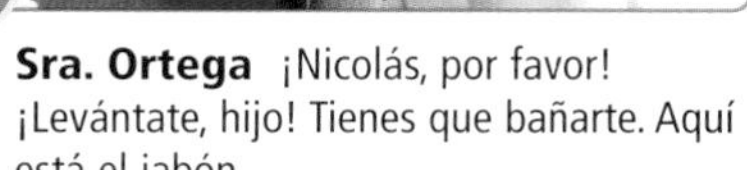

Lávate el pelo con el champú Estrella y ¡brilla como una estrella!

4 **Sra. Ortega** ¡Nicolás, por favor! ¡También tienes que lavarte el pelo! Aquí está el champú.

Sonrisa
Lávate los dientes con la pasta de dientes Sonrisa.

5 **Sra. Ortega** Nicolás, ¿no me oyes? Abre esta puerta, ¡ahora mismo! Sé que necesitas pasta de dientes... aquí está.

Nicolás, levántate, báñate, lávate el pelo y los dientes y ¡alístate!

6

Novela en video

A. Contesta

What's happening in the **Novela**? Answer these questions to make sure you understand.

1. Why does Sra. Ortega want Nicolás to get cleaned up? What is Nicolás doing in his room while she's talking to him?
2. What happens on the TV when Sra. Ortega holds up the soap? the shampoo?

¿Quién sera?

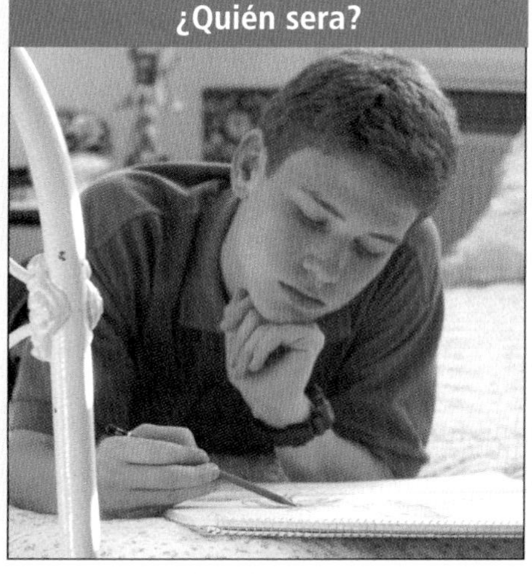

In Chapter 6, Sofía and her brother prepared a special anniversary dinner for their parents. In this episode, Nicolás has to get ready to attend a special birthday lunch for his grandmother. Nicolás, however, is busily working on his drawing. Nicolás's mother calls to him to get ready for the lunch, but he ignores her. As she tells him exactly what he needs to do to get ready, television advertisements with the products that he is to use flash onto his T.V. Thinking this is rather strange, he jumps from the bed and opens the door. His mother hands him the products. When he returns to his room, his mother is on the T.V. telling him what to do. He is surprised and rubs his eyes. The T.V. returns to normal. Later that morning Nicolás tells his grandmother that he's not feeling well, but he returns to working on his art. At the end of the episode Marcos is trailing the "candidate" from Argentina.

A. Contesta Answers

1. to attend the birthday lunch for his grandmother
2. a TV commercial for those products comes on

Gestures

Even though **Nicolás** doesn't say anything, we know he is a little annoyed that his mother is interrupting his creative brainstorming. What gestures and body language tell us about his feelings? Does his body language change when he opens the door for his mother? What gestures do you make when you are trying to ignore someone?

STANDARDS: 1.1, 2.1

B. Contesta Answers

1. His grandmother thinks he doesn't look well.
2. He says he's tired, cold, and has a headache.

Using the Strategy

Understanding a Character's Motives Ask students if they have identified Nicolas's motives in this episode. How does his motive influence his behavior, first with his mother, then with his grandmother, in the second part of the episode?

7 **Abuela** Nicolás, te veo cansado.
Nicolás Sí, abuela, estoy un poco cansado. Tengo frío y me duele la cabeza.

8 **Abuela** Anda, vete, acuéstate un rato. Te despertamos cuando esté listo el almuerzo.
Nicolás Gracias, abuela.

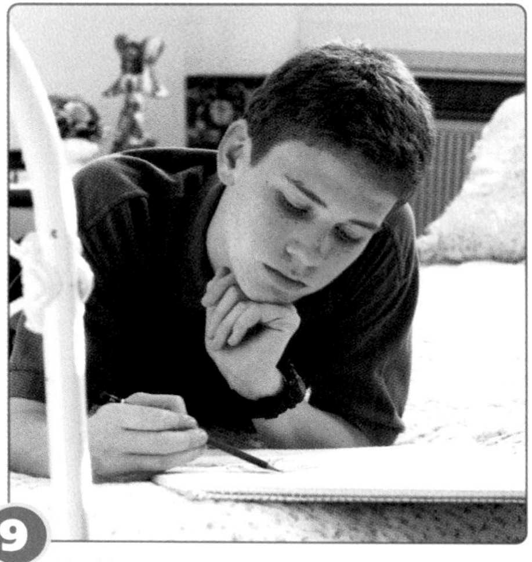

9 Nicolás se acuesta pero no descansa.

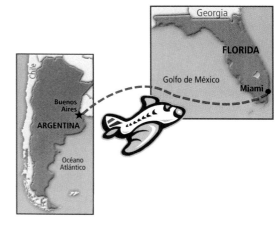

Georgia
FLORIDA
Golfo de México
Miami
Chile
Buenos Aires
ARGENTINA
Océano Atlántico

B. Contesta

1. What happens to Nicolás at his grandmother's house?
2. How does Nicolás say he feels?

Culminating Project

Para cuidarte mejor

1. Explain to students that they are going to create a poster about personal hygiene to present to children at an elementary school. The poster will demonstrate what a person should and should not do in order to develop good personal hygiene habits.
2. Divide the class into groups of four. Explain that two students will develop a list of what a person should do to have good hygiene, and the other two will develop a list of what a person should not do. Tell students that they must include at least five dos and five don'ts on their poster.
3. Have groups create their poster, writing out each piece of advice and illustrating it for the children. Remind students to be clear in their writing and drawing since the poster is meant for small children.
4. Have each group present their poster to an elementary class.

STANDARDS: 1.2, 3.2

Novela en video

Actividades

1 ¿Cierto o falso?

Tell whether each statement is **cierto** or **falso.** If it is **falso,** correct it.

1. La pasta de dientes se llama 'Estrella'.
2. Hoy es el cumpleaños de Nicolás.
3. Nicolás está cansado y tiene catarro.
4. En la cama, Nicolás descansa.

1. falso
2. falso
3. falso
4. falso

2 ¿Cómo se dice?

Find and write down the words and phrases in the **Novela** that . . .

1. Sra. Ortega uses to tell Nicolás to get up.
2. his grandmother uses to tell Nicolás that he looks tired.
3. Sra. Ortega uses to tell Nicolás to take a bath and wash his hair.
4. his grandmother uses to tell Nicolás to lie down.

1. ¡Nicolás, por favor! ¡Levántate, hijo!
2. Nicolás, te veo cansado.
3. Tienes que bañarte y lavarte el pelo!
4. Anda, vete, acuéstate un rato.

3 ¿Comprendes la Novela?

Check your understanding of the events in the story by answering these questions.

1. How can you tell from Nicolás's actions whether he wants to go to the birthday lunch?
2. What event in the story is Nicolás's fantasy?
3. Does he really not feel well at his grandmother's? How do you know?
4. What is Nicolás's motive for his actions throughout the episode?

Próximo episodio
Marcos has to go to Miami next. Can you predict what he might be doing there?
PÁGINAS 160–163

1 Actividades

1. falso; se llama Sonrisa
2. falso; es el cumpleaños de su abuela
3. cierto
4. falso; no descansa

2 ¿Cómo se dice?

1. ¡Nicolás, por favor! ¡Levántate, hijo!
2. Nicolás, te veo cansado.
3. Tienes que bañarte y lavarte el pelo!
4. Anda, vete, acuéstate un rato.

3 ¿Comprendes la novela?

1. He keeps ignoring his mother's requests to get ready.
2. his mother appearing on TV
3. He uses that as an excuse to work on his sketch.
4. He wants to get away and spend time drawing/working on his sketch.

Comunicación

Pair Work: Interpersonal

After students have seen the **Novela en video,** have them work in pairs to prepare for an event. Allow the students to choose who they want to be and what event they are going to attend. Have students switch roles after they have completed the scene one time.

Differentiated Instruction

ADVANCED LEARNERS

Challenge: Have students work in pairs to create a commercial advertisement for a personal care product (soap, shampoo, toothpaste) using phrases from the **Novela.** Ask them to give the product a Spanish name and to draw a picture of the product. Have them write out the commercial, including a description of the product, why consumers might want to buy it, and some commands that indicate how to use it. Ask pairs to present their commercials to the class, using their best dramatic voices.

SPECIAL LEARNING NEEDS

Students with Visual Impairments You might want to refer students with visual impairments to the online version of the **Novela** or give them extra time to watch the video/DVD version. If possible, have them view and listen to the **Novela** with a partner who can help describe the characters, action, and so forth as they are listening to the audio.

STANDARDS: 1.1

Resources

Planning:

Lesson Planner, pp. 65–67, 222–227

 One-Stop Planner

Presentation:

 Audio CD 7, Tr. 9

Practice:

Cuaderno de actividades, p. 32

Cuaderno para hispanohablantes, pp. 53–60

Reading Strategies and Skills Handbook, Chapter 7

¡Lee conmigo!

Applying the Strategies

For practice with drawing on background information, you might have students use the "Anticipation Guide" strategy from the *Reading Strategies and Skills Handbook.*

READING PRACTICE

Strategy: Anticipation Guide

Additional Practice

For more reading practice, use the **Literatura y variedades** reading for Chapter 7 on pages 268–269.

Heritage Speakers

If you have heritage speakers who have lived in another country, ask them whether or not gyms were popular in that country. Have them share what activities were popular for staying in shape in the country they lived in.

Leamos y escribamos

ESTRATEGIA

para leer Background knowledge is the information you already know about something. Before you read something, take a moment to recall what you already know about a topic. This will make it easier to guess the meaning of unknown words or phrases.

CD 7, Tr. 9

A Antes de leer

 Think about what you already know about health and diet. Now read the following article and try to infer the meanings of the words marked with a red asterisk by using context clues.

¡En buena salud!

Cecilia Mendoza, famosa entrenadora* y nutricionista argentina, contesta algunas preguntas sobre la salud y la dieta.

¿Qué es mejor para mantenerse en forma: levantar pesas o hacer aeróbicos?
Las dos actividades son buenas. Puedes hacer aeróbicos cuatro veces* por semana y levantar pesas dos veces por semana. Y recuerda[1], siempre debes estirarte después de hacer ejercicio.

¿Por cuánto tiempo se debe hacer una actividad aeróbica?
La intensidad de una actividad determina su duración. Si la actividad requiere más energía, no hay que hacerla por mucho tiempo.

¿Qué dieta recomiendas para bajar de peso?
Lo más importante es comer comida sana y prestar atención[2] a la cantidad* de comida que comes. Si reduces el tamaño* de las porciones y sigues las recomendaciones de la pirámide alimenticia, vas a bajar de peso.

Sufro[3] mucho de estrés durante el año escolar. ¿Qué puedo hacer?
Para reducir[4] el estrés, haz lo siguiente: duerme lo suficiente, haz ejercicio todos los días, come una dieta sana, no tomes bebidas con cafeína[5], maneja* bien tu tiempo, toma las cosas con calma y siempre respira[6] profundamente*.

1 remember 2 pay attention
3 I suffer 4 reduce
5 caffeinated beverages 6 breathe

Pirámide alimenticia

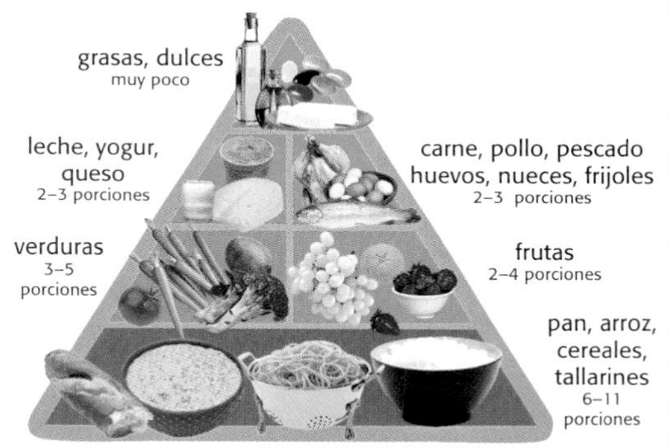

Core Instruction

TEACHING LEAMOS

1. Discuss the **Estrategia para leer** with students and have them share what they already know about healthful living. **(5 min.)**
2. Have students look at the format of **¡En buena salud!** and predict what will be in each section. Read the first paragraph as a class. **(5 min.)**
3. Have students continue with the rest of the article, stopping to monitor comprehension as needed. **(10 min.)**
4. Have students complete the **Comprensión** activities on page 119. **(10 min.)**

TEACHING ESCRIBAMOS

1. Discuss the **Estrategia para escribir** as a class. Go over the scenario with students to make sure they understand the assignment. **(5 min.)**
2. Have students complete step 1. **(10 min.)**
3. Have students complete step 2. Students might want to find their illustrations first to help them with their graphic organizers. **(20 min.)**
4. Have students complete steps 2 and 3 at home and then have volunteers share their results with the class. **(10 min.)**

STANDARDS: 1.2, 3.2

Visit Holt Online
go.hrw.com
KEYWORD: EXP1B CH7
Online Edition

B Comprensión

¿Son **ciertas** o **falsas** las siguientes oraciones? Corrige las oraciones falsas.

1. Cecilia Mendoza sólo *(only)* habla del ejercicio.
2. Para mantenerse en forma es necesario levantar pesas todos los días.
3. La intensidad de un ejercicio determina la cantidad de tiempo que debes hacerlo.
4. Para bajar de peso sólo es necesario seguir una dieta sana.
5. Para reducir el estrés es importante tener una vida sana.

C Después de leer

Which of Cecilia's recommendations do you already follow? How difficult would it be for you to follow all of her recommendations? Which ones would be the most difficult to follow? Why?

B Answers

1. falsa: También habla de la dieta; de cómo
2. falsa: Es necesario levantar pesas dos veces por semana.
3. cierta
4. falsa: Es necesario prestar atención a la cantidad de comida también.
5. cierta

Writing Assessment

To assess the **Taller del escritor,** you can use the following rubric.

Writing Rubric	4	3	2	1
Content (Complete—Incomplete)				
Comprehensibility (Comprehensible—Seldom comprehensible)				
Accuracy (Accurate—Seldom accurate)				
Organization (Well-organized—Poorly organized)				
Effort (Excellent effort—Minimal effort)				

18–20: A
16–17: B
14–15: C
12–13: D
Under 12: F

Interactive TUTOR

Taller del escritor

Clínica Fierro
¿Te duele...?
• ____________
• ____________
¿Estás...?
• ____________
• ____________

ESTRATEGIA

para escribir Graphic organizers can help you organize your thoughts visually and are especially helpful in designing posters and charts. Consider bulleted charts or cluster bubbles as you plan your poster.

El doctor te aconseja...

Imagine you are a doctor who believes that people should take a more active role in avoiding or curing their illnesses. Design a poster for the patients' waiting room listing common symptoms followed by your suggestions on how to avoid or cure the problem.

1 Antes de escribir

List the symptoms in question form: **¿Te duele la garganta? ¿Estás cansado(a)?** Then write one suggestion to solve each problem or illness.

2 Escribir y revisar

- Use a graphic organizer to plan where you'll write the symptoms and suggested solutions on a poster.
- Write down the symptoms.
- Write out suggestions telling patients what to do. Use expressions for giving advice as well as affirmative and negative commands.
- Read your poster of symptoms and advice to a classmate.
- Check for proper use of vocabulary, spelling, and punctuation.
- Revise your poster if needed.

3 Publicar

Illustrate your poster and show it to the class. Share one piece of advice from it.

Cuaderno para hispanohablantes, pp. 69–80

Differentiated Instructions

ADVANCED LEARNERS

Before visiting the doctor or joining a health club, you are often required to fill out a questionnaire about your current health. Ask each student to brainstorm questions that might appear on this type of questionnaire. For example, **¿Haces ejercicio? ¿Con qué frecuencia?** Write the questions on the board and have students copy them onto a piece of paper. After creating the questionnaire together, have volunteers complete it in Spanish, keeping in mind that some students might not want to share their health status.

SPECIAL LEARNING NEEDS

Students with Learning Disabilities Students with learning disabilities might have trouble visualizing the chart they are supposed to create for the **Taller del escritor.** Using examples from a health book or a fitness magazine, show students some models of what they will be working on. Have students work with a partner for steps 1–2.

Assess

Assessment Program
Prueba: Lectura, p. 49
Prueba: Escritura, p. 50
Test Generator

STANDARDS: 1.2, 1.3

Resources

Planning:

Lesson Planner, pp. 67–68, 224–225

One-Stop Planner

Presentation:

Video Program
Videocassette 4
DVD Tutor, Disc 2
Variedades

Teaching Transparencies
Situación, Capítulo 7
Picture Sequences, Chapter 7

Practice:

Activities for Communication, pp. 49, 67–68
TPR Storytelling Book, pp. 40–41
Video Guide, pp. 64–65, 70
Lab Book, pp. 21–22, 48
Audio CD 7, Tr. 11–14
Interactive Tutor, Disc 2

1 Answers

Miguelito: Tiene que ponerse los zapatos.
El señor Blanco: Tiene que afeitarse.
Elena: Tiene que maquillarse.

4 Answers

1. No seas perezoso. Busca un pasatiempo.
2. Acuéstate más temprano. No duermas en clase.
3. Come comida sana. No pidas muchos postres.
4. No veas tanta televisión. Compra lentes.

Prepárate para el examen

1 Vocabulario 1
- talking about your daily routine
- talking about staying fit and healthy

pp. 86–91

2 Gramática 1
- verbs with reflexive pronouns
- using infinitives
- review of stem-changing verbs

pp. 92–97

3 Vocabulario 2
- talking about how you feel
- giving advice

pp. 100–105

Repaso capítulo 7

1 Todos se preparan para salir. ¿Qué tiene que hacer cada persona para prepararse?

Miguelito

el señor Blanco

Elena

2 Completa el parráfo con las formas correctas de los verbos en paréntesis. **1.** duerme **2.** se levanta **3.** se viste **4.** entrenarme **5.** podemos **6.** juega **7.** me baño **8.** relajarme

Por la mañana, mi madre __1__ (dormir) hasta las seis. Luego, ella __2__ (levantarse) y __3__ (vestirse) antes de desayunar. Yo me levanto muy temprano para __4__ (entrenarse) antes de ir. Después de la escuela, mis hermanos y yo __5__ (poder) ver un poco de televisión antes de empezar la tarea. A veces mi hermana Maribel __6__ (jugar) videojuegos. Por la noche, (yo) __7__ (bañarse) y luego escucho música para __8__ (relajarse) un poco antes de acostarme.

3 Prepara una lista de consejos para un(a) amigo(a) usando las palabras de los cuadros.

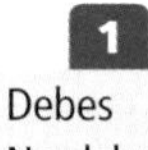

1	2	3
Debes	comer tanto dulce	si estás aburrido(a)
No debes	acostarte tarde	si siempre tienes catarro
	comer verduras	si no quieres subir de peso
	hacer yoga	si siempre tienes sueño
	buscar un pasatiempo	para mantenerte en forma
	entrenarte	para seguir una dieta sana
	cuidarte	para relajarte

Communities

Career Path

Ask students to list health and fitness-related careers. Have students choose one of the careers they have listed and imagine that it is their first day on the job. They have many Spanish-speaking clients. What Spanish words and phrases would students need to perform their job? Have partners write a short dialogue based on this scenario and present it to the class.

Preparing for the Exam

FOLD-N-LEARN
Folded Table

1. To help students prepare for the Chapter Test, have them create the **Fold-n-Learn** study aid as shown here, using a sheet of paper and a pen or pencil.

2. Once the Folded Table template is completed, ask students to create a useful study tool for reflexive pronouns. Students can use the first column for subject pronouns, the middle column for reflexive pronouns, and the last column for verb forms.

3. Have students use their templates to help quiz themselves while preparing for the Chapter Test.

STANDARDS: 1.2, 5.2

Repaso

4 Your friend has problems. Write informal commands using the verbs in parentheses to give advice to your friend.

1. No tengo nada que hacer después de clases. Estoy aburrido. (ser perezoso/buscar un pasatiempo)
2. Siempre me siento muy cansado en clase. (acostarse más temprano/dormir en clase)
3. Me duele el estómago después de comer en un restaurante. (comer comida sana/pedir muchos postres)
4. Me duelen los ojos y la cabeza. (ver tanta televisión/comprar lentes)

5 Contesta las preguntas.

1. What sport is practiced in July in Bariloche?
2. Name some foods that are popular in Argentina.
3. What is **mate**? How is it prepared?

CD 7, Tr. 11

6 Escucha la conversación entre Roberto y Laura. Luego di si las oraciones que siguen *(that follow)* son **ciertas** o **falsas.**

7 Mira los dibujos y con un(a) compañero(a), dramaticen la conversación. **1.** falsa **2.** cierta **3.** cierta **4.** falsa **5.** falsa

a.

b.

c.

d.

Visit Holt Online
go.hrw.com
KEYWORD: EXP1B CH7
Chapter Self-test

4 Gramática 2
- **estar, sentirse,** and **tener**
- negative informal commands
- object and reflexive pronouns with commands

pp. 106–111

5 Cultura
- **Comparaciones** **pp. 98–99**
- **Notas culturales** **pp. 90, 102, 104**
- **Geocultura** **pp. 80–83**

5 Answers
1. skiing
2. grilled meats, Spanish and Italian foods
3. hot water poured over dried **yerba mate**

6 Script
See script on p. 83F

AP Language Examination

PREPARACIÓN PRÁCTICA

7 Below is a sample answer for the picture activity.

—¿Qué tienes Rosa? ¿Te duele algo?

—Sí, me duele el brazo/hombro. Tengo un partido de béisbol.

—Debes acostarte temprano y descansar. Mañana debes estirarte antes del partido. Vas a sentirte mejor y a jugar bien.

Por la noche, Rosa se acuesta temprano y descansa. Duerme hasta tarde por la mañana y se siente mejor. No le duele el brazo/hombro. Rosa está contenta porque puede jugar en el partido de béisbol.

To display the drawings to the class, use the *Picture Sequences Transparency* for Chapter 7.

Oral Assessment

To assess the speaking activities in this section, you might use the following rubric. For additional speaking rubrics, see the *Alternative Assessment Guide.*

Speaking Rubric	4	3	2	1
Content (Complete—Incomplete)				
Comprehension (Total—Little)				
Comprehensibility (Comprehensible—Incomprehensible)				
Accuracy (Accurate—Seldom Accurate)				
Fluency (Fluent—Not Fluent)				

18–20: A 16–17: B 14–15: C 12–13: D Under 12: F

STANDARDS: 1.2, 1.3, 2.1, 4.1

Grammar Review
For more practice with the grammar topics in the chapter, see the *Grammar Tutor*, the *DVD Tutor*, the *Interactive Tutor*, or the *Cuaderno de vocabulario y gramática*.

GramaVisión

Online Edition 
Students might use the online textbook to practice the **Letra y sonido** feature.

Letra y sonido

Tell students "much softer" means the *g* is pronounced with a continuous flow of air, not exploded like the "hard *g*." Between vowels, Spanish speakers may drop it altogether. Try reading the **Dictado** scripts to students but dropping any *g* that falls between vowels. See if students can tell where the *g* was dropped.

Dictado Scripts

1. Me gusta jugar con juegos graciosos.
2. Los domingos hago dieta para mi estómago.
3. Como poca grasa, bebo jugo y hago yoga en grupo.
4. Mi amigo delgado sigue una dieta sana.
5. Muchas gracias, pero no tengo ganas de arreglar el garaje.
6. El gato negro está algo gordo.
7. A la muchacha guapa le duele la garganta.
8. Mis amigos son muy inteligentes y graciosos.

Gramática 1
- verbs with reflexive pronouns **pp. 92–93**
- using infinitives **pp. 94–95**
- review of stem-changing verbs **pp. 96–97**

Repaso de Gramática 1

Some verbs are used with reflexive pronouns if the subject and object of the verb are the same. For a list of such verbs, see page 92.

	lavarse		
me	lavo	**nos**	lavamos
te	lavas	**os**	laváis
se	lava	**se**	lavan

Use the infinitive of a verb after **acabar de, para, antes de, después de.**

Acabo de bañarme. Necesito una toalla **para** secarme.

For the forms of **acostarse** (**o** → **ue**), **encontrar** (**o** → **ue**), and **vestirse** (**e** → **i**), see page 96.

Gramática 2
- **estar, sentirse,** and **tener** **pp. 106–107**
- negative informal commands **pp. 108–109**
- object and reflexive pronouns with commands **pp. 110–111**

Repaso de Gramática 2

To describe mental or physical states or conditions use:

estar bien/mal/*adjective*
tener frío/calor/miedo/sueño
sentirse bien/mal/*adjective*

An object or reflexive pronoun goes just before the verb in **negative commands** and is attached to the end of an **affirmative command.**

fumar → **no fumes**
dormir → **no duermas**
levantarse → **no te levantes** (**levánta te**)
leer → **no lo leas**
dar → **no des**
ser → **no seas**
ir → **no vayas**

Letra y sonido (g) (gu)

La letra g CD 7, Tr. 12–14

- The letters **g** and **gu** sound like the "hard" *g* in *game* at the beginning of a phrase starting with **ga, gue, gui, go, gu, gr, gl** or when these follow **n:**
  gato, **gu**erra, **gu**itarra, ten**g**o, un **g**usto, ¡**G**rita!
- The letters **g** and **gu** sound much softer than the *g* in *game* when **ga, gue, gui, go, gu, gr, gl** follow a vowel or a consonant other than **n:**
  mi **g**ato, á**g**uila, al**g**o, mucho **g**usto, ne**g**ro

Trabalenguas

Tres tigres tragaban trigo en un trigal, y el más grande se puso a entigretar.

Contigo entró un tren con trigo un tren con trigo contigo entró.

Dictado

Escribe las oraciones de la grabación.

Chapter Review

Bringing It All Together

You might have students review the chapter using the following practice items and transparencies.

DVD Tutor

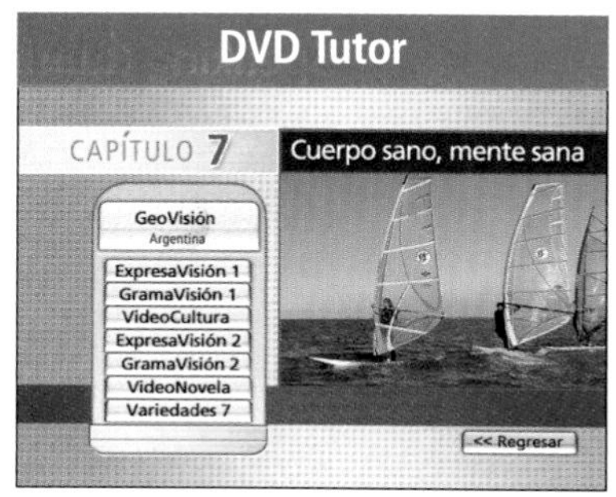

Interactive Tutor

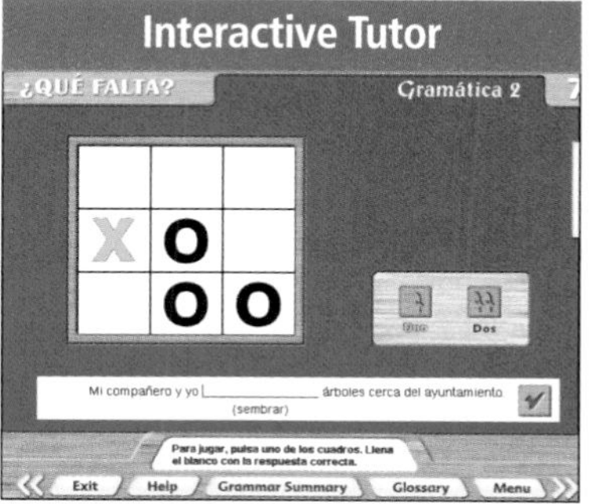

Repaso de Vocabulario 1

Talking about your daily routine

acabar de	*to just (have done something)*
acostarse (ue)	*to go to bed*
afeitarse	*to shave*
antes de	*before*
bañarse	*to bathe*
la boca	*mouth*
el brazo	*arm*
la cara	*face*
el cepillo de dientes	*toothbrush*
despertarse (ie)	*to wake up*
los dientes	*teeth*
encontrar (ue)	*to find*
entrenarse	*to work out*
la espalda	*back*
estar listo(a)	*to be ready*
estirarse	*to stretch*
los hombros	*shoulders*
el jabón	*soap*
lavarse	*to wash*
levantar pesas	*to lift weights*
levantarse	*to get up*
el maquillaje	*makeup*
maquillarse	*to put on makeup*
la nariz	*nose*
la navaja	*razor*
la pantorrilla	*calf*
la pasta de dientes	*toothpaste*
el pecho	*chest*
peinarse	*to comb your hair*
el peine	*comb*
la pierna	*leg*
el piyama	*pajamas*
ponerse	*to put on*
prepararse	*to get ready*
¿Qué te falta hacer?	*What do you still have to do?*
quitarse	*to take off*
la secadora de pelo	*hair dryer*
secarse	*to dry*
la toalla	*towel*
vestirse (i)	*to get dressed*

Talking about staying fit and healthy

mantenerse (ie) en forma	*to stay in shape*
¿Qué haces para relajarte?	*What do you do to relax?*

Repaso de Vocabulario 2

To talk about how you feel

bajar de peso	*to lose weight*
buscar un pasatiempo	*to find a hobby*
la cabeza	*head*
caminar	*to walk*
el cuello	*neck*
los dedos	*fingers*
dejar de fumar	*to stop smoking*
doler (ue)	*to hurt*
enojarse	*to get angry*
Es que...	*It's because/just that . . .*
estar aburrido(a)	*to be bored*
estar cansado(a)	*to be tired*
estar contento(a)	*to be happy*
estar enfermo(a)	*to be sick*
estar nervioso(a)	*to be nervous*
estar triste	*to be sad*
el estómago	*stomach*
la garganta	*throat*
hacer yoga	*to do yoga*
Le duele(n)...	*His (Her) . . . hurt(s).*
las manos	*hands*
Me duele(n)...	*My . . . hurt(s).*
el oído	*(inner) ear*
los pies	*feet*
¿Qué te pasa?	*What's wrong with you?*
¿Qué tiene...?	*What's the matter with . . . ?*
seguir (i) una dieta sana	*to eat a balanced diet*
sentirse (ie)	*to feel*
subir de peso	*to gain weight*
¿Te duele algo?	*Does something hurt?*
Te veo mal.	*You don't look well.*
tener catarro	*to have a cold*

To give advice

demasiado(a)	*too much*
dormir lo suficiente	*to get enough sleep*
ni	*neither*
No debes...	*You shouldn't . . .*
Para cuidarte la salud debes...	*To take care of your health, you should . . .*
Para cuidarte mejor...	*To take better care of yourself . . .*
tanta grasa	*so much fat*
tanto(a)	*so much, so many*
tanto dulce	*so many sweets*

For expressions with tener . . . . *See p. 106.*

Repaso

Repaso

Vocabulary Review

For more practice with the vocabulary in this chapter, see the *DVD Tutor*, the *Interactive Tutor*, or the *Cuaderno de vocabulario y gramática.*

Video/DVD

ExpresaVisión

Online Edition

For students to hear the vocabulary on audio, have them access the online textbook.

Game

El monstruo Ask students to draw a monster using the body parts in the **Vocabulario** (with two heads, three arms, etc.) Tell them not to let other students see what they draw. Then have them describe their monster to a partner, holding the drawing so the partner cannot see it. The student draws the monster his or her partner describes. They should then compare the two monsters and evaluate description, comprehension, and creative interpretation. You may wish to display students' artwork.

Online Edition

Transparency Vocabulario 7–1

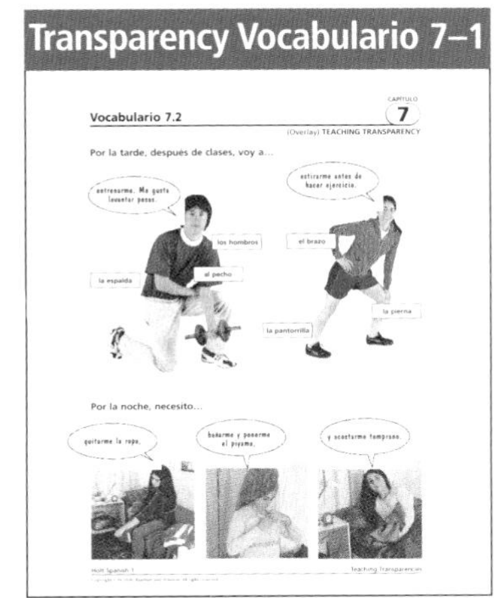

Transparency Situación 7–2

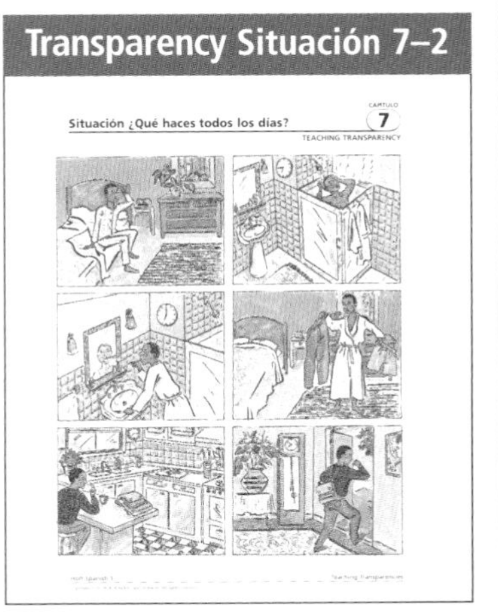

Assess

Assessment Program

Examen: Capítulo 7, pp. 145–155

Examen oral: Capítulo 7, p. 156

Alternative Assessment Guide, pp. 242, 250, 258

Audio CD 7, Tr. 18–19

Test Generator

STANDARDS: 1.2

Resources

Planning:

Lesson Planner, pp. 69, 226–227

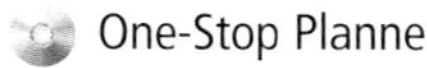 One-Stop Planner

Presentation:

 Teaching Transparencies Fine Art, Chapter 7

Practice:

Cuaderno de actividades, pp. 33–34

Audio CD 7, Tr. 15

Lab Book, pp. 21–22

Interactive Tutor, Disc 2

1 Script

1. Nuestra familia tiene la misma rutina todas las mañanas. Papá y mamá se despiertan a las seis. Mamá se lava la cara y se va a la cocina para preparar el desayuno.
2. Papá se afeita y luego se baña. Mi hermano y yo nos vestimos antes de comer.
3. Todos desayunamos juntos en el comedor. Hay pan, fruta y jugo de naranja.
4. Por fin salimos para el colegio.

2 Answers

1. industrious, hard-working
2. They like to go out, and they do not study.
3. She wants to go out with her friends.
4. She has too much homework.
5. To study for two or three hours
6. To go with her friends to a game or to a movie

Slower Pace Learners

2 For students who find Activity 2 challenging, you might have them work with a partner. Have them identify the key points in each letter and share them with the class. Then, have individuals complete items 1–5.

Integración

capítulos 1-7

CD 7, Tr. 15  **1** Escucha la descripción de una mañana típica en casa de los Muñoz. Escoge la foto correspondiente. 1. b 2. d 3. a 4. c

A

B
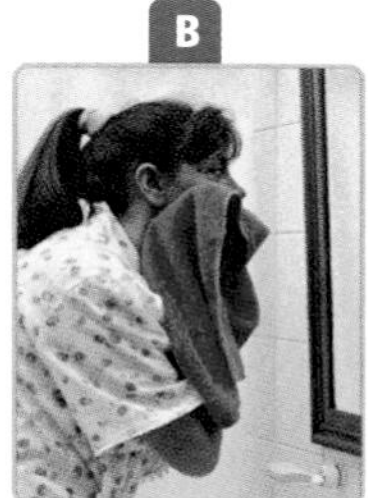

C

D

2 Read this letter to an advice columnist from a teen magazine. Then answer the questions in Spanish.

> *DameEsperanza...*
>
> Querida DameEsperanza:
> *Tengo muchas clases difíciles y soy muy trabajadora. Mis amigos prefieren salir y no estudiar. Quiero salir con ellos, pero no puedo porque tengo mucha tarea. ¿Qué debo hacer?*
>
> – Frustrada
>
> Querida Frustrada:
> ***Sí, debes estudiar, pero necesitas relajarte también. Puedes estudiar dos o tres horas cada noche. Entonces, los viernes y sábados puedes ir con tus amigos a un partido o al cine. ¡No necesitas pasar todas las noches en la biblioteca!***

1. How does Frustrada describe herself?
2. How does she describe her friends?
3. What does Frustrada want to do?
4. Why can't she do what she wants to?
5. What does the advice columnist tell Frustrada to do on weekdays?
6. Where does the columnist suggest Frustrada go on weekends?

Culture Project

Los deportes Have students research popular sports and activities in Argentina or another Spanish-speaking country they have studied at the library or on the Internet. They should select one sport or activity and research its origin. They should also identify why it is popular in that country and name some famous players of the sport or activity. Then, have students compare the popularity of the sport in the Spanish-speaking country versus its popularity in the U.S.

STANDARDS: 1.2, 1.3

Visit Holt Online
go.hrw.com
KEYWORD: EXP1B CH7
Cumulative Self-test

3 This painting shows a family traveling through the vast grasslands of Argentina in the 1860s. Imagine what their living conditions and health concerns might have been during this trip. Write five descriptive sentences about the people in the painting. Use the adjectives below and tell who might be feeling this way and why.

- cansado(a)
- aburrido(a)
- triste(a)
- nervioso(a)
- contento(a)

by Prilidiano Pueyrredón, 1823-70, Argentinian; The Art Archive / Museo Nacional de Bellas Artes Buenos Aires / Dagli Orti

Un alto en el campo, de Prilidiano Pueyrredón (1823–1870)

4 **Situación**

You're helping at your school's annual health fair by conducting a survey in Spanish. Write five or six questions to ask a classmate. Find out the following information.

- How does he or she stay in shape?
- What does he or she do to relax?
- Which foods does he or she typically eat?
- At what times does he or she go to bed and get up?
- How is he or she feeling right now?

After your partner answers your questions, suggest one thing that he or she could do to improve his or her health.

ACTFL Performance Standards

The activities in Chapter 7 target the communicative modes as described in the Standards.

Interpersonal	Two-way communication using receptive skills and productive skills	**Comunicación (SE),** pp. 89, 91, 93, 95, 97, 103, 105, 107, 109 **Comunicación (TE),** pp. 89, 91, 105, 107, 109, 115 **Situacíon,** p. 125
Interpretive	One-way communication using receptive skills	**Comparaciones,** pp. 98–99 **Comunicación (TE),** p. 91 **Novela en video,** pp. 114–117 **Leamos,** p. 118
Presentational	One-way communication using productive skills	**Comunicación (TE),** pp. 93, 95, 97, 103, 105

Fine Art Connection

Introduction In this chapter, students see the painting *Un alto en el campo* by Prilidiano Pueyrredón. You might share the following information with your students.

Prilidiano Pueyrredón (1823–1870) left Argentina at an early age, first to Río de Janiero and ultimately to Paris where he obtained a degree in engineering. He returned to Buenos Aires in 1854 and worked as an engineer, architect, and urban planner, in addition to producing a body of 232 paintings, which included 137 portraits. His style is characterized as naturalism, also influenced by European romanticism. Many of his other works featured the customs, people, and towns of the Argentine **pampas** and the coast of the **Río de la Plata.**

Analyzing To help students discuss and analyze the painting, you might use the following questions.

1. **¿Cómo viaja la gente hoy en día? ¿Cómo es un viaje en avión? ¿Cuáles son las dificultades de viajar hoy en día?**
2. **¿Qué hace la gente en la pintura?**
3. **¿Cómo viaja la gente? ¿Quiénes viajan?**
4. **¿Cómo es el viaje?**
5. **En tu opinión, ¿adónde van? ¿Por qué?**

Extension Have students work in groups of four or five to recreate the conversations and actions immediately preceeding the moment captured in the painting. Encourage students to use vocabulary and structures they have learned to create the dialogue. At the end of the dialogue, students should "freeze" in the poses shown in the painting.

STANDARDS: 1.1, 1.3

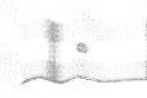

Resources

Planning:

Lesson Planner, p. xv

 One-Stop Planner

Presentation:

 Teaching Transparencies **Mapa 6**

Video Program, Videocassette 4
DVD Tutor, Disc 2
GeoVisión

Practice:

Video Guide, pp. 71–72

Lab Book, p. 49

Interactive Tutor, Disc 2

Atlas INTERACTIVO MUNDIAL

Have students use the interactive atlas at **go.hrw.com** to complete the Map Activities below.

Map Activities

1. Have students locate Florida on the U.S. map on the interactive atlas and name the bordering states. **(Georgia, Alabama)** What island country is the closest foreign neighbor to Florida? **(Cuba)**
2. Florida is a peninsula, surrounded by water except for a small land connection. What are the bodies of water that surround Florida? **(Océano Atlántico, Golfo de México)**

GeoVisión

Geocultura Florida

▲ **Cítricos** Florida is one of the world's largest exporters of citrus fruit. Spanish explorers first brought oranges to Florida in the 1500s.

Panama City

▼ **Miami** Many people from Spanish-speaking cultures live in the Miami area. Miami is on the Atlantic coast of Florida, only 322 kilometers (200 miles) northeast of Havana, Cuba.

Almanaque

Población
15.982.378

Capital
Tallahassee

Área
58.664 millas cuadradas (151.939 Km²)

Moneda
dólar estadounidense

Economía
manufactura, turismo, productos de frutas cítricas, pesca comercial, comercio con Latinoamérica

◀ **Florida** For its abundance of colorful flowers, the Spanish explorer **Juan Ponce de León** named this peninsula **Pascua Florida,** meaning *Flowery Easter.*

¿Sabías que...?

Spanish explorers founded St. Augustine, Florida, in 1565. It is the oldest European settlement in the United States still inhabited today. St. Augustine was founded 55 years before the Pilgrims landed at Plymouth Rock.

Background Information

 History

Several indigenous tribes lived in Florida before the arrival of the Spanish explorer Ponce de León in 1513. Throughout the 18th century, the Spanish fought attacks from the British and the French to defend their claim on Florida. In 1763, Florida was ceded to England. Spain took advantage of England's preoccupation with the American Revolution and again captured Florida, controlling it from 1783 to 1821. Florida became a U.S. state in 1845, but seceded in 1861 to the Confederacy.

Geography

St. Augustine is the oldest European city in the United States. It was settled by Pedro Menéndez de Avilés in 1565.

Florida was named by Ponce de León and means "full of flowers" in Spanish.

Calle Ocho, Little Havana's main street, buzzes with cafés and boutiques. Street vendors sell Cuban specialties such as **ceviche** and **churros.**

STANDARDS: 3.1

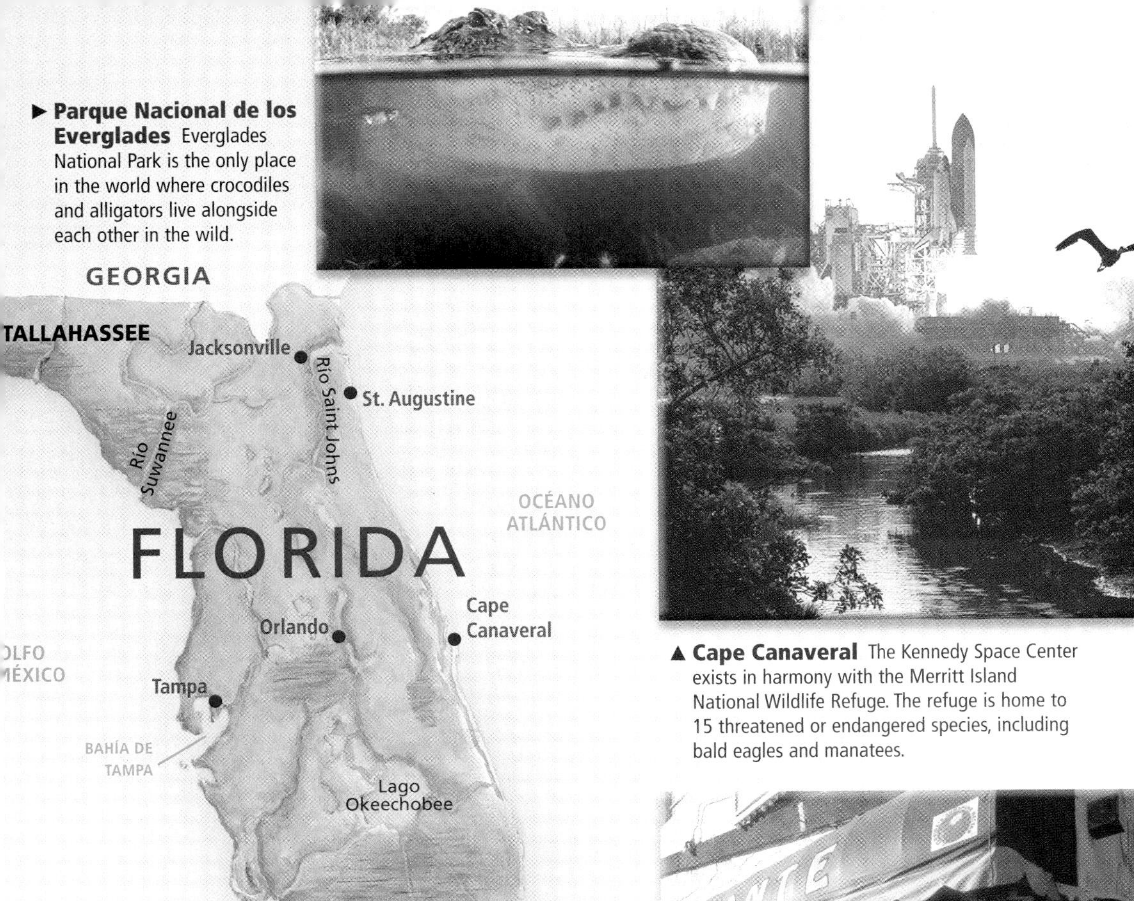

► **Parque Nacional de los Everglades** Everglades National Park is the only place in the world where crocodiles and alligators live alongside each other in the wild.

▲ **Cape Canaveral** The Kennedy Space Center exists in harmony with the Merritt Island National Wildlife Refuge. The refuge is home to 15 threatened or endangered species, including bald eagles and manatees.

▲ **La Pequeña Habana** Little Havana is a neighborhood in Miami where many Cuban Americans live and do business.

▼ **Los Cayos de Florida** The Florida Keys are a chain of islands connected by 42 bridges, including the famous Bahia Honda Bridge.

¿Qué tanto sabes?

How is Florida's economy a reflection of its geographic location?

Florida

Comparisons

Comparing and Contrasting

The state of Florida is mostly surrounded by water. Parasailing, surfing, windsurfing, snorkeling, and diving are some of the sports enjoyed on the coast. Enthusiasts enjoy fishing and canoeing in the streams, rivers, and marshes. International sea ports have helped make Florida's economy strong. Have students think about the implications of being surrounded by water. Ask them how far their region is from a water source. What water sports are practiced in the area? Does the water source have an impact on the local economy? In what way? Is that impact comparable to that experienced in Florida?

Communities

Celebrations

The **Festival de la Calle Ocho,** also known as **Carnaval de Miami,** is a ten-day celebration in mid-March. It is one of the largest block parties in the U.S., with the revelry spanning 23 city blocks. Colorful parades begin the festivities, which continue with nightly salsa dancing, live music, and brilliantly colored costumes. Every street is lined with vendors ready to sell many varieties of delicious Cuban specialties and delicacies. Thousands of people fill the streets for the **Carnaval** every year.

¿Sabías que... ?

Students might be interested in knowing the following facts about Florida.

- **Guayaberas** are loose fitting cotton shirts with short sleeves. These gauzy, front embroidered, and pleated shirts originated in Cuba, but are now a fashion statement in Miami.
- **La Revolución Cubana** triggered a wave of Cuban migration into Florida in the 1950s. About 350,000 Cubans entered Florida during that time.
- **Los pájaros de nieve,** or snow birds, are retired people who flock to the south to escape the cold northern winters.

Preguntas

You might choose to present these questions in English.

1. **¿Cómo y cuándo llegaron los primeros naranjos a Florida? (Con los exploradores españoles en el siglo XVI)**
2. **¿Dónde se encuentra Miami? (En la costa atlántica, a 381 kilómetros de Cuba)**
3. **¿Por qué es único el Parque de los Everglades? (Los cocodrilos y los caimanes cohabitan allí.)**
4. **¿Cómo se viaja entre los Cayos de Florida? (A través de 42 puentes)**

CNN enEspañol.com

Have students check the **CNN en español** website for news on Florida. This site is also a good source of timely, high-interest readings for students learning Spanish.

Cultures

Practices and Perspectives

Floridians have fused their many and various cultures into their own type of cuisine, **Floribbean.** Latin elements from the Caribbean are found side by side with Californian and Asian ingredients, creating altogether unique dishes, such as spicy sushi sauce with Peruvian **ceviche.** Central American street vendors sell their local specialties from small kiosks. Floridians, as well as the multitude of tourists that flock to the area each year, like to eat out, thus contributing to the large number of restaurants found in the state. Breakfasts tend to be light, and lunch is quick and often picked up on the street. The largest and most important meal of the day is dinner, for which the family gathers together around the table. Ask students to think about how typical dishes and meals are unique reflections of a culture.

Connections

Thinking Critically

Florida's population has grown over 40% in the last 30 years. Between the various waves of Central American, Cuban, and Haitian refugees, and the northern snowbirds, many native Floridians feel overwhelmed by the new population growth. Have students reflect on the enormous growth that Florida has seen in the last three decades. Imagine your community nearly doubling in size within ten years. How would it change your life? What would be some of the possible problems that could arise? What are possible solutions? Is such dramatic growth good for an area? Would students like to see such growth, or do they prefer their area the way it is?

A conocer Florida

La comida

▲ **Comida floribeña** "Floribbean" cuisine combines the flavors of traditional Caribbean dishes with foods native to Florida. Floribbean dishes often include seafood, tropical fruits, and zesty herbs and spices.

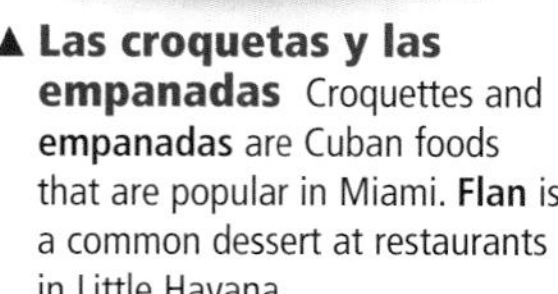

▲ **Las croquetas y las empanadas** Croquettes and **empanadas** are Cuban foods that are popular in Miami. **Flan** is a common dessert at restaurants in Little Havana.

El arte

▲ **Los seminoles** The Seminole people weave traditional baskets out of dried grasses from the Everglades wetlands.

▲ ***Calle Ocho*** This painting shows the heart of Miami's Cuban culture: a scene from the famous 8th Street, or **Calle Ocho**. The artist, Mildrey Guillot, was born in Havana, Cuba, and moved to Miami in 1962.

Interdisciplinary Links

La comida

Economics Link There are over 6,000 restaurants in Miami, ranging from traditional Spanish cuisine to New Age menus. The diversity in Florida's eating establishments covers the tastes of the world. Have students discuss why the restaurants reflect so many differing cultures. What types of dining are available in the students' area? Are their area's dining establishments driven by tourism or local population? What other influences might affect the types of restaurants that develop in an area?

El arte

Music Link Miami's Diaspora Vibe Art Gallery displays the city's greatest pieces of art by Caribbean, Latin American, and African-American artists. On the final Friday of the months of May through October, the gallery displays a new artist's works to the sounds of live music. Reflecting on the connection between music and the fine arts, have students choose an artist from Florida, perhaps one highlighted in the **Geocultura** section. After researching and viewing several pieces of art by this person, what type of music would they play at a showing to best capture the essence of the artist's work?

La arquitectura

Visit Holt Online
go.hrw.com
KEYWORD: EXP1B CH8
Photo Tour

¿Sabías que...?

During the 1960s, more than 260,000 Cuban refugees arrived in the United States. How does Cuban culture affect the arts, food, and festivals of Miami?

◄ **St. Augustine** The colonial architecture reflects St. Augustine's Spanish roots.

Las celebraciones

▲ **El Carnaval de Miami** The **Carnaval** of Miami in Little Havana includes the **Festival de la Calle Ocho,** a celebration of Miami's Hispanic culture.

▲ **El Festival de Jazz Latino** The Latin Jazz Festival is part of the Carnival of Miami. Latin jazz is a combination of American jazz with Afro-Cuban rhythms and percussion instruments.

La arquitectura

Art Link Miami's Art Deco District is one of the city's greatest tourist attractions. It wasn't always that way though. In fact, when historians pushed for saving the 50-year old buildings, many people didn't see their historic value and rallied for their demolition. Today the district has its own visitors center, and nearly 800 buildings are listed on the National Register of Historic Places. Have students research Art Deco architecture at the library or on the Internet. Where did this type of architecture originate? During what era was it popular? What are the major distinguishing features of Art Deco style?

Las celebraciones

Science Link Every February on the outskirts of the Everglades National Park, the small town of Florida City holds the Everglades Seafood Festival. People from all over flock to the festival for a two-day feeding frenzy of exotic dishes such as gator tails. Alligators, once an endangered species, have bounced back to substantial numbers due to effective conservation management, tourism, and farming. Have students reflect on the success of the alligator program and its link to tourism and celebrations such as the Everglades Seafood Festival.

Connections

Thinking Critically

Tourism is the most important asset in the Florida economy. More than 40 million tourists visit the state each year enjoying various theme parks, sun on the beaches, and the Kennedy Space Center. Almost all of these tourists eat in restaurants, sleep in hotels, and buy souvenirs to take home, spending around $22 billion a year. Tourism provides 79 percent of the state's gross annual product. Florida runs on a huge state budget. It is one of just a handful of states that has no individual state income tax. Nearly half of the state's functioning revenues come from its sales tax, which many visiting tourists contribute to. Many people move to Florida because of this lack of an individual state income tax. Ask students if tourism affects the economy where they live and why.

¿Comprendes?

You can use the following questions to check students' comprehension of the **Geocultura.**

1. Which flavors are combined in **comida floribeña**? (Caribbean and Floridian)
2. Where does the material for the Seminole baskets come from? (Everglades)
3. Where is the center of Miami's Cuban culture? (Little Havana, **Calle Ocho**)
4. What architectural elements in the St. Augustine streets resemble Spanish architecture? (wooden balconies)
5. What music styles are combined in Latin Jazz? (American jazz and Afro-Cuban rhythms)

Assess

Assessment Program

Prueba: Geocultura, pp. 155–156

Test Generator 

Capítulo 8

Vamos de compras

Overview and Resources

Overview and Resources

Chapter Section		Resources
Vocabulario en acción 1 • Asking for and giving opinions; asking for and offering help in a store, pp. 132–137 **¡Exprésate!** • To ask for an opinion; to give an opinion, p.133 • To offer and ask for help in a store, p. 136	Present	TPR Storytelling Book, pp. 42–43 Teaching Transparencies Video Program/DVD Tutor, **ExpresaVisión**
Assess Assessment Program • **Prueba: Vocabulario 1,** pp. 57–58 • Alternative Assessment Guide, pp. 243, 251, 259 Test Generator	Practice	Cuaderno de vocabulario y gramática, pp. 41–43 Activities for Communication, pp. 29–30 Video Guide, pp. 74–76 Lab Book, pp. 3, 23–26, 50 Teaching Transparencies Audio CD 8, Tr. 1 Interactive Tutor, Disc 2
Gramática en acción 1 • **Costar**, numbers to one million, p. 138 • Demonstrative adjectives and comparisons, p. 140 • **Quedar,** p. 142	Present	Video Program/DVD Tutor, **GramaVisión**
Assess Assessment Program • **Prueba: Gramática 1,** pp. 59–60 • **Prueba: Aplicación 1,** pp. 61–62 • Alternative Assessment Guide, pp. 243, 251, 259 Audio CD 8, Tr. 18 Test Generator	Practice	Grammar Tutor for Students of Spanish, Chapter 8 Cuaderno de vocabulario y gramática, pp. 44–46 Cuaderno de actividades, pp. 35–37 Activities for Communication, pp. 29–30 Video Guide, pp. 74–75 Lab Book, pp. 3, 23–26 Teaching Transparencies Audio CD 8, Tr. 2–4 Interactive Tutor, Disc 2

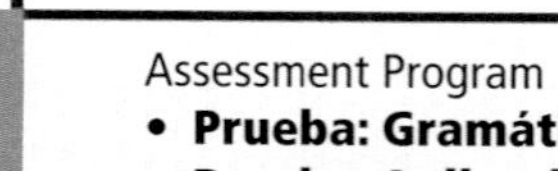

	Print	Media
Cultura • **Comparaciones,** pp. 144–145 • **Comunidad,** p. 145 • **Conexiones,** pp. 158–159	Cuaderno de actividades, p. 38 Cuaderno para hispanohablantes, pp. 61–68 Video Guide, pp. 74–75, 77 Lab Book, p. 51	Audio CD 8, Tr. 5–7 Video Program/DVD Tutor, **VideoCultura** Interactive Tutor, Disc 2
Novela en video • **Episodio 8,** pp. 160–163	Video Guide, pp. 74–75, 79 Lab Book, p. 53	Video Program/DVD Tutor, **VideoNovela**
Leamos y escribamos • **Una moneda de ¡Ay!,** pp. 164–165	Cuaderno de actividades, p. 42 Reading Strategies and Skills Handbook Cuaderno para hispanohablantes, pp. 61–68 ¡Lee conmigo! Assessment Program, pp. 69–70	Audio CD 8, Tr. 11

Lesson Planner with Differentiated Instruction, pp. 71–100, 228–255

One-Stop Planner® CD-ROM

Visit Holt Online
go.hrw.com
KEYWORD: EXP1B CH8
Online Edition

Chapter Section		Resources
Vocabulario en acción 2  • Saying where you went and what you did; talking on the phone, pp. 146–151 **¡Exprésate!** • To ask where someone went and what someone did; to respond, p. 147 • To talk on the phone, p. 150	Present	TPR Storytelling Book, pp. 44–45 Teaching Transparencies Video Program/DVD Tutor, **ExpresaVisión**
Assess Assessment Program • **Prueba: Vocabulario 2,** pp. 63–64 • Alternative Assessment Guide, pp. 243, 251, 259 Test Generator	Practice	Cuaderno de vocabulario y gramática, pp. 47–49 Activities for Communication, pp. 31–32 Video Guide, pp. 74–75, 78 Lab Book, pp. 3, 23–26, 52 Teaching Transparencies Audio CD 8, Tr. 8 Interactive Tutor, Disc 2
Gramática en acción 2  • The preterite of **–ar** verbs, p. 152 • The preterite of **ir,** p. 154 • The preterite of **–ar** verbs with reflexive pronouns, p. 156	Present	Video Program/DVD Tutor, **GramaVisión**
Assess Assessment Program • **Prueba: Gramática 2,** pp. 65–66 • **Prueba: Aplicación 2,** pp. 67–68 • Alternative Assessment Guide, pp. 243, 251, 259  Audio CD 8, Tr. 19  Test Generator	Practice	Grammar Tutor for Students of Spanish, Chapter 8 Cuaderno de vocabulario y gramática, pp. 50–52 Cuaderno de actividades, pp. 39–41 Activities for Communication, pp. 31–32 Video Guide, pp. 74–75 Lab Book, pp. 23–26 Teaching Transparencies Audio CD 8, Tr. 9–10 Interactive Tutor, Disc 2

	Print	Media
Repaso • **Repaso,** pp. 166–167 • **Gramática y Vocabulario,** pp. 168–169 • **Letra y sonido,** p. 168	Activities for Communication, pp. 50, 69–70 TPR Storytelling Book, pp. 46–47 Lab Book, pp. 23–26, 54 Assessment Program, pp. 173–183, 184 Alternative Assessment Guide, pp. 243, 251, 259 Standardized Assessment Tutor, pp. 33–36	Video Program/DVD Tutor, **Variedades** Teaching Transparencies Audio CD 8, Tr. 13–16 Interactive Tutor, Disc 2 Test Generator
Integración • Cumulative review, Chapters 1–8, pp. 170–171	Cuaderno de actividades, pp. 49–50 Lab Book, pp. 23–26	 Teaching Transparencies Audio CD 8, Tr. 17

Overview and Resources

Vamos de compras

Projects

La ropa tradicional

In this activity, students will research traditional clothing. For a multicultural approach, allow them to choose articles of clothing from any indigenous group in the world, or any clothing that has become popular worldwide. You may have students compare styles, materials, dyes, embroidery, weaving techniques, and other aspects of cloth manufacturing across cultures. Students will create a presentation for the class.

SUGGESTED SEQUENCE

1. Students do research on the Internet and/or at the library to select a type of clothing and obtain information about it. Types of clothing might include **gauchos, huipiles,** and **sarapes.**
2. Students document all Web sites or library sources they used to gather the information.
3. Students create posters, using magazine pictures or original personal drawings of the clothing. They might also bring in authentic costumes or fabrics. Students should address the clothing's origin, its material, and why it is worn. (climate, natural resources, aesthetics, to show marital status or origin). Or, instead of posters, students might prepare a PowerPoint slide show in Spanish on the item of clothing.
4. Students present their information to the class.

Grading the project

Suggested point distribution (100 points total)

Accuracy of information 40
Poster/Slide show 40
Presentation to class 20

e-community

e-mail forum:

Post the following questions on the classroom e-mail forum:

1. ¿Qué hiciste anoche? ¿Miraste la televisión? ¿Estudiaste?
2. ¿A qué hora te levantaste ayer?
3. ¿A qué hora te acostaste anoche?

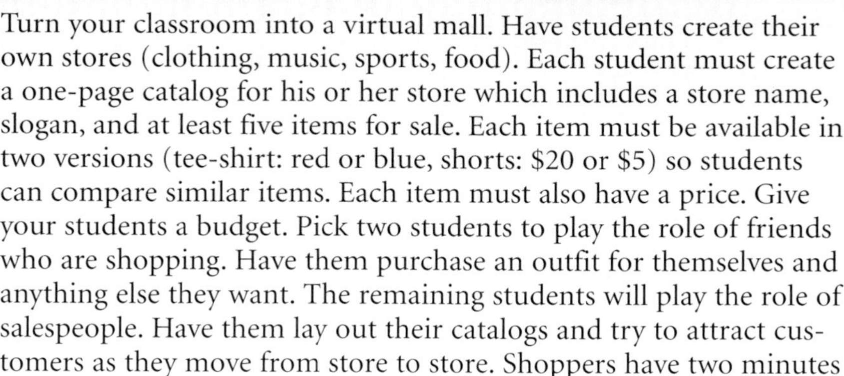

Partner Class Project

Turn your classroom into a virtual mall. Have students create their own stores (clothing, music, sports, food). Each student must create a one-page catalog for his or her store which includes a store name, slogan, and at least five items for sale. Each item must be available in two versions (tee-shirt: red or blue, shorts: $20 or $5) so students can compare similar items. Each item must also have a price. Give your students a budget. Pick two students to play the role of friends who are shopping. Have them purchase an outfit for themselves and anything else they want. The remaining students will play the role of salespeople. Have them lay out their catalogs and try to attract customers as they move from store to store. Shoppers have two minutes to shop, then another pair takes a next turn.

Game Bank

For game ideas, see pages T60–T63.

STANDARDS: 1.1, 1.3, 2.2, 4.2, 5.1

Traditions

Festivales

The annual **Calle Ocho Festival** in Miami's little Havana has become a major tourist attraction since its inception in 1977. This enormous block party, which takes place in March, celebrates Hispanic culture, food, and music. Salsa and merengue are especially highlighted during this festive event, and some of the most popular Latin musicians, including Celia Cruz and Gloria Estefan, have performed for crowds of up to a million people. To give your students a sample of the music one might hear in the streets of Little Havana, play ***Guantanamera*** on Audio CD 11, and ask the class to identify different instruments in the song. Have small groups of students make plans for a block party that would celebrate their own city or region. What representative songs, artists, and food would they choose and why?

Receta

Cuban cuisine is popular in South Florida, where many Cubans have settled. Cuba shares a Spanish and African cultural heritage with much of the rest of the Caribbean. Fried, baked, and puréed plantains are typical in Cuban and African cuisine. The following recipe is for fried sweet plantains, which make a delicious snack or dessert. You might have students make the following recipe as a class project or for extra credit.

Plátanos fritos

8 plátanos *(plantains)* muy maduros

aceite para freír

azúcar (opcional)

Use plátanos muy maduros (de color negro). Quíteles la piel y corte cada plátano en tajadas de una pulgada. Si quiere, puede revolverlos con el azúcar. Caliente el aceite para freír en una olla. Fría los pedazos de plátano, volteándolos hasta que se doren. Colóquelos en servilletas de papel para absorber el aceite.

Vamos de compras

For Student Response Forms, see the *Lab Book*, pp. 23–26.

Textbook Listening Activity Scripts

Vocabulario en acción 1

1 p. 134, CD 8, Tr. 1

1. —¿Qué te parece esta camisa?
   —Te queda muy bien.
2. —¡Qué cara es esta blusa!
   —Tienes razón. ¡Es un robo! No voy a comprarla.
3. —Cómo me queda el saco? Es una ganga, ¿verdad?
   —Me parece un robo. Te queda mal y cuesta mucho.
4. —Este vestido es muy bonito y te queda bien.
   —Sí, me gusta mucho. Voy a comprarlo.
5. —¿Te gustan estas botas?
   —No, son muy caras. Además, están pasadas de moda.
6. —¿Qué te parece esta chaqueta? Está a la última moda.
   —Es muy bonita y te queda bien.
7. —¿Qué te parece este sombrero?
   —¡Es feo! ¡Y cuesta mucho también!
8. —Este traje de baño es una ganga, ¿verdad?
   —Sí, es muy barato—y bonito también.
9. —¿Qué te parecen estos pantalones vaqueros?
   —Te quedan muy bien.
10. —Este abrigo es muy bonito, ¿no?
    —Si, y te queda muy bien. Debes comprarlo.

Answers to Activity 1
1. si; 2. no; 3. no; 4. si; 5. no; 6. si; 7. no; 8. si; 9. si; 10. si

Gramática en acción 1

11 p. 138, CD 8, Tr. 2

1. Esta camiseta cuesta cincuenta y siete dólares.
2. El abrigo cuesta ciento cuatro dólares.
3. La camisa de seda cuesta doscientos setenta y tres dólares.
4. El saco cuesta ciento treinta y dos dólares.
5. Las sandalias cuestan ochenta y cuatro dólares.
6. La chaqueta cuesta ciento veintiún mil dólares.
7. Las botas cuestan trescientos setenta y cuatro dólares.
8. Los pantalones vaqueros cuestan ciento treinta y ocho dólares.
9. La cama cuesta setecientos cuarenta y nueve dólares.
10. El sofá cuesta ochocientos sesenta y cinco dólares.

Answers to Activity 11
1. \$57; 2. \$104; 3. \$273; 4. \$132; 5. \$84; 6. \$121.000; 7. \$374; 8. \$138; 9. \$749; 10. \$865

15 p. 140, CD 8, Tr. 3

1. Mira este vestido negro. Es mucho más elegante que esa falda amarilla, ¿no?
2. Esta camisa blanca me gusta más que la camisa azul. La voy a comprar.
3. Estas botas cuestan más que los zapatos negros. Los zapatos cuestan diecisiete dólares. ¡Qué ganga!
4. Los pantalones vaqueros son menos caros que los pantalones cortos, pero los pantalones cortos están más a la moda. Voy a comprar los dos.
5. Este saco gris me parece tan bonito como esa chaqueta blanca. Me los compro.
6. Este traje de baño morado me queda más grande que el traje de baño anaranjado, y no hay una talla más pequeña. Voy a llevar el traje de baño anaranjado.

Answers to Activity 15
1. vestido negro; 2. camisa blanca; 3. zapatos negros: 4. las dos; 5. las dos; 6. traje de baño anaranjado

20 p. 143, CD 8, Tr. 4

1. Uso el diez y este vestido es el catorce. Me queda grande.
2. Esta camisa me queda grande. Necesito una talla más pequeña.
3. Estos pantalones me quedan bien.
4. Uso el número diez. Estos zapatos son del nueve.
5. —¿Qué te parece este saco?
   —No sé. Me parece que necesitas una talla más grande.
6. —¿Cómo me queda esta blusa?
   —Creo que te queda bien. Es tu talla, ¿verdad?

Answers to Activity 20
1. b; 2. b; 3. a; 4. b; 5. b; 6. a

Vocabulario en acción 2

23 p. 148, CD 8, Tr. 8

1. —¿En qué le puedo servir?
   —Busco una chaqueta.
2. —¿Vas a comprar todo aquí?
   —Sí, venden de todo y me gusta mucho.
3. —¿Qué te parecen estas botas?
   —Son bonitas y no cuestan mucho. ¡Son una ganga!
4. —Me gusta mucho esa pulsera.
   —A mí me gustan más los aretes.
5. —Busco el nuevo disco compacto de Shakira.
   —Aquí está.
6. —¿En qué le puedo servir?
   —Por favor, ¿dónde están las revistas de tiras cómicas?
7. —¿Te gusta el batido?
   —Sí, está muy rico.
8. —¿Qué vas a comer?
   —Quiero una ensalada con pollo.

Answers to Activity 23
1. tienda de ropa; 2. almacén; 3. zapatería; 4. joyería; 5. tienda de música; 6. librería; 7. heladería; 8. plaza de comida

Gramática en acción 2

34 p. 152, CD 8, Tr. 9

1. El sábado pasado fui de compras con mi mejor amiga, Magdalena.
2. Hoy fuimos al centro comercial y pasamos toda la tarde allí.
3. Esta vez mi hermana menor nos acompañó. No me gustó.
4. Prefiero ir a las tiendas de música a escuchar discos, pero a mi hermana le encantan las jugueterías.
5. La llevé a la juguetería Bebo donde ella miró las vitrinas por más de una hora.
6. Magdalena se cansó de mirar juguetes. Empezó a hablar de las tiendas de ropa.
7. Magdalena tiene ganas de comprar ropa y le encantan los zapatos.
8. En la zapatería Calzamás, pagué una fortuna por un par de sandalias.
9. Al final Magdalena y mi hermanita tomaron batidos en la heladería Dulce Vida. Yo tomé un jugo.

Answers to Activity 34
1. b; 2. b; 3. b; 4. a; 5. b; 6. b; 7. a; 8. b; 9. b

43 p. 156, CD 8, Tr. 10

1. Esta mañana Enrique y Lupita se levantaron temprano. Lupita se bañó y se maquilló. Enrique se afeitó.
2. Fueron al centro comercial donde miraron las vitrinas.
3. A Lupe le encanta la ropa y ellos fueron a la tienda de ropa donde Lupita compró un vestido, un suéter y una falda.
4. Después Enrique fue a la tienda de música donde compró muchos discos.
5. Regresaron a la casa por la tarde. Se entrenaron las piernas y se estiraron un poco.
6. Cenaron comida china y hablaron de sus amigos.
7. Enrique se relajó y miró la televisión hasta muy tarde.
8. Lupita estudió un poco y luego, se lavó la cara y se acostó.

Answers to Activity 43
c, d, e, a, f, g, b, h

Repaso capítulo 8

6 p. 167, CD 8, Tr. 13

1. El viernes voy a ir a la playa con mis amigos. Mi traje de baño me queda pequeño.
2. No me gusta llevar faldas ni vestidos.
3. No tengo diccionario para la clase de alemán.
4. Todos los días voy a correr y mis zapatos están viejos.
5. Me encantan los batidos de fruta.

Answers to Activity 6
1. un traje de baño; en la tienda de ropa; 2. pantalones; en la tienda de ropa; 3. un diccionario; en la librería; 4. zapatos de tenis; en la zapatería; 5. un batido; en la heladería

Dictado, p. 168, CD 8, Tr. 16
For script, see *Teacher's Edition*, p. 168.

Integración capítulos 1-8

1 p. 170, CD 8, Tr. 17

For script, see *Teacher's Edition*, p. 170.

Answers to Activity 1
1. a; 2. b; 3. b; 4. b; 5. a

Vamos de compras

50-Minute Lesson Plans

Day 1

OBJECTIVE
Asking for and giving opinions

Core Instruction
Chapter Opener, pp. 130–131
- See Using the Photo and **Más vocabulario,** p. 130. **5 min.**
- See Chapter Objectives, p. 130. **5 min.**

Vocabulario en acción 1, pp. 132–137
- See Teaching **Vocabulario,** p. 132. **30 min.**
- Play Audio CD 8, Tr. 1 for Activity 1, p. 134. **10 min.**

Optional Resources
- Common Error Alert, p. 132
- **También se puede decir,** p. 133
- Language Note, p. 133
- Special Learning Needs, p. 133 ●
- **Más práctica,** p. 134

HOMEWORK SUGGESTIONS
Cuaderno de vocabulario y gramática, pp. 41–43
Internet Activities

Day 2

OBJECTIVE
Asking for and giving opinions

Core Instruction
Vocabulario en acción 1, pp. 132–137
- Have students do Bell Work 8.1, p. 132 **5 min.**
- Show **ExpresaVisión,** Ch. 8. **10 min.**
- Review **Vocabulario 1** and **¡Exprésate!,** pp. 132–133 **15 min.**
- Present **Nota cultural,** p. 134. **5 min.**
- Have students do Activities 2–3, p. 134. **15 min.**

Optional Resources
- TPR, p. 133
- Advanced Learners, p. 133 ▲
- Fold-n-Learn, p. 134
- Slower Pace Learners, p. 135 ◆

HOMEWORK SUGGESTIONS
Cuaderno de vocabulario y gramática, pp. 41–43
Internet Activities

Day 3

OBJECTIVE
Asking for and giving opinions; asking for and offering help in a store

Core Instruction
Vocabulario en acción 1, pp. 132–137
- Have students do Activities 4–6, p. 135. **30 min.**
- See Teaching **¡Exprésate!,** p. 136. **20 min.**

Optional Resources
- **Más práctica,** p. 135
- **Comunicación,** p. 135
- Multiple Intelligences, p. 135
- Teacher to Teacher, p. 137

HOMEWORK SUGGESTIONS
Cuaderno de vocabulario y gramática, pp. 41–43
Internet Activities

Day 4

OBJECTIVE
Asking for and offering help in a store

Core Instruction
Vocabulario en acción 1, pp. 132–137
- Have students do Bell Work 8.2, p. 138. **5 min.**
- Review **¡Exprésate!,** p. 136. **10 min.**
- Have students do Activities 7–10, pp. 136–137. **35 min.**

Optional Resources
- Math Link, p. 136
- **Más práctica,** p. 137
- Slower Pace Learners, p. 137 ◆
- Special Learning Needs, p. 137 ●

HOMEWORK SUGGESTIONS
Study for **Prueba: Vocabulario 1.**

Day 5

OBJECTIVE
Vocabulary review and assessment

Core Instruction
Vocabulario en acción 1, pp. 132–137
- Review **Vocabulario en acción 1,** pp. 132–137. **30 min.**
- Give **Prueba: Vocabulario 1.** **20 min.**

Optional Resources
- **Comunicación,** p. 137
- Test Generator

HOMEWORK SUGGESTIONS
Preview **Gramática en acción 1,** pp. 138–143.

Day 6

OBJECTIVE
Costar, *numbers to one million*

Core Instruction
Gramática en acción 1, pp. 138–143
- See Teaching **Gramática,** p. 138. **30 min.**
- Play Audio CD 8, Tr. 2 for Activity 11, p. 138. **10 min.**
- Have students do Activity 12, p. 139. **10 min.**

Optional Resources
- Slower Pace Learners, p. 139 ◆
- Multiple Intelligences, p. 139

HOMEWORK SUGGESTIONS
Cuaderno de vocabulario y gramática, pp. 44–46
Cuaderno de actividades, pp. 39–42

Day 7

OBJECTIVE
Costar, *numbers to one million*

Core Instruction
Gramática en acción 1, pp. 138–143
- Have students do Bell Work 8.3, p. 140. **5 min.**
- Show **GramaVisión,** Ch. 8. **10 min.**
- Review **costar,** numbers to one million, p. 138. **15 min.**
- Present **Nota cultural,** p. 139. **5 min.**
- Have students do Activities 13–14, p. 139. **15 min.**

Optional Resources
- Teacher to Teacher, p. 139
- **Comunicación,** p. 139

HOMEWORK SUGGESTIONS
Cuaderno de vocabulario y gramática, pp. 44–46
Cuaderno de actividades, pp. 39–42

Day 8

OBJECTIVE
Demonstrative adjectives and comparisons

Core Instruction
Gramática en acción 1, pp. 138–143
- See Teaching **Gramática,** p. 140. **35 min.**
- Play Audio CD 8, Tr. 3 for Activity 15, p. 140. **10 min.**
- Present **Nota cultural,** p. 140. **5 min.**

Optional Resources
- Common Error Alert, p. 141
- **Comunicación,** p. 141

HOMEWORK SUGGESTIONS
Cuaderno de vocabulario y gramática, pp. 44–46
Cuaderno de actividades, pp. 39–42

To edit and create your own lesson plans, see the **One-Stop** Planner® CD-ROM

KEY
- ▲ Advanced Learners
- ◆ Slower Pace Learners
- ● Special Learning Needs
- ■ Heritage Speakers

Day 9

OBJECTIVE
Demonstrative adjectives and comparisons

Core Instruction
Gramática en acción 1, pp. 138–143
- Show **GramaVisión,** Ch. 8. **10 min.**
- Review demonstrative adjectives and comparisons, p. 140. **15 min.**
- Have students do Activities 16–18, p. 141 **25 min.**

Optional Resources
- Advanced Learners, p. 141 ▲
- Special Learning Needs, p. 141 ●

HOMEWORK SUGGESTIONS
Cuaderno de vocabulario y gramática, pp. 44–46
Cuaderno de actividades, pp. 39–42
Internet Activities
Interactive Tutor, Ch. 8

Day 10

OBJECTIVE
Quedar

Core Instruction
Gramática en acción 1, pp. 138–143
- See Teaching **Gramática,** p. 142. **20 min.**
- Have students do Activities 19–22, p. 142–143. **30 min.**

Optional Resources
- Slower Pace Learners, p. 143 ◆
- Multiple Intelligences, p. 143
- **Comunicación,** p. 143

HOMEWORK SUGGESTIONS
Study for **Prueba: Gramática 1.**
Interactive Tutor, Ch. 8

Day 11

OBJECTIVE
Grammar assessment

Core Instruction
Gramática en acción 1, pp. 138–143
- Review **Gramática en acción 1,** pp. 138–143. **30 min.**
- Give **Prueba: Gramática 1.** **20 min.**

Optional Resources
- Test Generator
- **Prueba: Aplicación 1**

HOMEWORK SUGGESTIONS
Assign Thinking Critically activity, p. 144.

Day 12

OBJECTIVE
Interviews from around the Spanish-speaking world

Core Instruction
Cultura, pp. 144–145
- Go over Thinking Critically activity, p. 144. **5 min.**
- See Teaching **Cultura,** #1–3, p. 144. **40 min.**
- Present and assign **Comunidad,** p. 145. **5 min.**

Optional Resources
- Map Activities, p. 144
- Slower Pace Learners, p. 145 ◆
- Multiple Intelligences, p. 145
- Practices and Perspectives, p. 145
- Community Link, p. 145

HOMEWORK SUGGESTIONS
Comunidad, p. 145
Community Link, p. 145
Cuaderno de actividades, p. 43

Day 13

OBJECTIVE
Saying where you went and what you did

Core Instruction
Vocabulario en acción 2, pp. 146–151
- Have students do Bell Work 8.5, p. 146. **5 min.**
- See Teaching **Vocabulario 2,** p. 146. **25 min.**
- Present **Nota cultural,** p. 148. **10 min.**
- Play Audio CD 8, Tr. 8 for Activity 23, p. 148. **10 min.**

Optional Resources
- **También se puede decir,** p. 147
- Language Note, p. 147
- Advanced Learners, p. 147 ▲
- Special Learning Needs, p. 147 ●

HOMEWORK SUGGESTIONS
Cuaderno de gramática, pp. 47–49

Day 14

OBJECTIVE
Saying where you went and what you did

Core Instruction
Vocabulario en acción 2, pp. 146–151
- Show **ExpresaVisión,** Ch. 8. **10 min.**
- Review **Vocabulario 2,** pp. 146–151. **15 min.**
- Have students do Activities 24–26, pp. 148–149. **25 min.**

Optional Resources
- TPR, p. 147
- Game, p. 148
- **Más práctica,** p. 149
- Special Learning Needs, p. 149 ●

HOMEWORK SUGGESTIONS
Cuaderno de gramática, pp. 47–49
Internet Activities

Day 15

OBJECTIVE
Saying where you went and what you did; talking on the phone

Core Instruction
Vocabulario en acción 2, pp. 146–151
- Have students do Activities 27–28, p. 149. **25 min.**
- See Teaching **¡Exprésate!,** p. 150. **15 min.**
- Have students do Activities 29–30, p. 150. **10 min.**

Optional Resources
- **Comunicación,** p. 149
- Slower Pace Learners, p. 149 ◆
- Extension, p. 150
- Heritage Speakers, p. 150 ■

HOMEWORK SUGGESTIONS
Cuaderno de gramática, pp. 47–49
Internet Activities

Day 16

OBJECTIVE
Talking on the phone; vocabulary review

Core Instruction
Vocabulario en acción 2, pp. 146–151
- Have students do Bell Work 8.6, p. 152. **5 min.**
- Review **¡Exprésate!,** p. 150. **10 min.**
- Have students do Activities 31–33, p. 151. **25 min.**
- Review **Vocabulario en acción 2,** pp. 146–151. **10 min.**

Optional Resources
- **Más práctica,** p. 151
- **Comunicación,** p. 151
- Advanced Learners, p. 151 ▲
- Special Learning Needs, p. 151 ●

HOMEWORK SUGGESTIONS
Study for **Prueba: Vocabulario 2.**

50-Minute Lesson Plans, continued

Day 17

OBJECTIVE
Vocabulary review and assessment; preterite of ***-ar*** *verbs*

Core Instruction
Vocabulario en acción 2, pp. 146–151
- Review **Vocabulario en acción 2,** pp. 146–151. 15 min.
- Give **Prueba: Vocabulario 2.** 20 min.

Gramática en acción 2, pp. 152–157
- See Teaching **Gramática,** #1–3, p. 152. 15 min.

Optional Resources
- Circumlocution, p. 150
- Test Generator
- Common Error Alert, p. 153

HOMEWORK SUGGESTIONS
Cuaderno de vocabulario y gramática, pp. 50–52
Cuaderno de actividades, pp. 44–47

Day 18

OBJECTIVE
Preterite of ***-ar*** *verbs*

Core Instruction
Gramática en acción 2, pp. 152–157
- Show **GramaVisión,** Ch. 8. 10 min.
- See Teaching **Gramática,** #4–5, p. 152 15 min.
- Play Audio CD 8, Tr. 9 for Activity 34, p. 152. 10 min.
- Have students do Activities 35–36, pp. 152–153. 15 min.

Optional Resources
- Special Learning Needs, p. 153 ●
- **Comunicación,** p. 153

HOMEWORK SUGGESTIONS
Cuaderno de vocabulario y gramática, pp. 50–52
Cuaderno de actividades, pp. 44–47
Internet Activities

Day 19

OBJECTIVE
Preterite of ***-ar*** *verbs; preterite of* ***ir***

Core Instruction
Gramática en acción 2, pp. 152–157
- Have students do Bell Work 8.7, p. 154. 5 min.
- Have students do Activity 37, p. 153. 15 min.
- Present **Nota cultural,** p. 152. 10 min.
- See Teaching **Gramática,** #1–3, p. 154. 20 min.

Optional Resources
- Advanced Learners, p. 153 ▲

HOMEWORK SUGGESTIONS
Cuaderno de vocabulario y gramática, pp. 50–52
Cuaderno de actividades, pp. 44–47

Day 20

OBJECTIVE
Preterite of ***ir***

Core Instruction
Gramática en acción 2, pp. 152–157
- Show **GramaVisión,** Ch. 8. 10 min.
- See Teaching **Gramática,** #4–5, p. 154. 10 min.
- Have students do Activities 38–41, pp. 154–155. 30 min.

Optional Resources
- Advanced Learners, p. 155 ▲
- Multiple Intelligences, p. 155

HOMEWORK SUGGESTIONS
Cuaderno de vocabulario y gramática, pp. 50–52
Cuaderno de actividades, pp. 44–47
Interactive Tutor, Ch. 8

Day 21

OBJECTIVE
Preterite of ***ir****; preterite of* ***-ar*** *verbs with reflexive pronouns*

Core Instruction
Gramática en acción 2, pp. 152–157
- Have students do Bell Work 8.8, p. 156. 5 min.
- Have students do Activity 42, p. 155. 15 min.
- See Teaching **Gramática,** p. 156. 20 min.
- Play Audio CD 8, Tr. 10 for Activity 43, p. 156. 10 min.

Optional Resources
- **Comunicación,** p. 155
- Slower Pace Learners, p. 157 ◆
- Special Learning Needs, p. 157 ●

HOMEWORK SUGGESTIONS
Cuaderno de vocabulario y gramática, pp. 50–52
Cuaderno de actividades, pp. 44–47
Internet Activities
Interactive Tutor, Ch. 8

Day 22

OBJECTIVE
Preterite of ***-ar*** *verbs with reflexive pronouns; grammar review*

Core Instruction
Gramática en acción 2, pp. 152–157
- Show **GramaVisión,** Ch. 8. 5 min.
- Have students do Activities 44–46, p. 157. 30 min.
- Review **Gramática en acción 2,** pp. 152–157. 15 min.

Optional Resources
- **Comunicación,** p. 157

HOMEWORK SUGGESTIONS
Study for **Prueba: Gramática 2.**
Interactive Tutor, Ch. 8

Day 23

OBJECTIVE
Grammar assessment; foreign currencies

Core Instruction
Gramática en acción 2, pp. 152–157
- Review **Gramática en acción 2,** pp. 152–157. 15 min.
- Give **Prueba: Gramática 2.** 20 min.

Conexiones culturales, pp. 158–159
- See Teaching **Conexiones culturales,** #1–3, p. 158. 15 min.

Optional Resources
- **Prueba: Aplicación 2**
- Test Generator

HOMEWORK SUGGESTIONS
Internet Activities
Interactive Tutor, Ch. 8

Day 24

OBJECTIVE
Foreign currencies; developing listening and reading skills

Core Instruction
Conexiones culturales, pp. 158–159
- See Teaching **Conexiones culturales,** #4–6, p. 158. 25 min.

Novela en video, pp. 160–163
- See Teaching **Novela en video,** #1–2, p. 160. 20 min.
- Discuss Gestures, p. 158. 5 min.

Optional Resources
- Thinking Critically, p. 159
- Advanced Learners, p. 159 ▲
- Multiple Intelligences, p. 159
- Visual Learners, p. 160

HOMEWORK SUGGESTIONS
Internet Activities
Culminating Project, p. 162

To edit and create your own lesson plans, see the **One-Stop** Planner® CD-ROM

KEY
- ▲ Advanced Learners
- ◆ Slower Pace Learners
- ● Special Learning Needs
- ■ Heritage Speakers

Day 25

OBJECTIVE
Developing listening and reading skills

Core Instruction

Novela en video, pp. 160–163
- See Teaching **Novela en video,** #3–4, p. 160 30 min.

Leamos y escribamos, pp. 164–165
- See Teaching **Leamos,** #1–2, p. 164. 20 min.

Optional Resources
- Practices and Perspectives, p. 161
- Comparing and Contrasting, p. 162
- **Comunicación,** p. 163
- Applying the Strategies, p. 164

HOMEWORK SUGGESTIONS
Read **Leamos** and finish Activity A, p. 164.
Cuaderno de actividades, p. 48

Day 26

OBJECTIVE
Developing reading and writing skills

Core Instruction

Leamos y escribamos, pp. 164–165
- See Teaching **Leamos,** #3–4, p. 164. 20 min.
- See Teaching **Escribamos,** #1–2, p. 165. 30 min.

Optional Resources
- Heritage Speakers, p. 165 ■
- Advanced Learners, p. 165▲
- Multiple Intelligences, p. 165

HOMEWORK SUGGESTIONS
Taller del escritor, p. 165
Cuaderno de actividades, p. 48
Additional Reading, pp. 270–271

Day 27

OBJECTIVE
Chapter review

Core Instruction

Leamos y escribamos, pp. 164–165
- See Teaching **Escribamos,** #4, p. 164. 10 min.

Repaso, pp. 166–167
- Have students do Activities 1–5, pp. 166–167. 40 min.

Optional Resources
- Fold-n-Learn, p. 166
- Reteaching, p. 166

HOMEWORK SUGGESTIONS
Internet Activities
Interactive Tutor, Ch. 8

Day 28

OBJECTIVE
Chapter review

Core Instruction

Repaso, pp. 166–167
- Play Audio CD 8, Tr. 13 for Activity 6, p. 167. 10 min.
- Have students do Activity 7, p. 167. 15 min.
- Play Game, p. 166. 10 min.
- Play Audio CD 8, Tr. 14–16 for **Letra y sonido,** p. 168. 15 min.

Optional Resources
- **Letra y sonido,** p. 168
- Teacher to Teacher, p. 169

HOMEWORK SUGGESTIONS
Study for Chapter Test.
Interactive Tutor, Ch. 8

Day 29

OBJECTIVE
Chapter review

Core Instruction

Integración, pp. 170–171
- Play Audio CD 8, Tr. 17 for Activity 1, p. 170. 10 min.
- Have students do Activities 2–4, pp. 170–171. 40 min.

Optional Resources
- Culture Project, p. 170
- Fine Art Connection, p. 171

HOMEWORK SUGGESTIONS
Study for Chapter Test.
Cuaderno de actividades, pp. 49–50

Day 30

OBJECTIVE
Assessment

Core Instruction

Chapter Test 50 min.

Optional Resources

Assessment Program:
- **Prueba: Lectura**
- **Prueba: Escritura**
- Alternative Assessment
- Test Generator

HOMEWORK SUGGESTIONS
Cuaderno de actividades, pp. 49–50, 82–83

Vamos de compras

90-Minute Lesson Plans

Block 1

OBJECTIVE
Asking for and giving opinions

Core Instruction

Chapter Opener, pp. 130–131
- See Using the Photo and **Más vocabulario,** p. 130. 5 min.
- See Chapter Objectives, p. 130. 5 min.

Vocabulario en acción 1, pp. 132–137
- Show **ExpresaVisión,** Ch. 8. 10 min.
- See Teaching **Vocabulario,** p. 132. 30 min.
- Present **Nota cultural,** p. 134. 10 min.
- Play Audio CD 8, Tr. 1 for Activity 1, p. 134. 10 min.
- Have students do Activities 2–4, pp. 134–135. 20 min.

Optional Resources
- Common Error Alert, p. 132
- **También se puede decir,** p. 133
- Language Note, p. 133
- Special Learning Needs, p. 133 ●
- **Más práctica,** p. 134
- Practices and Perspectives, p. 134
- Fold-n-Learn, p. 134
- Slower Pace Learners, p. 135 ◆

HOMEWORK SUGGESTIONS
Cuaderno de vocabulario y gramática, pp. 41–43
Internet Activities

Block 2

OBJECTIVE
Asking for and giving opinions; asking for and offering help in a store

Core Instruction

Vocabulario en acción 1, pp. 132–137
- Have students do Bell Work 8.1, p. 132 5 min.
- Review **Vocabulario 1** and **¡Exprésate!,** pp. 132–133. 20 min.
- Have students do Activities 5–6, p. 135. 25 min.
- See Teaching **¡Exprésate!,** p. 136. 20 min.
- Have students do Activities 7–9, pp. 136–137. 25 min.

Optional Resources
- TPR, p. 133
- Advanced Learners, p. 133 ▲
- **Más práctica,** p. 135
- **Comunicación,** p. 135
- Multiple Intelligences, p. 135
- Math Link, p. 136
- **Más práctica,** p. 137
- Special Learning Needs, p. 137 ●

HOMEWORK SUGGESTIONS
Study for **Prueba: Vocabulario 1.**
Cuaderno de vocabulario y gramática, pp. 41–43
Internet Activities

Block 3

OBJECTIVE
Vocabulary review and assessment; ***costar,*** *numbers to one million*

Core Instruction

Vocabulario en acción 1, pp. 132–137
- Have students do Bell Work 8.2, p. 138. 5 min.
- Have students do Activity 10, p. 137. 10 min.
- Review **Vocabulario en acción 1,** pp. 132–137. 15 min.
- Give **Prueba: Vocabulario 1.** 20 min.

Gramática en acción 1, pp. 138–143
- See Teaching **Gramática,** p. 138. 30 min.
- Play Audio CD 8, Tr. 2 for Activity 11, p. 138. 10 min.

Optional Resources
- Teacher to Teacher, p. 137
- Slower Pace Learners, p. 137 ◆
- **Comunicación,** p. 137
- Test Generator
- Slower Pace Learners, p. 139 ◆
- Multiple Intelligences, p. 139

HOMEWORK SUGGESTIONS
Cuaderno de vocabulario y gramática, pp. 44–46
Cuaderno de actividades, pp. 39–42
Internet Activities
Interactive Tutor, Ch. 8

Block 4

OBJECTIVE
Costar, *numbers to one million; demonstrative adjectives and comparisons*

Core Instruction

Gramática en acción 1, pp. 138–143
- Review **costar,** numbers to one million, p. 138. 10 min.
- Have students do Activities 12–14, p. 139. 25 min.
- Present **Nota cultural,** p. 139. 5 min.
- See Teaching **Gramática,** p. 140. 35 min.
- Play Audio CD 8, Tr. 3 for Activity 15, p. 140. 10 min.
- Present **Nota cultural,** p. 140. 5 min.

Optional Resources
- **GramaVisión,** Ch. 8
- Teacher to Teacher, p. 139
- **Comunicación,** p. 139
- Common Error Alert, p. 141
- **Comunicación,** p. 141

HOMEWORK SUGGESTIONS
Cuaderno de vocabulario y gramática, pp. 44–46
Cuaderno de actividades, pp. 39–42
Internet Activities
Interactive Tutor, Ch. 8

To edit and create your own lesson plans, see the One-Stop Planner® CD-ROM

KEY
- ▲ Advanced Learners
- ◆ Slower Pace Learners
- ● Special Learning Needs
- ■ Heritage Speakers

Block 5

OBJECTIVE
Demonstrative adjectives and comparisons; ***quedar***

Core Instruction

Gramática en acción 1, pp. 138–143
- Show **GramaVisión,** Ch. 8. **5 min.**
- Review demonstrative adjectives and comparisons, p. 140. **15 min.**
- Have students do Activities 16–18, p. 141 **25 min.**
- See Teaching **Gramática,** p. 142. **20 min.**
- Have students do Activities 19–22, p. 142–143. **25 min.**

Optional Resources
- Advanced Learners, p. 141 ▲
- Special Learning Needs, p. 141 ●
- Slower Pace Learners, p. 143 ◆
- Multiple Intelligences, p. 143
- **Comunicación,** p. 143

HOMEWORK SUGGESTIONS
Study for **Prueba: Gramática 1.**
Cuaderno de vocabulario y gramática, pp. 44–46
Cuaderno de actividades, pp. 39–42
Internet Activities
Interactive Tutor, Ch. 8

Block 6

OBJECTIVE
Grammar review and assessment; interviews from around the Spanish-speaking world

Core Instruction

Gramática en acción 1, pp. 138–143
- Have students do Bell Work 8.5, p. 146. **5 min.**
- Review **Gramática en acción 1,** pp. 138–143. **20 min.**
- Give **Prueba: Gramática 1.** **20 min.**

Cultura, pp. 144–145
- See Teaching **Cultura,** #1–3, p. 144. **40 min.**
- Present and assign **Comunidad,** p. 145. **5 min.**

Optional Resources
- Test Generator
- **Prueba: Aplicación 1**
- Thinking Critically, p. 144
- Map Activities, p. 144
- Slower Pace Learners, p. 145 ◆
- Multiple Intelligences, p. 145
- Practices and Perspectives, p. 145
- Community Link, p. 145

HOMEWORK SUGGESTIONS
Comunidad, p. 145
Community Link, p. 145
Cuaderno de actividades, p. 43

Block 7

OBJECTIVE
Saying where you went and what you did

Core Instruction

Vocabulario en acción 2, pp. 146–151
- Show **ExpresaVisión,** Ch. 8. **5 min.**
- See Teaching **Vocabulario 2,** p. 146. **25 min.**
- Present **Nota cultural,** p. 148. **10 min.**
- Play Audio CD 8, Tr. 8 for Activity 23, p. 148. **10 min.**
- Have students do Activities 24–28, pp. 148–149. **40 min.**

Optional Resources
- **También se puede decir,** p. 147
- Language Note, p. 147
- Advanced Learners, p. 147 ▲
- Special Learning Needs, p. 147 ●
- TPR, p. 147
- Game, p. 148
- **Más práctica,** p. 149
- Special Learning Needs, p. 149 ●

HOMEWORK SUGGESTIONS
Cuaderno de gramática, pp. 47–49
Internet Activities

Block 8

OBJECTIVE
Talking on the phone; preterite of ***-ar*** *verbs*

Core Instruction

Vocabulario en acción 2, pp. 146–151
- Have students do Bell Work 8.6, p. 152. **5 min.**
- Review **Vocabulario 1** and **¡Exprésate!,** pp. 146–147. **20 min.**
- See Teaching **¡Exprésate!,** p. 150. **15 min.**
- Have students do Activities 29–33, pp. 150–151. **35 min.**

Gramática en acción 2, pp. 152–157
- See **Teaching Gramática,** #1–3, p. 152. **15 min.**

Optional Resources
- **Comunicación,** p. 149
- Slower Pace Learners, p. 149 ◆
- Extension, p. 150
- Heritage Speakers, p. 150 ■
- **Más práctica,** p. 151
- **Comunicación,** p. 151
- Advanced Learners, p. 151 ▲
- Special Learning Needs, p. 151 ●
- Circumlocution, p. 150
- Test Generator
- Common Error Alert, p. 153

HOMEWORK SUGGESTIONS
Study for **Prueba: Vocabulario 2.**
Cuaderno de gramática, pp. 47–49
Internet Activities
Interactive Tutor, Ch. 8

90-Minute Lesson Plans, continued

Block 9

OBJECTIVE
Vocabulary assessment; preterite of ***-ar*** *verbs*

Core Instruction

Vocabulario en acción 2, pp. 146–151
- Review **Vocabulario en acción 2,** pp. 146–151. 15 min.
- Give **Prueba: Vocabulario 2.** 20 min.

Gramática en acción 2, pp. 152–157
- See Teaching **Gramática,** #4–5, p. 152 15 min.
- Present **Nota cultural,** p. 152. 5 min.
- Play Audio CD 8, Tr. 9 for Activity 34, p. 152. 10 min.
- Have students do Activities 35–37, pp. 152–153. 25 min.

Optional Resources
- Test Generator
- **GramaVisión,** Ch. 8
- Advanced Learners, p. 153 ▲
- Special Learning Needs, p. 153 ●
- **Comunicación,** p. 153

HOMEWORK SUGGESTIONS
Cuaderno de vocabulario y gramática, pp. 50–52
Cuaderno de actividades, pp. 44–47
Internet Activities
Interactive Tutor, Ch. 8

Block 10

OBJECTIVE
Preterite of ***ir****; preterite of* ***-ar*** *verbs with reflexive pronouns*

Core Instruction

Gramática en acción 2, pp. 152–157
- See Teaching **Gramática,** p. 154. 30 min.
- Have students do Activities 38–42, pp. 154–155. 40 min.
- See Teaching **Gramática,** p. 156. 20 min.

Optional Resources
- **GramaVisión,** Ch. 8
- Advanced Learners, p. 155 ▲
- Multiple Intelligences, p. 155
- **Comunicación,** p. 155

HOMEWORK SUGGESTIONS
Cuaderno de vocabulario y gramática, pp. 50–52
Cuaderno de actividades, pp. 44–47
Internet Activities
Interactive Tutor, Ch. 8

Block 11

OBJECTIVE
Preterite of ***-ar*** *verbs with reflexive pronouns; foreign currencies*

Core Instruction

Gramática en acción 2, pp. 152–157
- Have students do Bell Work 8.8, p. 156. 5 min.
- Show **GramaVisión,** Ch. 8. 5 min.
- Play Audio CD 8, Tr. 10 for Activity 43, p. 156. 10 min.
- Have students do Activities 44–46, p. 157. 30 min.

Conexiones culturales, pp. 158–159
- See Teaching **Conexiones culturales**, p. 158. 40 min.

Optional Resources
- Slower Pace Learners, p. 157 ◆
- Special Learning Needs, p. 157 ●
- **Comunicación,** p. 157
- Thinking Critically, p. 159
- Advanced Learners, p. 159 ▲
- Multiple Intelligences, p. 159

HOMEWORK SUGGESTIONS
Study for **Prueba: Gramática 2.**
Interactive Tutor, Ch. 8

To edit and create your own lesson plans, see the **One-Stop** Planner® CD-ROM

KEY

- ▲ Advanced Learners
- ◆ Slower Pace Learners
- ● Special Learning Needs
- ■ Heritage Speakers

Block 12

OBJECTIVE
Grammar assessment; developing listening and reading skills

Core Instruction

Gramática en acción 2, pp. 152–157
- Review **Gramática en acción 2,** pp. 152–157. 10 min.
- Give **Prueba: Gramática 2.** 20 min.

Novela en video, pp. 160–163
- See Teaching **Novela en video,** #1–2, p. 160. 40 min.

Leamos y escribamos, pp. 164–165
- See Teaching **Leamos,** #1–2, p. 164. 20 min.

Optional Resources

- **Prueba: Aplicación 2**
- Test Generator
- Gestures, p. 158.
- Visual Learners, p. 160
- Practices and Perspectives, p. 161
- Comparing and Contrasting, p. 162
- **Comunicación,** p. 163
- Applying the Strategies, p. 164

HOMEWORK SUGGESTIONS
Read **Leamos** and finish Activity A, p. 164.
Culminating Project, p. 162
Cuaderno de actividades, p. 48

Block 13

OBJECTIVE
Developing reading and writing skills; chapter review

Core Instruction

Leamos y escribamos, pp. 164–165
- See Teaching **Leamos,** #3–4, p. 164. 20 min.
- See Teaching **Escribamos,** #1–2, p. 165. 30 min.

Repaso, pp. 166–167
- Have students do Activities 1–5, pp. 166–167. 30 min.
- Play Audio CD 8, Tr. 13 for Activity 6, p. 167. 5 min.
- Have students do Activity 7, p. 167. 5 min.

Optional Resources

- Heritage Speakers, p. 165 ■
- Advanced Learners, p. 165 ▲
- Multiple Intelligences, p. 165
- Fold-n-Learn, p. 166
- Reteaching, p. 166
- Game, p. 166
- Teacher to Teacher, p. 169

HOMEWORK SUGGESTIONS
Study for Chapter Test.
Taller del escritor, p. 165
Cuaderno de actividades, p. 48
Additional Reading, pp. 270–271

Block 14

OBJECTIVE
Assessment

Core Instruction

Chapter Test 50 min.

Integración, pp. 170–171
- Play Audio CD 8, Tr. 14–16 for **Letra y sonido,** p. 168. 10 min.
- Play Audio CD 8, Tr. 17 for Activity 1, p. 170. 5 min.
- Have students do Activities 2–4, pp. 170–171. 25 min.

Optional Resources

- Teaching **Escribamos,** #4, p. 164
- **Letra y sonido,** p. 168
- Culture Project, p. 170
- Fine Art Connection, p. 171

Assessment Program:
- **Prueba: Lectura**
- **Prueba: Escritura**
- Alternative Assessment
- Test Generator

HOMEWORK SUGGESTIONS
Cuaderno de actividades, pp. 49–50, 82–83

Meeting the National Standards

Communication
Comunicación, pp. 135, 137, 139, 141, 143, 149, 151, 153, 155, 157

Situación, p. 171

Cultures
Comparaciones, pp. 144–145

Nota cultural, pp. 134, 140, 148, 152

Conexiones culturales, pp. 158–159

Connections
Background Information, pp. 126–127

Interdisciplinary Links, pp. 128–129

Language Note, pp. 133, 147

Math Link, pp. 136, 159

Thinking Critically, pp. 136, 159

Visual Learners, p. 160

Fine Art, p. 171

Comparisons
Comparaciones, pp. 144–145

Comparing and Contrasting, pp. 127, 162

Communities
Celebrations, p. 127

Comunidad, p. 145

Community Link, p. 145

Using the Photo
Read the caption and explain to students that Florida's mild climate allows people to shop and dine outside all year round. Have students look at the photo and compare this shopping scene with shopping in their region. Present the words in **Más vocabulario** and have students find each item in the photo. Ask students the questions under **¿Qué ves en la foto?**

Más vocabulario

la palmera	*palm tree*
el toldo	*awning*
el maniquí	*mannequin*
la sombrilla	*parasol*
la acera	*sidewalk*
la bolsa	*shopping bag*

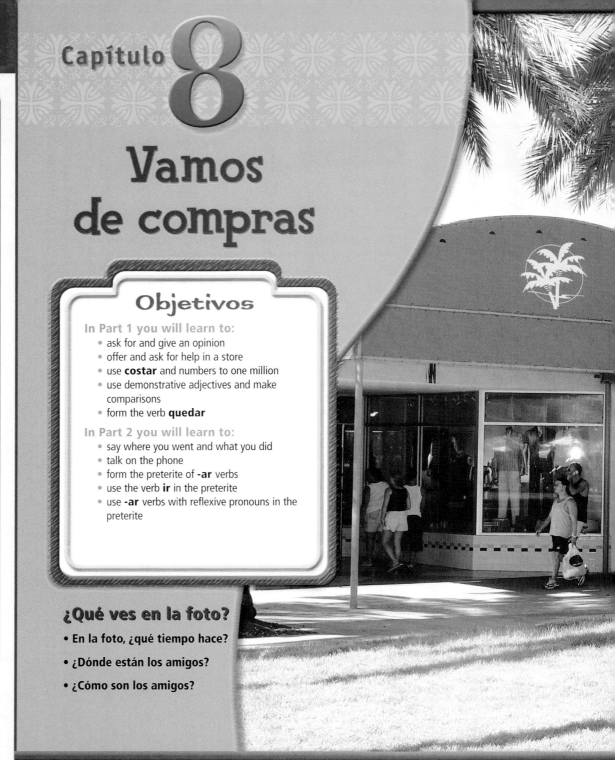

Capítulo 8
Vamos de compras

Objetivos

In Part 1 you will learn to:
- ask for and give an opinion
- offer and ask for help in a store
- use **costar** and numbers to one million
- use demonstrative adjectives and make comparisons
- form the verb **quedar**

In Part 2 you will learn to:
- say where you went and what you did
- talk on the phone
- form the preterite of **-ar** verbs
- use the verb **ir** in the preterite
- use **-ar** verbs with reflexive pronouns in the preterite

¿Qué ves en la foto?
- **En la foto, ¿qué tiempo hace?**
- **¿Dónde están los amigos?**
- **¿Cómo son los amigos?**

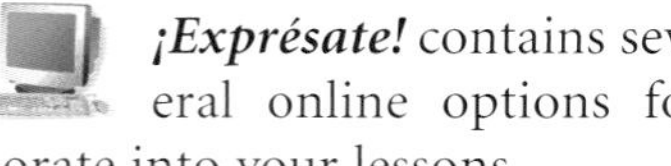

¡Exprésate! contains several online options for you to incorporate into your lessons.

***¡Exprésate! Student Edition* online at my.hrw.com**
On this site, you will find the online version of *¡Exprésate!* All concepts in the textbook are presented and practiced in this online version of your textbook. This online version can be used as a supplement to or as a replacement for your textbook.

Practice activities at go.hrw.com
These activities provide additional practice for major concepts presented in each chapter. Practice items include structured practice as well as research topics.

Teacher resources at www.hrw.com
This site provides additional information that teachers might find useful about the *¡Exprésate!* program.

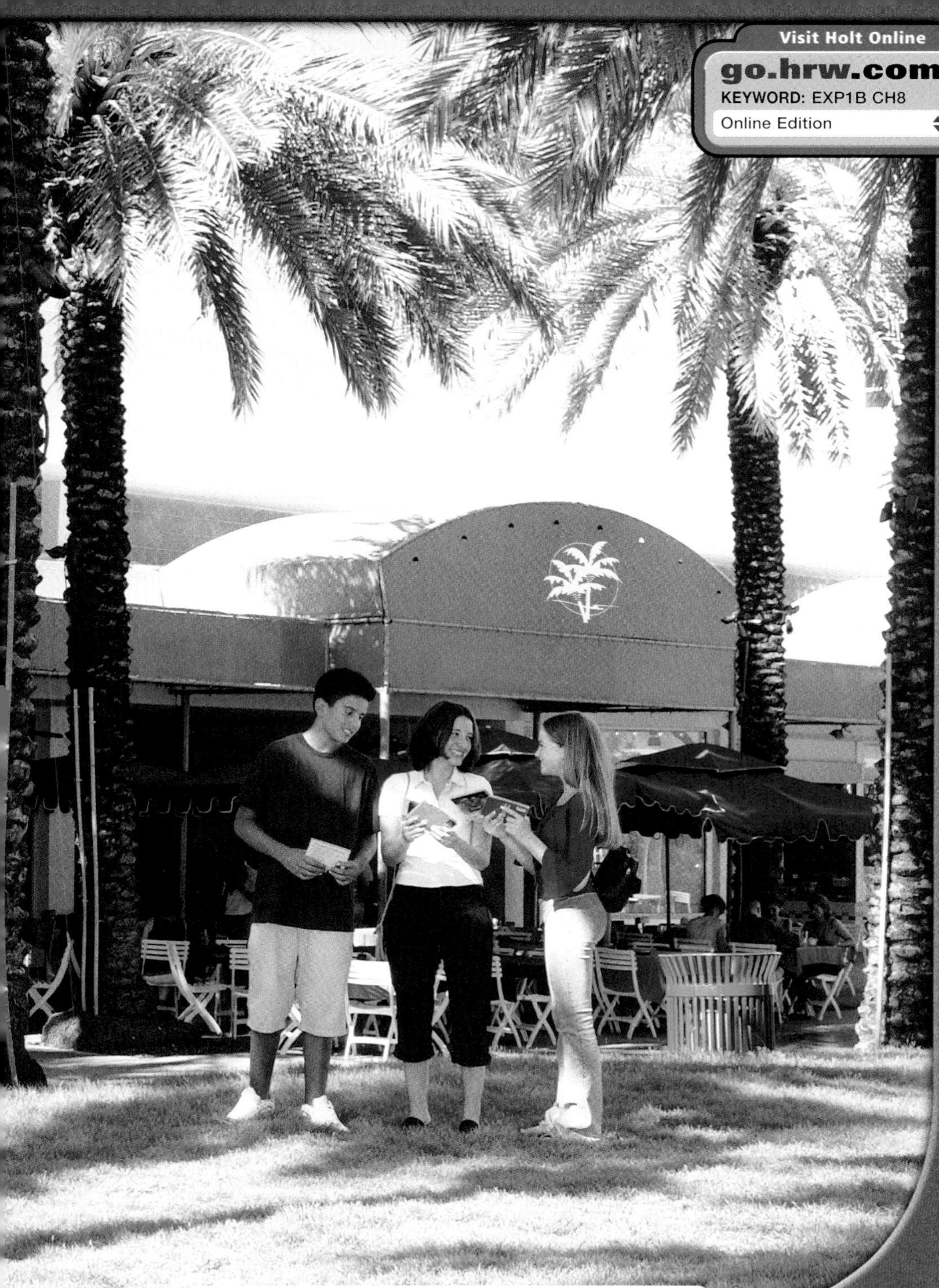

De compras en Miami, Florida

Chapter Opener

Learning Tips

Circumlocution Remind students that sometimes they don't know the exact word for something even in their native language. One way they can still get their message across is by describing what they want to say using circumlocution. Give students the phrase **Es una cosa que...** to help them practice the skill. Have students look around the classroom and pick three things they don't know how to say in Spanish. Have them describe the items to a classmate who will guess which objects are being described.

VIDEO OPTIONS

- **ExpresaVisión 1**
- **GramaVisión 1**
  Costar; numbers to 1 million; demonstrative adjectives and comparisons; **parecer, quedar,** and **costar**
- **VideoCultura**
- **ExpresaVisión 2**
- **GramaVisión 2**
  preterite of **–ar** verbs; preterite of **ir;** preterite of **–ar** verbs with reflexive pronouns
- **VideoNovela**
- **Variedades**

Pacing Tips

This chapter presents several key grammatical concepts, including the preterite, so you might choose to spend a few more days on this chapter. For complete lesson plan suggestions, see pages 129G–129N.

Suggested pacing:	Traditional Schedule	Block Schedule
Vocabulario 1/Gramática 1	11 days	5 1/3 blocks
Cultura	1 day	1/2 block
Vocabulario 2/Gramática 2	10 3/4 days	5 1/3 blocks
Conexiones culturales	1 day	1/2 block
Novela	3/4 day	1/3 block
Leamos y escribamos	1 1/2 day	1/2 block
Repaso	2 days	1/2 block
Chapter Test	1 day	1/2 block
Integración	1 day	1/2 block

Resources

Planning:

Lesson Planner, pp. 71–75, 228–233

One-Stop Planner

Presentation:

TPR Storytelling Book, pp. 42–43

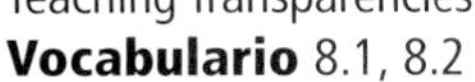
Teaching Transparencies **Vocabulario** 8.1, 8.2

Video Program
Videocassette 4
DVD Tutor, Disc 2
ExpresaVisión

Practice:

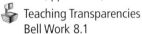

Cuaderno de vocabulario y gramática, pp. 41–43

Activities for Communication, pp. 29–30

Video Guide, pp. 74–76

Lab Book, pp. 23–24, 50

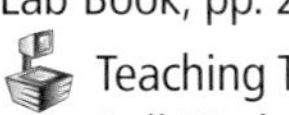
Teaching Transparencies
Bell Work 8.1
Vocabulario y gramática answers, pp. 41–43

Audio CD 8, Tr. 1

Interactive Tutor, Disc 2

Bell Work

Use Bell Work 8.1 in the *Teaching Transparencies,* or write this activity on the board.

Recommend a solution to each of these problems.

1. **A Álvaro le duele el cuello.**
2. **A Jorge y Patricia les duele el estómago.**
3. **A mí me duele la garganta.**
4. **A Ana le duele la cabeza.**
5. **A Ángela y a ti les duele el oído.**

COMMON ERROR ALERT
¡OJO!

Explain to students that a **blusa** *(blouse)* is worn by women. **Camisetas** and **camisas** are worn by men and women.

Objetivos
Asking for and giving opinions, offering and asking for help in a store

Vocabulario en acción 1

ExpresaVisión

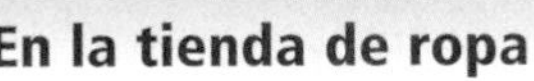
En la tienda de ropa

Más vocabulario...

Es...	*It's . . .*
de algodón	*made of cotton*
de lana	*made of wool*
de seda	*made of silk*
para hombres	*for men*
para mujeres	*for women*
para niños	*for children*

También se puede decir...

In Spain, you might hear **pantalones tejanos** as well as **pantalones vaqueros**. A sweater is called **un jersey** and tennis shoes are **zapatillas de tenis.**

Bluejeans are also known as **pantalones de mezclilla** and T-shirts are **playeras** in Mexico and Texas. Many Spanish speakers have borrowed the term **bluejeans** directly from English.

Core Instruction

TEACHING VOCABULARIO

1. Introduce the vocabulary using transparencies **Vocabulario 8.1** and **8.2.** Model the pronunciation of each word as you point to the appropriate picture. **(15 min.)**
2. Bring some clothing items to class. You might recycle **un reloj** and **unos zapatos** which students learned in **Capítulo 4.** Hold up items of clothing and make a comment about each one: **Me parece feo/a, bonito/a... Está a la moda.** As an alternative, you may point to various clothing items on the transparency. **(8 min.)**
3. Hold up an item of clothing and ask students yes/no questions such as **¿Está a la moda?** Finally, hold up an item and ask **¿Qué te parece...?** **(7 min.)**

ExpresaVisión

For a presentation of clothing vocabulary, use the video presenter. For interactive activities, see the *DVD Tutor.*

ExpresaVisión

Visit Holt Online
go.hrw.com
KEYWORD: EXP1B CH8
Vocabulario 1 practice

¿Qué ropa llevas hoy?

¿Qué color te gusta más?

rojo, azul, verde, amarillo, morado, blanco, negro, anaranjado, gris, café

¡Exprésate!

To ask for an opinion	To give your opinion
¿Qué te parece el traje de baño anaranjado? *What do you think of the orange swimsuit?*	**Me parece feo y cuesta mucho. ¡Es un robo!** *It's ugly and costs a lot. It's a rip-off!*
¿Cómo me queda el saco? *How does the sport coat fit me?*	**Te queda muy bien. Y está a la (última) moda.** *It looks good on you. And it's in (the latest) style.*
¿Y el/la...? ¡Cuesta ochenta dólares! *What about this . . .? It costs $80.00!*	**¡Qué caro(a)! Además, está pasado(a) de moda.** *How expensive! Besides, it's out of style.*
La bolsa es una ganga, ¿verdad? *The purse is a bargain, isn't it?*	**Tienes razón. Es muy barata.** *You're right. It's very inexpensive.*

Interactive TUTOR

Online
Vocabulario y gramática, pp. 41–43

▶ Vocabulario adicional — Ropa, p. R14

Vocabulario 1

TPR
Total Physical Response

Have students help you gather a variety of clothing items made of various fabrics. Ask individual students to respond to these commands.

Dale a... la camisa (amarilla,...).

Busca un suéter de lana.

Pon un par de botas junto con unos pantalones y una camisa.

Tráeme una bolsa que quede bien con estas sandalias.

Pon en esta mesa todos los calcetines.

Escoge un vestido o una falda (verde,...).

Muestra unos calcetines y unos zapatos que puedes llevar para ir a correr.

Encuentra un zapato, una bota o sandalia de número...

También se puede decir...

It is common to hear **ropa para damas** and **ropa para caballeros** as a more formal and polite variant of **para mujeres** and **para hombres.** In Peru, a sweater is called a **chompa.** In Mexico a **chamarra** is a jacket, and in Puerto Rico, a dress jacket is a **gabán.** Students may hear **traje** for dress in Puerto Rico and Argentina. Instead of **calcetines, medias** is used in Venezuela, Colombia, and Ecuador.

Differentiated Instruction

Advanced Learners

Bring several clothing catalogues to class and have students choose a page with an outfit that they like. Then tell them to describe the clothing. They can read the catalogue description to find out what the fabric is. You can place a picture and write an example on the board. **La mujer lleva pantalones negros de lana con una chaqueta roja y una blusa blanca de seda. Lleva sandalias. No lleva calcetines.**

Special Learning Needs

Students with Learning Disabilities/ Dyslexia These students may have difficulty with the concept of fabric type, without actual visual and tactile examples. Give students a swatch of the different materials (most fabric stores will give free swatches of fabric). Instruct them to write the Spanish names on sticky labels to attach to the back of each type of material.

Connections

Language Note

The origin of many clothing words tells us much about the meaning. **Abrigo** comes from the word **abrigar,** originally meaning *to warm with the heat of the sun.* The word **sombrero** comes from **sombra** meaning *shade.* Early usage of the word referred only to hats with very extensive brims.

STANDARDS: 1.2

 **Script**

See script on page 129E.

Cultures

Practices and Perspectives

Tell students the differences in the use of the comma and decimal points in numbers and prices. Ask them how to say 1.3 in Spanish.

Más práctica

1 Ask students to make a list of a favorite piece of clothing they own for each category listed in Activity 1. Then have them compare lists with a classmate and find people who have similar items. Ask them to talk about which clothing items they like best.

MODELO
(camisa) Tengo una camisa azul de algodón.
(blusa) No tengo blusas, no me gustan.
(saco) Tengo un saco de lana negro. Es bonito.

Nota cultural

Most Spanish-speaking countries use the metric system, so clothing and shoe sizes are different from sizes in the United States. The word for "size" also varies, depending on what you're buying. If you're looking for clothing, use **talla**. For shoes, use **número**. Look at the chart and compare the different sizes. What size shirt would you wear in Spain? What size shoes?

Tallas para hombres	USA	EUR	Tallas para mujeres	USA	EUR
Camisas	14	36	Blusas	8	36
	15	38		10	38
	16	40		12	40
Zapatos	7	40	Zapatos	5	36
	8	41		6	37
	9	43		7	38

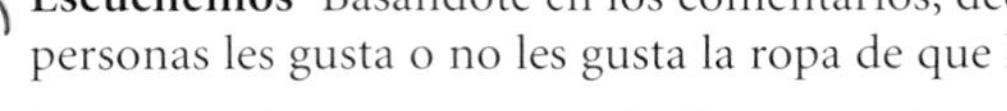

CD 8, Tr. 1

1 ¿Les gustan?

Escuchemos Basándote en los comentarios, decide si a las personas les gusta o no les gusta la ropa de que hablan.

1. la camisa sí
2. la blusa no
3. el saco no
4. el vestido sí
5. las botas no
6. la chaqueta sí
7. el sombrero no
8. el traje de baño sí
9. los pantalones vaqueros sí
10. el abrigo sí

2 La ropa nueva

Leamos Alicia is helping her sister Mónica shop for new clothes. Choose Alicia's best response for each of Mónica's comments.

1. d 2. c 3. b 4. a

Mónica	Alicia
1. ¿Cómo me queda la camisa?	a. Sí, está a la última moda.
2. ¿Qué te parece la blusa roja?	b. ¡Qué barato! ¡Es una ganga!
3. El abrigo cuesta doce dólares.	c. Es fea. No me gusta la roja.
4. ¿Está a la moda el saco de algodón?	d. Te queda muy bien.

3 ¿Qué te parecen?

Leamos Complete Mónica's and Alicia's conversation, based on the clothing pictured below.

Mónica	Alicia
—¿Qué te ___1___ la chaqueta negra?	—Es muy ___2___. Sólo cuesta $25.
—Los ___3___ verdes son una ganga, ¿no?	—¡ ___4___ ! Además, están pasados ___5___.
—¿ ___6___ me quedan los vaqueros?	—Te quedan muy ___7___. Están a la ___8___, también.
—¿Y el ___9___ amarillo? ¿Te gusta?	—Me parece ___10___ y cuesta mucho. ¡Es un ___11___ !
—La ___12___ roja es cara, ¿no?	—Sí, tienes ___13___. Es cara.

1. parece 2. barata 3. pantalones 4. Qué caros/Son un robo 5. de moda 6. Cómo 7. bien 8. (última) moda 9. traje de baño 10. feo 11. robo 12. camiseta 13. razón

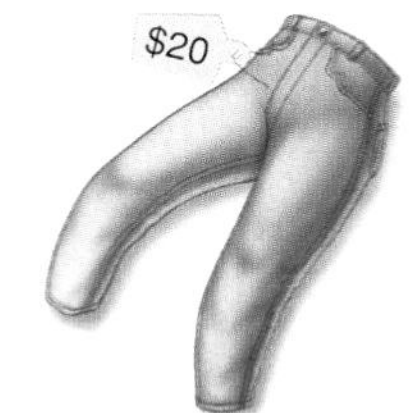

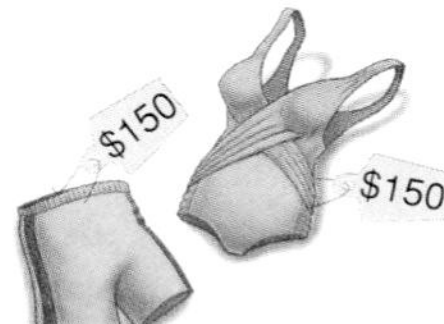

FOLD-N-LEARN

Four-page Booklet

1. Have students fold a sheet of paper in half from top to bottom, then from side to side. **2.** Students unfold the paper and cut a slit along the top-to-bottom creases from each edge to the side-to-side crease, leaving 1/4 inch in the center between the slits. **3.** Students refold the paper like in step 1 to make a four-page booklet. **4.** Students number the pages 1–8, starting with the cover. **5.** On each odd-numbered page students write sentences with colored illustrations of clothing that they would wear. For example: **Voy al gimnasio. Llevo...** Then they draw a cap, t-shirt, shorts, and tennis shoes, and color each drawing. **6.** On even-numbered pages, students write the vocabulary words that match their illustrations, including color. **7.** To study, students complete the sentences on the odd-numbered pages and flip to the even-numbered pages to check their answers.

STANDARDS: 1.2, 2.2, 4.2

4 ¿Qué ropa llevan?

Escribamos For each member of the Morelos family, write a list of his or her clothing. Include colors, possible fabrics, and adjectives of your choice.

MODELO **El señor Morelos tiene una camisa blanca de algodón y unos pantalones vaqueros.**

Comunicación

5 La familia Morelos

Hablemos In groups of five, play the roles of the members of the Morelos family from Activity 4. Introduce yourself to the class. Tell your name, family relationship, and age. Tell one thing you like to do. Then describe what you are wearing.

MODELO **Me llamo... Soy el padre. Tengo... años. Me gusta... Hoy llevo...**

6 En la tienda de ropa

Hablemos With a partner, play the roles of a clerk in a clothing store and a student shopping for clothes. Follow the format below. Then, switch roles.

El/La Dependiente	El/La Cliente
Greet the shopper and ask if you can help him or her.	Say you would like to buy a cotton shirt.
Ask what he or she thinks of the blue shirt and say it costs $50.	Say it is ugly and expensive.
Ask what he or she thinks of the red shirt and say it costs $15.	Say it is the latest style and is a bargain.

Vocabulario 1

4 Possible Answers

1. Carmen tiene una camiseta blanca y pantalones cortos anaranjados.
2. Sergio tiene un traje de baño morado.
3. La Sra. Morelos tiene una blusa amarilla de seda, una falda de café y unas sandalias.
4. Olivia tiene un traje de baño rojo, pantalones cortos azules, calcetines azules y zapatos de tenis blancos.

Más práctica

Collect pictures from clothing catalogs and glue them to sheets of construction paper. Show the pictures to the class and ask these questions:
¿Qué lleva esta persona?
¿Cómo es...(name a clothing item)?
¿Qué te parece...(name a clothing item)?
¿Está a la última moda?

Comunicación

Group Activity: Interpersonal

Divide students into groups of 6 to play the roles of the Morelos family and a clothing store clerk. Ask the members of the Morelos family to imagine they are going shopping for new clothes for school and work. As they enter the store, have the clerk greet them and ask what they are looking for. Then have each member of the Morelos family tell the clerk what type of clothing he or she wants. The clerk will then suggest an item and mention a price. Ask students watching this skit to write down what each family member buys, and how much it costs.

Differentiated Instruction

SLOWER PACE LEARNERS

3 Extension Have each student create a page for a clothing catalog by drawing or cutting items from a magazine. Ask them to put the pictures on an 8 1/2 x 11 sheet of paper, and to label each item with name, short description and price (**un sombrero negro, de lana, $250**). Then have them exchange pages with a partner and write a sentence for each item that gives an opinion of that item (**El sombrero negro es muy caro, y no está de moda**). Later you may want to bind all the pages together to create a Classroom Clothing Catalog.

MULTIPLE INTELLIGENCES

Bodily/Kinesthetic Ask students to imagine that they are fashion models and stage an impromptu fashion show. Have a volunteer go to the front of the classroom and model the clothes he or she has on, using exaggerated model movements. Ask another student to describe what the student is wearing and make comments about the outfit.

MODELO Hoy María tiene un vestido rojo y negro. ¡Qué bonito! También tiene zapatos negros y un suéter de lana. Me parece fenomenal. Está a la última moda. Gracias, María.

STANDARDS: 1.1, 1.2, 1.3, 2.2, 4.2

Resources

Planning:

Lesson Planner, pp. 71–75, 228–233

 One-Stop Planner

Presentation:

TPR Storytelling Book, pp. 42–43

 Teaching Transparencies **Vocabulario** 8.1, 8.2

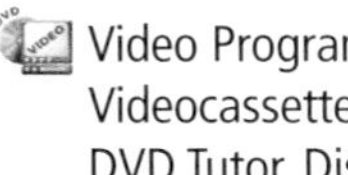 Video Program
Videocassette 4
DVD Tutor, Disc 2
ExpresaVisión

Practice:

Cuaderno de vocabulario y gramática, pp. 41–43

Activities for Communication, pp. 29–30

Video Guide, pp. 74–76

Lab Book, pp. 23–24, 50

 Teaching Transparencies **Vocabulario y gramática** answers, pp. 41–43

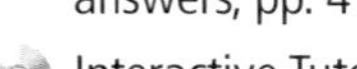 Interactive Tutor, Disc 2

Connections

Math Link

Ask students to figure out how much money they can save on the following items if they buy them on sale. Then have them calculate their total savings. On the board or on a transparency write the following:

Precios reducidos:	Originalmente:	Ahora
Sacos de seda	$225.00	$189.95
Camisas de algodón	25.95	25.95
Abrigos de lana	99.00	49.98

¡Exprésate!

To offer and ask for help in a store

Interactive TUTOR

¿En qué le puedo servir? *How can I help you?*	**Busco una camisa de seda.** *I'm looking for a silk shirt.* **Nada más estoy mirando.** *I'm just looking.* **Quiero devolver esta falda. La necesito en otro color.** *I want to return this skirt. I need it in another color.*
¿Qué número/talla usa? *What shoe/clothing size do you wear?*	**Uso el/la 8.** *I wear a size 8 in shoes/clothes.*
¿Cómo le queda la camisa? *How does the shirt fit you?*	**Me queda bien/mal. Necesito una talla más grande/pequeña.** *It fits well/poorly. I need a bigger/smaller size.*
¿A qué hora cierra la tienda? *What time does the store close?*	**Cierra a las siete.** *It closes at 7:00.*

Online Vocabulario y gramática, pp. 41–43

De tiendas en Florida

7 La camiseta perfecta

Leamos Read the conversation between **el dependiente** and Raúl. Answer the questions that follow.

DEPENDIENTE Buenos días. ¿En qué le puedo servir?
RAÚL Me gustaría comprar una camiseta.
DEPENDIENTE ¿Le gustan las camisetas de algodón?
RAÚL Sí, busco una camiseta blanca.
DEPENDIENTE ¿Qué talla usa?
RAÚL Me queda bien la talla grande. ¿Cuánto cuestan las camisetas?
DEPENDIENTE Las camisetas blancas cuestan siete dólares.
RAÚL ¡Qué baratas! ¡Son una ganga!
DEPENDIENTE ¿Busca más ropa?
RAÚL No gracias. ¿A qué hora cierra la tienda?
DEPENDIENTE Cierra a las nueve de la noche.

1. ¿Qué quiere comprar Raúl? una camiseta blanca
2. ¿Qué talla usa? grande
3. ¿Cuánto cuestan las camisetas blancas? siete dólares
4. ¿Es cara la camiseta? No, es barata.
5. ¿Quiere comprar algo más? No.
6. ¿A qué hora cierra la tienda? 9:00 P.M.

Core Instruction

TEACHING ¡EXPRÉSATE!

1. Use the expressions from **¡Exprésate!** to act out a conversation between a salesperson and a customer in a clothing store. You may wish to use puppets or stuffed animals to portray the different speakers. **(8 min.)**
2. Read aloud some of the expressions and ask students whether the speaker is most likely a salesperson or customer. **(3 min.)**
3. Show transparencies **Vocabulario 8.1** and **8.2.** Ask volunteers **¿En qué le puedo servir?** Point to a clothing item on the transparencies to cue their answers. **(4 min.)**
4. Bring magazine pictures of people in various clothing items and ask students how they fit the people. Cue their answers with a thumbs-up or thumbs-down gesture. As an alternative, you may wish to put on items that fit you poorly, over your outfit for the day, and ask students about the fit of those items. **(5 min.)**

STANDARDS: 1.2, 3.1

8 ¿Qué dices?

Escribamos Write this list of questions and statements. Then write a response to each using the clues given.

1. ¿En qué le puedo servir? *(I'm just looking.)* Nada más estoy mirando.
2. ¿Vas a comprar un vestido? *(No, I'm looking for a skirt.)* No, busco una falda.
3. ¿Qué talla usa? *(I wear a size 7.)* Uso la 7.
4. ¿Cómo le queda el abrigo? *(It fits poorly, I need a bigger one.)* Me queda mal. Necesito una talla más grande.
5. Busco unos zapatos. *(What size do you wear?)* ¿Qué número usa?
6. ¿A qué hora cierra la tienda? *(It closes at 8:30 P.M.)* Cierra a las ocho y media de la noche.
7. ¿Cómo le quedan los pantalones? *(They fit poorly, I need smaller ones.)* Me quedan mal. Necesito una talla más pequeña.
8. ¿Qué número de zapatos usa? *(I wear a size 12 in shoes.)* Uso el 12.

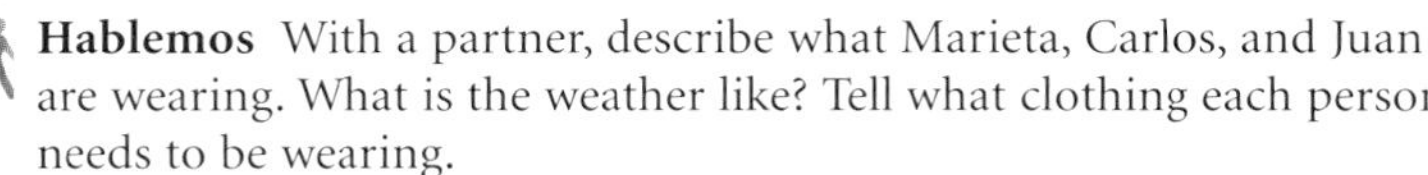

Comunicación

9 ¡Qué ropa tan rara!

Hablemos With a partner, describe what Marieta, Carlos, and Juan are wearing. What is the weather like? Tell what clothing each person needs to be wearing.

MODELO **Marieta lleva... Hace frío y nieva. Ella necesita llevar...**

1. Marieta

2. Carlos

3. Juan

10 Hablando de ropa

Hablemos Take turns with a partner asking and answering the following questions.

1. ¿Qué te parece la ropa de... *(famous person)*?
2. ¿Prefieres las camisas de seda o de algodón?
3. ¿Qué ropa está a la última moda?
4. ¿Qué ropa está pasada de moda?
5. ¿Cómo te queda la ropa de talla "extra-grande"?
6. ¿A qué hora cierra la tienda donde te gusta comprar ropa?

Teacher to Teacher

Paula Bernard
Sandy Creek High School
Fayette County, GA

I bring to class a suitcase packed with clothing items from the vocabulary and I unpack it, naming each item in Spanish. Students repeat the words. After completely unpacking, I randomly choose items of clothing and have students identify them. Finally, I repack, having students help me as I ask for the items in Spanish. You may vary this by packing unusual items, putting on some clothing, or asking what things may be missing.

Comunicación

Pair Activity: Presentational

Ask pairs of students to draw a person wearing some combination of clothing. Have them color the picture. Then have each pair tell the class about their person and include the following information:

- a description of the clothing
- how the person looks
- why the person is wearing that particular outfit
- where the person is going in that outfit

Differentiated Instruction

SLOWER PACE LEARNERS

Personalization Ask students to look at the clothing of teenagers in photos throughout this book and to compare it with the clothing they like to wear. Ask them to identify clothing styles that are popular both with them and with the Spanish-speaking teenagers. Do they notice any differences?

SPECIAL LEARNING NEEDS

Students with Auditory Impairments Create some visual aids by copying each phrase from **¡Exprésate!** on pages 133 and 136 onto a separate large index card. Use these cards to reinforce what is being said in skits and conversations for students with auditory impairments.

Assess

Assessment Program

Prueba: Vocabulario 1, pp. 57–58

Alternative Assessment Guide, pp. 243, 251, 259

Test Generator

STANDARDS: 1.1, 1.2, 1.3 3.1

Resources

Planning:

Lesson Planner, pp. 76–81, 232–239

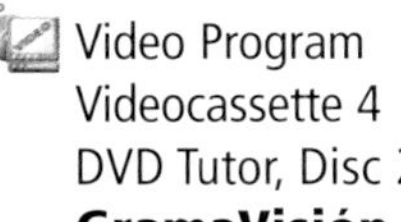
One-Stop Planner

Presentation:

Video Program
Videocassette 4
DVD Tutor, Disc 2
GramaVisión

Practice:

Grammar Tutor for Students of Spanish, Chapter 8

Cuaderno de vocabulario y gramática, pp. 44–46

Cuaderno de actividades, pp. 35–37

Activities for Communication, pp. 29–30

Video Guide, pp. 74–75

Lab Book, pp. 23–24

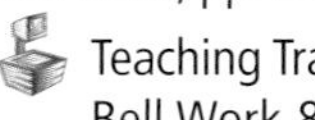
Teaching Transparencies
Bell Work 8.2
Vocabulario y gramática answers, pp. 44–46

Audio CD 8, Tr. 2

Interactive Tutor, Disc 2

Bell Work

Use Bell Work 8.2 in the *Teaching Transparencies,* or write this activity on the board.

Write for whom the following clothes would most likely be: **para hombres, para mujeres,** or **para niños.**

1. El vestido de seda es…
2. El saco de lana es…
3. Las sandalias número uno son…
4. La blusa amarilla es…
5. La falda de algodón es…

11 Script

See script on page 129E.

Objetivos
costar and numbers to one million, demonstrative adjectives and comparisons, **quedar**

Gramática en acción 1

GramaVisión

Interactive TUTOR

Costar, numbers to one million

1 Use the verb **costar (o ➝ ue)** to talk about what something costs. **Costar** is usually only used in the third person.

La blusa **cuesta** treinta dólares. Las botas **cuestan** setenta dólares.

2 To tell what something costs, you may need to use larger numbers.

100	cien	600	seiscientos(as)
101	ciento uno(a)	700	setecientos(as)
102	ciento dos	800	ochocientos(as)
200	doscientos(as)	900	novecientos(as)
300	trescientos(as)	1.000	mil
400	cuatrocientos(as)	2.000	dos mil
500	quinientos(as)	1.000.000	un millón (de)

3 Use **uno** when counting. **Uno** at the end of a number changes to **un** before a masculine noun and **una** before a feminine noun: **veintiún dólares, veintiuna faldas.**

Tengo **ciento un** dólares. Tengo **veintiuna** bolsas.

4 **Cien(to)** is used with both masculine and feminine nouns, but 200, 300, and so on agree with the noun they modify. **Mil** does not change.

cien dólares **ciento** tres dólares **doscientos** seis dólares **mil** dólares
cien sillas **ciento** dos sillas **doscientas** cuatro sillas **mil** sillas

5 **Un millón** changes to **millones** in the plural. Use **de** after **millon(es)** when it is followed by a noun.

3.520.312 = tres **millones** quinientos veinte mil trescientos doce
un millón de dólares **dos millones de** personas

Un supermercado en Miami

Online
Vocabulario y gramática, pp. 44–46 | Actividades, pp. 35–37

CD 8, Tr. 2

11 ¡Qué caro!

Escuchemos Escribe los números que corresponden a los precios. 1. $57 2. $104 3. $273 4. $132 5. $84 6. $121.000 7. $374 8. $138 9. $749 10. $865

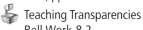

Core Instruction

TEACHING GRAMÁTICA

1. Go over Point 1. Write several numbers on the board. Be sure to use numbers under 99. Show transparencies **Vocabulario 8.1** and **8.2.** Ask students the prices of various items on the transparency: **¿Cuánto cuesta(n)…?** Cue their answers by pointing to the numbers you wrote on the board. **(5 min.)**
2. Go over Point 2. Then have students practice by counting from 100 to 1000 in increments of fifties, one hundreds, etc. **(10 min.)**
3. Read a number aloud in Spanish. Ask volunteers to write the number on the board. **(7 min.)**
4. Go over Points 3–5. Ask students how much money they have. Cue their answers by writing numbers on the board. **(8 min.)**

GramaVisión

For a video presentation of **costar** and numbers, use **el joven G.** For interactive activities, see the *DVD Tutor.*

GramaVisión

Visit Holt Online
go.hrw.com
KEYWORD: EXP1B CH8
Gramática 1 practice

12 Tenemos que pagar

Escribamos Write out each number in words.

MODELO $354
trescientos cincuenta y cuatro dólares

1. $2.168
2. $1.319.672
3. $1.550
4. $213.434
5. $11.721
6. $1.946

13 El inventario

Escribamos/Hablemos You have to write a clothing inventory list in the warehouse where you work. Use the list below to write sentences that tell how many of each type of clothing item are in stock.

MODELO botas 22.336
Tenemos veintidós mil, trescientos treinta y seis pares de botas.

zapatos	367.555	blusas	3.689
faldas	19.324	sombreros	475
pantalones	150.743	bolsas	2.079
camisas	4.597	camisetas	78.521

Comunicación

14 ¡Vamos de compras!

Hablemos With a partner, create a conversation between a clerk and a shopper as they talk about each item pictured below.

MODELO **—Quiero comprar el suéter de muchos colores. ¿Cuánto cuesta?**
—Cuesta doscientos nueve dólares.
—¡Es un robo! No voy a comprarlo.

12 Answers

1. dos mil ciento sesenta y ocho dólares 2. un millón trescientos diecinueve mil seiscientos setenta y dos dólares 3. mil quinientos cincuenta dólares 4. doscientos trece mil cuatrocientos treinta y cuatro dólares 5. once mil setecientos veintiún dólares 6. mil novecientos cuarenta y seis dólares

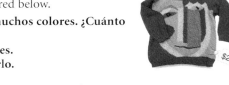

Teacher to Teacher

Bill Heller
Perry High School
Perry, NY

After dividing my class into teams of five, I prepare sets of large numerals 0–9 on tagboard. I use a different color for each set, and add extra zeros. Each student receives two cards in his or her team's color. I call out a number, and the students holding the digits in that number run to the front of the room and stand in order. The first team to form the number gets a point. Students return to their seats and a new number is called. The first team to reach five points wins.

Comunicación

Pair Activity: Interpretive

To practice numbers, prepare two lists of ten numbers of six digits. Give one student the first list of numbers. The student reads the numbers to a partner who writes it. Have students change roles using the second list.

Differentiated Instruction

SLOWER PACE LEARNERS

To help students understand when to use **cien, ciento, doscientos,** and **doscientas,** have them make a four-quadrant chart in which they list each of those forms, when to use each form, and examples. They can also add **un millón** and **dos millones** to their chart. Have them note how the plural **millones** does not use an accent.

MULTIPLE INTELLIGENCES

Logical-Mathematical Review the numbers twenty through ninety. Help students learn the numbers by writing them on the board in pattern sequences. Write out all the tens and have students count by tens. Orally review the hundreds in the box on page 138. Finally, write out all the thousands up to ten thousand. Have volunteers continue beyond ten thousand in their pattern sequences.

STANDARDS: 1.1, 1.3

Resources

Planning:

Lesson Planner, pp. 76–81, 232–239

One-Stop Planner

Presentation:

Video Program
Videocassette 4
DVD Tutor, Disc 2
GramaVisión

Practice:

Grammar Tutor for Students of Spanish, Chapter 8

Cuaderno de vocabulario y gramática, pp. 44–46

Cuaderno de actividades, pp. 35–37

Activities for Communication, pp. 29–30

Video Guide, pp. 74–75

Lab Book, pp. 23–24

Teaching Transparencies
Bell Work 8.3
Vocabulario y gramática answers, pp. 44–46

Audio CD 8, Tr. 3

Interactive Tutor, Disc 2

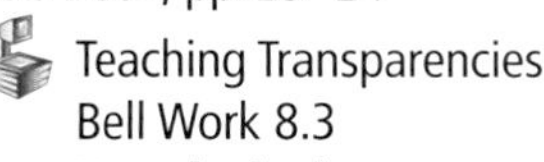

Bell Work

Use Bell Work 8.3 in the *Teaching Transparencies*, or write this activity on the board.

Match the numbers with their written equivalent.

1. sesenta y ocho mil veinticuatro
2. cuatrocientos setenta y cinco
3. un millón trescientos catorce mil doscientos sesenta y siete
4. doscientos cincuenta y cuatro mil seiscientos veintiuno
5. dos mil quinientos noventa y tres

a. 475
b. 254.621
c. 2.593
d. 1.314.267
e. 68.024

Interactive TUTOR

Demonstrative adjectives and comparisons

1 **Demonstrative adjectives** point out things. Use forms of **este** for things close to you. Use forms of **ese** for things farther away.

		Masculine	Feminine
this	SINGULAR	**este**	**esta**
these	PLURAL	**estos**	**estas**
that	SINGULAR	**ese**	**esa**
those	PLURAL	**esos**	**esas**

Me gusta **este** vestido, pero me gusta más **esa** falda.

2 Use these expressions with adjectives to compare things. The adjective agrees in gender and number with the object described.

más + *adjective* + que	*more . . . than*
tan + *adjective* + como	*as . . . as*
menos + *adjective* + que	*less . . . than*

Esta camiset**a** es **más bonita que** esa camiseta.
Esta camiset**a** es **tan bonita como** esa camiseta
Esta camiset**a** es **menos bonita que** esa camiseta.

3 These adjectives have irregular comparative forms.

bueno(a)	*good*	malo(a)	*bad*
mejor(es)	*better*	**peor(es)**	*worse*
joven	*young*	viejo(a)	*old*
menor(es)	*younger*	**mayor(es)**	*older*

Este disco compacto es **malo,** pero ese disco es **peor.**

4 Use **más que, menos que,** and **tanto como** to say if someone does something *more than, less than,* or *as much as* someone else.

Efraín compra **tanto como** Isabel.
Mis padres salen **menos que** mis abuelos.

Online
Vocabulario y gramática, pp. 44–46 | Actividades, pp. 35–37

Nota cultural

In Florida it is common to see men wearing **guayaberas,** embroidered short-sleeved cotton or linen shirts. These shirts originated in Cuba over 200 years ago. Ramón Puig, a Cuban immigrant in Miami, is famous for his guayabera shirts and has custom-made them for celebrities. What fashions were developed in the United States and imported to other countries?

CD 8, Tr. 3

15 **¿De qué habla?**

Escuchemos Escucha mientras estas personas dicen qué cosa prefieren. Escribe lo que prefieren en otro papel. Si les gustan las dos cosas igualmente, escribe **las dos.** 1. vestido negro 2. camisa blanca 3. zapatos negros 4. las dos 5. las dos 6. traje de baño anaranjado

Core Instruction

TEACHING GRAMÁTICA

1. Go over Point 1. Ask students which of two items they like, **¿Te gusta esa mochila o esta mochila?** Have them point as they answer to emphasize the things close to and far away from them. **(10 min.)**
2. Go over Point 2. Create a list of adjectives on the board that students might use to make comparisons: **bonito, feo, bajo, alto, grande, pequeño,** etc. Hold up or point to two items and ask students to compare them. **(10 min.)**
3. Go over Point 3. Ask students to compare bands, movies, television shows, and celebrities. **(7 min.)**
4. Go over Point 4. Ask students to compare the abilities of various celebrities. **(8 min.)**

GramaVisión

For a video presentation of demonstrative adjectives and comparisons, use **el joven G.** For interactive activities, see the *DVD Tutor.*

GramaVisión

STANDARDS: 1.2

16 Amigos

Leamos Read the descriptions of Bartolomé and Nidia. Then, complete the comparisons with **más ... que, menos ... que,** or **tan ... como** and the correct form of the adjective in parentheses.

Bartolomé tiene 12 años. Es alto, guapo y muy simpático. Es bastante serio y estudia mucho. Es muy buen estudiante. Le gusta pasar el rato solo y leer libros y revistas. No le gustan los deportes. Nidia tiene 13 años. Es baja, guapa y muy simpática. No le gusta estudiar y no es muy buena estudiante. Le gusta practicar deportes y salir con amigos.

MODELO **Bartolomé es ==== (serio) ==== Nidia.**
Bartolomé es más serio que Nidia.

1. Bartolomé es ==== (alto) ==== Nidia. más alto que
2. Nidia es ==== (guapo) ==== Bartolomé. tan guapa como
3. Bartolomé es ==== (simpático) ==== Nidia. tan simpático como
4. Nidia es ==== (atlético) ==== Bartolomé. más atlética que
5. Bartolomé es ==== (extrovertido) ==== Nidia. menos extrovertido que

17 Comparaciones

Escribamos/Hablemos Now compare yourself to the two people in Activity 16. *¿Se te olvidó?* Adjective agreement, p. 56

MODELO **Soy menor que Bartolomé. Él es más serio que yo, pero yo soy...**

Comunicación

18 Prefiero...

Hablemos Talk with a partner about these things you see in a store. Decide which item from each pair you prefer and say why.

MODELO **—¿Prefieres estos zapatos negros o esos...?**
—Prefiero los zapatos blancos. Son menos caros...

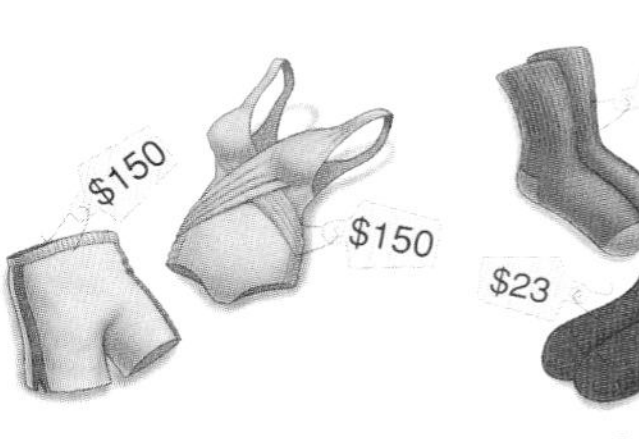

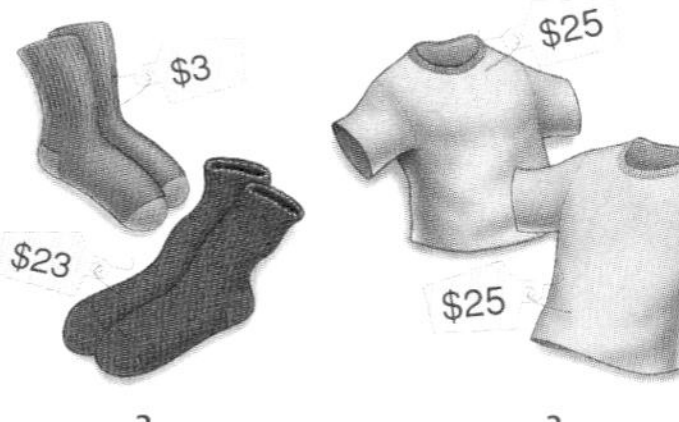

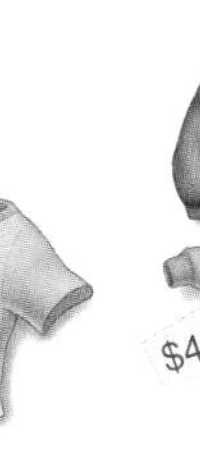

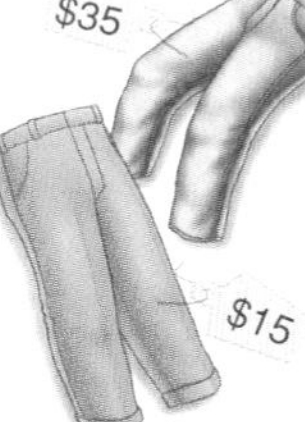

15 Script

1. Mira este vestido negro. Es mucho más elegante que esa falda amarilla, ¿no?
2. Esta camisa blanca me gusta más que la camisa azul. La voy a comprar.
3. Estas botas cuestan más que los zapatos negros. Los zapatos cuestan diecisiete dólares. ¡Qué ganga!
4. Los pantalones vaqueros son menos caros que los pantalones cortos, pero los pantalones cortos están más a la moda. Voy a comprar los dos.
5. Este saco gris me parece tan bonito como esa chaqueta blanca. Me los compro.
6. Este traje de baño morado me queda más grande que el traje de baño anaranjado, y no hay una talla más pequeña. Voy a llevar el traje de baño anaranjado.

15 Answers

1. vestido negro **2.** camisa blanca **3.** zapatos negros **4.** las dos **5.** las dos **6.** traje de baño anaranjado

COMMON ERROR ALERT ¡OJO!

Many students forget which demonstrative adjectives are used for things that are close and which are used for things that are not close. Tell them that the words that contain the letter "t" **(este, esta)** are the ones that are close enough to "touch."

Differentiated Instruction

ADVANCED LEARNERS

16 To prepare students for Activity 16, call two students to the front of the room. Using the adjective in number one of the activity, ask a student to compare the two students at the front. Continue calling two different students to the front and using the adjectives for items 1–7. As an extension you could also ask students to make a comparison using a different comparative adjective.

SPECIAL LEARNING NEEDS

16 Students with Learning Disabilities/ Dyslexia Students with learning disabilities might struggle to complete an activity that requires multiple tasks. First, make sure students understand the introductory paragraph. Have them take notes about the two subjects to help them remember the differences and similarities. To modify the items in Activity 16, give multiple choice answers for each of the seven items and have students circle the best answer for each question.

Comunicación

Pair Activity: Interpersonal

Have pairs of students role-play the following situation:
Para el cumpleaños del profesor, los estudiantes de la clase quieren comprar un artículo de ropa. Ustedes tienen opiniones diferentes sobre el regalo.

STANDARDS: 1.1, 1.2, 1.3

Resources

Planning:

Lesson Planner, pp. 76–81, 232–239

 One-Stop Planner

Presentation:

 Video Program
Videocassette 4
DVD Tutor, Disc 2
GramaVisión

Practice:

Grammar Tutor for Students of Spanish, Chapter 8

Cuaderno de vocabulario y gramática, pp. 44–46

Cuaderno de actividades, pp. 35–37

Activities for Communication, pp. 29–30

Video Guide, pp. 74–75

Lab Book, pp. 23–24

 Teaching Transparencies
Bell Work 8.4
Vocabulario y gramática answers, pp. 44–46

 Audio CD 8, Tr. 4

Interactive Tutor, Disc 2

Bell Work

Use Bell Work 8.4 in the *Teaching Transparencies*, or write this activity on the board.

Write a comparison for each of the combinations listed.

la falda $65
las sandalias $19
la chaqueta $127
los pantalones $65

1. la falda y la chaqueta
2. las sandalias y los pantalones
3. los pantalones y la falda
4. la chaqueta y los pantalones
5. las sandalias y la falda

Interactive TUTOR

Quedar

1 Use the verb **quedar** to say how something *fits* or *looks* on someone. **Quedar** works like **parecer** and **gustar.** Use **queda** when talking about one thing. Use **quedan** when talking about more than one thing.

(a mí)	me queda(n)	(a nosotros/as)	nos	queda(n)
(a ti)	te queda(n)	(a vosotros/as)	os	queda(n)
(a Ud., a él, a ella)	le queda(n)	(a Uds., a ellos, a ellas)	les	queda(n)

one thing
Esa blusa te **queda** bien. *That blouse looks good on you.*

more than one thing
Estas botas me **quedan** grandes. *These boots are too big for me.*

2 Adjectives like **grande** and **pequeño(a)**, as well as adverbs like **bien** and **mal**, can follow **quedar.** All adjectives must agree, but the adverbs don't change form.

agrees
Esta falda me queda **pequeña**. Me queda **mal**.
This skirt is too small for me. It fits me badly.

agrees
Estas botas me quedan **grandes**. No me quedan **bien**.
These boots are too big for me. They don't fit me well.

Online
Vocabulario y gramática, pp. 44–46 | Actividades, pp. 35–37

¿Te acuerdas?

The verb **parecer** *(to seem)* can be used like **gustar**.

Esa falda me **parece** fea.

¿Qué te **parecen** estos pantalones?

19 Comentarios

Leamos Graciela and Leonora are shopping. Read Graciela's comments and choose Leonora's probable response.

1. Me gustan esos zapatos. ¿Vas a comprarlos?
   (a.) No, me quedan grandes. **b.** Sí, te quedan muy bien.
2. Esa blusa es una ganga, ¿no te parece?
   (a.) Me parece muy cara. **b.** Le queda pequeña.
3. Prefiero los pantalones vaqueros a los pantalones cortos.
   a. Les gustan los pantalones vaqueros.
   (b.) Te quedan mejor que los pantalones cortos.
4. ¿Están estos pantalones a la última moda?
   a. Te quedan pequeños. (b.) Me parecen pasados de moda.
5. Me encantan estas sandalias rojas. Son número 6.
   (a.) Te quedan pequeñas. Usas el número 7, ¿no?
   b. Les parecen bonitas.
6. Necesito un regalo para Joaquín. Voy a comprarle un libro.
   a. Le queda bien. (b.) Me parece aburrido.

Core Instruction

TEACHING GRAMÁTICA

1. Go over **¿Te acuerdas?** Have each student write two sentences using **parecer** and **gustar.** Ask volunteers to write their sentences on the board for the class to check. **(7 min.)**
2. Go over Point 1. **(5 min.)**
3. Go over Point 2. Ask volunteers to describe the fit of various items of clothing. If you brought clothing items to school to present the vocabulary, you may wish to allow students to describe the fit of these items. **(8 min.)**

GramaVisión

For a video presentation of **quedar,** use **el joven G** from the *Video Program.* For interactive activities, see the *DVD Tutor.*

GramaVisión

CD 8, Tr. 4

20 **¿Cómo le queda?**

Escuchemos Escucha mientras varias personas hablan de ropa en una tienda. Para cada comentario, indica si el artículo de ropa **a**) le queda bien o **b**) le queda mal a la persona. 1. b 2. b 3. a 4. b 5. b 6. a

21 **¿Es bonita la ropa?**

Leamos/Escribamos Complete the conversation between Daniela and her mother. Use the correct form of **quedar** or **parecer** and the appropriate pronoun.

MODELO **A mí me queda grande esta falda. Además, me parece fea.**

—Mamá, me gusta ese vestido. A ti, __1__ muy bien. te queda

—Gracias, pero necesito otra talla. __2__ pequeño. ¿Qué __3__ esta blusa? Es bonita, ¿no? Me queda, te parece

—¡Uy!, __4__ fea. Además, cuesta una fortuna. me parece

—Daniela, ¿qué __5__ estas botas? Debo comprarlas para Raquel. te parecen

—Pero mamá, mira esas botas negras. No cuestan mucho y son muy bonitas. De verdad, __6__ feas las botas amarillas. No me gusta ese color. me parecen

—Bueno, a nosotras no __7__ bien nuestros zapatos viejos. ¿Quieres comprar unos nuevos? nos quedan

—¡Ay sí! Por ejemplo, estos zapatos negros __8__ muy bonitos. me parecen

Comunicación

22 **¿Qué te parece?**

Hablemos In pairs, give your opinion of the clothes that Luisa and Tomás are wearing. Do you like them? Are the clothes pretty? Ugly? Expensive? How do the clothes fit them? Take turns making comments.

MODELO **El sombrero de Luisa no me gusta. Es feo y caro. Le queda grande.**
Me gusta la camiseta de Tomás. Es muy bonita pero también es un poco cara.

20 Script

1. Uso el diez y este vestido es el catorce. Me queda grande.
2. Esta camisa me queda grande. Necesito una talla más pequeña.
3. Estos pantalones me quedan bien.
4. Uso el número diez. Estos zapatos son el nueve.
5. —¿Qué te parece este saco?
   —No sé. Me parece que necesitas una talla más grande.
6. —¿Cómo me queda esta blusa?
   —Creo que te queda bien. Es tu talla, ¿verdad?

Comunicación

Group Activity: Presentational

La pasarela Divide the class into teams of five and have them present a fashion show. Each student will model one outfit and describe one outfit, using the verb **quedar.** Have students plan for runway music, a theme, and simple decorations. You can give a creative twist to the presentation by setting the fashion show in the year 2050 or by doing an Out-of-Fashion show featuring disastrous clothing combinations and outfits. Students could also use dolls or tongue depressor puppets instead of modeling the outfits themselves. Individual students can be evaluated on their description of the outfits and on their contribution to the group.

Differentiated Instruction

SLOWER PACE LEARNERS

Because **quedar** functions in the same way as **gustar,** review the verb **gustar.** Write **Me gusta...** and **Me gustan...** on the board. Ask a student if he or she likes a certain clothing item, such as **pantalones de lana.** Write his or her answer using **gustar** on the board. Then, using the same clothing item, ask students to practice using the verb **quedar** in sentences describing how the clothing fits. Write **Me queda...** and **Me quedan...** on the board.

MULTIPLE INTELLIGENCES

Interpersonal/Bodily-Kinesthetic Have students bring crazy or fun dress-up clothes to class, or bring in some funny clothes, such as old costumes and out-of-date clothes. Give each student an 8 1/2″ piece of paper that they can tape to their back. Then, instruct students to write statements on the papers taped to their classmates' backs that gives opinions about articles of clothing that the classmates are wearing. They should use the verbs **quedar, parecer,** and **gustar.** (**Esa camiseta te queda mal. Estas botas te quedan grandes.**)

Assess

Assessment Program

Prueba: Gramática 1, pp. 59–60

Prueba: Aplicación 1, pp. 61–62

Alternative Assessment Guide, pp. 243, 251, 259

Audio CD 8, Tr. 18

Test Generator

Resources

Planning:

Lesson Planner, pp. 82, 238–239

 One-Stop Planner

Presentation:

 Teaching Transparencies **Mapa 6**

 Audio CD 8, Tr. 5–7

 Video Program Videocassette 3 DVD Tutor, Disc 2 **VideoCultura** 43

Practice:

Cuaderno de actividades, p. 38

Cuaderno para hispanohablantes, pp. 61–68

Video Guide, pp. 74–75, 77

Lab Book, p. 51

 Interactive Tutor, Disc 2

Connections

Thinking Critically

Ask students to look at the clothing of teenagers in photos in this book and in Spanish-language magazines. Have them compare what they see with what they like to wear. Ask them to identify similarities and differences.

Atlas INTERACTIVO MUNDIAL

Have students use the interactive atlas at **go.hrw.com.**

BY MAPQUEST.COM

Map Activities

Have students locate Miami and Madrid. Have them compare the cities to see how they differ in size and population.

Cultura

VideoCultura

Comparaciones

  CD 8, Tr. 5–7

De compras en la Pequeña Habana

¿Qué te gusta comprar cuando vas de compras?

Sin duda, vas de compras y tienes un lugar donde te encanta ir. ¿Qué diferencias hay entre un centro comercial, un almacén y un mercado al aire libre? En los países de habla hispana, la gente puede ir a grandes almacenes para comprar de todo. También es posible ir a tiendas pequeñas donde venden sólo un tipo de producto. De todos modos, parece que los jóvenes hispanohablantes van de compras con frecuencia. Estas personas nos dicen qué les gusta comprar y adónde van cuando tienen ganas de comprar algo nuevo. ¿Compras las mismas cosas?

Dayana
Miami, Florida

Dayana goes shopping first, then meets with a friend. How does this compare to your shopping habits?

¿Qué compras cuando vas de compras?

Cuando voy de compras, me gusta comprar CDs, zapatos, blusas, pantalones. Cosas así.

¿Adónde fuiste de compras la última vez?

La última vez que fui de compras fui a un centro comercial.

¿Qué clase de tienda es?

El centro comercial es... hay varias tiendas. Hay tiendas de discos, tiendas de películas, tiendas de zapatos, de todo tipo de ropa, vestidos. Cosas así.

¿Qué compraste?

Cuando fui de compras, compré unos discos, una película, unos aretes. Compré unos zapatos, unos pantalones y un vestido.

¿Qué más hiciste allí?

Fui a almorzar y me compré un helado. Después me encontré con una de mis amigas y charlamos.

Core Instruction

TEACHING CULTURA

1. Read and discuss the introductory paragraph as a class. Have students identify any points they do not understand. **(10 min.)**
2. Have students watch the two interviews on video using the *Video Program* or the *DVD Tutor*. Pause the video periodically and check for comprehension. **(15 min.)**
3. Have students answer the questions in the **Para comprender** section with a partner, then discuss **Para pensar y hablar as a class. (15 min.)**

VideoCultura

For a video presentation of the interviews as well as for additional interviews, see Chapter 8 **VideoCultura** on Videocassette or on DVD. For interactive practice, see the *DVD Tutor*.

VideoCultura

STANDARDS: 1.2, 4.2

Visit Holt Online
go.hrw.com
KEYWORD: EXP1B CH8
Online Edition

Miriam
Madrid, España

Miriam goes to a movie after shopping. What do you like to do after shopping?

¿Qué compras cuando vas de compras?
Pues, me gustar comprar pantalones ajustados, pantalones anchos, camisetas de colores y deportivas.

¿Adónde fuiste la última vez?
A «Tres Aguas», un centro comercial.

¿Qué clase de tienda es?
Pues, es de aire libre... muchas tiendas y mucho ocio.

¿Qué compraste?
Compré unos pantalones, una camiseta y unas deportivas.

¿Qué más hiciste allí?
Pues, después me fui con mis amigas al cine y a tomar una hamburguesa.

Cultura

Para comprender

1. ¿Qué compró Dayana la última vez que fue de compras?
2. ¿Qué compró Miriam la última vez que fue de compras?
3. ¿A quién le gusta comprar zapatos?
4. ¿Cómo es el centro comercial «Tres Aguas»?
5. ¿Quién fue a comer algo después de ir de compras?

Para pensar y hablar

Dayana and Miriam both enjoy shopping for clothes, among other things. When you go shopping, what do you like to buy? For both girls, a shopping trip means spending time with friends. With whom do you normally go shopping? Where do you go? What do you like or not like about shopping?

Cuaderno para hispanohablantes, pp. 81–92

Comunidad
Import stores

Imagine that your family is opening a clothing store that imports goods from a Spanish-speaking country. First choose a country. Use Internet sites in Spanish to find examples of typical clothing from that country. Create an advertisement flyer for your import store.

- Give your store a Spanish name.
- Include pictures (clipped or drawn) of the clothing you sell.
- Write product names and prices with each picture.
- Post your flyer in the classroom so you and classmates can compare stores.

La Alcaicería, Granada, España

Differentiated Instruction

SLOWER PACE LEARNERS

Advise students that they are going to hear interviews about shopping excursions that happened in the past. Tell them to focus on the vocabulary that they know. Explain that the verbs they hear are in the past tense and they will be learning the past tense in the next section of this chapter. Write the preterite forms of the verb **ir** on the board to help with the first interview and have students look for it in the text before listening to the audio or watching the video.

MULTIPLE INTELLIGENCES

Musical To expand the information presented in the **Comunidad,** have students work with a partner or in a small group to write and perform a short (30 seconds to one minute) television sales jingle for a particular shopping area, a store, or a certain type or item of clothing. As examples, you might show the class some ads for a popular clothing store, for a certain brand of jeans, or for a shopping mall. You might wait until the end of the chapter to complete this activity so they can incorporate all the information from the chapter.

Teacher Note

You might have students complete **Para comprender** after they have learned the preterite in **Gramática 2.**

Para comprender Answers

1. Compró unos discos, un DVD (una película), unos aretes, zapatos, pantalones y un vestido.
2. Compró unos pantalones, una camiseta y unas deportivas (zapatos de tenis).
3. A Dayana le gusta comprar zapatos.
4. Está al aire libre. Hay muchas tiendas.
5. Las dos chicas fueron a comer.

Communities
Community Link

Ask students to find out if there is a store in your community that sells items imported from a Spanish-speaking (or other) country. If possible have them visit the store with a parent or other relative. Encourage students to ask store owners or clerks where items come from and if the items are made by hand. Ask students to bring in a list of several items they found in the store and share the list with the class. Are there items that are popular with the students? What items would they most like to buy?

Cultures
Practices and Perspectives

People in Spanish-speaking countries do not use personal checks for purchases as often as people in the United States do. In Mexico, many people pay their utility bills with personal checks, but in Spain, bills are usually paid by direct withdrawal. Cash is universally accepted, and most stores also accept credit cards, especially in larger cities.

STANDARDS: 1.2, 4.2, 5.2

Resources

Planning:

Lesson Planner, pp. 83–87, 240–245

 One-Stop Planner

Presentation:

TPR Storytelling Book, pp. 44–45

 Teaching Transparencies **Vocabulario** 8.3, 8.4

Video Program
Videocassette 4
DVD Tutor, Disc 2
ExpresaVisión

Practice:

Cuaderno de vocabulario y gramática, pp. 47–49

Activities for Communication, pp. 31–32

Video Guide, pp. 74–75, 78

Lab Book, pp. 25–26, 52

 Teaching Transparencies
Bell Work 8.5
Vocabulario y gramática answers, pp. 47–49

 Interactive Tutor, Disc 2

Bell Work

Use Bell Work 8.5 in the *Teaching Transparencies*, or write this activity on the board.

Unscramble the words to write logical sentences about how these clothes fit.

1. **a / quedan / Andrés / pantalones / mal / le / los**
2. **mí / queda / me / la / bien / falda / a**
3. **te / no / la / mal / queda / blusa**
4. **quedan / Luisa / a / grandes / vestidos / le / los**
5. **pequeña / camisa / la / queda / me**

Objetivos
Saying where you went and what you did, talking on the phone

Vocabulario 2 en acción

Video/DVD
ExpresaVisión

Core Instruction

TEACHING VOCABULARIO

1. Introduce the vocabulary using transparencies **Vocabulario 8.3** and **8.4.** Model the pronunciation of each word as you point to the appropriate picture. **(12 min.)**
2. Tell students where you went yesterday and what you did at each place, using **Fui a... a comprar...** Use each of the shops at least once. **(5 min.)**
3. Ask students which store they go to in order to buy various items **¿Adónde vas a comprar...?** and which items they can buy at the various stores **¿Qué puedes comprar en ...?** **(8 min.)**

ExpresaVisión

For a presentation of stores and store items, use the video presenter. For interactive activities, see the *DVD Tutor.*

Video/DVD
ExpresaVisión

STANDARDS: 1.2

Visit Holt Online
go.hrw.com
KEYWORD: EXP1B CH8
Vocabulario 2 practice

Cuando voy de compras, me gusta...

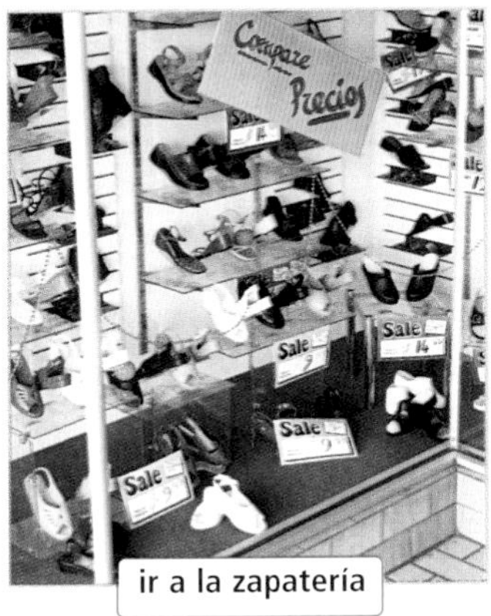

ir a la zapatería

unos juguetes
ir a la juguetería

mirar las vitrinas

ir a la plaza de comida

Más vocabulario...

ahorrar	*to save money*
el dinero	*money*
gastar	*to spend*
vender (de todo)	*to sell (everything)*

¡Exprésate!

To ask where someone went and what someone did	To respond
¿Adónde fuiste anoche/ayer/anteayer? *Where did you go last night/yesterday/the day before yesterday?*	**Fui a la heladería a tomar un batido.** *I went to the ice cream shop to have a milkshake.*
¿Qué hiciste el fin de semana pasado? *What did you do last weekend?*	**Fui al centro comercial y compré unos zapatos. Pagué una fortuna.** *I went to the mall and bought some shoes. I paid a fortune.*

Interactive TUTOR

Online
Vocabulario y gramática, pp. 47–49

▶ Vocabulario adicional — De compras, p. R11

Vocabulario 2

TPR
Total Physical Response

Set up posters at the front of the class, each with the name of one of the types of stores learned in this section. Then have students help you gather items or their representations that you might buy at each store.

Pon los aretes, anillos y pulseras en la joyería.

Busca los libros, tarjetas y cuadernos y ponlos en la librería.

Pon las sandalias, botas, zapatos y calcetines en la zapatería.

Pon los helados y los batidos en la heladería.

Pon un poco de todo en el almacén.

Arregla la vitrina de la zapatería aquí.

Ve al almacén a comprar unos zapatos de tenis, una pulsera y un disco compacto.

También se puede decir...

Students are likely to hear many words for **aretes** including **pantallas** (Puerto Rico), **pendientes** (Spain), **zarcillos** (Venezuela), and **aros** (Argentina). In addition to **anillos,** rings are also referred to as **sortijas.** Bracelets are often called **brazaletes.** In the Dominican Republic, it is common to hear **guillo** for bracelet. Puerto Ricans often refer to money as **chavos** and Venezuelans call it **reales.**

Differentiated Instruction

ADVANCED LEARNERS

To reinforce the vocabulary, bring in a bag of items, such as a book, a necklace, a CD, a greeting card, a shoe, a deck of cards, a shirt, etc. Write **¿Adónde fuiste ayer?** and **Fui...** on the board. Hold the bag in front of a student and tell them to blindly select an item. Then ask them **¿Adónde fuiste ayer?** Tell them to begin with **Fui** and complete the sentence with where they would have gone to find the item they have chosen. Continue until all students have had a turn.

SPECIAL LEARNING NEEDS

Students with Learning Disabilities/ Dyslexia It can be difficult for students with dyslexia to mentally categorize more than one concept at a time. To modify the organization of the new vocabulary, copy the blackline masters for transparencies **Vocabulario 8.3** and **8.4,** so that students can cut out the boldfaced phrases and the pictures. Have students glue or tape each individual phrase and its picture(s) onto a piece of paper to help establish mental sub-categories for each concept.

Connections

Language Note

Tell students that **pulsera** comes from the word **pulso** or *pulse,* as it is worn where the pulse can be sensed. **Arete** comes from the Portuguese and Spanish word **aro,** meaning *large ring of wood* or *metal.*

STANDARDS: 1.2

23 Script

1. —¿En qué le puedo servir?
   —Busco una chaqueta.
2. —¿Vas a comprar todo aquí?
   —Sí, venden de todo y me gusta mucho.
3. —¿Qué te parecen estas botas?
   —Son bonitas y no cuestan mucho. ¡Son una ganga!
4. —Me gusta mucho esa pulsera.
   —A mí me gustan más los aretes.
5. —Busco el nuevo disco compacto de Shakira.
   —Aquí está.
6. —¿En qué le puedo servir?
   —Por favor, ¿dónde están las revistas de tiras cómicas?
7. —¿Te gusta el batido?
   —Sí, está muy rico.
8. —¿Qué vas a comer?
   —Quiero una ensalada con pollo.

Circumlocution

Display transparencies **Vocabulario 8.3** and **8.4** or pictures of stores. Ask students to explain what each store is without using its root word. If you point to **la librería**, a student may not use the word **librería** to describe it. You might give them the following phrase to get them started: **En esta tienda, puedo comprar...**

Spanish speakers in the United States have amazing buying power. Retailers everywhere, but particularly in Florida and California, are marketing more to Spanish speakers. This group spends as much as or more than other Americans on food, clothing, telephone services, electronics, personal care products, public transportation, housing, and cleaning supplies. What products have you seen advertised in Spanish?

CD 8, Tr. 8

23 ¿Dónde están?

Escuchemos Escucha las conversaciones y determina dónde toma lugar *(takes place)* cada una. **1.** tienda de ropa **2.** almacén **3.** zapatería **4.** joyería **5.** tienda de música **6.** librería **7.** heladería **8.** plaza de comida

24 ¿Adónde fuiste?

Leamos Complete Ricardo's story about his trip to the mall with the best words from the box. **1.** librería **2.** discos **3.** pulsera **4.** juguetería **5.** vitrinas **6.** batido

batido	discos	juguetería
pulsera	librería	vitrinas

Primero fui a la __1__ a comprar un diccionario para mi clase de español. También compré unos __2__ compactos. Luego fui a la joyería a comprarle una __3__ a mi mamá. Pagué una fortuna por un videojuego en la __4__. Me gusta mirar las __5__ en el almacén pero no compré nada allí. Finalmente fui a la heladería a tomar un __6__ de chocolate.

25 Fui de compras

Hablemos/Escribamos Di adónde fuiste y qué compraste *(you bought)*.

MODELO **Fui a la tienda de música esta semana. Compré unos discos compactos.**

1.

2.

3.

4.

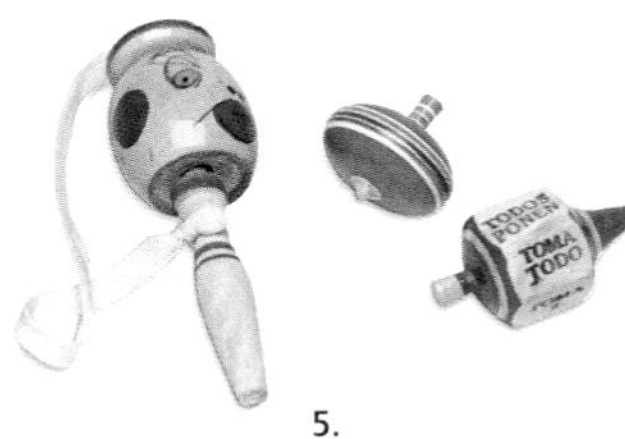

5.

6.

7.

8.

Game

La búsqueda

1. Make four lists of ten specific items from **Vocabulario 2,** pp. 146-147, and **Vocabulario 1,** pp. 132–133. Sample items might be: **una pulsera azul, una tarjeta de cumpleaños, un abrigo negro,** etc. You might also add some school supplies to the lists.
2. Divide the class into four groups.
3. Tell students that they are going on a timed scavenger hunt to search for the items on their group's list.
4. Give a list of items to each group and set the timer for five minutes. Students search their backpacks and the room. They may also ask other groups if they may borrow an item.
5. At the end of the five minutes, have each group hold up and describe the items on its list that they found. The group that found the most items on its list wins.

STANDARDS: 1.2, 2.2

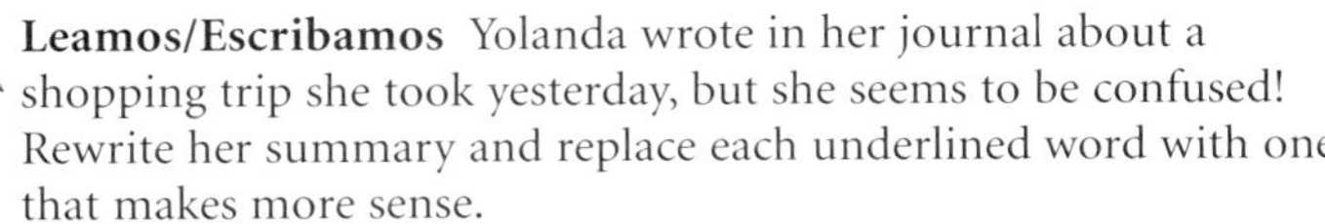

26 Yolanda en el centro comercial

Leamos/Escribamos Yolanda wrote in her journal about a shopping trip she took yesterday, but she seems to be confused! Rewrite her summary and replace each underlined word with one that makes more sense.

> <u>Mañana</u> fui al centro comercial. Fui a la <u>heladería</u> a comprar un DVD. Compré un juguete en la <u>tienda de ropa</u> y pagué una fortuna por <u>unas revistas</u> en la zapatería. En la plaza de comidas compré <u>pantalones vaqueros</u>. Luego fui a la <u>tienda de música</u> a comprar un anillo para mi hermana. También fui a la <u>librería</u> a comprar una camisa, unos zapatos y un sombrero. Al final fui a la <u>zapatería</u> a comprar una tarjeta para el cumpleaños de mi padre. ¡Me gusta <u>ahorrar</u> dinero!

Comunicación

27 ¿Adónde fuiste?

Hablemos With a partner, take turns asking each other if you went to the following places last weekend. When answering, mention something that you bought there.

MODELO —**¿Fuiste a la zapatería el fin de semana pasado?**
—**Sí, fui a la zapatería y compré...**

1. la zapatería
2. la tienda de música
3. el almacén
4. la joyería
5. la juguetería
6. la librería
7. la plaza de comidas
8. la heladería
9. la tienda de ropa

28 Una encuesta

Hablemos Working in groups of three or four, make a chart of the last three stores where you've bought something, and what you purchased. Be prepared to compare your findings with those of other groups.

MODELO —**¿Adónde fuiste de compras?**
—**Fui a 'Libromundo' y compré un libro.**

	Ricky	Monika	Luis
1	Libromundo: un libro		
2			
3			

Vocabulario 2

26 Answers

1. ayer, anoche
2. tienda de música
3. juguetería
4. unos zapatos, unas botas
5. *any food item*
6. joyería
7. tienda de ropa, almacén
8. librería
9. gastar

Additional Practice

26 Have students work in pairs to read aloud the corrected version of Yolanda's journal. Ask them to take turns, reading every other sentence.

Comunicación

Group Activity: Interpersonal

Have students work in groups of 3 to do a variation of Activity 27. Tell one student to begin by saying something he or she bought **(Compré una pizza y un jugo de naranja).** Instruct the student on the left to ask **¿Adónde fuiste?** and have the first student answer **(Fui a la plaza de comidas en el centro comercial).** Continue this pattern around the circle three times without repeating either store names or items purchased.

Differentiated Instruction

SLOWER PACE LEARNERS

Additional Practice Have students make mobiles that show store names with pictures of items to be purchased there. Follow these directions:

- Write a store name on both sides of a large piece of tag board.
- Cut out pictures of items for sale in the store and glue onto index cards.
- Attach pictures to bottom of tag board name with lengths of string.
- Hang from ceiling in classroom and use for vocabulary practice.

SPECIAL LEARNING NEEDS

Students with ADD Help students focus on Activity 25 by having each one work with a partner. Ask the partner to point to a picture and ask **¿Dónde compras...**(*name item*)**?** Then have the student answer using a complete sentence, naming the appropriate store. (**Compro...en ....**)

STANDARDS: 1.1, 1.2, 1.3, 2.2

Resources

Planning:

Lesson Planner, pp. 83–87, 240–245

 One-Stop Planner

Presentation:

TPR Storytelling Book, pp. 44–45

 Teaching Transparencies

Vocabulario 8.3, 8.4

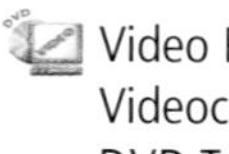 Video Program
Videocassette 4
DVD Tutor, Disc 2
ExpresaVisión

Practice:

Cuaderno de vocabulario y gramática, pp. 47–49

Activities for Communication, pp. 31–32

Video Guide, pp. 74–75, 78

Lab Book, pp. 25–26, 52

 Teaching Transparencies
Vocabulario y gramática answers, pp. 47–49

 Interactive Tutor, Disc 2

Heritage Speakers

Have heritage speakers share any other telephone expressions they might use in Spanish. Have them discuss other possible differences, such as the tone of the ringing, the tone for a busy signal, or the message given for a number that is not in service.

Extension

29 Have students work in pairs to act out the phone conversation. Then ask them to rewrite the conversation, this time assuming that Elena is not at home. Tell the student who makes the call to leave a message for Elena. Then have them switch roles and do the conversation again.

¡Exprésate!

To talk on the phone

Interactive TUTOR

Aló/Bueno/Diga.
Hello.

Hola. ¿Está Andrés?
Hi. Is Andrés there?

¿De parte de quién?
Who's calling?

Habla Felipe.
Felipe speaking.

Espera un momento, ya te lo (la) paso.
Wait a moment. I'll get him (her).

Gracias, señor(a) León.
Thanks, Mr. (Mrs.) León.

Lo siento, no está. ¿Quieres dejarle un recado?
I'm sorry. He's (She's) not here. Would you like to leave a message?

Sí, por favor, que me llame después.
Yes, please ask him to call me later.

No, gracias. Llamo más tarde.
No, thanks, I'll call back later.

Hola. ¿Está Felipe?

29 La llamada

Leamos Marta is calling her friend Elena at home. Elena's mother answers the phone. Reorder the sentences logically to recreate their conversation.

—Hola, señora Beltrán. ¿Está Elena? 2
—Espera, Marta, ya te la paso. 5
—Habla Marta. 4
—Bueno. 1
—Gracias, señora. Hasta luego. 6
—¿De parte de quién? 3

30 ¡Diga!

Leamos Choose a phrase from column B that is an appropriate response to the phrase in column A.

MODELO **—¿Está Amalia, por favor?**
—Un momento, por favor.

A	B
1. ¿De parte de quién, por favor? d	a. ¿Puedo dejar un recado?
2. El señor Chávez no está. a	b. Un momento, por favor.
3. ¿Está Omar, por favor? b	c. Bien, gracias, ¿y usted?
4. ¿Aló? f	d. Gustavo Muñoz.
5. Bueno, señora, llamo más tarde. e	e. Adiós.
6. ¿Cómo está? c	f. ¿Está la doctora Pérez?

Core Instruction

TEACHING ¡EXPRÉSATE!

1. Introduce the new expressions in **¡Exprésate!,** modeling the pronunciation of each new word and phrase. **(7 min.)**
2. Use the new expressions to act out both sides of a phone call. You may want to use puppets or stuffed animals to portray the participants in the conversation. **(4 min.)**
3. Randomly call out expressions from **¡Exprésate!** Ask students whether each expression would most likely be said by the person making the call, the person receiving the call, or either. **(4 min.)**

31 ¿Está mi mamá?

Escribamos/Leamos Pablo Delgado calls his mother at her office and the secretary answers. Write this conversation in order on your paper, filling in the blanks with words that make sense.

Srta. Cruz

Pablo Delgado

—__1__. Oficina de la señora Delgado. Aló/Bueno/Diga

—Hola, señorita Cruz. __2__ Pablo Delgado. Habla

—Hola, Pablo. ¿__3__ estás? Cómo

—Bien, gracias. ¿__4__ mi mamá? Está

—Espera un momento... Lo __5__, Pablo, tu madre no está. siento

—Ay, no...

—¿Quieres dejarle __6__? un recado

—Sí, por __7__. Que me __8__ más tarde. favor, llame

—Bueno. Adiós, Pablo.

—__9__ señorita Cruz. Adiós/Hasta luego

Comunicación

32 Otra llamada

Hablemos With a partner, act out the telephone conversation in Activity 31. This time pretend that Mrs. Delgado is in the office and can take the call from her son.

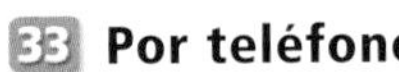

33 Por teléfono

Hablemos In groups of three, create a phone conversation involving two friends and the father of one of the friends.

- Call your friend; the father answers the phone.
- Greet the friend's father and ask to speak to the friend.
- Answer any questions politely.
- After the father passes the phone to your friend, ask what he or she did yesterday.
- Your friend will tell you that he or she went to a store and bought something.
- Exchange roles and create a new conversation.

Vocabulario 2

Comunicación

Pair Activity: Interpersonal

Ask students to call you at home to get a homework assignment. Tell them you will answer the phone in Spanish, or if someone else answers, tell them to ask for you in Spanish. Have students identify themselves, greet you and ask how you are, and then ask for the homework assignment. Then have them ask you one question before saying goodbye.

Más práctica

31 Have students act out the telephone conversation in pairs. Use telephones as props if possible, or have students sit back-to-back so they cannot see each others' faces.

Differentiated Instruction

ADVANCED LEARNERS

Extension Ask each student to think of a specific reason why he or she would call a friend (make an invitation to..., ask about homework, ask advice, talk about music...) Have them write the reason on a slip of paper and collect the slips in a container. Then have each student draw out a slip and act out a phone conversation with a partner based on the information on the slip.

SPECIAL LEARNING NEEDS

Students with Auditory Impairments When acting out any phone conversations, make sure you provide written scripts or prompts to students who may have auditory impairments. You might also want to let those students look at the partners they are talking to, instead of sitting back-to-back, when simulating telephone conversations.

Assess

Assessment Program

Prueba: Vocabulario 2, pp. 63–64

Alternative Assessment Guide, pp. 243, 251, 259

Test Generator

STANDARDS: 1.1, 1.2

Resources

Planning:

Lesson Planner, pp. 87–93, 242–251

 One-Stop Planner

Presentation:

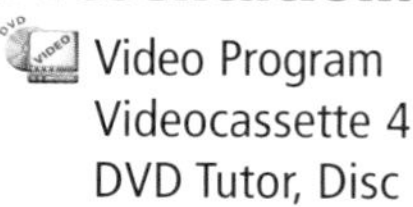
Video Program
Videocassette 4
DVD Tutor, Disc 2
GramaVisión

Practice:

Grammar Tutor for Students of Spanish, Chapter 8

Cuaderno de vocabulario y gramática, pp. 50–52

Cuaderno de actividades, pp. 39–41

Activities for Communication, pp. 31–32

Video Guide, pp. 74–75

Lab Book, pp. 25–26

 Teaching Transparencies
Bell Work 8.6
Vocabulario y gramática answers, pp. 50–52

 Audio CD 8, Tr. 9

 Interactive Tutor, Disc 2

Bell Work

Use Bell Work 8.6 in the *Teaching Transparencies*, or write this activity on the board.

Match each item with the store where you would most likely find it.

1. unos aretes
2. una revista
3. un juego de mesa
4. unas sandalias
5. un batido

a. la zapatería
b. la plaza de comida
c. la librería
d. la juguetería
e. la joyería

Objetivos
Preterite of **-ar** verbs, preterite of **ir**, preterite of **ar** verbs with reflexive pronouns

Gramática en acción 2

GramaVisión

Interactive TUTOR

Preterite of -ar verbs

1 Use the **preterite** tense to talk about what happened or what someone did at a specific point in the past. To form the **preterite** of **-ar** verbs, like **comprar,** add these endings to the verb stem.

yo	compr**é**	nosotros(as)	compr**amos**
tú	compr**aste**	vosotros(as)	compr**asteis**
Ud., él, ella	compr**ó**	Uds., ellos, ellas	compr**aron**

Compré un DVD ayer. *I bought a DVD yesterday.*

2 Note that the **nosotros** form of **-ar** verbs looks exactly like the present tense form. You will have to use context to decide whether the speaker is talking about the present or the past.

Isa y yo **gastamos** mucho ayer. Casi nunca **gastamos** tanto.
Isa and I spent a lot yesterday. We almost never spend so much.

3 The stem-changing **-ar** verbs do not have stem changes in the **preterite**.

Encontré una camisa bonita y la compré.

Online
Vocabulario y gramática, pp. 50–52 | Actividades, pp. 39–41

Nota cultural

In most Spanish-speaking countries people often shop at open-air markets. Unlike department stores or malls, customers are expected to **regatear,** or bargain with vendors. Bargaining is an art form in these markets and successful shoppers may bring the price of an item down considerably. Are there any open-air markets where you live? Do you bargain with the vendors?

CD 8, Tr. 9

34 ¿Pasado o presente?

Escuchemos Escucha lo que dice Alicia y decide si habla **a**) del presente o **b**) del pasado.

1. b 2. b 3. b 4. a 5. b 6. b 7. a 8. b 9. b

35 El fin de semana pasado

Escribamos Combine a word or phrase from each section to make six sentences that tell what people did last weekend.

Yo	hablar por teléfono	en el centro comercial
Mi familia y yo	mirar vitrinas	en la tienda de __?__
Mis amigos	escuchar música	en casa
Mi hermano(a)	comprar __?__	en la biblioteca
Mis amigos y yo	bailar	en una fiesta
Mis padres	estudiar	en la plaza de comida
	tomar un refresco	en la juguetería

Core Instruction

TEACHING GRAMÁTICA

1. Tell students they are going to learn the preterite. Go over point 1. Model the pronunciation of each form of the verb **comprar. (6 min.)**

2. Go over point 2. Have the class list words that will help them tell whether a sentence is in present or past tense: **ayer, hoy, este semana, este fin de semana… (4 min.)**

3. Go over point 3. Have students list stem-changing **-ar** verbs they have learned. **(5 min.)**

4. Call out a present or preterite form of an **-ar** verb. Have students raise their right hand if the verb is in present tense and their left if it is in past. **(10 min.)**

5. Ask students to add the preterite of **comprar** to the verb chart in their notebooks. **(5 min.)**

GramaVisión

For a video presentation of the preterite of **-ar** verbs, use **el joven G.** For interactive activities, see the *DVD Tutor.*

GramaVisión

STANDARDS: 1.2, 1.3, 4.2

Visit Holt Online
go.hrw.com
KEYWORD: EXP1B CH8
Gramática 2 practice

36 Roberto y sus amigos

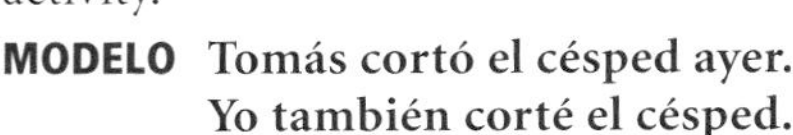

Escribamos/Hablemos Look at each photo and write what these people did. Then write if you also did the same activity.

MODELO Tomás cortó el césped ayer.
Yo también corté el césped.

Tomás

1. Sara/anteayer

2. ellos/el sábado pasado

3. tus amigas/ayer

4. Pablo y Mila/anoche

5. Carmela/ el martes pasado

6. Luis/ayer por la tarde

Comunicación

37 Ayer por la noche

Hablemos In small groups, ask your classmates if they did the following things last night.

MODELO —¿Estudiaste anoche?
—Sí, estudié mucho. (No, no estudié.)

cantar	hablar por teléfono	pasear
dibujar	comprar ropa	gastar dinero
escuchar música	montar en bicicleta	pasar el rato solo(a)
estudiar	nadar	alquilar un video

34 Script

1. El sábado pasado fui de compras con mi mejor amiga, Magdalena.
2. Hoy fuimos al centro comercial y pasamos toda la tarde allí.
3. Esta vez mi hermana menor nos acompañó. No me gustó.
4. Prefiero ir a las tiendas de música a escuchar discos, pero a mi hermana le encantan las jugueterías.
5. La llevé a la juguetería Bebo donde ella miró las vitrinas por más de una hora.
6. Magdalena se cansó de mirar juguetes. Empezó a hablar de las tiendas de ropa.
7. Magdalena tiene ganas de comprar ropa y le encantan los zapatos.
8. En la zapatería Calzamás, pagué una fortuna por un par de sandalias.
9. Al final Magdalena y mi hermanita tomaron batidos en la heladería Dulce Vida. Yo tomé un jugo.

COMMON ERROR ALERT ¡OJO!

The third person singular form of the preterite for **–ar** verbs often causes problems since students associate the **–o** ending with **yo.** Remind them that they must remember the accent, which distinguishes the preterite of the **él** form from the **yo** form of the present tense.

Comunicación

Pair Activity: Interpersonal

Prepare a list of fifteen activities with verbs ending in **–ar.** Distribute the lists to students. Tell them to select five activities they did the day before and write them down using the **yo** form. Then, instruct partners to take turns trying to guess the activities their partner did using **tú** in the preterite.

Differentiated Instruction

ADVANCED LEARNERS

37 To extend Activity 37, have students report on what the other people in their group did. Then, play a game in which you start on one side of the room and a student says what the person in front of him/her did. Then go to the next student who must say what the first person did, plus the person in front of him or her. Continue with the next student, adding an activity each time. If a student fails to remember what everyone did, he has broken the chain and is out.

SPECIAL LEARNING NEEDS

Students with Auditory Impairments In sign language, the past tense is represented using an open-to-closed palm-in hand motion that moves backwards in the air over the right shoulder, like a backwards wave. When introducing and teaching the preterite tense to students who use sign language, suggest that sign language interpreters spell out the conjugated verbs along with making the hand sign that signifies past tense, as a strategy for reinforcing that the conjugations are past tense.

STANDARDS: 1.1, 1.2, 1.3, 4.2

Resources

Planning:

Lesson Planner, pp. 87–93, 242–251

 One-Stop Planner

Presentation:

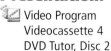

 Video Program
Videocassette 4
DVD Tutor, Disc 2
GramaVisión

Practice:

Grammar Tutor for Students of Spanish, Chapter 8

Cuaderno de vocabulario y gramática, pp. 50–52

Cuaderno de actividades, pp. 39–41

Activities for Communication, pp. 31–32

Video Guide, pp. 74–75

Lab Book, pp. 25–26

 Teaching Transparencies
Bell Work 8.7
Vocabulario y gramática answers, pp. 50–52

Interactive Tutor, Disc 2

Bell Work

Use Bell Work 8.7 in the *Teaching Transparencies*, or write this activity on the board.

Write the correct preterite form of the verb in parentheses to complete each sentence.

1. **El sábado pasado Tomás _____ (comprar) una chaqueta.**
2. **Anoche Amanda y Lenora _____ (estudiar) matemáticas.**
3. **Ayer tú _____ (mirar) vitrinas en el centro comercial.**
4. **Milagros y yo _____ (bailar) en la fiesta el viernes pasado.**
5. **Yo no _____ (hablar) con mis amigos ayer.**

Preterite of ir

1 To say where someone went at a certain time in the past, use **ir** *(to go)* in the **preterite**. Its preterite forms are irregular.

yo	fui	nosotros(as)	fuimos
tú	fuiste	vosotros(as)	fuisteis
Ud., él, ella	fue	Uds., ellos, ellas	fueron

2 Remember to use **adónde** to ask where someone went.

—¿**Adónde** fuiste ayer? *Where did you go yesterday?*
—Fui al cine. *I went to the movies.*

3 Use **a + infinitive** after **ir** to say why someone went somewhere.

Fuimos a la librería **a comprar** libros.
We went to the bookstore to buy books.

Online
Vocabulario y gramática, pp. 50–52 | Actividades, pp. 39–41

En el Festival de la Calle Ocho, Miami

38 De tienda en tienda

Leamos Choose the correct word in parentheses to complete the paragraph.

Ayer __1__ (fui/fuimos) con mi familia al centro comercial. Mi hermana Delia __2__ (fuiste/fue) al almacén a comprar pantalones. Mis padres __3__ (fuimos/fueron) a la librería y mi hermano __4__ (fue/fuiste) a la juguetería. Por fin todos __5__ (fuimos/fuiste) a la heladería a tomar un batido.

39 ¿Fuiste al festival este año?

Escribamos Combine a word or phrase from each section to make six sentences. Tell where these people went and what they did.

MODELO Fui al cine a ver una película.

yo	ir	al cine	a comprar
tú		al parque	a leer
mi mejor amigo(a)		al estadio	a comer
mi familia y yo		al almacén	a ver
mis padres		al restaurante	a jugar
mi profesora		a la biblioteca	a estudiar
mi hermano		a la librería	
		al colegio	

Core Instruction

TEACHING GRAMÁTICA

1. Go over point 1. Model the pronunciation of each form of **ir. (5 min.)**
2. Call out a subject pronoun and a tense and have students write a short sentence using the verb **ir.** Ask volunteers to write their sentences on the board for the class to check. **(9 min.)**
3. Go over point 2. Ask students where they went yesterday. **(6 min.)**
4. Go over point 3. Give students the beginning of a sentence and ask a volunteer to finish it. For example, for **Voy al cine** students might say **Voy al cine a ver una película. (6 min.)**
5. Ask students to add the preterite of **ir** to the verb chart in their notebooks. **(4 min.)**

GramaVisión

For a video presentation of the preterite of **ir,** use **el joven G.** For interactive activities, see the *DVD Tutor.*

GramaVisión

40 Contesta personalmente

Escribamos Contesta las preguntas según tus propias experiencias.

1. ¿Fuiste al colegio ayer?
2. ¿Fue al colegio ayer tu mejor amigo(a)?
3. ¿Fueron tus amigos y tú al centro comercial la semana pasada?
4. ¿Adónde fuiste anteayer?
5. ¿Adónde fueron tus amigos y tú el sábado pasado?
6. ¿Adónde fue tu familia el fin de semana pasado?

41 ¿Adónde fueron? ¿Qué compraron?

Escribamos/Hablemos María is saying where everyone went shopping and what they bought. Based on the photos, write what she says.

MODELO **Carlos y Carmen fueron a la juguetería. Compraron videojuegos.**

Carlos y Carmen

1. nosotros

2. papá

3. mis amigas

4. yo

5. Gabi y Rebeca

Comunicación

42 Tiendas y compras

Hablemos On a scrap of paper write down three stores you went to and what you bought there. Do not let your partner see what you write! Your partner will ask you questions and try to guess where you went and what you bought. Take turns guessing and answering.

MODELO **—¿Compraste un disco compacto?**
—No, compré unos audífonos.
—¿Fuiste a la tienda de música?
—Sí, fui a la tienda de música.

Tiendas	Cosas que compré
Muy de Moda	falda
Ropa y Más	sandalias
Joyería Sánchez	pulsera

Gramática 2

41 Answers

1. Nosotros fuimos a la joyería. Compramos una pulsera y unos aretes.
2. Papá fue a la tienda de música. Compró dos CDs.
3. Mis amigas fueron a la tienda de ropa y compraron dos vestidos.
4. Fui a la heladería y compré un helado.
5. Gabi y Rebeca fueron a la librería y compraron una revista de tiras cómicas.

Comunicación

Class Activity: Interpersonal

Rejoinders Review the expressions and grammar of the chapter with this class activity. Put a different question on enough index cards so that each student can ask a different question. For more structured questions, you may also write an appropriate answer in a different color ink so students can check their partner's response. Distribute the cards to students. Have the students circulate around the class asking their question and answering the questions of other students. This activity can be repeated several times in the next few days to review for upcoming chapter assessments.

MODELO:
¿Adónde fuiste a comprar el libro?
¿Qué número de zapato usas?
¿Qué hiciste anteayer?
¿Qué hiciste el verano pasado?

Differentiated Instruction

ADVANCED LEARNERS

41 As an extension to Activity 41, review vocabulary for school places and activities, then continue practicing the preterite of **ir** and **-ar** verbs. Write **la biblioteca, el salón de clase, el estadio, el auditorio,** and **la cafetería** on the board. Have students write or say sentences following the **Modelo** about what Carlos and Carmen did. For example: **Carlos y Carmen fueron a la biblioteca. Estudiaron matemáticas.** Change the subject to just Carlos or Carmen to practice the singular form of the verbs.

MULTIPLE INTELLIGENCES

39 **Linguistic** As an alternative to Activity 39, allow students with linguistic strengths to work with a partner and write and stage a mock interview between a well-known celebrity and a reporter about what the celebrity did over the weekend. Instruct them to use the verb **ir,** at least three of the different phrases from column 1, all of the phrases from column 3, and all of the phrases from column 4. Their interview should have at least six questions and answers.

STANDARDS: 1.1, 1.2, 1.3

Resources

Planning:

Lesson Planner, pp. 87–93, 242–251

 One-Stop Planner

Presentation:

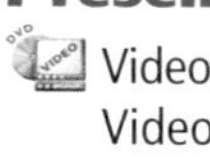 Video Program
Videocassette 4
DVD Tutor, Disc 2
GramaVisión

Practice:

Grammar Tutor for Students of Spanish, Chapter 8

Cuaderno de vocabulario y gramática, pp. 50–52

Cuaderno de actividades, pp. 39–41

Activities for Communication, pp. 31–32

Video Guide, pp. 74–75

Lab Book, pp. 26, 52–53

 Teaching Transparencies
Bell Work 8.8
Vocabulario y gramática answers, pp. 50–52

 Audio CD 8, Tr. 10

 Interactive Tutor, Disc 2

Bell Work

Use Bell Work 8.8 in the *Teaching Transparencies*, or write this activity on the board.

Write the correct preterite form of the verb **ir** in the blank.

1. Anoche Elisa _____ a la joyería.
2. Mi padre y yo _____ al partido de fútbol el viernes pasado.
3. ¿Tú _____ al concierto el miércoles?
4. Luisa y Estela _____ al cine ayer.
5. Yo _____ a la biblioteca a estudiar anoche.

43 Script

See script on page 129F.

Repaso Preterite of -ar verbs with reflexive pronouns

Interactive TUTOR

1 Use the **preterite** to talk about what happened at a particular point in the past and to narrate a sequence of events in the past. Use the correct form of the **reflexive pronoun** when necessary.

levantarse			
yo	**me** levanté	nosotros(as)	**nos** levantamos
tú	**te** levantaste	vosotros(as)	**os** levantasteis
Ud., él, ella	**se** levantó	Uds., ellos, ellas	**se** levantaron

Me levanté y **me** bañé. *I got up and took a bath.*

2 Stem-changing **-ar** verbs in the present tense don't have a stem-change in the **preterite**.

Ayer **me** desperté a las seis y **me** acosté a las diez.
Yesterday I woke up at six and I went to bed at ten.

Online
Vocabulario y gramática, pp. 50–52 | Actividades, pp. 39–41

CD 8, Tr. 10

43 ¡Qué día más ocupado!

Escuchemos Escucha lo que hicieron Enrique y Lupita ayer. Según *(according to)* lo que oyes, pon los dibujos en orden cronológico *(chronological order)*.

a. 4

b. 7

c. 1

d. 2

e. 3

f. 5

g. 6

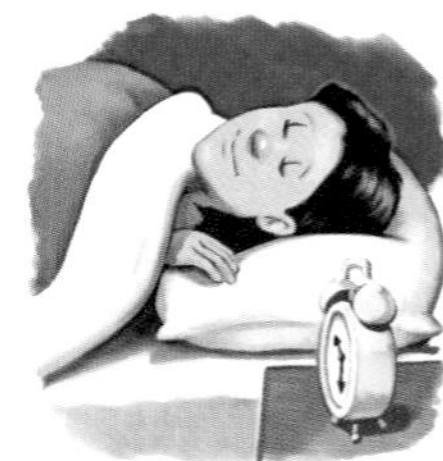
h. 8

Core Instruction

TEACHING GRAMÁTICA

1. Go over Point 1. Call out forms of **–ar** verbs or the verb **ir** in present or preterite tense. Have students raise their right hand if the verb is in present tense, and their left if it is in past. **(5 min.)**
2. Go over Point 2. Ask students to write down five things they did yesterday, using verbs with reflexive pronouns. Ask volunteers to read their sentences aloud. **(15 min.)**

GramaVisión

For a video presentation of preterite **-ar** verbs with reflexive pronouns, use **el joven G** from the *Video Program.* For interactive activities, see the *DVD Tutor.*

GramaVisión

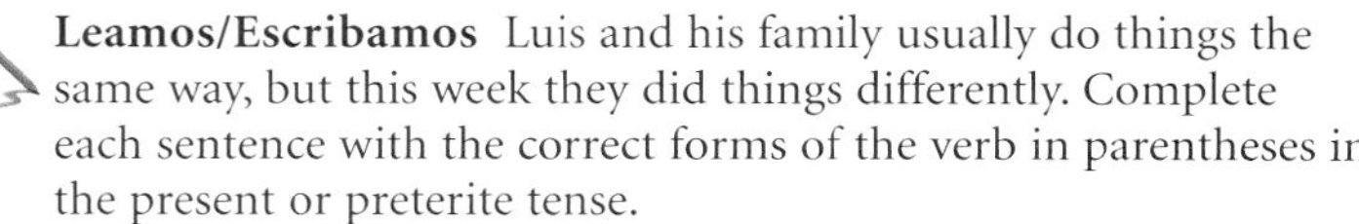

44 La familia de Luis

Leamos/Escribamos Luis and his family usually do things the same way, but this week they did things differently. Complete each sentence with the correct forms of the verb in parentheses in the present or preterite tense.

MODELO **Pili se baña por la mañana pero ayer se bañó por la noche.**

1. Papá ____ antes del desayuno, pero ayer no ____. (afeitarse) se afeita, se afeitó
2. Siempre ____ a las 8:00, pero el miércoles yo ____ a las seis para estudiar. (despertarse) me despierto, me desperté
3. Ana y yo ____ a las 3:30, pero ayer ____ a las 5:00. (regresar) regresamos, regresamos
4. Papá y mamá ____ la cena juntos, pero mamá trabajó tarde así que solamente la ____ juntos el jueves y el viernes. (preparar) preparan, prepararon
5. Patricia, tú ____ temprano por lo general, pero anoche ____ después de la medianoche. (acostarse) te acuestas, te acostaste

45 En mi familia

Hablemos Based on Activity 44, tell what you and your family usually do, and what you did differently this week. Use names from your family, and different verbs if you like.

MODELO **Generalmente me levanto a las 7:00, pero hoy me levanté a las 8:00.**

Comunicación

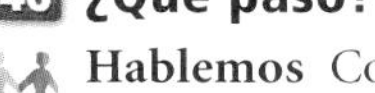

46 ¿Qué pasó?

Hablemos Con un(a) compañero(a), mira los dibujos y di adónde fueron Felipe y Cristina y qué hicieron. Luego, túrnense para crear una conversación entre ellos.

a.

b.

c.

Gramática 2

AP Language Examination

46 Below is a sample answer for the picture description activity.

Felipe y Cristina fueron al centro comercial a comer pizza en la plaza de comida. Después, fueron a la tienda de ropa. Cristina compró un vestido. Al final fueron a la librería. Felipe compró muchos libros de aventuras porque le encantan.

To display the drawings to the class, use the *Picture Sequences Transparency* for Chapter 8.

Comunicación

Pair Activity: Interpersonal

Instruct pairs to act out the following situation. If students require more structure, brainstorm a list of things that could have gone wrong.

Pasaste una mañana horrible en casa y ahora no vas a llegar a tiempo a una cita con un amigo o una amiga. Necesitas llamar a tu amigo o amiga para explicarle por qué no vas a llegar a tiempo. Representa el diálogo en una conversación por teléfono.

Differentiated Instruction

SLOWER PACE LEARNERS

43 Before listening to the audio for Activity 43, look at each of the pictures with the class. Ask students to describe them in Spanish. If they describe it in the present, have them change it to the preterite. Then ask them what they think the logical sequence of events would be. Stop the recording after each statement and allow students time to choose their answer. Play the entire audio without stopping after students have listened to each description.

SPECIAL LEARNING NEEDS

43 **Students with Learning Disabilities** To modify Activity 43, make copies of the Student Response Form and allow students to cut up each box and its letter before beginning the recording. As they listen, they can rearrange the boxes to put them in the correct chronological order. Once they've put the boxes into the correct order, play the audio a second time to verify and correct the sequence of the boxes.

Assess

Assessment Program

Prueba: Gramática 2, pp. 65–66

Prueba: Aplicación 2, pp. 67–68

Alternative Assessment Guide, pp. 243, 251, 259

Audio CD 8, Tr. 19

Test Generator

STANDARDS: 1.2, 1.3

Conexiones culturales

Resources

Planning:

Lesson Planner, pp. 93–94, 245–249

 One-Stop Planner

Connections

History Link

The persons depicted on the bills are important historical figures from the countries represented by the currency.

Lempira was a charismatic 16th century leader in what is now Honduras. He led a rebellion against the Spanish that lasted for three years.

Sor Juana Inés de la Cruz was a nun at the convent of San Jerónimo in Mexico City. Her convent cell, with its library of several thousand books, became an intellectual center of Mexico. She wrote poetry of simplicity and beauty, and some have called her the first feminist of her age (17th century).

Francisco Hernández de Córdoba led an expedition in 1524 that succeeded in establishing the first permanent settlement in Nicaragua. He was instrumental in the founding of the cities of León and Granada.

Simón Bolívar was a leader who helped many regions of South America win their independence from Spain. The **bolívar** is the national currency in Venezuela and the **boliviano** is the monetary unit of Bolivia.

Cristóbal Colón (Christopher Columbus) sailed west from Spain in 1492 seeking a new route to India. Instead, he made contact with the American continents. Today, the currencies in both Costa Rica and El Salvador are named **colón** in his honor.

1 Las figuras históricas

Many Latin American countries have pictures of important historical figures on their coins and paper bills, just as we have a picture of Abraham Lincoln on the five-dollar U.S. bill. Match the following people in Latin American history to the currencies that were named for them or that carry their pictures.

1. **Lempira,** the chief of the Lenca people, who fought heroically against the Spanish conquerors.
2. **Sor Juana Inés de la Cruz** (Juana de Asbaje), a nun who was a devoted scholar and poet in seventeenth-century Mexico.
3. **Francisco Hernández de Córdoba,** a Spanish explorer who founded the colonial cities of Granada and León.

A **córdoba:** Nicaragua

B **peso:** México

C **lempira:** Honduras

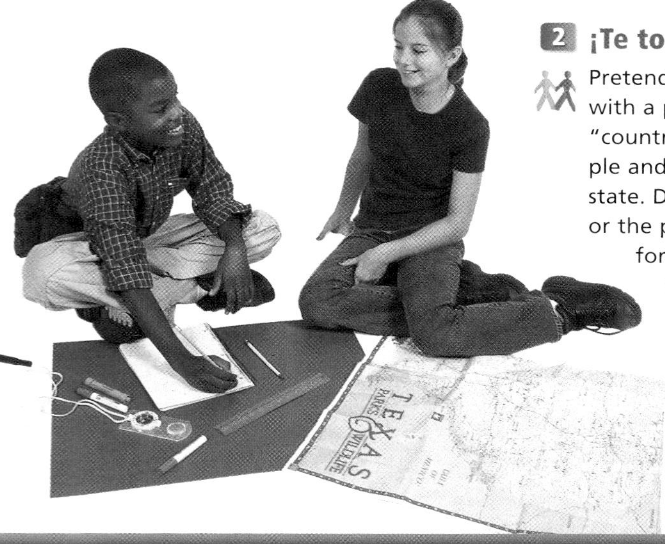

2 ¡Te toca a ti!

Pretend your state is actually a country. Work with a partner to create money for your "country." Include drawings of famous people and symbols that are important in your state. Draw examples of both sides of a coin or the paper money. Use the Spanish words for numbers to write the value of your coin or paper money. Present the money you designed to the class.

Can your classmates identify your symbols and colors and explain what they mean?

Core Instruction

TEACHING CONEXIONES CULTURALES

1. Begin by asking students questions about U.S. currency: Are all denominations of bills the same color? size? Who are pictured on the bills? Have they seen newer and older designs? **(5 min.)**
2. Do Activity 1 with class. How are these bills different from U.S. currency? **(5 min.)**
3. Present History Link. **(7 min.)**
4. You may want to assign Activity 2 as homework to be done in pairs, or plan it as a classroom project. Present Math Link. **(5 min.)**
5. Have students do Activity 3 individually. **(5 min.)**
6. Using a computer attached to a projector, guide the class in looking up the exchange rates of foreign currencies. **(15 min.)**

STANDARDS: 1.3, 2.2

Visit Holt Online
go.hrw.com
KEYWORD: EXP1B CH8
Online Edition

Conexión Matemáticas

3 De compras

In Spain and most Spanish-speaking countries, you can shop in neighborhood shops that specialize in one type of food or item. Large stores are common in big cities. Smaller shops and open markets are still popular, however, and they're within walking distance from most homes. Imagine you have 5.75€ (euros) to spend on fruit at the local fruit stand **(la frutería).**

1. Decide which kinds of fruit to buy.
2. Calculate how much change you will get back.
3. Where would you go to buy fruit in your hometown?

Mercado San Miguel, Madrid, España

las naranjas 2.00€/kg.

las fresas 1.30€/kg.

las manzanas 2.30€/kg.

el melón 3.00€/kg.

Conexiones culturales

Differentiated Instruction

ADVANCED LEARNERS

.Extension You may want to have students look up exchange rates for various countries' currency on the Internet or in a national newspaper. Have them figure out what the fruit depicted here would cost in various currencies. Also have them figure out the cost in foreign currency of some of the things that they buy often (music CDs, snacks...).

MULTIPLE INTELLIGENCES

Tactile Learners For students who may learn better with tactile experience, run off some play euros in various denominations to use in acting out Activity 3. Have students work in pairs, with one being the shopkeeper and the other playing the role of customer. Calculators would also be helpful for some students in making change.

Conexiones culturales

Connections

History Link

The currency unit of Spain used to be the **peseta,** but on January 1, 2002, Spain adopted the use of the **euro,** along with 11 other countries in Europe. The exchange rate of the euro at that time was approximately €1 = $1 U.S. (The symbol for the euro is €.)

Connections

Thinking Critically

Remind students that a store that sells shoes **(zapatos)** is called a **zapatería,** and that a store that sells games **(juegos)** is called a **juguetería.** Have students guess what a store is called that sells paper **(papel),** flowers **(flores),** watches **(relojes)** and **tortillas. (papelería, florería, relojería, tortillería)**

Math Link

Ask students, "How can we find out how much a dollar is worth in the money of another country today? What does knowing that tell us?" (Currency exchange rates are posted in national papers and on the Internet sites of national banks. The daily exchange rate varies according to supply and demand.) To teach students how to calculate the exchange rate, choose a set amount of U.S. money to be exchanged ($200.00, for example). Look up the daily exchange rate for the currency desired, and multiply that rate by the number of U.S. dollars. Assign each student a different currency and have them chart the daily exchange rate for a week and calculate how much a set amount of U.S. dollars would be worth each day. Have students post their findings on a classroom chart to compare the currency fluctuations of all the countries monitored.

STANDARDS: 3.2

Resources

Planning:

Lesson Planner, pp. 94–95, 250–251

 One-Stop Planner

Presentation:

 Video Program
Videocassette 4
DVD Tutor, Disc 2
VideoNovela

Practice:

Video Guide, pp. 74–75, 79
Lab Book, p. 53

Connections

Visual Learners

To help students better understand the two versions of the shopping trip in this episode of **Novela en video,** have them create comparative maps of each version. Draw two boxes on the board and label one **Versión de Sofía** and the other **Versión de Celeste.** Draw four or five spokes with circles on the end coming out of the boxes. Ask the students to fill in the circles with what each person says happened.

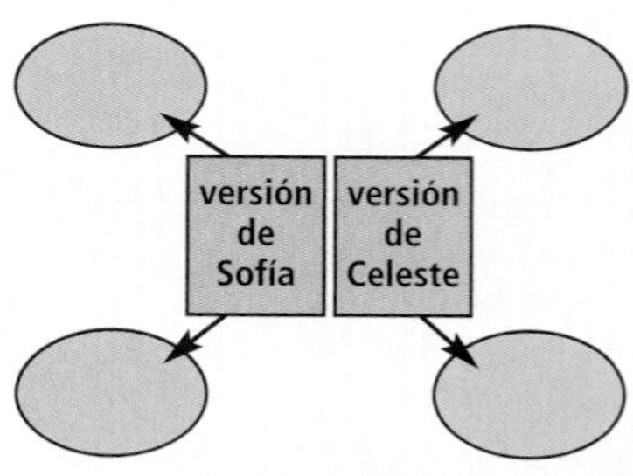

Gestures

Observing Sofía's and Celeste's body language and gestures in the two versions of the shopping trip will tell you a great deal about how each girl is feeling. Do the gestures and body language reflect what each girl says? Do you think these gestures are exaggerated in the girls' minds? Why do you think so?

Novela en video

¿Quién será?

Episodio 8

ESTRATEGIA

Recognizing different points of view When the same story is told from different points of view, it is important to keep track of who is telling what. This is because the same events can be interpreted in a completely different way by everyone who experienced them. The truth probably lies somewhere between the different versions. As you read the **Novela** or watch the video, keep track of whose view is being expressed, Sofía's or Celeste's. What do you think really happened?

En México

Estados Unidos
MÉXICO
Golfo de México
Ciudad de México
Océano Pacífico

Celeste habla con Sofía. Celeste quiere ir de compras a buscar ropa y zapatos para la fiesta del sábado.

1

Celeste Hola, Sofía. Necesito comprar una falda, una blusa y unos zapatos para la fiesta del sábado.

Sofía Está bien.

Celeste Perfecto. ¿Por qué no nos encontramos en Kulte a las diez y media?

Core Instruction

TEACHING NOVELA EN VIDEO

1. Have students scan the pictures of the **Novela.** Have them predict what they think is happening in this episode before reading the text. Have them give reasons to support their prediction. **(10 min.)**
2. Play the video stopping after scene four. Ask the comprehension questions from **A. Contesta.** Were any of the student's predictions correct? Are students surprised at the plot? **(10 min.)**
3. Play the rest of the video. Ask the questions in **B. Contesta.** In what ways did the plot take on a twist that the students had not inferred from the images? **(10 min.)**
4. In pairs, have students discuss the answers for the **Actividades** on page 163. Discuss their answers in class. **(10 min.)**

Captioned Video/DVD

As an alternative, you might use the captioned version.

STANDARDS: 1.2, 3.1

Novela

Visit Holt Online
go.hrw.com
KEYWORD: EXP1B CH8
Online Edition

Novela en video

La versión de Sofía

Fui con Celeste a Kulte, una tienda de ropa.

2

Celeste ¿Qué te parece esta falda azul? ¿Me queda bien?
Sofía No te queda nada bien. Te debes probar otra.
Celeste Ah, qué bueno que estás de acuerdo. Es muy bonita. Me gusta muchísimo.

No me hizo caso. Compró una falda horrible. Luego, se probó una blusa morada.

3

Celeste ¿Te gusta esta blusa morada? ¿Me queda bien?
Sofía No. ¡Está pasada de moda! Y debes probarte otra talla.
Celeste ¡Me queda perfecta! Y está a la última moda, ¿no crees?

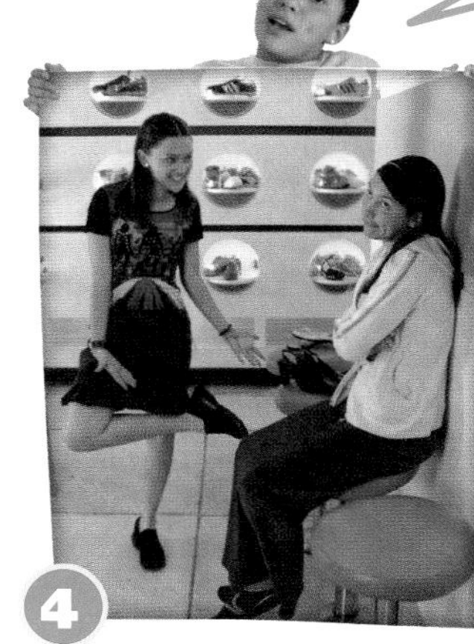

Traté de convencerla. Pero nada. Gastó su dinero en una blusa fea. Luego fuimos a la sección de zapatos.

4

Celeste ¿Qué piensas de estos zapatos? ¿Van bien con la blusa y la falda?
Sofía ¿Sabes qué? ¡Estás más loca que un zapato!
Celeste ¡Perfecto! Me voy a llevar estos zapatos. Ahora estoy lista para la fiesta del sábado. ¡Voy a estar a la última moda con mi nueva falda, blusa y zapatos!

A. Contesta

What is happening in the **Novela**? Check your understanding by answering the questions.

1. Why does Celeste call Sofía?
2. What does Sofía say about the skirt? the blouse? the shoes?
3. In Sofía's version, what does Celeste say about the things she bought?

¿Quién será?

In Chapter 7, Nicolás had to prepare for his grandmother's special birthday lunch. In this episode, Sofía goes on a shopping trip with her friend Celeste to help her get ready for a party. Unfortunately, the two friends have completely different versions of the shopping trip and its results. In Sofía's version all the clothing that Celeste tried on was horrible, didn't fit her, or was out of style. When Sofía attempted to tell her friend what she thought about the clothes, she was simply ignored. According to Celeste, Sofía was very coercive and persuaded her to buy all the clothing, even though she really didn't like it. In the end Celeste calls Sofía and asks her if she wants to go shopping again. It seems that her mother has told her that all of the clothing is wrong, and she has to take it back. Celeste blames Sofía, who is incredulous.

Using the Strategy

Recognizing different points of view To help students keep track of who says what in this episode (and to be able to answer #2 on page 163), it might help them to keep a chart of who says what in each version of the shopping trip.

A. Contesta Answers

1. She wants her to go shopping with her.
2. skirt: doesn't fit her, she should try another one; blouse: old-fashioned, not the right size for her; shoes: they are crazy—she shouldn't buy them
3. The skirt is pretty; she likes it very much. The blouse looks geat on her and is the latest style. She is going to buy the shoes to complete her perfect outfit.

Cultures

Practices and Perspectives

Although more and more urban cities have large discount stores and even an occasional mall, most shopping in Spanish-speaking countries is done in small, independently-owned boutiques. At these small stores, customers receive a high level of personal attention. Why do you think there are fewer large stores and more small stores in Spanish-speaking countries? What are some of the advantages of shopping at a small boutique? What are some of the possible disadvantages? Where would you prefer to shop?

STANDARDS: 1.2, 2.1, 3.2

B. Contesta Answers

1. The skirt is very pretty; it fits Celeste well. The blouse is the latest style and is a bargain. The shoes are the prettiest shoes in the world.
2. Because Sofía likes them so much.
3. Return everything

Comparison

Comparing and Contrasting

In many Spanish-speaking countries, people tend to purchase a few quality pieces that they can mix and match in many different ways. Rather than buy many inexpensive pieces, people often choose to buy just one or two expensive pieces of clothing that are unique, high quality, and durable. Is this different from shopping customs in the U.S.? What are some of the advantages of this philosophy of purchasing clothes? What are some of the possible problems? When you shop do you tend to shop for quality or quantity? Why?

La versión de Celeste

Fui con Sofía a Kulte. No me gustó mucho la falda azul, pero le gustó tanto a Sofía que la compré.

5

Celeste ¿Qué té parece esta falda azul? ¿Me queda bien?
Sofía ¡Te queda muy bien! ¡Muy bonita! Definitivamente debes comprarla.
Celeste ¿Estás segura? No sé.
Sofía ¡Te lo juro! ¡Te ves increíble!

Luego me probé una blusa morada. Gasté mi dinero en una blusa que no me queda bien.

6

Celeste ¿Te gusta esta blusa morada? ¿Me queda bien?
Sofía ¡Claro que sí! ¡Está a la última moda! Y es una ganga. ¡Mira el precio!
Celeste Pues, sí, tienes razón. Es muy barata. Pero...
Sofía ¿Pero qué? Hazme caso. Debes comprarla.

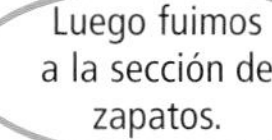
Luego fuimos a la sección de zapatos.

7

Celeste ¿Qué piensas de estos zapatos? ¿Van bien con la blusa y la falda?
Sofía ¡Amiga! ¡Estos zapatos son más bonitos que todos los zapatos en todo el mundo!
Celeste ¿De veras? Bueno, si te gustan a ti, los voy a comprar.

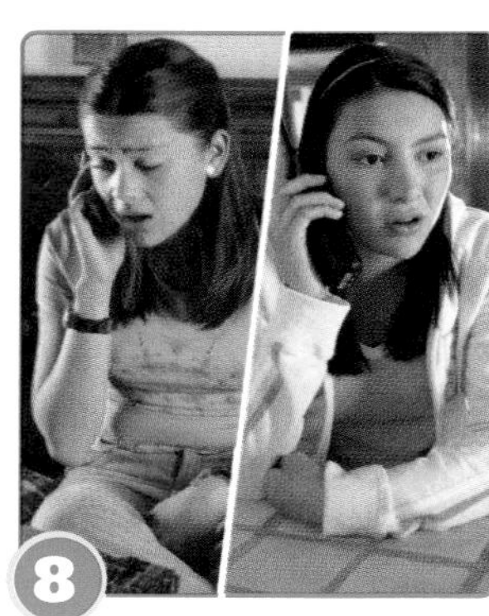

8

Celeste Sofía, tengo que regresar a Kulte. Tengo que devolver la falda, la blusa y los zapatos. ¿Vas conmigo?
Sofía Sí, pero ¿por qué tienes que devolver todo?
Celeste Mamá dice que me veo horrible en esa falda y esa blusa y que los zapatos son más horribles que la ropa. No sé por qué me dejaste comprarlos.

B. Contesta

1. In Celeste's version, what does Sofía say about the skirt? the blouse? the shoes?
2. According to Celeste, why does she end up buying the clothes and shoes?
3. What does Celeste's mother make her do?

Culminating Project

1. Tell students that they are going to write a script and present a mock fashion show. Students may choose to showcase contemporary or made-up fashions from another time period or planet. For example, they might show the latest clothing line from Mars.
2. Have students design an outfit that they will wear in the fashion show and write a complete description of the outfit, including fabric types and colors. Their outfit should include at least five different articles of clothing or accessories.
3. Students exchange scripts with a partner for editing. Students then rehearse reading the edited scripts while partners model the outfits.
4. Set a date for the fashion show and remind students to bring their outfits on that date.
5. Prepare a runway in the classroom and have partners present their outfits. You may wish to videotape the fashion show for students' portfolios.

STANDARDS: 4.2

Actividades

1 ¿Cómo lo diría?

Look through the story to find and write down Spanish words, phrases, and sentences that you could use to say the following.

1. It fits me well.
2. It's the latest style!
3. You should try on something else.
4. What do you think of this skirt?
5. It's a bargain!

1. Me queda bien.
2. ¡Está a la última moda!
3. Te debes probar otra.
4. ¿Qué te parece esta falda?
5. ¡Es una ganga!

2 ¡Opiniones!

The two girls don't seem to agree on Sofía's comments about the clothing that Celeste tried on. Look through the story to see how each girl remembers what Sofía said about each thing.

1. What advice does Sofía remember giving about . . .
   la falda?
   la blusa?
   los zapatos?
2. What advice from Sofía does Celeste remember hearing about . . .
   la falda?
   la blusa?
   los zapatos?

1. It doesn't fit you. You should try another one. It's old-fashioned, not the right size. crazy--she shouldn't get them
2. It fits you well. It's pretty. You should buy it. It's the latest style, and it's a bargain. They are the most beautiful shoes in the world.

3 ¿Comprendes la Novela?

Check your understanding of the events in the story by answering these questions.

1. Based on what you found in Activity 2, what could have led to two such different interpretations of the same events?
2. How would you respond to Celeste's statement, **No sé por qué me dejaste comprarlos?**

Próximo episodio
Marcos is going to another country. Where is he going? What do you think?
PÁGINAS 206–209

Novela en video

Comunicación

Pair Work: Interpersonal

After students have seen the **VideoNovela,** have them work in pairs to get ready for an event. Students can pretend to be two friends, a parent and a child, or two adults. One of the characters is unsure about what to wear and is feeling rather insecure. The other character is a fashion expert, and tells them how they feel about what they have chosen. The pairs should discuss at least five different articles of clothing before deciding on the final outfit. Have students switch roles after they have completed the scene one time.

3 Answers

1. Answers will vary. Possible answers: Celeste wanted to buy the things, so she heard what she wanted to. Or: later, when Celeste's mother didn't like the things, Sofía didn't want to admit that she had liked them.
2. Answers will vary. Possible answers: She listened to Sofía. Or: she didn't listen well enough to Sofía.

Próximo episodio:

research another student

Differentiated Instruction

SLOWER PACE LEARNERS

Have students select a Spanish-speaking country or area other than Florida and research typical shopping customs. Is bargaining popular in the country they selected? Are they more likely to find outdoor markets or larger shopping centers? Does that depend on whether the shopping is done in a larger city or in a rural area? How are the two similar or different?

MULTIPLE INTELLIGENCES

Logical-mathematical Have students use the Internet to find a specific store in the country they selected. Have them identify the store's hours of business, type of products sold, and the kinds of customers most likely to shop at such a store. Have them research the same topics for a similar store in their own city, compare the two stores, and then illustrate the resulting information in a bar chart. Have volunteers present the results of their research to the class.

STANDARDS: 1.1, 4.2

Leamos y escribamos

Resources

Planning:

Lesson Planner, pp. 95–97, 250–253

 One-Stop Planner

Presentation:

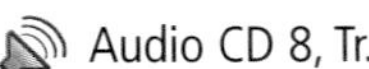 Audio CD 8, Tr. 11

Practice:

Cuaderno de actividades, p. 42

Cuaderno para hispanohablantes, pp. 61–68

Reading Strategies and Skills Handbook, Chapter 8

¡Lee conmigo!

Applying The Strategies

For additional practice, have students use the "Logographic Cues" strategy from the *Reading Strategies and Skills Handbook.*

READING PRACTICE

Strategy: Logographic Cues

STRATEGIES

Reading Skill	When can I use this strategy?		
	Prereading	During Reading	Postreading
Understanding Text Structure	✓	✓	✓
Analyzing Chronological Order		✓	✓
Making Generalizations and Understanding Text Structure		✓	✓

Strategy at a Glance: Logographic Cues

- Logographs are graphic representations of ideas. The **Logographic Cues** strategy uses simple pictures that represent or symbolize key ideas in a text.
- Students can use logographs to identify textual elements or organize and remember information.

Dr. Kylene Beers explains the **Logographic Cues** strategy with the following story.

I sat in the train station in Chaumont, France, wondering why I had taken Latin instead of French in high school and college. At that moment, I wanted to know if my train to Dijon was leaving when I thought it was. Blank stares and pitying shakes of the head were all I received when people realized that I was limited to English. Finally, I took out my map of the region, drew a train, circled my destination, and wrote the date and time of my departure. Underneath it all I put a big question mark. The clerk behind the window finally understood my question: Is the train from Chaumont to Dijon still departing today from this station at 3:48? "Oui," she said nodding her head.

Hours later, as I sat on the train, I realized that although I couldn't read French words, I *could* read musical notation, numbers, and international signs. I could read information that was presented logographically, but not information presented alphabetically. A Logographic Cue was worth a million French words.

"And why not?" I thought. Our first understanding of written language is a logographic understanding. Three- and four-year-olds who recognize their names in print rarely do so because they attach sounds to letters; instead, they simply recognize the shape of their printed names. Logographs, or picture cues, remain helpful when students are confronted with an alphabetic principle or text that they don't understand.

10 Reading Strategies and Skills Handbook — Logographic Cues

Additional Practice

For more reading practice, use the **Literatura y variedades** reading for Chapter 8 on pages 270–271.

ESTRATEGIA

para leer Visualizing what you read in a story helps you better understand it. As you read, create pictures in your mind of each scene or event. This will help you connect what you know to what you are reading and help you summarize the main events of the story.

A Antes de leer

CD 8, Tr. 11

Read the first paragraph of the story. Draw the picture that it brings to mind. What does this image tell you about the man and his servant? As you read the rest of the story, continue drawing pictures of how you imagine the events of each scene.

Una moneda[1] de ¡Ay!

En un pueblo, como muchos otros pueblos, vive un gran señor con muchos sirvientes. Pedro, el sirviente más nuevo, es un muchacho que al señor le parece un poco tonto. Para burlarse de él[2], lo llama, le da dos monedas y le dice:

—Pedro, vete al mercado y cómprame una moneda de uvas y otra de ¡Ay!

El pobre Pedro va al mercado y compra las uvas, pero cada vez que pregunta por la moneda de ¡Ay!, todos los vendedores se ríen de él[3].

Finalmente Pedro se da cuenta[4] que el señor quiere burlarse de él. Entonces decide poner las uvas en una bolsa[5] y sobre las uvas pone un manojo de espinos[6].

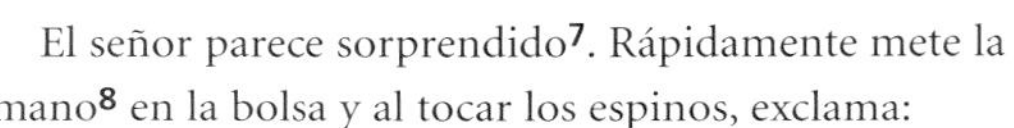

Cuando regresa a casa el señor le pregunta:

—¿Fuiste al mercado?

—Sí, señor.

—¿Y lo traes todo?

—Sí, señor. Todo está en la bolsa.

El señor parece sorprendido[7]. Rápidamente mete la mano[8] en la bolsa y al tocar los espinos, exclama:

—¡Ay!

—Y debajo están las uvas— le dice Pedro.

1 coin 2 to make fun of him 3 the vendors laugh at him 4 he realizes
5 a bag 6 handful of thorns 7 seems surprized 8 puts his hand in

Core Instruction

TEACHING LEAMOS

1. Discuss the **Estrategia para leer** with students and have them share what they already know about childhood stories. **(10 min.)**
2. Have students read the first paragraph and do the first part of Activity A. **(10 min.)**
3. Have students read the rest of the story, stopping to monitor comprehension as needed. **(8 min.)**
4. Have students complete the **Comprensión** activities on page 165. **(12 min.)**

TEACHING ESCRIBAMOS

1. Discuss the **Estrategia para escribir** as a class. Go over the scenario with students and have them give examples of clearly contrasting opinions. **(8 min.)**
2. Have students complete Activity 1. **(10 min.)**
3. Have students begin Activity 2. They might want to draw sketches of the imaginary clothes to help give them a reference when writing. Have students complete Activity 2 at home. **(12 min.)**
4. Have volunteers share their results with the class. **(10 min.)**

Visit Holt Online
go.hrw.com
KEYWORD: EXP1B CH8
Online Edition

B Comprensión

Contesta las siguientes preguntas con oraciones completas.

1. ¿Quién es Pedro? Pedro es el sirviente más nuevo.
2. ¿Qué debe comprar Pedro en el mercado? uvas y ¡ay!
3. ¿Por qué se ríen los vendedores de Pedro? Porque no hay ¡ay!
4. ¿Qué hay en la bolsa que Pedro le da al señor? espinos y uvas
5. ¿Cómo reacciona el señor cuando Pedro le dice que trae todo? Parece sorprendido.
6. ¿Qué hace el señor cuando mete la mano en la bolsa? Dice: ¡ay!

C Después de leer

Summarize the story using the drawings you made while reading it. Explain how you visualized each scene. What did each scene reveal about the characters? Did you find the ending of the story humorous? Why?

Ropa	Lo que (no) me gusta	Lo que (no) le gusta a mi amigo(a)

ESTRATEGIA

para escribir When you write about differing opinions, choose terms that show sharp, clear contrasts. Using charts can help you visualize and contrast differing points of view.

A mí me parece perfecto...

Imagine you are shopping for clothes with a friend. However, you can't agree about anything today! If you think something looks good and fits well, your friend says it looks awful. Write five things you're shopping for that you and your friend have different opinions about.

1 Antes de escribir

Make a chart. In one column, list at least five pieces of clothing. In the next column write what you like or don't like about each item. In the third column, write the differing opinions your friend has.

2 Escribir y revisar

Using your chart, write about your shopping trip. Include your and your friend's opinions about the clothes: how they fit, if they look good, or if they are in style. Include details to back up each opinion.

Read your draft at least two times, comparing it with your chart. Are the contrasting opinions clear? Check spelling and punctuation.

3 Publicar

Share your paragraph with the class. Ask your classmates to respond by giving their opinions or preferences regarding the clothing.

Online
Cuaderno para hispanohablantes, pp. 81–92

Leamos y escribamos

Heritage Speakers

Have heritage speakers discuss what they understand **¡Ay!** to mean and when it is used. Ask them in what contexts they have heard the expression (*Alas!*, or an exclamation of pain or grief). You might give students the expression **¡Ay de mí!** *(Alas, poor me!)*.

Writing Assessment

To assess the **Taller del escritor,** you can use the following rubric. For additional rubrics, see the *Alternative Assessment Guide.*

Writing Rubric	4	3	2	1
Content (Complete—Incomplete)				
Comprehensibility (Comprehensible—Seldom comprehensible)				
Accuracy (Accurate—Seldom accurate)				
Organization (Well-organized—Poorly organized)				
Effort (Excellent effort—Minimal Effort)				

18–20: A
16–17: B
14–15: C
12–13: D
Under 12: F

Differentiated Instruction

ADVANCED LEARNERS

In groups of three, have students write a short screenplay based on the reading. The cast of characters will be the **narrador, Pedro,** and **el señor.** Tell students that they are free to take liberty with the play and convert it into a contemporary version, for example. Allow time for groups to practice their play, and then have volunteers act it out for the rest of the class.

MULTIPLE INTELLIGENCES

Linguistic To extend the suggested reading strategy, give students the opportunity to rewrite the story as a children's book. Have them write one or two sentences per page and draw an illustration for each sentence or pair of sentences that shows what is being described. They should write the Spanish sentence on the top of the page. If students have a younger brother or sister at home, they can read the book to him or her.

Assess

Assessment Program
Prueba: Lectura, p. 69
Prueba: Escritura, p. 70
Test Generator 

STANDARDS: 1.2, 1.3, 3.1

Resources

Planning:

Lesson Planner, pp. 97–98, 252–255

One-Stop Planner

Presentation:

Video Program
Videocassette 4
DVD Tutor, Disc 2
Variedades

Teaching Transparencies
Situación, Capítulo 8
Picture Sequences, Chapter 8

Practice:

Activities for Communication, pp. 50, 69–70
TPR Storytelling Book, pp. 46–47
Video Guide, pp. 74–75, 80
Lab Book, pp. 25–26, 52
Audio CD 8, Tr. 13–16
Interactive Tutor, Disc 2

Reteaching

Hold up two magazine or catalog photos of clothing and make comparisons about them. Repeat with several pairs of pictures. Then, distribute catalogues or photos and have students continue this activity in small groups.

Game

¿Quién es? In small groups, one student names an item worn by one of his or her classmates. The other students try to identify the classmate by asking questions to get more details about the clothing item. The student who guesses correctly takes the next turn.

Prepárate para el examen

1 Vocabulario 1
- asking for and giving opinions
- offering and asking for help in a store

pp. 132–137

1 Tell what each item is, and what size and color you want or need.

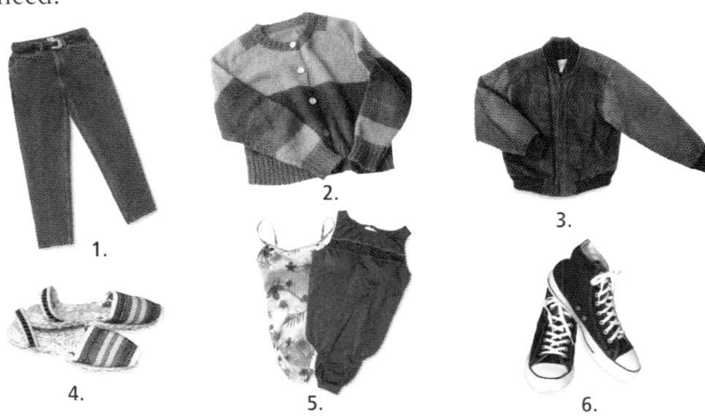

2 Gramática 1
- **costar,** numbers to one million
- demonstrative adjectives and comparisons
- **quedar**

pp. 138–143

2 Compare the prices of the following items with similar things you have at home. Begin with the correct form of **este(a).** Tell how much each thing costs.

1. mesa de plástico, $125/mi mesa
2. sofá de seda, $1.199/mi sofá
3. cama grande, $1.831/mi cama
4. cuatro plantas de seda, $45/mis plantas
5. refrigerador negro, ultra moderno, $2.057/mi refrigerador
6. teléfono azul y verde, $62/mi teléfono

3 Vocabulario 2
- saying where you went and what you did
- talking on the phone

pp. 146–151

3 Escoge la respuesta apropiada.

1. ¿Adónde fuiste el lunes por la noche? c
2. Hola. ¿Está Andrés? a
3. Compré aretes y un anillo. b
4. Lo siento, no está. ¿Quieres dejarle un recado? e
5. ¿Qué hiciste en la tienda de música? d

a. Espera un momento. Ya te lo paso.
b. ¿Fuiste a una joyería o a un almacén?
c. Fui a la biblioteca a estudiar.
d. Escuché muchos discos compactos.
e. Sí, por favor, que me llame después.

Preparing for the Exam

FOLD-N-LEARN
Four Corner Study Aid

1. To help students prepare for the Chapter Test, have them create a **Fold-n-Learn** study aid as shown here using a sheet of paper, scissors, and a pen or pencil.
2. Once the Four Corner template is completed, ask students to list a store type on each tab. Then, under each tab created, have students list the items you would buy at that store.
3. On the flip side of the Four Corner template, students can list expressions they would need to buy something at each store.
4. Have partners quiz each other using their new Four Corner study aids.

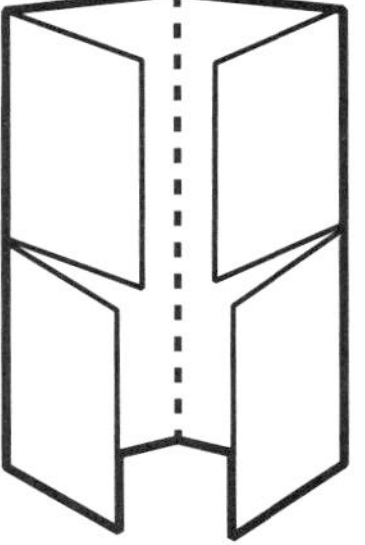

STANDARDS: 1.1, 1.2, 1.3

Repaso

Visit Holt Online
go.hrw.com
KEYWORD: EXP1B CH8
Chapter Self-test

4 Complete Carolina's description of her day, using the preterite of the verbs in parentheses.

Hoy __1__ (despertarse, yo) temprano para ir de compras con mi familia. __2__ (ir, nosotros) al centro comercial nuevo. Le __3__ (comprar, yo) una pulsera a mi abuela. Ignacio __4__ (mirar) las vitrinas, nada más. Mamá y papá __5__ (gastar) mucho dinero en DVDs. Por la tarde, mis padres __6__ (tomar) un batido y Federico __7__ (ir) al cine. Nosotros __8__ (regresar) a casa a las seis. Todos __9__ (acostarse) tarde. **1.** me desperté **2.** Fuimos **3.** compré **4.** miró **5.** gastaron **6.** tomaron **7.** fue **8.** regresamos **9.** nos acostamos

5 Contesta las siguientes preguntas.

1. How do you refer to clothing and shoe sizes in Spanish-speaking countries?
2. What are **guayaberas** and where did they originate?
3. Where would you likely see customers bargaining with vendors? Where wouldn't you?

CD 8, Tr. 13

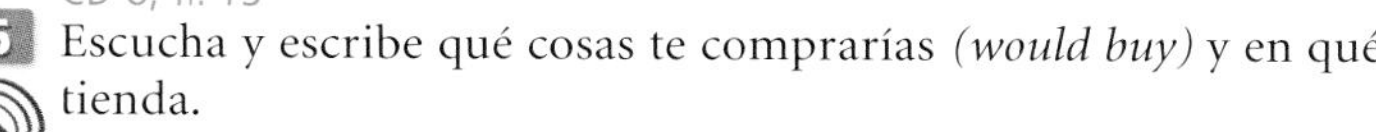

6 Escucha y escribe qué cosas te comprarías *(would buy)* y en qué tienda.

7 Describe lo que ves en los dibujos. En oraciones completas, di qué dicen Felipe y Cristina, y qué compraron.

a.

b.

c.

d.

4 Gramática 2
- preterite of **-ar** verbs
- preterite of **ir**
- preterite of **-ar** verbs with reflexive pronouns

pp. 152–157

5 Cultura
- **Comparaciones** **pp. 144–145**
- **Notas culturales** **pp. 134, 140, 148, 152**
- **Geocultura** **pp. 126–129**

Repaso

5 Answers
1. Using the words **talla, número,** and the metric system.
2. An embroidered shirt from Cuba
3. bargain in a market, but not in a mall

6 Script
1. El viernes voy a ir a la playa con mis amigos. Mi traje de baño me queda pequeño.
2. No me gusta llevar faldas ni vestidos.
3. No tengo diccionario para la clase de alemán.
4. Todos los días voy a correr y mis zapatos están viejos.
5. Me encantan los batidos de fruta.

6 Answers
1. un traje de baño; en la tienda de ropa
2. pantalones; en la tienda de ropa
3. un diccionario; en la librería
4. zapatos de tenis; en la zapatería
5. un batido; en la heladería

Preparación Práctica AP Language Examination

7 Below is a sample answer for the picture description activity.

—Felipe, ¿a qué hora cierra el centro comercial?
—Cierra a las nueve. Son las ocho ahora.
—¿Cómo me quedan la camisa y la blusa?
—Te quedan bien pero cuestan mucho.
—¿Cómo me quedan los pantalones?
—¡Ay, Felipe, te quedan mal! Necesitas una talla más grande.
—Sí, pero sólo cuestan $7,00. También voy a comprar el sombrero. Es barato.
—Y está pasado de moda.
—Bueno, ¿adónde vamos ahora?
—Quiero volver a casa.

To display the drawings to the class, use the *Picture Sequences Transparency* for Chapter 8.

Oral Assessment

To assess the speaking activities in this section, you might use the following rubric. For additional speaking rubrics, see the *Alternative Assessment Guide.*

Speaking Rubric	4	3	2	1
Content (Complete—Incomplete)				
Comprehension (Total—Little)				
Comprehensibility (Comprehensible—Incomprehensible)				
Accuracy (Accurate—Seldom Accurate)				
Fluency (Fluent—Not Fluent)				

18–20: A 16–17: B 14–15: C 12–13: D Under 12: F

STANDARDS: 1.1, 1.2, 1.3, 2.1, 2.2

Repaso

Grammar Review

For more practice with the grammar topics in the chapter, see the *Grammar Tutor*, the *DVD Tutor*, the *Interactive Tutor*, or the *Cuaderno de vocabulario y gramática*.

GramaVisión

Online Edition

Students might use the online textbook to practice the **Letra y sonido** feature.

Letra y sonido

For more practice with accents, read students a list of words that contain accents and have them write them down on their own paper while one student volunteer completes the activity on the board. Have students compare their answers with what is on the board and make corrections as needed.

Dictado Script

1. Es difícil cortar el césped del jardín.
2. El próximo sábado voy a mirar películas de ciencia ficción.
3. Después voy a comer atún y bróculi en el sofá.
4. También voy a escuchar música y a estudiar computación.
5. Tengo un lápiz y un bolígrafo para aprender matemáticas.
6. Este miércoles voy a comprar un suéter en el almacén.
7. Tienes razón, veo cosas pésimas en la televisión.
8. Además, el sándwich de jamón está riquísimo.

Gramática 1
- **costar** and numbers to one million **pp. 138–139**
- demonstrative adjectives and comparisons **pp. 140–141**
- **quedar** **pp. 142–143**

Repaso de Gramática 1

100	cien	600	seiscientos(as)
101	ciento uno(un)	700	setecientos(as)
102	ciento dos	800	ochocientos(as)
200	doscientos(as)	900	novecientos(as)
300	trescientos(as)	1.000	mil
400	cuatrocientos(as)	2.000	dos mil
500	quinientos(as)	1.000.000	un millón (de+*noun*)

singular subject / *plural subject*

La bolsa cuest**a** cien dólares. Las botas cuest**an** ciento veintiún dólares.

este/ese saco	**más**+*adj.*+**que**	**mejor(es)/mayor(es) que**
estos/esos sacos	**tan**+*adj.*+**como**	
esta/esa blusa	**menos**+*adj.*+**que**	**peor(es)/menor(es) que**
estas/esas blusas		

The verb **quedar** is used to say how something fits and is conjugated like **gustar: me/te/le/nos/os/les queda(n)**+*adjective/adverb.*

Gramática 2
- preterite of regular **-ar** verbs **pp. 152–153**
- preterite of **ir** **pp. 154–155**
- preterite of **-ar** verbs with reflexive pronouns **pp. 156–157**

Repaso de Gramática 2

The verb **comprar** has regular **preterite** forms; the verb **ir** is irregular.

compr**é**	compr**amos**
compr**aste**	compr**asteis**
compr**ó**	compr**aron**

fui	**fuimos**
fuiste	**fuisteis**
fue	**fueron**

The **preterite** is used to say what happened at a specific point in the past and to narrate a sequence of events. Verbs with **reflexive pronouns** in the **preterite** have the same preterite endings as other verbs.

Ayer **fui** al cine con mis amigos, **regresé** tarde a casa y **me acosté**.

Letra y sonido

El acento ortográfico CD 8, Tr. 14–16

- Words ending in a vowel, **-n**, or **-s** are usually stressed on the next-to-last syllable. Exceptions have an accent mark over the stressed vowel: niño, joven, compras, semáforo, almacén, jóvenes
- Words ending in a consonant other than **-n**, or **-s** are usuallly stressed on the last syllable. Exceptions have an accent mark over the stressed vowel: papel, ciudad, repetir, ángel, lápiz, Héctor

Trabalenguas

El célebre cerebelo del cerebro celebrará con celeridad una celebérrima celebración.

Dictado

Escribe las oraciones de la grabación.

Chapter Review

Bringing It All Together

You might have students review the chapter using the following practice items and transparencies.

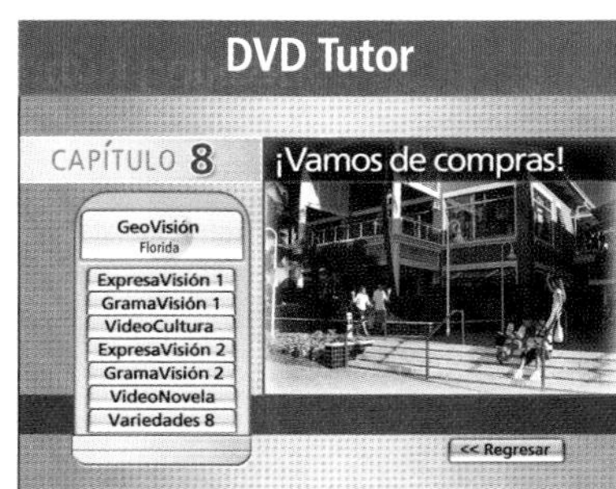

Repaso

Repaso de Vocabulario 1

Asking for and giving opinions

a la (última) moda	*in (the latest) style*
además	*besides*
barato(a)	*inexpensive*
caro(a)	*expensive*
costar (ue)	*to cost*
¡Es un robo!	*It's a rip-off.*
ese(a)	*that*
este(a)	*this*
feo(a)	*ugly*
la **ganga**	*bargain*
pasado(a) de moda	*out of style*
pequeño(a)	*small*
quedar bien/mal	*to fit well/badly*
tener razón	*to be right*

Colors . . . . *See p. 133.*

Asking for and offering help in a store

el **abrigo**	*(over)coat*
la **blusa**	*blouse*
la **bolsa**	*purse*
las **botas**	*boots*
los **calcetines**	*socks*
la **camisa**	*shirt*
la **camiseta**	*T-shirt*
cerrar (ie)	*to close*
la **chaqueta**	*jacket*
el/la **cliente**	*client, customer*
de algodón/lana/seda	*(made of) cotton/wool/silk*
devolver (ue)	*to return something*
el/la **dependiente**	*salesclerk*
¿En qué le puedo servir?	*How can I help you?*
la **falda**	*skirt*
llevar	*to wear*
Me gustaría...	*I would like . . .*
Nada más estoy mirando.	*I'm just looking.*
el **número**	*(shoe) size*
los **pantalones (cortos/vaqueros)**	*pants (shorts/jeans)*
un par de...	*a pair of . . .*
para hombres/mujeres/niños	*for men/women/children*
el **saco**	*sport coat*
las **sandalias**	*sandals*
el **sombrero**	*hat*
el **suéter**	*sweater*
la **talla**	*(clothing) size*
la **tienda de ropa**	*clothing store*
el **traje de baño**	*swimsuit*
usar	*to use, to wear*
el **vestido**	*dress*
los **zapatos (de tenis)**	*(tennis) shoes*

Numbers to one million . . . . *See p. 138.*
Demonstrative adjectives and comparisons . . . . *See p. 140.*

Repaso de Vocabulario 2

Saying where you went and what you did

ahorrar	*to save money*
el **almacén**	*department store*
el **anillo**	*ring*
anoche	*last night*
anteayer	*day before yesterday*
los **aretes**	*earrings*
los **audífonos**	*headphones*
ayer	*yesterday*
comprar	*to buy*
el **dinero**	*money*
el **disco compacto (en blanco)**	*(blank) CD*
el **DVD**	*DVD*
gastar	*to spend*
la **heladería**	*ice cream shop*
la **joyería**	*jewelry store*
la **juguetería**	*toy store*
los **juguetes**	*toys*
la **librería**	*bookstore*
mirar las vitrinas	*to window-shop*
pagar (una fortuna)	*to pay (a fortune)*
la **plaza de comida**	*food court in a mall*
la **pulsera**	*bracelet*
la **revista de tiras cómicas**	*comic book*
la **tarjeta (de cumpleaños)**	*greeting card (birthday card)*
la **tienda de...**	*. . . store*
tomar un batido	*to have a milkshake*
vender (de todo)	*to sell (everything)*
la **zapatería**	*shoe store*

Talking on the phone . . . . *See p. 150.*

Teacher to Teacher

Jackie Villalobos
Austin Academy
Garland, TX

First, I have the students copy a list of colors into their notes. Each word must be written in the appropriate color; for example, the word *green* must be written in green. Students use this list to study that night. The next day, I have student volunteers stand in front of the class and model the colors they are wearing. The class responds with the correct color in Spanish.

Vocabulary Review

For more practice with the vocabulary in this chapter, see the *DVD Tutor,* the *Interactive Tutor,* or the *Cuaderno de vocabulario y gramática.*

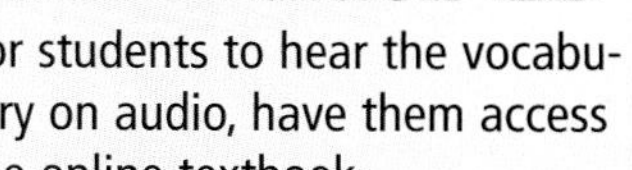

Online Edition

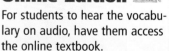

For students to hear the vocabulary on audio, have them access the online textbook.

Online Edition

Transparency Vocabulario 8.1

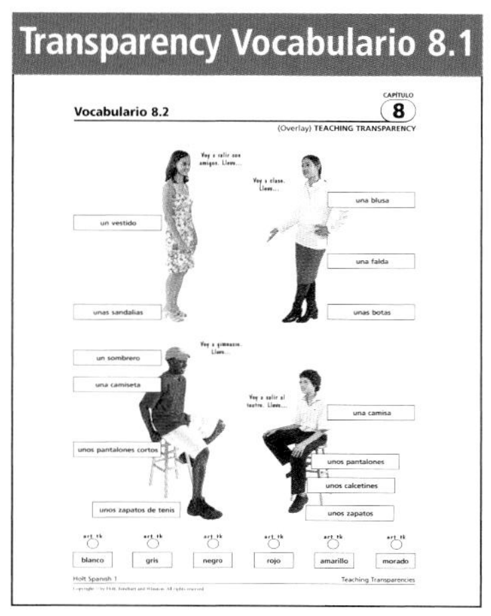

Transparency Situación Ch.8

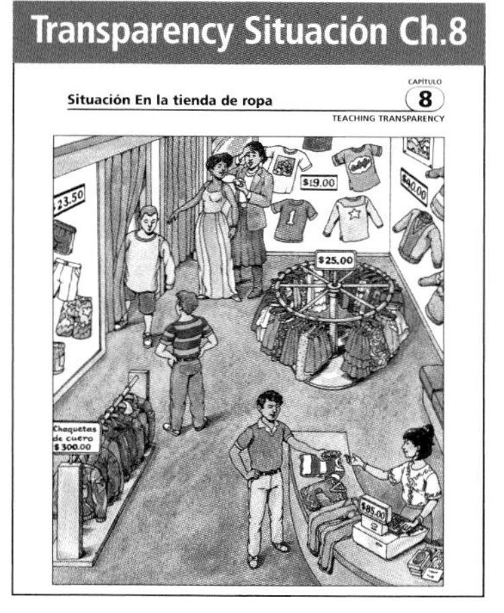

Assess

Assessment Program

Examen: Capítulo 8, pp. 173–183

Examen oral: Capítulo 8, p. 184

Standard Assessment Tutor, pp. 33–36

Audio CD 8, Tr. 20–21

Test Generator

STANDARDS: 1.2

Integración
capítulos 1-8

Resources

Planning:

Lesson Planner, pp. 99, 254–255

One-Stop Planner

Presentation:

Teaching Transparencies Fine Art, Chapter 8

Practice:

Cuaderno de actividades, pp. 43–44

Lab Book, pp. 25–26

Audio CD 8, Tr. 17

Interactive Tutor, Disc 2

CD 8, Tr. 17 

1 Escucha el anuncio y escoge la respuesta más apropiada.

1. Los audífonos son ____.
   a. de la más alta calidad b. muy caros
2. Esta tienda vende ____.
   a. pocos videos b. muchos videos
3. Casa Electrónica tiene ____.
   a. muchas cosas caras b. pocas cosas caras
4. Casa Electrónica nunca ____.
   a. tiene descuentos b. cierra
5. Según el anuncio, vas a ____.
   a. ahorrar dinero b. pagar mucho

1 Script

¿Todavía no tienes un DVD? Visita Casa Electrónica, la tienda con la mejor selección de aparatos electrónicos. Tenemos discos compactos de música Pop y Rock, de música clásica, jazz y… ¡mucho más! Ven y prueba nuestros audífonos. Son de la más alta calidad. También tenemos los DVD's más avanzados y toda clase de televisores. Aquí vas a encontrar más de mil videos clásicos y modernos. Ven a nuestra tienda, Casa Electrónica, donde vas a encontrar los mejores precios de toda la ciudad. ¡No pagues una fortuna en otras tiendas por los mismos productos! Ahorra mucho dinero con nosotros. Estamos en la Calle Colón, teléfono 956-800-2111. ¡Nunca cerramos! Abierta las 24 horas del día. Ven a visitarnos hoy. ¡Vas a estar super feliz!

2 Basándote en el anuncio, haz comparaciones entre las siguientes cosas, usando **más ... que, menos ... que** y **tan ... como.**

1. sandalias para mujeres/sandalias para hombres
2. blusas de seda/blusas de algodón
3. sombreros para hombres/sombreros para mujeres
4. pulseras/anillos y aretes
5. blusas para mujeres/camisas para hombres

2 Possible Answers

1. Las sandalias para mujeres son más bonitas que las sandalias para hombres.
2. Las blusas de seda son más caras que las blusas de algodón.
3. Los sombreros para hombres son tan baratos como los sombreros para mujeres.
4. Las pulseras son tan feas como los anillos y aretes.
5. Las camisas para hombres son tan baratas como las camisas para mujeres.

Culture Project

Have students select a Spanish-speaking country or area other than Florida and research typical shopping customs. Is bargaining popular in the country they selected? Are they more likely to find outdoor markets or larger shopping centers? Does that depend on whether the shopping is done in a larger city or in a rural area? How are the two similar or different?

Have students use the Internet to find a specific store in the country they selected. Have them identify the store's hours of business and type of products sold and figure out what kinds of customers most likely shop at such a store and how their shopping patterns are similar to or different from their own. Have volunteers present the results of their research to the class.

STANDARDS: 1.2, 3.2

Visit Holt Online
go.hrw.com
KEYWORD: EXP1B CH8
Cumulative Self-test

3 The woman in this painting has come to **el mercado** *(the market)* to buy **mangos, papayas, plátanos,** and **cocos**, all common tropical fruits. Write a conversation between the woman and the shopkeeper in Spanish.

- The people greet each other.
- The shopkeeper asks how he can help.
- The woman asks prices of various items.
- The shopkeeper answers with the prices, then compares two of the items.
- The woman decides what to buy.
- They say goodbye to each other.

After you have written your conversation, take turns acting it out with a partner.

Mercado caribeño, de la Dra. Dominica Alcántara

4 **Situación**

In small groups, create a department store in your classroom. Each group sets up a different department: clothing, accessories, school supplies, furniture, personal items (such as soap and shampoo), or food. Make signs for your department that show

- the items for sale
- their prices
- any special sales

After all the store departments are set up, play the roles of shoppers and clerks who buy and sell the merchandise.

Fine Art Connection

Introduction In this chapter, students see the painting *Mercado caribeño* by Dr. Dominica Alcántara. You might share the following information with your students.

Dr. Dominica Alcántara is an educator as well as an artist. She was born in the province of Las Villas, Cuba, and she is a descendent of a family from Spain. She is retired from the Miami Dade Public Schools System and presently is a professor teaching at Florida Memorial College. She has presented several exhibits in different local and foreign galleries.

Analyzing To help students discuss and analyze the photo, you might use the following questions.

1. **¿Te gusta ir de compras? ¿Qué te gusta comprar? ¿Te gusta ir al supermercado también?**
2. **¿Cuántas personas hay en la pintura?**
3. **¿Cómo es la muchacha? ¿Qué lleva la muchacha?**
4. **¿Qué lleva el vendedor?**
5. **¿Qué compra la muchacha?**

Extension Set up a still life **(naturaleza muerta)** arrangement of **artesanía** that you may have collected in your travels. Give students a 5 x 8 piece of white construction paper. If possible, circle the desks around the arrangement. Allow students to do pencil sketches of the objects displayed in the still life. This activity can also be done with colored pencils, crayons, or pastels if available.

ACTFL Performance Standards

The activities in Chapter 8 target the communicative modes as described in the Standards.

Interpersonal	Two-way communication using receptive skills and productive skills	**Comunicación (SE),** pp. 135, 137, 139, 141, 143, 149, 151, 153, 155, 157 **Comunicación (TE),** pp. 135, 141, 149, 151, 153, 155, 157, 163 **Situacion,** p. 171
Interpretive	One-way communication using receptive skills	**Comparaciones,** pp. 144–145 **Novela en video,** pp. 160–163 **Leamos,** p. 164
Presentational	One-way communication using productive skills	**Comunicación (SE),** pp. 137, 143 **Comunicación (TE),** p. 163

STANDARDS: 1.1, 1.3

La República Dominicana

Resources

Planning:

Lesson Planner, p. xv

One-Stop Planner

Presentation:

Teaching Transparencies
Mapa 4

Video Program
Videocassette 5
DVD Tutor, Disc 2
GeoVisión

Practice:

Video Guide, pp. 81–82

Lab Book, p. 55

Interactive Tutor, Disc 2

Atlas INTERACTIVO MUNDIAL

Have students use the interactive atlas at **go.hrw.com** to find out more about the geography of the Dominican Republic and to complete the activities below.

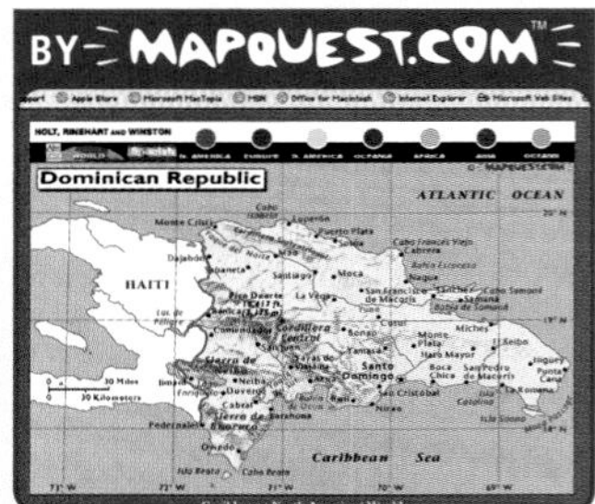

Map Activities

1. Have students locate the Dominican Republic on the interactive atlas and name the island to which it belongs. **(Hispaniola)** What other country shares this island? **(Haití)**
2. Several mountain ranges cross the Dominican Republic. The most prominent range is the **Cordillera Central.** Have students locate the **Cordillera Central.** What are the other ranges called? **(Cordillera Septentrional, Sierra de Neiba)**

GeoVisión

► **Concurso anual en Cabarete** A windsurfing competition takes place every June near the town of Cabarete.

Geocultura
La República Dominicana

▼ **Santo Domingo** The capital of the Dominican Republic, Santo Domingo, is located on the southern coast of the country at the mouth of the Ozama River.

Almanaque

Población
8.581.477

Capital
Santo Domingo

Gobierno
democracia representativa

Idioma oficial
español

Moneda
peso dominicano

Código Internet
www.[ ].do

¿Sabías que...?

Pico Duarte, a mountain in the Dominican Republic's Cordillera Central, is 3,087 meters high. It is the highest mountain in the Caribbean.

▼ **Niños dominicanos** These children reflect the mixed ethnic makeup of the Dominican Republic: 16% European origin, 11% African origin and 73% mixed.

Background Information

History

The indigenous group called the **Taíno** inhabited the island of Hispaniola for a thousand years before Christopher Columbus arrived in 1492. Around 500,000 **Taínos** lived on the island when the Spanish arrived. All of Hispaniola was a Spanish colony until 1697, when Spain signed the western third of the island over to France. In 1844, the Dominican Republic won independence from Spain, led by Juan Pablo Duarte. In 1966, a constitution was approved and the democratic process began.

Geography

La Costa de Ámbar, in the north of the island, is the world's richest supply of amber, the precious stone formed by pine resin and fossilized over millions of years.

Santiago is the nation's agricultural capital. It is in the Cibao Valley region **(la depresión del Cibao)**. The water from the **Río Yaque del Norte** irrigates the valley's crops.

La República Dominicana

◄ **El Parque Nacional de los Haitises** This park is in the province of **Samaná**. You can see low hills called **mogotes** in the waters of the **Bahía de Samaná**.

► **El Pico Duarte** The **Pico Duarte** was named for Juan Pablo Duarte, a 19th-century revolutionary.

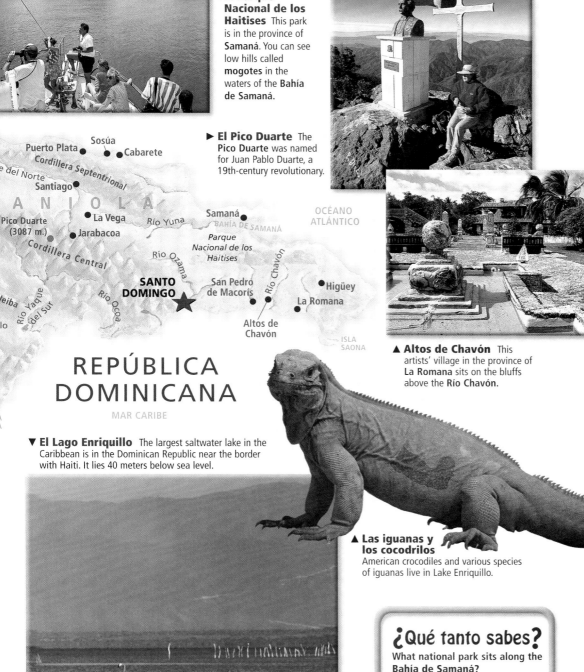

▲ **Altos de Chavón** This artists' village in the province of **La Romana** sits on the bluffs above the **Río Chavón**.

▼ **El Lago Enriquillo** The largest saltwater lake in the Caribbean is in the Dominican Republic near the border with Haiti. It lies 40 meters below sea level.

▲ **Las iguanas y los cocodrilos** American crocodiles and various species of iguanas live in Lake Enriquillo.

¿Qué tanto sabes?
What national park sits along the Bahía de Samaná?

Comparisons

Comparing and Contrasting

Apagones The high cost of fuel and slowed technological growth make **apagones,** or blackouts, a fairly common occurrence in the Dominican Republic. Each year parts of the nation suffer nearly 500 hours of power outages, or about twenty full days and nights without electricity! Entire cities go black and homes lose refrigeration. However, only half of the homes in the Dominican Republic are connected to electricity to begin with. Have students think about the implications of the **apagones,** and life without electricity. Are they aware of any towns or cities in the U.S. that have experienced blackouts?

Communities

Community Link

Celebrations For Dominicans, **Carnaval** is both a religious and patriotic celebration, combining the preparation for Lent and the celebration of independence. Throughout the Dominican Republic, communities express their identity through the crafting of their individual celebrations. In **Cotuí,** the expression of African culture dominates the celebration, with costumed characters such as the **Platanuses** and **Papeluses,** with costumes made with banana leaves, bee hives, termite nests, and other materials. In La Vega, Spanish colonial traditions are expressed with traditional dances and the **diablo cojuelo** masks. Have students think about how one of their community celebrations has developed its own identity.

CNN enEspañol.com
Have students check the **CNN en español** website for news on the Dominican Republic.

¿Sabías que... ?

Students might be interested in knowing the following facts about the Dominican Republic.

- **Quisqueya** was the **Taíno** name for the island of Hispaniola. Today many Dominicans affectionately refer to their country as **Quisqueya.**
- **Juan Pablo Duarte,** because of his wise and principled leadership, is considered the father of the Dominican Republic, even though he was in exile at the time of the revolution.
- **Bohíos** are small homes built from bamboo and palm leaves by agricultural workers.
- **Santo Domingo** is the oldest inhabited European city in the Americas.

Preguntas

You may wish to present these questions in English.

1. **¿Dónde está Santo Domingo? (En la costa sur)**
2. **¿Qué tipo de concurso tiene lugar cerca de Cabarete? (windsurfing)**
3. **Menciona dos animales que viven en el Lago Enriquillo. (las iguanas y los cocodrilos)**
4. **¿Cuál es el lago de agua salada más grande de las Antillas? (El Lago Enriquillo)**
5. **¿Qué se encuentra en los altos del Río Chavón? (Una majestuosa villa de artistas)**

Cultures

Practices and Perspectives

Dominican food is based on beans and rice, which are served at nearly every lunch and dinner. Dominicans like their food a little bit spicy, but not mouth-burning hot. Along with beans and rice, a typical meal might include plantains, bananas, cassava, sweet potatoes, and yams. **Sancocho,** a stew of cassava and plantains with chicken or pork, is a Dominican specialty. Beef is rarely eaten. Dominican families usually sit down together for all the meals of the day, unless a working parent can't make it home for the midday meal, which is the largest and most important meal of the day. The mother typically serves each plate, assuring that a proper portion is given to everyone in the family. In the cities, kitchens are usually modern, with stoves and ovens. But in the rural areas of the island where there is no electricity, women cook with wood and often haul their water from a river or stream. How does the practice of families eating together reflect family culture in the Dominican Republic?

Connections

Thinking Critically

Dominicans barter at markets, as well as with friends and neighbors, to get a good deal or exchange. Incredulous looks from both sides accompany the bartering. Dominicans always keep the bartering polite and friendly. Have students think about the concept of bartering. Do we barter for any products in the U.S. (like a new car)? What are some new means of bartering that have been widely accepted with technological advances? (e-bartering) Have students hold a market and barter prices.

A conocer la República Dominicana

La arquitectura

▲ **Casas de madera** Colorful wooden houses with sheet metal roofs are common in the Dominican Republic.

► **La Basílica de Higüey** This church has some of the most interesting modern architecture in the Dominican Republic. The concrete structure features a 75-meter-tall arch.

El arte

◄ ***El Once***
This painting is by the Dominican artist **Ramón Oviedo** (1924–). Oviedo is considered one of the most important modern painters in Latin America.

▼ **Mural cerámico** The Dominican artist Said Musa (1956–) is known for his many colorful murals. Musa created this public mural in Santo Domingo out of ceramic tile.

Interdisciplinary Links

El arte

Economics Link The Dominican government actively encourages the development of traditional crafts and has helped spawn the revival of many traditions that were being forgotten. The government is interested in keeping these artistic traditions alive to help the tourism industry, which is quickly becoming a major source of national income. Have students think about local folk art. How much does it contribute to the economy? Should a government be involved in promoting art? Does promotion of folk art for industry and tourism heighten its cultural significance?

La arquitectura

Science Link In the Dominican Republic, hurricanes are a way of life and a severe storm usually hits the island hard once every two years. Thousands of people are often left homeless because of the devastating effects of the storms. Have students research other areas, such as Florida and Texas, that contend with hurricanes as well. What technological and scientific developments have these communities put in place to combat the devastating effects of nature? What ways can buildings or sea walls be built differently to protect residents? What other natural disasters have caused architects to rethink building standards?

Visit Holt Online
go.hrw.com
KEYWORD: EXP1B CH9
Photo Tour

Las celebraciones

► **El Carnaval de Santo Domingo** In Santo Domingo, **Carnaval** is celebrated every February with parades and fantastic costumes.

▼ **El Festival del Merengue** **Merengue** is the national music and dance of the Dominican Republic.

¿Sabías que...?

The Dominican Republic is smaller than West Virginia, yet this island nation has an enormous variety of ecosystems and wildlife. In what ways can you see that nature is enjoyed and protected in the Dominican Republic?

La comida

▲ **El sancocho** A hearty meat and vegetable stew, **sancocho** is made on special occasions in the Dominican Republic.

◄ **Puesto de yaniqueque** **Yaniqueque** stands are common on beaches of the Dominican Republic. Similar to johnnycakes, **yaniqueques** are round, flat pieces of fried dough.

La República Dominicana

Cultures

Products and Perspectives

Sugar has been the backbone of the Dominican economy since colonial times. The sugar industry affects about 30% of the island's population. There are many seasonal cane cutters put to work at harvest time, as well as more workers who process the sugar. There are three major landholders in the sugar industry. The government-owned National Sugar Council produces 60% of the nation's sugar. What do students know about the production of sugar in the U.S.? Have them conduct some research and share their findings.

¿Comprendes?

You can use the following questions to check students' comprehension of the **Geocultura.**

1. What type of house is common in the Dominican Republic? (Colorful wooden houses with sheet metal roofs)
2. What is the artist Said Musa famous for? (his colorful murals)
3. What is the national music and dance of the Dominican Republic? (the **merengue**)
4. What is **sancocho?** (a hearty meat and vegetable stew served on special occasions)
5. What is **yaniqueque** and where is it sold? (round, flat pieces of fried dough; stands on beaches)

Las celebraciones

Music Link **Merengue** is the national dance and music of the Dominican Republic. Have students research **merengue** music at the library or on the Internet. What two types of music make up the **merengue?**(Spanish **pasodoble** and African tom-tom) When and where was the **merengue** born? What instruments are used to play the **merengue?** What are some of the typical themes that are sung about in **merengue** music?

La comida

History Link Dominican families gather for feasts at several times a year. **Lechón asado** *(roast pig)* and turkey are two holiday feast dishes. Traditionally a family may raise the young pig themselves, carefully feeding it certain foods to season it for the holiday meal. At the library or on the Internet, have students research one of their traditional holiday meals. Where does the traditional meal come from? What are some of the ways that it was traditionally prepared? How has the meal changed over the years? Have students write a brief paragraph in English to describe their meal.

Assess

Assessment Program
Prueba: Geocultura, pp. 175–176
Test Generator 

STANDARDS: 2.2, 3.1

Capítulo 9

¡Festejemos!

Overview and Resources

Chapter Section		Resources
Vocabulario en acción 1 • Talking about plans; asking about past holidays, pp. 178–183 **¡Exprésate!** • To ask about plans; to respond, p. 179 • To ask about past holidays; to respond, p. 182	Present	TPR Storytelling Book, pp. 48–49 Teaching Transparencies Video Program/DVD Tutor, **ExpresaVisión**
Assess Assessment Program • **Prueba: Vocabulario 1,** pp. 77–78 • Alternative Assessment Guide, pp. 244, 252, 260 Test Generator	Practice	Cuaderno de vocabulario y gramática, pp. 53–55 Activities for Communication, pp. 33–34 Video Guide, pp. 84–86 Lab Book, pp. 4, 27–30, 56 Teaching Transparencies Audio CD 9, Tr. 1 Interactive Tutor, Disc 2
Gramática en acción 1 • Preterite of **–er** and **–ir** verbs, p. 184 • Review of the preterite, p. 186 • **Pensar que** and **pensar** with infinitives, p. 188	Present	Video Program/DVD Tutor, **GramaVisión**
Assess Assessment Program • **Prueba: Gramática 1,** pp. 79–80 • **Prueba: Aplicación 1,** pp. 81–82 • Alternative Assessment Guide, pp. 244, 252, 260 Audio CD 9, Tr. 15 Test Generator	Practice	Grammar Tutor for Students of Spanish, Chapter 9 Cuaderno de vocabulario y gramática, pp. 56–58 Cuaderno de actividades, pp. 45–47 Activities for Communication, pp. 33–34 Video Guide, pp. 84–85 Lab Book, pp. 4, 27–30 Teaching Transparencies Audio CD 9, Tr. 2 Interactive Tutor, Disc 2

	Print	Media
Cultura • **Comparaciones,** pp. 190–191 • **Comunidad,** p. 191 • **Conexiones,** pp. 204–205	Cuaderno de actividades, p. 48 Cuaderno para hispanohablantes, pp. 69–76 Video Guide, pp. 84–85, 87 Lab Book, p. 57	Audio CD 9, Tr. 3–5 Video Program/DVD Tutor, **VideoCultura** Interactive Tutor, Disc 2
Novela en video • **Episodio 9,** pp. 206–209	Lab Book, p. 59 Video Guide, pp. 84–85, 89	Video Program/DVD Tutor, **VideoNovela**
Leamos y escribamos • **Las mañanitas, Canción de cumpleaños,** pp. 210–211	Cuaderno de actividades, p. 52 Reading Strategies and Skills Handbook Cuaderno para hispanohablantes, pp. 69–76 ¡Lee conmigo! Assessment Program, pp. 89–90	Audio CD 9, Tr. 8

Lesson Planner with Differentiated Instruction, pp. 101–130, 256–283

One-Stop Planner® CD-ROM

Visit Holt Online
go.hrw.com
KEYWORD: EXP1B CH9
Online Edition

Chapter Section		Resources
Vocabulario en acción 2 • Talking about preparing for a party; greeting, introducing others, and saying goodbye, pp. 192–197 **¡Exprésate!** • To ask about preparing for a party, p. 193 • To greet, introduce others, and say goodbye, p. 196	Present	TPR Storytelling Book, pp. 50–51 Teaching Transparencies Video Program/DVD Tutor, **ExpresaVisión**
Assess Assessment Program • **Prueba: Vocabulario 2,** pp. 83–84 • Alternative Assessment Guide, pp. 244, 252, 260 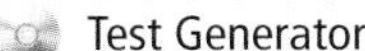 Test Generator	Practice	Cuaderno de vocabulario y gramática, pp. 59–61 Activities for Communication, pp. 35–36 Video Guide, pp. 84–85, 88 Lab Book, pp. 4, 27–30, 58 Teaching Transparencies Audio CD 9, Tr. 6 Interactive Tutor, Disc 2
Gramática en acción 2 • Direct object pronouns, p. 198 • **Conocer** and personal **a,** p. 200 • Present progressive, p. 202	Present	Video Program/DVD Tutor, **GramaVisión**
Assess Assessment Program • **Prueba: Gramática 2,** pp. 85–86 • **Prueba: Aplicación 2,** pp. 87–88 • Alternative Assessment Guide, pp. 244, 252, 260  Audio CD 9, Tr. 16  Test Generator	Practice	Grammar Tutor for Students of Spanish, Chapter 9 Cuaderno de vocabulario y gramática, pp. 62–64 Cuaderno de actividades, pp. 49–51 Activities for Communication, pp. 35–36 Video Guide, pp. 84–85 Lab Book, pp. 4, 27–30 Teaching Transparencies Audio CD 9, Tr. 7 Interactive Tutor, Disc 2

	Print 	Media 
Repaso • **Repaso,** pp. 212–213 • **Gramática y Vocabulario,** pp. 214–215 • **Letra y sonido,** p. 214	Activities for Communication, pp. 51, 71–72 Video Guide, pp. 84–85, 90 Lab Book, pp. 27–30, 60 TPR Storytelling Book, pp. 52–53 Assessment Program, pp. 185–195, 196 Alternative Assessment Guide, pp. 244, 252, 260 Standardized Assessment Tutor, pp. 37–40	 Video Program/DVD Tutor, **Variedades** 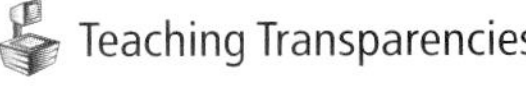 Teaching Transparencies  Audio CD 9, Tr. 10–13  Interactive Tutor, Disc 2  Test Generator
Integración • Cumulative review, Chapters 1–9, pp. 216–217	Cuaderno de actividades, pp. 53–54 Lab Book, pp. 27–30	 Teaching Transparencies Audio CD 9, Tr. 14

¡Festejemos!

Projects

Teatro guiñol

In this activity, students work in groups to create puppet shows about holiday celebrations. Each group researches the history, customs, and cultural importance of a different holiday. They then produce a brief puppet show that tells a story of the celebration.

SUGGESTED SEQUENCE

1. Explain the project and set due dates for research, a written script, and the show.
2. Divide the students into groups of four or five. Students decide on the holiday they would like to learn more about in groups.
3. Have students turn in rough draft scripts. Review and return the scripts.
4. Make puppets in class and allow students time to rehearse the shows.
5. Groups turn in a copy of their script and a short paragraph giving information about the celebration they researched.
6. Students present their shows to the class.

Grading the project

Suggested point distribution (100 points total)

Cultural Research	30
Scripts	20
Creativity	20
Puppet Show	30

Projects

e-community

e-mail forum:

Post the following questions on the classroom e-mail forum:

Location: http://spanish

1. ¿Te gusta recibir tarjetas electrónicas?
2. ¿Prefieres mandar o recibir tarjetas electrónicas?
3. ¿Prefieres recibir tarjetas por Internet o por correo tradicional? ¿Por qué?

Partner Class Project

Have your students go to one of the many Spanish-language electronic greeting card websites and choose a card to send to their keypal. It does not matter if there is a holiday at the time you are doing this, as such websites have cards for all occasions. In the card, students should tell which are their three favorite holidays and why. They should discuss what they are planning to do for one of those holidays this year and how they celebrated it last year. They should also find out similar information from their keypal. If they are writing to keypals in another country, they should also write about one typically American holiday, such as Thanksgiving or the Fourth of July.

Game Bank

For game ideas, see pages T60–T63.

STANDARDS: 1.1, 2.1, 5.1

Traditions

Danza

The **merengue** is the national dance of the Dominican Republic. There are many conflicting stories about its origin, but most scholars agree that it is a combination of European and African dances. The **merengue** first became popular in the middle of the nineteenth century among the people who lived in the countryside. For years it was scorned by the upper classes, but when the United States invaded the island in the early twentieth century, the **merengue** became a symbol of national unity against the foreign invader. The dance became known internationally when it was brought to Puerto Rico and New York by artists fleeing the Trujillo dictatorship that followed the U.S. invasion. By the late 1970's, it had displaced **salsa** as the most popular dance form in Latin America. Have students find instructions on how to dance the **merengue** on the Internet. After students have learned the dance, you might have students teach the dance to another language class.

Receta

Picadillo, a dish made with ground meat and spices, is a popular dish in the Caribbean. It is served over rice with ripe, fried plantains and an avocado salad to make a complete, delicious meal. Some cooks add capers, raisins, cubed potatoes, or even slivered almonds to add extra flavor. You might have students make this recipe as a class project or for extra credit.

Picadillo

para 4 personas

2 libras de carne molida

2 cebollas, bien picadas

1 pimiento verde, bien picado

2 dientes de ajo, bien picados

1 lata (15 onzas) de tomates (picados y con su líquido)

2 latas (8 onzas) de salsa de tomate

2 hojas de laurel

unas gotas de salsa Tabasco®

1 taza de aceitunas con pimientos, cortadas por la mitad

1 cucharadita de orégano

2 cucharaditas de comino

una pizca de nuez moscada

sal y pimienta al gusto

En una sartén grande, cocine la carne molida hasta que pierda su color rosado. Con una cuchara grande, saque toda la grasa que haya soltado. Agregue las cebollas, el pimiento verde, el ajo, la lata de tomates picados, las dos latas de salsa de tomate, las hojas de laurel, el Tabasco®, las aceitunas, el orégano, el comino y la nuez moscada. Sazone la mezcla con sal y pimienta. Cocínela a fuego lento, por 30 minutos, revolviéndola con frecuencia.

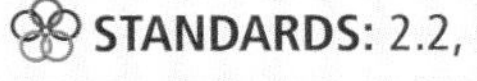

STANDARDS: 2.2, 5.1

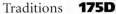

¡Festejemos!

For Student Response Forms, see *Lab Book*, pp. 27–30

Textbook Listening Activity Scripts 

Vocabulario en acción 1

8 p. 183, CD 9, Tr. 1

LUIS ¿Dónde pasaste el Día de Acción de Gracias? ¿Visitaste a tus abuelos?

ROSA No, vamos a ir a su casa en la Navidad. El Día de Acción de Gracias almorcé con mis padres en un restaurante y después fuimos al cine. Pasé la noche en la casa y ayudé a mi mamá a decorar la casa para la Navidad.

LUIS ¿Siempre pasas la Navidad en casa de tus abuelos?

ROSA Casi siempre. Por la mañana voy a misa con toda la familia. Después preparo la cena con mi abuela y mi mamá, y luego comemos y abrimos regalos. Por lo general, dormimos en su casa y regresamos al día siguiente.

Answers to Activity 8

1. ir a casa de los abuelos (va a ocurrir)
2. almorzar en un restaurante (ya ocurrió)
3. ir al cine (ya ocurrió)
4. pasar la noche en casa (ya ocurrió)
5. decorar la casa (ya ocurrió)
6. ir a misa (va a ocurrir)
7. comer y abrir regalos (va a ocurrir)
8. dormir en casa de los abuelos (va a ocurrir)

Gramática en acción 1

16 p. 186, CD 9, Tr. 2

1. Mis padres fueron a una cena romántica el Día de los Enamorados.
2. Mi familia va a misa de medianoche en la Navidad.
3. Mis tíos y primos comen con nosotros en casa de nuestros abuelos el Día de Acción de Gracias.
4. El cuatro de julio vimos fuegos artificiales en el parque.
5. Recibo muchas tarjetas el Día de los Enamorados.
6. Salí con mis amigos y no volvimos hasta muy tarde el 31 de diciembre.
7. Mi familia asistió a la iglesia tres veces durante la Semana Santa.
8. Mi abuela abrió muchos regalos el Día de la Madre.

Answers to Activity 16

1. b	3. a	5. a	7. b
2. a	4. b	6. b	8. b

Vocabulario en acción 2

29 p. 196, CD 9, Tr. 6

1. Nos vemos más tarde.
2. Tanto tiempo sin verte. ¿Cómo estás?
3. Hola. ¿Qué hay de nuevo?
4. Chao. ¡Que te vaya bien!
5. Te presento a mi compañera de clase.
6. Mucho gusto. Soy su hermano.
7. ¡Qué gusto verte!
8. Cuídate.

Answers to Activity 29

1. b	3. a	5. c	7. a
2. a	4. b	6. c	8. b

Gramática en acción 2

43 p. 202, CD 9, Tr. 7

1. Están nadando y jugando en la piscina.
2. Estamos comiendo y hablando.
3. Está preparando más sándwiches y galletas.
4. Estamos sirviendo la comida.
5. Están escuchando música de los años ochenta.
6. También están bailando.
7. Estamos limpiando un poco.

Answers to Activity 43

1. b	3. c	5. b	7. a
2. a	4. a	6. b	

Repaso capítulo 9

6 p. 213, CD 9, Tr. 10

¡Mi amigo Gerardo es un ángel! Me preparó un pastel de chocolate riquísimo y también ayudó a mis padres con todo antes de la fiesta. ¡Qué fiesta tan buena! Me cantaron "Feliz cumpleaños" y recibí muchos regalos. Las decoraciones están muy bonitas y la música fenomenal. Hay más de cincuenta personas en la casa. Algunas están en la sala y otras en el patio. Muchos amigos invitaron a otros amigos y no conozco a todas las personas. Por ejemplo, yo invité a Isabel y ella invitó a su hermana Maribel. Maribel invitó a Juan y a Miguel. Me gustan las fiestas pero creo que el próximo año vamos a tener una fiesta más tranquila. El año que viene pensamos tener una fiesta en la piscina de la casa de mis abuelos.

1. ¿Por que festejaron?
2. ¿Quién preparó el pastel antes de la fiesta?
3. ¿Qué tal estuvo la fiesta?
4. ¿Conoce Rita a todos los invitados?
5. ¿Cómo piensan celebrar el año que viene?

Answers to Activity 6

1. por el cumpleaños de Rita
2. Gerardo
3. muy buena, muy divertida
4. no, no conoce a todos
5. con una fiesta más tranquila

Dictado, p. 214, CD 9, Tr. 13

1. El miércoles, jueves y viernes va a hacer buen tiempo.
2. Siempre sales a pasear a las siete y cuarto.
3. Después de junio viene julio, no diciembre.
4. Cuatro y seis son diez.
5. A la tía rubia y seria le duele el oído.
6. El Día de Acción de Gracias es el aniversario de mi graduación.
7. Mi familia tiene una zapatería y una juguetería.
8. No sé la dirección de la joyería.

Integración capítulos 1-9

1 p. 216, CD 9, Tr. 14

1. Todos ayudan con los preparativos para la fiesta de cumpleaños. Adela está sirviendo el ponche.
2. Tenemos mucha prisa. La fiesta empieza en una hora y no estamos listos. Algunos amigos ayudan a decorar la casa mientras otros ponen la mesa.
3. Graciela prefiere no usar la computadora para preparar las invitaciones. Ella las está escribiendo. También le gusta dibujar cada invitación.
4. Me encanta cuando Adela me invita a su casa a comer. Su madre es una cocinera excelente. Ahora está preparando unas empanadas para la fiesta.

Answers to Integración Activity 1

1. b 2. d 3. c 4. a

¡Festejemos!

50-Minute Lesson Plans

Day 1

OBJECTIVE
Talking about plans

Core Instruction

Chapter Opener, pp. 176–177
- See Using the Photo and **Más vocabulario,** p. 176. 5 min.
- See Chapter Objectives, p. 176. 5 min.

Vocabulario en acción 1, pp. 178–183
- See Teaching **Vocabulario,** p. 178. 30 min.
- Have students do Activity 1, p. 180. 10 min.

Optional Resources
- Common Error Alert, p. 178
- **También se puede decir,** p. 179
- Language Note, p. 179
- Advanced Learners, p. 179 ▲
- Special Learning Needs, p. 179 ●

HOMEWORK SUGGESTIONS
Cuaderno de vocabulario y gramática, pp. 53–55
Internet Activities

Day 2

OBJECTIVE
Talking about plans

Core Instruction

Vocabulario en acción 1, pp. 178–183
- Show **ExpresaVisión,** Ch. 9. 5 min.
- Review **Vocabulario 1** and **¡Exprésate!,** pp. 178–179 15 min.
- Have students do Activities 2–4, p. 180–181. 30 min.

Optional Resources
- TPR, p. 179
- **Más práctica,** p. 180
- Extension, p. 180
- Communities, p. 180
- Fold-n-Learn, p. 180
- **Más práctica,** p. 181

HOMEWORK SUGGESTIONS
Cuaderno de vocabulario y gramática, pp. 53–55
Internet Activities

Day 3

OBJECTIVE
Talking about plans; talking about past holidays

Core Instruction

Vocabulario en acción 1, pp. 178–183
- Have students do Activity 5, p. 181. 20 min.
- See Teaching **¡Exprésate!,** p. 136. 15 min.
- Have students do Activities 6–7, p. 182. 15 min.

Optional Resources
- Slower Pace Learners, p. 181 ◆
- Multiple Intelligences, p. 181
- **Comunicación,** p. 181
- Teacher to Teacher, p. 182

HOMEWORK SUGGESTIONS
Cuaderno de vocabulario y gramática, pp. 53–55
Internet Activities

Day 4

OBJECTIVE
Talking about past holidays

Core Instruction

Vocabulario en acción 1, pp. 178–183
- Have students do Bell Work 9.2, p. 184. 5 min.
- Review **¡Exprésate!,** p. 182. 5 min.
- Present **Nota cultural,** p. 183. 10 min.
- Play Audio CD 9, Tr. 1 for Activity 8, p. 183. 10 min.
- Have students do Activities 9–10, p. 183. 20 min.

Optional Resources
- Practices and Perspectives, p. 183
- **Comunicación,** p. 183
- Advanced Learners, p. 183 ▲
- Multiple Intelligences, p. 183

HOMEWORK SUGGESTIONS
Study for **Prueba: Vocabulario 1.**

Day 5

OBJECTIVE
Vocabulary review and assessment

Core Instruction

Vocabulario en acción 1, pp. 178–183
- Review **Vocabulario en acción 1,** pp. 178–183. 30 min.
- Give **Prueba: Vocabulario 1.** 20 min.

Optional Resources
- Test Generator

HOMEWORK SUGGESTIONS
Preview **Gramática en acción 1,** pp. 184–189.

Day 6

OBJECTIVE
*Preterite of **-er** and **-ir** verbs*

Core Instruction

Gramática en acción 1, pp. 184–189
- See Teaching **Gramática,** p. 184. 25 min.
- Have students do Activities 11–13, pp. 184–185. 25 min.

Optional Resources
- **Comunicación,** p. 185

HOMEWORK SUGGESTIONS
Cuaderno de vocabulario y gramática, pp. 56–58
Cuaderno de actividades, pp. 51–54

Day 7

OBJECTIVE
*Preterite of **-er** and **-ir** verbs*

Core Instruction

Gramática en acción 1, pp. 184–189
- Have students do Bell Work 9.3, p. 186. 5 min.
- Show **GramaVisión,** Ch. 9. 10 min.
- Review preterite of **-er** and **-ir** verbs, p. 184. 15 min.
- Have students do Activities 14–15, p. 139. 20 min.

Optional Resources
- Slower Pace Learners, p. 185 ◆
- Multiple Intelligences, p. 185

HOMEWORK SUGGESTIONS
Cuaderno de vocabulario y gramática, pp. 56–58
Cuaderno de actividades, pp. 51–54

Day 8

OBJECTIVE
Review of the preterite

Core Instruction

Gramática en acción 1, pp. 184–189
- Show **GramaVisión,** Ch. 9. 5 min.
- See Teaching **Gramática,** p. 186. 20 min.
- Play Audio CD 9, Tr. 2 for Activity 16, p. 186. 10 min.
- Have students do Activities 17–18, pp. 186–187. 15 min.

Optional Resources
- Advanced Learners, p. 187 ▲

HOMEWORK SUGGESTIONS
Cuaderno de vocabulario y gramática, pp. 56–58
Cuaderno de actividades, pp. 51–54

To edit and create your own lesson plans, see the **One-Stop** Planner® CD-ROM

KEY
- ▲ Advanced Learners
- ◆ Slower Pace Learners
- ● Special Learning Needs
- ■ Heritage Speakers

Day 9

OBJECTIVE
Review of the preterite; ***pensar que*** *and* ***pensar*** *with infinitives*

Core Instruction
Gramática en acción 1, pp. 184–189
- Review the preterite, p. 186. 10 min.
- Have students do Activities 19–20, p. 187. 15 min.
- Show **GramaVisión,** Ch. 9. 10 min.
- See Teaching **Gramática,** p. 188. 15 min.

Optional Resources
- Special Learning Needs, p. 187 ●
- **Comunicación,** p. 187
- Common Error Alert, p. 188

HOMEWORK SUGGESTIONS
Cuaderno de vocabulario y gramática, pp. 56–58
Cuaderno de actividades, pp. 51–54
Internet Activities
Interactive Tutor, Ch. 9

Day 10

OBJECTIVE
Pensar que *and* ***pensar*** *with infinitives*

Core Instruction
Gramática en acción 1, pp. 184–189
- Have students do Bell Work 9.5, p. 192. 5 min.
- Review **pensar que** and **pensar** with infinitives, p. 188. 10 min.
- Present **Nota cultural,** p. 188. 10 min.
- Have students do Activities 21–23, p. 188–189. 25 min.

Optional Resources
- Slower Pace Learners, p. 189 ◆
- Multiple Intelligences, p. 189
- **Comunicación,** p. 189

HOMEWORK SUGGESTIONS
Study for **Prueba: Gramática 1.**
Interactive Tutor, Ch. 9

Day 11

OBJECTIVE
Grammar review and assessment

Core Instruction
Gramática en acción 1, pp. 184–189
- Review **Gramática en acción 1,** pp. 184–189. 30 min.
- Give **Prueba: Gramática 1.** 20 min.

Optional Resources
- Test Generator
- **Prueba: Aplicación 1**

HOMEWORK SUGGESTIONS
Read **Comparaciones,** pp. 190–191.

Day 12

OBJECTIVE
Interviews from around the Spanish-speaking world

Core Instruction
Cultura, pp. 190–191
- See Map Activities, p. 190. 10 min.
- See Teaching **Cultura,** p. 190. 35 min.
- Present and assign **Comunidad,** p. 191. 5 min.

Optional Resources
- Heritage Speakers, p. 191 ■
- Comparing and Contrasting, p. 191
- Language to Language, p. 191
- Slower Pace Learners, p. 191 ◆

HOMEWORK SUGGESTIONS
Cuaderno de actividades, p. 55
Multiple Intelligences, p. 191
Family Link, p. 191

Day 13

OBJECTIVE
Talking about preparing for a party

Core Instruction
Vocabulario en acción 2, pp. 192–197
- Show **ExpresaVisión,** Ch. 9. 5 min.
- See Teaching **Vocabulario 2,** p. 192. 35 min.
- Present **Nota cultural,** p. 194. 10 min.

Optional Resources
- TPR, p. 193
- Language Note, p. 193
- **También se puede decir,** p. 193
- Multiple Intelligences, p. 193
- Advanced Learners, p. 193 ▲

HOMEWORK SUGGESTIONS
Cuaderno de gramática, pp. 59–61
Internet Activities

Day 14

OBJECTIVE
Talking about preparing for a party

Core Instruction
Vocabulario en acción 2, pp. 192–197
- Review **Vocabulario 2** and **¡Exprésate!,** pp. 192–193. 20 min.
- Have students do Activities 24–27, pp. 194–195. 30 min.

Optional Resources
- Multicultural Link, p. 194
- Heritage Speakers, p. 194 ■
- Game, p. 194
- Products and perspectives, p. 195
- Practices and perspectives, p. 195
- **Comunicación,** p. 195
- Multiple Intelligences, p. 195

HOMEWORK SUGGESTIONS
Cuaderno de gramática, pp. 59–61
Internet Activities

Day 15

OBJECTIVE
Talking about preparing for a party; greeting, introducing others, and saying goodbye

Core Instruction
Vocabulario en acción 2, pp. 192–197
- Have students do Bell Work 9.6, p. 198. 5 min.
- Have students do Activity 28, p. 195. 20 min.
- See Teaching **¡Exprésate!,** p. 196. 15 min.
- Play Audio CD 9, Tr. 6 for Activity 29, p. 196. 10 min.

Optional Resources
- Advanced Learners, p. 195 ▲
- Special Learning Needs, p. 197 ●
- Advanced Learners, p. 197 ▲

HOMEWORK SUGGESTIONS
Cuaderno de gramática, pp. 59–61
Internet Activities

Day 16

OBJECTIVE
Greeting, introducing others, and saying goodbye

Core Instruction
Vocabulario en acción 2, pp. 192–197
- Review **¡Exprésate!,** p. 196. 10 min.
- Have students do Activities 30–34, pp. 196–197. 40 min.

Optional Resources
- **Más práctica,** p. 197
- Extension, p. 197
- **Comunicación,** p. 197

HOMEWORK SUGGESTIONS
Study for **Prueba: Vocabulario 2.**

50-Minute Lesson Plans, continued

Day 17

OBJECTIVE
Vocabulary review and assessment

Core Instruction
Vocabulario en acción 2, pp. 192–197
- Review **Vocabulario en acción 2,** pp. 192–197. 30 min.
- Give **Prueba: Vocabulario 2.** 20 min.

Optional Resources
- Test Generator

HOMEWORK SUGGESTIONS
Preview **Gramática en acción 2,** pp. 198–203.

Day 18

OBJECTIVE
Direct object pronouns

Core Instruction
Gramática en acción 2, pp. 198–203
- Show **GramaVisión,** Ch. 9. 5 min.
- See Teaching **Gramática,** p. 198. 25 min.
- Have students do Activities 35–37, pp. 198–199. 20 min.

Optional Resources
- Career Path, p. 199
- Special Learning Needs, p. 199 ●

HOMEWORK SUGGESTIONS
Cuaderno de vocabulario y gramática, pp. 62–64
Cuaderno de actividades, pp. 56–59
Interactive Tutor, Ch. 9

Day 19

OBJECTIVE
*Direct object pronouns; **conocer** and personal **a***

Core Instruction
Gramática en acción 2, pp. 198–203
- Have students do Bell Work 9.7, p. 200. 5 min.
- Review direct object pronouns, p. 198. 15 min.
- Have students do Activity 38, p. 199. 10 min.
- Present **Nota cultural,** p. 199. 5 min.
- See Teaching **Gramática,** p. 200. 15 min.

Optional Resources
- **Comunicación,** p. 199
- Slower Pace Learners, p. 199 ◆
- Multiple Intelligences, p. 201

HOMEWORK SUGGESTIONS
Cuaderno de vocabulario y gramática, pp. 62–64
Cuaderno de actividades, pp. 56–59
Internet Activities

Day 20

OBJECTIVE
Conocer** and personal **a

Core Instruction
Gramática en acción 2, pp. 198–203
- Have students do Bell Work 9.8, p. 202. 5 min.
- Present **Nota cultural,** p. 200. 5 min.
- Review **conocer** and personal **a**, p. 200. 10 min.
- Have students do Activities 39–42, pp. 200–201. 30 min.

Optional Resources
- **GramaVisión,** Ch. 9
- **Comunicación,** p. 201
- Advanced Learners, p. 201 ▲

HOMEWORK SUGGESTIONS
Cuaderno de vocabulario y gramática, pp. 62–64
Cuaderno de actividades, pp. 56–59
Interactive Tutor, Ch. 9

Day 21

OBJECTIVE
Present progressive

Core Instruction
Gramática en acción 2, pp. 198–203
- Show **GramaVisión,** Ch. 9. 5 min.
- See Teaching **Gramática,** p. 202. 35 min.
- Play Audio CD 9, Tr. 7 for Activity 43, p. 202. 10 min.

Optional Resources
- **Comunicación,** p. 203

HOMEWORK SUGGESTIONS
Cuaderno de vocabulario y gramática, pp. 62–64
Cuaderno de actividades, pp. 56–59
Internet Activities
Interactive Tutor, Ch. 9

Day 22

OBJECTIVE
Present progressive; grammar review

Core Instruction
Gramática en acción 2, pp. 198–203
- Have students do Activities 44–46, p. 203. 25 min.
- Review **Gramática en acción 2,** pp. 198–203. 25 min.

Optional Resources
- Advanced Learners, p. 203 ▲
- Special Learning Needs, p. 203 ●

HOMEWORK SUGGESTIONS
Study for **Prueba: Gramática 2.**

Day 23

OBJECTIVE
Grammar assessment; Arbor day in Venezuela

Core Instruction
Gramática en acción 2, pp. 198–203
- Review **Gramática en acción 2,** pp. 198–203. 10 min.
- Give **Prueba: Gramática 2.** 20 min.

Conexiones culturales, pp. 204–205
- See Teaching **Conexiones culturales,** #1–2, p. 204. 20 min.

Optional Resources
- **Prueba: Aplicación 2**
- Test Generator

HOMEWORK SUGGESTIONS
Multiple Intelligences, p. 205

Day 24

OBJECTIVE
Nature poem; developing listening and reading skills

Core Instruction
Conexiones culturales, pp. 204–205
- See Teaching **Conexiones culturales,** #3–6, p. 204. 25 min.

Novela en video, pp. 206–209
- See Teaching **Novela en video,** #1–2, p. 206. 20 min.
- See Thinking Critically, p. 207. 5 min.

Optional Resources
- Music Link, p. 205
- Advanced Learners, p. 205 ▲
- Visual Learners, p. 206
- Gestures, p. 206
- Comparing and Contrasting, p. 207

HOMEWORK SUGGESTIONS
Novela, pp. 206–209
Culminating Project, p. 208

To edit and create your own lesson plans, see the

One-Stop Planner® CD-ROM

KEY

- ▲ Advanced Learners
- ◆ Slower Pace Learners
- ● Special Learning Needs
- ■ Heritage Speakers

Day 25

OBJECTIVE
Developing listening and reading skills

Core Instruction

Novela en video, pp. 206–209
- Play **VideoNovela,** Ch. 9. 5 min.
- See Teaching **Novela en video,** #3, p. 206. 15 min.

Leamos y escribamos, pp. 210–211
- See Teaching **Leamos,** p. 210. 30 min.

Optional Resources

- Thinking Critically, p. 208
- **Más práctica,** p. 209
- Slower Pace Learners, p. 209 ◆
- Multiple Intelligences, p. 209
- Applying the Strategies, p. 210
- Slower Pace Learners, p. 211 ◆
- Special Learning Needs, p. 211 ●

HOMEWORK SUGGESTIONS
Cuaderno de actividades, p. 60

Day 26

OBJECTIVE
Developing writing skills

Core Instruction

Leamos y escribamos, pp. 210–211
- See Teaching **Escribamos,** p. 210. 50 min.

Optional Resources

- Process Writing, p. 211

HOMEWORK SUGGESTIONS
Review Chapter 9.

Day 27

OBJECTIVE
Chapter review

Core Instruction

Repaso, pp. 212–215
- Have students do Activities 1–5, pp. 212–213. 50 min.

Optional Resources

- Fold-n-Learn, p. 212
- Reteaching, p. 212

HOMEWORK SUGGESTIONS
Internet Activities
Interactive Tutor, Ch. 9

Day 28

OBJECTIVE
Chapter review

Core Instruction

Repaso, pp. 212–215
- Play Audio CD 8, Tr. 10 for Activity 6, p. 213. 10 min.
- Have students do Activity 7, p. 213. 10 min.
- Play Game, p. 215. 15 min.
- Play Audio CD 9, Tr. 11–13 for **Letra y sonido,** p. 214. 15 min.

Optional Resources

- Teacher to Teacher, p. 214

HOMEWORK SUGGESTIONS
Study for Chapter Test.
Interactive Tutor, Ch. 9

Day 29

OBJECTIVE
Chapter review

Core Instruction

Integración, pp. 216–217
- Play Audio CD 9, Tr. 14 for Activity 1, p. 216. 10 min.
- Have students do Activities 2–4, pp. 216–217. 40 min.

Optional Resources

- Culture Project, p. 216
- Fine Art Connection, p. 217

HOMEWORK SUGGESTIONS
Study for Chapter Test.
Cuaderno de actividades, pp. 51–62

Day 30

OBJECTIVE
Assessment

Core Instruction

Chapter Test 50 min.

Optional Resources

Assessment Program:
- **Prueba: Lectura**
- **Prueba: Escritura**
- Alternative Assessment
- Test Generator

HOMEWORK SUGGESTIONS
Cuaderno de actividades, pp. 84–85

¡Festejemos!

90-Minute Lesson Plans

Block 1

OBJECTIVE
Talking about plans

Core Instruction

Chapter Opener, pp. 176–177
- See Using the Photo and **Más vocabulario,** p. 176. 5 min.
- See Chapter Objectives, p. 176. 5 min.

Vocabulario en acción 1, pp. 178–183
- Show **ExpresaVisión,** Ch. 9. 5 min.
- See Teaching **Vocabulario,** p. 178. 30 min.
- Have students do Activities 1–5, p. 180–181. 45 min.

Optional Resources
- Common Error Alert, p. 178
- **También se puede decir,** p. 179
- Language Note, p. 179
- Advanced Learners, p. 179 ▲
- Special Learning Needs, p. 179 ●
- **Más práctica,** p. 180
- Extension, p. 180
- Communities, p. 180
- Fold-n-Learn, p. 180
- **Más práctica,** p. 181
- Slower Pace Learners, p. 181 ◆
- Multiple Intelligences, p. 181
- **Comunicación,** p. 181

HOMEWORK SUGGESTIONS
Cuaderno de vocabulario y gramática, pp. 53–55
Internet Activities

Block 2

OBJECTIVE
Talking about plans; talking about past holidays

Core Instruction

Vocabulario en acción 1, pp. 178–183
- Review **Vocabulario 1** and **¡Exprésate!,** pp. 178–179. 20 min.
- See Teaching **¡Exprésate!,** p. 136. 15 min.
- Have students do Activities 6–7, p. 182. 15 min.
- Present **Nota cultural,** p. 183. 10 min.
- Play Audio CD 9, Tr. 1 for Activity 8, p. 183. 10 min.
- Have students do Activities 9–10, p. 183. 20 min.

Optional Resources
- TPR, p. 179
- Teacher to Teacher, p. 182
- Practices and Perspectives, p. 183
- **Comunicación,** p. 183
- Advanced Learners, p. 183 ▲
- Multiple Intelligences, p. 183

HOMEWORK SUGGESTIONS
Study for **Prueba: Vocabulario 1.**
Cuaderno de vocabulario y gramática, pp. 53–55
Internet Activities

Block 3

OBJECTIVE
*Vocabulary review and assessment; preterite of **-er** and **-ir** verbs*

Core Instruction

Vocabulario en acción 1, pp. 178–183
- Review **Vocabulario en acción 1,** pp. 178–183. 20 min.
- Give **Prueba: Vocabulario 1.** 20 min.

Gramática en acción 1, pp. 184–189
- See Teaching **Gramática,** p. 184. 25 min.
- Have students do Activities 11–13, pp. 184–185. 25 min.

Optional Resources
- Test Generator
- **Comunicación,** p. 185

HOMEWORK SUGGESTIONS
Cuaderno de vocabulario y gramática, pp. 56–58
Cuaderno de actividades, pp. 51–54
Internet Activities
Interactive Tutor, Ch. 9

Block 4

OBJECTIVE
*Preterite of **-er** and **-ir** verbs; Review of the preterite*

Core Instruction

Gramática en acción 1, pp. 184–189
- Have students do Bell Work 9.3, p. 186. 5 min.
- Show **GramaVisión,** Ch. 9. 5 min.
- Review **preterite** of **-er** and **-ir** verbs, p. 184. 15 min.
- Have students do Activities 14–15, p. 139. 20 min.
- See Teaching **Gramática,** p. 186. 20 min.
- Play Audio CD 9, Tr. 2 for Activity 16, p. 186. 10 min.
- Have students do Activities 17–18, pp. 186–187. 15 min.

Optional Resources
- Slower Pace Learners, p. 185 ◆
- Multiple Intelligences, p. 185
- Advanced Learners, p. 187 ▲

HOMEWORK SUGGESTIONS
Cuaderno de vocabulario y gramática, pp. 56–58
Cuaderno de actividades, pp. 51–54
Internet Activities
Interactive Tutor, Ch. 9

To edit and create your own lesson plans, see the One-Stop Planner® CD-ROM

KEY
- ▲ Advanced Learners
- ◆ Slower Pace Learners
- ● Special Learning Needs
- ■ Heritage Speakers

Block 5

OBJECTIVE
Review of the preterite; ***pensar que*** *and* ***pensar*** *with infinitives*

Core Instruction
Gramática en acción 1, pp. 184–189
- Have students do Bell Work 9.4, p. 188. 5 min.
- Review the preterite, p. 186. 10 min.
- Have students do Activities 19–20, p. 187. 15 min.
- Show **GramaVisión,** Ch. 9. 10 min.
- See Teaching **Gramática,** p. 188. 15 min.
- Present **Nota cultural,** p. 188. 10 min.
- Have students do Activities 21–23, p. 188–189. 25 min.

Optional Resources
- Special Learning Needs, p. 187 ●
- **Comunicación,** p. 187
- Common Error Alert, p. 188
- Slower Pace Learners, p. 189 ◆
- Multiple Intelligences, p. 189
- **Comunicación,** p. 189

HOMEWORK SUGGESTIONS
Study for **Prueba: Gramática 1.**
Cuaderno de vocabulario y gramática, pp. 56–58
Cuaderno de actividades, pp. 51–54
Internet Activities
Interactive Tutor, Ch. 9

Block 6

OBJECTIVE
Grammar review and assessment; interviews from around the Spanish-speaking world

Core Instruction
Gramática en acción 1, pp. 184–189
- Review **Gramática en acción 1,** pp. 184–189. 10 min.
- Give **Prueba: Gramática 1.** 20 min.
- See Teaching **Cultura,** p. 190. 35 min.
- Present and assign **Comunidad,** p. 191. 5 min.

Vocabulario en acción 2, pp. 192–197
- See Teaching **Vocabulario 2,** #1, p. 192. 20 min.

Optional Resources
- Test Generator
- **Prueba: Aplicación 1**
- Map Activities, p. 190
- Heritage Speakers, p. 191 ■
- Comparing and Contrasting, p. 191
- Language to Language, p. 191
- Slower Pace Learners, p. 191 ◆
- Language Note, p. 193
- **También se puede decir,** p. 193
- Multiple Intelligences, p. 193

HOMEWORK SUGGESTIONS
Multiple Intelligences, p. 191
Family Link, p. 191
Cuaderno de actividades, p. 55

Block 7

OBJECTIVE
Talking about preparing for a party; greeting, introducing others, and saying goodbye

Core Instruction
Vocabulario en acción 2, pp. 192–197
- Review **Vocabulario 2,** pp. 192–193. 15 min.
- See Teaching **Vocabulario 2,** #2–3, p. 192. 10 min.
- Present **Nota cultural,** p. 194. 5 min.
- Have students do Activities 24–28, pp. 194–195. 45 min.
- See Teaching **¡Exprésate!,** p. 196. 15 min.

Optional Resources
- **ExpresaVisión,** Ch. 9
- TPR, p. 193
- Advanced Learners, p. 193 ▲
- Multicultural Link, p. 194
- Heritage Speakers, p. 194 ■
- Game, p. 194
- Products and perspectives, p. 195
- Practices and perspectives, p. 195
- **Comunicación,** p. 195
- Advanced Learners, p. 195 ▲
- Multiple Intelligences, p. 195

HOMEWORK SUGGESTIONS
Cuaderno de gramática, pp. 59–61
Internet Activities

Block 8

OBJECTIVE
Greeting, introducing others, and saying goodbye; direct object pronouns

Core Instruction
Vocabulario en acción 2, pp. 192–197
- Have students do Bell Work 9.6, p. 198. 5 min.
- Review **¡Exprésate!,** p. 196. 10 min.
- Play Audio CD 9, Tr. 6 for Activity 29, p. 196. 10 min.
- Have students do Activities 30–34, pp. 196–197. 40 min.
- See Teaching **Gramática,** p. 198. 25 min.

Optional Resources
- **Más práctica,** p. 197
- Extension, p. 197
- **Comunicación,** p. 197
- Special Learning Needs, p. 197 ●
- Advanced Learners, p. 197 ▲

HOMEWORK SUGGESTIONS
Study for **Prueba: Vocabulario 2.**
Cuaderno de vocabulario y gramática, pp. 62–64
Cuaderno de actividades, pp. 56–59
Internet Activities
Interactive Tutor, Ch. 9

90-Minute Lesson Plans, continued

Block 9

OBJECTIVE
Vocabulary review and assessment; direct object pronouns

Core Instruction
Vocabulario en acción 2, pp. 192–197
- Review **Vocabulario en acción 2,** pp. 192–197. 15 min.
- Give **Prueba: Vocabulario 2.** 20 min.

Gramática en acción 2, pp. 198–203
- Show **GramaVisión,** Ch. 9. 5 min.
- Review direct object pronouns, p. 198. 15 min.
- Have students do Activities 35–38, pp. 198–199. 30 min.
- Present **Nota cultural,** p. 199. 5 min.

Optional Resources
- Test Generator
- Career Path, p. 199
- **Comunicación,** p. 199
- Special Learning Needs, p. 199 ●
- Slower Pace Learners, p. 199 ◆

HOMEWORK SUGGESTIONS
Cuaderno de vocabulario y gramática, pp. 62–64
Cuaderno de actividades, pp. 56–59
Internet Activities
Interactive Tutor, Ch. 9

Block 10

OBJECTIVE
Conocer *and personal* ***a;*** *present progressive*

Core Instruction
Gramática en acción 2, pp. 198–203
- See Teaching **Gramática,** p. 200. 15 min.
- Present **Nota cultural,** p. 200. 5 min.
- Have students do Activities 39–42, pp. 200–201. 25 min.
- See Teaching **Gramática,** p. 202. 35 min.
- Play Audio CD 9, Tr. 7 for Activity 43, p. 202. 10 min.

Optional Resources
- **GramaVisión,** Ch. 9
- **Comunicación,** p. 201
- Multiple Intelligences, p. 201
- Advanced Learners, p. 201 ▲

HOMEWORK SUGGESTIONS
Study for **Prueba: Gramática 2.**
Cuaderno de vocabulario y gramática, pp. 62–64
Cuaderno de actividades, pp. 56–59
Internet Activities
Interactive Tutor, Ch. 9

Block 11

OBJECTIVE
Grammar review and assessment; Arbor Day in Venezuela

Core Instruction
Gramática en acción 2, pp. 198–203
- Review the present progressive, p. 202. 10 min.
- Have students do Activities 44–46, p. 203. 20 min.
- Review **Gramática en acción 2,** pp. 198–203. 20 min.
- Give **Prueba: Gramática 2.** 20 min.

Conexiones culturales, pp. 204–205
- See Teaching **Conexiones culturales,** #1–2, p. 204. 20 min.

Optional Resources
- **Comunicación,** p. 203
- Advanced Learners, p. 203 ▲
- Special Learning Needs, p. 203 ●
- **Prueba: Aplicación 2**
- Test Generator

HOMEWORK SUGGESTIONS
Multiple Intelligences, p. 205
Internet Activities

To edit and create your own lesson plans, see the **One-Stop** Planner® CD-ROM

KEY

▲ Advanced Learners
◆ Slower Pace Learners
● Special Learning Needs
■ Heritage Speakers

Block 12

OBJECTIVE
Nature poem; developing listening and reading skills

Core Instruction

Conexiones culturales, pp. 204–205
- See Teaching **Conexiones culturales,** #3–6, p. 204. 25 min.

Novela en video, pp. 206–209
- See Teaching **Novela en video,** p. 206. 35 min.

Leamos y escribamos, pp. 210–211
- See Teaching **Leamos,** p. 210. 30 min.

Optional Resources

- Music Link, p. 205
- Advanced Learners, p. 205
- Visual Learners, p. 206
- Gestures, p. 206
- Thinking Critically, p. 207
- Comparing and Contrasting, p. 207
- Thinking Critically, p. 208
- **Más práctica,** p. 209
- Slower Pace Learners, p. 209
- Multiple Intelligences, p. 209
- Applying the Strategies, p. 210
- Slower Pace Learners, p. 211 ◆
- Special Learning Needs, p. 211 ●

HOMEWORK SUGGESTIONS
Culminating Project, p. 208
Activity B, p. 211
Cuaderno de actividades, p. 60

Block 13

OBJECTIVE
Developing writing skills; chapter review

Core Instruction

Leamos y escribamos, pp. 210–211
- See Teaching **Escribamos,** p. 210. 40 min.

Repaso, pp. 212–215
- Have students do Activities 1–5, pp. 212–213. 25 min.
- Play Audio CD 8, Tr. 13 for Activity 6, p. 213. 10 min.
- Have students do Activity 7, p. 213. 5 min.
- Play Audio CD 9, Tr. 11–13 for **Letra y sonido,** p. 214. 10 min.

Optional Resources

- Process Writing, p. 211
- Fold-n-Learn, p. 212
- Reteaching, p. 212
- Teacher to Teacher, p. 214
- Game, p. 215

HOMEWORK SUGGESTIONS
Study for Chapter Test.
Interactive Tutor, Ch. 9

Block 14

OBJECTIVE
Assessment

Core Instruction

Chapter Test 50 min.

Integración, pp. 216–217
- Play Audio CD 9, Tr. 14 for Activity 1, p. 216. 10 min.
- Have students do Activities 2–4, pp. 216–217. 30 min.

Optional Resources

Assessment Program:
- **Prueba: Lectura**
- **Prueba: Escritura**
- Alternative Assessment
- Test Generator
- Culture Project, p. 216
- Fine Art Connection, p. 217

HOMEWORK SUGGESTIONS
Cuaderno de actividades, pp. 51–62, 84–85

Chapter Opener

Meeting the National Standards

Communication
Comunicación, pp. 181, 183, 185, 187, 189, 195, 197, 199, 201, 203
Situación, p. 217

Cultures
Nota cultural, pp. 183, 188, 194, 199
Comparaciones, pp. 190–191
Practices and Perspectives, p. 174

Connections
Thinking Critically, p. 175
Interdisciplinary Links, pp. 174–175
Fine Art, p. 217

Comparisons
Comparaciones, pp. 190–191
Comparing and Contrasting, pp. 173, 176, 191
Language Note, p. 179

Communities
Multicultural Link, p. 190
Comunidad, p. 191
Food, p. 180
Career Path, p. 199

Using the Photo

Tell students that the **Malecón** in Santo Domingo is a gathering place where parades are held and people stroll along the beach front. Point out the obelisk in the photo, then ask students what national monument in the United States is an obelisk.

Más vocabulario

You may want to use some of these words to discuss the photo.

la bandera *flag*
el ejército *army*
el soldado *soldier*
marchar *to march*
el malecón *sea wall; boardwalk*
el obelisco *obelisk*

Capítulo 9

¡Festejemos!

Objetivos

In Part 1 you will learn to:
- ask about plans
- ask about past holidays
- use the preterite of **-er** and **-ir** verbs
- use the preterite of **-ar** verbs (review)
- say what you plan to do using **pensar** with infinitives

In Part 2 you will learn to:
- ask about preparing for a party
- greet and introduce others
- say goodbye
- use direct object pronouns
- use **conocer** and personal **a**
- form and use the present progressive tense

¿Qué ves en la foto?

- ¿Quiénes son estas personas?
- En la foto, ¿qué llevan los muchachos?
- ¿Hace buen tiempo o mal tiempo?

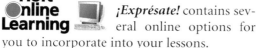

Holt Online Learning *¡Exprésate!* contains several online options for you to incorporate into your lessons.

***¡Exprésate! Student Edition* online at my.hrw.com**
At this site, you will find the online version of *¡Exprésate!* All concepts presented in the textbook are presented and practiced in this online version of your textbook. This online version can be used as a supplement to, or as a replacement for your textbook.

Practice activities at go.hrw.com
These activities provide additional practice for major concepts presented in each chapter. Practice items include structured practice as well as research topics.

Teacher resources at www.hrw.com
This site provides additional information that teachers might find useful about the *¡Exprésate!* program.

Visit Holt Online

go.hrw.com

KEYWORD: EXP1B CH9

Online Edition

El Malecón, Santo Domingo

Chapter Opener

Learning Tips

You might share the following learning tips with students. When students know an English word and want to find its Spanish equivalent, have them look up the English word in an English-Spanish dictionary. Make sure they read *all* of the meanings, since most words can mean several different things. For example, one can cut down trees with a *saw* or talk about a movie one *saw*. To choose the right meaning, students should think about how they're going to use the Spanish word.

- **ExpresaVisión 1**
- **GramaVisión 1**
  Preterite of **-er** and **–ir** verbs; review of the preterite. **pensar que** and **pensar** with infinitives
- **VideoCultura**
- **ExpresaVisión 2**
- **GramaVisión 2**
  Direct object pronouns; **conocer** and personal **a;** present progressive
- **VideoNovela**
- **Variedades**

Pacing Tips

In this chapter, there is more vocabulary in **Vocabulario 2** than in **Vocabulario 1,** so you might spend more time on **Vocabulario 2.** For complete lesson plan suggestions, see pages 175G–175N.

Suggested pacing:	Traditional Schedule	Block Schedule
Vocabulario 1/Gramática 1	10 1/2 days	5 1/3 blocks
Cultura	1 day	1/2 block
Vocabulario 2/Gramática 2	11 1/4 days	5 1/3 blocks
Conexiones culturales	1 day	1/2 block
Novela	3/4 day	1/3 block
Leamos y escribamos	1 1/2 days	1/2 block
Repaso	2 days	1/2 block
Chapter Test	1 day	1/2 block
Integración	1day	1/2 block

Resources

Planning:

Lesson Planner, pp. 101–105, 256–261

 One-Stop Planner

Presentation:

TPR Storytelling Book, pp. 48–49

 Teaching Transparencies **Vocabulario** 9.1, 9.2

 Video Program
Videocassette 5
DVD Tutor, Disc 2
ExpresaVisión

Practice:

Cuaderno de vocabulario y gramática, pp. 53–55

Activities for Communication, pp. 33–34

Video Guide, pp. 84–86

Lab Book, pp. 27–28, 56

 Teaching Transparencies
Bell Work 9.1
Vocabulario y gramática answers, pp. 53–55

 Interactive Tutor, Disc 2

Bell Work

Use Bell Work 9.1 in the *Teaching Transparencies,* or write this activity on the board.

Write the name of the store in which you would most likely buy the following items.

1. **una revista de tiras cómicas**
2. **unos zapatos**
3. **unos aretes**
4. **una blusa de seda**
5. **una tarjeta**

Objetivos
Talking about plans, asking about past holidays

Vocabulario en acción 1

Video/DVD
ExpresaVisión

Los días festivos

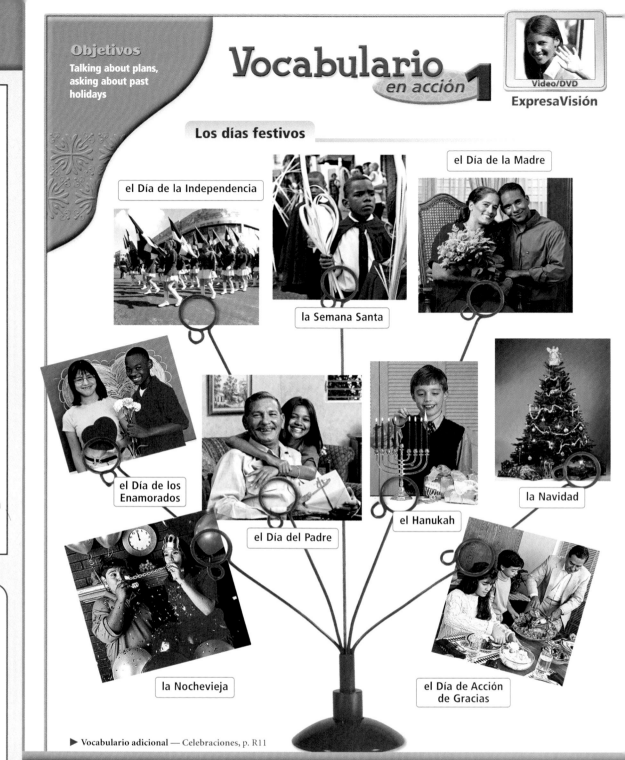

el Día de la Independencia

la Semana Santa

el Día de la Madre

el Día de los Enamorados

el Día del Padre

el Hanukah

la Navidad

la Nochevieja

el Día de Acción de Gracias

▶ **Vocabulario adicional** — Celebraciones, p. R11

Core Instruction

TEACHING VOCABULARIO

1. Introduce the vocabulary using transparencies **Vocabulario 9.1** and **9.2.** Model the pronunciation of each word as you point to the appropriate picture. **(15 min.)**
2. Ask students yes-no questions about the holidays, such as **¿Vas a ver fuegos artificiales en la Navidad?** Have students answer with **sí** or **no.** **(8 min.)**
3. Tell students your plans for two or three holidays using **Pienso...** Then ask students about their plans for various holidays, using **¿Qué vas a hacer...?** **(7 min.)**

ExpresaVisión

For a presentation of holidays and holiday preparations, use the video presenter from the *Video Program.* For interactive activities, see the *DVD Tutor.*

STANDARDS: 1.2

recibir regalos

ver fuegos artificiales

abrir regalos

mandar tarjetas

reunirse con (toda) la familia

¿Cómo lo festejaron?

Más vocabulario...

el Año Nuevo	*New Year's Day*
celebrar	*to celebrate*
decorar la casa	*to decorate the house*
invitar	*to invite*
ir...	
a misa	*to mass*
a la sinagoga	*to the synagogue*
al templo	*to the temple*

¡Exprésate!

To ask about plans	To respond
¿Qué vas a hacer el Día de la Independencia? *What are you going to do on Independence Day?*	**Pienso hacer una fiesta o tener un picnic.** *I plan to throw a party or have a picnic.*
¿Qué planes tienen para la Nochebuena? *What plans do you have for Christmas Eve?*	**Pensamos pasarla con mis abuelos, como siempre.** *We plan to spend it with my grandparents, as always.*

Interactive TUTOR

Online
Vocabulario y gramática, pp. 53–55

Vocabulario 1

TPR
Total Physical Response

Have the class respond to these commands after reviewing the expressions.

Levanta la mano si abres regalos en la Navidad o en el Hanukah.

Ponte de pie si te reúnes con la familia el Día de la Madre.

Párate en un pie si te gusta recibir tarjetas el Día de los Enamorados.

Levanta la mano si te gusta ver fuegos artificiales el Día de la Independencia.

Indica con los dedos cuántas tarjetas mandas en la Navidad.

To check comprehension, have students bring in items that are associated with each holiday.

Junta las cosas que se usan el Día de la Independencia.

Busca las cosas que necesitas para decorar la casa para la Navidad.

También se puede decir...

Students may hear **pascuas** used for Christmas. This can be confusing, as Easter is also referred to as **Pascua**. In Venezuela, Christmas cards may say **Felices pascuas** or **Feliz Navidad.** It is also common to hear **las Navidades,** referring to the Christmas season.

Differentiated Instruction

ADVANCED LEARNERS

Play a game with the class in which you describe what you do with your family during one of the holidays. Have students guess which holiday you are describing. The student that correctly guesses then chooses a holiday and describes what he or she does. Continue until all the students have had a turn describing their family traditions for at least one holiday.

SPECIAL LEARNING NEEDS

Students with Learning Disabilities These students might have trouble deciphering what these holidays mean simply by looking at the photos. Before presenting the new vocabulary, you might have students make a list of their favorite holidays during the year to activate their background knowledge on the subject. Also, in addition to using the photos, you might bring in props associated with each holiday in order to make the meaning clearer.

Connections

Language Note

Tell students that it can be useful to analyze the root of a word. **Festejar** derives from **fiesta** and **enamorado** from **amor.** This exercise also provides clues from similarities to English words. **Navidad** is an abbreviation of **natividad.** Ask students what English word is similar. *(nativity)*

STANDARDS: 1.2, 3.1

1 Answers
1. la Navidad
2. el Día de la Independencia
3. el Día de los Enamorados
4. el Día de la Madre
5. el Hanukah
6. la Nochebuena
7. el Día de Acción de Gracias
8. el Día del Padre
9. el Día de la Independencia

Más práctica

2 Have students work with a partner and tell each other what they give or make for their parents or other relatives on Mother's Day, Father's Day, or Christmas. Then have them tell each other what they receive from parents or relatives on their birthdays and on Christmas.

Extension

2 Have students play the role of Lili and write an answer to Jorge's letter. Ask them to include advice about what he can give each person, and also what they are giving their own parents for birthdays and parents' days.

Communities

Food

Tamales are a popular food throughout Mexico, Central America, and parts of the United States. Generally served on festive occasions, they may differ from place to place, and may be spicy or sweet. They are made with cornmeal dough spread on cornhusks or leaves, stuffed with fillings, and steamed. In Yucatán and Central America, they are made with plantain leaves. If you have a Spanish Club at your school, you might research to find different recipes, and then have a tamale taste-testing dinner to try out the different kinds of tamales.

Un desfile, Santo Domingo

1 Días festivos

Leamos/Hablemos Lee las siguientes oraciones y decide qué día festivo le corresponde a cada una.

1. Papá Noel trae muchos regalos.
2. Decoramos con los colores azul, blanco y rojo.
3. Muchas personas salen para una cena romántica.
4. Compramos algo especial para nuestra madre.
5. Muchas personas van a la sinagoga.
6. La gente va a misa a la medianoche.
7. Nos reunimos con la familia en noviembre para una comida especial.
8. Hacemos algo para nuestro papá.
9. La gente sale a ver fuegos artificiales.

2 ¿Qué hago?

Leamos Jorge le escribe un correo electrónico a Lili sobre sus planes para la próxima semana. Lee su correo electrónico y las oraciones a continuación. Di si cada oración es cierta o falsa.

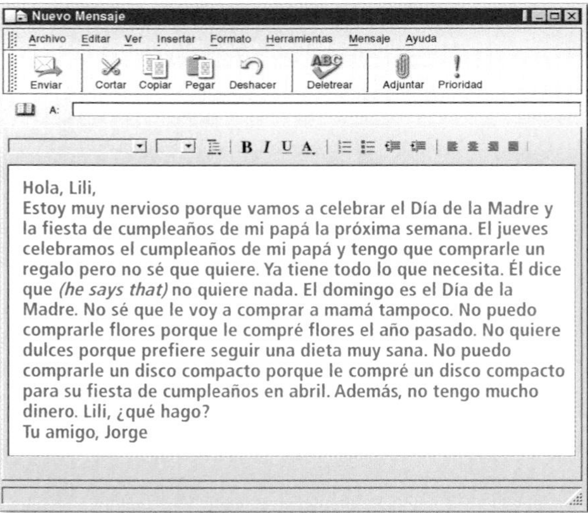

Hola, Lili,
Estoy muy nervioso porque vamos a celebrar el Día de la Madre y la fiesta de cumpleaños de mi papá la próxima semana. El jueves celebramos el cumpleaños de mi papá y tengo que comprarle un regalo pero no sé que quiere. Ya tiene todo lo que necesita. Él dice que *(he says that)* no quiere nada. El domingo es el Día de la Madre. No sé que le voy a comprar a mamá tampoco. No puedo comprarle flores porque le compré flores el año pasado. No quiere dulces porque prefiere seguir una dieta muy sana. No puedo comprarle un disco compacto porque le compré un disco compacto para su fiesta de cumpleaños en abril. Además, no tengo mucho dinero. Lili, ¿qué hago?
Tu amigo, Jorge

1. Jorge tiene todo listo para el cumpleaños de su papá y el Día de la Madre. falsa
2. El papá de Jorge dice que no quiere nada para su cumpleaños. cierta
3. Van a celebrar el cumpleaños del papá de Jorge el viernes. falsa
4. Jorge piensa comprarle flores a su mamá para el Día de la Madre. falsa
5. Jorge le compró un disco compacto a su mamá en abril. cierta

FOLD-N-LEARN

Tri-Fold

1. Have students fold a sheet of paper into thirds like a brochure. On the outside of the left side students write **¿Qué vas a hacer... ?** **2.** Students open the paper. On the left side, they draw nine illustrations to represent each of the holidays from **Vocabulario 1. 3.** In the middle section, they write the name of the holiday opposite the corresponding illustration.

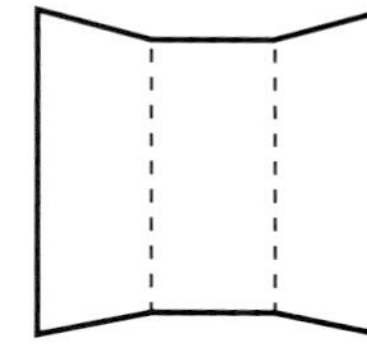

4. Students cover the middle section with the right side of the tri-fold. On the outside of the right side, students write **Pienso... 5.** On the inside of the right section, students write things that they might do to celebrate each of the holidays listed in the middle section. **6.** To study, students ask the question on the cover, completing it with a holiday prompted by an illustration and one of the things they listed in the right-hand section. They can lift the right side of the tri-fold to check their answers.

STANDARDS: 1.2, 5.1

3 Celebraciones

Escribamos Basándote en las fotos, describe cómo estas personas van a pasar los días festivos. Escribe por lo menos dos oraciones para cada foto.

MODELO **La familia celebra el Día de la Madre. Los hijos preparan comida especial para su madre.**

la familia

1. mis padres

2. mi familia y yo

3. mis hermanas

4. mis amigos

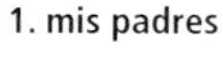

Comunicación

4 ¿Qué planes tienes para...?

Hablemos Work with three classmates to plan a party. Decide who you will invite, what kind of food you will have, and what music you will listen to. Also agree on a date, time, and place for the party. As you are talking about your plans, give your opinion using **me parece** or **(no) estoy de acuerdo.** Be prepared to present your plans to the class.

MODELO
—**¿Qué tal si invitamos a todos nuestros compañeros de clase?**
—**No estoy de acuerdo. Me parece mejor invitar a doce personas.**
—**Está bien, pero tenemos que invitar a...**

5 La invitación

Escribamos With a partner, write an invitation to a party. The invitation should say what is being celebrated, the date, time, and place of the party as well as anything your guests should bring. Exchange invitations with another pair of classmates and write a response. Say whether you can go to the party and what you will bring. If you can't go to the party, say why.

Vocabulario 1

3 Possible Answers

1. Mis padres celebran el Día de los Enamorados. Van a su restaurante favorito.
2. Mi familia y yo celebramos el Día de Acción de Gracias. Comemos en casa de mi abuelo.
3. Mis hermanas celebran la Navidad. Reciben regalos de mis padres y decoran la casa.
4. Mis amigos celebran la Nochevieja. Bailan en una fiesta grande.

Más práctica

3 Have students work in small groups to think of things that the people in the photos might be saying to each other. Ask them to write down at least one line for each person pictured. Then have volunteers play the roles of the people in the photos and have a short conversation.

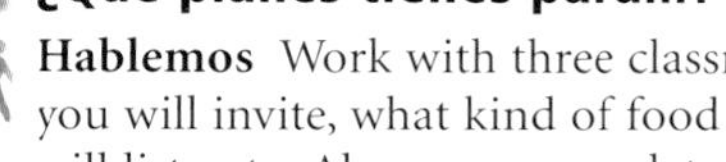

Comunicación

Pair Activity: Interpersonal

Ask students to work with a partner to talk about what their families do on certain holidays. Have them refer to the photos on page 178, and ask each other what they do on this holiday.

MODELO
—**¿Qué haces para celebrar la Semana Santa?**
—**Voy a la iglesia con mi familia y todos llevamos ropa nueva.**

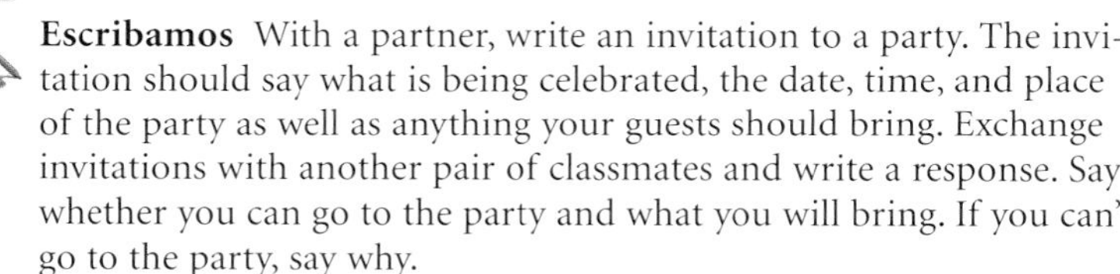

Differentiated Instruction

SLOWER PACE LEARNERS

Slower Pace Give students several minutes to work alone to make a list of things, events, or people associated with a specific holiday, without mentioning the name of the day. Then have several students read their lists aloud and have other students guess the holiday.

MULTIPLE INTELLIGENCES

Spatial Have students work in pairs or small groups to make holiday greeting cards for the next holiday on the calendar. They will need paper, pictures from magazines or handmade drawings, colored markers, glue, or tape. Allow them to use bilingual dictionaries. Have the class vote on the most colorful and creative cards.

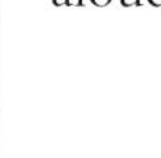

STANDARDS: 1.1, 1.2, 1.3

Resources

Planning:

Lesson Planner, pp. 101–105, 256–261

 One-Stop Planner

Presentation:

TPR Storytelling Book, pp. 48–49

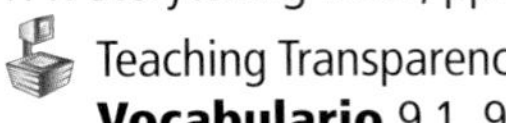 Teaching Transparencies **Vocabulario** 9.1, 9.2

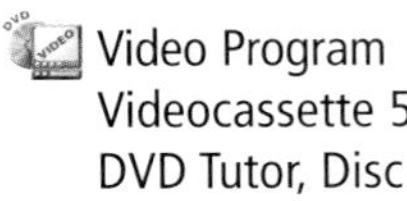 Video Program
Videocassette 5
DVD Tutor, Disc 2
ExpresaVisión

Practice:

Cuaderno de vocabulario y gramática, pp. 53–55

Activities for Communication, pp. 33–34

Video Guide, pp. 84–86

Lab Book, pp. 27–28, 56

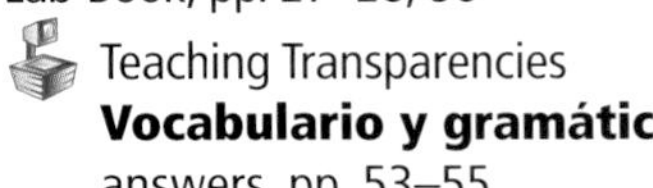 Teaching Transparencies **Vocabulario y gramática** answers, pp. 53–55

 Audio CD 9, Tr. 1

 Interactive Tutor, Disc 2

Teacher to Teacher

Sonia Burkart
Ruth Dowell Middle School
Sherman, TX

Use a scavenger hunt to familiarize students with holiday customs in Spanish-speaking countries. Create a worksheet with holiday images from several Internet sources. Insert a writing box next to each image and make a list of the URLs where the images reside at the end of the worksheet. Students search the sites for the images, read the information about the image, and write a summary of what they learned about the image on the worksheet.

¡Exprésate!

To ask about past holidays	To respond
¿Dónde pasaron la Navidad el año pasado? *Where did you spend Christmas last year?*	**La pasamos en casa de mis tíos.** *We spent it at my aunt and uncle's house.*
¿Qué tal estuvo? *How was it?*	**Estuvo a todo dar. Nos reunimos a comer.** *It was great. We got together to eat.*

Interactive TUTOR

Online Vocabulario y gramática, pp. 53–55

El Día del Padre

6 ¿Qué celebraron?

Leamos Escoge la actividad que le corresponde a cada día festivo.

1. Mis hermanos cocinaron una cena especial para mamá. Ella descansó todo el día. e
2. Los amigos mandaron muchas tarjetas, dulces y flores. f
3. Nos reunimos con la familia para una cena especial. c
4. Toda la familia le compró regalos para papá. Él descansó todo el día. b
5. Fuimos a una fiesta y no nos acostamos hasta la una o las dos de la mañana. g
6. La familia Rodríguez cenó en el parque para ver los fuegos artificiales. a
7. Compramos regalos para todos y toda la familia fue a misa. d

a. el Día de la Independencia
b. el Día del Padre
c. el Día de Acción de Gracias
d. la Navidad
e. el Día de la Madre
f. el Día de los Enamorados
g. la Nochevieja

7 Entre amigos

Leamos Pon en orden las oraciones de la siguiente conversación entre Lourdes y Manuel.

—¿Qué tal estuvo? 4
—¿Qué planes tienes para el Año Nuevo? 6
—Hola, Lourdes, ¿cómo estás? ¿Cómo pasaron la Navidad? 2
—Pues, la pasamos con mi familia en casa de los abuelos. 3
—¡Hola, Manuel! 1
—No sé, pero creo que lo voy a pasar con mis primos. 7
—Estuvo bien. Nos reunimos a decorar la casa, comer y abrir regalos. 5

Core Instruction

TEACHING ¡EXPRÉSATE!

1. Use the expressions from **¡Exprésate!** to act out a conversation between two friends about a holiday. You may wish to use puppets or stuffed animals to portray the different speakers. Use body language, gestures, and/or pictures to convey meaning. **(2 min.)**
2. Ask students where they spent various holidays, using **¿Dónde pasaron... el año pasado?** Have students answer with **La/Lo pasamos... (4 min.)**
3. Have students brainstorm logical answers to the question **¿Qué tal estuvo?** Write their answers on the board. (**Estuvo horrible, Estuvo a todo dar, Estuvo aburrido,...**) **(5 min.)**
4. Ask volunteers where they spent a recent holiday and how the holiday was. **(4 min.)**

STANDARDS: 1.2

CD 9, Tr. 1

8 **¿Pasado o futuro?**

Escuchemos Escucha la conversación entre Luis y Rosa. Indica si cada cosa ya *(already)* ocurrió el Día de Acción de Gracias o va a ocurrir el día de la Navidad.

	ya ocurrió	va a ocurrir
1. ir a casa de los abuelos		x
2. almorzar en un restaurante	x	
3. ir al cine	x	
4. pasar la noche en casa	x	
5. decorar la casa	x	
6. ir a misa		x
7. abrir regalos y comer		x
8. dormir en casa de los abuelos		x

9 **Mi día festivo preferido**

Escribamos Write a short paragraph about your favorite holiday. Explain how you celebrate the holiday and who celebrates the holiday with you. Also explain why it is your favorite holiday.

MODELO **Mi día festivo preferido es el Día de Acción de Gracias. Es mi día favorito porque toda la familia va a la casa de mi abuela y...**

Nota cultural

On February 27th, Independence Day, Dominicans celebrate **Carnaval**. In Santo Domingo, children and adults gather to watch a parade along **El malecón**, one of the main streets. The parade includes floats, marching bands, dancers, and **diablos cojuelos.** These figures wear brightly-colored, horned masks and costumes covered with toys, mirrors, and shiny objects. What celebrations in the United States or in other countries are similar to the Dominican **Carnaval?**

Comunicación

10 **¿Cómo lo van a pasar?**

Hablemos Ask a classmate which holiday is his or her favorite, how he or she celebrates that day, and what plans he or she has for this year's celebration. Also ask your classmate why that holiday is his or her favorite. Then your classmate should ask you the same questions.

MODELO **—¿Cuál es tu día festivo preferido?**
—Es la Nochevieja.
—¿Cómo celebran la Nochevieja tú y tu familia?
—Primero salimos con nuestros tíos y primos y luego...
—¿Por qué es la Nochevieja tu día festivo favorito?
—Es mi día festivo favorito porque...

8 Script

See scripts on p. 175E.

Cultures

Practices and Perspectives

La Navidad in Dominican Republic All public employees receive a **doble sueldo** *(double salary)* right before Christmas, a bonus that amounts to a full month's salary.
There are not any seasonal changes in the climate on this island, so the temperature at Christmas stays about 70°.
People spend the day visiting with family and friends.
Popular Christmas foods include roasted pork and **sancocho,** a soup made with pork, plantains, and vegetables.
People traditionally give children gifts on January 6, **el Día de los Reyes Magos** *(Three Kings' Day.)*

Comunicación

Pair Activity: Interpretive

Assign pairs of students one of the holidays listed on pages 178–179. Have them write a brief description of the holiday. Call on different pairs to read their descriptions. The other students guess which holiday is being described.

MODELO:
—Comemos una gran cena con la familia. Vemos partidos de fútbol americano en la televisión.
—el Día de Acción de Gracias

Differentiated Instruction

ADVANCED LEARNERS

Extension Have small groups of students research special holiday foods served in Spanish-speaking countries. Ask them to locate and bring in a recipe of a typical holiday food. If the recipe is in Spanish, make a translation in English. Make enough copies of the recipes so each student can have a set. Provide some class time for students to read the recipes and decide what they might like or dislike about each dish. If time allows, ask that students prepare one of the dishes and bring it to class for all to sample.

MULTIPLE INTELLIGENCES

Interpersonal Have students work with a partner to write a 4-question survey about favorite holiday foods and activities. Then have each pair ask their questions to two other pairs and report their findings to the class. What favorites do members of the class have in common?

MODELO
—¿Qué te gusta comer en la Navidad?
—¿Qué regalos te gusta recibir para tu cumpleaños?

Assess

Assessment Program

Prueba: Vocabulario 1, pp. 77–78

Alternative Assessment Guide, pp. 244, 252, 260

Test Generator

STANDARDS: 1.1, 1.2, 1.3, 2.1, 4.2

Resources

Planning:

Lesson Planner, pp. 106–111, 260–267

One-Stop Planner

Presentation:

Video Program
Videocassette 5
DVD Tutor, Disc 2
GramaVisión

Practice:

Grammar Tutor for Students of Spanish, Chapter 9

Cuaderno de vocabulario y gramática, pp. 56–58

Cuaderno de actividades, pp. 45–47

Activities for Communication, pp. 33–34

Video Guide, pp. 84–85

Lab Book, pp. 27–28

Teaching Transparencies
Bell Work 9.2
Vocabulario y gramática answers, pp. 56–58

Interactive Tutor, Disc 2

Bell Work

Use Bell Work 9.2 in the *Teaching Transparencies,* or write this activity on the board.

Match each person's activity with the most logical holiday.

1. Fui a misa.
2. Marcos compró una tarjeta roja.
3. El muchacho va a abrir muchos regalos.
4. Lola come un almuerzo grande con la familia.
5. Mi familia fue al parque para un picnic.

a. el Día de los Enamorados
b. el Día de Acción de Gracias
c. la Semana Santa
d. el Día de la Independencia
e. la Navidad

Objetivos
Using the preterite of -ar, -er, and -ir verbs; pensar with que and pensar with infinitives

Gramática en acción 1

GramaVisión

Interactive TUTOR

Preterite of -er and -ir verbs

1 The **preterite** is used to talk about what happened at a specific point in the past. To form the **preterite** of **-er** and **-ir** verbs, add these endings to the verb's stem.

	volver		escribir
yo	volví	yo	escribí
tú	volv**iste**	tú	escrib**iste**
Ud., él, ella	volv**ió**	Ud., él, ella	escrib**ió**
nosotros(as)	volv**imos**	nosotros(as)	escrib**imos**
vosotros(as)	volv**isteis**	vosotros(as)	escrib**isteis**
Uds., ellos, ellas	volv**ieron**	Uds., ellos, ellas	escrib**ieron**

—¿**Recibieron** la tarjeta? —Sí, la **recibimos** ayer. Gracias.

2 Regular **-er** and **-ir** verbs have the same endings in the **preterite**. Stem-changing **-er** verbs don't have a stem change in the **preterite**.

—¿Por qué no fuiste a la fiesta? —Porque me **dolió** la garganta.

3 The verb **ver** has regular **preterite** endings but without written accents.

yo	v**i**	nosotros(as)	v**imos**
tú	v**iste**	vosotros(as)	v**isteis**
Ud., él, ella	v**io**	Uds., ellos, ellas	v**ieron**

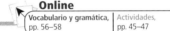

Online
Vocabulario y gramática, pp. 56–58 | Actividades, pp. 45–47

¿Te acuerdas?

To form the **preterite** of a regular **-ar** verb, add these endings to the verb's stem.

merend**é**	merend**amos**
merend**aste**	merend**asteis**
merend**ó**	merend**aron**

No **-ar** verbs have stem changes in the preterite.

11 La Navidad de Pablo

Leamos Escoge el verbo correcto entre paréntesis.

Pablo y sus padres ___1___ (salimos/salieron) muy temprano para la casa de sus abuelos el día de Navidad, donde ___2___ (se reunieron/me reuní) con toda la familia. Pablo ___3___ (vimos/vio) a unos tíos que viven lejos. Primero todos ___4___ (comí/comieron) y Pablo ___5___ (bebiste/bebió) tres vasos de limonada. Después de la comida ellos ___6___ (abrimos/abrieron) los regalos y a las cuatro ___7___ (fuimos/fueron) a misa.

Core Instruction

TEACHING GRAMÁTICA

1. Review **¿Te acuerdas?** Ask volunteers to tell the class something they did yesterday using only **–ar** verbs and **ir. (5 min.)**
2. Go over Point 1. Model the pronunciation of each preterite form of **volver** and **escribir. (5 min.)**
3. Go over Points 2 and 3. **(5 min.)**
4. Call out present and preterite forms of **–ir** and **–er** verbs. Have students raise their right hand if the verb is in present and their left hand if the verb is in preterite. **(5 min.)**
5. Have students add the preterite conjugation of an **–ir** verb and an **–er** verb to the verb conjugation chart in their notebooks. **(5 min.)**

GramaVisión

For a video presentation of the preterite of **–er** and **–ir** verbs, use **el joven G.** For interactive activities, see the *DVD Tutor.*

GramaVisión

Visit Holt Online
go.hrw.com
KEYWORD: EXP1B CH9
Gramática 1 practice

12 Ahora, ¿qué dice Pablo?

Escribamos Vuelve a escribir el párrafo de la Actividad 11 desde el punto de vista *(point of view)* de Pablo. ¿Qué dice él?

13 El Año Nuevo

Escribamos/Hablemos Mira las fotos y di quiénes hicieron estas cosas para celebrar el Año Nuevo según *(according to)* Marcos.

MODELO comer en un restaurante
Mis padres comieron en un restaurante.

mi hermano y yo

mis abuelos

mis padres

1. beber muchos refrescos
2. salir a un restaurante
3. beber café
4. comer pastel de chocolate
5. asistir a una fiesta
6. comer pizza
7. ver televisión
8. reunirse con la familia

Comunicación

14 La semana pasada

Hablemos Pregúntale a un(a) compañero(a) si hizo las cosas de la Actividad 13 la semana pasada.

MODELO —¿Fuiste a un restaurante?
—Sí, fui a un restaurante la semana pasada.

15 ¿Qué hiciste?

Hablemos Use the phrases in the word box to write four questions for a classmate about how he or she celebrated several holidays last year. Take turns answering each other's questions.

escribir tarjetas	reunirse con la familia	recibir regalos
ver fuegos artificiales	salir a comer	asistir a una fiesta

Gramática 1

12 Answers

Mis padres y yo salimos muy temprano para la casa de mis abuelos el día de Navidad, donde nos reunimos con la familia. Vi a unos tíos que viven lejos. Primero (nosotros) comimos y (yo) bebí tres vasos de limonada. Después de la comida abrimos los regalos. A las cuatro fuimos a misa.

13 Answers

1. Mi hermano y yo bebimos muchos refrescos.
2. Mis padres salieron a un restaurante.
3. Mis padres bebieron café.
4. Mis padres comieron pastel de chocolate.
5. Mi hermano y yo asistimos a una fiesta.
6. Mi hermano y yo comimos pizza.
7. Mis abuelos vieron televisión.
8. Mis abuelos se reunieron con la familia.

Comunicación

Class Activity: Interpersonal

Write regular verbs on 3x5 index cards, enough so that each student can have a different card. Students will poll their classmates on whether or not they did the activity on the card on the previous day using the preterite. On the back of the card, students should record the responses of their classmates by making two columns: **Sí** and **No,** and writing classmates' names in the column that best indicates their response. Have students report their responses to the class.

MODELO:
comer en un restaurante
—¿Comiste en un restaurante ayer?
—Sí, comí en un restaurante ayer.

Differentiated Instruction

SLOWER PACE LEARNERS

15 Point out to students that they will be writing all the questions for Activity 15 in the preterite verb form for the conjugation **tú.** Ask student volunteers to conjugate each verb before assigning the activity. Finally, remind students that when they give their answers to their partner's questions they will be using the **yo** form of the verbs in the preterite.

MULTIPLE INTELLIGENCES

15 Visual Allow students to draw a picture, either by hand or using a computer drawing tool, of each of the phrases in Activity 15. Then, with their partner, they can complete the activity using the images instead of the phrase box.

STANDARDS: 1.1, 1.2, 1.3

Resources

Planning:

Lesson Planner, pp. 106–111, 260–267

 One-Stop Planner

Presentation:

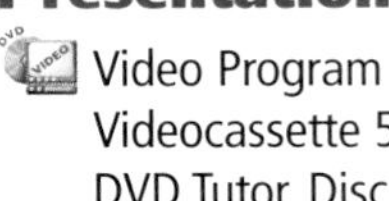 Video Program
Videocassette 5
DVD Tutor, Disc 2
GramaVisión

Practice:

Grammar Tutor for Students of Spanish, Chapter 9

Cuaderno de vocabulario y gramática, pp. 56–58

Cuaderno de actividades, pp. 45–47

Activities for Communication, pp. 33–34

Video Guide, pp. 84–85

Lab Book, pp. 27–28

 Teaching Transparencies
Bell Work 9.3
Vocabulario y gramática answers, pp. 56–58

 Audio CD 9, Tr. 2

 Interactive Tutor, Disc 2

Bell Work

Use Bell Work 9.3 in the *Teaching Transparencies*, or write this activity on the board.

Choose the logical verb for each sentence and write the correct preterite form.

abrir / escribir / asistir / ver / comer

1. **Yo no les _____ una carta a mis abuelos la semana pasada.**
2. **Mi hermana y yo _____ una película buena anoche.**
3. **Olivia y Paco _____ a la reunión del Club de ciencias la semana pasada.**
4. **Tu padre _____ poco en el restaurante.**
5. **Tú _____ los regalos de Navidad.**

Repaso The preterite

1 Compare the preterite forms of regular **-ar**, **-er**, and **-ir** verbs and the irregular verb **ir**.

	invitar	comer	salir	ir
yo	invit**é**	com**í**	sal**í**	**fui**
tú	invit**aste**	com**iste**	sal**iste**	**fuiste**
usted, él, ella	invit**ó**	com**ió**	sal**ió**	**fue**
nosotros(as)	invit**amos**	com**imos**	sal**imos**	**fuimos**
vosotros(as)	invit**asteis**	com**isteis**	sal**isteis**	**fuisteis**
ustedes, ellos, ellas	invit**aron**	com**ieron**	sal**ieron**	**fueron**

—¿**Saliste** con tus amigos?
Did you go out with your friends?

—Sí, **fuimos** a una fiesta.
Yes, we went to a party.

—¿A quiénes **invitaron** a la fiesta?
Who did they invite to the party?

—A todos. **Comimos** y **bailamos** mucho.
Everyone. We ate and danced a lot.

Online
Vocabulario y gramática, pp. 56–58 | Actividades, pp. 45–47

¿Te acuerdas?

Stem-changing **-ar** and **-er** verbs have no stem changes in the preterite.

El regalo c**o**stó veinte dólares.

No v**o**lvimos hasta *(until)* las once.

CD 9, Tr. 2

16 ¿Cuándo?

Escuchemos Escucha las oraciones y decide si la joven habla de **a)** lo que su familia siempre hace o de **b)** lo que hizo.

1. b **2.** a **3.** a **4.** b **5.** a **6.** b **7.** b **8.** b

17 ¿Qué tal estuvo?

Escribamos Indica qué hicieron las siguientes personas en varias fiestas. Luego di qué tal estuvo cada fiesta—a todo dar o aburrida.

MODELO **nosotros (no salir hasta muy tarde)**
No salimos hasta muy tarde.
La fiesta estuvo a todo dar.

1. su tía (cantar ópera)
2. yo (bailar toda la noche)
3. nosotros (comer muy bien)
4. sólo *(only)* cuatro personas (ir a la fiesta)
5. Laura y José (jugar al ajedrez)
6. muchas personas interesantes (hablar conmigo)
7. nosotros (pasar una noche fenomenal)
8. todos (salir temprano de la fiesta)
9. yo (ver a muchos de mis amigos)
10. mis primos (escribir tarjetas de Navidad)

Core Instruction

TEACHING GRAMÁTICA

1. Go over **¿Te acuerdas? (2 min.)**
2. Go over Point 1. **(6 min.)**
3. Ask students to write two sentences telling where they went and what they did last summer. One sentence should be true, and the other should be a lie, the more imaginative the better. Ask volunteers to read their sentences aloud. The class should decide which sentence is true. For example, if the volunteer says **Fui a Venus. Trabajé en el centro comercial;** the class would say **Trabajaste en el centro, pero no fuiste a Venus. (12 min.)**

GramaVisión

For a video presentation of the preterite, use **el joven G** from the *Video Program*. For interactive activities, see the *DVD Tutor.*

STANDARDS: 1.2, 1.3

18 Padres especiales

Escribamos Escribe tres oraciones para cada foto y di cómo festejó cada familia el Día del Padre y el Día de la Madre.

MODELO **Pasaron el Día de la Madre con la abuela.**

el Día de la Madre

el Día del Padre

19 El calendario de Arturo

Leamos/Escribamos Use the information from the calendar to write at least seven sentences about what Arturo did for each holiday. Then compare his activities with yours.

MODELO **El 4 de julio Arturo fue a la playa.**
No fui a la playa, pero sí comí en el parque.

14 de febrero	4 de julio	25 de diciembre	31 de diciembre
mandar tarjetas	ir a la playa	abrir regalos	ir a una fiesta
abrir regalos	ver fuegos artificiales	reunirse con la familia	bailar
comer chocolates	comer en el parque	ir a la iglesia	reunirse con amigos

Comunicación

20 ¿Y tú?

Hablemos Pregúntale a tu compañero(a) cómo celebró los días festivos de la Actividad 19.

MODELO **—¿Recibiste muchas tarjetas para el Día de los Enamorados?**
—Recibí muchas tarjetas y unos regalos también.

Differentiated Instruction

ADVANCED LEARNERS

17 As an extension to Activity 17, have students write a paragraph describing the last party they attended. Tell them to write at least six sentences using six different verbs in the preterite and six different subjects. Finally, have them conclude their paragraph with a summary sentence about whether the party was fun or not.

SPECIAL LEARNING NEEDS

20 Students with Learning Disabilities To offer more structure for Activity 20, have students make a list of the specific holidays they will ask their partner about. You might have students discuss only two or three of the holidays to make the task easier. Have them think about what they do for each holiday and make some notes on their list. Then, have them conduct the interview with their partner as described.

Gramática 1

16 Script

See script on p. 175E.

17 Answers

1. Su tía cantó ópera. La fiesta estuvo aburrida.
2. Bailé toda la noche. La fiesta estuvo a todo dar.
3. Comimos muy bien. La fiesta estuvo a todo dar.
4. Sólo cuatro personas fueron a la fiesta. La fiesta estuvo aburrida.
5. Laura y José jugaron al ajedrez. La fiesta estuvo aburrida.
6. Muchas personas interesantes hablaron conmigo. La fiesta estuvo a todo dar.
7. Nosotros pasamos una noche fenomenal. La fiesta estuvo a todo dar.
8. Todos salimos/salieron temprano de la fiesta. La fiesta estuvo aburrida.
9. Vi a muchos de mis amigos. La fiesta estuvo a todo dar.
10. Mis primos escribieron tarjetas de Navidad. La fiesta estuvo aburrida.

Comunicación

Individual Activity: Presentational

Think-Draw-Speak Give students a piece of 8 1/2 x 11 paper. Students have ten minutes to sketch pictures or symbols to represent 10 activities that took place at the last birthday party they attended. Then, have students use their drawings as cue cards to talk about their party experience. To help students connect their ideas, it may be helpful to brainstorm a list of time sequencing words and write them on the board or on a transparency for students to refer to during the activity. Give students 5 minutes to mingle and talk about their party experiences. To help students stay on task, have them ask each classmate with whom they speak to sign the back of their drawing.

Resources

Planning:

Lesson Planner, pp. 106–111, 260–267

One-Stop Planner

Presentation:

Video Program
Videocassette 5
DVD Tutor, Disc 2
GramaVisión

Practice:

Grammar Tutor for Students of Spanish, Chapter 9

Cuaderno de vocabulario y gramática, pp. 56–58

Cuaderno de actividades, pp. 45–47

Activities for Communication, pp. 33–34

Video Guide, pp. 84–85

Lab Book, pp. 27–28

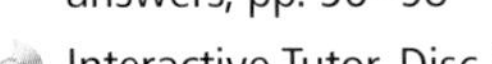Teaching Transparencies
Bell Work 9.4
Vocabulario y gramática answers, pp. 56–58

Interactive Tutor, Disc 2

Bell Work

Use Bell Work 9.4 in the *Teaching Transparencies,* or write this activity on the board.

Unscramble the words to write logical sentences.

1. la / fue / Arturo / fiesta / a / anoche
2. mi / en / estudió / Costa Rica / biología / tío
3. salí / amigos / mis / ayer / con / yo
4. ajedrez / Alana / la / jugó / toda / tarde / al
5. hermana / recibimos / y / en / muchos / Navidad / regalos / yo / mi / la

COMMON ERROR ALERT ¡OJO!

Remind students that **que** is not optional after forms of **pensar** when it means *to think (that) . . .*

Pensar que and pensar with infinitives

1 The **e → ie** stem-changing verb **pensar** means *to think.* When it's followed by **que,** it means *to think that . . .*

yo **pie**nso	nosotros(as) pensamos
tu **pie**nsas	vosotros(as) pensáis
Ud., él, ella **pie**nsa	Uds., ellos(as) **pie**nsan

Pienso que los invitados van a hablar y bailar toda la noche.
I think that the guests are going to talk and dance all night.

2 **Pensar** can also be followed by an **infinitive** to say what *someone plans* to do or *intends* to do.

—¿Qué **piensan hacer** para celebrar el Año Nuevo?
What do you plan to do to celebrate New Year's Eve?

—**Pensamos ir** a esquiar.
We plan to go skiing.

Online
Vocabulario y gramática, pp. 56–58 | Actividades, pp. 45–47

Nota cultural

Celebrations call for special foods. In the Dominican Republic, a food served during the Christmas season is **pasteles en hoja**. This dish is prepared by boiling and mashing green plantains. The mashed plantains are then spread onto plantain leaves. Next, the leaves are stuffed with ground beef or chicken. Finally, the stuffed leaves are folded, tied with string, and placed in a pot of boiling water. Which other cultures have dishes similar to this? Is there a similar dish in your culture?

21 Este año pienso...

Leamos/Escribamos Completa cada resolución de Año Nuevo *(New Year's resolution)* de manera lógica. Usa el verbo **pensar** y las siguientes palabras en tus respuestas.

relajarse más	seguir una dieta más sana
gastar menos en regalos	tomar una clase de francés
volver a la universidad	hacer más ejercicio
ir a la casa de los abuelos	pasar más tiempo en casa

MODELO Voy a comer más verduras.
Pienso seguir una dieta más sana.

1. Mi madre va a estudiar mucho.
2. Mi hermano y yo vamos a mantenernos en mejor forma.
3. Mi padre va a tomar menos café y no va a trabajar hasta tarde.
4. Vamos a reunirnos con todos mis tíos para la Navidad.
5. Mi madre va a estudiar francés.
6. Mis padres van a ahorrar dinero este año.
7. No voy a salir con mis amigos todos los sábados.
8. Mi hermana mayor no va a trabajar tanto.
9. Voy a pasar más tiempo con mis abuelos.

Core Instruction

TEACHING GRAMÁTICA

1. Go over Point 1. Model the pronunciation of each form of **pensar. (4 min.)**
2. Go over Point 2. **(2 min.)**
3. Ask students what they are planning to do after school and over the next weekend. **(5 min.)**
4. Have students add the conjugation of **pensar** to the verb conjugation chart in their notebooks. **(4 min.)**

GramaVisión

For a video presentation of **pensar que** and **pensar** with infinitives, use **el joven G** from the *Video Program.* For interactive activities, see the *DVD Tutor.*

GramaVisión

STANDARDS: 1.2, 2.1, 4.2

22 El Día de la Independencia

Escribamos/Hablemos Mira los dibujos e indica cómo piensan pasar el 4 de julio. Luego usa **pienso que** para dar tu opinión sobre los planes.

MODELO **Pienso ir a la playa con mis amigos. Pienso que va a ser muy divertido. Pienso que me voy a divertir mucho.**

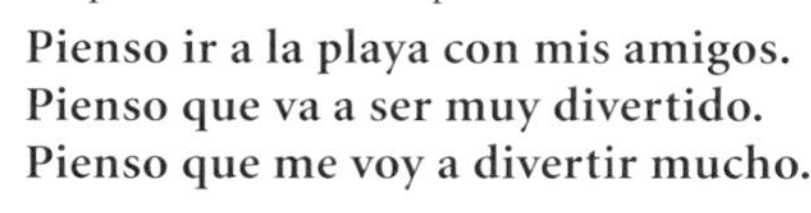
yo

1. mis amigos y yo

2. unos amigos

3. mis padres

4. mi hermana

5. por la noche, mis padres y yo

6. mis abuelos

Comunicación

23 ¡Ven a mi fiesta!

Hablemos With a classmate, talk about a party you are planning to have. You should talk about the reason for the party, where it will be, the guests, music, and food. You and your classmate can use phrases from the word box to ask questions and to respond.

Pienso que...	(No) estoy de acuerdo.	Prefiero...
fenomenal	pésimo(a)	divertido(a)
(No) me gusta(n).	¡Buena idea!	delicioso(a)

21 Answers

1. Mi madre (Ella) piensa volver a la universidad.
2. Pensamos hacer más ejercicio.
3. Mi padre piensa relajarse más.
4. Pensamos ir a la casa de los abuelos.
5. Piensa tomar una clase de francés.
6. Mis padres piensan gastar menos en regalos este año.
7. Pienso pasar más tiempo en casa con mis padres.
8. Mi hermana piensa relajarse más.
9. Pienso ir a la casa de los abuelos.

Comunicación

Class Activity: Presentational

Prepare 8 sentence starters asking students to give an opinion. **(Pienso que los profesores...)** Write one sentence at the top of each of 8 sheets of self-stick chart paper. Place the 8 sheets around the room. Divide students equally among the chart papers. Give 3 minutes for each group member to complete the sentence on the chart. Then, give a signal and have groups rotate clockwise to the next chart. Continue until all groups have had a chance to complete each sentence. The group takes the last chart they write on with them. Give each group five minutes to summarize the opinions expressed on the chart they've taken. Students can use **pensar** to report the opinions to the class.

Differentiated Instruction

SLOWER PACE LEARNERS

22 Explain to students that there are two parts to each item in Activity 22. The subject of the first part of the first item will be **mis amigos y yo,** followed by the correct form of **pensar** with an infinitive. Then, explain that the subject of the second part of the question will be **pensar** in the **yo** form, followed by **que** and their personal opinion about what the people are doing for the holiday. You might write this formula on the board: Part 1. subject of photo + correct form of **pensar** + infinitive; Part 2. **yo** form of **pensar** + **que** + personal opinion.

MULTIPLE INTELLIGENCES

Intrapersonal Students with intrapersonal skills are very good at identifying their own strengths and weaknesses. Give them an opportunity to make a list of ten of their own **resoluciones del Año Nuevo,** written in Spanish, for the New Year (or new month, if this is more applicable for your class schedule). Ask volunteers to share their resolutions with the class.

Assess

Assessment Program

Prueba: Gramática 1, pp. 79–80

Prueba: Aplicación 1, pp. 81–82

Alternative Assessment Guide, pp. 244, 252, 260

Audio CD 9, Tr. 15

Test Generator

STANDARDS: 1.1, 1.3

Cultura

VideoCultura

Planning:

Lesson Planner, pp. 112, 266–267

 One-Stop Planner

Presentation:

 Teaching Transparencies **Mapa 4**

Audio CD 9, Tr. 3–5

Video Program Videocassette 5 DVD Tutor, Disc 2 **VideoCultura**

Practice:

Cuaderno de actividades, p. 48

Cuaderno para hispanohablantes, pp. 69–76

Video Guide, pp. 84–85, 87

Lab Book, p. 57

 Interactive Tutor, Disc 2

Atlas INTERACTIVO MUNDIAL

Have students use the interactive atlas at **go.hrw.com.**

Map Activities

Using Map Transparencies 4 and 6, have students locate the cities of Santo Domingo and El Paso. Have them compare and contrast the size of the Dominican Republic and the state of Texas as well as their populations.

Teacher Note

Though Waldemar says he celebrates Mother's Day on May 14th, in general Mother's Day is celebrated in the Dominican Republic on the last Sunday in May.

Comparaciones

  CD 9, Tr. 3–5

Carnaval en la República Dominicana

¿Qué días festivos se celebran en tu país?

En los países hispanohablantes, los días festivos y los festivales son muy importantes. A veces los festivales son religiosos, y a veces son de sabor nacional o regional. De todos modos, toda la comunidad participa, y es común cerrar los colegios, tiendas y otros negocios para celebrar. Estas personas hablan de los días festivos en su país y de la manera en que se celebran. ¿Son días festivos que celebras también? ¿Los celebras igual que ellos? Si son festivales que no celebras, ¿te acuerdas de otros que sí celebras?

Waldemar
Santo Domingo, la República Dominicana

Waldemar talks about his favorite holiday, **Semana Santa.** What is your favorite holiday and how do you celebrate it?

¿Me puedes decir cuáles son dos o tres días festivos que se celebran en República Dominicana, y en qué fechas son?

Celebramos la Semana Santa, que es la segunda semana de abril. Celebramos el Día de la Madre, catorce de mayo. Y también celebramos las Navidades.

¿Cuál es tu día festivo favorito?

Me gusta mucho la Semana Santa.

¿Qué significa para ti la Semana Santa?

Es una semana muy espiritual.

¿Cómo pasaste la Semana Santa el año pasado?

Muy común. Como todo el mundo, fuimos a la iglesia mucho. Pasé mucho tiempo con mi familia.

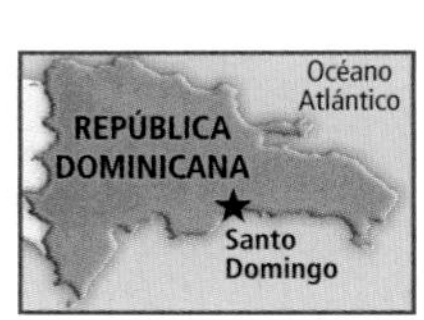

Core Instruction

TEACHING CULTURA

1. Play the introductory paragraph on Audio CD 9. Have students predict what holidays they might hear mentioned in the interviews. **(5 min.)**
2. Have students watch the two interviews on video using the *Video Program* or the *DVD Tutor.* Pause the video periodically and check for comprehension. **(15 min.)**
3. Have students answer the questions in the **Para comprender** section with a partner. Discuss **Para pensar y hablar. (15 min.)**

VideoCultura

For a video presentation of the interviews as well as for additional interviews, see Chapter 9 **VideoCultura** on Videocassette or on DVD. For interactive practice, see the *DVD Tutor.*

VideoCultura

STANDARDS: 2.1, 4.2

Visit Holt Online
go.hrw.com
KEYWORD: EXP1B CH9
Online Edition

Diana
El Paso, Texas

Diana shares a special meal with her family at Christmas. How do your holiday celebrations compare with hers?

¿Me puedes decir dos o tres días festivos que se celebran aquí en El Paso?

Claro, aquí en El Paso festejamos el Día de la Independencia de Estados Unidos, que es el cuatro de julio. También festejamos la Navidad, que es el veinticinco de diciembre, y el Día de Gracias, que es el último jueves de noviembre.

¿Qué día festivo es tu favorito?

Mi día festivo favorito es la Navidad.

¿Cómo pasaste la Navidad el año pasado?

Toda mi familia nos sentamos en la casa de los abuelos, y comimos pavo.

Cultura

Para comprender

1. ¿Cuáles son tres días festivos que se celebran en la República Dominicana?
2. ¿Dónde pasó Diana la Navidad el año pasado?
3. ¿En qué día se celebra el Día de Acción de Gracias en Estados Unidos?
4. ¿Adónde fueron Waldemar y su familia durante la Semana Santa?

Para pensar y hablar

Waldemar and Diana say that their favorite holidays are **Semana Santa** and **la Navidad.** Why do you think they chose those holidays as their favorites? Is the way they spend their holidays similar? What are your favorite holidays? Why are those days important to you?

Cuaderno para hispanohablantes, pp. 93–104

Comunidad
¿Cómo celebramos?

Individual countries often have unique holidays as well as holidays shared with people from other countries. Use resources from the library or the Internet to write a short report on a Latin American or Spanish holiday. Include the following information and present the report to the class.

- the name and date of the holiday
- special foods or activities associated with the holiday
- the history or origin of the holiday
- a song or poem related to the holiday

Fiesta de cumpleaños

Differentiated Instruction

SLOWER PACE LEARNERS

Have students make a list of holidays. You might give them prompts for holidays they forget to include on their lists. As they listen to the interview, advise students to put a "W" beside holidays that Waldemar mentions, and a "D" beside any holiday that Diana mentions. After listening to the interviews, allow students to use their lists when answering the comprehension questions and to help guide class discussion.

MULTIPLE INTELLIGENCES

Interpersonal Students with interpersonal strengths tend to enjoy opportunities to meet new people and begin new relationships. Give these students the opportunity to begin an online or traditional mail correspondence with a student from the Dominican Republic. Students can ask their pen pal the first question under **Para comprender** to practice the vocabulary from this chapter.

Para comprender Answers

1. la Semana Santa, el Día de la Madre y las Navidades (la Navidad)
2. Diana
3. el último jueves en noviembre
4. a la iglesia

Comparisons
Comparing and Contrasting

Ask students how many of them celebrate national holidays like the Fourth of July and Memorial Day. What events do these holidays commemorate? Have students research similar holidays of historic importance in other countries. Ask them to compare how people in different cultures celebrate their national history.

Heritage Speakers

Ask students from Spanish-speaking families whether they observe any holiday customs that originated in Hispanic countries. Students might be interested in researching how a particular holiday is celebrated in their family's country of origin and telling the class about it.

Comparisons
Language to Language

If you have students in your class that speak a language other than English or Spanish, have them tell how to express holiday greetings in other languages. In French, for example, you will hear **Joyeux Noël!** for *Merry Christmas!* Or, you might choose one or two holidays and have students try to find their names in as many languages as they can.

STANDARDS: 1.2, 2.1, 4.1, 4.2, 5.1

Resources

Planning:

Lesson Planner, pp. 113–117, 266–273

One-Stop Planner

Presentation:

TPR Storytelling Book, pp. 50–51

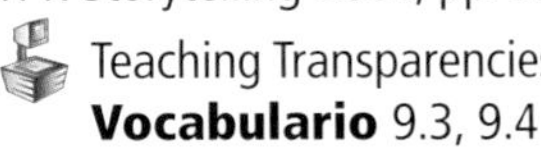
Teaching Transparencies **Vocabulario** 9.3, 9.4

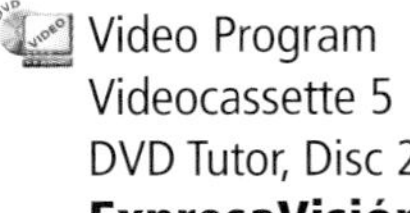
Video Program
Videocassette 5
DVD Tutor, Disc 2
ExpresaVisión

Practice:

Cuaderno de vocabulario y gramática, pp. 59–61

Activities for Communication, pp. 35–36

Video Guide, pp. 84–85, 88

Lab Book, pp. 29–30, 58

Teaching Transparencies
Bell Work 9.5
Vocabulario y gramática answers, pp. 59–61

Interactive Tutor, Disc 2

Bell Work

Use Bell Work 9.5 in the *Teaching Transparencies,* or write this activity on the board.

Using **pensar** followed by an infinitive, write what each person is thinking about doing according to the situation.

1. Es la una y tengo mucha hambre. Yo...
2. Es muy tarde y Jaime tiene un examen importante mañana. Él...
3. Hace mucho frío y nosotros llevamos blusas de seda. Nosotros...
4. No hay nada en la televisión y estás aburrido(a). Tú...
5. Elena quiere salir con sus amigos este viernes. Ella...

Objetivos

Asking about preparing for a party, greeting, introducing others, and saying goodbye

Vocabulario 2 en acción

Video/DVD
ExpresaVisión

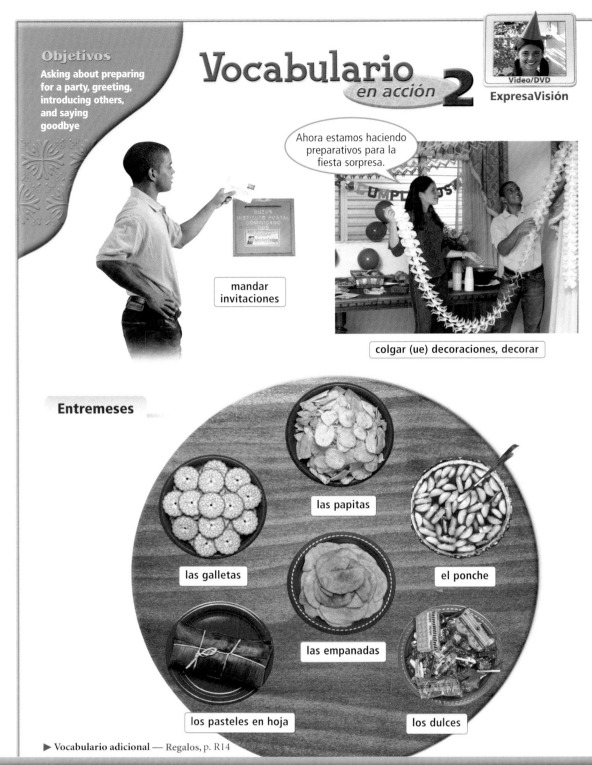

Ahora estamos haciendo preparativos para la fiesta sorpresa.

mandar invitaciones

colgar (ue) decoraciones, decorar

Entremeses

las papitas

las galletas

el ponche

las empanadas

los pasteles en hoja

los dulces

▶ **Vocabulario adicional** — Regalos, p. R14

Core Instruction

TEACHING VOCABULARIO

1. Introduce the vocabulary using transparencies **Vocabulario 9.3** and **9.4.** Model the pronunciation of each word as you point to the appropriate picture. **(20 min.)**
2. Call out various activities (**charlar, comprar las papitas**) and ask students to raise their right hand if the activity is something you would do to prepare for a party and their left hand if it is something you would do at a party. **(5 min.)**
3. Ask students if they have already done various things to prepare for the party, using **¿Está todo listo para la fiesta? ¿Ya...?** Give students a thumbs up or thumbs down to cue their response. **(5 min.)**

ExpresaVisión

For a presentation of party preparations, use the video presenter. For interactive activities, see the *DVD Tutor.*

Visit Holt Online
go.hrw.com
KEYWORD: EXP1B CH9
Vocabulario 2 practice

Vocabulario 2

Los invitados van a...

enseñar fotos

charlar

contar (ue) chistes

Más vocabulario...

Las fiestas

el aniversario	*anniversary*
la boda	*wedding*
el cumpleaños	*birthday*
el día de tu santo	*your saint's day*
la fiesta sorpresa	*surprise party*
la graduación	*graduation*
la quinceañera	*girl's fifteenth birthday*

También se puede decir...

In the Dominican Republic, finger foods are called **bocadillos** or **picaderas,** but they may also be called **tapas** in Spain, **botanas** in Mexico, **pasapalos** in Venezuela, or **bocas** in Costa Rica.

Some Spanish speakers in Mexico say **platicar** instead of **charlar.**

¡Exprésate!

To ask about preparing for a party	To respond
¿Está todo listo para la fiesta? ¿Ya terminaste con los preparativos? *Is everything ready for the party? Did you already finish the preparations?*	**Sí. Anoche compré las flores y preparé el ponche.** *Yes. Last night I bought the flowers and made the punch.*
¿Qué están haciendo los jóvenes ahora? *What are the young people doing now?*	**Están colgando la piñata.** *They are hanging the piñata.*

Interactive TUTOR

Online Vocabulario y gramática, pp. 59–61

TPR

Total Physical Response

Review the following commands before having students respond.

Dramatiza que te sirves y bebes un ponche que está muy frío.

Dramatiza que... es tu hermano(a) y te pide dulces pero no se los quieres dar.

Prepara una empanada.

Dramatiza que estás colgando decoraciones para la fiesta.

Prueba un tamal muy picante.

Dramatiza que acabas de llegar a tu fiesta sorpresa.

Dramatiza con... y... que se están contando chistes.

Connections

Language Note

The usage of **boda** differs slightly from the term *wedding.* It refers to both the ceremony and party or reception, whereas in English it would be common to say "wedding and reception." Although **empanadas** are consumed throughout much of the Spanish-speaking world, they vary significantly in traditional fillings, composition of the dough (flour or corn), and cooking means (frying or baking).

Differentiated Instruction

ADVANCED LEARNERS

To reinforce the vocabulary, bring in a bag of items such as an invitation, a balloon, a piece of candy, a small bag of potato chips, a cookie, a plastic cup, and photos. Write **¿Está todo listo para la fiesta?** and **Sí. Anoche...** on the board. Hold the bag in front of a student and tell him or her to blindly select an item. Then ask **¿Está todo listo para la fiesta?** Tell students to begin with **Sí. Anoche...** and complete the sentence using a preterite verb about what they did with the item they chose to prepare for the party.

MULTIPLE INTELLIGENCES

Bodily-Kinesthetic Instead of using the transparencies to present the new vocabulary, you might use the story and gestures from the *TPR Storytelling Book.* The gestures and story context will give students the opportunity to associate the new words with physical actions, helping them better retain the new content.

También se puede decir...

Students may hear many other words for candy including **caramelos** (often used in Venezuela), **golosinas,** and **bombones.** The plural **bodas** is often used in the context of wedding anniversaries such as in the usage **bodas de plata, de oro, de diamante.** Instead of **graduación,** students may hear **entrega de diploma,** and **entrega de título** (university).

STANDARDS: 1.2

24 Answers
1. cumpleaños
2. fiesta sorpresa
3. está listo
4. pasteles en hoja
5. decoraciones
6. piñata
7. invitados
8. ponche, empanadas
9. chistes

Connections

Multicultural Link

Ask students to research various coming-of-age celebrations around the world (Bat Mitzvah, Quinceañera, etc.). Have them work in pairs or small groups and use the library or Internet to get information. Ask them to write short reports that give the name of a celebration, the country of origin, and how it is celebrated. Have any students in the class attended any type of coming-of-age ceremony or celebration? Have volunteers share their experiences with the class.

Heritage Speakers

If any heritage speakers have been to a **fiesta de quinceañera,** have them write a report describing the event. If students have not been to a **quinceañera** but know someone who has had one, have them interview the person about the celebration.

Nota cultural

In many Spanish-speaking countries, a girl's fifteenth birthday is recognized with a special celebration. In some countries, this party is called a **quinceañera**. However, in the Dominican Republic, the word refers to the girl herself and not just the party. While the idea behind the custom has changed over time, **quinceañera** parties are still common in the United States among Spanish-speaking families, as well as in other countries. What is similar or different about coming-of-age parties or celebrations where you live?

24 ¡Vamos a festejar!

Leamos/Hablemos Completa las oraciones con la(s) palabra(s) apropiada(s).

decoraciones	ponche	está listo	invitados	fiesta sorpresa
empanadas	piñata	chistes	cumpleaños	pasteles en hoja

1. Hoy es el ═══ de mi primo Paco.
2. Esta noche hay una ═══. Va a ser muy divertida.
3. Todo ═══ para la fiesta.
4. Anteayer mi mamá, mis hermanos y yo preparamos los ═══.
5. Esta mañana limpiamos la casa y luego colgamos las ═══.
6. Ahora mi papá está colgando la ═══ en el patio.
7. En unas horas, los ═══ van a llegar a nuestra casa.
8. En la fiesta, vamos a beber ═══ y comer muchas ═══.
9. Voy a contar muchos ═══ también.

25 ¿Cuál palabra?

Leamos Read each list of words and phrases for holiday activities and decide which word or phrase does not belong with the others.

1. preparar el ponche/ir a la iglesia/colgar la piñata
2. ir a misa/contar chistes/celebrar el día de tu santo
3. mandar tarjetas y flores/celebrar El Día de los Enamorados/enseñar fotos
4. ir a la quinceañera/pasar el rato solo(a)/mandar invitaciones
5. mandar tarjetas/ir a la iglesia/asistir a la boda
6. celebrar la graduación/comprar regalos/ver fuegos artificiales

26 ¡Ya las compré!

Leamos/Escribamos Miguel is worried about the preparations for the party. Answer his questions by telling him that the preparations have already been done.

MODELO **—¿Compró las galletas Carlos?**
—Sí, Carlos ya las compró.

1. ¿Mandaste las invitaciones? Sí, ya las mandé.
2. ¿Colgaron las decoraciones Lili y Ana? Sí, Lili y Ana ya las colgaron.
3. ¿Compraron el pastel tú y Sara? Sí, ya lo compramos.
4. ¿Colgó la piñata María? Sí, María ya la colgó.
5. ¿Prepararon los tamales tus tíos? Sí, mis tíos ya los prepararon.
6. ¿Terminaste con los preparativos? Sí, ya los terminé.

Game

Un año de celebraciones

1. On index cards write verbs associated with having a party. Place the cards face down in a pile. On another set of index cards, write the names of all the celebrations listed in **Vocabulario 2,** pp. 192–193, and place the pile face down as well. Write the twelve months of the year in a column on the board. **2.** Divide the class into two teams. **3.** Call on a student from Team A to draw a card from each pile. He or she then creates a sentence mentioning the first month on the board (**enero**) as well as the event and the verb drawn. The verb should be conjugated in the preterite. For example, the student might draw **la boda** and **charlar.** He or she might then say **En enero mis primos y yo charlamos en la boda. 4.** If the student from Team A makes a logical sentence and conjugates the verb correctly, place an X by that month. A new member from Team A draws two more cards and tries to create a sentence for **febrero.** If Team A's sentence is not correct, then Team B gets an opportunity to make a sentence with the cards. **5.** The first team to complete a sentence for the most months wins.

STANDARDS: 1.2, 1.3, 4.1, 4.2

27 **La fiesta de Mila**

1. una graduación 2. Limpiaron la casa, prepararon comida, compraron y colgaron decoraciones. 3. La fiesta estuvo divertida. 4. Los invitados bailaron, charlaron, enseñaron fotos, comieron sándwiches y pastel, bebieron ponche y escucharon música.

Escribamos/Hablemos Contesta las siguientes preguntas básandote en el dibujo.

1. ¿Qué ocasión especial festejaron?
2. ¿Qué preparativos hicieron *(did they make)* antes de la fiesta?
3. ¿Qué tal estuvo la fiesta?
4. ¿Qué pasó en la fiesta?

Comunicación

28 **Historia de una fiesta**

Escribamos/Hablemos With two classmates, write a story about the preparations for a party, the party itself, and what happened after the party. Each member of the group should write one section of the story. Compare each part of the story carefully so that it makes sense when you read the three parts together. Be prepared to present your narrative to the class.

MODELO —**Antes de la fiesta compramos muchas cosas. Fuimos a la tienda y...**
—**El día de la fiesta empezó a llover. Los invitados llegaron tarde y...**
—**Después de la fiesta limpiamos la casa. Empezamos en la cocina y...**

Culture

Products and Perspectives

La piñata Breaking the **piñata** is a much anticipated activity in Hispanic family celebrations. A similar tradition was practiced in Italy in the 16th century. People made large clay pots, filled them with candies and hung them from ceilings for children to break open. That tradition traveled to Spain, and from there made its way to the Americas with Spanish settlers. Today **piñatas** are made from paper maché, in a wide variety of forms, and covered with colorful tissue paper fringe. Many stores in Latin America specialize in selling just **piñatas** and the candy and toys that go inside. Ask students if they have had a chance to participate in preparing or breaking a **piñata.**

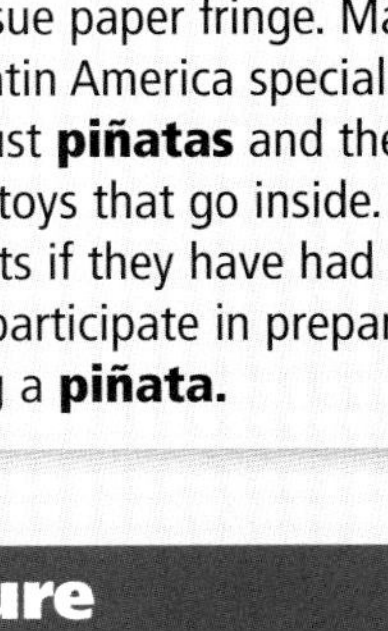

Culture

Products and Perspectives

Fiestas The Dominican Republic's Independence day is celebrated on February 27. On that day in the capital city of Santo Domingo, thousands of costumed people join a huge parade and march down **El Malecón** (see pages 176–177). The practice of using costumes to celebrate patriotic events dates back to before the island's independence, when the Spanish colony would hold **carnavales** and dress up as **moros y cristianos.**

Comunicación

Pair Activity: Interpersonal

Have pairs of students use the questions in Activity 27 to interview each other about a recent or favorite celebration.

Differentiated Instruction

ADVANCED LEARNERS

Challenge Have students create a greeting card to send to a grandparent or other relative on the next major holiday, or for a birthday. Let students use a bilingual dictionary for new words, if needed. Ask them to write a translation of the Spanish greeting on the back of the card. Have students bring a stamped, addressed envelope from home, and mail all the cards from school.

MULTIPLE INTELLIGENCES

Bodily/Kinesthetic Have students play "Holiday Activity Charades" in small groups. Use the phrases in Activity 25, page 194, writing each one on a slip of paper and placing them all in a container. Have one student from each group draw out a slip and act out the phrase for other members of the group to guess. You may want to set a time limit of 2 or 3 minutes for each Charade. Continue until all students have had a chance to act out a phrase.

STANDARDS: 1.2, 1.3

Resources

Planning:

Lesson Planner, pp. 113–117, 266–273

 One-Stop Planner

Presentation:

TPR Storytelling Book, pp. 50–51

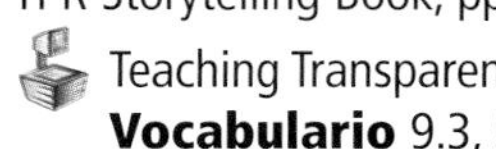 Teaching Transparencies **Vocabulario** 9.3, 9.4

 Video Program
Videocassette 5
DVD Tutor, Disc 2
ExpresaVisión

Practice:

Cuaderno de vocabulario y gramática, pp. 59–61

Activities for Communication, pp. 35–36

Video Guide, pp. 84–85, 88

Lab Book, pp. 29–30, 58

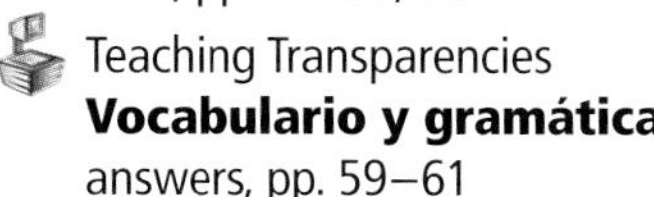 Teaching Transparencies **Vocabulario y gramática** answers, pp. 59–61

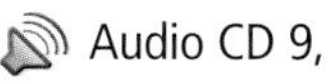 Audio CD 9, Tr. 6

Interactive Tutor, Disc 2

29 Script

1. Nos vemos más tarde.
2. Tanto tiempo sin verte. ¿Cómo estás?
3. Hola. ¿Qué hay de nuevo?
4. Chao. ¡Que te vaya bien!
5. Te presento a mi compañera de clase.
6. Mucho gusto. Soy su hermano.
7. ¡Qué gusto verte!
8. Cuídate.

¡Exprésate!

To greet, introduce others, and say goodbye

¡Qué gusto verte! *It's great to see you!*	**¡Tanto tiempo sin verte!** *Long time, no see!*
¿Qué hay de nuevo? *What's new?*	**Lo de siempre.** *Same as usual.*
Te presento a mis padres. *I'd like you to meet my parents.*	**Tanto gusto. ¡Feliz aniversario!** *So nice to meet you. Happy anniversary!*
Chao, te llamo más tarde. *Bye, I'll call you later.*	**Vale. Que te vaya bien.** *Okay. Hope things go well for you.*
	Cuídate. *Take care.*

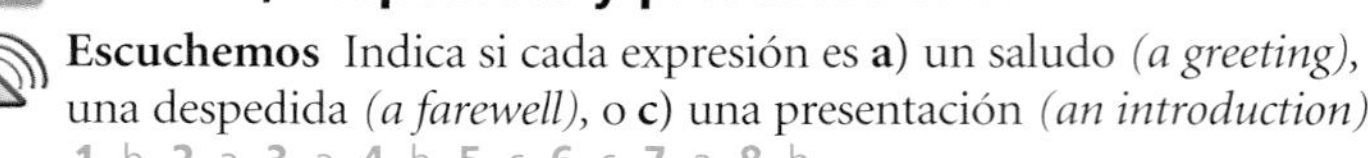

CD 9, Tr. 6

29 Saludos, despedidas y presentaciones

Escuchemos Indica si cada expresión es **a)** un saludo *(a greeting)*, **b)** una despedida *(a farewell)*, o **c)** una presentación *(an introduction)*.

1. b 2. a 3. a 4. b 5. c 6. c 7. a 8. b

30 ¡Qué gusto verte!

Leamos Escoge la mejor respuesta a cada oración.

1. Voy a llegar tarde. No puedo hablar ahora. c
2. Hasta luego. d
3. Te presento a mi hermano. f
4. Hoy es nuestro aniversario. b
5. ¿Qué hay de nuevo? a
6. Después de dos años, volví de África. e

a. Lo de siempre.
b. ¡Feliz aniversario!
c. Chao, te llamo más tarde.
d. Que te vaya bien.
e. ¡Tanto tiempo sin verte!
f. Tanto gusto.

31 ¿Qué dices?

Leamos/Hablemos Decide qué expresiones de **¡Exprésate!** puedes usar en estas situaciones.

1. Ves a un amigo después de tres años.
2. Acabas de presentar a dos amigos.
3. Estás con tus padres y ves a un amigo que no los conoce.
4. Vas a hablar por teléfono con un amigo más tarde.
5. Un amigo va a la República Dominicana por dos años.
6. Estás muy contento(a) de ver a un amigo.
7. Un amigo quiere saber qué hiciste ayer pero no hiciste nada nuevo.
8. Tu hermana va a pasar un año en China.

Possible answers:
1. ¡Tanto tiempo sin verte!
2. Tanto gusto.
3. Te presento a mis padres.
4. Chao, te llamo más tarde.
5. Que te vaya bien.
6. ¡Qué gusto verte!
7. Lo de siempre.
8. Cuídate.

Core Instruction

TEACHING ¡EXPRÉSATE!

1. Introduce the new expressions in **¡Exprésate!,** modeling the pronunciation of each new word and phrase. **(5 min.)**
2. Use the new expressions to act out both sides of a conversation. You may want to use puppets or stuffed animals to portray the participants in the conversation. **(5 min.)**
3. Randomly call out expressions from **¡Exprésate!** Ask students whether each expression would be used to greet, introduce, or say goodbye. **(5 min.)**

STANDARDS: 1.2

32 Te presento a...

Leamos Lili and José haven't seen each other for a while. Complete the conversation with appropriate phrases from **¡Exprésate!**

JOSE Hola Lili. ¡Tanto __1__! tiempo sin verte
LILI ¡Qué gusto verte! ¿Qué hay __2__? de nuevo
JOSE __3__. Lo de siempre
LILI José, __4__ a mi mamá. te presento
JOSE __5__. Tanto gusto.
SRA. LÓPEZ Igualmente.
LILI José, ¿quieres venir a una fiesta mañana?
JOSE Lo siento. No puedo ir. Mañana voy a Florida.
LILI Vale. __6__. Que te vaya bien.

Comunicación

33 ¿Qué dicen?

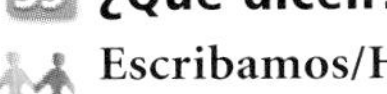

Escribamos/Hablemos Work with a partner. Choose two photos and write conversations based on each photo. Be prepared to role-play each conversation for the class.

1

2

3

4

34 Una reunion

Escribamos/Hablemos In groups of three role-play the following situation. Three years from now you meet a middle school friend at a party. You have come to the party with a new friend from high school. Introduce your new friend. Talk with both friends about the party and about what you are doing now in high school. Be prepared to present your role-play to the class.

Más práctica

32 Have students act out the conversation, using their own names in place of José, Lili, and Sra. López.

Extension

32 Divide students into groups of three to write and act out a new version of the conversation in Activity 32. Ask them to make the following changes:

- the invitation to the party is accepted and the person invited asks what time and where it is
- the mother is also invited to come
- the mother asks a question

Comunicación

Group Activity: Presentational

Divide the class into groups of two to four students and assign each group one of the scenarios in Activity 31, page 196. Give them 10 minutes to prepare and practice a short skit based on their particular scenario. Instruct them to have at least two speaking lines per person. After 10 minutes, have them present the impromptu skits to the class.

Differentiated Instruction

ADVANCED LEARNERS

Extension Have students bring magazine pictures that show people interacting at a party or celebration, or greeting or introducing someone. Then divide the class into small groups and ask them to create conversations for two of the pictures. Have them present one of the conversations to another group.

SPECIAL LEARNING NEEDS

Students with Learning Disabilities Allow extra time for students with LD to practice the phrases in **¡Exprésate!** on page 196. Write each phrase on an index card. Then have each student work with a partner to practice the expressions. You might have them match a statement or question with the appropriate response first, then act out the conversations with a partner, using the cards as prompts.

Assess

Assessment Program

Prueba: Vocabulario 2, pp. 83–84

Alternative Assessment Guide, pp. 244, 252, 260

Test Generator

STANDARDS: 1.1, 1.2, 1.3

Resources

Planning:

Lesson Planner, pp. 118–123, 272–277

 One-Stop Planner

Presentation:

Video Program
Videocassette 5
DVD Tutor, Disc 2
GramaVisión

Practice:

Grammar Tutor for Students of Spanish, Chapter 9

Cuaderno de vocabulario y gramática, pp. 62–64

Cuaderno de actividades, pp. 49–51

Activities for Communication, pp. 35–36

Video Guide, pp. 84–85

Lab Book, pp. 29–30

 Teaching Transparencies
Bell Work 9.6
Vocabulario y gramática answers, pp. 62–64

Interactive Tutor, Disc 2

Bell Work

Use Bell Work 9.6 in the *Teaching Transparencies*, or write this activity on the board.

Choose the correct ending to each sentence about Maite's party.

1. Tengo que mandar...
2. Necesito colgar...
3. Para comer mi madre prepara...
4. Para beber voy a preparar...
5. En la fiesta sólo quiero...

a. los pasteles en hoja.
b. las invitaciones.
c. charlar.
d. el ponche.
e. las decoraciones.

Objetivos
Using direct object pronouns, **conocer** and personal **a**, the present progressive

Gramática en acción 2

GramaVisión

Direct object pronouns

Interactive TUTOR

1 Direct objects are people or things that receive the action of a verb. To avoid repetition, the **direct object pronouns** can take their place.

Subject	Direct Object		Subject	Direct Object	
yo	**me**	*me*	nosotros(as)	**nos**	*us*
tú	**te**	*you*	vosotros(as)	**os**	*you*
usted (m.)	**lo**	*you*	ustedes (m.)	**los**	*you*
usted (f.)	**la**	*you*	ustedes (f.)	**las**	*you*
él	**lo**	*him*	ellos	**los**	*them*
ella	**la**	*her*	ellas	**las**	*them*

la stands for Paula

—¿Invitaste a **Paula?** —Sí, **la** invité. Ella viene.
Did you invite Paula? Yes, I invited her. She's coming.

2 When answering a question, remember to change the **direct object pronoun**, if necessary.

object me changes to te

—¿**Me** vas a llamar? —Sí, **te** llamo más tarde.
Are you going to call me? Yes, I'll call you later.

Online
Vocabulario y gramática, pp. 62–64 | Actividades, pp. 49–51

¿Te acuerdas?

The **direct object pronouns lo** *(him, it)*, **la** *(her, it)*, **los** *(them)* and **las** *(them)* can stand for things as well as people.

—¿Ya compraste **las flores?**
—Sí, ya **las** compré.

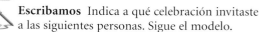

35 Invitaciones

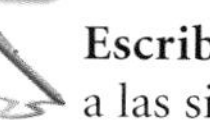

Escribamos Indica a qué celebración invitaste a las siguientes personas. Sigue el modelo.

MODELO La invité a la quinceañera.

Ana

1. a mis abuelos

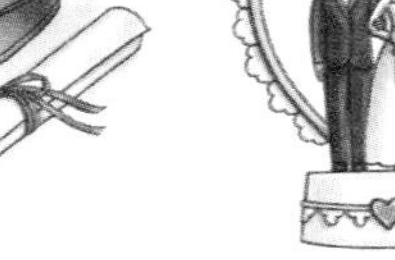
2. a mi profesora

3. a mis amigas

4. a mi primo

Core Instruction

TEACHING GRAMÁTICA

1. Go over **¿Te acuerdas?** If students need more review with this concept, see the *Grammar Tutor.* **(5 min.)**
2. Go over Points 1 and 2. **(10 min.)**
3. Ask students if they did various things yesterday. Have them answer with a direct object pronoun. For example, if you ask **¿Mandaste las invitaciones?**, students would answer **Sí, las mandé. (No, no las mandé.) (10 min.)**

GramaVisión

For a video presentation of direct object pronouns, use **el joven G** from the *Video Program.* For interactive activities, see the *DVD Tutor.*

GramaVisión

STANDARDS: 1.2, 1.3

Visit Holt Online
go.hrw.com
KEYWORD: EXP1B CH9
Gramática 2 practice

36 Una fiesta sorpresa

Escribamos/Hablemos Una amiga te ayuda con una fiesta para tu hermano José. Contesta las preguntas con un pronombre de complemento directo *(direct object pronoun)*.

¿Se te olvidó? Pronoun placement, p. 60

MODELO **Vas a llevar a *tu hermano* a la fiesta, ¿verdad? (sí)**
Sí, voy a llevarlo. (Sí, lo voy a llevar.)

1. ¿*Me* vas a llamar antes de la fiesta, ¿verdad? (sí)
2. José no debe ver *a los invitados* antes de entrar, ¿verdad? (no)
3. ¿Debo poner *los regalos* en la mesa del patio? (sí)
4. ¿Invitaste *a los estudiantes de su clase?* (sí)
5. ¿Él vio *las decoraciones?* (no)
6. ¿Tus padres *te* ayudaron a preparar todo? (sí)
7. ¿Tu hermano menor *nos* va a interrumpir durante los preparativos? (no)
8. ¿*Me* necesitas para mañana? (no)

37 ¡No nos fastidies!

Escribamos/Hablemos Usando un pronombre de complemento directo con el imperativo, dile a cada persona qué debe o no debe hacer.

¿Se te olvidó? Object pronouns and commands, p. 110

MODELO **Hablas con tus amigos y tu hermano los interrumpe.**
¡No nos interrumpas!

1. Un amigo que habla español nunca te ayuda a estudiar.
2. Hablas de algo secreto con un amigo y tu hermano los escucha.
3. El hermano menor de un amigo es antipático y tu amigo siempre lo trae cuando ustedes salen.
4. Tu mejor amigo no te llama.
5. Quieres comprar un regalo de cumpleaños para tu hermana y tu amigo la invita a ir de compras con ustedes.

Nota cultural

In most Spanish-speaking countries, including the Dominican Republic, dancing is an important part of any party. All kinds of music are played, food is served, and parties often do not end until the early morning hours. Spanish-speaking and Latin American countries have given us some of the most popular dances, including **merengue, salsa, samba, cha-cha-chá, tango, rumba,** and **cumbia.** Are these dances popular where you live?

1. ¡Ayúdame a estudiar! **2.** ¡No nos escuches! **3.** ¡No lo traigas! **4.** ¡Llámame! **5.** ¡No la invites!

Comunicación

38 Planes para una fiesta

Hablemos In pairs, talk about plans for a party. When will you have the party? Say who is going to help you with the preparations. What are you going to serve? What are you going to need and where are you going to put everything?

MODELO **—¿Cuándo quieres hacer tu fiesta de cumpleaños?**
—Quiero hacerla en dos semanas.

35 Answers

1. Los invité a la graduación.
2. La invité a la boda.
3. Las invité a la fiesta de cumpleaños.
4. Lo invité a la casa para celebrar la Navidad.

36 Answers

1. Sí, te voy a llamar antes de la fiesta. / Sí, voy a llamarte antes de la fiesta.
2. No, no debe verlos antes de entrar. / No, no los debe ver antes de entrar.
3. Sí, debes ponerlos en la mesa del patio. / Sí, los debes poner en la mesa del patio.
4. Sí, los invité.
5. No, no las vio.
6. Sí, me ayudaron a preparar todo.
7. No, no nos va a interrumpir. / No, no va a interrumpirnos.
8. No, no te necesito para mañana.

Communities

Career Path

Some people make a living as professional party planners. How would planners benefit from speaking Spanish? Have students imagine that they are able to hire a party planner for their next birthday or other significant celebration. Tell them to write a paragraph, in Spanish, describing the ideal party that the planner has designed for them.

Differentiated Instruction

SLOWER PACE LEARNERS

37 To prepare students for Activity 37, review the affirmative and negative informal command forms with the class. Remind students that the object pronouns are connected to the affirmative informal command and will often require a written accent to be added in order for the command to maintain proper pronunciation. The object pronoun must be placed before the negative command form. Read the sentences in class and decide which sentences will most likely be negative commands and which will be affirmative.

SPECIAL LEARNING NEEDS

Students with Visual Impairments These students might miss the opportunity for a visual explanation of how direct object pronouns can replace direct objects. When you define for students what a direct object is, you might change the pitch of your voice to indicate what the direct object is within a given phrase, giving the student an extra auditory clue when you might otherwise underline or circle the direct object. You might also display your examples in large handwriting on a transparency.

Comunicación

38 Individual Activity: Presentational

Ask students to prepare a written invitation for the party that they planned in Activity 38. You may show students authentic invitation cards from Spanish-speaking countries. Students may use computer page layout, printing or word-processing software to print a copy of their invitation.

Resources

Planning:

Lesson Planner, pp. 118–123, 272–277

 One-Stop Planner

Presentation:

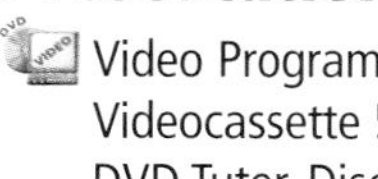 Video Program
Videocassette 5
DVD Tutor, Disc 2
GramaVisión

Practice:

Grammar Tutor for Students of Spanish, Chapter 9

Cuaderno de vocabulario y gramática, pp. 62–64

Cuaderno de actividades, pp. 49–51

Activities for Communication, pp. 35–36

Video Guide, pp. 84–85

Lab Book, pp. 29–30

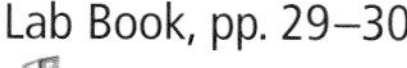 Teaching Transparencies
Bell Work 9.7
Vocabulario y gramática answers, pp. 62–64

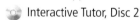

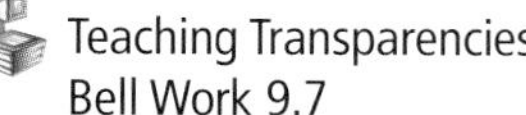 Interactive Tutor, Disc 2

Bell Work

Use Bell Work 9.7 in the *Teaching Transparencies*, or write this activity on the board.

Write the correct direct object pronoun to complete each sentence.

1. —¿Ustedes invitaron a Paula a su fiesta?
—Sí, _____ invitamos.
2. —¿Te llamó Juan Carlos?
—No, no _____ llamó.
3. —¿Tú y yo vamos a la fiesta también?
—No, no _____ invitaron.
4. —¿Por qué no traes las papitas a la mesa?
—Bueno, _____ traigo ahora.
5. ¿Viste los dulces para la piñata?
—No, no _____ vi.

Conocer and personal a

1 The verb **conocer** is used to say you know people or meet them, or that you are familiar with a place or a thing. It is irregular in the **yo** form.

yo	cono**zco**	nosotros(as)	conocemos
tú	conoces	vosotros(as)	conocéis
Ud., él, ella	conoce	Uds., ellos, ellas	conocen

—Aquí viene mi prima Claudia. ¿Quieres conocerla?
—Ya la **conozco**.

2 When a name or noun referring to a person is the **direct object** of **conocer** or other verbs, the word **a** comes before it. This **a** has no translation.

—¿**Conoces a mi hermano**?
—Sí, **conozco a toda tu familia**.

The preposition **a** combines with the definite article **el** to form the contraction **al.**

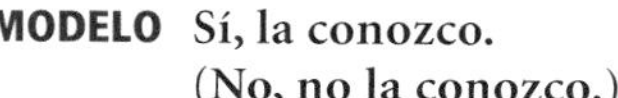
Online
Vocabulario y gramática, pp. 62–64 | Actividades, pp. 49–51

39 ¿Conoces sus obras?

Escribamos Indica si conoces o no las obras *(works)* de estos hispanos famosos. Usa un pronombre de complemento directo.

MODELO **Sí, la conozco.**
(No, no la conozco.)

la música de Andrés Segovia

1. las películas de Antonio Banderas

2. los libros de Isabel Allende

3. las canciones de Shakira

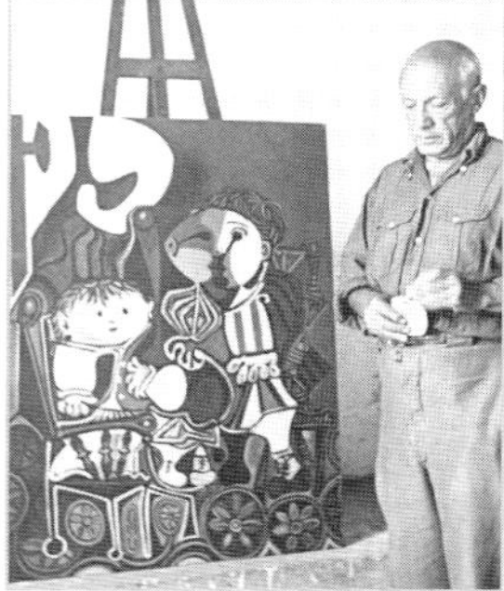
4. las obras de Pablo Picasso

Core Instruction

TEACHING GRAMÁTICA

1. Go over Point 1. Model the pronunciation of each form of **conocer. (2 min.)**
2. Go over Point 2. **(2 min.)**
3. Ask students if they know various people, students, teachers, or celebrities. Have them answer with **Sí, la/lo conozco** or **No, no la/lo conozco. (2 min.)**
4. Have students add the conjugation of **conocer** to the verb conjugation chart in their notebooks. **(3 min.)**

GramaVisión

For a video presentation of **conocer** and personal **a,** use **el joven G** from the *Video Program*. For interactive activities, see the *DVD Tutor.*

GramaVisión

STANDARDS: 1.2, 2.1, 2.2, 4.2

40 Presentaciones

Leamos Completa la siguiente conversación con las formas correctas de **conocer**, los pronombres de complemento directo o la palabra **a**.

SONIA Mario y Daniel, ¡qué gusto verlos! ¿ __1__ a mi hermano Carlos? Conocen

DANIEL No, no lo __2__. conocemos

SONIA Carlos, te presento __3__ mis amigos Mario y Daniel. Mario y Daniel, les presento __4__ mi hermano Carlos. a a

CARLOS Mario, ¿no eres el primo de Alberto Martínez?

MARIO Sí, soy su primo. ¿ __5__ conoces? Lo

CARLOS Sí, lo __6__ muy bien. Está en mi clase de historia y a veces jugamos al tenis después de clases. conozco

Un supermercado en la República Dominicana

41 ¿Se conocen?

Leamos/Escribamos Lee cada oración. Indica si estas personas conocen a las personas o las cosas entre paréntesis. Repite la respuesta usando un pronombre de complemento directo.

MODELO **Mis padres siempre invitan a mi mejor amigo a nuestra casa. (mi mejor amigo)**
Mis padres conocen bien a mi mejor amigo.
Mis padres lo conocen bien.

1. Juan habla con Sara todos los días. (Sara)
2. Mi tía sabe dónde están las tiendas, los restaurantes, el colegio, el correo y el cine. (la ciudad)
3. Mis abuelos quieren venir a mi colegio pero no saben dónde está. (el pueblo)
4. Mi mejor amigo viene a mi casa los fines de semana. (mi casa)
5. Mi madre quiere hablar con mi profesor de español pero no sabe cómo se llama. (mi profesor de español)
6. Lola está en mi clase de inglés. Es muy simpática. (Lola)

Comunicación

42 Un encuentro

Hablemos Imagine that you are at a party. In groups of four, take turns introducing two of your classmates to another person. You can use Activity 40 as model for your conversation.

39 Answers

Possible answers:
1. Sí, (No, no) las conozco.
2. Sí, (No, no) los conozco.
3. Sí, (No, no) las conozco.
4. Sí, (No, no) las conozco.

41 Answers

1. Juan conoce bien a Sara. La conoce bien.
2. Mi tía conoce bien la ciudad. La conoce bien.
3. Mis abuelos no conocen el pueblo. No lo conocen.
4. Mi mejor amigo conoce bien mi casa. La conoce bien.
5. Mi madre no conoce a mi profesor de español. No lo conoce.
6. Conozco a Lola. La conozco.

Comunicación

Class Activity: Interpersonal

Arrange the class into two concentric circles with students in the inner circle facing the students in the outer circle. Present a scenario in which the student in the inner circle has just met the new Spanish-speaking exchange student. The student in the inner circle asks the student in the outer circle if she or he has met the new student and give a description of the student. The students in the outer circle say that they have not yet met the student but wish to get to know him or her. Conclude the conversation with an invitation to meet. When students have completed the conversation, have the inner circle rotate two places and repeat the conversation again. Repeat several more times switching roles of students in the inner and outer circle. To check comprehension, call on several pairs to repeat their conversation or play a role in one of the conversations.

Differentiated Instruction

ADVANCED LEARNERS

39 As an extension to Activity 39, have students write down the name of their favorite artist (actor, writer, musician, or painter). Call on a student to ask the class if they know the work of that artist. Since they are addressing the class, tell them to use **Conocen...** Then call on a student to answer the question. Remind students to place the direct object in the correct position in the sentence.

MULTIPLE INTELLIGENCES

Interpersonal Have students cut out pictures of ten famous people to post on a poster board in the classroom. Each student should number their pictures, 1–10 for the first student, 11–20 for the second, and so on. Have the class write down whether or not they know each person. If they know the person, they should write, **Sí, la/lo conozco** and the name of the person. If they don't know the person, they should write **No, no la/lo conozco.** Then, let students tell the names of the people from their posterboard, in numbered order, and have other students check their results.

STANDARDS: 1.1, 1.2

Resources

Planning:

Lesson Planner, pp. 118–123, 272–277

One-Stop Planner

Presentation:

Video Program
Videocassette 5
DVD Tutor, Disc 2
GramaVisión

Practice:

Grammar Tutor for Students of Spanish, Chapter 9

Cuaderno de vocabulario y gramática, pp. 62–64

Cuaderno de actividades, pp. 49–51

Activities for Communication, pp. 35–36

Video Guide, pp. 84–85

Lab Book, pp. 29–30

Teaching Transparencies
Bell Work 9.8
Vocabulario y gramática answers, pp. 62–64

Audio CD 9, Tr. 7

Interactive Tutor, Disc 2

Bell Work

Use Bell Work 9.8 in the *Teaching Transparencies*, or write this activity on the board.

Use the correct form of **conocer** or **conocer a** to complete each sentence.

1. Luisa: Hola, Jaime. ¿Tú _____ mi amiga Nora?
2. Jaime: Sí, yo la _____. ¿Cómo estás, Nora?
3. Nora: Muy bien, gracias. Jaime y yo nos _____ muy bien. ¿Verdad?
4. Jaime: Sí. Mi madre _____ su madre por el trabajo.
5. Luisa: ¡Bueno! ¡Mis padres no _____ nadie!

43 Script

See script on p. 175E.

Present progressive

En inglés

In English, the present progressive can mean that something is happening right now, happens regularly, or will happen in the future.

Everyone *is celebrating* in the living room.

We *are spending* a lot of time together.

Tomorrow I *am leaving* for La Paz.

In Spanish, the present progressive can mean that something is happening right now or happens regularly. However, it is not used for events in the future. Instead, the simple present is used.

Todos **están** cantando.

Estamos pasando mucho tiempo juntos.

Mañana **salgo** para La Paz.

1 To say what is happening right now, use the present progressive. To form the present progressive, combine a conjugated form of **estar** with the present participle. Form the present participle by replacing **-ar** with **-ando** and **-er** or **-ir** with **-iendo**.

cantar → cant**ando**
Rosa **está** cant**ando**. *Rosa is singing.*
comer → com**iendo**
Estamos com**iendo**. *We are eating.*

2 When the stem of an **-er** or **-ir** verb ends in a vowel, form the present participle by changing **i** of -iendo to **y** (-yendo).

leer → le**y**endo
¿**Estás** le**y**endo? *Are you reading?*

3 The participles of stem-changing **-ir** verbs like **pedir, dormir,** and **servir** change **o** → **u** and **e** → **i**. There are no stem changes for **-ar** and **-er** verbs.

dormir → d**u**rmiendo   servir → s**i**rviendo

4 The verbs **ir** and **venir** are not usually used in the present progressive. Use the simple present tense instead.

—¿**Vienes** a la fiesta? *Are you coming to the party?*
—No, **voy** a la biblioteca. *No, I'm going to the library.*

5 **Direct object** and **reflexive pronouns** can go before the conjugated form of **estar** or can be attached to the end of the present participle. When you attach the direct object or reflexive pronoun to the end of the present participle, place an accent mark on the stressed vowel.

¿La tarea? **La** estoy haciendo. (Estoy haciéndo**la**)
¿Mis hijos? **Se** están bañando. (Están bañándo**se**.)

Online
Vocabulario y gramática, pp. 62–64 | Actividades, pp. 49–51

CD 9, Tr. 7

43 ¿Qué están haciendo?

Escuchemos Escucha las oraciones sobre la fiesta de Patricia y Roberto. Escoge las preguntas que le correspondan según el contexto.

a. ¿Qué están haciendo ustedes?
b. ¿Qué están haciendo los invitados?
c. ¿Qué está haciendo tu madre?

1. b 2. a 3. c 4. a 5. b 6. b 7. a

Core Instruction

TEACHING GRAMÁTICA

1. Go over **En inglés** and Point 1. **(4 min.)**
2. Pantomime an activity. The class will try to guess what you are doing. **¿Estás jugando al béisbol? (4 min.)**
3. Go over Points 2, 3, 4, and 5. Then, ask students if they are doing various things. Have them write their answers, using direct object pronouns when necessary. **¿Me estás escuchando? Sí, estoy escuchándote. (7 min.)**
4. Have students add notes about the present progressive to the verb chart in their notebooks. **(2 min.)**

GramaVisión

For a video presentation of the present progressive, use **el joven G** from the *Video Program*. For interactive activities, see the *DVD Tutor.*

GramaVisión

STANDARDS: 1.2

44 ¿Dónde están?

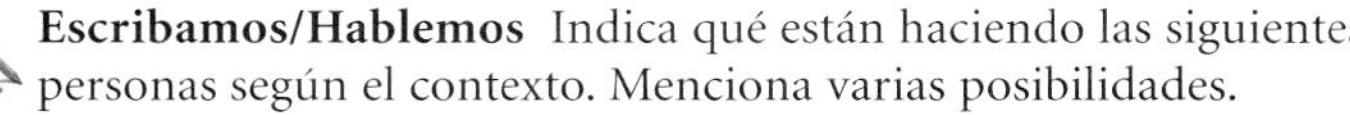

Escribamos/Hablemos Indica qué están haciendo las siguientes personas según el contexto. Menciona varias posibilidades.

MODELO **Consuelo está en su cuarto.** Possible answers:
Está durmiendo. Está estudiando.

1. Lupe está en la clase.
2. Juan y Carlos están en el parque.
3. Laura y José están en una fiesta de cumpleaños.
4. Mi hermana y yo estamos en la cocina.
5. Estás en una tienda.
6. Tu primo y tú están en un restaurante.

1. Está leyendo. Está escuchando a la profesora.
2. Están jugando al fútbol. Están corriendo.
3. Están escuchando música. Están bailando.
4. Estamos preparando comida. Estamos comiendo.
5. Estás comprando ropa. Estás probándote una camisa.
6. Están pidiendo algo de comer. Están comiendo y bebiendo.

Comunicación

45 Pantomimas

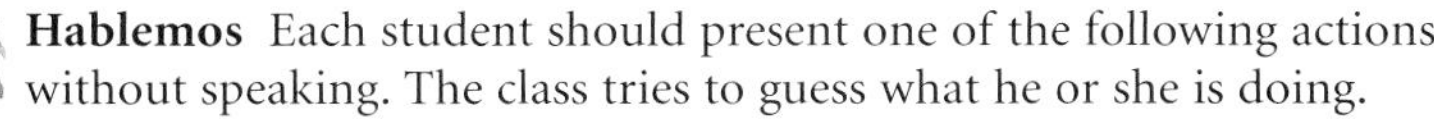

Hablemos Each student should present one of the following actions without speaking. The class tries to guess what he or she is doing.

hablar por teléfono	abrir un regalo	escribir una tarjeta
lavarse los dientes	secarse el pelo	maquillarse
peinarse	servir comida	acostarse

46 Una fiesta

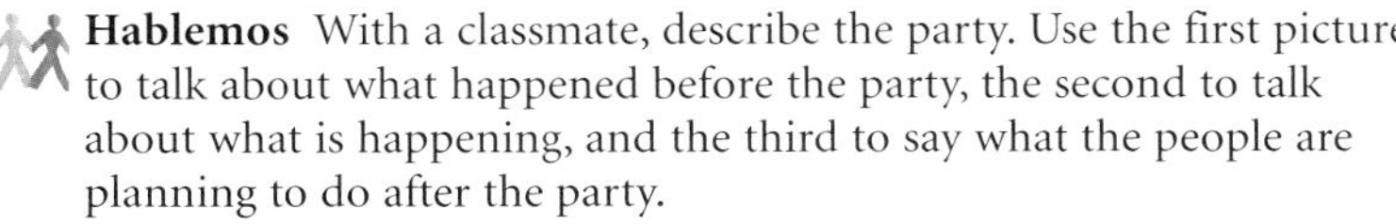

Hablemos With a classmate, describe the party. Use the first picture to talk about what happened before the party, the second to talk about what is happening, and the third to say what the people are planning to do after the party.

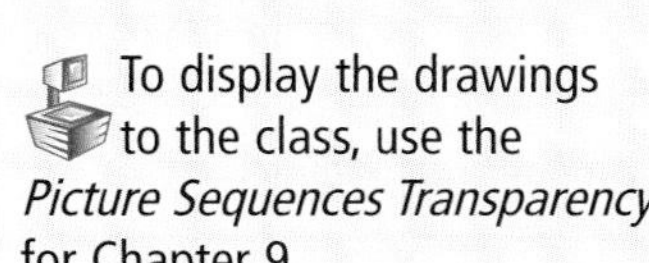

AP Language Examination

To display the drawings to the class, use the *Picture Sequences Transparency* for Chapter 9.

46 Below is a sample answer for the picture description activity.

Antes de la fiesta la mamá y la hija limpiaron la casa. Luego colgaron las decoraciones. Paco preparó la comida (un pastel) en la cocina. Ahora los invitados están comiendo y bebiendo. También están charlando y escuchando música. Después de la fiesta la familia piensa descansar y luego limpiar la casa. La mamá está durmiendo en el sofá, la hija está leyendo un libro y el hijo está viendo la tele.

Comunicación

Individual Activity: Presentational

Assign students to research and report about unique customs for celebrating holidays in various Spanish-speaking countries. As an alternative, students could report on unique traditions for celebrating holidays in their families.

Differentiated Instruction

ADVANCED LEARNERS

45 Add enough verbs or verb phrases to the list in the box of Activity 45 to equal the number of students in the class. Write each of the verbs on slips of paper to be randomly drawn from a bag. After each one has been used, set it aside and make sure that every student pantomimes a different activity. Additional possibilities are: **leer una revista, escuchar música, patinar, comer helado, beber ponche,** and **ver televisión.**

SPECIAL LEARNING NEEDS

44 **Students with Learning Disabilities** To modify Activity 44, convert items 1–6 to fill-in-the-blank answers. For further modification, you might also give students a word bank. **Lupe está ____. (estudiar)** Have students complete the activity with a partner.

Assess

Assessment Program

Prueba: Gramática 2, pp. 85–86

Prueba: Aplicación 2, pp. 87–88

Alternative Assessment Guide, pp. 244, 252, 260

Audio CD 9, Tr. 16

Test Generator

STANDARDS: 1.2, 1.3

Resources

Planning:

Lesson Planner, pp. 123–124, 276–279

 One-Stop Planner

Connections

Multicultural Link

Arbor Day and Earth Day are both spring holidays that promote a healthy environment. Arbor Day, on which people plant trees, began in 1872. The exact date on which it is celebrated varies from state to state and country to country. It is celebrated at the end of May in Venezuela. When is Arbor Day celebrated in your state?
Earth Day is celebrated on April 22. Celebrations on Earth Day revolve around heightening awareness about water conservation, air quality, recycling and other programs that help foster a healthy environment on earth. Are there any Earth Day celebrations in or near your area? How do people participate?

Biology Link

The **araguaney,** or *tecoma,* is the Venezuelan national tree. It is a flowering tree of the *Tabebuia* genus, a category of hardwood trees used for such varied ends as musical instruments, bridges, industrial flooring, and expensive furniture. Brainstorm with students how the **araguaney** trees benefit the ecology and economy of Venezuela. Have students research where the trees grow and how they benefit the region.

Conexiones culturales

1 El Día del Árbol

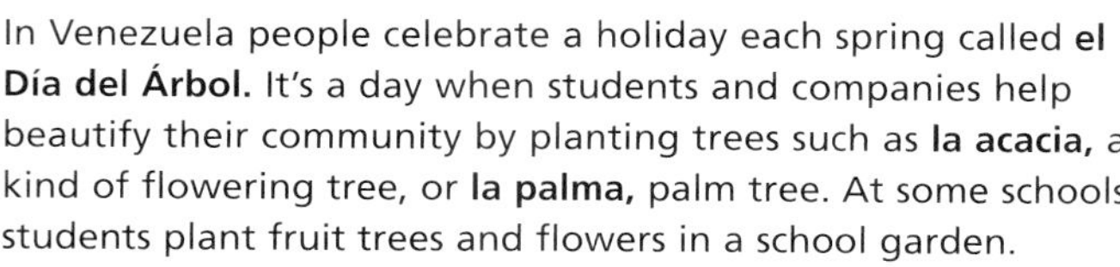

In Venezuela people celebrate a holiday each spring called **el Día del Árbol.** It's a day when students and companies help beautify their community by planting trees such as **la acacia,** a kind of flowering tree, or **la palma,** palm tree. At some schools students plant fruit trees and flowers in a school garden.

1. What kind of tree would you prefer to plant and why? How do trees help the environment?
2. If you plant a four-foot-tall palm tree this year that grows nine inches a year, how tall will it be when you're 18? when you are 50?
3. Is there a similar holiday where you live? Explain.

Possible answers:
1. avocado tree; could eat the avocadoes; Trees are important for shade, food, and clean air.
2. Possible answers: If the student is 13; 7'9" at 18 and 31'9" at 50
3. Arbor Day or Earth Day

Core Instruction

TEACHING CONEXIONES CULTURALES

1. Read aloud Activity 1 (**El día del árbol**). Present Multicultural and Biology Links. **(7 min.)**
2. Put students in small groups to answer the questions in Activity 1. Share answers in a class discussion. **(10 min.)**
3. To present Activity 2 (**La invitación**), do Thinking Critically on page 205. **(5 min.)**
4. Have students look for cognates and list them on the board. You may want them to look up meanings of unfamiliar words (**mundo, lejano, bosque**) and list them, also. **(10 min.)**
5. Read the poem and use the Teacher Note to clarify meaning. Do item 1. **(13 min.)**
6. Assign item 2 as homework.

STANDARDS: 2.1, 4.2

Visit Holt Online
go.hrw.com
KEYWORD: EXP1B CH9
Online Edition

Conexión Literatura

2 La invitación

Look at the following poem. See if you can guess what the poem is about before you begin reading. Make sure to use reading strategies such as thinking about the topic, looking for cognates, and looking for words you've already learned.

Sube a mi tronco
El árbol gigantesco te invita
El que bebe agua cristalina y canta aire azul
¡Ven! Sube a mis hombros, juega en mis brazos
¡Ven! Conoce el mundo desde un océano lejano
Descansa con la música verde de mis hojas
Baila conmigo el flamenco de mis flores
Y come la fruta rica del bosque
¡VEN!
SUBE
¡VEN!
SUBE
¡VEN!

1. What do you think the poem is about? What is the tree inviting someone to do? It's about climbing trees. It invites someone to climb it.
2. Write your own poem about your favorite park or your favorite holiday celebration. Play with the shape as shown in the poem above, and make your letters illustrate what you're describing.

Differentiated Instruction

ADVANCED LEARNERS

Personalization If students have been successful writing the poem in Activity 2, ask them to create another "shape" poem, this time about themselves. Have them draw a light pencil outline of one hand on a clean sheet of paper. Then ask them to create a poem, in which they describe themselves (their appearance, personality, likes, dislikes, and so on) and write it in pen in the outline of their hand. Finally, have them erase the pencil outline, and display the poems in class.

MULTIPLE INTELLIGENCES

Naturalistic Ask students to choose a state and find out what the state tree and flower are. Have them bring a picture of each to class and describe the plants to the other students. Would these trees and flowers grow in the area where you live? If possible, have them find the names of the plants in Spanish, also. Display the pictures on a **Día del Árbol** bulletin board.

Connections

Thinking Critically

2 As a pre-reading activity, ask students what the poem looks like (a tree). Ask them if they have ever climbed a tree. How did they climb it? How big was the tree? What was it like to be high above the ground? What did they see?

Teacher Note

The following are possible interpretations of the poem's metaphors **(metáforas):**
canta aire azul: The tree breathes air high in the blue sky.
juega en mis brazos: Play in my branches.
océano lejano: The leaves or the sky are an ocean far from the ground.
música verde de mis hojas: The sound of the leaves rustling.
Baila conmigo el flamenco de mis flores: Enjoy the wind blowing and swaying my branches and flowers.

Connections

Music Link

El flamenco The word **flamenco** refers to a style of music, song and dance that originated in Southern Spain. The music is characterized by guitars and emotional singing. The dancers use castanets **(castañuelas)** and rhythmic foot stomping. Flamenco performances are very colorful, with women wearing bright, long dresses with lots of ruffles.

STANDARDS: 1.2

Resources

Planning:

Lesson Planner, pp. 124–125, 278–279

 One-Stop Planner

Presentation:

 Video Program, Videocassette 5
DVD Tutor, Disc 2
VideoNovela

Practice:

Video Guide, pp. 84–85, 89
Lab Book, p. 59

Connections

Visual Learners

To help students better understand the confusion that occurs because of the dual action in this episode of **Novela en video,** have them create a flow chart of the action. Guide students through the chart, starting with the basic facts.

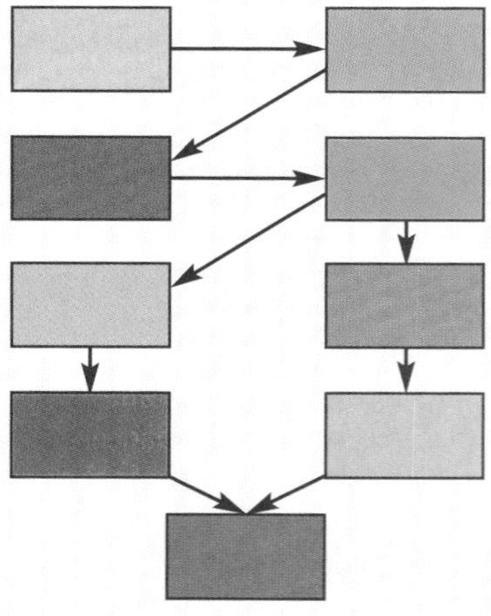

Gestures

Nicolás covers his face and bows his head when **Julia** and **Mateo** explain what happened at last year's party. What do these gestures mean? How do you think **Nicolás** is feeling when they tell everyone about the blunder? Are these gestures very different from how people react in the U.S. when they are embarrassed? What body language do you use when you feel embarrassed?

Novela en video

¿Quién será?

Episodio 9

ESTRATEGIA

Predicting When you plan an event, many things can go wrong. Before you read the **Novela** or watch the video, write a list of things that need to be done before a party. Write them in a logical sequence, then think about one or two things on your list that could go wrong. Compare your list with things mentioned in this episode. Based on the photos, predict what you think might go wrong in this episode. Read the **Novela** or watch the video to see how close your prediction was.

En Puerto Rico

Océano Atlántico
San Juan
PUERTO RICO
Mar Caribe

Nicolás hace los preparativos para la fiesta de cumpleaños de Mateo. Quiere la ayuda de su hermana Irene.

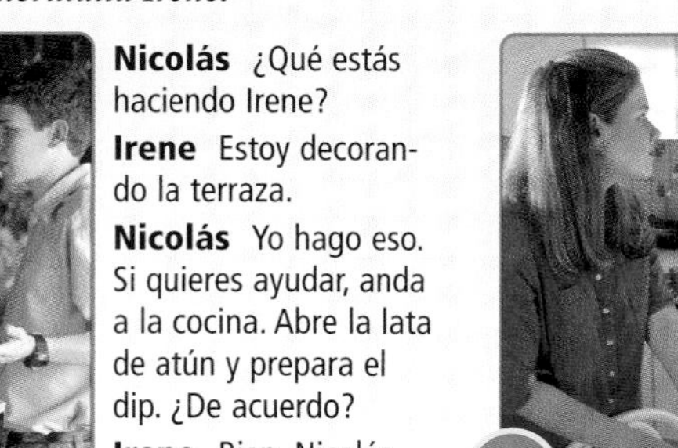

1 **Nicolás** ¿Qué estás haciendo Irene?
Irene Estoy decorando la terraza.
Nicolás Yo hago eso. Si quieres ayudar, anda a la cocina. Abre la lata de atún y prepara el dip. ¿De acuerdo?
Irene Bien, Nicolás.

2 **Mamá** Oye Irene, me parece que Picasso tiene hambe. ¿Quieres ponerle comida?
Irene Está bien, mamá.

3

4 **Julia** Hola Nicolás, ¿cómo te va? ¿Tú conoces a Mari?
Nicolás Claro que te conozco. ¿Qué tal, Mari? Esperen un momento. Voy a traer la comida.

Core Instruction

TEACHING NOVELA EN VIDEO

1. Play **Novela en video** stopping at the end of every scene. Read the conversation lines and have students repeat them, frame by frame. **(10 min.)**
2. After you have watched and read together the episode, play the video again, without stopping. Ask comprehension questions. **(5 min.)**
3. Have students read out loud the **Contesta** questions on pages 207–208. Call on student volunteers to answer the questions and discuss the answers as a class. **(5 min.)**

Captioned Video/DVD

As an alternative, you might use the captioned version.

STANDARDS: 1.2, 3.2

Visit Holt Online
go.hrw.com
KEYWORD: EXP1B CH9
Online Edition

5

Nicolás Bueno, por fin llegaste Mateo, el invitado de honor. Feliz cumpleaños. Este año va a ser una fiesta muy buena.

Mateo Mejor que la del año pasado.

Nicolás ¿Qué pasó el año pasado?

6

Mateo Julia mandó las invitaciones a todos, pero en la invitación no escribió en la casa de Nicolás. Escribió en la casa de Julia.

Nicolás Julia, Mateo y yo nos reunimos aquí, pero todos los invitados se reunieron en la casa de Julia.

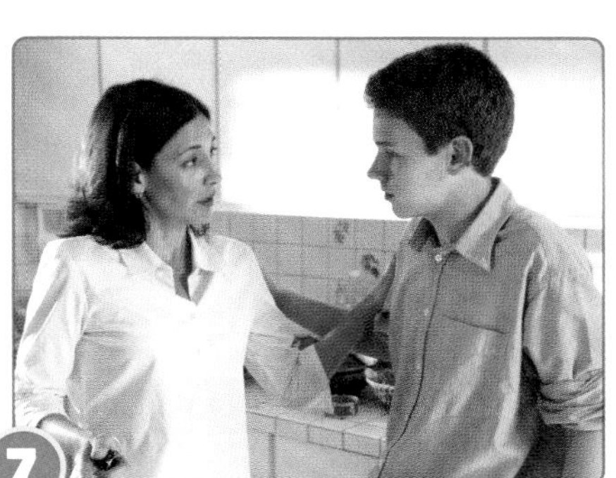

7

Mamá Nicolás, ¿cómo va todo?

Nicolás Muy bien, mamá. Todos están en la terraza. Están hablando. Acabo de poner la comida.

Mamá Muy bien. Voy a la casa de los abuelos por un rato. Te llamo más tarde, ¿eh?

Nicolás Gracias mamá.

8

Nicolás No puede ser. Ya lo están comiendo.

A. Contesta

1. What special occasion are the young people about to celebrate?
2. What does Nicolás want Irene to do?
3. What is the cat's name in the story?
4. What does Mamá ask Irene to do?
5. Where does Mamá go?

Novela en video

Answers
A. Contesta

1. Mateo's birthday
2. To help out in the kitchen
3. Picasso
4. To take out the trash and feed the cat
5. To visit the grandparents

Using the Strategy

Predicting Ask students if they have found clues, either in the text or visual clues, that might enable them to predict what is going to happen in the story. If not, direct them to frames 1, 3, and 8. Remind students of the importance of paying attention to visual clues when trying to predict the action in the **Novela.**

Connections

Thinking Critically

In Spanish-speaking countries, celebrations are often held at a public gathering place, rather than in a home. Ask students why friends might meet at their favorite coffee shop or restaurant to celebrate a special occasion. Where do they like to meet their friends?

Comparisons

Comparing and Contrasting

In some Spanish-speaking countries, the person who is celebrating his/her birthday is the one responsible for organizing the celebration. If family and friends gather in a restaurant, the celebrant picks up the tab. How is this different from birthdays in the U.S.? Would you like it? Why or why not?

¿Quién será? Episodio 9

In Chapter 8, Sofía and her friend Celeste went shopping. Unfortunately, the trip was a disaster and Celeste had to take back all of the clothing. In this episode of **Novela en video,** Nicolás experiences a different type of confusion due to lack of communication. His sister Irene is helping prepare the food for Mateo's birthday party, while Nicolás decorates. When the guests arrive we learn how important it is for Nicolás to throw a good party, because last year's party was a disaster. Nicolás wanders into the kitchen to get more food and discovers the can of food that he had asked Irene to use in the dip still unopened. Then he sees an identical looking can of cat food in the trash. He is horrified, and believes that his guests are eating cat food dip! In the end Nicolás and Irene talk and he learns that she got a can of tuna out of the cabinet.

STANDARDS: 4.2

B. CONTESTA
1. Tuna
2. Finishing the research on the candidates and making a final decision

Connections

Thinking Critically

Ask students to describe Nicolás, Mateo, and Julia based on previous episodes. Are they good friends, loyal, caring, and understanding? Are they easily offended, or do they have a sense of humor? Have students give descriptions and examples from previous episodes and list these on the board. Then explain that this episode is based on a misunderstanding. Tell students to look at the photos from this episode to see how the friends are interacting. Have students compare what they see in the photos with the descriptions and examples on the board. How well do they match?

9 **Mateo** Nicolás, ¿qué estás haciendo?
Nicolás Nada. ¿Por qué me lo preguntas?

10 **Nicolás** ¡¿Le pusiste comida de gato al dip?!
Irene ¿Qué dices? No, saqué una lata de atún del gabinete.
Nicolás Pensé que le pusiste comida de gato.

En España

La profesora considera los candidatos.

11 **Profesora** Nueve candidatos. Sólo falta uno y luego puedo tomar mi decisión final.

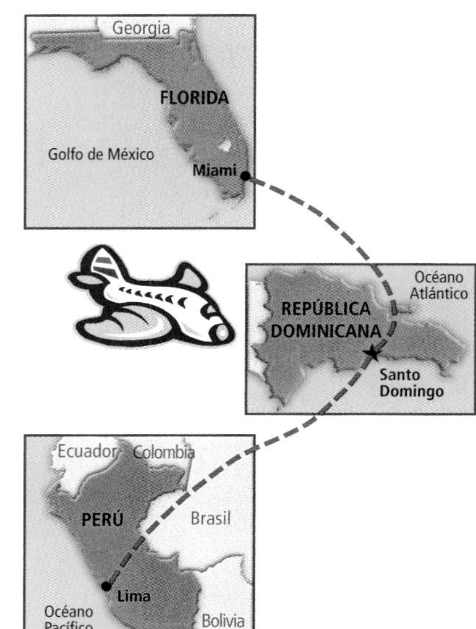

B. CONTESTA

1. What did Irene put in the dip?
2. What is **La profesora** looking forward to?

Culminating Project

Álbum de recortes

1. Explain to students that each of them is going to create a scrapbook for a real or imaginary holiday party or celebration. **2.** After students choose their holiday or celebration, they need to find at least six images for their scrapbook. Students may use a variety of visuals, such as magazine clippings, photos, illustrations, invitations, and cards. Students should then write a complete sentence in the preterite for each image to serve as a caption. The images and captions should describe the preparation for the party as well as the activities at the party. **3.** Set a date for students to turn in a rough-draft of the text for their scrapbooks. After you review the students' drafts, set a final date for completion of the scrapbooks. **4.** Students present their scrapbooks to the class and describe the party using the preterite.

STANDARDS: 1.3

Novela

Actividades

1 ¿Quién lo dijo?
Look at the story to help you remember who said each.
1. ¿Quieres ponerle comida?
2. Acabo de poner la comida.
3. ¡Ay! ¿Qué cosa? ¡No puede ser!
4. Estoy decorando la terraza.
5. Nicolás, ¿qué estás haciendo?

1. Mamá
2. Nicolás
3. Nicolás
4. Irene
5. Mateo

2 ¡Qué lío!
Mira la **Novela** para poner las oraciones en el orden correcto.
1. Julia y Mari llegaron a la fiesta.
2. Irene le puso *(gave)* comida a Picasso.
3. Nicolás pensó que los amigos comieron comida de gato.
4. Mamá salió para la casa de los abuelos.

correct order: 2, 1, 4, 3

3 ¿Comprendes la Novela?
Check your understanding of the events in the story by answering these questions.
1. What went wrong at Mateo's party last year?
2. Why is Nicolás so upset? What does he think happened?
3. Who straightens out the misunderstanding? What does she tell Nicolás?
4. Why does Nicolás look uneasy when Mateo asks him what he is doing?
5. What did you predict would happen?
6. Are the two things that went wrong realistic? Has anything like this ever happened to you?

Próximo episodio
La profesora is finally going to reveal what the ten candidates are for. Can you predict what will happen in the final episode?
PÁGINAS 252–255

Novela en video

3 Answers
1. The party was supposed to be at Nicolás' house, but the invitations gave Julia's address. Nicolás, Mateo, and Julia went to Nicolás' house. Everyone else went to Julia's house.
2. Nicolás thinks Irene put cat food in the dip.
3. Irene. She explains that she really put tuna in the dip.
4. He doesn't want him to know that he (Nicolás) thought everyone had been eating cat food.
5. Answers will vary.
6. Answers will vary.

Próximo Episodio:
Answers will vary.

Más práctica
3 Have students think of at least one example for the last question in Activity 3 and write about it. Tell them to include:
- who were the people involved in the misunderstanding
- the sequence of events and circumstances leading up to the misunderstanding
- who was affected by it and how
- whether it was resolved and why or why not

Comunicación
Group Work: Presentational
After students have seen the **Novela en video,** have them work in groups of three to create a scene about preparing for a party. Allow students time to create a short script and practice before having them present their skit to the class.

Differentiated Instruction

SLOWER PACE LEARNERS
Building on Previous Skills Have students imagine they attended Nicolás's party. Put them in groups of four and have them sit in a circle facing each other, then take turns giving information about the party using the preterite tense. Have them continue around the circle, adding sentences, until they have covered all aspects of the party.

MODELO
—Fui a la fiesta en casa de Nicolás anoche.
—Irene ayudó con las decoraciones....

MULTIPLE INTELLIGENCES
Interpersonal Have students imagine they are planning a party for a friend. Have them write down when and where the party will be, what decorations to put up, what foods to serve, who to invite, what music or games to have, and so on. Have them add to the list the names of family members or friends who would be responsible for different aspects of the party. Then, ask them to list things they definitely do not want at the party. Finally, have each student compare his or her party plans with those of a classmate.

STANDARDS: 1.2, 1.3

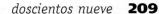

Resources

Planning:

Lesson Planner, pp. 125–126, 278–281

 One-Stop Planner

Presentation:

 Audio CD 9, Tr. 8

Practice:

Cuaderno de actividades, p. 52

Cuaderno para hispanohablantes, pp. 69–76

Reading Strategies and Skills Handbook, Chapter 9

¡Lee conmigo!

Applying The Strategies

For more practice, have students use the *Reading Strategies and Skills Handbook.*

READING PRACTICE

Strategy: Text Reformulation

Reading Skill	When can I use this strategy?		
	Prereading	During Reading	Postreading
Understanding Text Structure			✓
Analyzing Cause and Effect Relationships			✓

Strategy at a Glance: Text Reformulation

Additional Practice

For more reading practice, use the **Literatura y variedades** reading for Chapter 9 on pages 272–273.

Leamos y escribamos

ESTRATEGIA

para leer You can guess the meaning of many words by looking for context and grammatical clues. Look for the words you understand around an unknown word to determine its meaning. Also try to guess the meaning of the word by determining what part of speech it is (noun, verb, adjective, etc.) and by looking at its root, prefix, and suffix.

CD 9, Tr. 8

A Antes de leer

 Use the strategy to determine the meaning of the title of this song and the words in boldface. What clues helped you to determine the meanings?

Las mañanitas

Éstas son las mañanitas
que **cantaba** el Rey David;
a las muchachas bonitas
se las cantamos aquí.

Despierta mi bien despierta,
mira que ya **amaneció**.
Ya los pajaritos cantan,
la luna ya se metió[1].

Qué linda está la mañana
en que vengo a saludarte,
venimos todos con gusto
y placer[2] a **felicitarte**.

Canción de cumpleaños

Celebro tu cumpleaños
tan pronto veo **asomar** el sol
y en este día glorioso
pido tu dicha[3] al Señor,
porque lo he considerado[4]
como el regalo mejor.

Toma mi abrazo[5] que yo te doy,
y mucha felicidad.

1 already set 2 pleasure 3 happiness 4 I have regarded it 5 hug

Core Instruction

TEACHING LEAMOS

1. Discuss the **Estrategia para leer** with students. You might share examples of how they can use this strategy in English as well as in Spanish. **(2 min.)**
2. Before students read the text, play **Las mañanitas** and **Canción de cumpleaños** on Audio CD 9. Stop the recording and have students tell what they understand at this point. **(5 min.)**
3. Have students read the text with a partner. **(8 min.)**
4. Have students complete the activities on page 211. **(5 min.)**

TEACHING ESCRIBAMOS

1. Discuss the **Estrategia para escribir** as a class. Go over the scenario with students to make sure they understand the context. **(1 min.)**
2. Have students complete Step 1. Give examples of a cluster diagram that students can use as a model. See Process Writing, page 211. **(3 min.)**
3. Have students complete the first part of Step 2 individually before working with a partner. **(10 min.)**
4. Have students complete the presentations as outlined in Step 3. **(10 min.)**

STANDARDS: 3.2

Visit Holt Online
go.hrw.com
KEYWORD: EXP1B CH9
Online Edition

B Comprensión

Contesta las siguientes preguntas con oraciones completas.

1. ¿Qué se celebra con estas dos canciones?
2. ¿Qué hace en este momento la persona a quién se le dedican *Las mañanitas?*
3. ¿Cómo se describe el día de la celebración en las dos canciones?
4. ¿Por qué vienen las personas a cantar la serenata?
5. En la segunda canción, ¿qué se considera el "regalo mejor"?

C Después de leer

Can you think of other occasions that might be celebrated with a serenade? How do the songs compare to others you have heard to celebrate birthdays?

Mensaje Instantáneo
Archivo Editar Ver Herramientas Ayuda
Agregar nombre Advertir Bloquear Imprimir
A:
¿Cómo va la fiesta?
Enviar

ESTRATEGIA

para escribir Descriptions with interesting details can improve your writing. After choosing a topic, brainstorm adjectives and adverbs that will liven up the description or narrative.

¡Juy, qué desastre!

Last year you and your brothers planned a surprise party for your parents' anniversary. It went so well that you decided to do it again, but things aren't going as well this year. No one made the punch, so the guests are thirsty, and the dog is eating from people's plates. Your older brother couldn't come, but he's sent you an instant message asking for a report. Write back, comparing this party to last year's.

1 Antes de escribir

What were the highlights of last year's party? Which disasters from this year's party will you mention? Brainstorm and organize some descriptive details about each party using a cluster diagram.

2 Escribir y revisar

Use your cluster diagram to compare and contrast this year's party with last year's. Use details from the diagram to organize the comparison. You may want to ask your brother for advice. Read your draft twice, comparing it with your diagrams. Check spelling, punctuation, and verb usage. Have you used past-tense verbs to describe last year's party and the present progressive to talk about what's going on now? Then exchange papers with a classmate for a peer edit.

3 Publicar

Read the description of the party to the class. Have the other students give you advice about how to save the party.

Online
Cuaderno para hispanohablantes, pp. 93–104

Leamos y escribamos

B Answers

1. Se celebra un cumpleaños.
2. La persona está durmiendo.
3. La mañana está linda y el día está glorioso.
4. Las personas vienen a cantar, a felicitar y a darle un abrazo a la persona que cumple años.
5. Desear la felicidad de la persona que cumple años es el mejor regalo.

Process Writing

Cluster diagrams are a useful way to organize ideas and to see how different ideas and information about a topic are related. Have students use a cluster diagram to organize their ideas about the party. You might start a model on the board for students to follow.

Writing Assessment

To assess the **Taller del escritor,** you can use the following rubric. For additional rubrics, see the *Alternative Assessment Guide.*

Writing Rubric	4	3	2	1
Content (Complete—Incomplete)				
Comprehensibility (Comprehensible—Seldom comprehensible)				
Accuracy (Accurate—Seldom accurate)				
Organization (Well-organized—Poorly organized)				
Effort (Excellent effort—Minimal Effort)				

18–20: A
16–17: B
14–15: C
12–13: D
Under 12: F

Differentiated Instruction

SLOWER PACE LEARNERS

Have students point out the words that they do know in each song, including the ones glossed for them. Then, have them reread the songs and determine five words that they would need to know in order to understand the song. Have them first try to guess the meaning by the context, then give them the definitions, or have them use a dictionary to verify whether their guesses are correct.

SPECIAL LEARNING NEEDS

Students with Learning Disabilities To help answer the questions in Activity B, give a copy of the reading and questions to students. Suggest that students first translate the questions to guide them as they try to figure out the answers. Then, when students reread the passages to find the answers, instruct them to underline the part of the passage that answers each question, writing the number of the question in the margin next to its answer in the reading passage for reference.

Assess

Assessment Program

Prueba: Lectura, p. 89

Prueba: Escritura, p. 90

Standardized Assessment Tutor, pp. 37–40

Test Generator

STANDARDS: 1.1, 1.2, 1.3, 2.1, 4.2

Resources

Planning:

Lesson Planner, pp. 127–128, 280–281

One-Stop Planner

Presentation:

Video Program
Videocassette 5
DVD Tutor, Disc 2
Variedades

Teaching Transparencies
Situación, Capítulo 9
Picture Sequences, Chapter 9

Practice:

Activities for Communication, pp. 51, 71–72

TPR Storytelling Book, pp. 52–53

Video Guide, pp. 84–85, 90

Lab Book, pp. 29–30, 60

Audio CD 9, Tr. 10–13

Interactive Tutor, Disc 2

Reteaching

Have students invent and name an imaginary holiday **(El Día del Cine).** Ask them to come up with a date for their new holiday and to write a brief description of their holiday and how it is celebrated, incorporating as much vocabulary from the chapter as possible. Divide students into pairs and have them present their new holidays to each other.

1 Answers

Answers to second part will vary.
a. el Día de los Enamorados
b. el Día de la Independencia
c. la Nochevieja
d. el Hanukah
e. la Navidad
f. el Día de Acción de Gracias

5 Answers

1. **Carnaval, quinceañera, Navidad, Semana Santa**
2. a type of **tamal** made from plantains and meat; they are eaten at Christmas
3. a 15th birthday party for a girl or the 15-year old girl herself; **quinceañeras** occur in the U.S., as do debutante balls

Prepárate para el examen

Repaso capítulo 9

1 Vocabulario 1
- talking about plans
- talking about past holidays

pp. 178–183

1 Mira las fotos y decide qué día festivo representa cada foto. Luego di cómo se celebra el día donde vives y qué planes tienes.

1. 2. 3. 4. 5. 6.

2 Gramática 1
- preterite of **-ar, -er,** and **-ir** verbs
- **pensar que** and **pensar** with infinitives

pp. 184–189

2 Completa las oraciones con el verbo correcto en el pretérito.

—Hola, Vero. ¿Cómo estás? ¿Qué hiciste ayer?

—Bueno, como sabes, ayer fue el Día de la Madre. Por la mañana, yo __1__ (preparar/colgar) el desayuno para mi mamá. José y Beto __2__ (empezar/limpiar) y __3__ (decorar/comer) la sala. Por la tarde, nosotros __4__ (volver/ir) al parque para tener un picnic. Y tú, ¿cómo __5__ (pasar/mandar) el día?

—Yo __6__ (ir/invitar) a la iglesia con mi familia. Cuando (nosotros) __7__ (volver/merendar) a casa, mi mamá __8__ (pensar/abrir) sus regalos.

1. preparé 2. limpiaron 3. decoraron 4. fuimos 5. pasaste 6. fui 7. volvimos 8. abrió

3 Vocabulario 2
- asking about preparing for a party
- greetings, introductions, and goodbyes

pp. 192–197

3 Completa las oraciones con las palabras apropiadas.

1. Hoy es la ___ de Pablo y Carla. Es en la iglesia San Juan.
2. Hay más de cien ___ porque ___ muchas invitaciones.
3. Después de la ceremonia hay una ___.
4. Vamos a comer pastel y beber mucho ___.
5. En un año, ellos van a festejar su primer ___.
6. Ellos nos van a enseñar ___ de la ceremonia.

1. boda 2. invitados; mandaron 3. fiesta 4. ponche 5. aniversario 6. las fotos

Preparing for the Exam

FOLD-N-LEARN
Double Door

1. To help students prepare for the Chapter Test, have them create the **Fold-n-Learn** study aid as shown here, using a sheet of paper and a pen or pencil.
2. Once the Double Door template is completed, ask students to list holidays on the top door tab and their English equivalents or a short definition in Spanish underneath the tab.
3. On the bottom door tabs, have students list party preparations. On the bottom tab, have them list the English equivalents.
4. Have students use their templates to help quiz themselves while preparing for the Chapter Test.

STANDARDS: 1.2

4 Completa la siguiente conversación.

—¿Conoces __1__ Juan Antonio Machado? a

—No, no lo __2__. ¿Quién es? conozco

—Es mi primo. Muchas veces él __3__ ayuda con mi tarea de historia. __4__ puede ayudar a ti también si quieres. me Te

—Buena idea, gracias.

—¿Qué __5__ estudiando ustedes ahora en historia? están

—__6__ (Estar) estudiando la Guerra Civil. Estamos

—No te preocupes. Juan __7__ va a ayudar (a nosotros). nos

5 Answer the following questions.

1. Name some celebrations in the Spanish-speaking world.
2. What are **pasteles en hoja**? When are they eaten?
3. What is a **quinceañera?** Is there a similar event in the United States?

CD 9, Tr. 10

6 Escucha mientras *(while)* Rita habla de una fiesta. Luego contesta las preguntas.

7 Mira los dibujos. Escribe por lo menos seis oraciones describiendo lo que le pasa a Paco.

Visit Holt Online
go.hrw.com
KEYWORD: EXP1B CH9
Chapter Self-test

4 Gramática 2
- direct object pronouns
- **conocer** and personal **a**
- present progressive

pp. 198–203

5 Cultura
- **Comparaciones** **pp. 190–191**
- **Notas culturales** **pp. 183, 188, 194, 199**
- **Geocultura** **pp. 172–175**

Repaso

6 Script

See script on p. 175F.

6 Answers

1. para celebrar el cumpleaños de Rita
2. Gerardo
3. muy buena, muy divertida
4. no, no conoce a todos
5. con una fiesta más tranquila

To display the drawings to the class, use the *Picture Sequences Transparency* for Chapter 9.

7 Below is a sample answer for the picture description activity.

Paco va a una fiesta de cumpleaños. Él trae un regalo a la fiesta. Piensa que la fiesta va a ser muy divertida. Él piensa hablar con sus amigos, y comer y beber en la fiesta. Hay muchas personas en la fiesta. Paco y muchos de sus amigos están bailando. Les gusta mucho la música. Paco baila pero tiene mucha hambre. Quiere comer más pastel. Sus amigos están charlando y bailando. Paco no tiene ganas de bailar y come el pastel que está muy rico.

Oral Assessment

To assess the speaking activities in this chapter, you might use the following rubric. For additional speaking rubrics, see the *Alternative Assessment Guide.*

Speaking Rubric	4	3	2	1
Content (Complete—Incomplete)				
Comprehension (Total—Little)				
Comprehensibility (Comprehensible—Incomprehensible)				
Accuracy (Accurate—Seldom Accurate)				
Fluency (Fluent—Not Fluent)				

18–20: A 16–17: B 14–15: C 12–13: D Under 12: F

STANDARDS: 1.2, 1.3, 2.1, 2.2

Capítulo 9

Repaso

Grammar Review

For more practice with the grammar topics in the chapter, see the *Grammar Tutor*, the *DVD Tutor*, the *Interactive Tutor*, or the *Cuaderno de vocabulario y gramática.*

GramaVisión

Online Edition

Students might use the online textbook to practice the **Letra y sonido** feature.

Dictado Script

See script on p. 175F.

Teacher to Teacher

Carolyn Ostermann-Healy
Oakton High School
Vienna, VA

I have students prepare flashcards with the infinitive of a verb on one side and its present participle on the other. In groups of three, students place one set of ten cards, participle side up, on the desk. Two students face each other, while the third is the caller. The caller calls out an infinitive, and the first of the other two to pronounce the participle and slap the correct card keeps it. The student with the most cards after three minutes wins. I then have the winners become callers. This game can be altered to provide practice with other verb forms.

Gramática 1
- preterite of **-ar, -er,** and **-ir** verbs
  pp. 184–187
- **pensar que** and **pensar** with infinitives
  pp. 188–189

Repaso de Gramática 1

invitar		comer		salir	
invit**é**	invit**amos**	com**í**	com**imos**	sal**í**	sal**imos**
invit**aste**	invit**asteis**	com**iste**	com**isteis**	sal**iste**	sal**isteis**
invit**ó**	invit**aron**	com**ió**	com**ieron**	sal**ió**	sal**ieron**

The verb **ver** has regular **-er** endings but without written accents.

The verb **pensar** followed by **que** means *to think.* When it's followed by an **infinitive,** it means *to plan* or *to intend.*

Pienso que debes comprar un regalo.
Pienso comprar un regalo.

Gramática 2
- direct object pronouns
  pp. 198–199
- **conocer** and personal **a**
  pp. 200–201
- present progressive
  pp. 202–203

Repaso de Gramática 2

me	me	**nos**	us
te	you (familiar)	**os**	you (familiar)
lo	him, you (formal)	**los**	them, you (formal)
la	her, you (formal)	**las**	them, you (formal)

When the direct object of a verb like **conocer** *(to meet, to know, to be familiar with)* is a person, use the personal **a**.

No **conozco a** Juan.

The present progressive tense is formed by using a form of the verb **estar** and a **present participle** ending in either **-ando** for **-ar** verbs or **-iendo** for **-er** and **-ir** verbs.

Estamos celebrando el cumpleaños de mi hermano.
Raquel **está escribiendo** una carta.

Letra y sonido

CD 9, Tr. 11–13

Vocales fuertes (a, e, o) y débiles (i, u)
- Two **vocales fuertes** form two syllables:
  Rafael, teatro, traer, video, toalla
- One **vocal fuerte** and one accented **vocal débil** also form two syllables:
  día, tío, grúa
- One **vocal fuerte** and one unaccented **vocal débil** form one syllable where **i** sounds like *y* and **u** sounds like *w:*
  piano, salió, cuando, nuevo, bailar, auto, seis

Trabalenguas

Cómo quieres que te quiera
Si el que quiero que me quiera
No me quiere como quiero que me quiera.

Dictado

Escribe las oraciones de la grabación.

Chapter Review

Bringing It All Together

You might have students review the chapter using the following practice items and transparencies.

STANDARDS: 1.2

Repaso de Vocabulario 1

To talk about plans

el Año Nuevo	*New Year's Day*
celebrar	*to celebrate*
como siempre	*as always*
decorar la casa	*to decorate the house*
el Día de Acción de Gracias	*Thanksgiving Day*
el Día de la Independencia	*Independence Day*
el Día de la Madre	*Mother's Day*
el Día de los Enamorados	*Valentine's Day*
el Día del Padre	*Father's Day*
hacer una fiesta	*to have a party*
Hanukah	*Hanukkah*
invitar	*to invite*
la Navidad	*Christmas*
la Nochebuena	*Christmas Eve*
la Nochevieja	*New Year's Eve*
Pensamos...	*We plan to . . .*
¿Qué planes tienen para...?	*What plans do you have for . . .?*
la Semana Santa	*Holy Week*
tener un picnic	*to have a picnic*

To talk about past holidays

abrir regalos	*to open gifts*
el año pasado	*last year*
los días festivos	*holidays*
Estuvo a todo dar.	*It was great.*
festejar	*to celebrate*
La pasamos en casa de...	*We spent it at . . .'s house.*
mandar tarjetas	*to send cards*
la misa	*mass*
pasar	*to spend*
¿Qué tal estuvo?	*How was it?*
recibir regalos	*to receive gifts*
reunirse con (toda) la familia	*to get together with the (whole) family*
la sinagoga	*synagogue*
el templo	*temple*
ver fuegos artificiales	*to see fireworks*

Repaso de Vocabulario 2

To ask about preparing for a party

ahora	*now*
el aniversario	*anniversary*
anoche	*last night*
la boda	*wedding*
charlar	*to talk, chat*
colgar (ue)	*to hang (up)*
contar (ue) chistes	*to tell jokes*
el cumpleaños	*birthday*
las decoraciones	*decorations*
el día de tu santo	*your saint's day*
los dulces	*candy, sweets*
las empanadas	*turnover-like pastries*
enseñar fotos	*to show photos*
los entremeses	*appetizers*
¿Está todo listo para la fiesta?	*Is everything ready for the party?*
la fiesta sorpresa	*surprise party*
las flores	*flowers*
las galletas	*cookies*
la graduación	*graduation*
las invitaciones	*invitations*
los invitados	*guests*
los jóvenes	*young people*
mandar	*to send*
las papitas	*potato chips*
los pasteles en hoja	*Dominican tamales*
la piñata	*piñata*
el ponche	*punch*
los preparativos	*preparations*
¿Qué están haciendo?	*What are they doing?*
la quinceañera	*girl's fifteenth birthday*
terminar	*to finish*
ya	*already*

To greet, introduce others, and say goodbye

Chao, te llamo más tarde.	*Bye, I'll call you later.*
conocer	*to know, to meet, to be familiar with*
Cuídate.	*Take care.*
¡Feliz aniversario!	*Happy anniversary!*
Lo de siempre.	*Same as usual.*
¡Qué gusto verte!	*It's great to see you!*
¿Qué hay de nuevo?	*What's new?*
Tanto gusto.	*So nice to meet you.*
¡Tanto tiempo sin verte!	*Long time, no see!*
Te presento a...	*I'd like you to meet . . .*
Vale. Que te vaya bien.	*Okay. Hope things go well for you.*

Repaso

Repaso

Vocabulary Review

For more practice with the vocabulary in this chapter, see the *DVD Tutor*, the *Interactive Tutor*, or the *Cuaderno de vocabulario y gramática*.

ExpresaVisión

Online Edition

For students to hear the vocabulary on audio, have them access the online textbook.

Game

Ponga Ask students to prepare a grid as in a game of bingo, but not to write anything in the spaces. You will need to designate the number of spaces across and down. Then ask students to fill in the spaces at random with words or expressions from the Spanish vocabulary list. Call out each word or expression in English, and if students have the Spanish equivalent on their card, they place a mark on the space. The first student to mark a straight or a diagonal line of spaces is the winner. Students can also exchange cards with other students before play begins.

Online Edition

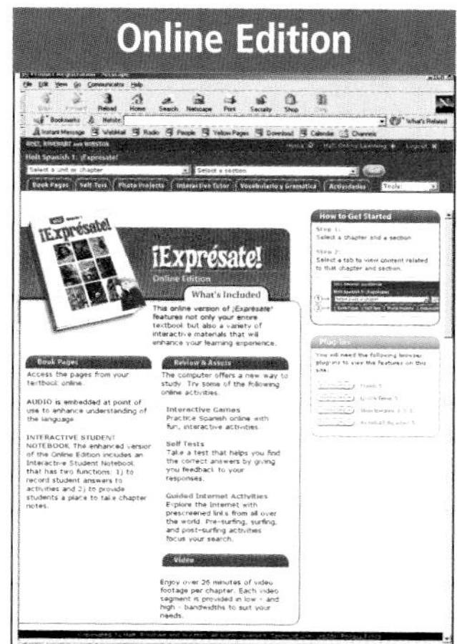

Transparency Vocabulario 9.1

Transparency Situación Ch. 9

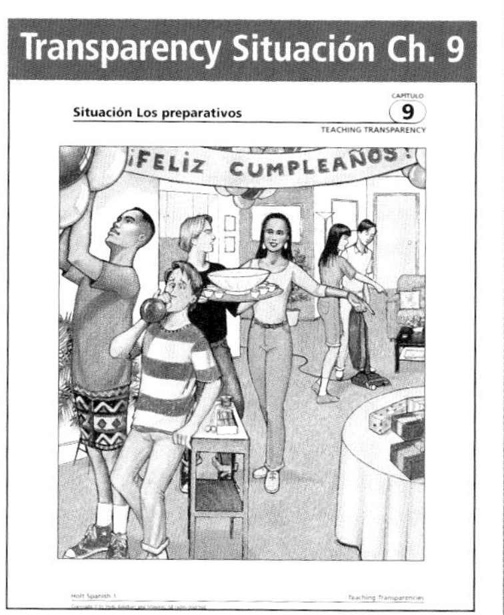

Assess

Assessment Program

Examen: Capítulo 9, pp. 185–195

Examen oral: Capítulo 9, p. 196

Alternative Assessment Guide, pp. 244, 252, 260

Standardized Assessment Tutor, pp. 37–40

Audio CD 9, Trs. 17–18

Test Generator

Resources

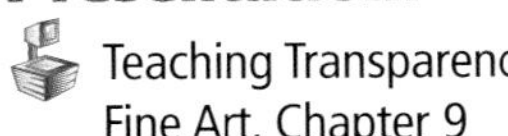

Planning:

Lesson Planner, pp. 129, 282–283

One-Stop Planner

Presentation:

Teaching Transparencies Fine Art, Chapter 9

Practice:

Cuaderno de actividades, pp. 53–54

Lab Book pp. 29–30

Audio CD 9, Tr. 14

Interactive Tutor, Disc 2

1 Script

1. Todos ayudan con los preparativos para la fiesta de cumpleaños. Adela está sirviendo el ponche.
2. Tenemos mucha prisa. La fiesta empieza en una hora y no estamos listos. Unos amigos ayudan a decorar la casa mientras otros ponen la mesa.
3. Graciela prefiere no usar la computadora para preparar las invitaciones. Ella las está escribiendo. También le gusta dibujar cada invitación.
4. Me encanta cuando Adela me invita a su casa a comer. Su madre es una cocinera excelente. Ahora está preparando unas empanadas para la fiesta.

2 Answers

1. falsa
2. cierta
3. falsa
4. cierta
5. falsa

Integración

capítulos 1-9

CD 9, Tr. 14

1 Escucha las descripciones y escoge la foto correspondiente. 1. b 2. d 3. c 4. a

A

B

C

D

2 Lee el anuncio y luego contesta las preguntas con **a) cierta** o **b) falsa**.

1. La especialidad de Fiesta Lala es comida mexicana. b
2. Fiesta Lala puede ayudar con tus celebraciones de lunes a domingo. a
3. La señora Quiñones tiene poca experiencia. b
4. Fiesta Lala puede organizar la boda de tu hermana. a
5. Fiesta Lala sólo ayuda con las fiestas de cumpleaños. b

Culture Project

Have students select a significant holiday celebrated by many Spanish-speaking countries (for example, Christmas Day, or Mother's Day). Then, have them research how the holiday is celebrated in at least three of the Spanish-speaking countries they have studied, or they might choose other Spanish-speaking countries they want to learn about. Have them prepare a short presentation in which they compare how the holiday is celebrated in the three countries. Have them tell what traditions they have in common and how the celebrations differ.

STANDARDS: 1.2, 3.2

3 Imagine you're at the party in this painting. First, write a story about two of the people you see. Include sentences and descriptions that tell

- the names of the people
- which holiday they're celebrating
- what they're doing now
- what each did earlier to prepare for the party

Then, with a partner role-play a conversation two people in the painting might have.

52 x 68cm (20.5" x 27") oil on cardboard, 1937; Bellapart Museum, Santo Domingo, Dominican Republic

Merengue, de Jaime Colson (1901–1975)

4 **Situación**

You have just arrived at a birthday party for a Spanish-speaking friend. You have lots of questions about the party. Take turns with a partner playing the roles of the guest and the friend celebrating his or her birthday.

- Say "Happy Birthday" to your friend.
- Ask who did the decorating.
- Find out who prepared the food.
- Ask if there is a **piñata**.
- Find out what everyone is going to do at this party.

Fine Art Connection

Introduction Jaime Colson (1901–1975) was a Dominican painter, designer, and muralist born in the province of Puerto Plata. At age 16, Colson left his homeland to study art in Madrid and in Paris. While in Europe, he was influenced by the cubist artists Pablo Picasso, Georges Braque, and Juan Gris. The work *Merengue* is displayed in the lobby of the Museo Bellapart in Santo Domingo. The musicians are seen playing the traditional instruments used in merengue music: the metal gourd, the drums, and the accordion. The colors are vibrant and very tropical.

Analyzing To help students discuss and analyze the painting, you might use the following questions.

1. **¿Qué hacen los jóvenes en una fiesta? ¿Hay música? ¿Bailan los invitados?**
2. **¿Qué hace la gente en la pintura?**
3. **¿Dónde están los invitados? ¿Por qué? ¿Cómo están?**
4. **¿Qué hacen los jóvenes en tu pueblo o tu ciudad para divertirse?**

Extension Have students research some of the paintings created by the famous cubist artists mentioned in the introduction. See if students can identify common elements across *Merengue* and the works of the Cubist artists mentioned above.

ACTFL Performance Standards

The activities in Chapter 9 target the communicative modes as described in the Standards.

Interpersonal	Two-way communication using receptive skills and productive skills	**Comunicación (SE),** pp. 181, 183, 187, 189, 197, 199, 201 **Comunicación (TE),** pp. 181, 185, 195, 201
Interpretive	One-way communication using receptive skills	**Comparaciones,** pp. 190–191 **Comunicación (SE),** pp. 195, 203 **Novela en video,** pp. 206–208 **Leamos,** p. 210
Presentational	One-way communication using productive skills	**Comunicación (SE),** pp. 181, 195, 197, 203 **Situación,** p. 217

STANDARDS: 1.1, 1.3, 3.1

Perú

Resources

Planning:

Lesson Planner, p. xv

 One-Stop Planner

Presentation:

 Teaching Transparencies
Mapa 3

Video Program
Videocassette 5
DVD Tutor, Disc 2
GeoVisión

Practice:

Video Guide, pp. 91–92

Lab Book, p. 61

 Interactive Tutor, Disc 2

Atlas INTERACTIVO MUNDIAL

Have students use the interactive atlas at **go.hrw.com** to find out more about the geography of Peru and to complete the activities below.

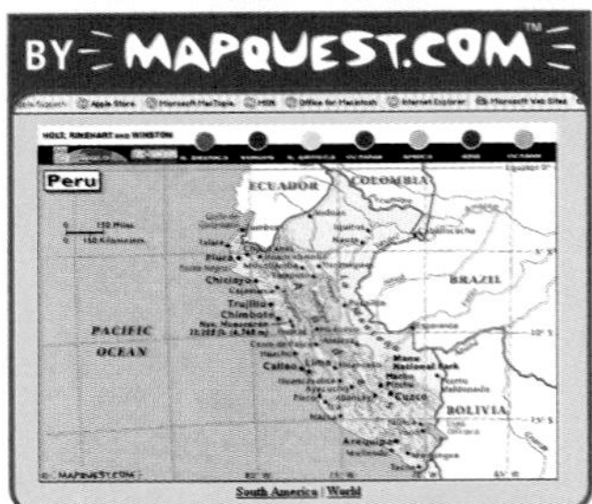

Map Activities

1. Have students locate Peru on the interactive atlas and name the bordering countries. **(Chile, Bolivia, Colombia, Brasil, Ecuador)** Ask students to identify any surrounding bodies of water. **(Océano Pacífico)**
2. The Andes Mountain range is actually two parallel ranges that run the length of Peru. Have students trace the Andes with their finger. Between the ranges lies the **Altiplano,** a high altitude grassland.

GeoVisión

Geocultura Perú

▲ **El río Amazonas** The Amazon River begins as a small mountain stream in the Andes of southern Peru. It then flows across the Peruvian rain forest and Brazil into the Atlantic Ocean.

Cerro Viej (3934 m

Chiclayo ● Caj

▼ **Lima** The capital lies on the coast in one of the driest regions of Peru. Here you can see Miraflores, the commercial district of Lima.

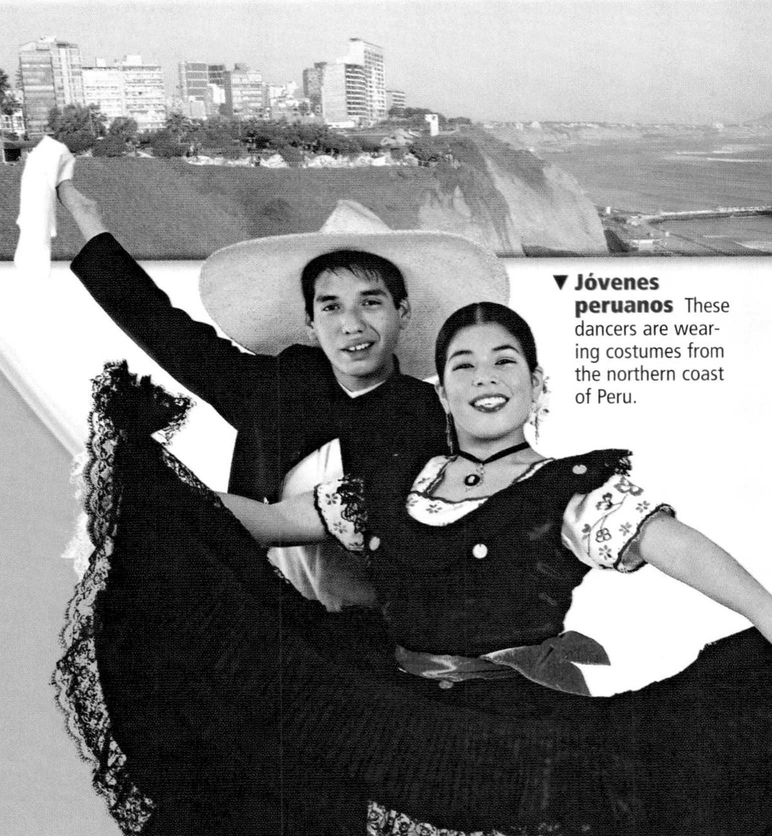

▼ **Jóvenes peruanos** These dancers are wearing costumes from the northern coast of Peru.

Almanaque

Población
27.949.639

Capital
Lima

Gobierno
república constitucional

Idiomas
español, quechua, aymara

Moneda
nuevo sol

Código Internet
www.[ ].pe

¿Sabías que...?
The Incas built a road network that was approximately 40,000 kilometers long. This system allowed for fast and efficient communication throughout the Incan Empire.

Background Information

History

Many indigenous groups settled in Peru. By the 13th century, the Inca had solidified power in the region, which extended from Ecuador to Chile. The Spanish explorer Francisco Pizarro conquered the Inca in 1532. Peru was a Spanish colony until 1821. Through the 19th century, Peru had many types of governments and presidents. In the 20th century, Peru has held democratic elections, although corruption and guerrilla groups continue to undermine national stability.

Geography

Manu National Park in Eastern Peru, covers 7,263 square miles, (18,811sq km). In the forested area as much as 156 inches of rain falls every year.

Las Islas Ballestas are traditionally home to millions of seabirds. In the 19th century, the export of their dung, or **guano,** brought economic wealth to Peru.

Huaca Rajada is a two thousand-year-old pyramid belonging to the Moche civilization. This site is full of precious jewelry and artifacts, fabricated well before the time of the Inca.

◄ **Los Andes** The Andes Mountains make up a large part of Peru. Some of the highest peaks are more than 6,000 meters high.

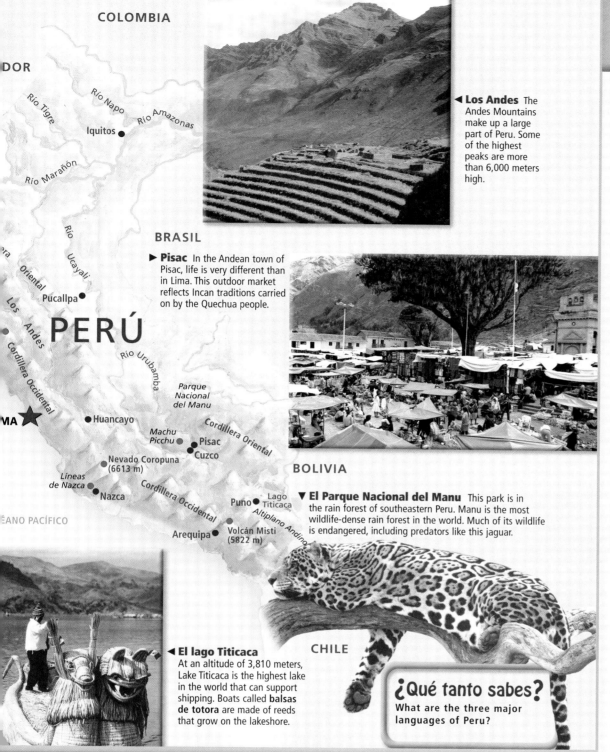

► **Pisac** In the Andean town of Pisac, life is very different than in Lima. This outdoor market reflects Incan traditions carried on by the Quechua people.

▼ **El Parque Nacional del Manu** This park is in the rain forest of southeastern Peru. Manu is the most wildlife-dense rain forest in the world. Much of its wildlife is endangered, including predators like this jaguar.

◄ **El lago Titicaca** At an altitude of 3,810 meters, Lake Titicaca is the highest lake in the world that can support shipping. Boats called **balsas de totora** are made of reeds that grow on the lakeshore.

¿Qué tanto sabes?
What are the three major languages of Peru?

Perú

Cultures

Practices and Perspectives

Las Huaringas For thousands of years the people of Peru have traveled to the beautiful, mystic lakes, or **las Huaringas,** in the north of the country. Traditional healers, or **curanderos,** accompany the travelers who journey to the lakes in search of cures and remedies for illnesses and problems. Each lake is known for its specific powers. Once at the lake a special ceremony, or **mesa,** is performed in which personal offerings are made, prayers are recited, and a ritual cleansing bath is taken in the lake. Have students reflect on this journey to the **Huaringas** lakes. Is there a place in their region or culture where people journey in search of help? What are some of the ways in which people in the U.S. use nature as a soothing or healing instrument?

Communities

Celebrations

In June the people of Peru celebrate the **Inti Raymi,** or Festival of the Sun. Beautifully colored floats parade through the streets of the town of Sacsayhuamán, where the principal parade takes place. The Quechua people of Peru dress with traditional Incan headgear and gowns. There are dances, feasts, and bonfires throughout the night. The main ceremony reenacts an offering to the sun god by the Incan emperor. The celebration, which lasts for a week, is the most important festival for Peru's indigenous people, particularly the Quechua.

CNN enEspañol.com

Have students check the **CNN en español** website for news on Peru. The site is also a good source of timely, high-interest readings for Spanish students.

¿Sabías que... ?

Students might be interested in knowing the following facts about Peru.

- **Peki-pekis** are small motor boats that serve as "river taxis" in the Amazon lowlands, where there are no roads.
- **Las vicuñas** are the smallest of the Andean camel family. **Vicuña** wool has been used for weaving since the times of the Inca.
- **El Niño,** a warm current of water that flows along the coast of Peru every two to six years, causes catastrophic climate change, including floods, torrential rains, and mud slides.

Preguntas

You might choose to ask students these questions in English.

1. **¿Dónde empieza el río Amazonas? (en los Andes peruanos)**
2. **¿Cómo se llama el lago navegable más alto del mundo? (el lago Titicaca)**
3. **¿Cómo se llama la gente indígena de la sierra peruana? (los Quechua)**
4. **¿Qué alturas alcanzan los picos de la Cordillera de los Andes? (más de 6.000 metros)**

STANDARDS: 3.1, 3.2, 4.2

Cultures

Products and Perspectives

Food Peruvian food is very varied and reflects the influence of many groups of immigrants including Africans, Japanese, Italians, and Chinese. Spanish settlers brought beef, pork, and goat meat to the region. On the coast, most people eat a lot of fish. In the mountains, the diet includes chicken, llama, beef, and guinea pig. Almost all Peruvian meals are served with **ají,** a thick sauce made of hot peppers, lemon juice, and oil. A native grain called **quinoa** has been eaten in the region since before the Incas ruled. It is high in protein, having twice that of the other cereal products of the area. Peruvian families and villages gather for a **pachamanca,** a meal prepared during an entire day, in an oven built underground. A large hole is dug and filled with wood. After the wood burns, food wrapped in banana leaves is placed on the hot stones, covered with more stones, and then covered with dirt. Ask students to discuss unique food preparations that they are familiar with from around the world.

Connections

Thinking Critically

Communal life On the small island of Taquile in Lake Titicaca, the residents live a very different way of life from the rest of the world. Everyone in the community has a different responsibility in farming, and this helps ensure that all types of food are grown. Women spin and weave the clothing for the community. Regular meetings of the entire community decide the rules of the island. Have students reflect on the way that the people of Taquile live. Is there any region or culture in the U.S. that participates in a communal lifestyle? What are some of the advantages? What are some of the problems that might arise?

A conocer Perú

La arquitectura

▲ **Machu Picchu** Located on a mountaintop near Cuzco, this city was abandoned by the Incas about 500 years ago. It was rediscovered in 1911 and is one of the most important archaeological sites in Peru.

▲ **Cuzco** The Spanish-built **Iglesia de Santo Domingo** sits on a massive Incan stone foundation. In the city of Cuzco, Spanish and Incan architecture are often found in the same building.

El arte

▲ **Los tejidos** Quechua people in the Andes region are famous for weaving and knitting colorful, intricate fabrics that are used for clothing. The finest material is made from alpaca wool.

▼ **Las famosas líneas de Nazca** The famous Nazca Lines are found in the desert near the southern coast of Peru. The lines form giant birds, people, and geometric designs that can only be seen clearly from the air.

Interdisciplinary Links

El arte

Art Link The Cuzco school of art taught native people to paint religious paintings in the Spanish style. But over the years, Peruvian artists began to add their own indigenous touches to the pieces. For example, Marcos Zapata painted a famous rendition of the Last Supper in which a guinea pig is on the central platter of Christ's dinner, and there are hot peppers and Andean cheese on the table. Tell students to pick a specific piece of art. How would they change it to reflect their own culture? What items would they include in the painting that would be a reflection of their lives?

La arquitectura

Engineering Link Incan architects were master masons. Many of the stone buildings that they built remain intact even after several earthquakes have toppled colonial and modern structures. Stones were cut and placed on top of each other without mortar or anything else to hold them together. Have students design a building or wall using stones, but no mortar. Should all of the stones be flat, or would some angles make the structure stronger? Have students experiment with blocks or stones. What theories can they think of to explain the strength of Incan engineering?

STANDARDS: 2.2, 3.1, 4.2

Las celebraciones

Visit Holt Online
go.hrw.com
KEYWORD: EXP1B CH10
Photo Tour

► **El Concurso Nacional de Marinera** A dance contest and festival is held every January in the coastal city of Trujillo. The festival celebrates **la marinera**, the national dance of Peru.

¿Sabías que...?

The walls of Incan buildings are made of heavy stones fitted together without mortar. The stones are so well cut that you cannot even fit a credit card into the seams. Why do you think many of these walls are still standing today?

► **El Concurso Nacional del Caballo Peruano de Paso** This horse show and competition centers on the Peruvian **Paso,** known as one of the finest horse breeds in the world.

La comida

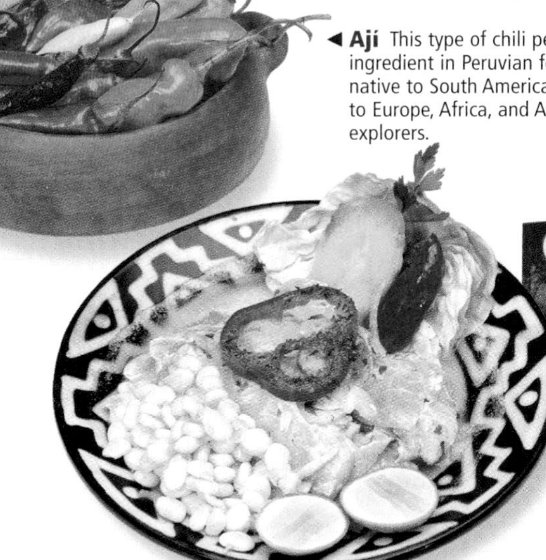

◄ **Ají** This type of chili pepper is a common ingredient in Peruvian food. Hot peppers are native to South America and were introduced to Europe, Africa, and Asia through Spanish explorers.

◄ **El ceviche** **Ceviche** is made of raw fish cured with lemon juice, onion, and **ají**. **Cevicherías,** restaurants that serve ceviche, are popular in Peru.

Las celebraciones

Music Link Andean music is an important part of celebrations. Traditionally, music was performed in ceremonies that worshiped the gods. Spanish and African influences have changed Andean music over the centuries. Have students research Andean music at the library or on the Internet. What are some of the instruments that are unique to this type of music? When and where is Andean music performed?

La comida

Science Link Cuy, or guinea pig, is a common meat source in Peru. It also serves various functions in folk medicine. Only black guinea pigs can be used in remedies. Have students research remedies that have been used in the past in the U.S., such as bleeding a patient. Are there similar remedies still being used today? Why do they think people still use traditional remedies?

Perú

Cultures

Products and Perspectives

The **cochineal,** a tiny insect that lives on the prickly pear cacti in the dry, southern desert of Peru, is harvested to produce a bright red substance called *carmine,* which is used as a dye. The insect is dried and sold at market, where it is highly valued as a dye for the brightly colored clothing of the Peruvians. It is also used to color lipstick, popsicles, and hot dogs. For centuries the **cochineal** has been valued by the cultures in the region. Today it is valued around the world. Peru is the largest world exporter of cochineal. Peru produces 700 tons of the dried insect each year and nearly half is destined for export. This tiny bug turns this dry region, that would otherwise be worthless economically, into a great benefit for the nation and the region.

¿Comprendes?

You can use the following questions to check students' comprehension of the **Geocultura.**

1. What are the three national languages of Peru? **(español, quechua, aymara)**
2. Where does the Amazon river begin? (as a small stream in the Andes of southern Peru)
3. What is a **balsa de totora** and where is it used? (a boat made of reeds; in the highest lake in the world, Lake Titicaca)
4. Name two foods typical of Peru. (**el ají,** a chili pepper; **el ceviche,** a fish dish)

Assess

Assessment Program
Prueba: Geocultura, pp. 111–112
Test Generator 

 **STANDARDS:** 2.1, 2.2

Capítulo 10

¡A viajar!

Overview and Resources

Overview and Resources

Chapter Section		Resources
Vocabulario en acción 1 • Asking for and giving information; reminding and reassuring, pp. 224–229 ¡Exprésate! • To ask for information; to give information, p. 225 • Reminding and reassuring, p. 228	Present	TPR Storytelling Book, pp. 54–55 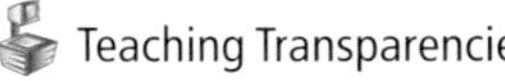 Teaching Transparencies Video Program/DVD Tutor, **ExpresaVisión**
Assess Assessment Program • **Prueba: Vocabulario 1,** pp. 97–98 • Alternative Assessment Guide, pp. 245, 253, 261  Test Generator	Practice	Cuaderno de vocabulario y gramática, pp. 65–67 Activities for Communication, pp. 37–38 Video Guide, pp. 94–96 Lab Book, pp. 5, 31–34, 62 Teaching Transparencies Audio CD 10, Tr. 1 Interactive Tutor, Disc 2
Gramática en acción 1 • Review of the preterite, p. 230 • Preterite of **-car, -gar, -zar** verbs, p. 232 • Preterite of **hacer,** p. 234	Present	Video Program/DVD Tutor, **GramaVisión**
Assess Assessment Program • **Prueba: Gramática 1,** pp. 99–100 • **Prueba: Aplicación 1,** pp. 101–102 • Alternative Assessment Guide, pp. 245, 253, 261  Audio CD 10, Tr. 17  Test Generator	Practice	Grammar Tutor for Students of Spanish, Chapter 10 Cuaderno de vocabulario y gramática, pp. 68–70 Cuaderno de actividades, pp. 55–57 Activities for Communication, pp. 37–38 Video Guide, pp. 94–95 Lab Book, pp. 5, 31–34 Teaching Transparencies Audio CD 10, Tr. 2–3 Interactive Tutor, Disc 2

	Print	Media
Cultura • **Comparaciones,** pp. 236–237 • **Comunidad,** p. 237 • **Conexiones,** pp. 250–251	Cuaderno de actividades, p. 58 Cuaderno para hispanohablantes, pp. 77–84 Video Guide, pp. 94–95, 97 Lab Book, p. 63	Audio CD 10, Tr. 4–6 Video Program/DVD Tutor, **VideoCultura** Interactive Tutor, Disc 2
Novela en video • **Episodio 9,** pp. 252–255	Video Guide, pp. 94–95, 99 Lab Book, p. 65	Video Program/DVD Tutor, **VideoNovela**
Leamos y escribamos • **Bienvenidos a la ciudad de Lima,** pp. 256–257	Cuaderno de actividades, p. 62 Reading Strategies and Skills Handbook Cuaderno para hispanohablantes, pp. 77–84 ¡Lee conmigo! Assessment Program, pp. 109–110	Audio CD 10, Tr. 10

Lesson Planner with Differentiated Instruction, pp. 131–160, 284–311

One-Stop Planner® CD-ROM

Visit Holt Online
go.hrw.com
KEYWORD: EXP1B CH10
Online Edition

Chapter Section	Resources
Vocabulario en acción 2 • Talking about a trip; expressing hopes and wishes, pp. 238–243 **¡Exprésate!** • Talking about a trip, p. 239 • Expressing hopes and wishes, p. 242	**Present** TPR Storytelling Book, pp. 56–57 Teaching Transparencies Video Program/DVD Tutor, **ExpresaVisión**
Assess Assessment Program • **Prueba: Vocabulario 2,** pp. 103–104 • Alternative Assessment Guide, pp. 245, 253, 261  Test Generator	**Practice** Cuaderno de vocabulario y gramática, pp. 71–73 Activities for Communication, pp. 39–40 Video Guide, pp. 94–95, 98 Lab Book, pp. 5, 31–34, 64 Teaching Transparencies Audio CD 10, Tr. 7 Interactive Tutor, Disc 2

Chapter Section	Resources
Gramática en acción 2 • Informal commands of spelling-change and irregular verbs, p. 244 • Review of direct object pronouns, p. 246 • Review of verbs followed by infinitives, p. 248	**Present**  Video Program/DVD Tutor, **GramaVisión**
Assess Assessment Program • **Prueba: Gramática 2,** pp. 105–106 • **Prueba: Aplicación 2,** pp. 107–108 • Alternative Assessment Guide, pp. 245, 253, 261  Audio CD 10, Tr. 18  Test Generator	**Practice** Grammar Tutor for Students of Spanish, Chapter 10 Cuaderno de vocabulario y gramática, pp. 74–76 Cuaderno de actividades, pp. 59–61 Activities for Communication, pp. 39–40 Video Guide, pp. 94–95 Lab Book, pp. 5, 31–34  Teaching Transparencies  Audio CD 10, Tr. 8–9  Interactive Tutor, Disc 2

	Print 	Media 
Repaso • **Repaso,** pp. 258–259 • **Gramática y Vocabulario,** pp. 260–261 • **Letra y sonido,** p. 260	Activities for Communication, pp. 52, 73–74 Video Guide, pp. 94–95, 100 Lab Book, pp. 31–34, 66 TPR Storytelling Book, pp. 58–59 Assessment Program, pp. 197–207, 208 Alternative Assessment Guide, pp. 245, 253, 261 Standardized Assessment Tutor, pp. 41–44	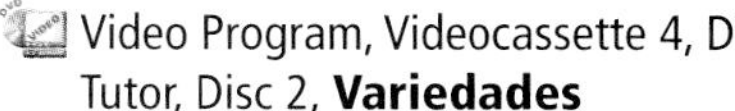 Video Program, Videocassette 4, DVD Tutor, Disc 2, **Variedades**  Teaching Transparencies  Audio CD 10, Tr. 12–15  Interactive Tutor, Disc 2 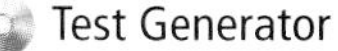 Test Generator
Integración • Cumulative review, Chapters 1–10, pp. 262–263	Cuaderno de actividades, pp. 63–64 Lab Book, pp. 31–34	 Teaching Transparencies Audio CD 10, Tr. 16

¡A viajar!

Projects

Collage de fotos

In this activity, students describe their ideal vacation spot and make collages to enhance their presentation.

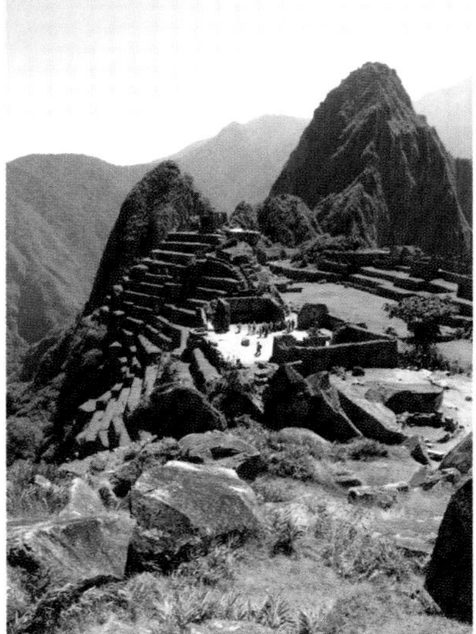

SUGGESTED SEQUENCE

1. Students decide on a vacation spot to illustrate. Ask students to search for information using reference books or the Internet. They might also consult travel agencies.
2. Have students gather drawings, photographs, magazine images, or small objects for their collages.
3. Have students decide on the final design of their collages. They should outline their presentation and exchange it with a classmate for peer review.
4. Have students present their collages to the class.

Grading the project

Suggested point distribution (100 points total)

Collage Information 40
Creativity 20
Presentation to class 40

e-community

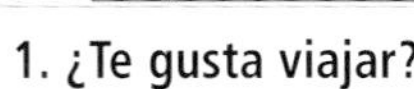

e-mail forum:

Post the following questions on the classroom e-mail forum:

Location: http://spanish

1. ¿Te gusta viajar?
2. Cuando estás de vacaciones, ¿prefieres viajar o quedarte en casa?
3. ¿Qué hiciste la última vez que viajaste?

Partner Class Project

Have students work in groups of three or four to create a skit in which they take a vacation abroad. Tell them that it is the third day of a week-long trip and today they are flying to meet their Spanish-speaking pen pal in his or her hometown. In their skit, they must check in at the airport, go through security before boarding, and upon arrival find their bags. When they arrive at their pen pal's, they should discuss how their flight was, how their trip is going, what they have done so far, and what they would like to do together. They should then videotape the skits and send the videos to their partner class. The partner class should then evaluate the skits for accuracy and creativity and return the videos with their comments.

Game Bank
For game ideas, see pages T60–T63.

STANDARDS: 1.1, 1.3, 5.1

Traditions

Tejidos

Andean textiles today reflect the 500-year-old weaving traditions of the Inca Empire. Inca women spun cotton and wool, colored the fabric with vegetable dyes, and made all of the clothing. The patterns, colors, and figures on fabrics identify the place of origin of each article. Andean women wear a **manta** *(shawl)* as a wrap or carry-all. Men and women wear different types of hats that indicate where they are from. The highland Incas wear **chullos** *(peaked caps with earflaps and colorful tassels)*. Have students research and draw colorful posters of some traditional Andean textiles or garments, and identify their place of origin.

Receta

Suspiro limeño is a custard served with floating spoonfuls of merengue on top. Have students research custard desserts from other Latin American countries and the United States. How are the desserts similar or different?

Suspiro limeño

para 6 personas

1 lata de leche condensada

2 latas de leche evaporada

1/2 taza de agua

5 yemas de huevo, batidas

1 taza de azúcar

1/4 taza de agua

3 claras de huevo

canela en polvo

Preparación:

Para hacer la crema, mezcle las dos leches, el agua y las yemas batidas. Cocine la mezcla a fuego moderado, revolviéndo la constantemente hasta que se espese. Añada la vainilla y deje que se enfríe. Vierta la crema en el plato hondo en que la va a servir. Para hacer el merengue, primero cocine el azúcar con 1/4 taza de agua en una cacerola hasta crear un almíbar. Segundo, bata las claras de huevo a punto de nieve. Vierta poco a poco el almíbar en las claras de huevo mientras continúe a batiéndolas. Siga batiéndolas hasta que se pongan más espesas y frías. Ponga cucharadas del merengue encima de la crema. Espolvoree la canela encima.

¡A viajar!

For Student Response Forms, see *Lab Book*, pp. 31–34

Textbook Listening Activity Scripts

Vocabulario en acción 1

1 **p. 226, CD 10, Tr. 1**

1. —¿Sabe usted a qué hora llega el vuelo 797?
   —No sé, pero lo puede ver en esa pantalla.
   —Gracias.
2. —¿Dónde puedo facturar mi equipaje?
   —Tiene que ir a ese mostrador y hacer cola.
3. —¿Me puede decir dónde están los servicios?
   —Sí, cómo no. Están a la vuelta.
4. —¿Sabe usted dónde está la aduana?
   —Lo siento, no sé.

Answers to Activity 1

a. 3
b. 1
c. 2
d. 4

Gramática en acción 1

12 **p. 230, CD 10, Tr. 2**

¡Qué viaje más difícil! Salí de la casa a las ocho pero dejé mi boleto. Regresé a casa para buscarlo. Fui al aeropuerto y me encontré con mis amigos Juan y Carlos. Fuimos al mostrador y la agente facturó el equipaje. Pasamos por el control de seguridad donde los agentes abrieron la maleta de Carlos. Después, Carlos y Juan fueron a la sala de espera y jugaron videojuegos. Fui a la librería y compré una revista. En la sala de espera, Juan perdió su tarjeta de embarque y regresó al mostrador para conseguir otra. Carlos y yo abordamos el avión pero Juan perdió el vuelo.

Answers to Activity 12

1. b
2. a
3. b
4. b
5. b
6. a

15 **p. 232, CD 10, Tr. 3**

1. Cuando viajo, siempre compro el boleto un mes antes de viajar.
2. Tengo todo muy organizado y hago las maletas dos o tres días antes del viaje.
3. La última vez que fui a Perú, compré el boleto sólo una semana antes.
4. Me preocupé un poco porque no encontré el pasaporte hasta el día de salir.
5. Comencé el viaje a las nueve de la mañana, pero no llegué a Lima hasta las cuatro de la tarde.
6. Normalmente almuerzo en el aeropuerto porque no me gusta la comida que sirven en los aviones.
7. Luego juego a los videojuegos en la sala de espera.
8. En ese viaje a Perú, almorcé en el avión.
9. No jugué a los videojuegos porque los dejé en casa.

Answers to Activity 15

1. a
2. a
3. b
4. b
5. b
6. a
7. a
8. b
9. b

Vocabulario en acción 2

23 **p. 240, CD 10, Tr. 7**

1. ¡El viaje fue horrible!
2. Perdimos el tren.
3. Paseamos en lancha y esquiamos en el lago.
4. Comimos en un restaurante muy bueno.
5. Nos quedamos en un hotel magnífico.
6. Dejé mi cámara en el autobús.

Answers to Activity 23

1. a
2. a
3. b
4. a
5. b
6. a

Gramática en acción 2

31 **p. 245, CD 10, Tr. 8**

1. —Estoy cansado y no quiero hacer nada hoy.
   —Quédate en el hotel y descansa.
2. —Quiero subir a la montaña y esquiar.
   —Ve al centro.
3. —Me gustaría hacer ejercicio.
   —No vayas de excursión.
4. —Quiero hacer un viaje pero no tengo dinero para un hotel.
   —Acampa.
5. —Hace muy buen tiempo y me gustaría tomar el sol.
   —Quédate en el hotel.
6. —Hace mal tiempo. Llueve mucho.
   —Ve al lago.
7. —No tengo cámara.
   —Saca muchas fotos.
8. —Hace mal tiempo y no tengo nada que hacer.
   —Pasa por el museo.

Answers to Activity 31

1. lógico 2. ilógico 3. ilógico 4. lógico
5. ilógico 6. ilógico 7. ilógico 8. lógico

34 **p. 246, CD 10, Tr. 9**

1. La voy a conseguir en el mostrador.
2. Las voy a llevar al centro.
3. Lo tengo que llamar desde el centro.
4. Quiero ayudarlas con sus maletas.
5. No los voy a abrir ni una vez.
6. La necesito para poder abordar el avión.
7. Las voy a ver hoy en el museo.

Answers to Activity 34

1. b 2. c 3. a 4. c 5. d 6. b 7. c

Repaso capítulo 10

6 **p. 259, CD 10, Tr. 12**

1. Paco, haz tu maleta. Sólo tenemos dos horas antes de ir al aeropuerto.
2. Señor, ¿me puede decir dónde está el mostrador?
3. ¿Dónde se puede encontrar el reclamo de equipaje?
4. Llegué tarde al aeropuerto. Corrí a la puerta pero fue inútil. Perdí el vuelo.
5. Primero factura tu equipaje. Luego ve a la sala de espera. Allí te espero.
6. Fuimos a conocer Machu Picchu. ¡Fue estupendo!

Answers to Activity 6

1. a 2. c 3. c 4. b 5. a 6. b

Dictado, p. 260, CD 10, Tr. 15

Escribe las oraciones de la grabación.

1. Paco y su primo practican deportes en la playa.
2. Mi tío tiene tres tiendas de camisas.
3. Quique toca el piano y come tacos y papitas.
4. La tía Teresa es atlética, intelectual y simpática.
5. Pepe Pidal trae tu correo de España.
6. Carlos se quita la chaqueta en el parque.
7. Quisiera un pastel pequeño de queso.
8. Tampoco hay quinientos papeles en el carro.

Integración capítulos 1-10

1 **p. 262, CD 10, Tr.16**

1. Jaime y Estela están en el aeropuerto, listos para sus vacaciones. Jaime va al mostrador para comprar el boleto y facturar el equipaje. La agente le pregunta a Jaime cuántas maletas tiene y él responde que lleva una.
2. Estela compró su boleto de avión el mes pasado así que ahora va directamente al mostrador y presenta su pasaporte. La agente le da a Estela su tarjeta de embarque.
3. Los dos van a la sala de espera, porque el avión sale a las dos y media de la tarde. Jaime se sienta y empieza a leer.
4. Son las doce y Estela tiene bastante tiempo para cambiar dinero. Ve que la oficina de cambio está cerca. Va allí y hace cola.

Answers to Activity 1

1. b 2. c 3. d 4. a

¡A viajar!

50-Minute Lesson Plans

Day 1

OBJECTIVE
Asking for and giving information

Core Instruction
Chapter Opener, pp. 222–223
- See Using the Photo and **Más vocabulario,** p. 222. 5 min.
- See Chapter Objectives, p. 222. 5 min.

Vocabulario en acción 1, pp. 224–229
- Show **ExpresaVisión,** Ch. 10. 5 min.
- See Teaching **Vocabulario,** p. 224. 25 min.
- Present **¡Exprésate!,** p. 225. 10 min.

Optional Resources
- TPR, p. 225
- **También se puede decir,** p. 225
- Advanced Learners, p. 225 ▲

HOMEWORK SUGGESTIONS
Cuaderno de vocabulario y gramática, pp. 65–67
Internet Activities

Day 2

OBJECTIVE
Asking for and giving information

Core Instruction
Vocabulario en acción 1, pp. 224–229
- Review **Vocabulario 1** and **¡Exprésate!,** pp. 224–225. 20 min.
- Have students do Activity 1, p. 226. 10 min.
- Play Audio CD 10, Tr. 1 for Activity 2, p. 226. 10 min.
- Have students do Activity 3, p. 226. 5 min.
- Present **Nota cultural,** p. 226. 5 min.

Optional Resources
- Social Studies Link, p. 226
- Fold-n-Learn, p. 226
- **Más práctica,** p. 227
- Special Learning Needs, p. 227 ●

HOMEWORK SUGGESTIONS
Cuaderno de vocabulario y gramática, pp. 65–67
Internet Activities

Day 3

OBJECTIVE
Asking for and giving information; reminding and reassuring

Core Instruction
Vocabulario en acción 1, pp. 224–229
- Have students do Activities 4–6, p. 227. 25 min.
- See Teaching **¡Exprésate!,** p. 228. 15 min.
- Have students do Activity 7, p. 228. 10 min.

Optional Resources
- **Comunicación,** p. 227
- Advanced Learners, p. 227 ▲
- Special Learning Needs, p. 227 ●
- **Más práctica,** p. 228

HOMEWORK SUGGESTIONS
Cuaderno de vocabulario y gramática, pp. 65–67
Internet Activities

Day 4

OBJECTIVE
Reminding and reassuring

Core Instruction
Vocabulario en acción 1, pp. 224–229
- Have students do Bell Work 10.2, p. 230. 5 min.
- Review **¡Exprésate!,** p. 228. 10 min.
- Have students do Activities 8–11, p. 228–229. 35 min.

Optional Resources
- **Comunicación,** p. 229
- Slower Pace Learners, p. 229 ◆
- Multiple Intelligences, p. 229

HOMEWORK SUGGESTIONS
Study for **Prueba: Vocabulario 1.**

Day 5

OBJECTIVE
Vocabulary review and assessment

Core Instruction
Vocabulario en acción 1, pp. 224–229
- Review **Vocabulario en acción 1,** pp. 224–229. 30 min.
- Give **Prueba: Vocabulario 1.** 20 min.

Optional Resources
- Test Generator

HOMEWORK SUGGESTIONS
Preview **Gramática en acción 1,** pp. 230–235.

Day 6

OBJECTIVE
Review of the preterite

Core Instruction
Gramática en acción 1, pp. 230–235
- See Teaching **Gramática,** p. 230. 30 min.
- Play Audio CD 10, Tr. 2 for Activity 12, p. 230. 10 min.
- Have students do Activity 13, p. 231. 10 min.

Optional Resources
- Advanced Learners, p. 231 ▲
- Special Learning Needs, p. 231 ●

HOMEWORK SUGGESTIONS
Cuaderno de vocabulario y gramática, pp. 68–70
Cuaderno de actividades, pp. 63–66

Day 7

OBJECTIVE
Review of the preterite

Core Instruction
Gramática en acción 1, pp. 230–235
- Have students do Bell Work 10.3, p. 232. 5 min.
- Show **GramaVisión,** Ch. 10. 10 min.
- Review the preterite, p. 230. 20 min.
- Have students do Activity 14, p. 231. 15 min.

Optional Resources
- Teacher to Teacher, p. 231
- **Comunicación,** p. 231
- Special Learning Needs, p. 231 ●

HOMEWORK SUGGESTIONS
Cuaderno de vocabulario y gramática, pp. 68–70
Cuaderno de actividades, pp. 63–66

Day 8

OBJECTIVE
*Preterite of **-car, -gar, -zar** verbs*

Core Instruction
Gramática en acción 1, pp. 230–235
- See Teaching **Gramática,** p. 186. 30 min.
- Play Audio CD 10, Tr. 3 for Activity 15, p. 232. 10 min.
- Have students do Activity 16, p. 232. 10 min.

Optional Resources
- **GramaVisión,** Ch. 10
- Career Path, p. 233
- Slower Pace Learners, p. 233 ◆

HOMEWORK SUGGESTIONS
Cuaderno de vocabulario y gramática, pp. 68–70
Cuaderno de actividades, pp. 63–66

To edit and create your own lesson plans, see the **One-Stop** Planner® CD-ROM

KEY
- ▲ Advanced Learners
- ◆ Slower Pace Learners
- ● Special Learning Needs
- ■ Heritage Speakers

Day 9

OBJECTIVE
Preterite of ***-car, -gar, -zar*** *verbs; preterite of* ***hacer***

Core Instruction
Gramática en acción 1, pp. 230–235
- Review the preterite of **-car, -gar, -zar** verbs, p. 232. 5 min.
- Have students do Activities 17–18, pp. 232–233. 15 min.
- See Teaching **Gramática,** p. 234. 30 min.

Optional Resources
- **Comunicación,** p. 233
- Special Learning Needs, p. 233 ●

HOMEWORK SUGGESTIONS
Cuaderno de vocabulario y gramática, pp. 68–70
Cuaderno de actividades, pp. 63–66
Internet Activities
Interactive Tutor, Ch. 10

Day 10

OBJECTIVE
Preterite of ***hacer***

Core Instruction
Gramática en acción 1, pp. 230–235
- Show **GramaVisión,** Ch. 10. 5 min.
- Review the preterite of **hacer,** p. 234. 10 min.
- Present **Nota cultural,** p. 188. 5 min.
- Have students do Activities 19–22, pp. 234–235. 30 min.

Optional Resources
- **Comunicación,** p. 235
- Slower Pace Learners, p. 235 ◆

HOMEWORK SUGGESTIONS
Study for **Prueba: Gramática 1.**
Multiple Intelligences, p. 235
Interactive Tutor, Ch. 10

Day 11

OBJECTIVE
Grammar review and assessment; interviews from around the Spanish-speaking world

Core Instruction
Gramática en acción 1, pp. 230–235
- Review **Gramática en acción 1,** pp. 230–235. 15 min.
- Give **Prueba: Gramática 1.** 20 min.

Cultura, pp. 236–237
- See Teaching **Cultura,** #1–2, p. 236. 15 min.

Optional Resources
- Test Generator
- **Prueba: Aplicación 1**
- Map Activities, p. 236
- Advanced Learners, p. 237 ▲
- Special Learning Needs, p. 237 ●

HOMEWORK SUGGESTIONS
Read **Comparaciones,** pp. 236–237.

Day 12

OBJECTIVE
Interviews from around the Spanish-speaking world; talking about a trip

Core Instruction
Cultura, pp. 236–237
- See Teaching **Cultura,** #3, p. 236. 15 min.
- Present and assign **Comunidad,** p. 237. 5 min.

Vocabulario en acción 2, pp. 238–243
- See Teaching **Vocabulario,** p. 238. 30 min.

Optional Resources
- Comparing and Contrasting, p. 237
- Language Note, p. 239
- **También se puede decir,** p. 239
- Multiple Intelligences, p. 239
- Advanced Learners, p. 239 ▲

HOMEWORK SUGGESTIONS
Community Link, p. 237
Cuaderno de gramática, pp. 71–73
Cuaderno de actividades, p. 67

Day 13

OBJECTIVE
Talking about a trip

Core Instruction
Vocabulario en acción 2, pp. 238–243
- Show **ExpresaVisión,** Ch. 10. 10 min.
- Review **Vocabulario 2** and **¡Exprésate!,** pp. 238–239. 25 min.
- Present **Nota cultural,** p. 240. 5 min.
- Play Audio CD 10, Tr. 7 for Activity 23, p. 240. 10 min.

Optional Resources
- TPR, p. 239
- Products and Perspectives, p. 240
- Game, p. 240

HOMEWORK SUGGESTIONS
Cuaderno de gramática, pp. 71–73
Internet Activities

Day 14

OBJECTIVE
Talking about a trip; expressing hopes and wishes

Core Instruction
Vocabulario en acción 2, pp. 238–243
- Have students do Bell Work 10.6, p. 244. 5 min.
- Have students do Activities 24–26, pp. 240–241. 30 min.
- See Teaching **¡Exprésate!,** p. 242. 15 min.

Optional Resources
- **Más práctica,** p. 240
- **Más práctica,** p. 241
- **Comunicación,** p. 241
- Slower Pace Learners, p. 241 ◆
- Multiple Intelligences, p. 241

HOMEWORK SUGGESTIONS
Cuaderno de gramática, pp. 71–73
Internet Activities

Day 15

OBJECTIVE
Expressing hopes and wishes

Core Instruction
Vocabulario en acción 2, pp. 238–243
- Review **¡Exprésate!,** p. 242. 10 min.
- Have students do Activities 27–30, p. 195. 40 min.

Optional Resources
- Teacher to Teacher, p. 242
- **Comunicación,** p. 243
- Advanced Learners, p. 243 ▲
- Multiple Intelligences, p. 243

HOMEWORK SUGGESTIONS
Study for **Prueba: Vocabulario 2.**

Day 16

OBJECTIVE
Vocabulary review and assessment

Core Instruction
Vocabulario en acción 2, pp. 238–243
- Review **Vocabulario en acción 2,** pp. 238–243. 30 min.
- Give **Prueba: Vocabulario 2.** 20 min.

Optional Resources
- Test Generator

HOMEWORK SUGGESTIONS
Preview **Gramática en acción 2,** pp. 244–249.

50-Minute Lesson Plans, continued

Day 17

OBJECTIVE
Informal commands of spelling-change and irregular verbs

Core Instruction
Gramática en acción 2, pp. 244–249
- Show **GramaVisión,** Ch. 10. 10 min.
- See Teaching **Gramática,** p. 244. 40 min.

Optional Resources
- Special Learning Needs, p. 245 ●

HOMEWORK SUGGESTIONS
Cuaderno de vocabulario y gramática, pp. 74–76
Cuaderno de actividades, pp. 68–71

Day 18

OBJECTIVE
Informal commands of spelling-change and irregular verbs

Core Instruction
Gramática en acción 2, pp. 244–249
- Have students do Bell Work 10.7, p. 246. 5 min.
- Review **Gramática,** p. 245. 15 min.
- Play Audio CD 10, Tr. 8 for Activity 31, p. 245. 10 min.
- Have students do Activities 32–33, p. 245. 20 min.

Optional Resources
- Heritage Speakers, p. 245 ■
- **Comunicación,** p. 245
- Slower Pace Learners, p. 245 ◆

HOMEWORK SUGGESTIONS
Cuaderno de vocabulario y gramática, pp. 74–76
Cuaderno de actividades, pp. 68–71
Interactive Tutor, Ch. 10

Day 19

OBJECTIVE
Review of direct object pronouns

Core Instruction
Gramática en acción 2, pp. 244–249
- See Teaching **Gramática,** p. 246. 35 min.
- Have students do Activity 34, p. 246. 5 min.
- Play Audio CD 10, Tr. 9 for Activity 35, p. 246. 10 min.

Optional Resources
- Show **GramaVisión,** Ch. 10. 5 min.
- Advanced Learners, p. 247 ▲

HOMEWORK SUGGESTIONS
Cuaderno de vocabulario y gramática, pp. 74–76
Cuaderno de actividades, pp. 68–71
Internet Activities
Interactive Tutor, Ch. 10

Day 20

OBJECTIVE
Review of direct object pronouns

Core Instruction
Gramática en acción 2, pp. 245–249
- Have students do Bell Work 10.8, p. 248. 5 min.
- Show **GramaVisión,** Ch. 10. 5 min.
- Review of direct object pronouns, p. 246. 15 min.
- Have students do Activities 36–37, p. 247. 10 min.
- Present **Nota cultural,** p. 247. 5 min.
- Have students do Activity 38, p. 247. 10 min.

Optional Resources
- **Comunicación,** p. 247
- Multiple Intelligences, p. 247

HOMEWORK SUGGESTIONS
Cuaderno de vocabulario y gramática, pp. 74–76
Cuaderno de actividades, pp. 68–71
Interactive Tutor, Ch. 10

Day 21

OBJECTIVE
Review of verbs followed by infinitives

Core Instruction
Gramática en acción 2, pp. 244–249
- See Teaching **Gramática,** p. 248. 30 min.
- Present **Nota cultural,** p. 248. 10 min.
- Have students do Activities 39–40, pp. 248–249. 10 min.

Optional Resources
- Slower Pace Learners, p. 249 ◆

HOMEWORK SUGGESTIONS
Cuaderno de vocabulario y gramática, pp. 74–76
Cuaderno de actividades, pp. 68–71
Internet Activities
Interactive Tutor, Ch. 10

Day 22

OBJECTIVE
Review of verbs followed by infinitives; grammar review

Core Instruction
Gramática en acción 2, pp. 244–249
- Review of verbs followed by infinitives, p. 248. 10 min.
- Have students do Activities 41–43, p. 249. 25 min.
- Review **Gramática en acción 2,** pp. 244–249. 15 min.

Optional Resources
- **Comunicación,** p. 249
- Special Learning Needs, p. 249 ●

HOMEWORK SUGGESTIONS
Study for **Prueba: Gramática 2.**

Day 23

OBJECTIVE
*Grammar assessment; **La Bahía Fosforesente** and the Arecibo Observatory*

Core Instruction
Gramática en acción 2, pp. 244–249
- Review **Gramática en acción 2,** pp. 244–249. 10 min.
- Give **Prueba: Gramática 2.** 20 min.

Conexiones culturales, pp. 250–251
- See Teaching **Conexiones culturales,** #1–3, p. 250. 20 min.

Optional Resources
- **Prueba: Aplicación 2**
- Test Generator

HOMEWORK SUGGESTIONS
Internet Activities

Day 24

OBJECTIVE
The Arecibo Observatory; developing listening and reading skills

Core Instruction
Conexiones culturales, pp. 250–251
- See Teaching **Conexiones culturales,** #4–6, p. 250. 25 min.

Novela en video, pp. 252–255
- See Teaching **Novela en video,** #1, p. 252. 20 min.
- See Gestures, p. 254. 5 min.

Optional Resources
- Advanced Learners, p. 251 ▲
- Multiple Intelligences, p. 251
- Visual Learners, p. 252
- Comparing and Contrasting, p. 253
- **Comunicación,** p. 253

HOMEWORK SUGGESTIONS
Culminating Project, p. 254

To edit and create your own lesson plans, see the

One-Stop Planner® CD-ROM

KEY

- ▲ Advanced Learners
- ◆ Slower Pace Learners
- ● Special Learning Needs
- ■ Heritage Speakers

Day 25

OBJECTIVE
Developing listening and reading skills

Core Instruction

Novela en video, pp. 252–255
- See Teaching **Novela en video,** #2–3, p. 252. 25 min.

Leamos y escribamos, pp. 256–257
- See Teaching **Leamos,** p. 256. 25 min.

Optional Resources

- Community Link, p. 254
- **Comunicación,** p. 255
- Advanced Learners, p. 255 ▲
- Special Learning Needs, p. 255 ●
- Applying the Strategies, p. 256
- Advanced Learners, p. 257 ▲

HOMEWORK SUGGESTIONS
Activities 1–3, p. 255
Cuaderno de actividades, p. 72

Day 26

OBJECTIVE
Developing writing skills

Core Instruction

Leamos y escribamos, pp. 256–257
- See **Teaching Escribamos,** p. 256. 50 min.

Optional Resources

- Process Writing, p. 257
- Special Learning Needs, p. 257 ●

HOMEWORK SUGGESTIONS
Review Chapter 10.

Day 27

OBJECTIVE
Chapter review

Core Instruction

Repaso, pp. 258–261
- Have students do Activities 1–5, pp. 258–259. 50 min.

Optional Resources

- Fold-n-Learn, p. 258
- Game Bank, pp. T60–T63

HOMEWORK SUGGESTIONS
Internet Activities
Interactive Tutor, Ch. 10

Day 28

OBJECTIVE
Chapter review

Core Instruction

Repaso, pp. 258–261
- Play Audio CD 10, Tr. 12 for Activity 6, p. 259. 10 min.
- Have students do Activity 7, p. 259. 10 min.
- See **Circumlocution,** p. 261. 15 min.
- Play Audio CD 10, Tr. 13–15 for **Letra y sonido,** p. 260. 15 min.

Optional Resources

- Interactive Tutor, Ch. 10
- Game Bank, pp. T60–T63

HOMEWORK SUGGESTIONS
Study for Chapter Test.

Day 29

OBJECTIVE
Chapter review

Core Instruction

Integración, pp. 262–263
- Play Audio CD 10, Tr. 16 for Activity 1, p. 262. 10 min.
- Have students do Activities 2–4, pp. 262–263. 40 min.

Optional Resources

- Additional Practice, p. 262
- Culture Project, p. 262
- Fine Art Connection, p. 263

HOMEWORK SUGGESTIONS
Study for Chapter Test.
Cuaderno de actividades, pp. 73–74

Day 30

OBJECTIVE
Assessment

Core Instruction

Chapter Test 50 min.

Optional Resources

Assessment Program:
- **Prueba: Lectura**
- **Prueba: Escritura**
- Alternative Assessment
- Test Generator

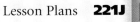

HOMEWORK SUGGESTIONS
Study for Final Exam.

¡A viajar!

90-Minute Lesson Plans

Block 1

OBJECTIVE
Asking for and giving information

Core Instruction

Chapter Opener, pp. 222–223
- See Using the Photo and **Más vocabulario,** p. 222. 5 min.
- See Chapter Objectives, p. 222. 5 min.

Vocabulario en acción 1, pp. 224–229
- Show **ExpresaVisión,** Ch. 10. 5 min.
- See Teaching **Vocabulario,** p. 224. 35 min.
- Present **¡Exprésate!,** p. 225. 10 min.
- Have students do Activity 1, p. 226. 10 min.
- Play Audio CD 10, Tr. 1 for Activity 2, p. 226. 10 min.
- Have students do Activity 3, p. 226. 5 min.
- Present **Nota cultural,** p. 226. 5 min.

Optional Resources

- Common Error Alert, p. 225
- **También se puede decir,** p. 225
- Advanced Learners, p. 225 ▲
- Multiple Intelligences, p. 225
- Social Studies Link, p. 226
- Fold-n-Learn, p. 226
- Variation, p. 227
- **Más práctica,** p. 227
- Special Learning Needs, p. 227 ●

HOMEWORK SUGGESTIONS
Cuaderno de vocabulario y gramática, pp. 65–67
Internet Activities

Block 2

OBJECTIVE
Asking for and giving information; reminding and reassuring

Core Instruction

Vocabulario en acción 1, pp. 224–229
- Review **Vocabulario 1** and **¡Exprésate!,** pp. 224–225. 20 min.
- Have students do Activities 4–6, p. 227. 25 min.
- See Teaching **¡Exprésate!,** p. 228. 15 min.
- Have students do Activities 7–10, p. 228–229. 30 min.

Optional Resources

- TPR, p. 225
- **Comunicación,** p. 227
- Advanced Learners, p. 227 ▲
- Special Learning Needs, p. 227 ●
- **Más práctica,** p. 228
- Slower Pace Learners, p. 229 ◆

HOMEWORK SUGGESTIONS
Study for **Prueba: Gramática 1.**
Cuaderno de vocabulario y gramática, pp. 65–67
Internet Activities

Block 3

OBJECTIVE
Vocabulary review and assessment; review of the preterite

Core Instruction

Vocabulario en acción 1, pp. 224–229
- Have students do Bell Work 10.2, p. 230. 5 min.
- Have students do Activity 11, p. 229. 10 min.
- Review **Vocabulario en acción 1,** pp. 224–229. 25 min.
- Give **Prueba: Vocabulario 1.** 20 min.

Gramática en acción 1, pp. 230–235
- See Teaching **Gramática,** p. 230. 30 min.

Optional Resources

- **Comunicación,** p. 229
- Multiple Intelligences, p. 229
- Test Generator

HOMEWORK SUGGESTIONS
Cuaderno de vocabulario y gramática, pp. 68–70
Cuaderno de actividades, pp. 63–66

Block 4

OBJECTIVE
*Review of the preterite; preterite of **-car, -gar, -zar** verbs*

Core Instruction

Gramática en acción 1, pp. 230–235
- Have students do Bell Work 10.3, p. 232. 5 min.
- Show **GramaVisión,** Ch. 10. 5 min.
- Review the preterite, p. 230. 20 min.
- Play Audio CD 10, Tr. 2 for Activity 12, p. 230. 10 min.
- Have students do Activities 13–14, p. 231. 20 min.
- See Teaching **Gramática,** p. 186. 30 min.

Optional Resources

- Teacher to Teacher, p. 231
- **Comunicación,** p. 231
- Advanced Learners, p. 231 ▲
- Special Learning Needs, p. 231 ●

HOMEWORK SUGGESTIONS
Cuaderno de vocabulario y gramática, pp. 68–70
Cuaderno de actividades, pp. 63–66
Internet Activities
Interactive Tutor, Ch. 10

To edit and create your own lesson plans, see the

One-Stop Planner® CD-ROM

KEY

- ▲ Advanced Learners
- ◆ Slower Pace Learners
- ● Special Learning Needs
- ■ Heritage Speakers

Block 5

OBJECTIVE

Preterite of ***-car, -gar, -zar*** *verbs; preterite of* ***hacer***

Core Instruction

Gramática en acción 1, pp. 230–235

- Review the preterite of **-car, -gar, -zar** verbs, p. 232. 10 min.
- Play Audio CD 10, Tr. 3 for Activity 15, p. 232. 10 min.
- Have students do Activities 16–18, pp. 232–233. 25 min.
- See Teaching **Gramática,** p. 234. 30 min.
- Present **Nota cultural,** p. 188. 5 min.
- Have students do Activities 19–20, p. 234. 10 min.

Optional Resources

- **GramaVisión,** Ch. 10
- Career Path, p. 233
- **Comunicación,** p. 233
- Slower Pace Learners, p. 233 ◆
- Special Learning Needs, p. 233 ●

HOMEWORK SUGGESTIONS

Study for **Prueba: Gramática 1.**
Cuaderno de vocabulario y gramática, pp. 68–70
Cuaderno de actividades, pp. 63–66
Internet Activities
Interactive Tutor, Ch. 10

Block 6

OBJECTIVE

Grammar review and assessment; interviews from around the Spanish-speaking world

Core Instruction

Gramática en acción 1, pp. 230–235

- Review the preterite of **hacer,** p. 234. 5 min.
- Have students do Activities 21–22, pp. 234–235. 15 min.
- Review **Gramática en acción 1,** pp. 230–235. 15 min.
- Give **Prueba: Gramática 1.** 20 min.

Cultura, pp. 236–237

- See Teaching **Cultura,** p. 236. 30 min.
- Present and assign **Comunidad,** p. 237. 5 min.

Optional Resources

- **Comunicación,** p. 235
- Slower Pace Learners, p. 235 ◆
- Test Generator
- **Prueba: Aplicación 1**
- Map Activities, p. 236
- Comparing and Contrasting, p. 237
- Advanced Learners, p. 237 ▲
- Special Learning Needs, p. 237 ●

HOMEWORK SUGGESTIONS

Multiple Intelligences, p. 235
Community Link, p. 237
Cuaderno de actividades, p. 67

Block 7

OBJECTIVE

Talking about a trip; expressing hopes and wishes

Core Instruction

Vocabulario en acción 2, pp. 238–243

- See Teaching **Vocabulario,** p. 238. 30 min.
- Present **Nota cultural,** p. 240. 5 min.
- Play Audio CD 10, Tr. 7 for Activity 23, p. 240. 10 min.
- Have students do Activities 24–26, pp. 240–241. 30 min.
- See Teaching **¡Exprésate!,** p. 242. 15 min.

Optional Resources

- TPR, p. 239
- Language Note, p. 239
- **También se puede decir,** p. 239
- Multiple Intelligences, p. 239
- Advanced Learners, p. 239 ▲
- Products and Perspectives, p. 240
- **Más práctica,** p. 240
- **Más práctica,** p. 241
- **Comunicación,** p. 241
- Slower Pace Learners, p. 241 ◆
- Multiple Intelligences, p. 241

HOMEWORK SUGGESTIONS

Cuaderno de gramática, pp. 71–73
Internet Activities

Block 8

OBJECTIVE

Talking about a trip; expressing hopes and wishes

Core Instruction

Vocabulario en acción 2, pp. 238–243

- Have students do Bell Work 10.6, p. 244. 5 min.
- Review **Vocabulario 2** and **¡Exprésate!,** pp. 238–239, 242. 20 min.
- Have students do Activities 27–30, p. 195. 40 min.
- See Teaching **Gramática,** #1–3, p. 244. 25 min.

Optional Resources

- **ExpresaVisión,** Ch. 10
- Game, p. 240
- Teacher to Teacher, p. 242
- **Comunicación,** p. 243
- Advanced Learners, p. 243 ▲
- Multiple Intelligences, p. 243
- Special Learning Needs, p. 245 ●

HOMEWORK SUGGESTIONS

Study for **Prueba: Vocabulario 2.**
Cuaderno de gramática, pp. 71–73
Internet Activities

90-Minute Lesson Plans, continued

Block 9

OBJECTIVE
Vocabulary review and assessment; informal commands of spelling-change and irregular verbs

Core Instruction
Vocabulario en acción 2, pp. 238–243
- Review **Vocabulario en acción 2,** pp. 238–243. 15 min.
- Give **Prueba: Vocabulario 2.** 20 min.

Gramática en acción 2, pp. 244–249
- Review informal commands of spelling change verbs, p. 244. 10 min.
- See Teaching **Gramática,** #4–5, p. 244. 15 min.
- Play Audio CD 10, Tr. 8 for Activity 31, p. 245. 10 min.
- Have students do Activities 32–33, p. 245. 20 min.

Optional Resources
- Test Generator
- Heritage Speakers, p. 245 ■
- **Comunicación,** p. 245
- Slower Pace Learners, p. 245 ◆

HOMEWORK SUGGESTIONS
Cuaderno de vocabulario y gramática, pp. 74–76
Cuaderno de actividades, pp. 68–71
Interactive Tutor, Ch. 10

Block 10

OBJECTIVE
Review of direct object pronouns; review of verbs followed by infinitives

Core Instruction
Gramática en acción 2, pp. 244–249
- See Teaching **Gramática,** p. 246. 35 min.
- Have students do Activity 34, p. 246. 5 min.
- Play Audio CD 10, Tr. 9 for Activity 35, p. 246. 5 min.
- Have students do Activities 36–37, p. 247. 10 min.
- Present **Nota cultural,** p. 247. 5 min.
- Have students do Activity 38, p. 247. 10 min.
- See Teaching **Gramática,** #1–2, p. 248. 20 min.

Optional Resources
- **GramaVisión,** Ch. 10
- **Comunicación,** p. 247
- Advanced Learners, p. 247 ▲
- Multiple Intelligences, p. 247

HOMEWORK SUGGESTIONS
Cuaderno de vocabulario y gramática, pp. 74–76
Cuaderno de actividades, pp. 68–71
Internet Activities
Interactive Tutor, Ch. 10

Block 11

OBJECTIVE
Review of verbs followed by infinitives; ***La Bahía Fosforesente*** *and the Arecibo Observatory*

Core Instruction
Gramática en acción 2, pp. 244–249
- See Teaching **Gramática,** #3–4, p. 248. 10 min.
- Present **Nota cultural,** p. 248. 5 min.
- Have students do Activities 39–43, pp. 248–249. 30 min.

Conexiones culturales, pp. 250–251
- See Teaching **Conexiones culturales,** p. 250. 45 min.

Optional Resources
- **GramaVisión,** Ch. 10
- Slower Pace Learners, p. 249 ◆
- **Comunicación,** p. 249
- Special Learning Needs, p. 249 ●
- Advanced Learners, p. 251 ▲
- Multiple Intelligences, p. 251

HOMEWORK SUGGESTIONS
Study for **Prueba: Gramática 2.**
Cuaderno de vocabulario y gramática, pp. 74–76
Cuaderno de actividades, pp. 68–71
Internet Activities
Interactive Tutor, Ch. 10

To edit and create your own lesson plans, see the **One-Stop** Planner® CD-ROM

KEY
- ▲ Advanced Learners
- ◆ Slower Pace Learners
- ● Special Learning Needs
- ■ Heritage Speakers

Block 12

OBJECTIVE
Grammar assessment; developing listening and reading skills

Core Instruction
Gramática en acción 2, pp. 244–249
- Review **Gramática en acción 2,** pp. 244–249. 5 min.
- Give **Prueba: Gramática 2.** 20 min.

Novela en video, pp. 252–255
- See Teaching **Novela en video,** #1, p. 252. 35 min.

Leamos y escribamos, pp. 256–257
- See Teaching **Leamos,** p. 256. 30 min.

Optional Resources
- **Prueba: Aplicación 2**
- Test Generator
- Visual Learners, p. 252
- Comparing and Contrasting, p. 253
- **Comunicación,** p. 253
- Gestures, p. 254
- Community Link, p. 254
- **Comunicación,** p. 255
- Advanced Learners, p. 255 ▲
- Special Learning Needs, p. 255 ●
- Applying the Strategies, p. 256
- Advanced Learners, p. 257 ▲

HOMEWORK SUGGESTIONS
Activities 1–3, p. 255
Culminating Project, p. 254
Cuaderno de actividades, p. 72

Block 13

OBJECTIVE
Developing writing skills; chapter review

Core Instruction
Leamos y escribamos, pp. 256–257
- See Teaching **Escribamos,** p. 256. 45 min.

Repaso, pp. 258–261
- Have students do Activities 1–5, pp. 258–259. 25 min.
- Play Audio CD 10, Tr. 12 for Activity 6, p. 259. 5 min.
- Have students do Activity 7, p. 259. 5 min.
- Play Audio CD 10, Tr. 13–15 for **Letra y sonido,** p. 260. 10 min.

Optional Resources
- Process Writing, p. 257
- Special Learning Needs, p. 257 ●
- Fold-n-Learn, p. 258
- Game Bank, pp. T60–T63

HOMEWORK SUGGESTIONS
Study for Chapter Test.

Block 14

OBJECTIVE
Assessment

Core Instruction
Chapter Test 50 min.

Integración, pp. 262–263
- Play Audio CD 10, Tr. 16 for Activity 1, p. 262. 10 min.
- Have students do Activities 2–4, pp. 262–263. 30 min.

Optional Resources
Assessment Program:
- **Prueba: Lectura**
- **Prueba: Escritura**
- Alternative Assessment
- Test Generator
- Additional Practice, p. 262
- Culture Project, p. 262
- Fine Art Connection, p. 263

HOMEWORK SUGGESTIONS
Study for Final Exam.
Cuaderno de actividades, pp. 73–74

Chapter Opener

Meeting the National Standards

Communication
Comunicación, pp. 227, 229, 231, 233, 235, 241, 243, 245, 247, 249, 253, 255
Circumlocution, p. 261
Situación, p. 263

Cultures
Products and Perspectives, pp. 220, 221
Nota cultural, pp. 226, 234, 240, 247
Practices and Perspectives, p. 240
Gestures, p. 254

Connections
Interdisciplinary Links, pp. 220–221, 226, 250–251, 263
Conexiones culturales, pp. 250–251

Comparisons
Comparaciones, pp. 236–237
Comparing and Contrasting, pp. 237, 253
Language Note, p. 239

Communities
Career Path, p. 233
Comunidad, p. 237
Community Link, pp. 237, 254

Using the Photo

The Incas farmed the land around Cuzco by cutting terraces into the sides of the mountains. Have students guess what the girl in the photo is pointing at. Use **¿Qué ves en la foto?** and **Más vocabulario** to extend the discussion.

Más vocabulario

Words to discuss the photo:

la muralla *wall*
antiguo *old*
la tierra *the ground*
el valle *valley*
señalar *to point out*
la terraza *terrace*

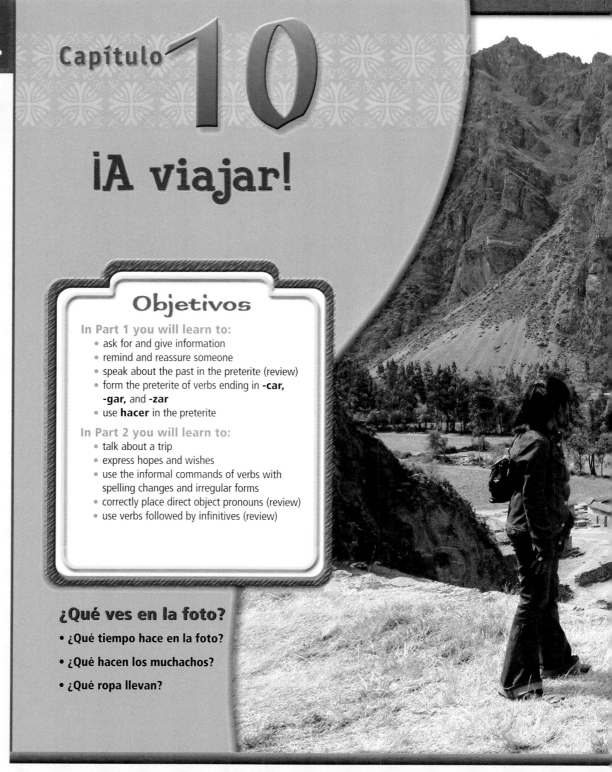

Capítulo 10

¡A viajar!

Objetivos

In Part 1 you will learn to:
- ask for and give information
- remind and reassure someone
- speak about the past in the preterite (review)
- form the preterite of verbs ending in **-car, -gar,** and **-zar**
- use **hacer** in the preterite

In Part 2 you will learn to:
- talk about a trip
- express hopes and wishes
- use the informal commands of verbs with spelling changes and irregular forms
- correctly place direct object pronouns (review)
- use verbs followed by infinitives (review)

¿Qué ves en la foto?

- **¿Qué tiempo hace en la foto?**
- **¿Qué hacen los muchachos?**
- **¿Qué ropa llevan?**

Holt Online Learning *¡Exprésate!* contains several online options for you to incorporate into your lessons.

***¡Exprésate!* Student Edition online at my.hrw.com**
On this site, you will find the online edition of *¡Exprésate!* All concepts presented in the textbook are presented and practiced in this online version of your textbook. You will also find audio and practice activities at point of use. The online pages can be used as a supplement to, or as a replacement for your textbook.

Practice activities at go.hrw.com
These activities provide additional practice for major concepts presented in each chapter. Practice items include structured practice as well as research topics.

Teacher resources at www.hrw.com
This site provides additional information that teachers might find useful about the *¡Exprésate!* program.

Visit Holt Online
go.hrw.com
KEYWORD: EXP1B CH10
Online Edition

Ruinas incaicas en Ollantaitambo, Cuzco

Chapter Opener

Learning Tips

Remind students of when they first started Spanish class. Have them think about all the progress they have made. Tell students that if they have a break between Spanish I and Spanish II, they should review their Spanish as much as possible to keep it fresh in their memory. Have them think about ways they can expose themselves to more Spanish over their holiday or summer break.

VIDEO OPTIONS

- **ExpresaVisión 1**
- **GramaVisión 1**
  Review of the regular preterite; preterite of **-car, -gar, -zar** verbs; preterite of **hacer**
- **VideoCultura**
- **ExpresaVisión 2**
- **GramaVisión 2**
  Informal commands of spelling-change and irregular verbs; review of direct object pronouns; review of verbs followed by infinitives
- **VideoNovela**
- **Variedades**

Pacing Tips

In this chapter, there is more review in **Gramática 2,** so you might spend more time on the concepts presented in **Gramática 1.** For complete lesson plan suggestions, see pages 221G–221N.

Suggested pacing:	Traditional Schedule	Block Schedule
Vocabulario 1/Gramática 1	10 1/2 days	5 1/3 blocks
Cultura	1 day	1/2 block
Vocabulario 2/Gramática 2	11 1/4 days	5 1/3 blocks
Conexiones culturales	1 day	1/2 block
Novela	3/4 day	1/3 block
Leamos y escribamos	1 1/2 days	1/2 block
Repaso	2 days	1/2 block
Chapter Test	1 day	1/2 block
Integración	1 day	1/2 block

Resources

Planning:

Lesson Planner, pp. 131–135, 284–289

 One-Stop Planner

Presentation:

TPR Storytelling Book, pp. 54–55

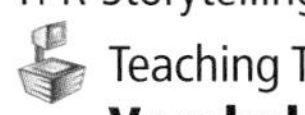 Teaching Transparencies **Vocabulario** 10.1, 10.2

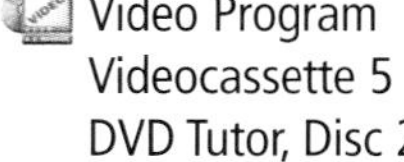 Video Program
Videocassette 5
DVD Tutor, Disc 2
ExpresaVisión

Practice:

Cuaderno de vocabulario y gramática, pp. 65–67

Activities for Communication, pp. 37–38

Video Guide, pp. 94–96

Lab Book, pp. 31–32, 62

 Teaching Transparencies
Bell Work 10.1
Vocabulario y gramática answers, pp. 65–67

 Audio CD 10, Tr. 1

 Interactive Tutor, Disc 2

Bell Work

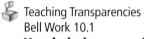

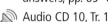

Use Bell Work 10.1 in the *Teaching Transparencies*, or write this activity on the board.

Match each person's activity with what he or she is most likely to do at the next party.

1. Ángel habla mucho. Va a...
2. Manolo es gracioso. Le gusta...
3. Eva es artística. Piensa...
4. Emilio siempre tiene sed. Va a...
5. A Lola le encanta la comida mexicana. Piensa...

a. contar chistes.
b. beber mucho ponche.
c. comer tamales.
d. charlar.
e. enseñar fotos bonitas.

Objetivos
Asking for and giving information, reminding and reassuring

Vocabulario en acción 1

ExpresaVisión

En el aeropuerto

Acabo de desembarcar. ¿Dónde puedo **recoger las maletas?**
Allí, en **el reclamo de equipaje.**
el reclamo de equipaje
las maletas

Core Instruction

TEACHING VOCABULARIO

1. Introduce the vocabulary on pp. 224–225, using transparencies **Vocabulario 10.1** and **10.2.** Model the pronunciation of each word as you point to the appropriate picture. **(10 min.)**
2. Pretend that you are going on a trip. Bring to class a bag full of items. Ask students if you have various items in your suitcase. **¿Tengo mi pasaporte?** Students will answer **sí** or **no,** depending on whether or not you have the item. **(10 min.)**
3. Ask students where you can do various things (**facturar el equipaje, recoger las maletas, cambiar dinero, comprar revistas**), using **¿Dónde se puede...? (14 min.)**
4. Ask students why you would normally use the **usted** form rather than the **tú** form to ask for directions or assistance. **(1 min.)**

ExpresaVisión

To teach the new terms related to airports and travelling, use the presenter from the *Video Program.*

ExpresaVisión

STANDARDS: 1.2

Vocabulario 1

Voy a **abordar** el
ión ahora. Tengo todo lo
ue necesito. No quiero
perder nada.

la bolsa

la billetera

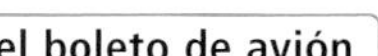

el boleto de avión

la tarjeta de embarque

el carnet de identidad

el pasaporte

Visit Holt Online
go.hrw.com
KEYWORD: EXP1B CH10
Vocabulario 1 practice

Más vocabulario...

cambiar dinero	*to change money*
comenzar (ie) un viaje	*to begin a trip*
encontrarse (ue) con (alguien)	*to meet up with (someone)*
hacer un viaje	*to take a trip*
irse	*to leave*
la llegada	*arrival*
la salida	*departure*
sentarse (ie)	*to sit down*
los servicios	*restrooms*

También se puede decir...

Some Latin American speakers say **la valija** instead of **la maleta.**

In Latin America, you will hear **chequear el equipaje** instead of **facturar el equipaje.**

El boleto is sometimes called **el billete, el ticket, la boleta, el tiquete,** or **el pasaje.**

¡Exprésate!

To ask for information	To give information
¿Me puede decir dónde está la oficina de cambio? *Can you tell me where the money exchange is?*	**Está a la vuelta.** *It's around the corner.*
¿Sabe usted a qué hora sale/llega el vuelo 954? *Do you know at what time Flight 954 leaves/arrives?*	**Lo puede ver allí en esa pantalla.** *You can see it there on that monitor.* **Sí, sale/llega a las cuatro en punto.** *Yes, it leaves/arrives at four on the dot.*
¿Dónde se puede conseguir un mapa? *Where can I get a map?*	**Lo siento, no sé.** *I'm sorry, I don't know.*

Interactive TUTOR

Online Vocabulario y gramática, pp. 65–67

▶ Vocabulario adicional — Vacaciones, p. R15

TPR
Total Physical Response

Have students help collect as many items as they can from the **Vocabulario.** Review the commands and then have students respond.

Pon el carnet de identidad en la billetera y pon la billetera en la bolsa.

Lleven el carnet de identidad y la tarjeta de embarque en la mano.

Ve a la oficina de cambio. Pon el dinero en la billetera.

Ve al reclamo de equipaje. Imagina que ves llegar tu maleta.

Connections
Language to Language

Billetera derives from ***billete*** and comes from the Latin word for *document.* The English word *bill* comes from the same word. **Equipaje** derives from **equipar** *(to equip, to provide what is necessary)* which comes through French from the ancient Scandinavian term used for equipping a boat. Ask students to identify any other words on page 225 that might have come into Spanish from another language. (For example, **pasaporte** comes from the French word ***passeport.)***

Differentiated Instruction

Advanced Learners

You might do the following activity after presenting the new terms. Write **Para preparar un viaje...** on the board and tell students to write a list describing the steps that a person would go through to prepare for a trip. After the students have completed their lists, ask volunteers to read them. Write the steps on the board. Then ask the class if there are any more steps that a person should take to prepare for a trip. Save each list for student portfolios.

Multiple Intelligences

Spatial/Bodily-Kinesthetic Some students might have never traveled by airplane. If possible, arrange an airport tour. Assign students terms or phrases to find at the airport. If a field trip is not possible, an alternative would be to have students take an online "virtual tour" of an airport. Students could print pictures from the tour to create a class poster.

Common Error Alert ¡Ojo!

Students will often try to use **para** or **por** after the verb **esperar.** Remind them that **esperar** means *to wait for* and that the preposition is included in the meaning of the verb.

También se puede decir...

Students may hear many words for restroom other than **servicios,** such as **el baño,** or **el excusado.**

STANDARDS: 1.2

1 Script

1. —¿Sabe usted a qué hora llega el vuelo 797?
—No sé, pero lo puede ver en esa pantalla.
—Gracias.
2. —¿Dónde puedo facturar mi equipaje?
—Tiene que ir a ese mostrador y hacer cola.
3. —¿Me puede decir dónde están los servicios?
—Sí, cómo no. Están a la vuelta.
4. —¿Sabe usted dónde está la aduana?
—Lo siento, no sé.

2 Answers

1. aeropuerto, **2.** cola, **3.** embarque, avión, **4.** vuelo, salida, **5.** seguridad, **6.** cambio, **7.** reclamo, **8.** perder

Connections

Social Studies Link

Have students find out more about Lake Titicaca in Southern Peru. Ask them to look on the Internet or in a travel guide book to find: the size and altitude of the lake, other islands in the lake in addition to Uros, mythology associated with the islands, typical daily life on the islands, and arts and crafts produced on the islands. Ask students to work in pairs to create a poster and/or report about their findings.

CD 10, Tr. 1

1 ¿Dónde están?

Escuchemos Mira las fotos y escucha las conversaciones. Decide qué foto corresponde a cada conversación.

A

3

B

1

C

2

D

4

Nota cultural

The Uros Islands on Lake Titicaca are man-made and constructed of *totora*, a reed-like grass that grows on the lake's bed. Though walking on the surface is like walking on a water bed, there are reed houses, schools, churches, and even a post office. The Uros people also make reed boats to travel to the mainland. What do you think life is like on these islands?

2 Definiciones

Leamos/Escribamos Completa las oraciones.

reclamo	embarque	seguridad	vuelo	salida
cola	cambio	avión	aeropuerto	perder

1. Un ___ es donde llegan y salen los aviones.
2. Una ___ es una línea de personas que esperan.
3. Necesitas una tarjeta de ___ para abordar un ___.
4. En la pantalla está el número del ___ y la hora de la ___.
5. El agente abre el equipaje en el control de ___.
6. Puedes cambiar dólares por soles en la oficina de ___.
7. Puedes recoger tus maletas en el ___ de equipaje.
8. Si llegas tarde puedes ___ tu vuelo.

3 Conversaciones

Leamos/Escribamos Completa las conversaciones con base en las fotos de la Actividad 1.

1. —¿Sabe usted dónde están ___? los servicios
—Sí, cómo no. Están ___. muy cerca
2. —¿Me puede decir a qué hora llega ___ 179? el vuelo
—Lo siento, ___. Pero lo puede ver allí en esa ___. no sé; pantalla
3. —¿Dónde puedo ___ el equipaje? facturar
—Tiene que ir a ese ___ y hacer ___. mostrador; cola
4. —¿Sabe usted dónde ___ la aduana? está
—Lo ___, no sé. siento

FOLD-N-LEARN

Four-door Fold

1. Have students fold a sheet of paper in half from left to right. Then they fold it in half again from top to bottom. **2.** Students open the paper, then fold each side of it to the center crease. **3.** Students cut slits on the horizontal creases of both flaps to form four doors. **4.** On each of the four doors, students sketch the four different areas in the airport from **Vocabulario 1**, p. 224. For example, on one door, they draw a waiting room. On another door, they draw a security checkpoint, and so on. **5.** On the inside of each door, students write all the vocabulary words that correspond to that area of the airport. **6.** To study, students choose a door, or area of the airport, and name all the vocabulary words that correspond to that area. They check their answers by looking behind the door.

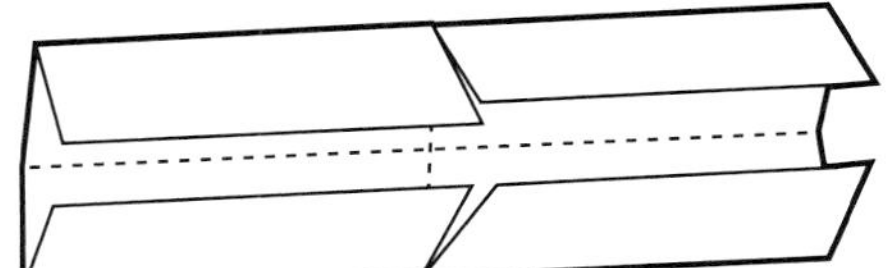

STANDARDS: 1.2, 2.1, 2.2, 3.2

4 ¿Para el viaje?

Leamos Complete these travel sentences by matching words in the first column with an appropriate ending in the second column.

1. Para abordar un avión... d
2. En la pantalla... a
3. Necesitas un boleto... e
4. Los pasajeros... b
5. Se pueden recoger las maletas... c

a. se pueden ver las salidas y llegadas.
b. hacen cola en el mostrador para hablar con el agente.
c. en el reclamo de equipaje.
d. necesitas una tarjeta de embarque.
e. para hacer un viaje en avión.

Comunicación

5 Un viaje de curso *(class trip)*

Hablemos Imagine your Spanish class is taking a trip to Peru! With a partner, take turns role-playing conversations you might have with an airport employee. Here are some topics to cover.

- What time does Flight 316 leave?
- Where do I check my bags?
- Where can I get a boarding pass?
- Where are the restrooms?
- Where can I get a map?
- Where can I pick up my bags?
- Where is the money exchange?

En el aeropuerto internacional de Lima

6 Consejos del profesor

Escribamos/Hablemos Your teacher is telling you what you need to do to get ready for the class trip. Work in groups of three to complete the instructions by turning the cues below into informal commands. Then take turns telling each other what to do.

MODELO cambiar/dinero **Cambia el dinero en el aeropuerto.**

1. comprar/un pasaporte y un boleto Compra un pasaporte y un boleto.
2. traer/el carnet de identidad Trae el carnet de identidad.
3. hacer cola/el mostrador Haz cola en el mostrador.
4. facturar/el equipaje con el agente Factura el equipaje con el agente.
5. esperar/la sala de espera Espera en la sala de espera.
6. abordar /con la tarjeta de embarque Aborda el avión con la tarjeta de embarque.
7. no perder/el vuelo No pierdas el vuelo.

Differentiated Instruction

ADVANCED LEARNERS

Building on Previous Skills Ask students to imagine that they have arrived in Peru and are writing home to tell their families about the trip. Have them refer to the topics in Activities 5 and 6, and write sentences in the past tense that tell what the trip was like.

MODELO

Facturé mis maletas en el mostrador, y luego esperé una hora en la sala de espera. El vuelo 316 salió a las 8:00 de la mañana...

SPECIAL LEARNING NEEDS

Students with Visual Impairments To help students who have visual impairments, you might want to assign a partner to work with each one to do the activities on pages 226–227. Have the partner read aloud all sentences, questions, and clues as the activity is being done. You might also ask the partner to write the material in large letters on construction paper to make it easier to read.

Variation

2 Ask students to work in pairs to turn Activity 1 into **cierto/falso** statements. Have them take turns reading each other the statements, placing a word in the blank. Tell them they may use the correct choice or an incorrect choice in the blank. Have the other partner listen carefully, then tell whether the statement was **cierto** or **falso.** If the answer is **falso**, the partner should correct the statement.

Más práctica

3 Ask students to work in pairs to read aloud the conversations in Activity 3.

Comunicación

Pair Activity: Interpersonal

5 Ask students to imagine that this **viaje de curso** is going to Peru in July, and that each student will be staying with a Peruvian family and will be going to the local school with the family's children. Have one student in each pair play the role of student, and one play the role of teacher. Instruct the student to ask six questions about the trip, and then have the teacher give an answer. Topics to cover: the weather, what clothes to take, what the host family is like, what town they will stay in and where it is located, what activities they will be doing, and what foods they will be eating. To make the information useful, you might want to have each pair prepare by researching a specific Peruvian town.

Resources

Planning:

Lesson Planner, pp. 131–135, 284–289

 One-Stop Planner

Presentation:

TPR Storytelling Book, pp. 54–55

Teaching Transparencies **Vocabulario** 10.1, 10.2

 Video Program
Videocassette 5
DVD Tutor, Disc 2
ExpresaVisión

Practice:

Cuaderno de vocabulario y gramática, pp. 65–67

Activities for Communication, pp. 37–38

Video Guide, pp. 94–96

Lab Book, pp. 31–32, 62

 Teaching Transparencies **Vocabulario y gramática** answers, pp. 65–67

Interactive Tutor, Disc 2

8 Answers

Already done: encontrar el pasaporte, hacer las maletas, poner la cámara en la maleta
Still to do: sacar el dinero, pasar por el cajero automático

Más práctica

7 Have students work in groups of three to read aloud the conversation in Activity 7. Then ask them to write another version of this conversation that might take place between Gabriela and her grandparents if Gabriela had not been so well prepared for her trip. Ask them to have the grandparents give advice and help her get ready. Have them practice, and then present their new conversation to the class.

¡Exprésate!

To remind and reassure

Interactive TUTOR

¿Ya sacaste el dinero? *Did you already get the money?*	**Sí, ya lo saqué.** *Yes, I already got it.* **No, todavía no. Debo pasar por el cajero automático.** *No, not yet. I need to go by the automatic teller machine.*
¿Ya hiciste la maleta? *Did you already pack your suitcase?*	**No, todavía tengo que hacerla.** *No, I still have to pack it.*
¡Ay, dejé la cámara en casa! *Oh, I left the camera at home!*	**No te preocupes. Puedes comprar una cámara desechable en cualquier tienda.** *Don't worry. You can buy a disposable camera at any store.*

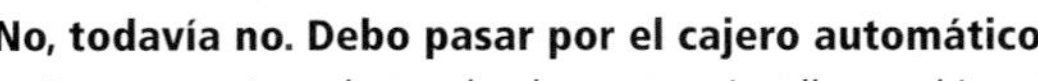

Online
Vocabulario y gramática, pp. 65–67

Una familia en Lima, Perú

7 El viaje de Gabriela

Leamos Gabriela has been visiting her grandparents in Lima, and is now saying goodbye to return to her school in the U.S. Complete their conversation using the best choice of words.

preocupes	hiciste	tengo	dejé
sale	sacaste	cajero	pasaporte

ABUELO ¿Encontraste tu __1__? pasaporte
GABRIELA Sí, abuelo, lo __2__ en mi bolsa. tengo
ABUELO ¿Y ya __3__ el dinero que necesitas? sacaste
GABRIELA No, todavía no. Debo pasar por el __4__ automático. cajero
ABUELA ¿__5__ bien las maletas? Hiciste
GABRIELA Sí, tengo todo mi equipaje.
ABUELA ¿Tienes tu cámara?
GABRIELA No te __6__, abuelita, no la __7__ en casa. La tengo en mi maleta. preocupes, dejé
ABUELO Bueno. El vuelo __8__ a las dos. Tenemos que salir para el aeropuerto. sale

8 ¿Qué más?

Escribamos On a separate piece of paper, make two columns. In the first column, write the things that Gabriela has already done. In the other, list the tasks she still has to do before the airplane takes off.

Core Instruction

TEACHING ¡EXPRÉSATE!

1. Use the expressions from **¡Exprésate!** to act out a conversation between two people preparing to go on a trip. You may wish to use puppets or stuffed animals to portray the different speakers. Use body language, gestures, and/or pictures to convey meaning. **(5 min.)**
2. Randomly read expressions from **¡Exprésate!** aloud. Ask students to raise their right hand if they would use the expression to remind and their left hand if they would use the expression to reassure. **(5 min.)**
3. Ask students if they have already done various things to prepare for a trip. Give them a thumbs-up or thumbs-down sign to cue their answers. **(5 min.)**

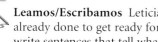

9 Una lista

Leamos/Escribamos Leticia has checked off the things she has already done to get ready for her trip to Peru. Read her list and write sentences that tell what she already did and what she still has to do.

Cosas por hacer:
sacar la tarjeta de embarque
√ encontrar el pasaporte
√ sacar dinero
√ comprar el boleto
facturar el equipaje
comprar revistas para el viaje

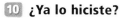

Comunicación

10 ¿Ya lo hiciste?

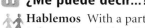

Hablemos With a partner play the roles of Leticia and her parent. The parent will ask Leticia if she has done the things on the list in Activity 9, and Leticia will answer.

MODELO MADRE O PADRE **¿Ya sacaste el dinero?**
LETICIA **Sí, pasé por el cajero automático ayer.**

11 ¿Me puede decir...?

Hablemos With a partner, take turns playing the roles of an airport information clerk and Spanish-speaking passengers in the following situations. Remember to be polite!

MODELO PASAJERA **¿Me puede decir dónde puedo comprar un mapa?**
TÚ **Sí, señora. Lo puede comprar en la tienda a la vuelta.**

1. A man has arrived from Chile and asks where the money exchange is. Give him directions.
2. A woman is looking for flight 394 to Mexico City. Point out the monitor to her.
3. Another traveler left his glasses at home and needs help reading the monitor. Help him find the flight number, when it leaves, and the gate it leaves from.
4. A woman from Venezuela is looking for the baggage claim and customs. Tell her where she should get in line.

Vocabulario 1

9 Possible Answers

1. Tiene que sacar la tarjeta de embarque en el aeropuerto.
2. Ya encontró el pasaporte en su bolsa.
3. Ya sacó dinero del banco.
4. Anteayer compró el boleto.
5. Necesita facturar el equipaje antes de viajar.
6. Tiene que comprar revistas en la librería para el viaje.

Comunicación

Class Activity: Interpersonal

Have students brainstorm to think of other travel situations, including problems that might occur. (lost passport or tickets, missing a flight, looking for a place to eat, can't find baggage, things left at home) Ask each person to write down on a slip of paper one situation, following the examples in Activity 11. Place all the slips in a container. Then assign two or three students roles as airline employees, and have them set up a counter to work behind. Other students draw a slip, read what's there, and approach one of the employees at the counter to present the situation or problem. Ask the employee to respond with appropriate advice or reassurance.

Differentiated Instruction

SLOWER PACE LEARNERS

9 Variation Have students plan an imaginary trip to Peru. Have them list things they need to do beforehand, including things they will pack, chores they need to do, and so on. After they put check marks by some items to indicate what they have already done, have them exchange lists with another student and talk about what each has already done and what still needs to be done.

MULTIPLE INTELLIGENCES

Bodily/Kinesthetic Set up an imaginary airport in the classroom. Place labels at various locations in the classroom: **los servicios, el mostrador, el reclamo de equipo, la sala de espera, el café, el control de seguridad, la aduana, la puerta, la librería.** Place one student at each location to act as the employee of that area. Have other students act as travelers, wandering around the airport and talking to at least five employees. Have students switch roles and do the activity again.

Assess

Assessment Program

Prueba: Vocabulario 1, pp. 97–98

Alternative Assessment Guide, pp. 245, 253, 261

Test Generator 

STANDARDS: 1.1, 1.2

Resources

Planning:

Lesson Planner, pp. 136–141, 288–295

 One-Stop Planner

Presentation:

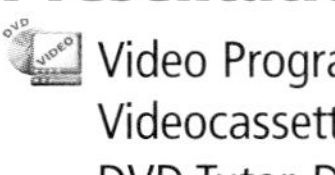 Video Program
Videocassette 5
DVD Tutor, Disc 2
GramaVisión

Practice:

Grammar Tutor for Students of Spanish, Chapter 10

Cuaderno de vocabulario y gramática, pp. 68–70

Cuaderno de actividades, pp. 55–57

Activities for Communication, pp. 37–38

Video Guide, pp. 94–95

Lab Book, pp. 31–32

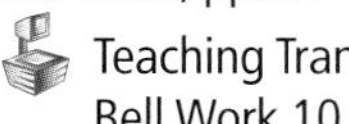 Teaching Transparencies
Bell Work 10.2
Vocabulario y gramática answers, pp. 68–70

 Audio CD 10, Tr. 2

 Interactive Tutor, Disc 2

Bell Work

Use Bell Work 10.2 in the *Teaching Transparencies*, or write this activity on the board.

Choose the logical verb for each sentence and write the correct form in the blank.

perder el vuelo hacer un viaje sentarse facturar el equipaje abordar

1. Ana María va a ____ a Puerto Rico.
2. En el aeropuerto Ana María lleva sus maletas al mostrador para ____.
3. Después ella ____ en una silla para esperar.
4. Ella no va a los servicios o de compras porque es importante no ____.
5. Por fin anuncian su vuelo y ella hace cola para____ el avión.

Objetivos
Review of the preterite; preterite of **-car, -gar, -zar** verbs; preterite of **hacer**

Gramática en acción 1

GramaVisión

Interactive TUTOR

Repaso The preterite

1 Use the preterite to talk about what happened at a specific point in the past and to narrate a sequence of events in the past.

Me levanté temprano, **comí** el desayuno y **fui** al aeropuerto.

2 You know how to form the preterite of all regular verbs. Remember that **-ar** and **-er** verbs do not have stem changes in the preterite.

	esperar	perder	abrir
yo	esper**é**	perd**í**	abr**í**
tú	esper**aste**	perd**iste**	abr**iste**
Ud., él, ella	esper**ó**	perd**ió**	abr**ió**
nosotros(as)	esper**amos**	perd**imos**	abr**imos**
vosotros(as)	esper**asteis**	perd**isteis**	abr**isteis**
Uds., ellos, ellas	esper**aron**	perd**ieron**	abr**ieron**

Esperamos una hora. — *We waited an hour.*
Perdí mi boleto. — *I lost my ticket.*

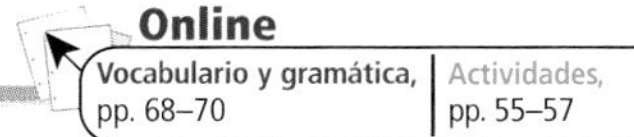

Vocabulario y gramática, pp. 68–70 | Actividades, pp. 55–57

¿Te acuerdas?

To say where someone *went*, use **ir** *(to go)* in the preterite.

fui	fuimos
fuiste	fuisteis
fue	fueron

CD 10, Tr. 2

12 ¡Qué viaje más difícil!

Escuchemos Jesse acaba de regresar de un viaje difícil. Escucha lo que dice y completa las oraciones con la respuesta correcta.

1. A las 8:00, Jesse ____.
   a. llegó al aeropuerto en taxi (b.) salió de la casa
2. Jesse regresó a casa porque ____.
   (a.) dejó el boleto allí b. olvidó sus lentes
3. Al llegar al aeropuerto, Jesse ____.
   a. compró un libro (b.) se encontró con sus amigos
4. En el control de seguridad, los agentes ____.
   a. facturaron el equipaje (b.) abrieron las maletas
5. Juan regresó al mostrador porque ____.
   a. recogió el equipaje (b.) perdió la tarjeta de embarque
6. Al fin, Carlos y Jesse ____.
   (a.) abordaron el avión b. perdieron el vuelo

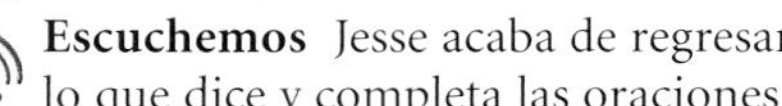

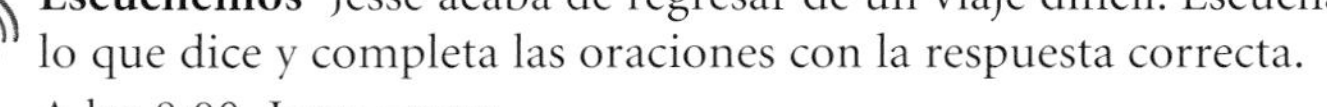

Core Instruction

TEACHING GRAMÁTICA

1. Go over **¿Te acuerdas? (1 min.)**
2. Go over Points 1 and 2. **(10 min.)**
3. Call out subject pronouns and verbs and have students raise their right hand if the verb is in present tense and their left hand if the verb is in preterite. **(5 min.)**
4. Have students play a chain game in which the first student tells something they did yesterday, (**Fui al colegio**). The second student repeats what the first student said, and adds a second activity to the list **Fui al colegio y monté en bicicleta. (14 min.)**

GramaVisión

For a video presentation of the preterite, use **el joven G** from the *Video Program*. For interactive activities, see the *DVD Tutor.*

GramaVisión

STANDARDS: 1.2

Visit Holt Online
go.hrw.com
KEYWORD: EXP1B CH10
Gramática 1 practice

13 ¿Qué pasó?

Escribamos/Hablemos Imagina que eres Daniela. Indica qué pasó el día en que ella y su familia fueron de viaje.

MODELO (yo) Me levanté temprano.

yo

1. nosotros

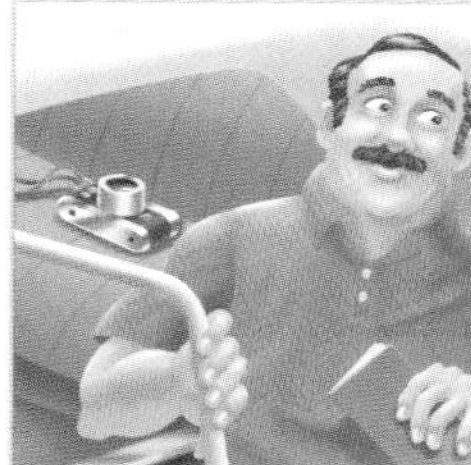
2. mi padre

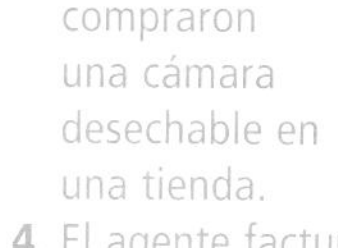

3. mis padres

4. el agente

5. los agentes

6. yo

1. Nosotros fuimos al aeropuerto en taxi.
2. Mi padre dejó su cámara en el taxi.
3. Mis padres compraron una cámara desechable en una tienda.
4. El agente facturó el equipaje.
5. Los agentes abrieron mi maleta.
6. Recogí mi maleta del reclamo de equipaje.

Comunicación

14 Un buen viaje

Hablemos In groups of three, act out the following situation. An exchange student calls his parents after he arrives in Lima, Peru. The parents ask questions about the trip and the student answers. Take turns playing the different roles, and use the verbs listed below.

MODELO —¿Esperaste mucho tiempo antes de abordar?
—No, no esperé mucho.

dejar	abordar	esperar	abrir
recoger	ir al mostrador	perder	encontrarse

Gramática 1

12 Script

See script on p. 221E.

Teacher to Teacher

Barbara A. Price
Bedichek Middle School
Austin, TX

Verb cards Pairs of students play a memory game using cards they create. First each student folds a 4x6 index card into eighths. Students write eight designated Spanish infinitives in the squares on one side of the card and cut the cards apart into eight pieces. Students create another eight cards with the verb in past tense and try to match the infinitive to its past tense; they can also create cards with the English translation to each infinitive; or they can create cards with a sentence using each infinitive. If the student is correct when playing the memory game, he or she keeps the matched pair. You can also use the infinitive cards for other games or activities.

Differentiated Instruction

ADVANCED LEARNERS

13 Have students sketch three pictures of events that would happen between item 5, (when Daniela checks her luggage) and item 6 (when she picks it up). Collect the drawings. Divide the class into groups and distribute the drawings. Have students write a sentence using the preterite to describe each of the drawings. Finally, tell the students to hold up their drawings and read the sentences. Have the artist confirm if they have correctly described what is happening. If not, the artist must state in Spanish what really happened.

SPECIAL LEARNING NEEDS

13 / 14 Students with Learning Disabilities/Language Impairments In Activities 13 and 14, students will be asked to act out scenarios in which they are someone else. Remind students that from this perspective, they will be using the first and second-person verb forms and not the third-person singular forms. You might begin each activity as a class to make sure that students understand the context.

Comunicación

Class Activity: Interpersonal

Arrange the class into two concentric circles with students in the inner circle facing the students in the outer circle. Present a scenario about travel problems for the students to role-play. When students have completed the dialogue, have the inner circle rotate two places and repeat the dialogue again. To check, call on several pairs to repeat their dialogue for the class. Move one of the circles again and repeat the procedure using a different scenario.

STANDARDS: 1.1, 1.3

Resources

Planning:

Lesson Planner, pp. 136–141, 288–295

One-Stop Planner

Presentation:

Video Program
Videocassette 5
DVD Tutor, Disc 2
GramaVisión

Practice:

Grammar Tutor for Students of Spanish, Chapter 10

Cuaderno de vocabulario y gramática, pp. 68–70

Cuaderno de actividades, pp. 55–57

Activities for Communication, pp. 37–38

Video Guide, pp. 94–95

Lab Book, pp. 31–32

Teaching Transparencies
Bell Work 10.3
Vocabulario y gramática answers, pp. 68–70

Audio CD 10, Tr. 3

Interactive Tutor, Disc 2

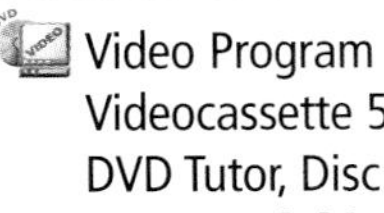

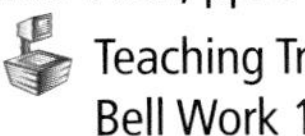

Bell Work

Use Bell Work 10.3 in the *Teaching Transparencies*, or write this activity on the board.

Write the correct preterite form of the verb in parentheses to complete each sentence.

1. **Esteban _____ (esperar) una hora en la cafetería a su amiga Lucía.**
2. **Lucía _____ (ir) a la biblioteca, no a la cafetería.**
3. **Por fin Lucía _____ (llegar).**
4. **Esteban y Lucía _____ (abrir) los libros para estudiar.**
5. **Pero yo _____ (venir) a charlar y no hicieron nada.**

Preterite of -car, -gar, -zar verbs

Interactive TUTOR

1 Verbs ending in **-car**, **-gar**, and **-zar** have a spelling change in the **yo** form in the preterite.

In **-car** verbs, the **c** changes to **qu**.	In **-gar** verbs, the **g** changes to **gu**.	In **-zar** verbs, the **z** changes to **c**.
sa**qué**	lle**gué**	comen**cé**
sa**caste**	lle**gaste**	comen**zaste**
sa**có**	lle**gó**	comen**zó**
sa**camos**	lle**gamos**	comen**zamos**
sa**casteis**	lle**gasteis**	comen**zasteis**
sa**caron**	lle**garon**	comen**zaron**

Comencé a las 8:00. **Llegué** al aeropuerto y **saqué** dinero.
I started at 8:00. I arrived at the airport and got money.

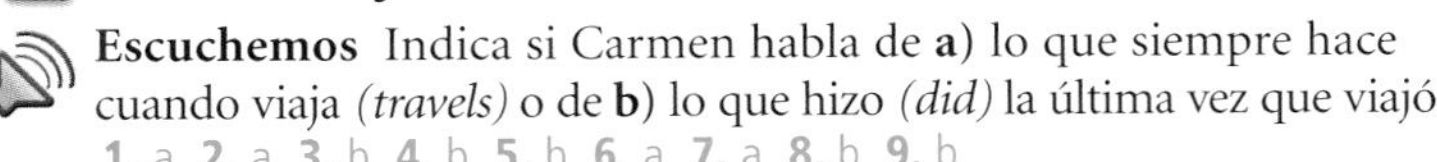

Online
Vocabulario y gramática, pp. 68–70 | Actividades, pp. 55–57

CD 10, Tr. 3

15 Cuando viajo...

Escuchemos Indica si Carmen habla de **a)** lo que siempre hace cuando viaja *(travels)* o de **b)** lo que hizo *(did)* la última vez que viajó.

1. a **2.** a **3.** b **4.** b **5.** b **6.** a **7.** a **8.** b **9.** b

16 La tarjeta postal

Leamos/Escribamos Completa la tarjeta postal que recibió Lili con la forma correcta del pretérito de los verbos.

encontrar	comenzar	buscar	llegar	almorzar
comprar	pagar	facturar	sacar	ir

1. comencé
2. fui
3. llegué
4. pagué
5. facturé
6. compré
7. saqué
8. Almorcé
9. busqué
10. encontré

Hola Liliana,

Ya sabes que __1__ el día a las 7:00 y que __2__ al aeropuerto en taxi. Cuando __3__, fui directamente al mostrador donde __4__ el boleto y __5__ el equipaje. Después, __6__ un mapa en la librería y __7__ dinero del cajero automático. __8__ un sándwich y __9__ una tienda para comprarte un regalo, pero no __10__ nada. Voy a buscarte algo en Cuzco.

Con cariño,
Tía Juana

Core Instruction

TEACHING GRAMÁTICA

1. Review the preterite of regular **–ar** verbs. **(5 min.)**
2. Go over Point 1. Ask students why they think these spelling changes occur. **(10 min.)**
3. Have students brainstorm a list of verbs they know that will have these spelling changes. (**buscar, practicar, sacar, secar, tocar, colgar, jugar, llegar, navegar, almorzar, comenzar,** and **empezar**) **(5 min.)**
4. Ask students to write two sentences using preterite forms of two of these verbs. **(5 min.)**
5. Ask students to add notes about the irregular **yo** forms in the preterite of **-car, -gar, -zar** verbs to their verb chart. **(5 min.)**

GramaVisión

For a presentation of the preterite with **–car, -gar,** and **–zar** verbs, use **el joven G.** For interactive activities, see the *DVD Tutor.*

GramaVisión

STANDARDS: 1.2

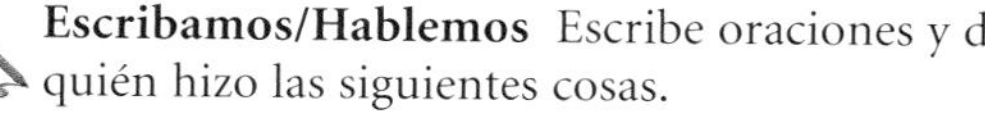

17 ¿Quién?

Escribamos/Hablemos Escribe oraciones y di quién hizo las siguientes cosas.

MODELO **llegar al aeropuerto**
Olivia llegó al aeropuerto a las siete.

Olivia

llegar al aeropuerto	levantarse	sacar dinero
pagar el boleto	buscar los servicios	almorzar en un restaurante

1. Ana

2. Felipe

3. Maricela y yo

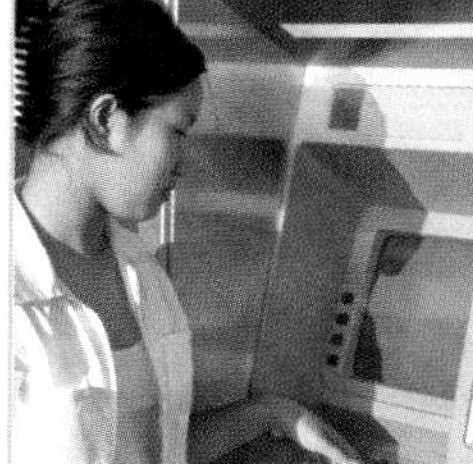
4. yo

5. Ricardo y Elena

6. yo

Comunicación

18 La fiesta de despedida

Hablemos Last night there was a going away party for a friend who is moving, but you couldn't go. Ask a classmate what happened at the party, using the verbs given below.

colgar decoraciones	comenzar la fiesta	llegar	jugar juegos de mesa
tocar instrumentos	contar chistes	bailar	preparar la comida

Differentiated Instruction

SLOWER PACE LEARNERS

15 Before playing the Activity 15 audio, explain to students that statements in the present tense will be marked **a,** whereas statements in the past tense will be marked **b.** Tell them to listen closely to the verb endings. Play the audio, pausing after each statement. Allow time for the students to write their answers.

SPECIAL LEARNING NEEDS

16 **Students with Visual Impairments** It may be difficult for students to decode text in an alternative font, such as the font in the letter in Activity 16. You might rekey the text in a different font that is larger and not stylized. When creating the letter in an alternative font, you might also increase the length of each answer line, so that students can actually write the correct form of each verb on the version you provide.

Gramática 1

15 **Script**

See script on p. 221E.

17 **Answers**

1. Ana se levantó temprano.
2. Felipe pagó su boleto.
3. Maricela y yo llegamos al aeropuerto a las nueve.
4. Yo saqué dinero del cajero automático.
5. Ricardo y Elena almorzaron en un restaurante/en el aeropuerto.
6. Yo busqué los servicios.

Communities

Career Path

Tourism is a major industry in many Spanish-speaking countries. Natural wonders, archeological sites, museums, and folk arts attract visitors from all over the world. Have students think about the tourist industry and brainstorm possible careers related to it. Have students select one or two places in which they would consider a career in tourism, and ask them how speaking Spanish would be beneficial. Ask for volunteers to share their thoughts with the class.

Comunicación

Group Activity: Interpersonal

Create a 5x5 square grid. In each space, write an activity that students may have done during the past school year, including: **jugar al fútbol, practicar un deporte, tocar un instrumento, organizar una fiesta,** and **llegar tarde a clase.** Instruct students to find classmates who have done these activities. Students should put the name of the classmate who responds affirmatively.

MODELO
—¿Sacaste buenas notas este año escolar?
—Sí, saqué buenas notas.
—Firma aquí, por favor.

Resources

Planning:

Lesson Planner, pp. 136–141, 288–295

One-Stop Planner

Presentation:

Video Program
Videocassette 5
DVD Tutor, Disc 2
GramaVisión

Practice:

Grammar Tutor for Students of Spanish, Chapter 10

Cuaderno de vocabulario y gramática, pp. 68–70

Cuaderno de actividades, pp. 55–57

Activities for Communication, pp. 37–38

Video Guide, pp. 94–95

Lab Book, pp. 31–32

Teaching Transparencies
Bell Work 10.4
Vocabulario y gramática answers, pp. 68–70

Interactive Tutor, Disc 2

Bell Work

Use Bell Work 10.4 in the *Teaching Transparencies*, or write this activity on the board.

Answer the questions using the preterite.

1. **¿Llegaste temprano al colegio hoy?**
2. **¿Comenzaste a estudiar para el examen de español?**
3. **¿Sacaste la tarea de la mochila?**
4. **¿Tocaste el piano por la mañana?**
5. **¿Almorzaste con la familia ayer?**

Preterite of hacer

1 The verb **hacer** *(to make, to do)* is irregular in the preterite. A question asked with **hacer** will often be answered using another **verb.**

yo	**hice**	nosotros(as)	**hicimos**
tú	**hiciste**	vosotros(as)	**hicisteis**
Ud., él, ella	**hizo**	Uds., ellos, ellas	**hicieron**

—¿Qué **hiciste** ayer? *What did you do yesterday?*
—**Fui** a la oficina de correo. *I went to the post office.*

2 To form the preterite of weather expressions with **hace**, replace **hace** with **hizo**. Use the preterite to say what the weather was like over a specific period or when telling how long conditions lasted. Use **nevó** for *it snowed* and **llovió** for *it rained.*

—¿Qué tiempo **hizo** ayer? —**Hizo** mal tiempo. **Llovió** todo el día.

El año pasado nunca **hizo** viento.

Online
Vocabulario y gramática, pp. 68–70 | Actividades, pp. 55–57

Nota cultural

The Incas called *quinoa* the Mother Grain. Every year the emperor planted the first seeds and on solstice, priests made quinoa offerings to Inti, the Sun. The Incan armies, which frequently marched for days at a time, ate war balls, a mix of quinoa and fat. Quinoa is still eaten in Peru and is imported to the United States for its high nutritional value. How do you think quinoa is used in recipes?

19 Antes de comenzar el viaje

Leamos Lee lo que dice Pablo e indica si **a)** habla de sí mismo *(himself)*, **b)** de sus padres, **c)** de él y sus amigos o **d)** del tiempo.

1. Antes de comenzar el viaje hicimos una fiesta en el Club Naval. c
2. Hice planes para encontrarme con ellos al volver. a
3. No hicieron las maletas hasta muy tarde. b
4. Hice las maletas anteayer. a
5. Hizo fresco e hizo sol. d
6. Al llegar al aeropuerto, hicieron cola delante del mostrador. b

20 ¿Qué hicieron ustedes?

Escribamos Indica si estas cosas pasaron o no la última vez que hiciste un viaje con tu familia en carro.

MODELO **mi madre/hacer las maletas**
Mi madre (no) hizo las maletas.

1. (yo)/hacer la maleta
2. mi hermano/hacer las camas antes de irnos
3. mis amigos/hacer una fiesta antes del viaje
4. (yo)/hacer la tarea en el carro
5. mis padres/hacer sándwiches y nosotros/comer en el carro
6. hacer buen tiempo
7. hacer frío

Core Instruction

TEACHING GRAMÁTICA

1. Go over Point 1. Model the pronunciation of each preterite form of **hacer.** **(5 min.)**
2. Go over Point 2. **(5 min.)**
3. Ask students what the weather was like yesterday. Hold up pictures of various weather conditions to cue their answers. **(10 min.)**
4. Ask students what they and various other people did yesterday. If you wish, cue their answers by holding up photos of activities or acting out the activities. **(10 min.)**
5. Ask students to add the preterite conjugation of **hacer** to the verb conjugation chart in their notebooks. **(5 min.)**

GramaVisión

For a video presentation of the preterite of **hacer,** use **el joven G.** For interactive activities, see the *DVD Tutor.*

STANDARDS: 1.2, 1.3, 2.2

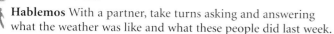

Comunicación

21 De vacaciones

Hablemos With a partner, take turns asking and answering what the weather was like and what these people did last week.

MODELO —**¿Qué tiempo hizo el lunes?**
—**Hizo calor y mucho sol.**
—**¿Qué hicieron Alicia y tú?**
—**Jugamos al tenis.**

lunes/Alicia y yo

1. lunes/yo

2. martes/mis hermanas

3. miércoles/mi madre

4. jueves/mi padre

5. viernes/María y Jorge

6. sábado/mis amigos y yo

7. sábado/mi hermano

8. domingo/mis padres

22 El fin de semana pasado

Hablemos In groups of three, take turns using the expressions in the word box to ask about who did these activities last weekend.

MODELO —**¿Hiciste un viaje el fin de semana pasado?**
—**Sí, hice un viaje./No, no hice un viaje.**

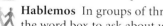

hacer un viaje	hacer cola en una tienda
hacer planes para salir con amigos	hacer la tarea de español
hacer el almuerzo para llevar al colegio	hacer la cama

Gramática 1

Teacher Note

For more information on **quinoa** and other Peruvian food, see page 220 of the *Annotated Teacher's Edition.*

Comunicación

Individual/ Group Activity: Presentational

Allow the students to interview you about a trip you took abroad. Give the students ten minutes to compose questions to ask you about the trip. Call on individual students to ask you their questions. Instruct the students to take notes on your answers. You can follow-up the interview by asking students to write a brief article about the interview for the Spanish Club newsletter or school newspaper.

20 Answers

1. (No) hice la maleta.
2. Mi hermano (no) hizo las camas antes de irnos.
3. Mis amigos (no) hicieron una fiesta antes del viaje.
4. (No) hice la tarea en el carro.
5. Mis padres (no) hicieron sándwiches y (no) comimos en el carro.
6. (No) hizo buen tiempo.
7. (No) hizo frío.

Differentiated Instruction

SLOWER PACE LEARNERS

21 Review weather expressions. Before beginning Activity 21, ask students **¿Qué tiempo hace?** for each drawing. Explain to them that they will be using the same weather expression for their conversation, but using the preterite tense.

MULTIPLE INTELLIGENCES

Naturalistic Allow students to plant **quinoa** seeds, or another plant seed, in either a small plot of land on the school grounds or in indoor planters. Have them keep a journal, in Spanish, of what the weather is like each day, using the correct form of the verb **hacer.** You might also have them write the size of the plants each week, once the seeds sprout. Have them use **Mide... centímetros (pulgadas).**

Assess

Assessment Program

Prueba: Gramática 1, pp. 99–100

Prueba: Aplicación 1, pp. 101–102

Alternative Assessment Guide, pp. 245, 253, 261

Audio CD 10, Tr. 17

Test Generator

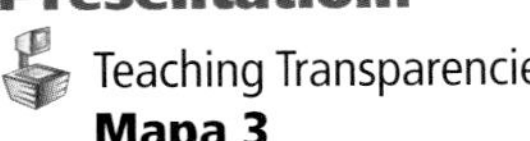

Resources

Planning:

Lesson Planner, pp. 141–142, 294–295

 One-Stop Planner, Disc 3

Presentation:

 Teaching Transparencies **Mapa 3**

Audio CD 10, Tr. 4–6

Video Program
Videocassette 5
DVD Tutor, Disc 2
VideoCultura

Practice:

Cuaderno de actividades, p. 58

Cuaderno para hispanohablantes, pp. 77–84

Video Guide, pp. 94–95, 97

Lab Book, p. 63

Audio CD 10, Tr. 4–6

Interactive Tutor, Disc 2

Atlas INTERACTIVO MUNDIAL

Have students use the interactive atlas at **go.hrw.com.**

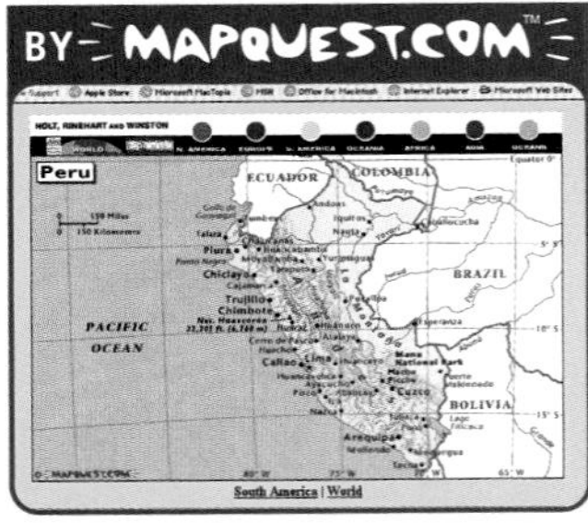

Map Activities

Using the interactive atlas or Map Transparency 3, have students locate Peru and its surrounding countries. Have them identify major cities in Peru and research the different types of vegetation and geographical features (mountains, rivers, etc.) that can be found in this country.

Cultura

VideoCultura

Comparaciones

  CD 10, Tr. 4–6

Terminal de autobuses, Lima, Perú

¿Adónde fuiste y qué hiciste la última vez que viajaste?

En Estados Unidos, la mayoría de la gente tiene carro, y es muy común viajar en coche. Si es un viaje de larga distancia, mucha gente viaja en avión. En Perú, es más común viajar en autobús, aunque *(although)* es posible ir en avión o en tren. Estas personas hablan de su último viaje y de lo que hicieron. ¿Cómo viajaron? ¿Qué hicieron al llegar a su destino *(destination)*? ¿Hacen las mismas cosas que tú haces cuando viajas? Compara sus viajes a tus propias experiencias.

Lisette
Lima, Perú

Lisette talks about the places she visits on vacation. Do you like to travel or stay at home during vacations?

Cuando vas de vacaciones, ¿en qué medio de transporte viajas?

Bueno, cuando voy de vacaciones, a mí me encanta viajar en ómnibus porque en el camino veo los paisajes y los animales.

¿Qué haces cuando vas de vacaciones?

Cuando voy de vacaciones, voy [y] visito a los lugares turísticos que me han recomendado.

¿Adónde fuiste de vacaciones la última vez?

Bueno, fui a Cajamarca.

¿Fuiste sola o fuiste con tu familia?

Fui con mi familia.

¿Qué hicieron allí?

Más que todo fuimos a visitar a los lugares turísticos y a algunos familiares.

Core Instruction

TEACHING CULTURA

1. Play the introductory paragraph on Audio CD 10. Have students discuss their travel experiences as a class. **(5 min.)**
2. Have students watch the two interviews on video using the *Video Program* or the *DVD Tutor*. Pause the video periodically and check for comprehension. **(10 min.)**
3. Have students answer the questions in the **Para comprender** section with a partner, then discuss **Para pensar y hablar. (15 min.)**

VideoCultura

For a video presentation of the interviews as well as for additional interviews, see Chapter 10 **VideoCultura** on Videocassette 5 or on DVD. For interactive practice, see the *DVD Tutor*.

VideoCultura

STANDARDS: 1.2, 4.2

Visit Holt Online
go.hrw.com
KEYWORD: EXP1B CH10
Online Edition

Paola
Lima, Perú

Paola visits her relatives during her vacation. Do you visit friends or relatives when you have a vacation?

Cuando vas de vacaciones, ¿en qué medio de transporte viajas?

Voy en bus mirando los paisajes.

¿Qué haces cuando vas de vacaciones?

Cuando voy de vacaciones, visito a mi familia, a mis amigos y los lugares turísticos.

¿Adónde fuiste de vacaciones la última vez?

Fui al departamento de Ica.

¿Fuiste sola o fuiste con tu familia?

Fui con mi familia.

¿Qué hicieron allí?

Visitamos a mi abuelita, primas, amigos y algunos lugares turísticos.

Para comprender

1. ¿Cómo le gusta viajar a Lisette?
2. ¿Qué hizo Lisette en su último viaje?
3. ¿Con quién viajó Paola a Ica?
4. ¿Qué hicieron Paola y su familia en su último viaje?
5. ¿Qué hacen Lisette y Paula cuando viajan en bus?

Para pensar y hablar

Both Lisette and Paola travel their country by bus. Do people in your community normally take the bus or other ground transportation when they travel somewhere? What other forms of transportation are common? What are two advantages of ground as opposed to air travel? What are two disadvantages?

Cuaderno para hispanohablantes, pp. 105–116

Comunidad

Spanish: Your World Passport

Plan an imaginary class trip to a country where Spanish is spoken. In small groups, research and present the following.

- Find the address of the tourism office for the selected country and write a letter in Spanish requesting tourist information.
- Each person finds out about one national or regional attraction to visit and writes a short paragraph in Spanish about it.
- Create a poster that shows typical foods or other attractions of the country.
- Display the completed posters and paragraphs in the classroom.

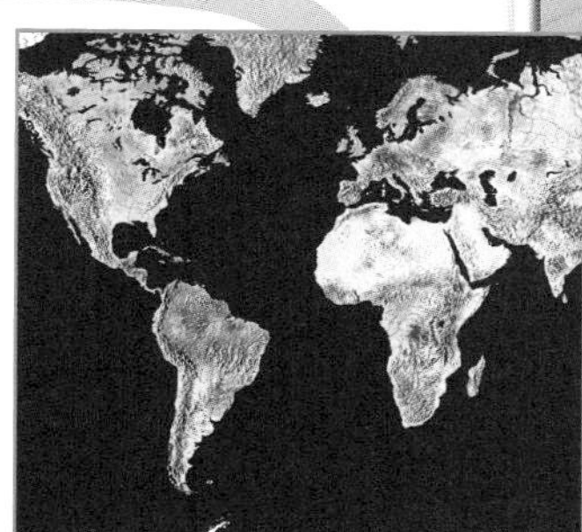

Mapa del mundo

Differentiated Instruction

ADVANCED LEARNERS

Tell students to jot down three or four things that one of the interviewees did on their vacation. After they have listened to all the interviews, tell them to write a brief paragraph comparing their last vacation with one of the student's vacations in the recording. Have them conclude with a statement as to whose vacation they think was better and why.

SPECIAL LEARNING NEEDS

Students with Visual Impairments If students have severe visual impairments and are not able to see the video screen clearly, have them access the video from the *Online Edition.*

Para comprender Answers

1. Le gusta ir por autobús porque puede ver el paisaje.
2. Fue con su familia a Cajamarca.
3. Viajó con su familia.
4. Visitaron a los primos y a unos amigos y a la abuela.
5. Miran los paisajes.

Comparisons

Comparing and Contrasting

In her interview, Paola mentioned that during her vacation, she went to the department of Ica. Ica is located south of Lima, along the coast. Founded by the Spanish in 1536, Ica suffered many natural disasters (floods and earthquakes), which explains why most of its colonial buildings have been replaced by more modern ones. Ica is close to the **Reserva Nacional de Paracas,** where wildlife can be observed, and also to Nazca and its famous geometric lines. Paola also mentioned that she visited her family during vacation. Have students compare Paola's vacation with a typical vacation they might have taken with their family. How are they similar and how are they different? Why?

Communities

Community Link

Have students ask their parents or other relatives to help them locate someone in the community who is from another country or who has visited or lived in another country. With parental permission, have students interview this person and ask her or him questions about international travel and living abroad. You might want to invite one or more of these people to visit the class and tell about their experiences. Prepare the students with appropriate questions to ask. As a follow-up, have students write a paragraph in Spanish about their interview.

STANDARDS: 1.2, 4.2, 5.1, 5.2

Resources

Planning:

Lesson Planner, pp. 142–146, 296–301

 One-Stop Planner

Presentation:

TPR Storytelling Book, pp. 56–57

 Teaching Transparencies **Vocabulario** 10.3, 10.4

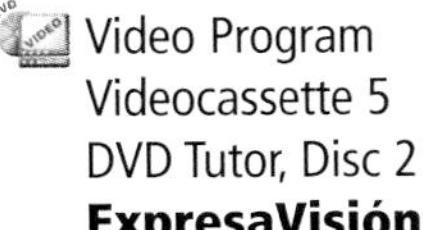 Video Program
Videocassette 5
DVD Tutor, Disc 2
ExpresaVisión

Practice:

Cuaderno de vocabulario y gramática, pp. 71–73

Activities for Communication, pp. 39–40

Video Guide, pp. 94–95, 98

Lab Book, pp. 33–34, 64

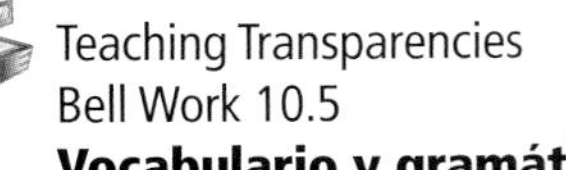 Teaching Transparencies
Bell Work 10.5
Vocabulario y gramática answers, pp. 71–73

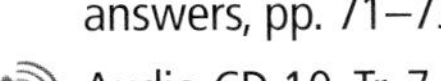 Audio CD 10, Tr. 7

Interactive Tutor, Disc 2

Bell Work

Use Bell Work 10.5 in the *Teaching Transparencies,* or write this activity on the board.

Unscramble the words and write logical sentences.

1. **hacer / tarea / yo / temprano / la**
2. **mi / una / hacer / fiesta / ayer / amigo**
3. **hacer / tú / viaje / la / pasada / un / semana**
4. **almuerzo / padres / ellos / para / el / hacer / sus**
5. **nosotros / todos / las / los / hacer / días / camas**

COMMON ERROR ALERT ¡OJO!

The expressions **¡Fue estupendo!** and **¡Fue horrible!** may confuse students since they have not yet seen the preterite of **ser.** They only know **fue** as the preterite of the verb **ir.**

Objetivos
Talking about a trip, expressing hopes and wishes

Vocabulario en acción 2

Video/DVD
ExpresaVisión

De vacaciones

Durante las vacaciones paseamos en lancha en el lago.
¡Qué divertido!

acampar

pasear en canoa

esquiar en el agua

ir de excursión

ir de pesca

pasear en bote de vela en el lago

Lugares de interés

el museo

el centro

el zoológico

el parque de diversiones

▶ Vocabulario adicional — Vacaciones, p. R15

Core Instruction

TEACHING VOCABULARIO

1. Introduce the vocabulary on pp. 238–239, using transparencies **Vocabulario 10.3** and **10.4.** Model the pronunciation of each word as you point to the appropriate picture. **(10 min.)**
2. Ask a volunteer to act out one of the activities or methods of transportation. The first student to identify the activity/mode of transportation correctly takes the next turn. **(10 min.)**
3. Introduce the expressions in **¡Exprésate!** by acting out a conversation between two people about a vacation. As you tell what you did on the vacation, act out each activity. **(10 min.)**

ExpresaVisión

To teach the travel-related vocabulary, use the presenter. For interactive activities, see the *DVD Tutor.*

Video/DVD
ExpresaVisión

STANDARDS: 1.2

Recorrí la ciudad en autobús. Luego tomé el tren a las ruinas.

Medios de transporte

Visit Holt Online
go.hrw.com
KEYWORD: EXP1B CH10
Vocabulario 2 practice

el metro

el tren

el taxi

el autobús

el barco

También se puede decir...

Mexicans call *the bus* **el camión**. In Puerto Rico and the Dominican Republic, they say **la guagua**. You'll hear **el colectivo** in Bolivia, Peru, and Ecuador.

Más vocabulario...

Expresiones

¡Ah, tuviste suerte!	*You were lucky!*
¡Qué bien!	*How great!*
¡Qué fantástico!	*How fantastic!*
¡Qué lástima!	*What a shame!*
¡Qué mala suerte!	*What bad luck!*

Actividades

quedarse en un hotel	*to stay at a hotel*
recorrer la ciudad/el país/la isla	*to tour the city/the country/the island*
tomar el sol	*to sunbathe*

¡Exprésate!

To talk about a trip

Interactive TUTOR

¿Qué tal el viaje? *How was the trip?*	**¡Fue estupendo!/¡Fue horrible!** *It was great!/It was horrible!*
¿Adónde fueron? *Where did you go?*	**Fuimos al campo y subimos a la montaña El Misti.** *We went to the countryside and went up Misti mountain.*
¿Qué hicieron? *What did you do?*	**Conocimos las ruinas y sacamos muchas fotos.** *We visited the ruins (for the first time) and took lots of pictures.* **Luego pasamos por la oficina de correos y por fin regresamos al hotel.** *Afterwards we stopped at the post office and finally we came back to the hotel.*

Online
Vocabulario y gramática, pp. 71–73

TPR
Total Physical Response

Review the following commands before having individual students respond.

Dramatiza que estás esquiando en el agua.

... y ... están caminando en un museo. Muestren con sus expresiones si les gusta lo que ven.

Enséñale a... cómo ir de pesca.

Dramatiza que paseas en bote de vela.

... y..., dramaticen que están acampando.

Súbete al metro con mucha gente.

Dramatiza que estás en un barco que sale de la isla.

Comparisons
Language Note

You might tell students that they can draw inferences about history and geography from the derivations of words. **Esquiar** comes from ***esquí,*** from the Norwegian word ***ski*** meaning wood or a cut tree trunk. Why does it make sense that this word would come from the Norwegian and not the Italian or Greek? (climate, much snow) **Museo** comes through the Latin from the Greek word for ***muse.*** Can students think of another word from this root? **(música)** What were the muses? (nine Greco-Roman deities representing the arts and letters)

Differentiated Instruction

Advanced Learners

Provide students with a wide array of travel brochures or visitor guides for the state and city in which you live. These materials are generally free, and can be obtained by contacting the visitor's bureau. Have students find and cut out as many pictures of the vocabulary as they can find and create travel posters with labels for each object and action. This will also expose them to travel reading materials, which will help them as they read sample text from a travel brochure later in the chapter.

Multiple Intelligences

Spatial To reinforce the vocabulary, divide the class into two or three teams. Call one representative from each team to come to the front. Explain to the class that each team's representative is going to draw a vacation activity. Without talking, point to one of the vacation activities in the book. Send each representative back to their group. When you say start, they begin drawing. Continue the drawing game until all vocabulary has been covered and each person on the team has had a chance to draw an activity.

También se puede decir...

Instead of **oficina de correos,** students may hear **correo** in Argentina, Cuba, or Venezuela, or **oficina postal** in Colombia. They may hear **crucero** instead of **barco** when referring to a cruise ship and **motora** in addition to **lancha.** Another expression for camping is **vivir en tienda de campaña.**

STANDARDS: 1.2

23 Script

1. ¡El viaje fue horrible!
2. Perdimos el tren.
3. Paseamos en lancha y esquiamos en el lago.
4. Comimos en un restaurante muy bueno.
5. Nos quedamos en un hotel magnífico.
6. Dejé mi cámara en el autobús.

Culture

Practices and Perspectives

Have students research the site of Machu Picchu and the people who lived there. Ask them to find answers to the following questions. When was Machu Picchu built and how long was it inhabited? What were the people like who lived there? What types of foods did they eat? Did they grow crops or get food from other areas? What others types of things did they produce? (pottery? textiles? tools?)

Más práctica

24 Have students write a narrative in first person form, recapping their adventures on the island in the drawing. Ask them to give the island a Spanish name and imagine that they did all the activities pictured. Instruct them to begin the narrative with any activity, then work their way through all the rest of the activities. Then pair students and have them read their narratives to each other.

MODELO
Fui a la Isla de Sueños *(dreams).* **Primero subí a la montaña. El próximo día, recorrí la isla y...**

Nota cultural

Starting in Cuzco, the train to Machu Picchu zigzags up the mountain to about 12,500 feet above sea level before starting its 7000-foot descent into the Urubamba Valley. In Peru passengers can request oxygen because trains may climb above 15,000 feet. Though meals are served on some trains, most travelers carry food with them and purchase a drink on board. How does this compare to train travel where you live?

CD 10, Tr. 7

23 ¿Qué dices?

Escuchemos Escucha los comentarios y escoge la mejor respuesta.

1. (a.) ¡Qué lástima! b. ¡Qué bien!
2. (a.) ¡Qué mala suerte! b. ¡Ah, tuviste suerte!
3. a. ¡Qué lástima! (b.) ¡Qué divertido!
4. (a.) ¡Qué bien! b. ¡Qué lástima!
5. a. ¡Qué horrible! (b.) ¡Qué fantástico!
6. (a.) ¡Qué mala suerte! b. ¡Ah, tuviste suerte!

24 En la isla

Leamos Para las siguientes oraciones, escoge la persona del dibujo que hizo cada actividad.

1. Tomó el sol en la playa. f
2. Sacó una foto de su amigo. b
3. Acampó en la playa. ¡Qué bien! e
4. Recorrió la isla con su mochila. c
5. Subió a la montaña. ¡Qué divertido! a
6. Paseó en bote de vela en el agua. g
7. Paseó en canoa. ¡Qué fantástico! d

Game

¿Qué tal el viaje?

1. Have students use words and expressions from **Vocabulario 2,** pp. 238–239, to write two sentences about an imaginary past vacation. One sentence should state something good that happened, and the other should state something bad. For example, students might write **Esquiamos en el lago. Fue muy divertido** and **Perdí el tren a las ruinas.** Collect the sentences. **2.** Divide the class into two teams. Write **¡Qué bien!** and **¡Qué lástima!** on the board. **3.** Read a sentence aloud, then call on a team member. He or she responds to the sentence with either **¡Qué bien!** or **¡Qué lástima!** **4.** If the response is logical, award his or her team a point. Play then moves to the other team. **5.** After reading all of the sentences, the team with the most points wins.

STANDARDS: 1.2, 1.3, 2.2, 4.2

25 El viaje de Carlos

Leamos/Escribamos Lee la tarjeta de Carlos. Después, usa las expresiones **primero**, **luego** y **por fin** y combina las palabras dadas para formar oraciones completas.

> Querida Carla,
> Aquí estoy en Perú. Es un país estupendo. Ayer me levanté temprano y desayuné en el hotel. Salí del hotel y fui al centro en autobús. Fui a una tienda para comprar una cámara y después recorrí el centro. Luego, almorcé en un restaurante. Después del almuerzo, tomé otro autobús y fui a las ruinas. Subí a la montaña y saqué muchas fotos. Regresé al hotel, cené en el restaurante de al lado y me acosté temprano. ¡Qué día tan magnífico!
>
> Abrazos,
> Carlos

MODELO **desayunar/salir/levantarse**
Primero, se levantó, luego desayunó y por fin salió.

1. ir al centro/comprar una cámara/ir a una tienda
2. recorrer el centro/almorzar/llegar al centro
3. sacar fotos/tomar el autobús a las ruinas/subir a la montaña
4. tomar el autobús al hotel/regresar a la ciudad/salir de las ruinas
5. acostarse/cenar en un restaurante/ponerse el piyama

Comunicación

26 Un viaje fantástico

Hablemos Talk with a partner about a real vacation you have taken or make up details of an imaginary vacation. First tell where you went and how you got there (plane, train, bus, or boat). Then your partner will ask questions to find out how the trip was, and what you saw and did there.

MODELO **—Fui a Puerto Rico en barco.**
—¿Qué tal el viaje? ¿Qué hiciste?
—El viaje fue bueno.

Más práctica

25 Rewrite the letter in Activity 25 as a cloze exercise, leaving out all the verbs. After students have completed Activity 25, pass out copies of the letter with blanks and ask them to try and fill in all the correct verb forms (with books closed). You might also want to prepare a version of the letter where you leave out random words—every 4th or 5th word—and see if students can add words that complete the letter in a way that makes sense.

Comunicación

Pair Activity: Interpersonal

Ask each student to write a list of five things that they did or that happened to them on a real or imaginary trip. They should list good as well as bad experiences. **(Tomé el sol en la playa. Perdí mi pasaporte en Machu Picchu.)** Pair students and have them read their lists of occurrences to each other. The partners respond to each statement with an appropriate phrase from pages 238–239 or previously-learned expression of emotion.

Pair Activity: Presentational

26 After completing Activity 26, ask each student to report to the class about their partner's trip. If needed, allow students first to repeat Activity 26 and take notes about what their partners say.

Differentiated Instruction

SLOWER PACE LEARNERS

25 **Variation** Have students use the elements listed in Activity 25 and imagine that they are making plans for a trip. Ask them to combine the elements to write sentences telling what they need to do, want to do, and are going to do.

MODELO

1. **Primero, voy a ir al centro. Necesito ir a una tienda. Quiero comprar una cámara.**

MULTIPLE INTELLIGENCES

Visual and Tactile Learners Ask students to collect from magazines, newspapers, scrapbooks, and other places items, or photos of items, that one would need while traveling. (photographs, tickets, passport, money, brochures, souvenirs) Have them create a summary of an imaginary trip where they used or collected all these items. Ask them to present their trip summary to the class and pass around the objects for students to see. You might encourage students who have traveled to talk about and use objects from a real trip.

STANDARDS: 1.1, 1.2, 1.3

Resources

Planning:

Lesson Planner, pp. 142–146, 296–301

 One-Stop Planner

Presentation:

TPR Storytelling Book, pp. 56–57

 Teaching Transparencies **Vocabulario** 10.3, 10.4

 Video Program
Videocassette 5
DVD Tutor, Disc 2
ExpresaVisión

Practice:

Cuaderno de vocabulario y gramática, pp. 71–73

Activities for Communication, pp. 39–40

Video Guide, pp. 94–95, 98

Lab Book, pp. 33–34, 64

 Teaching Transparencies **Vocabulario y gramática** answers, pp. 71–73

 Interactive Tutor, Disc 2

Teacher to Teacher

Jason Bryant
Duncanville High School
Duncanville, TX

Have students make a scrapbook of a fantasy trip using the Internet to find airplane tickets, hotels, maps, and entertainment in a Spanish-speaking location. They use the information to make a scrapbook of their "trip." Students also make an expense report that shows their exact spending in dollars and in the foreign currency.

¡Exprésate!

To express hopes and wishes

Interactive TUTOR

Algún día me gustaría viajar a Perú.
Some day I would like to travel to Peru.

Quiero conocer las ruinas de Machu Picchu.
I want to see the ruins at Machu Picchu.

Si tengo suerte, voy a visitar México.
If I'm lucky, I'm going to visit Mexico.

Espero ver las pirámides.
I hope to see the pyramids.

Online
Vocabulario y gramática, pp. 71–73

1. Algún 2. hacer 3. conocer 4. ir 5. ruinas 6. sacar 7. suerte 8. Quiero 9. museo 10. espero 11. recorrer 12. Qué

27 Me gustaría viajar

Leamos Paco y Ana están hablando de los viajes que quieren hacer. Completa su conversación con las palabras del cuadro.

sacar	suerte	recorrer	ir
hacer	Quiero	museo	Algún
ruinas	conocer	Qué	espero

PACO ___1___ día me gustaría ___2___ un viaje a Perú. Quiero ___3___ las montañas e ___4___ de excursión. Espero ver las ___5___ de Machu Picchu. Voy a ___6___ muchas fotos.

ANA Si tengo ___7___ voy a viajar a España. ___8___ ver el famoso ___9___ de arte en Madrid, El Prado. También ___10___ viajar por metro. Voy a ___11___ toda la ciudad en metro. ¡___12___ fantástico!

28 Espero...

Escribamos/Hablemos Reacciona a estas actividades con una expresión de **¡Exprésate!**

MODELO **Me gustaría ir de excursión. Espero ver...**

1 

2 

3 

4 

Core Instruction

TEACHING ¡EXPRÉSATE!

1. Introduce the new expressions in **¡Exprésate!,** modeling the pronunciation of each new word and phrase. **(5 min.)**
2. Tell students some things you wish or hope. Then ask students to write down two wishes or hopes for the future. Ask volunteers to write their wishes and hopes on the board for the class to check. **(10 min.)**

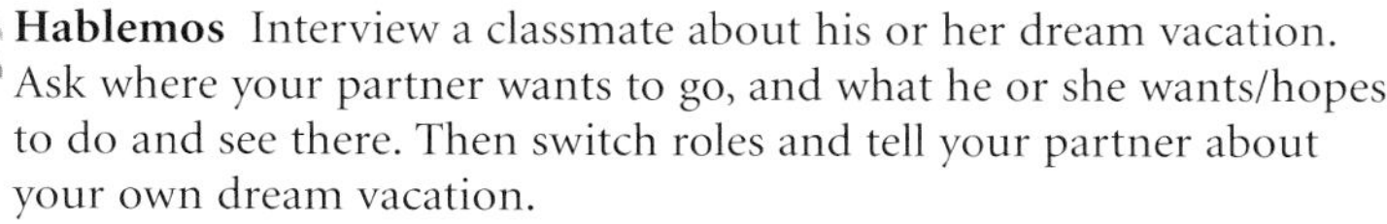

Comunicación

29 El viaje de tus sueños

Hablemos Interview a classmate about his or her dream vacation. Ask where your partner wants to go, and what he or she wants/hopes to do and see there. Then switch roles and tell your partner about your own dream vacation.

30 Hacer planes

Hablemos/Escribamos Work with two or three classmates to plan a school trip. Decide where you would like to go and how you want to travel. Talk about what you want to see and do there. On a sheet of paper, summarize the main points of your trip and be prepared to present them to the class.

MODELO **Algún día, nos gustaría viajar a...**
Queremos conocer...
Si tenemos suerte, vamos a...
Esperamos ver...

Comunicación

Individual Activity: Presentational

Think-Draw-Speak Give students a piece of 8 1/2 x 11 paper. Give students ten minutes to sketch pictures or symbols to represent ten activities that happened on a trip they took. Then, have students use their drawings as cue cards to talk with classmates about their trip. Encourage students to use vocabulary they know and to use circumlocution to communicate what they wish to say. To help students stay on task, have them ask each classmate with whom they speak to sign the back of their drawing. Call on a few students to show their drawings to the whole class.

Group Activity: Presentational

Ask students to work in small groups. Each group chooses one of the activities shown in Activities 28 or 29 about which to write a narrative. The narrative relates with whom and where the person went, what he or she did and saw, and whether or not the vacation was enjoyable. If time allows, encourage students to create a conversation between the people in the photos that illustrates how they are feeling about the vacation. Have each group tell another group the story it created, with each student responsible for telling part of the story.

Differentiated Instruction

ADVANCED LEARNERS

Extension Have students brainstorm and list on the board things there are to do and see in your town and nearby areas. (parks, museums, sporting events, restaurants, movies) Then ask each student to write a letter to an imaginary friend in Peru, inviting him or her to come to your town for a visit. Instruct them to include in the letter: places to visit, things to do, and things to see. The letter should end with the student asking the friend what there is to do and see in his or her town or area. Ask several students to read their letters to the class.

MULTIPLE INTELLIGENCES

Interpersonal Ask students to bring in photos from a real family vacation or visit to relatives, or photos of any outing they have taken with friends or family. Form small groups of students and have them show their pictures and talk in Spanish about the trips. Encourage students who do not bring photos to participate in the group activity by asking questions of the students who are showing photos.

Assess

Assessment Program

Prueba: Vocabulario 2, pp. 103–104

Alternative Assessment Guide, pp. 245, 253, 261

Test Generator 

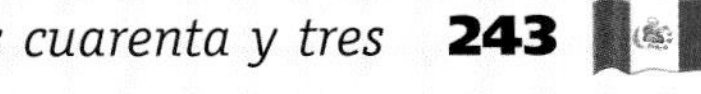

Resources

Planning:

Lesson Planner, pp. 147–153, 298–307

 One-Stop Planner

Presentation:

Video Program
Videocassette 5
DVD Tutor, Disc 2
GramaVisión

Practice:

Grammar Tutor for Students of Spanish, Chapter 10

Cuaderno de vocabulario y gramática, pp. 74–76

Cuaderno de actividades, pp. 59–61

Activities for Communication, pp. 39–40

Video Guide, pp. 94–95

Lab Book, pp. 33–34

 Teaching Transparencies
Bell Work 10.6
Vocabulario y gramática answers, pp. 74–76

 Audio CD 10, Tr. 8

 Interactive Tutor, Disc 2

Bell Work

Use Bell Work 10.6 in the *Teaching Transparencies,* or write this activity on the board.

Match each person with the appropriate vacation activity.

1. A Jorge le gustan los deportes.
2. Daniela estudia biología y le gusta ver animales.
3. Andrés pinta y dibuja mucho.
4. A Fernando le gusta caminar mucho.
5. Andrea quiere comprar muchas cosas.

a. Puede ir de excursión al campo.
b. Puede visitar el zoológico.
c. Tiene que ir al centro de una ciudad.
d. Debe ir al museo de arte.
e. Debe esquiar en el lago.

Objetivos
Using informal commands, direct object pronouns, verbs followed by infinitives

Gramática en acción 2

GramaVisión

Interactive TUTOR

Informal commands of spelling-change and irregular verbs

1 Verbs ending in **-ger, -guir, -car, -gar,** and **-zar** have spelling changes in some command forms.

	affirmative	negative
-ger	reco**g**e	no reco**j**as (*g changes to j*)
-guir	si**gu**e	no si**g**as (*gu changes to g*)
-car	bus**c**a	no bus**qu**es (*c changes to qu*)
-gar	lle**g**a	no lle**gu**es (*g changes to gu*)
-zar	empie**z**a	no empie**c**es (*z changes to c*)

Llega temprano al aeropuerto y **busca** a tus amigos. **No llegues** tarde.
Get to the airport early and look for your friends. Don't get there late.

2 Some verbs have irregular informal command forms.

	affirmative	negative
hacer	haz	no hagas
ir	ve	no vayas
poner	pon	no pongas
salir	sal	no salgas
ser	sé	no seas
tener	ten	no tengas
venir	ven	no vengas

Ve al aeropuerto en taxi.
Go to the airport by taxi.

No dejes nada en el taxi.
Don't leave anything in the taxi.

Online
Vocabulario y gramática, pp. 74–76 | Actividades, pp. 59–61

¿Te acuerdas?

Do you remember how to form affirmative informal commands?

tú piensa~~s~~ → piens**a**
tú come~~s~~ → com**e**
tú escribe~~s~~ → escrib**e**

Here's how to form negative informal commands.

yo piens~~o~~ → no piens**es**
yo com~~o~~ → no com**as**
yo escrib~~o~~ → no escrib**as**
yo veng~~o~~ → no veng**as**

Core Instruction

TEACHING GRAMÁTICA

1. Go over **¿Te acuerdas? (5 min.)**
2. Call out infinitives of verbs that have regular command forms and ask volunteers to give an affirmative or negative command using the verbs. **(10 min.)**
3. Go over Point 1. Have students brainstorm a list of **–ger, -gir, -guir, –car, -gar, -zar** verbs. **(10 min.)**
4. Go over Point 2. **(10 min.)**
5. Call out infinitives and ask volunteers to give an affirmative or negative command using the verbs. **(5 min.)**

GramaVisión

For a video presentation of informal commands, use **el joven G.** For interactive activities, see the *DVD Tutor.*

GramaVisión

STANDARDS: 1.2

CD 10, Tr. 8

31 ¿Es lógico?

Escuchemos Decide si los consejos que Enrique les da a sus amigos son lógicos o ilógicos. 1. lógico 2. ilógico 3. ilógico 4. lógico 5. ilógico 6. ilógico 7. ilógico 8. lógico

32 Consejos para los compañeros de viajes

Escribamos/Hablemos You are on vacation with friends who don't know what to do. Read what they say and make up one affirmative command and one negative command for each comment.

MODELO **—Salimos para Perú en tres horas y estoy listsa.**
—¡Sal inmediatamente! No llegues tarde al aeropuerto.

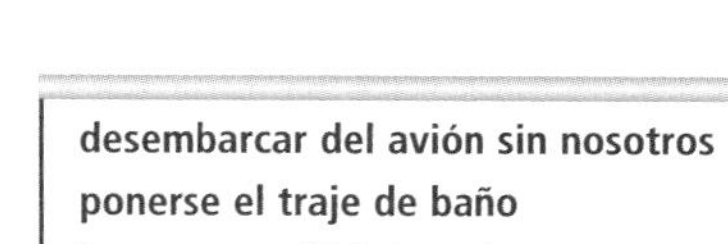

desembarcar del avión sin nosotros	ir de excursión
ponerse el traje de baño	ser puntual *(punctual)*
buscar un café Internet	salir inmediatamente
hacer cola en la aduana	comenzar el viaje tarde
ir al centro	tener miedo

1. Por fin llegamos a Lima. ¿Qué hago ahora en al aeropuerto?
2. Quiero ver las ruinas mañana, pero el autobús sale muy temprano.
3. No quiero recorrer el centro. Hace calor y quiero tomar el sol.
4. Mi hermana quiere esquiar en el agua. Tengo miedo.
5. Nuestros compañeros quieren jugar a los videojuegos esta tarde, pero no tengo ganas. Prefiero acampar.
6. No tengo mucho dinero y tenemos planes para comer en un restaurante caro.

Las ruinas de Machu Picchu, Perú

Visit Holt Online
go.hrw.com
KEYWORD: EXP1B CH10
Gramática 2 practice

Comunicación

33 ¡Ayúdame, por favor!

Hablemos Based on the photos, act out the following situation. Your partner is going on vacation and doesn't know what to do. Answer his or her questions and give some appropriate advice.

MODELO **—¿Cuándo hago la maleta?**
—Hazla un día antes de viajar. No lleves mucha ropa.

31 Script

1. —Estoy cansado y no quiero hacer nada hoy.
   —Quédate en el hotel y descansa.
2. —Quiero subir a la montaña y esquiar.
   —Ve al centro.
3. —Me gustaría hacer ejercicio.
   —No vayas de excursión.
4. —Quiero hacer un viaje pero no tengo dinero para un hotel.
   —Acampa.
5. —Hace muy buen tiempo y me gustaría tomar el sol.
   —Quédate en el hotel.
6. —Hace mal tiempo. Llueve mucho.
   —Ve al lago.
7. —No tengo cámara.
   —Saca muchas fotos.
8. —Hace mal tiempo y no tengo nada que hacer.
   —Pasa por el museo.

Heritage Speakers

Ask heritage speakers to write a journal entry about a trip, real or imaginary, that they made to visit a friend or relative. Or, have them interview an older friend or relative about a trip he or she has made and write about it. Review any spelling and writing skills you have targeted with your heritage speakers over the course of the school year and ask them to incorporate these skills in their reports.

Comunicación

Pair Activity: Presentational

Have pairs of students use affirmative and negative commands to develop a list of advice for travelers. Then, have pairs present their lists to the class.

Differentiated Instruction

SLOWER PACE LEARNERS

33 As a class, look at each of the photos in Activity 33. Brainstorm a list of questions that someone might have about what to do with the items in each photo. Write the questions on the board. Allow students to offer possible solutions. Finally, divide the class into pairs and tell them to take turns asking each other a question about what to do with the items in each photo. Explain that they must answer using the informal command forms from page 244.

SPECIAL LEARNING NEEDS

Students with Learning Disabilities These students might be overwhelmed by the number of spelling changes presented in **Gramática.** To help them understand the modifications, create a transparency or poster for each verb type. Color code the section of the verb that changes in the informal command form. Use a large font size and practice each verb type before moving on to the next type.

STANDARDS: 1.1, 1.2, 1.3

Resources

Planning:

Lesson Planner, pp. 147–153, 298–307

One-Stop Planner

Presentation:

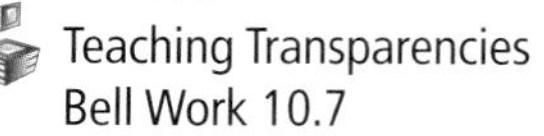

Video Program
Videocassette 5
DVD Tutor, Disc 2
GramaVisión

Practice:

Grammar Tutor for Students of Spanish, Chapter 10

Cuaderno de vocabulario y gramática, pp. 74–76

Cuaderno de actividades, pp. 59–61

Activities for Communication, pp. 39–40

Video Guide, pp. 94–95

Lab Book, pp. 33–34

Teaching Transparencies
Bell Work 10.7
Vocabulario y gramática answers, pp. 74–76

Audio CD 10, Tr. 9

Interactive Tutor, Disc 2

Bell Work

Use Bell Work 10.7 in the *Teaching Transparencies*, or write this activity on the board.

Write an affirmative or negative informal command to help prepare for the trip. Use the verb cues in parentheses.

1. No quiero perder el vuelo. (no salir tarde)
2. No encuentro mi pulsera. (buscar)
3. Tengo que facturar el equipaje. (ir al mostrador)
4. No sé si tengo todo. (hacer una lista)
5. Estoy nerviosa. (seguir con los preparativos)

Repaso Direct object pronouns

1 Direct object pronouns can go before the conjugated verb or be attached to the end of an infinitive.

—¿Ya conoces **la ciudad**?	*Do you already know the city?*
—No, todavía no **la** conozco.	*No, I don't know it yet.*
—¿Quieres recorrer**la** conmigo?	*Do you want to tour it with me?*

2 In affirmative commands, attach the pronoun to the end of the verb. Don't forget to add an accent mark when needed. In negative commands, place the pronoun before the conjugated verb.

Lláma**me** después de tu viaje, pero no **me** llames muy tarde.
Call me after your trip, but don't call me very late.

Online
Vocabulario y gramática, pp. 74–76 | Actividades, pp. 59–61

¿Te acuerdas?

Use these pronouns in the place of direct object nouns.

me	**nos**
te	**os**
lo	**los**
la	**las**

CD 10, Tr. 9

34 Para el viaje

Escuchemos Héctor habla de lo que va a hacer mientras está de vacaciones con su familia. Escucha las oraciones y decide de qué o de quién habla: **a**) su padre, **b**) su tarjeta de embarque, **c**) sus hermanas, **d**) sus libros de texto.

1. b 2. c 3. a 4. c 5. d 6. b 7. c

35 ¡Vamos al centro!

Leamos/Escribamos Completa las oraciones de la conversación entre dos amigos que están viajando juntos.

me	te	lo	la	los	las

—Mañana voy a visitar la ciudad. Voy a recorrer __1__ en autobús. Tengo ganas de visitar los museos del centro. ¿Quieres visitar __2__ conmigo?
—Sí, pero necesito dinero para la visita.
—Sáca __3__ del cajero automático aquí en el hotel.
—También tengo que mandar estas tarjetas. Puedo mandar __4__ mañana en el correo del centro, ¿no?
—Pues, ¿por qué no __5__ mandas desde el hotel? Oye, ¿tienes hambre? Me gustaría invitar __6__ a cenar conmigo.
—¡Con mucho gusto! ¿Quieres comer en el restaurante del hotel? No __7__ conozco.
—Es bueno, pero me gustaría probar la cocina regional. ¿Qué tal si __8__ probamos en el restaurante de al lado?

1. la 2. los 3. lo 4. las 5. las 6. te 7. lo 8. la

Core Instruction

TEACHING GRAMÁTICA

1. Go over **¿Te acuerdas? (1 min.)**
2. Go over Point 1. **(5 min.)**
3. Ask students if they are doing or going to do various things. Have them answer with a pronoun. For example, if you ask **¿Quieres escuchar la radio este fin de semana?**, students might answer **(No) la quiero escuchar/(No) quiero escucharla. (10 min.)**
4. Go over Point 2. **(5 min.)**
5. Write on the board several sentences using affirmative and negative commands. Have students rewrite the sentences using direct object pronouns. Ask volunteers to write their sentences on the board for the class to check. **(14 min.)**

GramaVisión

For a video presentation of direct object pronouns, use **el joven G.** For interactive activities, see the *DVD Tutor.*

GramaVisión

36 ¿Conoces tu ciudad?

Hablemos Construye oraciones y di si conoces estos lugares.

MODELO el centro
Lo conozco (muy) bien.

Possible answers:

1. el zoológico (No) lo conozco muy bien.
2. los museos (No) los conozco muy bien.
3. el centro comercial más cerca de tu casa (No) lo conozco muy bien.
4. la piscina más cerca de tu colegio (No) la conozco muy bien.
5. el lago más cerca de tu ciudad (No) lo conozco muy bien.
6. las tiendas del centro (No) las conozco muy bien.

Nota cultural

Peru's Manu rainforest has more than 1,000 species of birds and 300 species of trees. Many indigenous tribes also live there. Today Manu is a Biosphere Reserve composed of three parts: the Manu National Park, protecting the natural flora and fauna; the Manu Reserve Zone, for research and tourism; and the Manu Cultural Zone, for human settlement. Research animal or plant life in the forest.

37 Manito, llévame contigo

Hablemos Tu hermanito te hace muchas preguntas. Contesta las preguntas usando pronombres de complemento directo.

MODELO **—¿Piensas visitar las ruinas de Machu Picchu? (sí)**
—Sí, las voy a visitar. (Sí, voy a visitarlas.)

1. ¿Vas a visitar el Parque Nacional Manu? (sí)
2. ¿Me vas a llamar todos los días? (no)
3. ¿Vas a ver a los abuelos? (sí)
4. ¿Te puedo ayudar con las maletas? (sí)
5. ¿Vas a llevar tu cámara desechable? (sí)
6. Me vas a llevar contigo, ¿verdad? (no)

Comunicación

38 Las vacaciones de Araceli

Hablemos Ask a partner about the vacation that Araceli is going to take. Your partner should answer using direct object pronouns.

MODELO **—¿Cuándo va a hacer la maleta?**
—Ya la hizo anoche.

Gramática 2

34 Script

1. La voy a conseguir en el mostrador.
2. Las voy a llevar al centro.
3. Lo tengo que llamar desde el centro.
4. Me gusta ayudarlas con sus maletas.
5. No los voy a abrir ni una vez.
6. La necesito para poder abordar el avión.
7. Las voy a ver hoy en el museo.

37 Answers

1. Sí, lo voy a visitar. / Sí, voy a visitarlo.
2. No, no te voy a llamar todos los días. / No, no voy a llamarte todos los días.
3. Sí, los voy a ver. / Sí, voy a verlos.
4. Sí, me puedes ayudar con las maletas. / Sí, puedes ayudarme con las maletas.
5. Sí, la voy a llevar. / Sí, voy a llevarla.
6. No, no te voy a llevar conmigo. / No, no voy a llevarte conmigo.

Comunicación

Pair Activity: Interpersonal

Have students role-play a situation in which one friend checks up on a very forgetful friend about whether or not the forgetful friend has completed all of the necessary preparations for leaving on a trip the following day. Encourage students to use direct object pronouns as much as possible in responding to the questions. Dialogues should consist of at least four exchanges.

MODELO
—Enrique, ¿sacaste tu pasaporte?
—Claro. Lo saqué y está en mi mochila.
—Y Enrique, ¿compraste una cámara desechable?
—Sí, sí, la compré el fin de semana pasado.

Differentiated Instruction

ADVANCED LEARNERS

Using a complete Spanish sentence, have each student write about a place they would like to visit on their next vacation. For example: **Quiero visitar las playas de Acapulco.** Collect each of the sentences. Then walk around the room and have a student randomly choose a piece of paper. Ask them if they would like to visit that place and tell them to answer using a direct object pronoun. For example: **¡Sí, me gustaría visitarlas!**

MULTIPLE INTELLIGENCES

Spatial/Naturalistic In small groups, have students create ecotourism travel brochures, written in Spanish, for Peru's Manu rainforest. They should include pictures of the plant and animal life that is found in each zone of the rainforest. They should also describe the natural features of the area, the tribes who live there, and other interesting information that might appeal to visitors.

STANDARDS: 1.1, 1.2, 2.1

Resources

Planning:

Lesson Planner, pp. 147–153, 298–307

 One-Stop Planner

Presentation:

 Video Program
Videocassette 5
DVD Tutor, Disc 2
GramaVisión

Practice:

Grammar Tutor for Students of Spanish, Chapter 10

Cuaderno de vocabulario y gramática, pp. 74–76

Cuaderno de actividades, pp. 59–61

Activities for Communication, pp. 39–40

Video Guide, pp. 94–95

Lab Book, pp. 33–34

 Teaching Transparencies
Bell Work 10.8
Vocabulario y gramática answers, pp. 74–76

Interactive Tutor, Disc 2

Bell Work

Use Bell Work 10.8 in the *Teaching Transparencies,* or write this activity on the board.

Complete the sentences with the correct pronoun.

1. Elena piensa llamar_____ a ti para salir.
2. Mi hermano y yo perdimos las maletas. Vamos a buscar_____ en el reclamo de equipaje.
3. ¿Vas a visitar el museo? Tienes que ver_____.
4. Germán y Felipe van a los servicios. Búsquen_____, por favor.
5. A mí no_____ llames después de las diez, por favor.

40 Answers

1. piensan, 2. Tienen ganas, 3. le gustaría, 4. quiere, 5. tiene que, 6. espero

Repaso Verbs followed by infinitives

1 You can use certain **verbs** followed by **infinitives** to express what someone *wants, hopes,* or *plans* to do.

me (te, le...) gustaría + infinitive	*. . . would like to . . .*
me (te, le...) gustaría más + infinitive	*. . . would prefer to . . .*
querer (ie) + infinitive	*to want to . . .*
esperar + infinitive	*to hope to . . .*
pensar (ie) + infinitive	*to plan (intend) to . . .*

Me gustaría ir al lago.	*I'd like to go to the lake.*
Quiero pasear en bote.	*I want to go boating.*
Espero salir con amigos.	*I hope to go out with friends.*
Pienso hacer un viaje este año.	*I plan to take a trip this year.*

2 Remember to use **tener que** to talk about what someone *has to* do.

tener que + infinitive — *to have to . . ., must . . .*

Me gustaría ir de vacaciones, pero **tengo que** trabajar.
I'd like to go on vacation, but I have to work.

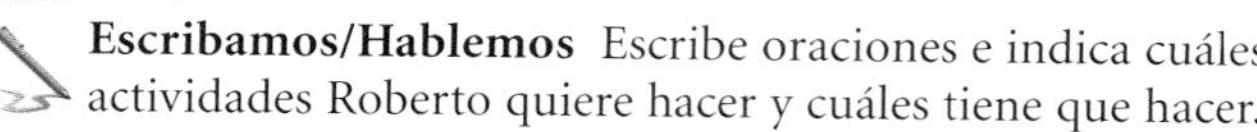
Online
Vocabulario y gramática, pp. 74–76 | Actividades, pp. 59–61

39 Proyectos

Escribamos/Hablemos Escribe oraciones e indica cuáles actividades Roberto quiere hacer y cuáles tiene que hacer.

MODELO viajar al Perú/estudiar
Quiere viajar a Perú. Tiene que estudiar.

1. acampar/trabajar
2. esquiar/limpiar el baño
3. hacer la tarea/ir al lago
4. tomar el sol/hacer la maleta
5. escribir cartas/salir con amigos

Isla Tequile en el Lago Titicaca, Perú

40 Lo que pensamos hacer es...

Leamos/Escribamos Completa el párrafo con la forma correcta del verbo más apropiado entre paréntesis.

Mi hermana mayor y su esposo __1__ (pensar/le gustaría) ir a Alaska para las vacaciones. __2__ (Tener ganas/Esperar) de ir de pesca y acampar. A mi padre __3__ (querer/le gustaría) acompañarlos pero mi madre __4__ (le gustaría/querer) viajar a Perú. El problema es que ella __5__ (tener que/tener ganas) trabajar y no tiene tiempo para viajar. En mi caso, (yo) __6__ (tener que/esperar) hacer un viaje a España algún día.

Core Instruction

TEACHING GRAMÁTICA

1. Go over Point 1. **(10 min.)**
2. Ask students to write three sentences about their hopes and plans. Have students exchange sentences and check their classmate's work. **(10 min.)**
3. Go over Point 2. **(5 min.)**
4. Ask students what they have to do after school and on weekends. **(5 min.)**

GramaVisión

For a video presentation of verbs followed by infinitives, use **el joven G** from the *Video Program.* For interactive activities, see the *DVD Tutor.*

GramaVisión

41 Planes

Escribamos Rosalinda habla de sus planes. Combina palabras de cada cuadro para hacer seis oraciones.

mis padres y yo	querer	ver los animales	en el lago
yo	esperar	pasear en bote	en el zoológico
mi hermana mayor	pensar	ir de excursión	del correo
mis abuelos	tener que	esquiar	en las montañas
¿Y tú?		mandar tarjetas	en el centro
		visitar el museo	en el hotel

Comunicación

42 Un día

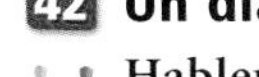

Hablemos Con un(a) compañero(a), túrnense para contestar estas preguntas.

MODELO **—Un día me gustaría visitar Lima. ¿Y a ti?**
—A mí me gustaría más visitar Barcelona.

1. ¿Qué ciudad te gustaría visitar un día?
2. ¿Cómo quieres ir a esa ciudad?
3. ¿Con quién quieres hacer el viaje?
4. ¿Cuántos días quieres quedarte?
5. ¿Piensas acampar, quedarte en un hotel, o quedarte en la casa de un(a) amigo(a)?
6. ¿Qué piensas hacer en esa ciudad?

43 ¿Qué quieren hacer? ¿Qué deben hacer?

Hablemos Con un(a) compañero(a), mira los dibujos y dramatiza la conversación entre Ana y Luis.

Gramática 2

AP Language Examination

Use the *Picture Sequences Transparency* for Chapter 10.

Sample answer:

—Ana, ¿qué quieres hacer para las vacaciones?
—Me gustaría ir a las montañas. Quiero acampar y subir a la montaña. Y tú, ¿qué quieres hacer para las vacaciones?
—Me gustaría ir al lago. Quiero ir de pesca y nadar. Pero no puedo. Tengo que quedarme en casa y ayudar a mis padres. Tengo que cortar el césped.
—Tengo que trabajar en casa también. Tengo que sacar la basura.

Comunicación

Group Activity: Interpersonal

Rejoinders To review the verbs followed by infinitives, give a different question on an index card to each student. Have them ask their question and answer the questions of other students.

MODELO

¿Qué debes hacer después de clases?

Differentiated Instruction

SLOWER PACE LEARNERS

40 Before assigning Activity 40, explain to students that they must look carefully for context clues to be able to decide which verb is the most appropriate. Review the structure of **gustar.** Tell them to watch for specific prepositions that only go with certain verb combinations, such as **tener ganas de.** Advise students to read each sentence slowly and determine the subject of the action. After they have done this, they should then choose and write their verb choice.

SPECIAL LEARNING NEEDS

43 Students with Visual Impairments Students with visual impairments might have trouble making out the small vacation activities in the thought bubbles presented in Activity 43. To help students, display the Picture Sequences Transparency for Chapter 10 to the class and go over the contents of the bubbles before students begin the activity.

Assess

Assessment Program

Prueba: Gramática 2, pp. 105–106

Prueba: Aplicación 2, pp. 107–108

Alternative Assessment Guide, pp. 245, 253, 261

Audio CD 10, Tr. 18 

Test Generator

STANDARDS: 1.1, 1.2

Resources

Planning:

Lesson Planner, pp. 153–154, 304–305

 One-Stop Planner

Connections

Biology Link

1 Tell students that although phytoplanktons are found at the sea surface, many species of bioluminescent marine life live deep underwater. Biologists have found that 90% of fish and marine organisms that live from 300 to 3,000 feet underwater glow. Some sea creatures use bioluminescence to camouflage themselves from predators. Their glow makes them invisible from below because they blend in with the background of sunlight.

Connections

Thinking Critically

2 As a follow-up to Activity 2, ask students what sources of light can be seen with the naked eye on a cloudy night. (light bulb, candle, flashlight) Which can be seen with the naked eye on a clear night from 500 miles or farther away? (city lights, stars, planets, the moon) Ask students to think of and name things that give off light. (lightbulbs, candles, lanterns, sun, stars) What is the source of light in these items? Then ask them to think of marine life forms that give off light. (lantern fish and some other fishes, some shrimp, some squid, some jellyfish, and many plantlike organisms) Have they ever seen any of these creatures? What do they think is the source of light in these organisms? You may wish to ask a science teacher to visit your class for a short guest lecture on this topic.

Conexiones culturales

1 De vacaciones en Puerto Rico

Many people in San Juan take vacations in La Parguera, a fishing village along **la Bahía Fosforescente,** or Phosphorescent Bay, on the southwest coast. Millions of tiny organisms (known as algae or dinoflagellates) glow in the water of this bay. Use Spanish resources from the Internet or the library to find out why these organisms produce light. When would a visitor be most likely to see the phosphorescent glow? Why?

a. on a moonless night with lots of big waves

b. in the middle of a stormy day

c. on a full moon night with calm water

a. A visitor is most likely to see the phosphorescent glow on a moonless night with lots of waves.

2 La luminiscencia

These glowing sea algae are *luminescent,* which means they give off light but not heat. All of the following generate light. Which are luminescent? c. A firefly is luminescent. The others give off both heat and light.

a. a star **b.** a lightbulb **c.** a firefly **d.** a candle

Core Instruction

TEACHING CONEXIONES CULTURALES

1. Present **Thinking Critically**, this page. Do Activity 1 with the entire class. Assign some additional time to research the light issue. **(5 min.)**
2. Present **Biology Link** and do Activity 2 with class. **(5 min.)**
3. Present **Thinking Critically**, page 251. Read **Conexión Astronomía** aloud. **(7 min.)**
4. Present **Science Links**. Encourage students to ask questions and share what they know about astronomy. **(10 min.)**
5. Divide the class into small groups to do Activities 3, 4, and 5. Lead a class discussion to go over the answers. **(10 min.)**
6. Present **Math Link** and write the formula on the board. Have students check their answers with other members of the class. **(3 min.)**

STANDARDS: 3.1

Many Puerto Ricans and tourists enjoy visiting the Arecibo Observatory, the largest and most sensitive single-dish radio telescope in the world. It is located ten miles south of the city of Arecibo. Galaxies, erupting stars, clouds of gas, pulsars, and quasars give off radio waves that are invisible to the naked eye, but that can be seen using radio telescopes. The Arecibo Observatory also uses planetary radar to study planets, moons, asteroids, and comets in our solar system. This is done by sending a powerful beam of radio energy at the object and analyzing the information about the radio echo that is reflected back to the Arecibo telescope.

3 El radar

Radio waves are used to study distant objects in our solar system because they can be used to "see" objects through clouds, darkness, and at a great distance. Radio waves were used by the Arecibo Observatory to map Venus. This use of radio waves is also known as radar. What other uses for radar do you know about?

4 Palabras científicas

Use a dictionary to find the Spanish words for *planet, asteroid, solar system, moon,* and *radar.* Most of these words are similar to the English words. Why do you think these words are similar?

5 ¡Qué grande!

The spherical reflector of the Arecibo radio telescope is 305 meters in diameter (measurement across). Calculate the diameter in feet. 1000.4 feet in diameter
(Hint: 1 meter = 3.28 feet) .

Conexiones culturales

4 Answers

el planeta, el asteroide, el sistema solar, el radar; Answers will vary, but the reason is because they all have their origin in ancient Greek—and became loan words in many European languages.

Connections

Science Links

3 In radio astronomy scientists use a large spherical reflector dish to collect natural radio energy that is emitted from pulsars, quasars, galaxies, erupting stars, and clouds of gas. Computers turn the radio waves into images that are displayed on a video monitor. Scientists study the radio waves to measure distances and study rotating stars (pulsars).

In planetary radar, a radar beam is sent to bounce off planets, moons, asteroids, comets, or other celestial bodies. After faint echoes of the radio waves are received by the reflector, computers turn them into images that are displayed on a video monitor. Scientists analyze the echo data to determine information about the size, shape, composition, rotation, and path of the target object.

Connections

Math Link

5 Have students calculate the circumference of the telescope noted in Activity 5 in meters and in feet. The formula is $2\pi r$ (957.7 meters / 3141.3 feet).

Differentiated Instruction

ADVANCED LEARNERS

Extension Have students research constellations on the Internet or in the library. Ask them to find out what stars and formations are visible in your area at this time of the year. Then have students check the sky at night for a few nights in a row and report what they see. Can they see the stars clearly in your area at night? If not, ask them to think of reasons why they cannot see them. (clouds, light pollution) If they can see the stars, ask them to describe the constellations that they observed.

MULTIPLE INTELLIGENCES

Mathematical Write the numerical representation of π on the board (3.14). Then review with students the formula for finding circumferences. Find some spherical or round objects in the classroom. (clock, globe, coffee cup, door knob, watches) Have each student work with a partner to find the circumferences of the items in inches or feet, and also in centimeters or meters. Provide the students with measuring tools that have both inches and centimeters. Have students compare answers with the class.

STANDARDS: 3.1, 4.1

Resources

Planning:

Lesson Planner, pp. 154–155, 306–307

 One-Stop Planner

Presentation:

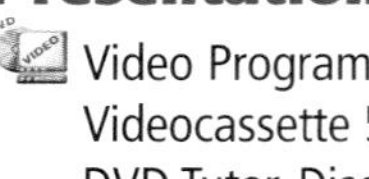 Video Program, Videocassette 5
DVD Tutor, Disc 2
VideoNovela

Practice:

Video Guide, pp. 94–95, 99
Lab Book, p. 65

A. Contesta Answers

1. about which candidates will win the scholarships
2. a foundation that promotes understanding among the Spanish-speaking countries
3. two of the ten will receive scholarships to come to Spain and study Spanish culture in the field of their choice

Connections

Visual Learners

To help students better understand the conclusion of **Novela en video,** have them create a concept map that guides them through the scholarship contest process, which they were secretly watching, without being aware. Start with the "Scholarship Contest" at the top, as the biggest, most important "umbrella" concept. Then keep reducing details of the contest until you reach the conclusion.

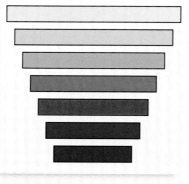

Novela en video

¿Quién será?

Episodio 10

ESTRATEGIA

Summarizing Before you read the **Novela** or watch the final episode of **¿Quién será?,** go back and summarize what has happened in the previous nine episodes. Pick only the most important moments that you think will help you understand the final episode. Write one or two sentences summarizing what happened in each episode. Do you see a pattern in your summary? Which characters appear the most often? Does summarizing in this way help you predict what might happen in the finale?

En España

Francia
Portugal
★ Madrid
ESPAÑA
Mar Mediterráneo
Marruecos
Argelia

La profesora está lista para tomar la decisión. ¿Quién será?

1 **Profesora Castillo** Ahora sí, ya están los diez candidatos. Dos deben recibir una beca para venir a estudiar en Madrid. Voy a tener que pensarlo muy bien.

Más tarde...Sofía y Nicolás reciben un e-mail.

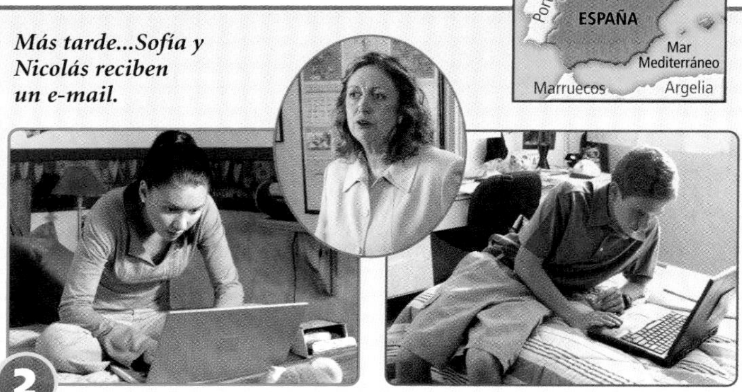

2 **Profesora Castillo** Soy Aurelia Castillo Velasco. Soy la directora de la Fundación para Cultivar las Relaciones entre las Culturas de Habla Hispana. Mi asistente y yo identificamos diez candidatos para las dos becas que vamos a otorgar este año.

A. CONTESTA

1. What is **La profesora** going to have to think about?
2. What kind of organization does she represent?
3. What will the candidates win?

Core Instruction

TEACHING NOVELA EN VIDEO

1. Have students read through the **Novela en video** and study the photos. Assign the parts of the characters to students to read out loud, and before viewing the video, skim through the text in class. Answer any student questions. **(20 min.)**
2. Play the entire video without stopping. Ask comprehension questions. In what ways was the video different from the classroom theatrics? If necessary play the video a second time. **(15 min.)**
3. Have students complete the **Actividades** on page 255 in writing for homework. **(2 min.)**

Captioned Video/DVD

As an alternative, you might use the captioned version.

STANDARDS: 1.2, 3.2

Visit Holt Online
go.hrw.com
KEYWORD: EXP1B CH10
Online Edition

En México

3

Es mi placer informarte de que vas a recibir una beca para estudiar en Madrid por un año.

¡Enhorabuena! Me da mucho gusto ver a alguien de tu inteligencia y dedicación conseguir tus sueños. Será un placer conocerte.

En Puerto Rico

Océano Atlántico
San Juan
PUERTO RICO
Mar Caribe

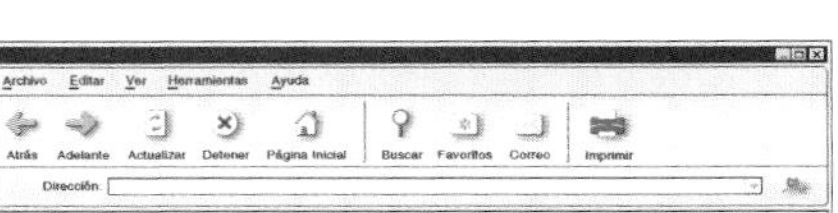

Es mi placer informarte de que vas a recibir una beca para estudiar en Madrid por un año.

¡Enhorabuena! Me da mucho gusto ver a alguien de tu inteligencia y dedicación conseguir tus sueños. Será un placer conocerte.

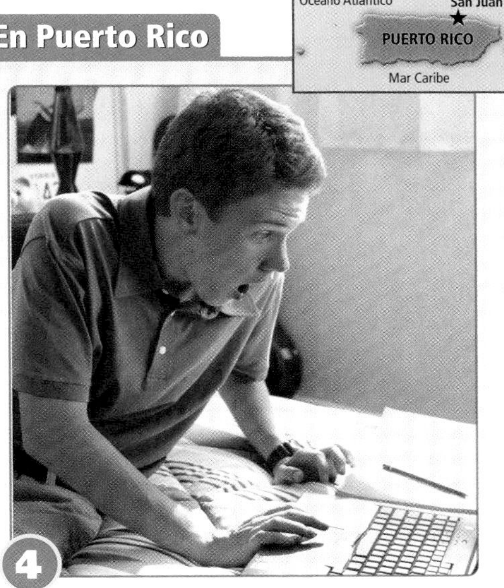

4

Novela en video

B. Contesta

1. What kind of scholarship has Sofía likely received?
2. What kind of scholarship has Nicolás likely received?

¿Quién será?

In this final episode of the **Novela en video,** we discover exactly who **La profesora** and Marcos, her assistant, are and what they have been up to. In streaming video, **La profesora** explains to Sofía and Nicolás that they have won scholarships to go to Madrid and study. **La profesora** is the director of a program to enrich relationships between Spanish-speaking cultures. Sofía will study dance, while Nicolás will study art. It seems that their true passions, which some adults and friends scoffed at, have earned them honor and recognition. In the end, poor Marcos takes a moment to rest and relax on the beach, after such an exhaustive search for just the right winners. Suddenly his cell phone rings. But Marcos isn't going to take any more stress, and he abandons his phone by the sea.

B. Contesta Answers

1. a scholarship to study dance in Spain
2. a scholarship to study art in Spain

Comparisons

Comparing and Contrasting

Sofía and Nicolás both are technologically savvy. Marcos doesn't seem to manage new technology as well. Ask students: Do you think this technological generation gap is also a reality in the U.S.? What kinds of technology do your parents use on a daily basis? What technological devices do you carry around with you?

Comunicación

Group Activity: Interpretive

To practice travel vocabulary, set up stations around the room representing the different stages of a trip by plane. Stations would include: **el mostrador, el control de seguridad, la puerta y la sala de espera, el avión, el control de pasaportes, el reclamo, la aduana.** Give small groups of students a list of activities that Sofia and Nicolás will do when they travel and instruct students to match the activities to the station at which they occur. Have students role-play at the stations.

STANDARDS: 1.1, 4.2

C. Contesta Answers

1. visit their children while they are in Spain
2. take a vacation, travel to an island, get some sun, rest
3. no

Using the Strategy

Summarizing Did students discover a pattern when they summarized the first nine episodes? (Summarizing probably helped them see that, even though the professor sent Marcos to ten different countries, the story continuously returned to Sofía and Nicolás. They were clearly the two strongest candidates.) Point out to students that summarizing the episodes helps them to recall what happened before and helps them focus on the most important aspect(s) of each episode—and that gives them insight into not only what is happening but why is it happening.

Gestures

Nicolás and Sofía are surprised and happy when they learn that they have won a scholarship to study in Madrid, Spain. Have students compare their reactions by studying their body language and gestures. What does Sofía do when she finds out? Where are her hands? What does Nicolás do when he finds out? Where are his hands? Are the expressions on their faces similar or different?

En México

5

Sofía ¿Lo pueden creer? Yo, ¿estudiando danza en Madrid?

Sra. Corona ¡Hija! ¡Qué bien! ¡Estoy muy orgullosa de ti!

Sofía Gracias, mamá. Van a venir a visitarme, ¿verdad?

Sr. Corona Claro que sí, hija. Me encantaría conocer Madrid.

En Puerto Rico

6

Nicolás ¿Lo pueden creer? Yo, ¿estudiando dibujo en Madrid?

Sra. Ortega ¡Hijo! ¡Qué bien! ¡Estoy muy orgullosa de ti!

Nicolás Gracias, mamá. Van a venir a visitarme, ¿verdad?

Sr. Ortega Claro que sí, hijo. Me encantaría conocer Madrid.

En España

En Perú

7

Profesora Castillo Marcos, ¡buen trabajo! Debes tomar unas vacaciones, viajar a una isla, tomar el sol, descansar… ¡Diviértete! Yo te llamo cuando estemos listos para empezar la investigación para el año próximo.

8

Después de investigar al candidato peruano, Marcos recibe el mensaje de la profesora. ¿Quiere trabajar en la investigación del año próximo?

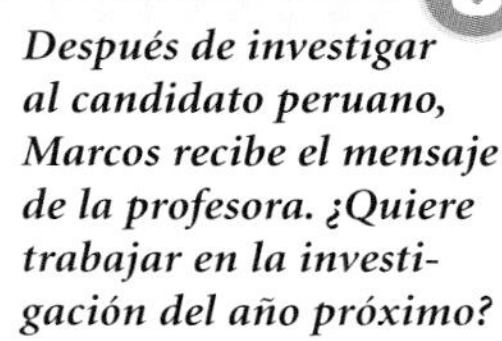

9

C. Contesta

1. What do both sets of parents agree to do?
2. What does **La profesora** suggest that Marcos do now?
3. Do you think Marcos is interested in working on another project like this again?

Communities

Community Link

Have students investigate vacation activities in Spanish-speaking areas that they have learned about in Chapters 1–9 by contacting local travel agents to request brochures or by having them do research on these places on the Internet. Ask students to list in Spanish the total estimated cost and the items they would need in order to complete each activity.

Culminating Project

Recorrido turístico

1. Explain to students that they will create a map of an imaginary city, and then write a script for a guide giving a tour of the city. **2.** Divide the class into groups of four. **3.** Have each group create a colored map of their city on poster board. Students should include at least five points of interest or places where tourists can enjoy different leisure activities, such as skiing on a lake. **4.** Have each group write a script to accompany the map. Students should include one interesting fact about each site on the map. They should also describe what each site looks like or what people usually do there. **5.** Groups present their maps to the class, pointing out the sites as they narrate the tour.

STANDARDS: 2.1, 5.1

Actividades

1 ¿Quién lo dijo?

Look at the story to help you remember who said each.

1. Voy a tener que pensarlo muy bien.
2. Yo, ¿estudiando danza en Madrid?
3. ¡Hija! ¡Estoy muy orgullosa de ti!
4. ¿Lo pueden creer? Yo, ¿estudiando dibujo en Madrid?
5. Claro que sí, hijo. Me encantaría conocer Madrid.
6. Será un placer conocerte.

1. La profesora
2. Sofía
3. Sra. Corona
4. Nicolás
5. Sr. Ortega
6. La profesora

2 ¡Qué lío!

Di si cada oración es cierta o falsa.

1. Marcos es el director de la fundación.
2. Sofía va a recibir una beca para estudiar baile en Madrid por dos años.
3. Nicolás va a recibir una beca para estudiar dibujo en Madrid por un año.
4. La señora Corona no quiere visitar a Sofía en Madrid.
5. Al señor Ortega le gustaría conocer Madrid.

1. falso
2. falso
3. cierto
4. falso
5. cierto

3 ¿Comprendes la Novela?

Check your understanding of the story.

1. Who is **La profesora?**
2. What was Marcos's role in the whole process?
3. Do the two students have similar reactions to the news? What is their reaction?
4. How did the parents of the two students react? Is this the reaction you might have expected?
5. Think about the ten episodes. Was there an episode when you suspected that Sofía and Nicolás were the winners? Explain when that happened.

Episodio final: *Now that you know what the ten candidates were for and which two of them won, can you understand the title of the video? Did the title ever help you predict what was going to happen?*

Novela en video

1 Answers

1. La profesora
2. Sofía
3. la Sra. Corona
4. Nicolás
5. el Sr. Ortega
6. La profesora

2 Answers

1. falso
2. falso
3. cierto
4. falso
5. cierto

3 Answers

1. She's the director of a foundation to promote understanding among the cultures of Spanish-speaking countries.
2. to observe and gather information about the candidates
3. surprised and very happy
4. They were happy. Answers will vary.
5. Answers will vary.

Comunicación

Pair Work: Interpersonal

After students have seen the **Novela en video,** have them work in pairs to talk in Spanish about winning a prize to do what they love the most. In the conversation one student should ask the other about his or her passion. Then, switch roles.

Differentiated Instruction

ADVANCED LEARNERS

Extension: Ask students to write a letter to **la profesora Castillo** to ask for a scholarship to study in Madrid. They should include in their letter their name, age, and address; what subject they would most like to study; a summary of what they are studying now in school; and reasons why they should receive a scholarship. Have them close and sign the letter appropriately. You might want to form a "scholarship committee" from another Spanish class to review the letters and decide on a winner.

SPECIAL LEARNING NEEDS

Students with Learning Disabilities: Allow students with learning disabilities extra time to spend with the *Online Edition* of the chapter. You might have them work with partners to listen to the audio portion of the conversations, then ask any questions they might have to their partners. Instruct the partners to help out with **CONTESTA** questions and **Actividades** by pointing out in the text where the answers might be found. Encourage your students also to repeat phrases they hear online for additional speaking practice.

STANDARDS: 1.1

Leamos y escribamos

Resources

Planning:

Lesson Planner, pp. 155–156, 306–309

 One-Stop Planner

Presentation:

 Audio CD 10, Tr. 10

Practice:

Cuaderno de actividades, p. 62

Cuaderno para hispanohablantes, pp. 77–84

Reading Strategies and Skills Handbook, Chapter 10

¡Lee conmigo!

Applying The Strategies

For practice with determining purpose, you might have students use the "Probable Passage" strategy from the *Reading Strategies and Skills Handbook.*

READING PRACTICE

STRATEGIES

Strategy: Probable Passage

Reading Skill	When can I use this strategy?		
	Prereading	During Reading	Postreading
Identifying Purpose	✓		✓
Making Predictions	✓		
Comparing and Contrasting			
Analyzing Chronological Order			✓

Strategy at a Glance: Probable Passage

- The teacher chooses key words or phrases from the text students will read, then develops categories for the words and writes the Probable Passage (a cloze passage with key words omitted).
- Before students read the text, they arrange the key words and phrases in the categories. Then they fill in the blanks in the cloze passage with the key words.
- After students read the text, they discuss how their passages were similar to or different from the actual text.

Many readers struggle because they don't predict what a selection might be about and don't think about what they already know about a topic. These students simply open a book, look at words, and begin turning pages. **Probable Passage** is a strategy that helps stop those poor reading habits by encouraging students to make predictions and to activate their prior knowledge about a topic.

Best Use of the Strategy

Probable Passage (Wood 1984) is a brief preview of a text from which key words and phrases have been omitted. The teacher chooses these key words from the text and presents them to the students. In some cases, it might be necessary to discuss the meaning of the words; many times, students can figure this out for themselves. Students arrange the words in categories according to their probable functions in the story (such as Setting, Characters, or Conflicts), then use the words to fill in the blanks of the Probable Passage. After reading the story, students compare it to their passages and discuss differences. As students work through this process, they use what they know about story structure, think about vocabulary, practice making predictions, and compare their predictions to the story line.

18 Reading Strategies and Skills Handbook — Probable Passage

Additional Practice

For more reading practice, use the **Literatura y variedades** reading for Chapter 10 on pages 274–275.

ESTRATEGIA

para leer When you read a brochure, it is important to read with a purpose. You need to decide first what kind of information you want. If you want an overview, then a quick, general reading may be all that is necessary. If you need specific information, however, a close reading will be required.

CD 10, Tr. 10

A Antes de leer

Read the title and subtitles of the following brochure. What kind of information does it contain? What specific facts would you expect to find under each subtitle?

¡Bienvenidos a la ciudad de Lima!
Aeropuerto Internacional Chávez

Transporte El servicio de transporte del aeropuerto a la ciudad y viceversa, se realiza por medio del[1] transporte público. Las compañías de taxis estacionan[2] sus vehículos en un área limitada, frente a la salida de las terminales nacional e internacional. La mayoría de hoteles cuentan con su propio[3] servicio de transporte.

Bancos
La moneda nacional de Perú es el nuevo sol. En los pasillos encontrará cajeros automáticos, los cuales aceptan tarjetas de crédito en moneda nacional y extranjera[4]. Las casas de cambio se encuentran en el pasillo principal[5] y en la zona de vuelos internacionales.

Información turística
En diversos lugares del aeropuerto encontrará módulos[6] con información sobre el arrendamiento[7] de coches, restaurantes, sitios turísticos de interés y una guía telefónica a los hoteles principales.

Otros servicios
En los pasillos encontrará teléfonos públicos que funcionan con monedas y tarjetas, las cuales se pueden conseguir en los diferentes quioscos[8] situados por todo el aeropuerto. Si necesita guardar[9] su equipaje por horas o por días, puede hacer uso del servicio de guardianía de equipajes, localizado en el pasillo principal.

1 by means of 2 park 3 have their own 4 foreign 5 main corridor 6 modules 7 rental 8 kiosk, stand 9 store

Core Instruction

TEACHING LEAMOS

1. Discuss the **Estrategia para leer.** Many students will not have previous experience with traveling, so you might discuss what one would expect to see in an article like this. **(5 min.)**
2. Have students skim the reading and the photos to get an idea of what the purpose of the brochure is. **(10 min.)**
3. Have students complete Activities B and C on page 257. **(10 min.)**

TEACHING ESCRIBAMOS

1. Review the **Estrategia para escribir** with students. Have students give examples of transitional phrases in English to check for comprehension. **(5 min.)**
2. Have students follow the steps as outlined on page 257. When students revise their partner's work, you might have them use the Peer Editing Rubric from the *Alternative Assessment Guide.* To help prepare students for the activity, see the Process Writing suggestion on page 257. **(45 min.)**

STANDARDS: 3.1

Visit Holt Online
go.hrw.com
KEYWORD: EXP1B CH10
Online Edition

Leamos y escribamos

B Comprensión

Basándote en la lectura, decide si las oraciones son **ciertas** o **falsas.** Corrige las oraciones falsas.

1. Los cajeros automáticos no aceptan tarjetas de crédito. falso
2. Todas las casas de cambio están en la zona internacional. falso
3. Los taxis se encuentran en frente de las terminales nacionales e internacionales. cierto
4. Hay información sobre los hoteles, las atracciones turísticas y el transporte público en los módulos de información. cierto
5. Puedes dejar tu equipaje por un fin de semana en la guardianía de equipajes. cierto

C Después de leer

Which services in the brochure might travelers arriving in Peru use? Do you think these same services are available in airports in the United States and other countries?

Leamos y escribamos

Interactive TUTOR

Taller del escritor

ESTRATEGIA

para escribir When writing about a series of events, use words such as **primero, luego, después,** and **por fin** to combine sentences.

Cartas del extranjero

You are writing home to friends to tell them about your first few days traveling abroad. Tell where you went and include five or six events that made your trip interesting, narrating them in order. End by mentioning your plans for the next day.

1 Antes de escribir

Make a list of the events you will report. Then brainstorm some phrases that will link them together logically **(primero, luego, después, por fin)**.

2 Escribir y revisar

Begin your letter with a greeting, then tell about your trip, focusing mainly on actions and events. Work in the linking phrases, being careful not to lose any clarity.

Exchange letters with a classmate. Read each other's letters checking for appropriate use of transitions and correct use of grammar, spelling, and punctuation.

3 Publicar

Write your letter on a large piece of paper or posterboard. On the other side illustrate one of the places you visited. Put your postcard up on the bulletin board. Which trip sounds most interesting to you?

Online
Cuaderno para hispanohablantes, pp. 105–116

B Answers

1. falso; Aceptan tarjetas de crédito en moneda nacional y extranjera.
2. falso; Hay casas de cambio en el pasillo principal y en la zona internacional.
3. cierto
4. falso; No hay información sobre el transporte público en los módulos. Sólo hay información sobre el arrendamiento de coches, los hoteles y las atracciones turísticas.
5. cierto

Process Writing

To help visual learners sequence events more easily, have students create a horizontal or vertical timeline of their vacation. Have students list the activities in the order that they were completed and note on the timeline where they will use transitional phrases.

Writing Assessment

To assess the **Taller del escritor,** you can use the following rubric.

Writing Rubric	4	3	2	1
Content (Complete—Incomplete)				
Comprehensibility (Comprehensible—Seldom comprehensible)				
Accuracy (Accurate—Seldom accurate)				
Organization (Well-organized—Poorly organized)				
Effort (Excellent effort—Minimal Effort)				

18–20: A
16–17: B
14–15: C
12–13: D
Under 12: F

Differentiated Instruction

ADVANCED LEARNERS

Tell students to imagine that an exchange student from Peru is coming to their city to visit for the first time. In groups of two or three, tell students to write a list with four pieces of advice that might help him or her get around in your local airport and city.

SPECIAL LEARNING NEEDS

Students with Learning Disabilities Since spelling and handwriting can be difficult for students with learning disabilities, allow these students to work on the **Taller del escritor** with a writing partner. Rather than exchanging letters with a single classmate, the pair can exchange their letter with another pair of students. Since students with learning disabilities often excel in creative activities, you might suggest that they work on drawings to depict the places mentioned in the letter, so that both students contribute to producing the final product.

Assess

Assessment Program

Prueba: Lectura, p. 109

Prueba: Escritura, p. 110

Standardized Assessment Tutor, pp. 41–44

Test Generator

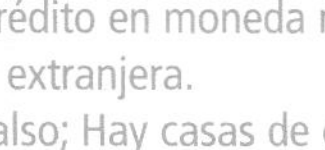

STANDARDS: 1.2, 2.2, 4.2

Resources

Planning:

Lesson Planner, pp. 157–158, 308–309

One-Stop Planner

Presentation:

Video Program
Videocassette 5
DVD Tutor, Disc 2
Variedades

Teaching Transparencies
Situación, Capítulo 10
Picture Sequences, Chapter 10

Practice:

Activities for Communication, pp. 52, 73–74

TPR Storytelling Book, pp. 58–59

Video Guide, pp. 94–95, 100

Lab Book, pp. 33–34, 60

Audio CD 10, Tr. 12–15

Interactive Tutor, Disc 2

1 Answers

1. Tengo que encontrar mi pasaporte. Necesito un pasaporte para viajar a otro país.
2. Tengo que buscar información sobre mi vuelo. No sé cuando sale.
3. Tengo que recoger mi equipaje.
4. Tengo que pagar mi boleto de avión. Tengo que hablar con el agente.
5. Tengo que pasar por el control de seguridad.
6. Tengo que ir a la oficina de cambio.

2 Answers

1. llegué
2. Me levanté
3. salió
4. Hice
5. Fui
6. llegué
7. Hice
8. comenzó
9. abordé

Prepárate para el examen

Repaso capítulo 10

1 Vocabulario 1
- asking for and giving information
- reminding and reassuring

pp. 224–229

1 Di lo que tienes que hacer según las cosas o lugares dados *(given)*.

1 

2 

3 

4 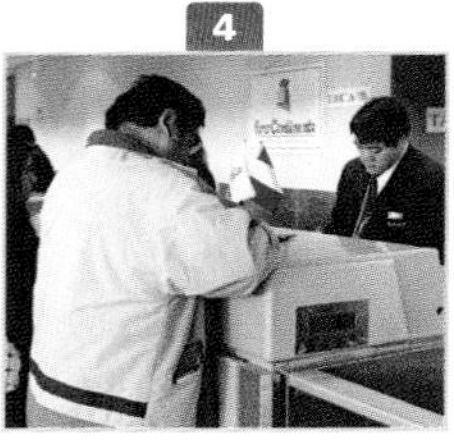

5 

6 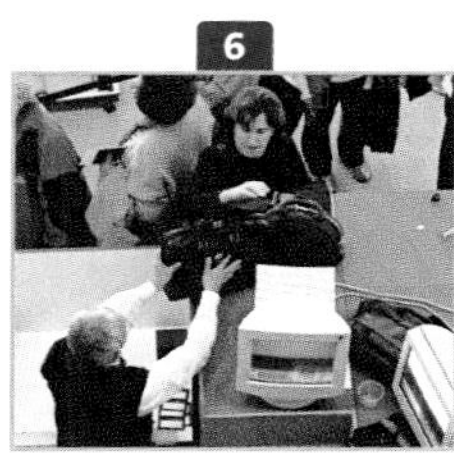

2 Gramática 1
- review of the preterite
- preterite of **-car, -gar, -zar** verbs
- preterite of **hacer**

pp. 230–235

2 Luis escribió una carta para su prima Ana sobre su viaje. Completa su carta con los verbos correctos en el pretérito.

> Querida Ana,
>
> Por fin estoy en Lima. ¡El viaje fue horrible! __1__ (Pasar/Ir) en taxi hasta el aeropuerto y __2__ (salir/llegar) allí temprano, a las seis de la tarde. __3__ (Hacer/Ir) cola en el mostrador. __4__ (Ver/Comprar) el boleto y la agente __5__ (facturar/hacer) la maleta. También __6__ (sacar/salir) la tarjeta de embarque. __7__ (Ir/Pasear) a la sala de espera. Entonces __8__ (comenzar/comprar) a nevar. ¡Por eso no __9__ (abordar/salir) el avión hasta las once. ¡Qué viaje más largo!
>
> Escribe pronto.
>
> Tu primo, Luis

3 Vocabulario 2
- talking about a trip
- expressing hopes and wishes

pp. 238–243

3 Escoge la respuesta que mejor completa cada oración.

1. Quiero ir de compras. Vamos al (correo/centro).
2. Fuimos a las ruinas, pero llovió. ¡Fue (estupendo/horrible)!
3. Quiero ir al lago. ¿Qué tal si (paseamos en lancha/vamos al centro)?
4. Perdí el autobús. ¡Qué (bien/mala suerte)!
5. Ana quiere ir a las islas Bermudas. Quiere ir en (barco/taxi).

Preparing for the Exam

FOLD-N-LEARN
Key Term

1. To help students prepare for the Chapter Test, have them fold a sheet of lined notebook paper in half from left to right. Then using scissors, they should cut along every third line from the right edge of the paper to the center fold to make tabs.
2. Ask students to list vocabulary terms and their English equivalents (or short Spanish definitions) on each slip.
3. Have students use their templates to help quiz themselves while preparing for the Chapter Test.

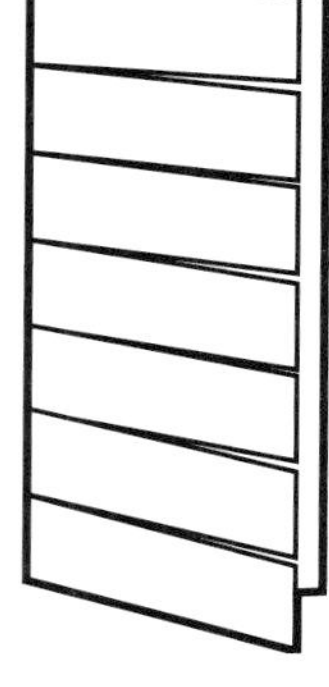

STANDARDS: 1.2

4 Complete the following conversation with an informal command, a direct object pronoun, or an infinitive.

—¿Conoces al profesor Augustino?

—No, no __1__ conozco. ¿Cómo es?

—Es interesante, pero tenemos que __2__ (estudiar) mucho. Hoy tengo que __3__ (leer) tres capítulos.

—Bueno, __4__ (empezar) a __5__ (leer) los capítulos.

—No tengo ganas de leer __6__. Tengo sueño.

—Pues, __7__ (descansar) y __8__ (leer) más tarde.

1. lo 2. estudiar 3. leer 4. empieza 5. leer 6. leerlo(s) 7. descansa 8. lee

5 Contesta las siguientes preguntas en español.

1. What material is used to build houses on the Uros Islands?
2. Name one unusual feature of trains in Peru.
3. How is the Manu rainforest in Peru preserved?

CD 10, Tr. 12

6 Escucha las siguientes oraciones. Decide si cada persona **a**) da un mandato, **b**) describe algo en el pasado o, **c**) busca información.

1. a 2. c 3. c 4. b 5. a 6. b

7 Crea *(create)* una conversación entre Ana y Luis sobre lo que hicieron durante las vacaciones.

Visit Holt Online
go.hrw.com
KEYWORD: EXP1B CH10
Chapter Self-test

4 Gramática 2
- informal commands of spelling-change and irregular verbs
- review of direct object pronouns
- review of verbs followed by infinitives

pp. 244–249

5 Cultura
- **Comparaciones** **pp. 236–237**
- **Notas culturales** **pp. 226, 234, 240, 247**
- **Geocultura** **pp. 218–221**

6 Script

See scripts on p. 221F.

5 Answers

1. **totora,** a reed-like grass that grows on the lake's bed
2. Passengers can request oxygen on trains.
3. Manu is a Biosphere Preserve divided into three parts; one for tourism, one for protecting plants and animals, and a third for settlement.

AP Language Examination

PREPARACIÓN PRÁCTICA

To display the drawings to the class, use the *Picture Sequences Transparency* for Chapter 10.

7 Below is a sample answer for the picture description activity.

—La primera parte de las vacaciones fuimos a un lago cerca de nuestra casa. Esquié en el lago todos los días. Hizo buen tiempo allí.

—Qué bien.

—Luego fuimos a Egipto a ver las pirámides. Hizo mucho sol y mucho calor pero fue divertido.

—¡Qué fantástico! Me gustaría ver las pirámides algún día. Yo fui a las montañas. Hizo fresco en las montañas. Acampamos y subí a la montaña. Fue muy divertido.

—Qué bien.

—Pero luego hizo mal tiempo. Llovió mucho y no hice nada. ¡Fue horrible!

—¡Qué mala suerte!

Oral Assessment

To assess the speaking activities in this chapter, you might use the following rubric. For additional speaking rubrics, see the *Alternative Assessment Guide.*

Speaking Rubric	4	3	2	1
Content (Complete—Incomplete)				
Comprehension (Total—Little)				
Comprehensibility (Comprehensible—Incomprehensible)				
Accuracy (Accurate—Seldom Accurate)				
Fluency (Fluent—Not Fluent)				

18–20: A 16–17: B 14–15: C 12–13: D Under 12: F

STANDARDS: 1.1, 1.2, 1.3, 2.1, 2.2

Grammar Review

For more practice with the grammar topics in the chapter, see the *Grammar Tutor,* the *DVD Tutor,* the *Interactive Tutor,* or the *Cuaderno de vocabulario y gramática.*

GramaVisión

Online Edition

Students might use the online textbook to practice the **Letra y sonido** feature.

Letra y sonido

For more practice with the consonants **c, p, q,** and **t,** have students pronounce words from the **Vocabulario** containing these consonants. As they do so, they should hold their hands in front of their mouths to see if they can feel a puff of air coming out as they say the words. Tell students that while they should feel the puff in English, they should not feel it when pronouncing the Spanish words.

Dictado Script

See scripts on p. 221F.

Gramática 1
- review of the preterite **pp. 230–231**
- preterite of **-car, -gar, -zar** verbs **pp. 232–233**
- preterite of **hacer** **pp. 234–235**

Repaso de Gramática 1

For the regular preterite forms of **-ar, -er,** and **-ir** verbs, see page 230. The preterite of **-car**, **-gar**, and **-zar** verbs have spelling changes.

sa**c**ar: yo sa**qué** lle**g**ar: yo lle**gué** comen**z**ar: yo comen**cé**

hacer			
yo	hice	nosotros(as)	hicimos
tú	hiciste	vosotros(as)	hicisteis
Ud., él, ella	hizo	Uds., ellos, ellas	hicieron

Gramática 2
- informal commands of spelling-change and irregular verbs **pp. 244–245**
- review of direct object pronouns **pp. 246–247**
- review of verbs followed by infinitives **pp. 248–249**

Repaso de Gramática 2

informal commands		
	affirmative	**negative**
-ger	reco**g**e	no reco**j**as
-guir	si**gu**e	no si**g**as
-car	bus**c**a	no bus**qu**es
-gar	lle**g**a	no lle**gu**es
-zar	empie**z**a	no empie**c**es

For a review of informal commands of irregular verbs, see page 244.
For a review of **direct object pronoun** placement see page 246.
Use these verbs followed by infinitives to say what someone *wants, hopes, plans,* or *has* to do.

esperar + infinitive
pensar (ie) + infinitive
querer (ie) + infinitive
tener que + infinitive
me (te, le...) gustaría (más) + infinitive

Letra y sonido c p q t

Las consonantes c, p, q, t CD 10, Tr. 13–15
- The letters **c, p, q, t** are not pronounced with a puff of air as in English *cat, pen, ten, quit:* **p**a**p**a, **p**atinar, **p**ar**q**ue, **c**ar**p**eta, **q**ueso, **C**uz**c**o
- The letter **t** is pronounced with the tip of the tongue right behind the teeth: **t**ía, **t**oalla, tris**t**e, **t**raje, **t**engo, **t**arde

Trabalenguas
Pablito clavó un clavito. ¿Qué clavito clavó Pablito?

Dictado
Escribe las oraciones de la grabación.

Chapter Review

Bringing It All Together

You might have students review the chapter using the following practice items and transparencies.

DVD Tutor

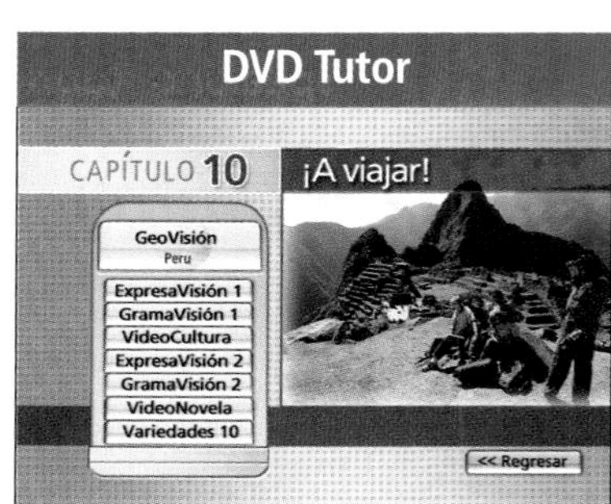

Interactive Tutor

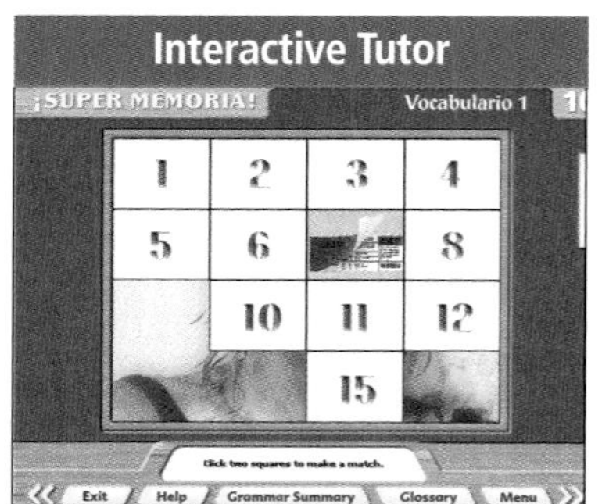

STANDARDS: 1.2

Repaso de Vocabulario 1

Asking for information

abordar	*to board*
la **aduana**	*customs*
el **aeropuerto**	*airport*
el (la) **agente**	*agent*
allí	*there*
el **avión**	*airplane*
la **billetera**	*wallet*
el **boleto de avión**	*plane ticket*
la **bolsa**	*travel bag, purse*
cambiar dinero	*to change money*
el **carnet de identidad**	*identity card*
comenzar (ie) un viaje	*to begin a trip*
conseguir (i)	*to get*
el **control de seguridad**	*security checkpoint*
desembarcar	*to disembark, to deplane*
¿Dónde se puede...?	*Where can one . . . ?*
encontrarse (ue) con	*to meet up with*
esperar	*to wait*
Está(n) a la vuelta.	*It's (They're) around the corner.*
facturar el equipaje	*to check luggage*
hacer cola	*to wait in line*
hacer un viaje	*to take a trip*
irse	*to leave*
la **llegada**	*arrival*
Lo siento, no sé.	*I'm sorry, I don't know.*
la **maleta**	*suitcase*
el **mapa**	*map*
¿Me puede decir...?	*Can you tell me . . . ?*
el **mostrador**	*counter*
la **oficina de cambio**	*money exchange*
la **pantalla**	*monitor, screen*
el (la) **pasajero(a)**	*passenger*
el **pasaporte**	*passport*
perder (ie)	*to miss, to lose*
la **puerta**	*gate*
el **reclamo de equipaje**	*baggage claim*
recoger	*to pick up*
la **sala de espera**	*waiting room*
la **salida**	*departure*
sentarse (ie)	*to sit down*
los **servicios**	*restrooms*
la **tarjeta de embarque**	*boarding pass*
el **vuelo**	*flight*

Reminding and reassuring. . . . . *See p. 228.*

Repaso de Vocabulario 2

Talking about a trip

acampar	*to camp*
¡Ah, tuviste suerte!	*You were lucky!*
el **autobús**	*bus*
el **barco**	*boat*
la **canoa**	*canoe*
el **centro**	*downtown*
durante	*during*
esquiar en el agua	*to water-ski*
¡Fue estupendo!	*It was great!*
ir de excursión	*to go hiking*
ir de pesca	*to go fishing*
la **isla**	*island*
el **lago**	*lake*
la **lancha**	*motorboat*
los **lugares de interés**	*places of interest*
los **medios de transporte**	*types of transportation*
el **metro**	*subway*
el **museo**	*museum*
la **oficina de correos**	*post office*
el **país**	*country*
el **parque de diversiones**	*amusement park*
pasar por	*to stop at/by*
pasear en bote de vela	*to go out in a sailboat*
¡Qué bien!	*How great!*
¡Qué fantástico!	*How fantastic!*
¡Qué lástima!	*What a shame!*
¡Qué mala suerte!	*What bad luck!*
quedarse en...	*to stay in . . .*
recorrer	*to tour*
las **ruinas**	*ruins*
sacar fotos	*to take pictures*
subir a la montaña	*to climb a mountain*
el **taxi**	*taxi*
tomar el sol	*to sunbathe*
tomar el tren	*to take the train*
el **tren**	*train*
viajar	*to travel*
el **viaje**	*trip*
el **zoológico**	*zoo*

Expressing hopes and wishes . . . . *See p. 242.*

Repaso

Vocabulary Review

For more practice with the vocabulary in this chapter, see the *DVD Tutor,* the *Interactive Tutor,* or the *Cuaderno de vocabulario y gramática.*

ExpresaVisión

Online Edition 

For students to hear the vocabulary on audio, have them access the online textbook.

Circumlocution

Ask students to explain the function of various vocabulary words in **Vocabulario 1** using the phrase(s), **Se usa(n) para... Es un lugar donde... Es una persona que...** Encourage students to use language they have learned in previous chapters.

Online Edition

Transparency Vocabulario 10.1

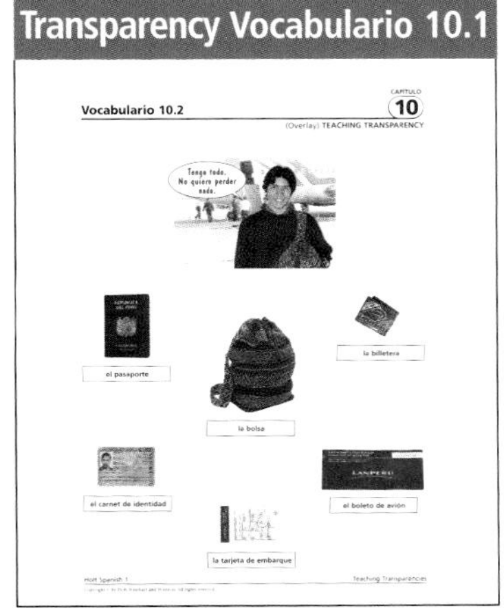

Transparency Situación Ch. 10

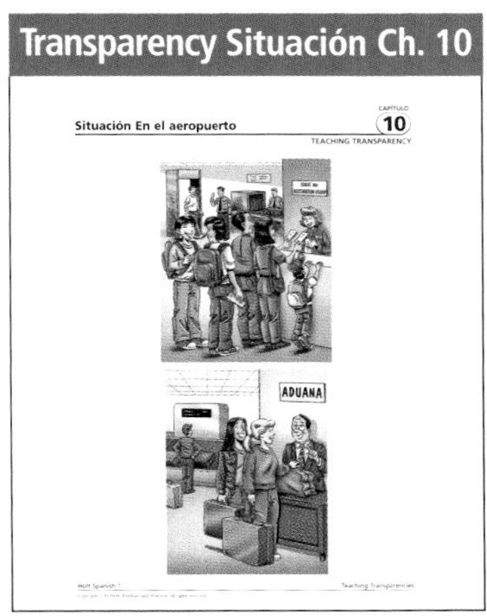

Assess

Assessment Program

Examen: Capítulo 10, pp. 197–207

Examen oral: Capítulo 10, p. 208

Examen final, pp. 209–223

Alternative Assessment Guide, pp. 245, 253, 261

Standardized Assessment Tutor, pp. 41–44

Audio CD 10, Trs. 19–20, 21–23

Test Generator

Resources

Planning:

Lesson Planner, pp. 159, 310–311

 One-Stop Planner

Presentation:

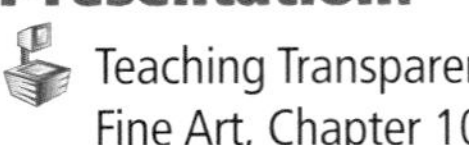 Teaching Transparencies Fine Art, Chapter 10

Practice:

Cuaderno de actividades, pp. 63–64

Lab Book, pp. 33–34

 Audio CD 10, Tr. 16

 Interactive Tutor, Disc 2

1 Script

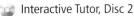

1. Jaime y Estela están en el aeropuerto, listos para sus vacaciones. Jaime va al mostrador para comprar el boleto y facturar el equipaje. La agente le pregunta a Jaime cuántas maletas tiene y él responde que lleva una.
2. Estela compró su boleto de avión el mes pasado así que ahora va directamente al mostrador y presenta su pasaporte. La agente le da a Estela su tarjeta de embarque.
3. Los dos van a la sala de espera, porque el avión sale a las 2:30 pm. Jaime se sienta y empieza a leer.
4. Son las 12:00 y Estela tiene bastante tiempo para cambiar dinero. Ve que la oficina de cambio está cerca. Va allí y hace cola.

Additional Practice

For students planning to travel to a Spanish-speaking country, learning to interpret flight information screens is an important skill. You might have students continue this type of activity using flight information posted on the Internet. You might also present students some examples of train and bus schedules in Spanish to see what they can understand. Have them use their prior knowledge and content to decipher words they do not know.

Integración

capítulos 1-10

CD 10, Tr. 16

1 Escucha las oraciones y escoge la foto correspondiente.
1. b 2. c 3. d 4. a

A

B

C

D

2 Hay cinco personas que buscan información sobre vuelos. Con base en la información de la pantalla, contesta las preguntas.

LLEGADAS INTERNACIONALES

HORAS	AEROLÍNEA	VUELO	ORIGEN	DESTINO	PUERTA
9:00	IBERIA	350	DALLAS	CUZCO	7
18:00	MEXICANA	119	SAN ANTONIO	LIMA	9
15:00	DELTA	230	NUEVA YORK	LIMA	11

SALIDAS INTERNACIONALES

HORAS	AEROLÍNEA	VUELO	ORIGEN	DESTINO	PUERTA
12:00	IBERIA	112	LIMA	NUEVA YORK	2
13:00	MEXICANA	256	LIMA	CIUDAD DE MÉXICO	5
8:00	DELTA	987	CUZCO	MIAMI	10

1. Nora quiere saber el número del vuelo de su amiga que llega a las 3:00 de la tarde de Nueva York.
2. Riqui tiene que recoger a su mamá que llega de Dallas. ¿A qué puerta va?
3. Susana viaja a Cuzco. ¿En qué aerolínea y vuelo viaja?
4. Tomás quiere saber a qué hora sale el vuelo para Nueva York.
5. Rosa pregunta cuántos vuelos hay entre Lima y Estados Unidos.

1. Es el vuelo 230. 2. La puerta 7 3. Iberia, 350
4. Sale a las 12:00. 5. Hay cuatro vuelos.

Culture Project

Have students imagine that they are travel agents and they are in charge of creating promotional materials for Spanish-speaking clients. Have them select one of the Spanish-speaking countries or areas they have studied this year and create a presentation in which they tell why their "clients" should select this country as a vacation destination. They might discuss unique customs and traditions, places and sights of interest to visit, and other fun vacation activities. Have them create a promotional poster to accompany their presentation with illustrations depicting the areas most interesting aspects.

STANDARDS: 1.2, 3.2

3 This painting shows a street vendor and townspeople in a Peruvian town, high in the Andes Mountains in South America. Imagine that this is a photo you took while on a visit there. Write a page for your travel journal about the day you took this picture.

- Tell how you traveled.
- What was the weather like?
- What did you see?
- Which foods did you eat?
- Where did you stay?

Exchange your journal entry with a classmate. After reading each other's description, ask a follow-up question of each other.

28h x 36w, oil; Columbine Galleries, Loveland CO

La vendedora de anticuchos, de Juan de la Cruz Machicado

4 **Situación**

Set up two tourist agencies in your classroom with two travel agents in each one. Make signs and posters in Spanish for different places to visit. Other students will play tourists who come in and ask about

- places they can visit
- prices
- necessary travel documents
- travel methods and schedules

The travel agents will answer with appropriate information and ask what the tourists hope to see and do on their trips.

Fine Art Connection

Introduction In this chapter, students see the painting *La vendedora de anticuchos* by Juan de la Cruz Machicado. You might tell the following information to your students.

Juan de la Cruz Machicado was born in Puno, Peru. He uses vibrant colors to show scenes from the city of Cuzco and the landscape of Southern Peru in a style that is characterized as abstract expressionism. His work is inspired by the myths and legends of his country and the colors of the changing of the seasons.

Anticuchos are beef hearts marinated in a spicy sauce grilled on skewers, sometimes with potatoes. It is a common dish in Peru.

Analyzing To help students discuss and analyze the painting, you might use the following questions.

1. **¿Cuáles son algunos platos típicos de nuestra región? ¿De dónde vienen estos platos originalmente?**
2. **¿Cómo es el pueblo en la pintura? ¿Cómo son las casas?**
3. **¿Cómo es la tierra? ¿Hay montañas?**
4. **En tu opinión, ¿cuál es el edificio blanco y alto en la distancia?**

Extension Set up a museum in the class. Put white paper behind the art transparencies of the paintings studied this year. Place the paintings around the room. Allow students to stroll around the "museum," making commentaries on the paintings. After the judging, gather the class to give their opinions and take a vote on the "Best in Show."

ACTFL Performance Standards

The activities in Chapter 10 target the communicative modes as described in the Standards.

Interpersonal	Two-way communication using receptive skills and productive skills	**Comunicación (SE),** pp. 227, 229, 231, 233, 235, 241, 243, 245, 247, 249, **Comunicación (TE),** pp. 227, 229, 231 **Situación,** p. 263
Interpretive	One-way communication using receptive skills	**Comparaciones,** pp. 236–237 **Comunicación (TE),** pp. 229 **Novela en video,** pp. 252–255 **Leamos,** p. 256
Presentational	One-way communication using productive skills	**Comunicación (TE),** pp. 243 **Comunicación (TE),** pp. 235, 241, 243, 245

STANDARDS: 1.1, 1.3, 3.1

Literatura y variedades

Meeting the National Standards

Cultures

Practices and Perspectives, p. 275

Products and Perspectives, pp. 267, 269

Connections

Thinking Critically, p. 271

Thinking Critically, p. 273

Using the Illustration

Have students look at the book titles and predict what types of readings they will find in **Literatura y variedades,** and from which countries they will come. See if they can recognize any of the structures in the background or at least say which countries they might represent. (Spain, Mexico)

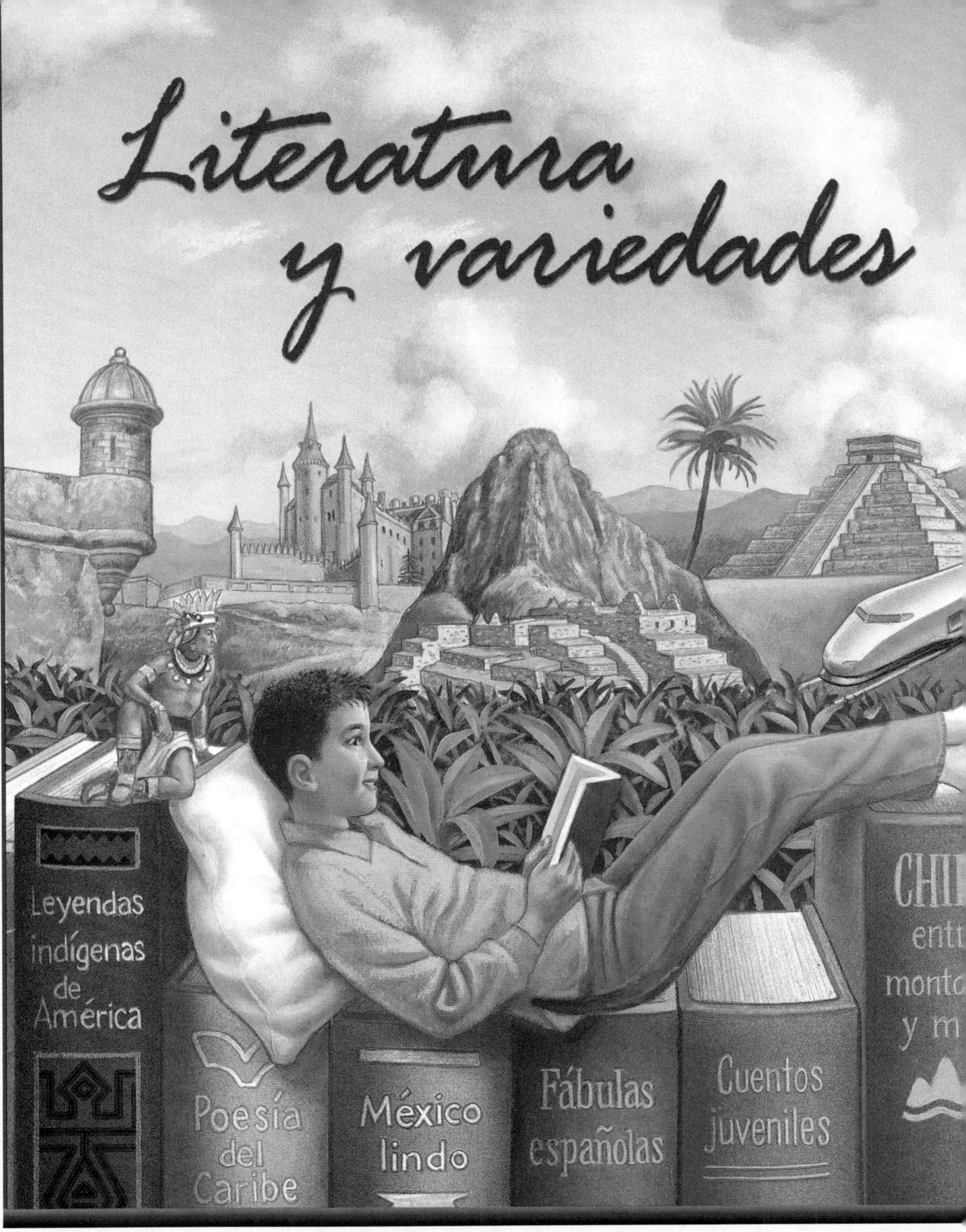

Holt Online Learning *¡Exprésate!* contains several online options for you to incorporate into your lessons.

***¡Exprésate! Student Edition* online at my.hrw.com**

On this site, you will find the online edition of *¡Exprésate!* All concepts presented in the textbook are presented and practiced in this online version of your textbook. You will also find audio and practice activities at point of use. The online pages can be used as a supplement to, or as a replacement of, your textbook.

Audio recordings of all readings at go.hrw.com

All of the texts in **Literatura y variedades** have been recorded and can be found in the online edition of this textbook.

Teacher resources at www.hrw.com

This site provides additional information that teachers might find useful about the *¡Exprésate!* program.

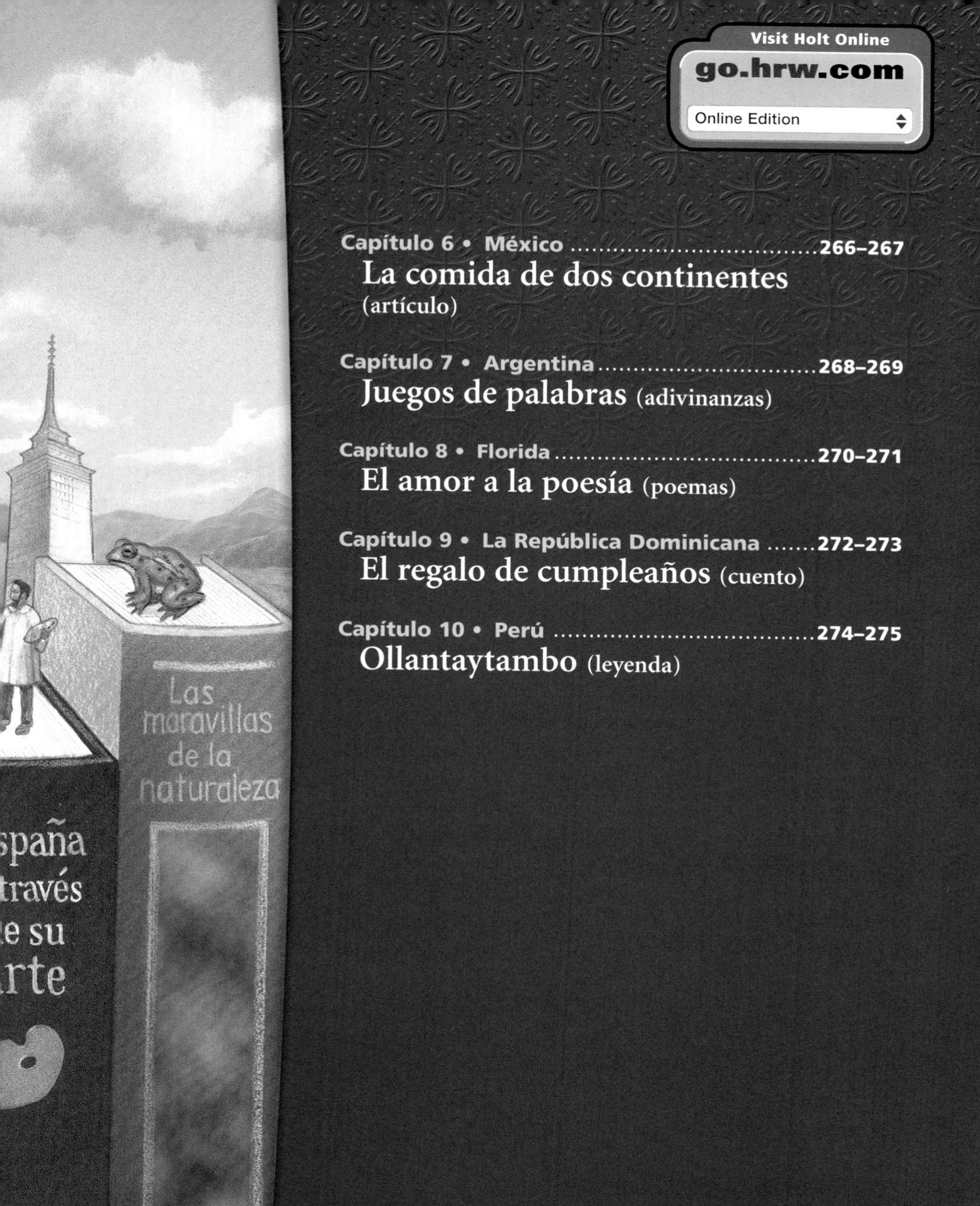

Literatura y variedades

The readings in this section of ***¡Exprésate!*** represent the ten different countries presented in the textbook, from Spain to Peru. The types of texts in this section include a museum brochure, two articles, an interview, commentary by a well-known Hispanic writer, another commentary by a renowned Hispanic painter, riddles, a poem, a story, and a legend. The difficulty increases somewhat in going from Chapter 1 to Chapter 10, but all of them are accessible to a Level 1 student who has successfully completed the core chapter reading. Each reading is accompanied by illustrations and a reading strategy to help students understand the text. These readings are meant to be fun—and to give students greater insight into the many cultures they encounter as they make their way through ***¡Exprésate!***

Using the Strategies

With every reading in **Literatura y variedades,** there are strategies designed to help students more easily understand the text. Some are pre-reading strategies that suggest techniques that students can apply before reading the text:

- identifying cognates
- activating background knowledge
- visualization
- using the title, photos, and so on to determine context
- thinking about the culture represented in the reading
- making predictions

Some of the strategies will be useful to students as they are reading the texts, such as using context to guess meaning and identifying the main idea and supporting details. Make sure students use the strategies to make these optional readings more accessible and therefore more enjoyable.

Resources

Planning:

Lesson Planner, pp. 93–94, 254–255

 One-Stop Planner

Presentation:

 Audio CD 6, Tr. 19

Practice:

Reading Strategies and Skills Handbook

¡Lee conmigo!

Applying the Strategies

For practice with finding the main idea, you might have students use the "Read, Rate, Reread" strategy from the *Reading Strategies and Skills Handbook.*

READING PRACTICE

STRATEGIES

Strategy: Read, Rate, Reread

Reading Skill	When can I use this strategy?		
	Prereading	During Reading	Postreading
Making Inferences		✓	
Identifying the Main Idea		✓	✓
Determining the Writer's Purpose			✓

Strategy at a Glance: Read, Rate, Reread

- Students read a short text three times, rating their understanding of the text and writing down any questions they have after each reading.
- After the third reading, students discuss with a partner or in a small group any unanswered questions. Then students rate their understanding a fourth and final time.
- As a class, students discuss how their ratings changed between readings, as well as asking any questions they still have.

Many struggling readers don't think reading the same passage or text again does them any good. That is partly because they operate under the misconception that other readers read something once, read it somewhat effortlessly, and "get it" every time, the first time. Rereading doesn't look any different from reading, so struggling readers don't see how many times proficient readers pause, loop back a few sentences, reread up to a point, reflect, start over completely, and then perhaps proceed slowly. Moreover, as we discuss texts with students, we rarely bring up the issue of *how* to understand; we are too busy focusing on *what* students understand. Therefore, struggling readers don't hear teachers or other students talk about the words—or even chapters—that they sometimes reread several times before formulating meaning. We need to help these students understand that rereading is something good readers do and that it is an important strategy to use when trying to understand a text.

Best Use of the Strategy

Use this strategy to offer students concrete evidence that comprehension does improve with repeated reading. We often tell students that rereading will increase their understanding of a text, but struggling readers need proof. They have years of evidence that reading does not work; therefore, they reason, why would rereading work any better? The structure provided by the **Read, Rate, Reread** strategy (Blau 1992)— the rating and questioning —provides the proof.

22 Reading Strategies and Skills Handbook — Read, Rate, Reread

Prereading

Discuss the **Estrategia** as a class. Tell students that one good way to discover the main idea of a selection is to make an outline that demonstrates what they think the main thought of each paragraph is. Under each main idea, have them write at least one detail that supports it. (You may want to review other strategies as well. For example, these paragraphs contain many cognates—have students look for them.)

México

La comida de dos continentes

 CD 6, Tr. 19

Much of the food that is consumed around the world today is made from ingredients that came originally from the Americas. Tomatoes, chocolate, corn, chile peppers, vanilla, pears, and potatoes are some of the foods that the Spanish conquistadors presented to the kings of Europe. Read the following article in order to learn more about the history of four of these foods.

ESTRATEGIA

When reading a text, look first for the main idea of each paragraph. After that, read carefully all the details that support the main idea. This wlll help you better understand the text.

El tomate

El tomate es originalmente de México. Cuentan[1] que cuando los exploradores llevan el tomate a Europa en el siglo XVI, ¡nadie lo quiere comer! Por su color rojo tan fuerte, todos piensan que es una fruta venenosa. Los exploradores aseguran que lo pueden comer sin problema y la gente poco a poco empieza a probarlo[2].

En la actualidad[3], el tomate es un ingrediente básico en la preparación de platos[4] alrededor del mundo.

El chocolate: ¿para beber o comerciar?

El chocolate es original de América Central. En México, los aztecas lo usaban *(used)* con varios propósitos[5]. Antes del trabajo, para el desayuno de los hombres por la mañana, hervido[6] con miel, agua y vainilla, y otra vez, por la tarde, después de la comida. Para el Gran Moctezuma, último líder de los aztecas, el chocolate era *(was)* su bebida diaria y además, un elemento importante en los ritos, en las ceremonias y para comerciar[7].

1 they say 2 to taste it 3 today 4 dishes 5 purposes 6 boiled 7 to trade

Core Instruction

TEACHING LITERATURA Y VARIEDADES

1. Before dividing students into work groups, brainstorm as a class the focus of each paragraph. If this is a reading about the history of certain foods, what questions might the text attempt to answer? (When was the food discovered? What people used the food first? When was it discovered by Europeans? What was the reaction at that time? How is the food used today?) **(5 min.)**
2. After reading the introductory paragraph, divide the class into four groups. Tell each group to read the paragraphs one at a time and try to find the answers you came up with together. One student might act as secretary for the group. An alternative might be to assign only one paragraph to each group, so that they have time to read the paragraph in more depth. **(5 min.)**
3. Have students share the details that they found in their paragraph with the other groups. **(4 min.)**
4. Have groups answer the questions in **Después de leer. (5 min.)**

STANDARDS: 1.1, 1.2, 1.3

El maíz: sustancia del hombre

Se dice que el maíz empieza a cultivarse[1] en América desde hace 10,000 años. Todos los miembros de la cultura maya comen maíz, desde el esclavo[2] hasta el rey. El *Popol Vuh*, libro religioso de los mayas, cuenta que el hombre mismo[3] se hace de[4] maíz. Cuando los exploradores españoles vienen a México prueban el maíz por primera vez en formas diferentes de tortillas y tamales.

Hoy en día, el maíz constituye un 20% de las calorías consumidas mundialmente[5]. En Estados Unidos se produce el 45% del maíz del mundo (mucho de éste destinado al ganado[6]) y en el continente de África el maíz es el grano que más se cultiva.

Los chiles: el picante del mundo[7]

Los chiles, sin duda, son el ingrediente más representativo de la comida mexicana en el mundo. En México hay más de cien variedades de chiles con nombres y sabores[8] diferentes. Algunos de los chiles más típicos son el serrano, el chipotle, el guajillo y el habanero, nativo de Yucatán y ¡muy picante!

Los grupos indígenas usan el chile para añadir sabor a los frijoles, las salsas, los arroces[9] y los moles.[10] Aunque el uso del chile no es tan popular entre los europeos, la llegada de éste a Asia cambia la cocina de la región para siempre. Hoy día se consumen más chiles en Tailandia que en cualquier otro país del mundo.

1 to grow 2 slave 3 man himself 4 is made of 5 worldwide 6 livestock
7 world's hot spice 8 tastes 9 rice dishes 10 sauces

Después de leer

1. Al principio, ¿por qué creen los europeos que el tomate es venenoso?
2. ¿Qué usos tienen los aztecas para el chocolate?
3. ¿Cómo preparan los aztecas su chocolate?
4. ¿De qué está hecho el hombre según los mayas?
5. ¿En qué región del mundo se consume la mayor cantidad de chiles?

Literatura y variedades

Answers

1. Creen que es venenoso por su color rojo tan fuerte.
2. Toman chocolate, le dan un lugar especial en los ritos y ceremonias religiosas y lo usan para comerciar.
3. hervido con agua, miel y vainilla
4. se hace de maíz
5. en Tailandia

Cultures

Products and Perspectives

It is said that Montezuma drank 50 cups a day of hot chocolate flavored with chili peppers. The drink was thought to have curative powers. The Aztecs also flavored their chocolate with vanilla, which comes from the bean of a tropical orchid plant. It wasn't until chocolate was brought back to Europe that people began sweetening the beverage with sugar to give it a more pleasant taste. Ask students if there are beverages unique to their own culture, and if so, why they are popular.

Postreading

Some other foods that originated in the Americas are vanilla, pears, and potatoes. Have students use the Internet to research these foods to see what interesting facts they can learn about them.

Differentiated Instruction

SLOWER PACE LEARNERS

Since the **Después de leer** questions are in Spanish, have students who might have difficulty with them read through the questions first and make sure they understand what is being asked before reading the selections. Doing this will help them understand what information they should watch for as they read each paragraph.

MULTIPLE INTELLIGENCES

Bodily-Kinesthetic Have students work in small groups to research a beverage that requires several steps to prepare (a special tea, juice, and so on). Have them make the beverage as a presentation to the class, explaining the steps in Spanish as they do each one.

STANDARDS: 2.2, 3.1

Resources

Planning:

Lesson Planner, pp. 109–110, 270–271

 One-Stop Planner

Presentation:

 Audio CD 7, Tr. 10

Practice:

Reading Strategies and Skills Handbook

¡Lee conmigo!

Applying the Strategies

For practice with visualizing a text, you might have students use the "Logographic Cues" strategy from the *Reading Strategies and Skills Handbook.*

READING PRACTICE

STRATEGIES

Strategy: Logographic Cues

Reading Skill	When can I use this strategy?		
	Prereading	During Reading	Postreading
Understanding Text Structure	✓	✓	✓
Analyzing Chronological Order		✓	✓
Making Generalizations and Understanding Text Structure		✓	✓

Strategy at a Glance: Logographic Cues

- Logographs are graphic representations of ideas. The **Logographic Cues** strategy uses simple pictures that represent or symbolize key ideas in a text.
- Students can use logographs to identify textual elements or organize and remember information.

Dr. Kylene Beers explains the **Logographic Cues** strategy with the following story:

I sat in the train station in Chaumont, France, wondering why I had taken Latin instead of French in high school and college. At that moment, I wanted to know if my train to Dijon was leaving when I thought it was. Blank stares and pitying shakes of the head were all I received when people realized that I was limited to English. Finally, I took out my map of the region, drew a train, circled my destination, and wrote the date and time of my departure. Underneath it all I put a big question mark. The clerk behind the window finally understood my question: Is the train from Chaumont to Dijon still departing today from this station at 3:48? "Oui," she said, nodding her head.

Hours later, as I sat on the train, I realized that although I couldn't read French words, I *could* read musical notation, numbers, and international signs. I could read information that was presented logographically, but not information presented alphabetically. A Logographic Cue was worth a million French words.

"And why not?" I thought. Our first understanding of written language is a logographic understanding. Three- and four-year-olds who recognize their names in print rarely do so because they attach sounds to letters; instead, they simply recognize the shape of their printed names. Logographs, or picture cues, remain helpful when students are confronted with an alphabetic principle or text that they don't understand.

10 Reading Strategies and Skills Handbook — Logographic Cues

Prereading

Read the introductory paragraph and discuss the **Estrategia** with students. Have students look at the images on these two pages and write down a guess about what the riddles are about. After they have read the texts, have them see how close their guess was.

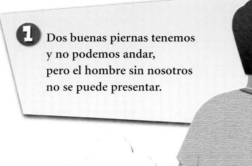

Argentina

Juegos de palabras

CD 7, Tr. 10

In Argentina, as in many places, word games are one of the favorite types of entertainment among children and adults. Here, two Argentinian authors present four easy riddles about common, everyday things. The first one and the last one are from the book ***Adivinanzas (Riddles)*** by Carlos Silveyna, teacher and author. The other two are riddles from the book ***Los rimaqué*** by Ruth Kaufman, who is also a teacher. See if you can guess the riddles.

ESTRATEGIA

Read the riddles aloud and think about the images that occur to you. Creating visual images in your mind will help you understand the text.

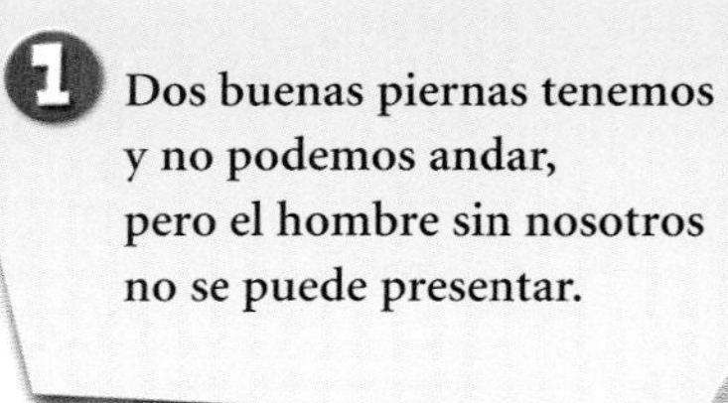

1

Dos buenas piernas tenemos
y no podemos andar,
pero el hombre sin nosotros
no se puede presentar.

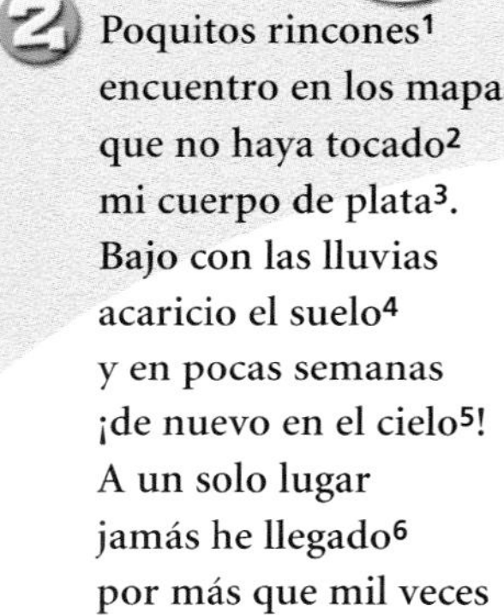

2

Poquitos rincones[1]
encuentro en los mapas
que no haya tocado[2]
mi cuerpo de plata[3].
Bajo con las lluvias
acaricio el suelo[4]
y en pocas semanas
¡de nuevo en el cielo[5]!
A un solo lugar
jamás he llegado[6]
por más que mil veces
lo haya intentado[7].
Le ruego[8] a las nubes
le suplico[9] al viento
¿por qué nadie quiere
llevarme al desierto?

1 corners
2 has not touched
3 silver
4 I touch the ground
5 sky
6 have never arrived
7 have tried
8 I beg
9 I implore

Core Instruction

TEACHING LITERATURA Y VARIEDADES

1. Remind students that in Spanish there may also be grammatical clues that may help them guess the answer. (In riddle 1, the word **nosotros** tells that the answer is a masculine plural noun. In riddle 4 the adjectives are feminine plural.) **(3 min.)**
2. Have students listen to the audio recording of these texts and read the riddles along with the recording. **(3 min.)**
3. Have students exchange the guesses for each riddle that they wrote on a piece of paper. Have them pass their papers around the room so they can read each other's ideas. After discussing the right answers, have students say how they figured each riddle out. **(4 min.)**
4. Have students answer the questions in **Después de leer** with a partner. **(5 min.)**

3 Se ponen las nubes
redondas y negras
de la tierra[1] sube
olor a tormenta[2].
Un fuerte estallido[3]
y volamos los dos:
hermanos mellizos[4]
relámpago[5] y yo.
Si juntos salimos
a andar por el mundo
¿por qué llego yo
siempre segundo?

1 earth 2 storm 3 crackling
4 twins 5 lightning

¡Yo primero, yo primero!

4 Siempre quietas[6],
siempre inquietas[7],
dormidas de día,
de noche despiertas[8].

6 still 7 restless 8 awake

Después de leer

1. En la primera adivinanza, ¿qué necesita el hombre?
2. ¿Adónde vuelven las lluvias que bajan a la tierra según la segunda adivinanza?
3. La segunda adivinanza habla de poca agua en un lugar. ¿Cuál es?
4. En la tercera, ¿cuál es el compañero del relámpago?
5. En la cuarta, ¿qué dice sobre el día y la noche?

Answers

1. sus pantalones
2. al cielo
3. el desierto
4. el trueno
5. que las estrellas y la luna están dormidas de día y de noche despiertan

Cultures

Products and Perspectives

Riddles have been around for centuries. Ancient Greek mythology tells of Oedipus who had to answer the riddle of the Sphinx or be killed. Her riddle was "What has four legs in the morning, two at noon, and three at night?" Oedipus gave the correct answer, "Man" who crawls on all fours as an infant, walks on two legs in his youth, and uses a cane in his old age. Have students think about why people might enjoy riddles and what part they play in any culture.

Postreading

Have students think of a riddle that they know in English and write it in Spanish. Have the other students in the class try to guess the answer.

Differentiated Instruction

ADVANCED LEARNERS

Advanced students may want to investigate other types of word games, such as crossword puzzles or anagrams. Have them try to make up their own puzzles and let the rest of the class try to solve them.

SPECIAL LEARNING NEEDS

Students with Learning Disabilities These riddles can be challenging due to their text structure and underlying meanings. Have students with learning disabilities work with a partner and work on only one of the three riddles. Have them make a list of each clue as they understand it before continuing on to the next clue.

Florida

Resources

Planning:

Lesson Planner, pp. 125–126, 286–287

 One-Stop Planner

Presentation:

Audio CD 8, Tr. 12

Practice:

Reading Strategies and Skills Handbook

¡Lee conmigo!

Applying the Strategies

For practice with understanding text structure, you might have students use the "Text Reformulation" strategy from the *Reading Strategies and Skills Handbook.*

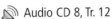

READING PRACTICE

Strategy: Text Reformulation

STRATEGIES

Reading Skill	When can I use this strategy?		
	Prereading	During Reading	Postreading
Understanding Text Structure			✓
Analyzing Cause-and-Effect Relationships			✓

Strategy at a Glance: Text Reformulation

- The teacher introduces **Text Reformulation** by having students reformulate a text they have read into a patterned story, such as an ABC story, or into another genre.
- The teacher models several types of reformulations.
- Either the teacher or the students choose which type of reformulation to do based on the desired learning objectives.

Sometimes by transforming a text into a different format—one that is more familiar or friendlier—students can understand it better. An example: reformulating an expository text structure to fit the narrative structure, in other words, taking what might be a difficult, even dry, expository text and retelling it as a story.

Text Reformulation, or **Story Recycling**, is a strategy in which students transform a text into another type of text.

Best Use of the Strategy

When students are having difficulty understanding a text, use the **Text Reformulation** (Feathers 1993), or **Story Recycling**, strategy to show them how to better understand the text by turning it into another type of text that is more familiar to them. Whether students turn expository texts into narratives, poems into newspaper articles, or short stories into patterned stories such as ABC books, reformulating texts encourages students to talk about the original texts.

54 Reading Strategies and Skills Handbook Text Reformulation

Prereading

Discuss the **Estrategia** as a class. Then, read the introductory paragraph about Marcel Mayor Marsán. You might locate more of her works to share with the class. Discuss some of the problems of being bilingual and bicultural.

El amor a la poesía

CD 8, Tr. 11

Maricel Mayor Marsán was born in Cuba but has spent most of her life living as an exile in the United States. She studied history and political science at the International University of Florida and discovered that she wanted to dedicate herself to writing. Even though she writes short stories and theatrical works, her true passion is poetry. She has published five books of poetry, including ***Un corazón dividido*** (1998), where she speaks of being bilingual and the difficulties of belonging to two cultures. Marsán lives in Miami.

ESTRATEGIA

In order to understand the main idea of a text, it is important to examine in detail each part. In poetry, for example, it is necessary to read and understand each stanza before deciding what the main idea of the poem is.

Apuntes° de un hogar° posmoderno

Yo como a las siete,
tú comes a las ocho,
el niño come a las seis
y la niña come a las nueve.
Queremos ser felices a toda costa°,
todos vemos televisión separados
en nuestras respectivas habitaciones
siempre a la misma hora,
siempre a las diez.

Title: Notes
home
5 no matter what

Core Instruction

TEACHING LITERATURA Y VARIEDADES

1. Have students read the first poem in its entirety. Then, have them write a short sentence or two about what the poem is trying to say about modern family life. Have a few volunteers share their sentences with the class. **(5 min.)**
2. Have students read along with the recording of ***Un corazón dividido.*** Tell them to reread the poem, looking for poetic devices such as simile (**como una canción/como el agua**). Ask them what the rhythm of the poem evokes (the beating of her heart as well as the movement of the waves). Ask students to find words that the poet uses to contrast aspects of her life (**aquí/ allá; saber/creer; caribeño/norteamericano**). What is the significance of these opposing words (her heart being pulled in two directions)? **(10 min.)**
3. Have students answer the questions in **Después de leer** with a partner. **(5 min.)**

STANDARDS: 1.1, 1.2

Un corazón dividido

El mío es un corazón de dudas°,
esfuerzos° que luchan entre el aquí y el allá.
Es el grito° continuo de mi ser interior.
Es "estar aquí" en sustancia°
pero el "estar allá" siguiéndote° a todas partes.
Es como una canción sin ritmo definido
que se va contigo sin terminar la tonada°.

Es ser una y otra a la vez.
Es ser una queriendo ser la otra
y la otra deseando ser la primera.
Es saber muy poco acerca
de aquellas cosas en las cuales crees.
Es saber menos acerca
de otras cosas que quieres expresar
pero tienes miedo reclamar°.
Es la transpiración de mi olor° caribeño
encima de la superficie de mi gel° norteamericano.

Es solamente mi corazón que late°
rápido e incesante
como las corrientes constantes del Golfo de México.

Es mi corazón dividido
secando° los finales del tiempo
como el agua de esas corrientes
sobre el Estrecho de la Florida.

---

1 doubts
2 efforts
3 scream
4 physically
5 following you
7 tune
15 to reclaim
16 *fig.* my soul
17 *fig.* my shell
18 beats
22 drying

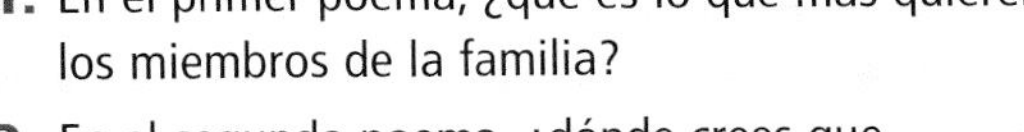

1. En el primer poema, ¿qué es lo que más quieren los miembros de la familia?
2. En el segundo poema, ¿dónde crees que está el "allá" referido en las líneas dos y cinco?
3. ¿Quién crees que es "la una" y "la otra"?
4. ¿Por qué crees que su corazón está dividido? Explica tu respuesta.

Literatura y variedades

Answers

1. ser felices a toda costa
2. Cuba y el Caribe
3. Answers will vary.
4. Answers will vary.

Connections

Thinking Critically

José Martí (1853–1895) was another poet who lived most of his life away from his native Cuba. He was exiled at the age of 17 for his political writings and was killed in one of the first battles in the war for Cuban Independence. Many of his ***Versos Sencillos*** express his love for his homeland and his longing to return there. Ask students how they think it might affect them to leave their homeland for political reasons and grow up in a different country. Do they know of any other writers or poets who left their country to live in America?

Postreading

Have students make a poster where they combine a poem with an illustration, similar to the one on page 396 that accompanies **Apuntes de un hogar posmoderno.** Have students present their poems and illustrations to the class.

Differentiated Instruction

ADVANCED LEARNERS

Have students try writing a short poem, perhaps expressing their feelings about modern family life as in the first poem they read. Though the poems do not necessarily have to rhyme, students should choose their words carefully and should attempt to establish some sort of rhythm with their poetry. Or, have students select a famous Spanish poet and present one of his or her poems to the class.

MULTIPLE INTELLIGENCES

Linguistic Have students recreate the poems in the form of a letter. They should imagine that they are the poet and that they are going to express the same ideas in the poem to a friend. Or, they might choose to act out the poem dramatically for the class.

STANDARDS: 1.2, 1.3, 2.2, 3.1

La República Dominicana

Resources

Planning:

Lesson Planner, pp. 141–142, 302–303

 One-Stop Planner

Presentation:

 Audio CD 9, Tr. 9

Practice:

Reading Strategies and Skills Handbook

¡Lee conmigo!

Applying the Strategies

For practice with making inferences, you might have students use the "It Says, I Say" strategy from the *Reading Strategies and Skills Handbook.*

READING PRACTICE

Strategy: It Says ... I Say

Reading Skill	When can I use this strategy? Prereading	During Reading	Postreading
Making Inferences		✓	
Making Generalizations and Drawing Conclusions			✓

Strategy at a Glance: It Says ... I Say

Prereading

Read the **Estrategia** as a class. Discuss the introductory paragraph and ask students what they know about the Dominican Republic and its culture.

El regalo de cumpleaños

CD 9, Tr. 9

Diógenes Valdez is a Dominican author who has written many acclaimed novels and short stories. In this story, the mother of David, a young Dominican, has spent years working in New York. In a letter to his mother, David tells her that everyone thinks that he should have more fun, that it is not good to be so sad, and that he must learn to smile. Read his mother's response and discover what the best gift is that she can give him.

ESTRATEGIA

In order to better understand a story, think about the culture that it represents. What do you know about the Dominican culture that can help you?

Querida mamá:

La abuela me ha dicho[1] que vendrás[2] pronto. Sé que dice esto para verme feliz, porque me paso mucho rato mirando tu fotografía y a veces los ojos se me llenan de lágrimas[3]. Comprendo que te fuiste a Nueva York a trabajar porque aquí cuesta mucho conseguir[4] un empleo.

En casa todos estamos bien, únicamente me preocupa[5] la abuela. Se pasa todo el día diciéndome que me divierta, que salga con los amigos, pero yo no siento deseos de hacerlo. Ha llegado a decirme que hace tiempo que no me ve sonreír[6], que parezco un niño viejo.

Sé que Nueva York es una gran ciudad y que allá se consigue de todo. Quiero que me traigas una sonrisa[7]. Estoy cansado de que me digan que no parezco feliz, sólo porque no sé sonreír.

Te quiere, tu hijo

David

Querido hijo:

Creo que tengo buenas noticias para ti. Voy a regresar pronto y aunque me pides algo que es difícil de conseguir[8], voy a hacer todo lo posible para complacerte[9]. Sé que costará mucho el conseguir esa sonrisa, pero puedes estar tranquilo. Espero estar contigo el mismo día de tu cumpleaños.

Tu madre que no te olvida,

Rebeca

1 has told me
2 you will come
3 tears
4 to get
5 I worry about
6 to smile
7 a smile
8 to get
9 to make you happy

Core Instruction

TEACHING LITERATURA Y VARIEDADES

1. Have students read David's letter and his mother's reply as you play the audio recording. After they have heard the recording, have them scan David's letter for words that will give them information about what David's mother is doing and how he feels about her absence. **(3 min.)**
2. Have students read the second page of the story as far as the word **Ábrelo,** then ask them to guess what David's mother might have brought him as a gift. **(7 min.)**
3. Have students finish reading the story to find out what his gift is. Have them compare the text with what they guessed in item two. **(3 min.)**
4. Have partners answer the questions in **Después de leer. (5 min.)**

Hoy es sábado 15 de agosto. Es el día del cumpleaños de David. En el aeropuerto, el niño mira los aviones[1] que despegan o aterrizan[2]. No se siente nervioso, ni emocionado. Contempla a su madre y tiene la esperanza de que en cartera[3], envuelta primorosamente[4], venga esa sonrisa. La ve salir y un nudo[5] se le forma en la garganta. Ella corre a abrazarlo[6] y por un momento David se olvida de todo.

¡Mamá!—exclama David.

¡Hijo mío! —responde la madre.

¿Has traído[7] mi sonrisa? —se atreve a preguntarle.

Ella abre la cartera y le entrega un paquetito primorosamente envuelto.

¡Aquí está!—le dice—¡Ábrelo!

David lo toma entre sus manos temblo rosas[8] y con los ojos llenos de lágrimas, responde:

¡Tengo miedo de hacerlo!

David comienza a abrir el pequeño paquete. Las manos le tiemblan cuando le quita la envoltura[9]. Abre la cajita, pero dentro tan sólo hay un papelito cuidadosamente doblado. Lo abre y lee:

"Querido hijo:

Mamá ha venido a quedarse definitivamente. Ya nunca más volverá a marcharse[10]."

Entonces David abrió los ojos y abrazó a su madre nuevamente. Sin darse cuenta comenzó[11] a sonreír.

1 airplanes
2 take off or land
3 purse
4 carefully wrapped
5 knot
6 to hug him
7 Have you brought
8 shaking
9 takes off the wrapping
10 I'll go away again
11 he began

Después de leer

1. ¿Por qué se fue a Nueva York la madre de David?
2. Según la abuela, ¿por qué debe divertirse David más? ¿A quién se parece?
3. ¿Qué le pide David a su madre?
4. En su carta, ¿cuándo dice que va a venir la madre de David?
5. ¿Cuál es el regalo que la madre le trae? Explica.

Literatura y variedades

Answers

1. a trabajar
2. no lo ve sonreír; un niño viejo
3. una sonrisa
4. pronto
5. Answers will vary.

Connections

Thinking Critically

Christopher Columbus landed on the island of Hispaniola in 1492. Today the island is divided into two countries, French-speaking Haiti on the west, and the Spanish-speaking Dominican Republic on the east. Santo Domingo, the capital of the Dominican Republic, is the oldest European settlement in the Americas. Baseball is a popular sport in the Dominican Republic. Many Major League players in the United States are Dominicans. Have students research other historical and popular connections between the United States and the Dominican Republic.

Postreading

Have students share with their classmates the best present that they ever received. If possible, they might bring the gift in and tell the class about it. Who gave it to them? Why is it special to them? Or, tell them to bring in a picture of a gift and explain why it would make them happy if they were to receive it.

Differentiated Instruction

SLOWER PACE LEARNERS

For this reading, you may want to pair students who are having difficulties with more advanced students who can help, since a variety of verb tenses are used. Have them make notes as they read about what they were able to understand.

MULTIPLE INTELLIGENCES

Bodily-Kinesthetic Have groups of students write a brief script and act out the story they just read. Have them bring props as needed in order to convey their meaning. You might divide the story into sections and assign each section to a different group.

STANDARDS: 1.3, 3.1, 3.2

Resources

Planning:

Lesson Planner, pp. 157–158, 318–319

 One-Stop Planner

Presentation:

 Audio CD 10, Tr. 11

Practice:

Reading Strategies and Skills Handbook

¡Lee conmigo!

Applying the Strategies

For practice with making predictions, you might have students use the "Probable Passage" strategy from the *Reading Strategies and Skills Handbook.*

READING PRACTICE

STRATEGIES

Strategy: Probable Passage

Reading Skill	When can I use this strategy?		
	Prereading	During Reading	Postreading
Identifying Purpose	✓		✓
Making Predictions	✓		
Comparing and Contrasting			
Analyzing Chronological Order			✓

Strategy at a Glance: Probable Passage

- The teacher chooses key words or phrases from the text students will read, then develops categories for the words and writes the Probable Passage (a cloze passage with key words omitted)
- Before students read the text, they arrange the key words and phrases in the categories. Then they fill in the blanks in the cloze passage with the key words
- After students read the text, they discuss how their passages were similar to or different from the actual text

Many readers struggle because they don't predict what a selection might be about and don't think about what they already know about a topic. These students simply open a book, look at words, and begin turning pages. **Probable Passage** is a strategy that helps stop those poor reading habits by encouraging students to make predictions and to activate their prior knowledge about a topic.

Best Use of the Strategy

Probable Passage (Wood 1984) is a brief preview of a text from which key words and phrases have been omitted. The teacher chooses these key words from the text and presents them to the students. In some cases, it might be necessary to discuss the meaning of the words; many times, students can figure this out for themselves. Students arrange the words in categories according to their probable functions in the story (such as Setting, Characters, or Conflicts), then use the words to fill in the blanks of the Probable Passage. After reading the story, students compare it to their passages and discuss differences. As students work through this process, they use what they know about story structure, think about vocabulary, practice making predictions, and compare their predictions to the story line.

18 Reading Strategies and Skills Handbook — Probable Passage

Prereading

Discuss the **Estrategia** as a class. Ask students what they know about legends. What is their purpose? What American legends do they know? Tell them to look at the pictures and try to make some predictions about the story that they are about to read.

Perú

Ollantaytambo

CD 10, Tr. 11

The Incan warrior Ollanta was made immortal thanks to the famous Peruvian writer Juan Espinoza Medrano, who wrote the drama *Ollantay* during the colonial period. Many years later, in 1780, the story was presented to the public with great success. Read about the Incan people and this famous warrior for whom the legend is named.

ESTRATEGIA

Making predictions helps prepare you to read a passage. Read the first four lines of the text and, thinking about other legends that you know, try to guess what is going to happen in this Inca legend.

Ollantay es el mejor guerrero[1] del imperio inca. Conquista regiones de la selva y lleva riquezas[2] al Inca Pachacútec.

Su casco de oro[3] le distingue como el más valiente. Todos lo admiran pero su corazón es de la princesa Cusi Coyllur.

Cuando Pachacútec se entera del amor entre el guerrero y la princesa se pone rojo de ira[4]. Castiga[5] a Ollantay y encierra a la princesa en una cueva[6].

Un día Ollantay se escapa y se convierte en jefe de los pueblos de los Andes. Gana todos los combates contra Rumiñahui, el general de Pachacútec.

Rumiñahui busca venganza[7]. Durante una fiesta emborracha[8] a los hombres de Ollantay y los hace prisioneros. El guerrero está ahora en manos del malvado Rumiñahui.

Pero en Cuzco hay un nuevo Inca, Tupac Yupanqui. Tupac es bueno y justo. Cusi Coyllur y Ollantay se casan al fin y viven en Tambo, una magnífica ciudad de piedra[9], levantada[10] al pie de la selva.

1 warrior 2 riches 3 golden helmet 4 hatred 5 He punishes 6 cave 7 revenge 8 he intoxicates 9 rock 10 raised

Core Instruction

TEACHING LITERATURA Y VARIEDADES

1. Before having students read the text, ask students what they know about the Incas and the ruins of Machu Picchu in Perú. Then have them read **Datos geográficos. (4 min.)**
2. Have students listen to the audio recording of the legend, reading along as they listen. Hearing the recording will help them pronounce the names correctly. As they listen, have them write down names they hear and identify names of places and names of people. **(4 min.)**
3. Have students read the legend with a partner. As they read, have them make a list of the characters in the legend and a short statement about who each one is. **(4 min.)**
4. Have students answer the questions in **Después de leer. (5 min.)**

STANDARDS: 1.1, 1.2

Datos geográficos

Ollantaytambo es un pueblo de la provincia de Urubamba, muy cerca de las famosas ruinas de Machu Picchu, al sur del Perú. En este pueblo todo ha permanecido[1] intacto y en sus casas siguen viviendo[2] los descendientes de sus primeros ocupantes. Allí se encuentra una antigua fortaleza inca, uno de los mejores ejemplos de la asombrosa[3] arquitectura de esta civilización. Muchas de las piedras en su construción, de más de 96 toneladas[4], fueron transportadas desde lugares lejanos, pero aún no se sabe cómo.

1 has remained 2 continue to live 3 astonishing 4 tons

Después de leer

1. ¿De quién está enamorado Ollantay?
2. ¿Qué hace el Inca Pachacútec al saber de ese amor?
3. ¿Qué hace Ollantay cuando se escapa de Pachacútec?
4. ¿Cómo se salva Ollantay del malvado Rumiñahui?
5. ¿Por qué es famoso hoy en día el pueblo Ollantaytambo?
6. ¿Cuál es el misterio de la construcción?

Answers

1. de la princesa Cusi Coyllur
2. Castiga a Ollantay y pone a Cusi Coyllur en una cueva.
3. Se convierte en el jefe de los pueblos de los Andes.
4. El nuevo Inca, Tupac Yupanqui, les deja libres.
5. Es uno de los mejores ejemplos de la arquitectura inca.
6. No se sabe cómo las piedras fueron transportadas.

Cultures

Practices and Perspectives

The city of Ollantaytambo is located in the Urubamba Valley near Cuzco and is known today as the "Sacred Valley". When the early Europeans arrived here, they thought the walls surrounding the city must have been built by giants because they were so high. Ask students what effect it has on modern Peruvians to have such a rich cultural heritage. Can students think of anything in their own culture that might be as impressive as the "sacred valley" was to the Europeans when they first saw it?

Postreading

Have students think of a legend or myth that they are familiar with and tell it simply in Spanish. If they prefer, have them make up a legend of their own.

Differentiated Instruction

ADVANCED LEARNERS

Have students, perhaps in pairs or small groups, rewrite the legend of Ollantay as a play to be presented to the class. They might bring in props to help convey the legend's meaning.

SPECIAL LEARNING NEEDS

Students with Learning Disabilities In order to make the legend easier to understand, prepare in advance a list of the characters in the legend along with a sentence or two, possibly in English, of identifying characteristics (Ollantay– best warrior of Incan empire). Have students skim the text for these characters and create a word web or other graphic organizer to help identify the relationships of the characters. Then, have them start reading, paying careful attention to the glossed words. Discuss these words as a group.

STANDARDS: 1.2, 2.1, 3.1, 3.2

Páginas de referencia

Secciones de referencia

La Península Ibérica

México

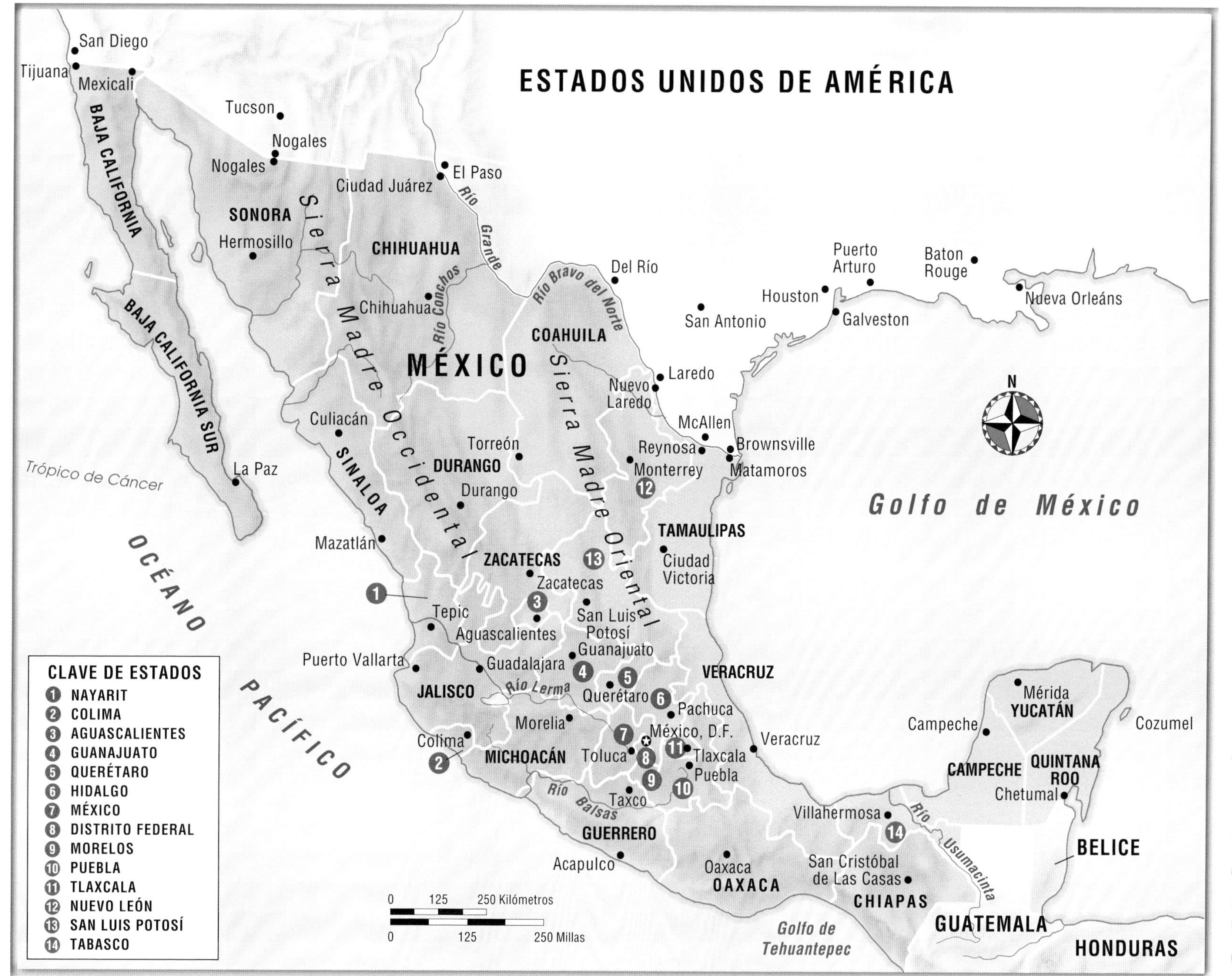

ESTADOS UNIDOS DE AMÉRICA
San Diego
Tijuana
Mexicali
Tucson
Nogales
Nogales
El Paso
Ciudad Juárez
Del Río
Laredo
Nuevo Laredo
San Antonio
McAllen
Reynosa
Brownsville
Matamoros
Houston
Puerto Arturo
Galveston
Baton Rouge
Nueva Orleáns
N
Golfo de México
BAJA CALIFORNIA
BAJA CALIFORNIA SUR
La Paz
SONORA
Hermosillo
CHIHUAHUA
Chihuahua
Río Grande
Río Conchos
Río Bravo del Norte
COAHUILA
Sierra Madre Occidental
Sierra Madre Oriental
MÉXICO
SINALOA
Culiacán
Mazatlán
DURANGO
Durango
Torreón
ZACATECAS
Zacatecas
Aguascalientes
Tepic
Puerto Vallarta
JALISCO
Guadalajara
Río Lerma
Colima
MICHOACÁN
Morelia
San Luis Potosí
Guanajuato
Querétaro
Monterrey
TAMAULIPAS
Ciudad Victoria
VERACRUZ
Pachuca
México, D.F.
Toluca
Tlaxcala
Puebla
Taxco
Veracruz
GUERRERO
Río Balsas
Acapulco
OAXACA
Oaxaca
Golfo de Tehuantepec
Villahermosa
San Cristóbal de Las Casas
CHIAPAS
Río Usumacinta
Campeche
CAMPECHE
Mérida
YUCATÁN
QUINTANA ROO
Chetumal
Cozumel
BELICE
GUATEMALA
HONDURAS
OCÉANO PACÍFICO
Trópico de Cáncer
0 125 250 Kilómetros
0 125 250 Millas
CLAVE DE ESTADOS
1 NAYARIT
2 COLIMA
3 AGUASCALIENTES
4 GUANAJUATO
5 QUERÉTARO
6 HIDALGO
7 MÉXICO
8 DISTRITO FEDERAL
9 MORELOS
10 PUEBLA
11 TLAXCALA
12 NUEVO LEÓN
13 SAN LUIS POTOSÍ
14 TABASCO

México

Estados Unidos de América

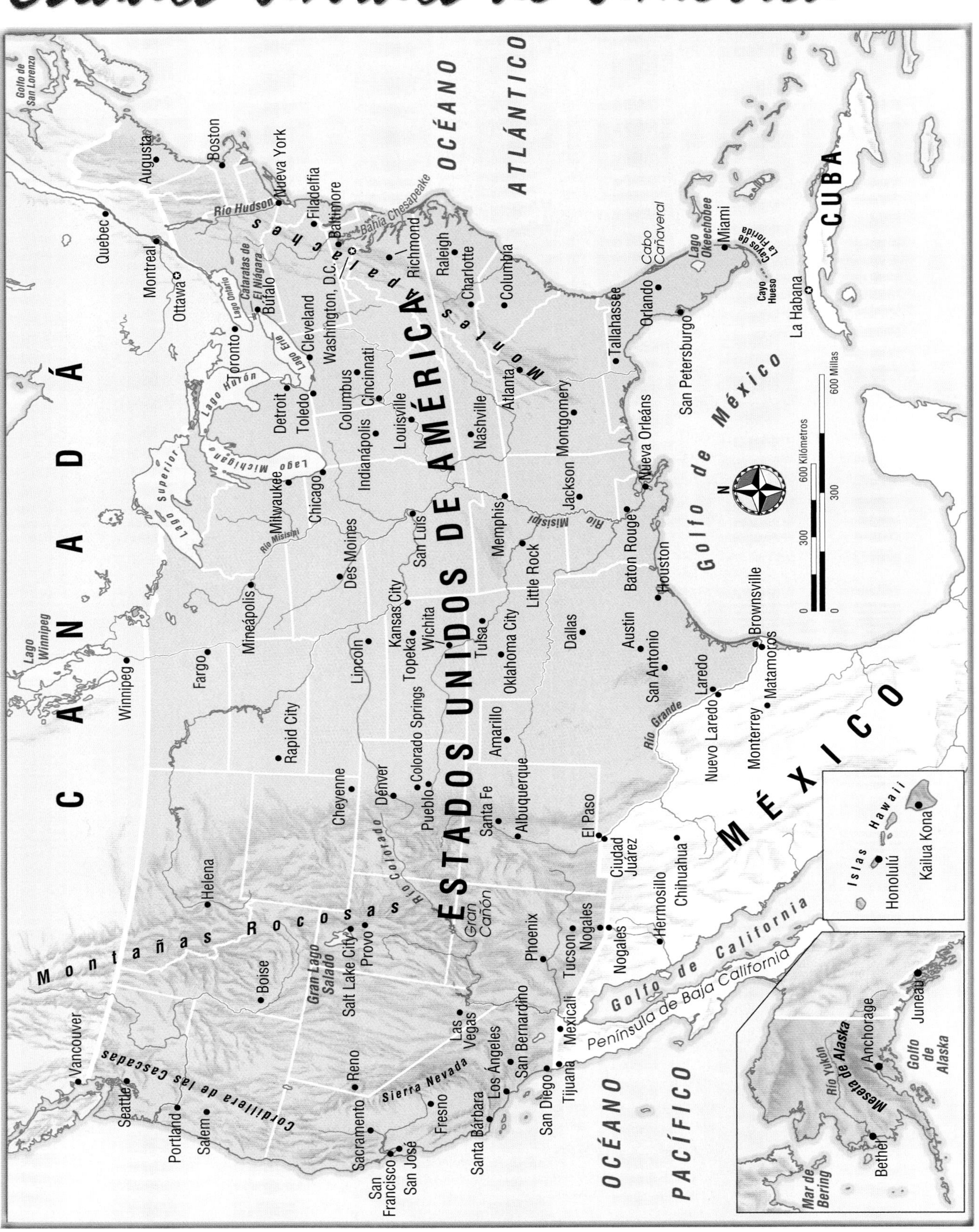

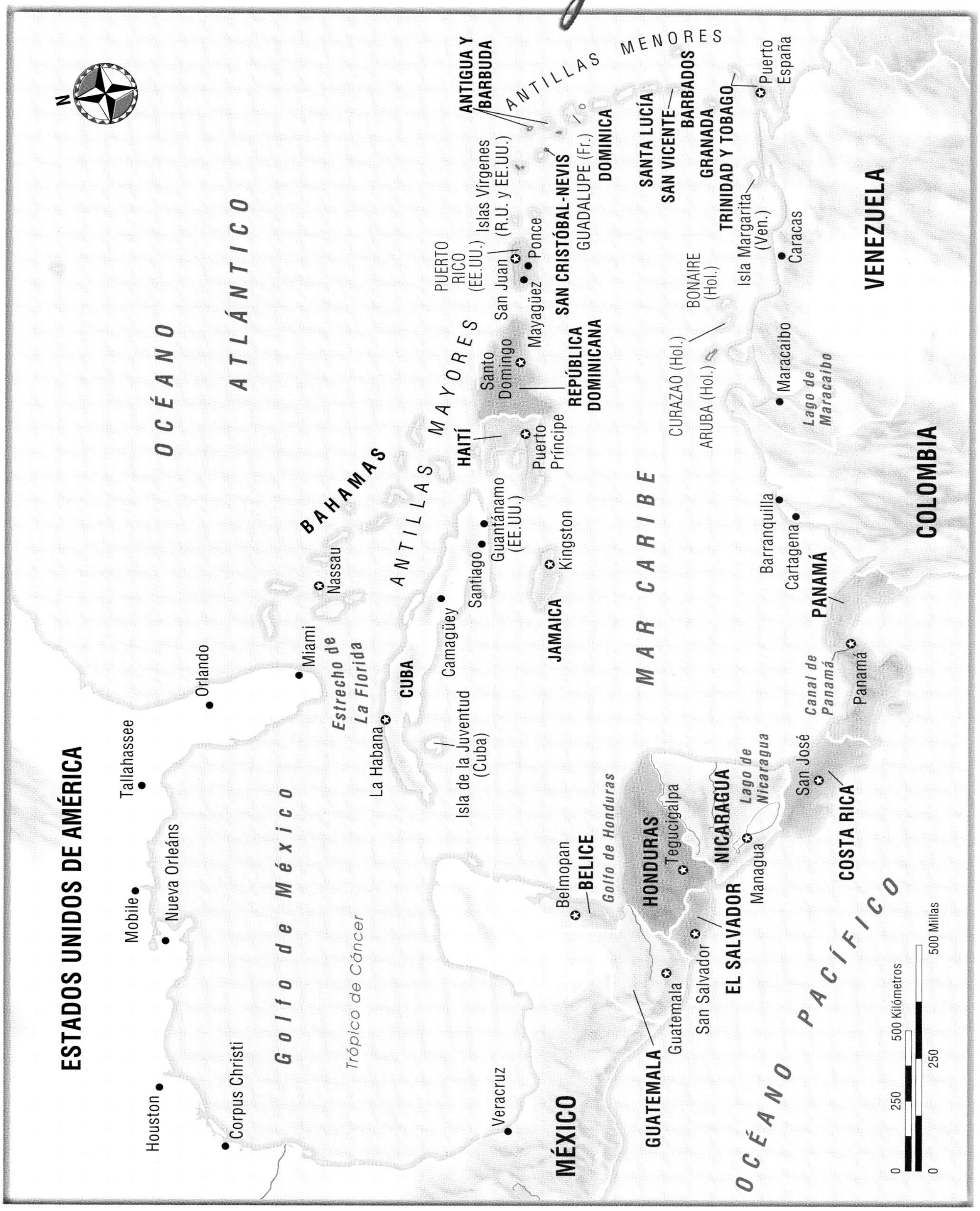

América Central y las Antillas

ESTADOS UNIDOS DE AMÉRICA
Houston
Corpus Christi
Mobile
Nueva Orleáns
Tallahassee
Orlando
Miami
Golfo de México
Trópico de Cáncer
Veracruz
MÉXICO
OCÉANO ATLÁNTICO
BAHAMAS
Nassau
Estrecho de La Florida
CUBA
La Habana
Isla de la Juventud (Cuba)
Camagüey
Santiago
Guantánamo (EE.UU.)
ANTILLAS MAYORES
JAMAICA
Kingston
HAITÍ
Puerto Príncipe
Santo Domingo
REPÚBLICA DOMINICANA
PUERTO RICO (EE.UU.)
San Juan
Mayagüez
Ponce
Islas Vírgenes (R.U. y EE.UU.)
ANTILLAS MENORES
ANTIGUA Y BARBUDA
SAN CRISTÓBAL-NEVIS
GUADALUPE (Fr.)
DOMINICA
SANTA LUCÍA
SAN VICENTE
BARBADOS
GRANADA
TRINIDAD Y TOBAGO
Puerto España
Isla Margarita (Ven.)
Caracas
VENEZUELA
BONAIRE (Hol.)
CURAZAO (Hol.)
ARUBA (Hol.)
Maracaibo
Lago de Maracaibo
COLOMBIA
Barranquilla
Cartagena
MAR CARIBE
PANAMÁ
Panamá
Canal de Panamá
COSTA RICA
San José
Lago de Nicaragua
NICARAGUA
Managua
HONDURAS
Tegucigalpa
Golfo de Honduras
BELICE
Belmopan
EL SALVADOR
San Salvador
GUATEMALA
Guatemala
OCÉANO PACÍFICO
0 250 500 Kilómetros
0 250 500 Millas
N

América del Sur

MAR DE LAS ANTILLAS
OCÉANO
ATLÁNTICO
América Central
Maracaibo
Caracas
Cartagena
VENEZUELA
Orinoco
Río
Ciudad Bolívar
GUAYANA
SURINAM
Medellín
Georgetown
Paramaribo
Cayena
COLOMBIA
GUAYANA FRANCESA
Bogotá
Cordillera de los Andes
Islas Galápagos
(Ecuador)
Río Putumayo
Quito
Ecuador
ECUADOR
Río Amazonas
Manaus
Belén
Guayaquil
Cuenca
BRASIL
Recife
PERÚ
Lima
Cuzco
Salvador
Brasilia
Lago Titicaca
La Paz
BOLIVIA
Sucre
OCÉANO
PARAGUAY
Río Paraná
Río de Janeiro
San Pablo
Asunción
Trópico de Capricornio
Tucumán
CHILE
ARGENTINA
PACÍFICO
Córdoba
URUGUAY
Valparaíso
Mendoza
Santiago
Montevideo
Buenos Aires
Río de la Plata
N
Bariloche
OCÉANO
ATLÁNTICO
0
500
1.000 Kilómetros
0
500
1.000 Millas
Estrecho de Magallanes
Islas Malvinas
(R.U.)
Punta Arenas
Tierra del Fuego
Cabo de Hornos

Repaso de Vocabulario

This list includes words introduced in *¡Exprésate!* Level 1A, Chapters 1–5. If you can't find the words you need here, try the Spanish–English and English–Spanish vocabulary sections beginning on page R29. You will also want to reference the review of functional expressions, beginning on page R17.

¿Adónde vamos? *(Where do we go?)*

el auditorio	*auditorium*
el baile	*dance*
la biblioteca	*library*
la cafetería	*cafeteria*
la casa de...	*. . .'s house*
el centro comercial	*shopping mall*
el cine	*movie theater*
el club de...	*the . . . club*
el colegio	*school*
el concierto	*concert*
el ensayo	*rehearsal*
el entrenamiento	*practice*
la fiesta	*party*
el gimnasio	*gym*
la iglesia	*church*
el parque	*park*
el partido de...	*the . . .(sports) game*
la piscina	*swimming pool*
la playa	*beach*
la reunión	*meeting*

Pasatiempos *(Pastimes)*

alquilar videos	*to rent videos*
bailar	*to dance*
cantar	*to sing*
comer	*to eat*
correr	*to run*
descansar	*to rest*
dibujar	*to draw*
escribir cartas	*to write letters*
escuchar música	*to listen to music*
estudiar	*to study*
hablar por teléfono	*to talk on the phone*
hacer la tarea	*to do homework*
ir de compras	*to go shopping*
leer	*to read*
montar en bicicleta	*to ride a bike*
nadar	*to swim*
navegar por Internet	*to surf the Internet*
pasear	*to take a walk*
patinar	*to skate*
salir con amigos	*to go out with friends*
tocar el piano	*to play the piano*
trabajar	*to work*
ver televisión	*to watch TV*

La casa/el apartamento *(House/Apartment)*

el baño	*bathroom*
el carro	*automobile*
la cocina	*kitchen*
el comedor	*dining room*
el escritorio	*desk*
el garaje	*garage*
el gato	*cat*
la habitación	*bedroom*
el jardín	*garden*
la mesa	*table*
el perro	*dog*
las plantas	*plants*
la puerta	*door*
la sala	*living room*
la silla	*chair*
el sofá	*couch*
la ventana	*window*

La comida *(Food)*

el almuerzo	*lunch*
la comida china (mexicana, italiana)	*Chinese (Mexican, Italian) food*
las frutas	*fruit*
las hamburguesas	*hamburgers*
el helado	*ice cream*
la pizza	*pizza*
las verduras	*vegetables*

Las cosas para el colegio *(Things for school)*

el bolígrafo	*pen*
la calculadora	*calculator*
la carpeta	*folder*
la computadora	*computer*
el cuaderno	*notebook*
el diccionario	*dictionary*
el lápiz/los lápices	*pencil/pencils*
la mochila	*backpack*
el papel	*paper*
la regla	*ruler*
el reloj	*watch/clock*

Calendario *(Calendar)*

abril	*April*
agosto	*August*
los días de la semana	*days of the week*
diciembre	*December*
los domingos	*on Sundays*
enero	*January*
febrero	*February*
los fines de semana	*on weekends*
el invierno	*Winter*
los jueves	*on Thursdays*
junio	*June*
julio	*July*
los lunes	*on Mondays*
los martes	*on Tuesdays*
marzo	*March*
mayo	*May*
los meses del año	*months of the year*
los miércoles	*on Wednesdays*
noviembre	*November*
octubre	*October*
el otoño	*Fall*
la primavera	*Spring*
la próxima semana	*next week*
los sábados	*on Saturdays*
septiembre	*September*
el verano	*Summer*
los viernes	*on Fridays*

¿Cuándo y con qué frecuencia? *(When and How often?)*

a tiempo	*on time*
a veces	*sometimes*
después de...	*after . . .*
luego	*then, next*
mañana	*tomorrow*
nunca	*never*
por la mañana	*in the morning*
por la noche	*at night*
por la tarde	*in the afternoon*
siempre	*always*
tarde	*late*
temprano	*early*
todos los días	*every day*

Los deportes y juegos
(Sports and Games)

el ajedrez	*chess*
el básquetbol	*basketball*
el béisbol	*baseball*
el fútbol	*soccer*
el fútbol americano	*football*
los juegos de mesa	*table games*
los videojuegos	*video games*
el volibol	*volleyball*

Descripciones *(Descriptions)*

alto(a)	*tall*
antipático(a)	*unfriendly*
bajo(a)	*short (height)*
bonito(a)	*pretty*
bueno(a)	*good*
callado(a)	*quiet*
canoso(a)	*grey-haired*
castaño(a)	*dark brown*
ciego(a)	*blind*
cómico(a)	*funny*
corto(a)	*short (length)*
delgado(a)	*thin*
fácil	*easy*
gordo(a)	*fat*
grande	*big*
guapo(a)	*handsome*
inteligente	*smart*
interesante	*interesting*
joven	*young*
largo(a)	*long*
mayor	*older*
menor	*younger*
moreno(a)	*dark-haired, dark-skinned*
pelirrojo(a)	*red-haired*
pequeño(a)	*small, little*
perezoso(a)	*lazy*
pésimo(a)	*awful*
rubio(a)	*blonde*
simpático(a)	*nice*
sordo(a)	*deaf*
viejo(a)	*old*

La familia *(Family)*

la abuela	*grandmother*
el abuelo	*grandfather*
el gato	*cat*
la hermana	*sister*
el hermano	*brother*
la hija	*daughter*
el hijo	*son*
la madre/mamá	*mother/mom*
la nieta	*granddaughter*
el nieto	*grandson*
el padre/papá	*father/dad*
el perro	*dog*
la prima	*female cousin*
el primo	*male cousin*
la sobrina	*niece*
el sobrino	*nephew*
la tía	*aunt*
el tío	*uncle*

Los gustos *(Things we like)*

los amigos	*friends*
los animales	*animals*
los libros (de aventura, amor)	*(adventure, romance) books*
la música (de...)	*music (by . . .)*
películas	*movies*
las revistas	*magazines*

Repaso de Vocabulario

Las materias *(School subjects)*

el alemán	*German*
el arte	*art*
la biología	*biology*
las ciencias	*science*
la computación	*computer class*
la educación física	*physical education*
el español	*Spanish*
el francés	*French*
la historia	*history*
el inglés	*English*
las matemáticas	*math*
la química	*chemistry*
el salón de clase	*classroom*
el taller	*workshop*

Números 0–100 *(Numbers 0–100)*

cero	*zero*
uno	*one*
dos	*two*
tres	*three*
cuatro	*four*
cinco	*five*
seis	*six*
siete	*seven*
ocho	*eight*
nueve	*nine*
diez	*ten*
once	*eleven*
doce	*twelve*
trece	*thirteen*
catorce	*fourteen*
quince	*fifteen*
dieciséis	*sixteen*
diecisiete	*seventeen*
dieciocho	*eighteen*
diecinueve	*nineteen*
veinte	*twenty*
veintiuno	*twenty-one*
veintidós	*twenty-two*
veintitrés	*twenty-three*
veinticuatro	*twenty-four*
veinticinco	*twenty-five*
veintiséis	*twenty-six*
veintisiete	*twenty-seven*
veintiocho	*twenty-eight*
veintinueve	*twenty-nine*
treinta	*thirty*
treinta y uno	*thirty-one*
treinta y dos	*thirty-two*
...	
cuarenta	*forty*
cincuenta	*fifty*
sesenta	*sixty*
setenta	*seventy*
ochenta	*eighty*
noventa	*ninety*
cien	*one hundred*

Los quehaceres *(Chores)*

arreglar el cuarto	*to pick up your room*
ayudar en casa	*to help out at home*
cocinar	*to cook*
cortar el césped	*to cut the grass*
cuidar a los niños	*to take care of children*
hacer la cama	*to make the bed*
lavar los platos	*to wash the dishes*
limpiar	*to clean*
pasar la aspiradora	*to run the vacuum*
sacar la basura	*to take out the trash*

Vocabulario adicional

This list includes additional vocabulary that you may want to use to personalize activities. If you can't find a word you need here, try the Spanish-English and English-Spanish vocabulary sections, beginning on page R29.

Materias *(School Subjects)*

el álgebra	*algebra*
el cálculo	*calculus*
la contabilidad	*accounting*
la física	*physics*
la geometría	*geometry*
el italiano	*Italian*
el japonés	*Japanese*
el latín	*Latin*
la literatura	*literature*
el ruso	*Russian*

Celebraciones *(Celebrations)*

el bautizo	*baptism*
la canción	*song*
El Día de los Reyes	*Three Kings Day*
la Pascua Florida	*Easter*
las Pascuas	*Christmas*
el Ramadán	*Ramadan*
Rosh Hashaná	*Rosh Hashanah*

Comida *(Food)*

el ají picante (el chile)	*hot pepper*
el aguacate	*avocado*
las arvejas	*peas*
el azúcar	*sugar*
la banana (el guineo)	*banana*
la batida	*milkshake*
la cereza	*cherry*
la coliflor	*cauliflower*
el champiñón (el hongo)	*mushroom*
los condimentos	*seasonings*
los fideos	*noodles*
el filete de pescado	*fish fillet*
la lechuga	*lettuce*
la mayonesa	*mayonnaise*
el melón	*cantaloupe*
la mostaza	*mustard*
la pimienta	*pepper*
la piña	*pineapple*
el plátano	*plantain*
la sal	*salt*
el yogur	*yogurt*

Computadoras *(Computers)*

arrastrar	*to drag*
la búsqueda	*search*
buscar	*to search*
comenzar la sesión	*to log on*
la contraseña, el código	*password*
el disco duro	*hard drive*
en línea	*online*
grabar	*to save*
hacer clic	*to click*
la impresora	*printer*
imprimir	*to print*
el marcapáginas, el separador	*bookmark*
el ordenador	*computer*
la página Web inicial	*homepage*
el ratón	*mouse*
la Red	*the Net*
la tecla de aceptación	*return key*
la tecla de borrar, la tecla correctora	*delete key*
el teclado	*keyboard*
terminar la sesión	*to log off*
la unidad de CD-ROM	*CD-ROM drive*
el Web, la Telaraña Mundial	*World Wide Web*

De compras *(Shopping)*

cobrar	*to charge*
el dinero en efectivo	*cash*
el descuento	*discount*
en venta	*for sale*
la rebaja	*sale, sale price*
regatear	*to bargain*
la tarjeta de crédito	*credit card*
el (la) vendedor, -ora	*salesperson*

Deportes y pasatiempos (Sports and Hobbies)

el anuario	*yearbook*
las artes marciales	*martial arts*
la astronomía	*astronomy*
el ballet	*ballet*
el boxeo	*boxing*
coleccionar sellos (monedas, muñecas)	*to collect stamps (coins, dolls)*
coser	*to sew*
el drama	*drama*
la fotografía	*photography*
la gimnasia	*gymnastics*
jugar a las cartas	*to play cards*
jugar a las damas	*to play checkers*
la orquesta	*orchestra*
el patinaje en línea, (sobre hielo)	*inline (ice) skating*

En el cine o el teatro (At the Movies or Theater)

el actor	*actor*
actuar	*to act*
la actriz	*actress*
aplaudir	*to applaud*
la butaca	*box seat*
la escena	*scene*
el escenario	*stage*
el espectáculo	*performance, show*
la estrella	*star*
la pantalla	*screen*
el telón	*curtain*

En el consultorio (At the Clinic)

la alergia	*allergy*
el antibiótico	*antibiotic*
darle a uno una inyección	*to give someone a shot*
el dolor	*pain*
los escalofríos	*chills*
estornudar	*to sneeze*
la gripe	*flu*
la medicina	*medicine*
las pastillas, las píldoras	*pills, tablets*
el síntoma	*symptom*
la tos	*cough*
toser	*to cough*

En el zoológico (At the Zoo)

el ave, las aves	*bird, birds*
el canguro	*kangaroo*
la cebra	*zebra*
el cocodrilo	*crocodile*
el delfín	*dolphin*
el elefante	*elephant*
el gorila	*gorilla*
el hipopótamo	*hippopotamus*
la jirafa	*giraffe*
el león	*lion*
la foca	*seal*
el mono, el chango	*monkey*
el oso	*bear*
el oso polar	*polar bear*
el pingüino	*penguin*
la serpiente	*snake*
el tigre	*tiger*

En la casa (Around the House)

la alfombra	*rug, carpet*
el ático	*attic*
el balcón	*balcony*
las cortinas	*curtains*
el despertador	*alarm clock*
las escaleras	*stairs*
el espejo	*mirror*
el estante	*bookcase, shelf*
el fregadero	*kitchen sink*
la galería	*porch*
la lámpara	*lamp*
el lavamanos	*bathroom sink*
la lavadora	*washing machine*
la mesita de noche	*nightstand*
los muebles	*furniture*
la secadora	*dryer*

el sillón	*easy chair*
el sótano	*basement*
el timbre	*doorbell*
el tocador	*dresser*

En las afueras y en la ciudad *(Places around Town)*

la autopista	*highway*
el banco	*bank*
la esquina	*street corner*
la estación de autobuses (trenes)	*bus (train) station*
la fábrica	*factory*
la ferretería	*hardware store*
la farmacia	*drugstore*
la gasolinera	*gas station*
el hospital	*hospital*
la mezquita	*mosque*
el mercado	*market*
la oficina	*office*
la parada de autobuses	*bus stop*
la peluquería	*barbershop*
el puente	*bridge*
el rascacielos	*skyscraper*
el salón de belleza	*beauty salon*
el semáforo	*traffic light*
el supermercado	*supermarket*

Instrumentos musicales *(Musical Instruments)*

el acordeón	*accordion*
el arpa, las arpas	*harp*
la armónica	*harmonica*
el bajo	*bass*
la batería	*drum set*
el clarinete	*clarinet*
la flauta dulce	*recorder*
la flauta	*flute*
la guitarra	*guitar*
la mandolina	*mandolin*
las maracas	*maracas*
el oboe	*oboe*
el saxofón	*saxophone*
el sintetizador	*synthesizer*
el tambor	*drum*
el trombón	*trombone*
la trompeta	*trumpet*
la tuba	*tuba*
la tumbadora	*conga drum*
la viola	*viola*
el violín	*violin*

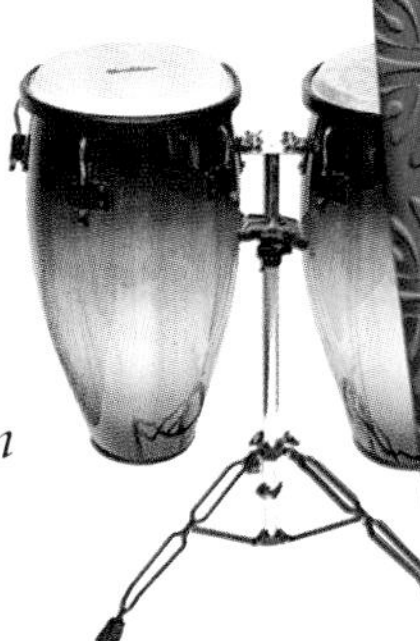

La familia *(Family)*

el (la) ahijado(a)	*godson, goddaughter*
el (la) bisabuelo(a)	*great-grandfather, great-grandmother*
el (la) biznieto(a)	*great-grandson, great-granddaughter*
el (la) cuñado(a)	*brother-in-law, sister-in-law*
el (la) hijastro(a)	*stepson, stepdaughter*
la madrina	*godmother*
la madrastra	*stepmother*
la nuera	*daughter-in-law*
el padrino	*godfather*
el padrastro	*stepfather*
el (la) suegro(a)	*father-in-law, mother-in-law*
el yerno	*son-in-law*

Palabras descriptivas *(Descriptive Words)*

amistoso(a)	*friendly*
la barba	*beard*
bien educado(a)	*well-mannered*
el bigote	*moustache*
calvo(a)	*bald*
la estatura	*height*
flaco(a)	*skinny*
lindo(a)	*pretty*
las pecas	*freckles*
las patillas	*sideburns*
el pelo lacio	*straight hair*
el pelo rizado	*curly hair*
pesar	*to weigh*
tranquilo(a)	*quiet*

Partes del cuerpo *(Parts of the Body)*

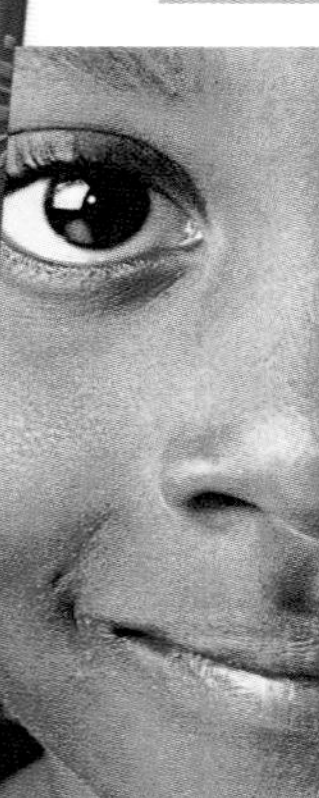

la barbilla	*chin*
las cejas	*eyebrows*
la cintura	*waist*
el codo	*elbow*
la frente	*forehead*
los labios	*lips*
la muñeca	*wrist*
el muslo	*thigh*
las pestañas	*eyelashes*
la rodilla	*knee*
la sien	*temple*
el tobillo	*ankle*
la uña	*nail*

Profesiones *(Professions)*

el (la) abogado(a)	*lawyer*
el (la) arquitecto(a)	*architect*
el (la) bombero(a)	*firefighter*
el (la) cartero(a)	*mail carrier*
el (la) cocinero(a)	*cook*
el (la) conductor, -ora	*driver*
el (la) constructor, -ora	*builder*
el (la) decorador, -ora	*interior decorator*
el (la) dentista	*dentist*
el (la) detective	*detective*
el (la) enfermero(a)	*nurse*
el (la) escritor, -a	*writer*
el hombre (la mujer) de negocios	*businessman, businesswoman*
el (la) ingeniero(a)	*engineer*
el (la) médico(a)	*doctor*
el (la) piloto(a)	*pilot*
el (la) (mujer) policía	*police officer*
el (la) secretario(a)	*secretary*

Regalos *(Gifts)*

la agenda	*agenda, daily planner*
el álbum	*album*
el animal de peluche	*stuffed animal*
los bombones	*chocolates*
el calendario	*calendar*
los claveles	*carnations*
la colonia	*cologne*
las flores	*flowers*
el llavero	*key chain*
el perfume	*perfume*
el rompecabezas	*puzzle*
las rosas	*roses*

Ropa *(Clothes)*

la bata	*robe*
la bufanda	*scarf*
el chaleco	*vest*
las chancletas	*flip-flops*
la corbata	*tie*
los guantes	*gloves*
las medias	*socks, stockings, hose*
las pantuflas, las zapatillas	*slippers*
el pañuelo	*handkerchief*
el paraguas	*umbrella*
la ropa interior	*underwear*
los tacones, los zapatos de tacón	*high heels*

Temas de actualidad *(Current Issues)*

el bosque tropical	*rain forest*
la contaminación	*pollution*
el crimen	*crime*
los derechos humanos	*human rights*
la economía	*economy*
la educación	*education*
la guerra	*war*

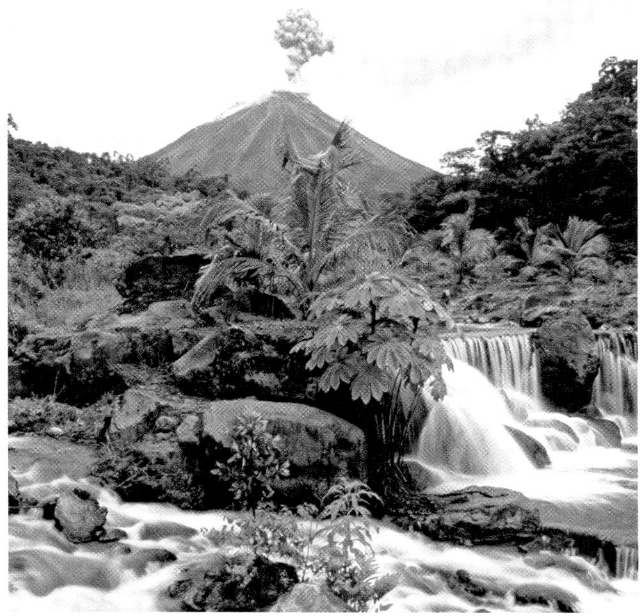

el medio ambiente	*environment*
el mundo	*world*
las noticias	*news*
la paz	*peace*
la política	*politics*
la tecnología	*technology*
la violencia	*violence*

Vacaciones *(Vacation)*

la agencia de viajes	*travel agency*
el andén	*train platform*
el asiento	*seat*
los cheques de viajero	*traveler's checks*
hacer una reservación	*to make a reservation*
el horario	*schedule, timetable*
el mar	*sea*
la parada	*stop*
el pasillo	*aisle*
reservado(a)	*reserved*
la ventanilla	*window*
la visa	*visa*
visitar los lugares de interés	*to sightsee*
volar	*to fly*

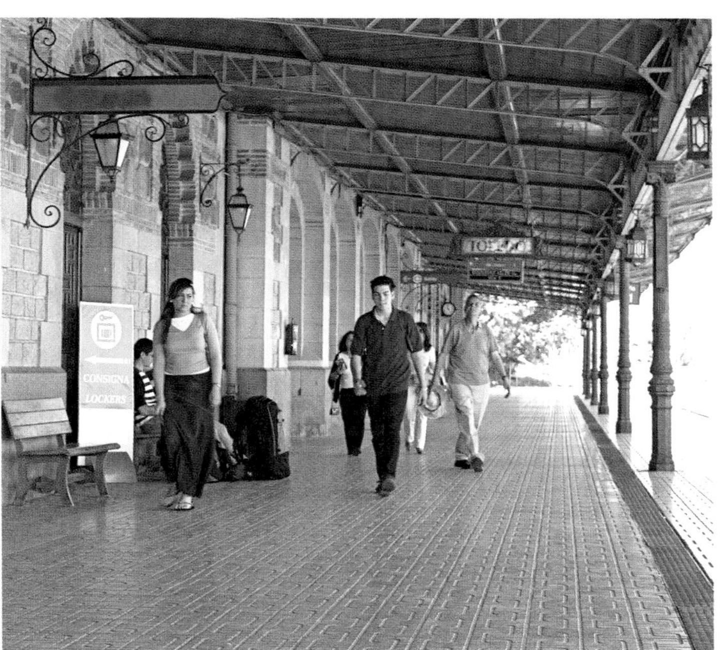

Refranes *(Proverbs)*

Más vale pájaro en mano que cien volando.
A bird in the hand is worth two in the bush.

Hijo no tenemos y nombre le ponemos.
Don't count your chickens before they're hatched.

Quien primero viene, primero tiene.
The early bird catches the worm.

Más vale tarde que nunca.
Better late than never.

El hábito no hace al monje.
Clothes don't make the man.

Más ven cuatro ojos que dos.
Two heads are better than one.

Querer es poder.
Where there's a will, there's a way.

Ojos que no ven, corazón que no siente.
Out of sight, out of mind.

No todo lo que brilla es oro.
All that glitters is not gold.

Caras vemos, corazones no sabemos.
You can't judge a book by its cover.

Donde una puerta se cierra, otra se abre.
Every cloud has a silver lining.

En boca cerrada no entran moscas.
Silence is golden.

Dime con quién andas y te diré quién eres.
Birds of a feather flock together.

Al mal tiempo buena cara.
When life gives you lemons, make lemonade.

Antes que te cases mira lo que haces.
Look before you leap.

Expresiones de ¡Exprésate!

Functions are the ways in which you use a language for particular purposes. In specific situations, such as in a restaurant, in a grocery store, or at school, you will want to communicate with those around you. In order to do that, you have to "function" in Spanish: you place an order, make a purchase, or talk about your class schedule.

Here is a list of the functions presented in ***¡Exprésate! 1A*** for Chapters 1–5 and in this book for Chapters 6–10 with the Spanish expressions you'll need to communicate in a wide range of situations. Following each function is the chapter and page number from the book where it is introduced.

Socializing

Greetings
Ch. 1, p. 8

Buenos días, señor.
Buenas noches, señora.
Buenas tardes, señorita.

Saying Goodbye
Ch. 1, p. 8

Adiós.	Hasta mañana.
Tengo que irme.	Nos vemos.
Hasta luego.	Hasta pronto.
Buenas noches.	

Asking how someone is and saying how you are
Ch. 1, p. 8

Hola, ¿cómo estás?	Estoy bien/regular/mal.
¿Cómo está usted?	¿Y usted?
¿Qué tal?	Más o menos.

Introducing people
Ch. 1, p. 10

Éste(a) es... Es un(a) compañero(a) de clase.	Encantado(a).
	Mucho gusto.
	Igualmente.
Ésta es... (Ella) es mi profesora de...	Éste es... (Él) es mi profesor de...

Inviting others to do something
Ch. 4, p. 158

¿Qué tal si vamos a...?
No sé. ¿Sabes qué? No tengo ganas.
Vienes conmigo a..., ¿no?
¡Claro que sí! Tengo mucha hambre.
Hay un concierto. Vas a ir, ¿verdad?
No, no voy a ir. Tengo que...

Talking on the phone
Ch. 8, p. 150

Aló/Bueno/Diga.	¿De parte de quién?
Hola. ¿Está...?	Habla...

Lo siento, no está. ¿Quieres dejarle un recado?
Sí, por favor, que me llame después.
No, gracias. Llamo más tarde.
Espera un momento, ya te lo (la) paso.

Greeting, introducing others, and saying goodbye
Ch. 9, p. 196

¡Qué gusto verte!	¡Tanto tiempo sin verte!
¿Qué hay de nuevo?	Lo de siempre.
Te presento a...	Tanto gusto.
¡Feliz...!	Chao, te llamo más tarde.
Cuídate.	Vale. Que te vaya bien.

Exchanging Information

Asking and giving names
Ch. 1, p. 6

¿Cómo te llamas?	¿Quién es...?
¿Cómo se llama usted?	Él (Ella) es...
	¿Cómo se llama él (ella)?
Me llamo... ¿Y tú?	Él (Ella) se llama...
Soy...	

Saying where you and others are from
Ch. 1, p. 11

¿De dónde eres?	¿De dónde es usted?
Soy de...	¿De dónde es...?
Es de...	

Asking and giving phone numbers
Ch. 1, p. 19

¿Cuál es tu teléfono?
Es tres-dos-cinco-uno-dos-tres-uno.
¿Cuál es el teléfono de...?
Es...

Saying what time it is
Ch. 1, p. 20

¿Qué hora es?
Son las seis y cuarto de la mañana.
Es la una en punto.
Son las... y trece de la tarde.
Son las... y media de la tarde.
Son las... menos cuarto.
Son las... menos diez de la noche.
Es mediodía.
Es medianoche.

Asking and giving the date and the day
Ch. 1, p. 21

¿Qué fecha es hoy?
Es el primero (dos, tres...) de enero.
¿Qué día es hoy?
Hoy es...

Asking how words are spelled and giving e-mail addresses
Ch. 1, p. 23

¿Cómo se escribe...?
Se escribe...
¿Cuál es tu correo electrónico?
Es...
¿Cuál es el correo electrónico de...?
Es eme punto ge-o-ene-zeta-a-ele-o arroba ere-e-de punto a-ere.

Describing people
Ch. 2, p. 49

¿Cómo es...?
... es moreno(a). También es... y un poco...
¿Cómo eres? ¿Eres cómico(a)?
Sí, soy bastante cómico(a).

Asking and saying how old someone is
Ch. 2, p. 52

¿Cuántos años tienes?
Tengo ... años.
¿Cuántos años tiene...?
... tiene ... años.
¿Cuándo es tu cumpleaños?
Es el 6 de mayo.
¿Cuándo es el cumpleaños de...?
Es el...

Describing things
Ch. 2, p. 66

¿Cómo es...?
Es muy...
Es bastante...
Es...
Es algo...

Talking about what you and others want to do
Ch. 3, p. 98

¿Qué quieres hacer hoy?
Ni idea.
¿Quieres ir a... conmigo?
Está bien.
No, gracias. No quiero ir a... hoy.

Talking about everyday activities
Ch. 3, p. 109

¿Qué haces los fines de semana?
Los sábados, cuando hace buen tiempo, voy...
¿Adónde vas...?
¿Qué hace... cuando hace mal tiempo?
Le gusta...
No va a ninguna parte.

Asking and saying how often
Ch. 3, p. 112

¿Con qué frecuencia vas a...?
Casi nunca. No me gusta...
¿Te gusta...?
Sí. Después de clases, casi siempre vamos a...
A veces vamos también a...

Talking about what you and others have or need
Ch. 4, p. 141

¿Necesitas algo para el colegio?
Sí, necesito muchas cosas.
No, no necesito nada.
¿Necesitas...?
Sí, necesito...
¿Tienes...?
Sí, tengo un montón.
No, no tengo.

Talking about classes
Ch. 4, p. 144

¿Qué clases tienes...?
Primero tengo... y después tengo...
¿Cuál es tu materia preferida?
Mi materia preferida es... Es fácil.
No me gusta la clase de... porque es difícil.

Talking about plans
Ch. 4, p. 155

¿Vas a ir a... en... el... por la...?
No, no voy a ir. El... tengo...
¿Qué vas a hacer el... próximo?
Por la tarde voy a... y después voy a ir a... Luego voy a...
¿A qué hora vas a llegar a...?
Voy a llegar temprano (a tiempo). No me gusta llegar tarde.

Describing people and family relationships
Ch. 5, p. 187
¿Cuántas personas hay en tu familia?
En mi familia somos... personas: mi...
¿Cómo son tus hermanos?
Todos usamos lentes. Somos... y tenemos... Mi... está en una silla de ruedas.
¿Cómo es tu...?
Es... Es una persona... y muy... Él (Ella) y mi... tienen... hijos pero no tienen...

Describing where someone lives
Ch. 5, p. 201
¿Dónde viven ustedes?
Vivimos en un apartamento. Está en un edificio grande de... pisos.
¿Cuál es tu dirección?
Mi dirección es calle..., número...
¿Cómo es tu casa?
Es bastante... Tiene... habitaciones, ...

Talking about your responsibilities
Ch. 5, p. 204
¿Qué haces para ayudar en casa?
A veces tengo que..., pero me parece bien. No es gran cosa.
¿Quién hace los quehaceres?
A menudo tengo que...
A... nunca le toca... Me parece injusto.
¿Qué te toca hacer a ti?
A mí siempre me toca... ¡Qué lata!

Commenting on food
Ch. 6, pp. 40–41
¿Qué vas a pedir?
¿Qué prefieres pedir para...?
Para tomar, puedes pedir...
En la mesa hay...
¿Qué tal si pruebas...? Son muy buenos(as) aquí.
¡Ay, no! Nunca pido... No me gusta.
Aquí preparan muy bien (mal)...
(No) estoy de acuerdo.
¡Qué ricos(as) están...!
Sí, me encantan.
¿Qué tal está(n)...?
Está(n) un poco...

Talking about meals
Ch. 6, p. 55
¿Qué desayunas?
Siempre desayuno...
¿Qué quieres hoy de almuerzo?
¿Qué tal si almorzamos...?
¿Qué hay de cena? Tengo mucha hambre.
Vamos a cenar...

Talking about your daily routine
Ch. 7, pp. 86–87
Por la mañana, tengo que...
Por la tarde, después de..., voy a...
Por la noche, necesito...
¿Estás listo(a)? ¿Qué te falta hacer?
¡Ay, no! Acabo de levantarme. Tengo que... antes de...
¿Qué tienes que hacer?
Tengo que..., pero no encuentro...

Talking about staying fit and healthy
Ch. 7, p. 90
¿Cómo te mantienes en forma?
... y... Entreno...
¿Qué haces para relajarte?
... También... o...

Offering and asking for help in a store
Ch. 8, p.136
¿En qué le puedo servir?
Busco...
Nada más estoy mirando.
¿Qué número/talla usa?
Uso el/la...
¿Cómo le queda(n)...?
Me queda(n) bien/mal.
Necesito una talla más grande/pequeña.
¿A qué hora cierra la tienda?
Cierra a las...

Saying where you went and what you did
Ch. 8, p. 147
¿Adónde fuiste ayer/anteayer/anoche?
Fui a... a buscar... (y compré)...
¿Qué hiciste el fin de semana pasado?
Pagué una fortuna por...

Talking about your plans
Ch. 9, p. 179
¿Qué vas a hacer...?
Pienso... o...
¿Qué planes tienen para...?
Pensamos pasarlo(la) con..., como siempre.

Talking about past holidays
Ch. 9, p. 182
¿Dónde pasaron... el año pasado?
Lo (la) pasamos en casa de...
¿Qué tal estuvo?
Estuvo a todo dar. Nos reunimos a...

Preparing for a party
Ch. 9, p. 193
¿Está todo listo para la fiesta?
¿Ya terminaste con los preparativos?
Sí. Anoche compré... y preparé...
¿Qué están haciendo...?
Están colgando...

Asking for and giving information
Ch. 10, pp. 224–225
¿Dónde puedo...?
Allí, en el...
Me puede decir dónde está(n)...?
Está(n) a la vuelta.
¿Sabe Ud. a qué hora sale/llega el vuelo...?
Lo puede ver allí en esa pantalla.
Sí, sale/llega a las...
¿Dónde se puede conseguir...?
Lo siento, no sé.

Reminding and reassuring
Ch. 10, p. 228
¿Ya sacaste el dinero?
Sí, ya lo saqué.
No, todavía no. Debo pasar por el cajero automático.
¿Ya hiciste la maleta?
No, todavía tengo que hacerla.
¡Ay, dejé... en casa!
No te preocupes. Puedes comprar... en cualquier tienda.

Talking about a trip
Ch. 10, pp. 238–239
¿Qué hiciste durante las vacaciones?
¡Qué divertido!
Recorrí la ciudad en... Luego, tomé... a...
¿Qué tal el viaje?
¡Fue estupendo!
¡Fue horrible!
¿Adónde fueron?
Fuimos a...
¿Qué hicieron?
Conocimos... y sacamos muchas fotos.
Luego pasamos por... y por fin...

Expressing Attitudes and Opinions

Talking about what you and others like
Ch. 2, p. 63

¿Te gusta(n)...?	Sí, me gusta(n) mucho.
No, no me gusta(n).	¿Te gusta(n) más... o...?
Me gusta(n) más...	Me da igual.

Talking about what you and others like to do
Ch. 3, pp. 94–95

A mis amigos y a mí nos gusta...	¿A... les gusta...?
	A mí me gusta...
¿Qué te gusta hacer?	Sí, porque les gusta...

Asking for and giving opinions
Ch. 8, p. 133
¿Qué te parece el (la)...?
Me parece... y cuesta mucho. ¡Es un robo!
¿Cómo me queda el (la)...?
Te queda muy bien. Y está a la (última) moda.
¿Y el (la)...? Cuesta... dólares.
¡Qué caro(a)! Además, está pasado(a) de moda.
El (La)... es una ganga, ¿verdad?
Tienes razón. Es muy barato(a).

Expressing hopes and wishes
Ch. 10, p. 242

Algún día me gustaría...	Espero ver...
Si tengo suerte, voy a...	Quiero conocer...

Expressing Feelings and Emotions

Talking about how you feel
Ch. 7, p. 101
Para cuidarte la salud, debes...
Te veo mal.
Es que estoy enfermo(a). Tengo catarro.
¿Qué te pasa? ¿Te duele algo?
Me siento (un poco)... y me duele(n)...
¿Qué tiene...?
Le duele(n)...

Persuading

Taking someone's order and requesting something
Ch. 6, p. 44

¿Qué desea (usted)?	¿Desea algo de postre?
Quisiera...	Sí, ¿me trae...?
¿Y para tomar?	¿Algo más?
Para tomar, quiero...	¿Nos trae..., por favor?

Offering help and giving instructions
Ch. 6, p. 58
¿Necesitas ayuda?
Sí, saca... y ponlo(la) en el horno/ el microondas.
¿Puedo ayudar?
Saca... del refrigerador.
¿Por qué no preparas...?
¿Pongo la mesa?
Sí, ponla, por favor.

Giving advice
Ch. 7, p. 104
¿Sabes qué? Comes muy mal. No debes comer tanto dulce ni grasa.
Para cuidarte mejor, debes... ¿Por qué no... más temprano?
No debes...

Síntesis gramatical

NOUNS AND ARTICLES

Gender of Nouns

In Spanish, nouns (words that name a person, place, or thing) are grouped into two classes or genders: masculine and feminine. All nouns, both persons and objects, fall into one of these groups. Most nouns that end in **-o** are masculine, and most nouns that end in **-a, -ción, -tad,** and **-dad** are feminine. Some nouns, such as **estudiante** and **cliente,** can be either masculine or feminine.

Masculine Nouns	Feminine Nouns
libro	casa
chico	universidad
cuaderno	situación
bolígrafo	mesa
vestido	libertad

FORMATION OF PLURAL NOUNS

	Add **-s** to nouns that end in a vowel.		Add **-es** to nouns that end in a consonant.		With nouns that end in **-z,** the **-z** changes to a **-c**.	
SINGULAR	libro	casa	profesor	papel	vez	lápiz
PLURAL	libro**s**	casa**s**	profesor**es**	papel**es**	ve**ces**	lápi**ces**

Definite Articles

There are words that signal the gender of the noun. One of these is the *definite article.* In English, there is one definite article: *the.* In Spanish, there are four: **el, la, los, las.**

SUMMARY OF DEFINITE ARTICLES

	Masculine	Feminine
SINGULAR	**el** chico	**la** chica
PLURAL	**los** chicos	**las** chicas

CONTRACTIONS

a + el → **al**
de + el → **del**

Indefinite Articles

Another group of words that are used with nouns are the *indefinite articles:* **un, una,** (*a* or *an*) and **unos, unas** (*some* or *a few*).

	Masculine	Feminine
SINGULAR	**un** chico	**una** chica
PLURAL	**unos** chicos	**unas** chicas

Pronouns

Subject Pronouns	Direct Object Pronouns	Indirect Object Pronouns	Objects of Prepositions	Reflexive Pronouns
yo	**me**	**me**	**mí**	**me**
tú	**te**	**te**	**ti**	**te**
él, ella, usted	**lo, la**	**le**	**él, ella, usted**	**se**
nosotros, nosotras	**nos**	**nos**	**nosotros, nosotras**	**nos**
vosotros, vosotras	**os**	**os**	**vosotros, vosotras**	**os**
ellos, ellas, ustedes	**los, las**	**les**	**ellos, ellas, ustedes**	**se**

ADJECTIVES

Adjectives are words that describe nouns. The adjective must agree in gender (masculine or feminine) and number (singular or plural) with the noun it modifies. Adjectives that end in -**e** or a consonant only agree in number.

		Masculine	Feminine
Adjectives that end in **-o** or **-a**	SINGULAR PLURAL	chico alt**o** chicos alt**os**	chica alt**a** chicas alt**as**
Adjectives that end in **-e**	SINGULAR PLURAL	chico inteligent**e** chicos inteligent**es**	chica inteligent**e** chicas inteligent**es**
Adjectives that end in a consonant	SINGULAR PLURAL	examen difícil exámenes difícil**es**	clase difícil clases difícil**es**

Demonstrative Adjectives

	Masculine	Feminine		Masculine	Feminine
SINGULAR PLURAL	**este** chico **estos** chicos	**esta** chica **estas** chicas	SINGULAR PLURAL	**ese** chico **esos** chicos	**esa** chica **esas** chicas

When demonstratives are used as pronouns, they match the gender and number of the noun they replace and are written with an accent mark: **éste, éstos, ésta, éstas, ése, ésos, ésa, ésas**.

Possessive Adjectives

These words also modify nouns and show ownership or relationship between people (*my* car, *his* book, *her* mother).

Singular		Plural	
Masculine	**Feminine**	**Masculine**	**Feminine**
mi libro	**mi** casa	**mis** libros	**mis** casas
tu libro	**tu** casa	**tus** libros	**tus** casas
su libro	**su** casa	**sus** libros	**sus** casas
nuestro libro	**nuestra** casa	**nuestros** libros	**nuestras** casas
vuestro libro	**vuestra** casa	**vuestros** libros	**vuestras** casas

Comparatives

Comparatives are used to compare people or things. With comparisons of inequality, the same structure is used with adjectives, adverbs, or nouns. With comparisons of equality, **tan** is used with adjectives and adverbs, and **tanto/a/os/as** with nouns.

COMPARISONS OF INEQUALITY

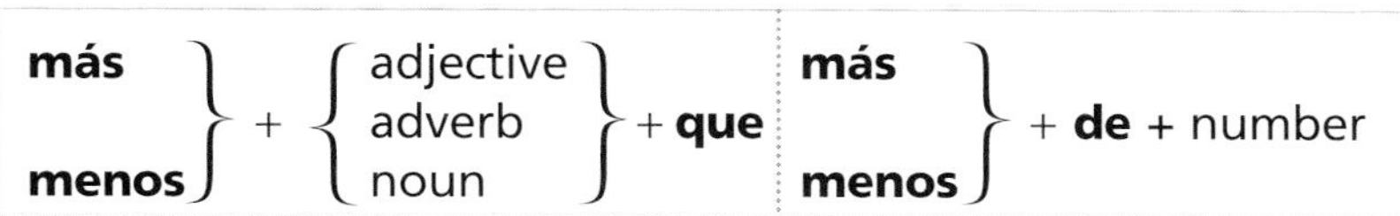
más / **menos** + adjective / adverb / noun + **que**
más / **menos** + **de** + number

COMPARISONS OF EQUALITY

tan + adjective or adverb + **como**
tanto/a/os/as + noun + **como**

These adjectives have irregular comparative forms.

bueno(a) *good*	malo(a) *bad*	joven *young*	viejo(a) *old*
mejor(es) *better*	**peor(es)** *worse*	**menor(es)** *younger*	**mayor(es)** *older*

Ordinal Numbers

Ordinal numbers are used to express ordered sequences. They agree in number and gender with the noun they modify. The ordinal numbers **primero** and **tercero** drop the final **o** before a singular, masculine noun. Ordinal numbers are seldom used after 10. Cardinal numbers are used instead: **Alfonso XIII, Alfonso Trece.**

1st	**primero/a**	**5th**	**quinto/a**	**9th**	**noveno/a**
2nd	**segundo/a**	**6th**	**sexto/a**	**10th**	**décimo/a**
3rd	**tercero/a**	**7th**	**séptimo/a**		
4th	**cuarto/a**	**8th**	**octavo/a**		

Affirmative and Negative Expressions

Affirmative	Negative
algo	**nada**
alguien	**nadie**
alguno (algún), -a	**ninguno (ningún), -a**
o ... o	**ni ... ni**
siempre	**nunca**

Interrogative words

¿Adónde?	**¿Cuándo?**	**¿De dónde?**	**¿Qué?**
¿Cómo?	**¿Cuánto(a)?**	**¿Dónde?**	**¿Quién(es)?**
¿Cuál(es)?	**¿Cuántos(as)?**	**¿Por qué?**	

Adverbs

Adverbs make the meaning of a verb, an adjective, or another adverb more definite. These are some common adverbs of frequency.

siempre	*always*	**casi nunca**	*almost never*
nunca	*never*	**a veces**	*sometimes*
todos los días	*every day*		

Prepositions

Prepositions are words that show the relationship of a noun or pronoun to another word. These are common prepositions in Spanish.

a	*to*	**debajo**	*under*	**hacia**	*toward*
al lado	*next to*	**delante**	*before*	**hasta**	*until*
antes de	*before*	**desde**	*from*	**para**	*for, in order to*
arriba	*over, above*	**detrás**	*behind*	**por**	*for, by*
con	*with*	**en**	*in, on*	**sin**	*without*
de	*of, from*	**encima**	*over, on top of*		

VERBS

Present Tense of Regular Verbs

In Spanish, we use a formula to conjugate regular verbs. The endings change in each person, but the stem of the verb remains the same.

Infinitive	habl**ar**		com**er**		escrib**ir**	
Present	habl**o**	habl**amos**	com**o**	com**emos**	escrib**o**	escrib**imos**
	habl**as**	habl**áis**	com**es**	com**éis**	escrib**es**	escrib**ís**
	habl**a**	habl**an**	com**e**	com**en**	escrib**e**	escrib**en**

Verbs with Irregular *yo* Forms

hacer		poner		saber		salir		traer	
hago	hacemos	**pongo**	ponemos	**sé**	sabemos	**salgo**	salimos	**traigo**	traemos
haces	hacéis	pones	ponéis	sabes	sabéis	sales	salís	traes	traéis
hace	hacen	pone	ponen	sabe	saben	sale	salen	trae	traen

tener		venir		ver		conocer	
tengo	tenemos	**vengo**	venimos	**veo**	vemos	**conozco**	conocemos
tienes	tenéis	vienes	venís	ves	veis	conoces	conocéis
tiene	tienen	viene	vienen	ve	ven	conoce	conocen

Verbs with Irregular Forms

ser		estar		ir	
soy	somos	estoy	estamos	voy	vamos
eres	sois	estás	estáis	vas	vais
es	son	está	están	va	van

Present Progressive

The present progressive in English is formed by using the verb *to be* plus the *-ing* form of another verb. In Spanish, the present progressive is formed by using the verb **estar** plus the -**ndo** form of another verb.

-ar verbs	**-er** and **-ir** verbs
hablar → estoy habl**ando**	comer → está com**iendo**
trabajar → estás trabaj**ando**	escribir → estamos escrib**iendo**

For **-er** and **-ir** verbs with a stem that ends in a vowel, the **-iendo** changes to **-yendo:**
leer → están le**yendo**

Stem-Changing Verbs

In Spanish, some verbs have an irregular stem in the present tense. The final vowel of the stem changes from **e** → **ie,** **o** → **ue,** **u** → **ue,** and **e** → **i** in all forms except **nosotros** and **vosotros**.

e → ie		**o → ue**		**u → ue**		**e → i**	
preferir		**poder**		**jugar**		**pedir**	
pref**ie**ro	preferimos	p**ue**do	podemos	j**ue**go	jugamos	p**i**do	pedimos
pref**ie**res	preferís	p**ue**des	podéis	j**ue**gas	jugáis	p**i**des	pedís
pref**ie**re	pref**ie**ren	p**ue**de	p**ue**den	j**ue**ga	j**ue**gan	p**i**de	p**i**den

Some **e → ie** stem-changing verbs are:		Some **o → ue** stem-changing verbs are:		Some **e → i** stem-changing verbs are:
empezar	**venir**	**almorzar**	**dormir**	**vestirse**
pensar	**merendar**	**llover**	**probar**	**servir**
querer	**calentar**	**encontrar**	**acostarse**	
nevar	**tener**	**volver**	**costar**	

Síntesis gramatical

The Verbs *gustar* and *encantar*

The verb endings for **gustar** and **encantar** always agree with what is liked or loved. The indirect object pronouns always precede the verb forms.

gustar (to like)		encantar (to really like or love)	
one thing:	more than one:	one thing:	more than one:
me, **te**, **le**, **nos**, **os**, **les** } **gusta**	**me**, **te**, **le**, **nos**, **os**, **les** } **gustan**	**me**, **te**, **le**, **nos**, **os**, **les** } **encanta**	**me**, **te**, **le**, **nos**, **os**, **les** } **encantan**

Verbs with Reflexive Pronouns

If the subject and object of a verb are the same, include the reflexive pronoun with the verb.

lavarse		ponerse		vestirse	
me lavo	nos lavamos	me pongo	nos ponemos	me visto	nos vestimos
te lavas	os laváis	te pones	os ponéis	te vistes	os vestís
se lava	se lavan	se pone	se ponen	se viste	se visten

Here are other verbs with reflexive pronouns.

acostarse	**bañarse**	**maquillarse**	**secarse**
afeitarse	**levantarse**	**peinarse**	**sentirse**

Preterite of Regular, Irregular, and Spelling-Change Verbs

The preterite is used to talk about what happened at a specific point in time.

Infinitive	Preterite of Regular Verbs	
habl**ar**	habl**é**	habl**amos**
	habl**aste**	habl**asteis**
	habl**ó**	habl**aron**
com**er**	com**í**	com**imos**
	com**iste**	com**isteis**
	com**ió**	com**ieron**
escrib**ir**	escrib**í**	escrib**imos**
	escrib**iste**	escrib**isteis**
	escrib**ió**	escrib**ieron**

hacer	ir	ser	ver
hice	fui	fui	vi
hiciste	fuiste	fuiste	viste
hizo	fue	fue	vio
hicimos	fuimos	fuimos	vimos
hicisteis	fuisteis	fuisteis	visteis
hicieron	fueron	fueron	vieron

sacar	llegar	comenzar
saqué	llegué	comencé
sacaste	llegaste	comenzaste
sacó	llegó	comenzó
sacamos	llegamos	comenzamos
sacasteis	llegasteis	comenzasteis
sacaron	llegaron	comenzaron

Imperative Mood

The imperative is used to tell people to do things. Its forms are sometimes referred to as *commands*. Regular affirmative commands are formed by dropping the **s** from the end of the **tú** form of the verb. For negative commands, switch the **-as** ending to **-es** and the **-es** ending to **-as.**

(tú) hablas → habla (no hables)	you speak → speak (don't speak)
(tú) escribes → escribe (no escribas)	you write → write (don't write)
(tú) pides → pide (no pidas)	you ask for → ask for (don't ask for)

Some verbs have irregular **tú** imperative forms.

tener → ten (no tengas)	ser → sé (no seas)
venir → ven (no vengas)	hacer → haz (no hagas)
poner → pon (no pongas)	salir → sal (no salgas)
ir → ve (no vayas)	decir → di (no digas)

The Verbs *ser* and *estar*

Both **ser** and **estar** mean *to be*, but they differ in their uses.

Use **ser:**

1. with nouns to identify and define the subject
   La mejor estudiante de la clase es Katia.
2. with **de** to indicate place of origin, ownership, or material
   Carmen es de Venezuela.
   Este libro es de mi abuela.
   La blusa es de algodón.
3. to describe identifying characteristics, such as physical and personality traits, nationality, religion, and profession
   Mi tío es profesor. Es simpático e inteligente.
4. to express the time, date, season, or where an event is taking place
   Hoy es sábado y la fiesta es a las ocho.

Use **estar:**

1. to indicate location or position of the subject
   Lima está en Perú.
2. to describe a condition that is subject to change
   Maricarmen está triste.
3. with the present participle (**-ndo** form) to describe an action in progress
   Mario está escribiendo un poema.
4. to convey the idea of *to look, to feel, to seem, to taste*
   Tu hermano está muy guapo hoy.
   La sopa está deliciosa.

Síntesis gramatical

Common Expressions

EXPRESSIONS WITH *TENER*

tener ... años	*to be . . . years old*	**tener (mucha) prisa**	*to be in a (big) hurry*
tener mucho calor	*to be very hot*	**tener que**	*to have to*
tener ganas de...	*to feel like . . .*	**tener (la) razón**	*to be right*
tener mucho frío	*to be very cold*	**tener mucha sed**	*to be very thirsty*
tener mucha hambre	*to be very hungry*	**tener mucho sueño**	*to be very sleepy*
tener mucho miedo	*to be very afraid*	**tener mucha suerte**	*to be very lucky*

EXPRESSIONS OF TIME

To ask how long someone has been doing something, use:
¿Cuánto tiempo hace que + present tense?

To say how long someone has been doing something, use:
Hace + quantity of time + **que** + present tense.
Hace **seis meses** que **vivo en Los Ángeles.**
You can also use:
present tense + **desde hace** + quantity of time
Vivo en Los Ángeles desde hace **seis meses.**

WEATHER EXPRESSIONS

Hace muy buen tiempo.	*The weather is very nice.*
Hace mucho calor.	*It's very hot.*
Hace fresco.	*It's cool.*
Hace mucho frío.	*It's very cold.*
Hace muy mal tiempo.	*The weather is very bad.*
Hace mucho sol.	*It's very sunny.*
Hace mucho viento.	*It's very windy.*
But:	
Está lloviendo mucho.	*It's raining a lot.*
Hay mucha neblina.	*It's very foggy.*
Está nevando.	*It's snowing.*
Está nublado.	*It's overcast.*

Vocabulario español-inglés

This vocabulary includes almost all words in the textbook, both active (for production) and passive (for recognition only). An entry in **boldface** type indicates that the word or phrase is active. Active words and phrases are practiced in the chapter and are listed on the **Repaso de gramática** and **Repaso de vocabulario** pages at the end of each chapter. You are expected to know and be able to use active vocabulary.

All other words are for recognition only. These words are found in exercises, in optional and visual material, in **Instrucciones** on pages xviii–xix, in **Geocultura,** which is referenced by chapter (1G), **Comparaciones, Leamos y escribamos, También se puede decir,** and **Literatura y variedades.** You can usually understand the meaning of these words and phrases from the context or you can look them up in this vocabulary index. Many words have more than one definition; the definitions given here correspond to the way the words are used in ***¡Exprésate!.***

Nouns are listed with definite articles and plural forms when the plural forms aren't formed according to general rules. The number after each entry refers to the chapter where the word or phrase first appears or where it becomes an active vocabulary word. This vocabulary index follows the rules of the **Real Academia,** with **ch** and **ll** in the same sequence as in the English alphabet.

Stem changes are indicated in parentheses after the verb: **poder (ue).**

a *to,* 3; *on,* 4; *at,* 8; a base de *based on,* 6; a continuación *that follows,* 7; a finales *at the end,* 10G; **a la (última) moda** *in the (latest) style,* 8; a la vez *at the same time,* 8; **a la vuelta** *around the corner,* 10; **A ...les gusta...** *They like to . . .,* 3; **a menudo** *often,* 5; **¿A qué hora vas a...?** *What time are you going to . . .?,* 4; **a tiempo** *on time,* 4; **a todo dar** *great,* 9; **Estuvo a todo dar.** *It was great.,* 9; a través de *through,* 5G; **a veces** *sometimes,* 3
abordar *to board,* 10
abrazar *to hug,* 9
el abrazo *hug,* 9
el abrigo *(over)coat,* 8
abril *April,* 1
abrir *to open,* 4; **abrir regalos** *to open gifts,* 9
la abuela *grandmother,* 5
el abuelo *grandfather,* 5
los abuelos *grandparents,* 5
aburrido(a) *boring,* 2; **estar aburrido(a)** *to be bored,* 7
acabar de *to just (have done something),* 7
acampar *to camp,* 3
acariciar *to caress,* 7
la acción *action,* 2
el aceite de oliva *olive oil,* 1G
el acento *accent,* 1; el acento ortográfico *written accent,* 8
acerca de *about,* 8
acompañar *to go with,* 6; *to accompany,* 1G; estar acompañada *to be accompanied,* 3
acordarse (ue) *to remember,* 9
acostarse (ue) *to go to bed,* 7
la actividad *activity,* 3
activo(a) *active,* 2
la actualidad *present time,* 6
el acuerdo *agreement;* **Estoy de acuerdo.** *I agree.,* 6; **No estoy de acuerdo.** *I disagree.,* 6
adaptado(a) *adapted,* 5G
además *besides,* 8
Adiós. *Good-bye.,* 1
adivinar *to guess,* 2
el adjetivo *adjective,* 5
la admiración *admiration,* 1
admirar *to admire,* 10
el adolescente *adolescent,* 3
¿adónde? *where?,* 8; **Adónde fuiste?** *Where did you go?,* 8; **¿Adónde vas...?** *Where do you go . . .?,* 3
la aduana *customs,* 10
el adulto *adult,* 7
los aeróbicos *aerobics,* 7; hacer aeróbicos *to do aerobics,* 7
el aeropuerto *airport,* 10
afeitarse *to shave,* 7
afuera *outside,* 3
las afueras *suburbs,* 5
la agencia inmobiliaria *real estate agency,* 5
el agente, la agente *agent,* 10
agitar *to shake,* 3
agosto *August,* 1
el agua *water,* 6
el águila *eagle,* 7
ahí *there,* 4
ahora *now,* 9
ahorrar *to save money,* 8
el aire *air,* 3; el aire central *central air conditioning,* 5; el aire libre *open air,* 8
el ajedrez *chess,* 1
el ají *hot pepper,* 10G
el ajo *garlic,* 6
ajustado(a) *tight-fitting,* 8
al (a + el) *to, to the,* 3; *upon,* 6; al fin *finally,* 10; **al lado de** *next to,* 5
la alberca *swimming pool,* 3
alcanzar *to reach,* 7G
la alcoba *bedroom,* 5
alegre *happy,* 2
el alemán *German,* 4
el alfabeto *alphabet,* 1
algo *something, anything,* 4; **algo** + adjective *kind of* + adjective, 2
el algodón *cotton,* 8; **de algodón** *made of cotton,* 8
algún día *one day,* 10
algunas *some,* 2
el alimento *food,* 6
alistarse *to get ready,* 7

Vocabulario español-inglés

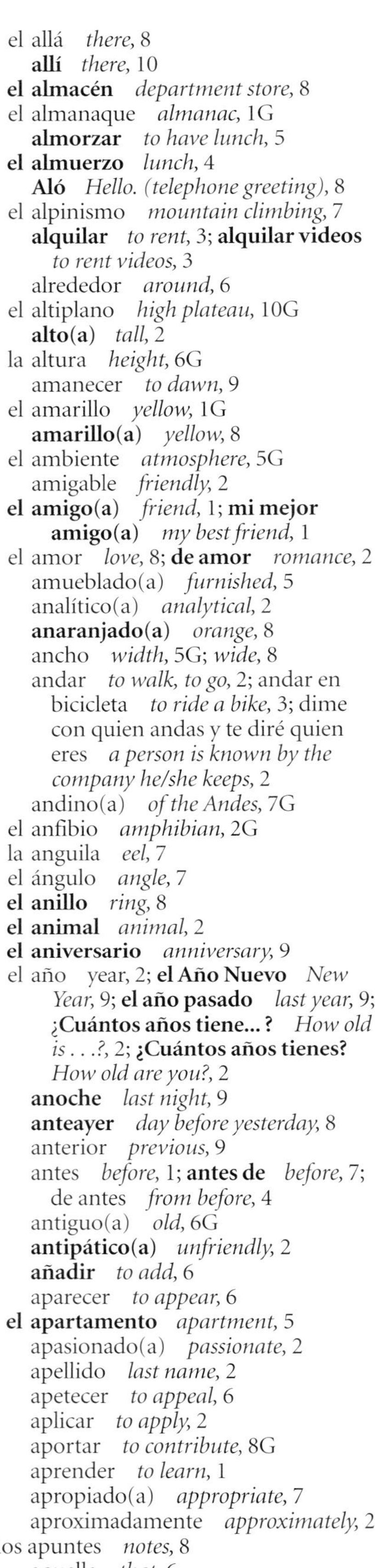

el allá *there,* 8
allí *there,* 10
el almacén *department store,* 8
el almanaque *almanac,* 1G
almorzar *to have lunch,* 5
el almuerzo *lunch,* 4
Aló *Hello. (telephone greeting),* 8
el alpinismo *mountain climbing,* 7
alquilar *to rent,* 3; **alquilar videos** *to rent videos,* 3
alrededor *around,* 6
el altiplano *high plateau,* 10G
alto(a) *tall,* 2
la altura *height,* 6G
amanecer *to dawn,* 9
el amarillo *yellow,* 1G
amarillo(a) *yellow,* 8
el ambiente *atmosphere,* 5G
amigable *friendly,* 2
el amigo(a) *friend,* 1; **mi mejor amigo(a)** *my best friend,* 1
el amor *love,* 8; **de amor** *romance,* 2
amueblado(a) *furnished,* 5
analítico(a) *analytical,* 2
anaranjado(a) *orange,* 8
ancho *width,* 5G; *wide,* 8
andar *to walk, to go,* 2; andar en bicicleta *to ride a bike,* 3; dime con quien andas y te diré quien eres *a person is known by the company he/she keeps,* 2
andino(a) *of the Andes,* 7G
el anfibio *amphibian,* 2G
la anguila *eel,* 7
el ángulo *angle,* 7
el anillo *ring,* 8
el animal *animal,* 2
el aniversario *anniversary,* 9
el año year, 2; **el Año Nuevo** *New Year,* 9; **el año pasado** *last year,* 9; **¿Cuántos años tiene... ?** *How old is . . .?,* 2; **¿Cuántos años tienes?** *How old are you?,* 2
anoche *last night,* 9
anteayer *day before yesterday,* 8
anterior *previous,* 9
antes *before,* 1; **antes de** *before,* 7; de antes *from before,* 4
antiguo(a) *old,* 6G
antipático(a) *unfriendly,* 2
añadir *to add,* 6
aparecer *to appear,* 6
el apartamento *apartment,* 5
apasionado(a) *passionate,* 2
apellido *last name,* 2
apetecer *to appeal,* 6
aplicar *to apply,* 2
aportar *to contribute,* 8G
aprender *to learn,* 1
apropiado(a) *appropriate,* 7
aproximadamente *approximately,* 2
los apuntes *notes,* 8
aquella *that,* 6
aquello *that,* 4
aquí *here,* 6
árabe *Arab,* 5G
el árbol *tree,* 1; la copa del árbol *top of the tree,* 4G
los aretes *earrings,* 8
la argamasa *mortar,* 10G
argentino(a) *Argentine,* 7
árido(a) *dry,* 10G
la armonía *harmony,* 2
armonizar *to harmonize,* 7G
el arquitecto *architect,* 3G
arquitectónico(a) *architectural,* 10G
la arquitectura *architecture,* 2G
arreglar *to clean up,* 5; **arreglar el cuarto** *to clean the room,* 5
el arrendamiento *rental,* 10
la arroba *@,* 1
el arroz *rice,* 6
el arte *art,* 4; las artes plásticas *sculpture,* 2
la artesanía *crafts,* 4
el artista, la artista *artist,* 1
artístico(a) *artistic,* 2
asegurar *to reassure,* 6
el asentamiento *colony, settlement,* 8G
el aseo *restroom,* 10
así *like this;* así que *so,* 8; Así es, *That's how it is.,* 2
asistente *assistant,* 10
asistir a *to attend,* 4
asomar *to peak out,* 9
el asterisco *asterisk,* 7
atlético(a) *athletic,* 2
el atole *Mexican drink made of cornmeal, milk or water, and flavoring,* 6
atraer *to attract,* 1G
atravesar *to cross,* 10G
atreverse *to dare,* 9
el atún *tuna fish,* 6
los audífonos *headphones,* 8
el auditorio *auditorium,* 4
aun *even,* 2
aún *still,* 10
aunque *even though,* 6
el autobús *bus,* 10
el autor *author,* 7
el autorretrato *self-portrait,* 6G
avanzado(a) *advanced,* 10G
el ave (pl. las aves) *bird,* 4G
la aventura *adventure,* 2
averiguar *to find out,* 10
el avión *airplane,* 10; por avión *by plane,* 10
¡Ay no! *Oh, no!,* 6
¡ay! *ouch!,* 8
ayer *yesterday,* 8
el aymara indigenous *language in Peru,* 10G
la ayuda *help,* 6
ayudar *to help,* 5; **ayudar en casa** *to help out at home,* 5; estamos ayudando *we are helping,* 3
el azúcar *sugar,* 6
el azul *blue,* 1G
azul *blue,* 5

la bahía *bay,* 8G
bailar *to dance,* 3; bailando *dancing,* 1; ponerse a bailar *to start dancing,* 3
la bailarina *dancer (fem.),* 3
el baile *dance,* 3
bajar *to descend,* 7; **bajar de peso** *to lose weight,* 7
bajo(a) *short,* 2
balanceado(a) *balanced,* 6
el balcón *balcony,* 5
balear *to shoot,* 5
el ballet *ballet,* 1
el baloncesto *basketball,* 3
bañarse *to bathe,* 7
la bandeja *platter,* 7G
la bandera *banner,* 9
el bandido *bandit,* 5
el baño *bathroom,* 5; *restroom,* 10
barato(a) *inexpensive,* 8
la barbacoa *barbecue,* 3G
el barco *boat,* 10; el barquito *little boat,* 5
la barranca *cliff,* 6G
el barrio *neighborhood,* 7G
básico(a) *basic,* 6
el básquetbol *basketball,* 3
basta *it's enough,* 5
bastante + adjective *quite, pretty* + adjective, 2
la basura *trash,* 5; **sacar la basura** *to take out the trash,* 5
la batalla *battle,* 3G
el batido *milkshake,* 8
el bebé, la bebé *baby,* 1
beber *to drink,* 4; **beber ponche** *to drink punch,* 9
la bebida *drink,* 6
la beca *scholarship,* 10
el béisbol *baseball,* 3
bello(a) *beautiful,* 2G
la biblioteca *library,* 4
la bicicleta *bike,* 3; **montar en bicicleta** *to ride a bike,* 3
bien *all right, fine,* 1; *really,* 2; bien dicho *well said,* 6; **está bien** *it's okay,* 3; **estoy bien** *I'm fine,* 1; **me parece bien** *it's all right/seems fine to me,* 5; **quedar bien** *to fit well,* 8; **Que te vaya bien.** *Hope things go well for you.,* 9
bienvenido *welcome,* 10
el billete *ticket,* 10

la billetera *wallet,* 10
la biología *biology,* 4
blanco(a) *white,* 8; **en blanco** *blank,* 8
el blanquillo *egg,* 6
la blusa *blouse,* 8
la boca *mouth,* 7
el bocadillo *sandwich* (Spain), 6, *finger food* (Dom. Rep.), 9
el bocadito *small servings of food,* 7G
las bocas *finger food* (Costa Rica), 9
la boda *wedding,* 9
la boleta *ticket,* 10
el boleto de avión *plane ticket,* 10
el bolígrafo *pen,* 4
la bolsa *purse,* 8; *bag,* 8; *travel bag,* 10
la bomba *music and dance style,* 2G
la bombilla *straw used for sipping* ***mate,*** 7
bonito(a) *pretty,* 2
el borde *edge,* 7G
el borrador *rough draft,* 1
el bosque *forest,* 2G; el bosque húmedo *rain forest,* 4G
la botana *finger food* (Mex.), 9
botar *to throw out,* 5
las botas *boots,* 8
el bote *boat,* 9G; **el bote de vela** *sailboat,* 10; **pasear en bote de vela** *to go out in a sailboat,* 10
el brazo *arm,* 7
brillar *to shine,* 7
brindar *to offer,* 5
el bróculi *broccoli,* 6
bueno(a) *good,* 2; **Buenas noches.** *Good evening., Good night.,* 1; **Buenas tardes.** *Good afternoon.,* 1; **Buenos días.** *Good morning.,* 1
Bueno. *Hello. (telephone greeting),* 8
burlarse de *to make fun of,* 8
el burro *donkey,* 1
buscar *to look for,* 7; **buscar un pasatiempo** *to find a hobby,* 7; búsquenme *look for me,* 3

el caballo de paso *horse with high-stepping gait,* 10G
caber *to fit,* 10G
la cabeza *head,* 7
el cacao *cocoa,* 6G
cada *each,* xxii; cada uno(a) *each one,* 6; cada vez *each time,* 8
el café *coffee,* 6; **el café con leche** *coffee with milk,* 6; *brown,* 1G; **de color café** *brown,* 5
la cafetería *cafeteria,* 4; *coffee shop,* 6
la caída de agua *waterfall,* 7G
el caimán *caiman (reptile),* 7G
la caja *box,* 9
el cajero automático *automatic teller machine,* 10
la calabaza *squash, pumpkin,* 6G; la calabacita *gourd used for* ***mate*** *tea,* 7G
los calcetines *socks,* 8; **un par de calcetines** *a pair of socks,* 8
la calculadora *calculator,* 4
la calefacción *heating,* 5; la calefacción central *central heating,* 5
el calendario *calendar,* 1
calentar (ie) *to heat up,* 6
caliente *hot,* 6
callado(a) *quiet,* 5
la calle *street,* 2G
el calor *heat,* 3; **Hace calor.** *It's hot.,* 3; **tener calor** *to be hot,* 7
la caloría *calorie,* 6
la cama *bed,* 5; **hacer la cama** *to make the bed,* 5
la cámara *camera,* 10; **la cámara desechable** *disposable camera,* 10
el camarero *waiter,* 6
cambiar *to change,* 4
cambiar dinero *to change money,* 10
el cambio *change,* 9
caminar *to walk,* 7
el camino *path,* 10G
el camión *bus (Mex.),* 10
la camisa *shirt,* 8
la camiseta *T-shirt,* 8; la camiseta deportiva *sport shirt,* 8
el camote *sweet potato,* 4G
el campo *countryside,* 5
la canción *song,* 8
candidato(a) *candidate,* 4
la canoa *canoe,* 10
el cañón *canyon,* 6G
canoso(a) *graying,* 5
cansado(a) *tired,* 7; **estar cansado(a)** *to be tired,* 7
cantar *to sing,* 3; cantaba *he sang,* 9
el cantar *singing,* 2
la cantidad *amount,* 2; *quantity,* 6; las cantidades *large numbers,* 6
el canto *song,* 1G
la capilla *chapel,* 3G
la capital *capital,* 1G
el capítulo *chapter,* 1
la cara *face,* 7; cara de tortilla *tortilla face,* 1
el carácter *character,* 5
la característica *characteristic,* 6
caracterizar *to characterize,* 5G
la cárcel *jail,* 8
caribeño(a) *Caribbean,* 4G
el cariño *affection; (addressing someone) dear, 3;* con cariño *affectionately,* 10
la carne *meat, beef,* 6; la carne de res *beef,* 6; la carne molida *ground beef,* 6
el carnet de identidad *ID,* 10
caro(a) *expensive,* 8
la carpeta *folder,* 4
la carreta *cart,* 4G
el carro *car,* 2
la carroza *float,* 9G
la carta *letter,* 3
la casa *house,* 5; **ayudar en casa** *to help at home,* 5; **la casa de...** *...'s house,* 3; **decorar la casa** *to decorate the house,* 9
el casabe *flat, dry bread made from manioc,* 9G
casarse *to get married,* 10
la cascada *waterfall,* 2G
la cáscara *shell,* 2G
casi *almost,* 3, **casi nunca** *almost never,* 3, **casi siempre** *almost always,* 3
el caso *case,* 2
castaño(a) *dark brown,* 5
las castañuelas *castanets,* 1G
el castellano *Spanish,* 1G
el castillo *castle,* 2G
el catalán *language from Catalonia, Spain,* 1G
el catálogo *catalog,* 8
la catarata *cataract, waterfall,* 7G
la catedral *cathedral,* 1G
catorce *fourteen,* 1
el cayo *key,* 8G
el cazador *hunter,* 7G
la cebolla *onion,* 10G
celebérrimo(a) *most famous,* 8
la celebración *celebration,* 1
celebrar *to celebrate,* 9; celebrará *will celebrate,* 8; se celebra *is celebrated,* 2G
célebre *famous,* 8
celeridad *speed,* 8
celta *Celtic,* 1G
la cena *dinner,* 6
cenar *to eat dinner,* 6
el centro *downtown,* 10; *center,* 3G
el centro comercial *mall,* 3
el cepillo de dientes *toothbrush,* 7
la cerámica *pottery,* 4
cerca de *close to, near,* 5
cercano(a) *close,* 5
los cereales *cereal,* 6
el cerebelo *cerebellum,* 8
el cerebro *brain,* 8
la ceremonia *ceremony,* 6
cero *zero,* 1
cerrado(a) *closed,* 1
cerrar (ie) *to close,* 8
el césped *grass,* 5
la cesta de paja *straw basket,* 8G
el ceviche *dish made with seafood, lemon, and seasonings,* 10G

chao *Bye,* 9
la **chaqueta** *jacket,* 8
charlar *to talk, to chat,* 9
el chayote *type of squash,* 4G
la chica *girl,* 8
chicano(a) *Mexican that has emigrated to the United States,* 3G
el chile *pepper,* chile en nogada *peppers in walnut and spice sauce,* 6
el chileno *Chilean,* 5
la chimenea *fireplace,* 5
el chiste *joke,* 9
el choclo *corn on the cob,* 5G
el chocolate *chocolate,* 6; *hot chocolate,* 6
el churro *sugar-coated fritter,* 6
el ciclismo *cycling,* 1
ciego(a) *blind,* 5
el cielo *heaven,* 3
cien *one hundred,* 2
la ciencia ficción *science fiction,* 2
las ciencias *science,* 4; **...de ciencias** *science . . .,*1
el científico *scientist,* 6
ciento un(o) *one hundred one,* 8
cierto(a) *true,* xxii
la cifra *number,* 8
la cima *mountain top,* 7G
cinco *five,* 1
cincuenta *fifty,* 2
el cine *movie theater,* 3
el cinturón *belt,* 8
el círculo *circle,* 3
el citrón *lemon,* 6
la ciudad *city,* 5
¡Claro que sí! *Of course!,* 4
claro(a) *clear,* 6G
la clase *class,* 3; **después de clases** *after class,* 3; **la clase de baile** *dance class,* 4
clasificar *to classify,* 6
clavar *to nail,* 10
el clavo *nail,* 10
el cliente, la cliente *client,* 8
el club de... *the . . . club,* 4
el cobre *copper,* 6G
cocer *to cook,* 3
el coche *car,* 10
la cocina *kitchen,* 5; *cooking,* 3G
cocinar *to cook,* 5
el coco *coconut,* 2G
el cocodrilo *crocodile,* 8G
el código *code,* 2G
cohabitar *to live together,* 8G
la cola *line,* 10
el colectivo *bus* (Bol., Perú, Ecuador), 10
el colegio *school,* 3
colgar *to hang,* 9
la colina *hill,* 9G
la colonia *colony,* 7G
el colonizador *colonist,* 6G
el color *color,* 5
el colorido *coloring,* 7G
colorido(a) *colorful,* 4G
la columna *column,* xxii
los combates *battles,* 10
la combinación *combination,* 1
combinar *to combine,* 5G
el comedor *dining room,* 5
comenzar(ie) *to start,* 10; **comenzar un viaje** *to begin a trip,* 10; comiencen *begin,* 8
comer *to eat,* 3; se comen *are eaten,* 2G
el comercio *commerce,* 3G
el comestible *food,* 3
cómico(a) *funny,* 2
la comida *food,* 2, *lunch,* 6; **la comida china (italiana, mexicana)** *Chinese (Italian, Mexican) food,* 2; la comida típica *traditional food,* 6
como *like,* 2; as, 9; **como siempre** *as always,* 9
cómo *how?, what?,* 1; **¿Cómo eres?** *What are you like?,* 2; **¿Cómo es...?** *What is . . . like?,* 2; **¿Cómo está(s)?** *How are you?,* 1; **¿Cómo me quedan...?** *How does . . . look?,* 8; **¿Cómo se escribe...?** *How do you spell . . .?,* 1; **¿Cómo se llama?** *What's his (her/your) name?,* 1; **¿Cómo te llamas?** *What's your name? (fam.),* 1
la compañera de clase *classmate (female),* 1; **una compañera de clase** *a (female) classmate,* 1
el compañero de clase *classmate (male),* 1; **un compañero de clase** *a (male) classmate,* 1
la comparación *comparison,* 1
comparar *to compare,* 8
compasivo(a) *compassionate,* 6
el complemento directo *direct object,* 6
completar *to complete,* xxii
completo *complete,* 6; por completo *completely,* 6
comprar *to buy,* 8; comprarías *you would buy,* 8
las compras *shopping,* 2; estar de compras *to be on a shopping trip,* 8; **ir de compras** *to go shopping,* 3
la comprensión *comprehension,* 10
comprender *to understand,* 2; nos comprendemos *we understand each other,* 2
la computación *computer science,* 4
la computadora *computer,* 4
común *common,* 9
comunicar *to communicate,* 5
la comunidad *community,* 1
con *with,* 3; con base en *based on,* xxii; **con mis amigos** *with my friends,* 3; **con mi familia** *with my family,* 3; con motivo de *on the occasion of,* 9; **¿Con qué frecuencia vas...?** *How often do you go . . .?,* 3; con relación a *in relation to,* 5
el concierto *concert,* 4
el concurso *competition,* 9G
el condominio *condominium,* 5
conectar *to connect,* 8G
confundido(a) *confused,* 4
confundir *to confuse,* 10
el conjunto *musical group,* 3G
conmemorar *commemorate,* 3G
conmigo *with me,* 3
conocer *to know (someone) or be familiar with a place,* 9; **conocimos...** *we visited . . .,* 10; **quiero conocer...** *I want to see . . .,* 10; se conoce *is known,* 2G
conocido(a) *known,* 2G
el conocimiento *knowledge,* 7
conquistar *to conquer,* 10
conseguir (i, i) *to get,* 10
el consejo *advice,* 7
conservar *to preserve,* 2G
considerar *to consider,* 2; *to regard,* 9
constituir *to make up,* 6
construir *to build,* 3G; construye *construct,* 10; fue construido *was built,* 3G
el consultorio médico *doctor's office,* 7
consumir *to consume,* 6; se consumen *are consumed,* 6
el consumo *consumption,* 6
contar *to count,* 1; *to tell,* 4; contando *counting,* 1; **contar chistes** *to tell jokes,* 9; contar con *to count on,* 10; cuenta *tells,* 6; cuentan *it is told,* 6
contemplar *to contemplate,* 9
contemporáneo *contemporary,* 1G
contener (ie) *to contain,* 10G; que contengan *that contain,* 10
contento(a) *happy,* 7; **estar contento(a)** *to be happy,* 7
contestar *to answer,* xxii
contigo *with you,* 3
el continente *continent,* 6
continuo *continual,* 8
contra *against,* 10
al contrario *to the contrary,* 6
la contribución *contribution,* 2G
contribuir *to contribute,* 8G
el control de seguridad *security checkpoint,* 10
controlar *to control,* 3G
el convento *convent,* 3G
la conversación *conversation,* xxii
convertirse *to become,* 10
el coquí *small tree frog,* 2G
el corazón *heart,* 7G
la cordillera *mountain range,* 2G
el coro *chorus,* 2
correcto(a) *right, correct,* xxii
corregir *to correct,* xxii

el correo electrónico *e-mail address,* 1; **¿Cuál es el correo electrónico de...?** *What is . . .'s e-mail address?,* 1; **¿Cuál es tu correo electrónico?** *What's your e-mail address?,* 1
correr *to run,* 3
la correspondencia *correspondence,* 1
corresponder *to correspond,* xxii; le corresponde *it falls to him,* 5; que le correspondan *that correspond to it,* 9
correspondiente *corresponding,* 8
la corriente *current,* 8
cortar *to cut,* 6; **cortar el césped** *to cut the grass,* 5
la Corte Suprema *Supreme Court,* 6
corto(a) *short,* 5
la cosa *thing,* 4; **necesito muchas cosas** *I need lots of things,* 4; **no es gran cosa** *it's not a big deal,* 5
coser *to sew,* 4
la costa *coast,* 3G
costar (ue) *to cost,* 8; costará *will cost,* 9
costeño(a) *coastal,* 10G
la costumbre *custom,* 5G
la creación *creation,* 3
crear *to create,* 7; creado por *created by,* 7G; fue creado *was created,* 3G
la creatividad *creativity,* 6G
creativo(a) *creative,* 2
crecer *to grow,* 9G; crecí *I grew up,* 3
creer *to believe,* 6; *to think,* 9
la crema *cream,* 6
la criatura *child,* 3
crudo *raw,* 10G
el cuaderno *notebook,* 4
la cuadra *block,* 5
cual: los cuales *which,* 10
el cuadro *box, chart,* xxii; *painting,* 1
¿cuál? *what?, which?,* 4; **¿Cuál es el correo electrónico de...?** *What is . . .'s e-mail address?,* 1; **¿Cuál es el teléfono de...?** *What's . . . telephone number?,* 1; **¿Cuál es tu correo electrónico?** *What's your e-mail address?,* 1; **¿Cuál es tu materia preferida?** *What's your favorite subject?,* 4; **¿Cuál es tu teléfono?** *What's your telephone number?,* 1
cualquier *any,* 10
cualquiera *whichever,* 6G
cuando *when,* 3
¿cuándo? *when?,* 2; **¿Cuándo es el cumpleaños de...?** *When is . . .'s birthday?,* 2; **¿Cuándo es tu cumpleaños?** *When is your birthday?,* 2
¿cuánto(a)? *how much?, 4*
¡cuántos! *so many!,* 4
¿cuántos(as) *How many . . .?,* 2; **¿Cuántos años tiene... ?** *How old is . . .?,* 2; **¿Cuántos años tienes?** *How old are you?,* 2
cuarenta *forty,* 2
cuarto *quarter,* 4; **menos cuarto** *a quarter to (the hour),* 4; **y cuarto** *quarter past,* 1
el cuarto *room,* 5; **arreglar el cuarto** *to pick up the room,* 5
cuatro *four,* 1
cuatrocientos *four hundred,* 8
cubierto(a) *covered,* 3
la cuchara *spoon,* 6
el cuchillo *knife,* 6
el cuello *neck,* 7
la cuenta *bill,* 6
el cuento *story,* 4
el cuerno *horn,* 2G
el cuerpo *body,* 7
el cuerpo de bomberos *fire department,* 2G
cuesta(n)... *cost(s) . . .,* 8
la cueva *cave,* 1G
el cuidado *care, 1;* ten cuidado *take care,* 6
cuidadosamente *carefully,* 9
cuidar *to take care of,* 5; **cuidar a mis hermanos** *take care of my brothers and sisters,* 5
cuidarse *to take care of oneself,* 7; **cuidarse la salud** *to take care of one's health,* 7; **para cuidarte la salud debes...** *to take care of your health, you should . . .,* 7; **Para cuidarte mejor, debes...** *To take better care of yourself, you should . . .,* 7; **Cuídate.** *Take care.,* 9
culinario(a) *culinary,* 6
cultivar *to cultivate,* 6
el cultivo *crop,* 4G
la cultura *culture,* 1
el cumpleaños *birthday,* 9; **¿Cuándo es el cumpleaños de...?** *When is . . .'s birthday?,* 2; **¿Cuándo es tu cumpleaños?** *When is your birthday?,* 2; **el cumpleaños de...** *birthday of . . .,* 2; **la tarjeta de cumpleaños** *birthday card,* 8
curioso(a) *odd, unusual,* 1
la curva *curve,* 3G

D

dado(a) *given,* 7
la danza *dance,* 1G
dar *to give,* 7; le dan *they give,* 7; **no des** *don't give,* 7; se da *is held,* 8G
darse cuenta *to realize,* 8
el dato *fact,* 10
de *of, from, in, by,* 1; *made of,* 8; **...de ciencias** *science . . .,* 1; **de color café** *brown,* 5; **¿De dónde eres?** *Where are you from? (fam.),* 1; **¿De dónde es usted?** *Where are you from? (formal),* 1; **¿De dónde es...?** *Where is . . . from?,* 1; de...en... *from . . . to . . .,* 8; **. . . de español** *Spanish . . .,* 1; **de la mañana** *in the morning,* 1; **de la noche** *at night,* 1; **de la tarde** *in the afternoon, evening,* 1; de nuevo *again,* 7; de nada *you're welcome;* **¿De parte de quién?** *Who's calling?,* 8; ¿de quién? *about whom?,* 1; de todo *everything,* 8; de todo tipo *all kinds,* 8; de todos modos *in any event,* 8; de veras *really,* 8
debajo *underneath,* 8; **debajo de** *underneath,* 5
deber *should,* 6; ¿Debo...? *Should I . . .?,* 8; **No debes...** *You shouldn't . . .,* 7; se debe hacer *should be done,* 6
los deberes *chores,* 5; *responsibilities,* 5
debido a *due to,* 7G
el decibel *decibel,* 2
decidir *to decide,* xxii
decir *to say,* 3; bien dicho *well said,* 6; di *say,* 4; dice *says,* 3; diciéndome *telling me,* 9; me han dicho *they have told me,* 6; se dicen adiós *they say goodbye,* 3; si lo hubiera dicho *if I had said it,* 6; te diré *I'll tell you,* 2; yo he dicho *I have said,* 6
declarar *to declare,* 6
la decoración *decoration,* 9
decorar *to decorate,* 9; **decorar la casa** *to decorate the house,* 9
dedicado(a) a *dedicated to,* 2G
dedicar *to dedicate,* 4; es dedicada *is dedicated,* 5; dedicación dedication, 10; se dedica is dedicated, 2G
el dedo *finger,* 7; *toe,* 4G
deducir *to deduce,* 7
la definición *definition,* 10
definido(a) *defined,* 8
definitivamente *definitely,* 8; *permanently,* 9
dejar *to allow,* 3; *to leave,* 10; **dejar un recado** *to leave a message,* 8
dejar de + infinitive *to stop doing something,* 7; **dejar de fumar** *to stop smoking,* 7
del (de + el) *of the,* 2
delante de *in front of,* 5
delgado(a) *thin,* 5
delicioso(a) *delicious,* 2
demasiado(a) *too much,* 7

demostrar (ue) *to show,* 10G
dentro *inside,* 9
el departamento *apartment (México),* 5; *district (Perú),* 10
el dependiente, la dependiente *salesclerk,* 8
los deportes *sports,* 2
deportivo(a) (adj) *sports,* 8
la derecha *right,* 1
el desarrollo *development,* 7G
el desastre *disaster,* 9
desayunar *to eat breakfast,* 6
el desayuno *breakfast,* 6
descansar *to rest,* 3
el descendiente *descendent,* 10
describir *to describe,* 5
descubrir *to discover,* 8; fue descubierto *was discovered,* 7G
desde *since,* 4; *from,* 10; ¿desde cuándo? *since when?,* 4; desde hace *since,* 6; desde joven *since her youth,* 8; desde luego *of course,* 7
desear *to want, to wish for, to desire,* 6; deseando *wanting to,* 8
desechable *disposable,* 10
desembarcar *to disembark, to deplane,* 10
desembocar *to flow,* 10G
el deseo *desire,* 9
desesperado(a) *desperate,* 6
el desfile *parade, procession,* 4G
el desierto *desert,* 5G
la despedida *farewell,* 9; la fiesta de despedida *goodbye party,* 10
despertarse (ie) *to wake,* 7
despierto(a) *awake,* 7
después *after,* 3; *afterwards,* 4; **después de** *after,* 7; **después de clases** *after class,* 3
destinado(a) *destined,* 6
el destino *destination,* 10
el detalle *detail,* 7
determinar *to determine,* 7
detrás de *behind,* 5
devolver (ue) *to return something,* 8
di *say,* 8
el día *day,* 1; **algún día** *one day,* 10; **el Día de Acción de Gracias** *Thanksgiving Day,* 9; **el Día de la Independencia** *Independence Day,* 9; **el Día de la Madre** *Mother's Day,* 9; **el día de la semana** *day of the week,* 1; **el Día de los Enamorados** *Valentine's Day,* 9; **el Día del Padre** *Father's Day,* 9; **el día de tu santo** *your saint's day,* 9; **el día festivo** *holiday,* 9; **¿Qué día es hoy?** *What day is today?,* 1
diablado(a) *devilish,* 5G
el diablo *devil,* 7G
el diálogo *dialogue,* xxii
diario(a) *daily,* 3G
dibujar *to draw,* 3
el dibujo *drawing,* xxii
el diccionario *dictionary,* 4
dice (inf. decir) *(he/she) says,* 4
la dicha *happiness,* 9
diciembre *December,* 1
el dictado *dictation,* 1
diecinueve *nineteen,* 1
dieciocho *eighteen,* 1
dieciséis sixteen, 1
diecisiete *seventeen,* 1
los dientes *teeth,* 7
la dieta *diet,* 7; **seguir una dieta sana** *to eat well,* 7
diez *ten,* 1
diferente *different,* 2
difícil *difficult,* 4; **Es difícil.** *It's difficult.,* 4
Diga. Hello. *(telephone greeting),* 8
el dinero *money,* 8
el dinosaurio *dinosaur,* 1
el dios *god,* 6; gracias a Dios *thank goodness,* 6
la dirección *address,* 5; **Mi dirección es...** *My address is . . .,* 5
directamente *directly,* 4
director (-a) *director,* 10
el directorio de teléfono *phone book,* 1
disciplinado(a) *disciplined,* 2
el disco *record,* 8
el disco compacto *compact disc,* 8; **el disco compacto en blanco** *blank compact disc,* 8
diseñar *to design,* 3G; fue diseñado(a) *was designed,* 3G
el diseño *design,* 5G
el disfraz *costume,* 9G
disfrazar *to wear a costume,* 4G
disfrutar *to enjoy,* 2G
disponible *available,* 7
dispuesto(a) *willing,* 6G
la distancia *distance,* 10
distinguirse *to distinguish oneself,* 10
distinto(a) *different,* 6G
la diversión *fun,* 2
diverso(a) *diverse,* 6
divertido(a) *fun,* 2; **¡Qué divertido!** *What fun!,* 10
divertirse *to have fun,* 1; diviértanse *have a good time* (pl.), 1; que me divierta *to have fun,* 9
doblado(a) *folded,* 9
doble *double,* 5
doce *twelve,* 1
el documento *document,* 1
el dólar *dollar,* 8
doler (ue) *to hurt,* 7; **Me duele(n)...** *My . . . hurt(s).,* 7; **¿Te duele algo?** *Does something hurt?,* 7
el domingo *Sunday,* 1; **los domingos** *on Sundays,* 3
dominicano(a) *Dominican,* 9
donde *where,* 8; *to the house of,* 9
¿dónde? *where?,* 5; **¿Dónde se puede...?** *Where can I . . .?,* 10
dorado(a) *golden,* 2
dormido(a) *asleep,* 7
dormir (ue) *to sleep,* 5; **dormir lo suficiente** *to get enough sleep,* 7
el dormitorio *bedroom,* 5
dos *two,* 1
dos mil *two thousand,* 8
dos millones (de) *two million,* 8
doscientos *two hundred,* 8
dramatizar *to dramatize, to role-play,* xxii
la duda *doubt,* 6; sin duda *without a doubt,* 6
dulce *sweet,* 7
el dulce *candy,* 9
la duración *duration,* 7
durante *during,* 10; *throughout,* 6G
durar *to last,* 10G
el durazno *peach*
el DVD *DVD,* 8

e *and,* 5
la economía *economy,* 3G; la economía doméstica *home economics,* 6G
la edad *age,* 2G; de más edad *the oldest,* 5
el edificio *building,* 5; **el edificio de... pisos** *. . . story building,* 5
la educación física *physical education,* 4
eficaz *efficient,* 10G
eficiente *efficient,* 2
el ejemplo *example,* 3G
el ejercicio *exercise,* 3; **hacer ejercicio** *to exercise,* 3
el *the* (masc.), 2
él he, 1; **Él es...** *He is . . .,* 1; **Él se llama...** *His name is . . .,* 1
el elefante *elephant,* 1
la elegancia *elegance,* 5G
elegante *elegant,* 2
el elemento *element,* 1
elevar *to raise,* 5G
la elite *elite,* 6
ella *she,* 1; A ella le gusta + infinitive *She likes to . . .,* 3; **Ella es...** *She is . . .,* 1; ella misma *herself,* 6; **Ella se llama...** *Her name is . . .,* 1
ellas *they (f.),* 1
ellos *they (m.),* 1
el elote *corn on the cob (Mexico),* 6
emitir *to emit,* 2
emocionado(a) *excited,* 9
la empanada *turnover-like pastry,* 9
el emparedado *sandwich,* 6

empezar (ie) *to start,* 5
el empleado, la empleada *employee,* 7
el empleo *job,* 9
emplumado(a) *feathered,* 6
en *on, in, at,* 1; en frente *in front,* 3G; **en blanco** *blank,* 8; en las cuales *about which,* 8; en negrilla *bold,* 9; **en punto** *on the dot,* 1; en que *in which,* 8; **¿En que le puedo servir?** *Can I help you?,* 8
enamorado(a) *in love,* 10
Encantado(a). *Pleased to meet you., Nice to meet you.,* 1
encantar *to really like, to love,* 6
encerrar *to lock up,* 10
encima de *on top of, above,* 5
encontrar (ue) *to find,* 7; encontrará *will find,* 10; se encuentra *is/it's located* 1G; se encuentran *they can be found,* 6
encontrarse con alguien *to meet up with someone,* 10
energético(a) *energetic,* 2
la energía *energy,* 2
enero *January,* 1
la enfermera *nurse,* 5
enfermo(a) *sick,* 7
enfrente *in front,* 10
enhorabuena *congratulations,* 10
enojado(a) *angry,* 7
enojarse *to get angry,* 7
enrollado(a) *rolled up,* 3
la ensalada *salad,* 6
el ensayo *rehearsal,* 3
enseñar *to show, to teach,* 4
enseñar fotos *to show photos,* 9
entender *to understand,* 5
enterarse *to find out,* 10
entonces *then,* 4
entrar *to enter,* 4
entre *between,* 2; *in, within,* 6; *among,* 7
entregar *to hand over,* 9
los entremeses *appetizers,* 9
la entrenadora *trainer,* 7
el entrenamiento *practice,* 3
entrenarse *to work out,* 7
la entrevista *interview,* 2
entrevistar *to interview,* 2
enviar *to send,* 1
la envoltura *wrapping,* 9
la época *era,* 6; la época colonial *Spanish colonial era,* 2G
el equipaje *luggage,* 10
el equipo *equipment,* 3G; *team,* 9G; el equipo de transporte *transportation equipment,* 3G
¿Eres...? *Are you . . .?,* 2
la erupción *eruption,* 6G
Es... *He (She, It) is . . .,* 2; **Es algo divertido.** *It's kind of fun.,* 2; **Es bastante bueno.** *It's rather good.,* 2; **Es de...** *He (She) is from . . .,* 1; **Es delicioso.** *It's delicious.,* 2; **Es el... de...** *It's the . . . of . . .,* 2; **Es facíl/difícil** *It's easy/hard,* 4; **Es el primero (dos, tres) de...** *It's the first (second, third) of . . .,* 1; **Es la una.** *It is one o'clock.,* 1; **Es pésimo.** *It's awful.,* 2; **Es que...** *It's because; It's just that . . .,* 7; **¡Es un robo!** *It's a rip-off!,* 8
ese(a) *that,* 5
escapar *to escape,* 5
la escena *scene,* 3
escoger *to pick,* 9; *to choose,* 6
escolar *school (adj.),* 4
esconder *to hide,* 4
escribir *to write,* 1; **¿Cómo se escribe...?** *How do you spell . . .?,* 1; escribamos *let's write,* 1; **escribir cartas** *to write letters,* 3; **se escribe...** *It's spelled . . .,* 1
el escritor, la escritora *writer,* 1
el escritorio *desk,* 5
escuchar *to listen,* 3; **escuchar música** *to listen to music,* 3; escuchemos *let's listen,* 1; has escuchado *have you heard,* 2; he escuchado *I have heard,* 2
la escuela *school,* 2; la escuela primaria *elementary school,* 5; la escuela secundaria *high school,* 9
el escultor *sculptor,* 4G
la escultura *sculpture,* 2G
ese(a) *that,* 8
eso *that,* 2
esos(as) *those,* 8
espacial *space,* 8G
la espalda *back,* 7
el español *Spanish,* 1
el español *Spaniard,* 6
esparcir *to spread,* 3; está esparciendo *is spreading,* 3
la especia *spice,* 8G
la especialidad *specialty,* 6
la especie *species,* 2G
específico(a) *specific,* 10
los espejuelos *glasses,* 5
la esperanza *hope,* 9
esperar *to wait,* 8; *to hope,* 10; *to expect,* 10; **Espera un momento.** *Hold on a moment.,* 8; **espero ver...** *I hope to see . . .,* 10
las espinacas *spinach,* 6
el espino *thorn,* 8
espiritual *spiritual,* 9
espontáneo(a) *spontaneous,* 2
la esposa *wife,* 9
el esposo *husband,* 5
esquiar *to ski,* 10; **esquiar en el agua** *to water-ski,* 10
Está a la vuelta. *It's around the corner.,* 10
ésta, éste *this (pron.),*1; **Ésta es.../la señora...** *This is . . . /Mrs. . . .,* 1; **Éste es.../el señor...** *This is . . . /Mr. . . .,* 1
establecer *to establish,* 8G, fue establecido *was established,* 8G
el establecimiento *colony,* 8G
estacionar *to park,* 10
el estadio *stadium,* 4
el estado *state,* 2G
los Estados Unidos *United States,* 1
estadounidense *pertaining to the United States,* 7
estar *to be,* 1; **¿Cómo está(s)?** *How are you?,* 1; **¿Está...?** *Is . . . there?,* 8; **Está bien.** *All right.,* 3; **Está nublado.** *It's cloudy.,* 3; **estar aburrido(a)** *to be bored,* 7; **estar bien** *to be (doing) fine,* 7; **estar cansado(a)** *to be tired,* 7; **estar contento(a)** *to be happy,* 7; **estar mal** *to be (doing) badly,* 7; **estar enfermo(a)** *to be sick,* 7; **estar enojado(a)** *to be angry,* 7; **estar en una silla de ruedas** *to be in a wheelchair,* 5; **estar listo(a)** *to be ready,* 7; **estar nervioso(a)** *to be nervous,* 7; **estar triste** *to be sad,* 7; **¿Está todo listo?** *Is everything ready?,* 9; **Estoy bien, gracias.** *I'm fine, thanks.,*1; **Estoy de acuerdo.** *I agree.,* 6; **Estoy mal.** *I'm not so good.,* 1; **Estoy regular.** *I'm all right.,* 1; **No está.** *He/She is not here.,* 8; **no estés** *don't be,* 7; **Estuvo a todo dar.** *It was great.,* 9; **No estoy de acuerdo.** *I disagree.,* 6
estas, estos *these (adj.),* 6
la estatua *statue,* 5G
éste *this (pron.),* 6
este(a) *this,* 8; **este fin de semana** *this weekend,* 4
el estilo *style,* 3G
estirarse *to stretch,* 7
el estómago *stomach,* 7
el Estrecho de la Florida *Strait of Florida,* 8
la estrella *star,* 5
el estrés *stress,* 7
estricto(a) *strict,* 4
el estruendo *noise,* 10
el estudiante, la estudiante *student,* 1; el estudiante de intercambio *exchange student,* 10
estudiar *to study,* 3
los estudios *studies,* 5; los estudios sociales *social studies,* 4
estupendo(a) *great,* 10; **fue estupendo** *it was great,* 10
la etapa *stage,* 2
el europeo *European,* 6G
el evento deportivo *sporting event,* 1
el examen *test,* 4; **presentar el examen de...** *to take a . . . test,* 4
exclamar *to exclaim,* 9
exclusivamente *exclusively,* 4
la excursión *hike,* 10; **ir de excursión** *to go on a hike,* 10
la excursión turística *to go on a trip,* 1

Vocabulario español-inglés

exigente *strict,* 5
existir *to exist,* 7
el éxito *success,* 10
la experiencia *experience,* 6
el explorador *explorer,* 5G
exponer *to display,* 4G
el exportador *exporter,* 8G
exportar *to export,* 1G
la exposición *exposition,* 5G, exhibition, 10G
expresar *to express,* 6G
la expresión *expression,* xxii; *saying,* 2
extender *to cover,* 3G; se extiende *it extends,* 5G
la extensión *length,* 10G
extranjero(a) *foreign,* 10
el extranjero *abroad,* 10
extraño(a) *strange,* 7G
extremo(a) *far,* 7G
extrovertido(a) *outgoing,* 2

fabuloso(a) *fabulous,* 6
fácil *easy,* 4; **Es fácil.** *It's easy.,* 4
facturar *to check,* 10; **facturar el equipaje** *to check luggage,* 10
la falda *skirt,* 8
falso(a) *false,* xxii
faltar *to be missing,* 1; nos faltan *we're missing,* 3
la fama *fame,* 5G
la familia *family,* 3; **En mi familia somos...** *There are . . . people in my family.,* 5; la Familia Real *Royal Family,* 1
familiar *pertaining to the family,* 7
famoso(a) *famous,* 2
fascinar *to love, to like very much,* 2
fastidiar *to annoy,* 9
favorito(a) *favorite,* 1
febrero *February,* 1
la fecha *date,* 1
la felicidad *happiness,* 9
felicitar *to congratulate,* 9
el felino *cat,* 10G
feliz (pl. felices) *happy,* 8; **¡Feliz...!** *Happy (Merry) . . .,* 9
fenomenal *awesome,* 2
feo(a) *ugly*
festejar to celebrate, 9
festivo *holiday* (adj), 9
la fibra de vidrio *fiberglass,* 3G
la fiesta *party,* 2; la fiesta patria *national holiday,* 5G; la fiesta patronal *feast celebrating the patron saint,* 4G; **la fiesta sorpresa** *surprise party,* 9; **hacer una fiesta** *to have a party,* 9
la figurita *shape, figurine,* 4

fijarse *to notice,* 7
el fin *end,* 9; al fin *finally,* 10
el fin de semana *weekend,* 3; **este fin de semana** *this weekend,* 4; **los fines de semana** *weekends,* 3
finales: a finales *at the end,* 10G
finalmente *finally,* 8
financiar *to finance,* 5
fino(a) *fine,* 2G
el flan *flan, custard,* 6
las flautas *rolled tortillas that are stuffed and fried,* 9
la flor *flower,* 1
las flores *flowers,* 9
las fogatas *campfires,* 3
el folleto *pamphlet,* 7
la forma *form,* xxii
formaba *formed*
la formación geológica *geological formation,* 7G
formar *to form,* 3
formidable *formidable,* 2
la fortaleza *fortress,* 10
la fortuna *fortune,* 8
la foto *photo,* xxii; **enseñar fotos** *to show photos,* 9; **sacar fotos** *to take photos,* 10
la fotografía *photograph,* 8
el fragmento *excerpt,* 5
el francés *French,* 4
la frase *phrase,* 8; *sentence,* 9
la frecuencia *frequency,* 8; con frecuencia *often,* 8; **¿Con qué frecuencia vas...?** *How often do you go?,* 3
frecuentado(a) *visited,* 1G
frente *front;* al frente *to the front,* xxii; en frente *in front,* 3G
el fresco cool, 3; **Hace fresco.** *It's cool.,* 3
el frijol *bean,* 2G
frío(a) *cold,* 6; **Hace frío.** *It's cold.,* 3; **tener frío** *to be cold,* 7
la frontera *border,* 7G
la fruta *fruit,* 2; la fruta cítrica *citrus fruit,* 8G
el fuego *fire,* 3
¡Fue estupendo! *It was great!,* 10
los fuegos artificiales *fireworks,* 9; **ver los fuegos artificiales** *to see fireworks,* 9
fuera *outside,* 7G
fuera (inf. ser) *was,* 6G
fuerte *loud,* 2; *strong,* 3G
fumar *to smoke,* 7; **dejar de fumar** *to stop smoking,* 7
el funcionalismo *functional architectural style,* 6G
funcionar *to work,* 10
fundado(a) *founded,* 2G
el fútbol *soccer,* 3
el fútbol americano *football,* 3
el futuro *future,* 3
futuro(a) *future,* 5

el gabinete *cabinet,* 9
las gafas *glasses,* 5
el gallego *romance language from Galicia, Spain,* 1G
la galleta *cookie,* 9
la gana *desire;* **tener ganas de** + infinitive *to feel like doing something,* 4
la ganadería *cattle raising,* 7G
el ganado *cattle,* 3G
ganar *to win,* 5G
la ganga *bargain,* 8
el garaje *garage,* 5
la garganta *throat,* 7
la garita *sentry box,* 2G
gastar *to spend,* 8
el gato, la gata *cat,* 5
el gazpacho *cold tomato soup*
la generación *generation,* 5
generalmente *generally,* 8
el género *genre,* 8G
generoso(a) *generous,* 6
la gente *people,* 3
la geografía *geography,* 1
geográfico(a) *geographical,* 10
geometriá *geometry,* 4
gigante *giant,* 6
el gimnasio *gym,* 3
el glaciar *glacier,* 5G
la gloria *heaven,* 3
glorioso *glorious,* 9
el gobierno *government,* 1G
el Golfo de México *Gulf of Mexico,* 8G
gordo(a) *fat,* 5
la gorra *cap,* 7
gótico(a) *gothic,* 3G
la grabación *recording,* 1
gracias *thank you,* 1, **Estoy bien, gracias.** *I'm fine, thanks,* 1; **no, gracias** *no thank you,* 8
gracioso(a) *witty,* 2
la graduación *graduation,* 9
gran *big,* 5; *great,* 5; *large,* 3
la granada *pomegranate,* 6
grande *big, large,* 5
el grano *grain,* 6
la grasa *fat,* 7
gratuito *free,* 1
gris *gray,* 8
gritar *to yell,* 7
la grúa *tow truck,* 9
el grupo *group,* 6
la guagua *bus (P.R., Dom. Rep.),* 10
los guandules *pigeon peas,* 6
guapo(a) *good-looking,* 2
guardar *to store,* 10
la guayabera *man's short-sleeved shirt,* 8
la guerra *war,* 7
la guía telefónica *telephone directory,* 10

guiar *to guide,* 10; *to drive,* 10
la güira *percussive instrument played by scratching with a stick across a rough surface,* 9G
el guiso *stew,* 6
la guitarra *guitar,* 2; la guitarra eléctrica *electric guitar,* 2
gustar *to like,* 2; **A ellos/ellas les gusta...** *They like . . .,* 3; **le gusta...** *he/she likes . . .,* 3; **Me gusta(n)...** *I like . . .,* 2; **Me gusta(n)... mucho.** *I like . . . a lot.,* 2; me gustaba *I liked,* 4; **Me gusta(n) más...** *I like . . . more.,* 2; **Me gustaría...** *I would like . . .,* 8; **Me gustaría más...** *I would prefer . . .,* 10; Me ha gustado... *I have liked . . .,* 4; **No, no me gusta(n)...** *No, I don't like . . .,* 2; **¿Te gusta(n)...?** *Do you like . . .?,* 2; **¿Te gusta(n) más... o...?** *Do you like . . . or . . . more?,* 2
el gusto *pleasure,* 9
los gustos *likes,* 2

haber *to have;* hubo *there was,* 10
las habichuelas *beans,* 2G
la habitación *bedroom,* 5
habitar *to inhabit,* 7G
el habla *speech,* 8
hablar *to talk, to speak,* 3; **Habla...** *. . . speaking (on the telephone),* 8; **hablar por teléfono** *to talk on the phone,* 3; hablemos *let's talk,* 1
hacer (-go) *to make, to do,* 4; **estamos haciendo** *we are making/doing,* 9; están haciendo *are making,* 3; **Hace buen (mal) tiempo.** *The weather is nice (bad).,* 3; **Hace calor.** *It's hot.,* 3; **Hace fresco.** *It's cool.,* 3; **Hace frío.** *It's cold.,* 3; Hace más de... años *It's more than . . . years ago,* 7G; **Hace sol.** *It's sunny.,* 3; Hace tanto... que... *It's so . . . that . . .,* 3; Hace tiempo. *It's been a long time.,* 9; **Hace viento.** *It's windy.,* 3; **hacer cola** *to wait in line,* 10; **hacer ejercicio** *to exercise,* 3; **hacer la cama** *to make the bed,* 5; **hacer la maleta** *to pack your suitcase,* 10; **hacer la tarea** *to do homework,* 3; **hacer los quehaceres** *to do the chores,* 5; **hacer una fiesta** *to have a party,* 9; **hacer un viaje** *to take a trip,* 10; **hacer yoga** *to do yoga,* 7; hacían *they made,* 4; **haz** *make, do,* 6; hizo *he/she did,* 9; **no hagas** *don't do,* 10; **¿Qué están haciendo?** *What are they doing?,* 9; qué hicieron *what they did,* 9; **¿Qué hiciste?** *What did you do?,* 8; se hace *is made,* 6
hallar *to find,* 7G
el hambre *hunger,* 4; **tener hambre** *to be hungry,* 4
la hamburguesa *hamburger,* 2
el Hanukah *Hanukkah,* 9
hasta *until,* 5; *up to,* 5; **Hasta luego.** *See you later.,* 1; **Hasta mañana.** *See you tomorrow.,* 1; **Hasta pronto.** *See you soon.,* 1
hay (inf. haber) *there is, there are,* 4; **Hay un(a)...** *There's a . . .,* 4
haz *make, do,* 6; Hazme caso. *Pay attention to me.,* 8
hecho(a) *made,* 2G
la heladería *ice cream shop,* 8
el helado *ice cream,* 2
la hembra *female,* 2
el hemisferio *hemisphere,* 7G
la herencia inheritance; la herencia alemana *German cultural tradition,* 7G; la herencia española *Spanish cultural tradition,* 10G
la hermana *sister,* 5
el hermano *brother,* 5
los hermanos *brothers, brothers and sisters,* 5
el héroe *hero,* 4G
la hierba *grass,* 8G; la hierba fina *herb,* 8G
la hija *daughter,* 5
el hijo *son,* 5
los hijos *sons, children,* 5
el hipo *hiccup,* 3; estar con hipo *to have hiccups,* 3
el hipopótamo *hippopotamus,* 1
hispano(a) *Hispanic,* 1
hispanohablante *Spanish-speaking,* 6
la historia *history,* 4
el hogar *home,* 3G
las hojas de maíz *cornhusks,* 3
hola *hi, hello* 1
el hombre *man,* 8; el hombre de negocios *businessman,* 5, los hombres *men, humans,* 6; **para hombres** *for men,* 8
el hombro *shoulder,* 7
el homenaje *tribute,* 1G
hondo(a) *deep,* 8G
el honor *honor,* 3
la hora *hour,* 1; **¿A qué hora vas a...?** *What time are you going to . . .?,* 4; **¿Qué hora es?** *What time is it?,* 1
el horario *schedule,* 3
la horchata mexicana *sweet rice drink,* 6
la hormiga *ant,* 6
el horno *oven,* 6; el horno microondas *microwave oven,* 6
horrible *horrible,* 2; **¡Fue horrible!** *It was horrible!,* 10
el hotel *hotel,* 10; **quedarse en un hotel** *to stay in a hotel,* 10
hoy *today,* 1; hoy en día *nowadays,* 6G; **Hoy es...** *Today is . . .,* 1; **¿Qué día es hoy?** *What day is today?,* 1
el huevo *egg,* 6
húmedo(a) *damp;* el bosque húmedo *rainforest,* 4G
el huracán *hurricane,* 3

la idea *idea,* 6; la idea principal *main idea,* 6
el idioma *language,* 1G; idioma oficial *official language,* 1G
identificar *to identify,* 10
la iglesia *church,* 3
igual que *same as,* 2
igualmente *equally,* 8
Igualmente. *Likewise.,* 1
la iguana *iguana,* 1
ilustrar *to illustrate,* 5
imaginar *to imagine,* 2
el imperativo *imperative,* 9
el imperio *empire,* 10G
imponente *imposing,* 6
importado(a) *imported,* 5G
la importancia *importance,* 6
impresionante *impressive,* 7G
incaico(a) *Incan,* 10G
incesante *without stopping,* 8
inclusive *including,* 8
incluso *including,* 8G
incomparable *incomparable,* 5
la independencia *independence,* 6G
independiente *independent,* 2
indicar *to indicate,* xxii
indígena *indigenous,* 6G
la influencia *influence,* 1G
Inglaterra *England,* 7G
el inglés *English,* 4
injusto *unfair,* 5; **Me parece injusto.** *I don't think that's fair; it seems unfair to me,* 5
inmediato(a) *immediate,* 10G
inmenso(a) *immense,* 6
el inmigrante *immigrant,* 7G
inmigrar *to immigrate,* 7G
el insecto *insect,* 2
inseparable *inseparable,* 3
inspirar *to inspire,* 1G

Vocabulario español-inglés

el instrumento *instrument,* 8G
intacto(a) *intact,* 10
intelectual *intellectual,* 2
inteligente *intelligent,* 2
la intensidad *intensity,* 7
el interés *of interest,* 10
interesante *interesting,* 2
internacional *international,* 6
interrumpir *to interrupt,* 4
el invasor *invader,* 4G
inventar *to invent,* 4
el inventario *inventory,* 8
inventivo(a) *inventive,* 2
la investigación *research,* 4G
el invierno *winter,* 3
inviolable *inviolable,* 5
la invitación *invitation,* 9; **mandar invitaciones** *to send invitations,* 9
el invitado *guest,* 9; el invitado de honor *guest of honor,* 9
invitar *to invite,* 9
ir *to go,* 2; **¿Adónde fuiste?** *Where did you go?,* 8; fue *went,* 8; fuimos *we went,* 8; **ir+ a +** infinitive *to be going to (do something),* 4; **ir de compras** *to go shopping,* 3; **ir de excursión** *to go hiking,* 10; **ir de pesca,** *to go fishing,* 10; **ir al cine** *to go to the movies,* 3; **no vayas** *don't go,* 7; **quiero ir...** *I want to go . . .,* 2; se va *leaves,* 6; **¿Vas a...?** *Are you going to . . .?,* 4; **Vas a ir, ¿verdad?** *You're going to go, aren't you?,* 4; **ve** go, 6
irse *to leave,* 10
la isla *island,* 10
italiano(a) *Italian,* 6
la izquierda *left*

J

el jabón *soap,* 7
el jamón *ham,* 6
el jardín *garden,* 5
el jefe *chief,* 10
el jersey *sweater,* 8
la jirafa *giraffe,* 1
joven *young,* 5
el joven, la joven *young person,* 9; **los jóvenes** *young people,* 9
la joyería *jewelry store,* 8
el juego *game, 3;* **el juego de mesa** *board game,* 3; el juego de palabras *word game,* 7
el jueves *Thursday,* 1; **los jueves** *on Thursdays,* 3
el jugador *player,* 2G
jugar (ue) *to play,* 3
eljugo *juice,* 6; **el jugo de** *. . . juice,* 6
el juguete *toy,* 8
la juguetería *toy store,* 8
el juicio *judgment,* 6
julio *July,* 1
junio *June,* 1
juntos(as) *together,* 1
justo(a) *fair, just,* 10

el karate *karate,* 1
el kilómetro *kilometer,* 3
el kiosko *stand or stall,* 9G

la *the* (fem. article), 2
la *you, it,* (pronoun), 6; *you,* 9
las labores *chores,* 5
el lado: por todos lados *everywhere,* 8G
el lago *lake,* 10
la lágrima *tear,* 9
la lana *wool,* 8; **de lana** *made of wool,* 8
la lancha *motorboat,* 10; **pasear en lancha** *to go out in a motorboat,* 10
el lápiz (pl. los lápices) *pencil,* 4
largo(a) *long,* 5
las *the* (pl. fem. article), 2
las *you, them* (pronoun), 6
la lástima *pity,* 8; ¡Qué lástima! *What a shame!,* 8
la lata *can,* 9
latinoamericano(a) *Latin American,* 1
lavar *to wash,* 5; **lavar los platos** *to do the dishes,* 5
lavarse *to wash,* 7
le *to/for him, her, you,* 2
la leche *milk,* 6
leer *to read,* 3; al leer *upon reading,* 6; antes de leer *before reading,* 1; leamos *let's read,* 1; leer en voz alta *to read aloud,* 6; se leen *are read,* 5; **leer revistas y novelas** *to read magazines and novels,* 3
el legado *legacy,* 8G
lejano(a) *distant,* 10
lejos *far,* 9; **lejos de** *far from,* 5la lengua *language,* 9
los lentes *glasses,* 5; **usar lentes** *to wear glasses,* 5
lento(a) *slow,* 4G
el león *lion,* 1
les *to/for you* (pl.), *them,* 2
levantar *to lift,* 7; **levantar pesas** *to lift weights,* 7
levantarse *to get up,* 7
la leyenda *legend,* 10
libre *free,* 6G
la librería *bookstore,* 8
el libro *book,* 2; **el libro de amor** *romance book,* 2; **el libro de aventuras** *adventure book,* 2
el líder, la líder *leader,* 2
el limón *lemon,* 6
limpiar *to clean,* 5; limpio(a) *clean,* 5
lindo(a) *beautiful, pretty,* 6
listo(a) *ready,* 7; **estar listo(a)** *to be ready,* 7; **¿Está todo listo?** *Is everything ready?,* 9
llamado(a) *called,* 9G
llamar *to call,* 9; **llamar por teléfono** *to make a phone call,* 8; **Llamo más tarde.** *I'll call back later.,* 8; **Te llamo más tarde.** *I'll call you later.,* 9
la llegada *arrival,* 10
llegar *to arrive, to get there,* 4; al llegar *upon arriving,* 6; ha llegado *she has come,* 9
llenar *to fill up,* 3
lleno(a) *full,* 9
llevar *to wear,* 8; *to take,* 6; lo llevó *took it,* 6G; lleva años trabajando *he has been working for years,* 9
llevarse *to get along,* 2
llover (ue) *to rain,* 3; **llueve (mucho)** *it rains (a lot),* 3
lo *him, it,* 6; *you,* 9; **lo siento** *I'm sorry,* 8
lo: lo de siempre *same as usual,* 9; lo que *what,* 6; lo que pasa *what is happening,* xxii
loco *crazy,* 5
lógico(a) *logical,* 2
el lonche *lunch (Southwest U.S.),* 6
los *the* (pl. masc.), 2
los *you, them* (pronoun), 6
luchar *to struggle,* 8; *to fight,* 4G
luego *then, later,* 4
el lugar *place,* 1G
los lugares de interés *places of interest,* 10
la luna *moon,* 9
lunes *Monday,* 3; **los lunes** *on Mondays,* 3
la luz *light,* 7G

el macho *male,* 2
la madera *wood,* 5G
la madre *mother,* 5
madrina *godmother,* 1
el maestro *master,* 7G
magnífico(a) *magnificent,* 4
el maíz *corn,* 6
majestuoso(a) *majestic,* 9G
mal *bad;* **Estoy mal.** *I'm not so good.,* 1; **Te veo mal.** *You don't look so well.,* 7
la maleta *suitcase,* 10
malo(a) *bad,* 2
malvado(a) *evil,* 10
la mamá *mom,* 5
el mamífero *mammal,* 4G
la mañana *morning,* 4; **por la mañana** *in the morning,* 4
mañana *tomorrow,* 4; **Hasta mañana.** *See you tomorrow.,* 1
mandar *to send,* 9; **mandar invitaciones** *to send invitations,* 9; **mandar tarjetas** *to send cards,* 9
el mandato *command,* 6
manejar *to manage,* 7
la manera *way,* 9
la mano *hand,* 7
el manojo *bunch,* 8
mantener *to preserve, to keep,* 6
mantenerse (ie) *to maintain,* 7; **mantenerse (ie) en forma** *to stay in shape,* 7
la manzana *apple,* 6
el mapa *map,* 10
el maquillaje *makeup,* 7
maquillarse *to put on makeup,* 7
marcado(a) *marked,* 7
marcar *to set, to dial,* 1
marcharse *to leave,* 9
el marisco *shellfish,* 5G
marítimo(a) *maritime,* 3G
marrón *brown,* 2; los ojos marrones *brown eyes,* 5
el martes *Tuesday,* 1; **los martes** *on Tuesdays,* 3
marzo *March,* 1
más *more,* 2; **Más o menos.** *So-so.,* 1; **más que** *more than,* 8; **más... que** more *. . . than,* 8
la masa *dough,* 3
la máscara *mask,* 2G
la mascarada *masquerade,* 4G
el mate *Argentine and Paraguayan tea,* 7
las matemáticas *mathematics,* 4
la materia *subject,* 4; las materias obligatorias *required subjects,* 4; las materias opcionales *elective,* 4
matutino(a) *(in the) morning,* 4
mayo *May,* 1
mayor(es) *older,* 5; *greater,* 3G
la mayoría *majority,* 4G
la mazorca *corn on the cob,* 6
me *to/for me,* 2; **Me da igual.** *It's all the same to me.,* 2; **Me duele(n)...** *My . . . hurt(s),* 7; **Me gusta(n)...** *I like . . .,* 2; **Me gusta(n) más...** *I like . . . more.,* 2; **Me gusta(n)... mucho.** *I like . . . a lot.,* 2; **Me llamo...** *My name is . . .,* 1; **No, no me gusta(n)...** *No, I don't like . . .,* 2; **Me parece bien.** *It seems fine to me.,* 5; **Me parece injusto.** *It's not fair.,* 5
me *me,* 9
mecánico *mechanic,* 5
la medalla *medal,* 5G
mediano(a) *medium,* 4
la medianoche *midnight,* 1
médico(a) *medical,* 7
medio(a) *half,* 4; **y media** *half past,* 1
los medios de transporte *means of transportation,* 10
el mediodía *midday, noon,* 1
medir (i) *to measure,* 5G
mejor(es) *better, best,* 7
el melocotón *peach,* 6
menor(es) *younger,* 5
menos *less,* 8; **menos cuarto** *a quarter to . . .,* 1; **menos que** *less than,* 8; **menos... que** *less . . . than,* 8
el mensaje *message,* 7G
la mente *mind,* 4
el mercado *market,* 6; el mercado al aire libre *open-air market,* 8
merendar (ie) *to have a snack,* 5
el merengue *music and dance style,* 9G
la merienda *snack,* 6
la mesa *table,* 5; **poner la mesa** *to set the table,* 6
los meses del año *months of the year,* 1
meter *to put in,* 8
meterse *to set,* 9
metódico(a) *methodical,* 2
el metro *meter,* 1G
el metro *subway,* 10
mezclar *to mix,* 6; mezcla *mixture,* 6
la mezquita *mosque,* 1G
mí *me,* 5; **A mí me gusta** + infinitive *I like to . . .,* 3; **a mí me toca...** *I have to . . .,* 5
mi(s) *my,* 1; **mi materia preferida es...** *my favorite subject is . . .,* 4 **mi mejor amigo(a)** *my best friend,* 1, **mi profesor(-a)** *my teacher,* 1
la miel *honey,* 6
el miembro *member,* 3
mientras *while,* 6
el miércoles *Wednesday,* 1; **los miércoles** *on Wednesdays,* 3
mil *one thousand,* 8; miles *thousands,* 2
la milla cuadrada *square mile,* 3
un millón (de) *one million,* 8; **dos millones (de)** *two million,* 8
mío *mine,* 8
mirar *to look,* 9; **Nada más estoy mirando.** *I'm just looking.,* 8; **mirar las vitrinas** *to window-shop,* 8
la misa *Mass,* 9
la misión *mission,* 3G
mismo(a) *same,* 6
el misterio *mystery,* 2
misterioso(a) *mysterious,* 2
la mitad *half,* 6G
la mochila *backpack,* 4
la moda *style, fashion,* 8; **a la última moda** *in the latest fashion,* 8; muy de moda *very fashionable,* 8; **pasado(a) de moda** *out of style,* 8
modelar *to shape,* 4
moderno(a) *modern,* 7
el módulo *module,* 10
el mogote *knoll,* 9G
el mole *sauce made with chiles and flavored with chocolate,* 6
el molino *windmill,* 1G
el momento *moment,* 6; **Espera un momento.** *Hold on a moment.,* 8
la monarquía parlamentaria *constitutional monarchy,* 1G
la moneda *currency,* 2; *coin,* 8
el mono *monkey,* 4G
la montaña *mountain,* 10; **subir a la montaña** *to go up a mountain,* 10
montañoso(a) *mountainous,* 7G
montar *to ride,* montar a caballo *to ride a horse,* 3G; **montar en bicicleta** *to ride a bike,* 3
un montón *a ton,* 4
el monumento *monument,* 1G
el morado *purple,* 1G
morado(a) *purple,* 8
moreno(a) *dark-haired; dark-skinned,* 2
morir (ue) *to die,* 5; murió *died,* 5
el moro *rice and beans,* 9G
el mosaico *mosaic,* 6G
el mosquito *mosquito,* 2
el mostrador *counter,* 10
mostrar (ue) *to show,* 1G
el movimiento *movement,* 4G
la muchacha *girl,* 1
el muchacho *boy,* 1
mucho *a lot (of),* 2; *much,* 4; **Mucho gusto.** *Pleased/Nice to meet you.,* 1
muchos(as) *a lot of, many,* 4
mudarse *to move,* 8G
mudéjar *Moslem,* 5G
la muerte *death,* 4G
la mujer *woman,* 8; **la mujer de**

negocios *business woman,* 5; **para mujeres** *for women,* 8
mundialmente *worldwide,* 6
el mundo *world,* 1G; todo el mundo *everybody,* 9
el mural *mural painting,* 6G
la muralla *wall, rampart,* 1G
el museo *museum,* 10
la música *music,* 2; **la música de...** *music of/by . . .,* 2; la música clásica *classical music,* 2G
el músico *musician,* 2
muy *very,* 2

nacer *to be born,* 7G; había nacido *had been born,* 7G; nacido(a) *born,* 8G
nacional *national,* 1
nada *nothing,* 4; *not anything,* 5
Nada más estoy mirando. *I'm just looking.,* 8
nadar *to swim,* 3
nadie *nobody, not anybody,* 5
la naranja *orange,* 6
el naranjo *orange tree,* 8G
la nariz *nose,* 7
la natación *swimming,* 7
nativo(a) *native,* 6
la naturaleza *nature,* 2
la navaja *razor,* 7
navegar *to sail,* 5; *to navigate,* 10; **navegar por Internet** *to surf the Internet,* 3
la Navidad *Christmas,* 9
la necesidad *necessity,* 7
necesitar *to need,* 4; **¿Necesitas algo?** *Do you need anything?,* 4; **Necesito muchas cosas.** *I need a lot of things.,* 4; **No, no necesito nada.** *No, I don't need anything.,* 4
negarse *to refuse,* 5
negociable *negotiable,* 5
el negocio *business,* 9
negro(a) *black,* 5
nervioso(a) *nervous,* 7
nevar (ie) *to snow,* 3
ni *neither, nor,* 7; **Ni idea.** *I have no idea.,* 3
el nido *nest,* 1
la nieta *granddaughter,* 5
el nieto *grandson,* 5
los nietos *grandsons, grandchildren,* 5
nieva *it snows,* 3
la niña *girl,* 1
ninguno(a) *no, none,* 10G; **ninguna parte** *nowhere,* 3; **no va a ninguna parte** *he/she doesn't go anywhere,* 3
el niño *male child,* 8
los niños *children,* 8
el nivel del mar *sea level,* 9G
no no, 3; *not, do not,* 5; **No debes...** *You shouldn't . . .,* 7; **No es gran cosa.** *It's not a big deal.,* 5; **No está.** *He/She is not here.,* 8; **No estoy de acuerdo.** *I disagree.,* 6; **no, gracias** *no thank you,* 8; **No sé.** *I don't know.,* 4; **No, no me gusta(n)...** *No, I don't like . . .,* 2; **No, no necesito nada.** *No, I do not need anything.,* 4; **No, no voy a ir.** *No, I'm not going to go.,* 4; **No seas...** *Don't be . . .,* 7; **No va a ninguna parte.** *He/She doesn't go anywhere.,* 3; **No vayas.** *Don't go.,* 7
¿no? *right?,* 4
la Nochebuena *Christmas Eve,* 9
la Nochevieja *New Year's Eve,* 9
nocturno(a) *(in the) evening,* 4
nombrado(a) *named,* 9G
el nombre *name,* 10
el noreste *northeast,* 2G
normalmente *normally,* 4
el noroeste *northwest,* 7G
el norte *north,* 5G
norteamericano(a) *North American,* 8
norteño(a) *northern,* 5G
Noruega *Norway,* 7G
nos *(to/for) us,* 2; **Nos vemos.** *See you.,* 1
nosotros(as) *we,* 1
la nota *grade,* 6
la noticia *news,* 9
novecientos *nine hundred,* 8
la novela *novel,* 3
noventa *ninety,* 2
noviembre *November,* 1
la nube *cloud,* 7
nuestro(a) *our,* 5
nuestros(as) *our,* 5
nuevamente *again,* 9
nueve *nine,* 1
nuevo(a) *new,* 2
la nuez (pl. las nueces) *nuts,* 6
el número *number,* 1; *shoe size,* 8
numeroso(a) *numerous,* 2G
nunca *never,* 5; **casi nunca** *almost never,* 3; nunca más *never again,* 6
la nutricionista *nutritionist,* 7

o *or,* 2
oaxaqueño *from the Mexican state of Oaxaca,* 6
el objetivo *objective,* 1
el objeto *object,* 1
la obra *work,* 7G; la obra de teatro *play,* 6G; la obra maestra *masterpiece,* 6G
observar *to observe,* 1
la ocasión *occasion,* 9
occidental *western,* 7G
ochenta *eighty,* 2
ocho *eight,* 1
ochocientos *eight hundred,* 8
el ocio *leisure time,* 8
octubre *October,* 1
el ocupante *occupant,* 10
ocupar *to occupy,* 7G
ocurrir *to occur;* ¿se te ocurren? *do they occur to you?,* 4
la oficina *office,* 5
la oficina de cambio *money exchange,* 10
la oficina de correos *post office,* 10
ofrecer *to offer,* 6
el oído *ear,* 7
oír *to hear,* 2; oyes *(you) hear,* 2; se oye *is heard,* 2
los ojos *eyes,* 5; los ojos borrados *hazel eyes,* 5; los ojos cafés *brown eyes,* 5; **tener los ojos azules** *to have blue eyes,* 5
la ola *wave,* 2G
la olla *pot,* 4G
olor *smell,* 7
olvidar *to forget,* 9; no te olvides *don't forget,* 8
once *eleven,* 1
la oportunidad *opportunity,* 5
la oración *sentence,* xxii
el orden *order,* 1; el orden cronológico *chronological order,* 8
ordenar *to organize,* 3; está ordenando *is organizing,* 3
organizado(a) *organized,* 2
organizar *to organize,* 10
orgulloso(a) *proud,* 6
oriental *eastern,* 10G
el origen *origin,* 6G
originalmente *originally,* 3G
os *(to/for) you* (pl.), 2
el oso *bear,* 1
el otoño *fall,* 3
otro(a) *other, another,* 8
otros(as) *other, others,* 8

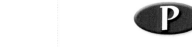

el paciente *patient,* 7
el padre *father,* 5
los padres *parents,* 5; los padres peregrinos *pilgrims,* 8G
pagar *to pay,* 8; **pagar una fortuna**

to pay a fortune, 8
la página *page,* xxii; la página Web *Web page,* 1
el país *country,* 6; el país de origen *native country,* 6
el paisaje *landscape,* 4G
el pájaro *bird,* 9
la palabra *word,* xxii; la palabra clave *key word,* 1
el palacio *palace,* 1
el pan *bread,* 6; **el pan dulce** *pastries,* 6; **el pan tostado** *toast,* 6
la pantalla *monitor, screen,* 10
los pantalones (vaqueros) *pants (jeans),* 8
los pantalones cortos *shorts,* 8
la pantomima *pantomime,* 9
la pantorrilla *calf,* 7
el papá *dad,* 5
el Papá Noel *Santa Claus,* 9
la papa *potato,* 6; **las papas fritas** *french fries,* 6
el papel *paper,* 4
las papitas *potato chips,* 9
el paquete *package,* 9
el par *pair,* 8
para *for,* 4; *to, in order to,* 7
el paraíso *paradise,* 8G
parecer *to seem,* 5; *to think,* 8; me parece *it seems to me,* 9; **Me parece bien.** *It's all right/seems fine to me.,* 5; **Me parece injusto.** *I don't think that's fair./It seems unfair to me.,* 5; No parezco. *I don't seem to be.,* 9; **¿Qué te parece...?** *What do you think of...?,* 8
parecido(a) similar, 2
la pared *wall,* 10G
la pareja *pair;* en parejas *in pairs,* xxii, *couple,* 3
el paréntesis *parenthesis,* 8
el pareo *matching,* 1
el pariente *relative,* 5
el parque *park,* 3; **el parque de diversiones** *amusement park,* 10
el párrafo *paragraph,* xxii
la parrilla *barbecue,* 7
la parrillada *Argentine barbecue,* 7G
la parte *part,* 6
participar *to participate,* 1
particular *particular,* 6
el partido de... *the . . . game,* 4
la pasa *raisin,* 6
el pasado *past,* 8
pasado mañana *day after tomorrow,* 4
pasado(a) *last,* 8; **el año pasado** *last year,* 9
pasado(a) de moda *out of style,* 8
el pasaje *ticket,* 10
el pasajero, la pasajera *passenger,* 10
el pasapalo *finger food (Ven.),* 9
el pasaporte *passport,* 10
pasar *to spend (time, occasion),* 9; con quien tú te pasas *who you spend time with,* 2; **la pasamos en casa de...** *we spent it at . . .'s house,* 9; lo que pasa *what is happening,* 9; **pasar el rato solo(a)** *to spend time alone,* 3; **pasar la aspiradora** *to vacuum,* 5; **pasar por** *to stop at/by,* 10; *to go through,* 2; qué pasa *what's happening,* 6
pasartelo(la) *to get someone for a telephone call,* 8
el pasatiempo *hobby,* 7; **buscar un pasatiempo** *to look for a hobby,* 7
pasear *to go for a walk,* 3; *to go out in,* 10; **pasear en bote de vela** *to go out in a sailboat,* 10; **pasear en lancha** *to go out in a motorboat,* 10
el pasillo *corridor,* 10
la pasta de dientes *toothpaste,* 7
el pastel *cake,* 6
el pastel en hojas *mashed plantain dough filled with meat and wrapped in plantain leaves,* 9
la patata *potato,* 1G; *sweet potato,* 6
el patinaje en hielo *ice skating,* 7
patinar *to skate,* 3
el patio *patio, yard,* 5
la patrona *patron,* 9G
la pava *kettle used to make* ***mate,*** 7
el pavo *turkey,* 6G
el payaso *clown,* 4G
el pecho *chest,* 7
pedir (i) *to order,* 6
peinarse *to comb your hair,* 7
el peine *comb,* 7
la película *film, movie,* 2; **(de ciencia ficción, de terror, de misterio)** *(science fiction, horror, mystery),* 2
el peligro de extinción *danger of extinction,* 8G
pelirrojo(a) *red-headed,* 2
el pelo *hair,* 5
la pelota *ball,* 9G
pensar (ie) *to think,* 8; **pensar** + inf. *to plan,* 9; **Pensamos...** *We plan to . . .,* 9
peor(es) *worse,* 8
pequeño(a) *small,* 5; **bastante pequeño(a)** *pretty small,* 5
la pera *pear,* 1
perder (ie) *to lose,* 10; *to miss,* 10; **perder el vuelo** *miss the flight,* 10; si me pierden *if you lose me*
perdido(a) *lost,* 10G
perdone *I'm sorry,* 1
el perezoso *sloth,* 4G
perezoso(a) *lazy,* 2
perfecto *perfect,* 8
el periódico *newspaper,* 8G
la perla *pearl,* 2G
permiso *excuse me,* 9
permitir *to allow,* 6
pero *but,* 5
el perro, la perra *dog,* 5
la persona *person,* 2
el personaje *character,* 1G; el personaje ficticio *fictional character,* 1G
la personalidad *personality,* 2
las pesas *weights,* 7; **levantar pesas** *to lift weights,* 7
la pesca *fishing,* 10; **ir de pesca** *to go fishing,* 10; la pesca comercial *commercial fishing,* 8G
el pescado *fish,* 6
pescar *to fish,* 10
pésimo(a) *very bad,* 2
el peso *weight,* 7
el pez *fish,* 1
la picadera *finger food (Dom. Rep.),* 9
el picante *spice,* 6
picante *spicy,* 6
el picnic *picnic,* 9; **tener un picnic** *to have a picnic,* 9
el pico *peak,* 1G
el pie *foot,* 7
la piedra *stone,* 5G
la pierna *leg,* 7
la pieza *bedroom,* 5; *piece,* 4
la pileta *swimming pool (Arg.),* 3
la piñata *piñata,* 9
el pingüino *penguin,* 7G
pintado(a) *painted,* 2G
pintar *to paint;* fue pintado *was painted,* 1
el pintor *painter,* 2G
pintoresco(a) *picturesque,* 7G
la pintura *painting,* 1; la pintura al óleo *oil painting,* 3G
la pirámide *pyramid,* 10; la pirámide alimenticia *food pyramid,* 7
la piscina *swimming pool,* 3
el piso *floor,* 5; **de... pisos** *. . . story,* 5
el piyama *pajamas,* 7
la pizza *pizza,* 2
el placer *pleasure,* 9
planes *plans,* 9; **¿Qué planes tienen para...?** *What plans do you have for . . .?,* 9
plano(a) *flat,* 7G
las plantas *plants,* 5
el plátano *plantain,* 8G
platicar *to chat,* 3
el plato *dish, plate,* 6; **lavar los platos** *to do the dishes,* 5; **el plato hondo** *bowl,* 6; el plato típico *traditional dish,* 2
la playa *beach,* 3
la playera *T-shirt,* 8
la plaza de comida *food court in a mall,* 8
la plena *music and dance style,* 2
la población *population,* 1G
poblado(a) *populated,* 4G
pobre *poor,* 8

Vocabulario español-inglés

poco(a) *few, little, not much,* 4; poco a poco *little by little,* 4; **un poco** *a little,* 2
pocos(as) *not many,* 4
poder (ue) *to be able to, can,* 6
el poema *poem,* 8
la poesía *poetry,* 8
el poeta, la poeta *poet,* 5G
el pollo *chicken,* 6; el pollo frito *fried chicken,* 2G
el ponche *punch,* 9
poner (-go) *to put,* 4; **no pongas** *don't put,* 10; **pon** *put,* 6; poner en orden *to put in order,* xxii; poner huevos *to lay eggs,* 2; poner la comida *to set out the food,* 9; **poner la mesa** *to set the table,* 6; tener puesto(a) *to have on,* 8
ponerse *to put on,* 7, *to get,* 6; ponerse *to start,* 7; ponerse a bailar *to start dancing,* 3; ponerse en contacto *to get in contact,* 5; ponerse rojo *to flush, to turn red,* 10
por in, by, 4; por ejemplo *for example,* 6G; por eso *that's why,* 6; por el estilo *of that sort,* 7; **por favor** *please,* 6; por fin *at last,* 8; **por la mañana** *in the morning,* 4; por la noche *at night,* 2; **por la tarde** *in the afternoon,* 4; por lo general *generally,* 8; por lo menos *at least,* 9; por más que *no matter how much,* 7; por medio de *by means of,* 10
¿por qué? *why?,* 2
la porción *portion, serving,* 7
porque *because,* 2
posible *possible,* 4
el postre *dessert,* 6
el pozole *soup made with hominy, meat, and chile,* 6
practicando *practicing,* 7
practicar deportes *to play sports,* 3
el precio *price,* 1; el precio de entrada *entry fee,* 1
precolombino(a) *of the New World era before the arrival of Europeans,* 2G
precoz *precocious,* 4
la preferencia *preference,* 3
preferido(a) *favorite,* 4
preferir (ie) *to prefer,* 6
la pregunta *question,* xxii
preguntar *to ask,* xxii
prehistórico(a) *prehistoric,* 7
preocuparse *to worry,* 9
preocuparse *to worry,* 10; **No te preocupes.** *Don't worry.,* 10
preparar *to prepare,* 6
prepararse *to get ready,* 7
los preparativos *preparations,* 9
la preposición *preposition,* 2
la presentación *introduction,* 9
presentar *to present,* 6; *to introduce,* 9; **presentar el examen** *to take an exam,* 4; se presentó *was performed,* 10; **te presento a...** *I'd like you to meet . . .,* 9
presentarse *to present oneself,* 6
el presente *present,* 9
prestar: prestar atención *to pay attention,* 7
el pretérito *preterite,* 8
la primavera *spring,* 3
el primero *first,* 1
primero(a) *first,* 4
el primo, la prima *cousin,* 5; el primo hermano, la prima hermana *first cousin,* 5
los primos *cousins,* 5
la princesa *princess,* 10
principal *main,* 4G; *primary,* 9G
la prisa *hurry;* **tener prisa** *to be in a hurry,* 4
el prisionero *prisoner,* 10
probar (ue) *to try, to taste,* 6
producir *to produce,* 1
el producto *product,* 3G; los productos petroleros *petroleum products,* 3G; los productos químicos *chemicals,* 3G
el profesor *teacher (male),* 1; **mi profesor** *my teacher,* 1
la profesora *teacher (female),* 1; **mi profesora** *my teacher,* 1
prometer *to promise,* 8
el pronombre *pronoun,* 6; el pronombre de complemento directo *direct object pronoun,* 9; el pronombre reflexivo *reflexive pronoun,* 7
pronto *soon,* 1; **Hasta pronto.** *See you soon.,* 1; tan pronto *as soon,* 9
la propiedad *property,* 5
propio(a) *own,* 4
el propósito *purpose,* 6
el provecho *benefit;* Buen provecho. *Enjoy your meal.,* 6
la provincia *province,* 10
próximo(a) *next,* 4; **la próxima semana** *next week,* 4; **el** *(day of the week)* **próximo** *next (day of the week),* 4
el proyecto *project,* 1
publicar *to publish,* 1
el pueblo *town, village,* 5; el pueblo natal *hometown,* 3
¿Puedo...? *Can I . . .?,* 6
el puente *bridge,* 8G
la puerta *door,* 5; *gate,* 10
el puerto *port,* 3G
el puesto *stall,* 9G
la pulsera *bracelet,* 8
el punto *dot,* 1
el punto de vista *point of view,* 9
puntual *punctual, on time,* 2
el puré de papas *mashed potatoes,* 6

que *that;* **que me llame después** *tell him/her to call me later,* 8; **Que te vaya bien.** *Hope things go well for you.,* 9
¡Qué...! *How . . .!;* **¡Qué bien!** *How great!,* 10; **¡Qué fantástico!** *How fantastic!,* 10; **¡Qué gusto verte!** *It's great to see you!,* 9; **¡Qué lástima!** *What a shame!,* 10; **¡Qué lata!** *What a pain!,* 5; **¡Qué mala suerte!** *What bad luck!,* 10
¿qué? *what?,* 1; **¿Qué clases tienes ...?** *What classes do you have . . . ?,* 4; **¿Qué día es hoy?** *What day is today?,* 1; **¿Qué están haciendo?** *What are they doing?,* 9; **¿Qué fecha es hoy?** *What's today's date?,* 1; **¿Qué hace...?** *What does . . . do?,* 3; **¿Qué haces para ayudar en casa?** *What do you do to help out at home?,* 5; **¿Qué haces...?** *What do you do . . .?,* 3; **¿Qué haces para relajarte?** *What do you do to relax?,* 7; **¿Qué hay de nuevo?** *What's new?,* 9; **¿Qué hiciste?** *What did you do?,* 8; **¿Qué hora es?** *What time is it?,* 1; **¿Qué planes tienen para...?** *What plans do you have for . . .?,* 9; **¿Qué quieres hacer?** *What do you want to do?,* 3; **¿Qué tal?** *How's it going?,* 1; **¿Qué tal...?** *How is . . .?,* 6; **¿Qué tal estuvo?** *How was it?,* 9; **¿Qué tal si...?** *How about if. . .?,* 6; **¿Qué tal si vamos a...?** *How about if we go to . . .?,* 4; **¿Qué te falta hacer?** *What do you still have to do?,* 7; **¿Qué te gusta hacer?** *What do you like to do?,* 3; **¿Qué te pasa?** *What's wrong with you?,* 7; **¿Qué te toca hacer a ti?** *What do you have to do?,* 5; **¿Qué tiempo hace?** *What's the weather like?,* 3; **¿Qué tiene...?** *What's the matter with . . .?,* 7; **¿Qué tienes que hacer?** *What do you have to do?,* 7; **¿Qué vas a hacer?** *What are you going to do?,* 4
el quechua *indigenous language in Peru,* 10G
quedar *to fit, to look,* 8; *to remain,* 3G; **¿Cómo me queda...?** *How*

does it fit?, 8; **quedar bien/mal** *to fit well/poorly*, 8
quedarse *to stay*, 9; **quedarse en...** *to stay in . . .*, 10
los quehaceres *household chores*, 5; **hacer los quehaceres** *to do chores*, 5
querer (ie) *to want to*, 3; *to love*, 9; **quiero conocer...** *I want to see . . .*, 10; queriendo *wanting to*, 8; **Quiero ir...** *I want to go . . .*, 3
querido(a) *dear*, 9
la quesadilla *tortillas with melted cheese*, 3G
el queso *cheese*, 6
¿quién? *who?*, 1; **¿De parte de quién?** *Who's calling?*, 8; **Quién es...?** *Who is . . .?*, 1; ¿de quién? *about whom?*, 1
¿quiénes? *who?* (pl.), 2
la química *chemistry*, 4
quince *fifteen*, 1
la quinceañera *girl's fifteenth birthday*, 9
quinientos *five hundred*, 8
el quiosco *stand*, 10
Quisiera... *I would like . . .*, 6
quitarse *to take off*, 7

las raciones *servings*, 6
la raíz (pl. las raíces) *root*, 1G
rallado *grated*, 6
la rana *frog*, 2
los rancheros *overalls*, 3
rápidamente *quickly*, 6
rápido(a) *fast*, 8
raro *add, strange*, 3
el rato *time*, 3; el rato libre *free time*, 4
reaccionar *to react*, 10
el realismo *realism*, 1
realizar *to carry out*, 10, ha realizado *has carried out*, 10G
el recado *message*, 8
la recámara *bedroom*, 5
recibir *to receive*, 9; **recibir regalos** *to receive gifts*, 9
reclamar *to reclaim*, 6G
el reclamo de equipaje *baggage claim*, 10
recoger *to pick up*, 10
la recomendación *recommendation*, 7
reconocido(a) *well-known*, 1G
recordar *to remember*, 6
recorrer *to tour*, 10
el recorrido *tour*, 4
el recreo *recreation time*, 4
la red *network*, 10G
redondo(a) *round*, 7
reducir *to reduce*, 7
referir *to refer*, 3; se refiere *refers*, 3G
reflejar *to reflect*, 1G
el refrán *proverb, saying*, 6
el refresco *soft drink*, 6
el refrigerador *refrigerator*, 6
el refugio de fauna *wildlife refuge*, 8G
el regalo *gift*, 9; **abrir regalos** *to open gifts*, 9; **recibir regalos** *to receive gifts*, 9
regatear *to bargain*, 8
la región *region*, 3
regional *regional*, 6
la regla *ruler*, 4
regresar *to return, to go back*, 4
regular *all right*, 1; **estoy regular** *I'm all right*, 1
regularidad: con regularidad *regularly*, 6
reírse *to laugh*, 8; ríe *he/she laughs*, 9; se ríen *they laugh*, 8
relajarse *to relax*, 7
religioso(a) *religious*, 1
el reloj *clock, watch*, 4
remodelado(a) *remodeled*, 5
remojar *to soak*, 3
remoto(a) *distant*, 5
el renacuajo *tadpole*, 2
el repaso *review*, 1
representar *to represent*, 3
representativo(a) *representative*, 6
la respuesta *answer*, xxii
la república *republic*, 5G
el res *beef*, 6
la reservación *reservation*, 6
requerir (ie) *to require*, 7
la resolución de Año Nuevo *New Year's resolution*, 9
resolver (ue) *to solve*, 7
respectivo(a) *respective*, 8
responder *to answer*, 9
la respuesta *answer*, 3
el restaurante *restaurant*, 6
el restaurante familiar *family restaurant*, 3
el retrato *portrait*, 1G
la reunión *meeting*, 3; *reunion*, 9
reunir *to bring together*, 1G
reunirse *to get together*, 9; **reunirse con (toda) la familia** *to get together with the (whole) family*, 9
revisar *to check, to revise, to correct*, 1
la revista *magazine*, 3; **la revista de tiras cómicas** *comic book*, 8
el revolucionario *revolutionary*, 9G
el rey *king*, 1
rico(a) *magnificent*, 9
ridículo(a) *ridiculous*, 8
riguroso(a) *harsh*, 5G
el río *river*, 3G
las riquezas *riches*, 10
riquísimo(a) *delicious*, 6
el ritmo *rhythm*, 5G; el ritmo del momento *the latest rhythm*, 1
el rito *ritual*, 6
el robo *rip-off*, 8; **¡Es un robo!** *It's a rip-off!*, 8
rodeado(a) *surrounded*, 1G
rodear *to surround*, 7G
el rodeo *rodeo*, 3G
rojo(a) *red*, 8
romántico(a) *romantic*, 2
el rompecabezas *puzzle*, 4
la ropa *clothes*, 4
rubio(a) *blond*, 2
las ruinas *ruins*, 10
la rutina *routine*, 2

el sábado *Saturday*, 1; **los sábados** *on Saturdays*, 3
saber *to know information*, 4; **saber de** *to know about*, 4; no sabe cómo *doesn't know how*, 9; **No sé.** *I don't know.*, 4; **¿Sabes qué?** *You know what?*, 4; Sé. *I know.*, 9
sacar *to take out*, 6; **sacar el dinero** *to get money*, 10; **sacar fotos** *to take photos*, 10; **sacar la basura** *to take out the trash*, 5; sacar una idea *to get an idea*, 4
el saco *sportscoat*, 8
sal *go out, leave*, 6
la sal *salt*, 6
la sala *living room*, 5; **la sala de espera** *waiting room*, 10; la sala de juegos *game room*, 5
salado(a) *salty*, 6
la salida *departure*, 10; *exit*, 10
salir (-go, ie) *to go out*, 3; *to leave*, 4; **no salgas** *don't leave*, 10; que salga *to go out*, 9; **sal** *go out, leave*, 6; salir bien *to work out well*, 7; **salir con amigos** *to go out with friends*, 3
el salón *room*, 1; **el salón de clase** *classroom*, 4
la salsa *sauce, gravy*, 6; **la salsa picante** *hot sauce*, 6
el salto *waterfall*, 2G
el salto en el tiempo *time warp*, 7
la salud *health*, 7
saludable *healthy*, 6
saludar *to greet*, 1
el saludo *greeting*, 9

Vocabulario español-inglés

salvarse *to save oneself,* 10
el salvavidas *lifeguard,* 1
el sancocho *stew made with meat, root vegetables and plantains,* 9G
las sandalias *sandals,* 8
el sándwich de... *. . . sandwich,* 6
los sanitarios *restrooms,* 10
sano(a) *healthy,* 7; **seguir una dieta sana** *to eat a balanced diet,* 7
el santo, la santa *saint,* 2G
la sarten, *frying pan,* 6
sé *be,* 6
la secadora de pelo *hair dryer,* 7
secarse *to dry,* 7
la sección rítmica *rhythm section,* 8G
seco(a) *dry,* 2G
secreto(a) *secret,* 1
la sed *thirst,* 4; **tener sed** *to be thirsty,* 4
la seda silk, 8; **de seda** made of silk, 8
seguir (i) *to follow,* 10; **seguir (i) una dieta sana** *to eat a balanced diet,* 7; sigue el modelo *follow the model,* xxii; siguiéndote *following you,* 8
según *according to,* 2
el segundo *second,* 4
segundo(a) *second,* 6
seis *six,* 1
seiscientos *six hundred,* 8
la selección *selection,* 6
la selva *jungle,* 10
la semana *week,* 4; **el día de la semana** *day of the week,* 1; **esta semana** *this week,* 4; **la próxima semana** *next week,* 4
la Semana Santa *Holy Week,* 9
el señor *sir, Mr.,* 1; *gentleman,* 8
el Señor *the Lord,* 9
la señora *ma'am; Mrs.,* 1
la señorita *miss,* 1
la sensación *feeling,* 1
sentarse (ie) *to sit down,* 10
sentir (ie) *to feel,* 9
sentirse (ie) *to feel,* 7
separados *separately,* 8
separar *to separate,* 1G
septiembre *September,* 1
ser *to be,* 1; **¿Cómo eres?** *What are you like?,* 2; **¿Cómo es...?** *What is . . . like?,* 2; No puede ser. *It can't be true.,* 9; **no seas** *don't be,* 7; **sé** *be,* 6; **será** *will be,* 10; **Soy...** *I'm . . .,* 2; **Soy de...** *I'm from . . .,* 1
el ser *being,* 8
la serenata *serenade,* 9
la serenidad *serenity,* 1
la serie *series,* 6G
serio(a) *serious,* 2
la serpiente *serpent,* 6
el servicio *restroom,* 10
la servilleta *napkin,* 6
servir (i) *to serve,* 6; **¿En qué le puedo servir?** *Can I help you?,* 8
sesenta *sixty,* 2
el seso *brain,* 4
setecientos *seven hundred,* 8
setenta *seventy,* 2
si *if,* 3; si no *otherwise,* 3
sí *yes,* 4; **Sí, necesito muchas cosas.** *Yes, I need a lot of things.,* 4; **Sí, tengo un montón.** *Yes, I have a ton of them.,* 4
siempre *always,* 5; **casi siempre** *almost always,* 3; **como siempre** *as always,* 9; **lo de siempre** *same as usual,* 9
la sierra *mountain range,* 10G
siete *seven,* 1
el siglo *century,* 3G
el significado *meaning,* 7
significar *to mean,* 2
siguiente *following,* 5; **lo siguiente** *the following,* 6
la sílaba *syllable,* 2
la silla *chair,* 5; **la silla de ruedas** *wheelchair,* 5
el símbolo *symbol,* 2
simpático(a) *friendly,* 2
simplemente *simply,* 6
sin *without,* 6; sin embargo *however,* 6
la sinagoga *synagogue,* 9
sincero(a) *sincere,* 2
sino *but also,* 6
los sirvientes *servants,* 8
el sistema *system,* 10G
el sitio *place,* 3; *site,* 7
la situación *situation,* 5
sobre *over,* 3; *on,* 4; *about,* 2
la sobrina *niece,* 5
el sobrino *nephew,* 5
los sobrinos *nephews, nieces and nephews,* 5
sociable *social,* 2
el sofá *sofa,* 5
el sol *sun,* 3; **Hace sol.** *It's sunny.,* 3
solamente *only,* 3G
el soldado *soldier,* 6G
soler *to usually do,* 5; suele *usually,* 5
sólido(a) *solid,* 6
sólo *only,* 4
sólo(a) *alone,* 3; **pasar el rato sólo(a)** *to spend time alone,* 3; **sólo** *only,* 7
el sombrero *hat,* 8
somos (inf. ser) *we are,* 5; **somos... personas** *there are . . . people,* 5
Son las... *It's . . . o'clock.,* 1
el sonido *sound,* 2G
la sopa *soup,* 6; **la sopa de verduras** *vegetable soup,* 6
sordo(a) *deaf,* 5
sorprendido(a) *surprised,* 8
Soy... (inf. **ser**) *I'm . . .,* 2; **Soy de...** *I'm from . . .,* 1
su(s) *his, her, its, their,* 5
suave *soft,* 7
subir *to rise,* 7
subir a la montaña *to climb a mountain,* 10; **subir de peso** *to gain weight,* 7
el subtítulo *subtitle,* 10
sucio(a) *dirty,* 6
el sudeste *south east,* 10G
Suele + inf. *He (She) usually + verb,* 10
el sueño *dream,* 1G
la suerte *luck,* 10; **si tengo suerte...** *if I'm lucky . . .,* 10; **Tuviste suerte.** *You were lucky.,* 10
el suéter *sweater,* 8
suficiente *enough,* 7; **dormir lo suficiente** *to get enough sleep,* 7
la sugerencia *suggestion,* 7
sugerir *to suggest,* 6
Suiza *Switzerland,* 7G
la superficie *surface,* 8
el sur *south,* 2G
sureño(a) *southern,* 7G
el surf a vela *windsurfing,* 9G
sus *his/her,* 4; *their, your,* 5
la sustancia *substance,* 6
suyo(a) *his,* 4G

Tailandia *Thailand,* 6
taíno(a) *belonging to the Tainos, Native Americans dominant in early Puerto Rico,* 2G
tal *such,* 7; tal vez *perhaps,* 4
la talla *(clothing) size,* 8
tallado(a) *carved, cut,* 10G
los tallarines *noodles,* 7
el taller *shop, workshop,* 4
la tamalada *gathering to make tamales,* 3G
los tamales *tamales,* 9
el tamaño *size*
también *also,* 2
la tambora *drum,* 9G
tampoco *neither, not either,* 5
tan *so,* 10G
tan sólo *only,* 9
tan... como *as . . . as,* 8
tanto *so much,* 7; *as much,* 1G; tanto... como... *both . . . and . . .,* 3G; **Tanto gusto.** *So nice to meet you.,* 9; **Tanto tiempo.** *It's been a long time.,* 1; **¡Tanto tiempo sin verte!** *Long time, no see.,* 9
la tapa *small servings of food,* 7G
tardar *to take;* ¿Cuánto tardas? *How long do you take?,* 4
la tarde *afternoon,* 4; **esta tarde** *this afternoon,* 4; **por la tarde** *in the*

afternoon, 4
tarde *late,* 4; **más tarde** *later,* 8
la tarea *homework,* 1; **hacer la tarea** *to do homework,* 3
la tarjeta *greeting card,* 8; *card,* 9; **mandar tarjetas** *to send cards,* 9; **la tarjeta de cumpleaños** *birthday card,* 8; la tarjeta de crédito *credit card,* 10; **la tarjeta de embarque** *boarding pass,* 10; la tarjeta postal *postcard,* 10
el tataranieto *great-great-grandson,* 10
el taxi *taxi,* 10
la taza *cup,* 6
te *(to/for) you,* 2; **¿Te duele algo?** *Is something hurting you?,* 7; **¿Te gusta(n)...?** *Do you like . . .?,* 2; **¿Te gusta(n) más... o...?** *Do you like . . . or . . . more?,* 2; **Te llamo más tarde.** *I'll call you later.,* 9; **Te presento a...** *I'd like you to meet . . .,* 9; **Te veo mal.** *You don't look well.,* 7
el teatro *theater,* 8
el techo de zinc *sheet-metal roof,* 9G
la tecnología *technology,* 4
tejano(a) *Texan,* 3G
el tejido *weaving,* 10G
la tele *TV,* 4
el teléfono *telephone number,* 1; *telephone,* 8; **¿Cuál es el teléfono de...?** *What's . . . 's telephone number?,* 1; **¿Cuál es tu teléfono?** *What's your telephone number?,* 1; **hablar por teléfono** *to talk on the phone,* 3; llamar por teléfono *to make a phone call,* 8; el teléfono público *pay phone,* 10
la televisión *television (TV),* 3; **ver televisión** *to watch TV,* 3
el tema *theme,* 6
temblar *to shake,* 9
tembloroso(a) *trembling,* 9
la temperatura *temperature,* 2G
templado(a) *temperate,* 2G
el templo *temple,* 9
temprano *early,* 4
ten *have,* 6
el tenedor *fork,* 6
tener (-go, ie) *to have,* 4; **Cuántos años tiene... ?** *How old is . . .?,* 2; **¿Cuántos años tienes?** *How old are you?,* 2; **Él (Ella) tiene... años.** *He's (She's) . . . years old.,* 2; **no tengas** *don't have,* 10; **ten** *have,* 6; tendrán que separarse *will have to separate,* 3; **tener calor** *to be hot,* 7; **tener catarro** *to have a cold,* 7; **tener frío** *to be cold,* 7; **tener ganas** *to feel like (doing something),* 4; **tener ganas de** + infinitive *to feel like doing something,* 4; **tener hambre** *to be hungry,* 4; **tener los ojos azules** *to have blue eyes,* 5; **tener miedo** *to be afraid,* 7; **tener prisa** *to be in a hurry,* 4; tener puesto *to have on,* 3; **tener que** + infinitive *to have to (do something),* 4; **tener razón** *to be right,* 8; **tener sed** *to be thirsty,* 4; **tener sueño** *to be sleepy,* 7; **tener suerte** *to be lucky,* 10; **tener un picnic** *to have a picnic,* 9; **Tengo que irme.** *I have got to go.,* 1; **Tengo... años.** *I am . . . years old.,* 2; **Tiene... años.** *He is (She is) . . . years old.,* 2; tuvo *had,* 7G
el tenis *tennis,* 3
el tentempié *snack,* 3G
el tercero *third,* 4
terminar *to finish,* 9
la terraza de comidas *food court in a mall,* 8
el territorio *territory,* 6G
el terror *horror,* 2
el testimonio *testimony,* 6G
el texto *text,* 6
ti *you (emphatic),* 3; a ti *to you,* 6; A ti te gusta + infinitive *You like . . .,* 3; para ti *for you,* 2
la tía *aunt,* 5
el tico *nickname for Costa Rican,* 4G
el tiempo *weather,* 3; *time,* 1G; **a tiempo** *on time,* 4; **cuando hace buen/mal tiempo** *when the weather's good/bad,* 3
la tienda de... *. . . store,* 8
tiene *he/she/it has,* 2; **Cuántos años tiene... ?** *How old is . . .?,* 2; **Él (Ella) tiene... años.** *He's (She's) . . . years old.,* 2; **Tiene... años.** *He's (She's) . . . years old.,* 2
tienes *you have,* 4; **¿Cuántos años tienes?** *How old are you?,* 2; **¿Tienes...?** *Do you have . . .?,* 4
la tierra *earth,* 6; *land,* 6G
el tigre *tiger,* 2
la tilde *wavy line above the ñ,* 1
tímido(a) *shy,* 2
la tinta *ink,* 10
el tío *uncle,* 5
los tíos *uncles, uncles and aunts,* 5
típico(a) *typical,* 2G
el tipo *type;* de todo tipo *all kinds,* 8; el título *title,* 5
la toalla *towel,* 7
tocar *to play,* 3; *to touch,* 8; **A mí siempre me toca...** *I always have to . . .,* 5; **A... nunca le toca...** *It's never . . .'s turn.; . . . never has to . . .,* 5; Le toca a él. *It's his turn.,* 9; **¿Qué te toca hacer a ti?** *What do you have to do?,* 5, Te toca a ti. *It's your turn.,* 6; **tocar el piano** *to play the piano,* 3; tocar la puerta *to knock on the door,* 3
el tocino *bacon,* 6
todavía *yet,* 10; *still,* 1G; **todavía no** *not yet,* 10
todo(a) *all, every,* 2; *whole,* 9; todo el mundo *everybody,* 9; de todo *everything,* 8; de todo tipo *all kinds,* 8; **todos(as)** *everyone,* 5; **todos los días** *every day,* 3
tomar *to drink,* 6; *to eat,* 8; *to take,* 9; siguen tomándolo *keep drinking it,* 6; *to take,* 7; **tomar el sol** *to sunbathe,* 10; tomar las cosas con calma *to take things calmly,* 7; tomar una decisión *to make a decision,* 9; **tomar un batido** *to have a milkshake,* 8
el tomate *tomato,* 6
la tonelada *ton,* 10
tonto(a) *dumb,* 2
el tornado *tornado,* 3
la toronja *grapefruit,* 3G
la torta *sandwich (Mexico),* 6
la tortilla *Spanish omelet,* 1G; *pancake-like bread made from corn,* 6
la tortuga *turtle,* 1
el tostón *fried green plantain,* 2G
trabajador(a) *hard-working,* 2
trabajar *to work,* 3
el trabajo *job,* 3; *work,* 4
el trabalenguas *tongue twister,* 1
la tradición *tradition,* 2
tradicional *traditional,* 1G
traer (-igo) *to bring,* 4; me trajo *he/she brought me,* 4; quiero que me traigas *I want you to bring me,* 9
el tráfico *traffic,* 3G
tragar *to swallow,* 2
el traje *suit,* 3; *dress,* 1G
el traje de baño *swimsuit,* 8
tranquilo(a) *quiet,* 5; *calm,* 9
la transpiración *perspiration,* 8
transportar *to transport,* 10; fueron transportadas *were transported,* 10
el transporte *transportation,* 10
el trasto *utensil, piece of junk,* 2
tratar *to try,* 10
travieso(a) *mischievous,* 5
trece *thirteen,* 1
treinta *thirty,* 1
treinta y cinco *thirty-five,* 2
treinta y dos *thirty-two,* 2
treinta y uno *thirty-one,* 1
el tren *train,* 10
tres *three,* 1
trescientos *three hundred,* 8
el trigal *wheat field,* 2
el trigo *wheat,* 2
triste *sad,* 7; **estar triste** *to be sad,* 7
el trozo *piece,* 6
tú *you,* 1
tu(s) *your,* 5
el turismo *tourism,* 8G

el turista *tourist,* 1G
turnarse *to take turns,* xxii
el turno *shift,* 4
tutear *to speak to someone informally,* 10
los tuyos, las tuyas *yours,* 9

último(a) *latest,* 8; la última vez *last time,* 8
el último, la última *last one,* 3
un(a) *a, an,* 4; **un poco** *a little,* 2; **un montón** *a ton,* 4
únicamente *only,* 9
único(a) *only,* 4G
la unidad *unity,* 3G
la universidad *university,* 5
uno *one,* 1
unos(as) *some,* 4
urgente *urgent,* 1
usar *to use, to wear,* 8; **usar el/la...** *to wear size . . .,* 8; **usar lentes** *to wear glasses,* 5; **usando** *using,* xxii
el uso *use,* 6
usted *you* (formal), 1
ustedes *you* (pl.), 1
los útiles escolares *school supplies,* 4
utilizar *to use,* 7
la uva *grape,* 1
¡Uy! *Oh!,* 1

Vale. *Okay.,* 9
valeroso(a) *brave,* 4G
valiente *brave,* 5
la valija *suitcase,* 10
el valle *valley,* 3G
vamos *let's go, we go,* 3
el vaquero *cowboy,* 3G
vaquero(a) *referring to cowboys,* 3G
los vaqueros *jeans,* 8
variado(a) *varied,* 7
varias *various,* 6G
la variedad *variety,* 6
vas *you are going,* 4; **¿Vas a (a la)...?** *Are you going to the. . .?,* 4; **Vas a ir, ¿verdad?** *You're going to go, aren't you?,* 4
el vasco *language from Basque Provinces, Spain,* 1G
la vasija *pot,* 4
el vaso *glass,* 6
ve *go,* 6
veces *times,* 7; **a veces** *sometimes,* 3; **hay veces** *there are times,* 4
veinte *twenty,* 1
veintiún *twenty-one,* 1
ven *come,* 6
vencido(a) *defeated,* 6; no se da por vencido *doesn't give up,* 6
el vendedor *vendor,* 8
vender *to sell,* 8; se vende *for sale,* 5; se venden *are sold,* 8; **vender de todo** *to sell everything,* 8
venir *to come,* 4; ha venido *has come,* 9; **no vengas** *don't come,* 10; **ven** *come,* 6; venga *will come,* 9; **vienes conmigo a...** *you're coming with me . . .,* 4
la ventana *window,* 5
el ventanal *large window,* 6G
la ventura *happiness,* 5
ver *to watch, to see,* 4; nunca ha visto *never has seen,* 6; **Te veo mal.** *You don't look well.,* 7; **ver televisión** *to watch television,* 3; vi *I saw,* 8
el verano *summer,* 3
el verbo *verb,* xxii
la verdad *truth,* 2
¿verdad? *right?,* 4
verde *green,* 5; verde mar *sea green,* 5G
las verduras *vegetables,* 2
vespertino(a) *(in the) afternoon,* 4
el vestido *dress,* 8
vestirse (i) *to get dressed,* 7
vete *go,* 7
vez *time,* 4; cada vez *each time,* 8; hay veces *there are times,* 4; la última vez *last time,* 8
viajar *to travel,* 10
el viaje *trip,* 10
el viajero *traveler,* 10
la vida *life,* 3G
el video *video,* 3; **alquilar videos** *to rent videos,* 3
los videojuegos *video games,* 2
los viejitos *older folks,* 3
viejo(a) *old,* 5
el viento *wind,* 3; **Hace viento.** *It's windy.,* 3
el viernes *Friday,* 1; **los viernes** *on Fridays,* 3; **el viernes próximo** *next Friday,* 4
el Viernes Santo *Good Friday,* 1
el violín *violin,* 1
visitar *to visit,* 6
la vista *view,* 5
la vitrina *shop window,* 8; **mirar las vitrinas** *to window-shop,* 8
vivir *to live,* 5
vivo(a) *bright,* 5G
el vocabulario *vocabulary,* xxii
volar *to fly,* 7
el volcán *volcano,* 4G
el volibol *volleyball,* 3
volver (ue) *to go or come back,* 5; nunca más volverá *never will do it again,* 9; se vuelve *it becomes,* 6
vosotros(as) *you* (plural; informal), 1
el vuelo *flight,* 10
vuestra(s) *your,* 5
vuestro(s) *your,* 5

el wáter *restroom,* 10
el windsurfing *windsurfing,* 7

y *and,* 1; **y cuarto** *a quarter past,* 1; **y media** *half past,* 1
ya *already,* 9
Ya te lo (la) paso. *I'll get him (her).,* 8
la yerba mate *herb used to make* ***mate,*** 7
yo *I,* 1
el yogur *yogurt,* 7
la yuca *yucca,* 8G

la zanahoria *carrot,* 6
la zapatería *shoe store,* 8
las zapatillas de tenis *tennis shoes,* 8
los zapatos *shoes,* 4; **los zapatos de tenis** *tennis shoes,* 8
la zona *area,* 4; la zona residencial *residential area,* 5
el zoológico *zoo,* 10
el zumo *juice (Spain),* 6

Vocabulario inglés-español

This vocabulary includes all of the words presented in the **Vocabulario** sections of the chapters. These words are considered active—you are expected to know them and be able to use them. Expressions are listed under the English word you would be most likely to look up.

Spanish nouns are listed with the definite article and plural forms, when applicable. If a Spanish verb is stem-changing, the change is indicated in parentheses after the verb: **dormir (ue)**. The number after each entry refers to the chapter in which the word or phrase is introduced.

To be sure you are using Spanish words and phrases in their correct context, refer to the chapters listed. You may also want to look up Spanish phrases in **Expresiones de ¡Exprésate!**, pp. R12–R14.

a little *un poco,* 2
a lot *mucho,* 2
a lot of, many *muchos(as),* 4
a ton *un montón,* 4
a, an *un(a),* 4
active *activo(a),* 2
to add *añadir,* 6
address *la dirección,* 5; **My address is...** *Mi dirección es...,* 5; e-mail address *correo electrónico,* 1
adventure *la aventura,* 2; **adventure book** *el libro de aventuras,* 2
after *después,* 3; *después de,* 7; **after class** *después de clases,* 3
afternoon *la tarde,* 4; **this afternoon** *esta tarde,* 4; **in the afternoon** *por la tarde,* 4
afterwards *después,* 4
agent *el agente, la agente,* 10
agree: I don't agree. *No estoy de acuerdo.,* 6; **I don't agree.** *Estoy de acuerdo.,* 6
airplane *el avión,* 10; **by plane** *por avión,* 10
airport *el aeropuerto,* 10
all *todas,* 1; *todo(a),* 2
all right *regular,* 1
to allow *dejar,* 3
almost *casi,* 3; **almost never** *casi nunca,* 3; **almost always** *casi siempre,* 3
alone *solo(a),* 3
alphabet *el alfabeto,* 1
already *ya,* 10
also *también,* 2
always *siempre,* 5; **almost always** *casi siempre,* 3; **as always** *como siempre,* 9
amusement park *el parque de diversiones,* 10
an *un, una,* 4
and *y,* 1
animal *el animal,* 2
anniversary *el aniversario,* 9
another *otro,* 8
any *cualquier,* 10
anything *algo,* 4; *nada,* 4
apartment *el apartamento,* 5
apple *la manzana,* 6
April *abril,* 1
Are you ...? *¿Eres...?,* 2
arm *el brazo,* 7
around the corner *a la vuelta,* 10
arrival *la llegada,* 10
to arrive *llegar,* 4
art *el arte,* 4
as ... as *tan...como,* 8
as always *como siempre,* 9
at *a(l),* 8; **@** *la arroba,* 1; *en,* 3
athletic *atlético(a),* 2
to attend *asistir a,* 4
auditorium *el auditorio,* 4
August *agosto,* 1
aunt *la tía,* 5
automatic teller machine *el cajero automático,* 10
awesome *fenomenal,* 2

back *la espalda,* 7, **I'll call back later** *Llamo más tarde,* 8; **to go (come) back** *volver (ue),* 5
backpack *la mochila,* 4
bacon *el tocino,* 6
bad *malo(a),* 2
bag *bolsa,* 8
baggage *el equipaje,* 10; **baggage claim** *el reclamo de equipaje,* 10
bargain *la ganga,* 8
baseball *el béisbol,* 3
basketball *el básquetbol,* 3
to bathe *bañarse,* 7
bathroom *el baño,* 5
be *sé,* 6
to be able to *poder,* 6
to be *estar,* 1; **How are you?** *¿Cómo está(s)?,* 1; **to be allright** *estar regular,* 1; **to be angry** *estar enojado(a),* 7; **to be bored** *estar aburrido(a)* 7; **to be familiar with** *conocer,* 9; **to be fine** *estar bien,* 1; **to be hungry** *tener hambre,* 4; **to be tired** *estar cansado(a),* 7; **to be happy** *estar contento(a)* 7; **to be sick** *estar enfermo(a)* 7; **to be in a hurry** *tener prisa,* 7; **to be in a wheelchair** *estar en una silla de ruedas,* 5; **to be ready** *estar listo(a),* 7; **to be nervous** *estar nervioso(a)* 7; **to be right** *tener razón,* 7; **to be sad** *estar triste,* 7; **to be scared** *tener miedo,* 7; **to be sleepy** *tener sueno,* 7; **to be lucky** *tener suerte,* 7; **to be thirsty** *tener sed,* 7; **don't be** *no estés,* 7
to be *ser,* 1; **don't be** *no seas,* 7
beach *la playa,* 3
because *porque,* 2
bed *la cama,* 5; **to make the bed** *hacer la cama,* 5; **to go to bed** *acostarse (ue),* 7
bedroom *la habitación,* 5
beef *la carne,* 6
before *antes de,* 7
behind *detrás de,* 5
besides *además,* 8
best *el/la/los/las mejor(es),* 1
better *mejor(es),* 7
big *grande,* 5
bike *la bicicleta,* 3; **to ride a bike** *montar en bicicleta,* 3
bill *la cuenta,* 6

biology *la biología,* 4
birthday *el cumpleaños,* 9; **When is . . .'s birthday?** *¿Cuándo es el cumpleaños de...?,* 2; **When is your birthday?** *¿Cuándo es tu cumpleaños?,* 2; **. . .'s birthday** *el cumpleaños de...,* 2; **birthday card** *la tarjeta de cumpleaños,* 8; **girl's fifteenth birthday** *la quinceañera,* 9
black *negro(a),* 5
blank *en blanco,* 8
blind *ciego(a),* 5
blond *rubio(a),* 2
blouse *la blusa,* 8
blue *azul,* 5; **to have blue eyes** *tener los ojos azules,* 5
board game *el juego de mesa,* 3
to board *abordar,* 10
boarding pass *la tarjeta de embarque,* 10
boat *el barco,* 10
book *el libro,* 2; **adventure book** *el libro de aventuras,* 2; **comic book** *la revista de tiras comícas,* 8; **romance book** *el libro de amor,* 2
bookstore *la librería,* 8
boots *las botas,* 8
boring *aburrido(a),* 2; **to be bored** *estar aburrido,* 7
bowl *el plato hondo,* 6
boy *el muchacho,* 1
bracelet *la pulsera,* 8
bread *el pan,* 6
breakfast *el desayuno,* 6
to bring *traer (-igo),* 4
broccoli *el bróculi,* 6
brother *el hermano,* 5
brothers, brothers and sisters *los hermanos,* 5
brown *castaño(a),* 5; *de color café,* 5
building *el edificio,* 5; **. . . story building** *el edificio de... pisos,* 5
bus *el autobús,* 10
but *pero,* 5
to buy *comprar,* 8; **you would buy** *comprarías,* 8
by plane *por avion,* 10
Bye *chao,* 9

cafeteria *la cafetería,* 4
cake *el pastel,* 6
calculator *la calculadora,* 4
calf *la pantorrilla,* 7
to call *llamar,* 9; **I'll call back later.** *Llamo más tarde.,* 8
camera *la cámara,* 10; **disposable camera** *la cámara desechable,* 10
to camp *acampar,* 10
can *poder,* 6
Can I . . .? *¿Puedo...?,* 6
Can I help you? *¿En que le puedo servir?,* 8
candy *el dulce,* 9
canoe *la canoa,* 10
car *el carro,* 2
card *la tarjeta,* 8
carrot *la zanahoria,* 5
cat *el gato, la gata,* 5
to celebrate *festejar,* 9
cereal *los cereales,* 6
chair *la silla,* 5; **wheelchair** *la silla de ruedas,* 5
to change money *cambiar dinero,* 10
to chat *charlar,* 9
to check *facturar,* 10; **to check luggage** *facturar el equipaje,* 10
checkpoint: security checkpoint *control de seguridad,* 10
cheese *el queso,* 6
chemistry *la química,* 4
chess *ajedrez,* 1
chest *el pecho,* 7
chicken *el pollo,* 6
children *los hijos,* 5; *los niños,* 8
chocolate *el chocolate,* 6
chores *los quehaceres,* 5
Christmas *la Navidad,* 9; **Christmas Eve** *la Nochebuena,* 9
church *la iglesia,* 3
city *la ciudad,* 5
class *la clase,* 3; **after class** *después de clases,* 3
classmate (female) *la (una) compañera de clase,* 1
classmate (male) *el (un) compañero de clase,* 1
to clean *limpiar,* 5
to clean the room *arreglar el cuarto,* 5
client *el cliente, la cliente,* 8
climb *subir,* 10
clock *el reloj,* 4
close to, *cerca de,* 5
to close *cerrar (ie),* 8
clothes *la ropa,* 4
cloudy *nublado,* 7
club *el club de...,* 4
coat *el abrigo,* 8
coffee *el café,* 6; **coffee with milk** *el café con leche,* 6; **coffee shop** *la cafetería,* 6
cold *frío(a),* 6; **It's cold.** *Hace frío.,* 3; **to be cold** *tener frío,* 7;
to have a cold *tener catarro,* 7
comb *el peine,* 7
to comb your hair *peinarse,* 7
to come *venir,* 4; **come** *ven,* 6; **don't come** *no vengas,* 10; **to come back** *volver,* 5; **you're coming with me to . . .** *vienes conmigo a...,* 4
comic book *la revista de tiras cómicas,* 8
compact disc *el disco compacto,* 8; **blank compact disc** *el disco compacto en blanco,* 8
computer *la computadora,* 4; **computer science** *la computación,* 4
concert *el concierto,* 4
to cook *cocinar,* 5
cookie *la galleta,* 9
cool *fresco,* 3; **It's cool.** *Hace fresco.,* 3
corn *el maíz,* 6
to cost *costar (ue),* 8; **costs . . .** *cuesta(n)...,* 8; **It will cost.** *Costará.,* 9
cotton *el algodón,* 8; **made of cotton** *de algodón,* 8
counter *el mostrador,* 10
country *el país,* 10
countryside *el campo,* 5
court: food court in a mall *la terraza de comidas,* 8
cousin *el primo, la prima,* 5
custard *el flan,* 6
customs *la aduana,* 10
to cut *cortar,* 6; **to cut the grass** *cortar el césped,* 5

dad *el papá,* 5
dance *el baile,* 3; **dance class** *la clase de baile,* 4
to dance *bailar,* 3; **dancing** *bailando,* 1; **to start dancing** *ponerse a bailar,* 3
dark: dark-skinned; dark-haired *moreno(a),* 2
date *la fecha,* 1
daughter *la hija,* 5
day *el día,* 1; **day after tomorrow** *pasado mañana,* 4; **day before yesterday** *anteayer,* 8; **day of the week** *el día de la semana,* 1; **Father's Day** *el Día del Padre,* 9; **holiday** *el día festivo,* 9; **Independence Day** *el Día de la Independencia,* 9; **Mother's Day** *el Día de la Madre,* 9; **Thanksgiving Day** *el Día de Acción de Gracias,* 9; **one day** *algún día,* 10; **Valentine's Day** *el Día de los Enamorados,* 9; **What day is today?** *¿Qué día es hoy?,* 1; **your saint's day** *el día de tu santo,* 9
deaf *sordo(a),* 5
December *diciembre,* 1
to decorate *decorar,* 9; **to decorate the house** *decorar la casa,* 9
decoration *la decoración,* 9

delicious *delicioso(a),* 2; *riquísimo(a),* 6
to delight *encantar,* 6
department store *el almacén,* 8
departure *la salida,* 10
to desire *desear,* 6
desk *el escritorio,* 5
dessert *el postre,* 6
destination *el destino,* 10
destined *destinado(a),* 6
detail *el detalle,* 7
to determine *determinar,* 7
dictionary *el diccionario,* 4
diet *la dieta,* 7; **to eat well** *seguir una dieta sana,* 7
difficult *difícil,* 4; **It's difficult.** *Es difícil.,* 4
dining room *el comedor,* 5
dinner *la cena,* 6
disc: compact disc *el disco compacto,* 8; **blank compact disc** *el disco compacto en blanco,* 8
to disembark *desembarcar,* 10
dish, *el plato,* 6
disposable *desechable,* 10; **disposable camera** *la cámara desechable,* 10
Do you like . . .? *¿Te gusta(n)...?,* 2
to do *hacer,* 4; **we are doing** *estamos haciendo,* 9; **to do homework** *hacer la tarea,* 3; **to do chores** *hacer los quehaceres,* 5; **to do yoga** *hacer yoga,* 7; **do** *haz,* 6; **don't do** *no hagas,* 10; **What are they doing?** *¿Qué están haciendo?,* 9; **What did you do?** *¿Qué hiciste?* 8
dog *el perro, la perra,* 5
door *la puerta,* 5
dot *el punto,* 1; **on the dot** *en punto,* 1
downtown *el centro,* 10
to draw *dibujar,* 3
dress *el vestido,* 8
dressed: to get dressed, *vestirvse (i),* 7
to drink *beber,* 4; **to drink punch** *beber ponche,* 9; *tomar,* 6
to dry *secarse,* 7
during *durante,* 10
DVD *el DVD,* 8

ear *el oído,* 7
early *temprano,* 4
earphones *los audífonos,* 8
earrings *los aretes,* 8
easy *fácil,* 4; **It's easy.** *Es fácil.,* 4
to eat a balanced diet *seguir una dieta sana,* 7; **to eat breakfast** *desayunar,* 6; **to eat dinner** *cenar,* 6; **to eat lunch** *almorzar (ue),* 6; 4 **to eat well** *seguir una dieta sana,* 7
to eat *comer,* 3; *tomar,* 8
egg *el huevo,* 6
eight *ocho,* 1
eight hundred *ochocientos,* 8
eighteen *dieciocho,* 1
eighty *ochenta,* 2
eleven *once,* 1
e-mail address *el correo electrónico,* 1; **What is . . .'s e-mail address?** *¿Cuál es el correo electrónico de...?* 1; **What's your e-mail address?** *¿Cuál es tu correo electrónico?,* 1
English *el inglés,* 4
enough *suficiente,* 7; **to get enough sleep** *dormir lo suficiente,* 7
evening *la tarde,* 1
everybody *todos (as),* 5
everyone *todos (as),* 5
everything *todo,* 8
to exercise *hacer ejercicio,* 3
to expect *esperar,* 9
expensive *caro(a),* 8
eyes *los ojos,* 5; **to have blue eyes** *tener los ojos azules,* 5

face *la cara,* 7
fall *el otoño,* 3
family *la familia,* 3; **There are . . . people in my family.** *En mi familia somos...,* 5
familiar: to be familiar *conocer,* 9
fantastic: How fantastic! *¡Qué fantástico!,* 10
fat (in food) *la grasa,* 7
fat (overweight) *gordo(a),* 5
father *el padre,* 5; **Father's Day** *el Día del Padre,* 9
favorite *preferido(a),* 4
flan *el flan,* 6
February *febrero,* 1
to feel *sentirse (ie),* 7; **to feel like doing something** *tener ganas de + infinitive,* 4
few *pocos(as),* 4
fifteen *quince,* 1
fifteenth: girl's fifteenth birthday *quinceañera,* 9
fifty *cincuenta,* 2
film *la película,* 2
to find *encontrar (ue),* 7; **to find a hobby** *buscar un pasatiempo,* 7
fine *bien,* 1; **I'm fine** *Estoy bien,* 1
finger *el dedo,* 7
finish *terminar,* 9
fireworks *los fuegos artificiales,* 9
first *el primero,* 1
first (adj) *primero(a),* 4
fish *el pescado,* 6
to fish *pescar,* 10
fishing *la pesca,* 10; **to go fishing** *ir de pesca,* 10
to fit *quedar,* 8; **How does it fit?** *¿Cómo me queda?,* 8
five *cinco,* 1
five hundred *quinientos,* 8
flight *el vuelo,* 10
floor *el piso,* 5
folder *la carpeta,* 4
to follow *seguir (i),* 10
food *la comida,* 2; **Chinese (Italian, Mexican) food** *la comida china (italiana, mexicana),* 2, **food court in a mall** *la plaza (terraza) de comida,* 8
foot *el pie,* 7
football *el fútbol americano,* 3
for *para,* 4
for example *por ejemplo,* 6G
fork *el tenedor,* 6
formidable *formidable,* 2
fortune *la fortuna,* 8
forty *cuarenta,* 2
four *cuatro,* 1
four hundred *cuatrocientos,* 8
fourteen *catorce,* 1
French *el francés,* 4
French fries *las papas fritas,* 6
frequency *la frecuencia,* 8
Friday *el viernes,* 1; **on Fridays** *los viernes,* 3
friend *el amigo* (male), *la amiga* (female), 1
from *de,* 1
fruit *la fruta,* 2
fun *divertido(a),* 2; **What fun!** *¡Qué divertido!,* 10

to gain weight *subir de peso,* 7
game: board game *el juego de mesa,* 3; **the . . . game** *el partido de...,* 4
garage *el garaje,* 5
garden *el jardín,* 5
German *el alemán,* 4
to get angry *enojarse,* 7
to get dressed *vestirse (i),* 7
to get off a plane *desembarcar,* 10
to get someone for a telephone call, *pasartelo(la),* 8
to get together *reunirse,* 9
to get up *levantarse,* 7
to get *conseguir (i, i),* 10
gift *el regalo,* 9
girl *la muchacha,* 1
girl's fifteenth birthday *la quinceañera,* 9

Vocabulario inglés-español

to give *dar,* 7; **don't give** *no des,* 7
glass *el vaso,* 6
glasses *los lentes,* 5; **to wear glasses** *usar lentes,* 5
go *ve,* 6
to go *ir,* 2; **Where did you go?** *¿Adónde fuiste?* 8; **to go shopping** *ir de compras,* 2; **to go to the movies** *ir al cine,* 3; **to go hiking** *ir de excursión,* 10; **don't go** *no vayas,* 7; **I want to go . . .** *quiero ir...,* 2; **Are you going to the . . .?** *¿Vas a...?,* 4; **You're going to go, aren't you?** *Vas a ir, ¿verdad?,* 4
to go back *regresar,* 4; *volver (ue),* 5
to go for a walk *pasear,* 3
go out *sal,* 6
to go out *salir,* 3; **to go out with friends** *salir con amigos,* 3; **to go out in a sailboat (motorboat)** *pasear en bote de vela (lancha),* 10
to go to bed *acostarse (ue),* 7
good *bueno(a),* 2; **Good evening., Good night.** *Buenas noches.,* 1; **Good afternoon.** *Buenas tardes.,* 1; **Good morning.** *Buenos días.,* 1
good-looking *guapo(a),* 2
Goodbye. *Adiós.,* 1
graduation *la graduación,* 9
grandchildren *los nietos,* 5
granddaughter *la nieta,* 5
grandfather *el abuelo,* 5
grandmother *la abuela,* 5
grandparents *los abuelos,* 5
grandson *el nieto,* 5
grandsons, grandchildren *los nietos,* 5
grass *el césped,* 5; **to cut the grass** *cortar el césped,* 5
gravy *salsa,* 6
gray *gris,* 8
graying *canoso(a),* 5
great *estupendo(a),* 10; *a todo dar,* 10; **it was great** *fue estupendo,* 10
green *verde,* 5
greeting card *la tarjeta,* 8
guest *el (la) invitado(a),* 9
guitar *la guitarra,* 2
gym *el gimnasio,* 3

hair *el pelo,* 5; **to comb your hair** *peinarse,* 7; **hair dryer** *la secadora de pelo,* 7
half *medio,* 1; **half past** *y media,* 1
ham *el jamón,* 6
hamburger *la hamburguesa,* 2
hand *la mano,* 7
hang *colgar (ue),* 9
Hanukkah *el Hanukah,* 9
happy *contento(a),* 7; **to be happy** *estar contento(a),* 7
Happy (Merry) . . . *¡Feliz...!,* 9
hard *difícil,* 4
hard-working *trabajador(a),* 2
hat *el sombrero,* 8
to have *tener (-go, ie),* 4; **have** *ten,* 6; **don't have** *no tengas,* 10; **to have a cold** *tener catarro,* 7; **to have a milkshake** *tomar un batido,* 8; **to have a picnic** *tener un picnic,* 9; **to have blue eyes** *tener los ojos azules,* 5; **to have to do something** *tener que + infinitive,* 4; **I have to . . .** *A mí me toca...,* 5
to have a party *hacer una fiesta,* 9; **to have a snack** *merendar,* 5; **to have lunch** *almorzar,* 5
he *él,* 1; **He is . . .** *Él es...,* 1
head *la cabeza,* 7
health *la salud,* 7
heat *el calor,* 3
to heat *calentar (ie),* 6
Hello. *Aló.; Bueno.; Diga.,* 8
help *la ayuda,* 6; **to help out at home** *ayudar en casa,* 5
hi, hello *hola,* 1
hike *la excursión,* 10; **to go on a hike** *ir de excursión,* 10
his *su(s),* 5
history *la historia,* 4
hobby *el pasatiempo,* 7; **to look for a hobby** *buscar un pasatiempo,* 7
holiday *el día festivo,* 9
Holy Week *la Semana Santa,* 9
homework *la tarea,* 3
Hope things go well for you. *Que te vaya bien.,* 9
horrible *horrible,* 2; **It was horrible!** *¡Fue horrible!,* 10
horror *el terror,* 2
hot *caliente,* 6; **hot sauce,** 6
hot chocolate *el chocolate,* 6
hotel *el hotel,* 10; **to stay in a hotel** *quedarse en un hotel,* 10
hour *la hora,* 1
house *casa,* 5; **. . .'s house** *la casa de...,* 3; **to decorate the house** *decorar la casa,* 9
household chores *los quehaceres,* 5
how *¿cómo?,* 1; **How are you?** *¿Cómo está(s)?,* 1; **How do you spell . . .** *¿Cómo se escribe…?,* 1; **How does it fit?** *¿Cómo me queda?,* 8; **How fantastic!** *¡Qué fantástico!,* 10; **How great!** *¡Qué bien!,* 10; **How many . . .** *¿cuántos(as)?,* 2; **how much?** *¿cuánto(a)?,* 4; **How often do you go . . .?** *¿Con qué frecuencia vas...?,* 3; **How old are you?** *¿Cuántos años tienes?,* 2
hunger *el hambre,* 4
hungry, to be *tener hambre,* 4
to hurt *doler (ue),* 7; **My . . . hurt(s)** *Me duele(n)...* 7; **Does something hurt?** *¿Te duele algo?,* 7

ID *carnet de identidad,* 10
I *yo,* 1
I agree. *Estoy de acuerdo,* 6; **I don't agree.** *No estoy de acuerdo.,* 6
I have no idea. *Ni idea.,* 3
I have to go. *Tengo que irme.,* 1
I want to see . . . *quiero conocer...,* 10
I would like . . . *Quisiera...,* 6
I'd like you to meet . . . *Te presento a...,* 9
I'll get him (her). *Ya te lo (la) paso.,* 8
I'm fine. *Estoy bien.,* 1
I'm sorry *lo siento,* 8
I'm . . . *Soy...,* 2; **I'm from** *Soy de...,* 1
I'm just looking. *Nada más estoy mirando.,* 8
I'm not so good. *Estoy mal.,* 1
ice cream *el helado,* 2
ice cream shop *la heladería,* 8
Independence Day *El Día de la Independencia,* 9
in front of *delante de,* 5
in the (latest) fashion *a la (última) moda,* 8
in, by *por,* 4
inexpensive *barato(a),* 8
intellectual *intelectual,* 2
intelligent *inteligente,* 2
interest *el interés,* 10
interesting *interesante,* 2
to interrupt *interrumpir,* 4
to introduce *presentar,* 9
invitation *la invitación,* 9
to invite *invitar,* 9
island *la isla,* 10
it *lo, la,* 6
It seems all right/fine to me. *Me parece bien.,* 5
It snows. *Nieva.,* 3
It's a rip-off! *¡Es un robo!,* 8
It's all the same to me. *Me da igual.,* 2
It's awful. *Es pésimo.,* 2
It's cold. *Hace frío.,* 3
It's cool. *Hace fresco.,* 3
It's delicious. *Es delicioso.,* 2
It's hot. *Hace calor.,* 3
It's kind of fun. *Es algo divertido.,* 2
It's not a big deal. *No es gran cosa.,* 5
It's okay. *Está bien.,* 3

It's pretty good/bad. *Es bastante bueno(a)/malo(a).*, 2
It's sunny. *Hace sol.*, 3
It's windy. *Hace viento.*, 3

jacket *la chaqueta*, 8; *el saco*, 8
January *enero*, 1
jeans *los vaqueros*, 8
jewelry store *la joyería*, 8
job *el trabajo*, 3
joke *el chiste*, 9; **to tell jokes** *contar chistes*, 9
juice *el jugo*, 6
July *julio*, 1
June *junio*, 1
to just (have done something) *acabar de*, 7

kitchen *la cocina*, 5
knife *el cuchillo*, 6
to know (facts) *saber*, 4; **I don't know** *no sé*, 4; **to know people** *conocer*, 9

lake *el lago*, 10
large *grande*, 6
last *pasado(a)*, 8; **last night** *anoche*, 9
late *tarde*, 4; **later** *más tarde*, 8; **latest** *último(a)*, 8
lazy *perezoso(a)*, 2
to leave *irse*, 10; *dejar*, 10; *salir*, 3; **leave** *sal*, 6; **to leave a message** *dejar un recado*, 8; **don't leave** *no salgas*, 10
leg *la pierna*, 7
letter *la carta*, 3
library *la biblioteca*, 4
lift *levantar*, 7; **to lift weights** *levantar pesas*, 7
to like *gustar*, 2; **I would like . . .,** *me gustaría*, 10
Likewise. *Igualmente.*, 1
line *la cola*, 10; **to wait in line** *hacer cola*, 10
to listen *escuchar*, 3; **to listen to music** *escuchar música*, 3
little (adv.) *poco*, 2; **a little** *un poco*, 2
live *vivir*, 5
living room *la sala*, 5
long *largo(a)*, 5; **Long time no see.** *¡Tanto tiempo sin verte!*, 9
to look *mirar*, 8
to look for *buscar*, 7
to lose weight *bajar de peso*, 7
to lose *perder*, 10
luck *la suerte*, 10
luggage *el equipaje*, 10
lunch *el almuerzo*, 4; *la comida*, 6; **to have lunch** *almorzar*, 5

ma'am; Mrs. *la señora*, 1
magazine *la revista*, 3
mail *el correo*, 7
to maintain *mantenerse(ie)*, 7; **to stay in shape** *mantenerse en forma*, 7
to make *hacer*, 4; **make** *haz*, 6; **to make the bed**, 5
makeup *el maquillaje*, 7
mall *el centro comercial*, 3
man *el hombre*, 6; **for men** *para hombres*, 8
many *muchos (as)*, 4
map *el mapa*, 10
March *marzo*, 1
Mass *la misa*, 9
mathematics *las matemáticas*, 4
May *mayo*, 1
me *mí*, 5; *me*, 9
meat *la carne*, 6
to meet *encontrarse (ue)*, 10
meeting *la reunión*, 3
Merry . . . *¡Feliz...!*, 9
message *el recado*, 8
midday, noon *el mediodía*, 1
midnight *la medianoche*, 1
milk *la leche*, 6
milkshake *el batido*, 8
million *un millón de*, 8
mischievous *travieso(a)*, 5
Miss *la señorita*, 1
to miss *perder(ie)*, 10
mix *mezclar*, 6
mom *la mamá*, 5
moment *un momento*, 8
Monday *lunes*, 3; **on Mondays** *los lunes*, 3
money *el dinero*, 8
money exchange *la oficina de cambio*, 10
monitor, screen *la pantalla*, 10
months of the year *los meses del año*, 1
month *mes*, 1
more *más*, 2; **more than** *más que*, 8; **more . . . than** *más... que*, 8
morning *la mañana*, 1
mother *la madre*, 5; **Mother's Day** *El Día de la Madre*, 9
motorboat *la lancha*, 10; **to go out in a motorboat** *pasear en lancha*, 10
mountain *la montaña*, 10
mouth *la boca*, 7
movie *la película*, 2
movie theater *el cine*, 3
museum *el museo*, 10
music *la música*, 2; **music by. . .** *la música de*, 2
my *mi(s)*, 1; **my best friend** *mi mejor amigo(a)*, 1; **my favorite subject** *mi materia preferida*, 4; **my teacher** *mi profesor(a)*, 1
mystery *el misterio*, 2

napkin *la servilleta*, 6
neck *el cuello*, 7
need *necesitar*, 4
neither, not either *tampoco*, 5; *ni*, 7
nephew *el sobrino*, 5
nervous *nervioso(a)*, 7; **to be nervous** *estar nervioso(a)*, 7
never *nunca*, 5; **almost never** *casi nunca*, 3
New Year's Eve *la Nochevieja*, 9
next *próximo(a)*, 4; **next to** *al lado de*, 5
nice *simpático(a)*, 2; **Nice to meet you.** *Encantado(a)*, 1; *Mucho gusto.*, 1
niece *la sobrina*, 5
nine *nueve*, 1
nine hundred *novecientos*, 8
nineteen *diecinueve*, 1
ninety *noventa*, 2
no *no*, 3
nobody, not anybody *nadie*, 5
noon *mediodía*, 1
nor *ni*, 7
nose *la nariz*, 7
not yet *todavía no*, 10
notebook *el cuaderno*, 4
nothing *nada*, 4
novel *la novela*, 2
November *noviembre*, 1
now *ahora*, 9
nowhere *ninguna parte*, 3
number *el número*, 1

October *octubre*, 1
Of course! *¡Claro que sí!*, 4
of the *del, de la, de las, de los*, 2
of *de*, 1
office: post office *oficina de correos*, 10
often *a menudo*, 5

Oh, no! *¡Ay, no!*, 6
Okay. *Vale.*, 9
old *viejo(a)*, 5
older *mayor(es)*, 5
on the dot *en punto*, 1
on time *a tiempo*, 4
on top of, above *encima de*, 5
one *uno*, 1
one day *algún día*, 10
one hundred *cien*, 2
one hundred one *ciento uno*, 8
one million *millón (de)*, 8
one thousand *mil*, 8
only *sólo*, 7; *no más*, 8
to **open** *abrir*, 4; **to open gifts** *abrir regalos*, 9
or *o*, 2
orange *la naranja*, 6; *anaranjado(a)*, 8
order *pedir (i)*, 6
to **organize** *organizar*, 10
our *nuestro(a)(s)*, 5
out of style *pasado(a) de moda*, 8
outgoing *extrovertido(a)*, 2
oven *el horno*, 6
overcoat *el abrigo*, 8

to **pack your suitcase** *hacer la maleta*, 10
pain: What a pain! *¡Que lata!*, 5
pair *el par*, 8
pajamas *el piyama*, 7
pants (jeans) *los pantalones*, 7
paper *el papel*, 4
parents *los padres*, 5
park *el parque*, 3; **amusement park** *el parque de diversiones*, 10
party, to have a *hacer una fiesta*, 9; **surprise party** *la fiesta de sorpresa*, 9
pass: boarding pass *la tarjeta de embarque*, 10
passenger *el pasajero, la pasajera*, 10
passport *el pasaporte*, 10
pastry *el pan dulce*, 6
patio *el patio*, 5
to **pay** *pagar*, 8
peach *el durazno*, 6
pen *el bolígrafo*, 4
pencil *el lápiz (pl. los lápices)*, 4
person *la persona*, 2
photo *la foto*, 9; **to show photos** *enseñar fotos*, 9; **to take photos** *sacar fotos*, 10
physical education *la educación física*, 4
to **pick up** *recoger*, 10
picnic *el picnic*, 9
piñata *la piñata*, 9
pizza *la pizza*, 2
place *el lugar*, 10
plane ticket *el boleto de avión*, 10
plans *planes*, 9
plants *las plantas*, 5
plate *el plato*, 6
to **play an instrument** *tocar*, 3; **to play the piano** *tocar el piano*, 3; **a game or sport** *jugar (ue)*, 3
to **play a game or sport** *jugar (ue)*, 3
to **play sports** *practicar deportes*, 3
please *por favor*, 6
Pleased to meet you. *Encantado(a).*, 1; *Mucho gusto.*, 1
pool *la piscina*, 3
porch *el patio*, 5
post office *la oficina de correos*, 10
potato *la papa*, 6; **potato chips** *las papitas*, 9
practice *el entrenamiento*, 3
to **prefer** *preferir (ie)*, 6
preparations *los preparativos*, 9
to **prepare** *preparar*, 6
pretty *bonito(a)*, 2
punch *el ponche*, 9
purple *morado(a)*, 8
purse *la bolsa*, 8
to **put** *poner*, 4; **put** *pon*, 6; **don't put** *no pongas*, 10; **to put on makeup** *maquillarse*, 7; **to put on** *ponerse*, 7
pyramid *la pirámide, 10*

quarter past (the hour) *y cuarto*, 1
quarter to (the hour) *menos cuarto*, 4
quiet *callado(a)*, 5

to **rain** *llover (ue)*, 3; **it rains a lot** *llueve mucho*, 3
rather *bastante* + adjective, 2
razor *la navaja*, 7
to **read** *leer*, 3; **to read magazines and novels** *leer revistas y novelas*, 3
ready *listo(a)*, 7; **to be ready** *estar listo(a)*, 7
to **receive** *recibir*, 9; **to receive gifts** *recibir regalos*, 9
red *rojo(a)*, 8
red-headed *pelirrojo(a)*, 2
refrigerator *el refrigerador*, 6
rehearsal *el ensayo*, 3
relax *relajarse*, 7
to **rent** *alquilar*, 3; **to rent videos** *alquilar videos*, 3
to **rest** *descansar*, 3
restaurant *el restaurante*, 6
restroom *el baño*, 5; *el servicio*, 10
to **return, to go back** *regresar*, 4; *volver*, 5
rice *el arroz*, 6
to **ride a bike** *montar en bicicleta*, 3
right? *¿no?*, 4; *¿verdad?*, 4; **to be right** *tener razón*, 8
ring *el anillo*, 8
rip off *el robo*, 8
romance book *el libro de amor*, 2
romantic *romántico(a)*, 2
room *el cuarto*, 5
ruins *las ruinas*, 10
rule *la regla*, 4
to **run** *correr*, 3

sad *triste*, 7; **to be sad** *estar triste*, 7
sailboat *el bote de vela*, 10; **to go out in a sailboat** *pasear en bote de vela*, 10
salad *la ensalada*, 6
salesclerk *el dependiente, la dependiente*, 8
salty *salado(a)*, 6
same as usual *lo de siempre*, 9
sandals *las sandalias*. 8
sandwich *el sándwich*, 6
Saturday *el sábado*, 1; **on Saturdays** *los sábados*, 3
sauce, gravy *la salsa*. 6; **hot sauce** *la salsa picante*, 6
to **save: to save money** *ahorrar dinero*, 8
school *el colegio*, 3
school supplies *los útiles escolares*, 4
science *las ciencias*, 4; **science fiction** *la ciencia ficción*, 2; **computer science** *la computación*, 4
security checkpoint *el control de seguridad*, 10
to **see** *ver*, 4; **See you tomorrow.** *Hasta mañana.*, 1; **See you.** *Nos vemos.*, 1
to **seem** *parecer*, 5
to **sell** *vender*, 8
to **send** *mandar*, 9
September *septiembre*, 1
serious *serio(a)*, 2
to **serve** *servir (i)*, 6
to **set** *poner (-go)*, 6; **to set the table** *poner la mesa*, 6
seven *siete*, 1
seven hundred *setecientos*, 8
seventeen *diecisiete*, 1
seventy *setenta*, 2

to shave *afeitarse,* 7
shirt *la camisa,* 8
shoe store *la zapatería,* 8
shoes *los zapatos,* 4; **tennis shoes** *los zapatos de tenis,* 8
shop window *la vitrina,* 8; **to window-shop** *mirar las vitrinas,* 8; **to go shopping** *ir de compras,* 2
short (height) *bajo(a), 2;* (length) *corto(a),* 5
shorts *los pantalones cortos,* 8
should *deber,* 6
shoulder *el hombro,* 7
to show *enseñar,* 4; **to show photos** *enseñar fotos,* 9
shy *tímido(a),* 2
sick: to be *estar enfermo(a),* 7
silk la seda, 8
silly *tonto(a),* 3
to sing *cantar,* 3
sir, Mr. *el señor,* 1
sister *la hermana,* 5
to sit down *sentarse,* 10
six *seis,* 1
six hundred *seiscientos,* 8
sixteen *dieciséis,* 1
sixty *sesenta,* 2
size, *la talla,* 8
to skate *patinar,* 3
to ski *esquiar,* 10; **to water-ski** *esquiar en el agua,* 10
skirt *la falda,* 8
to sleep *dormir,* 5; **to get enough sleep** *dormir lo suficiente,* 7
small *pequeño(a),* 5; **pretty small** *bastante pequeño,* 5
to smoke *fumar,* 7; **to stop smoking** *dejar de fumar,* 7
to snack *merendar (ie),* 5
to snow *nevar (ie),* 3
so-so *más o menos,* 1
so much *tanto,* 7
soap *el jabón,* 7
soccer *el fútbol,* 3
socks *los calcetines,* 8; **a pair of socks** *un par de calcetines,* 8
sofa *el sofá,* 5
soft drink *el refresco,* 6
some *unos(as),* 4
something *algo,* 4
sometimes *a veces,* 3
son *el hijo,* 5
soup *la sopa,* 6; **vegetable soup** *la sopa de verduras,* 6
Spanish *el español,* 1
to speak *hablar,* 3
to spend time alone *pasar el rato solo(a),* 3
to spend (money) *gastar,* 8; (time) *pasar,* 9
spicy *picante,* 6
spinach *las espinacas,* 6
spoon *la cuchara,* 6
sports *los deportes,* 2
spring *la primavera,* 3
stadium *el estadio,* 4
to start *empezar (ie),* 5; *comenzar (ie),* 10; **to start a trip** *comenzar un viaje,* 10
to stay *quedarse,* 10; **to stay in shape** *mantenerse (ie) en forma,* 7
stomach *el estómago,* 7
to stop doing something *dejar de + infinitive,* 7
store *la tienda de...,* 8
story *el piso,* 5; **. . .story building** *el edificio de . . .pisos,* 5
to stretch *estirarse,* 7
student *el estudiante, la estudiante,* 1
to study *estudiar,* 3
style *la moda,* 8; **in the latest style** *a la última moda* 8; **out of style** *pasado de moda,* 8
subject *la materia,* 4
suburbs *las afueras,* 5
subway *el metro,* 10
suitcase *la maleta,* 10
summer *el verano,* 3
to sunbathe *tomar el sol,* 10
Sunday *el domingo,* 1; **on Sundays** *los domingos,* 3
supplies: school supplies *los materiales escolares,* 4
to surf the Internet *navegar por Internet,* 7
surprise party *la fiesta de sorpresa,* 9
sweater *el suéter,* 8
sweet *dulce,* 7
to swim *nadar,* 3
swimsuit *el traje de baño,* 8
synagogue *la sinagoga,* 9

T

table *la mesa,* 5
to take care of *cuidar,* 5; **to take care of oneself** *cuidarse,* 7; **Take care.** *Cuídate.,* 9
to take off *quitarse,* 7
to take out *sacar,* 6; **to take out the trash** *sacar la basura,* 5
to take *tomar,* 9; **to take photos** *sacar photos,* 10; **to take a test** *presentar el examen,* 4
to talk *hablar,* 3; *charlar,* 10
tall *alto(a),* 2
tamales *los tamales,* 9
to taste *probar (ue),* 6
taxi *el taxi,* 10
teacher *la profesora* **(female),** *el profesor* **(male),** 1
teeth *los dientes,* 7
telephone number *el teléfono,* 1
television *la televisión,* 3; **to watch TV** *mirar la televisión,* 3
to tell jokes *contar chistes,* 9
temple *el templo,* 9
ten *diez,* 1
tennis *el tenis,* 3; **tennis shoes** *los zapatos de tenis,* 8
test *el examen,* 4; **to take a . . . test** *presentar el examen de...,* 4
Thanksgiving Day *el Día de Acción de Gracias,* 9
thank you *gracias,* 1
that *ese(a),* 8
the *el, la, los, las,* 2
their *su(s),* 5
them *los, las,* 6
then *luego,* 4
there *allí,* 10
there is, there are *hay,* 4
these *estos, estas,* 8
they *ellas, ellos,* 1
They like to . . . *A ...les gusta...,* 3
thin *delgado(a),* 5
thing *la cosa,* 4
to think *pensar (ie),* 8
thirst *la sed,* 4
thirteen *trece,* 1
thirty *treinta,* 1
this *ésta, éste,* 1; **this** *este(a),* 8; **this weekend** *este fin de semana,* 4
those *esos, esas,* 8
three *tres,* 1
three hundred *trescientos,* 8
throat *la garganta,* 7
Thursday *el jueves,* 1; **on Thursdays** *los jueves,* 3
ticket *el boleto,* 10; **plane ticket** *el boleto de avión,* 10
time *el rato,* 3
tired *cansado(a),* 7; **to be tired** *estar cansado,* 7
to/for me *me,* 2; **you** *te,* 2; **us** *nos,* 2; **him, her, you, them** *le(s),* 2
toast *el pan tostado,* 6
today *hoy,* 1
tomato *el tomate,* 6
tomorrow *mañana,* 4
ton: a ton of *un montón de,* 4
too much *demasiado(a),* 7
toothbrush *el cepillo de dientes,* 7
toothpaste *la pasta de dientes,* 7
to tour *recorrer,* 10
towel *la toalla,* 7
town *el pueblo,* 5
toy *el juguete,* 8
toy store *la juguetería,* 8
train *el tren,* 10
trash *la basura,* 5
to travel *viajar,* 10
trip *el viaje,* 10
to try, taste *probar (ue),* 6
T-shirt *la camiseta,* 8
Tuesday *el martes,* 1; **on Tuesdays** *los martes,* 3

tuna *el atún,* 6
turnover-like pastry *la empanada,* 9
twelve *doce,* 1
twenty *veinte,* 1
two *dos,* 1
two hundred *doscientos,* 8
two thousand *dos mil,* 8

ugly *feo(a),* 2
uncle *el tío,* 5
under, underneath *debajo (de),* 5
to understand *entender,* 5
unfair *injusto,* 5
unfriendly *antipático(a),* 2
until *hasta,* 5; **See you later.** *Hasta luego.,* 1; **See you tomorrow.** *Hasta mañana.,* 1; **See you soon.** *Hasta pronto.,* 1
up to *hasta,* 5
us *nos,* 2; *nosotros(as),* 3
usual: the usual *lo de siempre,* 9

to vacuum *pasar la aspiradora,* 5
vacuum cleaner *la aspiradora,* 4
Valentine's Day *el Día de los Enamorados,* 9
vegetables *las verduras,* 2
very *muy + adjective,* 2
very bad *pésimo(a),* 2
video *el video,* 3
video games *los videojuegos,* 2
village *el pueblo,* 5
volleyball *el volibol,* 3

to wait *esperar,* 8
waiting room *la sala de espera,* 10
to wake *despertarse (ie),* 7
to walk *caminar,* 7; **to go for a walk** *pasear,* 3
wallet *la billetera,* 10
to want *querer (ie),* 3
to wash *lavar,* 5; *lavarse,* 7; **to do the dishes** *lavar los platos,* 5
watch, clock *el reloj,* 4
to watch *ver,* 4; **to watch television** *ver televisión,* 3
water *el agua (f.),* 6; **to water ski** *esquiar en el agua,* 10
we *nosotros(as),* 1
to wear *llevar,* 8; **to wear glasses** *usar lentes,* 5
weather *el tiempo,* 3; **The weather is nice (bad).** *Hace buen (mal) tiempo.,* 3
wedding *la boda,* 9
Wednesday *el miércoles,* 1; **on Wednesdays** *los miércoles,* 3
week *la semana,* 4
weekend *el fin de semana,* 3; **weekends** *los fines de semana,* 3
weight el peso, 7; **to gain weight** *subir de peso,* 7; **to lose weight** *bajar de peso,* 7
weights *las pesas,* 7; **to lift weights** *levantar pesas,* 7
What? *¿Cómo?, ¿Qué?,* 1; **What a pain!** *¡Qué lata!,* 5; **What a shame!** *¡Qué lástima!,* 10; **What are you going to do?** *¿Qué vas a hacer?,* 7; **What bad luck!** *¡Qué mala suerte!,* 10; **What fun!** *¡Qué divertido!,* 10; **What are you like?** *¿Cómo eres?,* 2; **What day is today?** *¿Qué día es hoy?,* 1; **What did you do?** *¿Qué hiciste?,* 8; **What do you do to help out at home?** *¿Qué haces para ayudar en casa?,* 5; **What do you do to relax?** *¿Qué haces para relajarte?,* 7; **What do you have to do?** *¿Qué tienes que hacer?,* 7; **What do you like to do?** *¿Qué te gusta hacer?,* 3; **What do you still have to do?** *¿Qué te falta hacer?,* 7; **What do you want to do?** *¿Qué quieres hacer?,* 3; **What does . . . do?** *¿Qué hace...?,* 3; **What is . . . like?** *¿Cómo es...?,* 2; **What plans do you have for . . .?** *¿Qué planes tienen para...?,* 9; **What time are you going to. . .?** *¿A qué hora vas a...?,* 4; **What time is it?** *¿Qué hora es?,* 3; **What is . . .'s e-mail address?** *¿Cuál es el correo electrónico de...?,* 1; **What's . . . telephone number?** *¿Cuál es el teléfono de...?,* 1; **what?, which?** *¿cuál?,* 4; **What's his (her, your) name?** *¿Cómo se llama?,* 1; **What's new?** *¿Qué hay de nuevo?,* 9; **What's the matter with . . .?** *¿Qué tiene...?,* 7; **What's the weather like?** *¿Qué tiempo hace?,* 3; **What's today's date?** *¿Qué fecha es hoy?,* 1; **What's wrong with you?** *¿Qué te pasa?,* 7; **What's your name?** *¿Cómo te llamas?,* 1
wheelchair *la silla de ruedas,* 5; **to be in a wheelchair** *estar en una silla de ruedas,* 5
when *cuando,* 3
when? *¿cuándo?,* 2
Where did you go? *¿Adónde fuiste?,* 8
where? *¿dónde?,* 5; **Where can I . . .?** *¿Dónde se puede...?* 10; **Where do you go?** *¿Adónde vas?;* **Where did you go?** *¿Adónde fuiste?,* 8; **from where** *de dónde,* 1
white *blanco(a),* 8
whole *todo(a),* 9
Who's calling? *¿De parte de quién?,* 8
Who is . . .? *¿Quién es...?,* 1
why *¿por qué?,* 2
window *la ventana,* 5; **to window-shop** *mirar las vitrinas,* 8
winter *el invierno,* 3
to wish for *desear,* 6
with *con,* 3
with me *conmigo,* 3
with you *contigo,* 3
witty *gracioso(a),* 2
woman *la mujer,* 5
wool *la lana,* 8; **made of wool** *de lana,* 8
work *trabajar,* 3; *el trabajo,* 4
to work out *entrenarse,* 7
workshop *el taller,* 4
to worry *preocuparse,* 10; **Don't worry.** *No te preocupes.,* 10
worse *peor(es),* 8
to write *escribir,* 1; **How do you spell . . .?** *¿Cómo se escribe...?,* 1; **It's spelled . . .** *Se escribe...,* 1

yard *el patio,* 5
year *el año,* 2; **New Year** *el Año Nuevo* 9; **last year** *el año pasado,* 9
yellow *amarillo(a),* 8
yes *sí,* 4; **Yes, I need a lot of things.** *Sí, necesito muchas cosas.,* 4; **Yes, I have a ton of them.** *Sí, tengo un montón.,* 4
yesterday *ayer,* 8
yoga: to do yoga *hacer yoga,* 7
you *usted, ustedes,* (formal)1; *tú, vosotros(as),* (informal) 1; **You were lucky!** *Ah, ¡tuviste suerte!,* 10
young *joven,* 5
young people *los jóvenes,* 9
younger *menor(es),* 5
your *tu(s), su(s), vuestro(a)(s),* 5

zero *cero,* 1
zoo *el zoológico,* 10

Índice gramatical

Page numbers in boldface type refer to the first presentation of the topic. Other page numbers refer to grammar structures presented in the **¡Exprésate!** features, subsequent references to the topic, or reviewed in **Repaso de Gramática.** Page numbers beginning with R refer to the **Síntesis gramatical** in this Reference Section (pages R20–R27). The designations (IA) and (IB) following the page numbers refer to **¡Exprésate!** IA and **¡Exprésate!** IB.

Índice gramatical

Índice gramatical

Índice gramatical

Agradecimientos

STAFF CREDITS

Editorial
Barbara Kristof, Douglas Ward, Priscilla Blanton, Amber Nichols

Editorial Development Team
Marion Bermondy, Konstanze Alex Brown, Lynda Cortez, Janet Welsh Crossley, Jean Miller, Zahydée G. Minnick, Beatriz Malo Pojman, Paul Provence, Jaishree Venkatesan, J. Elisabeth Wright

Editorial Staff
Sara Anbari, Hubert W. Bays, Yamilé Dewailly, Virginia Dosher, Milagros Escamilla,
Rita Ricardo, Glenna Scott, Geraldine Touzeau-Patrick

Editorial Permissions
Ann B. Farrar, Yuri Muñoz

Book Design
Kay Selke, Marta Kimball, Marc Cooper, Robin Bouvette, José Garza, Sally Bess, Bruce Albrecht, Ed Diaz, Liann Lech

Image Acquisitions
Curtis Riker, Jeannie Taylor, Cindy Verheyden, Stephanie Friedman, Sam Dudgeon, Victoria Smith, Michelle Rumpf

Media Design
Richard Metzger, Chris Smith

Design New Media
Edwin Blake, Kimberly Cammerata

Production, Manufacturing, and Inventory
Beth Prevelige, Diana Rodriguez, Rose Degollado, Jevara Jackson, Rhonda Fariss, Jennifer Craycraft

New Media
Kenneth Whiteside, Lydia Doty, Jamie Lane, Chris Pittman, Cathy Kuhles, Nina Degollado

eLearning Systems
Beau Clark, Jim Bruno, Annette Saunders

ACKNOWLEDGMENTS

For permission to reprint copyrighted material, grateful acknowledgment is made to the following sources:

Children's Book Press, San Francisco, CA: "Baile en El Jardín" from *In My Family/En mi familia* by Carmen Lomas Garza, translated into Spanish by Francisco X. Alarcón. Text copyright © 1996 by Carmen Lomas Garza. "La Tamalada" from *Family Pictures/Cuadros de famila* by Carmen Lomas Garza, translated into Spanish by Rosalma Zubizarreta. Text copyright © 1990 by Carmen Lomas Garza. "La Montaña del Alimento" from *The Legend of Food Mountain/La Montaña del Alimento,* adapted by Harriet Rohmer, translated into Spanish by Alma Flor Ada and Rosalma Zubizarreta. Copyright © 1982 by Children's Book Press.

Dover Publications, Inc.: From "El Fracaso Matemático de Pepito" from First Spanish Reader: *A Beginner's Dual-Language Book,* edited by Angel Flores. Copyright © 1988 by Angel Flores.

Ediciones de la Fundación Corripio, Inc.: From "Regalo de Cumpleaños" by Diógenes Valdez from *Cuentos Dominicanos Para Niños,* vol. V. Copyright © 2000 by Ediciones de la Fundación Corripio, Inc.

Editorial Fundación Ross: "Dos buenas piernas tenemos..." and "Siempre quietas,..." from *Adivinanzas para mirar en el espejo* by Carlos Silveyra. Copyright © 1985 by Editorial Fundación Ross.

Editorial Sudamericana S.A.: "2" and "16" from *Los Rimaqué* by Ruth Kaufman. Copyright © 2002 by Editorial Sudamericana S.A.

HarperCollins Publishers: From "Una antigua casa encantada" from *Mi país inventado* by Isabel Allende. Copyright © 2003 by Isabel Allende.

Francisco J. Briz Hidalgo, www.elhuevodechocolate.com: "Una moneda de ¡Ay!" by Juan de Timoneda from *El huevo de chocolate* web site, accessed on September 10, 2003 at http://www.elhuevodechocolate.com. Copyright © by Francisco J. Briz Hidalgo.

Maricel Mayor Marsán: From "Un corazón dividido" from *Un corazón dividido/ A Split Heart* by Maricel Mayor Marsán. Copyright © 1998 by Maricel Mayor Marsán. From "Apuntes de un hogar postmoderno" from Impronta de los Rincones by Maricel Mayor Marsán. Copyright © by Maricel Mayor Marsán.

Museum of New Mexico Press: "Los Cuatro Elementos" from Cuentos: *Tales from the Hispanic Southwest,* selected and adapted in Spanish by José Griego y Maestas. Copyright © 1980 by Museum of New Mexico Press.

Scholastic Inc.: From "Ollantay Tambo" from *Ahora,* vol. 3, no. 2, September/October 1996. Copyright © 1996 by Scholastic Inc. From "Gustavo" from *Ahora,* vol. 4, no. 2, November/December 1997. Copyright © 1997 by Scholastic Inc.

PHOTOGRAPHY CREDITS

Abreviations used: c-center, b-bottom, t-top, l-left, r-right, bkgd-background.

AUTHORS: Page iii (Smith) Courtney Baker, courtesy Stuart Smith; (McMinn) courtesy John McMinn; (Madrigal Velasco) courtesy Sylvia Madrigal; (Humbach) courtesy Nancy Humbach.

TABLE OF CONTENTS: Page v (br) Don Couch/HRW; vi (b, c) Victoria Smith/HRW; (t) family photo in frame: ©Image100; photo by: Victoria Smith/HRW; vii (cr) Don Couch/HRW; (tr) ©Robert Frerck/Odyssey/Chicago; viii (cr) Don Couch/HRW; (tr) Michael Everett/D. Donne Bryant Photography; ix (cr, tr) Sam Dudgeon/HRW; x (cr, tr) John Langford/HRW; xi (cr) Don Couch/HRW; (tr) Digital Image copyright ©2006 PhotoDisc.

WHY STUDY SPANISH: Page xii (Argentina) ©Jeremy Woodhouse, digitalvision; (Chile Don) Couch/HRW; (Costa Rica) ©Buddy Mays/CORBIS; (Dominican Republic) John Langford/HRW; (Mexico) Corbis Images; (Peru) Don Couch/HRW; (Spain) Corbis Images; xiii (bl, tr) Alvaro Ortiz/HRW; (br, cart) Don Couch/HRW; (mural) John

Langford/HRW; xiv (b) Sam Dudgeon/HRW; (cl) ©Royalty-Free/CORBIS; (cr) Edward M. Pio Roda. (tm) & ©2003 CNN. An AOL Time Warner Co. All Rights Reserved; xv (br) ©Image 100 Ltd; (t) Alvaro Ortiz/HRW.

IN SPANISH CLASS: Page xvi (bl) HRW; (tr) ©Brand X Pictures. COMMON NAMES: Page xvii (bkgd) Alvaro Ortiz/HRW. DIRECTIONS: Page xviii (b) Digital Image copyright ©2006 PhotoDisc; xix (bl) Digital Image copyright ©2006 EyeWire; (br) Digital Image copyright ©2006 Artville; (tl) Randall Hyman/HRW; (tr) Sam Dudgeon/HRW. TIPS FOR LEARNING SPANISH: Page xx (b) Alvaro Ortiz/HRW; (cl, tr) ©Brand X Pictures; xxi (b, cr) Digital Image copyright ©2006 PhotoDisc; (cl) ©Royalty-Free/CORBIS; (tl) Don Couch/HRW; (tr) John Langford/HRW.

BRIDGE CHAPTER: Page xxii (all) Victoria Smith/HRW; 1 (b, t) John Langford/HRW; 2 (b) Alvaro Ortiz/HRW; (tl, tr) Don Couch/HRW; 3 (c, t) Alvaro Ortiz/HRW; 4 (1,2, 4) Martha Granger/Edge Video Productions/HRW; (3) Christine Galida/HRW; 5 (1, 2, 3, 5, Juan) Martha Granger/Edge Video Productions/HRW; (4) M. L. Miller/Edge Video Productions/HRW; 10 (all) Victoria Smith/HRW; 11 (b) John Langford/HRW; (t) Don Couch/HRW; 12 (all) Dennis Fagan/HRW; 13 (bailar) Martha Granger/Edge Video Productions/HRW; (básquetbol) Peter Van Steen/HRW; (béisbol) Michelle Bridwell/Frontera Fotos; (fútbol) David Young-Wolff/PhotoEdit; (hablar) ©Telegraph Colour Library/FPG International; (juegos) Victoria Smith/HRW; 16 (a, b) Corbis Images; (c, cl) Victoria Smith/HRW; (d) photographer/Painet Inc; (e) ©Nik Wheeler/CORBIS; 20 (all) family photo in frame: ©Image100; photo by: Victoria Smith/HRW; 21 (b) Don Couch/HRW; (t) John Langford/HRW; 22 (all insets) Victoria Smith/HRW; (bkgd) Don Couch/HRW; 23 (tl) Don Couch/HRW; 27 (1) Robert Fried Photography; (2) Sam Dudgeon/HRW; (3, 4) Michelle Bridwell/HRW; (5, 7) Michelle Bridwell/Frontera Fotos; (6, 8, cocinar) Christine Galida/HRW; 28 (bl) ©Comstock, Inc; (br) Peter Van Steen/HRW; (cl) Dennis Fagan/HRW; (cr) Digital Image copyright ©2006 EyeWire; (tl) Don Couch/HRW; 29 (1, 2) David Phillips/Words & Images; (3) Martha Granger/Edge Video Productions/HRW; (4) John Langford/HRW; (papá) Sam Dudgeon/HRW; 30 (br) ©Jan Butchofsky-Houser/CORBIS; (tl) Don Couch/HRW; 31 (c) ©Gabe Palmer/CORBIS; (tl) Don Couch/HRW; 32 (bl) Digital Image copyright ©2006 PhotoDisc; (br) David Young-Wolff/PhotoEdit; (cr) Alvaro Ortiz/HRW; 33 (br) Victoria Smith/HRW; (cr) David Phillips/Words & Images; (tl) ©Image100.

CHAPTER 6 All photos by Don Couch/HRW except: Page 34 (c) ©Danny Lehman/CORBIS; (tc) ©Getty Images/The Image Bank; 35 (bl, cr, tl) ©Robert Frerck/Odyssey/Chicago; (tr) Mark Newman/Bruce Coleman, Inc; 36 (b) ©Royalty-Free/CORBIS; (tl) ©Charles & Josette Lenars/CORBIS; (tr) ©Archivo Iconografico, S.A./CORBIS; 37 (cr) George H. H. Huey; (tl) Charlene E. Friesen/D. Donne Bryant Photography; 41 (cola) Victoria Smith/HRW; 43 (1) Sam Dudgeon/HRW; (tr , 5) Victoria Smith/HRW; 45 (3) Michelle Bridwell/HRW; (4) Victoria Smith/HRW; (5) Sam Dudgeon/HRW; 46 (bl) Victoria Smith/HRW; 47 (4, soup) Michelle Bridwell/HRW; 48 (bl) Victoria Smith/HRW; 49 (all) Victoria Smith/HRW; 50 (bl) Victoria Smith/HRW; 51 (tr) ©Robert Frerck/Odyssey/Chicago; 52 (tl) Victoria Smith/HRW; 53 (br) Gary Russ/HRW; (tl) John Langford/HRW; 55 (cl) Corbis Images; 60 (bl) John Langford/HRW; 61 (2) Digital Image copyright ©2006 PhotoDisc; (3) Victoria Smith/HRW; (t) Michelle Bridwell/HRW; 64 (br) © Scott Tevan/photohouston.com; 74 (br) Victoria Smith/HRW; 78 (A,B) Don Couch/HRW; (bl,C) Victoria Smith/HRW; (D) Digital Image copyright ©2006 PhotoDisc.

CHAPTER 7 All photos by Don Couch/HRW except: Page 80 (c) Peter Lang/D. Donne Bryant Photography; (cr) Jean Lee/AP/Wide World Photos; (tr) ©Tony West/PICIMPACT/CORBIS; 81 (bc) Luis Martin/D. Donne Bryant Photography; (br) ©Alissa Crandall/CORBIS; (cr) ©Hubert Stadler/CORBIS; (tr) Michael Everett/D. Donne Bryant Photography; 82 (bl) ©Hubert Stadler/CORBIS; (br) Museo Xul Solar; (tl) Peter Lang/D. Donne Bryant Photography; 83 (tl) ©Russell Gordon/Odyssey/Chicago; (tr) Victoria Smith/HRW; 89 (comb, makeup, shirt/jeans, soap, toothbrush, towels) Sam Dudgeon/HRW; (hairdryer) Digital Image copyright ©2006 PhotoDisc; (pajamas) Victoria Smith/HRW; (tr) Digital Image copyright ©2006 PhotoDisc; 90 (bl) Jean Lee/AP/Wide World Photos; 91 (1) Martha Cooper/Viesti Collection, Inc; (2, 6) Christine Galida/HRW; (3) Bob Daemmrich/Stock Boston; (4, 5) John Langford/HRW; 92 (bl) Elizabeth Grivs/TxDOT; 93 (1) John Langford/HRW; (2) ©John Foxx/Alamy Photos; (3) Bob Daemmrich/The Image Works; (4) Image Source/elektraVision/PictureQuest; (tr) Stockbyte/PictureQuest; 95 (cl, r) Dennis Fagan/HRW; (cr) ©Jose Luis Pelaez, Inc./CORBIS; (l, t) Peter Van Steen/HRW; 96 (bl) Victoria Smith/HRW; 99 (br) Isaac Menashe/Icon SMI/NewsCom; 107 (cl) ©Image Source; (cr, l) Peter Van Steen/HRW; (r) ©RubberBall Productions; 108 (bl) John Langford/HRW; 110 (all) ©2006 Radlund & Associates for Artville/HRW; 111 (all) http://www.latinosportslegends.com; 112 (ball, bat, glove) ©2006 Radlund & Associates for Artville/HRW;113 (br, cr) AP Photo/AP/Wide World Photos; 113 (tl) David Kohl/AP/Wide World Photos; 118 (bl) Peter Van Steen/HRW; 120 (tc, tl) Dennis Fagan/HRW; (tr) Peter Van Steen/HRW.

CHAPTER 8 All photos by Sam Dudgeon/HRW except: Page 126 (tr) ©Owaki - Kulla/CORBIS; 127 (bl) Werner Bertsch/Bruce Coleman, Inc; (br) ©Richard Bickel/CORBIS; (tc) Masa Ushioda/Bruce Coleman, Inc; (tr) Kennedy Space Center/NASA; 128 (br) ©Mildrey Guillot; (tl) ©Tony Arruza/CORBIS; 129 (cr) ©Latin Focus; (t) ©Robert Frerck/Odyssey/Chicago; 136 (bl) Michelle Bridwell/Frontera Fotos; 142 (bl) Alvaro Ortiz/HRW; 145 (br) Corbis Images; (t) Don Couch/HRW; 146 (anillo, aretes, pulsera) Victoria Smith/HRW; (audífonos, CD) Digital Image copyright ©2006 PhotoDisc; (tarjetas) Don Couch/HRW; 148 (2) Corbis Images; (4) Digital Image copyright ©2006 PhotoDisc; (5) Don Couch/HRW; (7 CDs,) Victoria Smith/HRW; 150 (cl) ©Arthur Tilley/Getty Images/Taxi; 151 (tl) Digital Image copyright ©2006 PhotoDisc; (tr) Martha Granger/Edge Video Productions/HRW; 153 (2, 3) Victoria Smith/HRW; (4) Image Source Ltd/Alamy; (5) Digital Image copyright ©2006 EyeWire; (6) Dennis Fagan/HRW; (t) Bob Daemmrich/The Image Works; 154 (l) ©Latin Focus; 155 (1, 2, tr) Victoria Smith/HRW; (5) Digital Image copyright ©2006 PhotoDisc; 158 (bl) Victoria Smith/HRW; (córdoba, lempira, peso) HRW file photo; 159 (euros) ©European Communities; (fresas, manzanas) Digital Image copyright © 2006 PhotoDisc; (melón) Corbis Images; (naranjas) ©Royalty-Free/CORBIS; 170 (all) Victoria Smith/HRW.

CHAPTER 9 All photos by John Langford/HRW except: Page 172 (c) ©Jeremy Horner/CORBIS; (tr) Martha Cooper/Viesti Collection, Inc; 173 (br) ©Giraud Philippe/Corbis Sygma; (cr, tl) Suzanne Murphy-Larronde; (tl) David Pou; (tr) Tom Bean; 174 (cl, tr) David Pou; 175 (br, tc) David Pou; (cl) age fotostock/Suzanne Murphy-Larronde, 2006; 178 (Acción de Gracias)

©Bob Daemmrich/Getty Images/Stone; (bkgd, t) Victoria Smith/HRW; (Enamorados) Christine Galida/HRW; (Hanukkah) Pam Ostrow/Index Stock Imagery/PictureQuest; (Navidad) Michael Matisse/Photodisc/PictureQuest; (Nochevieja) Christine Galida/HRW; (Semana Santa) Andres Leighton/AP/Wide World Photos; 179 (abrir, mandar, recibir) Sam Dudgeon/HRW; (fuegos) Corbis Images; (mandar) Victoria Smith/HRW; 181 (1, 4) Peter Van Steen/HRW; (2) ©Tom and Dee Ann McCarthy/Index Stock Imagery/ PictureQuest; (3) ©Creatas/PictureQuest; 185 (c, l) Peter Van Steen/HRW; (r) Victoria Smith/HRW; 186 (bl) Victoria Smith/ HRW; 187 (tl) Victoria Smith/HRW; (tr) Sam Dudgeon/HRW; 188 (bl) David Pou; 190 (br) Sam Dudgeon/HRW; 191 (br) Ric Vasquez/AP/Wide World Photos; (tl) Gary Russ/HRW; 192 (bkgd) Corbis Images; (galletas, papitas, ponche) Victoria Smith/HRW; (mailbox) Marta Kimball/HRW; 194 (l) Jose Carrillo/PhotoEdit Inc; 197 (all) Martha Granger/Edge Video Productions/HRW; 200 (1) The Kobal Collection; (2) Eric Risberg/AP/Wide World Photos; (3) The Kobal Collection; (4) ©Bettmann/CORBIS; (l) Courtesy of the Texas Folklife Festival ; (Segovia) ©Hulton-Deutsch Collection/CORBIS; 204–205 (various) Richard Hutchings/HRW; 204 (tl) Bob Daemmrich/ Stock Boston; 212 (1) ©Brand X Pictures; (2, 5) Digital Image copyright ©2006 PhotoDisc; (3-clock) ©Comstock; (3-hats, 4, 6) Corbis Images.

CHAPTER 10 All photos by Don Couch/HRW except: Page 218 (tr) ©Jack Fields/CORBIS; 219 (bl) Todd Wolf; (br) Erwin and Peggy Bauer/Animals Animals/Earth Scenes; (tc) ©Wolfgang Kaehler/CORBIS; 220 (bl) ©Diego Lezama Orezzoli/CORBIS; (tl) Digital Image copyright ©2006 PhotoDisc; 221 (cr) Ricardo Choy Kifox/AP/Wide World Photos; (tc) ©William Albert Allard/National Geographic Image Collection; 225 (t) Victoria Smith/HRW; 226 (tl) Robert Frerck/Woodfin Camp & Associates; 228 (l) Martha Granger/Edge Video Productions/ HRW; 229 (tl) Martha Granger/Edge Video Productions/HRW; 233 (1) Peter Van Steen/HRW; (2) Digital Image copyright ©2006 PhotoDisc; (4) Dean Berry/Index Stock Imagery, Inc; 248 (cl) Courtesy of Texas Highways Magazine; ©2006 PhotoDisc; 242 (1) ©Rick Doyle/CORBIS; (2, 4) ©Index Stock; (3) ©William Sallaz/CORBIS; (cr) Digital Image copyright ©2006 PhotoDisc; 243 (cl, cr) Martha Granger/Edge Video Productions/HRW; (tl) Ron Chapple/Thinkstock/PictureQuest; 244 (bl) Victoria Smith/HRW; 245 (br) Digital Image copyright ©2006 PhotoDisc; (cr) ©COMSTOCK, Inc; 247 (cr) ©Michael & Patricia Fogden/CORBIS; 249 (tr) Stephanie Maze/Woodfin Camp & Associates; 250 (c) Dr. Paul A. Zahl/Photo Researchers, Inc; (tr) Richard Rowan/Photo Researchers, Inc; 258 (tl) Digital Image copyright ©2006 PhotoDisc.

LITERATURA Y VARIEDADES: Page 271 (tl) Courtesy of Maricel Mayor Marsan; 272 (cr) Victoria Smith/HRW; 273 (cr) Victoria Smith/HRW; (tr) ©William James Warren/CORBIS; 274 (r) ©Bettmann/CORBIS; 275 (all) ©Wolfgang Kaehler/ CORBIS.

REVIEW VOCABULARY: Page R7 (bl) Digital Image copyright ©2006 PhotoDisc; (r) ©BananaStock; (tl) Sam Dudgeon/HRW; R8 (cl) Alvaro Ortiz/HRW; (cr) Don Couch/HRW; (t, tc) Digital Image copyright ©2006 PhotoDisc; R9 (bl) Don Couch/HRW; (br) Alvaro Ortiz/HRW; (cr, tr) Gary Russ/HRW; (tl) Sam Dudgeon/HRW; R10 (bl) Corbis Images; (cl) ©RubberBall/Alamy Photos; (cr) Digital Image copyright ©2006 PhotoDisc; (tl) ©Digital Vision; R11 (bl) Alvaro Ortiz/HRW; (br) ©Dennis Degnan/CORBIS; (tl) ©Buddy Mays/CORBIS; R11 (bl) Digital Image ©2006 PhotoDisc; (bl) Alvaro Ortiz/HRW; (br) ©Dennis Degnan/CORBIS; (r) ©BananaStock; (tl) Sam Dudgeon/HRW; (tl) ©Buddy Mays/CORBIS; R12 (cl) Alvaro Ortiz/HRW; (cr) Don Couch/HRW; (tc) Digital Image ©2006 PhotoDisc; R13 (bl) Don Couch/HRW; (br) Alvaro Ortiz/HRW; (cr) Gary Russ/HRW; (tl) Sam Dudgeon/HRW; (tr) Gary Russ/HRW; R14 (bc) Corbis Images; (cl) ©RubberBall/Alamy Photos; (cr) Digital Image ©2006 PhotoDisc; (tl) ©Digital Vision; R15 (bl) Alvaro Ortiz/HRW; (br) ©Dennis Degnan/CORBIS; (tl) ©Buddy Mays/CORBIS.

NOVELA STILL PHOTOS: Spain - Don Couch/HRW; Puerto Rico - John Langford/HRW; Mexico, Peru - Don Couch/HRW.

ICONS: (CULTURA) Don Couch/HRW; (VOCABULARIO 1) John Langford/HRW; (VOCABULARIO 2) Don Couch/HRW.

TE PHOTOGRAPHY CREDITS

Abbreviations used: c-center, b-bottom, t-top, l-left, r-right, bkgrd-background.

All photos by Don Couch/HRW except: page T5 (r) ©COMSTOCK, Inc.; T6 (b) ©Jeremy Woodhouse, digitalvision; (cl) John Langford/HRW; T8 (b) family photo in frame: ©Image100; photo by: Victoria Smith/HRW; (c, t) Victoria Smith/HRW; T9 (tr) ©Robert Frerck/Odyssey/Chicago; T10 (tr) Michael Everett/D. Donne Bryant Photography; T11 (b, tr) Sam Dudgeon/HRW; T12 (b, tr) John Langford/HRW; T13 (tr) Digital Image copyright ©2006 PhotoDisc; T15 (tr) HRW photo; T18 (bl) John Langford/HRW; (tl) Alvaro Ortiz/HRW; T19 (tl) Gary Russ/HRW; T21 (bl) Sam Dudgeon/HRW; (cl) PhotoDisc/gettyimages; (tl) John Langford/HRW; T22 (bl) ©Philip Coblentz, Brand X Pictures; T23 (cl) Sam Dudgeon/HRW; (tl) John Langford/HRW; T24 (cl) John Langford/HRW; T25 (tl) Gary Russ/HRW; T26 (tl) Alvaro Ortiz/HRW; T27 (bl) Gary Russ/HRW; (tl) John Langford/HRW; T30 (bl) ©Philip Coblentz, Brand X Pictures; (cl) ©Danny Lehman/CORBIS; T31 (bl) Art Resource, NY; (cl) ©Rob Lewine/CORBIS; (tl) ©Robert Landau/CORBIS; T32 (bl) Instituto Salvadoreno de Turismo; (cl) ©M. Timothy O'Keefe/Bruce Coleman, Inc.; (tl) ©2006 Brian A. Vikander; T33 (bl) ©Robert Francis/South American Pictures; (cl) Christine Galida/HRW; (tl) Chip & Rosa María de la Cueva Peterson; T34 (bl) ©Galen Rowell/Odyssey/Chicago; (cl) ©Bob Daemmrich/Stock, Boston; (tl) SuperStock; T35 (bl) ©2003 Estate of Pablo Picasso/Artists Rights Society (ARS), New York, Scala/Art Resource, New York. (cl) SuperStock; (tl) painting ©2003 Banco de México Diego Rivera & Frida Kahlo Museums Trust. Av. Cinco de Mayo No. 2, Col. Centro, Del. Cuauhtémoc 06059, México, D. F.; photo source The Granger Collection, New York; T46 (bl) © Dennis Galante/Taxi/Stone; (b) ©Luc Beziat/Getty Images/Stone; (c) PhotoDisc/gettyimages; (flamingos) Sam Dudgeon/HRW; (fountain) Alvaro Ortiz/HRW; (ruins) ©Robert Frerck/Odyssey/Chicago; T47 (#1-#4) Martha Granger/Edge Video Productions/HRW; (Chac Mool) ©Royalty-Free/CORBIS; (ExpresaVision) HRW photo; (GeoVision) ©Robert Francis/South American Pictures; (Video Novela) John Langford/HRW; T49 (b) PhotoDisc/gettyimages; T50 (c) John Langford/HRW; (tr) Sam Dudgeon/HRW; T52 (bc) John Langford/HRW; (cl) ©Royalty-Free/CORBIS; (cr) Corbis Images; T53 (c) Sam Dudgeon/HRW; T55 (Sandrock) courtesy Paul Sandrock; T56 (Beers) courtesy

Kylene Beers; T57 (Strickland) courtesy Cindy Strickland; (Tomlinson) courtesy Carol Ann Tomlinson; T58 (LeLoup) courtesy Jean W. LeLoup; (Ponterio) courtesy Robert Ponterio; T59 (Humbach) courtesy Nancy Humbach; T60 (b) ©COMSTOCK, Inc.; T61 (b, cr) PhotoDisc/gettyimages; (clock) ©Royalty-Free/CORBIS; (tr) Sam Dudgeon/HRW/SCRABBLE® is a trademark of Hasbro in the United States and Canada. ©2002 Hasbro, Inc. All Rights Reserved. T62 (b, c) PhotoDisc/gettyimages; (cr) John Langford/HRW; T63 (b) Sam Dudgeon/HRW; (cr) ©Bill Truslow/Getty Images/Stone; T61-T64 (border) PhotoDisc/gettyimages; T73C (tl) ©Jon Riley/Getty Images/Stone; T73D (b) ©Brian Hagiwara/Getty Images/FoodPix; (tr) RF Films; 37C (paella) William Koechling/HRW; 37D (br) Martha Granger/Edge Video Productions/HRW; (tr) Sam Dudgeon/HRW; 61 (Mahlmann) HRW photo; 63 (Vorrhees) HRW photo; 83D (br) Victoria Smith/HRW; (tr) Hubert Stadler/CORBIS; 93 (Bachman) courtesy Dena Bachman; 102 (Chadwick) courtesy Carol Chadwick; 115 (bl) John Langford/HRW; 129D (br) Beryl Goldberg Photography; (tr) Nik Wheeler/CORBIS; 137 (Bernard) HRW photo; 139 (Heller) Courtesy Bill Heller; 169 (Villalobos) HRW photo; 175C (tr) ©Bob Daemmrich/Getty Images/Stone; 175D (br) Scott Vallance/VIP Photo/HRW; (tr) John Langford/HRW; 182 (Burkart) courtesy Sonia Burkart; 207 (bl) John Langford/HRW; 214 (Ostermann-Healy) HRW photo; 221D (tr) Pablo Corral Vega/CORBIS; 231 (Price) HRW photo; 242 (Bryant) HRW photo.

ICONS: *e-community,* PhotoDisc/gettyimages; *Fine Art Connection* ©Stockbyte; *Game Bank,* PhotoDisc/gettyimages; *Holt Online Learning,* PhotoDisc/gettyimages; *Pacing Tips,* PhotoDisc/gettyimages; *Partner Class Project,* Steve Ewert Photography; *Projects,* Victoria Smith/HRW; *Traditions,* HRW photo.